Contemporary
Literary Criticism

Guide to Thomson Gale Literary Criticism Series

For criticism on	Consult these Thomson Gale series
Authors now living or who died after December 31, 1999	*CONTEMPORARY LITERARY CRITICISM (CLC)*
Authors who died between 1900 and 1999	*TWENTIETH-CENTURY LITERARY CRITICISM (TCLC)*
Authors who died between 1800 and 1899	*NINETEENTH-CENTURY LITERATURE CRITICISM (NCLC)*
Authors who died between 1400 and 1799	*LITERATURE CRITICISM FROM 1400 TO 1800 (LC)* *SHAKESPEAREAN CRITICISM (SC)*
Authors who died before 1400	*CLASSICAL AND MEDIEVAL LITERATURE CRITICISM (CMLC)*
Authors of books for children and young adults	*CHILDREN'S LITERATURE REVIEW (CLR)*
Dramatists	*DRAMA CRITICISM (DC)*
Poets	*POETRY CRITICISM (PC)*
Short story writers	*SHORT STORY CRITICISM (SSC)*
Literary topics and movements	*HARLEM RENAISSANCE: A GALE CRITICAL COMPANION (HR)* *THE BEAT GENERATION: A GALE CRITICAL COMPANION (BG)* *FEMINISM IN LITERATURE: A GALE CRITICAL COMPANION (FL)* *GOTHIC LITERATURE: A GALE CRITICAL COMPANION (GL)*
Asian American writers of the last two hundred years	*ASIAN AMERICAN LITERATURE (AAL)*
Black writers of the past two hundred years	*BLACK LITERATURE CRITICISM (BLC)* *BLACK LITERATURE CRITICISM SUPPLEMENT (BLCS)*
Hispanic writers of the late nineteenth and twentieth centuries	*HISPANIC LITERATURE CRITICISM (HLC)* *HISPANIC LITERATURE CRITICISM SUPPLEMENT (HLCS)*
Native North American writers and orators of the eighteenth, nineteenth, and twentieth centuries	*NATIVE NORTH AMERICAN LITERATURE (NNAL)*
Major authors from the Renaissance to the present	*WORLD LITERATURE CRITICISM, 1500 TO THE PRESENT (WLC)* *WORLD LITERATURE CRITICISM SUPPLEMENT (WLCS)*

ISSN 0091-3421

Volume 235

Contemporary Literary Criticism

Criticism of the Works
of Today's Novelists, Poets, Playwrights,
Short Story Writers, Scriptwriters, and
Other Creative Writers

Jeffrey W. Hunter
PROJECT EDITOR

THOMSON

GALE

Detroit • New York • San Francisco • New Haven, Conn. • Waterville, Maine • London

THOMSON
★
GALE

Contemporary Literary Criticism, Vol. 235

Project Editor
Jeffrey W. Hunter

Editorial
Kathy D. Darrow, Jelena O. Krstović, Michelle Lee, Thomas J. Schoenberg, Noah Schusterbauer, Lawrence J. Trudeau, Russel Whitaker

Data Capture
Frances Monroe, Gwen Tucker

Indexing Services
Laurie Andriot

Rights and Acquisitions
Edna Hedblad, Lisa Kincade, Timothy Sisler

Composition and Electronic Prepress
Gary Oudersluys

Manufacturing
Rhonda Dover

Associate Product Manager
Marc Cormier

LIBRARY OF CONGRESS CATALOG CARD NUMBER 76-46132

ISBN-13: 978-0-7876-9559-0
ISBN-10: 0-7876-9559-9
ISSN 0091-3421

Printed in the United States of America
10 9 8 7 6 5 4 3 2 1

Contents

Preface vii

Acknowledgments xi

Literary Criticism Series Advisory Board xiii

Preface

Named "one of the twenty-five most distinguished reference titles published during the past twenty-five years" by *Reference Quarterly*, the *Contemporary Literary Criticism* (*CLC*) series provides readers with critical commentary and general information on more than 2,000 authors now living or who died after December 31, 1999. Volumes published from 1973 through 1999 include authors who died after December 31, 1959. Previous to the publication of the first volume of *CLC* in 1973, there was no ongoing digest monitoring scholarly and popular sources of critical opinion and explication of modern literature. *CLC,* therefore, has fulfilled an essential need, particularly since the complexity and variety of contemporary literature makes the function of criticism especially important to today's reader.

Scope of the Series

CLC provides significant passages from published criticism of works by creative writers. Since many of the authors covered in *CLC* inspire continual critical commentary, writers are often represented in more than one volume. There is, of course, no duplication of reprinted criticism.

Authors are selected for inclusion for a variety of reasons, among them the publication or dramatic production of a critically acclaimed new work, the reception of a major literary award, revival of interest in past writings, or the adaptation of a literary work to film or television.

Attention is also given to several other groups of writers—authors of considerable public interest—about whose work criticism is often difficult to locate. These include mystery and science fiction writers, literary and social critics, foreign authors, and authors who represent particular ethnic groups.

Each *CLC* volume contains individual essays and reviews taken from hundreds of book review periodicals, general magazines, scholarly journals, monographs, and books. Entries include critical evaluations spanning from the beginning of an author's career to the most current commentary. Interviews, feature articles, and other published writings that offer insight into the author's works are also presented. Students, teachers, librarians, and researchers will find that the general critical and biographical material in *CLC* provides them with vital information required to write a term paper, analyze a poem, or lead a book discussion group. In addition, complete bibliographical citations note the original source and all of the information necessary for a term paper footnote or bibliography.

Organization of the Book

A *CLC* entry consists of the following elements:

■ The **Author Heading** cites the name under which the author most commonly wrote, followed by birth and death dates. Also located here are any name variations under which an author wrote, including transliterated forms for authors whose native languages use nonroman alphabets. If the author wrote consistently under a pseudonym, the pseudonym will be listed in the author heading and the author's actual name given in parenthesis on the first line of the biographical and critical information. Uncertain birth or death dates are indicated by question marks. Single-work entries are preceded by a heading that consists of the most common form of the title in English translation (if applicable) and the original date of composition.

■ A **Portrait of the Author** is included when available.

■ The **Introduction** contains background information that introduces the reader to the author, work, or topic that is the subject of the entry.

- The list of **Principal Works** is ordered chronologically by date of first publication and lists the most important works by the author. The genre and publication date of each work is given. In the case of foreign authors whose works have been translated into English, the English-language version of the title follows in brackets. Unless otherwise indicated, dramas are dated by first performance, not first publication.

- Reprinted **Criticism** is arranged chronologically in each entry to provide a useful perspective on changes in critical evaluation over time. The critic's name and the date of composition or publication of the critical work are given at the beginning of each piece of criticism. Unsigned criticism is preceded by the title of the source in which it appeared. All titles by the author featured in the text are printed in boldface type. Footnotes are reprinted at the end of each essay or excerpt. In the case of excerpted criticism, only those footnotes that pertain to the excerpted texts are included.

- A complete **Bibliographical Citation** of the original essay or book precedes each piece of criticism. Source citations in the Literary Criticism Series follow University of Chicago Press style, as outlined in *The Chicago Manual of Style,* 15th ed. (Chicago: The University of Chicago Press, 2003).

- Critical essays are prefaced by brief **Annotations** explicating each piece.

- Whenever possible, a recent **Author Interview** accompanies each entry.

- An annotated bibliography of **Further Reading** appears at the end of each entry and suggests resources for additional study. In some cases, significant essays for which the editors could not obtain reprint rights are included here. Boxed material following the further reading list provides references to other biographical and critical sources on the author in series published by Thomson Gale.

Indexes

A **Cumulative Author Index** lists all of the authors that appear in a wide variety of reference sources published by Thomson Gale, including *CLC*. A complete list of these sources is found facing the first page of the Author Index. The index also includes birth and death dates and cross references between pseudonyms and actual names.

A **Cumulative Nationality Index** lists all authors featured in *CLC* by nationality, followed by the number of the *CLC* volume in which their entry appears.

A **Cumulative Topic Index** lists the literary themes and topics treated in the series as well as in other Literature Criticism series.

An alphabetical **Title Index** accompanies each volume of *CLC*. Listings of titles by authors covered in the given volume are followed by the author's name and the corresponding page numbers where the titles are discussed. English translations of foreign titles and variations of titles are cross-referenced to the title under which a work was originally published. Titles of novels, dramas, films, nonfiction books, and poetry, short story, or essay collections are printed in italics, while individual poems, short stories, and essays are printed in roman type within quotation marks.

In response to numerous suggestions from librarians, Thomson Gale also produces an annual cumulative title index that alphabetically lists all titles reviewed in *CLC* and is available to all customers. Additional copies of this index are available upon request. Librarians and patrons will welcome this separate index; it saves shelf space, is easy to use, and is recyclable upon receipt of the next edition.

Citing *Contemporary Literary Criticism*

When citing criticism reprinted in the Literary Criticism Series, students should provide complete bibliographic information so that the cited essay can be located in the original print or electronic source. Students who quote directly from reprinted criticism may use any accepted bibliographic format, such as University of Chicago Press style or Modern Language Association (MLA) style. Both the MLA and the University of Chicago formats are acceptable and recognized as being the current standards for citations. It is important, however, to choose one format for all citations; do not mix the two formats within a list of citations.

The examples below follow recommendations for preparing a bibliography set forth in *The Chicago Manual of Style,* 15th ed. (Chicago: The University of Chicago Press, 2003); the first example pertains to material drawn from periodicals, the second to material reprinted from books:

Miller, Mae. "Patterns of Nature and Confluence in Eudora Welty's *The Optimist's Daughter." Southern Quarterly: A Journal of the Arts in the South* 35, no. 1 (fall 1996): 55-61. Reprinted in *Contemporary Literary Criticism.* Vol. 220, edited by Jeffrey W. Hunter, 304-09. Detroit: Thomson Gale, 2006.

Aronoff, Myron J. "Learning to Live with Ambiguity: Balancing Ethical and Political Imperatives." In *The Spy Novels of John le Carré: Balancing Ethics and Politics,* 201-14. New York: St. Martin's Press, 1999. Reprinted in *Contemporary Literary Criticism.* Vol. 220, edited by Jeffrey W. Hunter, 84-92. Detroit: Thomson Gale, 2006.

The examples below follow recommendations for preparing a works cited list set forth in the *MLA Handbook for Writers of Research Papers,* 5th ed. (New York: The Modern Language Association of America, 1999); the first example pertains to material drawn from periodicals, the second to material reprinted from books:

Miller, Mae. "Patterns of Nature and Confluence in Eudora Welty's *The Optimist's Daughter." Southern Quarterly: A Journal of the Arts in the South* 35.1 (fall 1996): 55-61. Reprinted in *Contemporary Literary Criticism.* Ed. Jeffrey W. Hunter. Vol. 220. Detroit: Thomson Gale, 2006. 304-09.

Aronoff, Myron J. "Learning to Live with Ambiguity: Balancing Ethical and Political Imperatives." *The Spy Novels of John le Carré: Balancing Ethics and Politics,* New York: St. Martin's Press, 1999. 201-14. Reprinted in *Contemporary Literary Criticism.* Ed. Jeffrey W. Hunter. Vol. 220. Detroit: Thomson Gale, 2006. 84-92.

Suggestions are Welcome

Readers who wish to suggest new features, topics, or authors to appear in future volumes, or who have other suggestions or comments are cordially invited to call, write, or fax the Associate Product Manager:

Associate Product Manager, Literary Criticism Series
Thomson Gale
27500 Drake Road
Farmington Hills, MI 48331-3535
1-800-347-4253 (GALE)
Fax: 248-699-8983

Acknowledgments

The editors wish to thank the copyright holders of the criticism included in this volume and the permissions managers of many book and magazine publishing companies for assisting us in securing reproduction rights. Following is a list of the copyright holders who have granted us permission to reproduce material in this volume of *CLC*. Every effort has been made to trace copyright, but if omissions have been made, please let us know.

COPYRIGHTED MATERIAL IN *CLC*, VOLUME 235, WAS REPRODUCED FROM THE FOLLOWING PERIODICALS:

The American Journal of Sociology, v. 109, March, 2004 for a review of Elizabeth Long's "Book Clubs: Women and the Uses of Reading in Everyday Life" by Judith A. Howard. Reproduced by permission of the author.—*American Scholar,* v. 70, summer, 2001; v. 74, winter, 2005. Copyright © 2001, 2005 by the respective authors. Both reproduced by permission.—*ARIEL,* v. 34, October, 2003 for "Routes of Identity In Conversation with Bharati Mukherjee" by Sharmani Patricia Gabriel. Copyright 2003 The Board of Governors, The University of Calgary. Reproduced by permission of the publisher and the author.—*Beijing Review,* v. 41, January 26, 1998. Reproduced by permission.—*Canadian-American Slavic Studies,* v. 33, 1999. Copyright © 1999 Charles Schlacks, Jr., and Arizona State University. Reproduced by permission.—*Change,* v. 32, May, 2000; v. 36, January-February, 2004. Copyright © 2000, 2004 by Helen Dwight Reid Educational Foundation. Both reproduced with permission of the Helen Dwight Reid Educational Foundation, published by Heldref Publications, 1319 18th Street, NW, Washington, DC 20036-1802.—*Contemporary Literature,* v. 40, spring, 1999. Copyright © 1999 by the Board of Regents of the University of Wisconsin System. Reproduced by permission.—*Contemporary Sociology,* v. 34, March, 2005 for a review of Elizabeth Long's "Book Clubs: Women and the Uses of Reading in Everyday Life" by Andrea L. Press. Copyright © 2005 American Sociological Association. Reproduced by permission of the publisher and the author.—*Critical Studies in Media Communication,* vol. 20, September, 2003 for "A Dialectic with the Everyday: Communication and Cultural Politics on Oprah Winfrey's Book Club" by Ted Striphas. Reproduced by permission of Taylor & Francis, Ltd., http://www.tandf.co.uk/journals and the author.—*Critique,* v. 39, spring, 1998. Copyright © 1998 by Helen Dwight Reid Educational Foundation. Reproduced with permission of the Helen Dwight Reid Educational Foundation, published by Heldref Publications, 1319 18th Street, NW, Washington, DC 20036-1802.—*The Explicator,* v. 54, spring, 1996; v. 55, winter, 1997; v. 56, fall, 1997; v. 62, winter, 2004; v. 64, winter, 2006. Copyright © 1996, 1997, 2004, 2006 by Helen Dwight Reid Educational Foundation. All reproduced with permission of the Helen Dwight Reid Educational Foundation, published by Heldref Publications, 1319 18th Street, NW, Washington, DC 20036-1802.—*Extrapolation,* v. 36, winter, 1995; v. 37, fall, 1996. Copyright © 1995, 1996 by The Kent State University Press. All reproduced by permission./ v. 43, summer, 2002; v. 44, winter, 2003; v. 45, winter, 2004.; v. 45, spring, 2004; v. 46, summer, 2005. © 2002, 2003, 2004, 2005 Extrapolation. All reproduced by permission.—*First Things,* v. 145, August-September, 2004. Copyright © 2004 Institute on Religion and Public Life. All rights reserved. Reproduced by permission.— *"Future Tense Visionary Legend Bradbury Going Strong,"* August 31, 2000. Copyright © 2000 Jim Cherry. Reprinted by permission of the author.—*Independent (London),* March 18, 2000; June 3, 2002. Copyright © 2000, 2002 Independent Newspapers (UK) Ltd. Both reproduced by permission.—*Independent on Sunday (London),* July 28, 2002. Copyright © 2002 Independent Newspapers (UK) Ltd. Reproduced by permission.—*Journal of Adolescent & Adult Literacy,* v. 39, November, 1995; v. 47, October, 2003. Copyright © 1995, 2003 International Reading Association. Both reproduced by permission of the International Reading Association.—*Journal of American Studies,* v. 28, August, 1994 for "The Flight from the Good Life: *Fahrenheit 451* in the Context of Postwar American Dystopias" by David Seed. Copyright © 1994 Cambridge University Press. Reprinted with the permission of Cambridge University Press.—*Journal of Commonwealth Literature,* v. 38, April, 2003. Copyright © 2003 by Sage Publications. Reproduced by permission of Sage Publications Ltd. www.sagepub.co.uk—*Journal of Popular Culture,* v. 35, fall, 2001. Copyright © 2001 Basil Blackwell Ltd. Reproduced by permission of Blackwell Publishers.—*Journal of Reading,* v. 31, May, 1988. Copyright © 1988 International Reading Association. Reproduced by permission of the International Reading Association.—*Journal of Southern History,* v. LXXI, May, 2005. Copyright 2005 by the Southern Historical Association. Reprinted by permission of the Editor.—*Library Journal,* v. 126, November 15, 2001; v. 127, May 15, 2002; v. 131, July 1, 2006. Copyright © 2001, 2002, 2006 by Reed Elsevier, USA. All reprinted by permission of the publisher.—*Library Quarterly,* v. 71, April, 2001. Copyright © 2001 by The University of Chicago. All rights reserved. Reproduced by permission.—*Magazine of Fantasy and Science Fiction,* v. 96, February, 1999 for a review of China Miéville's *King Rat* by Charles De Lint. Copyright 1999 Spilogale, Inc. Reproduced by permission of the author./ v. 110, April, 2006 for a review of China Miéville's *Looking for Jake,* by James Sallis. Reproduced by permission of the author./v. 104, March, 2003. Reproduced by permission.—

Thomson Gale Literature Product Advisory Board

The members of the Thomson Gale Literature Product Advisory Board—reference librarians from public and academic library systems—represent a cross-section of our customer base and offer a variety of informed perspectives on both the presentation and content of our literature products. Advisory board members assess and define such quality issues as the relevance, currency, and usefulness of the author coverage, critical content, and literary topics included in our series; evaluate the layout, presentation, and general quality of our printed volumes; provide feedback on the criteria used for selecting authors and topics covered in our series; provide suggestions for potential enhancements to our series; identify any gaps in our coverage of authors or literary topics, recommending authors or topics for inclusion; analyze the appropriateness of our content and presentation for various user audiences, such as high school students, undergraduates, graduate students, librarians, and educators; and offer feedback on any proposed changes/enhancements to our series. We wish to thank the following advisors for their advice throughout the year.

Contemporary and Historic Book Clubs

INTRODUCTION

Television personality Oprah Winfrey sparked a resurgence in the phenomenon of book clubs when she formed a club for viewers of her popular *Oprah Winfrey Show.* While some newcomers to the book club concept were surprised to learn that it is not a new idea (they were called salons in eras past), others saw the opportunity to utilize new technology, notably the Internet, to encourage the revitalization of this combination of intellectual development and social connection. Teachers and school counselors have also begun to use book clubs to inspire students to appreciate literature and even to rehabilitate adolescents struggling with reading, schoolwork, or other issues.

Book clubs are not exclusive to scholars, and they are no longer limited by geographic constraints or even real-time schedules. Winfrey's club, for example, has no specific meeting place or time (readers who miss the live episode discussing the book can read the highlights on Oprah.com), and the books she identifies for club members' perusal are universally available and matched to the reading level of most American adults. While some have criticized Winfrey's title selections as patronizing or overly reactionary to popular best-selling trends, many others have acknowledged that her spotlighting of classic works such as William Faulkner's *As I Lay Dying,* Leo Tolstoy's *Anna Karenina,* Toni Morrison's *The Bluest Eye,* and Gabriel García Márquez's *One Hundred Years of Solitude* has likely brought them to a previously inaccessible readership. This supposition is supported by *Oprah* viewers, who commonly report that, without Winfrey's encouragement, they would never have read these types of works.

While many book clubs are "virtual," the social component remains key for some. Inside jokes about people who won't read without the promise of a monthly buffet are common among book club devotees. For some people, the process of conversing with another person on the subject of a book is an ideal way to make a human connection; for others, the club's schedule with its implied deadlines provides the needed impetus to finally "get around to" reading.

REPRESENTATIVE WORKS

Ted Balcolm
Book Discussions for Adults: A Leader's Guide (nonfiction) 1992

Shireen Dodson
Mother-Daughter Book Club (nonfiction) 1997

Marcia Fineman
Talking about Books (nonfiction) 1997

Monique Greenwood, Lynda Johnson, and Tracy Mitchell-Brown
The Go on Girl! Book Club Guide for Reading Groups (nonfiction) 1999

Rachel W. Jacobsohn
Reading Group Handbook (nonfiction) 1998

Diana Loevy
The Book Club Companion (nonfiction) 2006

Elizabeth Long
Book Clubs: Women and the Uses of Reading in Everyday Life (nonfiction) 2005

Pat Neblett
Circles of Sisterhood: A Book Discussion Group Guide for Women of Color (nonfiction) 1996

Janice Radway
A Feeling for Books: The Book-of-the-Month Club, Literary Taste, and Middle-class Desire (nonfiction) 1997

Kathleen Rooney
Reading with Oprah: The Book Club That Changed America (nonfiction) 2005

Rollene Saal
New York Public Library Guide to Reading Groups (nonfiction) 1995

Ellen Slezak
The Book Group Book (nonfiction) 2000

Betty Holland Wiesepape
Lone Star Chapters: The Story of Texas Literary Clubs (nonfiction) 2005

THE BOOK CLUB PHENOMENON

Lee Mountain (essay date May 1988)

SOURCE: Mountain, Lee. "In Search of Book Lovers." *Journal of Reading* 31, no. 8 (May 1988): 754-55.

[*In the following essay, Mountain offers suggestions for finding like-minded reading aficionados.*]

You love to read, and you'd like to meet others who also love to read. Good idea! But suppose you already know the people in your library's Great Books Discussion Group, and you'd like to find some new friends who are avid readers. Surely there are other book lovers out there, even outside the teaching profession. Where can you go to spend an evening with these interesting people?

One place, in most large U.S. cities, is the Scrabble Club. Book lovers often have impressive vocabularies, so they gather where the word buffs go. If word play appeals to you, you can find thousands of kindred spirits though the national network of Scrabble Crossword Game Players, Inc., PO Box 700 Front Street Garden, Greenport NY 11944. This organization sponsors a national tournament biannually. It is the headquarters for local clubs which use numbers in their identification. The meeting format for most Scrabble Clubs involves three games during an evening. Your performance on the first game establishes your level of expertise; you are then matched with suitable competition for the other two games.

Another place to find lovers of literature is the Storytellers Guild. This organization, through its national, regional, and local groups, brings together lovers of folklore, tall tales, regional stories, and literature in the oral tradition. You can locate the group nearest you by writing NAPPS (National Association for the Preservation and Perpetuation of Storytelling), PO Box 309, Jonesborough TN 37659. The regional and local storytellers' meetings are becoming popular entertainment events in many states. Before the best storytellers compete at regional festivals, they polish their skills in front of appreciative local audiences. In these audiences, the readers of folklore can easily find each other.

Networking is equally convenient for readers who love drama, from Punch and Judy scripts to medieval and renaissance plays. The Punch and Judy group might find like-minded associates in a local puppetry guild affiliated with Puppeteers of America, 5 Cricklewood Path, Pasadena CA 91107. This organization publishes *The Puppetry Journal,* which is good reading material for teachers who recognize the classroom material of puppetry. The membership of the organization includes many groups besides teachers, however, and attracts an age range from teens to retirees.

Other drama enthusiasts can contact a national organization that brings together lovers of medieval and renaissance literature, The Society of Creative Anachronisms, PO Box 360743, Milipitas CA 94035. This society has guilds for minstrels, bards, dancers, and costumers. These special interest groups often help out with Renaissance Festivals staged in a variety of locations. These book lovers also enjoy fiction and nonfiction related to the medieval and renaissance periods.

For book lovers in remote locations, there is a mail-contact organization called the Single Booklovers of America, Box 117, Gradyville PA 19039. It attempts to put lovers of published language in touch with one another through its newsletter.

Many book lovers enjoy a variety of activities related to language, such as speaking (at Toastmasters Clubs) and writing (in authors' organizations). Avid readers also congregate in library associations and in groups that volunteer to help adult illiterates.

So if you love to read, and you want to meet others with a passion for books, you have a good chance of finding those others and getting to know them through organizations where book lovers congregate. Why not see which ones have chapters in your area?

James Flood and Diane Lapp (essay date April 1994)

SOURCE: Flood, James, and Diane Lapp. "Teacher Book Clubs: Establishing Literature Discussion Groups for Teachers." *Reading Teacher* 47, no. 7 (April 1994): 574-76.

[*In the following essay, Flood and Lapp present direction for teachers interested in starting a book club for colleagues.*]

Are you looking for something new to do for professional development at your school? Something that your colleagues will enjoy and take an active role in? Establishing a book club may be just what you're looking for.

In the past few years, book clubs have grown in popularity, both in the general public and in education circles. The March 11, 1990, *Chicago Sun-Times* reported, "These days, it's positively *de riguer* among baby-boom intelligencia to carve out a few hours once a month to pick apart a piece of literature and a buffet table"; and the March 13, 1992, edition of *The New York Times* reported on the efforts of one magazine to develop reading discussion groups among its readers by providing cards that inquired about readers' interest in forming book clubs. "More than 8,200 readers filled out the card that was included. The magazine matched them up by ZIP code and established 500 salons (reading discussion groups)" (Rabinovitz, 1992).

WHY IS THERE SO MUCH INTEREST IN BOOK CLUBS?

Book clubs are so popular because they provide an intellectual social forum where people can share ideas, thoughts, feelings, and reactions to a piece of literature.

The talk that takes place during book club meetings is often based on a personal response to literature in which participants read selections and share insights based on their own experiences with the text. Probst (1991) and others have argued for the reader-response approach to literature based on Rosenblatt's (1991) work, suggesting that competent, satisfied readers often define themselves against the background of the text and the text against the background they themselves provide. He and other educators (e.g., Purves, in press), however, have argued that this analysis must be done in a social context in which readers learn to pay attention to the critical influence of other people's responses about the meaning and significance they derive from a particular literary work. The interactions between the reader and the text and among the reader and other readers make book clubs an ideal tool for increasing awareness and understanding among book club participants.

How Do Book Clubs Function as a Professional Development Tool?

During the past 2 years, we have been involved in a book club with elementary school teachers in a local San Diego school in which the students come from many different cultural backgrounds. The purpose for our book club was to focus on the theme of multiculturalism in American society by reading contemporary fiction. We found that teachers and other staff members who participated in book clubs which focused on issues of multiculturalism often developed an awareness of other cultures by identifying similarities in their own lives with the lives of characters in stories. Participants often began to examine connections between their personal experiences and the text and to explore the function that they played, as readers, in the development of those connections (Flood, Lapp, & Ranck-Buhr, 1993). In addition to a growing understanding about issues related to multiculturalism, we realized that we also expanded our understanding about our own literacy processing as well as our understanding of teaching and learning.

Let's take a look at a group of teachers participating in a book club discussion about "Mexicans," a short story about a child's feelings toward the habits and rituals of her traditional grandmother, from the book *Woman Hollering Creek* by Sandra Cisneros (1991). One participant, Gil, a Euro-American male, remarked:

> I read it and I had some feelings. I read it again. I didn't write anything right away. I read it again. Then I wrote. I just wanted it to kinda work. I don't know if it was the mood I was in or what, I had this incredible opening of my childhood psyche by reading this. People would say this is Hispanic. You're not Hispanic. But I think it transcended all that . . .

Another participant, Jack, also a Euro-American male, noted, "I was most struck that you read it, you thought about it, you read it again, and you thought about it again."

In this example, Gil stated his belief that literature can be a vehicle for developing personal understanding and expanding views of other cultures—seeing similarities between different cultural groups. In addition, he also began to think about and analyze his own literacy processing, which allowed him to make connections between his life as a teacher and his life as a reader.

Other participants in the group saw the "realities" of their own cultures in the works and made connections from the text to their own lives. Alicia, a Hispanic female, remarked, "All that discipline stuff that happens in the story is very typical, certainly in Hispanic families . . . there is something there that is particular to certain cultures (certainly to my own experience)."

Through their interactions with the text and with one another, the members of the book club began to develop an awareness of similarities among themselves, their colleagues, and their students despite their different cultural backgrounds. As one Euro-American teacher commented, "These stories helped remind me that my students have a life beyond the classroom."

How Can a Book Club Become a Reality?

Getting Started

First, find out who is interested in participating in a book club. You might consider putting together an informative newsletter or memo to let other teachers know what a book club is and what purposes it can serve in your school.

Once you have a few people willing to participate, you should look at the following:

- the resources that will be needed;
- the amount of time that is available for the book club;
- the kind of space that is available;
- the materials that are available to you.

A portion of your time will also need to be spent on management issues involved in establishing a book club. Some of these include selecting books and making sure they are available in the necessary quantities.

Once you have the books, you will need to decide on a meeting place. It's best to find a location that has comfortable seating for all of the members of the book club. If your book club will be taking place at your school site, you might select a particular classroom, your library/media center, or the teachers' lounge.

How Do You Select Books?

Selecting books that will be used for book clubs is no different than selecting books for any other recreational reading activity. First, you will want to decide the type of materials you plan to read. Text length is a consideration for very busy professionals. When you start your book club, it might be best to start with short books or short stories that can be finished in brief periods of time. You will have time later to read long novels when participants have enough time for them and after participants can see how beneficial a book club can be. Once the book club is operating, encourage members to suggest new titles.

We have found that collections of short stories work well for several reasons: They provide reading material for several sessions, they are short enough to be read in one sitting, and they cover a wide variety of topics. The following is a list of books that we have used in our book club. The first four selections are collections of short stories and the others are short novels.

> *Woman Hollering Creek* by Sandra Cisneros (1991)
>
> *House on Mango Street* by Sandra Cisneros (1989)
>
> *The Assignation* by Joyce Carol Oates (1988)
>
> *Spider Woman's Granddaughters* edited by Paula Gunn Allen (1989)
>
> *The Bluest Eye* by Toni Morrison (1972)
>
> *Their Eyes Were Watching God* by Zora Neale Hurston (1991)
>
> *The Joy Luck Club* by Amy Tan (1989)

The First Meeting

After the organizational issues are out of the way and members have read the first selection, you will be ready for your first book club meeting. Book club meetings should be held for about an hour or an hour and a half. The number of times your book club meets each month may depend on the length of the reading selection. We try to meet once a month.

As you begin your discussion, you might ask the members, "What did you think about the book?" This question or a similarly broad one will encourage discussion. Once the discussion begins, it should be free flowing. If it isn't, you may want to ask, "What feelings did you have as you were reading the book? Did the story cause you to think about other experiences you've had?" Be sure to keep your questions very broad so that everyone feels free to contribute. Once a discussion begins, it tends to flow very easily, leaving little need for additional questions.

Journal Writing

Journal writing is an excellent method for encouraging members to reflect on their readings and on the discussions in which they've participated. Members may write their thoughts, feelings, and reflections about the reading in their journals when reading the selections on their own. You may want to encourage members to bring their journals with them to the book club meetings. Sometimes these writings spur discussions within the group. After the group discussion of the reading, members should be encouraged to write in their journals again. This repeated response procedure encourages members to reflect on changes in their ideas and responses to the literature after they've had the opportunity to discuss the reading with their colleagues and friends. We've found that our ideas are often enhanced after we hear the thoughts of others.

A Final Note

Literature discussion groups hold promise as effective tools for our personal development as teachers. The exchanges that result from discussions about literature create environments that welcome participation and the sharing of diverse points of view. As one social studies teacher, who participated in a book club, said about his exchanges with his colleagues: "[Before this] . . . at my school, when we did talk, we were so angry and worn out that all we did was complain or talk shop. [Then we had a book club and things changed.] I really enjoyed this" (Rabinovitz, 1992).

Note

The work that is reported in this column was supported, in part, by a National Reading Research Center project of the Universities of Georgia and Maryland (PR/Award No. 117A200071), as administered by the Office of Educational Research and Improvement, U.S. Office of Education. It was also supported, in part, by a grant from the Dean's Office, College of Education, San Diego State University.

References

Allen, P. G. (Ed.). (1989). *Spider woman's granddaughters.* New York: Ballantine.

Cisneros, S. (1989). *House on Mango Street.* New York: Random House.

Cisneros, S. (1991). *Woman hollering creek.* New York: Random House.

Flood, J., Lapp, D., & Ranck-Buhr, W. (1993, March). *A study of teachers' and preservice teachers' participation in contemporary multicultural fiction reading discussion groups.* Paper presented at the meeting of the American Educational Research Association, Atlanta, GA.

Hurston, Z. N. (1991). *Their eyes were watching God.* Urbana, IL: University of Illinois Press.

Morrison, T. (1972). *The bluest eye.* New York: Washington Square.

Oates, J. C. (1988). *The assignation.* New York: Harper & Row.

Probst, R. (1991). Response to literature. In J. Flood, J. Jensen, D. Lapp, & J. Squire (Eds.), *Handbook of research in the teaching of the English language arts* (pp. 655-663). New York: Macmillan.

Purves, A. (in press). Honesty in assessment and curriculum in literature. In J. Flood & J. Langer (Eds.), *Literature and instruction: Practice and policy.* New York: Scholastic.

Rabinvoitz, J. (1992, April 13). An attempted comeback for the literary salon. *The New York Times,* C15.

Rosenblatt, L. (1991). Literary theory. In J. Flood, J. Jensen, D. Lapp, & J. Squire (Eds), *Handbook of research in the teaching of the English language arts* (pp. 57-62). New York: Macmillan.

Tan, A. (1989). *The joy luck club.* New York: Putnam.

Margaret H. Hill and Leigh Van Horn (essay date November 1995)

SOURCE: Hill, Margaret H., and Leigh Van Horn. "Book Club Goes to Jail: Can Book Clubs Replace Gangs?" *Journal of Adolescent & Adult Literacy* 39, no. 3 (November 1995): 180-88.

[*Below, Hill and Van Horn recount the development of a successful rehabilitative book club, implemented at a juvenile detention center where youths were incarcerated.*]

"I know who stole the feast!" Anna yelled excitedly as graduate student/seventh-grade teacher Leigh entered the room for her second day of working with troubled youth. "We worked until late last night! We solved the mystery!"

Leigh smiled at her student, Anna, with enthusiasm, knowing the tremendous accomplishment of this statement. The mystery they had solved was *The Eleventh Hour* by Graeme Base.

Last summer, Leigh Van Horn, as part of her master's project, worked at a juvenile detention center where youth between the ages of 11 and 17 are incarcerated for up to 2 years for severe crimes, many of them gang related. This detention center is home to both girls and boys. During the day, public school teachers hold classes based upon the required district and state curriculum for secondary school. However, no regular classes were held during the month of July when Leigh proposed to initiate Book Club. Leigh spent 2 hours twice a week working with a group of students who ranged from good to strong readers, but reluctant writers. None were given the opportunity to read and discuss books freely in the regular academic program.

WHAT IS BOOK CLUB?

During the school year, Leigh is a seventh-grade reading teacher, but for her master's degree she wanted to research a different approach to reading that she could apply to her own seventh-grade classroom. She prepared herself by reading about literature response in the middle schools (Andrasick, 1990; Atwell, 1987; Beach, 1993; Marshall, Smagorinsky, & Smith, 1994; Purves & Beach, 1972; Rief, 1992), but when she discovered the Book Club model (Raphael, McMahon et al., 1991), she wanted to try the approach with the youth at the detention center, all of whom were at risk.

Briefly, Book Club is based on a social constructivist perspective which supports the interaction among reader, text, and the social context. This viewpoint is consistent with Vygotsky's (1986) focus upon the interaction of thought and language development, in which he argued that verbal thought develops as a result of the intersection of thought and language. In addition, as Rosenblatt (1978) argued, a literacy experience should unite personal experiences with text and thinking so that the reader will construct meaning from text. Raphael and McMahon (1994) indicated that Book Club evolved from this social constructivist stance linking learner and text through the intersection of literature-based reading instruction and student-led response groups. Its purpose was to investigate how literature-based instruction might be used to include reading comprehension and literature response through the processes of reading, writing, instruction, and discussion.

Book Clubs are student-led groups of three to six students who meet to discuss and write about what they have read. Book Club was developed for elementary-aged children (Raphael & McMahon, 1994; Raphael, Goatley et al., 1991), for culturally diverse populations (McMahon, 1992a, 1992b, 1992c; Pardo, 1992), and for special education populations (Goatley & Raphael, 1992). However, this model had not previously been applied to older students at risk, such as those at the juvenile detention center.

Leigh believed Book Club to be a powerful model as she investigated three questions. (a) How well would students at the juvenile detention center cooperate in group discussion? (b) How well would books help to stimulate student writing which stretched beyond journal responses to produce public pieces? (c) How might books help students gain a greater understanding of social justice? Her data collection contained her field notes, transcriptions of conversations, student journals and written work, and transcriptions of frequent debriefings with her supervisor.

CAN BOOK CLUB REPLACE GANGS?

Leigh wanted to extend the concept of Book Club at the juvenile detention center with youth who sometimes take pride in being aliterate (those who choose not to read or write). However, she was greatly surprised to find that the group of students who chose to work with her were strong readers and often used writing as a catharsis to help them through difficult emotional trials. She hypothesized that if youth were drawn easily into gangs, then they might also be drawn into a Book Club because it offered identity to students, established an environment for peer approval and recognition, and gave students a chance to excel in a way they hadn't before. During the 5-week course, Leigh spent 4 hours per week for 3 weeks (2 hours twice a week) with students at the detention center.

She prepared by reading everything she could about Book Club. And, even though Book Club is established for peer leadership, Leigh believed that initially the students at the detention center would need strong modeling from an adult facilitator waiting for the "teachable moment." Leigh served initially as facilitator but finally became a participant observer.

Book Club was strictly a volunteer program. Leigh explained the idea to all eligible students at the facility. About 20% of the residents indicated that they would like to join the club. Initially, two groups of five volunteered. Leigh started her group of five (three boys and two girls of middle school age whose names were changed for this article to protect their legal rights and confidentiality) by introducing herself and the books and magazines she liked to read (suspense and mystery) and the poetry and short stories she liked to write. Then she invited them to do the same. Because Anna was the most extroverted member of this Book Club, she broke the ice for them. "I like horror stories, mysteries, and romance. I just read Lois Duncan's *Don't Look Behind You*."

MYSTERY BECOMES THE HOOK

With the ice broken, others added what they had read recently. Vivian liked horror and Sweet Valley High novels. Steve liked V. C. Andrews, Danielle Steele, and R. L. Stine. Mark said he hadn't had much time for reading but he did own a book on World War II and had been reading about the Holocaust, although specific titles and authors did not come to mind. He spoke of a trip to the San Jacinto Monument where he saw names of some relatives inscribed on a plaque about World War II. Leigh wrote:

We continued around the circle throwing out titles and ideas. Talk turned to adventure mysteries and the name Indiana Jones came up. I commented about my fascination with the marker-symbol Indiana Jones uses to discover the location for the treasure in one of the stories. Mark commented that he liked the one where Indiana was searching for the Cup of Life. Anna corrected him by calling it the Holy Grail. The talk then turned to the methods used by Indiana—diaries of his father, hieroglyphics, other symbols.

Leigh pulled out her bag with multiple copies of Graeme Base's *The Eleventh Hour*. "My intention was to use this as an introduction to mysteries," she stated. She talked about Base, what he had written, and what kind of a person he was. Then she showed them the book and mentioned the many hidden clues in it. She let the students go through their own books and waited for a response.

Mark said, "It reads like a poem!"

Almost immediately the students began seeing the clues on the pages. She asked them what they could tell from the pencils around the border on the first page. Right away they read the words, "Drawing conclusions from sketchy clues may lead you astray. Sharpen your eyes and your wits. Get the point?"

One of them noticed the squares on the pencils with letters that spelled the words, "It was not Max!"

"They were off!" Leigh explained. "I could scarcely contain them."

As Leigh observed, she wrote, "Anna is highly organized. She wants to write everything we have found. Mark and Steve continue a heated dialogue, each asking questions and sometimes answering each other."

They noticed "Red Herring" spelled on croquet balls. Anna told the group a herring was a fish but not characteristically red. "This must mean that this was not a helpful comment—something like fishy or a fish out of water." The others respected her conclusion.

Mark worried about someone looking ahead and finding the answer. Steve speculated that the answer would be on the last page. But after they read the entire poem, they found that there were even more questions and many more clues.

For over 2 hours Leigh worked with them as they pondered the mystery, discussed, questioned, and developed strategies for problem solving. From this first day, Leigh had accomplished a tremendous amount of initial assessment of the students' reading interests and backgrounds and their ability to discuss an author's style, make predictions and inferences, draw conclusions, question, monitor, work within context, and set goals for their next meeting. After just one session, this group of five began to work together, to respect each other's literacy responses, and learn to trust each other.

Leigh wrote:

> Thanks to the teachable moment, we accomplished a great deal on the first meeting. I did not know that they would be so interested in mysteries. However, Anna began to talk about them. The others picked up on her interest and made their own connections to books and book topics. I had been prepared with a variety of genre and topics, but it was Base's mystery which not only helped solidify their focus and goals for the Book Club, but also united the group as they worked together to solve the mystery and establish a goal of working through more mysteries. Thus, with anticipation, both they and I waited for our next meeting.

But Will They Write?

Leigh's purpose during the second meeting was to encourage them to write a response rather than talk it. They were excited to discuss the mystery from *The Eleventh Hour* and tell how they worked together in their dorm to solve the mystery. What was interesting were the different ways in which they reached their conclusions. Sam was honest and said he had peeked at the information behind the seal. Anna said Sam had ruined it for her, but said that she had suspected Kilroy, the mouse, because of the clue, "Kilroy speaks the truth." Mark said he noticed the mouse was missing on one page, that the mouse was moving ahead in the sack race, and that he knew mice ate a lot. His journal was filled with notes, and he spent some time explaining how he had deciphered the clue on the bingo board, making notes as he explained. He tested his idea that it was Kilroy by deciphering the code on the back page. Leigh brought them copies of Morse code, and they experimented further with the code breaking. Then they talked about the hieroglyphics and other codes in the book.

Next, Leigh presented another mystery to them. In Van Allsburg's *The Wretched Stone,* strange things happen. Together they read and predicted what might happen and what was the stone. Then she gave each student a special journal and asked them to write down what their predictions were and why. Leigh wrote with them. Mark was hesitant, but when he saw her writing, he began to write too. Then they passed their predictions around and each wrote additional comments.

Anna's entry was a very powerful commentary on her thoughts and how they changed during the reading. She concluded that the stone was a symbol for television and that the story was a parable. They discussed the meaning of parable. Sam and Vivian both thought the stone was more magical and did not connect it to televi-sion. Mark thought the stone might reflect something of the story of evolution and that those who ignored it had evolved, while those who did not remained apes.

When Sam asked if they would read longer books, Leigh took the opportunity to introduce Avi and some of his books. They talked about Avi and what they had already read by him. Vivian said that she had read *The True Confessions of Charlotte Doyle.* She told the rest of the group about the book.

Sam read the back cover of *The True Confessions of Charlotte Doyle* and asked about Avi and his book about Poe. "Could you bring a book by Poe?" he asked Leigh. She made a note to bring in *The Tales of Edgar Allan Poe.*

Leigh introduced *Something Upstairs* by Avi. They looked at the cover and silently read the introduction. At the end of the introduction, Avi stated that he wrote the story as Kenny told it to him and that he believed it to be true. They read the first chapter silently and then discussed the setting, the problem, and possible solutions. This day ended with the group members setting their reading goal for Tuesday.

Are You Afraid to Work with Us?

Sam reminded the group members that none would have visitors over the weekend so that they would have time to read. Then he asked Leigh, "Aren't you afraid to be here?"

Leigh responded, "No." Then she asked Sam, "Why?"

Sam said bluntly, "We're criminals!"

Leigh then asked Sam and the rest if they thought they were criminals.

They all responded, "No!"

Leigh then asked if they were afraid.

Sam indicated that he was and that this was the first time he had been in trouble.

Leigh accepted and respected their feelings. She concluded her journal that day by saying, "I think they are all looking forward to the next meeting. I know I am!"

Book Club Makes Wider Connections

On Tuesday, Leigh arrived and the students were excited to see her. She had been met by the principal who indicated that Sam had already shared Avi's mystery with him. Vivian was excited because the bookmobile had come by, and she had found another book by Van Allsburg called *The Sweetest Fig.*

"Already they were making connections of their own and extending response groups outside of the Book Club," Leigh wrote.

This was a good moment to introduce other books by Van Allsburg. Leigh gave them each a planning sheet to use to help plan what they would talk about when they discussed each selection. The planning sheet directed the readers to decide what the author meant to say, whether they liked what they had read, what they liked about the book, what they would change, and the questions they might ask the author about his/her book. This was a modification of those suggested by Raphael, McMahon et al. (1991).

The interesting thing about the discussion was that they came to the conclusion that Van Allsburg's books all had a mystery or a message in them. Vivian's book began like a fable, so they knew to look for a moralistic message. At first, Sam was not able to see the meaning of his book, *The Stranger,* but then he began to point out clues. As he read them aloud to the group he answered his own questions. They talked about how thinking aloud helps. Leigh was then able to respond to Anna's request for another book like *The Eleventh Hour.* She gave her Arthur Geisert's *Pigs from A to Z.* Sam wanted something written by Poe, so she gave him a collection of his short stories along with Avi's *The Man Who Was Poe.*

Leigh then used Van Allsburg's *The Mysteries of Harris Burdick* to inspire further mystery reading. Each of the students chose an illustration to write about. Leigh also introduced them to Joan Lowery Nixon's *The Other Side of Dark.* Just as she had done with Avi, she talked about Nixon, the writer.

Book Clubs Might Replace Gangs

Several students discussed the importance of talking about books. Anna said that she looked forward to coming to Book Club. She said that she had a little sister and that when she was released from the detention center she would like to help her sister and friends establish a Book Club. She hoped that they would not join a gang. Sam said that he wanted to read some of Poe's short stories with others in his dorm. He liked the camaraderie that Book Club had brought to him and his friends. Anna offered to come to Leigh's class to help establish Book Club when she was released. Leigh welcomed her offer.

"When they left, they hugged me and said that they were glad I was there. So was I!" wrote Leigh.

It was during this meeting that Vivian shared her poem about power in education.

Power

I have power as an educated woman because people will
listen when I speak, not turn away.
When I show my intelligence, they will not look at my
body, but listen to my mind!
I will get respect for being me, not for what they see.
That is how I get power
by being an educated woman.

Writing Becomes a Catharsis

By the third Book Club session, students were responding through meaningful connections, writing poems and short stories of their own, and asking for response to their writing. They were already internalizing the process of group ownership and group responsibility.

Vivian also asked if Leigh would call Vivian's mother and share her work with her mother. Leigh did. Vivian's mother reported that Vivian was smiling during the last home visit and seemed to feel good about herself. She commented that Leigh was very important to Vivian and asked if Leigh would please call her before the Book Club ended for the summer.

On Thursday, they began by talking about the memories each book sparked. Leigh brought in some models of literacy journals from her students in school. The group was surprised to see that responses could be in the form of poems and art. This sparked a whole round of discussions of poetry and what the specific poems meant to them. Anna brought in her own book of poems to share. They took turns reading them, and Anna explained the process she went through in writing a poem as well as what poetry meant to her. She said that she usually wrote when she was angry or upset, and that someone reading her poems might think she was crazy.

Vivian disclosed that she had written poems while in a mental hospital and that the poems were a pathway into her mind. This conversation sparked a torrent of memories and concerns—attempted suicides, the deaths of friends, pregnancies, relationships with parents and friends. There was silence; then there were sighs.

Leigh added, "They seem to be torn between living the same life over and over, or making a change to the unknown. It is hard for them to think beyond the moment."

Then Sam indicated that he was ready to read Poe's "The Tell Tale Heart" (from Poe, 1991). He read with tremendous emotion and power. He stopped several times to tell us that he loved this story and pointed out details for us to notice. He thought it was humorous that someone would want to kill someone else because of the way his eye looked and that the author kept reminding the audience that he wasn't crazy, thus proving that he probably was crazy. When Sam finished, Anna seized the moment to insist that she do the reading at the next meeting. Vivian also wanted to prepare something to read to the group.

THE STUDENTS TAKE CONTROL OF BOOK CLUB

Leigh wrote, "They have taken control of their Book Club. They choose their own books, explain how they will discuss them, and look at extension activities. They are using me only as a resource at this point. They have become the experts of their books." By this time, they indicated that they would like Book Club to become a permanent fixture at the detention center.

At the following session, Leigh began by returning the responses she had written to them after reading their book responses. She also valued Mark's reentry. She planned to read *The Other Side of Dark,* but Mark had missed a time and had not had a chance to catch up. She emphasized to him that she greatly valued his input and that they would postpone the discussion until next time. Leigh also enjoyed watching as each student read her responses to them.

To Vivian she commented about her concise way of recording deep emotions. She complimented Sam's beautiful power of description. She praised Anna's prolific and analytical mind. She also had typed their poetry and gave each student clean copies so that they could appreciate the typed format and make final editing comments or changes.

Then Anna began reading Poe's short story "The Masque of the Red Death." Without prompting, Anna stopped every few paragraphs and explained what was going on. She explained that the Red Death probably was the Bubonic Plague.

Leigh concluded that day by reading an excerpt from "Sleeping Beauty," saying, "Sometimes I feel like the prince who has come within these walls to wake these sleeping beauties and help them to feel the power that comes with believing in themselves."

The summer session drew to an end. During the last session they read and responded to the pieces they had written for the Book Club anthology. They also made plans for the center newsletter. It was apparent they had become intensely aware of audience through these discussions and responses.

LEIGH'S MORAL DILEMMA

During the summer, Leigh supplied the group with many paperback books, but this day Vivian and Anna asked for Vincent Bugliosi and Curt Gentry's *Helter*

Skelter (1974). Leigh confided that all sorts of thoughts ran through her head about lying to them by saying the book was out of print, but finally decided to tell them the truth. Leigh just did not think that it was an appropriate book for them, and they accepted her comments. It was a book that they could read on their own if they so chose after they were released, but as a teacher, she felt that other books were more appropriate. They accepted her honesty as she reminded them that she was a teacher outside the center.

Vivian was a member of a gang and had a great deal of interest in reading about gangs. Leigh handed her S. E. Hinton's *The Outsiders.* Anna said, "It sounded like a *West Side Story* type of book." Leigh confirmed that it was similar. The alternatives satisfied the youth.

THEIR WRITING BECOMES PUBLIC

The last writing response involved found poems. Leigh's definition of found poems was finding favorite passages from a specific piece by another author and making it their own. Both Vivian and Mark had tremendous difficulty with their pieces, initially copying an entire passage that they liked. But Anna intervened to share hers and explained how she had constructed a piece from one line she copied from Base's *The Sign of the Seahorse.* In the end Vivian and Mark constructed pieces. Their surprised accomplishment created excitement within the group.

Leigh wrote about the last day, "Each day they surprise me. Today is no exception. Each member has acknowledged his or her achievement in both reading and original composition."

Leigh's final summary of her work with the five students indicated her growth as she came to understand the interconnections between reading and writing. Raphael and McMahon (1994) see writing in the Book Club Project as a means for students to respond to what they have read by creating character sketches, recording interesting dialogues, posing questions/comments they may have, and reflecting upon what has been read. Leigh wanted to extend this concept to include writing based upon the group's interaction and reaction to the text. Their writing included reaction to the text, feelings about what was read, found poems created through text interpretation and manipulation, and writings based upon illustrations taken from the text. For example, after reading *The Wretched Stone,* the students wrote to state their opinion of Van Allsburg's intent and their interpretation of the meaning of the stone. To create found poems, stories or poems were chosen at random, and students chose words and phrases that appealed to them. Then, they analyzed their choices for theme and mood. Students rearranged the text and added their own words to reinforce the previously determined central idea.

Students composed written pieces based upon illustrations using *The Mysteries of Harris Burdick.* They chose specific illustrations and composed poems after brainstorming their own list of words and thoughts which came to mind as they studied the illustrations. As noted by Raphael, McMahon et al. (1991) in their study, students were somewhat resistant to the idea of open-ended responses. These researchers suggested that this may be due to the students' long history in remedial classes with a subskill orientation. Leigh strengthened her students' instruction by modeling her own thinking as she wrote, but when students were invited to record their thoughts as they read outside of the group meeting, none took advantage of this opportunity. Leigh believed that their uncertainties would be alleviated through continued exposure to open-ended writing experiences over time. At the end of the 3-week period, the students seemed pleased with the writing they had done, although they still doubted their abilities.

COMPONENTS OF SUCCESS

ENTHUSIASM.

Leigh believed that enthusiasm was the key. However, it cannot be created but rather must be located and nurtured. The very things that motivate us also motivate students. Leigh valued them as individuals and celebrated and respected their opinions, thoughts, and writings. Also, she let them know that the things they did had impact beyond the classroom or their group into the world around them. "They are enthusiastic because they have discovered the wonder of the talent and ideas within themselves," she wrote.

INVOLVED AND RESPECTED DISCUSSIONS.

According to Raphael, McMahon et al. (1991), the discussion component of the Book Club is a culmination of all other components. Having read the material, students were given a forum in which they could talk about what they had read. Ideally this talk should be student generated and guided; however, students beginning a Book Club do need some instruction concerning discussion focus, listening, taking turns, and building upon the ideas of others. As predicted by Raphael, McMahon et al. (1991), these students began the process of discussion by waiting to see what Leigh would say. As might be expected, they were waiting for the one correct answer which they hoped Leigh would eventually supply. But, by giving them clues about how to begin and by going through repeated think-aloud simulations, Leigh was able to convey the idea that talk would be centered around their interests and discoveries of the text, not hers. Guidelines such as commenting on word choice, style, character, plot events, predictions, conclusions, and comparisons could be used by the students to formulate discussion.

In the beginning, the students were reluctant to state opinions and/or initiate discussion. Their comments were preceded by remarks such as "This is probably wrong, but . . ." and "I'm not really sure, but . . .". With encouragement and trust, the students began to generate their own topics and ideas, even to relate Book Club readings to outside readings. In addition, students made connections between the text and their own lives as they empathized with characters and used their own feelings to understand a deeper significance within the stories. Leigh believed that continued experiences of this nature would allow these students to extend their thinking. With regard to the format of their discussion, the students listened and took turns speaking about their own ideas, but were still reluctant to build upon the ideas of others. Again, Leigh felt that this was something which would develop through repeated exposure to discussion.

Leigh became a powerful learner/observer/model within this Book Club. Few people had given these youth the respect that Leigh had. She valued each expression, whether oral or written. At one point she wrote, "I feel as if every word they put down has potential, and it pains me to see any wasted." Leigh showed them respect by waiting until they could all be there for their discussions, by commenting on each journal entry, and by accepting their choice of reading/writing subject matter. She valued their thinking by helping them make links, by responding, and by extending further their thinking. She encouraged their problem-solving techniques as she realized the different avenues each took to solve mysteries. She offered advice when asked, and she asked them for their advice. Finally, she followed through on their ideas by offering books, short stories and poems and by sharing her pointed and supportive comments to their responses.

STUDENTS' SUCCESS ANSWERS RESEARCH QUESTIONS

Leigh's students had indeed answered her questions. First, they cooperated not only with her, but, more importantly, with each other. They suggested books to each other, they responded thoughtfully to each piece of writing read, and they supported a discussion of each piece with their own interpretations, reactions, and comments about others' interpretations and reactions.

Second, their written pieces proved to be thoughtful, varied, and insightful. Through reading-writing connections, they explored mood, character, and feelings. But most of all, they used what they read and discussed to help them with their own written responses, which extended far beyond their journals. Their pieces were ultimately published in an anthology.

Vivian wrote:

Freedom
To go where I choose
And to be
What I want to be.
Wish
What I want to wish,
And
Believe
What I want to believe.
Happiness
Can be
Anywhere
As long as you
Find it,
So . . .
Reach for the stars
And maybe
You'll find happiness.

Finally, Book Club became a way to help students explore their own minds, hearts, and feelings. One mentioned that Book Club might save her sister from gangs; another that Book Club helped her gain a new respect from her mother. One of the boys mentioned that it had given him respect among his peers, because he was now sharing his books in the dorm at night. Apparently Book Club reached beyond this group into the dorm. They had begun to share Book Club books with friends in the bookmobile, with their principal, and with their friends.

Reminiscent of learners in Fader's *The New Hooked on Books,* these very troubled youths tried hard to achieve a sense of success and self-worth through their reading and book talks. Leigh tried to show them the worth they already possessed through valuing them as humans who have an important contribution to make. And in the end, she reflected, as Rosenblatt (1978) had done so long ago, that the power of literature is truly the transaction between reader and text, which is always an individual matter. At the detention center, Leigh left the students feeling that their attempts with literature were important. Their transaction with text would provide them with a richer understanding of life—that life they were trying so desperately to construct for themselves.

Postscript: Book Club has continued at the detention center for the past year with a tremendous amount of success. Student involvement has tripled. Teachers are beginning to incorporate this model within their own classes. In addition Leigh implemented a very successful Book Club model with her own seventh-grade students in the public school.

References

Andrasick, K. (1990). *Opening text.* Portsmouth, NH: Heinemann.

Atwell, N. (1987). *In the middle: Writing, reading, and learning with adolescents.* Portsmouth, NH: Heinemann.

Beach, R. (1993). *A teacher's introduction to reader-response theories.* Urbana, IL: National Council of Teachers of English.

Fader, D. (1976). *The new hooked on books.* New York: Berkley Books.

Goatley, V. J., & Raphael, T. E. (1992). *Moving literature-based instruction into the special education setting: A book club with nontraditional learners* (Elementary Subjects Center Series No. 65). East Lansing, MI: Center for the Learning and Teaching of Elementary Subjects, Institute for Research on Teaching. (ERIC Document Reproduction Service No. ED 354 655)

Marshall, J. D., Smagorinsky, P., & Smith, M. W. (1994). *The language of interpretation: Patterns of discourse in discussions of literature.* Urbana, IL: National Council of Teachers of English.

McMahon, S. I. (1992a). *Book Club: Studying the written and oral texts of elementary children participating in a literature-based reading program* (Elementary Subjects Center Series No. 52). East Lansing, MI: Center for the Learning and Teaching of Elementary Subjects, Institute for Research in Teaching. (ERIC Document Reproduction Service No. ED 341 993)

McMahon, S. I. (1992b, April). *Classroom discourse during social studies: Students' purposes and topics of interest in peer-led discussion groups.* Paper presented at the annual meeting of the American Educational Research Association, San Francisco, CA. (ERIC Document Reproduction Service No. ED 351 262)

McMahon, S. I. (1992c). *Book Club discussions: A case study of five students constructing themes from literary texts* (Elementary Subjects Center Series No. 72). East Lansing, MI: Center for the Learning and Teaching of Elementary Subjects, Institute for Research on Teaching. (ERIC Document Reproduction Service No. ED 353 572)

Pardo, L. S. (1992, December). *Accommodating diversity in the elementary classroom: A look at literature-based instruction in an inner city school.* Paper presented at the annual meeting of the National Reading Conference, San Antonio, TX. (ERIC Document Reproduction Service No. ED 353 575)

Purves, A. C., & Beach, R. (1972). *Literature and the reader: Research in response to literature, reading interests, and the teaching of literature.* Urbana, IL: National Council of Teachers of English.

Raphael, T. E., & McMahon, S. I. (1994). Book Club: An alternative framework for reading instruction. *The Reading Teacher, 48,* 102-116.

Raphael, T. E., Goatley, V. J., McMahon, S. I., & Woodman, D. A. (1991). *Teaching literacy through student book clubs: A first-year teacher's experience*

(Elementary Subjects Center, Series No. 4). East Lansing, MI: Center for the Learning and Teaching of Elementary Subjects, Institute for Research on Teaching. (ERIC Document Reproduction Service No. ED 336 743)

Raphael, T. E., McMahon, S. I., Goatley, V. J., Bentley, J. L., Boyd, F. B., Pardo, L. S., & Woodman, D. A. (1991). *Reading instruction reconsidered: Literature and discussion in the reading program* (Elementary Subjects Center, Series No. 47). East Lansing, MI: Center for the Learning and Teaching of Elementary Subjects, Institute for Research on Teaching. (ERIC Document Reproduction Service No. ED 336 732)

Rief, L. (1992). *Seeking diversity: Language arts with adolescents.* Portsmouth, NH: Heinemann.

Rosenblatt, L. M. (1978). *The reader, the text, the poem: The transactional theory of the literary work.* Carbondale, IL: Southern Illinois University Press.

Vygotsky, L. (1986). *Thought and language.* (A. Kozulin, Ed. and Trans.). Cambridge, MA: MIT Press.

Literature Used in Book Club

Avi. (1988). *Something upstairs.* New York: Orchard, Franklin Watts.

Avi. (1990). *The true confessions of Charlotte Doyle.* New York: Orchard, Franklin Watts.

Avi. (1991). *The man who was Poe.* New York: Avon.

Base, G. (1989). *The eleventh hour: A curious mystery.* New York: Abrams.

Base, G. (1992). *The sign of the seahorse.* New York: Abrams.

Bugliosi, V., & Gentry, C. (1974). *Helter skelter.* New York: W. W. Norton.

Duncan, L. (1989). *Don't look behind you.* New York: Delacorte Press.

Geisert, A. (1986). *Pigs from a to z.* Boston: Houghton Mifflin.

Hinton, S. E. (1967). *The outsiders.* New York: Viking.

Nixon, J. L. (1986). *The other side of dark.* New York: Delacorte.

Poe, E. A. (1991). *The tales of Edgar Allan Poe.* New York: Morrow.

Van Allsburg, C. (1984). *The mysteries of Harris Burdick.* Boston: Houghton Mifflin.

Van Allsburg, C. (1986). *The stranger.* Boston: Houghton Mifflin.

Van Allsburg, C. (1991). *The wretched stone.* Boston: Houghton Mifflin.

Van Allsburg, C. (1993). *The sweetest fig.* Boston: Houghton Mifflin.

***Beijing Review* (essay date 26 January 1998)**

SOURCE: "Readers Clubs: A New Book Marketing Venue." *Beijing Review* 41, no. 4 (26 January 1998): 28-9.

[*The following essay offers a glimpse into the book club phenomenon in China.*]

The rising public interest in books has brought about a recent flourishing of China's publishing industry. An increasing number of bookstores and street bookstands have emerged, with numerous new titles coming off the presses each year. Readers clubs—a new bridge between publishers and readers—are springing up.

This type of reader's service facility first appeared in Germany more than a century ago. The form reappeared in a mature form some 50 years later in the United States and is now popular in many countries across the world.

Although operating under a variety of names and offering many diverse services, most readers clubs in China are striving to adopt the common operational practices found in similar international clubs. For instance, they offer memberships, invite experts to review and recommend new books, provide members with the latest book publishing information and sell books at preferential prices. Some well-operated clubs are evolving with unique features.

Jointly established by the All-China Federation of Trade Unions and *Workers' Daily* over two years ago, the China Workers Reading Service Network now has a membership numbering in the tens of thousands. According to Lu Hongliang, a leading member of the network, gaining success by solely relying on financial capability, experience or luck has become a thing of the past. To achieve their goals, business managers must possess advanced managerial expertise, says Lu. Therefore, books on modern management practices have done well in recent years.

To transform the trend of "blind buying" among its members, the network divides recommended books into three categories. One includes popular materials suitable for all workers in enterprises, such as *Talking about the Shareholding System with Colleagues.* Another category includes materials suited to mid-level managers, such as the *12-Hour Series,* including *12-Hour MBA.* The final category includes those best left to senior executives, such as *On Capital Operations* and

Famous Brand Strategies. By targeting specific audiences, the network helps members gain access to the materials best suited to their needs.

The Xi Shu Good Books Club, which has more than 10,000 members, was set up last July in Beijing. Its director, Li Zhenbang, says the club is operated by combining foreign experience with the reality of Chinese society. It practices direct marketing, as well as a membership system. According to Li, the club undertakes to provide its members with 12 special services.

The members receive free bimonthly issues of the club's journal, *Good Books.* They can also buy books at concessional rates, and can order purchases around the clock by phone or fax. Its Beijing and Shanghai branches are on call to deliver books directly to the homes of members. The club has invited more than 100 top experts and scholars nationwide to offer guidance on readings involving 16 subjects, such as literature, human studies, economics and health care. Through the club's journal, members become aware of new books and can read expert reviews. The club has established personal archives for each member, which allows it to offer proper services according to educational and work backgrounds of the members. In addition, the club regularly organizes gatherings, enabling members to directly exchange views with authors and experts.

"Buying books is no longer difficult," says Xu Guang, an employee of an audio-visual publishing house in Beijing and one of the first members of the Xi Shu Good Books Club. He says he is busy with work every day and has no time to visit bookstores. "The club's journal enables me to keep abreast of the latest books. When I want any, I just make a phone call, and someone will deliver them to my doorstep. It's convenient." Moreover, he can pick up the latest works at discount prices.

Bertelsmann, a world-famous German media group, established a joint venture readers club in Shanghai last year. It has its own editorial department. The group's main focus is on books concerned with daily life and practical sciences, biographies, children's books and literary works. Its membership now exceeds 100,000.

An increasing number of publishers agree that readers clubs are an important venue for book marketing. "Their significance is far beyond that," argues Xi Shu, founder of the Xi Shu Chain Bookstore now located in five major cities of China and in San Francisco of the United States. He notes that the club receives feedback from readers, which can serve as an important reference in forecasting publishing trends and planning and readjusting selected subjects.

In addition, Xi believes, an influential club can also play a positive role in international cultural exchange, book exports and copyright trade. He says his club is striving to enlarge its membership to more than 1 million within the next three to five years.

Lucy Kellaway (essay date 15 April 2000)

SOURCE: Kellaway, Lucy. "Novel Gazing." *Spectator* 284, no. 8958 (15 April 2000): 22.

[*In the following essay, Kellaway surveys the English take on book clubs.*]

Tonight, somewhere near you, they will be doing it: eight or ten consenting adults, crowded around a kitchen table, going at it hammer and tongs. The chances are they will be in earnest debate over *Disgrace,* last year's Booker prizewinner. Someone will be arguing that it was a grim, prophetic warning of the impending disintegration of South Africa. Someone else will be complaining that he didn't like the book at all: he couldn't empathise with any of the characters. Some Sauvignon blanc will be drunk, Kettle crisps eaten and, after a couple of hours, everyone will go home feeling well satisfied—another book under the belt.

Before they go, they will have jotted down in their notebooks, Filofaxes and Palm Pilots the name of the book they are going to talk about next time. *Captain Corelli's Mandolin* would be the perfect choice, only they've done that already. *Birthday Letters?* Done that too. American fiction? *As I Lay Dying, Humboldt's Gift, American Pastoral?* Or a return to the classics? *To the Lighthouse, What Maisie Knew, North and South?* Or, if all else fails, there is always Proust.

The book club is becoming educated, middle-class England's favourite night out, more so than the cinema, more than the theatre or opera or restaurants. 'To my mind the book club is the most fun a girl can have,' Kimberly Fortier, publisher of *The Spectator,* recently wrote in the *Times.* 'To get to the book club we have turned down a hefty roster of social and family events: a reception at Downing Street, a book launch, the in-laws' golden wedding anniversary.' She is not alone in her enthusiasm. People en masse are arranging babysitters for the pleasure of visiting the houses of those who are not necessarily friends to listen to their views on a book that they would not themselves have chosen to read.

Ten years ago these clubs were largely a women's thing. Mothers with young children would escape their brain-dead existence for an evening, when they could play out their former lives as educated people in an unthreatening environment. But now everybody is doing it. For every sex, age, special-interest and socio-economic group there is a book club. There are book clubs for oldies; book clubs for middle-aged men with a particular interest in biographies of historical figures; book clubs for New Labour groupies; book clubs for smug married couples; book clubs for Oxbridge-educated media people; book clubs for minor celebrities; book clubs for pushy career women; and, above all, book clubs for networkers, who will accost you in the office, at a party or by the school gates and say, 'I didn't know you knew so and so! They're in my book club.' Just in case there is anyone left who has neither been invited to join a book club nor has the organisational talent to start their own, there are scores of book clubs on the Internet to choose from. Or, as a last resort, there is James Naughtie's *Bookclub* on Radio Four.

The only people who are not enthusiastic members of book clubs seem to be the under-thirties. Presumably, their idea of an evening's entertainment consists of something more obviously entertaining. For them, the memory of doing English A-levels is fresh enough for the prospect of enforced discussion of a set book to hold no charms whatsoever. For the over-thirties, the popularity of this form of compulsory self-improvement is a puzzle.

There are three very good reasons why book clubs should be less popular now than before. For a start, we are too busy. Our lives are already jammed full of dates and obligations. Willingly to add to these seems folly. Second, there is so much else that we can pleasurably do with our small slice of free time. Never have there been more options and never have we had more money to indulge in whichever of them we like. Third, there is a glut of freely available advice on which books to read and what to think of them. Every newspaper and magazine is crammed with book reviews. Radio and television are full of this sort of thing too, the advantage being that if you don't like the views of the person you are reading or listening to, you simply stop, turn them off.

Yet each of these reasons, turned on its head, may be why these clubs are thriving. Take the question of time: it is because we are so busy that reading has been squeezed out. No one wants to admit to being a former reader and the only way of ensuring that reading gets done at all is to put it in the diary. Institutionalised as an exclusive social event, reading is cool again. It is also because of, rather than despite, the rival attractions that book clubs are so popular. Everyone can afford restaurants and opera. No one is impressed if you say you went to the River Café last night, but if you say you had a fascinating discussion about Mikhail Bulgakov's *The Master and Margarita* at your book club, and then drop some of the names in your group, that really

sets you apart from the crowd. Or it used to, before the crowd started doing the same thing. There is nostalgia at work too: the more pervasive technology becomes, and the more people feel tied to a life of wicked consumption, the more they long for an evening by the fireside reading a book, and possibly talking about it. There is something wistfully Victorian about the idea, and a book club is the closest they are able to get to it.

A third reason for the book-club craze is that it takes away choice. The more books that are published and reviewed, the more difficult it is to decide which ones to read. The beauty of the book club is that someone else mostly decides for you. Instead of passively flipping through book reviews, book-club members get the chance to become book reviewers themselves: every man his own Tom Paulin/Mark Lawson, every woman her own Germaine Greer/Allison Pearson. And this is where the fun starts. For one night a month, you can be reborn as a Booker judge. The downside is that you will have to listen to others pretending to be Booker judges too. In every group, there will always be a dominant one, a couple of bores, a few emoters and a driven, competitive one who has to win. All must be tolerated month in, month out. If the composition of the group were perfect, with a small handful (say six at most) of funny, clever people, then maybe a book club really would be the most fun a girl—or boy—could have. But, even then, I suspect I'd have more fun still with the same funny, clever people discussing whatever we liked in a restaurant. And afterwards, I could go home to bed and enjoy the solitary pleasure of a book.

Harold Orlans (essay date May/June 2000)

SOURCE: Orlans, Harold. "Selling Richard Wright." *Change* 32, no. 3 (May/June 2000): 8-10.

[*In the following essay, Orlans identifies censorship as a side effect of the Book of the Month Club's influence.*]

While writing *Native Son*, Richard Wright said, "I felt a mental censor . . . standing over me, draped in white. . . ." Hazel Rowley, Wright's biographer, adds, "and there were real censors."

In August 1939, *Native Son* was set in galleys ready for September publication by Harper & Bros., when editor Edward Aswell told Wright that the Book of the Month Club might adopt it if certain cuts were made. Adoption meant large sales, a large check, and great public attention.

In Rowley's opinion, cuts in the "longwinded" trial scene improved the novel. But the passages about Mary (the white daughter of black chauffeur Bigger Thomas's employer) making plain sexual overtures to Bigger were removed to make the book more palatable to club members.

In 1944, club judges told Wright they might adopt his autobiography, *American Hunger,* if the second part (attacking Chicago racism) were dropped and the first part (on his experience with Southern racist terror) ended more hopefully.

"[O]ne word of recognition" that some white Americans seek racial justice "would hearten all who believe in American ideals," judge Dorothy Canfield Fisher wrote. Wright did not write that word. Nonetheless, stripped of the second part, the book—retitled *Black Boy*—ended more hopefully than the original manuscript and sold twice as many copies as *Native Son.* Still, Howley thinks, "Wright must sometimes have felt he had sold his soul."

Kate Clifford Larson (essay date April 2001)

SOURCE: Larson, Kate Clifford. "The Saturday Evening Girls: A Progressive Era Library Club and the Intellectual Life of Working Class and Immigrant Girls in Turn-of-the-Century Boston." *Library Quarterly* 71, no. 2 (April 2001): 195-230.

[*In the following essay, Larson offers a detailed examination of a book club as change agent for poor immigrant women in the early twentieth century.*]

Introduction

When Dora Cohen stole out of the house on Friday evenings, she did so in direct defiance of her father. A devoted member of the Friday Evening Girls' Club, a junior group of the Saturday Evening Girls' Club in Boston's crowded, immigrant North End of the early 1900s, Dora would later recall, "I had to be one step ahead of my father to get out on the Sabbath, but to me it was worth it" [1, p. 10].[1] Dora was not unlike many of the other young women who belonged to the Saturday Evening Girls' Club (S.E.G.) and associated library clubs, who often had to hide their books and deceive their parents in order to participate. The Saturday Evening Girls' Club had been established in 1899 through the combined efforts of three women: Edith Guerrier (a librarian), her lifelong partner, Edith Brown (an artist), and their upper-class patron, Helen Osborne Storrow. Frustrated by the lack of opportunities for the educational, economic, and social advancement of immigrant and working-class women, Guerrier conceived of a "library club" program to provide educational, cultural, and social resources for the growing numbers of poor, young Jewish and Italian women living in the North End of Boston.

Held on Saturday evenings to accommodate young women who worked during the week, the Saturday Evening Girls' Story Hour was originally conducted at the North Bennet Street Industrial School (NBSIS), a charitable institution dedicated to providing social services, industrial and vocational training, and Americanization programs to immigrants in the North End. This story hour soon developed and expanded into eight library clubs, identified by the day and the time of day on which they met, each holding meetings for young women of different age groups. For almost twenty years, the Saturday Evening Girls and the other library clubs met weekly to discuss literature, economics, politics, music, art, and employment opportunities. At their peak in the mid-1910s, the clubs supported approximately 250 members, published a newspaper called the *S.E.G. News,* operated the Paul Revere Pottery, and struggled to improve their community and their own lives through education, economic opportunity, and independence. The Saturday Evening Girls' Club and its associated library clubs provide a rare opportunity to examine the intellectual life of immigrant and working-class women and the role of clubs and social reform organizations in advancing educational agendas and providing intellectual stimulation.

The Saturday Evening Girls and their mentors left behind a rare sampling of primary material, most notably the *S.E.G. News,* which documents their experiences in the club and their lives in the North End. Combined with oral histories conducted with surviving S.E.G.s during the mid-1970s, and subsequent interviews conducted with descendants and other relatives and friends of the S.E.G.s in the mid-1990s, these materials offer a remarkably consistent view of the important role that intellectual stimulation and opportunity played in the lives of these young women and girls. The library clubs, according to Fanny Goldstein, a Saturday Evening Girl who later went on to become the librarian of the West End Branch Library in Boston,[2] "offered a happy refuge and contrast. Here the doors of America literally opened up for them. They sought refuge from growing pains. They sought compatibility and understanding and companionship. They groped for the opportunity which America offered, without knowing and without understanding. Thus they drifted into the Library, fortunately . . . the Library offered a social haven. It was one of those psychological moments. A trinity of forces and elements—the need, the opportunity, the leader" (see fig. 1) [2, p. 22].

There has been much scholarship in the past fifteen years on the life experiences of immigrant women that focuses on the intractability of their experience in urban communities during the late nineteenth and early twentieth centuries.[3] Limiting the discussion of contact with American culture to work, labor activism, or the streets, historians have written little about clubs and organizations, particularly those conducted at the many settlement houses and community organizations across the country, which catered to the intellectual lives of immigrants, the working class, and their children. This is partly because of the absence of archival material that reflects the voices of nonelite women and girls. Karen J. Blair's work on the women's club movement [7] focuses almost exclusively on middle-class women's clubs, while Priscilla Murolo's recent scholarship on working girls' clubs [8] focuses primarily on postadolescent women and labor activism. Anne Ruggles Gere [9] offers a new look at women's club activities through a nuanced analysis of the textual practices employed in a variety of club settings, including those of elite, working-class, immigrant, and minority women. On the other hand, Kathy Peiss [10], and to a lesser degree, Elizabeth Ewen [6] both focus on dance halls, movies, and the streets as a major source of recreation for immigrant and working-class women and girls. Participation in the library clubs was a significant alternative to those leisure attractions. The clubs were a important venue for intellectual, social, professional, and economic advancement. Like the later Bryn Mawr Summer School for Women Workers (1921-38) and other worker education programs, education empowered and emboldened many working-class and immigrant women beyond society's expectations. Research into alternative programs like the Saturday Evening Girls offer scholars the opportunity to reexamine the lives of immigrant and working-class women and girls and their intellectual aspirations.

The S.E.G.s were overwhelmingly native born of immigrant parents, who often arrived in the late 1880s and early 1890s, though a significant number of S.E.G.s had older, foreign-born siblings.[4] Many of the S.E.G.s ultimately became middle-class housewives, a status that represented an enormous improvement over their mothers' lives. But the richness of their experience in the library clubs also enabled some of the S.E.G.s to pursue higher education and professional careers. Many of the Saturday Evening Girls went on to inspire and educate others through civic service, social service careers, teaching, the arts, and philanthropy. They became librarians, office and clerical workers, social workers, teachers, saleswomen, business owners, musicians, and artists. When the Saturday Evening Girls published a supplement to the *S.E.G. News* for a reunion in 1954, the women had been meeting formally and informally for fifty-five years. Many of them had become grandmothers, and in the bulletin they shared their memories and thoughts. This *S.E.G. News* supplement, the *Cherry Tree Edition,* included essays and biographical information from forty-three S.E.G.s [1]. Of the thirty-seven women who reported educational data for themselves, thirty-one, or 72 percent, graduated from at least high school. Twenty, or 54 percent of that group, took additional courses at colleges, universities, and other professional schools, including seven, or 19 percent, who graduated from college. These women went to schools such as Simmons, Radcliffe, Harvard,

Boston University, the Boston Conservatory, the New England Conservatory, the Museum School of Art, the Massachusetts Normal Art School, Boston Normal, and others. Only six, or 16 percent, reported graduating from grammar school and immediately going to work in a family business or factory [1].[5] This initial small sampling surpassed the expectations for higher education for women at the time (1900-20s). From 1900 to 1920, the percentage of all women eighteen to twenty-one years of age attending college rose from 2.8 percent to 7.6 percent [12, pp. 63-64]. At 54 percent, the level of post-high school education for the S.E.G.s in this sample was far greater than what was found in the general population.

For most immigrant families in the late nineteenth and early twentieth centuries, including those children who were native born of foreign-born parents, grammar school education was the norm. According to Jerry A. Jacobs and Margaret E. Greene's analysis of the 1910 U.S. census [13], immigrant teenagers were less likely to be enrolled in school after the age of fourteen, though younger children experienced school attendance at the same rate as native whites. Employment options after the age of fourteen altered the decision to stay in school. Parental literacy, foreign birth, the ability to speak English, and parental occupation also played a role in the persistence of education for children. "High school attendance remained low and high school completion remained exceptional in 1910" [13, pp. 212-13]. According to Jacobs and Greene, enrollment by native whites in the ten—thirteen year-old group was 92.9 percent; by Jews, 95.5 percent; and by Italians, 91.5 percent. In the following age group, fourteen—eighteen year-olds, typical high school ages, enrollment figures plunge dramatically to 59.1 percent for native whites, 47.4 percent for Jews, and 30.5 percent for Italians [13, p. 226]. Contrary to Jacobs and Greene's study, however, the situation in Boston may have been markedly different. According to a study conducted by the school committee in Boston in 1907, the percentage of all students completing elementary school was 50.3 percent, with 31.3 percent entering high school and only 11.5 percent completing a three-year course in high school [14, p. 38]. Though the study does not break down its sample by ethnic group, it is in this light then, that the S.E.G.'s successes can be seen as extraordinary.[6]

Progressive Era Boston

By the middle of the nineteenth century, the North End of Boston had become an elaborate community of immigrants and working poor whose interests and needs varied greatly. Long a settlement site for immigrants, it was a densely populated area of approximately one hundred acres, of which only 70 percent was used for housing. Of the total residents of the North End in 1860, approximately fourteen thousand were Irish, with the remaining twelve thousand predominantly Anglo-Saxon, and a few hundred Jews, Italians, Portuguese, and Greeks [16, pp. 21-22]. The 1880s brought a new tide of immigration to the United States. Political, economic, and natural disasters in Italy, combined with economic and political pogroms in Russia and other Eastern European countries, resulted in mass migrations out of those areas to America. By 1895, the North End was crowded with mostly eastern European Jews and southern Italians. The majority of Irish and Anglo-Saxons had left the community for other neighborhoods in the Boston area, leaving the crowded tenements for the newer and poorer immigrants.

Considered a neighborhood in itself by outsiders, those living within the community recognized that the North End was actually made up of several neighborhoods, all defined by racial, ethnic, regional, and religious identities. Of the approximately 23,800 residents of the North End in 1895, 32 percent were of Italian heritage, 28 percent Irish (down from 61.5 percent fifteen years earlier), 26 percent Jewish, 5 percent Anglo, and 3.7 percent Portuguese. By 1900, the population of the North End had grown to 28,000, with Italians representing over 60 percent of the population. In 1920 the population had burgeoned to 40,000, 95 percent of whom were Italian. By then, the Jews, Irish, Portuguese, and other ethnic groups had moved out of the North End into other areas of Boston, including the West End, Roxbury, Dorchester, and Hyde Park [16, pp. 22-24].[7]

The consequences of unrestricted immigration in the late nineteenth century into New England were manifold. Racial and ethnic groups crowded together in tenement neighborhoods where poverty was pervasive, and where immigrants were unfamiliar with the English language and unsure of American social and cultural customs and expectations. Divided by race, class, language, and religion, many immigrants kept within their own ethnic and racial spheres, separated by a street corner from another ethnic enclave. Residential segregation was a fact of life in the North End, with Italian families dominating certain streets, while Russian Jews dominated others, with some multiethnic border streets sprinkled about. Salem Street was one such street, populated by Jews and Italians, while Stillman Street housed mostly Jews and Hull Street mostly Italians. In 1910, at least thirty S.E.G.s lived on Salem Street alone, including four S.E.G. families who lived in an apartment building at 155 Salem Street [11]. Old, dilapidated housing, overcrowding, and inadequate sanitary conditions helped spread disease and ill health among families. Francis Rocchi, an S.E.G. who went on to run several businesses of her own in Portland, Oregon, lived on North Bennet Street, "in four crowded rooms with beds in every room, toilet in the cellar and plenty of bugs—a constant battle" [1, p. 23].

According to S.E.G. Sylvia Bacchini, the arrival in Boston from Europe was a confusing, frightening and at times, a dangerous experience: "It would be difficult to describe in detail a picture of the people pushing each other at the gang-plank to land in this promised land of health, wealth and prosperity" [17, p. 2]. The lengthy detention process and the examination of luggage and papers were just the beginning of the immigrants' reception in the land of opportunity. Trouble lurked for the "unwary 'Greenhorn,'" and, in particular, unsuspecting young girls, whom "kind gentlemen" sought to help. "If the girl knows the world, he may be told to attend to his own affairs, but on the other hand, simple and trusting aliens are often sadly misled" [17, p. 3].

A sense of urgency about the rampant overcrowding of the schools in eastern Massachusetts, resulting from the tremendous influx of immigrants, was palpable during the last quarter of the nineteenth century and the first two decades of the twentieth. Heavily burdened with thousands of young immigrant children, speaking dozens of languages from eastern and southern Europe, educators scrambled to accommodate and teach them. In horribly overcrowded schools, children struggled to learn English and the basics of compulsory elementary education. Boston schools suffered severe space shortages from the 1880s through 1910, creating unacceptable situations where children were turned away because of a lack of facilities [18, pp. 11-12]. Significant language barriers, poorly educated parents, and economic need also forced many children out of public schools and into the labor force prematurely.

The reformers of the Progressive Era recognized the perils of overcrowded neighborhoods and the stress placed on cities and their residents, both native born and immigrant. Through private and public programs and institutions, they sought to devise comprehensive ways of dealing with the many issues, needs, and problems of industrialization and the economic destabilization of the inner cities. Typically, however, many reformers also viewed immigrants' poverty as a function of their traditions, customs, and culture. By teaching American customs and ways of living, they believed immigrants would soon find financial security and improve their quality of life [19, pp. 131-32]. Organizations such as NBSIS sponsored many "Americanization" programs in their own facilities and public schools.[8] Viewed as agents of socialization, these programs were also a means of promoting conformity to white Protestant middle-class values.

It is clear that as the young S.E.G.s were pursuing intellectual stimulation, they were becoming Americanized. But the processes were complex and at times contradictory. According to Milton Gordon in *Assimilation in American Life* [20], in the late nineteenth century and early twentieth (before World War I) Americanization programs were moderate enough so that they showed some respect for immigrant culture. Throughout the period, however, there "were more prosaic instrumental programs of instruction in the use of the English language, elementary American history, the nature of American government, and so on" [20, pp. 100-101] that ultimately meant the abandonment of these connections to the immigrants' place of origin. Programs throughout the city of Boston during this time period were no different. The NBSIS was, in some ways, particularly sensitive to the cultural sensibilities of its neighbors because of the large number of individual ethnic groups living within the area. Yet, their ultimate goal was economic, political, and educational-vocational assimilation. Although aware of the "process of American assimilation" in their lives, some S.E.G.s believed that they had "retained [their] originality and racial traditions," in addition to white middle-class values and expectations [21, p. 2].

NORTH BENNET STREET INDUSTRIAL SCHOOL (NBSIS) AND EDUCATIONAL REFORM

It was during this time period that NBSIS developed and refined a variety of manual and industrial training programs to augment the public school programs in the city. Founded by Pauline Agassiz Shaw in the early 1880s, NBSIS represented a new trend in the development, use, and ideology of industrial and manual training during the late nineteenth century.[9] In 1880, Shaw had been asked by the Associated Charities of Boston to open a kindergarten and nursery school at the North End Industrial Home, a charitable organization established for the benefit of the North End's immigrants, at 39 North Bennet Street. Influenced by Elizabeth Peabody, Mary Garland, and Rebecca Weston, Shaw had already opened two kindergartens in 1877, one in Jamaica Plain and one in Brookline.[10] The Home provided classes in sewing and laundry to help poor women, particularly "widows, wives with sick husbands, and deserted wives" [23], learn necessary skills to earn extra income through piecework paid for by the Home. By 1881, Shaw maintained control of programming at the Home, expanding and changing its vision to helping not only poor women but their children and husbands as well. Under the direction of Mary Hemenway, the Boston Cooking School opened a branch in the building. A workroom was outfitted in the basement for carpentry classes for boys, and a print shop, library, and a "kitchen garden, where young girls twelve to fifteen are instructed in housework," were also established [23]. By 1883 the laundry and piecework were discontinued in favor of more expanded manual training programs in woodworking, printing, clay modeling, and leatherwork. By 1885, Shaw's management of NBSIS allowed the Associated Charities to quietly relinquish control of all programming. By the turn of the century,

Shaw's secular approach was instrumental in NBSIS's ability to reach into the community and offer its services to the many different cultures and religious groups living there.[11] Soon, courses were developed in cooperation with local private and public schools in Boston. Completely supported by private donations, the school maintained programs for public school children throughout the early part of the twentieth century, defining a new phenomenon of joint public and private initiatives that provided some manner of education and support for overcrowded, underrepresented, poor communities.

It was through club work, however, that many new ideas of social reform were played out. In 1889, NBSIS reported that with the growing demand for clubs and classes, "there is opportunity for more work and more workers. More lives might be brightened and ennobled, more weary bodies might be rested and refreshed, more rough manners made gentle, and the work would prove its own reward" [25, p. 25]. It was often through clubs that reformers capitalized on opportunities for "social intercourse" and "good citizenship" [26, p. 24]. By the turn of the century, however, maintaining an adequate number of devoted and reliable volunteers became increasingly difficult; older volunteers began to give way to young, unmarried middle- and upper-class women who were often not as philanthropic with their available time but were eager for more professional or paying positions. Through the newly emerging field of social work, college-trained professionals began to replace the multitude of volunteers that had staffed many charitable organizations throughout the nineteenth century. The NBSIS, for instance, actively pursued relationships with the emerging schools of social work in the Boston area, such as those at Simmons, Harvard, Boston University, Emerson, M.I.T., Wellesley, and Tufts, who used the North End location as a suitable site for the hands-on training of their schools' students. Radcliffe, the Winsor School, and the Women's Educational and Industrial Union placed many young girls and women either as volunteers or paid workers. Nevertheless, it was through the multitude of literary, debate, and athletic clubs for boys and young men, and sewing, cooking, and a few literary clubs for boys and young women that reformers and immigrants often experienced their first cross-class and cross-cultural exchanges [27].

While most clubs for girls generally centered on sewing, cooking, and other domestic duties, some clubs began to emerge that addressed the intellectual needs of girls and young women. By the mid-to-late 1890s, NBSIS had made a commitment to providing a library facility for the neighborhood. It was through this expansion of the library and its reading rooms that a new class of clubs for girls and young women began to take hold and flourish, offering girls an alternative club atmosphere to the monolithic domestic skills training clubs.

For Guerrier, Brown, and Storrow, providing a stimulating educational program through the library clubs recognized and honored the intellectual life of women. For women, particularly working-class and immigrant women, intellectual advancement was not a universally accepted concept. In an article in *Charities,* a social work magazine, the plight of the poor was seen largely the fault of poorly trained mothers:

> Nobody more than charity workers realize the great necessity for the training of girls in household duties. It would probably not be wide of the mark to say that a large number of cases of estrangement between husbands and wives among the poor is due to lack of ability on the part of the wife to make the home comfortable and attractive, to cook properly and to sew. If the home is to be the center and root of our civilization, it must be made a place worth while going to and spending time in. It is the girls who must be taught this lesson and aroused to the nobility of their calling . . . The men and women of thought are realizing the faults of education that looked well to filling the head with facts.
>
> [28]

By the turn of the century most of NBSIS's clubs for girls remained devoted to domestic activities, drama, music, and social entertainment. There were two embroidery clubs; several housekeeping clubs, including "Little Housekeepers" for girls aged twelve; assorted evening social clubs; the "Glover Club" for older Irish girls who were working; a "Current Events Club"; a "Miniature Music Club"; and the "Pauline Agassiz Shaw Club," which was established for teaching embroidery, beadwork, and machine stitching [29, p. 12]. There were only two literary clubs: the "Wiltse Club," a small club conducted by Sara Wiltse for young Jewish women; and the "Lily of the Arno Club," for Italian girls, which focused on Italian literature [30, pp. 9-10]. G. Stanley Hall, president of Clark University in Worcester, Massachusetts, prominent child psychologist and early childhood education proponent, believed that girls' education was ultimately dependent on their sex roles.

> The home should be served by every child, who should feel himself a useful and integral member of it with duties. Every girl should cook, sew, clean, polish, and, perhaps, wash; have something to do with flowers, develop some domestic taste and pride, in place of the shame so often felt by high-school girls for their lowly homes for which their education often breeds distaste. They should be reminded that too soft hands in the young suggest a soft brain; that hand and brain both grow and are educated together. The kitchen is the heart of the home; its industries, intelligently understood, are among the most educational of all possible influences; and to overcome the alienation school often breeds for home life in the modern American girl is one of our most serious problems. [28]

It is not surprising, then, that Guerrier, Storrow, and Brown were frustrated by the lack of interest in the intellectual advancement of young women. Guerrier had been deeply influenced by the great literary figures of nineteenth-century New England, and there is no doubt that she was determined to share this with other young women. Born in 1870 in New Bedford, Massachusetts, Guerrier was the granddaughter of Daniel Ricketson, a wealthy Quaker and active abolitionist who spent much of his time enjoying lively correspondence with prominent literary, social, and political leaders of his day. Guerrier's mother died when she was three years old, leaving her father, George Guerrier, grief-stricken and chaffing under the disapproving eye of his wife's family. With few resources of his own, Guerrier's father shuttled her from one relative to the next over the next ten years. Moving from the opulent parlors of her maternal grandfather's mansion in New Bedford and an aunt's drawing rooms in the middle-class South End of Boston to the poor household of a minister uncle and his family, Guerrier came to feel uncomfortable in both spheres. Only when she settled briefly with her mother's brother and sister, Walton and Anna Ricketson, did she find a sense of peace, security, and belonging [31].

The Ricketson family had been intimate with the literary circle of Concord, Massachusetts, of the mid-nineteenth century. Henry David Thoreau, Ralph Waldo Emerson, Bronson Alcott, and other literary giants were close friends of Guerrier's maternal grandfather. When Daniel Ricketson passed away, his two surviving children, Walton and Anna, maintained many of those relationships. Anna's closest friends were Louisa May Alcott and her sister, Anna Alcott Pratt.[12] When Guerrier wrote her autobiography in her eighties, she vividly remembered visiting the Alcott home; meeting the author of *Little Women* and being shown "May's" room left a lifelong impression [31, p. 19].[13] These women opened up a world of possibilities to Guerrier and offered her a model of womanhood that stretched beyond the domestic sphere to a world of independence, literature, and sisterhood.

Guerrier attended the Vermont Methodist Seminary and Female College in Montpelier, Vermont, where she enjoyed literature, music, art, and sports, and where she was introduced to the works of the latest social theorists, including John Ruskin [31, p. xxxi]. After graduating in 1891 with honors [34], Guerrier returned to Massachusetts and enrolled at the Museum School of Boston's Museum of Fine Arts [35] but soon found her needs for money so urgent that she had to give up pursuit of full-time artistic training and find paid work.[14] With a letter of introduction from William Lloyd Garrison II (a friend of her father's), she secured a position at Shaw's day nursery at NBSIS in the North End. She continued to take evening courses at the Museum School and soon became close friends with a talented young artist named Edith Brown. Self-conscious of her poverty, Guerrier felt intimidated by the more "prosperous" looking students. Longing for companionship, she searched for "someone of my own age who did not look prosperous" [31, pp. 64-68]. During a perspective class at the Museum School in 1893, Guerrier met Brown. They moved in together and started a lifelong personal and professional relationship that would span forty years of dedication to each other until Brown's death in 1932.

While working at the nursery at NBSIS, Guerrier was approached by Liliah Pingree, a close friend of Pauline Shaw's and a director of Shaw's various neighborhood nurseries [31, pp. 67-68].[15] She asked Guerrier to lead several girls' clubs that were being organized in various settlement houses and to maintain the reading room at NBSIS. In many cities, associations and clubs were formed for working-class women and girls that focused on "physical, industrial, mental, and moral" improvement [38, p. 340]. These clubs, it was believed, supplied a "common ground of meeting for young women who have had the privileges of education, money and leisure, with those who have had the privileges of self-denying, hard-working lives, and the benefits are mutual" [38 p. 340]. Guerrier, however, lacked the privileges of "money and leisure" and thought herself fortunate to have "had the real adventure of being ill-clad, ill-fed, ill-sheltered. . . . I am grateful for this experience, which makes it easier for me to get the point of view of the girl who is literally on her own" [31, p. 69]. Guerrier exemplified the growing population of well-educated single women, caught between their middle- or upper-class family identity and the economic realities of needing to support themselves. Pingree, however, recognized Guerrier's untapped abilities and promoted her on the first leg of her journey in the emerging career of librarianship for women.

The reading rooms at NBSIS had become so popular that Guerrier gave up all of her other club duties to work exclusively in the North End. In 1899, with the official opening of a Boston Public Library branch in the North End at NBSIS, daily deliveries of books were made to the Industrial School, which henceforth became known as Station W [39]. Guerrier's title was changed to custodian of the Station W of the Boston Public Library, and she was given a salary of forty dollars a month. Initially, however, Guerrier had been reluctant to choose library work as a life's profession:

> I did not wish to be responsible for giving to young people some of the trash I myself had obtained from public libraries. This qualm had been silenced by logical reasoning. I felt there was not as much trash in a public library as there was on a newsstand. Furthermore, there was always the opportunity of quietly offering the best, whether it was accepted or not. Again, who was I to set myself up as an infallible judge of good or bad literature. Perhaps my tastes were not sufficiently

> catholic. After all, I had read much trash and forgotten it; other young people would be pretty sure to do the same thing. [31, p. 78][16]

As head librarian, Guerrier continued directing several clubs in the library and was eager to transform them into something whereby young women could "find together the key to some secret garden in which we can profitably enjoy ourselves" [31, p. 68]. Burdened by the directive to "draw these girls in, from the perils of the street" [40, p. 4], Guerrier sought to organize the clubs along the same lines as the more literary and educational clubs that already existed for boys. These "perils" were a constant theme throughout the reform literature of the time period. Saloons, dance halls, and other "cheap" amusements were thought of as precursors to prostitution and the loss of morality. While the threat of prostitution and entrapment in white slavery was real for some vulnerable, single, poor, and immigrant women, middle-class observers' uneasiness with the explicit or potential sexuality of these young women created a tension that manifested itself as an assumption that all poor, immigrant women needed to be morally and physically protected.[17] In fact, many young immigrant women were also concerned with projecting an image of middle-class respectability and "social purity." The reality was that most Jewish and Italian parents would not allow their daughters out of the house in the evening without a chaperon, usually an older sibling (preferably male) or other relative. The reformers' language was, therefore, typical of the time period and the low expectations of moral character in immigrants but did not reflect the reality of these young women's lives.

The NBSIS felt, however, that girls were "sadly in need of every form of moral and mental enrichment" and that "strenuous effort" was made to introduce them to the joys of reading [40, pp. 12-13].[18] What the reformers at NBSIS may have interpreted as resistance may have actually been an issue of opposition from parents, who were fearful of education and Americanization for their daughters. The younger generation often learned English and accepted American lifestyles more readily than their parents. Many older immigrants viewed American culture as a threat to their own religious and cultural traditions. This view was particularly true for daughters, who were expected to remain under the control of their families until they married.[19] For some Saturday Evening Girls, attending meetings meant defying their parents. According to one S.E.G. daughter, some girls had to hide their books from their parents, lest they be scolded and prevented from visiting the reading rooms at North Bennet Street [45]. Another S.E.G. wrote, "the tragic gap between the first and second generation is the high price of assimilation" [46, p. 2]. Despite NBSIS staff's protestations that the "difficulty of leading the girls to read as seriously and continuously as the boys is not altogether overcome" [40, p. 5], they ignored their own statistics. In the Boy's Reading Rooms the average daily attendance from September 1897 to April 1898 was 97, and in the Girl's Reading Room, it was 110 [40, p. 8].

During the winter of 1901, the reading rooms at the library were "crowded to overflowing, and there is usually a crowd of children at the door, some of whom have to wait outside for an hour for a chance to come in and read quietly" [30, pp. 10-11]. Guerrier's efforts to interest more girls in reading had the effect of increasing the average daily attendance to 193 for girls (with a subsequent drop to sixty-four for boys) during the year, and the staff noted there was "a great need of a third reading room for the older girls" [30, pp. 10-11].[20] Interestingly, by 1905, however, the boys' library contained over one thousand volumes, and the girls' contained only six hundred [51, p. 13].

THE SATURDAY EVENING GIRLS AND OTHER LIBRARY CLUBS

Although Guerrier had started the Saturday Evening Girls' Story Hour in 1899, the first mention of the group appears in North Bennet Street's annual report for 1901. Commenting on the success of the group, the report noted that the group enjoyed readings and talks on various subjects by prominent people of the Boston community and that they "occasionally ended up with chocolate or lemonade" [29, p. 11]. Goldstein later wrote of Guerrier's motivations for establishing the library clubs for girls and young women. In a poem delivered at the thirtieth reunion of the Saturday Evening Girls in 1929, Goldstein wrote that Guerrier believed "the thing of great value is not brawn—but the mind. She looked at the churches, she looked at the schools. She looked at the streets, she looked at the tools, She looked at the club rooms, some twenty or more, And beheld with amazement—only boys—boys galore" [52, p. 4].

Hoping to extend opportunities for entertainment and education for working-class and immigrant girls and young women in the afternoons and evenings after school, Guerrier worked ceaselessly, writing "letters by the hundreds" to entice interesting and noteworthy individuals to come speak to the Saturday Evening Girls' club [52, p. 4]. Edward Everett Hale, Reverend Paul Revere Frothingham, Charles Eliot Norton, activists Philip Davis and Meyer Bloomfield, social reformers Vida Scudder and Robert Woods, and many doctors, lawyers, judges, librarians, artists, rabbis, clergy, performance artists, suffragists, business leaders, and writers spoke to the S.E.G. on a variety of classical and contemporary issues.

The S.E.G.s and the other library club girls met weekly to "take an intelligent individual, as well as collective, interest in civic, social, and economic affairs" [53, p.

4]. The program included courses in "English Literature, . . . Discussions on the fine art of living: work, recreation, study . . . Sociology, . . . City Government, . . . Economics, . . . all these subjects treated from three points of view, viz. Labor, Employer, Artists" [54, p. 3]. As the years passed, the library clubs expanded to include young girls from the fourth grade through high school and were also named after the days of the week that they met. By 1915 there were over 250 girls and young women in eight different library clubs. As the Saturday Evening Girls grew older and matured, they took over some of the responsibilities of conducting the other library club activities, the Monday Afternoon Girls group was for eighth graders; the Monday Evening Girls was for third- and fourth-year high schoolers; the Tuesday Afternoon Girls was for seventh graders; the Wednesday Afternoon Girls was for fifth and sixth graders; the Thursday Afternoon Girls was for first- and second-year high schoolers; the Thursday Evening Girls was for high school seniors and some working girls; and the Friday Evening Girls was for eighteen to twenty year-old working young women. The goal of most young library club girls was ultimately to become a Saturday Evening Girl. In June of each year, the Friday Evening Girls who were then over twenty years old were formally invited to join the S.E.G.s [55, p. 13].

Activities for the year 1915 are an example of the range of topics covered by the Library groups. The Monday Afternoon Girls studied Charles Dickens, "Comradeship," "Courtesy," "Loyalty," "Sincerity," and "School Visiting"; while the youngest groups studied Nathaniel Hawthorne's Tanglewood Tales, "The Prince and the Pauper," "The Lost Prince," and "Pinocchio," The Thursday Afternoon Girls "traveled in Europe . . . [a] different place was visited each week, and they all hope some day to 'really go over.'" The Thursday Evening Girls "had a most interesting series of talks on Current Events and have heard many fine talks on the War, the Mexican Situation, Suffrage, and Preparedness." The Friday Evening Girls discussed "our President, the Kaiser, and Alice Freeman Palmer" [56, pp. 4-6]. Much of the programming reflected Guerrier, Storrow, and Brown's influence, and middle-class white women would have recognized some of these programs as similar to their own club activities. For Vaine Casassa Bruno, however, membership in the S.E.G. Club became a substitute for a high school education she could not have:

> The S.E.G. talks that I have attended have helped me a great deal, in that I learned from them what other girls learned at high school, and I was thus given a general idea of the literature at different periods, civic and social problems in different countries, fine arts of living, etc. . . . Through the club I became connected with the Branch Public Library. During my work there I was able to help children and foreigners to read proper

books, and to handle them properly—to make them better citizens and scholars as well as increasing my knowledge of books and authors.

[57, p. 5]

The Saturday Evening Girls, in addition to monitoring and conducting many of the younger library club groups, spent the year investigating educational, social, and community organizations to foster cooperation among the different agencies for "better housing conditions, better schools, better local and civic administration" [56, p. 7]. The special needs and circumstances of living in a poor immigrant community, however, often dictated the clubs' programming and the members' responses. Reflecting not only the leaders' interests, the programming also spoke to the realities of living in an urban community. A course on city government became vital as the S.E.G. became enmeshed in community efforts to force municipal bodies to respond to a variety of urban issues, including sanitation, public health, education, and social services.

These clubs for girls and young women became an important part of the Americanization process, not only because of the programs that focused on civic and educational agendas but also because of their self-governing organizational structures. Inspired by Guerrier, a governing body of ten members was elected yearly by the oldest group, the Saturday Evening Girls. A house committee was formed that met on a weekly basis to generate policies and rules concerning the running of the clubhouse, and these were then voted on by the entire body of the clubhouse once a month [58, p. 5]. The girls and young women learned on a microlevel the concepts of a democratic government. They found discipline and confidence in a system whereby they could create an organization with rules and laws and could resolve problems and reach decisions based on a vote of the majority. By participating in the everyday running of the clubs, the members learned valuable lessons on responsibility and the use of power. This was particularly important for women and girls, who lacked opportunities—in the public sphere as well as the private sphere—to govern their own lives.

It was as a result of her appointment to the library service that Guerrier met Helen Osborne Storrow. Storrow was intrigued by Guerrier's work with the girls' clubs in the reading rooms at North Bennet Street. When they met at the turn of the century, Storrow was still a young woman, just emerging as an important philanthropic figure in the Boston community. They shared an understanding and appreciation for the disadvantages facing young women and girls. For Storrow, this was the beginning of her own personal "female dominion," unfettered by other powerful feminists, a place within which she could define and develop her own personal vision for independent womanhood [59]. Although Storrow continued to improvise and establish new programs at North Bennet Street for both boys and girls, her involvement with the Saturday Evening Girls developed into a more personal and lifelong relationship.

Storrow had joined the Board of Managers of North Bennet Street in 1898, and was a member of the Board of Visitors of the Boston Public Library. A Quaker, Storrow was the granddaughter of Martha Coffin Wright and grandniece of Lucretia Coffin Mott, ardent abolitionists and suffragists who, together with Elizabeth Cady Stanton, were among the small group that organized the first women's rights convention in 1848 in Seneca Falls, New York. Storrow's father was a successful manufacturer of farm equipment in Auburn, New York, and her mother, Eliza Wright Osborne, maintained her family's heritage of strong commitment to social and political reform [60]. Eliza's sister, Ellen Wright, married William Lloyd Garrison II and was also a prominent liberal reformer in her own right. Storrow's brother, Thomas Mott Osborne, became an outspoken supporter of prison reform, gaining notoriety as a controversial warden of Sing Sing prison in New York [61, p. 1].

Although her mother was an active suffragist, Storrow shied away from any prominent position in the movement. No doubt she experienced both the deference and disdain accorded her family by their Auburn neighbors. Lucretia Mott and Martha Wright were both frequent visitors to the Osborne household, and Eliza often entertained many of the suffrage movement's leaders, including Susan B. Anthony and Anna Howard Shaw. Harriet Tubman, a close friend of Lucretia and Martha's, lived only a few doors down South Street in Auburn where Storrow and her family lived when she was a child. As a young woman, Storrow shared the idealism of a community of activist women. It was, perhaps, her childhood experiences observing the network of powerful feminists of the mid- to late nineteenth century who flowed in and out of her childhood home that taught Storrow the value of female relationships. "Among her gifts, Mrs. Storrow has the faculty of establishing a common interest," an acquaintance once wrote. "As a rule, women have less of camaraderie than men, but . . . Mrs. Storrow has been able to draw it out" [62].

Helen Osborne married James Jackson Storrow, Jr., a prominent Boston lawyer and banker in 1891. Socially, politically, and financially secure, the Storrows continued her family's tradition of supporting social and political activism. They established or supported several charitable reform organizations, in addition to giving financial support to individual young women and men in their pursuit of higher education [63]. Unlike his business partner, Henry Higginson, who helped found the Immigration Restriction League in 1894, James J. Storrow renounced nativism and "never doubted that

America should remain the asylum for the downtrodden of the world" [64, p. 179]. Storrow's dedication to physical fitness and her experience working with the Saturday Evening Girls were instrumental in her pioneering work as a leader of the Girl Scouts in Boston in its early days [61, pp. 13-15].²¹ As the founder of the Women's City Club of Boston in 1913, Storrow promoted programs on suffrage, politics, reform, and more, often engaging leaders in the community to debate different sides of current issues. An enthusiastic dancer, she helped found the U.S. branch of the English Folk Dancing Society and the Country Dance and Song Society of America. In the late 1920s Storrow became a director of the Better Homes Association. She established Storrowton—a living museum of an eighteenth- and nineteenth-century New England village at the Eastern States Exposition in Springfield, Massachusetts—in 1927 and completed it in 1930. Storrow also participated in relief efforts during both world wars. Her vast connections throughout the community and the country allowed her to elicit the participation of some of the foremost national and international reformers, politicians, and leaders in industry, art, and society, as well as their opponents, in special forums, courses of study, and speaking engagements [65].²²

Storrow was extremely active during the first few years of her volunteer service at NBSIS. She is mentioned or quoted quite often in the reports of board meetings. Most notably, she readily volunteered to organize, lead, or support various committees that oversaw the multitude of programs at the school, and she was often responsible for initiating ideas and concepts for new programs, classes, clubs, and entertainment. She also reached out to members of Boston's social, artistic, and economic elite to become members of the school's advisory board or to offer services that in some manner supported the school and its programs. She was also instrumental in the establishment of the Boston Social Union, which was organized during the winter of 1904-5 at NBSIS to facilitate cooperation among the various social settlements, schools of social work, and charitable organizations in the city [66, p. 43]. Monthly meetings of prominent social workers and reformers in the city, including Woods, Mary Kenney O'Sullivan, Scudder. Mary Kehew, and others, were being held in North Bennet's Reading Rooms. It was no coincidence that the branch library at North Bennet had the largest selection of settlement and social work literature in the city.²³

THE POTTERY AND OTHER CLUB ACTIVITIES

For the first few years of 1900, the clubs, classes, and library at NBSIS expanded dramatically. The library was serving over eighty thousand requests a year, exhausting Guerrier and her small staff [69, pp. 93-94].²⁴ During 1906, Storrow sent Guerrier and Brown on a trip to Europe for a much-needed vacation [70].

During a stay in the Swiss Alps, the two women talked of ideas of starting an industry at which the young women in the library clubs could earn extra money. On visiting a "charming little pottery on the Lake of Thun," they realized the possibilities of starting their own pottery [71, p. 2]. "We spoke of making marmalade, or fruitcake, of hemming napkins and dishtowels, and finally, we spoke of pottery, of the charming peasant ware of Italy, of Holland, of Germany, and now of Switzerland. Since our club girls were almost all of peasant stock, why not start an art pottery and produce American peasant ware?" [31, p. 85].²⁵ Guerrier, Brown, and Storrow recognized that the need of these young women to contribute to family income conflicted with the pursuit of education beyond grammar school. While reformers in Boston, and all over the country, were providing educational, vocational, and Americanization programs, few were addressing the fact that many immigrant youths could not fully take advantage of these opportunities; their financial contribution to the family far outweighed any hopes of higher education. Establishing a commercial industry to provide financial resources, rather than just skills training, was a step toward resolving that problem.

Through Guerrier's help, Brown first started teaching at NBSIS while still studying at the Museum School during the late 1890s. Brown was hired to teach drawing on a part-time basis to various clubs and classes of boys and girls, including Guerrier's Saturday Evening Girls' Club. Her talent, popularity with the students, and interest in the modeling department eventually won her a full-time position at the school [72, pp. 11-12]. Brown was familiar with the making of pottery and the operation of a kiln, and her artistic training and background obviously played a major role in the decision to start a pottery.²⁶

It was not until 1908, however, that official pottery classes, as opposed to modeling, were conducted at NBSIS, and like the clay, wood, and stone modeling classes, these pottery classes were offered primarily for boys and young men [73]. Rarely, particularly talented young women or girls were allowed admittance to the modeling and pottery classes. In the many modeling classes conducted prior to 1910, only three girls are listed; two of them, Albina Mangini and Cecilia Leverone, were enrolled in a class of twenty-six boys; the other, Rose Dondero, was the only girl in a class of thirty-four boys [74]. Interestingly, all three young women were Saturday Evening Girls who went on to successful careers as decorators at the Paul Revere Pottery.

In the summer of 1907, with Storrow's approval and her donation of funds to purchase the equipment, the two Ediths started training in the specifics of pottery making. They hired a local potter and found a pottery chemist from the old Merrimac Pottery of Newburyport, Massachusetts, who "for a substantial consideration, parted with some of his formulas, which we found later on in a printed book of formulas in our own public library" [31, p. 86]. With great trepidation and excitement they fired their first "bright blue glazed tiles" in the cellar of Guerrier and Brown's Chestnut Hill home [58, p. 5]. By the summer of 1907, several S.E.G.s began to learn pottery making in Chestnut Hill. There they began to sign their pottery "S.E.G.," for Saturday Evening Girls, along with their initials; and the pottery works, or Bowl Shop as it was first known, was born. That fall, they moved the operations to West Gloucester with a plan to establish the pottery near the new S.E.G. Camp.[27] They quickly realized, however, that transportation was a problem—not only for equipment, clay, and other raw materials but also in the logistics of living there throughout the winter, which proved to be daunting [71].

No records exist that show what role, if any, NBSIS played in the establishment of the Paul Revere Pottery. In February 1908 a special meeting of the Board of Managers of North Bennet Street School was called to "hear an account of the work of the Library Department and Miss Guerrier's proposition for a pottery and bowl shop at the camp in West Gloucester" [76]. Held at Storrow's Beacon Street home, we can only speculate as to the discussion because the minutes of that meeting are no longer extant. We do know that NBSIS did not, apparently, consider this venture an opportunity the school ought to pursue or support. Interestingly, NBSIS's annual reports offer little recognition to the Saturday Evening Girls' work with the Paul Revere Pottery. The annual report for 1909 stated clearly that the school's newly organized pottery classes, which were specifically for boys, had been "maintained primarily for its recreational and cultural value. Its connection with industry is quite incidental" [77, p. 28]. By 1910, NBSIS claimed that "others have followed their lead in making pottery. . . . The Industrial School has again taken its place as a leader by showing others the possibilities in this field" [78, p. 32]. In its enthusiasm to celebrate its own accomplishments and to promote its vision of industrial training, NBSIS neglected to recognize the accomplishments of the Saturday Evening Girls. As a library group, the Saturday Evening Girls' activities had become an acceptable leisure activity. As a commercial venture, the S.E.G.s and their pottery works no longer fit into NBSIS's vision for the industrial training for girls and young women.[28] It is likely that there existed some level of tension between the two; for girls, classes in modeling at NBSIS remained elusive. As late as 1916, the school's executive committee vetoed a proposal to open the modeling program to girls [80].[29]

The prevailing attitude regarding the "most suitable" vocational training for elementary school and older girls was that of "two points of view . . . woman's relation to self support, and woman's relation to the home" [81, pp. 19-20]. During the winter of 1907, the Boston School Committee authorized fifty thirteen-year-old girls from the upper grades of the Hancock School to come to the NBSIS for ten hours of industrial training every week. The NBSIS recognized the pressures of girls' familial obligations and financial needs, and resistance on the part of parents to the advantages of additional educational opportunities. Although typical of the language of the time period, NBSIS's annual report for 1907 stated that this experiment was founded on the premise that "in the North End . . . (w)ith rare exceptions the girls leave school as early as the law permits. Whether they go at once into industrial or into home life, the training in hand and machine sewing, in domestic science and in textiles and design which we propose to give, will make a much needed connection between the school course and the life that follows" [82, p. 8].

By 1909, however, NBSIS reported that the experiment was not successful. "The class, on account of the age, mental capacity and development of the girls, and general attitude toward the work, was not a very encouraging one" [81, p. 19]. Because of the girls' lack of interest in this sort of "industrial" training, it was naturally assumed that they were intellectually not capable of developing the basic skills necessary "for housekeeping and housefurnishing" [81, p. 20]. What may have been fun in a social club atmosphere may have taken on an entirely different meaning for these young girls when incorporated into a course of study. Cooking, sewing, cleaning, textiles, and design, however, remained at the heart of the program. As one S.E.G. wryly noted, "the girls were the drudges in housework, and chore" [52, p. 4].

It appears then, that NBSIS was not an option for these women in their efforts to establish the pottery and train the S.E.G.s, Storrow, however, was so enthusiastic about the pottery that by early 1908 she had bought a four-story brick house on Hull Street in the North End to house the pottery and the library clubs. The building was located opposite Copps Hill Burying ground, near the Old North Church where Paul Revere had hung his famous lantern, and henceforth the pottery became known as the Paul Revere Pottery [71, pp. 2-3]. Officially called the Library Club House, it quickly acquired the name "Hull House." The two Ediths moved into the fourth-floor apartment of this building, and for the next seven years the Saturday Evening Girls, the other library clubs, and the Paul Revere Pottery flourished under their direction. Storrow's financial and emotional commitment to the group propelled the pottery venture forward at a rapid pace. The pottery continued to expand, gaining national recognition. The February 1912 edition of the *Craftsman* magazine noted that at the Fifth Exhibition of the National Society of Craftsmen in New York, "the most notable examples [of pottery] were the Paul Revere Pottery," propelling the modest venture into the international limelight [83].

Most Saturday Evening Girls and younger library club members, however, just worked a few hours on Saturday mornings, if only to sweep, clean, pack, or assist in the pottery, to earn their weekly-monthly club dues, pay for summer camp, and earn a few extra dollars to help them pursue higher education [54, p. 3].[30] A few worked either full-time or on a more regular part-time schedule [84]. Initially, the full-time workers earned three-four dollars per week, which quickly increased to ten, plus two weeks paid vacation, in addition to a hot lunch every day [85]. While they worked amid fresh flowers and bright light, the S.E.G.s were entertained by dramatic readings and soothing music performed by the daughters of some of Boston's social elite.

According to an article in *House Beautiful* in 1912, "the price of articles produced is fixed after careful consideration of the cost of production, including a fair living wage for the workers" [86]. In an undated advertising brochure, prices for the pottery ranged from $.75 for a small vase to $2.50 for a small bowl to $7.00 for a large pitcher to $18.00 for a large bowl to $31.00 for a lamp to $50.00 for a large, beautifully decorated "Chrysanthemum" vase [87]. At these prices, the wares were only accessible to middle- and upper-class families. As a result, not only did Storrow subsidize the pottery works, but the S.E.G.s were expected to help raise funds as well. Throughout the history of the library clubs, the members performed plays, operettas, and folk dancing to raise funds for their club work. They performed at NBSIS, the open-air theater at the Storrow's home in Lincoln, and the Vendome Hotel and many other Boston locations. Isabella Stewart Gardner offered her palace at Fenway Court on several occasions for their Shakespeare productions. "Mrs. John L. Gardner opened Fenway Court in March . . . for the presentation of *The Merchant of Venice* by the Saturday Evening Girls Club. The patronesses were the leading women of Boston, and the funds raised are to be for the pottery" [86]. Forty years later, the Saturday Evening Girls reminisced about how Mrs. Gardner "flew around behind the scenes and cautioned us North End actresses *not to* dare to touch the priceless tapestries," and about their "first glimpse of society ladies smoking—to us virtuous girls, a shocking glimpse of high life" [2, p. 29]. At the close of the evening, Gardner gave out small, six-inch bowls made by the pottery as party favors to her guests, and to the girls, she gave "cheap paper fans."[31]

Their plays and other productions were an important social and financial component of the clubs. The plays varied from comedies like "Mrs. Wiggs of the Cabbage Patch" to serious Shakespearean drama. The funds they collected from public performances enabled them to purchase "real costumes" and ultimately allowed them to expand their club work to include more young women and girls. According to Catherine Casassa, regardless of "the fun, work, or money, the plays did more than anything else in bringing us together, making good friends, helping us understand each other, and developing in all a fine spirit of comradeship. Together with this growth came the mental development, the broadening of intellect, and the beginning of our acquaintance with masterpieces in literature" [88, p. 7].

Shock and surprise often characterized the response of reformers and the native-born privileged classes to demonstrations of intelligence and eagerness to learn by immigrants and their children. Still, these attitudes informed the establishment of programs for education and training for immigrants and the poor, and also were used to social reformers' advantage when trying to raise funds for programs. In the North End, groups of "visitors," or tourists, were invited to NBSIS to view the work done by the students. Exhibitions were held every year to showcase the school's programs and the individual craft pieces made by the students, not only to celebrate their achievements but also to raise badly needed funds. Although the students were proud of their work, there was some resentment over these expectations of inferiority. In an *S.E.G. News* editorial, S.E.G. Goldstein admonished social workers, reminding them that the "poor . . . instinctively resent being patronized, investigated, meddled with, or put under a microscope as if they were some curious species of other life; for they, too, have intelligence" [89, p. 3]. In an interesting display of oppositional resistance, S.E.G. and Paul Revere Pottery artist Sarah Galner recalled that when tourists came to view the remarkable work these "illiterate . . . ignorant . . . immigrant girls" [85] were doing at the pottery on Hull Street, the girls acted out by feigning ignorance of English and exhibited a general lack of intelligence, all for the visitors' benefit. This performance by the girls, though funny to them, apparently infuriated Storrow, She may have clearly understood the irony of the S.E.G.s display; visitors ultimately walked away from their visit to the pottery with the image of the ignorant immigrant, an image that Storrow so desperately tried to dispel. For the girls, it may not have mattered; Storrow's vision and dedication to securing a future for them perhaps conflicted with their own ideas of identity, self-definition, and respect.

While money was extremely important in running these clubs, volunteer service ultimately made it all possible. Storrow taught folk dancing and provided continued inspiration and encouragement, while each S.E.G. and library club member contributed one hour per week of service, or "housetime," to the "Clubhouse." The S.E.G.s also ran a restaurant and continuously performed in plays, folk dances, operas, and recitals. By late 1914, the Saturday Evening Girls not only maintained financial responsibility by pledging $8.00 each to support the clubs for the seven groups of younger girls and women [58, p. 6] but also personally conducted "school visiting" in conjunction with NBSIS to "keep in touch with our own girls who fall behind in school" [55, p. 13]. According to Goldstein, "the older girls are the big sisters and associate workers. We always put special emphasis in the work with our groups on the cultural side of life and let them also unconsciously as we did before them, learn to establish their own ideals and to think for themselves" [90, p. 3].

Goldstein was one of the original Saturday Evening Girls who gathered with Guerrier in the reading rooms of NBSIS on Saturday evenings in 1899. Born in Russia around 1886, Goldstein was the oldest of five siblings. Goldstein began working at age ten to help support her family. When she was thirteen, her father died; her hopes of becoming a doctor ended. She barely finished grammar school, and the S.E.G. club became her main intellectual influence. Under the tutelage of Guerrier, Goldstein became an assistant in the library. According to Goldstein, "[an] examination for the post paying $35 a month was advertised at the school and [she] won the post, the first Jewish girl in history to receive this appointment. A number of volunteer socialites had tried it previously and some suffered nervous breakdowns . . . there was a gang of Italian and Jewish boys and girls who used the reading room and making them behave was not easy" [91]. In 1922, Goldstein was appointed head of the West End Branch of the Boston Public Library, the largest branch library at that time. In 1925 she founded "Jewish Book Week in America," which eventually became "Jewish Book Month." She lectured across the nation on immigration, library work, and interreligious and interethnic cooperation, and she was particularly interested in Jewish literature. In 1954 she was made curator of Judaica of the Boston Public Library. Because of her support, her brother and three sisters were able to attend high school. Throughout her career she was particularly interested in working with the "foreign born" [92]. She was convinced that the library had "every advantage over [social and educational] agencies, because it is the most free from political and religious influences." Lacking "academic degrees," Goldstein spent her life pursuing "educational opportunities which America had to offer the economically handicapped, . . . in spite of tremendous odds and discouraging experiences" [92]. Similar to other S.E.G.s, Fanny triumphed "by constant sacrifice and persistent application [and] developed an apprecia-

tion for the mental luxuries of life from mere fragments of a slight education, and (pardon the seeming egotism) have advanced to positions of trust and responsibility" [93, p. 2].

From 1912 to 1917 the Saturday Evening Girls published a newspaper entitled the *S.E.G. News,* of which Goldstein was editor in chief. The newspaper focused on contemporary issues related to immigration, education, the library, philanthropy, democracy, employment opportunities, literature, religion, community features, and social news, in addition to the basic subjects of literature, history, civics, economics, and social science. Guest contributors such as Storrow, Woods, and other business, political, educational, and reform leaders of the day often penned feature articles. The newspaper provided social news about the "girls," including engagements, marriages, elopements, births, and updates on the activities at neighborhood settlements. Their "Market" section reported on shipments coming into the docks on Boston's waterfront, noting that higher prices meant good news for fishermen, farmers, and shippers. It printed book reviews and listed "interesting articles" in popular magazines; it offered outlooks on certain career paths for young women, including social work, library work, secretarial and office work, retail, teaching, and nursing.

Many of the young women were in favor of woman's suffrage, though they rarely wrote about it in the *S.E.G. News.* Both Guerrier and Brown were members of the Boston Equal Suffrage Association for Good Government, and the "girls were being indoctrinated on the subject" [2, p. 27]. The NBSIS regularly hosted woman suffrage meetings. After a suffrage rally in Boston in 1913, one S.E.G. wrote, "I have been interested in the Suffrage movement but not in the Militant Method and on hearing Mrs. Pankhurst, my views changed" [94, pp. 4-5].[32] For the most part, however, the newspaper avoided controversial issues such as woman's suffrage, trade unionism, and other political issues, though Goldstein's editorials were often highly charged political statements about women's roles in society, social workers, and life in an immigrant community. She did not hesitate to voice her opinions about other issues of interest to young women. In response to the criticism at the time that "education and social work among the poor retard marriages," Goldstein wrote, "the thought of a mere mate for society's sake alone to any girl of intellect and independence becomes obnoxious . . . [and] the young woman, then, whom education has helped to be something more than a cat or a slave . . . is not selfish to remain single" [96, pp. 2-3]. In another editorial, Goldstein admonished social workers whose desire to "uplift" was derived from a sense of superiority: she argued that they "must teach people the things they want and need to know, and not the things which you think they ought to know" [89, p. 2]. In another editorial, Goldstein criticized reformers "addicted to the terrible hobby of 'Slumitis'" who spend their time making "microscopic studies . . . of the children of the slums" [97, p. 1], but who ignored the voices of the children themselves. The *S.E.G. News* became that voice. As Gere points out in her study of literacy practices in Progressive Era women's clubs, working-class women often employed "textual strategies" that helped them "resist definitions of urbanization that featured them as problems to be solved" [9, p. 64]. With the exception of guest contributors, the newspaper was written exclusively by the girls and young women of the various library clubs. The S.E.G.s published the newspaper in the hopes of having their voices heard as community members who had something to offer. Determined to make the newspaper "a medium of free speech and enlightenment on matters of importance in the North End" [98, p. 1], Goldstein summed up its importance to club members, "as a living voice of a living group, it is invaluable . . . we merely intend it as a medium of spreading the knowledge and benefits of our experiences where they may perhaps prove useful . . . our experiences in the many years that we have been receiving the bounty of so-called philanthropists and social workers ought to mean something. Together we have doubtless made many mistakes and the impressions gained along with these experiences are, together, ones of joy and sorrow" [99, p. 2].

By 1914, after much lobbying by Guerrier and the community, a North End Branch Library was officially opened in the remodeled St. John's Church on North Bennet Street. Because of other philanthropic and community commitments competing for her attention, Storrow decided at this time that she would no longer support all the library clubs and the pottery; the responsibility for supporting and running the clubs was turned over to the Saturday Evening Girls.[33] With the approval of the Board of Trustees of the Boston Public Library, the library clubs moved to the basement of the new branch library after Storrow paid for refurbishment of the space [100].

The S.E.G. and older library club members provided mentoring and guidance to younger members; they acted as living examples of the educational value of the library clubs and as role models for younger girls aspiring to something greater than the factory floor. Already self-governing, becoming self-supporting was the next step toward autonomy. While on the one hand the S.E.G.s resisted conforming completely to a white middle-class ideal of womanhood, they also embraced it. Convinced that they had not lost their ethnic traditions or identities in the process of Americanization, they found pride in having "grown from foreign little girls into American young women" [21, p. 2]. They thought that their work in the clubs had enabled them to do things for themselves, and they viewed Storrow,

Guerrier, and Brown as the "ideal[s] of American womanhood" [21, p. 2]. When Storrow passed the financial responsibility of the clubs to the Saturday Evening Girls in 1914, they were determined to live up to her example. According to Goldstein, the S.E.G.s hoped to "pass the ideal on to others. We shall endeavor to be better friends, better daughters, better wives, better mothers; and always pure and simple women, who, years hence, will look with pride upon this Association of American Daughters of North End Immigrants" [21, p. 2].

By 1915 the expanding library clubs and the growing Paul Revere Pottery were outgrowing the house at 18 Hull Street. The need for additional production, designing, glazing, and firing spaces for the pottery precluded Hull Street as a viable option for the expansion; the pollution from the kilns was adding to the dirt and filth in an already highly congested area. During the summer of 1915, with the funds provided from the sale of the building at 18 Hull Street, Guerrier and Brown moved the pottery to the nearby suburb of Brighton. Ultimately, the Paul Revere Pottery could not compete with mass-produced pottery, and its market remained limited. The overhead expenses that were charged to each piece of pottery priced them out of the mass market, and the pottery had to be continuously subsidized by Storrow.

Women reformers, like Guerrier, Brown, and Storrow, who supported the Saturday Evening Girls Club, were important to the lives of the thousands of immigrant families who crowded U.S. cities during the nineteenth century and early twentieth century. Their philanthropic efforts, financial or personal, deeply affected the lives of many families, in ways that would carry through to succeeding generations. By providing the "inspiration for a college education here . . . the opportunity for a career there, [and] a . . . livelihood" [101] for those associated with the Paul Revere Pottery, Guerrier, Brown, and Storrow helped some of the women of the North End move out of poverty and into the middle class.[34] In the aftermath of World War I, as the S.E.G.s aged and moved out of the North End, the structure of the clubs weakened. The individual library clubs consolidated, and thereafter they were all identified as Saturday Evening Girls. For many, the clubs became the bridge "between Jew and gentile, between rich and poor," and they "truly felt [themselves] to be citizens of a great and good world" [102]. The bonds that were created motivated many S.E.G.s to continue meeting on an irregular basis for the next fifty years, finally voting to dissolve in June 1969 [103].

Brown, the artistic director of the pottery for twenty-five years, died in 1932 after a long illness. The instability of the pottery was exacerbated by the Depression, and with the loss of Brown, the enthusiasm and inspiration was gone. The pottery finally discontinued its operations in 1942. After serving as supervisor of circulation and supervisor of branch libraries, Guerrier retired from the Boston Public Library in 1940 with forty-six years of library service. Having served as a volunteer director with the U.S. Food Administration during World War I, she went on to serve again, after her retirement, on the Committee for Public Safety during World War II.[35] In her autobiography, written in 1950 at the age of eighty, Guerrier wrote, "I could fill a book with the reminiscences of my friends around Hull Street, not one of whom lives there now. I have watched them emerge with pride and satisfaction. They serve on city committees and on educational boards, and are all for progress. They tell me the clubhouse meant much to them, I tell them it meant more to me" [31, p. 90]. In closing, she wrote, "I know some other worthwhile task is just around the corner, and I am waiting eagerly to welcome it" [31, p. 132]. She died in 1958 at the age of eighty-eight.[36]

Helen Storrow died in 1944, after forty-five years of personal commitment to the S.E.G.s. Storrow was often impatient with her upper-class associates and their preference for poetry and philosophy to philanthropy and other social activism [110]. Considered a "woman of many ideas and activities" [111], but entirely too democratic, Storrow was perhaps quietly tolerated by many of her upper-class acquaintances because of her wealth, family connections, and commanding energy. Storrow once wrote, "I expect to pass through this world but once. Any good, therefore, that I can do, or any kindness that I can show to any fellow creature, let me do it now. Let me not defer or neglect it, for I shall not pass this way again" [2, p. 1].

CONCLUSION

The Saturday Evening Girls' Club and the other library clubs emerged from an environment that was indifferent and at times even hostile to the educational and personal aspirations of immigrant and working-class girls and women. As the young women of the clubs were being challenged intellectually, they were in turn challenging systems that had institutionalized low expectations of them as women and as immigrants. Intellectual accomplishment and cultural and ethnic identities were merged, thus breaking down barriers that had traditionally prevented them from exploring educational and economic options. The S.E.G.s would not, therefore, simply accept vocational training for factory jobs or domestic responsibilities; they wanted more, above and beyond expectations of their gender, class, and ethnic groups. In the process of accepting the more appealing alternative promoted by Guerrier, Brown, and Storrow, the S.E.G.s became part of a modern movement toward greater options for women—educationally, politically, and economically. The S.E.G.s were surrounded, and perhaps even indoctrinated, with modern liberal ideas,

while at the same time they faced strong ethnic and old-world values and nineteenth-century Victorian ideals of women and their roles in the public and private spheres. The S.E.G.s demonstrated a determined resistance to the demands not only of industrialization but also of society's limited expectations for them as working-class women and as immigrants. According to Goldstein, "these girls were quite ordinary. In their ordinariness, they proved extraordinary" [2, p. 21].

Notes

1. The Friday Evening Girls' Club was the second club fashioned after the Saturday Evening Girls' Club. At age twenty, members of this club were inducted into the Saturday Evening Girls' Club.

2. Goldstein became the Branch Librarian of the West End in Boston in 1922. In 1925 she founded "Jewish Book Week in America," which eventually became "Jewish Book Month." Her collection of Judaica manuscript materials is located at the Boston Public Library Goldstein remained branch librarian at the West End Library until her retirement in 1958.

3. For a discussion of this phenomenon, see [3-6].

4. The 1910 United States Census of Population for the North and West Ends of Boston has been examined to compile data on the S.E.G.s and their parents and family members. Of the sixty-five young women located in the census, 77 percent were native and born to immigrant parents. They were overwhelmingly Russian Jews, at 78.5 percent, followed by 18.5 percent who were of Italian heritage. Over 90 percent of the S.E.G.'s parents were foreign born [11]. See also [1] for individual biographies of some of the women.

5. Thirty-two of the respondents reported having a total of sixty-seven children. Twenty-four of these S.E.G.s reported educational data for their children, for a total of fifty-two children, forty-seven of whom, or 90 percent, were enrolled in, or graduated (or assumed) from, college or other post-high school vocational or professional institutions. Their children became doctors, lawyers, librarians, artists, teachers, and more. See also [1].

6. The S.E.G.s represented a significant number of the graduates of the local girls' grammar school (Hancock) in the years 1902 through 1907 [15]. For graduation statistics of these years, please see table A1 in the appendix.

7. The advent of the railway and subway system in Boston enabled the growth of suburbs in Boston, as people could live outside the center of the city and still commute to jobs within the city.

8. These programs often included classes in English and citizenship, where immigrants were taught the basics of American history, the principles of a democratic government, and civic responsibilities.

9. Pauline Agassiz Shaw was the daughter of the famous nineteenth-century naturalist. Louis Agassiz, and the stepdaughter of Elizabeth Cary Agassiz, founder of Radcliffe College for women, in Cambridge, Massachusetts. For more information on Shaw and her family, see [22].

10. These women were pioneers in the kindergarten movement in the United States and founders of the Garland School for training kindergarten teachers in Boston.

11. According to the NBSIS minutes of the Executive Committee, November 18, 1909. "We have counted upon and secured the support of Catholics and non-Catholics alike and have intentionally ignored the possibility of a religious question concerning our work" [24].

12. Louisa May Alcott wrote several poems dedicated to "Our Anna," in which she and her sister rejoiced "in [Anna's] fireless kindness and thoughtfulness and friendship" [32].

13. Anna Pratt gave a pearl necklace to Edith, writing, "for my pearl was set on pleasing little Edith" [33].

14. Edith had apparently been interested in becoming an artist since she was a child [36].

15. Pingree was also an early proponent and supporter of the kindergarten movement in Boston, a member of the Boston School Committee from 1894 to 1906, and manager of the North Bennet Street Industrial School from 1883 to 1906 [37]. See also NBSIS Records.

16. Guerrier does not mention what type of literature she considered "trash."

17. For an expanded discussion of this point, see [41-42].

18. This is in direct contrast to many woman-centered reform organizations that actually assumed that reading and library rooms for women and girls were not only essential but much in demand by them. The Women's Educational and Industrial Union in Boston is a case in point.

19. There are many sources that describe this situation: see [3-6] and [43-44].

20. Under pressure from the trustees of NBSIS, Helen Storrow, and the community, the city of Boston eventually purchased a building for the purpose of establishing a permanent branch library in the North End in 1912 [47-50].

21. Many thanks to Pat Ross, curator of the Girl Scout Museum, Cedar Hill, Patriots Trail Girl Scouts, Waltham, Massachusetts.

22. She received an honorary Master of Arts from Smith College and a Doctor of Humanities in 1942 from Boston University for her commitment to social reform, the Girl Scouts, and pioneering preservation efforts.

23. By April 1905 NBSIS reported that the "Committee on co-operation reported the result of two meetings of delegates of other organizations at which was formed the Social Union of the North and West Ends" [67-68].

24. The library committee felt "that Miss Guerrier's salary is inadequate, considering that she gives all the time and strength she has to her work" [69].

25. Guerrier's association of "peasant stock" with "peasant ware" was typical of the time period. Many differentiated these late nineteenth and early twentieth century eastern European and southern Italian immigrants as peasants, in direct contrast to the earlier northern and western European and northern Italian immigrants, who were often better educated and more financially secure.

26. The NBSIS had installed a potter's wheel in the modeling room in 1902 and a kiln in 1903. Edith Brown is first noted here as a teacher in "modeling," and she is last listed as a teacher in the report for the year ending August 31, 1907, which coincides with the establishment of the Paul Revere Pottery. See [29].

27. In 1906. Helen Storrow purchased an acre of land in West Gloucester, Massachusetts, where she built a cottage with fourteen bedrooms, a living room, and a kitchen for the club's working "girls" for much needed summer vacations [31, p. 80]. Seventy-five years later. Gertrude Friederman would remember that her two weeks at the S.E.G. camp were one of the "great times" of her life [75].

28. The S.E.G.s are mentioned again in the annual report for the school in 1912, but there was no discussion of their commercial venture, only their work with the library clubs [79, pp. 47-48].

29. By 1918, however, the school was also offering classes in modeling, as well as printing, drafting, and telephone operating, in addition to its regular domestic skills training.

30. The club members were also responsible for raising the funds for their camp vacations. From 1913 to 1916 the cost to stay for a week at camp varied between approximately $5.50 and $6.20.

31. When I interviewed them (audio tapes in my possession), several descendants of S.E.G.s recalled their mothers telling them this. The Gardner Museum recently discovered several six-inch S.E.G. bowls, never used, of various colors and designs, on a top shelf in a kitchen cupboard.

32. Emmiline Pankhurst, militant English suffragette, spoke at the Tremont Temple in Boston in November 1913; see [2, p. 27] and [95, p. 7].

33. James Jackson Storrow offered to support the clubs for one year (through June 1915) to ensure a smooth transition: see [58, p. 5].

34. See also [1] and [2] for further information about the "uplifting" of these women into the middle class, from their own perspectives.

35. For more information on Guerrier's government work, see [104-105].

36. For more information on Guerrier's career and other accomplishments, see [31] and [106-109].

References

1. *S.E.G. News, Cherry Tree Edition,* 1954, Boston Public Library, North End Branch, Boston.

2. *S.E.G. News: 1899-1952 Reunion Edition,* 1952. Boston Public Library, North End Branch, Boston.

3. Seller, Maxine Schwartz. *Immigrant Women.* Philadelphia: Temple University Press, 1981.

4. Weinberg, Sydney Stahl. *The World of Our Mothers.* New York: Schoken, 1988.

5. Smith, Judith. *Family Connections.* Albany, N.Y.: SUNY Press, 1985.

6. Ewen, Elizabeth. *Immigrant Women in the Land of Dollars.* New York: Monthly Review, 1985.

7. Blair, Karen J. *The Clubwoman as Feminist: True Womanhood Redefined, 1868-1914.* New York: Holmes & Meier, 1980.

8. Murolo, Priscilla. *The Common Ground of Womanhood: Class Gender and Working Girl's Clubs, 1884-1928.* Urbana: University of Illinois Press, 1997.

9. Gere, Anne Ruggles. *Literacy and Cultural Work in U.S. Women's Clubs, 1880-1920.* Urbana: University of Illinois Press, 1997.

10. Peiss, Kathy. *Cheap Amusements: Working Women and Leisure in Turn of the Century New York.* Philadelphia: Temple University Press, 1986.

11. United States Bureau of the Census. Thirteenth Decenial Census of the United States, 1910, reels 615-16, Massachusetts, Suffolk County.

12. Solomon, Barbara Miller. *In the Company of Educated Women: A History of Women and Higher Education in America.* New Haven, Conn.: Yale University Press, 1985.

13. Jacobs, Jerry A., and Greene, Margaret E. "Race and Ethnicity, Social Class, and Schooling." In *After Ellis Island: Newcomers and Natives in the 1910 Census,* edited by Susan Cotts Watkins, pp. 212-26. New York: Russell Sage, 1994.

14. "School Document No. 16—1907." In *Annual Report of the School Committee of the City of Boston, 1907.* Boston: Municipal Printing Office, 1907.

15. "Statistics." In *Documents of the School Committee of the City of Boston.* Boston: Municipal Printing Office, 1908.

16. De Marco, William. *Ethnics and Enclaves: Boston's Italian North End.* Ann Arbor: University of Michigan Press, 1981.

17. Bacchini, Sylvia. "The Immigrant." *S.E.G. News* 3, no. 1, November 14, 1914, Boston Public Library, Fine Arts Department, Boston.

18. Lazerson, Marun. *Origins of the Urban School: Public Education in Massachusetts, 1870-1915,* Cambridge, Mass.: Harvard University Press. 1971.

19. Rothman, David J., and Sheila M., eds. *Sources of the American Social Tradition.* Vol. 2. New York: Basic, 1975.

20. Gordon, Milton M. *Assimilation in American Life: The Role of Race, Religion, and National Origin.* New York: Oxford University Press, 1964.

21. Goldstein, Fanny. "The Voice of Appreciation." *S.E.G. News* 3, no. 2, December 12, 1914, Boston Public Library, Fine Arts Department, Boston.

22. Tharp, Lonise Hall. *Adventurous Alliance.* Boston: Little, Brown, 1959.

23. "Report of the North Bennet Street Industrial Home." Records of North Bennet Street Industrial School. MC 269 (hereafter referred to as NBSIS Records), series 1.1.1. Schlesinger Library, Cambridge, Massachusetts.

24. Minutes of Executive Committee Meetings, November 18, 1909, Archives of the North Bennet Street School, North Bennet Street School, Boston.

25. *Annual Report, 1888-89,* NBSIS Records, series 1.1.1.

26. *Annual Report for the Year 1904-1905,* 25th anniversary ed., NBSIS Records, series 1.1.6.

27. Kingsbury, Susan, the Women's Educational and Industrial Union, to Dodd, Alvin, director, NBSIS organization, June 22, 1909, NBSIS Records, series 2, Aviii.32.

28. "Hands Need Training." *Charities* (August 23, 1902): 175.

29. *Annual Report, November 1901 to November 1903,* NBSIS Records, series 1.1.5.

30. *Annual Report, April 1901,* NBSIS Records, series 1.1.5.

31. Matson, Molly, ed. *An Independent Woman. The Autobiography of Edith Guerner.* Amherst: University of Massachusetts Press, 1992.

32. Alcott, Louisa May, to Ricketson, Anna. Anna Ricketson Papers, bois Am 1130.2, folders 1-3 and 17, Houghton Library, Harvard University, Cambridge, Massachusetts.

33. Pratt, Anna, to Ricketson, Anna, circa 1884. Anna Ricketson Papers, bois Am 1130.1, folder 5. Houghton Library, Harvard University, Cambridge, Massachusetts.

34. Graduation Program, Vermont Methodist Seminary and Female College, 1891, Ricketson Collection, SG 12 series D folder 1. New Bedford Whaling Museum/Old Dartmouth Historical Society, New Bedford, Massachusetts.

35. "Register of Pupils—School of Drawing and Painting. Museum of Fine Arts," September 1891, "Edith Guerrier," vertical file, School of the Museum of Fine Arts Archives, Boston.

36. The Massachusetts Normal Art School, 28 School Street, Boston (Commonwealth of Massachusetts, Department of Education), to George Guerrier, March 3, 1879, Ricketson/Guerrier Family papers, Liakos/Gentile Collection, series F., George P. Guerrier, 1865-1912, subseries 1, correspondence, 1865-1887, the Thoreau Society Archives and Collections, Concord Free Public Library, Concord, Massachusetts.

37. "Class Register," and "The Garland Kindergarten Alumnae Association Register, 1873-1923," Records of Garland Junior College, box 1, folder 1, series 1, MS 104, Simmons College Archive, Boston.

38. Meyer, Annie Nathan. *Women's Work in America.* New York: Holt, 1891.

39. "Public Library of the City of Boston, Records of the Corporation," Trustees Records, vol. 6, p. 260, Boston Public Library, Boston.

40. *Annual Report, 1897-1898,* NBSIS Records, series 1.1.4.

41. Peiss, Kathy. "'Charity Girls' and City Pleasures: Historical Notes on Working Class Sexuality, 1880-1920." In *Women and Power in American History,* edited by Kathryn Kish Sklar and Thomas Dublin, pp. 88-100. Englewood Cliffs, N.J.: Prentice Hall, 1991.

42. Peiss, Kathy. "Gender Relations and Working Class Leisure: New York City, 1880-1920." In *"To Toil the Live Long Day": America's Women at Work, 1780-1980,* edited by Carol Groneman and Mary Beth Norton, pp. 98-111. Ithaca, N.Y.: Cornell University Press, 1987.

43. Carson, Mina. *Settlement Folk.* Chicago: University of Chicago Press, 1990.

44. Howe, Irving. *The World of Our Fathers.* New York: Simon & Schuster, 1976.

45. Adelson, Mildred. Personal interview with author March 13, 1995.

46. Goldstein, Fanny. "Editorial." *S.E.G. News* 4, no. 3, January 8, 1916, Boston Public Library, Fine Arts Department, Boston.

47. Trustees Records, vol. 6. pp. 224, 256, 260, 403, Boston Public Library, Boston.

48. Trustees Records, vol. 7. pp. 126, 132, 346, Boston Public Library, Boston.

49. Trustees Records, vol. 8, p. 303, Boston Public Library, Boston.

50. Trustees Records, vol. 9, pp. 119, 185, 309, 311, 343, 448, Boston Public Library, Boston.

51. *Annual Report 1904-1905,* NBSIS Records, series 1.1.6.

52. *The Story of the Saturday Evening Girls,* Reunion, December 12, 1929, Boston Public Library, North End Branch, Boston.

53. Heiman, Rebecca G. "The Library Clubhouse." *S.E.G. News* 3, no. 1. November 14, 1914. Boston Public Library. Fine Arts Department, Boston.

54. Goldstein, Fanny. "The Story of the S.E.G. in Storytelling." *S.E.G. News* 3, no. 7. May 8, 1915, Boston Public Library, Fine Arts Department, Boston.

55. Heiman, Rebecca G. "The Library Clubhouse Report, 1916-1917." *S.E.G. News* 5, no. 8, June 9, 1917, Boston Public Library, Fine Arts Department, Boston.

56. Heiman, Rebecca G. "Report of the Library Clubhouse, September 15, 1915 to May 1916." *S.E.G. News* 4, no. 7, June 3, 1916. Boston Public Library, Fine Arts Department, Boston.

57. Bruno, Vaine C. "A Personal Letter," *S.E.G. News* 2, no. 1, November 8, 1913, Boston Athenaeum, Boston.

58. Guerrier, Edith. "A Brief Survey of the L.C.H. Group." *S.E.G. News* 3, no. 1, November 14, 1914, Boston Public Library, Fine Arts Department, Boston.

59. Muncy, Robyn. *Creating a Female Dominion in American Reform, 1890-1935.* New York: Oxford University Press, 1991.

60. Tucker, Sheila. "Lithgow Osborne Recalls Past, Looks Ahead." *Citizen Advertiser* (September 21, 1974): 12.

61. Ware, Leonard. *Helen Osborne Storrow, 1864-1944: A Memoir,* Helen Storrow vertical file, Schlesinger Library, Cambridge, Mass, 1970.

62. Bailie, Helen Tufts Journal Entries, 1915-1916, January 2, 1915, Sophia Smith Collection, Helen Tufts Bailie Papers, Smith College, Northampton, Massachusetts.

63. Pearson, Henry Greenleaf. *Son of New England: James Jackson Starrow, 1864-1926.* Boston: Todd, 1932.

64. Solomon, Barbara Miller. *Ancestors and Immigrants.* Boston: Northeastern University Press, 1989.

65. Records of the Women's City Club of Boston, Manuscript Collection M-55, Schlesinger Library, Cambridge, Massachusetts.

66. "Report of the Meetings of the Board of Managers, May 1904-April 1907," December 16, 1904, p. 43, NBSIS Records, series 1.2.15.

67. "Report of the Meetings of the Board of Managers, May 1904-April 1907," April 20, 1905, p. 71, NBSIS Records, series 1.2.15.

68. *Boston Transcript.* December 27, 1905, n.p. Scrapbooks, Archives, North Bennet Street School, Boston.

69. "Report of the Meetings of the Board of Managers, May 1904-April 1907," October 20, 1905, NBSIS Records, series 1.2.15.

70. "Report of the Meetings of the Board of Managers, May 1904-April 1907," Friday, May 18, 1906, NBSIS Records, series 1.2.15.

71. *The Story of the Paul Revere Pottery,* n.d., Boston Public Library, Boston.

72. "Report of the Meetings of the Board of Managers, May 1904-April 1907," Sept. 16, 1904, pp. 11-12, NBSIS Records, series 1.2.15.

73. Card Index: Kiln Record, 1908, NBSIS Records, series 2Bi.126.

74. "School Registers," NBSIS Records, series 4.2.42.

75. Oral history interview with Gertrude Friederman Levowich by Levowich family members, circa 1988, author's private collection.

76. Postcard, Ricketson/Guerrier Family Papers, the Liakos/Gentile Collection, Thoreau Society, Lincoln, Massachusetts.

77. *Annual Report, 1909-1910,* NBSIS Records, series 1.1.8.

78. *Annual Report, 1910-1911,* NBSIS Records, series 1.1.9.

79. *Annual Report, 1911-1912,* NBSIS Records, series 1.1.10.

80. "Executive Committee Meeting Minutes," April 16, 1916, Archives, North Bennet Street School, Boston.

81. *Annual Report, 1908-1909,* NBSIS Records, series 1.1.7.

82. *Annual Report, August 1907,* NBSIS Records, series 1.1.6.

83. "Fifth Exhibition of the National Society of Graftsman." *Graftsman* 21 (February 1912): 562-67.

84. "A Social and Business Experiment in the Making of Pottery." *Handicraft* 3 (February 1911): 415-16.

85. S.E.G. Sarah Galner Bloom, interview by Barbara Kramer, daughter of S.E.G. Ethel Epstein, spring of 1975, Kramer private collection.

86. Pendleton, Margaret. "Paul Revere Pottery." *House Beautiful* (August 1912): 74.

87. Undated Paul Revere Pottery brochure, circa 1920, author's private collection.

88. Carassa, Catherine, "The S.E.G. Dramatics." *S.E.G. News* 2, no. 4, February 14, 1914, Boston Athenaeum, Boston.

89. Goldstein, Fanny. "A Review of the S.E.G." *S.E.G. News* 3, no. 6, April 10, 1915, Boston Public Library, Fine Arts Department, Boston.

90. *S.E.G. News* 2, no. 5, March 14, 1914. Boston Public Library, Fine Arts Department, Boston.

91. Carberg, Warren. "In Library for Over 25 Years." Unidentified newspaper article, (circa 1934), n.d., n.p., Fanny Goldstein vertical file, West End Branch Library, Boston, Massachusetts.

92. Goldstein, Fanny, to Guggenheim Fellowship Committee, 1927. NBSIS Records, Series 2 Aix.44.

93. Goldstein, Fanny, "Editorial," *S.E.G. News* 4, no. 1, Boston Public Library, Fine Arts Department, Boston.

94. Goodman, Celia. "Mrs. Pankhurst at Tremont Temple." *S.E.G. News* 2, no. 2, December 13, 1913, Boston Athenaeum, Boston.

95. Heiman, Rebecca G. "House Notes." *S.E.G. News* 2, no. 7, May 16, 1914, Boston Athenaeum, Boston.

96. Goldstein, Fanny. "Editorial," *S.E.G. News* 4, no. 4, February 12, 1916, Boston Public Library, Fine Arts Department, Boston.

97. Goldstein, Fanny. "Editorial," *S.E.G. News* 4, no. 2, December 11, 1915, Boston Public Library, Fine Arts Department, Boston.

98. Goldstein, Fanny. "Editorial," *S.E.G. News* 2, no. 2, December 13, 1913, Boston Athenaeum, Boston.

99. Goldstein, Fanny. "Editorial," *S.E.G. News* 2, no. 8, February 14, 1914, Boston Athenaeum, Boston.

100. Trustees Records, vol. 10, p. 196, Boston Public Library, Boston.

101. Casassa, Catherine and Rose, to Guerrier, E., "Friendship Letters to Edith Guerrier from the S.E.G.," Sept. 20, 1950. Ricketson Collection, Mss 13, sg. 12, vol. 1, series A, New Bedford Whaling Museum and Old Dartmouth Historical Society, New Bedford, Massachusetts.

102. Letter to Edith Guerrier from Annie Krop Adelson, "Friendship Letters to Edith Guerrier from the S.E.G.," Sept. 20, 1950, "Ricketson Collection, Mss 13, Sg. 12, vol. 1, series A, New Bedford Whaling Museum and Old Dartmouth Historical Society, New Bedford, Massachusetts.

103. Minutes of the Saturday Evening Girls' Meetings, June 12, 1969, private collection.

104. Clark, Kellie D., and Richardson, John V. Jr., "Edith Guerrier: 'A Little [Warrior] Woman of New England,' 1870-1958." *Journal of Government Information* 28 (January/February 2001): in press.

105. Guerrier, Edith. *We Pledge Allegiance, A Librarian's Intimate Story of the United States Food Administration.* Stanford, Calif: Stanford University Press, 1941.

106. *Boston Transcript,* August 18, 1934, n.p., Edith Guerrier vertical file, West End Branch Library, Boston, Massachusetts.

107. *Christian Science Monitor* (February 16, 1954), n.p., Edith Guerrier vertical file, West End Branch Library, Boston, Massachusetts.

108. Usher, Sarah M. "In Memoriam: Edith Guerrier." In *The Question Mark.* Boston: Boston Public Library Staff Association, 1958, pp. 3-4, Edith Guerrier vertical file, West End Branch Library, Boston, Massachusetts.

109. Beal, George Brinton. "Retired Hub Librarian: 52nd Anniversary Meeting of Group She Started to Make Girls Read Books." *Boston Post Magazine* 3 (February 1952): n.p., Edith Guerrier vertical file, West End Branch Library, Boston, Massachusetts.

110. Bryant, Louise Stevens, to Rose Kerr, December 31, 1944, Louise Stevens Bryant Papers, Sophia Smith Collection, Smith College, Northampton, Massachusetts.

111. Bailie, Helen Tufts. Journal entries, August 8, 1916, Helen Tufts Bailie Papers, Sophia Smith Collection, Smith College, Northampton, Massachusetts.

Jacques Barzun (essay date summer 2001)

SOURCE: Barzun, Jacques. "Three Men and a Book." *American Scholar* 70, no. 3 (summer 2001): 49-57.

[*In the following essay, Barzun relates the history of book clubs in America and his role in developing one.*]

The book club is not a twentieth-century invention, unless turning a thing upside down is inventiveness. In the eighteenth and nineteenth centuries, small groups of people clubbed together to buy books because they were expensive. In colonial New York, for example, five or six men formed the New York Society Library for such a purpose in 1754, and it has had an uninterrupted existence to this day. It is now a large collection open to the public. Around the same time, the Boston Library Society thrived, and by joining another society became the present Boston Athenaeum, which combines a grand museum with a vast library and is now expanding its quarters.

The book club of the mid-twentieth century was no such grassroots affair with a noble future. It started from the business end of things, its purpose being to increase the sale of books. This need had been made acute by the practice of letting booksellers return to the publisher any unsold copies. With the enormous output of books annually and the competing agencies of film, radio, and television, the publishing industry found itself producing more than it could distribute in the ordinary way of chancy announcements through reviews. Advertising is too expensive to waste on works that do not take flight on their own. The result is that by far the greater number issued—good, bad, or indifferent—are hustled to the remainder house. Incidentally, the book jacket is a by-product of this return policy; it protects the object on its multiple comings and goings. The simple days are over when the printer-publisher sold his wares on a stall outside the press, direct to the passerby.

In this country, the Literary Guild inaugurated the distribution of popular novels to people who agreed to buy every month—or nearly—a book chosen for them by the Guild. Next, the Book-of-the-Month Club offered in the same way works of a more intellectual cast, and several other organizations catered to the tastes of people interested in a single subject, such as history or popular science. In England, the Book Society was for the generalist, and the Left Book Club for Soviet sympathizers. All these enterprises succeeded in materially extending the dissemination of new books. In both countries, such success showed up the publishing industry's incapacity to sell what it made; the buyers were there, but nobody had found the means of reaching them steadily as individuals.

Book clubs achieved this purpose by offering each month a fairly wide choice of books, together with a share of the usual publishers' discount. This lowered by 25 to 30 percent the list price of books, which fifty years ago ranged from six to eight dollars. If a club member did not return the card enclosed in the bulletin by a certain date, he received the main selection automatically. Consent and absentmindedness were on a par.

* * *

Among the American clubs serving the public in this way, one had a different origin from all the rest. Instead of being the offspring of salesmanship, the Readers'

Subscription was founded in September 1951 to create an audience for books that the other clubs considered to be too far above the public taste. The Book-of-the-Month Club had somewhat lowered its original goal and the specialist caterers also looked for the safely popular. The idea of going beyond these limits and supplying readers with books of solid intellectual merit arose in a conversation between Lionel Trilling and his former student in Columbia College, Gilman Kraft. He was the brother of the future political journalist Joseph Kraft, who had been a student of mine and who vouched to me for Gilman's intelligence and integrity.

Trilling and I were then teaching together a seminar for Ph.D. candidates, and when he asked me to serve with him as coeditor of the venture, I agreed. But I urged that we needed a third, not only to resolve possible differences in making the selections, but also to offset the appearance of exclusively academic judgment, I suggested a poet and proposed W. H. Auden. He and I shared a strong interest in music and used to go together to Richard Franko Goldman's classical band concerts in Central Park. Auden accepted "editing" with us, and we were off with controlled enthusiasm.

Gilman Kraft was a good organizer. He found the needed resources and used them prudently: no large staff or sumptuous offices, but two modest rooms on Broadway, a typist, and a handyman, a charming, gentle, efficient soul, who turned out to be the brother of the novelist James Baldwin. To help Kraft write the briefer notices of alternative choices and occasional recordings, we had young Leo Raditsa, later a distinguished scholar and teacher at St. John's College. The mailing of materials and other relations with members—the shipment of books, billing, and bookkeeping—were handled by one of the two or three firms that called themselves "fulfillment" companies, a title that soon took on the hue of irony.

The name Readers' Subscription was chosen after a long discussion in the Trillings' living room on Claremont Avenue. Gilman Kraft was present, but not Auden. It was Diana Trilling who coined the formula. I thought it inaccurate; a club member is not locked in like a magazine subscriber; he can choose a substitute for the month's offering or refuse it altogether. This disagreement was, I am happy to say, the last on any important matter. At that same session, it was Gilman Kraft who baptized the future bulletin *The Griffin*. The body of a lion and the head of an eagle is perhaps an apt description of the species Critic.

At the first editorial meeting, the three judges tackled a large pile of books that Kraft had solicited from publishers or that had been sent after the public notice of our existence. We each chose half a dozen for reading at home and briefly scanned and discussed possible others.

We did this every month, or rather every four weeks, making a year of thirteen months and thirteen books. At a second meeting each month, we reported, chose the main selection and several alternates, and decided which of us would write the lead reviews. The discussions were remarkably urbane. I recall no dispute, not even unpleasant vehemence. Nor was there ever a two-to-one decision.

By good luck, we were all three incredibly punctual and faithful. It took the flu to keep one of us away, and this happened only a few times in the 139 months of our service. Wystan Auden, who may have begun with a little apprehension about trading literary opinions with a pair of professors, soon saw that Lionel and I had long forgotten our Ph.D.'s and were at ease with each other—as shortly were the three of us.

This good understanding was desirable, because each review was mailed by its author to the other two and changes or additions freely suggested by phone. Sometimes the book that one of us particularly favored had to be postponed one month to make room for another; timing was governed by the need to offer a book as soon as possible after publication. On occasion, we were outbid by the Book-of-the-Month Club, where Clifton Fadiman, that highly qualified judge, evidently shared our estimate of a new work and persuaded the rest of his panel.

It goes without saying that the tone and twists of blurbery were automatically avoided. The reviews were indeed always favorable; the book would not have been chosen if it had not pleased us all. As to our range, it had no preshrunk limits about viewpoint or subject. We offered E. M. Forster's essays on politics and society and the plays of Bertolt Brecht, the poems of Cavafy and Proust's first novel, *Jean Santeuil*. *The Griffin* might in addition feature a letter from an author, or a poem, or a guest reviewer for a second book. Among these visitors I recall Peter Gay, Alan Pryce-Jones, and Edmund Wilson. Forster dropped us a line when working on the libretto of *Billy Budd*. First and last, we recommended works by authors as far apart in opinion as Günter Grass, James Baldwin, Lawrence Durrell, Eleanor Clark, William Golding, Norman O. Brown, Harold Rosenberg, James Agee, William Burroughs, Cesare Pavese, Claude Lévi-Strauss, Muriel Spark, Iris Murdoch, and J. R. R. Tolkien.

Some of our authors were at the start of their renown, but to bring out Flaubert's *Bouvard and Pécuchet* (with its annex, *The Dictionary of Accepted Ideas,* for the first time in English) or Berlioz's dramatized music criticism, *Evenings with the Orchestra,* was tantamount to offering our readers unknown "first works." It was not surprising that some who enjoyed our painstaking essays (each of us had two critics always at his elbow) should suggest reprinting the best pieces. Lionel Trilling yielded to the entreaty and made from among his reviews the now well known *A Gathering of Fugitives,* published in 1956.

But there hung over us another obligation, unexpected and, unlike the rest, a chore. That hopeful word "fulfillment," applied to the mechanics of distribution, turned out a delusion and betrayal. Fairly soon, friends, colleagues, or strangers who knew us through our writings sent us pathetic or indignant letters about their running battle with Fulfillment. They had received no book or the wrong book or the main book when they had declined it; they had been billed for it or billed twice or the wrong amount—or rather, they had been unable to get these misdeeds remedied after repeated letters and phone calls. We the editors were the court of last resort and we had to reply, expressing regrets coupled with promises we hardly believed in. We switched firms, but errors continued to bedevil us.

* * *

The Readers' Subscription succeeded beyond the editors' expectations—we had been a trio of cultural skeptics. But after eight years the club did not meet Gilman Kraft's financial hopes or needs, and one day in early 1959 he told us that he had reluctantly decided to leave for greener pastures. He gave us time to find his replacement. For his new venture he bought *Playbill,* made it profitable, and enlarged it while improving its literary quality. We missed him. He was always calm, friendly, and solicitous about our wants. He never offered an opinion on books unless we asked him for one, for he was a thoughtful person whose Columbia College education had given him a solid grounding in literature and history.

Remembering those book-centered discussions tempts me to suggest the atmosphere in which they took place. We enjoyed ourselves. We expressed our preferences, our prejudices freely, often turning them into sources of entertainment. No tricks of thought or manner were frequent enough to annoy, even though we were strongly marked characters, forced to meet face-to-face every two weeks and settle points of style and literary judgment by phone in between. Our work was, in fact, a long conversation heading toward endless decisions. But unlike the Supreme Court's sober weighing of wire-drawn arguments, our discussions were interwoven with jokes, puns, and parodies. We behaved like friends talking over what to recommend to other friends.

To make a point about something—I no longer remember what—Lionel invented "A History of English Literature from B. O. Wulf to Virginia Woolf" and parodied the textbook style. Wystan would utter a clerihew he thought apposite, and he and I got into the habit

of matching clerihews by way of touching off the proceedings. For those who do not know what a clerihew is, here are one of his and one of mine: "Joseph Haydn / Never read Dryden. / Nor did Dryden / Ever hear Haydn." "Henry James / Did not name names, / But all the Bostonians knew / Who was who." Later, Auden published two collections of these ink-spot biographies. About one element of our work we all groaned in unison: the galleys. In those days, books were circulated before publication in unpaged proofs on sheets nearly two feet long and unbound. Turning over these streamers, carrying them folded in half in a duffel bag (a briefcase would not hold six or eight sets), and marking one's place or trying to find an earlier passage were as irritating as locating the set wanted, since when one had read halfway through, it bore no mark on its back.

As critics we had one trait in common: none of us applied a theory or system. Apart from this unifying mode, our tendencies and backgrounds differed widely, surely a desirable diversity for the purposes of the club. Trilling has latterly been dubbed a disciple of Matthew Arnold because he wrote a classic work on the subject, but it is a misjudgment. In youth Lionel had been a Marxist, later he was a good Freudian, and although something of these influences remained visible in his work, he was nobody's follower; his original thought outweighs the derived elements, as is true of every genuine thinker. What is more to the point than influence, he knew no foreign languages, but drew all his critical principles from absorption in English and American literature, including the great critics.

This happy single-mindedness set him apart from his two colleagues. Auden, partly because of his pride in ancestry, which his given name Wystan signalized, fell deep interest in things Germanic. He and I had had a classical education strongly colored by Greek and Latin, but he rejoiced that Oxford had compelled him to learn Anglo-Saxon. During his years with the club he was reading the Icelandic Eddas and detailing their merits to us. After many summers spent in Italy, he came to prefer life near Vienna, and he died there. His intellectual rapport with Hannah Arendt confirmed this sympathy with Germanic culture, as did his coolness toward French literature and ideas. For some reason he hated Racine almost as much as he hated the works of A. A. Milne.

That Wystan and I were good friends was no doubt a tribute to my Americanization. My antecedents contrasted with those of my fellow reviewers. The intellectual imprint of a French lycée should have made me a disciple of Descartes and a devotee of seventeenth-century literature, but early in life music had been an antidote and made me value the Romanticists in art and letters—this in the teeth of contemporary opinion, both French and American. Since I had grown up among the artists of the next wave, the Cubists and their peers, I was resistant to the anti-Romantic prejudice. My masters in criticism were Gautier, Hazlitt, and Poe, Goethe and Nietzsche. Trilling being untouched by them, and Auden disdainful of things French, our reviews in *The Griffin* were in an effortless way independent.

* * *

What emerges from this sketch of our inclinations is the principle of what Trilling was the first to call "cultural criticism," that is, criticism inspired by whatever is relevant to the work. Its genesis, form, and meaning have roots in the culture where it appears, and it is also unique through its author's own uniqueness. To us, none of this was new. We were cultural critics with no need of a doctrine, for the essence of culture is inclusiveness. And here Matthew Arnold properly enters again. It was he who said: "The men of culture are the true apostles of equality. They have a passion for diffusing, for making prevail, for carrying from one end of society to the other, the best ideas of their time."

It is clear in retrospect that not we alone but the mid-century as a whole, particularly in the United States, made a many-sided effort to carry out the Arnoldian mandate. The hope of a collective enjoyment of the best in thought and art was still strong. It was manifest in the drive to send the young to college, in the foundations for the advancement of one of another cultural good and the free public libraries, in the many series of classics in cheap, well-edited form, and not least, in the book clubs.

Ours continued without a break after Gilman left us. Trilling found a successor in Sol Stein, another former student. He was Kraft's opposite in temper—buoyant, expansive, and as a budding novelist, consciously literary. He had found a sponsor for buying the Readers' Subscription, the well-to-do Arnold Bernhard. Soon we were in more spacious offices emphatically on the East Side, served by a larger staff, including the elegant and businesslike Patricia Day, who later formed with our executive the publishing firm of Stein and Day.

Aware, perhaps, of the pressure of the times, we chose as the name of our second club the Mid-Century. It was that of the monthly bulletin as well. The kind of books we chose and the way we presented them remained the same, but nearly everything else about the society was different. I have mentioned Sol Stein's princely ways and the classier offices. The atmosphere changed with them. For one thing. Stein took part in our discussions, which lengthened them to little perceptible advantage, because he introduced considerations of pricing and of favors to and from publishers—elements we had known nothing about before and from which we firmly remained aloof.

We were happy to have, in replacement of Leo Raditsa, a recent Harvard Ph.D., John Simon. He was a broadly educated young man with whom it was a pleasure to work. His career since then as a leading critic of theater, film, music, and language confirms the judgment that brought him into our midst forty years ago and made him so congenial a helper.

In this new incarnation of our purpose, I remember fewer appeals from distraught readers angry about bills. Fulfillment had gained somewhat in its Manichaean battle with Frustration. But not long after the change-cover, a worse preoccupation began to cloud our work. It started with a suggestion from Sol Stein that the editors should become part owners of the society, on what terms was not clear. My fellow editors expressed interest, coupled with a vague alarm, which I shared. I was reluctant, both because I thought a financial interest inappropriate to our role as judges and because I foresaw additional time being used up for present negotiations and future business meetings.

They began right away and proved a kind of commitment. We were soon spending afternoons in parleyings. Then came what we had all half-detected: the society was in financial trouble. Overhead and costs exceeded revenue. When the truth was out, we became well acquainted with our backer, whose emergency help Sol Stein was soliciting. Arnold Bernhard was the founder and head of ValueLine, the highly regarded and profitable financial newsletter. Mr. Bernhard was a cultivated gentleman, whose intentions in entering our small domain were entirely altruistic. His interest was in literature and, as head trustee of the University of Bridgeport, in the spread of general education. He straightened out our current troubles and was further intent on making the editors part owners at no cost to them.

But Mr. Bernhard made one mistake, as he was the first to say when the collapse occurred. His rescue of the company had given him in double measure the right to oversee its operations and he thought of delegating the task to one of his aides at ValueLine. But he deferred to Stein's assurances and forbore, leaving the ship to its fate. After a lapse of twenty years, in November 1985, just before his death, Arnold Bernhard and I met at lunch, and soon our conversation turned to the old subject. Without any word from me, he mentioned his deep regret that he had not set a watch on the Mid-Century.

* * *

The end of the club in 1963 was not a decline and fall. The membership had risen from about thirty-five thousand to a little over forty thousand. This formidable surge was attributed to advertising. Arnold Bernhard believed that with the company's proper handling and publicity this number could be at least doubled. The Readers' Subscription had used only mailings. Now readers of the *New York Times Book Review* and the *Herald-Tribune Books* could see the three editors in arranged poses that showed the intensity of their conferrings; journalistic realism was at work in our behalf. We also appeared on television on David Susskind's program, *Open End,* meaning that once we started talking, nothing could stop us, We forgathered one evening about eleven o'clock, and after a vague briefing went on the airwaves, seated on camp chairs and divided by a table on which were several pots and mugs, Lionel and I had coffee pots, Wystan one for tea, but the brownish liquid that flowed from his was whiskey.

Our host, Mr. Susskind, had collected a good many reviews of our published works and arranged them, folded, in three little piles. He took up one at a time, glanced at it, and with a rising inflection quoted a sentence or two. Thus goaded we were presumably to start a discussion, but after two or three such prods from the little piles (our host looked as if he were playing solitaire) nothing really got going. We had to jerry-build a conversation, unavoidably leaving him out. His voice, though, cut in at short intervals with commercials. One of them touted a brokerage firm: "I tell you, these people are integrity-ridden." Some of our listeners, half-asleep, took this encomium to be about us. Kenneth Tynan reviewed our session adversely, and quite right he was. We had tried hard to be serious and had been defeated. Trilling, in his later review of Tynan's *Curtains,* rose to our defense, claiming jocularly that Tynan "deals with [our] performance with no comprehension of its genre: he takes it to have been a problem drama, when actually it was wild, grim comedy."

That second half-life, I hasten to add, was not wholly spoiled by money matters and legal confabs. Besides the reading-and-choosing, which continued to spark good conversation, there were Wystan's birthday parties. These were held on February 21 at his apartment on St. Mark's Place. The house was a fine old specimen, *really* old. The floors curved downward, and when his thirty or forty guests stood on them, glass in hand, anyone who walked could test the degree of flexibility underfoot.

Wystan's invitations were formal, typed and multigraphed, and they bore in the lower left corner: "Carriages at eleven." About that hour on one of these occasions, the Mid-Century gang went in a body to the back room where the overcoats were piled on a couch. It was a freezing cold night and powdery snow was falling. Arnold Bernhard could not find his coat. We helped him to search again: it was gone. Arnold made no comment, thanked Wystan without mentioning the loss, and

walked out with us as if all parties ended this way. Fortunately, several of us had mufflers; we wrapped them around his throat and torso, and he suffered no harm. A couple of days later a muffler arrived in the mail.

The end came suddenly, by telephone and without details. The new deficit was greater than Arnold Bernhard cared to make up. When the three of us met again for mutual solace, we agreed that there would have come a time, not indefinitely far off, when we would have wanted to cease and desist. And any successors of ours would have made something different of the society, perhaps more popular but not so ecumenical. The title Readers' Subscription had in fact been acquired for a club still in being today.

The close of ours, although abrupt, should not be called premature. In our eleven years and six months of existence, we had made a point about books and readers, publishers and their methods. For my part certainly, I was glad to be free of the burden of reading, meeting, and writing; but at the time I had a special cause of annoyance: my ultimate review, for February 1963, got lost in the breakup of the office. Wystan had sent it in after phoning me to say that he particularly liked it because of the parallels in it. The book was Henry Miller's autobiographical *Tropic of Cancer,* which I had compared with *Werther* for its hero and with Henry James's *Ambassadors* for its setting, which is Paris. The terms of these comparisons, like the loss, I have magnanimously forgotten.

William McGinley and Katanna Conley (essay date fall 2001)

SOURCE: McGinley, William, and Katanna Conley. "Literary Retailing and the (Re)making of Popular Reading." *Journal of Popular Culture* 35, no. 2 (fall 2001): 207-21.

[In the following essay, McGinley and Conley note publishing companies' responses to the book club phenomenon.]

Talk is no longer cheap. Moreover, according to most major book publishers and retailers it's been downright difficult to find in most communities across the country—that was, at least, until the recent rise in the popularity of book clubs. Although the origins of this renewed popularity are difficult to trace fully, book publishers have responded to this growing interest among readers with various forms of promotional support. Demonstrating that talk, like text, "has its price," publishers and book retailers are peddling the "fine art of conversation" through hundreds of "Reading Group

Discussion Guides" similar to the one composed for Margaret Atwood's novel *The Robber Bride* which begins with the following excerpt:

> Remember the days when you could spend hours talking with friends over coffee about an idea—before the numbing effect of too much television, and too little time, when the excitement of discovering a new writer was something you just couldn't wait to share? . . . The discussions went on over lunch, between meetings, and in the elevators. Great, lively talk about men, women, war, sex, childhood, lies, truth; it was all there, just waiting to be explored. . . . These pleasures are returning for thousands of Americans, as the fine art of conversation makes a comeback in living rooms and bookstores across America. The evidence is the near explosive growth of book groups and salons from coast to coast.
>
> (1)

As forecasted in the above excerpt, the "fine art of conversation" has certainly made a comeback of sorts in communities across the country where growing numbers of men and women gather regularly in homes and bookstores with fellow community members to talk with one another about the books they have read. As Elizabeth Long tells us in "Women, Reading, and Cultural Authority," these community-based book club gatherings provide insight into how at least one segment of the reading public "responds to the economic power of the modern book industry and to the cultural authority of the critical establishment" (591). Elsewhere, Long has argued for the need to recognize some of the ways that such cultural and institutional authorities shape "popular" reading practices by officially outlining what books are worth reading as well as how to read them:

> [T]his authoritative framing has effects on what kinds of books are published, reviewed, and kept in circulation in libraries, classrooms and the marketplace, while legitimating, as well, certain kinds of literary values and correlative modes of reading. Academics tend to repress consideration of variety in reading practices due to our assumptions that everyone reads (or ought to) as we do professionally, privileging the cognitive, ideational, and analytic mode. Further, recognizing the importance of the collective activity . . . inevitably brings into view both the commercial underside of literature and the scholar's position of authority within the world of reading.
>
> ("Textual Interpretation" 192)

It is this "commercial underside" of literature, the scholar's position of authority, and the specific nature of the pedagogical routines the book industry sponsors or authorizes for "everyday" readers through "Reading Group Discussion Guides" that we wish to explore. Norman Fairclough explains that we live in times where the culture of American educational and social life is increasingly colonized by the discourse practices of

marketization and commodification. The social and cultural changes to which Fairclough refers "very often manifest themselves discursively through a redrawing of boundaries within and between orders of discourse" (56). Our study of book club guides sheds light on this sort of redrawing—offering an occasion to examine one component of the processes through which the discourse of "popular reading" is perhaps redefined and redistributed by the corporate book industry.

As reading in book clubs has become an increasingly popular practice in many communities, we set out to examine the kinds of "literature lessons" the modern book industry has to offer this growing population of readers who once read and wrote in school classrooms. We did so by documenting the instructional perspectives or "recommended" ways of reading found in a wide range of commercially produced "Reading Group Discussion Guides"—the "popular" reading manuals that major book publishers have recently provided for book club readers everywhere. Our work provides insight into this industry as a source of cultural authority among the reading public, and sheds light on the potential processes through which particular ways of reading enter the stock of authoritative or "official" knowledges at hand for an ever growing number of the popular reading public.

Conversation Makes a Comeback

In discussing the renewed popularity of book clubs in America, Walter Kirn's article, "Rediscovering the Joys of Text," noted that reading in book clubs may be "to the 1990's what gym-going was to the 80's: something we plan to do, something we *want* to do and, by all appearances, something everyone else is doing, even Oprah viewers" (102). Moving into homes, apartments and even TV studios, contemporary book clubs have perhaps moved into "the social vacuum created by the decline of Tupperware parties while appealing to some of the same higher yearnings as 12 Step groups" (102).

Notwithstanding the rich and unquestionably diverse collection of personal motivations and occasions for participating in a contemporary book club, this return to text is not without its own literary leadership—a small but willing "faculty" anxious to provide whatever lessons in literature the new reading public might need. This "comeback of conversation," as it is formulated by the publishing industry, has received attention and support from such television personalities as Oprah Winfrey and Bill Moyers. Most notably, in developing and producing her own brand of literature-based entertainment, Oprah has fashioned an entirely new genre of talk show—a kind of "talk literature" programming complete with book recommendations, commercial reading guides for book club members, and LIVE readers modeling "approved" ways of interacting and discussing an Oprah-endorsed book with one another. Meanwhile, in the PBS special *Genesis: A Living Conversation,* Moyers brought together biblical scholars, writers, teachers, lawyers, psychotherapists, scientists, journalists, clergy members, college presidents, and translators for several televised discussions of the "Genesis" stories. In a sort of book club "mini-series," viewers/readers were treated to a collection of "lively and thought-provoking" conversations on these "timeless stories." For those wishing to do more than watch, Moyers and company also created the *Bill Moyers Genesis Website* which promises to help interested readers experience the same discussions by providing them with instructions on such things as "How to start a Genesis group," and "How to be a good Genesis group member."

Although we do not discount the value of reading or the potentially significant contributions that Winfrey, Moyers, and other celebrity readers have made to the personal and social lives of many readers, book club discussions have not always been such public affairs. Nor have they been so closely linked to the commercial interests and economic wellbeing of the entertainment industry. Sometimes referred to as "study groups," book clubs have long played a role in the literate practices of American readers dating back more than one-hundred years to the development of women's literary societies of the progressive era. Such groups, many scholars suggest, often provided women with a means to discover the eloquence of their voices and the strength of their convictions; and very quickly these literature study circles became a forum for addressing more public issues of progressive reform and democratic public life (e.g., Blair, Gere, Long, Martin). As Gere notes, "Clubwomen wanted different things, depending on their social locations, but for all clubwomen literacy connected with social and political struggles to transform the goals and conditions of their lives" (53).

In contrast, members of today's book clubs are increasingly under the influence of numerous corporate and commercial interests who compete for the cash and consciousness of potential readers. In what has fast become a "classroom," the size of which only a marketing executive could imagine teaching, the modern book industry has virtually set up shop in living rooms of potential readers from San Diego to Staten Island. One large book seller in the metropolitan Denver area, for example, estimates sponsoring approximately 200 to 300 book clubs located throughout neighboring suburban communities. Although the nature and extent of their "sponsorship" in these community-based clubs varies widely, they currently support a staff of seven part-time employees who perform a variety of organizational tasks for the club readers in addition to providing more specific instructional activities for these members. One of the primary mechanisms through which

instructional/promotional support occurs is the commercially produced "Reading Group Discussion Guide."

Simultaneously serving as an pedagogical tool as well as a marketing mechanism for the book industry, discussion guides range in format from a simple tri-fold pamphlet to a more elaborate brochure with a glossy front cover and design features resembling a small book. "Book companions," as they are also called, are available at no cost to readers and are often prominently displayed at check-out counters or in specially designated book club centers that have recently begun to appear in many bookstores. In addition to their obvious impact as a marketing strategy, such commercially produced guides are intended to function as a kind of literary primer—a book club "teacher's manual" if you will, with the goal of providing relevant literary information designed to "enhance your groups reading" of a particular book. Guides frequently contain a variety of discussion questions for group members, as well as a range of other book- or author-related information. At any given time, it is customary for some larger retail stores to have such guides on hand for approximately 400 different fiction and non-fiction texts representing a wide range of topics and themes.

OFFICIAL KNOWLEDGE AND OFFICIAL READING

As sociologist E. Doyle McCarthy explains, knowledge of social life and social reality is increasingly "disparate and dispersed," prepared and distributed for us in "variety packs" across a wide range of settings from internet sites to perfumed magazine advertisements (24). In her recent book *Knowledge as Culture,* McCarthy draws upon work from classical and contemporary sociology, Marxist theory, anthropology, American pragmatism, and feminist theory in an attempt to reintroduce at the forefront of the sociology of knowledge the issue of the function of knowledge in public life and in politics. In brief, McCarthy explains that recent interest in the function of knowledge within society has developed along with the idea that "social reality is not a phenomenon that exists in its own right but one that is produced and communicated" through "knowledges" that render it real for us (17).

Doubtless, many of the social realities of modern life are made known to us through the diverse venues or social "languages" of the popular press (e.g., books, newspapers, television, etc.), as well as the authorized reports of social scientists, government commissions, political groups, professional organizations, and other agencies. Today's knowledge is expressed, experienced, and negotiated virtually everywhere and in a wide range of settings wherein cultural production takes place (e.g., TV programs, movie theaters, bookstores, law offices, shopping malls, classrooms, health clubs, hospitals, police stations, and internet sites). The popularity of these "texts" provide insight into the nature of knowledge in society, as well as the sources of knowledge that we have come to identify as authoritative.

In light of these circumstances, it should come as little surprise to learn that "reading," and the knowledges that define it, also come to us in "variety packs"—in our case, the reading group discussion guides—that legitimize particular literate identities and reading practices deemed to be more or less appropriate within a given social and historical context (e.g., Greenfield, Heath, Morgan, Tompkins, Willinsky). As Robert Morgan makes clear, "legitimate" reading "always shifts in concert with the changing nature of institutional arrangements and the dominate social discourses of a period" (328). In conceptualizing reading as a social or discursive practice, we distance ourselves from many of the pedagogical models which hierarchize ways of reading literature as more or less "sophisticated," "tasteful," or "refined." As a discursive practice, reading is understood for its contingent and socially constructed nature "as a constantly changing form of cultural production" (Morgan 323).

It follows from the above perspectives that all ways of reading books (or literature, more specifically) are also socially produced and communicated through knowledges that reproduce the viewpoints of particular individuals or institutions. In short, no "reading" is ever entirely one's own. Rather, the meaning of any story-reading event is always subject to one or more discursive framings or interpretations as a function of the variety of related texts (i.e., book reviews, related films, public readings, advertisements, curriculum materials, etc.) and other readers that help to determine its meaning (e.g., Fish, Hunter, Morgan). In their analysis of certain texts of popular culture, Bennett and Wollocott explain that the meaning of any text is always a function of the specific contextual influences which "bear in upon" and shape the nature of a given reading experience (64). They describe these configurations as socially-based "reading formations" or those specific determinations which bear in upon, mould and configure the relations between texts and readers in determinant conditions of reading (64). Relations between readers and texts are never pristine encounters. Rather, they are always subject to various forms of social mediation through the other texts (i.e., author biographies, book reviews, scholarly critiques, advertisements, magazines, etc.) and readers that "locate" a book in a particular way and define the experience of reading it within a particular time and place.

Commercially produced book club discussion guides represent yet another, more contemporary type of "determing texts" that function in a similar fashion to constitute and define the nature of a given reading experience for a growing portion of the reading public.

With this in mind, we set out to understand the nature of the discursive training that reading guides provide, assessing their payoffs and their limitations; examining the kinds of readers and specific ways of reading literature that they legitimize; exploring what counts as "reading" from their point of view.

AUTHORIZING READERS, WRITERS, AND THE ACT OF READING

Our inquiry into the content of book club guides was informed by Fairclough's recent work in critical discourse analysis. Fundamental to this perspective is the idea that language is both socially shaped and socially shaping, or constitutive. As such, any text can be understood as "interweaving, 'ideational,' 'interpersonal,' and 'textual' meanings" (Fairclough 136). According to this perspective, language (as it is deployed in book club guides) always produces particular reader identities, social relations among readers and texts, and knowledge frameworks related to literature reading—each in varying degrees. Moreover, this language has the capacity to be constitutive both in socially reproductive and in socially transformative ways, with more salience given to one or the other depending on the circumstances.

We selected "Reading Group Discussion Guides" from several commercial booksellers over the course of a year to represent a broad range of texts, as well as a wide range of genres and narrative styles including mysteries, historical fiction, romance, horror, feminist, and "contemporary" fiction. Specifically, we conducted critical text-based analyses of the organizational structure, style, vocabulary, and specific content of approximately one-hundred twenty guides representing roughly 26 different publishers. Our focus, in this regard, was on the particular reader identities constituted by such texts, as well as the discursive construction of "popular" reading they sought to produce and market.

Although some reading guides were far more elaborate than others, they were often comprised of some combination of plot summaries, specific literary information, historical backgrounds, author biographies and autobiographies, critical essays, author interviews, questions for discussion, supplementary literature such as poetry, and suggestions for further reading. Producing, and perhaps doing its part to police the boundaries of popular reading, the presence of such literary prefaces, commentaries, and questions have the potential to act in a rather preemptive way, legitimizing a sort of highly formal "English class" version of reading in everyday social life. The attention to narrative styles and techniques, historical background, literary criticism, biography, authorial intent, and so forth suggest an approach to literature wherein "appropriate" reading begins with, and is necessarily built upon, attention to formalist ways of reading and understanding "the-text-in-itself." It is unclear, for example, how such an approach might lead readers to experience many of the "life-informing" or critical functions of reading that many literacy educators and researchers have described as essential to engaging in lifelong reading (e.g., Coles, Rosenblatt, Wolf, and Heath).

Packaged as a kind of neutral pedagogical complement designed to assist all readers in their understanding of a book, at first glance, such guides seem to assist only academically inclined readers in achieving a very specialized type of understanding. Indeed, like the primers, "teacher's companions," and "School Readers" of an earlier time, reading guides seem to outline a rather constraining "textual" space. To paraphrase Morgan, texts such as these construct this a space by identifying and authorizing a specific "cultural network" into which a book should be placed, circumscribing the ways of reading and discussing it within a specialized "literary" discourse. Such a practice has the effect of further limiting what other kinds of texts and wider social discourses one might connect with any instance of popular reading.

This sort of re-drawing of "academic reading" as "popular reading" is further accomplished through the construction and marketization of particular academic aesthetic dispositions and literary tastes as evidenced in the promotional discourse related to books, authors, and potential readers. This promotional discourse is an interesting mix of elements from the discourse of more traditional literary studies alongside features of a commodity advertising genre. In highlighting the overall plot and general content of their respective *books,* these descriptions often drew readers' attention to specific aesthetic or stylistic features of presumed interest:

> "a profound and redemptive symphony of god and indifference" (guide to *Reservation Blues*)

> "It is a novel whose compactness, narrative simplicity, and unadorned voices mask a complex structure and a tragic moral vision." (guide to *Littlejohn*)

> "poetically nuanced portraits of character and place" (guide to *Snow Falling on Cedars*)

> ". . . a novel whose eloquence, thematic richness, and moral resonance have called forth comparisons to the work of Richard Wright, James Baldwin, and William Faulkner" (guide to *A Lesson Before Dying*)

> ". . . spellbinding tale of genius and obsession, winner of the 1997 Pulitzer prize for fiction." (guide to *Martin Dressler*)

As an approach to reading, or to books more generally, the guides do not "market" a simple or vernacular gaze for prospective readers. Rather, they recommend that books be approached through a particular aesthetic lens

defined by attention to form, style, and generally in terms of formal literary features that would seem to discourage or even deny more colloquial enjoyment or facile involvement with books, and perhaps with other readers.

Similar to the discursive framing of books, the particular cultural identity of authors promoted in reading guides is formulated through an interdiscursive mix of elements from a formal literacy aesthetic discourse with elements from the genres of commodity and prestige advertising. In reference to authors, the guides imply that "their" readers are a special or prestigious breed who possess the knowledge to understand and appreciate some of the more "intellectual" components of an author's writing style and ability, as well as the importance of his or her professional literary reputation:

> "a master strategist, moving her characters around the gameboard" (guide to *The Robber Bride*)

> "Roddy Doyle pulls off a radical shift in narrative and mood that establishes him as one of the most technically accomplished writers at work today" (guide to *Paddy Clark Ha Ha Ha*)

> "He entered the Iowa Writer's Workshop on the GI Bill, where writers Alan Gurganus and T. Coraghessan Boyle were among his classmates." (guide to *Atticus*)

> "Do you see *A Map of the World* as a great thematic and stylistic departure from your first novel . . . ?" (guide to *A Map of the World*)

> "How did you arrive at your unique solution to the challenge of Dante's terza rima?" (guide to *The Inferno of Dante*)

As these excerpts pertaining to authors suggest, the reader's eye is not only focused on a more academic understanding of an author's craft, but is also granted the ability to *see* in these specialized ways. In essence, readers are promised a kind of intellectual-turned-commodity "gift" of being able to apprehend and appreciate the importance of fictional styles, stylistic dilemmas, literary reputation, authorial background, and authorial intention. The commodity, in this case, is an academic account of what counts as "good" writing. The prestige, although implied, lies in the assumption of, and promise that, Joe and Jane Reader will view authors and their writing in ways similar to those endorsed in the guides. Taken together, reading guides seamlessly assume and promise a readerly identity that embodies a very specific kind of cultural competence—one that has the consequence of ultimately distinguishing them from more colloquial or "everyday" readers.

Such a "scholarly" or even privileged identity is further evident in the more explicit descriptions of readers and the practice of reading that such guides recommend. This is once again accomplished through an interdiscursive mix of elements from both educational and commodity-driven discourses through which popular reading and popular readers are reformulated and promoted. An obvious promotional element is the presence of catchy statements of commodity advertising genre mixed with a discourse of personal qualities and prestige that bestows on chosen readers the disposition to appreciate books in a highly prescriptive way:

> "Some books are meant to be read, others are meant to be savored. *Range of Motion* is both—a book to treasure and to share with old friends and new, and a book tailor made for discussion." (guide to *Range of Motion*)

> "Remember the days when you could spend hours talking with friends over coffee about an idea? . . . when the excitement of discovering a new writer was something you just couldn't wait to share? . . . fans lined up, begging for an early look. . . . The discussions went on over lunch, between meetings, and in the elevators." (guide to *The Robber Bride*)

> "One comes to the end of *The Cunning Man* reflecting on the sheer pleasure of reading a novel by a writer who has lived a full life. . . . What a delight to be again in the hands of a master storyteller." (guide to *The Cunning Man*)

> [You'll read this book] "for the clarity and eloquence of its prose, for its bold and perceptive ideas, and for the sheer delight in discovering a long lost treasure by a beloved author." (guide to *A Long Fatal Love Chase*)

Readers, as they are formulated by the corporate book industry, do more than simply *read* books. To the contrary, they *savor* them, as well as analyze them for their aesthetic qualities. Readers discuss books "between meetings and in elevators" with friends, as well as with other readers like themselves in a world that almost presupposes a kind of elective distance from some of the necessities of social life. Although the "popular" readerly identity or literary journey promised in reading guides is certainly appropriate, it does not appear to be the sort of "coast to coast" excursion that just any ordinary reader is capable of purchasing. Not only do these guides displace or re-draw popular reading in favor of more academic or "school-like" reading practices, but in the process, they effectively commodify and colonize the academic practices and identities they seek to encourage. Under the promotional pen of the modern industry, the academic reader is formulated as a cultural elite—a distinguished reading superior, who in their almost exclusive preference for the "scholarly," ends up denying the commonplace. Pierre Bourdieu, in *Distinction: A Social Critique of Judgment and Taste*, explains this:

> The denial of lower, coarse, vulgar, venal, servile—in a word, natural—enjoyment, which constitutes the sacred sphere of culture, implies an affirmation of the superiority of those who can be satisfied with the sublimated, refined, disinterested, gratuitous, distinguished pleasures forever closed to the profane. That is why art and

cultural consumption are predisposed, consciously and deliberately or not, to fulfill a social function of legitimating social differences.

(7)

"Consciously and deliberately or not," reading guides promote a version of school-like reading for the popular reading public that is refracted through the promotional and market discourses of the corporate book industry. In discursive terms, the recommended "Questions for Discussion" that comprise such a significant part of all guides can also be understood "as the generalization of promotion as a communicative function—discourse as a vehicle for 'selling' goods, services, organizations, ideas, or people—across order of discourse" (Fairclough 141). In this case, literary questions, and the kinds of knowledge they provide about novels, stories, poems, and plays, are re-visioned as a form of commodity advertising wherein a particular approach to reading is assigned special status. In recommending such questions, the corporate book industry draws upon a collection of academic discursive practices and pedagogical routines while they also makeover and appropriate these routines in reconstructing and promoting "the popular reader."

To effect this sort of reconstructing, book guides pose questions for discussion that focus on the academic qualities of several aspects of the novels they are designed to accompany. For example, book guides typically asked many questions designed to engage readers in some form of character analysis or an examination of the techniques through which an author developed his or her characters. Additionally, they ask readers to describe the beliefs, values, or moral disposition of characters; to summarize the nature of relationships among characters; and/or to interpret the meaning of specific character experiences or decisions:

> "How does Spiegelman establish his characters?" (guide to *Maus 1*)

> "Laura's on-again off-again relationship with her lover, Q., is a central theme. In the beginning, Laura says, 'Q. threads through my life like an unusual color in a tapestry or a swatch in a cape of many colors.' How would you describe the character of Q?" (guide to *The Fatigue Artist*)

> "Throughout the novel, Laf is writing a story about Dale and Theresa. . . . Discuss Dale's change of character in terms of Laf's change of character." (guide to *Love Warps the Mind a Little*)

> "Cunningham takes us through 40 years of different characters' lives. Are his characters dynamic or do they remain the same? How do Mary, Susan, and Billy grow? Do you feel the characters find what they are seeking? What does each see, and more importantly, what does each find?" (guide to *Flesh and Blood*)

Nearly as common as character-specific questions were those that encouraged readers to interpret text by identifying and examining a range of narrative techniques. Such questions instructed readers to interpret or evaluate the meaning of specific narrative techniques within a text (e.g., symbolism, metaphor, irony, allusion, flashback, theme, lyricism, literary voice, point of view, setting, plot structure); to discuss or evaluate an pre-identified theme as a function of particular events; and/or to discuss the extent to which various themes were present in a novel:

> "Where and to what purpose does Faulks use images of birds?" (guide to *Birdsong*)

> "What is symbolically suggested by the motif of doubling, with reference to the ideas about identity? Fate?" (guide to *Atticus*)

> "What techniques does Munro use in this story to evoke the sense of time passing?" (guide to *Open Secrets*)

> "The setting of the novel can almost be looked upon as another character. How does the bleak Maine landscape contribute to the tension of the novel?" (guide to *A Brother's Blood*)

> "Describe the structure of *Bucking the Sun*. Discuss Doig's literary voice, as well as his use of flashback." (guide to *Bucking the Sun*)

To a lesser extent, reading guides also provided readers with questions designed to involve them in analyzing text both through and in relation to other literary works, and/or in relation to "official" meanings that the publisher often provided in the context of specific questions. This way of reading, wherein particular questions suggest that the meaning of a text can be best understood as a function of related literary works, or an already accepted account, is illustrated in the following questions:

> "All of the characters' names are carefully chosen and layered with meaning. What is the significance behind the following names: [list of character names] (Clues to the last three [names] may be found in the poetry of Tennyson, Yeats, and Coleridge cited below)." (guide to *Possession*)

> "Like Faulkner and Joyce, Wolfe has been acclaimed for his evocation of place. What details in *Look Homeward, Angel* evoke its setting, and what is the relation between its setting and its themes?" (guide to *Look Homeward, Angel*)

> "Do you see Nigel as a comment on the 'type' of the Romantic hero—Heathcliff or Byron?" (guide to *Babel Tower*)

> "How does the story resemble the biblical parable of the prodigal son? How does it mirror another biblical parable, Absalom?" (guide to *Cry, the Beloved Country*)

CONCLUSION

Taken together, with a few important exceptions, the recommended pedagogical routines of the modern book industry, as embodied in book club guides, reflect a rather analytic and text-based literary ancestry: the image of the everyday reader as a sort of solitary, scholar-anchorite or academic analyst. Such an academic framing of book club reading, while certainly securing the scholar's position of authority within the world of reading, raises important questions about the potential consequences of authorizing this sort of reading for the popular reading public. Specifically, in fashioning an "official" status for a rather shorthand collection of academic reading practices, book club guides suppress not only other popular modes of thinking and reading, but other types of "less-refined" or less "schooled" readers. In the end, as Catherine Greenfield argues, the neutralization and subsequent naturalization of such pedagogical routines effectively denies their fundamentally political nature rendering them "self-evident unities" in the eyes of the reading public as opposed to being understood as "discursive objects of particular training" (136).

In contrast to the street-based literature curriculums of the working class men and women of nineteenth century England (Willinsky), the vernacular expressions of hope and struggle implicit in the "literature" of the blues in early twentieth century America (e.g., Baker, Murray), or the transformative reading practices of women's literary societies of the progressive era (e.g., Blair, Gere, Long, Martin), the curriculum of the book guide promises a much different sort of reading for a very specialized reader—text-intensive, ideational, and analytical. At the core of the pedagogical practices of reading guides is an entire literature "curriculum" refracted through the reading discourses of a rather elite, academic literary infrastructure appropriated and made over in the promotion language of commodity advertising. Ironically, in offering such an identity, this formulation of the "book club reader" stands in direct contrast to the kinds of readers and modes of reading that book groups have historically made possible. Long explains this in reference to her analysis of the history of such groups and their use of stories as "equipment for living":

> The process of "living" other stories than one's own may be crucial for confronting times of individual or social change, in part because it is then that such "equipment for living" is especially needed. . . . A socially negotiated process of cultural reflection makes these groups [book clubs]—when functioning well— sites for insight and innovation in the arena of identity, values, and meanings.

> ("Textual Interpretation" 200-2)

As both products and producers of literate culture, the conceptual frames put forth by book club guides provide only a partial account of the nature of reading, and offer a rather limited view of the possibilities that might be associated with reading in the world. Equally important, however, is that reading guides represent a sort new kid on the literature-reading block—a new mechanism for competing with a range of other social and commercial organizations for positions of cultural authority among the reading public. Doubtless, the prize accompanying such a competition is the power to persuade book club readers to see the approaches endorsed by the book industry as the natural, if not the most prestigious, way of proceeding with books. One specific side-effect of these circumstances is the descendent or lesser cultural status bestowed to more "popular" readers and ways of reading. Indeed, in the reading world imagined by the producers of commercial reading guides, readers inclined to take up more personal or colloquial forms of engagement with stories are simply not invited to the discussion.

Notwithstanding this rather obvious dismissal of everyday readers as well as other ways of approaching literature, it is not our intention to suggest that the pedagogical routines of such guides are without merit. Nonetheless, we contend that book club guides represent a relatively new social mechanism through which the modern book industry is capable of authorizing not only "preferred" books for the reading public, but also "preferred" ways of reading and responding to such books in the company of other readers. Although our understanding of this relationship and its consequences for the reading public is a partial one, it raises important questions about the influence of modern book industry on the practices and consciousness of the popular reading public.

Works Cited

Atwood, Margaret. *The Robber Bride*. New York: Doubleday, 1993.

Baker, Houston. *Blues, Ideology, and Afro-American Literature: A Vernacular Theory*. Chicago: U of Chicago P, 1984.

Bennett, Tony, and Janet Woollacott. *Bond and Beyond: The Political Career of a Popular Hero*. New York: Methuen, 1987.

Blair, Karen. *The Clubwoman as Feminist: True Womanhood Redefined, 1868-1914*. New York: Holmes & Meier, 1980.

Bourdieu, Pierre. *Distinction: A Social Critique of the Judgment of Taste*. Trans. Richard Nice. Cambridge: Harvard UP, 1984.

Coles, Robert. *The Call of Stories: Teaching and the Moral Imagination*. Boston: Houghton Mifflin, 1989.

Fairclough, Norman. "Critical Discourse Analysis and the Marketization of Public Discourse: The Universities." *Discourse & Society* 4 (1993): 133-68.

Fish, Stanley. *Is There a Text in This Class? The Authority of Interpretive Communities*. Cambridge: Harvard UP, 1980.

Gere, Anne. *Intimate Practices: Literacy and Cultural Work in U.S. Women's Clubs, 1880-1920*. Chicago: U of Illinois P, 1997.

Greenfield, Catherine. "On Readers, Readerships and Reading Practices." *Southern Review* 16.1 (1983): 121-42.

Heath, Shirley. "Being Literate in America: A Sociohistorical Perspective." *Issues in Literacy: A Research Perspective*. Ed. Jerome Niles and Rosary Lalik. New York: Holt, Rinehart & Winston, 1985.

Hunter, Ian. "The Concept of Context and the Problem of Reading." *Southern Review* 15 (1982): 80-91.

Kirn, Walter. "Rediscovering the Joys of Text." *Time* 149.16 (1997): 100-3.

Long, Elizabeth. "Women, Reading, and Cultural Authority: Some Implications of the Audience Perspective in Cultural Studies." *American Quarterly* 38 (1986): 591-612.

Long, Elizabeth. "Textual Interpretation as Collective Action." *The Ethnography of Reading*. Ed. J. Boyarin. Berkely: U of California P, 1992. 180-211.

Martin, T. P. *The Sound of Our Own Voices: Women's Study Clubs, 1860-1910*. Boston: Beacon, 1987.

McCarthy, E. Doyle. *Knowledge as Culture: The New Sociology of Knowledge*. New York: Routledge, 1996.

Morgan, Robert. "Reading a Discursive Practice: The Politics and History of Reading." *Beyond Communication: Reading Comprehension and Criticism*. Ed. Deanne Bogdan and Stanley B. Straw. Portsmouth: Heinemann, 1990. 319-36.

Murray, Albert. *Train Whistle Guitar*. Chicago: Northwestern UP, 1974.

Nussbaum, Martha. "The Literary Imagination in Public Life." *New Literary History* 22 (1991): 877-910.

Rosenblatt, Louise. *Literature as Exploration*. New York: Modern Language Association, 1983.

Tompkins, Jane. *Reader Response Criticism: From Formalism to Post-structuralism*. Baltimore: Johns Hopkins P, 1980.

Willinsky, John. *The Triumph of Literature and the Fate of Literacy: English in the Secondary School Curriculum*. New York: Teacher College P, 1991.

Wolf, Shelby, and Shirley Heath. *The Braid of Literature*. Cambridge: Harvard UP, 1992.

Mary K. Chelton (essay date fall 2001)

SOURCE: Chelton, Mary K. "When Oprah Meets E-mail: Virtual Book Clubs." *Reference & User Services Quarterly* 41, no. 1 (fall 2001): 31-6.

[*In the following essay, Chelton discusses the rise of Internet-based book clubs.*]

One of the interesting phenomena of the Information Age is the simultaneous growth of super bookstores and adult reading groups with the rise of the Internet and other forms of instant, technological connectivity. Libraries are hosting many of these groups, mostly still in person, but many others are meeting elsewhere in communities or are creating their own communities in cyberspace.

The following article takes a look at the differences between face-to-face and computer mediated book clubs, giving a good overview of the strengths and weaknesses of both to help organizers decide which might be best for them and their readers. Resources for any kind of readers group are also included from a working public librarian with frontline experience with such groups. If the article makes no other point, the fact that information technology can augment the reader's advisory as well as the much more touted reference service environment should inspire imitators of the projects described.

There is no question that many a library book club owes its inception to Oprah Winfrey. Of course, there were plenty of library-sponsored and private reading groups in existence before Ms. Winfrey discovered the joys of reading and sharing, but when Oprah picks up a new hobby, so does a nation.

The hobby isn't a new one, either, but a rediscovered pastime. Literary discussions reach back to the French salons of the eighteenth century. In the United States, the origin of book groups can be traced to the early nineteenth century, "when spirited New England women met to discuss the issues addressed in serious poetry, nonfiction, and publications of the day. By the turn of the century, reading groups were flourishing."[1] Today's book clubs can be as intellectual as the French salons or as casual as a coffee chat. All that is required for a successful book discussion group is a love for reading and a desire to share thoughts about the selected title.

The character of a book club will evolve over time. Some reading groups are very social with participants meeting monthly over a meal and discussing the assigned book in relation to members' own lives. The Mostly, We Eat Book Club (www.mostlyweeat.org) is this type of reading group. Other groups adopt a scholarly approach, meeting to analyze the work using reviews, literary criticism, or biographical information of the author. The Great Books Foundation (www.greatbooks.org) and the Kansas Humanities Council's Talk about Literature in Kansas (www.ukans.edu/kansas/khc) programs both promote reading groups with a more serious focus on book discussion.

This surge in the popularity of book clubs is encouraging for library staff everywhere. Established library reading groups are operating at capacity. Book discus-

sion group leaders are forming off shoot clusters to accommodate the public's rediscovered interest in reading and sharing. Newly formed reading groups are experimenting with the format by exploring specific themes or genres in literature. Mysteries prove to be a perennial favorite among book clubs, as are biographies, classics, children's literature, and travelogues.[2]

Library book groups also experiment with time frames. Some groups may meet on a regular schedule, others may meet for a couple of months or a season to explore books with a specific theme, then disband, only to reform with old and new members when the next thematic book group is organized.

There are many ways to operate a book discussion group, and forming and maintaining a library-sponsored book club has never been easier. There are more guides for starting a reading group, both in and out of the library, than ever before, both in print formats and on the Internet.[3] The Morton Grove (Ill.) Public Library (MGPL) offers the premiere Web site for devoted readers, covering all aspects of reading, including discussion groups both online and off-line (www.webrary.org/rs/rslinks.html). There is even an association devoted to book clubs, the Association of Book Group Readers and Leaders, based in Highland Park, Illinois.

Publishers have recognized the financial potential in this reading boom by making discussion guides available on Web sites. The Book Group Corner (www.randomhouse.com/resources/bookgroup) offers "reader's companions" for a number of novels published by Bantam, Broadway, Dell, and Doubleday. Time-Warner (www.twbookmark.com/books/reading_guides.html), Houghton Mifflin (www.houghtonmifflinbooks.com/readers_guides), and HarperCollins (www.harpercollins.com/hc/readers/fiction.asp) all have Web sites with reading group guides. Some trade paperbacks are being published with discussion topics and questions printed in their endpapers. *Where the Heart Is* by Billie Letts, *White Oleander* by Janet Fitch, and *While I Was Gone* by Sue Miller include author statements and discussion questions. It is no surprise that all of these books have been recent selections of Oprah's Book Club and are likely to be picked up by other book clubs.

READING AND THE INTERNET

It did not take long for wired readers to discover there are just as many places on the Internet to talk about books as there are in their own communities and in most cases, there are more. Listservs, bulletin boards, and chatrooms all devoted to book lovers, abound on the Internet.

Romance Readers Anonymous (RRA-L) (subscribe: rra-llistserv.kent.edu) and Dorothy-L (www.iwillfollow.com/dorothyl) are two extremely active and popular discussion lists devoted to romance and mystery novels, respectively. Members primarily post mini-reviews and recommendations or short opinions on books they have recently read. The standard reviewlet usually isn't more than a few lines stating, "This book was great and kept me reading all weekend!" Contributors may go on to talk about the characters, plot, and writing style when asked by other list members what was enjoyed most about a book. Rarely do the contributors engage in formal analysis; however, discussion of a book's subject or characters can bloom into a prolonged conversation.

RRA-L introduced the idea of a scheduled discussion of a prechosen title in the mid-1990s. A list member volunteers to select a couple of books, all available in mass-market paperback, and members who are interested vote on a title and a date is agreed upon for discussion to begin. Contributors are instructed to insert spoiler alerts in the subject line or body of the message. A recent discussion of *This Heart of Mine* by Susan Elizabeth Phillips yielded subject headings with "book chat" in bold letters and "spoiler alert" sprinkled throughout the message. It is understood among the list members that a book chat will include discussion of all aspects of the book, including plot twists and endings.

All messages are posted to the list for all members to read, whether or not members have read the book, and book discussions usually don't last more than two weeks. Members of this RRA-L subgroup sample various subgenres of romance for their discussions (i.e., regencies, time-travel, or futuristic romances) each month.

Dorothy-L members simply post mini-reviews or brief opinions and build on each other's responses without employing a structured book discussion. The message board rec.arts.books and its adherents are catchall forums for diverse topics regarding books, but none of the threads are structured. Subjects addressed include, "What is the answer to the Lewis Carroll riddle, 'Why is a raven like a writing desk'?" and, "Where do ISBNs come from?" For readers who need more structure to their discussions than RRA-L or rec.arts.books can provide, there are online book clubs, modeled after the in-person book clubs conducted by libraries, bookstores, private citizens, and Oprah.

Book Clubs Get Wired

While there is no way to determine when the first formal virtual book club was formed, nor how many there are, it is safe to say that online reading groups started springing up not long after Oprah launched her TV-based book club. A *Publishers Weekly* article printed in 1996 offers a profile of some of the first virtual book discussion groups. Most of these new groups were situated at Book Central, an AOL site (keyword: BC) created by iProd, a division of Franklin Spear Advertising.[4]

Ostensibly geared toward readers who cannot find the time to attend a formal book club meeting, there are numerous reasons for readers to join a wired book club. An online book group offers convenience of location, mobility, and schedule, in addition to a cloak of anonymity that some readers may find appealing. Virtual groups give participants the opportunity to read and discuss books at their leisure and give them a variety of formats from which to choose: e-mail, message boards, or chat rooms.

There's nothing more convenient than accessing a book club from the comfort of home, especially if transportation is an issue. Erratic schedules can make attending an offline book club almost impossible. Online book clubs are not hampered by meeting times and places; readers can post comments any time of day or night.

Some readers may not be aware of the established book clubs in a community. If a local library isn't sponsoring a reading groups a list of community discussion groups accompanied by a reading schedule might be made available there since public libraries are a likely resource for members of an existing book club doing research on the next title. However, the privately run reading groups may be operating at capacity with no room for new members. The Mostly, We Eat Book Club makes it very plain on its Web site it is not soliciting new members.

Publicly run book clubs, such as those offered by libraries or bookstores, rarely turn away interested members. None of the libraries in the Kansas City area put a cap on the attendance of their reading groups unless the group is a special one, such as Great Books. Jean Hatfield, Program Services Manager for Johnson County (Kans.) Libraries, says, "We limit Great Books discussion because we have to order the books. We take a waiting list for that and when slots open up we call and let people know that they can come. Most of our groups are pretty small so we haven't had to turn anyone away from our general interest groups."[5] At Mid-Continent (Independence, Mo.) Public Library, Adult Specialist Marlena Boggs encourages book groups to split into two if the attendance level is more than fifteen people. She acknowledges that this can be difficult if the group doesn't want to divide itself or there is no other staff to lead the group.[6] Authorities on maintaining reading groups set the optimal group membership at no more than fifteen.[7]

The looser structure of a cyber reading group allows for as many members as have computers. Contributors may all be speaking up at one time, electronically, but each contribution can only be accessed one at a time. Virtual book clubs will also appeal to the readers who feel they are stronger writers than orators and prefer to share their opinions in writing rather than orally in public.

VIRTUAL READING GROUPS VIA E-MAIL,
BULLETIN BOARDS, AND REAL-TIME CHAT

Most online book clubs employ e-mail or bulletin boards as the forum for their reader members. For e-mail clubs, such as Book Lovers or Bookies Too, participants must have an e-mail account in order to join, submit a subscription request, and are accepted to the list. Books can be chosen by the list owner or moderator or suggested by and voted upon by the list members. Members then read the selected books on their own and e-mail their comments at their convenience. Sometimes there is a set date on which to begin discussion.

Discussion topics are usually posted in advance and readers may or may not choose to address their comments to these topics. Most groups select at least two titles per month with discussion lasting for two weeks to a month before a new book is discussed. Bookies-Too, a lively online book club, also utilizes the bulletin board method of threaded discussions. Since its server's untimely demise, BookiesToo has graduated from a simple e-mail network to a Yahoo! group, complete with message board and digest-format e-mail capability.

Some established "name brand" Web sites host book clubs. Salon.com hosts the Table Talk Reading Group where meetings are held on a regular monthly schedule at a specific message board. Threaded discussions include books as diverse as Thomas Pynchon's *Crying of Lot 49* and comic books, and topics as varied as "Best-Selling Authors in Need of an Editor" and African-American poetry.

Operation of a Web-enhanced book club is similar in some respects to an e-mail group. Books are chosen in advance, members may or may not complete reading by the agreed upon date and will post their comments as they find time. Joining a message board also requires participants to register with an e-mail address at the specified site.

Some online book clubs are hosted as live chats using Internet Relay Chat or some other real time medium. The drawbacks to a real-time virtual book club are similar to the scheduling difficulties faced by actual book clubs—selecting a time at which the maximum number of readers will find it convenient and participate. Notes Anne Coviello—Simon and Schuster online community manager, home of SimonSays, a Web site for numerous online book groups—"S&S has been careful not to go up against NBC's Thursday night 'Must See TV.'"[8] A recent visit to the SimonSays site found no real time chats scheduled for any books, but numerous message boards for the discussion of cookbooks, children's books, romance, and general fiction.

LIBRARIES AND CYBER BOOK CLUBS

How can libraries use this popular book discussion format to promote reading, and is it worth the time and effort? As of this writing only two library-supported virtual book clubs show any sign of activity: Book Clique, sponsored by the Tippecanoe County (Ind.) Public Library (TCPL), and the Virtual Book Club, sponsored by the Baltimore County Public Library (BCPL).[9] Of the two, BCPL's Virtual Book Club is the most active, but it has also been in existence since 1998 as opposed to newcomer Book Clique, established in May 2000.

Both clubs use the e-mail format of conducting discussion. Participants are not required to be cardholders at either library; they must, however, possess an e-mail address and adhere to the standard behavior policies set forth by the libraries' book clubs and e-mailed out to each member after subscribing.

Both reading groups choose to moderate discussions. BCPL has one staff member who informally moderates the messages and occasionally this leads to outside groups promoting events to post a message that would be deemed inappropriate if read in advance. TCPL rotates moderator duties among staff members.

Books for discussion are chosen by staff at both libraries. TCPL staff select books for six months in advance; BCPL follows a similar pattern using a team of four people to select titles for three months in advance—the fourth month is devoted to a theme, a recent one being "favorite childhood book."[10]

TCPL offers some unique features to its online reading group. Messages are archived chronologically and participants use the title of the selected reading in the subject line of each message in order to make the archives more accessible. TCPL also asks readers to give each book a rating and then uploads the rating along with an image of the book's cover on a Previous Selections page.

Aside from initial startup work, the time and tools required to maintain the book clubs is manageable. Exact details could not be obtained from TCPL, but Karen Quinn-Wisniewski, moderator of BCPL's Virtual Book Club, monitors messages, uploads book cover images and text, and maintains the Virtual Book Club Web site.[11]

Time will tell if TCPL's Book Clique can match the success of BCPL's Virtual Book Club. Just over a year old, Book Clique's singular features of searchable archives and members' book ratings should help keep it afloat. However, like most in-person activities that are translated to the Internet, when a reading group is adapted to cyberspace, some things are lost, some things are gained, and some things remain the same.

VIRTUAL VS. ACTUAL

While there is no set formula for forming an in-person book club, there are certainly more resource guides than there are for the cyber book clubs. Once formed, however, the amount of maintenance required differs greatly between the two.

The face-to-face reading group will require meeting space, numerous copies of the book, a prepared book group leader, and a limited amount of time for discussion. An online club requires only the necessary amount of bandwidth to support an e-mail discussion, a few discussion questions posted to the group and limitless discussion time. Participants are responsible for obtaining their own copies of the selected title.

Membership in both groups can be unpredictable, but more so online.[12] The point and click atmosphere of the Internet does not lend itself to viewing one Web site for long periods of time. E-mail is also a quick-time activity and many users are in the habit of dashing off replies in as little time required as necessary.

On the positive side, with a cyber book club, there is no need for concern about a group's personality mix. It doesn't matter online if a reader wants to compose a long diatribe about the latest selection, or if the reader is obnoxious while doing it. As long as proper modes of e-mail and bulletin board netiquette are observed, the reader's conversational style is a moot point. There is less chance discussion will wander off on tangents involving the personal histories of participants or the meeting turning into group therapy. Moreover, unless conversation gets heated, there is little for a moderator to do.

Exchanges between readers can rely solely on the reading matter in a wired book club. However, the social and emotional aspects of an in-person reading group are valuable ones. Reader delight at discovering a new favorite author, or understanding a previously overlooked idea in the book, is lost on the Web. The immediacy of an offline book club encourages the rapid-fire exchange of insights and personal reflections. Readers who experience strong emotions while reading a book want to share them with other group members and find validation in their feelings. This emotional sharing may bond an in-person reading group in a way that cannot be matched by an online reading group with members who never see each other's faces and are not all logged in at the same time. Tones of voice and facial expressions lend more depth to opinions expressed in an in-person book club. Emoticons (those little strings of text characters that form faces when viewed sideways, that is, ;-) or :-( ) may help online reading group members express their feelings about a book, but cannot match an excited voice or an animated face.

In wired book clubs, "discussion of a single book can last for weeks, not for the hour or two a month typical of face-to-face groups."[13] Time enough to cover all issues raised upon the reading of an especially hefty book is not a concern online, although it is one with real-time book clubs. There is also time for all members to contribute their thoughts and opinions on a reading selection. For a larger-than-average book club (more than fifteen members), discussing a book that has provoked all the readers, and providing everyone enough time to express themselves can be very difficult, especially if the meeting room is reserved for only ninety minutes. Online reading group members can contribute whenever and wherever they choose, on lunch hours at the office or at home in the middle of the night.

Time to prepare for a book discussion is also more flexible in cyberspace than in real time. Pressure to have a book read before the next book club meeting can either prevent attendance or cut down on discussion. Attendees of an in-person reading group usually feel compelled to admit if they have not finished reading a book and may feel reluctant to contribute to the discussion—if they show up. With a virtual book group, readers can not only contribute to the discussion without admitting they haven't finished the book, but attendance at the discussion, if it is conducted through e-mail and message boards, doesn't feel compulsory to members.

Although both kinds of book clubs have the same goals—to get members reading and talking about books—they seem to be entirely unrelated programs in the eyes of participants. Questions posed to the moderator and members of BCPL's Virtual Book Club about both types of reading groups elicited intriguing answers.

The Virtual Book Club has no connection to any library sponsored in-person book club and there is more moderating than facilitating. Quinn-Wisniewski notes that "the club discusses whatever they want." It is not known at BCPL if participation in the Virtual Book Club has affected attendance at real-time book clubs. The BCPL Virtual Book Club selection team limits featured titles to those owned by BCPL in multiple copies. The members of the online club are also informed if a selected title is available in large print or nonprint formats.[14]

When asked what prompts participation in the online group, all respondents mention time and scheduling constraints. All respondents have an interest in an in-person book club, but find the virtual reading group more convenient. None feel obligated to follow the reading selections, as one respondent notes, "no one notices if I don't read the book." Another member states she did not want to be "pressured into spending time reading a book because of a book-club's requirement."

All members like the atmosphere of the Virtual Book Club. Discussions are described as "reasonably free-wheeling": "People usually shoot off a short paragraph or two with [an] overall impression of a brief description of what they liked or didn't like." "Very seldom a sustained dialogue about a book." Mention was made of discussions coming up about different books or book related topics. A couple of respondents note that the *Virtual Book Club* has expanded reading horizons by selecting books neither would have chosen outside of a discussion group.

An interesting related thread at BCPL involves debating whether or not book selections should be voted upon by the members of the Virtual Book Club. To date the majority is voting against voting. Most readers enjoy the fact that a team of library staff select books and compile annotations and format availability, and do not want their time taken up by voting on prospective titles.

Inasmuch as libraries are still and will always be, in part, about promoting reading, the establishment of a cyber book club is an idea worth exploring. The target audience for such a program appears to be decidedly different from those readers who prefer to talk about their books in person and are already finding time to do so. It may be that an online book club would encourage crossover attendance. But this program is only viable, of course, if the staff time and interest and library resources allow for it. Libraries and readers' advisors have always been in the best positions to know what the public is reading and discussing. After all, whether the reader is a member of a virtual or veritable reading group, usually the first stop for the next book club title is the library.

Notes

1. Rachel W. Jacobsohn, *The Reading Group Handbook: Everything You Need to Know to Start Your Own Book Club,* rev. ed. (New York: Hyperion, 1998).

2. Donna Davis. "Libraries and Book Clubs," *Mississippi Libraries* 64 (spring 2000): 7-9.

3. Ted Balcolm, *Book Discussions for Adults: A Leader's Guide* (Chicago ALA, 1992), Marcia Fineman, *Talking about Books: A Step By Step Guide for Participating in a Book Discussion Group* (Rockville, Md.: Talking about Books, 1997); David Laskin and Holly Hughes, *The Reading Group Book* (New York: Plume, 1995); Ellen Slezak, ed., *The Book Group Book,* 3d ed. (Chicago: Chicago Review Pr., 2000).

4. Bridget Kinsella, "Book Groups Get Wired," *Publishers Weekly* 243 (Nov. 18, 1996); 46-47.

5. Jean Hatfield. e-mail to the author, May 9, 2001.

6. Marlena Boggs, e-mail to the author, May 9, 2001.

7. Balcolm. *Book Discussions for Adults: A Leader's Guide,* 12.

8. Kinsella. "Book Groups Get Wired," 46.

9. Michelle Bradley. "The Book Clique: Creating and Running a Book Discussion Group Online," *Public Libraries* 39 (Sept/Oct. 2000): 244-45.

10. Ibid., 245; Karen Quinn-Wisniewski, e-mail to the author, Apr. 18, 2001.

11. Quinn-Wisniewski, e-mail to the author.

12. Pamela LiCalzi O'Connell. "Online Book Clubs: Everything but Food," *New York Times* 148 (Mar. 18, 1999): G4

13. Ibid.

14. Quinn-Wisniewski, e-mail to the author.

Selected Web Sites for Online Book Clubs

Baltimore County Virtual Book Club

www.beplonline.org/centers/library/bookclub.html

Book Lovers

http://mindmills.net/booklovers

BookiesToo

www.geocities.com/athens/aegean/2515

Morton Grove Public Library's Webrary Reader's Services www.webrary.org/rs/rslinks.html

Rachel's Compendium of Online Book Discussions

www.his.com/-allegria/clubs.html

Reader's Club www.readersclub.org

Reading Group Choices www.readinggroupchoices.com

Salon's Virtual Book Group http://tabletalk.salon.com

SimonSays www.simonsays.com

Tippecanoe County (Ind.) Public Library's The Book Clique www.tepl.lib.in.us/ref/bookgroup.html

ADDITIONAL RESOURCES FOR BOOK GROUPS

Association of Book Group Readers and Leaders, P.O. Box 885, Highland Park, IL 60035.

Balcolm, Ted. *Book Discussions for Adults: A Leader's Guide.* Chicago: ALA, 1992.

Book Lover's Guide to Reading Groups. Special advertising supplement to *The New Times.* June 22, 1997.

Craughwell, Thomas. *Great Books for Every Book Lover.* New York: Black Dog & Levanthal, 1998.

Dodson, Shireen. *Mother-Daughter Book Club: How Ten Busy Mothers and Daughters Came Together to Talk Laugh and Learn through Their Love of Reading.* New York: HarperCollins, 1997.

Fineman, Marcia. *Talking about Books: A Step by Step Guide for Participating in a Book Discussion Group* 3d ed. Rockville, Md.: Talking about Books, 1997.

Greenwood, Monique, Lynda Johnson, and Tracy Mitchell-Brown. *The Go on Girl! Book Club Guide for Reading Groups.* New York: Hyperion, 1999.

Jacobsohn, Rachel W. *Reading Group Handbook: Everything You Need to Know to Start Your Own Book Club.* Rev. ed. New York: Hyperion, 1998.

Laskin, David, and Holly Hughes. *Reading Group Book,* New York: Plume/Penguin, 1995.

McMains, Victoria Golden. *Readers' Choice: 200 Book Club Favorites* New York: Quill/HarperCollins, 2000.

Neblett, Pat. *Circles of Sisterhood: A Book Discussion Group Guide for Women of Color.* New York: Writers & Readers, 1996.

Pearlman, Mickey. *What to Read: The Essential Guide for Reading Group Members and Other Book Lovers.* Revised and updated. New York: HarperCollins, 1999.

Reading Group Choices: Selections for Lively Book Discussions. Nashville: Paz and Associates, annual.

Rubel, David. *The Reading List: Contemporary Fiction: A Critical Guide to the Complete Works of 440 Authors.* New York: Holt, 1998.

Saal, Rollene. *New York Public Library Guide to Reading Groups,* New York: Crown, 1995.

Slezak, Ellen. *The Book Group Book: A Thoughtful Guide to Forming and Enjoying a Stimulating Book Discussion Group.* 3d ed. Chicago: Chicago Review Pt., 2000.

Mary Kooy (essay date October 2003)

SOURCE: Kooy, Mary. "Riding the Coattails of Harry Potter: Readings, Relational Learning, and Revelations in Book Clubs." *Journal of Adolescent & Adult Literacy* 47, no. 2 (October 2003): 136-45.

[*In the following essay, Kooy feels encouraged at the surge in adolescent reading provoked by the Harry Potter books and suggests attaching book clubs to this momentum.*]

Once upon a time, in a city far, far away, people eagerly awaited the arrival of a star. Newspapers reported the banner event. A buzz spread across the land. Everywhere people were talking of little else. At long last, when tickets became available, the people came from far and wide—they descended upon the city and formed a line kilometers long. They clambered to get tickets and, within minutes, the event was sold out! Many went home empty-handed and disappointed.

Then organizers put their heads together. "What shall we do?" they asked. Finally, a practical woman in sensible shoes spoke up: "Let's find a bigger space—a venue large enough so more can come and participate in this great, once-in-a-lifetime appearance!" So they found a huge arena—one that could hold thousands of fans. Again tickets sold out in minutes. Few celebrities achieve such notoriety, such brilliance, that they generate actual frenzies. Such was the atmosphere and excitement surrounding this event.

At long last, the day arrived for the star to appear. Thousands upon thousands of people came from near and far. They packed the arena. Splotches of color dotted the scene—waves of bright blues and reds. They sat, waiting, restless, absolutely bubbling with anticipation. The atmosphere was charged.

When the master of ceremonies announced the arrival of the star, he didn't have to say her name—people leapt to their feet and erupted into spontaneous, thunderous applause. Above the deafening wave of sound, the star shouted into the microphone: "I feel like I should be leading a revolution." One ardent fan shouted back, "You are!" (Graham, 2000). The star said only a few words—enough to remind everyone in the stadium why they were there—and then everyone went silent as she began to read.

When she finished, the lights came up to reveal the entire audience on its feet cheering again. As the lights bathed the seats of the arena, the splashes of bright blues and reds took the shape of wizards in capes and hats; there were Hermiones and Rons and any number of witches. Many sported lightning bolt scars on their foreheads. All too soon, the master of ceremonies bid them farewell and urged them to "Read, read, read."

MAGIC, MYSTERY, AND MAYHEM: READING AS EXPERIENCE

Though presented as an imaginative tale, the event I just described actually occurred. J. K. Rowling's appearance at Toronto's Skydome in Canada drew 20,000 reading fans, setting a record in the Guinness Book of World Records for a live reading of a book. The magic of the "lived-through experience" (Rosenblatt, 1938) gripped the audience. I sometimes wonder what happened in the Skydome: Was it merely hoopla and hype that drew the myriad young book wizards to the J. K. Rowling reading? If so, why was it such a success? By all reports, Rowling *is* a terrific reader who does full justice to her material. She knows how to bring characters to life and color to the descriptive passages with just the right amount of verbal spin. Throngs of readers, many armed with their own copies of her books, read along, mimed the words, or became caught up in the sheer force of Rowling's magic world. All this, mind you, before the advent of Harry Potter calendars, movies, and soft drink endorsements. The books alone provided the magnetic force that drew real readers to the Skydome.

Rowling has, as one reporter observed, "a completely honest connection to her writing, and communicates it so clearly that every kid in the dome could get the point" (Ouzounian, 2000, p. A27). When young fans exclaimed "I wished it could have lasted longer," "She really knows how to capture kids' attention," and "She used a different voice for every character. I *heard* them talking" (Ouzounian, 2000, p. A27), magic must have been in the air.

Before Rowling came, Sheena, a graduate student in one of my teacher education classes at the University of Toronto, told me about the author's upcoming visit. Tickets, she explained, ran up to CAN$50 apiece. Sheena taught in the Jane/Finch corridor of Toronto—the heart of the inner city—and lamented that her students couldn't afford the tickets. She envied Patricia, a fellow graduate student and teacher in an exclusive girls' school where all the girls had tickets to the grand event.

A week later, Sheena bounced into the class and proclaimed triumphantly, "Magic lives! By some miracle, my class got free tickets to hear J. K. Rowling read." Her excitement gave me goose bumps.

Ouzounian (2000) concluded his article with the following comments:

> I have one memory I'll take away from the day, and it has nothing to do with record-breaking crowds. A young boy, maybe 10, sat between his mother and his sister. He wore no costume and made no fuss, but he carried a copy of *Harry Potter and the Goblet of Fire* [Rowling, 2000]. As Rowling read, he followed along. The first time she spoke a line as Harry, he broke into an enormous grin. A reader and a writer making contact. That's more powerful than a thunderbolt, and it was wonderful to see.
>
> (p. A27)

If literacy levels are dipping lower and children don't read like they used to, what explains such a record-making event? What explains lineups at bookstores that begin before dawn in anticipation of a shipment of the next Harry Potter installment? If the grim stories about literacy among children today perpetrated by the media

and politicians were actually true, perhaps Rowling would still be sitting in a little café scribbling plots on napkins, because books need readers.

READING STORIES AND STORIES OF READING

I am dazzled by graphic demonstrations of people in love with books (Burke, 1999; Marshall, Smagorinsky, & Smith, 1995; Schwartz, 1996). In time, I began to wonder why and how the Harry Potter phenomenon occurred in an increasingly technological age where political agendas thrive on abysmal literacy scores. (According to an article in *The Atlantic Monthly* [Schrag, 1997], no U.S. politician can gain political office without using the failing education system as a primary agenda item during the election process.) I wondered about the power of the shared experience. As I reflected, I remembered that within a month of my move to Toronto I invited five relative strangers to form a book club that remains intact today (Marshall et al., 1995; Miller & Legge, 1999; Sorenson, 1998). These issues and my own "personal practical knowledge" (Clandinin & Connelly, 1991) led me to think about and wonder whether possible links between preservice teachers' knowledge of their own reading processes and the experiences of shared reading were foundational for them to become teachers of reading.

REHEARSING READING: LITERACY AUTOBIOGRAPHY IN LANGUAGE EDUCATION CLASSES

At the beginning of each methods course, I assign my teacher education students a literacy autobiography. In this work, they detail their reading journeys and get in touch with their reading knowledge—a critical step in their teacher development (Yero, 2002). My students reflect on how they became readers (or not), what reading means to them, which germinal texts shaped their thinking, their reading preferences and frequencies, their favorite authors and books, and school reading experiences. In addition to writing, some students include pictures, school projects, stories, poems, awards, or book covers.

Some students identify themselves as "a voracious reader," "not a reflective reader," or "not a reader." They begin telling stories of school reading: "I hated always being told what to read and what to think about my reading." Some find the journey challenging: "I've never thought about *how* I read a book. This is extremely hard to do." Others describe rich and full reading lives: "If I am really enjoying a book, I think about the characters all the time, meaning I sometimes wonder what they would be like in our world."

Exchanging the literacy autobiographies stimulates lively, meaningful, and vibrant conversations about reading processes, the canon, literacy and illiteracy, problem readers, choice of texts, and budgets for representational texts in increasingly multicultural contexts. Most students critically examine and deconstruct their own reading and reading knowledge (Yero, 2002). Knowing what they know situates and prepares the ground for further learning (Smith, 1986; Vygotsky, 1992; Weaver, 1998) because to develop knowledge requires knowing other things first (Dewey, 1938; Kant, 1929; Vygotsky, 1992). That is, establishing what learners know (Vygotsky's "zone of proximal development") connects to, builds on, and opens the way for creating new knowledge. When students talk like professionals—like teachers—they situate themselves as potential teachers in a professional community.

BOOK CLUBS ENTER ENGLISH AND LANGUAGE EDUCATION CLASSES

Book clubs have crept into my English language education classes (Forest, 1994; Grumet, 1991; Heft & O'Brien, 1999; Kooy, 1999; Kooy & Wells, 1996; Marshall et al., 1995; Miller & Legge, 1999; Sumara, 1996). Like Rowling's Skydome appearance, book clubs clearly model and confirm the value and power of shared reading experiences, knowledge, and membership. They are a natural follow up to the literacy autobiography that examines a reader's past. Book club experiences ask students to explore the present through an *applied* reading experience that operationalizes the practices of the language arts—reading, writing, talking, and listening.

My students begin by choosing a text. I distribute a list of 10 titles. Genres vary each year—from multicultural to young adult or Canadian literature. Students rank the titles from 1 (most interesting) to 10 (least interesting), compare their rankings with their peers, and then rethink their rankings by weighing additional information (summary statements about each book). Needless to say, sometimes the first is relegated to last and the last becomes first. After each activity, lists and choices are compared, discussed, argued, and reasoned, and sometimes they are changed again. When the dust settles, students sign up for their first choice and form a book club.

Reading responsibilities include preparing a log during the reading (Kooy, 1999; Kooy & Wells, 1996; Trimmer, 1997) to "keep a finger on the pulse" of the reading process and prepare for the book club meeting. Students bring books and logs to class. They read one another's logs and begin to "talk story." The writing in the logs feeds the dialogue and grows as readers add their impressions of generating the logs while reading, trace their changing understandings, explain their reading processes, describe the group talk, and speculate about anticipated teaching approaches. Almost without exception, they note that while the log disrupts the read-

ing, it is effective for preparing for and informing discussion, preserving memory, and heightening learning.

Significant for me is the developing awareness of students' reading processes and practices. The recognition that they enter a text with some expectations and awareness that clarifies or changes significantly as the reading progresses (Chambers, 1996; Kooy, 1999; McMahon, Raphael, Goatley, & Pardo, 1997) mirrors most learning experiences. Learning begins with a vague sense of the topic, and knowledge or skills are refined through application and experience (e.g., learning to write or ski). It's more like, as one student relayed to me, a developing photograph negative—vague hints evolve into a clear picture.

Often, this developing knowledge leads readers to question conventional and linear story reading in school. Such stories fly in the face of their awareness and experience (Dewey, 1938) and are based on commonly held assumptions that knowledge develops first with literal details and becomes more complex (similar to the hierarchical view represented in Bloom's [1956] taxonomy). Where and how does learning begin and evolve? Even young children recognize and prepare for a certain reading experience when the text begins with "Once upon a time" (a fairy tale of princes and princesses who live happily ever after, for instance). Other texts provide fewer familiar markers and challenge understanding. A grade 9 student, asked to write her way through Robert Cormier's *I Am the Cheese* (1985) during the reading, opened her reading log with "I hate this book. I don't understand a thing. All I can do is ask questions." About two thirds of the way through, she wrote, "I am a detective. I am gathering up the clues and all the pieces are coming together" (Kooy, 1999). In effect, she taught herself how to read this complex text.

Calling on their reading knowledge and book club experiences, preservice teachers can begin to release their imaginations and envision possibilities in the books they are reading. This proves particularly important for those students who made few, if any, claims to an active reading life. Many tell me they benefit from negotiating, in the book clubs, ways of approaching and understanding reading on the basis of their own practical knowledge. The metacognitive "stock taking," both oral and written, results in solid convictions overturned, connections made, and understandings altered.

This resounding and repeated affirmation of book clubs led me to expect—prematurely—that the process would therefore (causally) move into these preservice teachers' future classrooms. But even practical experience, I learned, does not magically transform into school practice. I puzzled over the gap in the transitional process (from student to teacher) and what I should be doing to transfer and trace the effects of the book club experience from preservice to inservice. How, I wondered, will preservice teachers act upon their new knowledge gained in book clubs to inform their planning and practice?

EXPLORING AND EXTENDING BOOK CLUBS FOR TELLING STORIES IN SCHOOL

What stories of reading, teaching, and learning are being constructed as preservice students make the transition to inservice teachers? Do they fantasize about being J. K. Rowling in the English classroom, bringing students to their feet at the prospect of shared readings? Do they envision developing vital and dynamic reading lives for every student? Or will they, instead, find themselves slipping uneasily into the long-held stories of teaching deeply embedded in school cultures and English and language arts departments? Will they "play school" as a survival strategy? Will they maintain a reading life apart from or parallel to the texts used in their teaching?

Virtually no work exists that explores the relationship between preservice experiences (e.g., sharing literary texts in book clubs) and the development of professional knowledge and practices in the classroom. The literacy autobiography, reading, and book club experiences seem to alter perceptions of reading and reading practices and, thus, could play a critical role in developing and enriching the practical knowledge of reading for preservice students.

Opportunities to address these questions arrived in the form of a Social Sciences and Humanities Research Council of Canada grant. It was serendipitous that at the same time a group of nine women in my language arts methods class inquired about ways to continue their reading and relationships once class was over. They suggested including them in the research by forming a second book club. This opportunity proved too good to miss. I could hear firsthand about teacher induction experiences and actively investigate my questions related to experiences and transitions from preservice to inservice—at least as they might apply to the lives of active, lifelong teachers and readers. I wondered how J. K. Rowling and all her Harry Potter fans, the book clubs in the pre-service classes, our personal and professional reading lives, and our experiences might be implicated in these teachers' identities and knowledge.

In the autumn of 2000, after each member accepted a secondary English/language arts position, we initiated our book club meetings. We agreed to meet three to four times a semester (Saturday mornings approximately every five weeks), select mutually agreed-on books,

respond in some form during the reading, and come prepared to talk. Research funds covered the costs of brunch and books.

Needless to say, I asked why anyone, in the midst of a new and challenging teaching position, would voluntarily add another commitment. Over the last two years, I have read and heard three consistent and key reasons: (a) books and reading, (b) social and relational experiences, and (c) personal and practical knowledge.

BOOKS AND READING

Members, intent on maintaining an active reading during their teacher induction, opened the initial book club session with talk of summer days spent with books, reading under the covers with flashlights, reading daily (even if only a page or two), getting "lost" in books, and book discussions with friends. These readers understood what it was to be captivated and even changed by their reading. Most had read the Harry Potter books and grasped their magnetic draw on young readers. They, too, would stand in line to hear J. K. Rowling. They know what reading *is* because they know what reading *does*.

Reading entered these teachers' lives mostly through parents who read to them and bought them books. One book club member, Rachel, said, "I remember loving the feeling of owning books." Without exception, stories captivated them. Marnie said, "I think I became a reader because I love stories." Hillary wrote, "I don't remember learning to read; I just always did." Rachel added, "My sisters are both avid readers." From the start, reading played a significant role in these teachers' lives. Influences around books and reading also included teachers, friends, and particular authors and key texts. Their desire to keep a robust reading profile made my students' participation relevant for a dynamic reading life and identity.

This passion for reading cannot go unchecked; it cannot be dropped casually into the teacher staff room or left at the book club sessions. Their love for reading is so profoundly woven into their identities that the resulting knowledge reaches into all the corners of these teachers' lived experiences—in and out of schools (Clandinin & Connelly, 1991).

SOCIAL AND RELATIONAL EXPERIENCES

"I'm ready. I need to compare interpretations and experiences," Emily said after reading a book. This common urge to share stories of books and reading is the raison d'être of the book club. It's a social, relational thing. Even youngsters who share their reading experiences of the Harry Potter books know "club membership" has its privileges. On a recent Halloween evening when a young Hermione showed up at our door, she proudly announced her identity. "Have you read Harry Potter?" I asked. She replied "Yes, all four of them!" Surprised by the response, I asked, "How old are you?" "Eight," she responded. Even in that brief exchange, we shared a discourse—we both knew Harry Potter. Participating in talk around texts offers readers identity and membership in a community. It is a shared adventure.

The book club phenomenon has not gone unnoticed in research literature, even though research on book clubs often relates to elementary school teaching and experiences (e.g., Marshall, 2000, 2001, 2002; Raphael, Florio Ruane, & George, 2001; Raphael, Pardo, Highfield, & McMahon, 1997). Those focusing on teachers and parents (Zaleski, 1999) and adults (Smith, 1996; Marshall et al., 1995) explore opportunities to "know and enjoy books and each other" (Zaleski, p. 120). Other works offer guidelines to establish book clubs (Flood & Lapp, 1994; Jacobsohn, 1998; McMahon et al., 1997). Still others focus on book clubs as professional development using young adult or children's literature or multicultural texts with an eye to direct implications for classroom practice (Goldberg & Pesko, 2000).

I investigated the book club as (a) integral to teacher preparation in English and language arts, (b) a support structure during the induction period, and (c) ongoing professional development. I participated in the book club as a reader and member, learned through the other members' stories (which inform a graduate course I teach entitled From Student to Teacher: Professional Induction), and witnessed the members' evolution and development as teachers. Members described the importance of the meetings as a "safe space" for sharing book experiences, relating school stories, and relational learning. Rachel noted that she joined "because I knew I would be in the company of expert readers who are also fabulous women with brilliant minds, I guess the reading, camaraderie, and thoughtful discussions were the main tugs." The social context of book clubs allows members to negotiate, challenge, and rethink the knowledge they carry and interactively and collaboratively construct new stories for teaching and learning.

PERSONAL AND PRACTICAL KNOWLEDGE OF TEACHING AND LEARNING

Book club sessions often open with members zeroing in on teaching issues that, at times, consume them. Hillary opened one session with a school story:

HILLARY:

> Well, I had a complete meltdown in my class the day before yesterday. I was so upset. I was still upset yesterday. I lost it, totally freaked out on my kids. I need to do stress management. It was too much, and I think I just had it.

LAUREN:

> But you have to have the room for it.

HILLARY:

> But I don't have the time for it. I don't know how to balance it. And so I know an element is being new and inexperienced, but it's also the system. I was really upset because I thought it was so unprofessional of me, the way I reacted.

MARNIE:

> Hillary, don't feel bad. I've freaked out on my kids and then said "I can't teach you," and I walked around the school. But then I came back, and I was listening at the door. I'd shut the door behind me, and they're saying, "Why don't you ever shut up?" and the kids were yelling at each other. I could hear them arguing with each other, saying, "You're so mean. Why don't you ever shut up? She's just trying to teach you," and on, and on, and on.

KELLY:

> And then they start to police each other and. . . .

MARNIE:

> Yeah, and they did.

Through such conversations teachers create a space to tell their stories; explore their thinking; and relate events that cannot be revealed, perhaps, to their department head, assigned mentor, or even colleagues. The best mentoring, ironically, seems to occur with other new teachers. The social context, exchanges, interactions, and the stories in the texts and of their professional lives result in new stories and interpretations.

The discussion transcripts clearly reveal that members are drawn—almost magnetically—to educational contexts and practices in the books we read (see also, Pelletier, 1993; Raphael, 1999). Often, textual issues or incidents prompt classroom stories. Sapphire's *PUSH* (1997), where Precious overcomes illiteracy through an inspiring teacher in an alternative school, prompted such a discussion:

EMILY:

> Isn't it wonderful—the very first day she [Precious] comes, she gets a journal.

MARNIE:

> And she doesn't know the alphabet.

SABRINA:

> Yeah. And she has to write in it.

LAUREN:

> I wanted to hug that teacher. I wanted to be there with her.

RACHEL:

> And then that way of writing back; I loved that.
> And the way that the teacher did not, at any time,
> show any judgement of what she said.

EMILY:

> If you look at this book, literacy is the savior. If
> that's the case, then how do we dare withhold it?

On the heels of this short exchange, members began questioning one another about writing in their own classes. Marnie said, "I have students who've been writing journals at least twice a week, and they still will write only one sentence. I give them 10 minutes." Her peers offered a range of options. "OK, then do 'the Derby' [have them write nonstop] and use a timer," "Start in pairs," and "Get them to doodle," they suggested. The discussion continued for several more minutes, bouncing back and forth between questions and suggestions.

Captured by the texts and eager to learn and share, the novice teachers generate new stories of books, reading, teaching, and learning. The discussions move reciprocally between life and the text. The stories become heuristics for sorting out complex problems. Connelly and Clandinin's (1998) research confirmed the force of drawing on and (re)constructing experiences in and out of the classroom to create new knowledge: "For each of us, the more we understand ourselves and can articulate reasons why we are what we are, do what we do, and are headed where we have chosen, the more meaningful our curriculum will be" (p. 11). However, the stories are not, as Geertz (1977) noted, prescriptions for practice so much as materials with which to think.

The *personal, practical knowledge* cultivated and pruned in these book club sessions emphasizes the fact that we do not simply tuck our reading experiences and knowledge in our book bags or deposit them in the hallway before we enter our classrooms. Our reading experiences stay with us whether we acknowledge them or not. Capitalizing on book clubs for English and language arts teachers encourages multiple stories of teaching and learning—of reading and living—that become a catalyst for building teacher knowledge and identity. Equipped with book club experiences, novice teachers can prepare the grounds for raising reading explorations, possibilities, and pleasures as pedagogy.

BRINGING BOOK CLUBS INTO CLASSROOMS

As we listen to the voices resonating on the literacy landscape—what it is, how it is taught, and who gets membership in the club—we hear from naive idealists ("just connect book and child"), to doomsayers ("kids can't read or write or even spell these days"), and those

in between. How do literacy teachers make reasoned and productive choices among such arguments? Do they abandon hope, accept the hype, forge ahead?

Teachers in Canada are unaccustomed to—even suspicious of—assuming professional responsibilities that reach beyond the more clinical, analytic features represented in government documents and programs. They've been handed the curriculum, tests, and provincial exams (different versions with each new political party) and are expected to implement and endorse them as well as raise test scores. Teachers are increasingly expected to follow orders. Such overt moves back toward traditional models of teaching that rely exclusively on "playing school" (read the chapters, answer the questions, or the initiate-respond-evaluate model of questioning) widen the gap between text and pleasure—between pedagogy and reading experience. Professionalism has been compromised so often that teachers have become uncertain of their abilities to act upon their personal, professional knowledge.

From book club experiences, teachers know and invest in the power of stories for and with their students. They "ride the coattails of Harry Potter" to get back to the basics of reading and, in the process, invigorate their reading and the reading lives of their students. Story upon story, a life in books for individuals and groups emerges through book clubs (Trimmer, 1997).

Time and again, teachers have joined forces with words on a page. They have all gone—as Carrier (2001) heard from a 9-year-old reader—"to places where my feet can't take me." Teachers can use what they know about reading, along with their personal, practical knowledge of teaching and learning (Clandinin & Connelly, 1991), to invite students into a life in books.

What teachers do with books and reading in school matters. Students learn what reading is, what books are, and why anyone should read at all from their lived experiences with books—much of it in school. If those readers attending the Harry Potter reading by J. K. Rowling had been handed a discussion guide with summaries of plot, theme, conflict, setting, and characterization followed by questions, vocabulary definitions, and a brief biography of the author to prepare for the reading, think how their lusty enthusiasm might have been affected. Indeed, the students who attended seemed to grasp intuitively that *real* reading is more, much more, than accumulating facts, and they wanted in on that action. They wanted a part in constructing meaning and making sense of the world of that text (Kooy, 1991; Kooy & Wells, 1996; Miller & Legge, 1999; Sumara, 1996).

It seems logical that narratives are at the heart of what we make sense of and understand. Stories can be read, heard, told, and talked about. Stories bring on other stories—they draw people together through shared experiences. In the end, as teachers, we must ask ourselves, "How does being a reader infuse and transform reading practices in this classroom?" We have to discover how our students respond to invitations to be members of the literacy club (Smith, 1986). To cultivate a community of readers, we have to show anyone entering our classrooms what occupies us there—in that place we read. Alone, together, on pillows, on the floor, on a sagging sofa, or around a table in a book club, we actively cultivate a life in books.

To maintain an active reading life in our classroom, we must continue to develop our own reading lives in teacher book clubs. We journey alone in the classroom, but in a book club we can journey together. As a result, we can feel as J. K. Rowling did in Toronto and proclaim that "we feel like we should be leading a revolution." I hope our students will respond, "You are!"

References

Bloom, B. S. (Ed.). (1956). *Taxonomy of educational objectives: The classification of educational goals: Handbook I, cognitive domain.* Toronto: Longmans, Green.

Burke, J. (1999). *I hear America reading.* Westport, CT: Heinemann.

Carrier, R. (2001, February). *Growing readers.* Paper presented at the Potential for Greatness Conference on Literacy, Victoria, BC, Canada.

Chambers, A. (1996). *Tell me: Children, reading and talk—How adults help children talk well about books.* York, ME: Stenhouse/Heinemann.

Clandinin, J., & Connelly, M. (1991). Narrative and story in practice and research. In D. Schon (Ed.), *The reflective turn: Case studies in and of educational practice* (pp. 258-281). New York: Teachers College Press.

Connelly, M., & Clandinin, J. (1988). *Teachers as curriculum planners: Narratives of experience.* New York: Teachers College Press.

Cormier, R. (1985). *I am the cheese.* New York: HarperCollins.

Dewey, J. (1938). *Experience and education.* Toronto: Collier's Macmillan.

Flood, J., & Lapp, D. (1994). Teacher book clubs: Establishing literature discussion groups for teachers. *The Reading Teachers, 47,* 574-576.

Forest, L. (1994). Teachers reading, writing and responding together: A story. In B. Corcoran, M. Hayhoe, & G. Pradl (Eds.), *Knowledge in the making: Challenging the text in the classroom* (pp. 149-162). Portsmouth, NH: Boynton/Cook Heinemann.

Geertz, C. (1977). *The interpretation of cultures.* New York: Basic.

Goldberg, S., & Pesko, E. (2000). The teacher book club. *Educational Leadership, 57*(8), 39-41.

Graham, J. (2000, October 25). Fans spellbound by "regular mom." *The Toronto Star,* p. A26.

Grumet, M. (1991). Lost places, potential spaces and possible worlds: Why we read books with other people. *Margins, 1*(1), 35-53.

Heft, H., & O'Brien, P. (1999). *Build a better book club.* Toronto: Macmillan Canada.

Jacobsohn, R. (1998). *The reading group handbook: Everything you need to know to start your own book club.* Framingham, MA: Hyperion.

Kant, I. (1929). *Critique of pure reason* (N. K. Smith, Trans.). Hampshire, England: Macmillan. (Original work published 1788)

Kooy, M. (1991). *The effects of implementing transactive teaching strategies on oral and written responses to the novel in secondary English classrooms.* Unpublished doctoral dissertation, Simon Fraser University, Burnaby, BC, Canada.

Kooy, M. (1999). Constructing literary landscapes: Reading logs in literature classes. In M. Kooy, T. Janssen, & K. Watson (Eds.), *Fiction, literature and media* (pp. 77-88). Amsterdam, The Netherlands: Amsterdam University Press.

Kooy, M., & Wells, J. (1996). *Reading response logs: Inviting students to explore novels, short stories, plays, poetry and more.* Toronto: Pembroke.

Marshall, G. (2000). Researching the implementation of faculty book clubs in an urban middle school. *ALAN Review, 28*(1), 22-25.

Marshall, G. (2001, April). *Teachers learning together: Faculty book clubs as professional development in an urban middle school.* Paper presented at the annual conference of the American Educational Research Association, Seattle, WA.

Marshall, G. (2002). Professional development for a literature-based middle school curriculum. *The Clearing House, 75,* 327-331.

Marshall, J., Smagorinsky, P., & Smith, M. (1995). *The language of interpretation: Patterns of discourse in discussions of literature.* Urbana, IL: National Council of Teachers of English.

McMahon, S., Raphael, T., Goatley, V., & Pardo, L. (Eds.). (1997). *The book club connection: Literacy, learning and classroom talk.* Englewood, CO: Teachers College Press.

Miller, S., & Legge, S. (1999). Supporting possible worlds: Transforming literature teaching and learning through conversations in the narrative mode. *Research in the Teaching of English, 34*(1), 10-64.

Ouzounian, R. (2000, October 25), J. K. Rowling delivers a wiz of a reading. *The Toronto Star,* pp. A1, 27.

Pelletier, C., (1993, April). *Professional development through a teacher book club.* Paper presented at the annual meeting of the American Educational Research Association, Atlanta, GA.

Raphael. T. (1999). The book club plus network. What counts as teacher research? *Language Arts, 77*(1), 48-52.

Raphael, T., Florio Ruane, S., & George, M. (2001). Book club plus: A conceptual framework to organize literacy instruction. *Language Arts, 79*(2), 159-169.

Raphael, T., Pardo, L., Highfield, K., & McMahon, S. (1997). *Book club: A literature-based curriculum.* St. Lawrence, MA: Small Planet Communications.

Rosenblatt, L. (1938). *Literature as exploration.* New York: Appleton-Century.

Rowling, J. K. (2000). *Harry Potter and the goblet of fire.* New York: Scholastic

Sapphire. (1997). *PUSH.* New York: Random House.

Schrag, P. (1997). The near-myth of our failing schools. *The Atlantic Monthly, 280*(4), 72-80.

Schwartz, L. (1996). *Ruined by reading: A life in books.* Boston: Beacon Press.

Smith, F. (1986). *Insult to intelligence: The bureaucratic invasion of our classrooms.* New York: Arbor House.

Smith, M. (1996). Conversations about literature outside classrooms: how adults talk about books in their book clubs, *Journal of Adolescent & Adult Literacy, 40,* 180-186.

Sorenson, N. (1998) *Making sense for our lives: Women's collaborative reading of fiction,* Unpublished doctoral dissertation, University of Toronto, Toronto, ON, Canada.

Sumara, D. (1996). *Private readings in public: Schooling the literary imagination.* New York: Peter Lang.

Trimmer, J. (1997). Telling stories about stories. In J. Trimmer (Ed.), *Narration as knowledge: Tales of the teaching life* (pp. 51-60). Portsmouth, NH: Boynton/Cook Heinemann.

Vygotsky, I., (1992). *Thought and language.* Cambridge, MA: MIT Press.

Weaver, C. (Ed.). (1998), *Practicing what we know: Informed reading instruction.* Urbana, Il.: National Council of Teachers of English.

Yero, J. (2002). *Teaching in mind: How teacher thinking shapes education.* Hamilton, MT: Mindflight.

Zaleski, J. (1999), Parents and teachers as readers: The book club as meeting place. *Language Arts, 77*(2) 118-124.

Patricia Fry (essay date October-November 2003)

SOURCE: Fry, Patricia. "Bonding with Books." *Reading Today* 21, no. 2 (October-November 2003): 26.

[*In the following essay, Fry examines the growing phenomenon of parent/child book clubs.*]

When Connie Th'ng visits the library with her 12-year-old daughter, they often check out the same book. Other mothers and daughters in the area are checking out that book too.

The same thing is happening in many other communities—mothers and daughters across town are picking a book and reading it. And all of them will meet soon to discuss what they're reading—many of them inspired by a woman who once swore that she would never read another book for pleasure.

Shireen Dodson earned a law degree at night while working full time in the day, and when she graduated she swore that she would never read another book. That was more than 20 years ago. Her desire to read for pleasure grew back after a few years, and her family was growing too.

Seeking a way to spend more "special time" with her daughter, Dodson developed an activity for them and for other mothers and daughters like them that was described in her 1997 book *The Mother-Daughter Book Club: How Ten Busy Mothers and Daughters Came Together to Talk, Laugh and Learn Through Their Love of Reading.*

Since then, hundreds of mothers and daughters like Th'ng have been reading together, having a special time with each other while learning about themselves, each other, and the world.

"I had always read to my daughter from the time she was a baby," says Th'ng. "Around third grade, she started reading books to herself at bedtime. I really missed the reading connection with her."

Families in some of the many book clubs across the United States have reestablished the bedtime reading ritual. As one mother says, "My 9-year-old daughter and I take turns reading to each other at bedtime in preparation for the next book club discussion."

Yapha Mason is the librarian at Brentwood School in Los Angeles. She facilitates a mother-daughter book club for 4th- through 6th-grade girls. "It not only exposes parents and children to the wonderful array of children's literature that is out there, but it gives them something to discuss and explore together," she says. She describes the club as "a playing field where all participants are on equal levels and everyone's opinion counts."

Marion Chamberlain at Seminole Community Library in Seminole, Florida, operates two mother-daughter book clubs for two different age groups: grades 1-2 and grades 3-5. She also ran a father-son book club for boys in grades 1-5 for a while. "The significance of the club is sharing some quality time exploring books together," Chamberlain says. "It's a great way for parents and children to bond."

CHOOSING HOW TO CHOOSE

At least as important as spending quality time together is the choice of books. The book selection process differs from club to club. In Th'ng's book club, they select the books a year in advance. "We have a party and each mother and daughter recommends whatever book they want," she says. "We put the titles in a hat and we read them in the order that they're drawn."

While most book clubs have one book selection per meeting, participants in Chamberlain's younger mother-daughter club and the father-son club read different books. She selects a topic and the kids choose their own book to read. "Topics for the boys might include adventure, scary, sports, westerns," she says. "Girls had poetry week, fairy tales, etc. At the meeting, the child will share the book with the others, reading excerpts, showing pictures, and answering questions. I have definitely seen kids get involved in reading new things because of the book club."

Th'ng says that in her club, whoever recommends the book for the next meeting automatically becomes the facilitator. "This person is encouraged to share whatever they find online about the author or the book," she says, "We discuss the book. Did we like it? What was our favorite part?"

While mother-daughter book clubs are thriving, leaders have been hard pressed to keep a father-son book club going. Mason learned that finding free time was a problem. "The only thing that kept the parent-son club from succeeding was the abundance of after-school commitments," she says. "Between homework, sports, and other activities, it's hard to carve a space."

The average age for the girls in mother-daughter reading groups is fourth through sixth grades. This works well for clubs operated through schools and public libraries. But when a mother and daughter start a neighborhood or community book club, it can grow with them. Nancy Zimble and her daughter launched a mother-daughter book club with friends and neighbors in Los Angeles when the girls were just 7. The club changes as the girls grow.

SNACKS AND BATTLES

In many clubs they serve snacks, and some go so far as to relate the snacks to the theme of the book. Th'ng says that at the last meeting she attended, "the book was *Wise Child* by Monica Furlong. She writes of fresh bread, milking cows, and making cheese. So we baked bread in a breadmaker and brought butter, cheese, honey, and milk. For *Ella Enchanted,* we made giant chocolate chip cookies because the book has a giant's wedding feast in it."

They may also occasionally have a craft project or an activity. "We had a water balloon fight after we read *Redwall,* which had battle scenes in it," Th'ng says. "We made magic wands for *Harry Potter* and for *Juniper* we made essential oils." These mother-daughter pairs have also planted sunflower seeds and learned how to spin wool.

Kirstin Arnett is youth coordinator at University Place Library in Tacoma, Washington. She meets with an average of eight mothers and daughters in grades 3 through 6 one Saturday morning each month. She uses publishers' websites to help formulate questions that provoke discussion.

"The girls often remember details that most of the adults have long forgotten after reading the book," Arnett says. "And the moms tend to reflect a lot on 'when I was young.' It's a wonderful opportunity for the girls to learn more about their own mothers."

According to Arnett, the books and the discussions not only establish and reinforce values and the enjoyment of literature, but also build a stronger communication link between the mothers and daughters at a time when they might otherwise start drifting apart.

"As the girls reach adolescence," Arnett says, "the communication gap begins to widen and parent-child quality time is less of a priority—for the girls, anyway. The girls face numerous pressures to fit in, deal with puberty, deal with gaining independence and sustaining their self-esteem as strong girls. The book club allows them to continue with an already strong relationship, discuss some issues in a safe zone relating to books that also relate to their changing lives."

The moms and daughters in the University Place reading group have discussed some serious and sensitive issues through-books, including death in the family, divorce, extended family member relationships, family history, sibling relationships, disabilities, and the elderly.

DEFEATING DISTANCE

One mother and daughter pair share books from a distance. Deb Beck operates a mother-daughter book club at Plymouth Library in Plymouth, Indiana. While their core membership is 16 members, not every participant attends meetings. "We have one member whose mother lives in another state," Beck says, "so she tells her the book and they are able to read it together and discuss it over the phone."

Do the girls enjoy the book club, or is this something they do to appease their mothers? "I've heard numerous times from the mothers that their daughters can't wait to come and they talk about the book all week prior to our meeting," Arnett says.

Beck's own daughter's enthusiasm sums up the feelings of most of the girls in parent-child reading groups. "After the meeting on the way home," Beck says, "my daughter will blurt out, 'I love these meetings!' So I know it is working well."

Suggested Titles for Mother-Daughter Book Clubs

The Giver by Lois Lowry

Eli by Bill Myers

The Shepherd of the Hills by Harold Bell Wright

Running Out of Time by Margaret Peterson Haddix

The Junkyard Dog by Erika Tamar

Love from Your Friend, Hannab by Mindy Warshaw Skolsky

Ella Enchanted by Gail Carson Levine

How Do You Spell Geek? by Julie Anne Peters

Yang the Third and Her Impossible Family by Lensey Namioka

Walk Two Moons by Sharon Creech

Suzanne Freeman (essay date winter 2005)

SOURCE: Freeman, Suzanne. "End of Discussion: Why I'm Leaving My Book Group." *American Scholar* 74, no. 1 (winter 2005): 138-42.

[*In the following essay, Freeman recounts how she came to realize that book clubs are not for her.*]

At *Book Browse.com,* there is an online forum that's set up for people who want to talk about the problems in their book clubs. Most of the gripes posted are about the difficult personalities who spoil the fun at book club meetings: the member who regularly shows up drunk, the one who is bossy and controlling, the one who won't shut up, the one who steers every discussion to the topic of her own sex life.

It occurred to me as I scrolled through these plaints that the next phenomenon might be group therapy for book groups. It also occurred to me that my own book club

lacks even a single one of these colorful troublemakers. Probably, by default, this makes me our group's difficult personality. I'm afraid that I am the dubious one, the recalcitrant one, the mope. I'm the one who disdains much of the assigned reading and the one who balks at using those Discussion Questions or Reading Group Guides so helpfully provided by the publishers at the back of some books. Certainly I am the one who has begun seizing upon the flimsiest of excuses (e.g., thunderstorm warnings) to avoid going to the meetings.

There is a definite pattern in my family of not being successful at clubs, beginning with my mother, who managed to get ousted from her Brownie troop in Montclair, New Jersey, at age eight for roller-skating through the room during a meeting. But a book club seemed like such a safe bet. In many ways, it's difficult to avoid being a member of a book club these days, especially if you're female. Almost all of my women friends belong to one, and some to more than one. Nobody can say for sure just how many of these groups there are across the country, but the estimated number has quadrupled, from 250,000 ten years ago, to a million or more today. If, by some miracle, you have managed to miss this bandwagon, there are now all kinds of self-styled experts who are ready to help you hop aboard.

You can buy a variety of how-to books that will instruct you on the fine points of setting up your own club. Other books provide lists of what your group ought to read—or, at least, what everybody else is reading. You can hire book group consultants, such as an outfit called Good Books Lately, which offers its services anywhere in the nation, promising, for a fee, to "enhance and energize" your reading and discussion. If your group has no natural leaders, you can turn to the Association of Professional Book Club Facilitators, which boasts more than a thousand members. Finally, you can learn from *BookBrowse.com* how to break the ice at your first club meeting by organizing everybody to play games called Pass the Hat, Pair Share, and Human Twister.

* * *

Evidently, the twelve women who gathered in the Quincy, Illinois, home of Sarah At-water Denman to start a literary society on November 16, 1866, were able to manage without any professional facilitating or human twisting. This was a group that got right down to business. The first book they chose to read was *The History of the Rise and Influence of the Spirit of Rationalism in Europe,* a two-volume tome by the Irish historian W. E. H. Lecky. Among other topics, this book led them through the study and discussion of Greek idolatry, the art of Persia, Galileo, Paracelsus, Spinoza, Descartes, Martin Luther, the French Revolution, Suarez's *De Fide,* slavery, the industrial system, and mercantile theory.

Next, the women devoted twenty-nine weeks to reading aloud and pondering Lydia Maria Child's *Progress of Religious Ideas, Through Successive Ages.* After that, according to the club's records, "the pages of Plato were laid open and were not again closed for two successive winters." This group called itself Friends in Council; it was among the earliest of the women's clubs—reading circles, civic clubs, art leagues, and, eventually, suffragette groups—that began to crop up in cities and towns all over America after the Civil War. Because women in this era rarely had the chance to go on to higher education, they banded together to form these clubs, serious organizations with agendas of "social good" and "mental stimulation."

The Friends in Council's early ideals were so pure and hopeful and steeped in longing that they could almost break your heart. Its members spoke in terms of illumination, generosity, and a widening of the spirit that would be reached through intellectual growth. They pledged to meet every Tuesday, to read and to talk about such subjects as Hegel, Goethe, Charlemagne, chivalry, and the education of women. They would aim "in the direction of whatever is noble, beautiful, just, and true."

If you thumb through any of the contemporary how-to guides for book groups, you'll notice that most of them invoke those nineteenth-century women's literary societies as direct ancestors of today's new book clubs. But I wonder if Sarah Atwater Denman and her Friends in Council would recognize as their progeny groups with names like The Book Babes, The Book Bimbos, and The Hardback Hussies. What would they make of The Happy Bookers of Linn, Missouri, who in an online interview give their motto as "You Never Know What You'll Find Between the Covers"? Or of the book club in Winona, Minnesota, whose members wore witch hats and capes on the night they were discussing *Harry Potter* and, on another occasion, went together to see the movie *Bridget Jones's Diary* all dressed in their pajamas?

I think it's fair to say that the lineage is less than direct. For one thing, it's pretty clear that the actual descendants of the Friends in Council are, well, the Friends in Council. This group, which can claim to be the oldest continuous literary society in the nation, still meets on Tuesdays in Quincy, Illinois, and, remarkably, seems to retain its sweet, solemn sense of purpose. Many of its members are daughters and granddaughters of earlier members. They may no longer devote two winters to reading Plato, but they spend a year studying a single topic—ethical dilemmas, Nobel Peace Prize winners, immigration, banned books. Each member is assigned to write a lengthy research paper on some aspect of the topic and present it at a meeting. After producing twenty-five of these scholarly reports, she can retire from paper-writing and become an associate member.

"Associate member?" a friend of mine said when I told her about this. "After twenty-five papers, I'd demand a Ph.D."

There are thousands of other longtime reading groups around the country—many of them affiliated with libraries or churches—that have met without fanfare over the years and also stem from those nineteenth-century roots. But the new slew of book clubs comes from a discrete family tree. To chart that, you don't have to go back very far—only as far as Oprah.

Winfrey's audience is vast and worshipful, and it's not hard to see why—she manages to be all heart and brains and clout at the same time. More important, she's always had a preternatural understanding of what American women want next: Dr. Phil, an Enell Serious Support bra, a brand-new Pontiac G6. Who knew? Oprah knew.

When she launched her televised book club, in 1996, one other thing Oprah knew was that most women no longer cared about getting a higher education from a club. They didn't need to—women outnumber men in American universities these days. They demand real Ph.D.'s. What Oprah offered, with the titles she selected and the tone she set, was not self-improvement but solace. This would be a club for the weary, the wounded, and the overworked. It would be a balm for busy lives. It was, of course, an instant hit. Oprah's idea not only put every single book she picked on the best-seller list but also touched off the epidemic of new book groups that began to meet monthly in living rooms and coffee shops around the country.

Because of all her visible success, it's often claimed that Oprah Winfrey "got women reading." I don't think so. I give her credit for many things, but it seems logical to me that most of the women who flocked to join her book club were already readers. Non-gardeners, after all, don't tend to sign up for a garden club—nor do they rush out by the millions to buy a trowel just because a celebrity holds one up on television. What Oprah did was organize women as a reading force. She legitimized their taste by choosing the same kinds of books that many of them were already buying and reading. She showed them how they could find time to bond with other overscheduled women simply by reading the same book at the same time—or even a little bit of the book. In her list of tips on hosting a book group, Oprah is a forgiving taskmaster. Try, she advises, to make sure "everyone has read at least one chapter."

The bonding part has clearly worked. In interviews filed on *ReadingGroupGuides.com,* you'll find enthusiastic accounts of book clubs whose members travel to the beach together, plan spa weekends, gamble in Las Vegas, bolster one another through messy divorces and regimens of chemotherapy, baby-sit for one another's kids, exchange confidences, share in-jokes, and play pranks. It can be almost too easy to mock the things women will do—wear pajamas and tiaras, for instance—under the guise of a book club, but there's an insistent and poignant theme to the interviews, too. In these clubs, the women say again and again that they've found a place to "let go" and "kick back" and "come out of their shells." They've found a place where they can drink some wine and wave magic wands and, if they want to, brand themselves babes or divas or hussies for a while. They've found a place, finally, to just get together and have some fun.

* * *

An odd truth about women, though, is that many of us are not so good at sustaining fun once we've found it. We just can't keep it simple. We up the ante until we're exhausted again. A friend of mine called recently to tell me that she'd shopped, cleaned, cooked, and then set and re-set the table twice in preparation for hosting her book club—and still she was worried that things wouldn't measure up to the level of entertaining they've come to expect. BookBrowse, in its column of trouble-shooting tips, warns of the tendency to turn meetings into "gourmet extravaganzas," with each member trying to outdo the others until it all "gets out of hand." There are clubs where members have routinely come to count on party favors, elaborate decorations, and food that relates to the theme of the reading. One New Jersey group is particularly unabashed about this. The name of their book club is "Mostly We Eat." They maintain an up-to-date Web site that lists their own favorite food/book pairings, such as "The Human Stain, food theme: foods that leave a stain"; "Mrs. Dalloway, food theme: a stream of appetizers"; or, "A Lesson Before Dying, food theme: Cajun and Southern." Scrolling through this extensive list can make you see your own bookshelves in a new light. Beowulf, food theme: smorgasbord! A Field Guide to the Birds of Eastern and Central North America, food theme: worms and more!

The recently published *Book Club Cookbook* takes this idea a step further, offering actual recipes solicited from book groups around the nation. It suggests, for example, eggplant caponata to accompany a discussion of *Bel Canto* and lemony goat cheese tart as the right dish to go with *Galileo's Daughter*. Or perhaps you'd like a little homemade Irish soda bread along with your *Angela's Ashes*. "[M]y book club ate jam sandwiches and hard-boiled eggs just like the picnicking couple in Margaret Atwood's riveting *Blind Assassin*," reports critic Sacha Zimmerman in *The New Republic*. "Thank goodness we didn't read *Hannibal*." And thank goodness, too, that Sarah Atwater Denman never had to whip up two years' worth of souvlakis and moussakas to go

with all that Plato. The Friends in Council, according to current member Laura Gerdes Ehrhart, have never bothered with refreshments at their regular Tuesday meetings.

* * *

When you pare away food and funny hats, the book is still the core of any book group. There is plenty of reading going on in these clubs and plenty of passion about that reading. Publishers have taken note. Overall trade-book sales in this country have not risen much in years, but when book groups latch on to a particular title or author that they love, they tend to pass the word to other groups, and the result can be a nice big boost for certain books. These days, almost all of the major publishing houses are courting book clubs through their Web sites. They offer enticements in the form of newsletters, reading guides, downloadable excerpts of new books, snippets from authors' diaries, bookmarks, and, of course, recipes. They've set up contests for book groups to win advance copies of new novels and even the chance to have an "author chat"—a phone call to your club from a real, live writer (whose latest book you will, naturally, all have just read).

It has become doubly important for publishers to get their authors known to smaller book groups because they've already missed their shot at the big time with Oprah. She deals only in dead writers now. After critics sniffed at her book choices for dwelling too much on themes of trauma, hardship, and loss, Winfrey closed down her club completely for a while and then reincarnated it in an all-classics mode. Her loyal television audience has gamely stayed with her, putting titles like *Anna Karenina, East of Eden,* and *The Heart Is a Lonely Hunter* onto the best-seller list (and, presumably, reading at least one chapter). These books may be the stuff of a college syllabus, but Oprah's critics aren't appeased—now they point out that the classics she has chosen deal preponderantly with trauma, hardship, and loss. This is probably the time to remind ourselves that, ever since the Bible started the trend, almost all books have relied, in some measure, on trauma, hardship, and loss.

* * *

It took me a while to understand what was bothering me about being in a book club. When my mother skated her way out of Brownies, she knew what she was doing. She wanted no more of whittling soap or peddling cookies or singing the song about the Brownie smile. But I didn't have such clear complaints. There are many things to like about my book group. We have no name. We're only sporadically organized. Setting up a meeting always involves several rounds of e-mails and more than one rescheduling. This suits me. There are seven of us—writers, teachers, a lawyer. We agree on important things; politics (progressive), pets (dogs), war (against), and wine (for). We compare notes on our children, our doctors, our hair colorists. We have never traveled anywhere together, but we could. I cannot picture us around a blackjack table at Caesar's Palace, but a beach weekend would not be out of the question. Nobody has suggested that we attempt book-based meals, but, if it happened, I would give it a try. If only to banish the thought of "food theme: Cajun," I would serve okra and rice, a pork chop, cornbread, some ice cream in a cup, and a Moon Pie—the plain, transcendent last meal that Ernest Gaines's Jefferson asks for in *A Lesson Before Dying*. Really, I would do a lot of things with this group, but I do not want to sit around with them and talk about books.

When I finally figured out why, it was mostly thanks to Laura Bush. "Books are not just for reading—they are for sharing, and talking about," the First Lady told an audience at one of her national book festivals. "Finishing a book is like saying good-bye to an old friend; we need support groups for that. That's why book clubs were invented."

And that is the big problem. For me, books and support groups do not really mix. When we make them mix, it is the book that loses. Right away, we turn it into something it wasn't: an assignment, a lesson, a chore. We use it as a menu maker and a party favor. Worst of all, we'll put it into the hands of a consultant or a facilitator who will almost make us believe there is some special trick to all this, something more than what we've always known by heart: find a book; open it; read.

In groups, we kill books with kindness and confabulation. We discuss them to death. I'm tired of all this talking and sharing—and where does it even take us? In your luckiest moments of reading, it seems to me, what you find is something to keep quiet about. You find something to hoard. You come upon one of those inexplicable places in a book that touches you so deeply you don't even have the words to say why. And you should not have to. These places belong to you. Others can just go find their own.

If only a book group would never assign or talk about books. Then I could stay. But that, of course, won't happen. A book is the badge of any book group—everyone knows that. Without it you are only a group of women in a living room, talking about fabrics or face cream or the mysteries of the universe and, God forbid, having fun.

Barbara Fister (essay date summer 2005)

SOURCE: Fister, Barbara. "'Reading as a Contact Sport': Online Book Groups and the Social Dimensions of Reading." *Reference & User Services Quarterly* 44, no. 4 (summer 2005): 303-09.

[*In the following essay, Fister discusses the highly important social element of book clubs.*]

Though reading is often perceived as a sedate and solitary activity, the popularity of reading groups suggests that reading is very much a social experience. Readers—women, in particular—have been coming together for generations to share their responses to books as an occasion for social engagement. That engagement can have a profound, if sometimes unappreciated, effect on our culture. For example, the majority of public libraries in the United States were founded by women who found an opportunity to create positive social change through their cultural associations.

More recently, reading groups gained a high profile during the heady days of Oprah's Book Club, when for a few years, a relatively obscure novel anointed by the popular talk show host would become an instant bestseller. Some members of the literary establishment took exception to a television celebrity being so strongly identified with book culture. When Jonathan Franzen expressed reservations that his novel *The Corrections* would be labeled with the Oprah logo—and therefore risked being shunned by highbrow and male readers, if embraced by middle-class women—the high-stakes juggernaut came to a sudden halt. But Sedo has pointed out that there is "life after Oprah," that the success of the talk show book club was merely a well-publicized version of an unquenchable thirst for talking about books.[1]

The power of a television celebrity to influence reading practices has made some critics worry that book groups, often supported by chain bookstores and big publishers, are commodifying reading—that we are witnessing a corporate takeover of literary practices that engages readers in formulaic, shallow analysis of texts.[2] Others see the burgeoning of reading groups as a grassroots appreciation of books that can teach us much about the relationship of readers and texts. Hall has noted that "the classroom study of literature sometimes dims the joy of reading," and popular literacy practices encouraged by Oprah offered attractions that academics should take seriously.[3] Strip has found in Oprah's invitation to relate books to everyday lives a feminist reclamation of reading as an act of transformation.[4]

Radway and Long have both explored the ways reading and talking about books enriches women's lives in a manner that academic approaches to literary analysis often disparage.[5] According to Long, a sociologist whose curiosity about women's reading groups was considered a peculiarly trivial research subject by many of her colleagues, "literature requires a broad base of readers to flourish" and, thanks to new channels available for forming book groups, "books are still closely tied to moments of experiential insight and still show a stunning ability to make people, in discussion, feel part of a significant book-related community."[6]

Paralleling the rapidly increasing numbers of face-to-face book clubs, the Internet has become home to thousands of book discussion groups. Critics of online communication, including Robert Putnam and Clifford Stoll, suggest time spent in online communities leads to isolation and social disengagement.[7] An examination of one online book discussion group contests that claim. This analysis draws on the discussion practices of one online group and off-list interviews with members to explore the experience of reading together in a virtual community. An active online discussion among committed readers can reveal much about how readers choose and respond to books, what role reading for pleasure plays in their lives, and how sharing responses to books can enrich the reading experience—and indeed, our lives.

BOOKS AT THE CENTER

An unusually successful reading list, 4_Mystery_Addicts (4MA) was founded in late 1999 by a dedicated group of mystery fans who wanted to create an online forum for readers to share their reading experiences through organized book discussions. It is not the oldest or largest of online mystery discussion groups. That distinction most likely belongs to DorothyL, a discussion group founded by librarians at a 1991 Association of Research Libraries meeting that currently has more than three thousand members. But 4MA is surely one of the most active, with more than six hundred members who together post between fifteen hundred and three thousand messages a month. Although many of these messages are marked "OT" for "off topic" and long-running inside jokes and personal observations pepper the daily diet of lively conversation, the focus is kept on books through three well-organized monthly book discussions and regularly scheduled opportunities to share reading experiences.

When a new member joins, the focus on books is clearly announced: they are asked to introduce themselves to the group by discussing who their favorite mystery authors are and what they've enjoyed reading lately. New members are welcomed by the group, with members responding specifically to their reading tastes but also describing the nature of the group as a social entity. One member does a particularly good job of capturing the character of the community in this

welcome post. This quote and all following quotes from 4MA come from list postings or interviews and personal communications with the author during fall 2004.

> Stick around long enough and somebody will have danced with a ladder, left their unmentionables someplace, gotten locked in a bathroom, gotten stuck in a stair railing, fainted, fell, ate something, rode something, broke something, that will have you falling out of your chairs with hysterical laughter. (We assume no liability for the damage done to keyboards and mice if you insist on reading 4MA posts while you are eating or drinking). You'll hear about stalking authors, nicknaming authors, plans for book heists, hijacking the 4MA website, wild get togethers in NYC, conventions and somewhere in the midst of all that, you will occasionally hear about books and authors that you won't usually find on the bestsellers lists but should be. And if you hang in there long enough you will find that we just like to laugh, have fun, read and eat chocolate, not necessarily in that order.

Though this post emphasizes the fun aspects of the list, her statement that you will "occasionally hear about books and authors" is intentionally ironic. In fact, one of the group's prime functions is to help avid mystery readers decide what to read next. In the middle of each month members are prompted to report on what they are reading. At the end of the month they post reviews of the books they have read. Members value these tips. As one member put it, "I have my reading list made to order." Another said:

> I tend to be a bit 'traditional' and stick to authors I know I like. If I'm looking at unfamiliar authors, I skim through the summary and if it doesn't sound interesting, I generally don't try it. I've found a number of authors I probably would not have found if they hadn't been suggested by a 4MA member. I also find I now keep a list of books/authors suggested by other readers that I know like many of the same authors that I particularly like.

In fact, many members have "reading twins" whose tastes are so similar they take special note of each others' recommendations.

Ross has pointed out the process of choosing what to read is not a trivial matter, particularly for beginners. "Each book read contributes to the bulk of reading experience that enhances the reader's ability to choose another satisfying book. Conversely, each unsuccessful choice decreases the beginning reader's desire to read, which in turn reduces the likelihood of further learning based on interaction with books."[8] Sharing information about what to read next—or what to avoid—is a key function of 4MA. As members pool their vast knowledge of the genre, they constitute an ongoing readers' advisory service of great depth.

As self-described "addicts," running out of books to read is a shared concern. One member joked about her need for a mountainous TBR—common shorthand for books "to be read":

That's why most of us are here I think—none of my co-workers read much and they think I'm bats and the family is constantly wondering aloud if the third signature for committal proceedings is overdue. I just don't seem to be able to explain to any of them that a Mt TBR of less than fifty books is a source of mild panic.

The solidarity of a group of like-minded avid readers is also a source of comfort (and amusement) for this on-line group.

Most people have stopped asking me why I need so many books (because I've taken to peering at them and asking in a very loud voice "you mean you don't!!!!!!!") but they still sigh and pointedly move stacks of books around so they can "sit comfortably" . . . I've often contemplated banning anyone from the house who doesn't have an emergency book in the glove box of their car when they arrive.

FILLING THE SPACES AROUND BOOKS

All of the members who were interviewed off-list commented on the warmth and friendliness of the community, and several had stories about times when the group provided emotional support. One member said:

I came aboard after coming out of hospital and in the first throes of dealing with an incurable disease that prevents me from doing lots of things I could before . . . few of my friends share my love for mysteries or books, at least to the degree I do, So finding 4MA was a double bonus for me. I found kindred spirits, I could finally discuss the books I loved to read, and I found a whole parallel community from all over the world (or close enough) who have supported me personally all through the last years.

"4MA has soul," another member said. "We are friends who read books—some of us are best friends even though we have never met each other; there is even a sub-group which emotionally supports a fellow member in times of sadness or illness," referring to the "sunshine club," an off-list group of volunteers who see to it that members who are going through a difficult time get letters, small gifts, phone calls, and other forms of support. Even members who don't post messages to the list appreciate reading the messages of more active members. One "lurker" wrote off list to assure me 4MA was an important part of the lives of even those who are invisible participants.

"It's a weird thing that you can end up having a sense of community with people you are never ever likely to meet," one member who lives in a rural area commented, which she finds an advantage. "I'm not really a face-to-face people person, to be honest." One felt the community was "there for her" after her husband suffered a heart attack, providing support that was "social and intellectual at the same time." Another said, "I joined 4MA shortly after losing my dad, whose death left a big hole in my life. I was looking for some way to fill the time I had spent with him without falling into depression and joining 4MA did just that. As well as helping to fill a void in my life, I have met some truly wonderful people on the list . . . I look forward to reading each day's posts to see who has done what, as well as who has read what." Members often contact each other off list, make efforts to visit each other in person or meet as a group at mystery conventions such as Left Coast Crime and the Harrogate Festival.

Though all of the members enjoy mysteries, there is enormous diversity in the membership of 4MA, which is considered a strength. "Online book groups take you beyond color, race, religion, and sex—you all love books" one member said. Indeed, the 4MA membership offers great variety in terms of physical disabilities, educational attainment, income, age, gender, and sexual orientation. Though the majority are from the United States, the United Kingdom, Canada, and Australia, the membership is drawn from six continents, and for several active posters English is not their primary language.

This diversity makes for lively book discussion. One member contrasted the narrower range available in her face-to-face group: "we know each other so well (we studied together for the same career forty years ago) that the discussions follow a familiar pattern. In 4MA there is always a fresh view of things." She added, "we get to like other members because we like their minds, not because they are good looking or have lovely manners or move in the best circles." Another member described 4MA as "very non-judgmental and supportive . . . Worldwide perspective and lots of mutual respect." Though political discussions are discouraged as potentially divisive, the sensitivity to international perspectives allows for cross-cultural analysis of criminal justice systems and social issues brought out in mysteries. One member said some discussion lists have "a very American-centric view which I find decidedly rankling, very closed and insular and very off-putting," though she added, demonstrating a "communication work" gambit typical of the list, "That could just be me, of course."

One of the moderators put it especially well:

People respect each other's opinions but go way beyond that and support each other. True friendships have bloomed. Lots of small and not so small gestures have happened—books sent to members who don't have the resources to buy some books for example . . . Over the years, this list has grown into a full blown community where the books are still the center but the people and their lives fill all the space around them.

MAKING AND MAINTAINING A COMMUNITY

As Bird has commented, creating successful online communities takes work and "being subscribed to a list doesn't result in community, any more than just living in a neighborhood makes that a community.'"[9] Though some online book discussion lists are beset by discord—one even has a list of "forbidden topics" posted on its Web site—4MA members only rarely need a gentle reminder that some issues have the potential to upset other members. "Let's remember we're at a party and that politics and religion and causes are subjects that should always be avoided to ensure a peaceful, successful party," one of the moderators recently posted when members wandered into an area that invited discord. Another member used the party metaphor, but described a somewhat rambunctious event:

> This is like a cocktail party where we schmooze the room and maybe make some friends and have heated conversations when we disagree. If you use your imagination you can see this group or that hanging around in clumps, never stopping the focus of why we're gathered in the first place. A room with mystery book lovers of all types getting along just fine, maybe checking this dress or that suit out or the dressing gowns or jeans . . . we are all here for our love of mysteries and good writing. The point being is I like to schmooze my way through what's out there to read and thereby add to my daily being something different now and then.

Though controversial issues often surface in the discussion of a book, since social conflict and troubling ethical issues are so commonly the subject matter of crime fiction, members generally are careful to focus their comments on interpreting the texts to minimize any potential to cause offense.

Symptomatic of the group's self-reflective humor, along with gently worded rules sent to new members and posted in the group's files, there is a spoof of list rules that includes the following:

> • No member shall submit more than sixty-two posts per day.
>
> • If you are wittier than the list leaders, you will be appointed as the CEO of something or other and given a very nasty job to do.
>
> • If you insist on sending BSP [authors indulging in "blatant self-promotion"], we will send the BS back to you and dispel the P.
>
> • If any of these rules are not adhered to, we will infect your computer with one of those nasty worm viruses who will eat all of your "t"s. -ry -yping a pos- wi-hou- using -he le—er -. No- easy, is i-?

Several moderators divide up the maintenance tasks designed to keep the monthly discussions going, such as organizing nominations for group reads and recruiting discussion leaders, but the task of enforcing polite behavior is not onerous. The focus and tone of the list was carefully shaped by its founders when it was launched, and members work to retain its cordial and informal nature. One moderator told me, "we very, very

seldom have to intervene. This list is incredible for its self-policing." Though some online discussions are closely identified with a single moderator, the sharing of list "ownership" among moderators from several countries has added to the welcoming diversity of the group and avoids the group being too dependent on one person's tastes and list management style.

Though off-topic posts are welcome, the list never wanders far from the subject of mysteries. In addition to sharing personal reading experiences, three books are chosen for group discussion each month. These books are selected through a voting process that involves members making nominations, a period during which readers comment in support of (ISO) nominated books they would like to read, followed by a voting process from which the two top scoring books are chosen for group discussion. For variety, there is a moderator's choice month, one devoted to other cultures and a classics month, in which nominated books must have been published at least forty years ago. The middle of the month is reserved for serial readers, a group discussion of the first three books in a mystery series, spread across three months.

READING PRACTICES

The discussions themselves are led by volunteer question maestros, who develop a set of five to ten question to be posted to the list over the course of ten days, giving readers time to compose their own responses and comment on each other's posts. Often, general questions are included so those who were not able to obtain the discussion book, or did not have time to read it, can participate. Spoilers—information about the endings of books or twists in the plot—are allowed. The discussion questions for each group are archived so novice discussion leaders have models for their questions, as are responses for those who came late to the conversation and want to revisit the discussions about particular books.

Some question maestros go to special lengths to enrich discussion by pointing out Web sites for background information, finding apt lyrics of songs to preface questions, or even contacting and interviewing the authors of books under discussion. From time to time a brave author will join the group for discussion, though that does not prevent readers responding frankly and forthrightly about aspects of the book they disliked. Though some books generate less participation than others, the careful planning, routine maintenance, and sensitive communication work done by moderators and members alike keep the discussions focused and lively. The depth of analysis is no doubt influenced by the fact the membership is unusually well-read in the genre, with members pointing out plot holes, clichés, and factual errors that evade most professional reviewers and many editors. Members feel comfortable stating radically different opinions because it is understood that reactions to books vary widely, and that different responses are to be expected and even enjoyed. At the same time, having someone respond the same way can be reaffirming. Quite often, after a dissenting opinion is posted, a member will say "I'm so glad you said that; I thought I was the only one who felt that way."

Becoming more adept at reading critically is a member benefit. "I have never been part of any book discussion group," a member told me. "Except for high school and college literature courses, I have never had the opportunity to discuss a book in depth with many people . . . I am viewing many of the books I read more critically and therefore I often have a greater appreciation of many of them. I find that many times I really think about what I reading and not just escaping into another world." Unlike in a classroom, the development of critical skills is not tied to grades. As another member put it, "the book discussions are wonderful. I am forced to consider why I enjoy or reject a book. I am grateful for the opportunity to voice my opinions, even if I consider them half-baked or incomplete. 4MA is invariably kind—no opinion is too stupid. Reading the opinions of others makes me think of the book in new ways."

The importance of these opportunities to tackle books with other readers is often underestimated by outsiders. "I was talking to a coworker today," one member told me, "and mentioned this and he was amazed that we actually discuss three books a month. I think he thought it was a group of people who chatted about silly things." Yet the group can also parody the high purpose of some book discussion groups. A new member was welcomed with this message:

> We are just a nice quiet bunch of sedate readers . . . we're very strict about the rules and never get off topic, we're quite a serious bunch . . . If this sounds like you—You are on the wrong list! LOL! We're a rowdy, crazy bunch of readers who spend our waking hours, reading books, trying to keep up with all the posts on this list . . . justifying that last book purchase, entering book give-aways, drooling over the latest book from our favorite author and trying to figure out if we can get by without using the oven, so we can use it for book storage.

Though deepening one's understanding of books and of the genre is a function of the discussions, members do not forget to have fun while they are doing it.

RESISTING CULTURAL CATEGORIES

Sedo points out that cultural studies scholars have not studied reading groups because they are not considered "oppositional" enough to be interesting, but rather are perceived as groups of middle- and upper-class readers, chiefly women with sufficient leisure to form such groups, who are susceptible to commercial and cultural messages about books.[10] Though certainly chain bookstores and publishers have paid more attention to book clubs than scholars have, the assumption that book group members are by nature complacent and gullible is not borne out by the evidence.

In the case of 4MA, members challenge dominant notions of the worth of books in two significant ways. First, there is a strong resistance to marketing messages. One highly touted but poorly written debut thriller led to the creation of the "Buzzhoff Award," given to amateurishly written books with big marketing budgets. Nominees are proposed from time to time with snippets of particularly bad prose. Though mysteries and thrillers dominate the fiction bestseller lists, 4MA members tend to pay relatively little attention to big-name authors. Discovering and supporting good mid-list authors is a shared and clearly articulated value among list members.

Second, the focus is on genre fiction, and the membership frequently offers spirited defenses of fiction not considered literary. Unlike the romance readers in Radway's study of reading for pleasure as a form of concealed resistance, 4MA members make no apologies for their taste and do not see reading crime fiction as a guilty pleasure but a worthwhile activity.[11] Indeed, they frequently argue that the issues tackled in mysteries and the overall quality of writing in the genre makes it superior to most literary fiction. Reviewers who describe books as "transcending the genre" come in for a regular drubbing.

Though all members love mysteries, they like different ones and are savvy about the differences. Several files at the group's Web site offer humorous definitions and examples of different types of mysteries. A number of these parodies were written by Donna Moore, a talented Scottish writer whose witty posts to a variety of discussion lists caught the eye of a British publisher who encouraged her to try her hand at a full-length mystery. Her affectionate spoof of the genre, featuring every annoying plot device known to mystery readers, *Go to Helena Handbasket,* will be published by Point Blank Press in 2005. A 4MA quiz helps readers determine their reading tastes based on five descriptions of subgenres. They range from "mysteries with a quilt making heroine and a quilt pattern and recipe for something wholesome every three pages," to "All the good guys have packed up their smiles and left town . . . The good guy usually wins, but becomes a little less good in the process." Adding up the score identifies the reader as Classy (a cozy lover), Splasher (sometimes cozy, sometimes hard-boiled) or Badass (hard-boiled). Though the taxonomies of subgenre are well understood, the membership is broad-minded; of the nearly two hundred members who have taken the poll, Splashers are in the majority.

When asked what they get out of reading mysteries, entertainment and escape were often mentioned by 4MA members, but so was learning new things. "I like the way I can get lost in a good mystery and I feel like I learn something from the best of them, be it about a geographical area, or some aspect of science or technology, or just about people of different cultures or backgrounds," one member told me. Another said, "Reading has always been my saving grace. As the eldest of nine children escaping to a corner with a book was my way of coping with life in general. Even though I have always read many different types of books, from historical to romances to nonfiction history and biography, mysteries have long been my favorite genre . . . Maybe it's the psychology involved in trying to understand the villain or maybe it's escaping my problems by reading about someone else's."

One member began by pointing out she enjoys the puzzle, but added "What's kept me interested in mysteries is the constant spotlight on the human condition. Even the more gory, extreme books that I've managed to finish have provided an insight into humanity and its frailties that I just don't get with mainstream literature anymore." Another agreed, saying "the genre tends to be more grounded in the traditions of social realism and permits a greater interplay between characters and the social surround than do other genres." Though this may mean reading about uncomfortable subjects at times, that encounter can be informative. "If it makes people stop and think about issues then it's a positive thing," one member said. "I keep remembering the discussion we had on Rebecca Pawel's *Death of Nationalist* and the issues it raised about war, human nature and how nothing is black and white. I think that's probably the most interesting book discussion I've ever participated in."

One discussion thread concerned "parents as readers," For some members, reading was not modeled at home. One member noted both her mother and grandmother read in secret because it was considered self-indulgent when there was work to be done. In other cases, reading was encouraged by parents. One member from Argentina told of her widowed grandmother emigrating from Spain with two children and a trunk full of books. "One of the first things I remember is my Father and my Grandmother discussing the battles of WW II with their newspapers open. And my Grandmother reading or telling me some tales from her books. I was a voracious reader since before I could read. Loved the printed word even before it took a meaning." Encouraging adolescents to continue reading is a common concern, often prompting book suggestions for particular interests, and getting a reluctant reader or a family member with learning disabilities hooked on books is grounds for communal celebration.

Above all, reading is not seen as a passive activity. One member called the encounter between reader and writer a "contact sport."

> Reading is an *active* process for me, not something I passively do—brain engaged, heart open, willing to be stomped on or thrilled or hurt or helped, or all of the above. It perhaps explains my anger when an author disappoints or, even worse, deliberately "trifles with my emotions," promising but not delivering, manipulating for sensation only, "playing with my affections". <grin> . . . And oh, the wonder, the joy, the almost physical satisfaction when an author unexpectedly delights you, charms you, pulls you away from the mundane and "the usual". Brings you into their world, truly welcomes you there, makes you feel a part of it, *invested* in it, as if it truly matters for you what happens to those people, that place, this occasion, THAT's writing!

Not only is it an interaction, the relationship between book and reader can be an emotionally intense and personal one:

> Reading a good book is a lot like a love affair, admittedly short-term, but nonetheless intense for all that. Some lovers become boring very quickly, others can be endlessly fascinating, with new sparkles coming to light at surprising moments, shining in the sun when you least expect it. But it always takes two, and even the ultimately sad ones "grow" you in some way, as long as they touch you where it matters.

Given that members of this group are activist readers, they are comfortable articulating their responses to books even when they disagree, making for lively and impassioned discussions. In fact, the books that meet with the greatest divergence of opinion are often the best choices for conversation. It's not surprising that each year, as members submit their "tops and bottoms"—the ten books they liked most and least—that the same title will often be found in both categories.

"BOOK HEAVEN"

One member commented that, though the librarians she encountered as a child fit the stereotype of spinsters with tight buns found in the film *It's a Wonderful Life,* they provided something important to her: "several of them were the warmest and nicest people I'd ever met, and they turned part of my difficult childhood into a beautiful imaginary world, gave me gifts I didn't understand until many years later, helped me realize that the life I—or they—had wasn't all there might be." She added, with tongue firmly in cheek, "But obviously I'm a disturbed personality—I consider 'librarian' to be a noble title! And I have a tweed suit . . ."

Though most members of 4MA have extensive personal book collections, and those who can afford to buy books make a point of supporting their favorite authors, many rely heavily on their public libraries. As one measure of the need for extensive library service, a member lives in a city in which the branch libraries limit the number of books that can be checked out at one time. She managed to overcome that liability by obtaining seven library cards in various family members' names from different branches!

Recently, when a member reported moving from a rural location without a strong public library system to a community with a good library collection, helpful librarians, and virtually no waiting lists for books, she added, "I won't tell you where I live, or you all will want to move here. And there will go my 'no wait list' for books I want to read." The response was immediate: "Where is this book heaven that you've moved too?! We want to know, right now!" Members began planning a retirement community for 4MA, describing the restaurants, pubs, tea shops, and bookstores they wanted located nearby. For this group, a dream community starts with a good library.

The needs and practices of the common reader, largely ignored by scholars of cultural studies and literary criticism, are also neglected in library science literature. For the most part, provision of information (whatever that might mean) is valorized, while pleasure reading is seen as a popular but far less culturally significant function. Information literacy, a cause that academic librarians in particular find urgent, is framed around a process that begins with identifying and satisfying information needs; lifelong learning—the ultimate aim of information literacy efforts—is presumed to depend on continuing patterns of information-seeking established in the school or college years. The Association of College and Research Libraries Information Literacy Competency Standards for Higher Education makes no mention of reading without a specific purpose in mind, even though readers report learning a great deal through pleasure reading that is not driven by an information need.[12] Ross makes a strong case for librarians taking more seriously the role of encountering information in popular fiction and the significant impact reading has on people's lives.[13] She points out that understanding readers and their needs not only leads to better collection development, but better reference and readers' advisory service—not to mention a broader understanding of the uses of libraries, including those considered merely recreational.

Though 4MA is a virtual group, with its members scattered across the globe, it has succeeded in becoming a true community for serious mystery readers who never take themselves too seriously. As a knowledgeable group of dedicated and critically acute readers, 4MA members provide an extraordinary readers' advisory service for one another through regularly scheduled and impromptu sharing of reading lists and ad hoc reviews,

forming a worldwide network of friends in the process. As a resource for avid readers, online discussion groups can enhance readers' horizons and provide a sense of community with books at the center. For librarians, virtual book discussion groups offer extraordinary insights into the social nature of reading and its importance in the everyday lives of readers.

Notes

1. DeNel Rehberg Sedo, "Predications of Life After Oprah: A Glimpse at the Power of Book Club Readers," *Publishing Research Quarterly* 18, no. 3 (2004): 11-22.

2. Dennis Barron, "I Teach English—and I Hate Reader's Guides," *Chronicle of Higher Education* 49, no. 6 (2002): B5; William McGinley and Katanna Conley, "Literary Retailing and the (Re)Making of Popular Reading," *Journal of Popular Culture* 35, no. 2 (2001): 207-21.

3. R. Mark Hall, "The 'Oprafication' of Literacy: Reading 'Oprah's Book Club'," *College English* 65, no. 6 (2003): 665.

4. Ted Striphas, "A Dialectic with the Everyday: Communication and Cultural Politics on Oprah Winfrey's Book Club," *Critical Studies in Media Communication* 20, no. 3 (2003): 295-316.

5. Janice A. Radway, *Reading the Romance: Women, Patriarchy, and Popular Literature* (Chapel Hill: Univ. of North Carolina Pr., 1984); Elizabeth Long, *Book Clubs: Women and the Uses of Reading in Everyday Life* (Chicago: Univ. of Chicago Pr., 2003).

6. Ibid., 217-218.

7. Robert D. Putnam, *Bowling Alone: The Collapse and Revival of American Community* (New York: Simon & Schuster, 2000); Clifford Stoll, *Silicon Snake Oil: Second Thoughts on the Information Highway* (New York: Doubleday, 1995).

8. Catherine Sheldrick Ross, "Making Choices: What Readers Say about Choosing Books to Read for Pleasure," *Acquisitions Librarian* no. 25 (2001): 9.

9. S. Elizabeth Bird, *The Audience in Everyday Life: Living in a Media World* (New York: Routledge, 2003), 157.

10. DeNel Rehberg Sedo, *Badges of Wisdom, Spaces for Being: A Study of Contemporary Women's Book Clubs.* Ph.D dissertation, Simon Fraser University, 2004.

11. Radway, *Reading the Romance.*

12. Association of College and Research Libraries, "Information Literacy Competency Standards for Higher Education," 2000. Accessed Oct. 30, 2004, http://www.ala.org/ala/acrl/acrl standards/informationliteracycompetency.htm.

13. Catherine Sheldrick Ross, "Finding without Seeking: What Readers Say about the Role of Pleasure Reading as a Source of Information," *Australasian Public Libraries and Information Services* 13, no. 2 (2000): 72-80.

Barbara Hoffert (essay date 1 July 2006)

SOURCE: Hoffert, Barbara. "The Book Club Exploded." *Library Journal* 131, no. 12 (1 July 2006): 34-7.

[*In the following essay, Hoffert surveys library-based book clubs.*]

One leader, 12 readers, and a few well-thumbed copies of Jane Austen's *Pride and Prejudice.* That's all a book club once required. No more. The runaway popularity of book clubs has brought with it a whole new set of possibilities. Thematic discussion? A fiction/nonfiction mix? Videoconferencing? Multimedia exploration? With these and other approaches, librarians nationwide are successfully restructuring chitchat about beloved classics or recent best sellers to deliver a richer and more vibrant experience for everyone.

One Topic, Lots of Books

Take the monthly book club at East Palestine Memorial PL, OH. Says Director Lisa Rohrbaugh, who selects the material and then leads the discussion, "Sometimes we all read the same book, sometimes the same genre, sometimes the same subject," Writers whose works have been considered as a whole include Ivan Klíma, Naghib Mafhouz, and Jorge Luis Borges. Broader reading has encompassed foreign travel literature, Eastern European fiction and nonfiction, and author or musician biographies. And a few imaginative forays have taken in books about the sun as well as essays by Montaigne and Emerson. For these thematic discussions, participants aren't necessarily reading the same titles, but by reading related material they each bring valuable information and a unique perspective to the proceedings.

Folks at Upper Merion Township Lib., King of Prussia, PA, also enjoy thematic discussions but approach them differently, with two yearly five-book series led by two popular and dedicated English professors from nearby West Chester University. Everyone reads the same five books, one every other week, with topics like "The Cultural Fabric of America" (e.g., David Guterson's *Snow Falling on Cedars,* Richard Rodriguez's *Hunger of Memory,* and poetry by Gwendolyn Brooks, Langston Hughes, and Rita Dove), "Family: The Battle with the Past" (e.g., Paul Monette's *Becoming a Man,* Julia Alvarez's *How the Garcia Girls Lost Their Accents,* and Eugene O'Neill's *Long Day's Journey into Night*),

and "The Family and Working America" (e.g., Willa Cather's *The Professor's House,* Tillie Olsen's *Yonnodio,* and Russell Baker's *Growing Up*).

Chesterfield Cty. PL, VA, is experimenting with having a book club follow a theme over several months, too, though like East Palestine Memorial it will encourage participants to read different titles. The first theme planned is World War II, and other themes will likely include the Civil War, African American literature, and the immigrant experience, supported by a We the People Grant from the National Endowment for the Humanities. New Canaan PL, CT, offers yet another approach, including among its four groups an "Eighteenth Century Club," which considers only works written in or about the 1700s. (The mystery book club, another subject-specific type, is especially popular nationwide.) In addition, discussion at New Canaan's "Reader's Choice" club has veered toward topics like "Biographies To Winter By" and "Family Relationships." A different member chooses the book for each meeting, and even when a title isn't theme-based, topical thinking is contagious. "There is always some kind of tie-in with a previous book," notes assistant director Cynde Bloom Lahey.

The Advantages Stack Up

Once you start counting them, the advantages of a thematic approach to book discussion really add up. Instead of rushing to secure 22 copies of a single title through purchase or interlibrary loan, librarians can pull different titles already on the shelves, saving effort and money while exploiting the riches of the collection. Thematic discussions aren't as likely to grind to a halt after a few observations of the "I liked it" or "It bored me" variety, instead flowing from book to book and meeting to meeting.

Working by theme enriches the conversation by allowing readers to cross genres and approach the discussion from different perspectives, thus getting a better sense of an author, idea, or culture. It can also shake up reader complacency, attracting new people who might be intimidated by or uninterested in book clubs generally but who find a topic appealing. "Everyone who is part of planning our new project is really excited," observes Chesterfield's Neal Wyatt, "because it breaks up the deadlock groups have right now and invites other people in."

Those coming in are not just new people but a new demographic, notes Donna Bettencourt, Mesa County PL, CO. "Teen groups seem to like theme-based book discussions, reading different fiction and nonfiction titles and discussing all the books. Reading one book with a series of questions just doesn't appeal." A topical mix of fiction and nonfiction may attract more male readers, too, who have tended to shy away from the fiction-dominated book groups of the past. "It's assumed that a book for discussion has to be an Oprah book," observes Brian DeLuca, Hartford County PLs, CT, "which won't draw in men at all."

Mixing Up the Media

If a book club can conjure up more engaged and engaging discussion by linking several titles, often mixing fiction and nonfiction, poetry and plays, it's just as illuminating to mix books with other media. After reading one of the Bard's plays, the book club at Kingstowne Community Library, Fairfax County PL, VA, bounded into Washington, DC, to see a live performance at the Shakespeare Theatre. East Palestine Memorial's book club often spices its discussions with talk of movies and not just remakes of a book. Intriguing pairs that have allowed participants to explore ideas in multiple contexts include Truman Capote's *The Thanksgiving Guest* and the movie *The Piano Lesson* and John Gardner's *Sunlight Dialogues* and the film *House of Sand and Fog*.

Kansas City PL, MO, also encourages exploration, supporting other reading forums tied to special library exhibits or citywide events in addition to hosting its popular book clubs at ten locations. Book clubs make homier links, too. Members often combine discussion with a meal, especially one that reflects scenes from the book or the author's culture. (Butterbeer, anyone? Or perhaps a delicious mole sauce to accompany Laura Esquivel's *Like Water for Chocolate*?)

Chesterfield's Wyatt would go in another direction, combining reading with knitting. "It's huge where I am," she says of the craft, "as I'm sure it is everywhere. We've had one success, when people came and just knitted and talked. I want to ramp that up to chick lit and knitting because the same audience checks out both. We're trying to work with yarn stores in the area."

The Power of Authors

If attending an author lecture is a pleasure, having the author participate in a book discussion seems like a dream. It's not as hard to arrange as one may think. "Authors love libraries," exclaims New Canaan's Lahey. "They tell us with every visit." Author visits can be arranged through a publisher's publicity department, and though one can ask for any author, catching someone who's young and hungry or just out the door with a new title probably works best, (A dedicated library marketer will be especially helpful in arranging a visit; for a list, see *LJ* Web Exclusive info, p. 37, and www.authorsatyourlibrary.org). These days, however, many authors are visiting book clubs without setting foot in the library.

A good book, an avid group of readers, and an author on a speakerphone: that's the perfect formula for an exciting book discussion, as Lahey discovered in 2004 when Khaled Hosseini (*The Kite Runner*) was invited to speak at the library. "It was at the peak of his popularity, and we had over 200 people attend," she recalls. "The sound was great, he was articulate, and the Q&A went well."

Smaller groups are doubtless better for real one-on-one discussions, but librarians working with groups of any size can check out publisher web sites to see what authors might be available for phone chats. Many Random House imprints will even pay for the call. Librarians can join Random's reader's group advisory list to receive galleys, backup materials, and a monthly e-newsletter by emailing libraryrandomhouse.com. HarperCollins, whose "Invite the Author" lottery initially targeted consumers, has recently extended it to libraries and bookstores and will even lend out a speakerphone.

A Person on the Screen

Librarians who like the idea of phone chats might go one step further and consider videoconferencing. That's what Kathleen Degyansky did at Queens Borough PL, NY. Saddled with donated videoconferencing equipment never used for remote meetings as intended, the library's director challenged staff to come up with a few good ideas. Degyansky landed the job of coordinating the videoconferencing initiative and immediately thought of author visits. In short order, books clubs in Queens were booking up with Gary Soto (*Baseball in April and Other Stories*) in California, Chris Bohjalian (*Midwives*) in Vermont, and Mark Spragg (*An Unfinished Life*) in Red Lodge, MT, who was chatting with a Michigan group at the same time. Queens Borough has also hosted authors, beaming Michael Cunningham (*The Hours*) to a library in California.

In videoconferencing, the author can both see and hear book club members, and members can both see and hear him or her. "Sort of like the Jetsons and Rosie," explains Degyansky. For that reason, she considers videoconferencing superior to webcasting, in which the only opportunity for exchange with the speaker comes in the form of emailed queries. Authors aren't likely to have their own videoconferencing equipment, of course, but many local institutions will; Spragg spoke from a telemedicine clinic ten minutes from his home. "If Red Lodge, MT, has videoconferencing equipment, every town has videoconferencing equipment somewhere," asserts Degyansky, who points to community colleges, hospitals, and business centers as likely sites. In fact, since videoconferencing equipment doesn't come cheap, librarians interested in trying it might first ask to use a nearby college's equipment, hook up with Spragg at the Red Lodge clinic, and see how they like it.

It's about Content

Degyansky's advice for videoconferencers could apply to anyone doing a phone chat as well: "Some work can figure out the technology; stay centered on the content, which is what everybody really cares about." In fact, the technology is not unduly challenging. A bigger challenge for Degyansky is making sure that she lands an author willing to take a chance at something new, so she heeds publisher recommendations carefully. Publicists know their authors and can identify the mavericks. They can also tell anyone trying to arrange a visit, whether high or low tech, which authors will jump into conversation and which are cold fish who'd rather stay home in their garrets (or mansions). Observes Sarah Pucillo, Random's library marketing coordinator, "You want authors who want to promote their books, which not all authors will agree to do."

Technology promises to transform the book club experience, and many librarians are intrigued if cautious. "I'll support anything that connects authors and readers—if a library has the personnel to do it," says Kathleen Sullivan, Phoenix PL. Concurs Kansas City's Bob Lunn, "I would be interested in experimenting with any of these approaches. The problem for me comes with trying to juggle everything that needs doing, plus the nagging fear of technology failure." Time will tell how popular phone chats and videoconferencing will become, though they will probably flourish with a generational changing of the guard. Even now, online book clubs have had mixed results—except among teenagers, who, as many librarians happily report, are actively engaging in library-sponsored book blogs.

A Real Community

With book clubs bursting out all over, some thanks are due Oprah Winfrey, "Oprah got many more people comfortable talking about books," says Michele McGraw, Southdale Library, Hennepin County PL, MN. But she goes on to cite another, deeper reason for book club euphoria: "People are looking for a chance to connect, and the library's book club is a real community."

Indeed, many librarians consider book clubs an important part of their mission, bringing back lapsed users, hauling in new ones, providing enhanced service to regulars, and promoting the value of reading to the community at large. "Book discussion groups support the idea that libraries harbor communities of readers," observes Kansas City's Lunn. "If someone visiting the library goes away with that impression, who knows where it might end?"

Club in a Kit

Some libraries are so committed to book clubs that they offer members special collections or kits. Hennepin County's 150 kits, which are generally checked out by a single member for the entire group, include ten copies of the book, plus discussion questions and background information on the author. Several years ago, New Canaan opted to purchase multiple copies of any title a book club wanted, realizing that other clubs would likely line up for the book as well. Now, with local clubs numbering several hundred, these book club collections have created a spurt in circulation.

Seattle PL's ten-year program is even more ambitious. Catering to more than 400 book groups, which must register with the library, the book group collection offers multiple copies (generally numbering 24) of more than 400 titles. Users don't even need to check out the particular passel of books, which are typically packed up by librarians for the clubs; the packages almost always come back intact. "We look for books that are good for discussion and with broad enough appeal for a variety of groups," explains Christine Hagashi, "We make a lot of friends with this collection." Librarians interested in checking out the list—clearly a great source for book club suggestions—should go to www.spl.org/pdfs/ RecommendedBooksforDiscussion.pdf for a 30-page extravaganza.

Bonuses Abound

Like Hennepin County PL, many libraries with book club kits offer bonus materials because, as Chesterfield's Wyatt says, "Readers love to know more about the author." Wyatt's wish list for good bonus materials includes questions (though not ponderous ones like "How is the color red used?"), plus an author interview, a list of readalikes, and a list of read-abouts—"that's my version of nonfiction readalikes so that all those good nonfiction titles will support a book," she explains. Many publishers currently have online reading guides, and Crown is launching a program called "Ask Another Author," online interviews of a book's author by a colleague, which should offer special insight into the writing process.

Exploiting the newest technology, HarperCollins has just begun creating podcasts that can be downloaded to an iPod from the HarperPerennial.com web site and heard later. The original programming on these podcasts includes author interviews and even musical scores, suggesting what music was wafting in the background as the author wrote the book. "If a librarian is thinking of suggesting a book, the podcast can give a little more background," explains HarperPerennial marketing director Amy Baker. "For reading groups themselves, it supplies more fuel to fire the discussion."

A Good Book

What finally drives a good book group discussion is the right book, and librarians have plenty of opinions on that subject. Most agree that publishers overemphasize literary fiction in the reading guide sweepstakes, ignoring reader hunger for simply a good story, "Just because it's literary doesn't mean it's discussable, and just because it's popular and heavily plotted doesn't mean it's not," asserts Wyatt. The discussable book lets sparks fly instead of inspiring consensus and leaves readers wrestling with complexity and nuance. "In a good book group book, not everything is wrapped up and answered for you," explains Seattle's Hagashi.

Hagashi also praises books that feature characters "dealing with life issues we can identify with, who make decisions that sometimes make sense and sometimes don't." Her comment obviously applies to fiction, the favorite of most book clubs. At New Canaan, Lahey finds that nonfiction does have its advantages: "Readers who have not finished the book can still share in the discussion, and fiction is much more personal to discuss." Still, many librarians agree with Upper Merion County director Karl Helicher that selling nonfiction to the book club crowd can be a chore. "Perhaps, in scary times, people gravitate toward fiction," he says. "There is not a lot of good nonfiction, other than memoir, that can be read as quickly as fiction."

PICKING NONFICTION

The scattered resistance to nonfiction is unfortunate, since a good true-to-life account adds depth to any book club roster, and some librarians are desperate to find such works. In general, briefer, more focused titles seem to work best, and narrative nonfiction—nonfiction that reads like fiction, in today's lingo—has the broadest appeal. Juicy biography or history with a real story always elicits conversation, though at Queens Borough PL, Degyansky has had good luck with really nitty-gritty how-to books: one successful discussion featured several works on skin care.

Good resources include the web site of libraries like Seattle PL and New Canaan PL, which offer extensive book club recommendations, and anyone interested in a thematic approach should know that Wyatt's World on www.libraryjournal.com often features nonfiction. In fact, following the trend of mixing genres for thematic discussion is an effective way to introduce nonfiction to book club skeptics.

Buffed, blended, and hooked up to other media or to video-conferencing equipment, the current book club looks nothing like yesterday's modest tea party. As book clubs keep booming, more and more libraries will become happy hosts. The book club is not just a way to satisfy a few hard-reading patrons. It helps polish the library's image and build bridges to the entire community. Whoever said talk is cheap? In today's library, with groups large or small, book club talk is priceless.

OPRAH WINFREY'S BOOK CLUB

Francine Fialkoff (essay date 15 November 2001)

SOURCE: Fialkoff, Francine. "Franzen: Too Highbrow for Oprah?" *Library Journal* 126, no. 19 (15 November 2001): 52.

[*In the following essay, Fialkoff recounts author Jonathan Franzen's snubbing of Oprah's Book Club.*]

"Book bait." That's what young adult librarians once called the selection of adult books they compiled to entice young readers. The last edition of *Book Bait* (American Library Assn.) was published in 1988, but the concept began several generations earlier, built on the wisdom of public librarians who understood that it doesn't matter what young adults read as long as they do read. The "habit of reading" is "indispensable. That habit once established, it is a recognized fact that readers go from poor to better sorts of reading," wrote F. B. Perkins in 1876 in the *Special Report on Public Libraries in the United States*. "[T]hose who intend to organize a library for the public, for popular reading, and who intend to exclude 'trash,' might as well stop before they begin. . . . What is trash to some is . . . stimulus . . . to others."

If only Jonathan Franzen, author of the critically acclaimed and best-selling novel *The Corrections,* were familiar with library history and philosophy. He might not have been so beset by contradictory feelings when his book, already a nominee for this year's National Book Award (and by the time you read this, perhaps a winner), was selected as the 43rd Oprah Book Club selection.

Certainly Oprah's selections are not "trash," and even Franzen would agree that a number of the authors—Joyce Carol Oates, Andre Dubus III, Isabel Allende, Bernhard Schlink—fit into the "high-art literary tradition" where he situates himself. Nevertheless, many of Oprah's choices are clearly middlebrow. "She's picked some good books," Franzen told Powell's bookstore in Portland, OR, "but she's picked enough schmaltzy, one-dimensional ones that I cringe, myself, even though I think she's really smart and she's really fighting the good fight."

Franzen had misgivings on other fronts, too. The Oprah logo on his book smacked of "corporate ownership," he told the Portland *Oregonian* (notwithstanding that his publisher, Farrar, Straus & Giroux, is part of the same German conglomerate that owns St. Martin's and Henry Holt) and might frighten some highbrow readers away. Most of Oprah's followers are women, and they might be disappointed by the book (though it is not clear why). Conversely, men might be put off, since Oprah's picks seem to be geared toward her mostly female viewers.

In the frenzy of his misgivings, however, Franzen blew the opportunity to bridge the gap between popular, or middlebrow, fiction and his own "high-art literary tradition." Oprah has disinvited him to appear on her show, saying, "It is never my intention to make anyone uncomfortable or cause anyone conflict. . . . [w]e're moving on to the next book." The doyenne of daytime television may have acted out of pique, but to her credit, the book is still an Oprah selection.

All of this is somewhat ironic in light of an essay Franzen wrote for *Harper's* in 1996. In it he bared his soul about "succumbing . . . to despair" at our consumer- and television-obsessed society, which had "killed the novel of social reportage" and his own ability to write his third novel which became *The Corrections*). Ultimately, Franzen describes emerging from his depression, and his self-imposed isolation, and concludes the essay on a note of hope as he begins writing "about the things closest to me . . . the characters and locales I loved" and in doing so also addresses "the bigger social picture."

Given the concerns he expressed in his essay about the demise of the social novel, the novel of manners, how wonderful it would have been had Franzen appeared on Oprah's show to talk about just such a novel. Librarians have shown us that one way to create highbrows out of middlebrows is to give readers avenues they can be comfortable with: that is what Oprah's Book Club does. The Oprah appearance would have given Franzen access to an even broader readership than he already has, and it may have helped elevate the reading tastes of some of those viewers. What a triumph that would have been for the once-despairing novelist.

Francine Fialkoff (essay date 15 May 2002)

SOURCE: Fialkoff, Francine. "12 Good Books: Despite Oprah's Careless Words, There Are Dozens of Books Worthy of Attention." *Library Journal* 127, no. 9 (15 May 2002): 76.

[*In the following essay, Fialkoff criticizes Oprah Winfrey for declaring the world devoid of inspiring books.*]

They're stacked high on my nightstand, waiting to be read: backlist books, frontlist titles, new galleys, old classics. Oprah Winfrey, as you've all heard, can't find any books to inspire her with the desire to read and to share what she's read with her viewers. In the damning statement she released last month as she dropped her

show's book club, she said, "It has become harder and harder to find books on a monthly basis that I feel absolutely compelled to share."

When Winfrey was honored at the National Book Awards several years ago for the impetus she and her book club had given books and reading—not to mention publishers' sales and library circulation statistics—she emphasized the impact of reading on her life and the importance of books for all. Now, she can't find even a dozen books to keep her book club going.

It's certainly Winfrey's prerogative to end the book club. But her choice of words rankles. Notwithstanding the soul-searching that goes on on her show and in her magazine, Winfrey isn't given much to soul-searching in her press statements regarding books. She disinvited Jonathan Franzen (*The Corrections*) from her show with another blunt, pithy statement. In that instance her coolness may have been justified. In this case, her words are profoundly thoughtless.

To give her credit, Winfrey jumped on the book group phenomenon and popularized it as only she and her show could. Certainly, libraries had hosted book groups long before Winfrey launched her club in fall 1996. Nevertheless, she brought some new authors into the mainstream culture and resurrected some backlist titles. By enticing hundreds of thousands of viewers to read the same book at the same time, her club may have been, in a sense, the precursor of the One City, One Book concept.

Her impact on libraries was not insignificant either, though some librarians may rue the number of holds her books generated. She brought new patrons into libraries who had never been there before. With pressure from the American Library Association (ALA), distributors, and the library media, Winfrey's producers agreed to give libraries and library distributors the same advance warning about her picks that booksellers got. Moreover, Winfrey requested that the publisher of each book club selection donate 10,000 books to libraries; many of these books went to institutional members of ALA.

Ingram established a standing order plan for her books and shipped titles automatically and in advance to their library customers so they could have them on their shelves when booksellers did. Long before the *Harry Potter* mania had librarians shelving books at midnight before publication day, Winfrey forced librarians to think about ordering many more copies and getting them into libraries and out to patrons much faster.

Happily, despite the demise of Winfrey's book club, there is no sign that book groups are on the wane. Nancy Pearl, *LJ*'s Reader's Shelf columnist, director of the Washington Center for the Book, and founder of One City, One Book, notes, "Book groups aren't at all a passing fad. More and more people are finding how much there is to be gotten from well-run book groups." (For this issue's installment of Reader's Shelf, which focuses on book group titles from the immigrant experience, see p. 152.) Three new national clubs have been launched via the *Today* show, *USA Today,* and *Regis and Kelly.*

There is some irony in Winfrey's selection of Toni Morrison's *Sula* as her final book club choice. True, Morrison is one of her favorite authors, having been chosen four times altogether. But Morrison, in her writings and in the brilliant speech she gave when she was awarded the Nobel Prize in Literature in 1993, attests to the power of language "as an agency . . . an act with consequences . . . the choice word, the chosen silence, unmolested language surges toward knowledge, not its destruction." Would that Oprah Winfrey had thought more about her favorite writer's words before she issued her own.

Ted Striphas (essay date September 2003)

SOURCE: Striphas, Ted. "A Dialectic with the Everyday: Communication and Cultural Politics on Oprah Winfrey's Book Club." *Critical Studies in Media Communication* 20, no. 3 (September 2003): 295-316.

[*In the following essay, Striphas profiles the influence of Oprah Winfrey's book club.*]

> The Oprah Book Club did something extraordinary. I don't think there's been anything ever like it. When a beloved television personality persuades, convinces, cajoles, hundreds of thousands of people to read books, it's not just a revolution, it's an upheaval.
>
> —Toni Morrison, Nobel Prize winning author, also selected for Oprah's Book Club (Oprah's book club anniversary party, 1997, p. 17)

> Come on, people; Oprah isn't a literary critic, or a family therapist, or a priest. She's a talk-show host. Some perspective here, please.
>
> —Abby Fowler (2001, p. 21), letter to the editor, *Newsweek*

When Oprah Winfrey announced on the September 17, 1996 installment of *The Oprah Winfrey Show* that she wanted "to get the whole country reading again" (Oprah's book club anniversary party, 1997, p. 1), few would have predicted the daytime television talk-show personality's extraordinary influence on bibliographic taste and patterns of book buying in the United States. Yet her first selection for the newly-formed Oprah's Book Club, Jacquelyn Mitchard's (1996) hitherto

modestly successful novel *The Deep End of the Ocean,* proceeded to sell more than 700,000 copies and shot to number one on the *New York Times* bestseller list. The sudden, intense interest in the book, and by extension the Book Club, prompted the *Washington Post* less than two weeks later to profile the Club in a cover story (Streitfeld, 1996). The significance of the *Post's* coverage was not lost on Winfrey, who noted that the Book Club enjoyed "an even bigger start than Watergate" in its pages (Newborn quintuplets, 1996, p. 15). Over the next six years, all 48 of Oprah's Book Club selections followed a similar pattern of success. Each typically sold a further half a million to one million copies or more after being chosen by Winfrey (Gray, 1996; Ticker, 2000; Touched by an Oprah, 1999). She even was awarded a gold medal at the 1999 National Book Awards, the Oscars of the book industry, in recognition of the Book Club's ability to stimulate interest in and demand for books and reading. Despite Winfrey's decision in May 2002 to discontinue Oprah's Book Club as a mainstay of *The Oprah Winfrey Show,* her selections continue to figure prominently in most retail bookstores and non-book outlets (such as supermarkets, department stores, pharmacies, and so on).[1]

Oprah's Book Club was and continues to be a complexly mediated cultural phenomenon, combining printed books, television programs, letters, emails, and face-to-face conversations, among other media and forms of communication. At the heart of this study, then, lies a concern for the specific communicative processes through which books are produced, distributed, exchanged, and consumed (Darnton, 1995). It both insists on and explores the role of communication with respect to the apparent success and popular appeal of Oprah's Book Club in the late 1990s and early 21st century. More specifically, it considers how communication about the selections for Oprah's Book Club affected how individuals and groups engaged with the texts by asking: How have those who orchestrated and participated in Oprah's Book Club together negotiated the purpose and value of books and reading?

The success and popularity of Oprah's Book Club did not, of course, insulate it from controversy; in fact, the club's extremely high profile probably attracted and intensified it. During its six year tenure Oprah's Book Club elicited an array of responses from authors, readers, publishers, professional and lay literary critics, booksellers, and others. As the quotations above attest, critical appraisal ran the gamut from outright exuberance to unmitigated contempt. Opponents of the Book Club were at a particular loss to explain how a stark, ambiguous German novel like Bernhard Schlink's *The Reader* (1997) could sit side-by-side in the Oprah's Book Club catalog with Breena Clarke's *River, Cross My Heart* (1999), which one journalist dismissed as "a poorly written, sentimental novel from a diversity bureaucrat at Time, Inc." (McNett, 1999, para. 5), let alone four selections by Nobel Prize winning author Toni Morrison—*Song of Solomon* (1977), *Paradise* (1997), *The Bluest Eye* (1970), and *Sula* (1973).

Feelings of contempt for the club came to a head in September 2001 when author Jonathan Franzen publicly divulged his misgivings about Winfrey's selecting his highly acclaimed novel, *The Corrections* (2001), for the Book Club. Winfrey has "picked some good books," Franzen remarked upon hearing the news, "but she's picked enough schmaltzy, one-dimensional ones that I cringe myself, even if I think she's really smart and she's really fighting the good fight" (quoted in Kirkpatrick, 2001, p. C4). Franzen worried, in other words, that so-called serious readers might cease taking his book, well, seriously, given its association with a host of books of putatively lesser caliber. His public comments earned him the dubious distinction of being the only author ever to have an invitation to *The Oprah Winfrey Show* rescinded. Despite—or perhaps because of—the controversy, his novel went on to win the coveted National Book Award in December 2001.

These and other critics have repeatedly thrown their hands in the air trying to explain how high art so easily could commingle with mass culture, let alone how millions of *Oprah* viewer/readers were unfazed by this seeming contradiction. Thus, not only is it worth considering how specific communication practices relate to the Book Club's popularity, but also how members of the Book Club challenged normative economies of cultural value through their participation in it. This struggle becomes all the more salient when one considers that women between the ages of 18 and 54 make up both the primary audience for *The Oprah Winfrey Show* and the largest aggregate book reading public in the United States (Dortch, 1998; Gabriel, 1997; Kinsella, 1997; Radway, 1984). Reproachful responses to Oprah's Book Club, in other words, provide a kind of cover under which are smuggled demeaning attitudes towards women and the cultural forms they tend to engage.

Thus, this essay critically reads women's conversations about and modes of engaging with the selections for Oprah's Book Club, bearing in mind these negative appraisals and the ways in which patriarchal assumptions inflect them. Both the success of and controversies surrounding the Book Club, I maintain, flowed in part from the ways in which Winfrey, *Oprah Winfrey Show* producers, and participants in the club together articulated the value of books and book reading specifically for women. The first part of this essay, therefore, both reflects on and situates Oprah's Book Club within the context of feminist responses to mass culture. Here, I argue that the club offered a set of symbolic and material resources with which feminist cultural producers might begin piecing together a feminist aesthetics. In

addition to teasing out the logic by which selections were made for the Book Club, in the next section I show how women's patterns of engaging with Oprah books as material artifacts paralleled the ways in which groups of women have been shown to employ specific categories of popular literature (such as romance novels) to escape temporarily from conservative gender role expectations. In the third section, I reverse course to consider how conversations about the narrative content of Oprah books prompted women to move closer to and interrogate the determinate conditions of their everyday lives and experiences. As such, I argue, Oprah's Book Club advanced a particular protocol for engaging with popular literature, a dialectic with the everyday, whereby women were encouraged to use books and book reading as vehicles both to step outside of and to interrogate critically values and routines. Finally, this essay concludes by assessing the club's actual and potential relationship to a feminist cultural politics, recognizing how, as a club, it may have opened possibilities for dialogue and collective political action.

FEMINIST RESPONSES TO MASS CULTURE: A CRITICAL FRAMEWORK

Condemnations of Oprah's Book Club follow a long line of condescending responses to media genres and mass cultural forms targeted toward and consumed primarily by women. At least since Tania Modleski's (1982) path-breaking book *Loving with a Vengeance: Mass-Produced Fantasies for Women,* feminist scholars have challenged both popular and scholarly accounts that at best are dismissive of, and at worst openly hostile to, women and their relationships to mass culture. This line of research thus has focused on a host of media genres, including romance and gothic novels (Light, 1999; Modleski, 1982; Radway, 1984, 1999b), young women and girls' magazines (McRobbie, 1991), popular music and dance (McRobbie, 1994), soap operas (Modleski 1982, 1998), prime time television sitcoms featuring women (Dow, 1996), and literature, television programming, and films geared toward women of color (Bobo, 1995; Bobo & Seiter, 1997). Without diminishing the significant differences across these studies, they (and this essay) share at least two attributes in common: first, a recognition that demeaning attitudes toward these mass cultural forms and women's engagements with them reflect larger patriarchal assumptions about the value of women in society, and second, an abiding commitment to taking seriously these and other mass cultural forms, with the intention of assessing their effects and political possibilities.

Modleski (1982, 1998) recognizes that the narratives and fantasy structures of romance novels, gothics, and daytime soap operas produced in the 1970s and early 1980s surely reinforced highly circumscribed understandings of women's place in society. Despite their conservatizing impulses, however, she maintains that feminist scholars should resist flatly condemning them. "It is useless to deplore [mass cultural] texts for their omissions, distortions, and conservative affirmations," she argues. "It is crucial to understand them: to let their omissions and distortions speak, informing us of the contradictions they are meant to conceal and, equally importantly, of the fears that lie behind them" (1982, p. 113). Thus Modleski, Janice A. Radway (1984), and numerous feminist scholars who have followed them have enjoined researchers to engage the thorny question of why women are drawn to such texts, the nature of the pleasures they derive from them, and the relationship of these texts to women's everyday lives.

Together, Modleski (1982, 1998) and Radway (1984) maintain that the pleasure and popularity of romance novels, gothics, daytime soap operas, and other texts derive at least partly from the ways in which they achieve both a symbolic and practical fit with the everyday lives and experiences of women living in patriarchal societies. As Modleski (1982, p. 14) puts it, the "enormous and continuing popularity" of these types of texts "suggests that they speak to the very real problems and tensions in women's lives." Similarly, Radway (1984, p. 45) asserts, "the meaning of the romance-reading experience may be closely tied to the way the act of reading fits within the middle-class mother's day and the way the story itself addresses anxieties, fears, and psychological needs resulting from her social and familial position." While both Modleski and Radway are cautious not to overestimate the progressive political possibilities that may follow from women's engagements with mass culture, both underscore how "contemporary mass-produced narratives for women contain elements of protest and resistance underneath highly orthodox plots" (Modleski, 1982, p. 25; see also Radway, 1984, pp. 17, 220). In other words, mass entertainment and feminist politics are not, perforce, antithetical.

The challenge facing feminist scholars of mass culture, then, is what to do with these pleasures, these small kernels of protest which, at some level, may challenge patriarchal values, assumptions, and power structures, albeit within the constraints of capitalist production? Modleski (1982, p. 25) observes that, in most circumstances, these challenges are neither obviously nor explicitly feminist. Yet she also maintains that they can provide the rudiments of a more sustained and broadranging critique of patriarchy. "Clearly," she states, "women find soap operas eminently entertaining, and an analysis of the pleasure that soaps afford can provide clues not only about how feminists can challenge this pleasure, but also how they can incorporate it" (1979/1997, p. 43). She goes on to propose the project of recovering a "feminist aesthetics" from the specific media genres and mass cultural forms targeted to women. This feminist aesthetics would "rechannel and make explicit the criticisms of masculine power and masculine pleasure implied in the narratives of soap operas" and other mass cultural forms involving a predominantly female audience (Modleski, 1979/1997, p. 46), with the larger goal of amplifying these criticisms and articulating them back into the sphere of cultural production.

Critical responses to daytime television talk shows further confirm the rule that mass cultural texts intended for and consumed primarily by women tend to attract condemnation. Popular, scholarly, and lay critics alike routinely impugn these shows for spectacularizing the profane and/or for offering a surfeit of popular psychological quick-fixes to recalcitrant social problems. Among scholarly critics, Janice Peck (1994) and Dana L. Cloud (1996) have argued respectively that talk on *The Oprah Winfrey Show* and popular biographies about Winfrey both turn on and reinforce a classically liberal notion of the autonomous individual subject. By advancing an ethic of individual responsibility and personal psychological healing, they maintain, the Oprah Winfrey text denies the necessity of contesting structural forms of oppression through collective political action.

On a more optimistic note, Peck (1994, p. 115) concedes that *The Oprah Winfrey Show* is "haunted by traces of social egalitarian values, democratic strivings, and desires" to transform "social worlds." Some feminist scholars have engaged various Oprah Winfrey texts hoping to recover these traces and let them speak, thereby cobbling together a feminist aesthetics from the raw materials of mass culture. Corinne Squire (1997), for example, argues that although the show's persistent focus on women's victimization may prove disarming for some viewers, it still manages to weave together a complex, shifting narrative of women's experiences of gender, race, and class. As such, the show consistently illuminates "the contradictions that traverse our [women's] subjectivities" (p. 109). Against those who would claim that *Oprah* merely reduces structural social inequities to personal psychological problems, moreover, sustained viewing of the show suggests a recurrence of specific psychological motifs. As more and more *Oprah* guests attest to their reality, Squire claims, they aggregate or "begin to shed [their] individual psychological character and start to look like . . . social, political, or religious fact[s]" (p. 110). She concludes, therefore, that *The Oprah Winfrey Show* possesses "some modest feminist value" owing to its narrative structure (p. 109; see also Masciarotte, 1991; Shattuc, 1999).

This essay continues the project of recovering a feminist aesthetics vis-à-vis Oprah Winfrey's Book Club, by investigating why women were drawn en masse to a specific category of popular literature. Methodologically, it consists of a close reading of transcripts of all 45 episodes of *The Oprah Winfrey Show* featuring Oprah's Book Club.[2] These materials, at minimum, provide a reasonably accurate and accessible public record of how Winfrey, *Oprah Winfrey Show* producers, authors, and viewers invited to join them on the air conceived of and regularly talked about the value of specific books and books in general, in addition to particular norms and protocols for engaging with them.[3] Indeed, the transcripts provide some evidence of how approximately 200 club members publicly discussed the selections in relationship to their daily lives[4]—with the important caveat that these conversations were strategically planned, organized, edited, and arranged, given the conventions of commercial television and the producers' understandings of what might appeal to *The Oprah Winfrey Show*'s television audience.

All viewers invited to discuss Book Club selections on the air distinguished themselves by taking the time to write in to *The Oprah Winfrey Show*. In other words, they demonstrated a level of interest and practical involvement setting them apart from the majority of readers who presumably decided not to write in. Thus, their comments are not necessarily typical of the club as a whole. These voices are significant, nevertheless, because those invited to participate on air were considered by the show's producers to be ideal readers whose relationships to the book(s) under discussion, they hoped, would resonate with the broadest possible audience.

The question, which is best left open for the time being, is whether the responses of these ideal readers reflect a reasonably diverse cross-section or an essentializing amalgam of women's experiences engaging with Book Club selections. Indeed, as Charlotte Brunsdon (1999, p. 361, emphasis in original) notes, "the personae and positions" offered by mass cultural texts, and which often serve as the taken-for-granted analytical categories for feminist critics (such as "the 'female spectator,' 'reading as a woman,' 'women of color,' 'we,' 'the ordinary woman'"), are "*historical* identities, the contradictory sites and traces of political arguments and exclusions." The mode of address of *The Oprah Winfrey Show* and the Book Club selections is thus worth scrutinizing, insofar as it may reflect normative assumptions about, and perhaps challenges to, proper female subjectivity.

"No Dictionary Required"

According to some critics, Oprah Winfrey's emergence as a key arbiter of cultural value and authority bordered on absurdity. The *Wall Street Journal,* for instance, claimed (through a thinly disguised veil of indignation) that "no dictionary is required for most" of Oprah's Book Club selections, "nor is an appreciation for

ambiguity or abstract ideas. The biggest literary challenge of some Oprah books is their length" (Crossen, 2001, p. W15). As the primary spokesperson for the club, the *Journal* took Winfrey to task for failing to challenge readers with the apparent literariness of Book Club selections, or, alternatively, for failing to challenge readers with titles that were sufficiently literary at all. The *Journal,* however, made no effort to understand the Book Club's decision-making on its own terms.

The televised Book Club discussions admittedly tended to shy away from even the most basic vocabulary employed in literary criticism (tone, imagery, metaphor, symbolism, allusion, and so on). Thus, the *Journal* was right to point out that length was a more important criterion for selecting titles for the club than were traditional literary considerations. Almost every on air announcement of new Oprah's Book Club selections, in fact, included at least some mention of each book's total number of pages. Why then did page length play such a crucial role in the selection process?

The selection of Barbara Kingsolver's (1998) *The Poisonwood Bible* is telling. When Winfrey announced the book in June 2000, just prior to *The Oprah Winfrey Show*'s summer recess, she described it as "a walapalooza of a book. . . . It's 500 and some pages. . . . [A]ctually, it's—yeah, 546, 546, which is wonderful for the summer, because I didn't want you to, like, just breeze through it and then have to complain to me because you didn't have enough to read." Winfrey then went on to admonish her audience to "take your time with it. Read one of the . . . chapters, come back, let that settle in with yourself, come back and read another chapter" (Oprah's book club, 2000, June 23, p. 17). She concluded the broadcast by reiterating that it was a "great, great, great book for the summer, 546 pages" (p. 18).

Winfrey framed other selections almost identically. At the beginning of a June 1997 broadcast, Winfrey stated: "Today we're announcing a big—I mean B-I-G book" (Book club finale, 1997, p. 1). Later, when she revealed the selection, she explained (p. 17):

> I knew back last year when we first started this Book Club that this was the book that you should be reading for the summer, because it is 740 pages long. Now for a lot of you, that's—that'll be your first time with a book that big—a big accomplishment, OK? So our big book for the summer is *Songs in Ordinary Time* by Mary McGarry Morris.

Winfrey used virtually the same language to frame the June 1998 selection, Wally Lamb's (1998) *I Know This Much Is True*—"a great, big book for the summer," she called it, at 897 pages (Oprah's book club, 1998, June 18, p. 17). Jane Hamilton's (1988) *The Book of Ruth*, in contrast, appears to have been selected in December

1996 in part because of its brevity. "You have two months to finish . . . and it's not even a whole lot of pages. . . . [I]t's only 328 pages in paperback," Winfrey explained. She then commented on the possible significance of the book's length: "The next Book Club airs Wednesday, January 22nd of next year, 1997. We gave you extra time over the holidays so you don't have to read at the Christmas table, OK?" (Behind the scenes, 1996, pp. 20-21).

The language Winfrey used to frame every one of these books suggests that her selections for the club were not made on the basis of her tastes alone. That she repeatedly referred to specific selections as summer books, holiday books, and so forth indicates that both time and page length were carefully considered criteria by which specific books were selected. Longer books often were timed to coincide with the summer months, when *Oprah* viewers presumably had more time to spend reading. Shorter books, on the other hand, often coincided with months when women were assumed to have more responsibilities and thus less time to read (such as around the winter holidays). Oprah's Book Club producers were sensitive, in other words, to how books and reading could be made to fit into the routines of women's lives, rather than placing the burden on women to adjust their schedules to accommodate books and reading.

In one respect, then, women's patterns of engaging with the selections for Oprah's Book Club can be said to mirror those of women who consume other categories of popular literature. Among the women whom Radway (1984, p. 213) interviewed, for example, reading romance novels functioned in part as "a 'declaration of independence' and a way to say to others, 'This is my time, my space. Now leave me alone.'" Romance novel reading, in other words, allowed these readers to construct imagined—albeit effective—spatial and temporal barriers with which to modulate their heterosexual partnerships, the needs of their children and, more broadly, the everyday demands they faced as women living in a patriarchal society. Similarly, women used Oprah's Book Club selections to create spaces and thus remove themselves both symbolically and practically from their domestic, female role-assigned duties.

Indeed, women featured on Oprah's Book Club highlighted how these kinds of responsibilities posed formidable challenges to their finding personal time. The August 2000 Book Club program, for example, included an audio excerpt of a letter explaining how one woman was moved by *The Poisonwood Bible* (Kingsolver, 1998), a novel chronicling a pious American family's mission in the Belgian Congo and the Congolese struggle for independence. "As a stay-at-home mom, I often feel caught up in the world of children, conversations with children, conversations about children. I loved this book. It brought me out of the world I live in" (Oprah's book club, 2000, August 23, p. 23). Karen, another Book Club participant, likewise explained: "My children now are trained that when they see Mom with a book, they just don't bother me. . . . And on Saturday and Sunday mornings, my husband knows I'm going to get up early at five to read, fall back to sleep, and wake up again and read some more. . . . I get up about 1:00 in the afternoon to start my day, because I love to just lay there and read" (Letters to Oprah's book club, 2001, para. 271). Like Radway's (1984) romance novel readers, these women affirmed how the reading of popular literature could help them both to justify and to enact a desire to step outside and away from the sometimes tedious and unfulfilling role expectations placed upon them as women, if only temporarily.

Although women may have turned to Oprah's Book Club for this reason, its extraordinary success cannot be reduced to that alone. Many women featured on Oprah's Book Club attributed their inability to read books to their responsibilities at home, yet equally as many women indicated never having developed an interest in books or book reading at all prior to their involvement with the club.

For example, the September 1997 Oprah's Book Club program featured an interview with Candy Siebert, who had written in to *Oprah* explaining her newfound interest in the Book Club:

WINFREY:

    Candy Siebert wrote us to say . . . she's never read a book in her entire life. Not one?

SIEBERT:

    Not one. [. . .]

WINFREY:

    Until?

SIEBERT:

    Until—I kept watching the Book Club. . . . And finally I bought my first book, and I bought it so I would have to read it. And I did it. I—[Wally Lamb's 1992] *She's Come Undone*—and I—I cried at the end and it was because I finished it and it was a great book.

WINFREY:

    It was the first book you read at 40 years old?

SIEBERT:

    Yes.

WINFREY:

    I could weep for you.

       (Oprah's book club anniversary party, 1997, p. 4)

The same program also featured videotaped excerpts from previous episodes of *Oprah,* in which one unidentified woman testified to not having read a novel in two decades; another shared that she had not read any books at all in about a dozen years. Similarly, the October 1996 Book Club discussion included an audio excerpt of a letter from an unidentified woman who stated: "I am 46 years old. And until this past year, I have not read more than five books" (Newborn quintuplets, 1996, p. 15).

Candy Siebert's provocative statement that something about Oprah's Book Club compelled her to take up books and book reading raises an important question: What about the club moved women to engage with and read books for the first time in many years, perhaps even for the first time in their lives?

Some critics have expressed dismay over the range of titles chosen for Oprah's Book Club. "Taken individually," the *Wall Street Journal* reported, "Oprah's books run the gamut from absorbing to vacuous" (Crossen, 2001, p. W15). The *Journal* was troubled, in other words, by the seemingly inconsistent demands Oprah's Book Club placed on participants in terms of the degree of difficulty of club selections, which fluctuated between arguably straightforward books like A. Manette Ansay's (1994) *Vinegar Hill* and Alice Hoffman's (1997) *Here on Earth,* to more intricate, lyrical titles such as those of Toni Morrison and Bernhard Schlink. Perhaps those who had not read books in many years were drawn to Oprah's Book Club precisely because of this apparent inconsistency.

Indeed, *Oprah Winfrey Show* producers demonstrated remarkable sensitivity to the range of reading abilities of both actual and potential club members, and this sensitivity was reflected in the timing and relative degree of difficulty of titles chosen for the Book Club. Anticipating that readers might encounter difficulty with *Paradise* (Morrison, 1997), club members were granted seven, rather than the customary four weeks between the announcement of the book and its discussion (Book club: Toni Morrison, 1998).[5] Beyond merely acknowledging and making allowances for the fact that certain titles might prove more challenging for readers than others, the choice of books often was influenced directly by the relative difficulty of the preceding one. *The Reader* (Schlink, 1997) was followed by Anita Shreve's (1998) *The Pilot's Wife,* which Winfrey described repeatedly as a "quick read" in contrast to the previous selection (Oprah's book club, 1999, March 31, p. 21). *The Poisonwood Bible* (Kingsolver, 1998) similarly was followed by Elizabeth Berg's *Open House* (2000). "[A]s I've been saying," Winfrey revealed, *Open House* "is really going to be a breeze. I thought after reading over 500 pages, we needed something lighter" (Oprah's book club, 2000, August 23, p. 20).

The intense frustration many members of Oprah's Book Club felt towards the September 1999 selection, Melinda Haynes' (1999) *Mother of Pearl,* provides by far the richest example illustrating how the relative difficulty of club selections affected the choice of subsequent books. When announcing *Mother of Pearl* in June 1999, Winfrey anticipated some of the difficulties readers might encounter with the book but encouraged them to persevere. *Mother of Pearl* "is layered," she observed, "which means that in the beginning you're thinking, 'Where is this going?'" (Oprah's book club: *White Oleander,* 1999, pp. 14-15). At the conclusion of the program she re-emphasized: "It's not a fast read, again. The first few chapters may challenge you, so stay with it until the flood. Hang in there until the flood, OK? You've got all summer to read it" (p. 17). When the Book Club reconvened in September, Winfrey reiterated her caveats. "I warned you-all," she stated, "it wasn't an easy book, but my feeling was that you have the whole summer. There are no deadlines. You can take your time" (Oprah's book club, 1999, September 9, p. 8).

Still, Winfrey's warnings did not manage to defuse readers' strong reactions to the book. Rather than trying to conceal the fact that many club members disliked *Mother of Pearl,* producers of *The Oprah Winfrey Show* opted instead to air readers' frustrations in an audio montage:

WINFREY:

> Some people didn't make it beyond the first word before getting frustrated.

UNIDENTIFIED WOMAN #1:

> Why is Even's name Even? I am so confused.

WINFREY:

> Others got stuck a little later in the book. [. . .]

UNIDENTIFIED WOMAN #7:

> Half the time I'm not sure what the characters are talking about. Will it get better or should I just wait for the next book? [. . .]

WINFREY:

> One reader even used it as a sleep aid.

UNIDENTIFIED WOMAN #12:

> It was a great book to read before going to bed because I always fell asleep quickly.
>
> (Oprah's book club, 1999, September 9, p. 9)

Airing readers' negative reactions was an extremely clever strategy by which to reframe the confusion and frustration many women felt toward *Mother of Pearl* from a personal failure to an error on the part of the

Book Club. What this incident reveals is that on Oprah's Book Club reading did not connote the act of humbling oneself before the genius of an intractable book, as it may in a more traditional economy of literary instruction. Rather, it connoted, on the one hand, doing one's best to engage with challenging books, and on the other, recognizing that one's dissatisfaction with specific selections stemmed not from a personal intellectual defect but rather from Winfrey and her producers' failure to choose a book that met the needs, tastes, and desires of the club.

Like other longer and more complex books, *Mother of Pearl* was followed by what Winfrey characterized as a far easier and quicker selection. "Now if *Mother of Pearl* was too challenging for you," she stated, "I've got the ideal one to bring you back, really" (Oprah's book club, 1999, September 9, p. 6). Her remark acknowledged that *Mother of Pearl* alienated many members of the Book Club, and that the subsequent selection was chosen precisely to help them to re-engage. When Winfrey finally revealed the selection at the end of the program, Maeve Binchy's (1998) *Tara Road,* she reiterated: "OK. Now some of you might have felt a little challenged with our summer book but I've got a new book to bring you back. It is a fast read—far, far away from the Deep South" (the setting of *Mother of Pearl*). She continued: "It's a thick book. It's a thick book but a really fast read. I promise you" (p. 19).

This is not to suggest, however, that members of the Book Club were unanimously turned off by *Mother of Pearl* and that faster reads like *Tara Road* were the only fare that appealed to them. Indeed, several women expressed how much they enjoyed *Pearl* during the September 1999 Book Club broadcast. "A friend asked me if I was leaving this planet, what three books would I take with me," one woman shared. "My second choice was *Mother of Pearl*" (Oprah's book club, 1999, September 9, p. 9). Similarly, a second woman revealed: "*Mother of Pearl* is the only book that when I finished reading it, I immediately began rereading it because I was captivated" (p. 20). At the end of the broadcast, Winfrey asked a guest in the studio audience who belonged to a women's book club to share some of the group's favorite selections. "Truthfully," she said, "*Mother of Pearl,* we all agreed was . . . four-star. We loved it. We would read passages just to anyone walking by that's how much we loved it" (p. 20).

There was no single level, then, at which members of Oprah's Book Club read, and indeed their range of reading interests and abilities was reflected in the seemingly inconsistent profile of the titles chosen for the club. Winfrey and her producers, deliberately made and timed selections to appeal strategically to a broad range of women/readers and to welcome newcomers to the club, some of whom may have felt intimidated by books and book reading.

"It's More About Life"

In the previous section, I explored how women involved in Oprah's Book Club used specific selections to create spatio-temporal barriers, which allowed them to regulate the incursions of children and heterosexual partners. This pattern of use is consistent with the findings presented in Radway's (1984) study of romance novel readers. Yet the foregoing analysis explored only how the very fact of the Oprah books as material artifacts occasioned the construction of these barriers. How, then, did Oprah's Book Club articulate the content of specific selections? It is worth pointing out that Radway's romance readers employed both the actual, physical books and the narrative content to distance themselves and/or to escape from the everyday/patriarchal demands they faced as women. The narratives of "failed" romances, in fact, "tread[ed] too close to the terrible real in ordinary existence" (Radway, 1984, p. 72). In contrast, women routinely turned to the narrative content of the selections for Oprah's Book Club to reflect on the conditions of their lives and experience—to engage more intensively with and to interrogate everyday life.

The March 2001 Book Club discussion included an intriguing message from Winfrey directed to those who had and had not read that month's selection, Joyce Carol Oates's (1997) *We Were the Mulvaneys.* "Don't worry if you haven't read . . . *We Were the Mulvaneys,*" she stated, "because as with all our Book Club shows, it's more about life than about a novel" (Oprah's book club: *We Were the Mulvaneys,* 2001, p. 1). What this statement suggests, and what emerged time and again on episodes of Oprah's Book Club, is that the content of specific books was perceived to be valuable by Winfrey and viewer/readers to the extent that it shared a clear connection with life, or that it resonated with their everyday interests, personal experiences, and concerns.

One way in which the Book Club both established and maintained this connection to life was through its constant emphasis on the actuality—not merely the realism—of the settings, events, and people featured in each book. Nearly every episode of Oprah's Book Club thus included interviews in which the author related her or his creative process, which almost always highlighted how she or he drew significant inspiration from existing people and places. This pattern began at least as far back as the beginning of the club's second season, when the Book Club featured Morris's (1996) *Songs in Ordinary Time.* "Even though the people were made up, some of the places in Atkinson, Vermont [the setting of *Songs*] are not far from Mary's hometown" of Rutland, Vermont, Winfrey explained. The program then cut to a videotaped segment of Morris touring Rutland:

There is so much of Atkinson, Vermont in Rutland, Vermont. . . . On the corner is the funeral home I imagined when I was writing the funeral of Sonny Stoner's wife, Carol. And I naturally thought of this little restaurant when I was writing the book. This is the Rutland Restaurant. It's been here since 1917. . . . The character of Sam is very much like my father. He—he was a very intelligent man, an educated man, who was cursed with the disease of alcoholism. . . . I've created my own Rutland, I guess.

(Oprah's book club anniversary party, 1997, p. 17)

Similarly, the January 2001 Book Club episode focused on the inspiration behind Andre Dubus III's (1999) *House of Sand and Fog.* The author shared how he drew the book's premise from an article he had read in the *Boston Globe,* in which a young woman, like the lead character Kathy Nicolo, was wrongly evicted from her house for failing to pay an erroneous tax bill (Oprah's book club, 2001, January 24). Dubus also disclosed that the other main character, Massoud Amir Behrani, was based on the life of a friend's father who had been a colonel in the Iranian Air Force before the Shah was deposed and who, like Behrani, lost nearly everything upon emigrating to the United States. Dubus went on to note that the man who had purchased the house in the *Globe* article was of Middle Eastern descent, prompting him to wonder, "What if my colonel bought this house?"—a question that summarizes the book's basic storyline (Oprah's book club, 2001, January 24, p. 13).

Because the characters, settings, and so forth to which specific Oprah books refer sometimes no longer were there, however, producers of *The Oprah Winfrey Show* turned to authors, invited guests, and particular textual elements to bear witness to their actuality. For example, the November 1999 program on Clarke's (1999) *River, Cross My Heart* dwelled extensively on the actuality of the novel's setting and main character. The story takes place in 1920s Georgetown, DC, when the neighborhood consisted largely of working class African Americans (in contrast to its far whiter, petite-bourgeois population of today). In order to demonstrate the actuality of "black Georgetown," the episode included a videotaped interview with 100-year-old Eva Calloway, whom Winfrey described as "one of the last living witnesses" of the old community (Anne Murray, 1999, p. 11). Calloway's witnessing was clearly meant to actualize a Georgetown that once existed. The episode also featured an on-camera interview with Edna Clarke, the author's mother, whom Winfrey revealed "was the inspiration behind 12-year-old Johnnie Mae," the novel's main character (Anne Murray, 1999, p. 10).

The videotaped interview with Lalita Tademy, author of the September 2001 Book Club selection *Cane River* (2001), likewise bore witness to the disappearance of people and places while underscoring their actuality.

Spanning the years 1834-1936, *Cane River* chronicles the lives of four generations of Louisiana Creole slave women, all of whom were Tademy's ancestors whom she came to know after conducting exhaustive genealogical research (Oprah's book club: *Cane River,* 2001). Although *Cane River* is a novel, the videotaped author interview stressed again and again how the book blurred the boundaries between fiction and nonfiction (without using those exact words).

Like the videotaped interview with Morris, the Tademy interview included a segment in which she toured locations that had inspired scenes in the book. "Cane River is a real place," Tademy began. But in contrast to the Morris interview, very few of the places Tademy described in the book still existed. "I began to go and visit Cane River, and I would just walk along unmarked sites just trying to get the feel of the place. [. . .] A lot of the areas that were plantations that I talk about in the book no longer exist. For one thing, so much of it was burned during the Civil War" (Oprah's book club: *Cane River,* 2001, p. 3). Tademy's videotaped tour of Cane River thus provided evidence of the absence of the places featured in *Cane River.* Near the end of the Book Club discussion, Winfrey also noted the photographs included in the book. "[T]hat's one of the fascinating things, didn't you all think, about the book?" she asked the studio audience. "When you turn the page, there are the pictures of the people you've been reading about" (p. 15). Winfrey drew attention specifically to the indexicality of these photographs: they could not have been produced without the women and places of *Cane River* actually having been present. Together, the videotaped author tour and the photographs invited participants in the Book Club to think about the characters and setting of *Cane River* as actual, despite their novelization.

The Oprah's Book Club catalog consists almost entirely of novels, save for two works of nonfiction and three short children's books. Bracketing the children's books, the preceding discussion suggests that the reified classificatory scheme of fiction versus nonfiction does not adequately account for the logic underlying the selections for Oprah's Book Club; it relies on a predetermined literary distinction that may have been inappropriate from the standpoint of the club, even if those closely associated with it occasionally employed that distinction themselves (Salute to mothers, 1997). Put another way, the two nonfiction books selected for Oprah's Book Club, Maya Angelou's (1981) *The Heart of a Woman* and Malika Oufkir's (2001) *Stolen Lives,* may seem anomalous alongside the 40-plus novels chosen for the Book Club. Yet, the repeated stress producers of *The Oprah Winfrey Show* placed on the actuality of the novels suggests a rupturing of the distinction between fiction and nonfiction on Oprah's Book Club. *Heart of a Woman* and *Stolen Lives* indeed made perfect sense alongside the novels chosen for the club; virtually all of them were portrayed as stories that actually happened, even if book publishers, booksellers, and critics persisted in classifying, marketing, and talking about these selections simply as works of fiction or nonfiction.

Thus Oprah's Book Club producers and participants were further able to connect books with life by troubling this most basic bibliographic distinction. Collectively, they articulated Book Club selections—novels especially—from the realm of the imagined to the actual, or perhaps it would be more accurate now to say from the fantastic to the everyday. For the everyday, as Michèle Mattelart (1997, p. 25) observes, "represent[s] a specific idea of time within which [both] women's social and economic role is carried out" and "the fundamental discrimination of sex roles is expressed." Similarly, Henri Lefebvre (2002, p. 11) notes that women tend to bear a disproportionate burden of "the weight of everyday life" owing to the ways in which patriarchy and capitalism inflect one another, yet he adds that this very burden opens possibilities for the "active critique" (p. 223) and transformation of these structures given the gendered contradictions, inconsistencies, and double standards they inevitably produce.

Indeed, the televised Oprah's Book Club broadcasts regularly went beyond framing the selections as stories that actually happened, by highlighting how the characters, events, and themes corresponded with and provoked women to question their everyday lives. During the first anniversary episode of the Book Club, Winfrey remarked: "I love books because you read about somebody else's life but it makes you think about your own" (Oprah's book club anniversary party, 1997, p. 2). She reaffirmed this point 18 months later: "We love books because they make you question yourself" (Oprah's book club, 1999, March 31, p. 13). Reading books was valued on Oprah's Book Club, then, because it provoked critical introspection or, more strongly, provided women with symbolic and practical resources with which to challenge reified conceptions of their subjectivities.

Herein lies the Book Club's dialectic with the everyday. Following Mikhail Bakhtin (1981), dialectic denotes any two opposing yet dynamically interdependent elements whose tense relationship can provoke change. On Oprah's Book Club, the very fact of the books themselves provided at least some women with time and space away from their daily obligations as partners, mothers, and professionals, while the content of the books encouraged just the opposite. In other words, club members valued the reading of Book Club selections not only because it helped them to create distance from their everyday responsibilities and routines as women. On the contrary, it also enabled them to move

closer to and interrogate their everyday lives as women via the characters and events in the books.

The way in which the December 1999 selection, Ansay's (1994) *Vinegar Hill,* was discussed and framed on *The Oprah Winfrey Show* is illustrative of this dialectic with the everyday. The novel turns on the tensions between a married couple and their in-laws, and more specifically on the main character Ellen Grier's struggle to assert herself after she, her husband James, and their two young children are forced to move in with James's overbearing parents. *Vinegar Hill,* Ansay explained, was born of actual events; she and her parents moved in with her paternal grandparents briefly when she was five, and she drew some of the scenes in the book directly from that experience (Oprah's book club, 1999, December 3). Although Ansay claimed that Ellen was not her mother per se, she did reveal that her "mother's own story inspired Ellen's transformation" (p. 15). The program thus stressed how *Vinegar Hill* was grounded in the events and experiences of a woman who had overcome unreasonable expectations resulting from her heterosexual partnership.

For the remainder of the broadcast, *Oprah* producers broke with the tradition of inviting four or five guests to discuss the book over dinner with Winfrey and the author, opting instead to invite married women and their mothers-in-law to the studio to share how their relationships with one another and their families had been affected by living together. One guest, Valerie, explained that she was "amazed at how similar Ellen's experience was to something that happened to [her] 18 years ago," when she was forced to move in with her mother-in-law while her husband completed a degree (Oprah's book club, 1999, December 3, p. 14). Another guest, Cherie Burton, also identified with Ellen Grier. "I wouldn't say it feels like a prison here," she stated, describing the experience of living with her in-laws for the past eight months, "but there are some moments where I do feel trapped" (p. 6).

Indeed, *The Oprah Winfrey Show* routinely featured letters and stories from women who connected the narratives/characters of specific Book Club selections directly to their own everyday lives. One viewer/reader named Connie, for instance, wrote in to the show after reading Morris' (1996) *Songs in Ordinary Time* to express how she felt while reading the book:

WINFREY:

> Now, didn't you write me that you thought at one point reading it that Mary [McGarry Morris] had changed the names of the characters to protect your privacy?

CONNIE:

> Yes. Yes. Exactly. I—I—that was my first impression. Marie was 35. I was 34 when my experience happened. My children were the exact same age

as Alice, Norm, and Benjy. And as I read, I just thought, "This is my story." . . . I should be writing this book.

(Oprah's book club anniversary party, 1997, p. 16)

She's Come Undone (Lamb, 1992) generated a similar response from C. C., who was invited to join the videotaped conversation about the book. "[T]his was my life," she stated. "My father—after my mother died, even though I lived in the same house with him, he was never there. . . . [H]e would be gone for days at a time to his girlfriend's house, he would be away on business or whatever, and he loved me with food the same way Dolores' [the main character] father did" (*Third Rock from the Sun*, 1997, p. 12). Likewise, *Here on Earth* (Hoffman, 1997) resonated strongly with Cynthia, a participant in the April 1998 Book Club discussion. Cynthia was drawn to March Murray, the main character, who early on in the book struggles over whether to leave her husband Richard, whom she considers to be a bland but otherwise agreeable partner. Richard "reminded me of my . . . ex-husband, just a really great guy," Cynthia observed. "He met my checklist: good looking, athletic, good family, smart, educated, and all of that. But he was the wrong good guy. And, as a woman, I grew up thinking that the only way you would leave a man or should leave a man is if he beats you or if he's abusive or if he's an alcoholic. . . . But how do you leave a good man?" (Oprah's book club, 1998, April 9, p. 17). Identifying with characters and events in specific Oprah's Book Club selections thus allowed these participants to interrogate some of their everyday assumptions and routines.

The March 2001 program on *We Were the Mulvaneys* (Oates, 1997) provided some of the most moving examples of this process of identification and self-reflection. Winfrey indicated that numerous readers had written in to the show explaining how they had seen themselves and their families in the book. "[W]hat's so exciting about *We Were the Mulvaneys*," Winfrey observed, was that "we've gotten so many letters from . . . people who were members of families who say, 'We were the Grants,' or 'We were the Pullmans.' 'We were'—a lot of people started their letters that way" (Oprah's book club: *We Were the Mulvaneys*, 2001, p. 6). The broadcast also included a poignant videotaped interview with the Hanson family who, like the Mulvaneys, were ostracized from their community after they filed suit against a young man who had raped their daughter Susan.[6] As Jayne Hanson, Susan's mother explained, "[I]t dawned on me reading this book, we have all been—we've all been raped" (p. 7).

Collectively, all of these women recognized themselves and their everyday lives in the characters and situations presented in specific Book Club selections. Their engagements with the books, therefore, facilitated not only their breaking temporarily from their everyday lives or the normative expectations placed on them as women living in a patriarchal society, but also their interrogating and perhaps even challenging the social pressures implicated in, for example, heterosexual partnerships, families, intimacy, beauty, body image, and gendered violence.

Interestingly, the one novel in which Winfrey promised "a total escape from your own life—escape, escape, escape" (Oprah's book club, 2000, November 16, p. 21), *House of Sand and Fog* (Dubus, 1999), met with significant resistance on the part of readers invited to participate in the videotaped discussion.[7] All but one of the guests was particularly disgusted by the character Kathy Nicolo, whose lying, promiscuity, theft, substance abuse, racism, and inattention to her daily responsibilities disturbed them deeply. While the exact source of their distress remains unclear, it may have been at least partly a function of the book's escapist tenor. Its deeply tragic conclusion—the five principal characters wind up either dead or imprisoned—may have further reinforced this sense of disconnect. *House of Sand and Fog* may have upset these readers precisely because it failed to tell a story that resonated sufficiently with their own daily lives.

Conclusion: Toward a Feminist Aesthetics

The success of Oprah's Book Club may help to temper the often-repeated charges about declining interest in books and book reading, which typically authorize critics to make heady claims about the dumbing down of United States culture in an era supposedly dominated by electronic media (Gitlin, 1997; Postman, 1986). The sudden, intense interest in the Book Club and its communicative efforts to bring in non-readers at all levels suggests that an extensive yet largely untapped book reading public existed in the United States prior to the club's formation, particularly among women; indeed, many more of these nascent publics may exist today. Thus, critics who attribute an apparent disinterest in books and book reading to an intellectual downturn in United States culture or to the putatively deleterious effects of electronic media may overlook a far more mundane explanation for these phenomena. The communicative strategies employed on Oprah's Book Club throw into relief the global book publishing industry's general ineffectiveness at communicating the relevance of books and book reading to specific social groups using anything other than the most traditional of aesthetic/literary labels.

But make no mistake: Winfrey, her producers, and the members of Oprah's Book Club were engaged in the work of distinction. Within the context of *The Oprah Winfrey Show*, Winfrey, her producers, and the members of the Book Club together rearticulated received categories into a highly sophisticated—and markedly different—economy of cultural value in which proximity and pertinence to women's everyday lives superceded what Pierre Bourdieu (1984, p. 34) calls the "icy solemnity" of decrepit aesthetic labels. The work of the Book Club consisted not just of finding good books, in other words, but more importantly books that fit—an intractable alchemy that has vexed the book industry for a century.

This understanding may help to contextualize condescending responses to Oprah's Book Club. They belong, as Radway (1999a) observes, to a long line of phobic reactions to specific reading practices, mass cultural forms, and regimes of cultural value that challenge their hegemonic counterparts. "Reading induces phobic responses," she argues, "precisely because it contains such rich potential for social disorder and disarray" (p. 24). Indeed, the vociferous public outcry generated by Oprah's Book Club was and remains symptomatic of the club's challenge to a regime of cultural value that has consistently excluded, or at the very least marginalized, hundreds of thousands and perhaps millions of women/readers. Future research would do well to assess the extent to which communication on Oprah's Book Club has helped to construct a broader, creative, and politically progressive set of codes, vocabularies, and practices for these and other women and, if so, to chart their circulation in and beyond the *Oprah Winfrey Show*. The growth of and access to such symbolic and material resources, as Celeste Condit (1989) reminds us, is a necessary condition for textually-related strategies to take on a larger political significance.

For now, I merely want to ask if the economy of cultural value articulated on Oprah's Book Club, its dialectic with the everyday, indeed contributes to Modleski's (1979/1997) project of developing a feminist aesthetics. Doubtless, *The Oprah Winfrey Show* tended to imagine and address the women who watched and participated in the Book Club using very traditional categories: as wives, mothers, victims of gendered violence, and so forth. While it may be too strong to call this mode of address essentializing, given the ways in which race, class, and other factors routinely complicate these subject positions on the show (Squire, 1997), it would be fair to characterize it as normative and quite circumscribed with respect to gender.

That said, it is important not to underestimate the feminist possibilities of the Book Club. While *The Oprah Winfrey Show* may have performatively reiterated key subjectivities through which patriarchal oppression is enacted at the level of the everyday, the selections for the Book Club and women's conversations about them nevertheless were powerful vehicles for helping them to step outside of those positions, to deny and disrupt, however briefly and temporarily,

everyday life's profound gravitational pull. In addition, the ways in which narrative content was discussed on the show encouraged women/readers to engage more intensively with these normative subjectivities—not simply to reinforce them, but also to scrutinize them, to interrogate them, to complicate and challenge their apparent self-evidence. Oprah's Book Club thus helped women to transform the everyday from a locus of banal patriarchal routine to one rife with antagonism and creativity, a project consistent with a progressive feminist politics.

Of course, all that says next to nothing about the effectiveness of these challenges. Can individual acts of book reading and television viewing really short-circuit patriarchy and other forms of oppression? They certainly cannot. Imagining that patriarchy can be overcome in this way merely reaffirms a therapeutic model of politics (Cloud, 1996, 1998), in which individual acts of oppression are abstracted from their enabling conditions and individual psychological healing is posited erroneously as the only viable locus of change. Then again, it is crucial not to lose sight of the fact that Oprah's Book Club was what it was—a club, which, by definition, implies some level of sociality or, more optimistically, a willingness on the part of viewer/readers to engage the social problems addressed in the selections, discussed on *The Oprah Winfrey Show*, and manifested in readers' everyday lives collectively. These inequities, injustices, and brutalities, however, remain stubbornly and undeniably part of women's everyday lives. The larger political challenge, then, may be to find ways both to broaden and to intensify these kinds of collective relations and engaged conversations—to refuse to close the book, as it were, on Oprah's Book Club.

Notes

1. Winfrey announced in February 2003, that she will be restarting the Book Club. Rather than focusing monthly on contemporary literature by living authors, however, the new Oprah's Book Club will feature only literary classics, presumably by dead authors, three to five times per year.

2. In two instances Winfrey chose more than one book for the monthly Book Club selection, hence the disparity between the number of Book Club programs and the total number of Book Club selections.

3. The word "public" is absolutely crucial here. One potential limitation of the research for this essay is that it relies only on public transcripts, while on the whole bracketing the hidden transcripts which, for various reasons, typically are excluded from the public record. Further research would do well to take up these hidden transcripts and revisit/rework my hypotheses about Oprah's Book Club in light of them.

4. I would caution the reader to differentiate between four forms of belonging to the club. Some members simply might have read each month's selection; others might have read and tuned into the televised discussions on *The Oprah Winfrey Show*; others might not have read the books at all but watched the Book Club programs anyway; and still others may have read the selections in conjunction with their local book clubs, with or without having watched *Oprah*.

5. Interestingly, the timing of Morrison's *Paradise* coincided with the infamous lawsuit brought against Winfrey by a group of Texas cattle producers, in response to an April 1996 episode of *The Oprah Winfrey Show* about beef and the dangers of mad cow disease. For weeks Winfrey was away in Amarillo, Texas observing and participating in the trial, and *The Oprah Winfrey Show* was moved there temporarily. One has to wonder to what extent, if any, these events influenced the selection of a challenging book like Morrison's *Paradise* and the conferral of extra time for readers to grapple with it. I wonder, moreover, what members of the Texas beef industry would think if they realized that they not only lost their suit against Winfrey but also indirectly may have encouraged more people to read Toni Morrison!

6. In contrast to the character Marianne Mulvaney, the Hanson's daughter Susan tragically committed suicide.

7. Interestingly, during the program in which *The Poisonwood Bible* was discussed, Winfrey and several women reported feeling transported to Congo while reading. I would argue, however, that the book overall tended not to be considered an escape by the women featured on the show, since many observed how, upon reading the book, they became increasingly aware of and thankful for their domestic accoutrements, such as dishwashers, soap, and so on (Oprah's book club, 2000, August 23).

References

Anne Murray and her daughter's battle with anorexia. (1999, November 10). *The Oprah Winfrey Show* [Transcript]. Livingston, NJ: Burrelle's Information Services.

Bakhtin, M. M. (1981). *The dialogical imagination: Four essays by M. M. Bakhtin* (Ed. M. Holquist, Trans. C. E. Emerson & M. Holquist). Austin: University of Texas Press.

Behind the scenes at Oprah's dinner party. (1996, December 3). *The Oprah Winfrey Show* [Transcript]. Livingston, NJ: Burrelle's Information Services.

Bobo, J. (1995). *Black women as cultural readers.* New York: Columbia University Press.

Bobo, J., & Seiter, E. (1997). Black feminism and media criticism: The women of *Brewster Place*. In C. Bruns-

don, J. D'Acci, & L. Spigel (Eds.), *Feminist television criticism: A reader* (pp. 167-183). Oxford: Oxford University Press.

Book club finale. (1997, June 18). *The Oprah Winfrey Show* [Transcript]. Livingston, NJ: Burrelle's Information Services.

Book club: Toni Morrison. (1998, March 6). *The Oprah Winfrey Show* [Transcript]. Livingston, NJ: Burrelle's Information Services.

Bourdieu, P. (1984). *Distinction: A social critique of the judgment of taste* (Trans. R. Nice). Cambridge: Harvard University Press.

Brunsdon, C. (1999). Pedagogies of the feminine: Feminist teaching and women's genres. In M. Shiach (Ed.), *Feminism and cultural studies* (pp. 343-367). Oxford: Oxford University Press.

Cloud, D. L. (1996). Hegemony or concordance? The rhetoric of tokenism in "Oprah" Winfrey's rags-to-riches biography. *Critical Studies in Mass Communication, 13,* 115-137.

Cloud, D. L. (1998). *Control and consolation in American culture and politics: Rhetoric of therapy.* London: Sage.

Condit, C. M. (1989). The rhetorical limits of polysemy. *Critical Studies in Mass Communication, 6,* 103-122.

Crossen, C. (2001, July 13). Read them and weep: Misery, pain, catastrophe, despair . . . and that's just the first chapter. *The Wall Street Journal,* p. W15.

Darnton, R. (1995). Communication networks. In R. Darnton, *The forbidden best-sellers of pre-revolutionary France* (pp. 181-197). New York & London: W. W. Norton.

Dortch, S. (1998, May). Ready readers, reluctant readers. *American Demographics, 8,* 10-13.

Dow, B. J. (1996). *Prime-time feminism: Television, media culture, and the women's movement since 1970.* Philadelphia: University of Pennsylvania Press.

Fowler, A. (2001, November 19). Saying no to Oprah. *Newsweek,* p. 21.

Gabriel, T. (1997, March 17). Women buy fiction in bulk and publishers take notice. *The New York Times,* p. D1.

Gitlin, T. (1997, March 17). The dumb-down. *The Nation,* p. 28.

Gray, P. (1996, December 2). Winfrey's winners. *Time,* p. 84.

Kinsella, B. (1997, January 20). The Oprah effect: How TV's premier talk show host puts books over the top. *Publishers Weekly,* pp. 276-278.

Kirkpatrick, D. D. (2001, October 24). Winfrey rescinds offer to author for guest appearance. *The New York Times*, p. C4.

Lefebvre, H. (2002). *Critique of everyday life. Vol. 2. Foundations for a sociology of the everyday* (Trans J. Moore). London: Verso.

Letters to Oprah's book club. (2001, July 6). *The Oprah Winfrey Show* [Transcript]. Available online at *http://www.oprah.com*. Accessed February 2, 2002.

Light, A. (1999). "Returning to Manderley": Romance fiction, female sexuality, and class. In M. Schiach (Ed.), *Feminism and cultural studies* (pp. 371-394). Oxford: Oxford University Press.

Masciarotte, G.-J. (1991). C'mon girl: Oprah Winfrey and the discourse of feminine talk. *Genders, 11*, 81-110.

Mattelart, M. (1997). Everyday life (excerpt). In C. Brunsdon, J. D'Acci, & L. Spigel (Eds.), *Feminist television criticism: A reader* (pp. 23-35). Oxford: Oxford University Press.

McNett, G. (1999, November 12). Reaching to the converted. *Salon* [Online]. Available at http://www.salon.com/books/feature/1999/11/12/oprahcon/print.html. Accessed December 13, 2000.

McRobbie, A. (1991). *Feminism and youth culture: From Jackie to Just Seventeen*. London: Macmillan.

McRobbie, A. (1994). *Postmodernism and popular culture*. London & New York: Routledge.

Modleski, T. (1982). *Loving with a vengeance: Mass-produced fantasies for women*. London: Routledge.

Modleski, T. (1997). The search for tomorrow in today's soap operas: Notes on a feminine narrative form. In C. Brunsdon, J. D'Acci, & L. Spigel (Eds.), *Feminist television criticism: A reader* (pp. 36-47). Oxford: Oxford University Press. (Original work published 1979)

Modleski, T. (1998). *Old wives' tales and other women's stories*. New York: New York University Press.

Newborn quintuplets come home. (1996, October 18). *The Oprah Winfrey Show* [Transcript]. Livingston, NJ: Burrelle's Information Services.

Oprah's book club. (1998, April 9). *The Oprah Winfrey Show* [Transcript]. Livingston, NJ: Burrelle's Information Services.

Oprah's book club. (1998, June 18). *The Oprah Winfrey Show* [Transcript]. Livingston, NJ: Burrelle's Information Services.

Oprah's book club. (1999, March 31). *The Oprah Winfrey Show* [Transcript]. Livingston, NJ: Burrelle's Information Services.

Oprah's book club. (1999, September 9). *The Oprah Winfrey Show* [Transcript]. Livingston, NJ: Burrelle's Information Services.

Oprah's book club. (1999, December 3). *The Oprah Winfrey Show* [Transcript]. Livingston, NJ: Burrelle's Information Services.

Oprah's book club. (2000, June 23). *The Oprah Winfrey Show* [Transcript]. Livingston, NJ: Burrelle's Information Services.

Oprah's book club. (2000, August 23). *The Oprah Winfrey Show* [Transcript]. Livingston, NJ: Burrelle's Information Services.

Oprah's book club. (2000, November 16). *The Oprah Winfrey Show* [Transcript]. Livingston, NJ: Burrelle's Information Services.

Oprah's book club. (2001, January 24). *The Oprah Winfrey Show* [Transcript]. Livingston, NJ: Burrelle's Information Services.

Oprah's book club anniversary party. (1997, September 22). *The Oprah Winfrey Show* [Transcript]. Livingston, NJ: Burrelle's Information Services.

Oprah's book club: *Cane River*. (2001, September 24). *The Oprah Winfrey Show* [Transcript]. Available online at http://www.oprah.com. Accessed February 2, 2002.

Oprah's book club: *We Were the Mulvaneys*. (2001, March 8). *The Oprah Winfrey Show* [Transcript]. Livingston, NJ: Burrelle's Information Services.

Oprah's book club: *White Oleander*. (1999, June 15). *The Oprah Winfrey Show* [Transcript]. Livingston, NJ: Burrelle's Information Services.

Peck, J. (1994). Talk about racism: Framing a popular discourse of race on *The Oprah Winfrey Show*. *Cultural Critique, 27*, 89-126.

Postman, N. (1986). *Amusing ourselves to death: Public discourse in the age of show business*. New York: Viking Press.

Radway, J. A. (1984). *Reading the romance: Women, patriarchy, and popular literature*. Chapel Hill, NC: University of North Carolina Press.

Radway, J. A. (1999a). On the importance of reading: Book history and the possibilities for rethinking the social. Unpublished manuscript.

Radway, J. A. (1999b). Romance and the work of fantasy: Struggles over feminine sexuality and subjectivity at century's end. In M. Shiach (Ed.), *Feminism and cultural studies* (pp. 395-416). Oxford: Oxford University Press.

Salute to mothers. (1997, May 9). *The Oprah Winfrey Show* [Transcript]. Livingston, NJ: Burrelle's Information Services.

Shattuc, J. M. (1999). The Oprahification of America: Talk shows and the public sphere. In M. B. Haralovich & L. Rabinovitz (Eds.), *Television, history, and American culture: Feminist critical essays* (pp. 168-180). Durham, NC: Duke University Press.

Squire, C. (1997). Empowering women? *The Oprah Winfrey Show*. In C. Brunsdon, J. D'Acci, & L. Spigel (Eds.), *Feminist television criticism: A reader* (pp. 98-113). Oxford: Oxford University Press.

Streitfeld, D. (1996, September 26). On *Oprah:* People who read. *The Washington Post,* p. 1A.

Third Rock from the Sun. (1997, February 28). *The Oprah Winfrey Show* [Transcript]. Livingston, NJ: Burrelle's Information Services.

Ticker (2000, April). *Brill's Content,* p. 84.

Touched by an Oprah. (1999, December 20). *People,* pp. 112-116.

OPRAH'S BOOK CLUB SELECTIONS

Angelou, M. (1981). *The heart of a woman.* New York: Random House.

Ansay, A. M. (1994). *Vinegar hill.* New York: Avon Books.

Berg, E. (2000). *Open house.* New York: Random House.

Binchy, M. (1998). *Tara road.* New York: Delacorte Press.

Clarke, B. (1999). *River, cross my heart.* Boston: Little Brown & Company.

Dubus III, A. (1999). *House of sand and fog.* New York: Vintage Books.

Franzen, J. (2001). *The corrections.* New York: Farrar, Straus, & Giroux.

Hamilton, J. (1988). *The book of Ruth.* New York: Ticknor & Fields.

Haynes, M. (1999). *Mother of pearl.* New York: Hyperion.

Hoffman, A. (1997). *Here on Earth.* New York: Berkley Books.

Kingsolver, B. (1998). *The poisonwood bible.* New York: HarperPerennial.

Lamb, W. (1992). *She's come undone.* New York: Pocket Books.

Lamb, W. (1998). *I know this much is true.* New York: Regan Books.

Mitchard, J. (1996). *The deep end of the ocean.* New York: Viking Press.

Morris, M. M. (1996). *Songs in ordinary time.* New York: Penguin Books.

Morrison, T. (1970). *The bluest eye.* New York: Washington Square Press.

Morrison, T. (1973). *Sula.* New York: Knopf.

Morrison, T. (1977). *Song of Solomon.* New York: Plume.

Morrison, T. (1997). *Paradise.* New York: Plume.

Oates, J. C. (1997). *We were the Mulvaneys.* New York: Plume.

Oufkir, M. (2001). *Stolen lives: Twenty years in a desert prison* (Trans. R. Schwartz). New York: Hyperion.

Schlink, B. (1997). *The reader* (Trans. C. B. Janeway). New York: Vintage Books.

Shreve A. (1998). *The pilot's wife.* Boston: Little, Brown, & Company.

Tademy, L. (2001). *Cane river.* New York: Warner Books.

Edward Wyatt (essay date 23 September 2005)

SOURCE: Wyatt, Edward. "Oprah's Book Club Reopening to Writers Who'll Sit and Chat." *New York Times* (23 September 2005): A1.

[*In the following essay, Wyatt reports the re-expansion of Oprah Winfrey's book club with the ill-fated* A Million Little Pieces.]

Oprah Winfrey said yesterday that she was expanding her highly influential television book club to include the works of contemporary authors, reversing a policy of choosing only classic novels and once again offering authors and their publishers the hope of huge sales resulting from her picks.

"I wanted to open the door and broaden the field," Ms. Winfrey said in an interview. "That allows me the opportunity to do what I like to do most, which is sit and talk to authors about their work. It's kind of hard to do that when they're dead."

As her first selection under the new criteria, Ms. Winfrey chose *A Million Little Pieces,* by James Frey, a harrowing 2003 memoir about the author's stay in a treatment center to address his alcoholism and drug addiction.

From 1996 to 2002, a book's selection for Oprah's Book Club typically resulted in sales of more than a million copies, a boon to authors and publishers in a business where selling 20,000 copies of a literary novel is considered a success. Her picks drew readers both to well-regarded authors like Toni Morrison and to relative unknowns like Wally Lamb and Anita Shreve.

Ms. Winfrey abandoned the book club in 2002 but restarted it a year later in a different form, choosing only classic novels, mostly by authors long dead. While sales soared for some of her classic picks, like *East of Eden* by John Steinbeck, others did not reach expectations, most notably this summer's selection of three novels by William Faulkner.

In an interview, Ms. Winfrey, who does not profit from the sales of the books she chooses, acknowledged that some recent selections did not draw the enthusiasm of some of her early ones. In a break with the past, no shows this summer were devoted to the Faulkner books; rather, she had extensive materials available on her Internet site (www.oprah.com).

Ms. Winfrey said she intended to widen her choices to an array of genres, including history, biography and historical fiction, to give herself more room to follow her instincts about what makes a positive reading experience.

"For six years, I couldn't really read any nonfiction or biography because I thought I was wasting my time" by spending hours on a book that did not fit her book club format, she said. "Now, when I read something really interesting or promising, I can find a way to introduce it to the public." Her aides say she alone reads potential selections and makes the choice.

Publishers were quick to welcome the announcement yesterday.

"It is fabulous news," said Jane Friedman, the chief executive of HarperCollins. "I think her impact will be as great if not greater than it was initially," when she began her book club shows in 1996.

Sonny Mehta, the chairman of the Knopf Publishing Group at Random House Inc., which has published more than a third of the 58 books chosen for Oprah's Book Club, said the book club had "brought the act of reading home to people in a way that publishers have not always been successful at doing."

"The fact that she had 300,000 people reading William Faulkner over the summer—she should be given a cabinet post," he added.

But Ms. Winfrey's recent emphasis on classics has contributed to a drop in her book club's popularity, said Kathleen Rooney, the author of *Reading with Oprah: The Book Club That Changed America* (University of Arkansas Press, 2005).

"There wasn't the widespread enthusiasm that was evident when she was picking contemporary fiction and nonfiction" for the club, Ms. Rooney said.

That led a group of mostly female writers to send a petition to Ms. Winfrey this year, asking her to return to her advocacy of contemporary writing and citing evidence that sales of fiction began to drop about the time her book club went on hiatus in 2002.

Meg Wolitzer, a novelist who was one of the early signers of the petition, said Ms. Winfrey's effect on authors, particularly novelists, "was to make us feel relevant," whether they were chosen for the club or not.

"To have somebody with a really loud mouth and a lot of power saying to people, 'You need to read this,' is important," she added.

Ms. Winfrey said she was aware of the petition and was moved by it. When she stopped choosing contemporary books, Ms. Winfrey said she was struggling to find enough titles that she felt compelled to share with her viewers, a statement that angered many publishers. But the change also followed by a few months a highly public quarrel with Jonathan Franzen, whose novel *The Corrections* was chosen by Ms. Winfrey in September 2001.

After Mr. Franzen made public comments suggesting that her choices were unsophisticated and appealed mainly to women, she revoked an invitation for him to appear on her show.

Ms. Winfrey dismissed the notion that his remarks influenced her decision to drop the book club. "Jonathan Franzen was not even a blip on the radar screen of my life," she said. "I didn't think one day about it."

Mr. Frey, whose memoir was published by Anchor Books, said he received a call about a month ago asking if he would appear on a show about drug rehabilitation. After he accepted, Ms. Winfrey got on the phone and told him her intention to recommend the book.

"I was shocked and thrilled and had this sort of amazing and surreal moment," he said.

Mr. Frey and Ms. Winfrey then conspired to have Mr. Frey's mother, who he said had given him copies of many of Ms. Winfrey's picks in the past, in the audience for yesterday's show. When Ms. Winfrey started talking about her son's book, the author's mother started to scream, "That's my son!"

Edward Wyatt (essay date 19 January 2006)

SOURCE: Wyatt, Edward. "It's a Matter of Timing." *New York Times* (19 January 2006): E7.

[*In the following essay, Wyatt relates the impact book clubs can have on publications' success or failure.*]

The announcement of a new pick for Oprah's Book Club is usually greeted with great enthusiasm in the publishing business, even by those publishers who do not have the rights to the latest pick.

But at Bantam Books, the announcement on Monday that Oprah Winfrey had chosen Elie Wiesel's *Night* as her next recommendation set off a different reaction: more like feeling all the air go out of the room.

Since April 1982, Bantam, an imprint of Random House Inc., had held the paperback rights to *Night*. But that license expired at the end of December, and Bantam officials said they did not learn of Ms. Winfrey's selection in time to print more copies of their version, a pocket-size paperback that sells for $5.99.

Hill & Wang, a division of Farrar, Straus & Giroux that was the original American publisher of *Night,* told Bantam last summer that it would not renew the paperback license, Barb Burg, a senior vice president at Bantam said on Tuesday. Farrar, Straus & Giroux did not renew the license because it was planning its own new translation. Because *Night* is popular in academic markets and the newly translated version was not expected to be on sale until April, Bantam printed enough copies to carry it through the academic year. Then came Ms. Winfrey's announcement.

Bantam can still sell the copies it has in print, and on online best-seller lists this week the Bantam paperback was ranked close behind the new Hill & Wang paperback, which has a list price of $9 but which the major online retailers were offering for $6.30.

"We are honored to have sold 6 million copies of Elie Wiesel's book over the last 24 years," Ms. Burg said. But with one to two million more copies of *Night* likely to be sold in the coming months alone, thanks to Ms. Winfrey, Bantam could be feeling the sting for years to come.

Sarah Lyall (essay date 29 July 2006)

SOURCE: Lyall, Sarah. "The British Version of Oprah's Book Club." *New York Times* (29 July 2006): B7.

[*In the following essay, Lyall examines the popularity and power of the* Richard and Judy *television show compared to* The Oprah Winfrey Show.]

The reviews for *The Righteous Men,* a thriller published last summer, were not universally ecstatic.

While popular tabloids and magazines seemed to like the novel, higher-brow publications scoffed at it. "It isn't much of a book," sniffed *The Observer* of London.

A gossip item in *The Times* of London referred mean-spiritedly to the fact that the author, Sam Bourne, was really Jonathan Freedland, a columnist at a rival newspaper, *The Guardian,* writing under a pseudonym. Like many such novels that appear to have little to distinguish them from the great mass of published works, *The Righteous Men* sold passably well, then began fading quietly from view.

Until Richard and Judy came along.

That would be Richard Madeley and Judy Finnigan, the married hosts of *Richard & Judy,* a live talk show broadcast each weekday afternoon on Channel 4 here. The pair put *The Righteous Men* on their list this year of six Summer Reads, paperbacks they recommend every summer as light, entertaining and enthralling vacation reading. And all of a sudden, the book's fortunes changed.

The week that Richard and Judy (like Cher or Sting, they are thought of as virtually surname-free) first praised *The Righteous Men*—merely in passing—on the show, the book sold 17,164 copies. The next week, when it was the featured book, it sold 30,624 copies, jumping straight to the top of the fiction bestseller lists, where it remained until knocked from the No. 1 spot by Victoria Hislop's *Island,* another *Richard & Judy* pick.

Like Oprah Winfrey in the United States, Richard and Judy are hugely influential in the world of books in Britain. Selection on one of their two annual lists—there is a separate winter book club, with 10 works discussed over 10 weeks—virtually guarantees that a book will become a best seller.

Amanda Ross, joint managing director of Cactus TV, which produces *Richard & Judy,* said that inclusion on the list has turned at least eight authors into multimillionaires, and that in the past two years, the books on the reading lists have, all told, sold some eight million copies among them.

"I think I just have the knack of choosing what's popular," said Ms. Ross, who recently was put at No. 1 on *The Observer* of London's list of the most influential people in British publishing. Defining a heavy book buyer in Britain as "someone who buys 12 books a year," she said she selected books for their entertainment value and their likelihood of provoking an interesting conversation.

The *Richard & Judy* approach differs significantly from Oprah's. While Ms. Winfrey invites a selected author into the studio for a discussion that is part interview, part cheerleading, the *Richard & Judy* authors never meet their hosts. For the summer reads, minor celebrities like soap opera stars, socialites and comedians describe the books while filmed on vacation posing (and occasionally reading) in a variety of spots: on the beach, by the pool, in the Jacuzzi.

Then the segment cuts to the studio, where Richard and Judy are joined by a panel of celebrities who discuss the book as if they were regulars in a monthly book club. "They are never experts and never book critics," Ms. Ross said. "I want people to feel like it's a group of friends chatting."

Mr. Madeley said: "We talk about the books in a way that we think that ordinary people would. The books are there to be read and enjoyed and talked about sensibly, not in the rarefied way of a wine buff or a food critic, but in the way the rest of the world does."

The couple stressed that they have nothing to do with the books' selection; that is all the work of Ms. Ross, helped by a panel of advisers. They both read the book for the first time when she gives it to them, and they don't always agree: Mr. Madeley thought highly of *The Lovely Bones* by Alice Sebold, while his wife hated it. "It's important that we come to the books with clean hands," Ms. Finnigan said.

Publishers, of course, are thrilled when their books are selected by *Richard & Judy*. "It's a very dynamic form of literary criticism," said Nigel Newton, the chief executive of Bloomsbury Publishing.

Jim Lynch's *Highest Tide*, a Bloomsbury book about a 13-year-old boy in the Pacific Northwest who becomes an unlikely media star after discovering a giant squid, made the list this summer, and the effect was immediate, Mr. Newton said, as it has been for every Bloomsbury book selected. For instance, he said, *The Gathering Light*, by Jennifer Donnelly, sold more than a quarter of a million copies after appearing on a *Richard & Judy* list.

Publishers are so eager for their books to be selected that they are willing to cede to Ms. Ross's publishing suggestions.

HarperCollins said it published the paperback edition of *The Righteous Men* this summer instead of October, as originally scheduled, because Ms. Ross made it clear she would consider only paperbacks. A couple of years ago, HarperCollins also agreed to change the cover of Cecelia Ahern's *PS, I Love You*, the tale of a young widow recovering from her husband's death, to blue from pink after Ms. Ross said that pink would turn off male readers.

The winter books tend to be more highbrow than the summer ones; this year's list included Geraldine Brooks's *March*, which went on to win the Pulitzer

Prize for fiction, and *Arthur and George*, the latest novel by Julian Barnes, which was shortlisted for the Man Booker Prize. The year before, it included David Mitchell's *Cloud Atlas*, a challenging tour de force of a novel told by multiple narrators, which went on to win the "Best Read of the Year" award at the British Book Awards. (It is a measure of the influence of *Richard & Judy* that the Best Read nominees are the 10 books on its winter list.)

Authors whose works are selected for the lists say that because so many reviews tend to condescend to readers, and because simply picking a book from so many choices can be so difficult, Richard and Judy perform an invaluable service.

"It is overwhelming when you go into a bookshop and see thousands of books lying there, and aren't sure what to go for," said Ms. Hislop, whose novel, *The Island*, is a rich romance about secrets, lies and love set partly in the forbidding world of a now-deserted leper colony off the Greek coast. "But people trust Richard and Judy, and are guided by their selections."

The bookstores trust them, too: chains like Waterstone's promote *Richard & Judy* books with special displays and discounts.

Mr. Freedland, author of *The Righteous Men*, said that the *Richard & Judy* experience had been eye-opening, from his perspective as both an author and an occasional reviewer.

"It was meant to be a thriller," he said of his book. "It was meant to be gripping and riveting and exciting; it wasn't meant to be *Anna Karenina*. What Richard and Judy did was to take the book on its own terms."

By the same token, he said: "When I write reviews, sometimes I make all these points about new ideas, or interesting experiments with form. But actually if I was asked, 'Would I recommend it?,' the answer would be no. The *Richard & Judy* thing is great because it gets right to the point: would you give this to someone to read?"

REVIEWS OF BOOKS ABOUT BOOK CLUBS

Harold Orlans (essay date January-February 2004)

SOURCE: Orlans, Harold. "Books of the Month." *Change* 36, no. 1 (January-February 2004): 6-7.

[*In the following essay, Orlans discusses the workings of the Book of the Month Club.*]

[In *A Feeling for Books,*] Duke literature professor Janice Radway examines the Book of the Month Club (BMC) as she encountered it from 1963 onward, in her school years, when she avidly read its offerings, and subsequently, when she saw it through the thick lens of literary theory. The latter view may be professionally obligatory, but the former is more informative.

In graduate school, Radway confesses, "I had learned to disparage the club as a middle-brow operation offering . . . bestsellers to people who wanted only to be told what to read in order to look appropriately cultured." Yet, initially, she liked the club's books (*Marjorie Morningstar*; *Gods, Graves, and Scholars*; *Kon-Tiki*; *The Wall*; *Sexual Politics*) "a lot more than the books I read for my classes" (Henry James, Faulkner, Pound, Joyce, William Carlos Williams).

In time, she realized that BMC defined itself against academic standards of "high culture." Using *academic* as literature professors used *middlebrow*, "to dismiss books they did not like," its editors selected books that were well-written, instructive, yet entertaining and, if possible, with literary merit. Their standards differed both from those of academics, unconcerned with readability, and popular best-sellers, which were merely readable, with little literary or educational value.

BMC catered to the growing population of persons hoping to continue the education they had started in college. Four-fifths had attended (not all completed) college: 60 to 65 percent were women. In 1926, its first year, the club had 46,500 members; in 1929, membership was 110,600; in 1958, it had risen to 500,000. BMC recruited from lists of educated persons with a good income and interested in culture, like the New York Social Register and college alumni; many members were young professional people—lawyers, dentists, doctors, managers, professors, teachers, secretaries.

Two novel devices furthered the club's success. A committee of prominent critics and writers selected the books. Initial members were Henry Seidel Canby, chairman; Heywood Broun; Dorothy Canfield; Christopher Morley; and William Allen White. In 1985, the judges were Clifton Fadiman, chairman; David McCullough; Gloria Norris; Mordecai Richler; and Wilfrid Sheed. Though their selections were attacked by highbrow critics (Dwight Macdonald said, "the best that can be said [for the quality of selections] is that it could be worse"), the judges helped to keep BMC from becoming just another marketer of popular books.

At the outset, monthly selections were mailed to all members, who could return any they did not want. The volume of returns threatened disaster until a shrewd policy was adopted; subscribers were given a review of the books and two weeks to return a card saying, do NOT send the book, or, send an alternative selection. Since many subscribers did not get around to returning the card, this "negative option" reduced returns and helped the club estimate the number of copies to order.

BMC editors feared the mergers and mass marketing that transformed the book industry. Commercial factors had always affected selections, but the club's 1977 purchase by Time, and the Time-Warner merger a decade later, made them the prime factor. Critics who had berated BMC's middlebrow values now mourned the demise of its standards and viewed the 1994 dissolution of its book selection committee as the final triumph of marketing.

Today, each of four judges chooses a different book. BMC is one of over 40 book clubs with 8.5 million members that belong to Booksonline, a Web-based BMC-Doubleday Book Club partnership. Time, which owns BMC, is itself a unit of AOL Time-Warner (recently renamed Time-Warner). Seventeen times a year BMC offers members up to 200 alternate choices, including omnibus editions, "multi-volume . . . classics," and "up-and-coming writers," or a main selection that is sent to members who do not e-mail "No."

Judith A. Howard (review date March 2004)

SOURCE: Howard, Judith A. Review of *Book Clubs: Women and the Uses of Reading in Everyday Life,* by Elizabeth Long. *The American Journal of Sociology* 109, no. 5 (March 2004): 1203-05.

[*In the following review, Howard recommends Elizabeth Long's* Book Clubs: Women and the Uses of Reading in Everyday Life.]

Instance 1.—Recent trips to my sociology department mailbox have brought me Ann Patchett's *Taft* (Houghton Mifflin, 1994), and this week, *The Full Catastrophe* (Linden Press, 1990), by David Carkeet. The colleague who left these for me found in her mailbox my copy of Yann Martel's *The Life of Pi* (Harcourt, 2001), and more recently, Monique Truong's *The Book of Salt* (Houghton Mifflin, 2003). I see this colleague no more than once a quarter for lunch; our communication is more frequent, and possibly richer, through our literary reciprocity.

Instance 2.—After several years of "we really should," my colleagues in the Department of Women Studies, which I currently chair, have initiated a reading group in which we read chapters, books, even utopian excursions, directed toward how to define and practice women's studies, feminist methodology, and transnationalism.

The reading in these two situations entails different sorts of books, different purposes, different ways of exchanging reactions, indeed, different pleasures. But both instances speak to the power of reading and the power of reading for women. This is the central theme of *Book Clubs: Women and the Uses of Reading in Everyday Life.* In this book Elizabeth Long traces the results of several years of observing and participating in a number of different book clubs in Houston, Texas. Although men, and even women, have read for centuries (despite the best attempts to trivialize women's reading, as Long's historical introduction makes abundantly clear), book clubs have only existed for approximately the past century. Book clubs could not flourish until book publishing made inexpensive books widely available. (There are some wonderful gems in this history; for example, that early women's book clubs were critical to the establishment of public libraries, establishing about three-quarters of the public libraries in the nation.) Most recently, book clubs have been put on the map of most U.S. readers and television viewers alike through the efforts of Oprah Winfrey. Celebrity aside, book groups have become a major cultural phenomenon. As Long observes, in an era in which it seems every adult feels overscheduled, the fact that reading group activity flourishes is remarkable.

What *is* a book club—is it just a group that gets together once a month or so to read and talk about a book? At one level, that is a book group. But book groups accomplish a good deal more than discussion of a text, and it is those accomplishments that are the heart of Long's analysis. Long traces the motivation for this project in her preface: her male colleagues' reaction to the topic: "You want to study what? Why on earth would you want to do that?" Their infuriating reaction mobilized Long to conduct this fascinating study, the scope of which surprised even her. Anticipating perhaps a dozen reading groups in the greater Houston area, she and her team identified over 120 such groups. It was in part these sheer numbers that led Long to decisions that do circumscribe the contributions of this research. Given that she did not have the resources to study all of these groups, she elected to study only white women's groups. Her choice of women's groups is partly pragmatic: many more existing groups are formed by women than by men. Explaining her choice to focus only on groups of white women, Long states "I did not want to make an inadequate or tokenist comparison between black and white women's groups, or appropriate the experiences of African American women within categories of knowledge that worked for white women" (p. xv). At the same time, she observes that her racial difference from members of black women's groups encouraged the posing of different research questions than those were posed in her work with white women's groups. This speaks to the importance of conducting precisely this analysis in her future research. Long is clearly

sensitive to these limitations: "Literacy and the practices of reading it produces in our society can never be divorced from questions of power, privilege, exclusion, and social distinction" (p. 16).

After a historical discussion of the beginnings of women's reading groups in the Houston area, Long analyzes the social characteristics of the contemporary groups, including how each began and why people join. She addresses the organizational details, including varied membership, discussion rules, book selection practices, questions of group identity, and, in an especially intriguing chapter, the content of group discussions. A remarkable number of groups spend very little time actually discussing the assigned books. Rather, they use the discussion of books as a jumping off point to talk about themselves, their lives, and social and political phenomena. Long argues that the best book groups can lead members toward creative appraisals of social others as well as of their own historical situations and life choices. Long thus turns a finding that in the hands of some researchers could be used to further trivialize women's book groups (that discussions often have little to do with the books) into an insightful commentary about the significant identity work and social criticism these groups enable. Evidence of such social criticism is Long's observation that in many of these groups members often disregard the cultural authority that labels some books classics and other books "light reading." As she puts it, "Reading is a variable practice, [and] reveals the give and take between literature and life experience by which audiences dismantle and reinscribe the seemingly stable hegemony of the evaluative hierarchy" (p. 128).

If you have ever been a member of a book group, whether formal or informal, you should read this book. If you study or teach sociology of culture, you should read this book. If you think of book groups as beneath the terrain of cultural studies, you especially should read this book. And perhaps you can get a group together to discuss it.

Andrea L. Press (review date March 2005)

SOURCE: Press, Andrea L. Review of *Book Clubs: Women and the Uses of Reading in Everyday Life,* by Elizabeth Long. *Contemporary Sociology* 34, no. 2 (March 2005): 160-61.

[*In the following review, Press praises* Book Clubs *as a significant reinforcement of the legitimacy of women's intellectual pursuits.*]

In a world increasingly defined by mass media, we hear constantly of the death of the written word. Therefore it is refreshing to read [Elizabeth] Long's in-depth study of readers, *Book Clubs.* Long studied organized groups of women readers who live and meet in the Houston area. Exhaustively researched over a period of years, *Book Clubs* discusses in careful detail the way women's reading, and their discussions about it, help them to work out areas of conflict in their lives and particularly in their identities as women, or, as Long puts it, to "narrate the self." What role, she asks, does reading, and especially, talking about reading, play for women grappling with perplexing issues? Do books help to empower women as they write or speak their stories? These are the ambitious questions Long seeks to investigate in this impressive work.

In fact, Long argues, there are many different types of book groups that can play different roles in the lives of very different women. Some of the women in her study have remained in book groups that were organized when their children were young even as their children are grown and off on their own. For these women, their book groups may contain their oldest and dearest friends, women whose philosophies of childrearing, marriage, and life often closely match their own. Other women enter book groups temporarily, to cope with transitions in their lives, or to fill the intellectual gap left when they leave school or work to stay home with young children. Still others use book groups as a way to cement their social positions in Houston society. Some groups tolerate conflicts of ideas and opinions, others take pains to minimize it, or avoid it altogether. Some groups admit men, others have strict rules not to do so. The only rule when examining book groups is that there is an impressive variety of formats and functions for these historically important organizations, and Long's historical chapter documents the longevity of these organizations, and the important role they have played throughout the last two centuries in women's lives in the United States.

All book groups have rules by which books are selected and meetings are run. These rules vary in that some yield a more "intellectual" or canon-bound selection of books, and others less so. How women discuss critical evaluations of the books they read, for example, how they negotiate their relationship to the established intellectual "canon" of literature, makes for some of the most interesting reading in the book. While some groups are tied to these evaluations and take them very seriously as guides for their own choices of books to read and their concomitant assessment of these books, others find them off-putting and even make a policy of avoiding books sanctioned by canonical methods of evaluation. Sometimes these disputes center around feminist issues: Some groups pursue books that discuss topics of particular interest from a feminist perspective, while others avoid like the plague any "women in pain" books, as books focusing on women's subjective experience are sometimes disparagingly labeled.

I found especially enlightening Long's extended discussion of various women's reactions to Jane Austen's novels in one of the groups she herself attended. As a feminist academic who is also a huge fan of Austen's work, it was fascinating to see how women struggled with her language, and with trying to relate to the world of the eighteenth and nineteenth century British leisure classes Austen describes. It certainly gave me some insights into popular perceptions of classic literature, perceptions often shared by the university students we teach. Many of the women persevered through their struggles to develop an appreciation of this early feminist author. Some found her world, language, and experience simply too alien to enlighten life in our times. Their variety of responses probably parallel the range of historical processes through which some literary works are forgotten, while others are canonized, remembered, and widely considered important.

Theoretically, Long's book makes a significant contribution to feminist theories of the public sphere. By elaborating a space that few have acknowledged or described, she helps all of us to understand how women reflect and act upon the world in the semi-public setting that is the book group. Twenty years after this literature has pointed out the need to investigate these kinds of spaces that women occupy, there remain scandalously few other empirical studies that contribute to our knowledge of them. In this respect, Long's book addresses a crucial gap in our theoretical literature. She also includes a useful analysis of Bourdieu and mentions that she is attempting to illustrate how people become subjectively engaged with culture, a type of discussion that adds an important dimension to Bourdieu's work. *Book Clubs* is an important addition to the sociology of culture, and to the gender and culture literature, and can be useful in classes that fall into either category.

Crista DeLuzio (review date May 2005)

SOURCE: DeLuzio, Crista. Review of *Lone Star Chapters: The Story of Texas Literary Clubs,* by Betty Holland Wiesepape. *Journal of Southern History* 71, no. 2 (May 2005): 490-91.

[*In the following review, DeLuzio concludes that Betty Holland Wiesepape has succeeded in providing narrative histories of Texas' significant book clubs in* Lone Star Chapters.]

During the early twentieth century, literary clubs across Texas offered participants opportunities to practice creative writing and to share their literary endeavors. Betty Holland Wiesepape's *Lone Star Chapters: The Story of Texas Literary Clubs* examines four of these organizations, all founded during the 1920s and 1930s. Her careful examination of the Manuscript Club of Wichita Falls, the Makers of Dallas, the Panhandle Pen Women of Amarillo, and the Border Poets of Kingsville makes use of a variety of sources. Intending to counter stereotypes of Texas as a "cultural wasteland" and of literary club members themselves as so-called pink tea poets, she convincingly documents the contributions of these clubs to cultural development in the state and to the enhancement of the national reputation of Texas writers (p. 40).

These clubs facilitated contacts among writers within communities and across the state, sponsored events that exposed local citizens to major literary figures of the day, and fostered connections between academic institutions and local communities. Some members helped to further literary education as creative writing teachers. Several participated in statewide arts organizations. Others became editors and publishers on the regional and national level. A handful of club members went on to earn national acclaim as authors. Perhaps most importantly, she argues that the clubs "encouraged the growth of a community of readers," whose enthusiasm and respect for literature fostered a fertile cultural climate "that could eventually support and enable the work of ensuing generations of Texas writers" (pp. 11, 138).

Weisapape's goal is to provide narrative histories of these clubs rather than "theoretical argument" (p. 9). She succeeds admirably at this, offering engaging stories about the founding of the clubs, information about historical context, biographical sketches of key members, detailed accounts of club proceedings, and thoughtful descriptions of members' publications. There is, however, room for more analysis. She introduces

some intriguing questions about gender that would be worth exploring further. Given that more women than men participated in these clubs yet received less recognition for their work, what meaning did women writers bring to club membership and to the role of cultural development? She might also have deployed a more critical usage of the term *culture*. To what extent did club members think of themselves as "individuals of superior intellect, education, and refinement" (p. 3), bringing "cultural advancement" (p. 5) to a "backward frontier" (p. 95)? Work by Laura Hamner on the history of the people of West Texas and by Frank Goodwyn on Hispanic folklore, for example, suggests that participation in the process of cultural development was more complicated than this statement implies. Wiesepape recognizes that "many additional chapters" need to be written on the history of literary societies in Texas and in the nation (p. 139). Her book offers a good place to start.

FURTHER READING

Criticism

Hall, R. Mark. "The 'Oprahfication' of Literacy: Reading Oprah's Book Club." *College English* (July 2003): 646-67.

> Provides an analysis of the impact of Oprah Winfrey's book club.

Smith, Michael W. "Conversations about Literature outside Classrooms: How Adults Talk about Books in Their Book Clubs." *Journal of Adolescent & Adult Literacy* 40, no. 3 (November 1996): 180-87.

> Provides a study demonstrating the importance of the social aspect of book clubs.

Ray Bradbury
1920-

(Full name Raymond Douglas Bradbury; also wrote under the pseudonyms D. R. Banat, Leonard Douglas, William Elliott, Douglas Spaulding, Leonard Spaulding, and Brett Sterling) American novelist, short story writer, and screenwriter.

The following entry presents an overview of Bradbury's career through 2006. For further information on his life and works, see *CLC*, Volumes 1, 3, 10, 15, 42, and 98.

INTRODUCTION

Bradbury considers himself a fantasy writer, despite persistent association with the science-fiction genre, and is credited with elevating science fiction into a more sophisticated style. Often described as economical yet poetic, Bradbury's fiction conveys a vivid sense of place in which everyday events are transformed into unusual, sometimes sinister situations. In a career that has spanned more than half a century, Bradbury has written crime and mystery stories, supernatural tales, poetry, and screenplays, as well as fantasy and science fiction. His works are imbued with optimism and values that support humankind's highest good, and his stories startle with depictions of what could potentially transpire if such qualities erode in a widespread manner.

BIOGRAPHICAL INFORMATION

Bradbury was born August 22, 1920, in Waukegan, Illinois. His mother kept him highly sheltered, a result, Bradbury has opined, of the deaths of two siblings. Nonetheless, he was able to experience the world of literature, largely through the influence of his Aunt Neva, an artist ten years older than Bradbury who lived next door to him when he was a boy. He began writing short stories at age 12 and was 19 when his first published story, "It's Not the Heat, It's the Hu-," appeared in *Script* magazine in 1939. He continued to publish short stories in magazines such as *Weird Tales,* and his first book-length collection, *Dark Carnival,* was published by Arkham House in 1947. His sophomore effort, however, became Bradbury's "big break." *The Martian Chronicles* (1950) was accepted by Doubleday, which paid an advance of $750, a then-handsome sum that was acquired before the arrival of his first child

with his wife, Maggie. Over the course of his career, Bradbury has distinguished himself as a prolific author who is also accessible, having consented to more than 300 interviews. Now an octogenarian and stroke survivor, Bradbury continues to publish.

MAJOR WORKS

The publication of *The Martian Chronicles* established Bradbury's reputation as an author of sophisticated science fiction. This collection of stories is connected by the framing device of the settling of Mars by humans and is dominated by tales of space travel and environmental adaptation. Bradbury's themes reflect many important issues of the post-World War II era in which the stories were written—racism, censorship, technology, and nuclear war. Bradbury's later short story collections, in which he shifted his focus from outer space to more familiar earthbound settings, are generally considered less significant than *The Martian Chronicles* and *The Illustrated Man* (1951), despite the author's later use of many similar techniques employed in these two collections.

Dandelion Wine (1957) focuses on the youth of a semi-autobiographical protagonist, Douglas Spaulding, a midwesterner. *A Medicine for Melancholy* (1959), *The Machineries of Joy* (1964), *I Sing the Body Electric!* (1969), and *Long after Midnight* (1976), contain stories set in Bradbury's familiar outer space or midwestern settings and explore his typical themes. Several short story collections have been published more recently and include some stories written decades before. Many of Bradbury's stories have been anthologized or filmed for such television programs as *The Twilight Zone, Alfred Hitchcock Presents,* and *Ray Bradbury Theater.*

Bradbury's first novel, *Fahrenheit 451* (1953), is the only work he will acknowledge as science fiction, a genre which he defines as being about things that could happen, as opposed to fantasy, which is about the impossible. *Fahrenheit 451* concerns a future society in which books are burned because they are perceived as threats to societal conformity. The book became, and remains, a lightning rod for debate over censorship, and some consider it Bradbury's most important work. In the novel *Something Wicked This Way Comes* (1962), a father attempts to save his son and a friend from the sinister forces of a mysterious traveling carnival. The optimistic ending of this story was deemed simplistic by some reviewers and uplifting by others. *From the Dust Returned* (1998) brings together the Elliott family, three ghoulish characters who appeared individually in previously published stories and who are based on family members including Bradbury's beloved Aunt Neva.

Farewell Summer was published in 2006 and was dubbed a sequel to *Dandelion Wine*, but Bradbury revealed that the two novels were originally one large work written in 1955. When he submitted it to Doubleday for publication, the tome was deemed too long and only the first half was published, as *Dandelion Wine*. Some of Bradbury's early short stories were of the detective fiction genre and were later collected in *A Memory of Murder* (1984). A trilogy of detective novels followed. *Death Is a Lonely Business* (1985) features Douglas Spaulding, the protagonist of *Dandelion Wine*, as a struggling writer for pulp magazines. Bradbury has acknowledged that this work, set in Venice, California, in 1949, contains many autobiographical elements. *A Graveyard for Lunatics* (1990), the sequel to *Death Is a Lonely Business,* gives voice to the author's disapproval of the film industry for what he considers its wholesale disregard of literary integrity. *Let's All Kill Constance* (2003), the third title in this trilogy, features a character who died in the first book but, Bradbury noted, refused to stay dead.

CRITICAL RECEPTION

Bradbury's accolades have accumulated apace with his ever-burgeoning oeuvre. Among the most notable of his awards are the Grandmaster Nebula Award for lifetime achievement from the Science Fiction and Fantasy Writers of America, the National Book Foundation Medal for Distinguished Contribution to American Letters, and the National Medal of the Arts. Bradbury's appeal has been acknowledged even beyond the literary world with a star on the Hollywood Walk of Fame. While Bradbury's popularity is universally acknowledged, many critics find the reasons for his success difficult to pinpoint. Some believe that the tension Bradbury creates between fantasy and reality is central to his ability to convey his visions and interests to his readers. In a genre in which futurism and the fantastic are usually synonymous, Bradbury stands out for his celebration of the future in realistic terms and his exploration of conventional values and ideas. As one of the first science fiction or fantasy writers to convey his themes through a refined prose style replete with subtlety and humanistic analogies, Bradbury has helped make science fiction a more respected literary genre and he is widely admired by the literary establishment.

PRINCIPAL WORKS

Dark Carnival (short stories) 1947; revised edition, 1948; published as *The October Country,* 1955

The Martian Chronicles (novel) 1950; revised edition published as *The Silver Locusts,* 1965; anniversary edition published as *The Martian Chronicles: The Fortieth Anniversary Edition,* 1990

The Illustrated Man (short stories) 1951

The Golden Apples of the Sun (short stories) 1953

Fahrenheit 451 (novel) 1953

Moby Dick [adaptor; from the novel *Moby-Dick* by Herman Melville] (screenplay) 1956

Dandelion Wine (short stories) 1957

A Medicine for Melancholy (short stories) 1959; revised edition published as *The Day It Rained Forever,* 1959

R Is for Rocket (juvenilia) 1962

Something Wicked This Way Comes (novel) 1962

The Machineries of Joy (short stories) 1964

S Is for Space (juvenilia) 1966

I Sing the Body Electric! (short stories) 1969

Old Ahab's Friend, and Friend to Noah, Speaks His Piece: A Celebration (poetry) 1971

Zen and the Art of Writing, and the Joy of Writing (essays) 1973

Long after Midnight (short stories) 1976

Where Robot Mice and Robot Men Run Round in Robot Towns (poetry) 1977

A Memory of Murder (short stories) 1984

Death Is a Lonely Business (novel) 1985

The Coffin (teleplay) 1988

A Graveyard for Lunatics: Another Tale of Two Cities (novel) 1990

Yestermorrow: Obvious Answers to Impossible Futures (essays) 1991

Green Shadows, White Whale (novel) 1992

Quicker Than the Eye (short stories) 1996

From the Dust Returned: A Family Remembrance (novel) 1998

Let's All Kill Constance (novel) 2003

The Cat's Pajamas (short stories) 2004

Farewell Summer (novel) 2006

CRITICISM

David Seed (essay date August 1994)

SOURCE: Seed, David. "The Flight from the Good Life: *Fahrenheit 451* in the Context of Postwar American Dystopias." *Journal of American Studies* 28, no. 2 (August 1994): 225-40.

[*In the following essay, Seed places* Fahrenheit 451 *in context with other dystopian novels, including Aldous Huxley's* Brave New World *and Kurt Vonnegut's* Player Piano.]

Surveying the American scene in 1958, Aldous Huxley recorded his dismay over the speed with which *Brave New World* was becoming realized in contemporary developments: "The nightmare of total organization, which I had situated in the seventh century After Ford, has emerged from the safe, remote future and is now awaiting us, just around the next corner."[1] Having struck a keynote of urgency Huxley then lines up a series of oppositions between limited disorder, individuality and freedom on the one hand, and order, automatism and subjection on the other in order to express his liberal anxieties that political and social organization might hypertrophy. Huxley sums up an abiding fear which runs through American dystopian fiction of the 1950s that individuals will lose their identity and become the two-dimensional stereotypes indicated in two catch-phrases of the period: the "organization man" and the "man in the grey flannel suit." William H. Whyte's 1956 study diagnoses the demise of the Protestant ethic in American life and its replacement by a corporate one which privileges "belongingness." The result might be, he warns, not a world controlled by self-evident enemies familiar from *Nineteen Eighty-Four,* but an antiseptic regime presided over by a "mild-looking group of therapists who, like the Grand Inquisitor, would be doing what they did to help you."[2] Whyte endorsed the social insights of Sloan Wilson's 1955 novel *The Man in the Grey Flannel Suit* which dramatizes the conflicts within the protagonist between individual advancement and self-location within a business hierarchy, Despite being an apparently successful executive Thomas Rath registers a tension between satisfaction and its opposite which recurs throughout fifties dystopias.

One crucial sign of this issue is the fact that the protagonists of dystopias are usually defined in relation to organizational structures. Walter H. Miller's 1952 short story "Conditionally Human" is typical of the genre in centring on an official. The action takes place in an America of the near future which has become "one sprawling suburb" ruled over by "Uncle Federal." Because the inexorable rise in the population is clearly threatening the promise of the "good life" the regime introduces draconian limits to the birth rate and the government-sponsored organization Anthropos Inc. designs baby substitutes called "neutroids", chimp-like creatures produced by the radioactive mutation of reproductive cells. The central character Norris has the job of an updated dog-catcher, rounding up stray "neutroids" to his wife's disgust. Already we can see the key generic motifs emerging: the problem of homogeneity, the disparity between restriction and avuncular government, the risk of technology exceeding its moral bounds, and—within the Norris couple—the debate between acceptance and dissatisfaction. When questioned by his wife, Norris characteristically pleads helplessness by appealing to the necessities of the system: "And what can I do about it? I can't help my Placement Aptitude score. They say Bio-Authority is where I belong, and it's to Bio I have to go. Oh, sure, I don't *have* to work where they send me. You can always join the General Work Pool, but that's all the law allows, and GWP'ers don't have families. So I go where Placement Aptitude says I'm needed."[3] Psychometrics has become institutionalized into a narrow series of legally enforced prescriptions which induce an acquiescence in Norris reflected in the key verb "belongs."

The adjustment of the individual's notion of appropriateness to officially measured norms evident in the story just quoted also figured prominently in the sociologist Mordecai Roshwald's examination of American society in the late fifties. Viewing developments with the special clarity of a newcomer (Roshwald was born in Poland and lived in Palestine before he took up permanent residence in the USA), he applied David Riesman's notion of other-directedness and located a resultant tendency to "imitation and uniformity." His 1958 article "Quo Vadis, America?" concludes with an indignant polemic against the complacency of imagining that the only danger confronting society is the external physical threat of atomic war. Not so. "The loss of individual norms in moral issues, the admiration of unjust power, the lack of tradition" and a host of other dangers present themselves just as urgently, and Roshwald here opens up a potential purpose for the writer of dystopias: "to warn against these and to fight them may be a second front in the fight for human survival. . . ."[4] Roshwald was in fact already contributing to that fight by working on his own dystopian novel *Level 7* (1959) which transposed the streamlined production systems of *Brave New World* on to the self-contained mechanized environment of a nuclear defence bunker. The inordinate reliance on technology and bland interchangeability of American manners which "seemed to point to a uniformly happy, efficient and self-sufficient society, verging on automata or robots," finds its expression in the novel as an ironic implication that the operative-protagonist is an extension of his machines instead of vice versa.[5] As happens with Montag in *Fahrenheit 451,* X-127, known only by his functional label, comes gradually to realize the consequences of his participation in a system, here of nuclear destruction, but with the added irony that his realization comes too late to make any difference even to his own fate. Roshwald's original title for this work was *The Diary of Push-Button Officer X-127* which appropriately stressed the issue of robotization, partly problematizing the individual's relation to technology and partly using that technology as a metaphorical expression of the individual's conformity to prescribed roles.[6] Quite independently Erich Fromm identified the emergence of exactly the same social type, declaring: "Today we come across a person who acts and feels like an automaton; who never experiences anything which is really his; who experiences himself entirely as the person he thinks he is supposed to be."[7]

Ray Bradbury's *Fahrenheit 451* (1953) goes one step farther. Not only is the protagonist Montag initially a robot too, he is also a member of the state apparatus which enforces such prescriptions by destroying the books which might counteract the solicitations of the media. The regime of the novel masks its totalitarianism with a facade of material prosperity. Montag's superior Beatty explains its coming-into-being as a benign process of inevitable development, everything being justified on the utilitarian grounds of the majority's happiness: "technology, mass exploitation, and minority pressure carried the trick, thank God." A levelling-down is presented as a triumph of technological know-how and of system; above all it was a spontaneous transformation of society not a dictatorial imposition ("it didn't come from the Government down").[8] Bradbury's description of the media draws on *Brave New World* as confirmed by postwar developments in television. Observing the latter boom in America, Huxley commented: "In *Brave New World* non-stop distractions of the most fascinating nature . . . are deliberately used as instruments of policy, for the purpose of preventing people from paying too much attention to the realities of the social and political situation." He continues in terms directly relevant to the world of Bradbury's novel: "A society, most of whose members spend a great deal of their time . . . in the irrelevant other worlds of sport and soap opera . . . will find it hard to resist the encroachments of those who would manipulate and control it."[9] Where Beatty minimizes the firemen's role as benevolent guardians of the status quo, Huxley refuses such a tendentiously spontaneous account in order to pinpoint political purpose.

The result of this process in *Fahrenheit 451* is a consumer culture completely divorced from political awareness. An aural refrain running through the novel is the din of passing bombers which has simply become background noise. This suggests a total separation of political action from everyday social life and correspondingly when Montag's wife Millie and her friends agree to "talk politics" the discussion revolves entirely around the names and appearances of the figures concerned. In other words the latter have become images within a culture dominated by television. "The Fireman" (the first version of *Fahrenheit 451*) summarizes the typical programmes as follows:

> . . . there on the screen was a man selling orange soda pop and a woman drinking it with a smile; how could she drink and smile simultaneously? A real stunt! Following this, a demonstration of how to bake a certain new cake, followed by a rather dreary domestic comedy, a news analysis that did not analyze anything

and did not mention the war, even though the house was shaking constantly with the flight of new jets from four directions, and an intolerable quiz show naming state capitals.[10]

The very tempo of this list, a rapid sequence of short items, has been explained by Beatty as economy ("the centrifuge flings off all unnecessary, time-wasting thought") but the discourse of production has now become contradictory as it has been displaced onto consumption. If commercial efficiency notionally releases workers to enjoy new leisure opportunities, the aim of the new media is to fill that leisure time not to economize on it.

The novel significantly magnifies the references to TV which occur in "The Fireman" on to a larger scale. Montag's living room has become a 3-D televisual environment for his wife who dreams of adding a fourth wall-screen so that the house will seem no longer theirs but "exotic people's." One of Montag's earliest realizations in the novel is that his house is exactly like thousands of others. Identical and therefore capable of substitution, it can never be his own. That is why the clichéd designation by the media of Millie as "homemaker" is so absurdly ironic because at the very moment when the television is promoting one role it is also feeding her with desires which push in the opposite direction, ultimately inviting her to identify with another place preferable to her more mundane present house. *Fahrenheit 451* dramatizes the effects of the media as substitutions. Millie finds an ersatz intimacy with the "family" on the screen which contrasts markedly with her relation to Montag. Again and again the dark space of their bedroom is stressed, its coldness and silence; whereas Millie's favourite soap operas keep up a constant hubbub and medley of bright colours.

Millie and her friends are defined entirely by their roles as consumers, whether of sedatives, soap-operas, or fast cars. Bradbury anticipates Marshall McLuhan by presenting the media which stimulate this consumption as extensions of faculties (the thimble anticipations of Walkmans) or their substitutes (the toaster has hands to save her the trouble of touching the bread). A bizarre passage Bradbury planned to include in the novel pushes the dehumanizing effects of the media to Gothic extremes:

> They sat in the room with the little electronic vampires feeding silently at their throats, touching at their jugulars with great secretness. Their faces were masked over with black velvet, and their bodies were draped in such a way as not to prove whether man or woman sat there beneath. And the hands were gloved with thickened, sexless material, and only the faintest gleam showed in the slits of their eyes, in the half dark twilight room.

Here dress performs a near total erasure of feature and even gender, replacing skin with an insulating patina. Bradbury's application of the vampire myth stresses loss of vitality whereas Marshall McLuhan draws on the story of Narcissus: "This extension of himself by mirror numbed his perceptions until he became the servomechanism of his own extended or repeated image."[11] The result in both cases is immobility and the creation of a closed system between the individual and technology which, in the Bradbury passage quoted above, drains off the sociability of the gathering described. Mildred's house combines all the electronic gadgetry associated with the fifties "good life." But these things have a cost. Bradbury further anticipates McLuhan in rendering television as an aggressive medium: "Music bombarded him at such an immense volume that his bones were almost shaken from his tendons," and then, as it quietens down, "you had the impression that someone had turned on a washing-machine or sucked you up in a gigantic vacuum."[12] The experience of one consumable can only be understood through comparison with another, and here the individual is put into a posture of maximum passivity as subjected to machines, not their controller. McLuhan explains the television in far more positive terms, but still ones which partly echo Bradbury's. Thus "with TV, the viewer is the screen. He is bombarded with light impulses." And because TV is no good for background it makes more demands on the viewer than does radio: "Because the low definition of TV insures a high degree of audience involvement, the most effective programs are those that present situations which consist of some process to be completed."[13] Bradbury burlesques this notion of audience participation as no more than an electronic trick whereby an individual's name can be inserted into a gap in the announcer's script (and even his lip-movements adjusted).

The media in Bradbury's novel then induce a kind of narcosis. There is both a continuity and an analogy between Millie watching the wall-screens and then taking sleeping pills. Similarly in *Brave New World* the opiate some has become the religion of the people. Huxley subsequently explained that "the soma habit was not a private vice; it was a political institution."[14] Bradbury's emphasis on the consumer end of the cycle of production was shared by, for example, Ann Warren Griffith whose 1953 story "Captive Audience" portrays an America dominated by the Master Ventriloquism Corporation which specializes in placing aural advertisements in consumables. The Corporation's influence on Congress and the Supreme Court has been so successful that any resistance to their sales techniques has been declared illegal.[15] The Writer who most successfully dramatized the political power of business combines in this period was however Frederik Pohl. His collaboration with Cyril Kornbluth, *The Space Merchants* (1953), rewrites the Cold War across a commercial grid. The world has been almost taken over by a massive American-based multinational named Schocken Associ-

ates which is locked into a struggle with its main rival, not only for the world market but also to develop Venus commercially. Working against Schocken is an organization of subversive Conservationists known as "Consies." Mitchell Courtenay functions happily as an advertising executive within Schocken until a complex series of events displace him into the alien contexts at the opposite extremes of the social spectrum, so that he experiences a series of discoveries about the nature of manual labour and consumerism. It is the impetus of the plot itself which carries Courtenay towards social awareness and therefore towards disenchantment with his company, whereas we shall see that Montag's flight from his culture is more willed.

The essential trigger to that flight is supplied by an alienation not only from suburban monotony but also from Montag's consumer-wife. He contemplates her as if she has ceased to be a human being: ". . . he saw her without opening his eyes, her hair burnt by chemicals to a brittle straw, her eyes with a kind of cataract unseen but suspect far behind the pupils, the reddened pouting lips, the body as thin as a praying mantis from dieting, and her flesh like white bacon."[16] Millie here fragments into disparate features transformed by dye, cosmetics or dieting. Instead of being the consumer she is now consumed by commercially induced processes. The passage points backwards to an original state which is no longer recoverable and in that respect the images approach the free-floating state of simulation described by Jean Baudrillard. In the contemporary phase of capitalism, he argues, abstraction and simulation now involve the "generation by models of a real without origin or reality: a hyperreal." Signs now become substitutions for the real, at their most extreme bearing no relation to any reality. It is the penultimate phase of the image or sign, however, which best glosses Bradbury's novel, namely when the image "masks the *absence* of a basic reality" (Baudrillard's emphasis).[17] The adjective "reddened" only appears to suggest a physical state prior to make-up. Later in the novel when Millie flees from the house without lipstick her mouth is simply "gone," as if the adjective has grotesquely taken over actuality from its referent.

Montag clearly functions as a satirical means for Bradbury to question the impetus of consumerism and passages like the one just quoted estrange Montag from an environment he has been taking for granted. Frederik Pohl likewise exploits estrangement effects in "The Tunnel under the World" (1954). Here the executive-protagonist goes to the office on what seems to be a perfectly normal morning, normal that is until small differences begin to strike him like the fact that he is offered a new brand of cigarettes. Guy Burckhardt's routine, even his sense of reality, has been determined by an accumulation of such details: brand names, consumer objects, and advertising jingles. To his understandable horror Burckhardt discovers that a local company Contro (control?) Chemicals has concealed a massive industrial accident by building a replica of his town and has even housed the brains of the few survivors—Burckhardt's included—in anthropoid robots. The story in other words presents a grim parable of the extent to which commerce can construct the consumer's reality, appropriately reflecting Kingsley Amis's claim that Pohl's characteristic work is the "satirical utopia."[18]

Where Pohl briefly surveys the control of a whole environment Bradbury sets up contrasts between different kinds of social space in *Fahrenheit 451,* particularly between interiors and exteriors. A 1951 short story, **"The Pedestrian,"** anticipates these themes and describes a point of transition just before the uniformity of the novel is finally established. The subject is simple: a pedestrian is arrested for walking the streets at night. The opening paragraph introduces an iterative account of what the protagonist has been doing for ten years:

> To enter out into that silence that was the city at eight o'clock of a misty evening in November, to put your feet upon that buckling concrete walk, step over grassy seams and make your way, hands in pockets, through the silences, that was what Mr. Leonard Mead most dearly loved to do. He would stand upon the corner of an intersection and peer down long moonlit avenues of sidewalk in four directions, deciding which way to go, but it really made no difference; he was alone in this world of 2053 A.D. . . .[19]

Bradbury's infinitives and then his use of the hypothetical second person draw the reader into a pattern of action which turns out to be a rhetorical cul-de-sac because Mead, it transpires, is the last of his line pursuing a habit which has become obsolete. The unusual opening phrase destabilizes our distinction between interior and exterior space and the description then draws on post-romantic survival narratives like Mary Shelley's *The Last Man* to suggest an ultimate state of isolation. But Mead stands in ironic proximity to a new species of citizens who, in anticipation of Millie, fill their leisure time watching television. Even the police car which arrests Mead (since there are no officers inside it is literally the car which does the arresting) is the last of its line since there is no longer any urban crime, and the story concludes with Mead being taken away to the "Psychiatric Center for Research On Regressive Tendencies," thereby signalling the demise of a social possibility. When Bradbury worked this story into his novel it became part of the regime's past, helping to explain why in *Fahrenheit 451,* the nocturnal streets are either deserted or used as improvised race tracks.

It is of course a truism that the dystopias of the fifties base themselves on the premise that dissatisfaction with the prevalent regime will be registered sooner or later by their protagonists. In order to accelerate this process of realization some novelists use catalyst-figures whose role is to function as a productive irritant in the protagonist's consciousness. So Clarisse, the niece it turns out of Leonard Mead, fascinates and disturbs Montag because she seems wilfully to stand outside social norms. Neither child nor woman, she introduces herself as a social misfit ("I'm seventeen and I'm crazy") and challenges Montag to confront awkward questions such as whether he is happy. In Kurt Vonnegut's *Player Piano* (also published temporarily under the title *Utopia 14*) Finnerty also performs the role of misfit. He is an old friend of Paul Proteus but his appalling manners repeatedly disrupt the decorum of the rituals which bond together that novel's managerial elite. Like Montag Proteus envies the apparent freedom of the other: "It was an appalling thought, to be so well-integrated into the machinery of society and history as to be able to move in only one plane, and along one line. Finnerty's arrival was disturbing, for it brought to the surface the doubt that life should be that way. Paul had been thinking of hiring a psychiatrist to make him docile, content with his lot, amiable to all."[20] As in *Brave New World* the factory system once again sets coordinates for the self and Proteus feels himself to be tugged in two directions: On the one hand Finnerty lifts his level of dissatisfaction, on the other a psychiatrist— again a typical detail of the genre—would encourage acquiescence to the regime in the name of "adjustment."

Fahrenheit 451 and *Player Piano* both narrate a dual process of learning and disengagement where the protagonist's field of consciousness supplies the ground of the action, indeed even becomes the central issue within that action. At one point Clarisse declares "this is the age of the disposable tissue," a strategic pun on Bradbury's part which relates directly to Vonnegut's novel also since both writers are describing acts of resistance towards social and economic systems where human beings have become dispensable material. Characters accordingly are grouped oppositionally around the protagonists. Finnerty's niggling influence on Proteus is counter-balanced by those representatives of his managerial group who warn him what he might lose. In *Fahrenheit 451* Clarisse and then later an English professor named Faber stimulate Montag towards overt resistance, whereas Beatty functions as antagonist. From a very early stage in the novel Montag internalizes Beatty's voice as a censorious or punitive force, the voice of the superego resisting taboo thoughts or actions. Every scene where Beatty figures then becomes charged with ambiguity as if he is accusing Montag of crimes. When the latter comes down with a "fever" Beatty visits him without being called, explaining that he could foresee what was going to happen. In a simulation of a doctor's visit Beatty tries to deindividualize Montag's problem as a typical case which will pass. If we visualize Montag being addressed on the one side by Beatty and on the other by Faber like a morality play, although the latter occupies the moral high ground, Beatty represents a far more sinister presence by his uncanny knack of predicting what Montag will think. Francois Truffaut described the action as "une forme de lutte contre l'autorité" and Montag must kill Beatty as the personification of that authority however euphemistically the latter presents his power.[21]

The key progression in this process is a shift from the latent to the overt, from the implicit to the explicit. Montag discovers an inner voice which he has been suppressing and his previously unified self fractures into dissociations of mind from body and limb from limb: "His hands had been infected, and soon it would be his arms. He could feel the poison work up his wrists and into his elbows and his shoulders, and then the hump-over from shoulder-blade to shoulder-blade like a spark leaping a gap. His hands were ravenous. And his eyes were beginning to feel hunger. . . ."[22] The metaphor of poison encodes Montag's dissidence within the ideology of a regime devoted to maintaining the so-called health of the body politic; but the displaced hunger of his other limbs suggests a desire that will take him out of that dominant ideology. We can see from this passage how the issue of authority pervades the very style of the novel. In his 1968 article **"Death Warmed Over"** Bradbury mounts a spirited defence of classic horror movies and fantasy fiction by contrasting two broad artistic methods: the accumulation of fact and the use of symbolism. He condemns the former as being appropriate to another discipline altogether: "We have fallen into the hands of the scientists, the reality people, the data collectors." And he goes on to propose selective resonance as an alternative. "The symbolic acts, not the minuscule details of the act, are everything."[23] Retrospectively this article helps to explain the method of *Fahrenheit 451* which, like the other dystopias of the period, uses the dissatisfaction of one individual to reflect on the general inadequacies of a regime perceived as in some sense totalitarian. This dissatisfaction is articulated through an intricate series of symbols and images which support the action at every point. The repeated syntagmatic metaphors always run counter to the fixity and therefore the values of the official discourse of the state.

The most prominent example of such symbolism occurs in the references to fire. Donald Watt has argued that "burning as constructive energy, and burning as apocalyptic catastrophe, are the symbolic poles of Bradbury's novel" and certainly the antithesis of extremes could not be stronger between fire as destructive and fire as transforming or life-giving.[24] The range of signification is introduced in the astonishing first paragraph of the novel:

IT WAS A PLEASURE TO BURN.

It was a special pleasure to see things eaten, to see things blackened and *changed*. With the brass nozzle in his fists, with this great python spitting its venomous kerosene upon the world, the blood pounded in his head, and his hands were the hands of some amazing conductor playing all the symphonies of blazing and burning to bring down the tatters and charcoal ruins of history. With his symbolic helmet numbered 451 on his stolid head, and his eyes all orange flame with the thought of what came next, he flicked the igniter and the house jumped up in a gorging fire that burned the evening sky red and yellow and black.

The opening sentence leaves an ambiguity about how active the verb is, suggesting at once an intransitive state which looks forward to Montag's "fever" of disobedience, and also suggesting an absent object. Although we know that Montag is a fireman the description shifts voice to place him in the position of a spectator rather than an agent. The true object of "burn" is deferred until Part III of the novel where Montag destroys first his house and then Beatty. Already the political theme of the regime's attempted erasure of the past has been established and also the quasi-sexual intoxication of power. The latter implication came out more strongly in Bradbury's original version of the passage where the third sentence read: "With his symbolic number 451 on his earnest head, with his eyes all orange fire with the very thought of what was to come, he let the boa-constrictor, the pulsing fire-hose in his fists spray the highly incandescent fluid upon the flanks of the ancient building."[25] Here sex and work have become more firmly identified in a depiction of orgasmic destruction and the passage (in either version) articulates a preliminary state of mind where Montag is totally engrossed by his work. Questioning comes later.

Symbolism of course is historically determined and vulnerable to political manipulations and fire symbolism is no exception. On the night of 10 May, 1993 Nazi followers destroyed piles of books in German university towns. As the flames rose in the square opposite the University of Berlin the Propaganda Minister Dr. Goebbels praised the gathered throng for ending the "age of extreme jewish intellectualism" and ushering in the new German era: "From these ashes there will rise the phoenix of a new spirit . . . The past is lying in flames. The future will rise from the flames within our own hearts."[26] The equivalent of such utterances in Bradbury's novel are slogan-like statements by Beatty ("fire is bright and fire is clean") but the symbolism has become even more rigidly codified in the uniforms and equipment of the firemen. It would be wrong to suggest any direct application by Bradbury of such historical occurrences because his novel does not explicitly identify the country being described. On the other hand, like Mordecai Roshwald in *Level 7*, he positions the reader so as to be able to infer connections with the

USA. In a retrospective article on the novel Bradbury comments on the Nazi book-burning: "when Hitler burned a book I felt it as keeply, please forgive me, as his killing a human, for in the long sum of history they are one and the same flesh."[27] And he has since confirmed that the main burnings he had in mind were those which took place in Soviet Russia and Nazi Germany, adding: "fortunately, nothing of the sort in the United States. Minor altercations with town censors, mayors, politicians, which have all blown away in the wind."[28] In fact the situation in the United States was serious enough for the American Library Association to issue a manifesto in 1953, the same year as Bradbury's novel, which proclaimed that "the freedom to read is essential to our democracy" and which set out to protect exactly those rights which have disappeared in *Fahrenheit 451*:

> Private groups and public authorities in various parts of the country are working to remove books from sale, to censor textbooks, to label "controversial" books, to distribute lists of "objectionable" books or authors and to purge libraries. These actions apparently rise from a view that our national tradition of free expression is no longer valid; that censorship and suppression are needed to avoid the subversion of politics and the corruption of morals.[29]

The document rails against the encroaching power of officialdom to prescribe taste which the "firemen" are doing without any constraint.

The state control of the printed word has been a major concern in modern dystopias. Yevgeny Zamyatin's *We* describes the use of the *Gazette of the One State* to induce the individual's subservience to collective civic purposes ("the beauty of a mechanism lies in that which is undeviating and exact").[30] *Brave New World* polarises literary expression between the minimal expressive needs of the present and the library of "pornographic old books" locked away in the safe of the Controller, himself a precursor of Beatty. And *Nineteen Eighty-Four* collapses together "every conceivable kind of information, instruction, or entertainment" in the Records Department of the Ministry of Truth so that newspapers, text books, and novels all function on the same level of representation.[31] In these three classic dystopias the state reduces printed output to a utilitarian minimum, whether in the name of political efficiency or the supposed happiness of the greatest number. By depicting a regime where *all* books are banned, however, Bradbury implicates the reader from the very start in illegality, in an oppositional relation to the regime. Automatically then Montag's resistance becomes privileged as he learns to cherish books, as he appropriates the official fire-symbolism to his own purposes (reading it as suggestive of renewal), and most importantly as he gradually refuses the state separation of books from humans. One draft for the novel has Be-

atty describe the destruction of the former as an execution ("Books are dinosaurs, they were dying anyway. We just gave them the bullet behind the ear"), whereas Bradbury has summed up the novel as revolving round a "book-burner who suddenly discovers that books are flesh and blood."[32] What Bradbury draws our attention to here is the insistent series of humanizing metaphors in his novel which revitalise books and which prevent them from being regarded as inanimate objects.

The last part of *Fahrenheit 451* traces out the consequences of Montag's estrangement from his society. His physical flight expresses in terms of action a disengagement which has already taken place in his mind. Here again Bradbury is following a generic pattern. We have already noted the displacement of the protagonist in *The Space Merchants*. Vonnegut's Paul Proteus also has to transgress the boundaries of his city Ilium which have been erected to separate personnel from machines, managerial elite from workers. Where Proteus crosses a literal and metaphorical bridge between these domains Montag undergoes a rite of passage which involves the death of his old self (spuriously enacted on the TV by the authorities) and rebirth by water (the crossing of a river). Just as the city of Ilium is destroyed in an attempted putsch so Montag's city is laid waste by atomic bombing out of which emerges a strange new beauty: "gouts of shattered concrete and sparkles of torn metal" compose into a "mural hung like a reversed avalanche."[33]

Both Bradbury and Vonnegut refute their regimes' claims of progress by investing a special value in the past. The eponymous object which gives *Player Piano* its title is a historical throwback to an earlier period and is also a machine played by the ghost of a craftsmanship which has become obsolete. Proteus attempts to enact his disillusionment with modern automation by taking possession of an old farmhouse but this solitary gesture proves to be futile. Montag by contrast discovers a whole social group devoted to preserving books through memory, thereby actualising Bradbury's earlier metaphors of books-as-people. Similarly in Walter M. Miller's *A Canticle for Leibowitz* (1959) a surviving remnant from a nuclear holocaust preserves the few surviving books through "book-leggers" who smuggle them to safety or through "memorizers."[34] One critic has complained that the last section of Bradbury's novel is "vague in political detail" but the national references are clear and specific.[35] The hoboes gathered round their campfires and constantly moving on to avoid a threatening state authority recall the unemployed transients of the Depression (even the rusting railway line strengthens this echo). And the leader of the campers is named after the Granger Movement which flourished in the USA in the late 1860s and 1870s. This movement made a collective protest against the encroachments of large-scale capitalism and asserted the values of the local agrarian community. Its Declaration of Purposes asserted the aim "to labor for the good of our Order, our Country, and mankind"; and the movement set up reading pro-grammes for farming families among other measures.[36] Although Montag rediscovers the communal space of the campsite and although the campers do possess contemporary technology, all the appeal of place and community lies in its appeal to the past. Personal memory and collective history blur together as the novel concludes with an attempted exercise in radical conservation which plays on the reader's own historical memory of a lost agrarian past.

Concluding her 1957 survey of utopian thought from the Enlightenment through romantic despair and Christian fatalism Judith N. Shklar pronounces what is in effect an obituary on the very notion of utopia: ". . . radicalism in general has gone totally out of fashion. Radicalism is not the readiness to indulge in revolutionary violence; it is the belief that people can control and improve themselves and, collectively, their social environment. Without this minimum of utopian faith no radicalism is meaningful."[37] While it is certainly true that fifties dystopias situate their protagonists in relation to regimes which have apparently concentrated power on a massive scale, the result is by no means simple acquiescence. These are works with as it were a double gaze on the reader's present and on the hypothetical future. As Vonnegut declares in his foreword to *Player Piano*, "this book is not a book about what is, but a book about what could be." The direction taken by social change is repeatedly depicted as an erasure of the known and it is here that a polemical edge emerges in the dystopias.

Notes

1. Aldous Huxley, *Brave New World Revisited* (1958; rept. New York: Harper and Row, 1965), 4.

2. William H. Whyte, *The Organization Man* (1956: rept. Harmondsworth: Penguin, 1960), 33. The term "belongingness" was first used in the 1930s by the behavioural psychologist E. L. Thorndike. Its earliest postwar citations by the *O.E.D.* are by David Riesman (a contribution to A. W. Loos's *Religious Faith and World Culture,* 1951) and Whyte's *Invisible Man.*

3. Walter M. Miller, Jr., *Conditionally Human* (1962; rept. London: Science Fiction Book Club, 1964), 8.

4. Mordecai Roshwald. "Quo Vadis, America?" *Modern Age,* 2.ii (1958), 195, 198.

5. Roshwald, letter of 1988, quoted in H. Bruce Franklin, "Afterword," *Level 7,* by Mordecai Roshwald (Chicago: Chicago Review Press, 1989), 190. This edition corrects errors which appeared in the original 1959 edition of the novel.

6. Letter from Mordecai Roshwald, 29 April, 1993. I have discussed these themes in greater detail in "Push-Button Holocaust: Mordecai Roshwald's *Level 7,*" *Foundation,* 57 (Spring 1993), 68-86.

7. Eric Fromm, *The Sane Society* (London: Routledge and Kegan Paul, 1956), 16.

8. Ray Bradbury, *Fahrenheit 451* (1953: rept. London: Rupert Hart-Davis, 1967), 81.

9. Huxley, 37.

10. Bradbury, "The Fireman," *Galaxy Science Fiction,* (Feb. 1953), 33.

11. *Fahrenheit 451* papers, California State University, Fullerton, second folder, unnumbered 1953; Marshall *McLuhan, Understanding Media: The Extensions of Man* (London: Routledge and Kegan Paul, 1964), 41.

12. Bradbury *Fahrenheit 451,* 46, 47.

13. McLuhan, 313, 319.

14. Huxley, 69.

15. This story is collected in Martin Harry Greenberg and Joseph D. Olander, eds., *Tomorrow, Inc.: S.F. Stories about Big Business* (London: Robson, 1977), 67-79.

16. Bradbury, *Fahrenheit 451,* 49.

17. Jean Baudrillard, *Selected Writings,* ed. Mark Poster (Stamford: Stamford University Press, 1988), 166, 170.

18. Kingsley Amis, *New Maps of Hell* (London), 119. Relevant critical commentary on this aspect of Pohl's work is also given by R. Jeff Brooks. "The Dystopian American Futures of Frederick Pohl," *Journal of the American Studies Association of Texas,* 4 (1973), 55-64.

19. Bradbury, *The Golden Apples of the Sun* (1953: rept. St. Albans: Granada, 1981), 9. "The Fireman" dates its narrative similarly at 2051.

20. Kurt Vonnegut, *Player Piano* (1952; rept. St. Albans: Granada, 1977), 38.

21. Anne Gillain, *Le Cinéma selon Francois Truffaut* (Paris: Flammarion, 1988), 176.

22. Bradbury, *Fahrenheit 451,* 43.

23. Bradbury, "Death Warmed Over," *Playboy,* (Jan. 1968), 252.

24. Donald Watt, "*Fahrenheit 451* as Symbolic Dystopia," in M. H. Greenberg and Joseph D. Olander, eds., *Ray Bradbury* (Edinburgh: Paul Harris, 1980), 196.

25. *Fahrenheit 451* papers, second folder.

26. Jeremy Noakes and Geoffrey Pridham, eds., *Documents on Nazism, 1919-1945* (London: Jonathan Cape, 1974), 345.

27. Bradbury, "At What Temperature Do Books Burn?" *The Writer,* 80 (July 1967), 19.

28. Letter from Ray Bradbury, 2 Sept. 1992.

29. *The Freedom to Read* (Chicago: American Library Association, 1953), 1, 4.

30. Yevgeny Zamyatin, *We,* transl. Bernard Gilbert Guerney (1970; rept. Harmondsworth: Penguin, 1980), 173.

31. George Orwell, *Nineteen Eighty-Four,* corrected ed. (1987; rept. Harmondsworth: Penguin, 1989), 45.

32. *Fahrenheit 451* papers, second folder; Bradbury "At What Temperature Do Books Burn?", 20.

33. Bradbury, *Fahrenheit 451,* 153.

34. Miller's application of Bradbury's notion is also presented as a kind of revival, this time of the Church's lost role as guardian of literacy. The purpose is likewise one of preservation: "The project, aimed at saving a small remnant of human culture from the remnant of humanity who wanted it destroyed, was then underway": Walter M. Miller, Jr., *A Canticle for Leibowitz* (1959; rept. London: Weidenfeld and Nicolson, 1984), 74.

35. Watt, 213.

36. Solon Justus Buck, *The Granger Movement* (Cambridge, Mass.: Harvard University Press, 1933), 64.

37. Judith N. Shklar, *After Utopia: The Decline of Political Faith* (1957; rept. Princeton: Princeton University Press, 1969), 219.

Kevin Hoskinson (essay date winter 1995)

SOURCE: Hoskinson, Kevin. "*The Martian Chronicles* and *Fahrenheit 451*: Ray Bradbury's Cold War Novels." *Extrapolation* 36, no. 4 (winter 1995): 345-59.

[*In the following essay, Hoskinson suggests that both* Fahrenheit 451 *and* The Martian Chronicles *are enhanced when read as complementary works.*]

In a discussion about the thematic content of *The Martian Chronicles* with interviewer David Mogen in 1980, Ray Bradbury stated, "*The Martian Chronicles* and *Fahrenheit 451* come from the same period in my life, when I was warning people. I was *preventing futures*" (83). In this pairing of the two books, Bradbury suggests a deep kinship between the pieces and indicates the probability that they are more than just successive novels in his overall body of work.[1] Though the two fictions are usually read as separate entities, if read as complementary works, they provide a more comprehensive view of a larger whole. As consecutive arrivals in Bradbury's postwar publications, and in their mutual attraction to similar major themes of the cold war era, *The Martian Chronicles* and *Fahrenheit 451* distinguish themselves as Bradbury's "cold war novels."

The two works are on the surface entirely different kinds of fiction. *The Martian Chronicles* is a collection of twenty-six chapters (most originally published as short stories), written between 1944 and 1950 and linked primarily by their setting on the planet Mars between the years 1999 and 2026. Since many of the stories were separately conceived, most of the characters in the finished book are contained within their initial tales and do not cross over into other chapters. And though Mars itself is in many ways the centerpiece of the book, and its treatment by the humans is "chronicled" over a twenty-seven-year period, there is no "protagonist" in the pure sense of the term, nor is there a "plot" common to the separate sections. In contrast, *Fahrenheit 451* is structured as a novel, divided into three chapters; it is set on Earth; it is the story of one central protagonist, Guy Montag; and the plot of the novel—Montag's liberation from Captain Beatty and his acceptance of a new purpose in a new civilization—is carefully mapped out.

These surface differences of structure, character, and setting notwithstanding, *The Martian Chronicles* and *Fahrenheit 451* share a distinction as "cold war fiction" because in them, much more deliberately than in earlier or later publications, Bradbury deals with subjects and issues that were shaped by the political climate of the United States in the decade immediately following World War II.[2] A number of significant events during these years transformed the character of America from a supremely confident, Nazi-demolishing world leader to a country with deep insecurities, one suddenly suspicious and vigilant of Communist activity within its citizenry. First, Joseph Stalin's immediate and unchecked occupation of Eastern European countries at the close of World War II left many Americans wondering if the United States and the Roosevelt administration hadn't foolishly misjudged Soviet intentions at the Yalta Conference in 1945. Second, the Soviet Union's subsequent acquisition of atomic weapons technology by 1949 would reinforce this position; it would also end the U.S. monopoly on thermonuclear weapons and raise questions about Communist agents in high-level government positions. Third, Senator Joseph McCarthy's public accusations of Communist activity in the State Department in 1950 (together with the inflammatory tactics of J. Edgar Hoover, the FBI, and a host of other right-wing government agencies) planted seeds of paranoia and subversion in the American culture that would blossom into fear and irrationality throughout the 1950s. As David Halberstam points out, "It was a mean time. The nation was ready for witch-hunts" (9). Through his examination of government oppression of the individual, the hazards of an atomic age, recivilization of society, and the divided nature of the "Cold War Man," Ray Bradbury uses *The Martian Chronicles* and *Fahrenheit 451* to expose the "meanness" of the cold war years.

During the Truman years of the early cold war, when the administration attempted to reverse the image of the Democratic party as being "soft" on communism, the U.S. government attempted to silence individuals who were thought to be "potentially disloyal" through various offices such as the Justice Department and the Loyalty Review Board. Truman himself released a press statement in July 1950 that granted authority over national security matters to the FBI. The statement expressed grave concern over "the Godless Communist Cause" and further warned that "it is important to learn to know the enemies of the American way of life" (Theoharis 141-42). For Bradbury, such government-supported conformism amounted to censorship and ultimately led to the fostering of what William F. Touponce labels "mass culture" (46) and what Kingsley Amis calls "conformist hell" (110). We see Bradbury's strong distrust of "majority-held" views and official doctrine positions in several places in *The Martian Chronicles*; these areas of distrust, moreover, recur in *Fahrenheit 451*.

In the seventh chapter of *Chronicles*, "**—And the Moon Be Still as Bright**" (originally published in 1948), the fierceness of the individual and the official will of the majority clash violently in the persons of Jeff Spender and Captain Wilder. Spender is a crewman on the Fourth Expedition to Mars who feels a sense of moral outrage at the behavior of his fellow crewmen upon landing. While Biggs, Parkhill, and others break out the liquor and throw a party upon their successful mission, Spender is revolted at their dancing and their harmonica playing on the Martian landscape and at Biggs's throwing of wine bottles into canals and vomiting on the tiled city floors. Spender marvels at Martian literature and ancient art forms, and he views the others' actions as sacrilegious, lamenting that "We Earth Men have a talent for ruining big, beautiful things" (73). Like Spender, Captain Wilder also perceives the beauty of the cities; but as the officer of the crew, he does not allow his sympathies with Spender to override his need as commander in chief to preserve authoritative control of the mission. He doles out a perfunctory fifty-dollar fine to Spender for punching Biggs and orders Spender to "go back [to the party] and play happy" (74); later, following Spender's desertion and mutinous killing of several crewmen, Wilder acknowledges that he has "too much earth blood" to accept Spender's invitation to stay on Mars without the others (88).[3] Wilder is convinced by this time that he must stop Spender, but he is tormented by an uncertainty over whether he is stopping him because he believes Spender is wrong or whether he simply lacks Spender's individual conviction to lash out against the will of the majority: "I hate this feeling of thinking I'm doing right when I'm not really certain I am. Who are we, anyway? The majority? Is that the answer? . . . What is the majority and who are in it? And what do they think and

how did they get this way and will they ever change and how the devil did I get caught in this rotten majority? I don't feel comfortable" (90). In order to preclude the disintegration of the mission, Wilder shoots Spender before Spender can kill anyone else. But the issue of individuality vs. conformity that has been raised by Spender's mutiny has not been resolved for the captain. The next day, Wilder knocks out Parkhill's teeth after Parkhill has shot out the windows of some of the buildings in a dead city. Wilder here releases his inner rage at his own ambivalent compliance with a "government finger point[ing] from four-color posters" described in the book's next chapter, "The Settlers" (94). On the one hand, he has eliminated the disruptive presence of an outlaw; on the other hand, in so doing he has taken the Official Position and removed from the expedition the value of "the most renegade of Bradbury's frontiersmen" (Mogen 85) as well as the one other individual who valued art and creative expression.

Bradbury picks up this theme of distrust for the officially endorsed view again in "**Usher II,**" the seventeenth chapter of *Chronicles* (originally published in 1950 prior to the publication of the full book). In this chapter William Stendahl designs a replica of Edgar Allan Poe's House of Usher on Mars. The intent is twofold: to pay tribute to Poe and "to teach [the Clean-Minded people a fine lesson for what [they] did to Mr. Poe on Earth" (135), which was to burn his works (along with the works of others who wrote "tales of the future") in the Great Fire of 1975. Here again Bradbury rejects the will of the majority through Stendahl's speech to Bigelow, the architect of Usher II. Stendahl sermonizes to Bigelow that the Great Fire came about because "there was always a minority afraid of something, and a great majority afraid of the dark, afraid of the future, afraid of the past, afraid of the present, afraid of themselves and shadows of themselves" (134). Another neurosis Bradbury places in Stendahl's litany of fears has roots in the "red scare" policies enacted through McCarthyist tactics in 1950s America: "Afraid of the word 'politics' (which eventually became a synonym for Communism among the more reactionary elements, so I hear, and it was worth your life to use the word!) . . ."[4] Later, at the party Stendahl throws for his invited guests, the Moral Climates people, Stendahl kills all the "majority guests" with different approaches to murders seen in Poe's stories.[5] At the end of the chapter, Stendahl mortars up Moral Climates Investigator Garrett into a brick wall because Garrett "took other people's advice that [Poe's books] needed burning" (147). In contrast with "**—And the Moon Be Still as Bright,**" where the individual is martyred by the majority, the individual in "**Usher II**" enjoys a sinister triumph over the majority.

In *Fahrenheit 451* Bradbury resumes his attack on government-based censorship encountered earlier in

"Usher II." Set on Earth rather than on Mars, this novel follows the metamorphosis of Guy Montag, a fireman (a starter of fires in this future dystopian society) who comes to question and break free of the government that employs him to burn books. The novel opens with Montag having just returned to the firehouse after igniting another residence, "grinn[ing] the fierce grin of all men singed and driven back by flame" (4). He is clearly of the majority at this point, loyal to his job and proud of wearing the salamander and the phoenix disc, the official insignia of the Firemen of America. But seventeen-year-old Clarisse McClellan, who is dangerous in Beatty's eyes because "she [doesn't] want to know *how* a thing [is] done, but *why*" (60), points out some disturbing facts that Montag cannot escape: he answers her questions quickly without thinking; he can't remember if he knew there was dew on early-morning grass or not; he can't answer the question of whether he is happy or not. A growing unrest with his own lack of individual sensibilities creeps into Montag at Clarisse's challenges. As Donald Watt observes, Clarisse is "catalytic" and "dominant in Montag's growth to awareness" (197); her role for Montag parallels the role of Spender for Captain Wilder, planting the seed of doubt that enacts a process of critical self-examination. These doubts about the government he is serving accumulate through the latest suicide attempt by Montag's wife, Mildred (and her casual acceptance of this attempt after she is resuscitated); through his witnessing of a book-hoarding woman who chose to ignite her own home rather than flee in the face of the firemen's flamethrowers; through the government's systematic elimination of Clarisse; through his own growing need to read and understand books.

Montag ultimately realizes that he cannot return to the firehouse. At this point he rejects both the realm of the majority and his association with Chief Beatty, who professes to "stand against the small tide of those who want to make everyone unhappy with conflicting theory and thought" (62). Montag's liberation from the Firemen of America is augmented when he locates Faber (a former English professor and current member of the book-preserving underground), who offers Montag moral counsel and employs him as an infiltrator at the firehouse. Mildred, in the meantime, breaks her silence and sounds a fire alarm at the Montag residence. In a dramatic confrontation of Individual vs. State, Montag refuses Beatty's orders to burn his own house and instead turns the flamethrower on Beatty. This revolt severs Montag from the majority permanently; he then joins the underground movement to preserve books for the future as global war descends on the city.

Another theme of the cold war years Bradbury takes up in both novels is the precariousness of human existence in an atomic age. The eventual "success" of the Manhattan Project in 1945, which resulted in the development of the atomic bomb, came about only after several years' worth of blind groping toward the right physics equations by some of the brightest physicists in the world.[6] The scientists were literally guessing about how to detonate the bomb, how big to make the bomb, and, most significantly, how strong the bomb would be. The project itself, in the words of Lansing Lamont, was "a bit like trying to manufacture a new automobile with no opportunity to test the engine beforehand" (50). After studying various reports on a wide range of explosions in known history, the Los Alamos physicists determined that the atom bomb's force would fall somewhere in between the volcanic eruption of Krakatau in 1883 (which killed 36,000 people and was heard 3,000 miles away) and the 1917 explosion of the munitions ship *Mont Blanc* in Halifax Harbor, Nova Scotia (killing 1,100)—"hopefully a lot closer to Halifax," Lamont notes, "but just where [the scientists] couldn't be sure" (51-52). The subsequent explosions at Hiroshima and Nagasaki made Americans more "sure" of the bomb's potential but not sure at all about whether the knowledge of its potential was worth the price of having created it in the first place. As a line of military defense against the spread of nazism, the bomb became a prime example of how science unleashed can, according to Gary Wolfe, produce "the alienation of humanity from the very technological environments it has constructed in order to resolve its alienation from the universe" (128).

It is difficult to comprehend the depth to which the atom bomb terrified the world, and America specifically, in the early cold war era. Richard Rhodes, author of the *The Making of the Atomic Bomb*, writes that "A nuclear weapon is in fact a total-death machine, compact and efficient" (746) and quotes a Japanese study that concludes that the explosions at Hiroshima and Nagasaki were "the opening chapter to the annihilation of mankind." More than any single technological development, the atomic bomb made people think seriously about the end of the world. As a passport to Wolfe's icon of the wasteland, the bomb "teaches us that the unknown always remains, ready to reassert itself, to send us back to the beginning" (147).

Bradbury first captures the general sense of anxiety felt in a new atomic age in the fifth chapter of *The Martian Chronicles,* **"The Taxpayer."** This short chapter identifies fear of nuclear war as an impetus for leaving Earth; the chapter also establishes itself as one of several in *Chronicles* that serve as precursors to *Fahrenheit 451* and centralize many of the early cold war themes Bradbury resumes in the second book: "There was going to be a big atomic war on Earth in about two years, and he didn't want to be here when it happened. He and thousands of others like him, if they had any sense, would go to Mars. See if they wouldn't! To get away from wars and censorship and statism and conscription and government control of this and that, of art and science!" (47).

Once the fear-of-nuclear-holocaust theme is introduced in the book, Bradbury structures the story-chapters so that references to the bomb and to atomic war in *Chronicles* are periodically repeated, thus sustaining anxiety throughout the novel. One of Jeff Spender's fears in **"—And the Moon Be Still as Bright,"** for example, is that war on Earth will lead to "atomic research and atom bomb depots on Mars"; he is willing to kill off the members of the Fourth Expedition in order to keep Earth from "flopping their filthy atom bombs up here, fighting for bases to have wars" (84-85). **"The Luggage Store,"** a later bridge chapter that echoes the points made in **"The Taxpayer,"** picks up the theme of atomic war on Earth in the year 2005. In discussing whether or not members of the Earth society transplanted on Mars will return to Earth when the war begins. Father Peregrine explains to the proprietor of the luggage store man's inability to comprehend atomic war from millions of miles away: "[Earth is] so far away it's unbelievable. It's not here. You can't touch it. You can't even see it. All you see is a green light. Two billion people living on that light? Unbelievable! War? We don't hear the explosions" (164). The expanse of the physical distance between Earth and Mars in his dialogue mirrors the uneasy diplomatic distance the United States and the Soviet Union managed to somehow sustain throughout the cold war years, which kept atomic war in the abstract then as well.

In November 2005, however, the Mars inhabitants receive a light-radio message in **"The Watchers"**: "AUSTRALIAN CONTINENT ATOMIZED IN PREMATURE EXPLOSION OF ATOMIC STOCKPILE. LOS ANGELES, LONDON BOMBED. WAR" (180). The resulting picture of Mars—and Earth—for the remaining forty-two pages of the novel is desolate and, for the most part, apocalyptic. Viewers on Mars could point a telescope at Earth and see New York explode, or London "covered with a new kind of fog" (181). Bradbury also employs humor in driving home the gravity of nuclear catastrophe. In one of the novel's more ironic and darkly humorous chapters, **"The Silent Towns,"** Walter Gripp believes himself the only man left on Mars following the wartime emigration back to Earth by most of the planet's inhabitants. Never having found "a quiet and intelligent woman" to marry when Mars was fully inhabited, Walter is shocked by the sound of a ringing phone. On the other end is the voice of Genevieve Selsor. Ecstatic, he arranges to meet her and conjures up a beautiful woman with "long dark hair shaking in the wind" and "lips like red peppermints" (187). When he meets her and sees that she in fact has a "round and thick" face with eyes "like two immense eggs stuck into a white mess of bread dough" (189), he endures a painful evening with her before fleeing for a life of solitary survivalism. Though the chapter provides a moment of levity compared to the ruined civilization chapters that follow and close out the book, the humor in **"The Silent Towns"** is carefully crafted toward nervousness. It is in the vein of comedy Donald Hassler identifies in *Comic Tones in Science Fiction: The Art of Compromise with Nature* that "refuse[s] to be tragic and yet [is] filled with pathos because [it] represents *just* survival" (27). The story's humor serves primarily to deromanticize the last-man-on-earth motif: though atomic war may have made Walter Gripp a master of all he surveys, it has also perpetuated and intensified his isolation.

"There Will Come Soft Rains," the novel's penultimate chapter, restores the tone in *The Martian Chronicles* to grimness, depicting the "tomb planet" character of Mars alluded to one chapter earlier in **"The Long Years"** (193). The "character" in this chapter is an ultramodern home on post-atomic war Earth in 2026, equipped with turn-of-the-twenty-first-century gadgetry. A voice-clock repeats the time of day each minute, and a kitchen ceiling reads off the date. The automatic kitchen cooks breakfast for four; the patio walls open up into bridge tables; the nursery walls glow and animate themselves at children's hour; the beds warm their own sheets; and the tub fills itself with bath water. This technology wastes away mindlessly, however, for "the gods had gone away" (207). This is the wasteland of thermonuclear destruction: the home is "the one house left standing" in a "ruined city" whose "radioactive glow could be seen for miles" (206). The only signs of life (other than the various "small cleaning animals, all rubber and metal") are a dying dog and the evidence of a family vaporized by atomic explosion: "The entire west face of the house was black, save for five places. Here the silhouette in paint of a man mowing a lawn. Here, as in a photograph, a woman bent to pick flowers. Still farther over, their images burned on wood in one titanic instant, a small boy, hands flung into the air; higher up, the image of a thrown ball, and opposite him, a girl, hands raised to catch a ball which never came down." The chapter ends with the house endlessly spinning out its daily mechanical routine to the ghosts of its vaporized inhabitants. It is perhaps the most vivid image Bradbury's cold war novels offer of the synthetic hell man makes for himself from the raw materials of science, technology, and irrationality.

Fahrenheit 451 resumes the examination of precarious existence in an atomic age that Bradbury began in *The Martian Chronicles*. Fire as the omnipotent weapon in *Fahrenheit 451* finds metaphoric parallels in the notion of the bomb as the omnipotent force in the cold war years. The early tests of the Los Alamos project, for example, paid close attention to the extreme temperatures produced by the fissioning and fusioning of critical elements. J. Robert Oppenheimer, Niels Bohr, and Edward Teller based key decisions in the atomic bomb (and later the hydrogen bomb) designs on the core temperatures created at the moment of detonation.[7] Montag and the Firemen of America, likewise, are ever conscious of the key numeral 451 (the temperature at which books burn), so much so that it is printed on their helmets. The linking of hubris with the attainment of power is evident in both the Los Alamos scientists and the Firemen as well. As the Manhattan Project was drawing to a close, the team of physicists who designed the bomb came to exude a high degree of pride in their mastery of science, but without an attendant sense of responsibility. As Lamont explains, the bomb "represented the climax of an intriguing intellectual match between the scientists and the cosmos. The prospect of solving the bomb's cosmic mysteries, of having their calculations proved correct, seemed far more fascinating and important to the scientists than the prospect of their opening an era obsessed by fear and devoted to the control of those very mysteries" (144). *Fahrenheit 451* opens with Montag similarly blinded by his own perceived importance: "He knew that when he returned to the firehouse, he might wink at himself, a minstrel man, burnt-corked, in the mirror. Later, going to sleep, he would feel the fiery smile still gripped by his face muscles, in the dark. It never went away, that smile, it never ever went away, as long as he remembered" (4). Like the engineers of atomic destruction, the engineer of intellectual destruction feels the successful completion of his goals entitles him to a legitimate smugness. The work of the cold war physicists, in retrospect, also shares something else with Montag, which Donald Watt points out: "Montag's destructive burning . . . is blackening, not enlightening; and it poses a threat to nature" (198).

Fahrenheit 451 also expands on the anxiety over the atomic bomb and fear of a nuclear apocalypse introduced in *Chronicles.* In *Fahrenheit,* Beatty endorses the official government position that, as "custodians of our peace of mind" (59), he and Montag should "let [man] forget there is such a thing as war" (61). Once Montag has decided to turn his back on the firehouse, however, he tries conveying his personal sense of outrage to Mildred at being kept ignorant, hoping to incite a similar concern in her: "How in hell did those bombers get up there every single second of our lives! Why doesn't someone want to talk about it! We've started and won two atomic wars since 1990!" (73). Mildred, however, is perfectly uninspired and breaks off the conversation to wait for the White Clown to enter the TV screen. But Montag's unheeded warning becomes reality; the bombs are dropped once Montag meets up with Granger and the book people, just as they became reality in **"There Will Come Soft Rains,"** and Montag's horrific vision of the bomb's shock wave

hitting the building where he imagines Mildred is staying captures a chilling image of his ignorant wife's last instant of life:

> Montag, falling flat, going down, saw or felt, or imagined he saw or felt the walls go dark in Millie's face, heard her screaming, because in the millionth part of time left she saw her own face reflected there, in a mirror instead of a crystal ball, and it was such a wild empty face, all by itself in the room, touching nothing, starved and eating of itself, that at last she recognized it as her own and looked quickly up at the ceiling as it and the entire structure of the hotel blasted down upon her, carrying her with a million pounds of brick, metal, plaster, and wood, to meet other people in the hives below, all on their quick way down to the cellar where the explosion rid itself of them in its own unreasonable way.

> (159-60)

Perhaps Bradbury's own sense of fear at a future that must accommodate atomic weapons had intensified between *The Martian Chronicles*'s publication in 1950 and *Fahrenheit 451*'s completion in 1953; perhaps what David Mogen identified as Bradbury's inspiration for the book, Hitler's book burnings, affords little room for the comic (107). For whatever reasons, unlike *Chronicles,* which intersperses the solemnity of its nuclear aftermath chapters with a bit of lightness in the Walter Gripp story, *Fahrenheit* sustains a serious tone to the end of the book, even in its resurrectionist optimism for the future of the arts.

This optimism for the future—this notion of recivilization—is the thin common element between *The Martian Chronicles* and *Fahrenheit 451* that has early cold war connections. Given such nihilistic phenomena of the cold war era as its tendencies toward censorship, its socially paranoid outlook, and its budding arms race, it may seem a strange period to give rise to any optimism. However, one of the great ironies of the period was a peripheral belief that somehow the presence of nuclear arms would, by their very capacity to bring about ultimate destruction to *all* humans, engender a very special sort of cautiousness and cooperative spirit in the world heretofore not experienced. Perhaps there was a belief that Hiroshima and Nagasaki had taught us a big enough lesson in themselves about nuclear cataclysm that we as humans would rise above our destructive tendencies and live more harmoniously. One very prominent figure who espoused this position was Dr. J. Robert Oppenheimer, the very man who headed the Los Alamos Manhattan Project. Oppenheimer would emerge as one of the most morally intriguing characters of the cold war. He was among the first in the scientific community to encourage restraint, caution, and careful deliberation in all matters regarding the pursuit of atomic energy. "There is only one future of atomic explosives that I can regard with any enthusiasm: that they should never be used in war," he said in a 1949 address before the George Westinghouse Centennial Forum (5). He also refused to participate in the development of the hydrogen bomb following Los Alamos calling such a weapon "the plague of Thebes" (Rhodes 777).[8] In one of his most inspired addresses on the cooperation of art and science, Oppenheimer stated that "Both the man of science and the man of art live always at the edge of mystery, surrounded by it; both always, as the measure of their creation, have had to do with the harmonization of what is new with what is familiar, with the balance between novelty and synthesis, with the struggle to make partial order in total chaos. They can, in their work and in their lives, help themselves, help one another, and help all men" (145).

Such a spirit of hope for renewed goodwill among men of all vocations is the optimistic vein through which society is reenvisioned following the atomic devastation of the Earth in **"The Million-Year Picnic,"** the final chapter of *The Martian Chronicles.* Several days in the past, a rocket that had been hidden on Earth during the Great War carried William and Alice Thomas and their children, Timothy, Michael, and Robert, to Mars, presumably for a "picnic." The father admits to his inquisitive sons on this day, however, that the picnic was a front for an escape from life on Earth, where "people got lost in a mechanical wilderness" and "Wars got bigger and bigger and finally killed Earth" (220-21). The father literally plans a new civilization: he blows up their rocket to avoid discovery by hostile Earthmen; he burns up all the family's printed records of their life on earth; and he now awaits, with his family, "a handful of others who'll land in a few days. Enough to start over. Enough to turn away from all that back on Earth and strike out on a new line" (221). When his son Michael repeats his request to see a "Martian," the father takes his family to the canal and points to their reflections in the water. The book's last line, "The Martians stared back up at them for a long, long silent time from the rippling water" (222), is optimistic without being didactic. It suggests that this new society has in fact already begun, that it is already "making partial order out of total chaos," as Oppenheimer suggests the cold war future needs to do. William F. Touponce believes that it is "an altogether appropriate ending" that "summarizes the experience of the reader, who has seen old illusions and values destroyed only to be replaced with new and vital ones" (38). It also offers an image that invites the reader to extrapolate on the father's vision of "a new line" and trust the will of the colonizers for once.

Bradbury's optimism for a recivilized world is also evident in the conclusion of *Fahrenheit 451.* The seed for an optimistic ending to this dystopian work is actually planted just before the bombs strike. As Montag makes his way across the wilderness, dodging the pursuit of the mechanical hound and the helicopters, he spots the campfire of the book people. His thoughts reflect an epiphany of his transformation from a destroyer of civilization to a builder of it: "[The fire] was not burning. It was *warming.* He saw many hands held to its warmth, hands without arms, hidden in darkness. Above the hands, motionless faces that were only moved and tossed and flickered with firelight. He hadn't known fire could look this way. He had never thought in his life that it could give as well as take" (145-46). This spirit of giving, of creating from the environment, is emphasized throughout the speeches given by Granger, the leader of the book preservers. In his allusion to the phoenix, which resurrects itself from the ashes of its own pyre, Granger's words reflect the new Montag, who can now see the life-sustaining properties of fire as well as its destructive powers; hopefully, Granger's words also contain hope for the American response to Hiroshima and Nagasaki: "we've got one damn thing the phoenix never had. We know the damn silly thing we just did. We know all the damn silly things we've done for a thousand years and as long as we know that and always have it around where we can see it, someday we'll stop making the goddamn funeral pyres and jumping in the middle of them" (163). The book ends with Montag rehearsing in his mind a passage from the Book of Revelation, which he says he'll save for the reading at noon. Peter Sisario sees in this ending "a key to Bradbury's hope that 'the healing of nations' can best come about through a rebirth of man's intellect" (205); Sisario's interpretation of *Fahrenheit*'s ending and Oppenheimer's interpretation of mankind's necessary response to the cold war share a belief in the triumph of the benevolent side of humans.

A fourth theme in Bradbury's cold war novels that has a historical "objective correlative" is the dichotomous nature of the Cold War Man. The Cold War Man is a man antagonized by conflicting allegiances—one to his government, the other to his personal sense of morals and values—who is forced by circumstance to make an ultimate choice between these impulses. This Bradbury character type has roots in cold war political tensions.

During the early cold war years, the United States's international stance frequently wavered between a policy of military supremacy and one of peacetime concessions. One historian notes this phenomenon in the about-face many Americans took toward Theodore Roosevelt's role in the shifting of global powers following World War II: ". . . both policy and attitude changed with the Truman administration. The rationale behind Yalta—that a negotiated agreement with the Soviet Union was possible and that the development of mutual trust was the best means to a just and lasting peace—was now rejected in favor of the containment policy and superior military strength" (Theoharis 70).

These contradictory stances of peace and aggression in our nation's outlook occasionally found expression in the form of a single man during the early cold war. The figure of Dr. J. Robert Oppenheimer again becomes relevant. Though primarily remembered for his contribution to physics, Oppenheimer also had strong leanings toward the humanities; as a youth and in his years as a Harvard undergraduates, he developed a range of literary interests from the Greek classicists to Donne to Omar Khayyam (Lamont 19). David Halberstam observes, "To some he seemed the divided man—part creator of the most dangerous weapon in history—part the romantic innocent searching for some inner spiritual truth" (33). For a government-employed physicist, however, this "division" would turn out to be something of a tragic flaw in the cold war years. When Oppenheimer would have no part of the U.S. government's decision to pursue the hydrogen bomb in its initial phase of the arms race with the Soviets, the government began an inquiry into his past. It was "determined" in June of 1954 that Oppenheimer was guilty of Communist associations that jeopardized national security.[9] He was then stripped of his government security clearance, and his service with the Atomic Energy Commission terminated. Thus, in Oppenheimer was a man whose pacifistic sympathies eventually triumphed over his capacity for aggression—and in the early cold war years he was punished for it.

The Oppenheimer figure finds interesting parallels in Bradbury's cold war novels. In **"—And the Moon Be Still as Bright"** in *The Martian Chronicles,* Spender is torn between the need to serve his Earth-based government (in his participation with the expedition crew on Mars) and the deep personal need to preserve the remains of the native Martian culture, which he believes is threatened by the very kind of expedition he is serving: "When I got up here I felt I was not only free of [Earth's] so-called culture, I felt I was free of their ethics and their customs. I'm out of their frame of reference, I thought. All I have to do is *kill you all off* and *live my own life*" (85; emphasis added). Spender's surrender to the personal impulse to defend Mars from Earth corruption over the impulse to follow the government-entrusted group leads to his death. Wilder is forced to shoot Spender when he threatens more killings, and his death-image symbolically reinforces his divided self: "Spender lay there, his hands clasped, one around the gun, the other around the silver book that glittered in the sun" (92). The gun, which is entrusted to him as a member of the expedition and the book, which he found in his walks through the Martian ruins, emblematize Spender's divided allegiances. The image is curiously akin to the image Lansing Lamont provides of Oppenheimer's dichotomous self: "With balanced equanimity he could minister to a turtle and select the target cities for the first atomic massacres" (285). Wilder also exudes characteristics of the dichotomous Cold

War Man. The captain's sympathies toward the arts and toward Spender's appreciation of them lead him to bury Spender with an aesthetic touch. Finding a Martian sarcophagus, Wilder has the crew "put Spender into a silver case with waxes and wines which were ten thousand years old, his hands folded on his chest" (93). The scene immediately changes from Spender's ornate sarcophagus to the captain's catching Parkhill in one of the dead cities and knocking his teeth out for shooting at the Martian towers. Wilder's coexistent propensity for violence and aesthetic sensibilities mark his dichotomous cold war sides as well. Stendahl in "Usher II" further reflects both sides of this Cold War Man. He possesses the aesthetic appreciation of a literature devotee, a man with an architectural vision of Usher II, specifying to Bigelow the need for colors precisely "desolate and terrible," for walls that are "bleak," for turn that is "black and lurid," for sedge that is "gray and ebon" (132-33). Yet this same man furnishes his home with all of Poe's macabre instruments of death: an ape that strangles humans, a razor-sharp pendulum, a coffin for the nailing up of a live woman, and bricks and mortar for sealing up a live victim.

The dichotomous Cold War Man theme is again treated in *Fahrenheit 451* Both Montag and Beatty are simultaneously capable of the destructive and appreciative of the artistic. As Donald Watt remarks of Montag, "Burning as constructive energy, and burning as apocalyptic catastrophe, are the symbolic poles of Bradbury's novel" (196). Montag's divided self is clearly displayed by Bradbury at moments when his character is being influenced by the intellectually stimulating presences of Clarisse and Faber. Early in the book, when Montag is just beginning to wrestle with his identity as a fireman, Clarisse tells him that being a fireman "just doesn't seem right for you, somehow" (24). Immediately Bradbury tells us that Montag "felt his body divide itself into a hotness and a coldness, a softness and a hardness, a trembling and a not trembling, the two halves grinding one upon the other." Later, after offering his services to Faber and his group, Montag considers the shiftings of his own character that he has been feeling in his conflicting allegiances: "Now he knew that he was two people, that he was, above all, Montag, who knew nothing, who did not even know himself a fool, but only suspected it. And he knew that he was also the old man who talked to him and talked to him as the train was sucked from one end of the night city to the other" (102). Fire Chief Beatty also suggests aspects of the Cold War Man. In spite of his wearing the role of the Official State Majority Leader as the fire chief and relentlessly burning every book at every alarm, Beatty acknowledges that he knows the history of Nicholas Ridley, the man burned at the stake alluded to by the woman who ignites her own home. He gives Montag the reply that most fire captains are "full of bits and pieces" (40); however, when he later warns Montag against succumbing to the "itch" to read that every fireman gets "at least once in his career," he further adds an ambiguous disclosure: "Oh, to *scratch* that itch, eh? Well, Montag, take my word for it, I've had to read a few in my time to know what I was about, and the books say *nothing!* Nothing you can teach or believe" (62). Though Beatty has an alibi for having some knowledge of literature, Bradbury urges us to question just what Beatty may *not* be telling us. Montag's later certainty over Beatty's desire to die at Montag's hands (122) raises even more questions about Beatty's commitment to the destructive half of his duality.

Through *The Martian Chronicles* and *Fahrenheit 451,* Ray Bradbury has created a microcosm of early cold war tensions. Though the reader will perceive a degree of Bradbury's sociopolitical concerns from a reading of either novel, it is only through the reading of both as companion pieces that his full cold war vision emerges. From the perspective that America has wrestled itself free of the extremism of the McCarthyists and, thus far, has escaped nuclear war as well, Bradbury's cold war novels may have indeed contributed to the "prevention" of futures with cold war trappings.

Notes

1. There is a lack of decisiveness among Bradbury scholars as to whether *The Martian Chronicles* is a novel or a collection of short stories with an epicenter of a common world. Much attention has been paid to Bradbury's 1949 encounter with Doubleday Publishing, during which an editor asked Bradbury to piece together his Mars stories and see what happened; no consensus has been reached as to whether the resulting book is a novel or short stories. Mogen describes it both ways, ultimately classifying it in his selected bibliography section of Bradbury's primary sources as a "novel"; Johnson argues for a collection of short stories "adapted and linked together by bridge passages." Bradbury himself has compared the work to Sherwood Anderson's *Winesburg, Ohio,* but he has also called it a novel in other places, suggesting that the distinction is significant only to critics. I prefer the "novel" classification because it seems a more fitting descriptor for a fictional history of Mars than does "short story collection." For a fuller examination of the issue, see Mogen, *Ray Bradbury* 82-93; Johnson, *Ray Bradbury*; and Gallagher, "The Thematic Structure of 'The Martian Chronicles.'"

2. It has been asserted in many places among Bradbury scholarship that the Mars created in *The Martian Chronicles* is in one way or another a metaphor for twentieth-century America. Two of the more clearly articulated views on this belong to McNelly and Pell.

3. "Earth" in Bradbury most often equals "Americans." See Rabkin 115 and Slusser 55.

4. For two enlightening discussions of the subversive tactics employed by many 1950s right-wing government organizations, see Halberstam and Theoharis.

5. This organization is strongly suggestive of the House Committee on Un-American Activities, a group Halberstam maintains "included a large number of the most unattractive men in American public life—bigots, racists, reactionaries, and sheer buffoons" (12).

6. These minds were, ironically, "true science fictionists" in the Bradbury sense. Bradbury said in 1976 that "science fiction deals with any 'idea' which is not yet born, which wants to come to birth." The atomic bomb became an idea wanting birth in 1939 when Hungarian physicist Leo Szilard solicited Albert Einstein's help in drafting a letter to President Roosevelt, advising the president that, since Hitler's Germany had successfully produced atomic fission (under Otto Hahn and Fritz Strassman), it would be wise to establish the necessary research to develop a nuclear defense weapon. Los Alamos was conceived of at that point, and science fiction moved closer to science fact. See Jacobs 19 and Lamont 23-25.

7. In fact, the design of the hydrogen bomb was slowed by William Teller's inaccurate calculations regarding the temperature produced when igniting deuterium. The inaccuracy involved the difference between 40 million and 400 million degrees fahrenheit. See Rhodes 418-20.

8. The explosion of one hydrogen bomb is the equivalent of 500 atomic bombs. See Rhodes 418.

9. The actual conviction was one of "'susceptibility' to influences that could endanger the nation's security." Such vagueness pervades the course of the hearings with Oppenheimer. See Lamont 258-91 and Halberstam 342-54.

Works Cited

Amis, Kingsley. *New Maps of Hell.* London: Lowe and Brydone, 1960.

Bradbury, Ray. *Fahrenheit 451.* New York: Ballantine, 1953.

———. *The Martian Chronicles.* Garden City, NY: Doubleday, 1950.

Gallagher, Edward J. "The Thematic Structure of *The Martian Chronicles.*" In Olander and Greenberg 55-82

Halberstam, David. *The Fifties,* New York: Villard, 1993.

Hassler, Donald. *Comic Tones in Science Fiction: The Art of Compromise with Nature.* Westport, CT: Greenwood, 1982.

Jacobs, Robert. "The Writer's Digest Interview." *The Writer's Digest* 55 (Feb. 1976): 18-25.

Johnson, Wayne L. *Ray Bradbury.* New York: Frederick Ungar, 1980.

Lamont, Lansing. *Day of Trinity.* New York: Atheneum, 1965.

McNelly, Willis E. "Two Views." In Olander and Greenberg 17-24.

Mogen, David. *Ray Bradbury.* Boston: Twayne, 1986.

Olander, Joseph D., and Martin Harry Greenberg, eds. *Ray Bradbury.* New York Taplinger, 1980.

Oppenheimer, J. Robert. *The Open Mind.* New York: Simon and Schuster, 1955.

Pell, Sarah-Warner J. "Style Is the Man: Imagery in Bradbury's Fiction." In Olander and Greenberg 186-94.

Rabkin, Eric S. "To Fairyland by Rocket: Bradbury's *The Martian Chronicles.*" In Olander and Greenberg 110-26.

Rhodes, Richard. *The Making of the Atomic Bomb.* New York: Simon and Schuster 1986.

Sisario, Peter. "A Study of the Allusions in Bradbury's *Fahrenheit 451.*" *English Journal* 59 (1970): 201-05, 212.

Slusser, George Edgar. *The Bradbury Chronicles.* San Bernardino: Borgo Press, 1977.

Theoharis, Athan. *Seeds of Repression: Harry S. Truman and the Origins of McCarthyism.* Chicago: Quadrangle, 1971.

Watt, Donald. "Burning Bright: *Fahrenheit 451* as Symbolic Dystopia." In Olander and Greenberg 195-213.

Wolfe, Gary. *The Known and the Unknown: The Iconography of Science Fiction.* Kent, OH: Kent State UP, 1979.

Rafeeq O. McGiveron (essay date spring 1996)

SOURCE: McGiveron, Rafeeq O. "Bradbury's *Fahrenheit 451.*" *Explicator* 54, no. 3 (spring 1996): 177-80.

[*In the following essay, McGiveron examines Bradbury's use of hands as a symbolic device in* Fahrenheit 451.]

Ray Bradbury's 1953 *Fahrenheit 451* contains a number of interesting stylistic devices. Robert Reilly praises Bradbury for having a style "like a great organ. . . ." (73). David Mogen comments on the novel's "vivid style" (110). Peter Sisario applauds the "subtle depth" of Bradbury's allusions (201), and Donald Watt pursues Bradbury's bipolar "symbolic fire" (197) imagery. In recent articles I discussed Bradbury's use of mirror imagery and nature imagery.

In addition, throughout *Fahrenheit 451* Bradbury uses imagery of hands, making them significant reflectors of conscience. The hands of the misguided are deceptively calm, reflecting the complacency of self-righteousness. At the same time, the hands of the character struggling for right seem to do good almost of their own volition, even before the mind has been consciously decided. Finally, once characters are committed to positive action, their hands become an unambiguous force for good.

As the novel opens, "fireman" Guy Montag joyously goes about his job of burning down a house found to contain books, and Bradbury describes Montag's hands with ironic majesty. According to Bradbury, "his hands were the hands of some amazing conductor playing all the symphonies of blazing and burning to bring down the tatters and charcoal ruins of history" (3). This early in the story Montag does not yet recognize the true destruction of his profession; indeed, he finds it "a pleasure to burn" (3). Montag's conscience is blithely clear—or perhaps pathetically blank—and his self-confident, self-aggrandizing hands are a reflection of this emptiness.

Montag, however, has from time to time been taking books from the forbidden libraries he burns. When we finally witness this. Montag's hands reflect the unacknowledged dictates of conscience:

> Montag's hand closed like a mouth, crushed the book with wild devotion, with an insanity of mindlessness to his chest.
>
> Montag had done nothing. His hand had done it all, his hand with a brain of its own, with a conscience and a curiosity in each trembling finger, had turned thief. Now it plunged the book back under his arm, pressed it light to sweating armpit, rushed out empty. . . .
>
> He gazed, shaken, at that white hand.
>
> (37-8)

His hand, of course, is not possessed by "an insanity of mindlessness." On the contrary, Montag has "a conscience and a curiosity . . ." but, still unwilling to recognize them, he projects them into his hands.

Soon Montag visits Faber, a former literature professor, to try to enlist the old man's help. When Faber initially refuses, Montag holds out a Bible and "lets" his hands shock Faber into action:

> Montag stood there and waited for the next thing to happen. His hands, by themselves, like two men working together, began to rip the pages from the book. The hands tore the flyleaf and then the first and then the second page.
>
> . . . Montag . . . let his hands continue.
>
> (88)

Again Montag's hands express what his consciousness scarcely can recognize. He has no real wish to damage the old Bible, but his conscience apparently understands that Faber's help is even more important.

Once Montag returns to the firehouse, his hands feel restless under the gaze of Fire Captain Beatty, his superior:

> In Beatty's sight, Montag felt the guilt of his hands. His fingers were like ferrets that had done some evil. . . . [T]hese were the hands that had acted on their own, no part of him, here was where the conscience first manifested itself to snatch books. . . .
>
> (105)

Though Montag still has trouble accepting responsibility for breaking away from the thoughtless destruction which had been his way of life, Bradbury significantly uses the word conscience again. Just as his hands first manifested his new *conscience,* now they reflect his nervousness at possible discovery.

Captain Beatty leads the quivering Montag through a series of literary allusions, yet while Montag's hands reflect his precarious mental position, when the mocking Beatty reaches out to check Montag's guiltily racing pulse, his "graceful fingers" (107) reflect a dogged self-righteousness. Bradbury employs such ironic imagery to show that Beatty is still able to possess the kind of clear (or blank) conscience which the nervous Montag fortunately no longer has. Beatty unwittingly may be the novel's best spokesperson against the stifling anti-intellectualism of his society, but he refuses to let any doubts interfere with his work; unlike Montag's, his hands never waver.

Bare minutes after the tense firehouse scene, Beatty forces Montag to burn down his own house. As Beatty berates him and threatens to track down Faber, Montag finds himself "twitch[ing] the safety catch on the flame thrower" (119). Again, Bradbury has the conscience drive the hands onward even before the conscious mind has reasoned out the situation: "Montag . . . himself glanced to his hands to see what new thing they had done. Thinking back later he could never decide whether the hands or Beauty's reaction to the hands gave him the final push toward murder" (119).

Even when Montag finally kills the taunting Beatty, Bradbury displaces him syntactically from the center of the action. Describing Beatty, Bradbury writes, "And then he was a shrieking blaze, a jumping, sprawling, gibbering mannikin, no longer human or known, all writhing flame on the lawn as Montag shot one continuous pulse of liquid fire on him" (119). While Bradbury does identify the actor as Montag rather than as his disembodied hands, the abrupt transformation of Beatty and the placement of Montag toward the end of the sentence emphasize the spontaneity of the action. Should any doubts remain about the correctness of the action of Montag's conscience-driven hands, Bradbury has Montag think moments later in his flight, *"Beatty wanted to die"*; (122). Though Montag would not have killed Beatty willingly, his hands expressed what he consciously understands only later: "[B]urn them or they'll burn you. . . . Right now it's as simple as that" (123).

When Montag escapes into the wilderness and joins a group of book-memorizing intellectuals, his first glimpse of them shows only "many hands held to [the campfire's] warmth, hands without arms. . . ." (145). After several pages of highly didactic conversation with the group's leader. Montag helps put out the campfire: "The men helped, and Montag helped, and there, in the wilderness, the men all moved their hands, putting out the fire together" (154). Certainly putting out the fire is symbolic of stopping society's book burning, but Bradbury's explicit mention of hands seem equally symbolic, for now hands are revealed as an unambiguous force for good.

Montag shows this again when he realizes that the future will "come out our hands and our mouths" (161). Good thus comes not only from thinking and talking but from actually *doing* as well. Bradbury reiterates this important point when Montag thinks, "I'll hold onto the world tight someday" (162); just as hands may carry out deeds of conscience before the mind has fully decided, once the decision has been made, the conscience-driven hands must then follow though.

With his imagery of hands, Bradbury seems to suggest that actions may indeed speak louder than words. It is doubtful that our hands will ever simply reflect the conscience as Montag's so conveniently do, but it is equally doubtless that they should. Though blind self-righteousness may be most comfortable. Bradbury shows that the uncertainty of following one's conscience is morally preferable.

Works Cited

Bradbury, Ray. *Fahrenheit 451.* 1953. New York: Del Ray. 1991.

McGiveron. Rafeeq O. "'Do You Know the Legend of Hercules and Antaeus?' The Wilderness in Ray Bradbury's *Fahrenheit 451.*" Forthcoming in *Extrapolation* 38 (1997).

———. "'To Build a Mirror Factory': The Mirror and Self-Examination in Ray Bradbury's *Fahrenheit 451.* Forthcoming in *Critique.*

Mogen, David. *Ray Bradbury.* Twayne's United States Authors Series 504. Boston: Twayne. 1986.

Reilly, Robert. "The Art of Ray Bradbury." *Extrapolation* 13 (1971): 64-74.

Sisario, Peter. "A Study of the Allusions in Bradbury's *Fahrenheit 451.*" *English Journal* Feb. 1970: 210+.

Watt, Donald. "Burning Bright: *Fahrenheit 451* as Symbolic Dystopia." *Ray Bradbury.* Writers of the 21st Century Series. Ed. Martin Harry Greenberg and Joseph D. Olander. New York: Taplinger, 1980. 195-213.

Rafeeq O. McGiveron (essay date fall 1996)

SOURCE: McGiveron, Rafeeq O. "What 'Carried the Trick'? Mass Exploitation and the Decline of Thought in Ray Bradbury's *Fahrenheit 451.*" *Extrapolation* 37, no. 3 (fall 1996): 245-56.

[*In the following essay, McGiveron argues that mass exploitation, the least discussed cause of censorship in* Fahrenheit 451, *is actually the most important.*]

There is an interesting dichotomy in Ray Bradbury's 1953 *Fahrenheit 451,* a noticeable gap between the message that the author and we the readers receive from the novel and the message that the text actually seems to support. While I realize that some see little use for such old-fashioned attention to the text itself, *Fahrenheit 451* is such an overtly didactic work that it almost invites such examination. Surely even the staunchest reader-response critic would agree that Bradbury is trying to sell the readers on ideas that he has put into his story. Yet there is a discrepancy between the ideas the author is selling—and readers are buying—and the ideas he has let the whole rest of the text support. I suggest this not necessarily to label it as a weakness but to show that the novel is thereby just a little bit richer and probably truer to life than many have supposed.

The discrepancy lies in the book's subtle treatment of the relationship between mass exploitation and the decline of thought. Fire Captain Beatty, the novel's chief book-burner, explains that "technology, mass exploitation, and minority pressure carried the trick" of supplanting independent thought with conformity and leading to censorship (58). Clearly Bradbury wants us to notice these three culprits in his fictional world and to beware of them in our own society as well. Often, however, readers have a tendency to miss the real textual centrality of mass exploitation, focusing instead on the minority pressure that Bradbury makes so much more apparent.

Technology allows for the existence of mass culture in the novel, and minority pressure helps enforce conformity, but the mass exploitation of easy gratification is the fundamental threat to thought, for this exploitation begins earlier than minority pressure, requires the participation of a far greater majority of the population, and has a more direct effect on the decline of thought. In Bradbury's work controllers of mass communication and other producers of entertainment exploit the public's desire for easy gratification by disseminating only mindless escapism, which the exploited willingly consume to the exclusion of independent thought. People grow unwilling to give up their pleasures, even momentarily, by thinking deeply about anything, and they also become unwilling to violate the norms of society by expressing any original thought. Recognizing this role of mass exploitation in the decline of thought is important because the lesson applies both in *Fahrenheit 451* and in the real world as well.

Robert Reilly claims that the novel is "a frightening picture of how the products of science can destroy persons and human values" (67), but this is an unfortunate simplification. Although it helps maintain the conformist mass culture of *Fahrenheit 451,* technology itself does not cause the decline of thought, for people still make the important decisions. Controllers of mass communication and other producers of entertainment decide which ideas they will censor and which they will disseminate, and the public decides what it will enjoy, what it will believe, and how it will act. Fire Captain Beatty contrasts the "pastepudding norm" of modern mass communication with books, which once "appealed to a few people, here, there, everywhere . . . [and] could afford to be different" (54). He is unable, however, to support the idea that technology itself causes people to abandon independent thought in favor of simple conformity. Beatty claims, for example, that when zippers replace buttons "a man lacks just that much time to think while dressing at dawn" (56), yet he avoids the obvious fact that the man is making the decision about what and when to think. Willis E. McNelly is correct when he writes that the novel "is not . . . about the technology of the future" (19), and so is Marvin E. Mengeling, who finds that "Bradbury is no reactionary, antimachine 'nut'" (98).

Faber, the old, former literature professor, explains the primacy of human choice to Guy Montag, the unsettled "fireman" who no longer wants to burn books: "The same infinite detail and awareness [which books have] could be projected through the radios and televisors, but are not" (82). According to Faber, "you can't argue with the four-wall televisor. Why? The televisor is 'real.' It is immediate; it has dimension. It tells you what to think and blasts it in. It *must* be right. It *seems* so right. It rushes you on so quickly to its own conclusions your mind hasn't the time to protest, 'What nonsense!'" (84). Yet despite the fact that Faber, "with all [his] knowledge and skepticism, . . . [has] never been able to argue with a one-hundred piece symphony orchestra, full color, three dimensions, and being in and part of those incredible parlors" (84), he still has a small television he can "blot out with the palm of [his] hand" (132), and so do the book-memorizing intellectuals whom Montag later meets after his flight from the city (147-49). Clearly Bradbury is not simply attacking technology in general or even electronic mass communication in specific. Though technology can be used to brainwash people, Professor Faber and the other intellectuals show that people themselves are responsible for the condition of their own intellects.

Unlike technology, intolerant minority pressure that seeks to stifle ideas instead of arguing against them is a major cause of the decline of independent thought in *Fahrenheit 451.* Walter E. Meyers refers to this when he claims that "the danger to ideas and to their embodiment in books" comes from "a desire not to offend" and from "the unofficial sanctions of the appropriately named 'pressure groups'" (503). My teaching experience with the book suggests to me that this is a very common thing for readers to think. It is easy to see why, for the unity and explicitness of the passage dealing with minority pressure make that pressure the single most noticeable and memorable cause of the decline of thought in the novel.

Beatty explains to Montag that in the past intolerant pressure groups were influential in stifling free expression, fostering the conformity that eventually allowed the government to begin its own censoring:

> Bigger the population, the more minorities. Don't step on the toes of the dog lovers, cat lovers, doctors, lawyers, merchants, chiefs, Mormons, Baptists, Unitarians, second-generation Chinese, Swedes, Italians, Germans, Texans, Brooklynites, Irishmen, people from Oregon or Mexico. The people of this book, this play, this TV serial are not meant to represent any actual painters, cartographers, mechanics anywhere. The bigger your market, Montag, the less you handle controversy, remember that! All the minor minor minorities with their navels to be kept clean. Authors, full of evil thoughts, lock up your typewriters. They *did.* Magazines became a nice blend of vanilla tapioca. Books . . . were dishwater.
>
> (57)

Beatty thus not only directly claims minority pressure as a cause of intellectual self-censorship and conformity but also emphasizes its pervasiveness with his rhetoric, listing fully twenty-one pressure groups organized by ethnicity, religion, geography, occupation, and even pet preference. He shows that from the major to, in the case of dog lovers and cat lovers, the ridiculously "minor minor," each narrow pressure group pares down free expression of individuals' thoughts a little more.

Beatty's reiteration of the idea just over a page later is similar in purpose, although its rhetoric is slightly more restrained. He explains, "You must understand that our civilization is so vast that we can't have our minorities upset and stirred" (59): "Colored people don't like *Little Black Sambo.* Burn it. White people don't feel good about *Uncle Tom's Cabin.* Burn it. Someone's written a book on tobacco and cancer of the lungs? The cigarette people are weeping? Burn the book. Serenity, Montag. Peace, Montag. Take your fight outside. Better yet, into the incinerator" (59). The mesmerizing Beatty again shows how intolerance for opposing ideas helps lead to the stifling of individual expression, and hence of thought.

While it is not actually part of the novel itself, Bradbury's postscript **"Coda"**—which between 1979 and 1982 was called the Afterword—likewise emphasizes the dangers of minority pressure. Commenting on the text, Bradbury claims that "Fire-Captain Beatty . . . describe[s] how the books were burned first by minorities, each ripping a page or a paragraph from this book, then that, until the day came when the books were empty and the minds shut and the libraries closed forever" (177). Here, in the author's own explanation of his work, he reminds readers that the pressure of intolerant minorities is the "first" and presumably most important cause leading to the decline of thought.

Bradbury also repeats Beatty's idea of the dangers of minority pressure in relation to the real world: "There is more than one way to burn a book. And the world is full of people running about with lit matches. Every minority, be it Baptist/Unitarian, Irish/Italian/Octagenarian/Zen Buddhist, Zionist/Seventh-day Adventist, Women's Lib/Republican, Mattachine/Four Square Gospel feels it has the will, the right, the duty to douse the kerosene, light the fuse" (176-77). Like Beatty, he emphasizes the pervasiveness of the problem by defining the pressure groups with ridiculous improbability.

In addition to the evidence of the text itself and of Bradbury's coda, we are more likely to see the dangers of minority pressure in the novel because of the widespread perception that such dangers exist in our own society. In the 1950s readers might have thought of McCarthyism or perhaps the pious efforts to "clean up" comic books. Today adult readers are aware of various pressure groups' campaigns against sexually explicit music, the burning of the American flag, or sex and violence on television. Moreover, the current debate about political correctness also helps shape how we read Bradbury. Awareness of these controversies is certain to make us even more aware of Bradbury's treatment of minority pressure.

The threat of "mass culture" has been recognized by Peter Sisario (201), John Huntington (136), and David Mogen (107-08), and the idea, though not the term, has also been used by Donald Watt (212), Kingsley Amis

(111-12), and Charles F. Hamblen (819). No one, however, has followed up with an investigation of the real importance of mass exploitation, especially in relation to Beatty's overemphasized scapegoat, minority pressure.

Despite the obvious role of intolerant minority pressure in the decline of thought, the text actually shows mass exploitation to be the more serious problem. Whereas Beatty's discussion of minority pressure is explicit and highly coherent, comprising mainly most of a paragraph over half a page long, his discussion of mass exploitation is less explicit and is diluted through eight pages. Yet Beatty himself cites mass exploitation as a problem that began even earlier, and both his exposition and the rest of the text show that mass exploitation requires the participation of a far greater majority of the population and replaces thought with conformity even more directly than does minority pressure.

Mass exploitation in the novel begins long before minority pressure, as soon as technology allows for the development of mass communication and mass culture. According to Beatty, the trends leading up to censorship "really got started around a thing called the Civil War," when modern technology, beginning with photography, enabled communication "to have *mass*" (54). Presumably this metaphorical use of "mass" refers to the greater amount of information carried; whereas earlier oral and printed communication still left much information to the imagination of the audience, photography and, later, moving pictures shifted this "mass" from the audience to the means of communication themselves. Rather than challenge audiences, controllers of communication chose to rely on "mass" to sell, thereby simplifying the ideas being transmitted: "'And because they had mass, they became simpler,' said Beatty. 'Once, books appealed to a few people, here, there, everywhere. They could afford to be different. The world was roomy. But then the world got full of eyes and elbows and mouths. Double, triple, quadruple population. Films and radios, magazines, books leveled down to a sort of pastepudding norm'" (54). Although technology makes this change possible, technology itself is not the cause, as Faber's understanding of technology's capacity for projecting "infinite detail and awareness" (82) indicates. Minority pressure is also not responsible for this reduction of communication to the "paste-pudding norm," for Beatty does not even bother to bring that last problem into the discussion for another three pages. The more important problem is the preexisting mass exploitation of easy gratification.

The responsibility for the decline of thought this exploitation causes belongs to a great majority of the population. Because the damage of minority pressure is caused primarily by intolerant pressure groups and secondarily by the controllers of communication who

follow their wishes, the public is far less responsible; people for the most part may be unaware that pressure groups influence what they watch, hear, and read. Mass exploitation is very much different, however, for it is the result of the public's active desire to avoid controversy and difficult thought in favor of easy gratification and, eventually, intellectual conformity. Beatty tells Montag that the pressure for censorship and the abandonment of thought at first "didn't come from the Government down" (58), and this is especially true of mass exploitation. The disseminators of mindless escapism are to some extent to blame, and the consumers of this escapism are guilty as well.

Bradbury names the exploiters only once. According to Beatty, they are the "publishers, exploiters, broadcasters" who "whirl man's mind around about so fast . . . that the centrifuge flings off all unnecessary, time-wasting thought" (55). Phrased another way, the exploiters are the controllers of mass communication who appeal solely to the public's desire for pleasure. Although Beatty does not say it, the exploiters are also those who design and market the dangerously powerful automobiles and drugs that the society consumes. They are those who encourage the acceptance of, as Granger, the leader of the book-memorizers, says, "dream[s] made or paid for in factories" (157). Knowing that the public prefers easy gratification to difficult contemplation and evaluation, the exploiters "empty the theaters save for clowns and furnish the rooms with glass walls and pretty colors running up and down the walls like confetti or blood or sherry or sauterne" (56). Beatty's imagery here, effective as always, mirrors the triviality, violence, and intoxication of the four-wall televisions. While Beatty explicitly identifies the exploiters only once, their effect on society is apparent throughout the novel.

Although the exploiters bear some responsibility for the decline of thought, the exploited are at least as guilty, for they are willingly exploited. Faber remembers that "the public stopped reading of its own accord" (87) and that when the newspapers died out "no one *wanted* them back. No one missed them" (89). Because he did not speak out when he could have, Faber even considers himself to be guilty as well (82). He explains to Montag that after half a century of the vigorous pursuit of easy gratification, the book-burning firemen are "hardly necessary to keep things in line. So few want to be rebels any more" (87). According to Faber, who paraphrases very closely from Henrik Ibsen's 1882 *An Enemy of the People,* "the most dangerous enemy to truth and freedom" is neither technology nor minority intolerance but "the solid unmoving cattle of the majority" (108). This important statement seems to refer to the public's acceptance of and even craving for mindnumbing mass exploitation and the comfort of its resulting intellectual conformity.

Beatty shows a similar understanding when he notes that the public, "knowing what it want[s], spin[s] happily" (57). He explains the motivation to Montag: "Ask yourself, What do people want in this country, above all? People want to be happy, isn't that right? Haven't you heard it all your life? I want to be happy, people say. Well, aren't they? Don't we keep them moving, don't we give them fun? That's all we live for, isn't it? For pleasure, for titillation? And you must admit our culture provides plenty of these" (59). Beatty thus blames—or, according to his view, credits—not only the exploiters but the willingly exploited.

According to Clarisse, the inquisitive seventeen year old who helps Montag learn to question and wonder, people no longer really think or talk about anything important: "No, not anything. They name a lot of cars or swimming pools mostly and say how swell. But they all say the same things and nobody says anything different from anyone else" (31). The public is happy to think of pleasure and brand names and talk in clichés.

One of the most pathetic examples of the public's willingness to allow itself to be exploited is not its attraction to obviously seductive pleasures but its automatic acceptance of even the least attractive things that the televisions and radios present. People are so accustomed to enjoying mindless mass communication that they also enjoy the accompanying commercials. While riding on the subway, Montag sees people "tapping their feet to the rhythm of Denham's Dentifrice, Denham's Dandy Dental Detergent, Denham's Dentifrice Dentifrice Dentifrice, one two, one two three, one two, one two three . . . mouths . . . faintly twitching the words Dentifrice Dentifrice Dentifrice" (79). The masses are unwilling to break with conformity and relinquish even this least attractive "pleasure" by thinking for themselves.

Mass exploitation hastens the decline of thought even more directly than does intolerant minority pressure, for while pressure groups may make people avoid controversy, easily gratifying entertainment actually provides a seductive alternative to any and all difficult thought. Beatty neatly sums up the philosophy embodied by the mass exploitation of easy gratification: "Life is immediate, the job counts, pleasure lies all about after work. Why learn anything save pressing buttons, pulling switches, fitting nuts and bolts?" (56) While minority pressure comes from a comparative few members of the public, the impetus for this exploitation comes instead from an overwhelming majority. "Publishers, exploiters, broadcasters" sense the public's desire for relaxation and pleasure and exploit this for profit by producing only entertainment which is easily gratifying, and the willingly exploited enjoy their freedom from independent thought.

Four main kinds of this exploitation exist in the novel: the simplification of intellectual challenges, competitive diversions, drug use, and commodifed physicality. Referring to such pleasurable distractions, Beatty says, "So bring on your clubs and parties, your acrobats and magicians, your daredevils, motorcycle helicopters, your sex and heroin, more of everything to do with automatic reflex" (61). Easy gratification is to be pursued to the exclusion of independent thought.

Although, as Bradbury says in the coda, books may have been "burned first by the minorities" (177), works of art with the potential to be challenging were simplified even earlier. Beatty shows that this exploitation of easy gratification began "around a thing called the Civil War" and rapidly accelerated in the twentieth century with the increasing sophistication of mass communication technology, when "films and radios, magazines, books leveled down to a sort of paste-pudding norm" (54). Beatty explains that intellectually challenging works were made easier so that they would appeal to a larger audience: "Classics cut to fit fifteen-minute radio shows, then cut again to fill a two-minute book column, winding up at last as a ten- or twelve-line dictionary resume. . . . [M]any were those whose sole knowledge of *Hamlet* . . . was a one-page digest in a book that claimed: *now at last you can read all the classics; keep up with your neighbors*" (54-55). In this example the exploitation is two-fold in that publishers play both on the public's desires for shorter and easier readings and on desires to "keep up with [the] neighbors" as well.

After such exploitative cutting, books and magazines were watered down still farther so that by the time of the novel only "comics, the good old confessions, [and] trade journals" survive (58). Drama on television has been simplified to the level of the "Clara Dove five-minute romance" (95) and pointless serials featuring a "gibbering pack of tree apes that [say] nothing, nothing, nothing and [say] it loud, loud, loud" (44). Presumably films are similar. Radio is simply "an electronic ocean of sound, of music and talk and music and talk" that figuratively drowns the listener (12). In a more visceral metaphor, radio "vomit[s] . . . a great tonload of tin, copper, silver, chromium, and brass . . . pound[ing listeners] into submission" (79). Most sinister of all, Bradbury describes the ubiquitous thimble-sized ear radios rather ominously as "hidden wasp[s]" (12), "electronic bees" (18), and "praying mantis[es]" (48). The novel's equivalent of music videos on the "musical wall" are now "only color and all abstract," and even such musical art as previously existed in record-playing machines has been so drained of emotion and changed in form that the machines have gradually become merely "joke boxes" (31). Moreover, Clarisse says that in what passes for modern museums, art is "*all* abstract," paintings refusing to "[say] things or even [show] people" (31) and thereby risk making people think. The public wants easily gratifying entertainment, the exploiters help make the situation worse by producing only that which requires no original thought to enjoy, and thought is gradually abandoned.

Moreover, education is simplified as "school is shortened, discipline relaxed, philosophies, histories, languages dropped, English and spelling gradually neglected, finally almost completely ignored" (55). Clarisse tells Montag that school now stifles thought rather than encouraging it: "An hour of TV class, an hour of basketball of baseball or running, another hour of transcription history or painting pictures, and more sports, but do you know, we never ask questions, or at least most don't; they just run the answers at you, bing, bing, bing, and us sitting there for four more hours of film teacher" (29). To ensure that children do not grow up to ask what Beatty calls "embarrassing" questions, the government has "lowered the kindergarten age year after year until now [it is] almost snatching them from the cradle" (60). Even to parents school is simply a place to "plunk" the children in nine days out of ten" (96).

This reflects and reinforces the conformity already manifested in the public's acceptance of simplified entertainment, for children who are never taught to think about anything challenging are unlikely to want to be challenged by their entertainment or by anything else. According to Beatty, when "school turn[s] out more runners, jumpers, racers, tinkerers, grabbers, snatchers, fliers, and swimmers instead of examiners, critics, knowers, and imaginative creators, the word 'intellectual,' of course, [becomes] the swear word it deserve[s] to be" (58). Thus the simplification of education reinforces the public's existing desire to avoid difficult thought, reteaching the lesson already taught by mass entertainment: thoughtless conformity is simple and pleasurable.

Just as the simplification of intellectual challenges helps stifle independent thought by catering to and encouraging intellectual apathy, so does an emphasis on competitive diversions. Beatty shows how an overemphasis on sports can take the place of thought: "More sports for everyone, group spirit, fun, and you don't have to think, eh? Organize and organize and superorganize super-super sports" (57). Beatty is even more explicit about the mindlessness of contests: "Give the people contests they win by remembering the words to more popular songs or the names of state capitals or how much corn Iowa grew last year. Cram them full of noncombustible data, chock them so damned full of 'facts' they feel stuffed, but absolutely 'brilliant' with information. Then they'll feel they're thinking, they'll get a *sense* of motion without moving" (61). Feeling stuffed with unimportant facts thus replaces actual thinking. Likewise, Faber reminds Montag that most people are satisfied if they can "dance faster than the White Clown, shout louder than 'Mr. Gimmick' and the parlor 'families'" (87). Both sports and contests emphasize a simple competitiveness leading away from individual thought.

A more dangerous type of thought-destroying mass exploitation is socially condoned drug use. Heroin is the most powerful drug in the novel, and Beatty's reference to it is casual enough to suggest that its use is not uncommon (61). Although the sleeping pills prevalent in the society could be used responsibly, the book shows only escapist overuse. When Montag's wife, Millie, overdoses, perhaps accidentally, by taking "thirty or forty" pills (19), the medical technicians who detoxify her and replace her blood tell Montag that the problem is common: "We get these cases nine or ten a night. Got so many, starting a few years ago, we had the special machines built" (15). Millie also shows that alcohol abuse is still widespread, for when she wakes in the morning with a headache and no memory of the previous night, her first thought is that she has a hangover from "a wild party or something" (19). Just as people flee difficult thought with simplified challenges and competitive diversions, they also occupy their time with mind-altering drugs that, presumably, are marketed without care for their dangerous effects.

The most common of the distracting drugs is nicotine, which Bradbury often presents the enemies of thought as using. Beatty smokes compulsively (33, 53-59). Bradbury's conspicuous imagery of flame and smoke certainly reflects the destructive burning of Beatty's profession, but the act itself also reveals the nervous behavior of a mind mechanically avoiding thought; later Bradbury shows Beatty smoking automatically, lighting up habitually without any fanfare (105). The medical "handymen" who save Millie's life, "the men with the cigarettes in their straight-lined mouths," are able to stand "with the cigarette smoke curling around their noses and into their eyes without making them blink or squint" (15-16). Millie's imbecilic friends are similar, for when Guy turns off the television walls the women sit nervously "lighting cigarettes, blowing smoke" (95). Later Montag tells Granger that when he tries to remember his wife, one of the only things he can see is that "there's a cigarette in [her hands]" (156). Montag smokes early on in the novel (24), but as he grows more thoughtful Bradbury simply lets this habit disappear. For the others, however, the ritual of smoking fills the time that might otherwise be used for thought and self-reflection.

The final type of mass exploitation speeding the decline of thought is commodified physicality, both actual and vicarious. People can "head for a Fun Park to bully people around, break windowpanes in the Window Smasher place or wreck cars in the Car Wrecker place with the big steel ball" (30). Powerful "beetle cars" are designed, and probably marketed, for "driving a hundred miles an hour, at a clip where you can't think of anything else but the danger" (84). Millie often drives "a hundred miles an hour across town . . . hearing only the scream of the car" (46), and late at night she likes to "get it up around ninety-five and . . . feel wonderful" hitting rabbits and dogs out in the country (64). Children as young as twelve might go "playing 'chicken' and 'knock hubcaps'" (30) or go "out for a long night of roaring five or six hundred miles in a few moonlit hours, their faces icy with wind, . . . coming home or not coming at dawn, alive or not alive" (128). Violence and danger thus crowd out original thought.

Even dramatic entertainment contains a small element of actual physicality that helps replace emotional and intellectual content. Beatty reveals this when he says, "If the drama is bad, if the film says nothing, if the play is hollow, sting me with the theremin, loudly. I'll think I'm responding to the play when it's only a tactile response to vibration. But I don't care. I just like solid entertainment" (61). Like Beatty's hypothetical play, Millie's insipid television serials use irresistibly climactic "thunderstorm[s] of sound" that alone give the impression of plot resolution "even though the people in the walls of the room [have] barely moved" (45).

Vicarious physicality provides a seductive alternative to thought just as the more dangerous actual physicality does. Vicarious physicality also comes in many forms in the novel, from entertainment of what Professor Faber calls "passionate lips and the fist in the stomach" (89) to "the three-dimensional sex magazines" (57-58), from the graphic violence of the animated White Clown cartoons to the televising of fatal jet car demolition derbies (94). Common people also go to such races (9). "Nights when things [get] dull, which [is] every night," the firemen "let loose rats . . . and sometimes chickens, and sometimes cats that would have to be drowned anyway" and bet on which will be the first killed by their eight-legged Mechanical Hound (24-25). Occasionally the public voyeurs of violence are treated to television coverage of "dangerous" criminals being similarly hunted down (124, 133-39, 147-49).

Even while Bradbury in the coda warns of intolerant minority pressure, he apparently cannot help but also attack the first type of mass exploitation, that of the simplification of challenges. Most of the coda discusses the way pressure groups threaten free thought by "ripping a page or a paragraph from this book, then that" (177), but some also concerns the simplification of challenging entertainment by exploiting editors. The motive for editors' censoring is sometimes ideological, but it is also sometimes simply economic:

> How do you cram 400 short stories by Twain, Irving, Poe, Maupassant and Bierce into one book?

> Simplicity itself. Skin, debone, demarrow, scarify, melt, render down and destroy. Every adjective that counted, every verb that moved, every metaphor that weighed more than a mosquito—out! Every simile that would have made a sub-moron's mouth twitch—gone! Any aside that explained the two-bit philosophy of a first-rate writer—lost!

> Every story, slenderized, starved, bluepenciled, leeched and bled white, resemble[s] every other story. Twain read[s] like Poe read[s] like Shakespeare read[s] like Dostoevsky read[s] like—in the finale—Edgar Guest. Every word of more than three syllables [has] been razored. Every image that demand[s] so much as one instant's attention—shot dead.

> (176)

The economic rather than ideological motive shown in this impassioned passage is important to recognize. Although the rest of the coda attacks the intolerance of minority pressure groups, including editors who have censored the "controversial" ideas of Bradbury himself, in this instance the motive of the editors is simply to remove anything requiring even "one instant's attention." This exploits readers' desires for easy gratification just as do the "digests-digests, digests-digests-digests" (55), which Beatty in the novel cites as one of the first examples of simplified challenges.

Certainly present-day American society abounds with examples of the exploitation Bradbury discusses: the simplification of challenges, both artistic and educational; an overemphasis of competitive diversions like sports and contests; rampant drug use; and commodified physicality, both actual and vicarious. All of these pleasurable pursuits interest us so much that they threaten to replace independent thought. If it were not for the controversies over censorship and political correctness, the numerous examples of mass exploitation in American society might make readers wonder why Bradbury attacks the real but lesser problem of intolerant pressure groups so much more vehemently.

Professor Faber says that "books are to remind us what asses and fools we are" (86). Ray Bradbury's *Fahrenheit 451* certainly fulfills this goal, for it shows readers more than forty years after its first publication how individual thought can so easily be supplanted by thoughtless conformity. Bradbury's warning about the dangers of intolerant minority pressure is perceptive and important, but it should not overshadow his subtler but more important warning about mass exploitation. Despite the ease of recognizing the problems of minority pressure in the book, mass exploitation begins earlier, requires the participation of a far greater majority of the population, and has a more direct effect on the decline of thought. This should remind us that even more dangerous than the pressure groups that attempt to peck away at the freedom of expression and, eventually, thought is our own desire for easy gratification. The "publishers, exploiters, broadcasters" have great economic incentive to exploit this desire, and when we allow such pleasurably escapist mass exploitation to replace our thoughtful interest in the real world, we abnegate our intellectual and moral responsibilities as human beings.

Works Cited

Amis, Kingsley. *New Maps of Hell: A Survey of Science Fiction*. 1960. New York: Arno, 1975.

Bradbury, Ray. *Fahrenheit 451*. 1953. New York: Ballantine, 1991.

Greenberg, Martin Harry, and Joseph D. Olander, eds. *Ray Bradbury*. Writers of the 21st Century Series. New York: Taplinger, 1980.

Hamblen, Charles F. "Bradbury's *Fahrenheit 451* in the Classroom." *English Journal* (Sept. 1968): 818-19ff.

Huntington, John. "Utopian and Anti-Utopian Logic: H. G. Wells and his Successors." *Science-Fiction Studies* 9 (1982): 122-46.

McNelly, Willis E. "Ray Bradbury—Past, Present, and Future." Greenberg and Olandor 17-24.

Mengeling, Marvin E. "The Machineries of Joy and Despair: Bradbury's Attitudes toward Science and Technology." Greenberg and Olander 83-109.

Mogen, David. *Ray Bradbury*. Twayne's United States Authors Series 504. Boston: Twayne, 1986.

Reilly, Robert. "The Artistry of Ray Bradbury." *Extrapolation* 13 (1971): 64-74.

Sisario, Peter. "A Study of the Allusions in Bradbury's *Fahrenheit 451*." *English Journal* (Feb. 1970): 201-05ff.

Touponce, William F. *Ray Bradbury and the Poetics of Reverie*. Studies in Speculative Fiction 2. 1981. Ann Arbor: UMI, 1984.

Watt, Donald. "Burning Bright: *Fahrenheit 451* as Symbolic Dystopia." Greenberg and Olander 195-213.

Rafeeq O. McGiveron (essay date spring 1998)

SOURCE: McGiveron, Rafeeq O. "'To Build a Mirror Factory': The Mirror and Self-Examination in Ray Bradbury's *Fahrenheit 451*." *Critique* 39, no. 3 (spring 1998): 282-87.

[*In the following essay, McGiveron identifies several characters and techniques representative of the mirror metaphor in* Fahrenheit 451, *finding Clarisse to be the most effective.*]

In *Fahrenheit 451* Ray Bradbury creates an unthinking society so compulsively hedonistic that it must be atom-bombed flat before it ever can be rebuilt. Bradbury's clearest suggestion to the survivors of America's third atomic war "started . . . since 1990" (73) is "to build a mirror factory first and put out nothing but mirrors . . . and take a long look in them" (164). Coming directly after the idea that they also must "build the biggest goddamn steam shovel in history and dig the biggest grave of all time and shove war in and cover it up" (164), the notion of the mirror factory might at first seem merely a throwaway line. Indeed, John Huntington suggests, with no little justification, that the whole passage is "confuse[d]" by its "vagueness, ambiguity, and misdirection" (138). Despite that, however, Bradbury shows throughout *Fahrenheit 451* the necessity of using a metaphorical mirror, for only through the self-examination it makes possible can people recognize their own shortcomings.

The novel's first use of the mirror, a failed one, emphasizes the need for self-examination. After a book burning, Guy Montag, the unsettled "fireman," knows "that when he return[s] to the firehouse, he might wink at himself, a minstrel man, burnt-corked, in the mirror" (4). Montag's winking acceptance of himself here is not reflective but reflexive, for his glance is superficial rather than searching. Montag has the opportunity truly to examine himself, and if he did, he might see a glorified anti-intellectual stormtrooper. However, the situation, the surroundings, and even the mirror itself are too familiar, and he does not see himself as he really is. Instead of recognizing the destructiveness of his book-burning profession, his gaze is merely one of self-satisfaction.

Bradbury uses Clarisse, Guy's imaginative and perceptive seventeen-year-old neighbor, as a metaphorical mirror to begin reflecting truths that Montag otherwise would not see. The imagery of mirrors and reflection is very clear:

> He saw himself in her eyes, suspended in two shining drops of bright water, himself dark and tiny, in fine detail, the lines about his mouth, everything there, as if her eyes were two miraculous bits of violet amber that might capture and hold him intact.
>
> (7)

Montag thinks of Clarisse again:

> How like a mirror . . . her face. Impossible, for how many people did you know who refracted your own light to you? . . . How rarely did other people's faces take of you and throw back to you your own expression, your own innermost trembling thought?
>
> (11)

William F. Touponce suggests that Montag thereby receives "a tranquil affirmation of his being" (90); those passages bear that out.

But Clarisse's mirror imagery serves another function. Seeing himself in the mirror of Clarisse helps Montag realize that he merely "[wears] his happiness like a mask . . ." (12). He imagines that Clarisse has "run off across the lawn with the mask . . . (12). It would, however, be more accurate to say that Montag himself throws away the poorly fitting mask after Clarisse shows, or reflects to him, the truth underneath. Clarisse's game of rubbing a dandelion under his chin to determine whether he is in love (21-2) "sum[s] up everything" (44), showing Montag an aspect of his emptiness he otherwise could not see. Her curiosity about why he and his wife have no children (28-9) is another example of her mirror function. Perhaps most important, Clarisse asks about Montag's job: "How did it start? How did you get into it? How did you pick your work and how did you happen to think to take the job you have? . . . It just doesn't seem right for you, somehow" (23-4). With each little observation, game, or question, Clarisse reflects a previously unseen truth for Montag to examine and, in the words of Robert Reilly, "show[s] him how empty his existence is" (68).

In addition to serving as a mirror reflecting Montag himself, Clarisse also serves as a mirror held up to the rest of society. Her perspective helps Montag see that his contemporaries, as Clarisse says, really neither talk nor think about anything; "No, not anything. They name a lot of cars or clothes or swimming pools mostly and say how swell! But they all say the same things and nobody says anything different from anyone else" (31). That should be as familiar to Montag as the cloying stench of kerosene (of which Montag blithely observes, "You never wash it off completely" (61). Yet really to notice and examine those too-familiar facts he needs to see the situation reflected in the mirror of Clarisse.

Clarisse is a mirror not simply because she informs readers about the state of society. Each of the characters does that. If informing were the sole criterion for being a mirror, then even the most minor character would qualify—and so would most of the novel's narrative description. The metaphor would be so all-inclusive as to be meaningless. Clarisse is a mirror because she is so mirrorlike in her informing. She "talk[s] about how strange the world is" (29), reminding Montag that "everyone . . . is either shouting or dancing around like wild or beating up one another" (30), but she has no ideological agenda. For the most part Clarisse does not interpret or offer suggestions; she merely draws Montag's attention to facts he should already understand but does not. Like a mirror, Clarisse guilelessly reflects the truth into Montag's eyes.

Guy's wife, Millie, is another mirror, although Bradbury has not set her up with imagery like Clarisse's. Like the firehouse mirror, however, she is such a part of Guy's routine that he cannot seem to see what she

reflects. In the beginning of the novel, Guy may find it "a pleasure to burn" books (3) and may honestly claim that "[k]erosene . . . is nothing but perfume to me" (6), but Millie finds even more pleasure in the burning. She compulsively watches her three-wall television and begs Guy for a fourth wall that would cost one-third of his yearly salary (20-1). When not entranced by the television, she wears "thimble radios tamped tight" (12) in her ears, even in bed. Sometimes while her husband sleeps she drives all night out in the country, "feel[ing] wonderful" hitting rabbits and dogs (64). She has begun to overdose on sleeping pills but still maintains in bland disbelief, "I wouldn't do a thing like that" (18). Millie shows the superficiality and emptiness of the novel's society, yet Guy misses her mirror function. He finally recognizes her as "a silly empty woman" (44) who is "really bothered" (52), but he never seems to understand that she reflects an entire culture. As with the firehouse mirror, Montag has not looked carefully enough.

Beatty and Faber—chief book burner and former literature professor, respectively—both explain to Montag how the society of the past has turned into the inhumane world of *Fahrenheit 451.* Yet neither of those men is a mirror, for unlike Clarisse and Millie, they are overtly didactic. Each tries to sway Montag with a different interpretation of the past. Beatty wants Montag to "stand against the small tide of those who want to make everyone unhappy with conflicting theory and thought" (61-2), whereas Faber has no plans but at least wants Montag to think. Although the two characters provide important historical and sociological information, they are teachers more than mirrors. As Donald Watt notes, Beatty and Faber articulate the ideas that Millie and Clarisse live (197). They reflect society to some extent, but more often they evaluate and advise— tasks of the viewer and thinker, not the mirror.

The book contains other important mirrors. After a week of daily talks with Clarisse, Montag is ready to look into one of them. This time he takes more initiative, for the mirror is one he must visualize himself. After ten years of simple acceptance, Montag finally sees himself by looking into the mirror of the other firemen:

> Montag looked at these men whose faces were sunburnt by a thousand real and ten thousand imaginary fires, whose work flushed their cheeks and fevered their eyes. These men who looked steadily into their platinum igniter flames as they lit their eternally burning black pipes. They and their charcoal hair and soot-colored brows and bluish-ash-smeared cheeks where they had shaven close. . . . Had he ever seen a fireman that didn't have black hair, black brows, a fiery face, and a blue-steel shaved but unshaved look? These men were all mirror images of himself!
>
> (33)

Montag is "appalled" (Watt 199), for this mirror invites a disquieting self-examination.

After looking into the ready-made mirror of Clarisse and recognizing an unflattering image mirrored by the other mindless firemen, Montag begins holding up his own mirror to society. The first attempt, when he and Millie look through the books he has stolen (66-74), is a comparative failure. Guy tells Millie, "[Books] just might stop us from making the same damn insane mistakes [people have always made]!" (74), but he cannot find a text that mirrors his own society clearly enough to provide either criticisms or solutions. Montag reads, "'It is computed that eleven thousand persons have at several times suffered death rather than submit to break their eggs at the smaller end'" (68). Swift's *Gulliver's Travels* may be, as Peter Sisario claims, "an excellent one for him to choose" (203), but it is excellent for the well-read reader, not for Montag. The firehouse mirror and the mirror that is Millie are missed opportunities because Montag does not look hard enough, but this book-mirror may be too subtle for him even to recognize.

Despite that failure, Professor Faber reminds Montag that mirrors are all around him. Although he does not speak in terms of mirrors, the idea of the reflection of truths fills his discussion:

> It's not books you need, it's some of the things that once were in books. The same things could be in the [televised] parlor families' today. The same infinite detail and awareness could be projected through the radios and televisors, but are not. No, no, it's not the books at all you're looking for! Take it where you can find it, in old phonograph records, old motion pictures, and in old friends; look for it in nature and look for it in yourself. Books were only one type of receptacle where we stored a lot of things we were afraid we might forget. There is nothing magical in them at all. The magic is only in what the books say, how they stitched the patches of the universe together into one garment for us.
>
> (82-3)

Bradbury uses more than one type of imagery here, but the idea of the mirror could easily encompass them all. Throughout his talk Faber stresses examining the individual and society as reflected in a metaphorical mirror.

Faber says that books "can go under the microscope. You'd find life under the glass, streaming past in infinite profusion. The more pores, the more truthfully recorded details of life per square inch you can get on a sheet of paper, the more 'literary' you are" (83). Reiterating that idea, he says that books "show the pores in the face of life" (83). In other words, the microscope—or mirror—reflects important truths that otherwise would be missed. In that passage, Faber focuses on books; but his earlier discussion shows that a mirror can be found almost anywhere.

Finally, of course, Bradbury lets Montag stumble on a literary mirror that he, and even others, can recognize. When Guy reads Matthew Arnold's "Dover Beach" to Millie's friends, he holds up a mirror that reflects all too clearly:

> "'Ah, love, let us be true
> To one another! for the world, which seems
> To lie before us like a land of dreams,
> So various, so beautiful, so new,
> Hath really neither joy, nor love, nor light,
> Nor certitude, nor peace, nor help for pain;
> And we are here as on a darkling plain
> Swept with confused alarms of struggle and flight
> Where ignorant armies clash by night.'"
>
> (100)

Beatty calls American civilization "our happy world" (62), but families are hollow and loveless, suicide is commonplace, violence is endemic on the streets and in broadcast entertainment, and jet bombers circle ominously in the night. The poem's bleak conclusion rings so true that it makes the mindless Mrs. Phelps cry (100).

Just as Mrs. Phelps begins to get a glimmering of what it truly means to look in the mirror, Bradbury finally seems to allow Millie the same experience. As the bombs of one of the faceless enemies of an America that is "hated so much" abroad (74) begin to fall on the city from which he has fled, Guy's fancy conjures up a most significant image:

> Montag . . . saw or felt, or imagined he saw or felt the [television] walls go dark in Millie's face, heard her screaming, because in the millionth part of time left, she saw her own face reflected there, in a mirror instead of a crystal ball, and it was such a wildly empty face, all by itself in the room, touching nothing, starved and eating of itself that at last she recognized it as her own.
>
> (159-60)

Guy's peculiar little fantasy, of course, may not actually happen to Millie, but its existence demonstrates the crucial importance of the mirror. Unlike her husband, the imagined Millie of that passage recognizes its importance too late.

In the very last scene of the novel, Montag holds up the Bible as a mirror in which to see the world from a different perspective:

> And when it came his turn, what could he say, what could he offer on a day like this, to make the trip a little easier? To everything there is a season. Yes. A time to break down, and a time to build up. Yes. A time to keep silence, and a time to speak. Yes, all that. But what else? Something, something. . . .
>
> (165)

Ecclesiastes is a mirror providing some comfort, but Montag senses that Revelation is an even better one: "And on either side of the river was there a tree of life, which bore twelve manner of fruits, and yielded her fruit every month; And the leaves of the tree were for the healing of the nations" (165), Like Mrs. Phelps, he sees his own situation reflected in a piece of literature, but there the mirror brings hope rather than despair. without the mirror of the Bible, however, Montag would be hard pressed to see any positive "truths" in his post-nuclear world.

Granger, leader of the book-memorizing intellectuals whom Montag meets after his flight from the city, ties together all the other uses of mirror imagery. "Come on now, we're going to build a mirror factory first and turn out nothing but mirrors for the next year and take a long took in them" (164). The suggestions reaffirms the necessity of using mirrors for self-examination. Just as Montag struggles to use figurative mirrors to discover the shortcomings in himself and in society, the survivors must use them in striving for a humane future. If they successfully use the mirrors, perhaps they can avoid making "the same damn mistakes."

Considered along with the other mirrors in *Fahrenheit 451,* Granger's suggestion begins to make metaphorical sense. Perhaps Bradbury's mirror imagery is not used as carefully as it could be; certainly it is possible to imagine its being more consistently employed or more fully articulated. Yet throughout the book, mirrors of a kind are missed and found, seen and used. With Montag's failures and successes, Bradbury shows that all of us, as individuals and as a society, must struggle to take a long, hard look in the mirror. Whether we look at ourselves from another's perspective or from the perspective of a good work of art, we need this self-examination to help avoid self-destruction.

Works Cited

Bradbury, Ray. *Fahrenheit 451.* 1953. New York: Ballantine, 1991.

Huntington, John. "Utopian and Anti-Utopian Logic: H. G. Wells and his Successors." *Science-Fiction Studies* 9 (1982): 122-46.

Reilly, Robert. "The Artistry of Ray Bradbury." *Extrapolation* 13 (1971): 64-74.

Sisario, Peter. "A Study of the Allusions in Bradbury's *Fahrenheit 451.*" *English Journal* Feb. 1970: 200+.

Touponce, William F. *Ray Bradbury and the Poetics of Reverie. Studies in Speculative Fiction* 2. 1981. Ann Arbor: UMI, 1984.

Watt, Donald A. "Burning Bright: *Fahrenheit 451* as Symbolic Dystopia." In *Ray Bradbury. Writers of the 21st Century Series.* Ed. Martin Harry Greenberg and Joseph D Olander. New York: Taplinger, 1980. 195-213.

Ray Bradbury and Jim Cherry (interview date 31 August 2000)

SOURCE: Bradbury, Ray, and Jim Cherry. "Future Tense Sci-Fi Legend Bradbury Going Strong." In *Conversations with Ray Bradbury,* edited by Steven L. Aggelis, pp. 191-93. Jackson, Miss.: University Press of Mississippi, 2004.

[*In the following interview originally published in the August 31, 2000, issue of* Arizona Republic, *Bradbury answers questions regarding spirituality, genre, and the life of a writer.*]

[*Cherry:*] *You lived in Arizona as a boy?*

[Bradbury:] I lived there when I was six in 1926, and for a year when I was twelve. I was a curious kid. When I was six and lived in Tucson, I was on the university grounds all the time, especially the natural science building, which was full of snakes and tarantulas and Gila monsters. They used to throw me off campus, and I'd creep back and hide. Tucson's a very special place to me.

Do you think your peripatetic childhood had an impact on your becoming a writer?

I think that I was born to be a writer—it was genetic. You can't teach that; what you can teach is good habits. When you read my books you can't imagine anyone else writing them.

There seems to be a spiritual quality that runs through your work. Do you subscribe to the Eastern idea of an impersonal God or the Western idea of a personal one?

I have a delicatessen religious outlook—"I'll take some a' deez, some a' doze and some a' deez." I believe in American Indian ideas, ideas of the Far East; they're all fascinating and nothing is proved.

Do you "write drunk and revise sober" or compose everything carefully in your mind before setting it down?

It's got to be an explosion. I get an idea and then, bang! I'm at the typewriter, and two hours later it's done. All of my short stories have taken two or three hours.

You don't consider yourself a science-fiction writer. Instead, you're a fantasy writer, is that correct?

Correct.

There's a timelessness to your work.

It's mythological—I write Greek myths, Roman myths, Egyptian myths. It's metaphorical, but there's no science in them. The only book I've written that's science fiction is *Fahrenheit 451.* That's political and psychological science fiction.

In that way, your book is like A Clockwork Orange.

Oh, don't say that! That's a sick book! I hate *A Clockwork Orange.* It's so vulgar. The characters don't lift you up in any way.

Do you have any idea how many copies of **Martian Chronicles** *you've sold?*

Oh, I don't know, it's never been a bestseller. It only sold five thousand copies its first year. But, it's been a cumulative bestseller. You sell fifty thousand to one hundred thousand paperbacks a year for fifty years and you have quite a few million. None of my books sell worth a damn when they first come out.

How many movies have been made from your books?

Oh, four or five. **Illustrated Man,** which is no good; **Something Wicked This Way Comes,** which was very good. **Fahrenheit 451,** which had things missing but was still a good job. **Martian Chronicles** on TV was a bore, but we're going to do it over next year as a theatrical movie.

Do you hand the book over to the movie studio and let them do their thing?

No, I have to be in there, or I won't let them do it.

Did you see computers and the Internet coming?

I could see them coming, but nobody could predict some of the problems that would be connected to that.

Such as?

Well, all this business with Napster, and stealing all that music—thieving millions of dollars of music away from people without paying for it. That's ridiculous. They should be destroyed. They're behaving like the Russians and Chinese, who've been stealing my books for forty years.

What do you think of alien visitors and UFOs?

No such, no way. It's ridiculous; there's absolutely no proof anywhere, at any time.

You've never driven a car?

I never learned. I was too poor. Writers can't afford things like that. My wife and I didn't have enough money to buy a car till we were thirty-seven and thirty-eight—then she learned to drive. Becoming a writer is a very slow process and there's not much money in it for a long time.

Your musical **Dandelion Wine** *is set to play in L.A.*

I did it first at Lincoln Center thirty years ago; now we're bringing it back, at the Colony Theater in Burbank.

What are you working on now?

I have a new book of essays called *A Chapbook for Burnt-Out Priests, Rabbis and Ministers,* a book of philosophic essays, a new book called *One More for the Road,* a novel *From the Dust Returned,* and a book of poetry. That's more than enough, don't you think?

Ray Bradbury and Ben P. Indick (interview date 22 October 2001)

SOURCE: Bradbury, Ray, and Ben P. Indick. "Ray Bradbury: Still Talking and Still Listening." *Publishers Weekly* 248, no. 43 (22 October 2001): 40.

[*In the following interview, Bradbury remarks on the completion of a project in progress for over fifty years.*]

Ray Bradbury may be 81 and recovering from a stroke, but he is not yet ready to be mummified like a Thousand Times Great Grand-Mère, a star among the eccentric stars of his latest novel, *From the Dust Returned.* Bradbury looks thin, and his voice is a bit hollow, but he talks. And laughs. On the wall of his living room, where it has been hanging for 50 years, is a painting by Charles Addams, the great *New Yorker* cartoonist, showing an eerie Victorian gothic haunted house inhabited by a family of lovable freaks, the Elliotts, who are featured in some of Bradbury's best-loved stories and take center stage in *From the Dust Returned.* Originally intended to grace the cover of the long-planned novel, the painting is finally being put to use.

Bradbury was a brash, broke and confident 26-year-old living in New York when *Weird Tales* magazine rejected **"Homecoming,"** his first Elliotts story. *Weird Tales* was his first serious publisher, paying him $20 apiece for **"The Jar"** and **"Skeleton,"** but **"Homecoming"** wasn't traditional enough for the editors, who wanted stories imitating Poe and Lovecraft. So he submitted the story to *Mademoiselle,* where Truman Capote, then an editor, accepted it for the Halloween issue. Addams was chosen to do the artwork. Bradbury decided to do a book based on the story and illustrated by Addams after he and the artist became close. "But he wandered off to do his Addams Family [inspired by the Elliots], and I wandered off and did my other Family stories on my own. Along the way I bought the painting from him for $200 when I couldn't afford it and paid by the month. It took me three or four months."

It took another 55 years for the book to appear, but it still seems remarkably fresh, as vibrant as any of Bradbury's earlier work. The reason, insists the writer, is that "all of my books surprise me. I'm writing them all the time."

Bradbury's first foray into the world of writing came in 1939, when the Waukegan, Ill., native was 19 and working as a newsboy in Los Angeles. Setting himself up as the publisher of a fanzine, *Futuria Fantasia,* he managed to recruit an impressive lineup. "Forrie Ackerman paid for it. Henry Kuttner and Robert Heinlein wrote for it and Hannes Bok drew for it," he says. His first published story was **"It's Not the Heat. It's the Hu-"** (sic), which appeared in *Script* magazine in Beverly Hills: "no money but a lot of free copies." After his success with *Mademoiselle,* the editors of *Weird Tales* accepted his strange and unique stories, "but they kept fighting me. 'Do real ghost stories!'"

He published his first book, the story collection **Dark Carnival,** with Arkham House in 1947, but his breakthrough came in 1949, when he sold **The Martian Chronicles** to Doubleday. He needed the money, because by then he was married to Maggie McClure and expecting their first child. The book's origin was near miraculous. "I was writing it for four or five years, but I didn't know it. It took a Doubleday editor, Walter Bradbury (no relation to me), to point out I had written a novel. He told me to go back to the YMCA where I was staying and write an outline. We had no money. Maggie was pregnant. He told me, 'Bring it to the office and if it's any good I'll give you $750.' I stayed up all night and wrote the outline of a novel I didn't know I had written and took it to the office of Doubleday the next day. Walter Bradbury looked at it and said, 'That's it, here is $750.' So I was rich, because in 1949 that paid our rent for a whole year in Venice, Calif. It paid for our first baby, too, because babies in those days only cost about $100."

Although he is often called to appear on TV as a science fiction writer, he insists he is not one. "Only **Fahrenheit 451** is science fiction. **The Martian Chronicles** is fantasy. There is no such place as Mars. It's based on the dreams I had as a child, on the photographs taken at the Lowell Observatory and the sketches by Schiaparelli and the Martian books by Edgar Rice Burroughs."

His second love has always been the theater. After working for seven months on the screenplay for *Moby Dick,* one morning he looked into the mirror and "there was Herman Melville. He assumed my identity." John Huston had told him that he wanted the interpretation of the story to be Bradbury's and then unjustly took co-credit for the film. Still, the work in Ireland paid off in his Irish one-act plays, **"The Anthem Sprinters."** He recalls, several years ago, a production in San Francisco and the marquee read, "Two Irish plays tonight, by Sean O'Casey and Ray Bradbury. Isn't that great, huh?" After a pause, he adds, "I cried."

Waukegan has appreciated Bradbury, who returns annually and visits the ravine where "I used to play. . . .

They've renamed it 'The Ray Bradbury Park.'" Asked about another famous Waukeganite, Jack Benny, he says, "We used to appear on concert programs together. I introduced him, and he would play the violin. We were known as 'The Boys from Waukegan.' He was a very nice gentleman." Ray chuckles as he recalls a Steven Spielberg story. The great filmmaker was asked in an interview, "If you could make God say something, what would it be?" Spielberg answered, "Thanks for listening." Bradbury laughs. "Isn't that beautiful? God whispered to Spielberg to tell him to become Spielberg, and whispered to me to become Bradbury, and I listened."

Concerning the recent terrible terrorist events, he refers to a recent essay in which he wrote, "Mankind is too soon from the cave, too far from the stars, we are the in-between generation, not having accepted the gift of life completely. We diminish it by such acts. Not by war, hatred and greed, but then we recover and do good things. We are half and half people. We need forgiveness. We have to move forward, go back to the moon, go to Mars, on into the universe, meantime struggling with the two halves of ourselves. The events of recent weeks have been a real struggle not to go crazy."

Walter J. Mucher (essay date summer 2002)

SOURCE: Mucher, Walter J. "Being Martian: Spatiotemporal Self in Ray Bradbury's *The Martian Chronicles.*" *Extrapolation* 43, no. 2 (summer 2002): 171-87.

[*In the following essay, Mucher examines elements of* The Martian Chronicles *which exemplify his phenomenological interpretation of the novel.*]

> . . . the ego constitutes itself for itself, so to speak, in the unity of a [hi]story.
>
> —Edmund Husserl

During the Late Modern[1], the question of identity has been more of a psychological program than a physical one. It has questioned the realm of the Absolute and its transcendental nature as adjudicated by the ideas of Time and Space proposed by Early Modern thinkers such as René Descartes and Sir Isaac Newton. Early empirical scholars, such as John Locke and David Hume, questioned the process by which all sentient beings acquire knowledge of the external. Others, like Immanuel Kant, proposed the idea of truth on an *a priori* reality known by humans given its all-encompassing design. What is somewhat clear is that for the Late Modern, identity is, in some manner, a mental construct of those experienced spaces and those experienced times brought into review post-experientially by the mind

(Henri Bergson, William James and Edmund Husserl). And, in such a review of experienced moments (i.e. the mental combination of particular experiences of Time and Space), there is an expected end, the phenomenological construction of an identity to be brought to fulfillment, not by nature, but by choice. Still, one must somewhat contend that the program might be p/rewritten, as Edmund Husserl notes in *The Phenomenology of Internal Time-Consciousness* [*PITC*] and that the conscious individual follows course until finally reaching the telos of his self.

In this spirit Ray Bradbury's *The Martian Chronicles* (1958) can be understood as the historical reading made by the protagonists as they re-create a "diary" of their lives and loves in their quest for Mars. It reflects the Late Modern's incursion into a psychological and phenomenological humanism in which, in their search for a new self, the protagonists re-create a world of multiple readings which re-trace their exploits, moving forward while continuously looking back over their own experiential shoulders. Bradbury's overall structure posits each story as an entry of a universal consciousness, which retains the memory of a world gone by as well as the prophecy of a world to be.[2] His narrative represents the temporality of Martianness, that is, in a Lacanian sense, it represents the space in which Martianness may be attainable, for it opposes a "thing," the "Martian self," as "one that has not yet been made a symbol . . . [but] has the potential of becoming one" (Lacan 46). Furthermore, as David Carr may declare, one could conclude that in Bradbury's *The Martian Chronicles*," to be a human individual is to instantiate a special sort of relationship to time" (94). This is because the diary-like narrative reminds us that "at the bottom it is, to be sure, to be always 'located' in an ever changing now, and thus to be subjected, like everything else, to temporal sequences" (Carr 94). Key to this is that Bradbury's protagonists do not just "undergo or endure or suffer this sequence as it comes, one thing at a time" (Carr 94). But, in fact, what is central to my discussion is that the protagonists, eventually, will come to realize that "Whatever else it is, to exist as a person is to experience and to act" (Carr 95).

This idea of spacetime incurred during the period of the Late Modern is reflected especially in Edmund Husserl's phenomenological proposal that knowledge of our world is determined by our psychic interpretation of the experienced world. Husserl would come to see time as an inner sense of ordering and understanding the world as given in first impressions. For Husserl, time structures the constituting synthesis of perceiving the phenomena, itself a step toward re-establishing a crucial link between Being and Time. As such, being is defined, by all accounts, as the end result of a subjective act of self-definition, one located in space by its differentiating time sequence. This means that the subject of the

Late Modern is determined by the very act of reading its own history, which, eventually, is imposed upon the events in question by the protagonist/reader him-, her-, and/or it-self. "History," according to Claude Lévi-Strauss, "has replaced mythology and fulfills the same function" (43). With it, historic narratives ensure and maintain the proper relation between man's past, present and future within space, a space which, in its narrative, temporally contains the "unity of life." As Helga Nowotny notes, the Late Modern "was rather a question of defining time and space anew for the greatest possible— and for the first time democratic—variety of perspectives and points of views, of positions and subjective experiences" (20). And, in that experience, of life itself.

The creation of a self during the period of the Late Modern, a period that could well be defined as an industrially and early technologically centered age, required total dominion of the ego over spacetime. Preluding Jean-François Lyotard's work. *The Postmodern Condition,* Lewis Mumford defines this preoccupation of the Late Modern as an empowerment over spacetime:

> The new bourgeoisie, in counting house and shop, reduced life to a careful, uninterrupted routine: so long for business; so long for dinner: so long for pleasure— all carefully measured out, as methodical as the sexual intercourse in Tristam Shandy's father, which coincided, symbolically, with the monthly winding of the clock. Timed payments: timed contracts: timed work: timed meals: from this period on nothing was quite free from the stamp of the calendar or the clock. Waste of time . . . one of the heinous sins.
>
> (34)

As Mumford notes, for the bourgeoisie experiential spacetime had to be useful. Like Jules Verne's Phinneas Phogg (*Around the World in Eighty Days*), man began to set their lives to the beat of a watch's second hand. Between 1880 and 1918 "technological, artistic and scientific achievements . . . converged to break down the well-rehearsed spatial and temporal structures of social perception and transform them into a broad experiential field . . ." (Nowotny 19). The Late Modern deemed it necessary to exteriorize and reify the internal wants and needs of the self by rewriting its history, and with it the way man interacts with his and/or her historical self.

Husserl's phenomenological concept of "internal time-consciousness" represents the essence of this historical spacetime. "The idea of an 'event,'" writes David Carr, "is already that of something that *takes* time, has temporal thickness, beginning and end; and events are experienced as the phases and elements of other larger-scale events and processes" (Carr 24). As Carr notes, it is in his *Cartesian Meditations* that Edmund Husserl proposes "that the ego 'constitutes itself for itself, so to speak, in the unity of a *Geschichte*'; or, as one could say, in one possible translation of *Geschichte,* the unity of a *life*" (74; my emphasis). Furthermore, "The idea of a purely phenomenological psychology," writes Husserl, "does not have just the function . . . of reforming empirical psychology. For deeply rooted reasons, it can also serve as a preliminary step for laying open the essence of a transcendental phenomenology" ("Phenomenology" 27). Husserl's claim against empiricism lies in redirecting his inquiry toward the intentionality of the world, as understood by Descartes. Husserl reminds us that for Descartes the world presents itself as existing "for us, [it] exists only as the presentational content of our presentations" ("Phenomenology" 27). As such, the world exists because we exist.

Husserlian time-consciousness basically argues against the precariousness and uncertainty with which the sequence of events were described by empirical psychologism of the sixteenth and seventeenth century, such as that of John Locke and David Hume:

> When we speak of the analysis of time-consciousness, of the temporal character of objects of perception, memory, and expectation, it may seem, to be sure, as if we assume the Objective flow of time. What we accept, however, is not the existence of a world-time, the existence of a concrete duration, and the like, but time and duration appearing as such.
>
> (*PITC* 23)

Husserl points to the false assumption of Locke that our perceptions are the impressions upon our minds of a real, static and absolute world, which lies outside of ourselves. Empiricists such as Locke and Hume, according to Husserl, had argued for this "Objective flow of time" which confidently expresses the "concrete" world as given by the repetitive sensory perceptions of causal events from the external world. But for Husserl, this time perception is truly the intentional perception of our internal senses. "To be sure," adds Husserl, "we also assume an existing time; this, however, is not the time of the world of experience but the *immanent time* of the flow of consciousness" (Husserl 23). In a word, all consciousness is, eventually, the content or object (*noema*) of the consciousness of something. And for Husserl this something was our own perceptive act, and not an original perception in itself. "Thus," Joan Stambaugh remarks in her introduction to Martin Heidegger's *On Time and Being,* "there is no such thing *as* a worldless subject (exemplified by Descartes' *res cogitans*), nor is there a world in any meaningful, phenomenological sense of that word without human being" (viii). That is, a world independent of our own conscious act of perceiving and describing what we perceive.

Husserl lays claim to two creative principles of perception which make up the perception of the now: that is (1) retention, or the just-pastness of an event, and (2)

protention, that is, the just-future of an event. Husserl's celebrity consists in describing how retention and protention differ from recollection and expectation of the future respectively.[3]

Consider Husserl's example of the hearing of a sequence of tones, that is, "we hear a melody . . . we perceive it. . . . While the first tone is sounding, the second comes, then the third, and so on. Must we not say that when the second tone sounds I hear *it,* but I no longer hear the first, and so on?" (*PITC* 43) For Husserl, though, this act is not so simple. For though it is true that the particular tone expires as the next arises to take its place, its objective reality is still maintained due to primary memory, and to the expectation of its successor (*PITC* 43).

Perception of a melody demands, first, that there be present a "primal impression" which constitutes the tonal now, that is, the immediately sounding tone of the melody. Secondly, there is at the same time as the perceived tone, an existing peripheral tonal experience active in the constituted conscious act of perceived tonal now. This "fresh" or "primary memory" which holds near to the perceiving now the just-past tone in consciousness is known as retention. As such "when the tonal now, the primal impression, passes over into retention, this retention is itself again a now, an actual existent. While it itself is an actual (but not an actual sound), it is the retention of a sound that has been" (*PITC* 50).

Retention constitutes the living horizon of the now; I have in it a consciousness of the "just past." But what is originally constituted thereby—perhaps in the retaining of the tone just heard—is only the shoving back of the now-phase or the completed constituted duration, which in this completeness is no longer being constituted and no longer perceived. (*PITC* 66)

Finally there is the expectation, or protention expressed by the tonal now as it opens into receiving its tonal successor in the melody. With it a new tonal now is poised, pushing the "present" tonal now back into the no-longer (that is, the just-pastness) of the tone. Husserl referred to it as projected phantas:

> . . . every act of memory contains intentions of expectation whose fulfillment leads to the present. Every primordially constitutive process is animated by protentions which voidly *[leer]* constitute and intercept *[auffangen]* what is coming, as such, in order to bring it to fulfillment.
>
> (*PITC* 76)

The foreground is nothing without the background; the appearing side is nothing without the non-appearing. It is the same with regard to the unity of time-consciousness—the duration reproduced is the foreground; the classifying intentions make us aware of a background, a temporal background. (*PITC* 78)

Furthermore, Husserl states that an "expectational intuition is an inverted memorial intuition, for the now-intentions do not go 'before' the process but follow after it" (*PITC* 79). Thus, the perception of the totality of the melody depends on the capacity to consciously pre-perceive the following tonal now as a protentive constitutive reality of the "present" tonal now and of retentive tonal now.

This sequence of tonal experiences constitutes "modes" or a "continuous flux" of sequential now-points:

> Every temporal being "appears" in one or another continually changing mode of running-off, and the "object in the mode of running-off" is in this change always something other, even though we still say that the Object and every point of its time and this time itself are one and the same.

(PITC 47)

For Husserl, spatiotemporal being, as David Carr notes, follows this relation between retention and protention by which they are taken together to make up what may be referred to as a "field of occurrence," that is, where the present may stand out from amidst its surroundings (23).

But it would be wrong to say that retention and protention are just empty forms of experience. They are not to be considered as mere crucibles to be filled by recollections or dreams, as empiricists might claim. It is impossible to conceive an act which is devoid of a past or of a future, that is, of retention and protention.

David Carr correctly translates this relational act between retention, protention and the primal now to mean that "to be conscious temporally is to 'constitute' these phenomena from an ever changing now-perspective through our protentive-retentive grasp" (Carr 95). But it is clear that this "constitution," as Carr proposes, is still just a cognitive act reminiscent of the empirical perceptive acts Husserl himself condemns. "As these notions are understood by Husserl," writes Carr, "without past and future there can be no present and thus no experience at all" (Carr 29). It is evident that Husserl, and Carr, believe in a world ruled by sequential spacetime: that is, by causal events. Husserl's perceptive act presupposes that the world is a sequential given, such as in a film strip or a musical score, where each event *is* followed eventually and necessarily by its following successor: for example, as in a movie where each film cell is followed by its succeeding film cell, or in a musical score where each tone is followed by its successor, all in a pre-scribed order. As such, Husserl's phenomenological spacetime

maintains league with the transcendentalism of Newton, the rationalism of Descartes and empiricism of Locke and Hume. Its only difference lies in treating and establishing the perceptive act of consciousness as an active constitutive event itself.

Bradbury's narrative in *The Martian Chronicles,* on the other hand, questions not these theories, but, rather, questions the Late Modern's influence upon the self's social journey of hope into the future, especially as it parallels the colonizing and expansionism of the Americas, and the socio-ethnic problems in said act by an industrial and post-industrial community which had no regards for the other. This is compounded by the need to re-invent a self-identity that could be harmonious to these new possibilities, a shucking of the old in search for a new and improved self (such as that represented by Nietzsche's superman in *Also Sprach Zarathustra* and the nihilistic process exposed in *Der Wille zur Macht*).

Three moments in *The Martian Chronicles* are focal to the phenomenological reading of spacetime that I propose, and that may even hint at the cyclical self-reflective nature expressed by a Late Modern conceptualization of spacetime. They are: 1) **"February 1999: Ylla," "August 1999: The Summer Night," "August 1999: The Earth Men," and "April 2000: The Third Expedition"**; 2) **"August 2002: Night Meeting"**; and 3) **"October 2026: The Million-Year Picnic."** These moments are focal in understanding my argument that, as laid out by the Late Modern, man's re-collection of spacetime is retentive/protentive, rather than presentive. Spacetime is still a collection of Aristotelian "now-moments." But, instead of being recognized at its surfacing, they are reflexively construed as conscious remembrances of the "just-past." What is more, the game of self-identity played out by Bradbury is one pertaining to the future as the horizon of the expected. As I stated before, the text, a diary-like narrative, basically asks who or what is the Martian. It is only in retrospect, by reaching the last entry of the chronicle, that one can see how the solution to this problem follows Husserl's concept of time-consciousness. As Husserl contends about the perception of time-consciousness, the solution was always there, in the horizon, like a melody, waiting to be played out fully before providing the answer. Like a musical score, diaries or chronicles contain all the scores ready to be played.[4]

In *The Martian Chronicles,* each entry in the colony's diary leads, ultimately, to revealing the historical score of Martian identity, as it becomes obvious once one reaches **"The Million-Year Picnic."** It is by realizing each entry, and by recollecting such entries from the perspective of their succeeding entries, that the full value of Bradbury's narrative is realized. Each entry is a date in a calendar, as each musical note is a tone in a musical score, or each cell is a scene in a film; they all follow a prescribed sequence which, in retrospect, reveals a given whole.

In **"February 1999: Ylla"** Mr. K's implicit hatred toward the arrival of the first Earth expedition to Mars is fueled by his fear of loss of identity, as a (Modern) male and as a Martian. The Earthmen bring with them a decentering lust—in the form of the industrial and technological marvels of the Late Modern—as witnessed by Mr. K's wife's dreams (3-4, 8). But this un-eventful arrival is of a double nature, for it occurs only in the wantonness of Mrs. K's dreams. In reality, the objectified knowledge of this arrival is covered and denied by Mr. K's murder of the Earth crew. Mr. K's actions are fueled by a need to safeguard himself and the Martians from losing their idyllic—Victorian—identities as Martians, After all, his wife was lusting for foreigners that, by all accounts, contradicted Martian (Modern) norms, and especially his own self.

But the damage had already been done. The Martians had been infected telepathically by the overriding intentions of the Earthmen's self. The Martians found themselves singing rhymes in languages they did not know (**"August 1999: The Summer Night"** 15). The premonition, or, rather, the fulfillment of the end is given early, when the Martian women wake-up with screaming fear.

> [Martian women] "Something terrible will happen in the morning."
>
> [Martian husbands] "Nothing can happen, all is well with us."
>
> [Martian women] A hysterical sobbing, "It is coming nearer and nearer and *nearer!*"
>
> (**"August 1999: The Summer Night"** 16)

This dialogue between the Martian women and their husbands forms the essence for what Margaret Lee Zoreta identifies as the "*monologic* attitude toward alterity," that is, "the obliteration of the other" (57). Zoreta identifies this attitude as standing against Bakhtin's concept of the dialogic, that is, as Zoreta states, as

> a polyphonic coexistence of "understanding as the transformation of the other's into 'one's own/another's'"
>
> (57)

This imperialistic attitude against the other fuels the fear of not only the Martians, as noted above by the cry of the Martian women, but also the fear of the Earthlings of not succeeding in their quest for Mars.

As the narrative of the next two expeditions reveals, the Martians, in an act of preserving their sanity and, eventually, their identity, decide to eliminate the threat

to their identities by eliminating the expeditions. In particular, the second expedition, **"August 1999: The Earth Men,"** deals with the psychic stability of the Martian self. Arriving in a world wracked by mass psychosis, the Earthmen are shuffled from one Martian to another, to end locked-up in a mental institution. In the same manner that Mrs. K suffered from the maddening illusiveness of her dreams, the Martian population has been infected with an unexplainable telepathic psychosis of an other which threatens their society: Martians now believe that they are Earthlings (25). Their only recourse is to eradicate the source of such deviations from the established societal norm.

> Yes. You know, such cases as yours need special 'curing'. The people in that hall are simpler forms. But once you've gone this far, I must point out, with primary, secondary, auditory, olfactory, and labial hallucinations, as well as tactile and optical fantasies, it is pretty bad business. We have to resort to euthanasia.
>
> (**"The Earth Men"** 27-28)

Reality is a construction of primary and secondary sensory perceptions that the human mind orders into a working reality. Thus the description made by the Martian psychologist, Mr. Xxx, of the psychosis suffered by the Martians can be defined simply as cognitive experience. The experiential act is basically the collective sum of what British empiricists, such as Locke and Hume, have described as "primary, secondary, auditory, olfactory, labial, tactile and optical" perceptions. The Martian psychologist could have been reading either Locke or Hume, for he describes the mental faculty of forming the real, as British empiricists in the seventeenth and eighteenth century proposed. But, in this case, these perceptions are the perceptions of an other's reality, and, at that, one menacing to the stability of Martian reality. For a people who have found a sounder form of living, these intruding multiple sensorial acts merely complicate the Martians' definition of being. Not because they are real, but because they are somebody else's "real." The Late Modern, somewhat founded on these empirical tenets, embodies the same definition for reality as that offered by the Martian psychologist. But the Industrial Modern, represented by the Earth expeditions, endangers the continuance of these simple tenets of Martian living. Eventually, the Martian psychologist falls victim to the same insanity of which he accused the Earthlings. And as indicated, his only recourse is to eradicate the source of his infection by killing himself. It is here that the consequence of the industrial world merges with the surfacing of the new dangers of the global world as reflected in the last chapter of *The Martian Chronicles*: **"The Million Year Picnic."**

In **"April 2000: The Third Expedition"** Bradbury extends this idea of an identity based on memory and imagination, and plays upon a sense of telepathy and hypnosis as a constitutive act between experiential subjects, and not merely as an individual act. As Captain John Black tries restlessly to sleep he wonders how a Martian city can be so similar to an Earth town.

> Suppose all these houses aren't real at all, this bed not real, but only figments of my own imagination, given substance by telepathy and hypnosis through the Martians, thought Captain John Black.
>
> What if the Martians took the memories of a town *exclusively* from *my* mind?
>
> ("The Third Expedition" 46)

Reminiscent of Descartes' argument of an evil genie, introduced in his *First Meditations,* Captain Black questions the reality that surround him as an illusion created for his benefit, in his, and his crew's, minds. But, after the Earthmen are killed by the population, the Martians still hold Earth forms, and as their masks melt, one must question: what is the reality that Bradbury wanted the reader to see (47-48)? For the psychosis seems to have greater hold on the Martians this time around. No longer is the Martian's psychosis a mere psychosis, as in the second expedition where the Earthmen were a mental sickness, now it is a physical virus that eats away at the physical as well as the mental self of the Martians.

It is the last chapter of *The Martian Chronicles,* "October 2026: The Million-Year Picnic,"[5] which offers to the reader the open closure of being by retrospectively questioning, as well as answering, the beginning of the ordeals on Mars as well as the end of the true lunacy on Earth. It also reflects back to the fears expressed by the Martian women in "The Summer Night." The story deals with a family that goes to Mars for a picnic. But it will reveal itself as the last hope for the race, for Earth, in its narrow mind, has destroyed itself. Faced with the horrors of the past, the father's last act is one of defiance against what he had held as true: he burns copies of texts which once defined the human race and the individual self.

> I'm burning a way of life, just like that way of life is being burned clean of Earth right now. . . . Science ran too far ahead of us quickly, and the people got lost in a mechanical wilderness, like children making over pretty things, gadgets, helicopters, rockets; emphasizing the wrong items, emphasizing machines instead of how to run the machines.
>
> (179-180)

Fire is the purifying element of creation. But left to the incapable hands of man, it becomes a dangerous toy. For such reasons one remembers a shooting star, the first conscious viewing of electricity at work, or the simple act of viewing a movie. When the father destroys all links to the past he is burning all that was burned before him: "All the laws and beliefs of Earth were

burnt into small hot ashes which soon would be carried off in a wind" (180). The father is looking back one last time, looking up at the remembrance of what is, and must be, lost for his family to continue. It is that spirit of annihilation and re-birth that he takes a last wistful glance toward the Earth, an intense search "for Earthian logic, common sense, good government, peace, and responsibility" (173). All the virtues of the Modern. But the father knew that in its enthusiasm to be heralded as the great hope of a technological driven society, the world sent itself aflame in nuclear smoke.

Bradbury's last piece is in fact his first piece. Written well before all the other stories included, or not, in *The Martian Chronicles,* it becomes the motivating telos of the collection. The narrative's theme seems to become clear: to establish the identity of the true Martians. Until now the narrative had demonstrated the "colonizing" process that identity suffers by denying, to break its links with the past, in this case its identification with Earth/Old World. But "The Million-Year Picnic" attempts to break with the past, as the father burns the last physical links with the Old World (i.e. the rocket they came in and the documents). Here "Earth," writes Gary K. Wolfe, "has become less a planet in his mind than a way of life to be rejected" (47). In a Heraclitean move the father takes his family down one of the Martian canals. When asked by his son, Robert, how far down the river they have to go, the father answers "a million years" (172). Time and space are brought together in their being on the river. It is not enough just physically to go down the river, but they must also denude themselves of their "past."

This transposition of time over space reflects how one must deal with their "new" identity. A total annihilation of their past self is demanded for them to carry on, as Nietzsche would expect. To establish the new self, all ties to the past must be broken.

The truth is that neither the past nor the futures are unlinked, as it would seem. For the opened ending of "The Million-Year Picnic" is not only a view forward toward a new Martian self, but it is also a retrospect of the Martian past. A million years is to travel back to the Martian beginning and to the apocalyptic dreams of the Martian women in "The Summer Night." Foreseeing the end of the Martian civilization, the women had unknowingly foreseen the coming of the Earthlings, and the end of their civilization. What Ylla had lustily foreseen in her waking dreams earlier, in those strange forms and sound, had become the feared nightmares and psychotic experiences of a dying Mars. A waking dream, as the oracles would call it, for it foretold the end of the old civilization and the beginning of the new.

In a similar fashion, the father of "The Million-Year Picnic" foresees the coming of his Earthlings, the family with which he expects to repopulate Mars. "Now we're alone. We and a handful of others who'll land in a few days. Enough to start over" (180). But these Earthlings would not be the menace that Mr. K and the Martian women dreaded. Bradbury comes full circle by linking this last hope with Ylla's vision of the Earthmen's first coming. Interestingly, the end of the Martian race becomes the subliminal catalyst that foresees the end of the Human race.

In the **"Night Meeting" ("August 2002")**, Tomás Gomez meets with a Martian, Muhe Ca. This piece is central to this idea of joining ends, for it ties together the nature of time and space played out in the chronicle. It is the meeting of past and future, somewhat similarly to Husserl's meeting of the horizons in the present. But just whose past and whose future are we talking about? For both characters are as real to each as they are phantoms to the other. Like Husserl's time-consciousness of music, each character is the other character's next tone. Each one reflects the just pastness of the other's reality. And each has a future horizon, to which they can lay claim, as the becoming of the other's past: "Tomás put out his hand. The Martian did likewise in imitation. Their hands did not touch; they melted through each other" (86). Not only do their physical bodies melt through each other's, but their identities as well. Concrete opposition within givens establishes identity, and at this point all empirical givens have melted away with their hands.

Past and present do not meet. Rather, they melt into a present without really touching each other. What is cannot come into contact with what is not. In theory, the meeting of matter and anti-matter produces the annihilation of all. And in a sense, the present can be seen as this annihilation, for it loses all sense of past and all sense of future. As Spender had discovered earlier, it just is:

> The Martians discovered the secret of life among animals. The animal does not question life. It lives. Its very reason for living *is* life; it enjoys and relishes life.
>
> **("June 2001:—And the Moon Be Still as Bright"** 66)

Spender's sympathy toward Martian life is echoed by the old man to whom Tomás had spoken at the gas station before meeting up with the Martian Muhe Ca.

> You know what Mars is? It's like a thing I got for Christmas seventy years ago—don't know if you ever had one—they called them kaleidoscopes, bits of crystal and cloth beads and pretty junk. You held it up to the sunlight and looked in through it, and it took your breath away. All the patterns! Well, that's Mars. Enjoy it. Don't ask it to be nothing else but what it is.
>
> **("Night Meeting"** 79)

And what "it" [Mars] is, is the simplicity of being. The multiple colorings of the self as one attempts to describe the soul through its own body. The Martians had sup-

posedly understood the kaleidoscope effect of life. But Earthmen had opted for the complications of explaining away, and, eventually, of controlling the real through science and technology. As such, it is not the Martian who is the Other, as Earth would have us believe. Rather, it is the intruding Earthness, which shows its otherness previously concealed by its imperialistic superiority.

Simplicity in being, as the Martians discovered, seems to be what the human identity lacks. In the need to reflect and create an identity, the truth of the human being denies its own simple and uncomplicated self. Spender understands the totemic representations of "primitive" people. In adopting the image of animals, the spirit is free to commune and enact its primal being. But more than that, Spender's act, as sympathetic identification with the Martian, reflects the secret of phenomenological spacetime, that is, it is *not* simple. Rather, phenomenological spacetime avoids the simplicity of just being by continuously emphasizing the relation between past and future, or just-past and just-future.

Tomás and Muhe, Earthling and Martian, are the two poles of this identity dyad. Each represents the other's reality by projecting its negation unto the other. But this reality is not to be taken as an objective reality. Rather it proposes a subjective power, which establishes each other's experienced reality. Descartes would have described it as a divine power. But Bradbury's protagonists follow empiricist modes and, as such, mirroring somewhat Husserl's phenomenological act of perceiving, they establish a less divine source for their perceptions.

Realities, then, are memories projected into our conscious being. As Captain Black had earlier predicted in **"The Third Expedition,"** the Martians had tapped into the unconscious chamber of memories creating, thus, "the ability to keep me under this dreaming hypnosis all of the time" (46). These memories are what sustain our very own self, for they are the contents of past as well as future being, as Tomás and Muhe would come to argue later. And Time will somehow be key to this being:

> [Muhe Ca] "This can only mean one thing. It has to do with Time. Yes. You are a figment of the Past!"
>
> "No, you are from the Past." said the Earth Man, having had time to think of it now.
>
> "You are so *certain*. How can you prove who is from the Past, who from the Future? What year is it?"
>
> **("Night Meeting"** 85)

Not surprisingly, neither wants to be the past of the other, so they accuse each other of being his past. The fear of not being translates into each one's desire to be the other's future. Existentially, it is easier to be the other's future, rather than his past, for without this illusion of futurity, they would no longer find a reason in living. And resorting to dates offers no solution for each has his own arbitrary way of keeping time. "The result of the meeting," according to Edward J. Gallagher, "is a distinct feeling of simultaneous reality, mutual fate, and mutual (spiritual) communion" (68). Intentions aside, whether figments of our past or figments of our future, the present is the meeting place of all our hallucinations, both those that we expect, as well as those that invade and contradict our every sense of reason.

> The task of projecting your psychotic image into the mind of another via telepathy and keeping the hallucinations from becoming sensually weaker is almost impossible.
>
> ("**The Earth Men**" 29)

But it is done. The Earth Men's perceptive act, reminiscent of Husserl's cognitive act as I described earlier, is a continuous hallucinatory act. And the narrator, as a psychotic genius, is responsible for infecting us with the virus of imagination. To tell a story is to make one feel the story, the place, and the time. These acts illustrate phenomenological spacetime. Sensory hallucinations are the basis for our known selves. Who we are and who we pretend to be are just figments of a long movie script. In the narrative act, these hallucinations are transferred, transformed and eventually adapted into our very own being. The world that surrounds us is a conscious confection of our interpreted world. Who or what surrounds us become definitions of our comprehension. And as such, they form part of the sound stage and supporting cast which help narrate our self.

As I stated above, "**The Million-Year Picnic**" ends with an open closure. In their plight to escape the savage destruction of Earth, the father promises his boys that he will show them Martians. What the boys do not expect is how familiar those Martians will seem to them.

> They reached the canal. It was long and straight and cool and wet and reflective in the night.
>
> "I've always wanted to see a Martian," said Michael. "Where are they, Dad? You promised."
>
> "There they are." Dad said, and he shifted Michael on his shoulder and pointed straight down.
>
> The Martians were there. Timothy began to shiver.
>
> The Martians were there—in the canal—reflected in the water. Timothy and Michael and Robert and Mom and Dad.
>
> The Martians stared back up at them for a long, long silent time from the rippling water. . . .
>
> ("**The Million Year Picnic**" 181)

This is the Father's startling revelation to his children in "**The Million Year Picnic**" which marks a new phase, by accentuating the father's assertion that they are the Martians, both by choice and by accident. This "desire" which, from a beginning, is represented as a desire to impose Earthness upon Mars, has now been transformed into a desired fulfillment of abandoning one identity for another. Similar to Lacan's description of the three mirror phases of an infant's self-cognization, the Earth family now look upon the waters of the Martian canal to reveal a new diverted reality: the Martianness in all of us. Looking back at "**—And the Moon Be Still as Bright**" we can identify the first mirror phase of self awareness when Spender's neurotic identification with the sought "Other" (the Martians) leads towards the desired fulfillment of being safe expressed in the Earthmen's desire mimed by the "blankness" of the Earth (Martian) town of "**The Third Expedition.**" This desire becomes a mimicked reality in its second mirror phase as the first Earth colony battles its fears fulfilling their desires upon the shape shifting form of the "last" Martian in "**The Martian.**" As Brenda K. Marshall notes in *Teaching the Postmodern,* "The subject's identity is the image of itself that the subject forms by identifying with other's perceptions of it" (93). This opened form shifts its site of being as it runs from center to center (the different desires of the people of the town, as projected upon the Martian's chameleonic form) until, in its final act of decentering, it becomes all and none of the sites, breaking its veil and washing away any recognizable form from the sight of the colonists. A new reality is now a must, for the colonists desired safeguards, their constructed realities, now are shattered pieces of their othering mirror.

"**The Million Year Picnic**" tries to pick up the pieces without recreating it. It is the third mirror phase of self-cognization, when the infant sees itself as the self that sees its reflection. The family, seeing their reflecting forms on the waters of the traversed canal, passes from desiring the "Other" towards an understanding of its own "Otherness." It is this new Martian identity that allows the family to be present with it/self.

The transcourse of time and the change of space have led these remnant beings to re-establish their self-identity. They had a choice, and, in retrospect, their choices were forced upon them. Yet the question of spacetime brings out the reality of how the chronicle brings to light the creation of the self, as did Greece and the religious books in the Middle Ages. The epic as well as the religious story trace, in their own ways, the beginnings of a people and of a society. In the same way, they explicate the process by which the individual self, as well as the collective self, is molded. Santayana once said that those who did not learn from their histories were condemned to repeat it. As the future is open, yet restrictively expected by a past that "proph-ecizes" its coming into fulfillment, so the identity of the self is openly desired, yet somewhat preconditioned by the body's alterity

The future follows a text to its "conclusion," temporally, since it recycles itself, as Bradbury seems to allude by leaving the ending suspended by an ellipsis (181). "One key to the story [**"The Million-Year Picnic"**] is the children. Mars will be given to the children who are still capable of wonder . . ." as we are foretold earlier by the old man in **"Night Meeting"** (181). Optimisti-cally, through the father's eyes Bradbury sees a hope for a better future. As in Genesis, Mars is the new land of the twenty-first century Adam and Eve, who with their sons await the daughters from Nod, as well as the birth of their future sister. Such children are not continu-ations of the Old Order, or so Bradbury seems to hope. As Heraclitus once stated, "Time is a child playing a game of draughts; the kingship is in the hands of a child" (in Freeman frg. 52). In this manner, these "new Martians" could be the inheritors of a new playground free of any legacy. Like the kaleidoscope, the dead cit-ies light up the children's faces with the splendor of the new unknown.

Bradbury's narrative represents the temporality of Mar-tianness, that is, it represents the space in which Mar-tianness may be attainable for it opposes the Martian self to a "thing as one that has not yet been made a symbol, . . . [but] has the potential of becoming one" (Lacan "Desire" 46). In this sense, the desire demon-strated by Spender to *be* a Martian, and the desire of the boys to *see* a Martian are themselves two opposing desires of the fulfillment of the Martian. This "pres-ence" in the desire, or the desired, is outside time. "The fantasy of perversion (of Martianness) is namable. It is in space. It suspends an essential relationship. It is not atemporal but rather outside time" (Lacan "Desire" 17). Furthermore, this desire "creates the space of discourse, the possibility of dialogue . . . and in so doing engenders (or represents) the space of temporality" (Schleifer 880). But, as hopeful as this project sounds, these children are not yet the children of the postmod-ern, and even less the children of Nietzsche. For Brad-bury hides them from that important transition through which the self has to reveal itself: to face the future, as Heidegger would probably say, in one's death. This transition is the transitional relationship between the individual and death expressed as an "in-between" that operates as a spatiotemporal constitutive of the self. And that is theme for another Time and another Space.

Notes

1. For the sake of argument in this essay I identify the Early Modern as that period between the 1500s and 1850s and the Late Modern as that period between the 1850s and the late 1960s.

2. Look especially in such stories as "The Summer Night," "The Meeting" and "The Million-Year Picnic."

3. Husserl lays claim to two creative principles of perception which make up the perception of the now: that is (1) retention, or the just-pastness of an event, and (2) protention, that is, the just-future of an event. For Husserl the distinction between recollection and retention is one of proximity to the event (the same applies to the distinction between expectation of the future and protention). Recollection of the past is to remember an act or an event that is no longer occur-ring: but retention is maintaining "present" the just-pastness of the act in relation to its successive act. Of import is that contrary to empiricists, Husserl proposes continuity in the succession of perceptive acts. Consciousness of the present (the perceptive act) presupposes the consciousness of its "comet trail of retentions," that is, of the trail it leaves behind. In the same way, protentional act differs from expecta-tion of the future in that the expectation of the future is one's intentionality towards some far future act or event (one plans for it, dreads its coming, or looks forward to its becoming), while protention is the implicitly anticipated immediate future envisioned as the horizon of the present. Protention, then, is the conscious knowledge that an act occurs only to be replaced by its succeeding act. In this manner, hu-man time-consciousness is understood as "past-retention-event-protention-future."

4. Bradbury wrote another possible ending which could be seen as complementary yet oppositional to this one. See "Dark They Were, and Golden Eyed." First published as "Naming the Names" in *Thrilling Wonder Stories* (August 1949). In this story the transformation of the family into Martians is due to the environment, and not by choice.

5. In *Jacques Lacan* Anika Lemaire explains: During the [first] mirror phase of the child's development it "recognizes" itself as distinct from the outside world. The term "mirror phase" refers to the awareness of the subject of itself as separate from the mother, for example . . . [it is] an identification with an imaginary (because imagined) . . . autonomous self. [Second phase] the child recognizes him/herself as separate in the mirror phase, but at this phase also identifies him/herself with equal-age peers, reimagin-ing these peers as they replicate the image he/she has seen in the mirror "of the human form" (91).

Works Cited

Bradbury, Ray. *The Martian Chronicles*. Garden City, NY: Doubleday, 1958.

Carr, David. *Time, Narrative, and History*. (1986) Stud-ies in Phenomenology and Existential Philosophy. Bloomington and Indianapolis: Indiana UP, 1991.

Freeman, Kathleen. *Ancilla to the Pre-Socratic Philoso-phers*. Boston: Harvard University Press, 1983.

Gallagher, Edward J. "The Thematic Structure of *The Martian Chronicles*." In Greenberg and Olander 55-82.

Greenberg, Martin Harry, and Joseph D. Olander. "Ray Bradbury." *Writers of the 21st Century.* Edinburgh: Paul Harris Publishing, 1980.

Grudin, Robert. *Time and the Art of Living.* New York: Ticknor and Fields, 1982.

Guffey, George R. "The Unconscious, Fantasy, and 'Science Fiction': Transformations in Bradbury's *Martian Chronicles* and Lem's *Solaris*." In Slusser, *Bridges of Fantasy* 142-159.

Heidegger, Martin. *On Time and Being.* (1969). Trans. by Joan Staumbaugh, NY: Harper Torchbooks [Harper and Row], 1972.

Husserl, Edmund. *Husserl: Shorter Works.* Peter McCormick and Frederick Elliston, editors. Foreword by Walter Biemel. Notre Dame, Indiana: University of Notre Dame Press; Great Britain: The Harvester Press, 1981. 18-35.

———. *The Phenomenology of Internal Time-Consciousness.* [*PITC*] Edited by Martin Heidegger. Trans. James Churchill. Bloomington, IN: Indiana University Press, 1973.

Johnson, Wayne L. *Ray Bradbury.* New York: Frederick Ungar, 1980.

Lacan Jacques. "Desire and the Interpretation of Desire in *Hamlet*." Trans. James Hulbert. *Yale French Studies,* 55/56 (1977).

Lemaire, Anika. *Jacques Lacan.* Trans. David Macy. Boston: Routledge & Keegan Paul. 1977.

Lévi-Strauss, Claude. *Myth and Meaning.* New York: Schocken Books, 1979.

Marshall. Brenda K. *Teaching the Postmodern: Fiction and Theory.* New York/London: Routledge. 1992.

Mogen, David. *Ray Bradbury.* Twayne's United States Authors Series, 504. Boston: Twayne, 1986.

Mumford, Lewis. *Technics and Civilization.* Quoted in Jean-François Lyotard, *The Postmodern Condition.* Trans. G. Bennington and B. Massumi: Minneapolis: University of Minnesota Press, 1984.

Nowotny, Helga. *Time: The Modern and Postmodern Experience.* Trans. Neville Plaice, Cambridge: Polity Press, 1994.

Schleifer, Ronald. "The Space and Dialogue of Desire. Lacan, Greimas and Narrative Temporality." *Modern Language Notes* Vol. 98 no. 5 (Dec 1983): 871-890.

Slusser, George E., et. al. *Bridges of Fantasy: Alternatives.* Carbondale: Southern Illinois University Press, 1992

Wolfe, Gary K. "The Frontier Myth in Ray Bradbury." In Greenberg 33-54.

Zoreta, Margaret Lee. "Bakhtin, Blobels and Philip Dick." *Journal of Popular Culture.* Vol. 28.3 (Winter 1994): 55-61.

Ray Bradbury and Steven L. Aggelis (interview date 9 October 2002)

SOURCE: Bradbury, Ray, and Steven L. Aggelis. "Conversation with Ray Bradbury." In *Conversations with Ray Bradbury,* edited by Steven L. Aggelis, pp. 194-202. Jackson, Miss.: University Press of Mississippi, 2004.

[*In the following interview, conducted October 9, 2002, Bradbury reveals the influence of his childhood in a number of his works.*]

[*Aggelis:*] *You've been interviewed numerous times. I've got a bibliography of 335 interviews. If you could interview anyone, living or passed on, who would you interview, and why?*

[Bradbury:] George Bernard Shaw. He was the greatest playwright of our century. There was no one anywhere near him when it came to play writing. And his book of prefaces, which I have two copies of, is around three or four thousand pages of the essays he wrote introducing his plays, on any subject you want to name. So, if I were to interview anyone, it would be George Bernard Shaw.

What's the latest on your work in film?

There's nothing going on except one project, *A Sound of Thunder,* which started filming in Prague, in October. And on all the other films or events, I have no news.

What were some of the problems you were having with **A Sound of Thunder***?*

Well, the director who had been on the project for a year, all of a sudden, said: "Why don't we get rid of the butterfly?" When I tell that story people say: "The butterfly? Good Grief! That's the center of the story. If you get rid of the butterfly, there's no story." So, we fired him. We have another director now.

I would like to discuss your latest short-story collection, **One More for the Road.**

OK.

The story "One More for the Road" addresses plagiarism and censorship, and also mentions the city of Tallahassee. I contacted you from Tallahassee in February

2002 about the Conversations with Ray Bradbury *project and, over the ensuing few months, we discussed the issue of plagiarism. When did you write this story and what was your motivation?*

Ho ho! I can't remember. Once the writing process is back, I really can't remember.

You said Tallahassee stuck out in your mind. One time you had car trouble there.

I was down . . . twenty years ago, I was going for the opening of EPCOT, the Disney project in Florida, and I lectured in New Orleans one day, and the next day I was supposed to leave on the train for Miami, and they canceled all the trains. So, I had to hire a limousine driver in order to go south for the opening of EPCOT. Well, I wound up with this limousine with a driver, a colored driver who was about twenty years older than myself (I think he was seventy-five years old, at least, and I was in my early sixties.), and we started out on the road to head south into Florida. And at Tallahassee we blew a tire in the middle of the freeway. So, you can imagine what fun it was to change a tire right out in the middle of the freeway, with the cars whizzing by. And we finally got the spare put on, but it was not a good spare. It only lasted a few miles. So, we pulled into Tallahassee, and we tried to find a place that carried a different sized tire. Limousine tires aren't the same size as ordinary tires. So, it took us two hours of prowling around until finally we got decent tires for the limousine. And we got on the road, and a couple of hours later the engine of the limousine broke, and we drifted into a motel, and the car died right there in the motel parking lot. And I moved into the motel for the night with two six-packs of beer for the last night of the World's Series. And the next morning, the damn limousine was dead forever, and there was no way of getting further south for the opening of EPCOT. So, I called the local taxi cab company—I still had about 150 miles to go to get down to EPCOT. Well, the taxi driver showed up, and he turned out to be the town sheriff as well as being the cab driver. So, the town sheriff took me the rest of the way down to EPCOT. And I got a full lecture on the splendors and the glories of Florida on the way, and it cost me an additional $200 to get to EPCOT. So, Tallahassee is burned into my mind from that splendid day when the car blew a tire there. These things happen, and I write a story within minutes of it happening. I never brood over anything.

In "First Day," four elderly gentlemen are stationed around their alma mater's flag pole, because of a pact they made to meet on the first day of school, fifty years after their graduation. They do not speak, but wave to each other and leave. Charles Douglas, the protagonist, concludes that they were to meet on the last *day of school, not the first, but, when he returns home, he tells*

his wife, Alice, "We talked our heads off!" What exactly is the moral of this particular story?

The moral, of course, is you mustn't plan things like that. It's a romantic idea. It actually happened to me on the last day of school, back in 1938. All my buddies, all my best pals, we all promised each other that fifty years later we'd all get together and have a reunion. Well, I'm the only one who remembered, I think, and that's why I wrote the story—because I'm a born romantic, hopelessly sentimental. And of all the people who took that oath, I was the only one who remembered. I didn't go there on that day, but I thought about it. So, naturally, I wrote the story, because I was sad remembering our friendship and the fact that we would never get together again.

The story "Beasts" seems to address the effect of pornography on personal relationships and society. The story depicts men wading through the sewers for flesh, like lemmings swimming to their destruction. Is this an accurate take on the story? Please elaborate.

What happened is that many years ago I belonged to a gymnasium, and you get to talking to all kinds of people. And there was a gymnast there—I used to swim, and then lie out in the sun and take some sunlight, and you get to talking to people when you belong to the gymnasium—and he told me about a phone number I could call. And it was a combination of numbers that fused, you could hear voices from around the city and around the country, of people calling in with terrible needs. Phone sex. All sorts of strangers who took that way of connecting with people—not meeting them, but having this sort of terrible meeting on the telephone. I never called the number. I never had enough courage. I didn't want to know that truth about people. I thought it was horrible such a number existed, and that people would be using it—tens of thousands of them, or hundreds of them, or dozens of them. So, the story was born out of knowing that such a number really existed, and that kind of phone pornography occurred in the world. It's a metaphor that connects with the phone. That's all.

"Fore!" and "Well, What Do You Have to Say for Yourself" both deal with marital infidelity, but are handled quite differently. In "Fore!" Glen Foray, the golf driving range manager, acts on behalf of Mr. Gingrich by punching Gingrich's adulterous wife in the mouth. In "Well, What Do You Have to Say for Yourself," the couple resolves their differences between themselves. Do certain circumstances justify specific reactions, or should Glen Foray go to jail for assault?

Ha! It's only a story!!

It's a purging; it's a way to get the hairball out.

That's right. But, you mustn't read too much into a story like that. You read it because it's the sort of thing you would like to have happen in the world, if there was any justice.

"The Cricket on the Hearth" seems to lead the reader to accept government surveillance in personal households. Was this your intention?

No, no, not for a moment. It's a thing that actually happened about fifty years ago during the McCarthy era. I had a writer friend, a lady friend, whose husband, James Wong Howe, was the most important cinematographer in movies. I knew Jimmy very well. They had been in love for many years, but they were not allowed to marry because there was a law in California up until 1949 or 1950 that Chinese were not allowed to marry Americans. That law was changed, and they were able to marry at last. During the same period, they were under surveillance because she was, on occasion, I believe, a member of the Communist Party, so they thought that their home was bugged. And she told me about it, and I said, "Are you sure?" And she said, "Yes." There were these mysterious sounds on the telephone, and that was a bad period, around 1952 or 1953, when almost anything was possible. And I knew a lot of people who were temporarily involved with Communism and were not what you would call "diehard." They were people with good hearts who thought Communism promised them a good future. All of us at one time or another, when we were young, fall into that category—not necessarily Communism. I belonged, when I was nineteen, to Technocracy Incorporated. They had a good heart, and had a wonderful plan, but it was completely impractical. I belonged to it for about a year, and then I realized I was boring the hell out of everybody, by lecturing them. Anyway, when Sanora told me about this possible bug, a cricket on the hearth, I was so upset I wrote the story. So, the story is very old. I never sold it. And I finally took it out of my file forty-eight years later. So, censorship is nothing I approved of, ever.

It almost seemed, when I read the story, that the couple's behavior changed after the "cricket" was gone, that the wife, particularly, missed it.

She's being semi-facetious, or sometimes a certain kind of threat or almost danger becomes part of our lives, and when it's gone, we get bored. While it was there, it was more stimulating, and when it was gone, they missed it, because it was stimulating.

"My Son, Max" addresses homosexuality. Was the husband justified in shocking his wife because she had defended her son's position, versus her husband's stance, over the last year, since Max came out of the closet?

The father there is a man who's had the future taken away from him, when he realized there could be no future if his son turned out the way his son said. It means there would be no grandchildren. So, the shock of realizing the family was destroyed caused him to behave that way. It's very natural. I was very fortunate in raising four daughters, and I have four grand-daughters and four grandsons. But, if someone had said to me at a certain point, fifty-two years ago, "You're not going to have any grandchildren," that would have been a terrible shock. And God knows how I would have reacted to it. So, what the father does is perfectly natural, to put himself on some sort of even keel with the world, now that the future has been destroyed.

Stepping out of **One More for the Road,** *and looking at your collection* **Long after Midnight,** *there were a couple of stories that dealt with homosexuality (Bradbury laughs "Ha!"), and both are compassionate representations of a particular culture—***"Long after Midnight,"** *the story of the apparent suicide of a transvestite, and* **"The Better Part of Wisdom,"** *the story of a grandfather who happens upon his grandson in a homosexual relationship.*

That one story where the grandfather comes to visit his grandson, the memory he has of his childhood—there was a thing that happened to me when I was twelve. I had a friendship with a boy who moved in next door, and we were great pals. We wandered everywhere, like gypsies, totally innocent, you know. When you're twelve years old, you don't know anything about the world. You don't know about sex, you haven't discovered your body. So, your feelings are pure—absolutely pure. And two boys wandering around with their arms over each other's shoulders. The world is glorious; it's simply glorious. And the grandfather remembers this, and that makes him a little bit more tolerant of his grandson, and realizing that the same thing could have happened to him, but never did. He had that one summer where he wandered around with his best pal. The best pal went away forever, and that was it. But it was absolutely pure and complete. So, I thought it would be wonderful to build a story around a real memory I had of childhood, and place it forward in relation to a grandson.

The transvestite in **"Long after Midnight,"** *it seemed to me that it was a suicide, but I had someone read it and say, "How do you know that someone didn't pick this person up and find out who it was and then lynched this person?"*

That story's based on a real story that was in the *L.A. Times,* and it so saddened me to think that someone would commit suicide by hanging himself. And then the next day they discover it wasn't a girl after all. It was a man dressed like a woman, who must have had, God knows, an unhappy life and killed himself by hanging. So, the terrible irony of the story is in the fact that you have the police sympathetic in one moment because they think they're taking down the body of a girl, and then later discover it's not a girl at all. So, you have a shift in feelings implied, and you, the reader, then suffer the difference.

According to some literary critics such as Michel Foucault, a work should be thought of as author-less—that what really matters is the relationship between the reader and the text. And the skillful writer uses this principle to intentionally create gaps so that the reader must fill them in, thus acting as a co-creator, actively participating in the creation of the story. What would you say about this? Can Ray Bradbury stories be read without being aware of Ray Bradbury?

Oh, dear me! That's too complicated. I don't believe in theories like that. If you thought of that sort of thing, you would write self-conscious stories that wouldn't be any good. You can't think about what you're doing. Just get the story down.

Just put it on paper.

Yes, that's all. And whatever people think about, let them think. Because you, yourself, don't know when you're writing it why, exactly, you're doing it, but you write the story.

One of the last stories I want to discuss from **One More for the Road** *is "Where All Is Emptiness, There Is Room to Move," which sounds Eastern in its orientation. What was your inspiration and moral for that story?*

When I was in Mexico fifty-seven years ago, traveling around, I was supposed to go down the coast to Vera Cruz. And there was a harbor there that had been silted in with sand. And the sand had collected in such a way to build a barrier, so that ships couldn't get in or out. Well, the people couldn't afford to clear the sand barrier, and the port died. And the ships that were in the port stayed there, and the ships that were outside could never come in. So, you had a ghost town. The town eventually was evacuated by the people, who went elsewhere. It's a perfect town for someone to use as a bombing target for a motion picture. So, there's an irony there of Hollywood taking advantage of an actual disaster that occurred to the town, and moving in to further destroy it. So, that's basically what the story is.

Was Jackie Robinson's entry into professional baseball the inspiration for **"The Big Black and White Game"**?

No. That's a true story that happened to me when I was twelve years old. I saw that game, and I saw the cakewalk at the end of the day, that evening in the big tavern there at the lakefront in Wisconsin. All the colored people got together. The women in those most beautiful gowns, and all the colored men in tuxedos. And there must have been—oh, forty or fifty couples, a hundred colored people, dancing the cakewalk there, in the tavern, that night, after the big black and white game. So, the memory of it stayed with me for all those years, and I finally had to write about it. Everything in that story is the truth. So, it wasn't inspired by anything else—only that time when I was twelve.

Were both **"The Golden Kite, The Silver Wind"** *and* **"The Meadow"** *pro United Nations pieces?*

No. Starting when I was thirteen, I hung around Paramount Studios, Columbia, United Artists, MGM, and I saw them building and destroying the sets. So, I remembered that when I was twenty-six years old—and I wrote a short story then, based on the destruction of those sets. And they were metaphorically representative of the world. But, that's mainly it. It wasn't about politics at all.

What would you say to one's assertion that, in **Dandelion Wine,** *Leo Auffman and his "Happiness Machine" are fashioned around the story of Philo T. Farnsworth and his electronic transmission of images, his television?*

No, I didn't know anything about him till later in life. I still don't know all that much. But, when I was young, of course, I had no way of knowing what he was up to because very few articles appeared anywhere—I believe there were one or two articles in *Popular Mechanics,* that sort of place. So, no, I knew nothing of him.

Henry Adams compared the dynamo to a cathedral. How much Henry Adams is in **"Powerhouse"**?

I didn't read him till later. I lived in Venice, California, with my parents, from 1942 on the powerhouse property. We had a little bungalow and right next door across the wire fence was this powerhouse. I would go over on occasion and look at the various electrical devices humming there. It was a small place, where the power came to be reduced to a smaller voltage before it was sent back out. I was amazed at my feelings there at night, that the interior of the powerhouse felt like a church. It reminded me of the interior of a cathedral, a small metaphor for something very large. So, I wrote about it because I lived next door to it.

I'd like to ask you a couple of questions about films. I know you're very much a film person.

I've seen every film made. I'm a super expert.

Which films over the last few years do you consider fabulous works of art and why?

A film came out about five years ago called *As Good As It Gets*, with Helen Hunt and Jack Nicholson, and directed by Brooks who wrote the fabulous screenplay. It had incredible performances. And it achieved an impossible goal, because you start with a man who is completely unpleasant, played by Nicholson, and you begin by not liking him at all, maybe even hating him. And over a period of two hours you get to love him and understand him and his relationship with the waitress that he falls in love with. So, if you haven't seen it, I think it had twelve Academy nominations and won eight Oscars. Everyone in the film, and the film itself, and the screenplay won Academy awards. And that's fabulous. Have you seen it?

I enjoyed the film. I have yet to see A Beautiful Mind. *My professor has really encouraged me to see that film.*

No. I turned it off. We have a copy here, but it was too self-conscious. I hate films that are "good" for you. I don't like people who set out to do me a favor: "Look at this film and it will do good for you." See, *Fahrenheit* does good for you without trying. And the important thing about *Fahrenheit* is that I wrote a James Bond adventure, but the core of it has a lot to do with my love of reading and libraries, and about book burning. But, I don't hit you over the head with it, at least I don't think I have. I don't recommend my book or my film of *Fahrenheit* because it will do you good. That would be terrible. I don't want to do good for anyone. I want the good to come incidentally.

On the flipside, which films over the last few years do you consider worthless works of art and why?

Well, most of them. I mean, films that have won Academy awards the last few years—like *American Beauty* is filled with terrible people. They all deserve to die. The one person who does something decent, the husband, at the end, when he refuses to go to bed with his stupid daughter's girlfriend, he's rewarded with a bullet through the brain. Well, come on! So, I hated that film. And it got all kinds of Academy awards. Same way with *The English Patient*. It's a story of a dreadful man who destroys everyone. He destroys his best friend, who commits suicide, by trying to kill him. He kills his mistress, indirectly. She dies in a plane crash. He's carrying her dead body back across enemy lines. He's shot and burned, and finally commits suicide. So, it's a real happy story, isn't it? And it got all kinds of Academy awards.

Well, Mr. Bradbury, is there anything, a question, I haven't asked you (Bradbury laughs "Ha!") that you would like to respond to?

If I start doing that, we'll be here all night. Bye bye.

Michael Angelotti (essay date 2002)

SOURCE: Angelotti, Michael. "Afraid of the Dark: Censorship, Ray Bradbury, and *The Martian Chronicles.*" In *Censored Books II: Critical Viewpoints, 1985-2000,* edited by Nicholas J. Karolides, pp. 296-304. Lanham, Md.: Scarecrow, 2002.

[*In the following essay, Angelotti rates the vulnerability of* The Martian Chronicles *to public-school censorship.*]

> They began by controlling books of cartoons and detective books and, of course, films, one way or another, one group or another, political bias, religious prejudice, union pressures; there was always a minority afraid of something, and a great majority afraid of the dark, afraid of the future, afraid of the past, afraid of the present, afraid of themselves and shadows of themselves.
>
> *The Martian Chronicles* 105

Ray Bradbury wrote **"April 2005: Usher II,"** one of twenty-six chapters in *The Martian Chronicles* (1950), in the style of Edgar Allan Poe. It is the futuristic story of Mr. William Stendahl, a Poe zealot who "delicately contrived" on Mars the House and atmosphere of Usher to intricately replicate Poe's fictional creation. Stendahl further embellished the House and grounds by adding horrific touches from many of Poe's other works, particularly "Murders in the Rue Morgue," "The Cask of Amontillado," and "The Masque of Red Death." His object was deadly revenge against the government censors and like-minded "Moral Climate" people who had burned all of Poe's works in the "Great Fire" of 1975, and ten years later, Stendahl's entire illegal library of 50,000 books. [Please see Bradbury's *Fahrenheit 451* (1953) for the infernal details.] Specifically, Stendahl invited prominent censors, citizens, and members of the "Society for the Prevention of Fantasy" to a "costume ball" at the House of Usher II, during which he subjected his victims to grotesque deaths perpetrated by Stendahl's mechanical manifestations of Poe's ironic fictional motifs; for example, one killed by a robotoid gorilla, another in a pit by a swinging pendulum, a large group by the red death, and whoever somehow survived to evening's end, by the swift and crushing collapse of the House of Usher II upon itself.

As a reader who also happens to admire the works of Poe, I could relish the ironies and literary allusions to Poe's works. They were abundant and cleverly worked into this story. No doubt, Bradbury had at least as much fun writing this piece as did I reading it; although I must admit that at times I was aghast at the fiendish slaughter of forty-something human beings, fictional or not, censors or not. The very idea! Surely Stendahl was insane. But, then again, that was one of Bradbury's intentions, wasn't it? Nevertheless, I appreciated Bradbury's excellent literary craftsmanship, the interplay of his own style and content with Poe's style and content. Clearly, this story is a quality piece of writing. And I never once confused Bradbury, the author, and Stendahl, the fictional character, nor thought Bradbury a criminal for creating this story nor felt a single impulse to imitate Stendahl's actions in real life. That is, I was not moved to censor the book because of the possible harm it could inflict upon an impressionable reader.

But why was this story written as it was in this book? To make a unique and interesting "chronicle" that in itself engages the reader in story while moving along the larger narrative while restating one of its major themes? Done. Which theme? The politics of government versus human rights? Of government and censorship? At least those. The lead quote to this chapter was spoken by Stendahl near the end of his impassioned recounting of the history of a continuing censorship nightmare born in the second half of the twentieth century as projected by a Ray Bradbury writing in the late forties very much aware of the brutal promise of Senator McCarthy's Un-American Activities Committee to wreak havoc on the U. S. artistic community. Assuming that Stendahl speaks for Bradbury, the author's position on censorship leaves little to the reader's imagination. And given the publication of *Fahrenheit 451* in the midst of the McCarthy paranoia, one cannot help but admire Bradbury's courage under fire (not to pun).

Throughout *The Martian Chronicles* Bradbury questions the ethics, actions, and moral character of governments, I think fairly put, over the history of humankind, but especially those so characterized as "colonial," who conquered, plundered, and arrogantly erased the identities of whole peoples, without conscience, often in the name of pious religious orders.

The Martian Chronicles was Bradbury's futuristic story of a Mars inhabited by an ancient, dying civilization, hastened to its extinction, erased, in body and artifact, by Earth "colonizers." Yes, as reader, one can marvel at his writing. Yes, as reader, one can become more aware, become more deeply sensitive to the earthbound issues he so powerfully raises, think differently, even be persuaded to condemn, act against, such action by his or her own government. And yes, Bradbury includes, rather blatantly, the U. S. government of the time of the novel as a primary evildoer. And, yes, extreme acts of censorship and book burning have been part of world history, even United States history. But in this book and others it is the scale of it, the extinction by fire, the bibliocide of all works of fantasy and imagination that raise consciousness.

Again, there is not much of a stretch between the brewing communist witch-hunts of Senator McCarthy's Committee on Government Operations of the Senate of the late 1940s and early 1950s and Bradbury's depic-

tions of extreme acts of censorship in those of his works immediately preceding and following McCarthy's Committee. Nor does he omit callous environmental destruction and crimes against indigenous peoples. Whether extreme literary censorship or suppression of political beliefs, governmental paranoia is governmental paranoia. And usurped individual freedoms is the result. Strong anti-government political statement? Yes. Portrayal of grotesque acts of violence by human beings upon human beings? Yes. Excellent literary writing worth preserving, fighting for? Yes.

So, how censorable is this story? This book? If history serves, not very to the general public readership to this point in the twenty-first century. Like Shakespeare, its literary value and continuing interest to readers protect it. But the public school arena provides different risks. There, recent and troublesome challenges have occurred. What is their nature? And what can be done to protect accessibility to *The Martian Chronicles* for teachers who may freely choose to teach it and those students who may freely choose to read it?

To address the question of the vulnerability of *The Martian Chronicles* to censorship at this writing, I will discuss it in the context of data provided by the Office for Intellectual Freedom (OIF), the American Library Association's censorship database website, and a recent censorship case illustrating in some detail how one school and teacher responded in all the right ways to a parental challenge of her teaching of *The Martian Chronicles* to her eighth grade students.

The "OIF Censorship Data Base 1990-1999" recently graphed three sets of data on its website depicting challenges to book accessibility, which indicate that (1) in terms of numbers of recorded *challenges by institution being challenged*—schools (2925), school libraries (2013), public libraries (1462), and museums/galleries (43) were the four institutions most challenged during this period; (2) in terms of numbers of recorded *challenges by type*—sexually explicit (1446), offensive language (1262), unsuited to age group (1167), occult/satanism (773), violence (630), homosexuality (497), religious viewpoint (397), nudity (297), and racism (245) were the nine most frequently challenged targets during this period; and (3) in terms of numbers of recorded *challenges by initiator of challenge*—parent (3427), patron (878), administrator (541), board member (206), teacher (169), and pressure group (163) were the six most frequent initiators of challenges during this period. Interestingly, religious organization (107) and clergy (89) taken together represent the fourth most frequent initiator, and there were only ten recorded challenges during this period by elected officials.

Of importance is the statement by the OIF that "Research suggests that for each challenge reported there are as many as four or five which go unreported."

Assuming that the relative positions of more to less frequent items in each group would remain the same with unreported challenges factored in, one might conclude from the data taken as a whole that the most likely challenge would come from a parent concerned about sexually explicit content or offensive language or material unsuited to an age group (or some combination of these) and that the challenge would be directed to a school or school library. In fact, that is the nature of a 1998 challenge of the teaching of *The Martian Chronicles* reported by the Edison, New Jersey, *Star-Ledger* in its April 9, 1998, edition.

The article reports that the issue centered on a chapter in *Chronicles*, **"June, 2003: Way in the Middle of the Air,"** which tells the story of a group of southern blacks gathering to fly to Mars to establish their own settlement. They are harassed by a viciously racist southern white man who frequently degrades them individually and as a race and often uses the term "nigger" to accentuate his rancorous language use. The point of the story is to make a strong statement against racism and project a sympathetic, positive image of African Americans.

The students in question were eighth graders, among whom were two African American students. The mother of one of the African American students claimed that the oral reading of the story "humiliated" her daughter and its offensive language was inappropriate for the maturity level of eighth graders. The teacher had carefully prepared herself and the students in advance of the teaching, and the book was among those on the school district's approved list. The mother presented her case to appropriate school and district personnel. Ray Bradbury, in a telephone interview, noted the positive portrayal of African Americans and thought it "ridiculous, at this late date, to criticize the use of the word. It was a different time." University experts strongly defended the book. The district had in place American Library Association Guidelines, was opposed to censorship, and supported the teacher's position. The mother, also opposed to censorship, per se, engaged the press. The district relented, and upon further study and the subsequent recommendation of the middle school English department chair, moved the book from the eighth grade to the tenth grade on the grounds that the story in particular and the book in general required a more mature reader than eighth-grade students.

In a related story, the teacher wrote a letter about the case to the National Coalition Against Censorship (NCAC), which printed a "shortened version" of the letter in its Censorship News Online, "Issue #70: Censorship and Ray Bradbury's *The Martian Chronicles,* Summer 1998." In the introduction to the letter "excerpts," NCAC notes that the teacher chose *Chronicles* "for its relevance to the science and social

studies curriculum" and "In preparation, she read articles on science fiction, critical essays of Bradbury's work, and teaching materials from the Center for Learning for use with the novel." In the version of the letter provided by NCAC the teacher wrote that:

> Because of its use of the word "nigger," I briefly considered skipping the chapter, but I felt that was a cowardly thing to do. . . . I decided . . . to do a guided reading of the chapter. . . . As soon as we started the novel, we were engaged in discussions of social criticism—environmental issues, gender issues, colonization issues, etc. For the controversial chapter, I created a worksheet. . . . I told my students that this was a controversial chapter . . . , that we would meet a character who would use the word "nigger" several times, as well as curses. We then discussed the author's purpose in creating this character. The students correctly concluded that the reader was supposed to hate Teece, and that Bradbury was trying to illustrate the evils of racism, prejudice, and discrimination. . . . I felt that I had established a safe environment in my classroom and that my students were ready for this material. I read the chapter aloud to the class, stopping frequently for discussion. . . . The mother of one of my African-American students objected to my reading of the chapter aloud and especially to my saying "nigger" instead of saying "the n-word" or skipping the word entirely. . . . The mother went to the principal, my department head, and the assistant superintendent of curriculum. All supported my use of the book and teaching methods. She was advised that she could file a complaint against the book. Instead she went to the *Star Ledger.* . . . After much discussion in which using an expurgated version, dropping the book altogether, or shipping it to the high school was debated, the decision was made to move the book to the tenth grade (where Bradbury's *Fahrenheit 451* is also taught). . . . My district wanted the issue to go away, and I knew that although they supported what I did, they would not fight for the book. I was afraid that they would go the expurgated route (I informed my department head that I would not teach that version). . . . But what disturbs me even more is the fact that the far-reaching repercussions of this incident are not being addressed. Teachers in the seventh grade are now reluctant to recommend, much less teach, *Sounder* and *The Autobiography of Miss Jane Pittman* (both Board approved books). Copies of Art Spiegelman's *Maus II* were removed from a Scholastic book fair and students were only permitted to purchase it after they returned a letter signed by their parents acknowledging the "mature content" of this book.

What strikes me first about this case is that the behaviors of teacher and district were admirable, appropriate, and consistent with professional guidelines. First and foremost, they seemed thorough in their readiness for and response to this challenge. If asked, I would advise the teacher and district to do approximately what they did do, except, perhaps, not make the final decision to move the book to the high school. As far as I know, the teacher's employment was never threatened. The issue was the book and its appropriateness for eighth-grade students. Still, this case makes clear that you can do all the right things as a teacher—perform rationally, sensitively, even heroically—and still lose. In sum:

> 1. She selected a book of solid literary quality characterized by elements integral to the learning potential of her students, her teaching agenda, and her school program of study.

> 2. She researched the book thoroughly, consulted with colleagues, developed a teaching plan, and prepared her students for the experience well in advance of teaching it.

> 3. She reacted to the challenge according to the established school and district procedures, which were consistent with the ALA guidelines.

> 4. She responded according to her sense of personal ethics, even refusing to teach an expurgated version.

> 5. She published her take on the case to the profession at large.

As I wonder about this case, an absolute conclusion is impossible for me simply because I was not there and do not know the context intimately. Certainly, there may be more here than the relentless drive of a parent for her child. But according to the teacher's letter, five classes of eighth graders apparently engaged in a productive study of the book—a study that had been available to fifteen previous years of eighth graders. The department chair was quoted as making the final decision after further study. Maybe her decision was purely professional and apolitical, although one would think that during that fifteen years *Chronicles* would have been assessed many times for its "appropriateness" for eighth graders. But maybe cases like this also suggest that something more fundamental than avoiding school-community conflict should drive instructional materials selection. And it is a tough place to go. But there is the issue of honest choices in book selection appropriate for the student audience versus book selection to avoid censorship on whatever grounds, which is in itself censorship.

What becomes clear regarding censorship and book selection is that easy, guilt-free, decisions are hard to come by, particularly when one weighs possible consequences. Book selection in a school setting comes before the fact. Any choice of one book for all, de facto, denies all other books for all—at least for the moment. Is it really the literary quality or complexity or reading level or maturity level that is at issue, or is it the chance that the content or language use or point of view might be offensive to someone real or imagined? What of matters of courage, professional integrity, job security, school politics, teacher comfort level with text? That is, is the selection purely driven by personal ethics and pedagogy or not? Most elections, in my experience,

have reflected a mix of pedagogic and other influences to arrive at the most contextually appropriate choice. What has not been acceptable to me is that avoiding the best piece of literature available for a particular group of students does not matter—that literature is literature. That attitude insults the needs of student and teacher alike.

I wonder about the student and the parent at the center of the Edison controversy. If the student continues on to the local high school, she likely will encounter *Huckleberry Finn* and *To Kill a Mockingbird*. What then? And what of the teacher who so strongly defended her personal ethic against censorship and her professional privilege to select books for her students? How will she approach the next challenge? Will she unconsciously or consciously precensor to avoid challenge? And what of the effects on other teachers? Students? Where does the censorship of one book end?

In the case of classroom use of *Chronicles,* questions are easy to raise. Answers are slippery and so related to context. In the end, the best answer resides in the heart and judgment of the professional teacher: knowledgeable of students, content, and teaching methodologies; aware of context; confident in abilities. Even then, as the Edison case points out, there is the body politic. So my answer is not one a teacher frustrated by challenges to book selections or the threat of challenges wants to hear. There is no magic formula to solve the problem. There is only doing the best you can do based on the best information available in readiness for and delivery of work with literature and kids. And trusting in self and the continuing effort to engage your students and yourself in the most enjoyable, productive literary experiences possible. If challenges occur, you do like our Edison teacher—the best you can. If you should lose, you go on, strengthened, but not diminished, by the experience. Faith in self and faith in the kids must save the day. Maybe that is the answer you want to hear after all. Maybe that is my rationalization for the way I tell it to myself.

Finally, what has Ray Bradbury, himself, written about censorship? Of course, one could accurately say, everything he writes or has written is a defense of absolute freedom to write what he wants. But what does he think outside of the words he puts inside of the mouths of his characters? Listen to these excerpts from his revised (1979) **"Coda,"** an addendum to *Fahrenheit 451.* Sound familiar?

> The point is obvious. There is more than one way to burn a book. And the world is full of people running about with lit matches. Every minority . . . feels it has the will, the right, the duty to douse the kerosene, light the fuse. Every dimwit editor who sees himself as the source of all dreary blanc-mange plain porridge unleavened literature, licks his guillotine and eyes the

neck of any author who dares to speak above a whisper or write above a nursery rhyme. . . . In sum, do not insult me with the beheadings, finger-choppings or the lung-deflations you plan for my works. I need my head to shake or nod, my hand to wave or make into a fist, my lungs to shout or whisper with. I will not go gently onto a shelf, degutted, to become a non-book. . . . And no one can help me. Not even you.

(175-179)

And so we end, where we began, like the incessant cycles of censorship itself, with a second quote from **"April 2005: Usher II"** as Stendahl finds retribution in the bricking in of Garrett (as per Poe's "Cask of Amontillado") in the wine cellar of Usher II for his leading role as "Investigator of Moral Climates" in the burning of great literary works, in particular those of Poe:

"Garrett?" Called Stendahl softly. Garrett silenced himself. "Garrett," said Stendahl, "do you know why I've done this to you? Because you burned Mr. Poe's books without really reading them. You took other people's advice that they needed burning. Otherwise you'd have realized what I was going to do to you when we came down here a moment ago. Ignorance is fatal, Mr. Garrett."

(118)

And so, once again we confront humankind's greatest literary sin: "ignorance." And the most powerful argument against censorship: to ensure that humankind does not fall to the inexcusable sin of Ignorance. And we confront again the censor's mortal enemy: imagination. Arguably, Ray Bradbury's imaginative works themselves carry within, perhaps, the richest commentary on censorship in literature today. And they are written with honesty and courage (some may say arrogance). To now, censors attacks on Bradbury's works have been relatively modest. At some point, censors may take them more seriously. Then we shall see.

Works Cited

American Library Association—Office for Intellectual Freedom (OIF). 2000. "OIF Censorship Database 1990-1999: Institution Being Challenged, Challenges by Type, Initiator of Challenge." http://www.ala.org/ala/oif/index.html.

Bradbury, Ray. *Fahrenheit 451*. New York: Ballantine, 1953 (Eighty-first printing 1990, with revised "Coda" 1979, and "Afterword" 1982).

———. *The Martian Chronicles*. Bantam: New York, 1950 (Bantam paperback edition, 1979).

National Coalition Against Censorship (NCAC)—CENSORSHIP NEWS ONLINE. 2000. "Issue #70: Censorship and Ray Bradbury's *The Martian Chronicles*." Summer, 1998. http://www.ncac.org/cen_news/cn70bradbury.html (Edison case, teacher letter).

The *Star-Ledger* Archive. "Mom wants Edison school to pull sci-fi book." 1998. http://search.starledger.com/cgi-bin/.

———. "Edison ditches old version of classic book." http://search.starledger.com/cgi-bin/.

NOTE: Please see the following sources for extensive assistance and free materials related to censorship and responding to challenges:

American Library Association—Office of Intellectual Freedom publication "Coping with Challenges: Strategies and Tips for Dealing with Challenges to Library Materials" at http://www.ala.org/oif/copinginf.html.

National Council of Teachers of English (NCTE), *Guidelines for Selection of Materials in English Language Arts*. An NCTE Standards Document available at http://www.ncte.org/censorship/guide.shtml.

George E. Connor (essay date winter 2004)

SOURCE: Connor, George E. "Spelunking with Ray Bradbury: The Allegory of the Cave in *Fahrenheit 451*." *Extrapolation* 45, no. 4 (winter 2004): 408-18.

[*In the following essay, Connor demonstrates his assertion that* Fahrenheit 451 *is ideal for the examination of a confluence of literature and philosophy.*]

According to Holtsmark, "for reasons of plot, character, and allusion, among others, myth is a central feature of ancient Greek literature, [and] it has appeared tacitly axiomatic from the time of antiquity that myth informs most narrative literature" (2001, 24). Greek authors turned to myth "at those crucial points at which pure reason seem[ed] unable to advance further" (Kirk 1970, 259). Foremost among the mythic themes in Greek literature is the word *katabasis*, which "literally means 'a going down, a descent,' capturing the imagined physical orientation of the other world relative to this one" (Holtsmark 25). Obvious manifestations of this theme can be found in the Homeric journeys of the *Odyssey* (1996) and the *Iliad* (1991). In both books, Homer utilizes physical caves to accent the literary descent. Although he rejected certain literary applications of myth, especially among the poets, Plato "reasserted the role of myth in his own practice" (Kirk 1970, 250). In particular, Plato asserted the role of myth in the dialogue of the *Republic* when "reason seemed unable to advance further."

The *katabasis* tradition is introduced into the *Republic* at the beginning of Book VII when Socrates asks Glaucon to "make an image of our nature in its education and want of education, likening it to a condition of the following kind. See human beings as though they were in an underground cave-like dwelling" (1968, 514a). This passage is the opening line of Plato's Allegory of the Cave. With little question, scholars agree that the Allegory "is the keystone of the dialogue" (Sandoz 1971, 62). The textual relevance of the Allegory for Ray Bradbury's *Fahrenheit 451* is obvious in Montag's hope that "[m]aybe the books can get us half out of the cave" (1953, 74). Perhaps less obvious, the following analysis demonstrates that Plato's Allegory is the central metaphor for the novel. More specifically, the Allegory provides a template by which Bradbury's characters can be analyzed and distinguished.

Initially, this analysis rests upon the explicit linkage between literature and political philosophy. With respect to literature, Zuckert insists that novels can be "forms of political thought" (1990, ix). Reflecting her subtitle, *Political Philosophy in Novel Form,* Zuckert examines the perspective of the author and suggests, "novelists' often differing theoretical reflections have led them nevertheless to agree on the need for literary political teaching" (ix). With respect to the audience, she suggests that "aware of readers' antipathy to arguments by authority, novelists appeal to readers' own experience by enlisting their sympathies through empathetic identification with the protagonists of the stories" (247). Complementing Zuckert's view, Strauss maintains that "[t]he study of the literary question is an important part of the study of what philosophy is" (1964, 52). Using *Fahrenheit 451* as an example, science fiction author Frederik Pohl similarly argues "there is very little science fiction, perhaps no good science fiction at all, that is not to some degree political" (1997, 7). The linkage between the two fields rests upon the fact that "[p]olitical theorists and science fiction writers alike are continually aware of the role of language" (Hassler and Wilcox 1997, 1).

With respect to language, the significance of metaphor is probably the single most analyzed aspect of Bradbury's fiction: Mogen (1986), Watt (1980, 2000), McNelly (1980), Mengeling (1980), Wolfe (1980) McGiveron (1996), and Sisario (1970). Scholarly attraction to the concept is best explained by McNelly: "For Bradbury, a metaphor is not merely a figure of speech, it is a vital concept, a method he uses for comprehending one reality and expressing it in terms of another; it permits the reader to perceive what the author is saying" (1982). Nevertheless, for all the attraction to the concept, whether scholars use the term metaphor, imagery, symbol, or, like Mogen, allegory, they do not discuss *the* Allegory. Only Pell (1980), who links Bradbury's imagery to Aristotle, and Spencer (1999), who discusses Bradbury in the context of Plato's *Phaedrus,* address Bradbury's relationship to his ancient Greek predecessors. However, neither Pell nor Spencer link Bradbury or *Fahrenheit 451* to Plato's Allegory.

Finally, the present application of the Allegory is rooted in Morson's (1981) discussion of "combined genres" and his delineation of the utopian "masterplot." Like Zuckert, Morson argues that writers "exploit an audience's favorable disposition" (95) and exploit the "readers' willingness to think in unfamiliar or nonhabitual ways" (94). However, unlike Zuckert's broader discussion of novels, Morson narrows his application to a discussion of a more particular genre. Although he admits that he is not concerned with "defining" (ix), Morson initially labels *Fahrenheit 451* as "anti-utopia" (117). Later, he settles on dystopia: "Whereas utopias invite their readers to contemplate a world in which they would at last be at home, dystopias invite their readers to contemplate one in which they would have 'no place' at all" (141-142). Morson concludes that "combined genres are not in principle incompatible" and "it is quite possible to read *Fahrenheit 451* as both science fiction and anti-utopia" (117). Broadening the idea of "combined genres" a bit further, Sargent proposes a more inclusive definition that encompasses both "anti-utopia," or dystopian, literature and utopian literature: "Whatever we label these works—be it utopias, social science fiction, or tales of the future— they are part of the utopian tradition since they do present fairly detailed descriptions of nonexistent social systems" (1975, 144). This approach allows scholars to avoid the tangle of definition and classification so evident in the literature on *Fahrenheit 451* (Reid 2000, 7-13).

Definitional questions aside, it is Morson's application of the Allegory that undergirds his analysis. Although earlier scholarship linked Dostoevsky to the Allegory (Sandoz 1971, xiv), Morson broadened this linkage to suggest that Plato's Allegory, as well as the counterplots of "the madman" and "escape," provide the "masterplot" for the entire genre of utopian fiction (38). He maintains "most utopias describe a similar journey from darkness to light, followed by a real or imagined return" (89). With specific reference to dystopias, Morson notes that because "[a]n anti-generic work must parody a target genre," the *Republic* serves as a "negative model" for *Fahrenheit 451.* However, Morson's reference to *Fahrenheit 451* is related to Plato's "suspicion of poetry" and not specifically to the Allegory. Whereas Morson could not, in a single volume, address the myriad applications of his theory, this analysis reexamines and expands Morson's theory in a characterdriven discussion of Bradbury's *Fahrenheit 451.*

In short, Bradbury's *Fahrenheit 451* provides a venue for an interdisciplinary examination of the linkage between literature and philosophy, the concept of metaphor, and the application of a unifying theory that places the book into a broader context.

The Allegory

Morson's delineation of the Allegory is limited to the "masterplot" and the counterplots of "the madman" and "escape." While this three-part discussion was adequate for Morson's purpose and consistent with what is defined as "the thematic simplicity, almost shallowness, of most Greek myths (Kirk 1970, 187), the discussion below is based upon a six-part division that focuses specifically on the cave's inhabitants: Those who are bound in the cave; the cave's puppeteers; the madman; those who escape from the cave; those who help the escapees; and those who would return to the cave.

The Allegory begins with those who are bound in the cave. "They are in it from childhood with their legs and necks in bonds so that they are fixed, seeing only in front of them," seeing nothing "other than the shadows cast by the fire on the side of the cave facing them" (514a, b, 515a). Socrates concludes that "[s]uch men would hold that the truth is nothing other than the shadows of artificial things" (515c). Behind those who are bound are the cave's puppeteers. "Human beings carrying all sorts of artifacts, which project above the wall, and statues of men and other animals wrought from stone, wood and every kind of material; as is to be expected, some of the carriers utter sounds while others are silent" (514c, 515a). Third, is the component that Morson identifies as the "madman" subplot: "[i]f they were somehow able to get their hands on and kill the man who attempts to release and lead up, wouldn't they kill him?" (517a).

The next distinction is the one Morson labels as the "escape." "[I]f someone dragged him away from there by force along the rough, steep, upward way and didn't let him go before he had dragged him out into the light of the sun" (515e). The discussion below divides this escape into two parts. Morson focuses on the reaction of the person being dragged up. If they were "release[d] from bonds and folly" and "compelled to stand up, to turn his neck around, to walk and look up toward the light." Socrates argued that he would be "distressed" and this would all be done "in pain because he is dazzled," and he would "be unable to see even one of the things now said to be true" (515c, 515e, 516a). While the reaction is important, a character-driven analysis should also consider the "someone" who does the dragging. This "someone" is described by Bloom as a "guide" (1968, 403). The final aspect of the Allegory consists of the return to the cave. Here again, this analysis departs from Morson by subdividing the "madman" subplot. When faced with the choice of returning to the shadows of the cave, Glaucon concludes that the former inhabitant of the cave "would prefer to undergo everything rather than live that way" (516d).

Morson argues, "works of this highly determined genre repeat that plot, either in part or in its entirety." The discussion below examines how Bradbury's *Fahrenheit 451* repeats the six parts of the Allegory in their entirety. Touponce noted "the complaint that utopian novels are more concerned with ideas than characters, and present characters who are simply one-dimensional spokesmen the author's social hypothesis, is often voiced." He concluded that, "this charge [cannot] be brought successfully against *Fahrenheit 451*" (1984, 110). For example, scholars have explored the multi-dimensionality of Montag. Hoskinson discusses "Montag's liberation from Captain Beatty" (1995, 345). Similarly, but perhaps a bit more philosophical, Zipes maintains that Montag "begins to assume command of his own destiny" (2000, 131). Nevertheless, a narrow focus on Montag's evolution from cave dweller/puppeteer to guide, although reasonably within the metaphor of the cave, diminishes the literary value of Bradbury's other characters. While the number of named and un-named characters is not large, each one finds his or her own place in the Allegory.

Allegorical Application

Amis maintains, "Bradbury's is the most skillfully drawn of all science fiction's conformist hells" (2000, 96). Montag's conformist colleagues find themselves bound in the cave and testifying to shadows in response to Montag's question about the history of firemen. "Stoneman and Black drew forth their rule books, which also contained brief histories of the Fireman of America." "Established, 1790, to burn English-influenced books in the Colonies. First Fireman: Benjamin Franklin" (34). While Stoneman and Black acknowledge the shadows they have been shown, Montag's wife, Mildred, epitomizes Socrates' conclusion that the inhabitants of the cave "would hold that the truth is nothing other than the shadows of artificial things." Mildred has her sleeping tablets (13), electric bees (18), seashell (42), and thimble (48). Most importantly, Mildred has her "walls" (44). Here she has her own "part" (20) in a fictional "family" (77). Here, "Three White Cartoon Clowns chopped off each other's limbs to the accompaniment of immense incoming tides of laughter" (94). Mildred has become so engrossed in her shadow "family" that she cannot remember when she and Montag met and concludes, "it doesn't matter" (43).

Captain Beatty is the best single character to represent the "human beings carrying all sorts of artifacts." Unlike those bound in the cave, these puppeteers know that the figures on the wall are mere "shadows of artificial things." In short, the puppeteers know the truth about the cave and Beatty knows the truth about the world around him. He is both a representative of the "exploiters" (McGiveron 1996, 249) and a defender of "a consumer culture completely divorced from political awareness" (Seed 1994, 228). Unlike Stoneman and

Black, the Captain knows the secret history of their profession and he tells Montag, "I'll let you in on it" (54). Quoting Dr. Johnson, he tells Montag, both in a dream and in person, "He is no wise man that will quit a certainty for an uncertainty" (106). And Beatty knows the certainties. They are defined in people like Mildred. The certainties of this world are 3-D sex magazines, sex, heroin, and noncombustible data (57-58, 61).

A casual reading of the text might suggest that Guy Montag fulfills the role of Morson's "madman." The real and televised pursuit of Montag is illustrative of the inhabitants of the cave rising up against one "who attempts to release and lead up." "Police alert. Wanted: Fugitive in city. Has committed murder and crimes against the State. Name: Guy Montag. . . . watch for a man alone, on foot" (124). However, Montag lives. A more intriguing illustrator of the madman subplot would be Clarisse McClellan. Unlike the drivers racing down the highways, Clarisse knew what grass, flowers, and dew were (9). She let raindrops fall on her face (21) and she "smelled old leaves" (29). Montag exclaims, "She saw everything. She didn't do anything to anyone" (114). This statement is, of course, untrue because Clarisse's "madness" was to go down into the cave and lead Montag up. Her eventual fate, however, is something that Bradbury only gradually reveals. At first, Montag simply notices that "Clarisse was gone" (32). Later, Mildred suggests that she was "[r]un over by a car." "I don't know. But I think she's dead" (47).

With Montag unable to remember her face, Captain Beatty intones that the "poor girl's better off dead" (60). It is not until the final confrontation between Beatty and Montag, that a more sinister end is suggested. Catching Montag's wistful glance "Beatty snorted." "Oh, no! You weren't fooled by that little idiot's routine, were you?" (113). "She chewed you around, didn't she? One of those damn do-gooders with their shocked, holier-than-thou silences, their talent making others feel guilty" (114). Although Bradbury does not make it explicit, the text suggests that, unlike the "madman" Montag, who lives, the "madman" Clarisse is killed by the inhabitants of the cave (Sisario 1970, 203; Hoskinson 1995, 348).

Although the death of the "madman" is a significant component of the Allegory, Plato's text does allow for the successful release of the cave's inhabitants. Here this analysis turns to the "someone" who drags the inhabitant "into the light of the sun." The choice of illustrative characters, Faber and Granger, is fairly simple. Faber admits that "we *do* need knowledge" (86) but he is initially reluctant to join Montag. Later, he continues the work of Clarisse by helping Montag escape. In the novel, Faber helps Montag escape from the police. In the metaphor, he helps Montag escape from the cave. "I feel like I'm doing what I should've done a lifetime ago. For a little while I'm not afraid. Maybe it's because I'm doing the right thing at last" (131). Continuing the work of Faber, and helping Montag on his journey out of the city and out of the cave is Granger. Their world, their cave, had been destroyed in an instant. In the aftermath, there would be "a lot of lonely people" (164). These survivors would be trying to find their own path "along the rough steep, upward way." Granger and his companions "can be of some use in the world" (152) by leading them into the light. Strauss argues, "the *Republic* never abandons the fiction that the just city as a society of human beings is possible" (1964, 129). While Granger thinks they "will win out in the long run," the text also suggests that he has his doubts about the future of humanity: "But even when we had the books on hand, a long time ago, we didn't use what we got out of them. We went right on insulting the dead. We went right on spitting in the graves of all the poor ones who died before us" (164). Bloom maintains that the one who drags people out of the cave and into the light "can only lead a few" (1968, 403). Similarly Granger argues that "[w]e pick up a few more people every generation" (163).

Socrates maintains that the person dragged into the light of the sun would be "distressed" (515e). Jowett (Plato 1948) translates this passage as "suffer sharp pains." The conflict between truth and shadow in ***Fahrenheit 451*** is equally painful. When confronted by Montag, Faber exclaims, "I care so much I'm sick." This same physical distress is revealed when Montag's reading of *Dover Beach* struck a long-buried nerve in Mrs. Phelps. "She sobbed uncontrollably" and "her faced squeezed itself out of shape" (100). These examples notwithstanding, it is Montag himself who best illustrates the physical dimensions of facing the truth. After burning the unnamed neighbor of Mrs. Blake, Montag "had chills and fever in the morning" (48) and "suddenly the odor of kerosene made him vomit" (49). Thrust into moderating a debate between Faber and Beatty, his "head whirled sickeningly" (107). Just before the death of Beatty, Montag feels an earthquake "shaking and falling and shivering inside him and he stood there, his knees half bent under the great load of tiredness and outrage" (118). After Beatty's death, "Montag kept his sickness down long enough" (120).

The choice of characters representing those "would prefer to undergo everything rather than live that way" is, in one case, textually obvious. The unnamed neighbor of Mrs. Blake didn't simply die in the firemen's inferno; she committed suicide. She would not be forced to live in a world that contained only shadows. "The woman on the porch reached out with contempt to them all and struck the kitchen match against the railing" (40). Montag himself suggests the second example of refusing to go back into the cave: "Beatty wanted to die" (122). In the climatic scene between Beatty and Montag, Beatty's can no longer bear the role of puppeteer. In fact, Beatty dares Montag to kill him: "There is no terror, Cassius, in your threats, for I am arm'd so strong in honesty that they pass me as an idle wind which I respect not." "Go ahead now, you second-hand litterateur, pull the trigger" (119). In the end, Faber's thought that Beatty "could be one of us" (91) was closer to the truth than either he or Montag ever imagined.

KIRK SUGGESTS

Kirk suggests that Greek myths "can hardly be understood in isolation" (v). As the discussion above demonstrates, the same should be said about Ray Bradbury's *Fahrenheit 451.* While Plato's Allegory of the Cave is the defining metaphor for *Fahrenheit 451,* it must be recognized that the Allegory itself is part of the larger *katabasis* tradition and that that tradition is itself part of an even larger tradition in Greek literature. Kirk maintains "the detailed study of mythical themes in the literature of the classical period in Greece is essential for the understanding of the whole culture" (1). This analysis suggests that a detailed study of the mythical themes in *Fahrenheit 451* is essential for the understanding of Bradbury. Moreover, by examining the linkage between literature and philosophy, the role of metaphor, and the application of Morson's theory, this analysis transcends traditional disciplinary boundaries.

Khanna asserts that the "disjunction between theory and praxis, literature and politics, art and life, or text and body is exactly what the utopian enterprise denies" (39). Keeping in mind Sargent's inclusive approach to the "utopian enterprise," this analysis suggests that Bradbury's *Fahrenheit 451* provides ample evidence for Khanna's assertion on all counts. While one could analyze the relationship between theory and praxis, art and life, and text and body within the novel, *Fahrenheit 451* best exemplifies the *conjunction* of literature and politics as defined by the literary theories of Zuckert and Strauss. Moreover, *Fahrenheit 451* illustrates the centrality of the role of language in the science fiction genre.

Bradbury's use of metaphor is, as was demonstrated above, central to the role of language in *Fahrenheit 451.* In the same way that Plato inserted myth into the *Republic,* Bradbury borrowed the "masterplot" of the Allegory of the Cave. In substituting metaphor for reason, like Plato, Bradbury may have sought to "replace opinion about the nature of political things by the knowledge of the nature of political things" (Strauss 1959, 11-12). There is, however, one key difference between Bradbury's cave and Plato's cave. In assessing the Platonic model, Strauss insists, "the *Republic* never abandons the *fiction* that the just city as a society of human beings is possible" [emphasis added]. Strauss

argues that "[t]he just city is impossible. It is impossible because it is against nature. It is against nature that there should ever be a 'cessation of evils.'" (1964, 129; 127). Unlike Strauss, Bradbury has hope for a "cessation of evils" and, unlike Plato's *Republic, Fahrenheit 451* was not constructed solely for contemplation.

According to Bloom's analysis of the *Republic,* "[t]he philosopher does not bring light to the cave, he escapes into the light and can lead a few to it; he is a guide, not a torchbearer" (1968, 403). Consistent with Bloom's analysis, Faber, Granger and Montag serve as Platonic guides in the text and, in fact, only lead a few to the light. Regardless of the role of these characters *in the text,* it can be demonstrated that *through the text* Bradbury himself relished the role of torch-bearer in his quest to lead the cave dwellers to enlightenment. Here, again, Morson's theory helps to define the voice of the author in utopian fiction.

If, as was argued above, neither Montag nor any other single character is a spokesman for the author, how is the author's voice revealed? Morson inquires, "[i]nasmuch as literary utopias are either entirely or mostly fictional, and the 'fictional contract' suspends authorial responsibility for statements represented rather than made, it may be asked how is it possible to say what the author advocates." His query is answered in that "[t]he conventions of utopia provide that if the work contains a nonfictional section, its statements are to be taken as authoritative" (Morson 76). Of course, many editions of *Fahrenheit 451* contain nonfictional sections such as Bradbury's **"Afterword"** or **"Coda."** Here, like Bellamy's "Postscript" to *Looking Backward* (1986), Bradbury speaks for himself: "For it is a mad world and it will get madder if we allow the minorities, be they dwarf or giant, orangutan or dolphin, nuclear-head or water-conservationalist, pro-computerologist or Neo Luddite, simpleton or sage, to interfere with aesthetics" (178). Obviously, Bradbury's message is not in Montag or, as Touponce indicated, any single one-dimensional character. Bradbury's message is in the entire text and in the reader's response to it. In answer to the question "can books convert dystopia into utopia," Bradbury said "I feel that what I had to say in *Fahrenheit 451* is valid today and will continue to be valid here and in other countries in other years" (Spencer 2000, 104). He was right.

Works Cited

Amis, Kingsley. 2000. "A Skillfully Drawn Conformist Hell." *Readings on Fahrenheit 451,* Ed. Katie de Koster. San Diego, CA: Greenhaven Press, Inc., 93-99.

Bellamy, Edward. 1986. *Looking Backward.* New York: Penguin Books.

Bloom, Allan. 1968. "Interpretive Essay." *The Republic.* Translated by Allan Bloom. New York: Basic Books Inc., Publishers.

Bradbury, Ray. 1953. *Fahrenheit 451.* New York: Ballantine Books.

Hassler, Donald M. and Clyde Wilcox. 1997. "Introduction: Politics, Art, Collaboration." *Political Science Fiction.* Eds. Donald M. Hassler and Clyde Wilcox. Columbia, SC: University of South Carolina Press, 1-6.

Holtsmark, Erling B. 2001. "The Katabasis Theme in Modern Cinema." *Classical Myth & Culture in the Cinema.* Ed. Martin M. Winkler. New York: Oxford University Press.

Homer. 1996. *The Odyssey.* Translated by Robert Fagles. New York: Viking.

Homer. 1991. *The Iliad.* Translated by Robert Fagles. New York: Penguin Books.

Hoskinson, Kevin. 1995. "The *Martian Chronicles* and *Fahrenheit 451*: Ray Bradbury's Cold War Novels." *Extrapolation* Vol 36 # 4 345-359.

Khanna, Lee Cullen. 1981. "The Reader and *Looking Backward.*" *Journal of General Education* 33 (spring): 69-79.

Kirk, G. S. 1970. *Myth: Its Meaning and Functions in Ancient and Other Cultures.* Berkeley, CA: University of California Press.

McNelly, Willis E. 1982. "Ray Bradbury." *Science Fiction Writers: Critical Studies of the Major Authors from the Early Nineteenth Century to the Present Day.* Ed. E. F. Bleiler. New York: Charles Scribner's Sons, 171-178.

McNelly, Willis E. 1980. "Ray Bradbury—Past Present, and Future." *Ray Bradbury.* Eds. Martin Harry Greenberg and Joseph D. Olander. New York: Taplinger Publishing Company, 17-24.

McGiveron, Rafeeq O. 1996. "What 'Carried the Trick'? Mass Exploitation and the Decline of Thought in Ray Bradbury's *Fahrenheit 451.*" *Extrapolation* Vol. 37 # 3, 245-256.

Mengeling, Marvin E. 1980. "The Machineries of Joy and Despair." *Ray Bradbury.* Eds. Martin Harry Greenberg and Joseph D. Olander. New York: Taplinger Publishing Company, 83-109.

Mogen, David. 1986. *Ray Bradbury.* Boston: Twayne Publishers.

Morson, Gary Saul. 1981. *Boundaries of Genre: Dostoevsky's Diary of a Writer and the Traditions of Literary Utopia.* Austin, TX: University of Texas Press.

Pell, Sarah-Warner J. 1980. "Style Is the Man: Imagery in Bradbury's Fiction." *Ray Bradbury.* Eds. Martin Harry Greenberg and Joseph D. Olander. New York: Taplinger Publishing Company, 186-194.

Plato. 1968. *The Republic.* Translated by Allan Bloom. New York: Basic Books Inc., Publishers.

Plato, 1948. *The Portable Plato: Protagoras, Symposium, Phaedo, and The Republic.* Translated by Benjamin Jowett. New York: Viking Press.

Pohl, Frederick. 1997. "The Politics of Prophecy." *Political Science Fiction.* Eds. Donald M. Hassler and Clyde Wilcox. Columbia, SC: University of South Carolina Press, 7-17.

Reid, Robin Anne. 2000. *Ray Bradbury: A Critical Companion.* Westport, CT: Greenwood Press.

Sandoz, Ellis. 1971. *Political Apocalypse: A Study of Dostoevsky's Grand Inquisitor.* Baton Rouge, LA Louisiana State University Press.

Sargent, Lyman T. 1975 "Utopia: The Problem of Definition." *Extrapolation* 16 (May): 137-48.

Seed, David. 1994. "The Flight from the Good Life: *Fahrenheit 451* in the Context of Postwar Dystopias." *Journal of American Studies Vol.* 28 # 2, 225-240.

Sisario, Peter. 1970. "A Study of the Allusions in Bradbury's *Fahrenheit 451.*" *English Journal* Vol 59, # 2, 201-205, 212.

Spencer, Susan. 2000. "Can Books Convert Dystopia into Utopia?" *Readings on Fahrenheit 451.* Ed. Katie de Koster. San Diego, CA: Greenhaven Press, Inc., 100-106.

Spencer, Susan. 1999. "The Post-Apocalyptic Library: Oral and Literate Culture in *Fahrenheit 451* and *A Canticle for Leibowitz.*" *Extrapolation* Vol 32 #4 331-142.

Strauss, Leo. 1959. *What Is Political Philosophy? And Other Studies.* Glencoe, IL: The Free Press of Glencoe.

Strauss, Leo. 1964. *The City and Man.* Chicago: University of Chicago Press.

Touponce, William F. 1984. *Ray Bradbury and the Poetics of Reverie: Fantasy, Science Fiction, and the Reader.* Ann Arbor, MI: UMI Research Press.

Watt, Donald. 2000. "The Use of Fire as a Multifaceted Symbol." *Readings on Fahrenheit 451.* Ed. Katie de Koster. San Diego, CA: Greenhaven Press, Inc., 44-54.

Watt, Donald. 1980. "Burning Bright: *Fahrenheit 451* as Symbolic Dystopia." *Ray Bradbury.* Eds. Martin Harry Greenberg and Joseph D. Olander. New York: Taplinger Publishing Company, 195-213.

Wolfe, Gary K. 1980. "The Frontier Myth in Ray Bradbury." *Ray Bradbury.* Eds. Martin Harry Greenberg and Joseph D. Olander. New York: Taplinger Publishing Company, 33-54.

Zipes, Jack. 2000. "*Fahrenheit 451* Is a Reflection of 1950s America." *Readings on Fahrenheit 451.* Ed. Katie de Koster. San Diego, CA: Greenhaven Press, Inc. 124-133.

Zuckert, Catherine. 1990. *Natural Right and the American Imagination.* Savage, MD: Rowman & Littlefield Publishers, Inc.

Steven L. Aggelis (essay date 2004)

SOURCE: Aggelis, Steven L. Introduction to *Conversations with Ray Bradbury,* edited by Steven L. Aggelis, pp. xi-xxv. Jackson, Miss.: University Press of Mississippi, 2004.

[*In the following essay, Aggelis examines the influence of life experiences on Bradbury's writing.*]

Ray Bradbury considers himself a child of his time. He was born Ray Douglas Bradbury on August 22, 1920, in Waukegan, Illinois, and began reading voraciously at the age of eight, about the time Hugo Gernsback's pulp magazine *Amazing Stories* first appeared. He came to maturity just prior to World War II, when the V-1 and V-2 rockets were used against the British, and began writing in the nascency of the space age. Since his first professional sale in 1941 of **"Pendulum,"** written with Henry Hasse for *Super Science Stories,* Bradbury has written and published hundreds of essays, short stories, novels, dramas, operas, teleplays, poems, and screenplays. Over the course of his career, he has been interviewed more than 335 times.

The Bradbury family's American roots run back three hundred years. The early Bradbury immigrants came from a little community outside London, England, and settled around 1630 in Salisbury, Massachusetts. Later, members of the family moved to Illinois. Bradbury's father's full name is Leonard Spaulding Bradbury. Ray combined his middle name and his father's to create one of his pseudonyms, Douglas Spaulding, also the name of one of his characters. Bradbury's great-grandfather in Waukegan was involved in the printing trade, making up small booklets and doing odd printing jobs at the same time that he was editor and publisher of two newspapers. Much of the Bradbury family money was lost by his paternal grandfather's ill-fated expeditions, including his desperate enterprises in gold and silver mining in Canada and Nevada. Bradbury's childhood was filled with such stories of family misadventure.

Esther Marie Moberg, Bradbury's mother, was two when her family migrated to America from Stockholm, Sweden, as part of the movement of the Swedes to the steel mills in Worcester, Massachusetts. When steel and iron foundries moved into the vicinity of Chicago, her family migrated there. In Illinois, Esther met Leonard, and they were married in Waukegan, where Bradbury and his older brother Leonard were born. Bradbury had

another brother, Leonard's twin, Samuel, who died in the Asian flu epidemic in 1918, two years before Ray's birth. This tragedy was followed by the death of a sister, Elizabeth, in 1927, when Ray was only seven. Consequently, Esther Bradbury was overcautious in rearing Ray, making him, he readily admits in a video biography, *Ray Bradbury: An American Icon,* a "mama's boy," who was bottle-fed until the age of six and spoon-fed until he was thirteen or fourteen years old. Bradbury did not leave the nest until he was twenty-seven years old.

The early deaths of these siblings most assuredly contributed to Bradbury's fascination with death, one of his major themes. In the 1962 Harvey interview, Bradbury comments on how he came to see the value of horror films such as *Dracula* as a way of "making do with death." According to Bradbury, Count Dracula is a symbol for death and the unknown, and the stake, cross, and Bible are symbols used to conquer death. With these sure-fire vampire-extinguishing symbols, the reader or filmgoer can self-project into the text or film and release his or her tension about the horror of the unknown, in much the same way that the people of Mexico laugh at death in its face in their celebration of El Día de los Muertos (the Day of the Dead), on which Bradbury based his 1947 short story **"El Día de Muerte,"** the English title for which is **"The Day of Death."**

Bradbury credits two people, his Aunt Neva and his father, for his literary interests. Aunt Neva—a painter, artist, dress designer, and, above all, a great lover of books, who was only ten years older than Bradbury—lived next door to him in his grandmother's house when he was a boy. Bradbury thoroughly enjoyed her company and conversation, at times looking upon her as a kind of surrogate mother. His natural mother was not particularly interested in literary things, and he went to his aunt for artistic stimulation. Of Aunt Neva, Bradbury says that she "helped bring me up in a world of let's-pretend, in a world of masks and puppets that she made, in a world of stages and acting, in a world of special Christmases and Halloweens. It was she who read me my first fairy tales, she who read Poe aloud to me when I was seven and taught me all about fabulous mythological country from which I never quite emerged" (*Show*).

His father's reading habits also influenced Bradbury. As he informs us in the 1961 recordings in his home by Craig Cunningham, compiled in the unpublished manuscript entitled *The Dogs That Eat Sweet Grass,* as the young Bradbury matured, the sight of his father "constantly sitting in the front room with a book in his hand" served as inspiration (4). Seeing his father "night after night in the living room, like a statue, saying very little to the family," contributed to Bradbury's picking up books and magazines and reading them throughout his developmental years. Throughout the interviews in this book, Bradbury is critical of the public educational system in the United States. He came to reflect in the 1999 Klein interview, surely drawing upon his own childhood experiences, that the developmental years, especially kindergarten and the first grade, demand the attention of anyone who wishes positive reform in education. "It's the teachers who have to do the job in kindergarten and first grade. Once you teach them to read and write, then the students will be curious. But the education system has failed, and all the money that Washington sends out in the next two years has got to go to local schools, first grade, and kindergarten. Then we can cure the problem." Bradbury's 1999 thinking had not strayed from his belief expressed nearly two decades earlier that if children do not know how to read and write certainly by the third grade, then they're not going to know how to think—since "the only way that you can learn to think is by knowing how to write" (Newcomb).

Films, comics, and books, all stimulations Bradbury loved, have been part of his writing, beginning with *The Hunchback of Notre Dame,* starring Lon Chaney, in 1923 when he was a mere three years old and *The Phantom of the Opera* when he was five. These two films set Bradbury off on a great, lifelong love affair with the cinema. Buck Rogers arrived in eight-year-old Bradbury's life, and he "lived in a state of near hysteria waiting for the comic to slap onto my front porch each night in the evening paper" (*Show*). With Buck Rogers came Tarzan and John Carter, Warlord of Mars, created by Edgar Rice Burroughs. He borrowed the Burroughs books from his Uncle Bion, read them numerous times, and virtually committed them to memory, chapter and verse. Aunt Neva's huge bookcase next door to him supplemented Bradbury's Burroughs readings with Lyman Frank Baum's "Oz" books. Bradbury reminisces, "Long before I went to the regular library, I picked up on those elements of fantasy which I think influenced me and changed my life" (Dorf). Later on, he prowled the Waukegan town library for volumes of Jules Verne, Robert Louis Stevenson, and H. G. Wells. Says Bradbury, "The library was the greenhouse in which I, a very strange plant indeed, grew up, exploding with seeds" (*Show*).

The young Bradbury kept moving from excitement to excitement. When Blackstone the Magician came to town, "that was incredible, too," says Bradbury. "I could hardly wait. I'd just go right out of my head waiting for Blackstone to show up. So all of that energy and passion and madness went right into my writing when I began to do it at the age of twelve" (Dorf). Bradbury decided to become a magician at the age of ten after Blackstone gave him his first live rabbit. The young

Bradbury's meeting with Mr. Electrico was also inspirational. This meeting is recounted in the video biography, *Ray Bradbury: An American Icon.* When he was twelve, he attended Mr. Electrico's performance when the Dill Brothers Combined Shows set up their tents just outside Waukegan. With a charged sword, Mr. Electrico reached out and touched the boy Bradbury on both shoulders and then on his nose, and commanded him to "Live forever!" The following day, the enthralled Ray returned and met Mr. Electrico in his uncharged state, who revealed to Bradbury the behind-the-scenes mysteries of the carnival, introducing him to some of the carnival figures, such as the strong man and the fat woman. Then he told the boy they had had a memorable meeting in a previous incarnation during the battle of the Ardennes forest in France. Bradbury's extraordinary encounter with Mr. Electrico and his consequent insider's glimpse into carnival life loom large in his short stories such as **"The Black Ferris,"** first published by *Weird Tales* in 1948, and **"The Illustrated Man,"** released two years later, as well as his popular 1962 novel ***Something Wicked This Way Comes.*** For example, in the first of these works, the slick carnival man Mr. Cooger appears, dressed in sharp, bright clothes with a carnation in his lapel, his hair greased with oil, and a brown derby on his head.

Bradbury's inspiration to be a writer solidified at age twelve, when he began writing his first stories by hand on butcher paper. He was determined that his first "book" should be a sequel to a Mars volume by Burroughs. Bradbury's young talents not only included burgeoning writing skills, but also his thespian interests in performing magic shows and reading comics to children over radio air waves on Saturdays. Thus, Bradbury fused his passion for magic and comics and drama, which still flourishes. John J. McLaughlin, theater critic for *The Nation,* wrote the following in the January 25, 1965, edition about "The World of Ray Bradbury," an evening of three one-act plays: "The appearance of a theatrical company dedicated to producing his own work represents more than dabbling in a new literary form for Bradbury. It is a full commitment to put time, energy, and money into the theatre. He spent $20,000 out of his own pocket, gathered a professional group of actors and stage technicians, and set out to establish a permanent theatre where his plays can be staged for as long as he cares to write them" (92-93).

Continuing his writing and thespian propensities, at Los Angeles High School Bradbury studied short story writing under Jennet Johnson, whom he describes in the 1964 *Show* interview as "a kindly, patient, warm, and very human woman, whose influence must weigh heavy on the scales [of his development as a writer]. After her, my teachers were all established writers in the science-fiction field." At his high school, Bradbury became a scriptwriter, producer, and director of the school's *Roman Review*. During his senior year, he joined the Los Angeles Science Fiction League, founded in 1935 as a chapter of Gernsback's Science Fiction League, and he began friendships with Ray Harryhausen, Forrest J. Ackerman, Robert Heinlein, Hannes Bok, Jack Williamson, Edmond Hamilton, Henry Kuttner, and Leigh Brackett. The League met in Clifton's Cafeteria, where free meals were provided if someone was short of money. Heinlein, Hamilton, Kuttner, and Brackett, at one time or another, worked with Bradbury on refining his craft. Brackett, particularly, met with him every Sunday afternoon for about four years in Santa Monica. Bradbury soon reached the point where he was able to write well enough to chart his own direction.

In June 1939, when he was nineteen and had saved enough money, Bradbury traveled four days and nights in a Greyhound bus to the First World Science Fiction Convention in New York, where successful writers and editors in the field convened. On this trip, he acted as agent for Hannes Bok, a member of the League who was also an artist and whose illustrations Bradbury carried with him. Bradbury showed Bok's many oil paintings and illustrations to *Weird Tales, Astounding Science Fiction,* and similar magazines and was directly responsible for selling his friend's work. Bok continued doing artwork for the covers and interior illustrations for science-fiction magazines in the years following.

This 1939 trip to New York proved pivotal for Bradbury's professional ambitions. Beyond the thrill of meeting central figures in the science-fiction field and successfully promoting his friend Bok's illustrations, Bradbury was able to further his own writing career, sharing samples of his short stories and receiving editors' encouragement to continue writing his stories. In particular, the editor Walter Bradbury, no relation to Ray, planted the thematic seed that eventually germinated and became ***The Martian Chronicles.*** On this same trip Bradbury also formed a friendship with Julius Schwartz, who later became his first agent in the pulp field and was editor at DC comics starting in 1944. When "Julie" read his work for the first time, he told Bradbury it was not good enough, and he rejected Bradbury as a client. Bradbury was twenty-one before he presented a short story that met Mr. Schwartz's standards. **"Pendulum,"** a collaborative effort with Henry Hasse, was sold to *Super Science Stories* and was Bradbury's first move into the pulp field for real money.

On Bradbury's momentous 1939 trip to New York, he also visited the New York World's Fair, which fueled his energies, imagination, and creativity with its exhibits of the future. Presented to him was a holistic view of a future community, complete with freeways and cloverleaf intersections, a fabulous concept to behold in that day. This fascination with the future and technology continued throughout Bradbury's writing, though, ironically, in his private life he has avoided driving, preferring to ride a bicycle, and has shunned e-mail in favor of more human, handwritten letters. Bradbury's rapture with things future is manifest in his involvement in city planning, including his participation in the development of Disney World's Experimental Community of Tomorrow (EPCOT) and Horton Plaza in San Diego. Bradbury's penchant for urban planning, which is a prevalent concern for him throughout his interviews, was framed by his philosophy to be part of the solution, not part of the problem. He perceives the active leadership role of the corporations, such as Walt Disney, in the development of ideal cities as the panacea for urban ills: "[T]he failure of cities is the failure of chambers of commerce and the failure of the mayors and the city councils who don't understand what cities are," he believes. "They're in for political power, they're not in to recreate the city, and make it better for everyone. So my dream has been, if they won't do it, some sort of corporate effort has to do it" (Couteau). This remedy-focused philosophical bent attracted Bradbury to the problem-solving genre of science fiction.

Unfortunately, amid the grand promises of what the world could be, within a few months of his New York trip, the United States was plunged into World War II. Poor eyesight kept Bradbury from the front lines, but his writing appeared in the major pulp magazines of the period: *Weird Tales, Famous Fantastic Mysteries, Thrilling Wonder Stories, Planet Stories, Super Science Stories, Detective Book Magazine, New Detective Magazine, Dime Mystery Magazine,* and *Astounding Science Fiction.* The pulp press is not without merit, he avowed to the *Show* interviewer: "Long before mass media began publishing or broadcasting material on the color problem, science fiction acted out such problems in the pulp magazines. I wrote a story in which the Negroes picked up and went off to Mars, leaving the entire South in the lurch, way back in 1949."

A major milestone occurred in Bradbury's writing in 1943, when he wrote **"The Lake,"** which he considers to be his first story of literary value. It recorded a disturbing incident from his childhood, when he built sand castles with a little girl on the shore of a lake. She went for a swim and never returned. He trusted his subconscious and allowed his emotions to write the story, and as a result was able, at least partially, to purge from his system a demon that had long haunted him, the memory of her death. Bradbury has relied on his muse ever since, and he advises those who wish to be writers to follow their emotions, rather than economics. He discourages writers from being directed by profit, because "the cleansing process, the therapeutic process that should be going on between the writer and his typewriter, or his pen and ink, is cut across, then, by this commercial function. And he begins to lie. And as soon as he begins to lie in his work, it becomes noncreative, nontherapeutic to himself, and non-therapeutic to anyone that reads him" (Harvey). Paradoxically, Bradbury has become one of the most financially successful writers in America, sometimes by repackaging his works in different collections for redistribution.

Two events in 1947 proved monumental for Mr. Bradbury. He married Marguerite "Maggie" McClure and became a client of literary agent Don Congdon. Both relationships have persevered to this day. During the '40s, five of Bradbury's stories brought him critical acclaim. **"The Big Black and White Game," "Powerhouse," "The Meadow," "I See You Never,"** and **"Homecoming"** were selected for prestigious awards. The latter became the nucleus of his 1998 novel *From the Dust Returned.* In John C. Tibbetts's March 20, 1991, interview with Bradbury for the *Christian Science Monitor,* which, regrettably, does not appear in this collection, Ray recalled how his story **"Homecoming"** was sold in the slick magazine market. *Mademoiselle* and *Vogue* "were women's magazines with fine story editors who published work by Katherine Anne Porter, Carson McCullers, and Eudora Welty," he remembered. "A young assistant at *Mademoiselle* found one of my stories in the 'slush pile.' It was about a family of vampires, called **'The Homecoming.'** He gave it to the story editor and said, '. . . you must publish this!' That young man was Truman Capote, and *Mademoiselle* ended up changing the whole magazine to fit the story!" (17).

If the decade of the '40s solidified Bradbury's reputation in the pulp tradition with a scattering of prize-winning, non-pulp short stories, then the '50s introduced Bradbury to the major slick magazines. His work appeared in *Senior Scholastic, Maclean's, Esquire,* the *Saturday Evening Post, Argosy, Charm, Life,* and *Playboy.* Approaching the '50s, Bradbury's short works made the transition to hardcovers and paperbacks as compilations. His first hardcover collection, **Dark Carnival,** was published in 1947. The 1950 publication of **The Martian Chronicles,** a collection of short stories with the common thread of planet Mars accounts, which shed light on contemporary issues, established Bradbury's reputation in the sophisticated, speculative fiction field.

The literary critic Christopher Isherwood rendered the first major review of a Bradbury work when he critiqued **The Martian Chronicles** in *Tomorrow* magazine. Isherwood's analysis placed Bradbury more in the fantasy tradition, one of Poe's genres, than in the science-fiction

field. Bradbury admits, "I'm not a science-fiction writer. I've only written one book that's science fiction, and that's *Fahrenheit 451.* All the others are fantasy." Bradbury is careful to differentiate between the two: "Fantasies are things that can't happen, and science fiction is about things that can happen" (Klein). Bradbury agrees with the critics' charge that he relies too much on fantasy and not enough on science to be labeled a science-fiction writer. He says in his 1996 *Playboy* interview with Kelley, "I use a scientific idea as a platform to leap into the air and never come back. This keeps them angry at me. They still begrudge my putting an atmosphere on Mars in *The Martian Chronicles* more than forty years ago." As evidence of this grudge by readers, Juliet Grimsley's essay in the December 1970 *English Journal* cites a student's response to Bradbury's Mars: "When an author can make his reader believe his story, I feel he is then a good writer. Ray Bradbury did this to me, and it makes me a bit angry to think I believed his 'fakey' story without any question" (1239).

Many critics point to Bradbury's prose collections of the '50s as among his best. **The Illustrated Man** was published in 1951, and like **The Martian Chronicles** it is a collection of short stories linked by a framing device, a tattooed man whose illustrations come alive to tell their stories. In 1953 Bradbury published his most influential and widely read work on censorship, **Fahrenheit 451,** a revision and expansion of his fifty-six-page novella, **"The Fireman,"** which first appeared in *Galaxy.* **Fahrenheit** was sold to Hugh Hefner's new magazine, *Playboy,* in three installments. In the May 1954 edition of *Playboy,* readers' reactions to the **Fahrenheit** installments in "Dear Playboy" varied from "I've read a lot of stories in my day but this one is the worst. It *stinks!*" to "Ray has been a good friend for a number of years and gifted me with the original manuscript to **F.451** a few months back. At that time I termed it a classic in the field and upon re-reading the first installment in your magazine my opinion seems justified." That accolade was made by William F. Nolan, whose interview with Bradbury is included in this collection. *Playboy* continued to publish Bradbury's fiction, essays, and poetry throughout his career.

Fahrenheit 451 is the quintessential fictional masterpiece on censorship and is discussed numerous times in Bradbury's interviews. Even though he abhors censorship, "when government controls things, and you cannot publish or sell or find in a library the books that you want" (Gasior), Bradbury paradoxically believes government may and should use discretion in selecting the art it wishes to fund, without being considered tyrannous: "[Government is] just saying that they're funding you just as a gallery does; a gallery has the right to choose what it wants to hang on its walls. That's not censorship—that's selectivity" (Albright).

As special interest groups and political correctness gained influence, Bradbury came to view these forces as menacing as despotism and the malleable masses, and he expanded his views on censorship. "So whereas back then [the early '50s] I wrote about the tyranny of the majority, today I'd combine that with the tyranny of the minorities. These days, you have to be careful of both. They both want to control you" (Kelley). "If we listened to all these groups then we wouldn't have anything to read or anything to look at. It's okay for them to speak up, but you don't have to listen to them 'cause if we censor all the things the gays want changed and all the women's lib things changed and all the Jewish groups want changed and all the Catholic groups, after a while you have empty shells" (Albright).

Bradbury's output for the rest of the '50s included *The Golden Apples of the Sun* and *The October Country,* both published in 1953, the latter containing many of the stories from *Dark Carnival* with some additions, and *A Medicine for Melancholy,* released in 1959. Each of these volumes gathered stories written from 1945 to 1959. In 1957 he also produced his semi-autobiographical novel, *Dandelion Wine,* which contains many previously published individual short stories. In his review of *Dandelion Wine,* literary critic Robert O. Bowen commented in the September 7, 1957, issue of the *Saturday Review* that "no other writer since Mark Twain has caught the vitality and innocence of smalltown American youth with as fine and mature perception as Ray Bradbury's (18). In 1971 the Apollo 15 crew named a section of the moon Dandelion Crater after the title of this Bradbury novel.

Bradbury's work in 1954 crafting the screenplay for John Huston's film *Moby Dick* established him as a permanent fixture in Hollywood. *Moby Dick* set a conspicuous precedent for Bradbury's presence in television, cinema, and stage, and, no doubt, contributed to his financial success. In addition to his works appearing on all the major networks—ABC, CBS, NBC, BBC, and PBS—sixty-five of his teleplays for *The Ray Bradbury Theater* were produced for Home Box Office (HBO) and USA Network from 1985 through 1992. HBO viewers tuned into Bradbury's familiar description of the genesis of his ideas: "People ask 'Where do you get your ideas?' Well, right here [pointing to his cluttered 'office' that brings to mind the 'fabled attic or basement storehouse' he uses in the *Show* interview as a metaphor for the source of his *Dandelion Wine*]. All this is my Martian landscape. Somewhere in this room is an African veldt. Just beyond, perhaps, is a small Illinois town where I grew up. And I'm surrounded on

every side by my magician's toy shop. I'll never starve here. I just look around, find what I need, and begin. I'm Ray Bradbury, and this is *The Ray Bradbury Theater.* Well, then, right now what shall it be? Out of all this, what do I choose to make a story? I never know where the next one will take me. The trip—exactly one half exhilaration, exactly one half terror."

In 1961 Bradbury composed the voice-over narration for the movie *King of Kings.* The following year saw the release of *Icarus Montgolfier Wright,* an eighteen-minute animated film conceived by Bradbury and the co-written with George C. Johnson. The film was nominated for an Academy Award as the best animated short subject of the year and received a Golden Eagle Film Award. Bradbury's first drama collection, *The Anthem Sprinters and Other Antics,* appeared in 1963, and director François Truffaut's film adaptation of *Fahrenheit 451* was released in 1966.

Though predictably critical of film versions of his works, Bradbury said in his 1972 interview with Kunert: "I thought François Truffaut did a fine job with *Fahrenheit 451.* I loved the adventure, the chase, the way he handled his actors." According to Bradbury, the film improves with multiple viewings: "There are many fine little throwaway items that one often misses on the first viewing. Truffaut probably didn't have the city congested with people, for example, because he wanted to suggest that everyone was inside—watching television." Bradbury regards many of the film's scenes as poignant: "For example, the first night that Montag reads a book, sitting by the television set, and using the light from the set to read is a great touch. That isn't even in my book. And the careful articulation of the words from Dickens, running his finger over every word, stumbling. This is a *great* scene." Bradbury counted the conclusion of the film among the most beautiful in the history of film: "These people at the ending of the film only articulate as walking metaphors what *we* are as people. Each of us has some part of some book in our heads. Some of us have good memories. Some of us have poor memories. But we all have memories of a book and how it changed our lives. So to me, that ending is beautiful. It's a lovely movie. It's a haunting movie."

Bradbury's *Something Wicked This Way Comes,* a novel which includes many autobiographical episodes, was published in 1962 and was subsequently popularized in film by Walt Disney Studios in 1983. Its thirteen-year-old Will Halloway is essentially Douglas Spaulding from *Dandelion Wine.* Throughout the '60s Bradbury published several repackaged anthologies of previously written and compiled material, including *R Is for Rocket, The Machineries of Joy, The Vintage Bradbury, S Is for Space,* and *Twice 22.* Of *The Machineries of Joy,* literary critic Martin Levin writes in the February 16, 1964, *New York Times'* Reader's Report: "Mr. Bradbury is a smooth pitchman for his versatile collection, luring you into each story with a well-thrown narrative hook, and then confronting you with whatever exhibit takes his fancy" (38). The decade culminated in a 1969 collection of new Bradbury fiction, *I Sing the Body Electric!*

With the nation's successes in its space program in the late '60s, Bradbury shifted from thinking about space as a concept to thinking about it as a definite reality, and he welcomed the theological implications of such "blasphemies." "We are refashioning God into a new image so that He will stay conveniently out of the way. So that we can get the work done of going into space, of landing on God's moon, of landing on God's Mars, and going places where, a hundred years ago if we had tried to go there, we would have been burned at the stake for doing the job" (Berton). Bradbury believes in the divinity of man and not in the anthropomorphic God: "Man is a fusion of the human and the divine. I believe that the flesh of man contains the very soul of God, that we are, finally, irrevocably and responsibly, God Himself incarnate, that we shall carry this seed of God into space" (Nolan). In response to William B. Allen's query regarding whether "one finds much of Walt Whitman or Ralph Waldo Emerson in Bradbury," Ray admits, "Not too much. I read Emerson so many years ago that I can't really say that he rubbed off that much. Little of Whitman, and I was very young. But Whitman could have come to me through other people; people like Norman Corwin or Thomas Wolfe. I'm not sure how much Whitman Thomas Wolfe read; but there are echoes. Emerson could have come to me through other people too. But if I really listed influences, I don't think I would put them on the list anywhere."

Little new Bradbury fiction appeared in the '70s and '80s. Instead, Bradbury turned his energy towards publishing poetry—*When Elephants Last in the Dooryard Bloomed, Where Robot Mice and Robot Men Run Round in Robot Towns, The Haunted Computer and the Android Pope,* and *The Complete Poems of Ray Bradbury,* released from 1973 through 1982. During this period, drama also received more of his attention. *Madrigals for the Space Age, Pillar of Fire, Dandelion Wine, Leviathan '99,* and *The Martian Chronicles* were all staged from 1973 through 1976, and *Pillar of Fire and Other Plays for Today, Tomorrow, and Beyond Tomorrow* came to print in 1975.

The three Bradbury short story collections released in the '70s and '80s, *Long after Midnight, The Stories of Ray Bradbury,* and *The Toynbee Convector,* gather the stories Bradbury wrote from 1943 through the '80s. Ralph A. Sperry in the December 1976 *Best Sellers* book review of *Long after Midnight* describes the story

"The Better Part of Wisdom" as "the most sensitive, most restrained, most graceful treatment of homosexuality I've ever read, ought to be required reading for all gay writers." The critic Orson Scott Card, writing in the November 2, 1980, *Washington Post Book World,* said concerning *The Stories of Ray Bradbury*: "It is not the characters he expects you to identify with. Rather, he means to capture you in his own voice, expects you to see through his eyes. And his eyes see, not the cliché plot, but the whole meaning of the events; not the scenes or the individual people, but yourself and your own fears and your own family and the answer, at last, to the isolation that had seemed inevitable to you" (5).

Bradbury delved into the crime and detective genre early in his writing career, and these stories were collected in *A Memory of Murder,* released in 1984. In 1985 he published a second work within this genre, *Death Is a Lonely Business.* Set in 1949 Venice, California, this work contains many autobiographical dimensions. Bradbury admits that the crazy kid in the novel is a portrayal of Bradbury himself as a struggling writer for pulp magazines: "Events in my past life are in there, some people that I knew" (Couteau). The November 3, 1985, review of the book in the *Washington Post Book World* focuses on its romantic style: "Ray Bradbury's writing remains as rich and ripe as ever," Ross Thomas writes. "When describing a woman he has his Young Writer hero think of her as being 'a lovely chess game carved and set in a store window when you were a kid. She has a freshly built girl's gym, with only the faintest scent of the noon tennis dust that clings to golden thighs.'" The book is dedicated to the memory of "hard-boiled" writers Raymond Chandler, Dashiell Hammett, James M. Cain, and Ross Macdonald, among others.

The sequel to *Death Is a Lonely Business, A Graveyard for Lunatics,* was inspired by an incident in Bradbury's life, when he sailed to Europe and for four or five days observed a man with a horribly disfigured face. He began to write the book with the plot revolving around the man with the ruined face. The work is critical of the film industry for such things as control over the writer's material, because "once you sell those things to the studio, they can do anything with it that they want" (Klein). *Let's All Kill Constance,* Bradbury's 2002 novel, is the latest in this series. As Bradbury explains to Jason Marchi in a 1998 interview preceding the publication of this work, Constance has "been in my first two murder mysteries, and I killed her off in the first one. As I was revising that first murder mystery she came back and knocked on the door and said, 'I refuse to stay dead. Put me back in.' So I put her back in and now she's in three books." His murder mystery characters are paranoids, schizophrenics, neurotics, and perverts—all representative of the underbelly of mass culture.

Over the last decade, in addition to his late murder mysteries, Bradbury has published two novels—*Green Shadows, White Whale* (1992), a mosaic of his experiences in Ireland while working on the *Moby Dick* screenplay for John Huston, and *From the Dust Returned* (1998), a tapestry of exploits by the ghouls of his imagination. The Elliott family, featured in the latter novel, is based on Ray's childhood memories of his grandmother, his Aunt Neva, and his favorite Swedish uncle, Einar. The individual characters in the Elliott family threesome appear elsewhere in previously published short stories. Three compilations of short stories, written from 1947 through 2001, were published from 1996 through 2002—*Quicker Than the Eye, Driving Blind,* and *One More for the Road. Publishers Weekly* said of the twenty-one stories in *Driving Blind:* "Despite bizarre actions and abstract twists, all are grounded in the everyday. Here are sketches, vignettes, strange tales, colorful anecdotes, little tragedies, hilarious lies, and metaphysics too" (72). Hanna-Barbera Studios' animated version of Bradbury's *The Halloween Tree* earned an Emmy in 1993, and Walt Disney Studios released *The Wonderful Ice Cream Suit* on video in 1998. Bradbury wrote the screenplay for this movie and considers it "the best film I've ever made, and there's not one curse in the whole film. And it's about people who could very easily curse, you see? But you don't need those swear words" (Klein).

At eighty-three Mr. Bradbury continues to work from his wheelchair, his post-stroke command center. In a May 7, 2002, communication to me, he reminded me of his circumstances: "During the last two-and-a-half years, I've been recovering from a stroke. Not long ago I went completely blind in my left eye and my right eye is behaving poorly. I've had to learn to write again and to speak clearly, and there are many other medical problems that have occurred in recent months." At the time of my interview with him, he was awaiting the release of the remaking of his short story **"A Sound of Thunder"** in production in Prague and other Hollywood projects. His plays continue to be presented on the stage.

Of all the accolades Bradbury has received over his illustrious career, most notably the Nebula Grandmaster Award for his lifetime achievements and the National Book Foundation's 2000 Medal for Distinguished Contribution to American Letters, Bradbury would best like to be remembered as a teller of tales. In his own words, from the 1964 *Show* interview, he sends himself "on a journey back through the ages in a time machine.

Arriving in Baghdad I would walk through the marketplace and turn down a street where sit the old men who are the tellers of tales. There, among the young who listen and the old who say aloud, I would like to take my place and speak when it is my turn. It is an ancient tradition, a good one, a lovely one, a fine one. If some boy visits my tomb a hundred years from now and writes on the marble with a crayon: He Was a Teller of Tales, I will be happy. I ask no more name than that." And Bradbury has most solidly earned that epigraph.

The interviews in this collection span more than five decades and appear in chronological order as they were conducted. Obvious grammatical and spelling errors have been silently corrected. Bradbury's responses to interviewers, over the years, are well crafted and generally consistent, with exceptions, some of which I have highlighted. This uniformity is due, in large part, to repetitive or similar questions being posed and his typically well-rehearsed responses. Some duplication of questions and answers occurs in the different interviews, but I have made every effort to cover the gamut with as little redundancy as possible. It is impossible to offer all the available interviews in one volume, but I wanted to assemble the "major," most representative, and most difficult-to-access interviews.

A number of people helped me with this project: Seetha Srinivasan and Walter Biggins from the University Press of Mississippi; Dr. R. Bruce Bickley Jr. and Dr. William T. Lhamon Jr., members of my doctoral committee, and Dr. Elisabeth Logan, associate dean and professor of library and information studies, Florida State University; Margaret J. Kimball, Stanford University archivist; Jon Edmondson, public services manager, UCLA Southern Regional Library Facility; Alva Moore Stevenson, UCLA Oral History Program; Dr. Peter Schramm, Ashland University; Dr. William B. Allen, Michigan State University; William F. Nolan, acclaimed author and Bradbury bibliographer; Jason J. Marchi, New Century Cinema Group; Arnold Kunert, retired communication arts teacher; Dr. Jonathan Eller, a Bradbury scholar, University of Indiana and Purdue University, Indianapolis; Donn Albright, professor in communications, Pratt Institute, and author of *The Ray Bradbury Bibliography,* and Shel Dorf, former lettering man on Milton Caniff's *Steve Canyon* comic-strip, who has two interviews with Milton Caniff included in the University Press of Mississippi's *Milton Caniff: Conversations,* edited by Robert C. Harvey, and who graciously served as my ambassador to personally meet and talk with Mr. Bradbury in San Diego. Special credit is given to my wife, Kitty Jo, and my mother, Zola Belle, for their professional assistance and continuing support.

Last, but not least, I am deeply grateful to Ray Douglas Bradbury, who made a personal commitment to my project and also granted me access to Craig Cunningham's interview with him entitled *The Dogs That Eat Sweet Grass,* 1965, maintained by the University of California Los Angeles Oral History Program. Echoing the words of Mr. Electrico to the young Ray Bradbury, my wish is that he may "Live forever!" And, indeed, he will—in the hearts and minds of his readers.

Jonathan R. Eller and William F. Touponce (essay date 2004)

SOURCE: Eller, Jonathan R., and William F. Touponce. "Fathering the Carnival: *Something Wicked This Way Comes.*" In *Ray Bradbury: The Life of Fiction,* pp. 256-309. Kent, Ohio: Kent State University Press, 2004.

[In the following essay, Eller and Touponce give an extended explication of Bradbury's Something Wicked This Way Comes.*]*

Bradbury's first Simon and Schuster title remains the most filmic of his major fictions. The evolution of **Something Wicked This Way Comes**—as well as its legacy—is deeply tied to film history; in fact, in 1983 it would become the first feature film of a Bradbury work produced from a Bradbury screenplay. Fathering this work extended over seventeen years; it was his first full-length novel, emerging (unlike the shorter and more focused **Fahrenheit 451**) from materials for a novel dating back to 1945. The project metamorphosed through plans for an experimental graphic novel and blossomed into a full screenplay before reaching print as a book in 1962. The referent for his title—the arrival of a supernatural carnival with nightmare rides—projected his memories of traveling carnival shows of his Midwest youth from nostalgic reality into the dark fantastic. As a novel, it culminates the most productive period of his fiction and sets out in strongly emotional terms his own most heartfelt notions of life, death, and creativity. In this work he reached a peak of character development that he would rarely attain again. By the early 1980s, Stephen King would observe that **Something Wicked,** while certainly not Bradbury's best-known or most acclaimed novel, is arguably his best.[1]

But during the 1940s, Bradbury held back almost every image of this dark carnival from his earliest successes in a new kind of supernatural fiction that, as Darrell Schweitzer has pointed out, "defined the direction in which horror fiction would go, away from haunted English country houses, dark forests, and monsters (Lovecraftian or traditional), toward big cities and their suburbs, and into the mind." Bradbury would soon be an influence on Charles Beaumont and the "California School" of horror and mystery writers that gathered around him, including Richard Matheson, George Clayton Johnson, Chad Oliver, and William F. Nolan. Clive

Barker considers the early stories collected by Bradbury in **Dark Carnival** (1947) as central to the continuing tradition of the fantastic in contemporary literature. King proclaimed **Dark Carnival** "the *Dubliners* of American fantasy," and William F. Nolan believes that every major writer of supernatural fiction has encountered Bradbury's distinctive early work.[2] The history of **Something Wicked** clearly begins here with Bradbury's weird tales, but the historical trail quickly leads to an intertextual mystery: why is the dark carnival absent from **Dark Carnival**?

BRADBURY'S TEXTS

Surviving notes from the period 1945-1946 show that Bradbury's ideas for a dark carnival novel are inextricably linked to the evolving concept of his first story collection. The history of **Dark Carnival** is full of clues: an early 1945 outline containing the story title "Carnival" and two possible volume titles, THE DARK CARACEL [*sic*] and DARK CARNIVAL [. . .]; the definition of a dark carnival developed in a letter to his editor, August Derleth; and his two word-pictures of a dark-carnival dust jacket, one presented on the outline of contents and one in a letter to Derleth, which adds a child to the jacket composition:

> The cover jacket might possibly illustrate a small carnival that has set up its merry-go-round and side-show tent and banners in a dark green woodland glade at twilight—the entire atmosphere of the picture would be one of remoteness, of a carnival in the wilderness going full steam, but with no one in sight except one small boy in the foreground, tiny, very alone, staring at the moving carousel and the high banners. And on the banners instead of portraits of Fat Ladies, Thin Men and Tattooed Freaks would be pictures of strange, nebulous creatures. And on the carousel, instead of horses sliding up and down the gleaming brass poles, would be other impossible, vaguely, disturbingly delineated creatures of such indistinct cast and line that ones [*sic*] imagination could make them anything in the whole universe.[3]

The impressionistic and misty scenes of this dark carnival are very similar to the dim glances off the midway into terrifying menageries and freak tents that Bradbury would perfect seventeen years later in his novel. In all, the visual images of the imaginary carnival described in his papers of this period are most striking and suggest that he was well on the way to seeing the full potential of carnival to illuminate the secrets of life, death, and creativity. But Bradbury was already developing the germ of a novel from these images, and he held story-length glimpses of the sinister shows out of **Dark Carnival** completely. The early content outlines instead contain weird tales inspired by memories outside of his carnival experiences; seven of these were pulled into **Dark Carnival** from **The Small Assassins,** the Ur-novel from which **Dandelion Wine** and his two unpublished Green Town novel projects descend. His early idea for a full section of stories on carnival simply disappeared as his first collection evolved. The final dust-jacket design was refocused on masks, themselves a symbol of the carnivalesque, but Bradbury deliberately left one direct visual clue in the center of this collage of masks: a carousel horse. It would prove to be a talisman of things to come.[4]

Bradbury continued to move stories in and out of *Dark Carnival* even after he submitted copy to August Derleth in June 1946. But none of these changes brought the carnival back into that collection. Instead, Bradbury was working simultaneously on a novel that seemed to blend his carnival fantasies with the detective fiction he had been publishing successfully during the final years of World War II. An undated outline survives with the title, "DARK CARNIVAL a novel of 70,000 words," prepared on the coarse-wove manila paper he used during the mid-1940s. A two-page opening fragment suggests that the plot idea involved a journey on a carousel into the past to prevent a murder from occurring in the present. The nineteen chapter titles found on the outline have elements in common with the detective stories he had already tired of, and there is no evidence that this form of the novel went any further.

The true origins of *Something Wicked* survive in a much larger nest of materials from this same period, saved in a more contemporary three-prong yellow binder subsequently titled by Bradbury as "Original Materials 'Dark Carnival' which became 'Something Wicked T. W. C.'" The date, also in his hand, reads "Summer 1945 and 1946." The binder contains more than thirty pages of fragments, sketches, and chapter openings for a dark carnival novel that no longer echoes his detective fiction at all.[5] These fragments are also distinctly different from the weird tales he was simultaneously assembling in *Dark Carnival*. They do, however, seem to share the same setting of *The Small Assassins*; eventually, this setting would develop more fully and define *Something Wicked* as a companion Green Town novel to *Dandelion Wine,* but the evolution of contents is distinctly separate for these two books (table 12). The chapter fragments show Bradbury working on early forms of the carnival's supernatural aspects and its effects on the people of his small Midwestern town. There are partial sketches and chapter openings centering on the carnival's arrival and canopy raising, the carnival freaks (including Mr. Electrico), the tunnel of love, the calliope, arcade games, the mirror maze, the Ferris wheel, and the carousel. In nearly every fragment these rides and games, common to so many of the carnivals from Bradbury's youth, have sinister features that can turn deadly without warning. There are three variations on a mirror maze that can trap the viewer in the frozen future of old age and three more variations on husbands who go to the carnival and

return home as either old men or young children. Bradbury would develop both of these conceits into major horrors of the final novel.

The story fragments of man-to-boy transformations inspired the first germ of the novel to reach print. In 1948 Bradbury decided to offer an opening episode of the larger concept for publication. **"The Black Ferris"** presents an evil carnie who rides the Ferris wheel forward and backward to change his age so that he can pose as a child while he preys on the people of the town. This story, which also introduces two local boys—Pete and Hank—who take control of the Ferris and age the carnival master into oblivion, appeared in the May 1948 issue of *Weird Tales.*[6] But the larger carnival fiction would soon languish as Bradbury and Congdon focused on winning a book contract beyond the niche market that *Weird Tales* and Derleth's Arkham House could command. The novel materials, as well as his plan to expand and novelize the vampire stories from his *Dark Carnival* collection, moved to the background as Bradbury's science fiction and wider-market fantasies were transformed into *The Martian Chronicles, The Illustrated Man,* and *The Golden Apples of the Sun. Fahrenheit 451* and his nine-month European excursion to write the *Moby Dick* screenplay took all of 1953 and the first half of 1954.

Even so, the carnival was never far away. In 1952 Bradbury was just beginning his long-term publishing relationship with California artist Joe Mugnaini, whose shadowy drawings and dreamlike paintings would provide illustrations and cover art for some of the writer's most enduring titles. Bradbury would later recall, "Joe Mugnaini and I planned to do the *Dark Carnival, Black Ferris, Something Wicked this Way Comes* complex as an illustrated book with no text, a novel in pictures." A single worksheet for the cover and title survives [. . .]; Bradbury's light sketch of the carnival train crossing a trestle bridge was made from "The Caravan," a Mugnaini wax and oil painting that, a decade later, would inspire the dust jacket of the British first edition.[7]

Other aspects of this project never moved beyond the planning stage, but it is clear that Bradbury was developing visual images of the novel's plot elements even while the prose remained dormant. Perhaps the most significant of these planned but now lost images was a merry-go-round, for Bradbury's early vision of the carousel as the centerpiece of the carnival had never waned. None of his three 1945-1946 chapter fragments on the carnival's ability to alter age reveals which ride (carousel or Ferris) offers the enchantment. He now saw the carousel, rather than the Ferris wheel of his 1948 trial story, as the device the evil carnival owner would use to cycle back and forth through the aging process. This was no doubt a development of his own "novel in

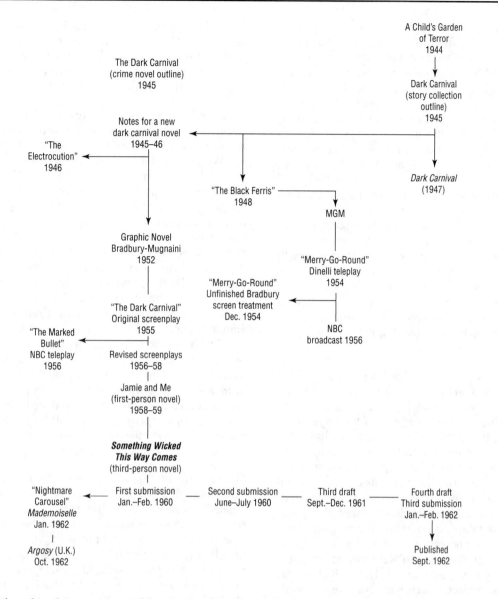

pictures" project, but the next stage of inspiration would come, quite unexpectedly, from the pen of a Hollywood scriptwriter.

Film and television adaptations of a half-dozen Bradbury stories were produced between 1951 and 1953, prompting Samuel Goldwyn Jr. to buy the rights to **"The Black Ferris"** for MGM. He hired Mel Dinelli to write the script, a writer who already knew where Bradbury was going with the plan for the dark carnival novel. In 1949 Dinelli, introducing himself to Bradbury as both a fan and fellow writer, had visited Bradbury at home and received a copy of **Dark Carnival.** During this visit, Bradbury explained to him the curious absence of the carousel from his first story collection, imparting his vision of this ride as the central device of his developing novel. Five years later Dinelli, working with Goldwyn, developed a parallel evolution in the form of a short television script. It aired locally on the *Starlight Summer Theater,* but Goldwyn had difficulty

finding a sponsor for national broadcast. During this time, Bradbury returned from overseas work on production of **Moby Dick,** and in early December 1954 Goldwyn showed him the broadcast piece. Bradbury immediately saw the potential for a feature-length film and within two days produced a fifty-page treatment expanding Dinelli's core teleplay along the lines of his own notes for the novel. Dinelli's teleplay was eventually aired on July 10, 1956, as a series pilot for NBC's *Sneak Preview* under the title **"Merry-Go-Round."**[8] No more came of this project, and Bradbury's expansion of the teleplay remains unlocated. But within a few months, another MGM giant would inspire Bradbury to write a completely original full-length film treatment of the evolving novel.

Once again, the catalyst would be visual.[9] Gene Kelly had recently wrapped production of *Invitation to the Dance,* and in 1955 he arranged a screening for the new film at MGM. The Bradburys had known Kelly for several years and were invited to the screening; they covered the two miles from their Clarkson Road home by bus and greatly enjoyed the movie's three interwoven storylines. The film, and in particular the carnival sequence that opened it, reawakened the long line of Bradbury's circus and carnival experiences, dating back to his childhood viewing of Lon Chaney Sr.'s *Laugh, Clown, Laugh.* The Bradburys had plenty of time to think about the experience that evening—the bus never came, and they decided to walk home. As they walked, Bradbury's wish for a chance to work with Kelly led Maggie to challenge him to find something in his files that could be extended into a screenplay. Within a few days Bradbury was composing his own screen treatment of the now almost fully evolved dark carnival storyline: once Pete and Jim (Hank in **"The Black Ferris"**) have destroyed one of the carnival owners in his own evil device, they become fugitives in their own town as the surviving owner searches them out for revenge. This opening, as well as stored images from his notes and the "novel in pictures" project, quickly grew into a detailed screen treatment.

Two distinct drafts survive in Bradbury's papers, both titled **"The Dark Carnival."** The earliest form is a forty-page typewritten draft on legal-size pages that carries the action through to the capture of the boys in the town library by the surviving co-owner, an illustrated man whose tattoos control the tormented carnival freaks who work for him. This typescript is paginated but undated, though discards include dates running from late January through mid-March 1955. A second draft developed from these materials runs to eighty-six pages and is nearly complete. It contains inserts from 1956 and 1957, but it undoubtedly served as the basis for an unlocated typescript submitted to Kelly sometime in the late spring or early summer of 1955. Kelly was fascinated by the project, which was tailor-made for his acting and directing talents, and committed to make it his next film. He soon left for London and Paris to secure backing.

Meanwhile, Bradbury, still intending to work with his actor-friend, explored options for independent backing for the collaboration if MGM failed to support the project at home. There was interest at Columbia, but Kelly was aware that this would jeopardize his own participation; on August 8 he cabled Bradbury with his blessing to proceed with any deals of his own but offered a strong Irish hunch that he could bring in backing from overseas. Bradbury quickly cabled back: "Believe in Irish hunches. . . . No doubt in my mind that Kelly is the man to do it." Unfortunately, Kelly's early 1950s success with such films as *An American in Paris* was fading; *Invitation to the Dance* had not been successful at the box office, and he returned from Europe in September without securing the finances. Bradbury was honored that Kelly had even tried and

knew that the project the actor had rekindled could be polished further. Dated inserts in the second draft, as well as discarded pages, show that Bradbury worked on at least one subsequent draft in the middle of 1956; the opening eight pages are dated April 29, 1957.

Bradbury's correspondence reveals that he did indeed circulate revised versions of the Kelly screen treatment through his film and television agent Ben Benjamin of the West Coast-based Famous Artists Agency. Disney declined in December 1955. In May 1957 Hecht-Hill-Lancaster returned it as too fantastic for wide audiences; Bradbury would work in Hollywood and London on retainer with H-H-L through much of 1957 and turn out an excellent screenplay for Carol Read based on **"And the Rock Cried Out"** (it remains one of the best unproduced Bradbury screenplays). While in London he sent **"The Dark Carnival"** to Hammer Films, suggesting (through the Peters Agency) that the screenplay would fit in with the studio's recent run of horror films. Hammer executives declined, so in 1958 Bradbury offered **"The Dark Carnival"** to Twentieth Century Fox, but they were still smarting from an inability to come to terms with him for a film version of *The Illustrated Man* and refused the unpublished property.[10] Bradbury would continue to work on unproduced film and television options (primarily involving *The Martian Chronicles*) for two more years, but none of these screenplays were ever produced.

One significant byproduct of **"The Dark Carnival"** screenplay did make it to television. In 1955 Bradbury created a standalone half-hour teleplay about the bullet trick, a common sideshow illusion where the artist appears to catch a bullet fired by a volunteer from the crowd. Bradbury added the suspense of a deadly love triangle to this game and sold the teleplay to the producers of *Jane Wyman Presents.*[11] It aired as **"The Marked Bullet"** on November 20, 1956, with Jane Wyman in the role of the illusionist. The love triangle closely followed the plot of **"The Electrocution,"** his 1946 story about an electric-chair illusion in a side-show. This variation once again demonstrated the intertextual nature of his cross-media authorship—his transfer of storyline from one sideshow act to another is similar to his transfer of the central attraction from Ferris wheel to carousel as **"The Dark Carnival"** evolved from story to screenplay to novel. Bradbury never published **"The Marked Bullet"** as a short story; instead, he would write yet another variation on this act into the developing novel. Clearly, the Hollywood interlude had been pivotal—he now had a detailed plot and a great deal of dialog for **"The Dark Carnival"** project and began to transform these materials into his first full-length novel. The transformation was not continuous—he moved away from the material for six months at a time during 1958 and 1959, eventually finding time to run out a first-person variation of the novel titled *Jamie and Me.*

During the first months of 1960, he moved the narrative back into the third person and completed a first draft of the entire novel.[12] This draft would prove to be an ending as well as a beginning—it was the last original work he would ever write for his longtime publisher, Doubleday. In fact, his Doubleday editors would never even see the second draft.

Bradbury experienced growing frustration with Doubleday during the 1950s. His relationship with Walter Bradbury was always trusting and cordial, but periodically Ray Bradbury and his agent, Don Congdon, would point out the failure of Doubleday to increase the relatively small advertising budget and limited review contacts as Bradbury continued to gain popularity among mainstream readers at home and abroad. But by early 1960, other issues needed to be resolved as well. Doubleday was still taking 50 percent of the paperback sales and royalties; any leverage Bradbury had gained in securing full paperback profits from Ballantine for *Fahrenheit 451* (1953) and *The October Country* (1955) was countered in Doubleday's view by Bradbury's vulnerability on two unspoken points: first, that Ballantine, primarily a paperback publisher, could never offer Bradbury large hardback printings or guarantee long-term hardback reprint opportunities; and second, that Bradbury's preference for the short-story form, and his consequent need to periodically publish in the always market-risky short-story-collection format, would put him at a disadvantage with nearly any publisher. Furthermore, Doubleday was growing increasingly weary of Bradbury's move away from science fiction; when he proposed another fantasy collection along the lines of *The Golden Apples of the Sun,* his editors were not willing to offer a better deal. In fact, Bradbury and Congdon had to settle for a two-book deal similar to his earlier contract for *Golden Apples* and *Dandelion Wine*—that is, committing to produce a novel in order to publish another story collection. The contract was signed in the spring of 1958, but Congdon was only able to negotiate a slight increase in the hardback royalty scale and an approval clause for reprints.[13]

But the biggest issue would be the long-term marketing of his titles. Bradbury was still trying to understand how Doubleday let *The Martian Chronicles* hardback edition go out of print in 1957 just as *Sputnik* seemed to launch the *Chronicles* as the great American space-age novel. He secured a new printing with a new introduction by Clifton Fadiman the following year, but Bradbury was frustrated at Doubleday's decision to deny him a new (reset) edition, which would have allowed him to make much-desired changes in content. By 1959, *The Golden Apples of the Sun* was out of print in both hardback and paperback, and the new fantasy collection, released as *A Medicine for Melancholy,* was being advertised on a scale that seemed, from Bradbury's perspective, to assure the same fate in

an even shorter period of time. The biggest blow came when Walter Bradbury moved to Henry Holt and Company during the spring of 1959. This move, along with Stanley Kauffmann's move from Ballantine to Knopf, led Bradbury to consider both houses as potential alternatives to Doubleday. But Congdon advised his client to wait and see if these moves by trusted editors of the past would prove to be long-term opportunities for the future.[14] As it turned out, neither Walter Bradbury nor Kauffmann would be able to work with their respective new publishers and could not provide a stable alternative to Doubleday.

By October 1959 Bradbury was determined to force either a renegotiation of the two-book contract (and thus pave the way for better deals in the future) or a release from the agreement. Again Congdon urged caution. From an agent's perspective, the best strategy to get earlier Bradbury titles back in print would be to present Doubleday (or any potential rival press) with a new book that would clearly move him to a higher sales plateau. Congdon sensed that *The Dark Carnival* could be just that book and urged Bradbury to complete the first draft as soon as possible. In November Congdon sounded out Walt Bradbury's successor, Tim Seldes, and discovered that Doubleday held a similar view— delivery of the new novel would indeed open a window for renegotiation. Spurred on by Congdon's advice and embassies, Bradbury began a final period of sustained activity; on April 4, 1960, he sent the first draft of the novel, now titled *Something Wicked This Way Comes,* to Congdon for review. The letter of transmittal for the 377-page, 43-chapter typescript reveals the intensity of the creative process; for the first time in their relationship, Bradbury was sending Congdon a book-length manuscript that was, in large part, unrevised: "Half of the book is first draft, half of it second. . . . The main thing, which I'm sure you're prepared for, is that perhaps never before in the last 13 years, have I sent you a story or book manuscript in quite this almost-but-not quite born state. As you read, I know you will mentally cut some of the more florid metaphors which always encrust my first and second drafts. Sometimes I give myself, on a single page, 4, 5, or 6 similes which, by the fifth draft, dwindle down to one or two really good ones, for proper emphasis."[15]

Congdon wanted a reading from Doubleday as soon as possible and immediately sent a copy to Seldes. In late May Congdon passed along the editor's initial comments to Bradbury, noting that the surface praise and lightly handled suggestions for revision masked the position that Doubleday saw nothing more or less than the usual Bradbury craftsmanship. The implication, from Congdon's viewpoint, was that renegotiation would net no major concessions. But he also felt that the new novel, once revised, would be a book that could command a new level of attention from publishers other than Doubleday. He now urged Bradbury to make his case in writing to Seldes.[16]

On June 2 Bradbury wrote Seldes asking for an editorial board decision on his future with the publishing house. He noted the warm response to his work offered by Walter Bradbury and Seldes over the last eleven years but felt that few others at Doubleday shared their enthusiasm. He cited a need for increased advertising and promotion budgets for the new novel as well as renewed efforts to reprint and promote his earlier titles as fictional forerunners of the space age, which had now become reality. It took Seldes nearly a month to confer with vacationing colleagues, and this was not a good sign. His response went to Congdon with a copy for Bradbury on July 1; it offered to give Bradbury more control of advertising copy and agreed to promote his earlier titles. But Doubleday's initial advertising budget for the new book would only be three thousand dollars, and editorial ideas for republication of the out-of-print titles focused on paperback options and omnibus consolidations of the story collections. Doubleday was a large house with many authors, and it was now clear to Bradbury that his editors were not willing to move him to the next level of marketing visibility. On July 8, after consulting with Congdon, he wrote Seldes to ask for his release from the second half of the current two-book contract: "After eleven years, I think it is time for me to leave Doubleday and to try to find a new publisher who will see me and this fantastic and exciting new Space Age with the same high-spirits in which I approach it. I feel very much like a person who, throwing confetti, serpentines, and my hat to the sky, finds he is the lone celebrant at a party. I need a whole company of people to celebrate and be really excited with me about an Age I believe is the greatest man ever lived in."

Bradbury's use of carnival images was not merely rhetorical. Through its many complex manifestations, carnival expressed his whole approach to writing—and to life. From his point of view, a life worth living requires a crowd of participants, not just spectators. Bradbury needed a high-energy, carnivalized relationship with his chosen genre, his publisher, and his readers. But Walter Bradbury was gone, and Tim Seldes alone did not have the power to increase Doubleday's support. His publisher had become a spectator, and it was time to find a new company of editorial celebrants.

Seldes soon arranged an amicable release. The entire exchange had been carefully developed between author, agent, and editor without acrimony, and the terms of release merely reflected the differing business needs of both parties. He was free to offer his new novel elsewhere, and his advance would be covered by future royalties on his earlier titles and his share of the continuing paperback royalty split on those books. Brad-

bury would never leave an editor on bad terms and, in fact, would continue to work with Doubleday on derivative anthologies, including two young-adult titles—*R Is for Rocket* (1962) and *S Is for Space* (1966)—and *Twice-22* (1966), an omnibus edition of *The Golden Apples of the Sun* and *A Medicine for Melancholy*. But Bradbury would never again contract new work with Doubleday.

During June and July he worked from a carbon of the initial 377-page submission to produce a new 425-page, 40-chapter typescript of the novel. Meanwhile, Congdon continued to evaluate potential new publishers and soon found high interest where he himself had once worked—Simon and Schuster. He reviewed the new draft in mid-August and then sent it on to Robert Gottlieb at his old firm. Events moved quickly from that point; strong support from the other editors led Gottlieb to offer a contract by mid-September 1960.[17] Simon and Schuster was still a close-knit operation where a commitment to an author brought all departments together to develop an effective marketing strategy. The gifted advertising director Nina Bourne, as well as Bradbury fanatics Peter Schwed and Dick Grossman, were part of Gottlieb's plan to provide what Bradbury needed from a publishing house. On September 9, he outlined his plan for Congdon:

> I understand—and I've made it clear to the others— exactly what it is that Bradbury and you want and expect from a new publisher. You want extra effort. We will give it to you, and it will be an intelligent effort too (I hope). In our favor: Nina is fascinated with the problem of extending the cult-feeling about Bradbury to a much larger public; and Dick Grossman, who's in charge of marketing (which really means co-ordinating sales with promotion and publicity) is a violent Bradbury-lover and is already conniving. Also in our favor: this particular novel, which seems to combine the best features of Bradbury's different themes and manners, is very promotable. Most in our favor: we want to do it well. Both out of respect for his writing, and out of a healthy desire to do better with a writer than anyone else could do.[18]

This attitude had been a Simon and Schuster hallmark since the 1930s, and it was clearly in tune with Bradbury's own carnival vision of authorship. Gottlieb was a fairly young sponsoring editor, but he offered the first real chance to put Bradbury's reputation with the book-buying public on par with his mainstream reputation as a major-market magazine favorite. And Gottlieb, like Congdon, felt that this new project was a book that merited a higher level of marketing support than Bradbury had ever before experienced. The contracts were completed before the end of the month; Bradbury received a five-thousand-dollar advance on signing, but nearly a year and a half would pass before he was finished revising his new novel.

During the fall of 1960 Bradbury's revisions were interrupted by interference from a most unlikely source—

the head of MGM Studios, Samuel Goldwyn Jr.[19] By now, Goldwyn knew that the novel was under contract and felt that the studio still owned rights to the plot elements that had evolved from **"The Black Ferris"** story and from the **"Merry-Go-Round"** teleplay. He renewed his option for a film version based on these properties and took the position that these rights would limit Bradbury's ability to market a screenplay based directly on the new novel. His position was ambivalent. At times Goldwyn seemed willing to engage Bradbury for a new screenplay; their earlier work on expanding the Dinelli script had been enjoyable, and the fully developed novel promised an even richer cinematographic experience. But both Congdon and Bradbury knew that this kind of film was not really in Goldwyn's line and that he had never recovered his investment from the unsuccessful pilot teleplay. It soon became apparent that, between the lines, he preferred a buyout—either directly or through a share in Bradbury's future sale of a new screenplay to another studio.

Goldwyn went so far as to ask that plot elements carried over from the story and teleplay be removed from the novel as well. Character names such as Cooger, the carnival owner, could be changed if necessary, but Bradbury knew that the aging effect of the carnival ride was the central conceit of the novel. In his story and Dinelli's teleplay, it allows Cooger to assume the appearance of a child in order to prey on Miss Foley, and it proves to be the means of his own destruction. As Bradbury's novel developed, the carousel grew into the central symbol of the evil that empowers the carnival masters and enslaves anyone who comes under its influence. On Congdon's advice, Bradbury presented his position to MGM through his own West Coast film and television agent, Ben Benjamin. Bradbury agreed not to use the carousel in any future screenplays as long as Goldwyn maintained his option for an MGM film. But he refused to remove it from the novel. He recounted the whole history of his vision of the carousel as the central image of his dark carnival, his own influence on Dinelli's vision of the work, and his own creative jump from Ferris wheel to merry-go-round as the dark agent of immortality while he worked with Joe Mugnaini on the graphic-novel project. Bradbury noted that these developments predated the Dinelli teleplay and made this clear in his instructions to Benjamin: "These discussions took place in 1952 and were common knowledge among my friends, and in these discussions with Joe we planned on the wonderous merry-go-round which now is in my novel."

Goldwyn maintained his option for the time being and in 1961 contracted Robert Bloch for a feature-length screenplay expansion of the Dinelli teleplay. Bloch delivered the screenplay, but it was never filmed, and Goldwyn eventually allowed his option to lapse. In the meantime Bradbury spent the first half of 1961 working on three very successful teleplays—a dramatization of Stanley Ellin's **"The Faith of Aaron Menefee"** for NBC's *Alfred Hitchcock Presents* and dramatizations of two new stories of his own, **"The Jail"** for ABC's *Alcoa Premiere* and **"I Sing the Body Electric"** for CBS's *The Twilight Zone*. These projects eased the frustration of the unproduced screenplays of earlier years, but Bradbury was turning more and more to adapting his stories to the stage. The previous spring he had transformed his award-winning 1947 radio play **"The Meadow"** into a stage play for Hollywood's Huntington Hartford Theatre. Veteran stage and screen actors James Whitmore and Strother Martin were part of the project, and they soon convinced Bradbury to bring more of his stories to the stage. Bradbury spent the first half of 1961 dramatizing stories, preparing his first collection of plays for press, and planning **R Is for Rocket,** the first of two young-adult anthologies derived from his older work. This period of activity marked a turning point in the nature of Bradbury's authorship—from now on he would spend less time writing stories as he turned more and more to stage, television, and film adaptations of his work. The decision was not a conscious one; he still wrote a few stories a year and outlined ideas for novels. What he could not know at the time was that a quarter century would pass before he would finish another major novel. But one thing he knew for sure was that he had to publish the one novel he had in hand. By late summer 1961, Congdon and Gottlieb finally persuaded him to return to his revisions for *Something Wicked This Way Comes.*

Bradbury was all too aware that the books based on his Illinois youth seemed the hardest to revise for publication. His first Green Town novel, *Summer Morning, Summer Night,* had wrestled him to a draw; after seven long years under contract, he had only been able to extract the stories of *Dandelion Wine* from that manuscript. Skillful bridging had created a very successful and nearly seamless story cycle, but only a few glimpses of the remaining novel manuscript, now called *Farewell Summer,* would ever reach print. *Something Wicked* represented a similar challenge; he had submitted a long and largely unrevised typescript in early 1960, and his second draft later that year was even longer. Bradbury now faced the most crucial phase of revision and would work from August into December 1961 in an effort to bring the dark carnival to life.

His lifelong conviction that fiction has a life of its own is perhaps most evident in the composition and revision of *Something Wicked.* He had admitted to Congdon that his initial April 1960 submission was in an "almost-but-not quite born state." Bradbury had never submitted work in this state before, but he had also never tried to bring the long-neglected Renaissance tradition of carnival in literature back to life before. He found himself reviving the folk carnival as a literary subject and, in the process, linked himself (and for the first time in a sustained way) to the carnivals he knew so well as a young man. Carnival has always been on the border between art and life, and Bradbury's own close identification with the subject allowed for very little distance between author and narrative. The result is intensity of effect; indeed, effect outshines event in every draft as well as the finished novel. Bradbury's text is itself a carnival. He throws the reader into the hyperbolic play of carnival language—no one is addressed as a mere spectator.

From the beginning of the novel phase of the project, Bradbury allowed for a great deal of textual play and did not impose the conventional narrative control of the novelist on his material. The rational cause-and-effect plot relationship demanded by the narrative code is only a loosely structuring element here. But the explosion of metaphor in *Something Wicked* is as intense as one finds anywhere in Bradbury's fiction, allowing him to create a nonlinear symbolic code where time and logic are reversible. Fathers can be dethroned from positions of authority; fathers can even become sons. Bradbury found the resulting ambivalence both comfortable and vital as he developed this literary equivalent of carnival. He simply did not pass judgment on the evolving work and in a sense let the novel write itself through several difficult stages of revision. In submitting the first draft, his last words to Congdon were "Anyway, the baby is on the way to you. Old Dad? He's just going to sit here in the sun, with his shoes off, for the rest of the day, feeling good."[20]

The material he took up again in the fall of 1961 was quite massive. Bradbury's second submission from the year before totaled 425 pages; it had evolved from a half-first-, half-second-draft original submission of 377 pages and an even earlier 357 pages of discarded variant chapters. The earliest grouping of variants included nearly 100 pages of first-person narrative in young Will's voice, grouped under the running title *Jamie and Me*. In these pages the influence of the *Dandelion Wine* period is evident. Bradbury had read a number of books during 1955-1956, including *Huckleberry Finn,* to enrich his own sense of place and nostalgia as he fashioned *Dandelion Wine* from his larger Green Town manuscript. The initial *Jamie and Me* fragment forms a smooth bridge between the screenplay material and what (in a longer form) would become the final novel, but it also represents an experimental storytelling approach in the tradition of Mark Twain's Huck and Tom narratives. This opening fragment predates all known drafts—a surviving outline of future novels (subsequently dated 1956 or 1957 by Bradbury) schedules *Jamie and Me* for 1959, and holograph revisions show him recasting the narrative in the third person for expansion into the first full draft of the novel.

The remaining discards appear to be the first (third-person) draft of roughly the first half of the novel. Two of these discards contain another alternate title, **The Autumn People.** But Bradbury soon settled on the name provided by Shakespeare, his own literary father figure, who dominates over other authors in the library episode at the center of the novel. In fact, the discards also contain an uncanceled series-title page that instantiates the title in an even larger vision of autobiographical fiction:

The Illinois Trilogy

Dandelion Wine
Farewell Summer
Something Wicked This Way Comes

Dandelion Wine had recounted the nostalgic summer events of 1928. **Farewell Summer** was the new title for the **Summer Morning, Summer Night** novel manuscript from which **Dandelion Wine** had been carved; its still largely unpublished episodes recount fictional events from the summer of 1929 in much the same way. **Something Wicked** is clearly the culminating volume in the trilogy; the boys of this novel, two variations on Bradbury's own final Green Town years, are nearly fourteen, a bit older than Bradbury was when in 1932 he encountered the Dill Brothers Combined Traveling Shows and Mr. Electrico dubbed him with the carnival blessing "live forever."[21]

By the fall of 1961 the fiction that had evolved out of fact now ran as follows. Advance posters tell of a strange off-season carnival that will arrive Halloween week, and friends Will and Jim witness the late-night arrival of the carnival train and the supernatural encampment of Cooger and Dark's Pandemonium Shadow Show. They survey the show and sense that venues such as the mirror maze and the carousel can entrap the unwary in their own subconscious fears and desires. As the story unfolds, their suspicions are confirmed: Cooger reverses the carousel (which is always "out of order" for paying customers) to become a boy and pass himself off as a guest in town; he flees back to the carousel when Will and Jim find him out; and the boys jam it in full throttle as Cooger tries to regain his proper age, leaving him little more than a living skeleton. Mr. Dark, Cooger's partner, afterward seeks to take the boys into the carnival, where they will join all the other freaks enslaved from other towns to serve the two supernatural carnival masters, but the boys are aided by Mr. Ellis, the clownish philosopher-custodian of the town library. Will's father also tries to help the boys, but the other parents and townspeople are unaware of the enslaving powers of the carnival. Dark takes the boys from the library, nearly killing Ellis in the process; but the custodian learns how to combat evil through laughter and enlists Will's father to help save the boys. They rescue Will after beating a deadly version of the bullet trick and escaping from the devouring self-images of the mirror maze. Cooger, who has been artificially preserved in Mr. Electrico's chair, blows apart in the wind before he can be revived on the carousel; Dark tries to lure Jim into a ride on the carousel that will make him the new junior partner in the show. But Dark fails, and he is destroyed along with the enslaving power of his tattoos; the carnival blows away; and the two boys and two men walk home to family and friends who will never guess the truth. Bradbury had worked out much of this plot in writing and revising his first complete screenplay in 1955. The *Jamie and Me* manuscript of 1959 had been a transitional working out of method, and the first two drafts of the novel as a third-person narrative (1960) had been packed to capacity with details of effect and description.

Congdon may not have seen the first-person *Jamie and Me* experiment, but he had carefully read the third-person narratives of the first and second submissions. His August 1960 suggestions for the second submission included a recommendation to differentiate between the boys in order to point up more clearly what is at stake for everyone as the dark carnival settles nearby the small town. The suggestions were practical as well—there are times in the early drafts and discards where it is impossible to tell which boy is speaking.[22] In the evolving third draft, Bradbury did, in fact, carefully delineate the boys, developing Will Halloway more consistently in his words and actions as the practical, well-balanced boy who intuitively gravitates toward traditional patterns of interaction with family and town life. Bradbury also stabilized Jamie as Jim Nightshade, now a fatherless boy living next door with his mother, drawn to the darker mysteries of life and impatient to grow up. In the first two drafts (and in the earlier screen treatments), the boys had shared a common protective source of wisdom—Mr. Ellis, the erudite elderly custodian at the public library. In the third draft Bradbury made his most significant single revision by subsuming Ellis into the character of Charles Halloway, Will's father. Charles Halloway becomes the thoughtful protector of both boys, but he is nevertheless the natural father of only one. By splitting the circumstances of the two boys in these ways, Bradbury clarified and dramatically advanced a central motivation of the novel: why the carnival has such an irresistible appeal for Jim Nightshade.

But Bradbury was also careful to retain just enough in common between the boys to make their adventures both believable and compelling. Will also enjoys small-town adventures, and he is also curious, in a much more cautious way than Jim, about the strange appearance of the carnival and the dangers it brings to everyone. Even the natural protection provided by Will's father is vulnerable—Charles Halloway, as developed in the third draft, is an older man, and both he and Will sense that they have not really connected as father and son. All these refinements of relationship worked to good effect. The fusing of the two good father figures eliminated the often heavy-handed philosophizing of the clownlike janitor and reduced the overcrowded field of protagonists from four to three. It also made Charles Halloway a believable father. Instead of an archetype of the ideal father, he is debased by all-too-common human frailties—he is an aging man in a humble profession, worries about the present, and fears for the future.

These substantial changes in the third draft brought Will's father into focus as a major character who, along with Cooger and Dark, must fight to win true fathership of the boys. The struggle is one of crowning and decrowning in the traditional sense of literary carnival—by convention, the decrowning of the king represented the central moment in the carnival literature of the Renaissance. The novel itself is deliberately set off into three acts that echo the movement of the crowd at any carnival: "Arrivals," "Pursuits," and "Departures." The first phase of this struggle for control of the boys centers on Cooger and dominates the first third of the novel. The dark-carnival masters have been passing through the same small towns at long intervals, returning when the only evidence of their supernatural longevity is locked away in the dusty library files of old newspapers. When Will and Jim unintentionally endanger this cycle by spinning Cooger around in his own protean device until he's nothing more than a living bag of bones, they have decrowned one of the dark fathers of the carnival. The boys run away in horror, but when they return to the carousel with medics and the police, they find that Dark and the other carnies have stabilized Cooger's failing body in Mr. Electrico's chair. The final scene of "Arrivals" is a carnivalesque parody of a father's blessing; instead of wishing them long and prosperous lives, Cooger showers the boys with sparks from Mr. Electrico's prop sword and curses them to a short, sad life. Figure 13 shows how Bradbury revised the central moment of this scene from the *Jamie and Me* variant, eliminating Will's first-person narrative but retaining the full effect of Cooger's naming "his" boys: "I dub thee—asses and fools. I dub—thee—Mr. Sickly and Mr. Pale. Mr. Scream—ssss—and Mr. Yell." Cooger literally wants to put fear back in the boys with his curse, and screams and yells are, of course, the very manifestation of fear. In all the complete drafts, Bradbury eliminated the final names "Scream" and "Yell"—perhaps to make the reader work a bit harder to "hear" the fear that controls the dark carnival.

The carnivalesque decrowning of Cooger has made him laughable, but he can still invoke fear. The final scene of "Arrivals" is polarized between these two extremes, for there are no neutral terms in a contest with evil. "Pursuits," the second and largest section of the novel, shows Charles Halloway's own decrowning; he uses his self-taught research skills to discover the library archives that document the timeless evil of the carnival, and he tries bravely to bring all his literary knowledge to bear in his fight to save the boys from Dark's revenging hand. But he loses them to Dark in the library, and his own fear paralyzes further action as Dark orders the Dust Witch in for the kill: "The janitor's clock. Stop it." The section ends with Halloway's rediscovery of himself and his realization that laughter can fight fear. Discards from the first draft show how carefully Bradbury worked with this key passage to strengthen its power. His notes for these revisions survive on a remarkable sheet of light blue scratch paper preserved with the discards [. . .]. His note to check the doubled use of "senseless" in his description of the blind Dust Witch as she gestures to stop the heart of Charles Halloway, who has closed his eyes in fear, is bracketed by two equally important notes about laughter: "Don't give away effect of laughter *too soon*" and "Strengthen laugh discovery growing power & *hope*."

The comments are framed by faces and eyes directed toward a small man. The figure may represent disconnected doodling, Halloway, or perhaps the author playfully reflecting on the effect of carnival, both in real life and in his novel. The happy caricature is unexpected; these are, after all, notes for a horror novel, and one would expect fear to be central to it. Yet fear is entirely banished by laughter—in the author's life and in his art. Particularly evident is the joyous relativity brought on by carnival laughter, which levels social hierarchies and class distinctions. These drawings certainly stand in sharp contrast to the derisive faces and haunted figure found with Bradbury's unpublished *Masks* manuscript of the late 1940s [. . .]. The more upbeat notes and figures found in the first-draft discards of *Something Wicked* suggest Bradbury was working toward a more carefully paced revelation of laughter as the great leveling device in the carnival of life, and his success is best seen through a comparison of the September 1962 published version of this passage with the version as it stood in the discards of early 1960. (Note that Mr. Ellis has been replaced by Charles Halloway in the third draft; his left hand has been broken by Mr. Dark, and the Dust Witch has almost stopped his tired heart in a dark corner of the library.)[23]

Successive bursts of laughter drive the Dust Witch out of the library, disoriented and barely able to join Dark and the captive boys back at the carnival. It is the beginning of the end for Dark and his powers of enslave-

First-Draft Discard
(January 1960)

And then, for no reason at all, for a last look around, perhaps, Mr. Ellis opened his eyes.

He saw the Witch. He saw her fingers tickling the air, tickling at his sight, tickling toward his heart as her lips twitched and her swamp breath inundated him. There was something about her folded flesh, something about her nose, her chin, her dusty ears, her skinny fingers that . . . that . . . that . . .

Mr. Ellis giggled.

Quickly, the thought jumped up in his head, why am I doing this now? The witch pulled back the merest inch, as if suddenly feeling the pain from the old man's hand.

The old man saw but did not see this, sensed but did not consider this.

Again, senselessly, he found himself smiling and then letting a little careless laugh out.

"Slow!" cried the Witch, angrily.

He did note her anger.

But still the important thing was, nothing really mattered, life, in the end, was an immense joke of such size you only stood back toward the very end to see it stretch away, and you in its shadow. With death this close he thought of a million silly things he had done in his time, as a boy, boy-man, man, and idiot old goat. He had gathered them up like toys and now, between the stacks, in an instant, the toys of his life (continued)

First-Edition Text
(September 1962)

And then for no reason, save perhaps for a last look around, because he *did* want to get rid of the pain, and sleep was the way to do that . . . Charles Halloway opened his eyes.

He saw the Witch.

He saw her fingers working at the air, his face, his body, the heart within his body, and the soul within the heart. Her swamp breath flooded him while, with immense curiosity, he watched the poisonous drizzle from her lips, counted the folds in her stitch-wrinkled eyes, the Gila monster neck, the mummy-linen ears, the dry-rivulet river-sand brow. Never in his life had he focused so nearly to a person, as if she were a puzzle, which once touched together might show life's greatest secret. The solution was in her, it would all spring clear this moment, no, the next, no, the next, watch her scorpion fingers! hear her chant as she diddled the air, yes, diddled was it, tickling, tickling, "Slow!" she whispered. "Slow!" And his obedient heart pulled rein. Diddle-tickle went her fingers.

Charles Halloway snorted. Faintly, he giggled.

He caught this. Why? Why am I . . . giggling . . . at such a time!?

The Witch pulled back the merest quarter inch as if some strange but hidden electric light socket, touched with wet whorl, gave shock.

Charles Halloway saw but did not see her flinch, sensed but seemed in no way to consider her withdrawal, for almost immediately, seizing the initiative, she flung herself forward, not touching, but mutely gesticulating at his chest as one might try to spell an antique clock pendulum.

"Slow!" she cried.

Senselessly, he permitted an idiot smile to balloon itself up from somewhere to attach itself with careless ease under his nose.

"Slowest!"

Her new fever, her anxiety which changed itself to anger was even more of a toy to him. A part of his attention, secret until now, leaned forward to scan every pore of her Halloween face. Somehow, irresistibly, the prime thing was: nothing mattered. Life in the end seemed a prank of such size you could only stand off at this end of the corridor to note its meaningless length and its quite unnecessary height, a mountain built to such ridiculous immensities you were dwarfed in its shadow and mocking of its pomp. So with death this near he thought numbly but purely upon a billion vanities, arrivals, departures, loomed, among them the largest silliest toy of all, this woman who called herself witch, tickling, tickling, that's what she's doing, just tickling the air, what a fool, didn't she know what she was doing, tickling the air, tickle . . .

He opened his mouth and let the blast of hilarity out.

The Witch was flung back by his laugh.

idiot excursions of boy, boy-man, man and old-man goat. He had gathered and stacked all manner of foibles, devices, playthings of his egotism and now, between all the silly corridors of books, the toys of his life swayed. And none more grotesque that this thing named Witch Gypsy Reader-of-Dust, tickling, that's what! just *tickling* the air! Fool! Didn't she know what she was *doing!*

He opened his mouth.
Of itself, like a child born of an unsuspecting parent, one single raw laugh broke free.
The Witch swooned back.

ment. The revised and greatly expanded text provides a more believable pace for Halloway's saving insight into life, and the additional metaphors support rather than detract from the development of this central passage of the novel.

The various stages of revision also allowed Bradbury to develop sophisticated characterizations to an extent he had rarely attempted previously. Although Halloway and Mr. Dark, developed as two rival father figures, are clearly "prosaic" allegorical types of humanity because of the carnival masks they wear, they are not for that reason flat characters. On the contrary, both are capable of surprising us. Their struggle over the boys and the carnival, over who will "father" the carnival, creates many moments of thematic inversion (explored in detail below). They have a special complexity and multilayeredness that derives from their roles in the carnival chronotope (roughly fool-clown and devil). Among other things, Mr. Dark (the Illustrated Man) surprises Halloway (and the reader) with his ability to handle and mock the Bible, and Halloway himself goes through a surprising revolution in his worldview when he encounters the grotesque in the form of the Dust Witch and understands that life itself is an immense prank being played on him. He comes to accept the darker aspects of life, though only in the right proportion. Evil no longer dominates character out of hand, and this is certainly not what one expects to encounter in a traditional horror novel.

As the final section, "Departures," begins, Halloway is no longer controlled by his book-learned seriousness and his fear of the carnival. Through the insight of his near-death experience, he has been restored as a father who stands a chance of winning back the boys from Dark's control. He now stands in sharp contrast to the carnival owner as a father figure. Despite his seductive appeal, Dark is finally revealed as the "devilish" limiting authority he really is. In cultural terms he is Freud, the threatening contested father of the modern fantastic, who fights with the boys and wrestles for control of

their destinies. Charles Halloway has cast off his fear and armed himself with the laughter that destroys seriousness. He is now a father who embraces all of life: the grotesque, the beautiful, and the sublime. In the final contest he is able to decrown Dark and break his control over Will, Jim, and the souls trapped for ages in his carnival.

The freeing of the trapped souls will only come with the destruction of Dark and his enslaving illustrations. Dark's last act of magic proves to be his undoing—while Will and his father attempt to revive Jim, who has nearly lost his soul to the temptation of instant adulthood offered by the carousel, Dark reverses the ride and tries to pass himself off as a lost little boy. Halloway knows him for what he is, though, and senses Dark's plan to murder him. The two would-be fathers play out the final drama in character. Halloway cleverly offers the boy-man the love of a father, a proposition he knows Dark cannot abide. Dark expires in his loving embrace, his body and tattoos blowing away with the rest of the dark carnival on the sudden predawn wind. Halloway revives Jim through the same laughing celebration of life that he experienced in the library and introduces "his" boys to the more balanced carnival of real life that comes with every Green Town dawn.

This fundamental use of carnival's decrowning rituals to restore balance to life is found in the two earlier submissions, but in combining the janitor-father into a single character for the third draft, Bradbury was able to bring the central philosophical illumination of the book into sharper focus. This change also tightened a narrative that sometimes wandered off into a maze of characters and an explosion of metaphors. He completed the third draft by December 1961, and Simon and Schuster tentatively scheduled a summer 1962 release.[24] The final fifty-four-chapter structure was now in place, and the narrative had been tightened to 380 pages. But Bradbury held it back over the holidays and soon began a final sequence of revisions. Between February 12 and 22, 1962, he finalized (in ink) many minor revisions and cuts throughout the typescript. He mailed the fourth and final draft (now 340 pages) directly to Bob Gottlieb in two installments during the final two weeks of February. Gottlieb had to delay the production schedule, but he was pleased to find a tighter narrative that retained the same power of the earlier drafts.

Bradbury soon learned to work effectively with his new editor.[25] At first he expected to make his usual extensive revisions in the galleys, but Gottlieb convinced him to work from his carbon of the final typescript while a Simon and Schuster copyeditor made a light styling pass through the original to save time. During March, Bradbury made final cuts in the descriptions of the ancient Cooger-Mr. Electrico and the other carnival freaks that protect him from too much scrutiny by the police and the boys in the closing scene of "Arrivals." Gottlieb suggested some trimming in "the father scenes," his shorthand for the detailed library introspections of Will's father at the philosophical center of the novel. Bradbury may have made these changes in the galleys, which he went over closely from April 21 to May 14. Nearly three months had elapsed from his submission of the final draft, and publication was rescheduled for September to provide enough time for reviewers to prime the pump. Bradbury was juggling no less than three other book projects, and this contributed to the minor delays. His first volume of plays, *The Anthem Sprinters* (Dial), and the young-adult collection *R Is for Rocket* (Doubleday) were also scheduled for fall release, and he had already submitted *The Machineries of Joy,* his next story collection, to Gottlieb for review. He was also deeply involved with design issues and was delighted with the dust jacket for *Something Wicked* developed by well-known cover illustrator Gray Foy. Bradbury's good eye for cover art and front-matter design led the production department to make a few changes to color values on the jacket and alter layout of the title page, all to good effect.

Despite these delays, Gottlieb was able to get the text to reviewers well ahead of publication. He sent a number of bound galleys out even before proofs were ready; this way he was able to give Gilbert Highet enough time to read the galleys and write a timely review-article for the September issue of *Book-of-the-Month Club News*. Highet and the other BOMC editors did not select *Something Wicked* as a monthly feature, but his review was very positive and reached a large cross-section of grassroots readers. Congdon's parallel effort for advance publicity began more than a year earlier as he worked closely with Bradbury to place an excerpt with a major-market magazine. Will and Jim's fateful encounter with Cooger and the carousel still had enough of the freestanding structure of the original 1948 **"Black Ferris"** story to form a publishable excerpt; in early February 1961 Congdon found interest but not a commitment from *Life* editor Ralph Graves, but the agent soon placed the opening excerpt with *Mademoiselle*.[26] This venue had been instrumental in Bradbury's quick rise to mainstream magazine prominence in the mid-1940s, publishing similar Bradbury fantasies each year from 1945 to 1947. During the summer of 1961, Congdon secured a first-serial agreement using an excerpt from the first or second draft, thinking that book publication would be based on this stage of the work. It appeared as **"Nightmare Carousel"** in the January 1962 issue of *Mademoiselle,* without the significant third- and fourth-draft revisions but recognizable as material that would subsequently appear as chapters 16, 18-19, and 21 of the finished novel.

Bradbury isolated two other excerpts for serial publication but was never able to place them. In late 1960 *Good Housekeeping* rejected one, which was extracted from the complex and introspective library discussions between Charles Halloway and the two boys. In February 1961 Graves of *Life* rejected the other, which consisted of Halloway's library encounter with the Dust Witch bracketed by a new standalone opening and ending designed to work as a Halloween story. *Harper's* declined both in October 1961. Editors at the *Saturday Evening Post* were very interested but, after three separate reviews in the spring and summer of 1962, decided against publication. In September 1962 Bradbury tried *Life* again, where he had enjoyed major national attention for his speculative essay on space, **"Cry the Cosmos,"** earlier in the year. Its editors again declined, noting that there was no time to place a serial excerpt before release of the book. But the real issue was structural—the novel simply had no other self-contained episodes beyond **"Nightmare Carousel."** And as the publication date approached, it was no easier for advertisers or reviewers to categorize the book itself. Gottlieb and Nina Bourne had faced a similar challenge the year before as they launched *Catch-22* into the literary marketplace. The irreverent satire, dark humor, and experimental structure of Joseph Heller's World War II narrative had demanded an innovative advertising approach. For Heller, Simon and Schuster ran mysterious advertisements containing only the paper soldier from Paul Bacon's dust-jacket design and the title *Catch-22*. A year later Gottlieb and Bourne took the same approach with Bradbury. The *New York Times Book Review* for September 16, 1962, contained a three-column page-length ad featuring Gray Foy's glowing dust devil from the book jacket above the words "Ray Bradbury's long-awaited major novel." The dust devil, spelling out *Something Wicked This Way Comes,* points to a single word at the top of the black background: "Tomorrow." On the eighteenth, the daily *Times* featured the same ad, but the headline now read "Today."[27]

These advertisements exemplified the new level of marketing Gottlieb had promised, and follow-up ads on both coasts picked up on lines from the better reviews.[28] Gottlieb's point was to tell the story of the book, to bring the public in on the publishing event. It was the perfect strategy for Bradbury, who once again had a publisher willing to participate in the carnival of his fiction. Gottlieb understood just what Bradbury was trying to do with this novel, but it was a tougher proposition for some of the critics. On September 19 the influential Orville Prescott, who had praised *Fahrenheit 451* nearly a decade earlier, came down hard on *Something Wicked* in the *New York Times*. He called Bradbury "the uncrowned king of science-fiction writers" but found his latest fantasy to be overwritten and unengaging. Prescott took the central insight—the leveling, unmasking power of laughter—far too seriously, calling it a "clumsy effort to be significant about the eternal conflict between good and evil." He wanted the traditional enslavement of the horror reader: "if the author does not instantly enslave the reader's imagination he is likely to seem like a little boy wearing a mask and shouting 'Boo!'"[29] These assumptions could not be further from Bradbury's broader philosophical purpose. Good and evil are "transvalued" by the book; it is not evil, but the inner phantasmagoria of fear that evil instills in people and feeds on, that is the focus of Bradbury's thematics.

The weekly *New York Times Book Review* for November 4 featured another harsh blow, this time delivered by an obscure horror and crime writer named Lillian De La Torre. She also wanted to squeeze the plot into a story-length work, maintaining that the barrage of supernatural effects and the unrestrained style were too off trail and too off putting for serious fantasy readers. And like Prescott, she attacked Bradbury's treatment of the genre. Not surprisingly, this instinctive defense of the genre was also at the center of private responses from such close friends and fellow writers as Charles Beaumont and William F. Nolan. Both were uncomfortable with Bradbury's approach to the presence of evil. Beaumont took issue with what he saw as the point of the novel: that evil can be laughed out of the world. Nolan took this line of reasoning even further: "I just flat don't believe that you can deal with true Evil by laughing it out of existence, by fighting a force of darkness with a smile. It is a nice symbolic idea—but the reality of the defeat of Evil did not come across to me with any real force or conviction in the book."[30] Nolan's stance is that of the quintessential horror and mystery writer, and this position is also explicit in both of the *New York Times* reviews. It is the horror genre seen in naturalistic terms—how can laughter defeat the physical manifestation of the supernatural? Laughter confronts fear, laughter wins. A good horror writer cannot suspend disbelief in such a situation.

Most critics and genre writers expected horror pure and simple from *Something Wicked,* not a carnivalization of horror. The genre has always been a literature of fear; one can never put evil away for good. But Bradbury was never a traditional horror writer, and in *Something Wicked* his strategy became downright subversive. His elimination of fear runs counter to the horror writer's need to keep fear central to the tale. Laughter becomes the key to a whole new outlook on life, a philosophy where evil is given its due but is degraded and made laughable through carnivalization. Evil normally separates people from life, but in *Something Wicked* it is relativized, brought down, and reintegrated into life. The evil carnival is no longer taken seriously. In this way laughter is also philosophical and represents a more balanced way of looking at both the light and the dark elements of life. In short, Bradbury gives readers a broader view of life, embraces more of life, than the genre permits. This was hard for most horror writers to accept at the time, but Stephen King's unqualified endorsement suggests that the genre masters of more recent times may be warming to *Something Wicked*—a book that has never been out of print. It makes sense, then, that more favorable reviews initially came from critics and writers who were comfortable judging the novel outside the bounds of the horror tradition.

Gilbert Highet's favorable review for the Book-of-the-Month Club was soon reinforced by Anthony Boucher's remarkable essay headlining the September 16 issue of the *New York Herald Tribune*'s weekly *Books* magazine. Boucher, writing under his house pseudonym of H. H. Holmes, offered a major two-page assessment of the science fiction genre, culminating in a look at Bradbury's almost unique ability to carry science fiction into mainstream literature. His point was that Bradbury, already "consistently recognized as an ambassador and almost as a symbol of S.F. . . . , never really wrote science fiction at all." The essay, which privileges Bradbury's range above that of all other major science fiction writers, ends with a balanced and insightful review of *Something Wicked.* Boucher, a legendary mystery editor and reviewer himself, could not quite see all that operated within Bradbury's carnivalesque exploration of good and evil. But he nevertheless managed to take the longer view that Bradbury implicitly asks of all his readers and found this first full-length novel "superb as pure fantasy narrative." None of the initial reviewers were able to place the book in its true niche. Boucher was certain that it was not an allegory, thus avoiding the trap that snared the *Christian Science Monitor*'s enthusiastic reviewer a few months later. Bradbury offers no philosophical abstractions of good and evil in the tradition of an allegory, for as noted, *Something Wicked* does not follow conventional notions of good and evil. Faith Baldwin, observing in a personal note to Bradbury that the author had simply written truth, perhaps came closest to locating this novel as a complex variation on the moral fables one finds in much of Bradbury's other book-length fictions.[31]

Something Wicked remained a steady seller through a hectic fall season complicated by the unprecedented international anxiety of the Cuban missile crisis. By November, Bradbury had only seen a dozen reviews in major media venues, the fewest for any of his major books to that time. It might have fared better with the earlier summer release that Gottlieb had hoped for—the crowded fall book market and international affairs may have been responsible—but Bradbury never knew for sure. Yet most of the reviews were very good; only the *New Yorker* came across with the same complaints as the two *Times* reviews.[32] Advance orders topped 6,000, prompting Gottlieb to add a second printing of 4,000 to the initial print run of 7,500 before the September 18 release. At the same time, he was able to secure an excellent paperback contract for Bradbury. Despite Bradbury's break with Doubleday, Bantam's Marc Jaffe and Oscar Distel were keen to continue a paperback publishing relationship that had made *The Martian Chronicles, The Illustrated Man,* and *Dandelion Wine* perennial sellers. Jaffe initially offered a $5,000 advance on the new novel. Gottlieb negotiated patiently and eventually secured Bradbury's best terms with Bantam so far: a $12,000 guaranteed advance on the first 300,000 copies sold and $4,800 on every additional 100,000 sold. These numbers were based on sales of a sixty-cent book, but Bradbury's demonstrated value as a long-term seller allowed Gottlieb to secure a proportional raise in the payments as paperback prices increased. Congdon was pleased with the Simon and Schuster negotiating effort: "Not only is the advance guarantee decidedly bigger than any of the Doubleday negotiations, but the royalty is approximately 7% for the first 300,000 copies and 8% thereafter—compared with the usual 4% and 6%."[33] This development signified to Bradbury that his new book was continuing to get the level of financial recognition and promotion that he felt his books deserved. Gottlieb's deal with Bantam was particularly gratifying, for Bradbury's paperback editions were now all back in print and were continuing to have a major mass-market presence in homes and schools across America.

October brought Simon and Schuster hardback sales topping eight thousand and a strange letter from Charles Finney, who felt that *Something Wicked* infringed on his own well-known 1930s horror novella, *The Circus of Dr. Lao.* The assertion was really the result of Finney's frustration over his own declining career, for the two works have little in common. Bradbury had been very careful to avoid influences in his fiction, and his own successful 1961 case against CBS and Playhouse 90 for an unauthorized adaptation of *Fahrenheit 451* had helped clarify the application of plagiarism laws to literature.[34] He had known of Finney's strange tale of an Arizona town's confrontation with a macabre circus since the late 1940s. Robert Bloch had recommended it to him in 1947, but Bradbury shied away from it while his own carnivals began to take shape. His eventual reading of Finney's tale resulted from his own growing reputation as an editor. Bradbury's successful edition of Bantam's *Timeless Stories for Today and Tomorrow* (1952) led Bantam's Saul David to plan an anthology of weird tales around another Bradbury introduction. Early in 1953 the new anthology began to take shape around "The Circus of Dr. Lao" as the title story, but Bradbury was busy with *Fahrenheit 451* and the *Moby Dick* screenplay and could not turn attention to the Bantam project until the end of 1954. By this time, the spark of creativity generated by the Goldwyn teleplay and the Gene Kelly screen treatment had grown

into a fire, and he delayed work on the anthology until he had the fully developed screenplay for **"The Dark Carnival"** in the form that he would novelize as *Something Wicked.* With this work behind him, Bradbury finally read Finney's novella and sent Bantam the long-awaited introduction for *The Circus of Dr. Lao and Other Stories* in January 1956.[35]

Finney, of course, knew nothing of Bradbury's independent development of a very different kind of novel; he only knew the sequence of publication. Bradbury related the underlying textual history to Gottlieb, adding that he had found Finney's novella to be very different in approach from his own work and, in fact, an imaginative letdown for him as a reader; this view is also evident in the qualified endorsement he included in his 1956 introduction.[36] Bradbury's own experience with the CBS case, which had been settled in his favor just short of the Supreme Court, offered a clear basis of comparison. There was little similarity in idea and no similarity in incident or plot sequence: "the only resemblance between Finney's novel and mine is he wrote one about a Circus, I wrote one about a carnival. Beyond that gapes the Abyss." His letter to Gottlieb also contains very significant views on originality in authorship, quoting in part from the briefs written in his own successful case:

> The whole thing boils down to: Ideas cannot be copyrighted or protected, but "sequences of texture, sequences of events, based on an Idea, *can.*" For instance, I can write a story tomorrow called TO BUILD A FIRE, using Jack London's title and idea, as long as I challenge my hero differently, and adventure him in such a way that all the textures and details are different and in no way resemble "in sequence" or "any inferred sequence" London's story. Just because London wrote a story about a man freezing to death in the wilds doesn't mean all writers after him must give up trying to write about death by freezing . . . It means they must find fresh ways to use that idea, so as not to infringe on his sequential originality (ellipses Bradbury's).[37]

This note clearly shows how Bradbury situated himself in relation to his dearly loved literary influences. He was confident in his own creative authorship and avoided borrowing. Instead, he tended to bring his masters into his own fiction overtly, using them or their works as actual characters in the play of his fantasies. The living books of *Fahrenheit 451* provide the most celebrated example. In *Something Wicked* the key to understanding Bradbury's carnival comes from Shakespeare's stage, not from any superficial resemblance to Finney's circus. Charles Halloway uses the library and its vast archive of literary traditions to build a defense against the dark carnival. He arranges books in a "great literary clock on a table, like someone learning to tell a new time." Many titles relating to the occult are mentioned, but it is impossible to decode the chronotope—the specific spatio-temporal generic matrix—of the carnival because the clock has no hands, no place in real human time. As Halloway begins to think about the language and freakish faces of the carnival, he realizes that *"Physiognomonie. The Secrets of the Individual's Characters as Found in His Face,"* the book whose pages he is turning, is not the master key to unlocking the "personality" of the carnival either. Men cannot be judged by their faces—a fact enunciated by Duncan in Shakespeare's *Macbeth,* the most phantasmagoric and imaginative of all the Bard's plays. So in the middle of the clock of books, Bradbury writes the title of his book, taken from the witches of *Macbeth.* The key to understanding this literary dark carnival is indeed in Shakespeare's lines (so vague, yet so immense), but they must be reimagined, textualized anew. Thus, although Shakespeare can be said to have invented the modern notion of personality, Bradbury must find fresh ways to use textuality in understanding the character of his carnival of evil. Because of its use of masks, the carnival (as analyzed in the thematics section below) is as much a character in the novel as anyone else.[38]

In its originality of events, sequences, and textures, *Something Wicked* is as different from *The Circus of Dr. Lao* as it is from Philip Barry's *Send in the Clowns.* It is not clear if Finney ever realized this fundamental distinction, but there is no evidence that he ever pursued the matter further. Gottlieb was satisfied with Bradbury's position, and the incident was soon forgotten. Hardbound sales continued to do well, and in December *Something Wicked* made the *New York Herald Tribune*'s list of the best books of 1962. Gottlieb and Bradbury were already at work on the submitted stories for *The Machineries of Joy* (1964), which had been welcomed by Simon and Schuster. It was clear that his new publisher was willing to consider story collections as the normal vehicle for Bradbury's unique brand of fiction. It was a nice contrast to Doubleday: as Bradbury's story output turned more and more to fantasy in the 1950s, Doubleday had come to view his story collections merely as a price one had to pay for the occasional novelesque story cycle. The move to Simon and Schuster tied Bradbury to a publisher who could appreciate the major-market author he had become rather than the niche-market science fiction author he had once been labeled.

Bradbury and Congdon hoped to see the same process unfold in England, even if it meant, once again, breaking a long association with a publisher. Bradbury had a solid following in the United Kingdom, and British intellectuals on both sides of the Atlantic read him— including Graham Greene, Christopher Isherwood, Aldous Huxley, Kingsley Amis, Gerald Heard, Lord Bertrand Russell, Somerset Maugham, Stephen Spender, and W. H. Auden. But the British market was relatively small, and even with overseas commonwealth distribu-

tion, his contracts with Rupert Hart-Davis were not yet in proportion to his reputation. In April 1962 Hart-Davis read a typescript of *Something Wicked* and offered a £150 advance on signing.[39] Congdon's London agents at A. D. Peters were able to get the advance offer up to £250 but cautioned against any hope for further progress. Both Pete Peters and his associate, Margaret Stephens, enjoyed the novel as much as Hart-Davis did, but they also shared his sense that this was not the book to take Bradbury to the higher level in British sales that his long-term reputation warranted. Bradbury and Congdon had heard this from Doubleday two years earlier and asked Peters to shop the novel to three other London publishers (beginning with Gollancz) to see if there was interest. Bradbury also informed Hart-Davis of his plans, for the two men were friends and had no trouble speaking frankly on such issues.

On May 22 Hart-Davis wrote back to affirm his willingness to go higher on the advance but made it clear that this in no way changed his belief that sales would remain problematic. Peters, Stephens, and Hart-Davis all sensed that English readers, expecting what had usually been promoted there as Bradbury's special brand of science fiction, would not know what to do with this long, carnivalesque horror novel. Bradbury wrote again to make his position perfectly clear. For Bradbury, it was not a matter of money upfront or of best-seller status; it was a matter of long-term promotion:

> As for best sellerdom, I don't kid myself that I will ever have that, in the larger degree. But I do believe my books, all of them, could have done better, if more had been done with them. Why do I believe this? Because, everywhere I go in America I find my fans growing up in legions in the schools, not as the result of my hardcover books, but of my softcovers that followed. I find an acceptance, belatedly, on all intellectual levels, for my work, and each time, here in the USA, I have had to go out on my own, and make suggestions, and follow through, in much of the campaigning for my books, on my own.[40]

In his final paragraph he used a military metaphor to show Hart-Davis the kind of participation he wanted from his good friend and long-time British publisher: "I hope you will sympathize with my point and buy the book and go into battle for me. Again, the advance money, while welcome, is not the whole point, but the promotion of the book is." It was, essentially, a variation on his carnival cry to readers and publishers to participate in the creation of the literary work and its cultural success—no one is a spectator. For Bradbury, the advance money was simply a measure of the publisher's commitment to promote, to believe in, the author's book. Hart-Davis responded to the essential issue; in addition to raising the advance offer to £500, he also doubled the promotional budget for *Something Wicked*.[41] Bradbury and Congdon accepted the offer, and his first full-length novel was on its way to release in England.

English release was previewed in October 1962 with British *Argosy*'s reprint of the January 1962 *Mademoiselle* excerpt **"Nightmare Carousel."** *Argosy* had been a steady market for Bradbury since the late 1940s and welcomed the chance to provide the first view of the novel in England.[42] At the last minute, Bradbury realized that the novel had gone through several significant stages of revision since *Mademoiselle* had purchased the excerpt in the summer of 1961, and in June 1962 he wrote *Argosy* to offer the final version of those chapters forming the excerpt. But the publication had already set the October issue, and **"Nightmare Carousel"** appeared once again as a preliminary form of the novel's first horrifying adventure.

The British edition of *Something Wicked* was released in March 1963, and once again the critics tried to force-fit the new novel into a traditional genre niche. By that standard, the English critics were just as disappointed as their American counterparts. The *New Statesman* noted, "Ray Bradbury turns from Science Fiction to Gothick fantasy; but it isn't well sustained." The reviewer felt that "the nightmare pursuit and capture of two boys is impressive" but in the final analysis found "too little good horror, and a lot that just suggests the machinations of a black Disney." The *Times Literary Supplement* proclaimed that "[Bradbury] has hit on a finely sinister idea" but considered the horror effect diminished by predictable stylistic effects. "Overwriting has always been Mr. Bradbury's weakness, as though he felt a little ashamed of his chosen genres, horror and science fiction, but hoped that by making them literary enough he would automatically establish their claim to literature."[43] Ironically, none of the critics chose to define or follow the way that Bradbury used the older carnivalesque traditions of literature to level or relativize the effect of fear and thus break out of genre conventions. But his readership in England remained loyal, and Hart-Davis was able to keep *Something Wicked* and most of his earlier titles in print throughout the 1960s.

In the mid-1960s *Something Wicked* received a boost in Britain when Corgi agreed to buy U.K. paperback rights to both of Bradbury's Green Town books. Corgi had published British paperback editions of his science fiction titles and finally agreed to bring out paperbacks of both **Dandelion Wine** and **Something Wicked** in 1965. Meanwhile, the 1963 Bantam paperback edition became a steady seller (and remains in print). As always, Bradbury's hardbound editions eventually

slipped out of print, but further moments of market prominence were to come. Once again, he would have to rely on his own promotional skills. Review copies of the novel went out to Harold Prince, who felt that a stage treatment was impossible but that Ingmar Bergman could make an excellent film of it. Bradbury also sent a copy to English director Jack Clayton, who had impressed him with *The Innocents,* a 1961 adaptation of Henry James's master horror novella *The Turn of the Screw.* During the next two decades, he would write three more screenplays of **Something Wicked,** selling the first to Twentieth Century Fox and almost pulling in Clayton to make the film. In the 1970s Bradbury wrote another screenplay that was sold to the Bryna production company of Kirk Douglas. Rights were eventually optioned to his son, Peter Douglas, and under this arrangement Bradbury tried for several years to get Sam Peckinpah, who was deeply interested, to direct the film; again, a deal was never finalized. In 1980 Bradbury's third screenplay was purchased by Disney and lined up to be one of the first films produced under Disney's Touchstone subsidiary. Steven Spielberg was interested in the project but was sidetracked by his whimsical *1941.* Instead of Spielberg, Bradbury was able to lure Jack Clayton out of retirement to make the movie. Substantial post-production reshoots delayed release to 1983, when **Something Wicked** became the third Touchstone film (after *Tron* and *Splash*).[44]

In 1968 Gottlieb had become vice president at Knopf and paved the way for Bradbury to become a Knopf author the following year. The release of the 1983 film persuaded Gottlieb, by then the top executive at Knopf, to bring out a new hardbound edition of **Something Wicked.** But in the late 1980s, Gottlieb moved on to become editor in chief of the *New Yorker,* and it became harder for Bradbury to keep hardbound editions of his books in print with any of his present or past publishers. With the Bantam and Ballantine paperbacks in print, there was little incentive for publishers to bring out hardbound editions except for special projects. Bradbury's 1994 move to Avon led to cloth reprints of the key titles and handsome trade-paper editions of most of the rest. In 1999 Avon released its hardbound edition, but a year earlier **Something Wicked** became the lone mass-market paperback edition in the Avon list of Bradbury titles, joining the Bantam mass-market paperback as an accessible and very popular text of the novel. Despite its long and complicated prepublication history, **Something Wicked** has remained a very stable text in print. All subsequent editions radiate from the Simon and Schuster first edition, which was carefully edited under Bradbury's close supervision. Only the dedication has changed. Leaving his original dedication, which included his two inspirational high school English teachers, in the ever selling Bantam edition, he rededicated both of the new Avon editions to Gene Kelly, who inspired Bradbury with his films and his very personal encouragement so many years ago.

More than any of his major fictions, *Something Wicked* demonstrates in its textual history Bradbury's long-standing ties to the film industry. He began to write for studios in the early 1950s, and over the years this work often focused on one version or another of *Something Wicked.* Publication of the book also marked the beginning of a long period away from sustained story or novel writing. His productivity as a story writer dropped off significantly after 1962 as he turned more and more to writing stage versions of his stories and screenplays of his major fictions. His next book-length work, *The Halloween Tree,* was itself a novella developed out of a deferred animated film project in 1972. In all, nearly a quarter century would intervene between *Something Wicked* and release of another major novel. And many of the publications of his later years would emerge from ideas born in the richly creative midcentury period of his career (1942-62) that culminated in *Something Wicked.* In the best work of this period, he affirmed that laughter is the great unmasking of the seriousness of life. As seen in the thematics discussion below, carnival in *Something Wicked* becomes a master metaphor for Bradbury's life of fiction.

Themantics

Something Wicked This Way Comes raises issues of interpretive reading as no other book by Bradbury does. Critics are divided into those who want to read it as a Christian allegory and those who want to read it as bearing Freudian symbolic or archetypal meanings. The one exception to this rule is Stephen King's deft appreciation of the book in his *Danse Macabre,* which manages to weigh the merits of both readings while suggesting other, more complex ways of understanding it.[45] We do not propose to repeat the details of King's analysis here, but surely this kind of reading of Bradbury's fantasy is an advance over others that try to "decide" on the book's meaning in terms of one interpretive scheme or another as if a fantasy novel were a monologue expressing only one point of view (usually identified with the author of the interpretation). In fact, as we have been at pains to point out earlier in this book, Bradbury's fundamentally carnivalistic view of the fantastic presupposes the ambivalence of themes and the dialogic interaction of metaphors, myths, and masks. This is especially true of *Something Wicked,* which is carnivalized on every level of thematic meaning.

Something Wicked is one of Bradbury's most densely coded books. It uses many "reduced" or indirect forms of laughter, such as parody, irony, jokes, and mocking

sarcasm, as well as direct laughter itself. Bradbury's style in this novel piles metaphor upon metaphor, building dense matrices of meaning where codes intersect (the polyphonic musical code alone crosses church music and carnival music with popular tunes) until any literal ground of meaning becomes problematic. These excesses of style—if they can be called that; we think that their function is to evoke the hyperbolic language of carnival—do not mean, however, that the book has become "poetic," losing sight of the prosaic world of everyday life. On the contrary, central to the novel's thematics is the need for building "common cause" with others. In fact, on one level of meaning (the symbolic), it is a concerted attack on the individualistic and romantic (that is, Freudian) use of masks employed by the dark carnival.

Mikhail Bakhtin has demonstrated how profoundly the development of the novel was affected by the adoption of three carnival figures—the rogue, the clown, and the fool—as narrators or central characters. Historically, these "uninvented" figures were needed because of the problem of authorship in the novel genre, which really has no inherent set-and-fixed way to coordinate the authorial position with regards to its narrative's represented world and its public, the readers. Bradbury's authorial position in this novel is complex and needs to be explored in depth, so summarizing it will wait until the end of the chapter. But here let it be noted that, while *Something Wicked* uses the carnival mask of the fool in its main character, the father-fool Charles Halloway, it also invites us to laugh at the fool in all of us.[46] It especially invites us to laugh (with some sympathy) at those "unconnected fools" who are the harvest of the dark carnival. The book takes a stand against lonely, isolated individualism and argues for a collective laughter at everything that is exclusively serious in life (this much is explicitly stated in chap. 39).

King's reading, while acknowledging the role that the "admiring laughter" of the father plays in the book with regard to its sons and recognizing the capacity of Bradbury's "myth-children" to enjoy their terror, does not analyze the all-important role of laughter (in the collective sense belonging to authentic carnival) in this fantasy. Nor does it examine the ways in which the spirit of laughter—increasingly evident in Bradbury's writing from this book onward—might be related to a transvaluation of values. King is content to call the book a "moral horror tale" not so much different from Pinocchio's scary encounter on Pleasure Island, where boys who indulge in their baser desires (smoking cigars and playing snooker, for instance) are turned into donkeys.[47] For King, Bradbury's carnival represents a false freedom to its myth-children, William Halloway and Jim Nightshade; it is a taboo land made magically portable, traveling from place to place and even from time to time with its freight of freaks and its glamorous attractions.

It could be argued that King has read his own moral concerns as a writer of horror—concerns that always involve a threat to normalcy—into **Something Wicked,** but that is not the main concern here. Beyond the obvious appeal of the book's temptation theme and the father-son relationships that are strong in it, laughter—which has such a primal, visceral function for Bradbury as a sign of the capacity to affirm and to enjoy life—is the key to understanding it, for laughter is the primary means by which the fearsome carnival with its evil sideshows is unmasked, defeated, and transformed. Laughter is also the means by which we experience, in the book's third part, a transvaluation of values in which our conventional notions of fatherhood, bad conscience, guilt, and remorse are transformed. What follows is a reading of **Something Wicked** with the intent of showing how laughter, fathership-authorship, and the carnivalization of genre are all interrelated themes in the book.

The first part of **Something Wicked This Way Comes** presents the invasion of a small town in the American Midwest by the denizens of a supernatural traveling carnival, or, more precisely, Cooger and Dark's Pandemonium Shadow Show. Ostensibly, the town with its rules and laws is considered the norm, and the fantasy involves an intrusion of creatures (or ideas) that ordinarily would be confined to some other outside realm of existence.[48] The fortune-telling Dust Witch, for example, embodies our superstitious fear of fate and subjection to chance. As a literary topos, this carnival shares in the notion of a Dionysian eruption or tearing of the social fabric.

In addition to the father-fool as its central interpretive character, Bradbury's carnival still bears many popular-festive carnival images (especially grotesque body images) but is itself double or ambivalent. We hesitate between its two versions. During the day, it acts like a normal carnival that offers the kind of excitement and escape traditionally associated with such entertainments. Yet at night Bradbury's carnival is a machine that runs on bad conscience and regret, evil certainly, but equally pious and serious about itself. It is a paranoid machine run by Mr. Dark, an "illustrated man," who acts as a kind of father to all the freaks. He is clearly a cultural embodiment of the punishing superego of Freudian psychology, which basically defines his role in the internalized Gothic of the novel. The body images of the freaks are imprisoned as magic tattoos on his skin, but he also wears a "brambled suit" of thorns intermina-

bly itching, which suggests his relationship to an ascetic ideal.[49] One should remember here that, in its historical origins, carnival was a festive response to the seriousness of the church and official culture of the Middle Ages, which emphasized sin and the punishments of hell and upheld an ascetic ideal for humanity, this world being nothing more than a vale of tears. It was a world of fear and piety that excluded laughter. Mr. Dark's stinging suit is a reminder that he comes from that world, the anti-carnival, not the true carnival.

We soon learn that it is the function of the mirror maze, which operates during the day, to lure people back to the carnival at night by showing them reflections of a part of themselves that they once were or would wish to be so that they are plunged into aching despair. It represents, then, the whole world of interiority and regret—exposed by Friedrich Nietzsche in *On the Geneology of Morals* as the source of all higher values—that can threaten or destroy our capacity to affirm our lives. To the mirror maze is linked the carousel, which seems to run only at night. It can be run at a supernormal speed, forward or backward, and whoever rides it adds or subtracts a year of life per revolution. The carousel offers to repair the damage revealed in the mirror maze by providing maturity or youth—but at a price. The buyer of the ticket becomes a slave to Mr. Dark's shadow show.

Bradbury's fantasies often approach the issue of values by inverting them and then having the reader search for the reasons behind the inversion (*Fahrenheit 451* has firemen lighting fires instead of putting them out). At the outset we are presented with a reversed-image carnival:

> A carnival should be all growls, roars like timberlands stacked, bundled, rolled and crashed, great explosions of lion dust, men ablaze with working anger, pop bottles jangling, horse buckles shivering, engines and elephants in full stampede through rains of sweat while zebras neighed and trembled like cage trapped in cage.

> But this was like old movies, the silent theater haunted with black-and-white ghosts, silvery mouths opening to let moonlight smoke out, gestures made in silence so hushed you could hear the wind fizz the hair on your cheeks.[50]

This carnival—compared to a movie screen that stages desire—sets itself up in the darkest hours of the night. Why does Bradbury reverse the traditional associations belonging to this literary chronotope? We have to remember that he is writing *after* Freud, in a culture that has internalized the Gothic to an extraordinary degree. Tzvetan Todorov has indicated, in a statement that has provoked some controversy, that there is no literature of the fantastic in the twentieth century because psychoanalysis has taken over its themes.[51] This assertion has been largely confirmed, though inadvertently, by recent studies of the American Gothic, such as Mark Edmundson's *Nightmare on Main Street*. Edmundson does not consider the possibility, however, that fantastic literature could take revenge on psychoanalysis for this encroachment by making psychoanalysts figures of fun (or even serial killers themselves; the stories of Clive Barker or films like Brian DePalma's *Dressed to Kill* manifest this widespread tendency) in stories that discredit their authority or show their theories to be fictions. That is the cultural process—carnivalization—that is happening in *Something Wicked.*

Bradbury carnivalizes each genre in which he works. Here it is a question of the horror, or dark fantasy, genre whose themes have been dominated by Freud and based on Oedipal and familial fears. But in *Something Wicked* Bradbury's strategy is less direct than in his short stories and poems. There is no psychoanalyst overtly represented in the literal story. But the carnival itself, because it functions by feeding off the desires of people for lost objects, their guilt and sense of debt, and especially their narcissism, is similar to the psychoanalytic machine as parodied in some recent Nietzschean-inspired anti-Freudian polemics: "the psychoanalyst parks his circus in the dumbfounded unconscious, a real P. T. Barnum in the fields."[52]

Another interpretative issue to be dealt with, then, is the fact that *Something Wicked* speaks to us in the language of images derived from carnival that are indirect and often have a metaphorical and even allegorical significance.[53] But carnival should not be translated into a language of abstract concepts. Instead, one must investigate how carnival laughter, symbols, and its sense of change can be figured by literature and, through understanding them, again regain some sense of participation in it, the authentic use of the carnival being identified, according to Bakhtin, with our sense of carnival having *only just* been transformed into literature. Everything in Bradbury's text, its discourse and themes, strives to achieve this effect.

Here we want to mention that Bradbury conducts his critique of the Freudian view of man (as driven by unconscious desires he can never fulfill and by self-punishment for having those very desires) by the technique of carnivalizing the carnival and by masking his main character as a fool who, because of his "outsidedness," is able to resist its temptations. Fearful things such as Mr. Dark must also be masked in Bradbury's aesthetic. This is not to suggest, however, that *Something Wicked* is purely an allegory. Although his

name suggests some such function, Mr. Dark does not represent the abstract allegorical *idea* of the evil father. His image is, in fact, quite ambivalent and derived from carnival images that in origin parodied the ascetic ideal. Mr. Dark is only one of several fathers in the book. It is Cooger whose name comes first in that of the carnival, and he is its (crowned-decrowned) king.

Mr. Dark is, however, the main spokesman for the sinister carnival. His language conveys something of the carnival's attractions, with his talk about life surviving "wildly" in it. He is figured in the novel as an inscribed body that has to be interpreted by Halloway (and Halloway's reading is itself a carnivalized history, a Nietzschean genealogy). In the story the main struggle consists in trying to stop Mr. Dark from "Oedipalizing," or fathering, the entire town. Initially, only the two boys stand in the way of the carnival. Jim Nightshade's father has apparently died. The attraction that Mr. Dark offers him is sexual maturity, the chance to become his own father by riding the nightmare carousel into the future and ruling the carnival with him. Jim is fascinated by the "bramble suit" long before he is seduced by Dark's tattoo images (at least some of them seem to be of phallic origin; Jim hesitates but says he saw a "snake" on Mr. Dark's arm).[54] Will Halloway, Jim's best friend, is able to resist such a temptation because he does have a father—the quiet, scholarly, middle-aged janitor of the local library who has a weak heart.

Will, as his shortened name suggests, has the will to command and obey himself, a prime Nietzschean virtue. He runs because running is its own excuse. Jim runs because "something's up ahead of him," according to Mr. Halloway, who has a deep sympathy with the boys, understanding them from the point of view of the adolescent he once was.[55] But of course, Mr. Halloway is an adult, worried that his age and weak heart do not allow him to be a proper father to Will. The carnival tempts him with restored sexual potency and vitality. Together, Will and his father—who emerges as the real hero of the story—must defeat the carnival and rescue Jim Nightshade from its clutches.

Early in the novel, one of the carnival workers, distributing advertising and putting up posters in the town, shows Halloway what can only be the image of female genitalia on the palm of his hand, which is "covered with fine black silken hair." He leaves a block of ice in an unrented, empty store. This ice block represents "The Most Beautiful Woman in the World." Halloway gazes into it, and Bradbury writes the "truth" about desire staged as lack:

> And yet this vast chunk of wintry glass held nothing but frozen river water.

No. Not quite empty.

Halloway felt his heart pound one special time.

Within the huge winter gem was there not a special vacuum? a voluptuous hollow, a prolonged emptiness which undulated from tip to toe of the ice? and wasn't this vacuum, this emptiness waiting to be filled with summer flesh, was it not shaped somewhat like a . . . woman?

Yes.

The ice. And the lovely hollows, the horizontal flow of emptiness within the ice. The lovely nothingness. The exquisite flow of an invisible mermaid daring the ice to capture it.[56]

Charles Halloway wants to leave but instead stands looking for a long time. The desire being staged in this passage, with its emphasis on the captured gaze, suggests that the ice itself is a kind of mirror (and Halloway's name seems to be an echo of the word "hollow"). We are asked to imagine both the representation of a nothingness and something else that flows exquisitely outside that representation, daring desire to capture it. The flow provokes a reverie of warm summer water imprisoned in ice, which eventually suggests the absence of a supernatural mermaid who left behind her voluptuous form.

In the psychoanalytic sense the desire Halloway feels is based precisely on nothing, a feminine void (that is, castration). The fantastic representations of the carnival want to ensnare him in such emptiness. Yet psychoanalytic desiring and the themes of sex and age do not explain everything here. Another, different type of desiring based on the plenitude of the material imagination (of water, which flows outside of forms in this instance) is also present in this passage. The text illustrates very clearly that Bradbury's use of fantastic representation is profoundly ambivalent. There is always life amid death, the lure of beautiful Apollonian forms and the Dionysian flow outside them.

Halloway's views about life at this point are fairly consonant with Christian notions of sin, guilt, and the need for grace. At fifty-four he feels the weight of the world, the spirit of gravity. He is shocked by Jim, who cannot understand the Christian allegorical import of Dante (but Bradbury manages a pun on "Alighieri" and "allegory"), but who is instead fascinated by the literal hell as illustrated by Gustave Doré. At this stage of valuing, Halloway represents classical—and conventional—aesthetic attitudes. His understanding of the carnival is limited initially to the beautiful, as in the figure of the woman, and the sublime. Indeed, the carnival's impending arrival brings with it a sense of the sublime, a "terrified elation" as Bradbury describes

it. In response Halloway recites to himself a traditional Christmas carol ("God is not dead, nor doth he Sleep!"), which gives expression to his feelings.

But the mermaid is also a figure, half-human and half-fish, of the "grotesque realism" (the term is Bakhtin's) of carnival. In our interpretation of her image, we can already see that Halloway's experiences with the carnival will not be limited to the classical dualism of the beautiful and the sublime. In the book's second part, Halloway will have to experience and interpret the body of the carnival, which in turn will lead to his rebirth and revaluation of it and its meanings. Halloway will defeat the carnival through an appropriation of its (hidden) laughter, which enables the ambivalent fathering or destruction of Cooger and Dark in the book's third part.

But before that can happen, the reader needs to be dramatically "horrified" by what the carnival can do. Among the supernatural events in the first and early second parts of the book, none is more fully realized and terrifying than the capture of Miss Foley, the boys' seventh-grade schoolteacher. Described as a little woman lost somewhere in her gray fifties, she is nearly drowned in the fathoms of reflections in the mirror maze but is rescued by Jim and Will. Her desire-as-lack is to have once been beautiful. After her experiences with the mirror maze, her house seems haunted by mirrors that threaten her with "billionfold multiplications of self, an army of women marching away to become girls and girls marching away to become infinitely small children."[57] Miss Foley's final metamorphosis into a frightened girl beneath a tree in the cold autumn rain is Bradbury's own image of hell—to be trapped as an adult inside a child's body, unknown even to oneself, with no way to tell the strangeness to anyone. Miss Foley gets more than she desires from the carnival, but in getting it, she severs all ties of love and human time with the community. Even the boys she once taught are unable to do anything about her situation.

The evil agent in this punishment is Mr. Cooger, who is changed into a semblance of her nephew, Robert, by the carousel; changed and crowned by a ruse of Mr. Dark's into Mr. Electrico; and finally decrowned when the freaks cannot get him back to the carousel in time to revive him. The boys spy on this transformation and are aware of his intention to lure Miss Foley back to the carnival to ride on it also. Jim wants to meet the transformed Mr. Cooger out of sheer curiosity, but Will responds to the danger of the situation. What Will sees in Miss Foley's comfortable living room (in the final version, on the right, below) is a quintessential romantic-Freudian mask:[58]

Jamie and Me discards (1959)	*Something Wicked* (1962)
Something was standing on the porch looking out at the town. I felt Jamie flinch one way, then another, undecided. I grabbed him tighter. The something on the porch could have been the man, could have been the boy. I smelled the man somehow, and saw the boy a moment later come out in the streetlight. There was his face, round and smooth as a peach. But there were the man's eyes looking out like through the slits of a Sleeping Beauty mask at Hallowe'en. At any moment I expected a crack to appear in the top of the boy's chestnut hair and move down cracking his face in half, splitting his nose, his chin, cleaving like an ax had chopped him down through the neck, the chest, to let a great wet moth heave out beating its wings in the porch dark, a moth big enough to carry us both away from the town forever into hills that never ended. That's how much I felt the other thing inside the thing that said it was a boy that said it was good that never shaved but was all tarantula hair inside.	And it was wild and crazy and the floor sank away beneath for there was the pink shiny Halloween mask of a small pretty boy's face, but almost as if holes were cut where the eyes of Mr. Cooger shone out, old, old, eyes as bright as sharp blue stars and the light from those stars taking a million years to get here. And through the little nostrils cut in the shiny wax mask, Mr. Cooger's breath went in steam came out ice. And the Valentine candy tongue moved small behind those trim white candy-kernel teeth. Mr. Cooger, somewhere behind the eye slits, went *blink-click* with his insect-Kodak pupils. The lenses exploded like suns, then burnt chilly and serene again.

The final passage emphasizes the eyes of the mask, which have no part in the comic masks of carnival that are meant to dispel fear and hide nothing.[59] It expresses, in sweetened images of candy, the individual disconnected human life, not the grotesque body of carnival, which is open to the world [. . .]. Although it too contains a reference to eyes—in fact, in the earlier version the face beneath the mask is compared to a molting tarantula, a striking image of the fear of dehumanization. In the final version the horror is that the boys can see through the mask. They are not taken in by the ruses of the carnival. The pink, shiny Halloween mask is also linked to another popular-festive holiday, Valentine's Day, which is often celebrated in schools.

Nonetheless, ruses and dissimulation are the laws of life in the romantic carnival, which could not survive if it did not don the mask of the forces against which it struggles. Cooger's mask is scary because, to the boys anyway, it does not entirely hide the horror of chaos beneath it. On the contrary, it lets this stare through in a glance of cold command. And because his eyes are compared to stars and the vast distances traveled by light from sources that may no longer exist (and whose origin is forever unknown), we have the eerie sensation of being looked down upon by a force that is much larger than ourselves. Nephew Robert only seems obedient; actually it is Miss Foley who obeys. Cooger's face appears to have beauty, the sweetness of candy, but underneath lies an abomination of nature, an abyss, which is why Will feels the floor sliding away beneath him.

Soon after this scare, the boys return to the carnival, Jim because he wants to go forward on the carousel, Will because he wants to stop him. Accidentally, while they are fighting, Will pushes the lever forward, and Mr. Cooger is metamorphosed in a shower of electrical sparks into an old, old man. Later, seeking revenge, the carnival comes on a parade through town. For the first time, Will's father is convinced that something wicked has arrived when he has an ominous confrontation with Mr. Dark and the Dust Witch.[60] The parade scene is also the first time we are given an indication that the carnival has a weak spot: its unrelenting seriousness. (It had played church music when it first arrived, another sign of its seriousness.)

During this episode, Mr. Halloway's prankish behavior with a cigar—he is something of a rogue in this scene, pretending not to know who the boys are—causes the Dust Witch to recoil from "the concussion of his fiercely erupted and overly jovial words," which also cause Mr. Dark to go rigid with anger. We are given a strong indication that the carnival cannot abide any attack on its seriousness and "piety," especially the enjoyment of life in an expenditure without reserve. When Mr. Halloway puffs a cigar, everything goes up in smoke of enjoyment; nothing, save his enjoyment, remains. But the carnival, we may infer, wants to make human pain and negativity a resource, to make it work for them. Mr. Dark talks openly later in the book about "investing in our securities" and offers ostensibly free tickets to the boys.[61] Here, the reader begins to suspect, however, that there is something deceptive about the economy of the carnival that needs to be unmasked.

The unmasking occurs in the books interpretive chapters. Following the parade through town, Mr. Halloway repairs to the library with an invitation to Mr. Dark to come and find him there. The setting is already symbolic of reading and interpretation. By the end of the book's second part, we are astonished not by supernatural events, but by the eight full chapters set in the town's library that are devoted to interpretation of the carnival (chaps. 37-44). These argue against our seeing the carnival as an allegory of abstract ideas, urging us rather to interpret it as a body with a certain history.

When the boys arrive and give a precise summary of the fantastic events in the plot thus far (that now become "facts" to interpret), we enter into what Mr. Halloway calls a "history of the carnival." Actually, it is no conventional history at all but approximates a Nietzschean genealogy that examines the emergence and descent of things one normally thinks of as being without history—negative emotions such as fear and unhappiness, conscience and regret, and instincts. According to Michel Foucault, Nietzschean genealogy is "history in the form of a concerted carnival."[62] Halloway's history of the carnival does not, in fact, trace in the carnival a gradual curve of evolution from an origin or describe a linear development in the conventional historical sense. Rather, it is sensitive to the carnival's periodic invasions of the "real" world, its struggles, plunderings, disguises, ploys, and above all its recurrence, in the process isolating different scenes where it engaged in different roles. It is best understood as a carnivalized history:

> The stuff of nightmare is their plain bread. They butter it with pain. They set their clocks by death-watch beetles, and thrive the centuries. They were the men with the leather-ribbon whips who sweated up the Pyramids seasoning it with other people's salt and other people's cracked hearts. They coursed Europe on the White Horses of the Plague. They whispered to Caesar that he was mortal, then sold daggers at half-price in the grand March sale. Some must have been lazing clowns, foot props for emperors, princes, and epileptic popes. Then out on the road, Gypsies in time, their populations grew as the world grew, spread, and there was more delicious variety of pain to thrive on. The train put wheels under them and here they run down the long road out of the Gothic and baroque; look at their wagons and coaches, the carving like medieval shrines, all of it stuff once drawn by horses, mules, or, maybe, men.[63]

This entire highly engaging genealogical analysis by Halloway—of which we have only reproduced a small sample here—proceeds through a series of what Nietzsche calls emergences *(Entstehung),* moments of arising. An emergence is an entry of forces onto the scene of history through a play of dominations. It designates a place of confrontation that later becomes stabilized in social forms such as rituals, in meticulous procedures that impose rights and obligations. Thus these "autumn people" (as Halloway earlier calls them) become "foot props for emperors, princes, and epileptic popes." But no single unified origin is posited as giving rise to the carnival, nor is there a fall into sin or a promise of redemption. On the contrary, throughout this history, Halloway stresses the strategies of the weak against the strong, not good against evil. (Could the carnival of evil have had the same values in such different historical periods as the Gothic and the baroque?) A form of the dark carnival arises whenever and wherever people begin to feed on what Nietzsche calls man's progressive internalization of instinct, giving rise to bad conscience and even higher morality, especially ascetic ideals.[64] Interestingly, the carvings on the wagons are described as "medieval shrines," making the dark carnival allude to the pious seriousness of the Middle Ages.

The genealogy begins with the simple prehistoric *Schadenfreude,* the malicious delight of one man in another's misfortune, and thereafter (passing from father to son—an Oedipal structure is suggested) grows until it takes on the qualities of a machine threatening to dominate the earth. As Halloway patiently explains to Jim in the passage immediately preceding this, the carnival is not evil but bad, for from it comes "nothing for something," nothingness in return for the investment of desire. (A similar deconstructive analysis of the binary oppositions, for example, "good" and "bad," that structure our moral values can be found in Nietzsche's *On the Geneology of Morals,* which we suggest as an intertext here.)

The second part of Halloway's genealogy takes the form of a descent *(Herkunft)* that is involved with the body and everything that touches it: diet, climate, soil. Something of this is already evident in the passage quoted above, which is strongly phrased in such metaphors ("The stuff of nightmare is their plain bread. They butter it with pain"). But the body metaphor becomes dominant in the next chapter (forty), in which the bodily image of the carnival is analyzed, and where the soul itself becomes a kind of body that oxidizes need, want, and desire. Halloway here gives an instinctive Nietzschean analysis of the "black candle-power" of the carnival, whose fuel is "the raw stuffs of terror, the excruciating agony of guilt, the scream from real or imagined wounds."

In Foucault's analysis descent "attaches itself to the body," inscribing itself in the nervous system, in the temperament.[65] Descent establishes marks of its power and engraves memories on things, creating stigmata that can be read by the genealogist. Through his analysis of its descent, Halloway is able to interpret the carnival as a machine that inscribes desires, failings, and errors on the bodies of its victims, the people who join it, abandoning wives, husbands, and friends. In Halloway's interpretation—which he stresses is incomplete and subject to a lot of guesswork—the carnival becomes a body and the freaks are read as ironic inscriptions on an inscribed surface of events. The mirror maze transforms these individualized people who want a "change of body, change of personal environment" into freakish living images of their "original sins." The primary sins are narcissism and not bothering to form common causes with others. For instance, the lightning-rod salesman, whom the boys meet at the beginning of the novel, is figured as someone who never stays around with others to face the storms. The carnival turns him not into a boy, but into a dwarf, "a mean ball of grotesque tripes, all self-involved."

A few comments on the nature of the carnival body as it develops in the novel is necessary at this point, for that body represents collectivities and crowds whose nature may be misunderstood. At the end of the novel's first section, we see how Mr. Dark's body bears the living tattoos, the illustrations of all the stories of the freaks he dominates. Although they are described as a collective identity, as a "picture crowd flooded raw upon his chest," the freaks are not allowed to speak in their own voice, to tell their own stories.[66] They have to serve the evil of Mr. Dark's narrative monopoly:

> Mr. Dark came carrying his panoply of friends, his jewel-case assortment of calligraphical reptiles which lay sunning themselves at midnight on his flesh. With him strode the stitch-inked *Tyrannosaurus rex* which lent to his haunches a machined and ancient wellspring mineral-oil glide. As the thunder lizard strode, all glass-bead pomp, so strode Mr. Dark, armored with vile lightening scribbles of carnivores and sheep blasted by that thunder and arun before storms of juggernaut flesh. It was the pterodactyl kite and scythe which raised his arms almost to fly the marbled vaults. And with the inked and stenciled flashburnt shapes of pistoned or bladed doom, came his usual crowd of hangers-on, spectators gripped to each limb, seated on shoulder blades, peering from his jungled chest, hung upside down in microscopic millions in his armpit vaults screaming bat-screams for encounters, ready for the hunt and if need be the kill.[67]

The passage goes on for another lengthy sentence. On the whole it evokes a sense of Mr. Dark's tyrannical and predatory power over the carnival. It is composed of dinosaur metaphors and metaphors of metaphors. The narrative of events is halted by the outbreak of a profusion of bodily metaphors—consider the series pterodactyl-kite-scythe, which signifies by resemblance the deadly mechanisms that lift Mr. Dark's stitch-inked arms. Everything happens on the surface of a fantasized body that Dark has somehow made appealing to the boys, who he knows are interested in dinosaurs. (Earlier, stripped bare to the navel, he is seen stinging himself with a tattoo needle, adding a picture to his left palm, undoubtedly the image of Jim's face.)[68]

The crowds depicted on this social body, though they seem full of life, are not really free. In true carnivals no one is just a spectator. No one is outside the play of carnival, everyone is a participant in its life and subject to it. The freaks should be able to speak with their own true voices to each other, yet they appear as themselves only as masked by their sins. Because his body contains so many "spectators," Mr. Dark is thus the *author* of the carnival, one who seeks to master and control all of its narrative meanings. Bradbury wants very much to defeat this notion of authorship in all its seriousness with the notion of the author as someone who creates himself and sees himself created as self and other, as both man and mask. (Julia Kristeva describes the notion

of carnivalesque authorship in exactly these terms.)[69] In intellectual terms the Illustrated Man, as Dark prefers to call himself, is a congeries of inscribed images, a text threatening to dissociate itself, held together by the appropriative force of his will.

Mr. Dark tries to tempt Halloway with restored youth and vitality if he will tell him where the boys are hiding in the library. Halloway refuses, but his heart is too weak to put up a fight. His attempt to do battle with Dark among books, he now realizes, has not really amounted to much in terms of action, and Dark taunts him with this knowledge. When Halloway asks him if he has read the Bible, Dark takes the copy from him with ease: "Do you expect me to fall away into so many Dead Sea scrolls of flesh before you? Myths, unfortunately, are just that. Life, and by life I could mean so many fascinating things, goes on, makes shift for itself, survives wildly, and I not the least wild among many. Your King James and his literary version of some rather stuffy poetic materials is worth about *this* much of my time and sweat."[70] Dark then throws the Bible into the wastebasket.

Because Mr. Dark can read the Bible and discard it as if it were rubbish—a still shocking act of carnivalization, decrowning what was for many centuries the center of our literary culture—we understand that words, not even the Word of God in the soaring poetic cadences of the King James Version, are going to be sufficient to defeat the carnival. There is no question either of any genealogical word of "truth" that would make Dark's body fall away into textuality, into "Dead Sea scrolls of flesh." As Halloway realizes that he is being mocked and debased in his efforts to understand the carnival as both book and text, he lies helpless on the floor of the library, thrown down by Mr. Dark's power. Dark then goes off in search of the boys, "my two precious human books," so he can turn their pages. Having caught them and sealed their lips with a magic dragonfly spell, he leaves Halloway in the unsavory company of the Dust Witch, who has been instructed to stop his heart.

At this point something rather unexpected, though not entirely unprepared for, happens. Looking up at the wizened Dust Witch's mask, at her "Halloween face" with an intense scrutiny as she tries to kill him "as if she were a puzzle, which once touched together might show life's greatest secret" (in the last revised draft, Bradbury had originally typed "hidden values" but wrote "life's greatest secret" over it, which indicates that he was thinking of a transvaluation of values in this scene), Halloway is still trying to interpret what that secret may be when—and the phonetic resemblance between "Halloway" and "Halloween" may also be a dialogic jest on his own mask here—he begins to spontaneously and uncontrollably giggle.

The central passage from chapter 44 cited above in compared texts is highly significant in terms of its carnivalized thematics and requires extensive comment. First of all, it is the literal turning point of the novel, the pivot around which the story changes because, as the penultimate sentence indicates, laughter and freedom are breaking free and turning the tide against a "grotesque" horror. When raw laughter is born from Halloway, its "unsuspecting parent" (in the last revised draft, Bradbury had written "unsuspecting father," which makes the birth directly related to fathering the carnival), we sense a reappropriation of the true function of folk carnival, which had become perverted by Mr. Dark. Of great significance is the fact that the laughter is described as "raw." It is not undergoing sublimation of any sort, neither religious, mystical, nor philosophical. It has not been filtered through the corrupted institutions of the dark carnival that prey on isolated individuals. This laughter remains outside of official falsification and lies, exploding and ripping away masks and pretensions. The passage goes on to register Halloway's acute awareness of a "joke" rushing through his body, "letting hilarity spring forth of its own volition along his throat . . . , whipping shrapnel in all directions." As Lionel Trilling has observed (in a quote reproduced in the front matter), no great novel exits that does not have a joke at its very heart.

Bradbury's use of laughter and the joke is still more complex. According to Bakhtin, the themes of carnival laughter were expressed in a number of characteristic comic images. Always in them can be discerned "the defeat of fear presented in a droll and monstrous form, the symbols of power and violence turned inside out, the comic images of death and bodies gaily rent asunder. All that was terrifying becomes grotesque." Furthermore, Bakhtin goes on to add, in carnival even death becomes pregnant. In the true carnival symptoms of pregnancy or of procreative power are not hidden but abound, and a joyous recreation of an Earth without fear is expected. At the end of the novel, Halloway and the boys experience the world "as it must have been in the first year of Creation, and Joy not yet thrown from the Garden."[71] This "final" victory over fear is not its abstract elimination, however.

Bradbury has adapted these carnivalesque images to our modernist sensibilities about meaning. The Dust Witch, the embodiment of human desires to understand such serious notions as fate, desire, and fortune, seems funny to Halloway because she is blind to her own interpretive activities. By tickling and interpreting Halloway, she is trying to give him a heart attack, but instead she only makes him laugh. All the reading and interpretive activities he has engaged in, all those books, seem like "playthings of his egotism and swaying toys of his life"

now. As the Illustrated Man points out to Halloway, biblical images of him as the Devil are myths, and myths, unfortunately, are just that. As interpretations, they cannot help Halloway defeat the carnival. Life, however, "goes on, makes shift for itself, survives wildly." In other words, a myth or a metaphor simply *is* a mask of the play of interpretive forces. Mr. Dark can see, touch, and even read from the Bible, a fact that surprises Halloway. Life as the will to power interprets, using any number of masks. This is the "great secret of life" that Halloway learns and appropriates from the carnival.

Second, Halloway begins to see himself, it is clear, not as a stable person who is either good or evil, but as a succession of arrivals and departures (the names of *Something Wicked*'s first and last sections). Having gained this radical perspective, this "joyful relativity" from the carnival itself, Halloway realizes that the only thing possible to do at this extreme moment is to push this ridiculous masquerade to its limits, to risk a revaluation of all values. In looking so closely at the witch's mask and at her efforts to stop his heart by negating his love of life, Halloway at least realizes that he too, although "good," must give up any claims to substantial identity, to a metaphysical essence that defines reality once and for all.

It is important to realize that Halloway *has* gone beyond conventional notions of good and evil in this passage. He no longer believes in these or in the specter of Christian guilt. Therefore, the carnival, which represents the whole world of interiority and regret, can have no claim on him any longer. It is not normalcy that is restored at the end (as in King's reading of the novel, in which the Dionysian only disrupts and threatens normalcy that is then restored, missing entirely the ambivalence of carnival). Halloway ends up believing in a kind of pure exteriority of meaning, in the playful surfaces of things instead of the profound "depths" of meaning, an appreciation that is brought to him though his intense scrutiny of the Dust Witch's mask. Through saying "yes" to life's essential meaninglessness and suffering and to death itself, he overcomes the carnival and himself. Halloway realizes he has been granted this power "all because he accepted everything at last, accepted the carnival, the hills beyond, the people in the hills, Jim, Will, and above all himself and *all of life,* and, accepting, threw back his head for a second time tonight and showed his acceptance with sound" (emphasis added).[72] Laughter, not meaning, will defeat the carnival.

Laughter brings the serious things of life—which usually occupy a position above us—close at hand so that they can be mocked. Laughter has brought Halloway to understand the partial nature of all one-sided ideological positions. His actions after this transformative experience disrupt the restrictive economy of the master-slave dialectic on which the carnival runs. Making use of the unsuspected Dionysian power of laughter, Halloway bursts apart the carnival at its seams, shattering the mirror maze with its anguish of petty narcissism, which is the very motor of the carnival's machine, which gives nothing (it seems the very spirit of Hegelian negation) for something. Eventually, he slays the Dust Witch with a bullet on which he has marked his smile. No aspect of displaced carnivalesque humor is too "childish" or baroque for Bradbury to appropriate and use in his war against the internalized Gothic and its regime of guilt and self-punishment.

The laughter that is born from the Dust Witch's "tickling" is not just a physiological response. It opens up a new philosophical understanding of the world, revealing the joyful relativity of all structure and order, of all authority and hierarchical positions. In Nietzschean terms it would mark the birth of the overman and a more joyous and higher psychic life. To laugh at "evil" requires discipline and strength, an entire method that understands evil's byways and techniques and actively appropriates them: "Not by wrath does one kill, but by laughter. Come, let us kill the spirit of gravity!"[73] In Nietzsche's later philosophy, laughter is an antidote for afflictions produced by the spirit of gravity that makes life a burden. So in Bradbury's text also, when the Dust Witch comes with her "weights and pressures of despair" to read his pain and regret and to make him part of the carnival, Halloway laughs, prompted by her ticklings. Actually, he does more than simply laugh: he laughs hysterically, guffaws, and hollers with mirth. His laughter is the deeply primal bodily laughter of the carnival reborn and released in all of its ambivalent life.

After these Dionysian insights, Halloway is no longer an interpreter of literary myths in the library, but someone who experiences a rebirth through the ambivalent death of the carnival (he had, in fact, told the boys earlier that "Death doesn't exist; it never did, it never will" but explained to them that the carnival feeds off of the fear of death). As a Dionysian father, however, he has to teach young Will the value of laughter for life. Will must learn to affirm life; he must abandon will-negating moods brought on by the carnival. Only then can he and Will bring Jim back to life with mirth, harmonica playing, and mimic dancing—all true aspects of carnival culture. Halloway even kills Mr. Dark, who has transformed himself into a boy, Jed, with a loving fatherly embrace. Halloway literally kills with kindness. Before he dies, Jed groaningly accuses Halloway of being "evil" in a nice carnivalesque reversal of perspectives.

Mr. Dark's illustrations disperse and melt away, leaving the freaks with no body in which to recognize themselves any longer, with no "common cause" to unite them. This dispersal of the romantic-Freudian machine that was Cooger and Dark's Pandemonium Shadow Show is in itself a rather dismal affair, for it seems we will never know who the freaks really were as they are liberated into intensities and differences, for they disappear in all directions like shadows, Miss Foley and the others captured from Green Town leaving with them. The true horror of Miss Foley's transformation is that she is no longer connected to a social body in human lived time.

We know that the carnival of interiority is finished, though it may return again under different masks. The haters and despisers of life will always be around, Halloway seems to imply: "The fight's just begun." Indeed, Bradbury will struggle again with such "autumn people" and "pessimist" thinkers in *Death Is a Lonely Business*. But laughter will be available also as a principle that affirms life, as a balm that makes light of our wounds. "We *can't* take them seriously," Halloway tells his son, "them" being the "night people" of the carnival in whatever form they may take.

Although expressed in carnival images, Bradbury's authorial position (a notion that encompasses the author-hero relationship in the world of the novel and also the relationship of the author to his readers) in this novel is complex and philosophical. Fathering the carnival with a fool character and his laughter does not mean that Bradbury's position of authorship dispenses with seriousness altogether. Bradbury still wants to be taken seriously as an author, but it is a question of an "open" seriousness, one that eschews the dogmatic and the hierarchical notion of author represented by Mr. Dark. Some readers of this novel cannot understand how evil can be defeated so easily by laughter alone. But it is not evil as a metaphysical essence that Bradbury is out to destroy. What he wants to destroy is the fear on which evil feeds. With this book, Bradbury serves his readers "official" fair warning that henceforth those who read him without laughter, without finding the joke at the very heart of his works, might as well not be reading him at all.

Through the ambivalence of carnival—it has always represented both death and life for him since he met the real Mr. Electrico (who curses the boys in this novel instead of giving them a blessing, [. . .])—Bradbury addresses his own authorship of the fantastic. The father-fool's ritual debasement by the carnival and the Dust Witch gives birth to a new and world-embracing "raw" laughter outside of the need for social masks that hide the person inside. It now seems entirely appropriate for Halloway as Nietzschean father to kill this "son" Jed, who represents the poisoned ruses and formal disguises of psychoanalysis insofar as they have penetrated the horror and dark fantasy genre. By making his fantasy responsive to the situation of the fantastic after Freud, by carnivalizing the whole tragic nature of interiority (repression, guilt, anguish) that Freud's work represents in our literary culture for him, Bradbury has written a new chapter in the history of laughter. *Something Wicked This Way Comes* remains his favorite book and is (in our judgment) his best use of metaphor, myth, and mask to create a literary carnival. Because of its intense focus on carnivalization on all levels of the text, and especially because of its use of laughter, the novel exists on the boundary between art and life as if carnival itself had *only just* come to claim its rights in literature.

Something Wicked is the culmination of Bradbury's aesthetics of carnival in the fantasy genre. But he went on to use the mask of the fool to transform the detective genre as well.

Notes

1. Stephen King, *Danse Macabre* (New York: Berkley, 1983), 324. "But I believe that *Something Wicked This Way Comes,* a darkly poetic tall tale set in the half-real, half-mythical community of Green Town, Illinois, is probably Bradbury's best work—a shadowy descendant from that tradition that has brought us stories about Paul Bunyan and his blue ox, Babe, Pecos Bill, and Davy Crockett."

2. Darrell Schweitzer, "Ray Bradbury's Horror Fiction," in *Fantasy Review* 10, no. 2 (1987): 18, 16; William F. Nolan, interview by Jonathan R. Eller, Los Angeles, Mar. 13, 2002; Clive Barker, afterword to *Dark Carnival,* by Ray Bradbury (Springfield, Penn.: Gauntlet, 2001); King, *Danse Macabre,* 326. The California Group is listed by Schweitzer and described in detail in Christopher Conlon, "California Sorcerers," introduction to *California Sorcery,* ed. William F. Nolan and William Schafer (New York: Ace, 2001). Nolan attributes the group's name to critic Robert Kirsch; see "Remembering 'The Group,'" preface to *California Sorcery.*

3. Bradbury to Derleth, Mar. 8, 1945, Madison; a variant draft also survives in Bradbury's personal papers.

4. Bradbury also left a blurred area in the jacket's center to suggest the motion of the carousel. He would later recall this strategy in a letter to his film and television agent, Ben Benjamin, written in late 1960.

5. This folder of materials, containing thirty-one pages of text and a title page indicating that Don Congdon

read the selections while at Simon and Schuster, has been published as bonus material in a special collector's print run of Gauntlet's 2001 limited-edition *DC.*

6. *Outré*'s 1997 reprint of "The Black Ferris" includes an excellent introduction by William F. Nolan that summarizes the history of this story and its germinal relationship to *SW.*

7. Bradbury to Ben Benjamin, n.d. [Dec. 1960], carbon copy, personal papers. The original oil painting is included in Jerry Weist's tribute to Bradbury's book, magazine, and comic illustrators; see *Ray Bradbury: An Illustrated Life* (New York: William Morrow, 2002), 76.

8. Bradbury related portions of these events as they were unfolding in a letter to his Doubleday editor, Walter Bradbury; R. Bradbury to W. Bradbury, Jan. 27, 1955, Lilly. A more retrospective summary is contained in Bradbury to Benjamin, n.d. [Dec. 1960].

9. The following account of the Bradbury-Kelly relationship and the screen treatment that resulted is derived from Bradbury, interviews by Jonathan R. Eller, Los Angeles, Mar. 11-12, 14, 2002; and Gene Kelly to Bradbury, telegrams, Aug. 8 and 10, 1955, personal papers; a draft of Bradbury's response to the August 8 telegram also survives in his personal papers. King's *Danse Macabre* includes an account of these events from an undocumented letter by Bradbury, but the excerpt misstates the year as 1958. Both the 1998 Avon paperback and the 1999 Avon hardbound editions of *SW* contain afterwords by Bradbury that recount variations of these events.

10. Walt Disney to Bradbury, Dec. 2, 1955; Bernard Smith (Hecht-Hill-Lancaster) to Bradbury, May 20, 1957; David Brown (Twentieth Century Fox) to Bradbury, Aug. 11, 1958; and John Montgomery (Peters Agency) to Bradbury, Aug. 6, Dec. 12, 1958, personal papers. A number of letters to Bradbury during 1957 relate to the Reed-Bradbury collaboration; reasons for the collapse of this project are best summarized in Bradbury to August Derleth, July 8, 1958, Madison. The filming of Nevil Shute's novel *On the Beach* (1958), which focuses on themes central to "And the Rock Cried Out," also worked against the Bradbury-Reed venture. Bradbury to Congdon, Sept. 27, 1960 (Butler).

11. The initial teleplay, "The Bullet Trick," was turned down by the producers of both the *GE* and *Star Stage Shows.* Revue Productions to Bradbury, Dec. 28, 1955, personal papers. Bradbury's fascination with the bullet trick dates from his reading about Ching Ling Soo, the Oriental magician killed while performing the trick in 1910.

12. The dates of all four major drafts, as well as the surviving preliminary draft runs and discard sheets

of the first draft, are dated from Bradbury's notes on the boxes containing these drafts of the novel. All four drafts are in the Albright Collection.

13. Congdon to Walter Bradbury (copy to Ray Bradbury), May 15, 1958, Congdon to R. Bradbury, May 28, 1958, personal papers.

14. Congdon to Bradbury, Apr. 15, Oct. 22, 1959, personal papers.

15. Bradbury to Congdon, Apr. 4, 1960, Butler. Bradbury wrote a five-page discussion of concerns in a letter intended for Seldes, Sept. 29, 1959. Instead, he forwarded it to Congdon, who persuaded Bradbury to withhold it (Butler). Congdon's three-page letter of October 22, 1959, contains a detailed rationale for postponing a confrontation with Doubleday. The publisher's parallel view regarding reprints with the release of a new book is reported in Congdon to Bradbury, Nov. 6, 1959, personal papers.

16. The break with Doubleday is documented in the follow sequence of letters: Congdon to Bradbury, May 23, 1960, personal papers; Bradbury to Seldes, June 2, 1960, Lilly; Seldes to Bradbury, June 7, 24, 1960, personal papers; Seldes to Congdon (copy to Bradbury), July 1, 1960, personal papers; Bradbury to Seldes, July 8, 1960, Lilly (asking for release); and Congdon to Seldes, July 13, 1960, Lilly (transmitting Bradbury's release request). Five letters finalize the release: Congdon to Bradbury, July 21, 1960, personal papers; Seldes to Bradbury, July 27, 1960, personal papers; Congdon to Bradbury, July 28, 1960, personal papers; Bradbury to Congdon, July 29, 1960, Butler; and Seldes to Bradbury, Sept. 26, 1960, personal papers (correcting the terms of the release).

17. Bradbury to Congdon, July 12, 24, 1960 (Butler); Congdon to Bradbury, July 28, Sept. 8, 13, 16, 1960, personal papers.

18. Gottlieb to Congdon, Sept. 9, 1960, Butler.

19. The discussions with Goldwyn are described in a detailed five-page letter, Congdon to Bradbury, Nov. 23, 1960, personal papers. Bradbury's position is summarized in a letter to his film agent, Bradbury to Ben Benjamin, n.d. [Dec. 1960], copy in personal papers.

20. Bradbury to Congdon, Apr. 4, 1960, Butler.

21. Bradbury's most detailed account of his encounter with Mr. Electrico and the Dill Brothers Show is in "Mr. Electrico," *Guideposts Magazine* (1991), rpt. *Wonder: The Children's Magazine for Grown-Ups,* 8 (Spring 1994): 8-9.

22. Congdon's three-page typed review of the second submission is dated Aug. 24, 1960. He returned the first two submissions so that Bradbury could make revisions with a cover letter dated June 6, 1961.

23. Compared texts from first draft discards (Albright Collection) and *SW* (New York: Bantam, 1963), 168-69, reset without variation from the first edition (1962).

24. Bradbury to Gottlieb, Nov. 28, 1961, copy, personal papers. The subsequent delays in submission and scheduled release are discussed in Gottlieb to Bradbury, Nov. 30, 1961, Jan. 3, Feb. 8, 28, 1962, personal papers; Congdon to Bradbury, Feb. 6, 1962, personal papers; and Bradbury to Gottlieb (copies), Feb. 17, Mar. 6, 1962. Further details of the final revision process are annotated on the box containing the final submission.

25. Editor-author discussions about postsubmission revisions, design issues, and promotion of the novel are found in Gottlieb to Bradbury, Mar. 8, 23, Apr. 24, May 14, June 12, July 5, 13, 1962, personal papers; Bradbury to Gottlieb (copy), Apr. 21, 1962, personal papers.

26. Gilbert Highet to Bradbury, June 13, 1962, personal papers; *Life* (Graves) to Congdon, Feb. 9, 1961, Butler.

27. Responses to the second set of excerpts include Congdon (by Rina Shulman) to Bradbury (re: *Good Housekeeping*), Nov. 23, 1960, personal papers; *Harper's* (Joyce Bermel) to Congdon, Oct. 19, 1961, Butler; *Saturday Evening Post* (Stuart Rose) to Congdon, Apr. 16, July 9, 1962, Butler; and *Life* (Ralph Graves) to Bradbury, Sept. 25, 1962, personal papers. For Simon and Schuster's advertising campaign for Heller's novel, see Jonathan Eller, "Catching a Market: The Publishing History of *Catch-22,*" *Prospects* 17 (1992).

28. For correspondence regarding promotion and advertising, see Bradbury to Gottlieb (copy), July 16, 1962, personal papers; Gottlieb to Bradbury, July 20, Aug. 21, Sept. 11, 17, 1962, personal papers; and Congdon to Bradbury, Sept. 11, 1962, personal papers.

29. Orville Prescott, "Books of the Times," *New York Times,* Sept. 19, 1962, 37. Prescott mistakenly assumed that Bradbury had written Dinelli's "Merry-Go-Round" teleplay, which predisposed him to think of the novel in terms of that uneven production. Bradbury sent Prescott a tactful correction and a copy of *The Martian Chronicles.* See Prescott to Bradbury, Sept. 26, 1962, personal papers.

30. Beaumont to Bradbury, Oct. 3, 1962, personal papers; Nolan to Bradbury, July 6, 1962, personal papers.

31. H. H. Holmes [Anthony Boucher], review of *SW, New York Herald Tribune Books,* Sept. 16, 1962, 3; Baldwin to Bradbury, Oct. 30, 1962, personal papers.

32. An untitled review in the "Briefly Noted" section of "Books," *The New Yorker,* Oct. 27, 1962, 216.

33. The details of the negotiation are contained in Gottlieb to Bradbury, Sept. 11, 1962; and Congdon to Bradbury, Sept. 11, 1962.

34. The plagiarized adaptation of *Fahrenheit* is discussed in Bradbury to Congdon, Oct. 14, 1957, May 30, June 25, July 18, 1959 (Butler). Gottlieb's letter of transmittal for the unlocated Finney letter is dated Oct. 30, 1962 (personal papers). For Bradbury's detailed response summarizing how the *Fahrenheit*-CBS case helped define the guidelines for film and television adaptations of literature, see Bradbury to Gottlieb (copy), Oct. 31, 1962, personal papers.

35. Bloch to Bradbury, n.d. [Spring/Summer 1947], personal papers. The letters concerning the long-delayed *Dr. Lao* anthology are Saul David to Bradbury, Mar. 27, June 8, 1953, June 29, Sept. 1, 28, 1954, Dec. 13, 1955, Jan. 17, 1956, personal papers. David was clearly not aware that Bradbury's parallel work on "The Dark Carnival" screenplay was keeping him from reading *Dr. Lao*. Bradbury's criticisms of *Dr. Lao* in the anthology introduction are discussed in David to Bradbury, Jan. 17, Feb. 9, 1956, personal papers.

36. Finney's letter to Simon and Schuster has not been located, but his frustration with Bradbury's success may have originated with the lukewarm introduction and Bantam's cover design for the 1956 anthology, which fails to link Finney's name to the title story at all.

37. Bradbury to Gottlieb (copy), Oct. 31, 1962.

38. Harold Bloom writes: "Personality, in our sense, is a Shakespearean invention, and it is not only Shakespeare's greatest originality but also the authentic cause of his perpetual pervasiveness. Insofar as we ourselves value, and deplore, our own personalities, we are the heirs of Falstaff and of Hamlet, and all the other persons who throng Shakespeare's theater of what might be called the colors of the spirit." Harold Bloom, *Shakespeare: The Invention of the Human* (New York: Riverhead, 1998), 4. Bloom also asserts of Shakespeare's characters that they were the first in literature who overhear themselves speaking, interpret what they have said, and so garner the power to change. These dialogic aspects of character are exhibited prominently by Charles Halloway in the book's central interpretive chapters, which, incidentally, Bradbury claims are his favorite chapters.

39. The three-way negotiations between Bradbury-Congdon, the London-based A. D. Peters Agency, and Rupert Hart-Davis appear in Hart-Davis to Bradbury, Apr. 24, May 22, June 5, 1962, personal papers; Bradbury to Hart-Davis, May 27, 1962, copy, personal papers; Margaret Stephens (of Peters) to Congdon, Apr. 25, Sept. 7, 1962, Butler; A. D. Peters to Congdon, May 25, June 20, 1962, Butler; Congdon to Stephens, May 9, June 19, 1962, copies, personal papers; and Congdon to Bradbury, May 4, 1962, personal papers.

40. Bradbury to Hart-Davis, May 27, 1962.

41. A last-minute misunderstanding over the advance delayed the contract signing until September 1962. Both Peters and Hart-Davis felt that Bradbury's May 27 assertion that promotion meant more than money upfront superseded Congdon's request for the advance increase to £500. Bradbury and Congdon pursued the higher amount as a pledge of better promotion. Since Margaret Stephens of Peters had already negotiated a paperback deal on the novel with Corgi for Hart-Davis, the publisher agreed to increase the advance. Congdon to Stephens (copies), Aug. 17, 23, 1962, Butler; Stephens to Congdon (copy), Aug. 21, 1962, personal papers; Congdon to Bradbury, Aug. 22, 1962, personal papers; Bradbury to Congdon (copy), Aug. 26, 1962, personal papers.

42. The British *Argosy* publication negotiations are recorded in Fleetway Publications (Peggy Sutherland) to Bradbury, Mar. 16, 1962; (Joan Stevenson), May 2, 14, 1962, personal papers.

43. Robert Taubman, review of *SW, New Statesman*, Mar. 1, 1963, 312; London *Times Literary Supplement*, Mar. 15, 1963, 189.

44. Harold Prince to Don Congdon, May 25, June 19, 1962, Butler. Copies also went to West Coast studios, including MGM. Milton Beecher to Bradbury, Sept. 17, 1962, personal papers. For an extensive discussion of the film and the evolution of the successive Bradbury screenplays, see "Ray Bradbury's Something Wicked This Way Comes," in *Cinefantastique* (June-July 1983): 28-49.

45. King, *Danse Macabre*, 324-38. King claims that his first experience with real horror came when he heard a radio broadcast of Bradbury's "Mars Is Heaven!" ("The Third Expedition," *MC*) in 1951. Although he now finds Bradbury's style, so attractive to him as an adolescent because of its rhetorical excesses, to be a bit oversweet, he still finds *SW* to be a powerful book of childhood remembered in myth. Interestingly, King tries to understand this myth in terms of a thematics of Apollonian norm and Dionysian invasion. On a personal level, Bradbury has indicated to King that the book was an unconscious tribute to his father, who died in 1957. In terms of the life of fiction we are here investigating, we can only repeat Bradbury's own words in that same letter to King: "[In *SW*] I said all and everything, just about, that I would ever want to say about my younger self and how I felt about that terrifying thing: Life, and that other terror: Death, and the exhilaration of both." King, *Danse Macabre*, 327.

46. Mikhail Bakhtin, "Forms of Time and Chronotope in the Novel," in *Dialogic Imagination,* 162-63. Our analysis acknowledges that *SW* is structured by fathers, living and dead, literary and real, in all of its versions. Bradbury makes Shakespeare the center of his interpretive clock in chapter 37, and the title of the book comes from *Macbeth.* For many romantic thinkers, and certainly for Bradbury too, Shakespeare was the greatest of artists because he overcame the limitations of classical aesthetics and embraced the grotesque realism of carnival as a necessary part of life. For Bradbury, Shakespeare embodies the totality of life, culture both high and low.

47. King, *Danse Macabre,* 329.

48. See ibid., 330-31.

49. *SW,* chap. 18, 52.

50. Ibid., chap. 12, 38.

51. Todorov, *The Fantastic,* 160.

52. Deleuze and Guattari, *Anti-Oedipus,* 298. In a programmatic sense, Deleuze and Guattari are carrying out a carnivalization of Freud's theories and their dogmatic seriousness. They even use one of Bradbury's story, "The Nursery" (*IM*), in arguing that some forms of fantasy are nonfamilial and that psychoanalysis has failed utterly to take them into account. Ibid., 47.

53. Bakhtin, *Dialogic Imagination,* 161-612.

54. *SW,* 54, 55.

55. Ibid., 14.

56. Ibid., 20-21.

57. Ibid., throughout chap. 15, 89.

58. Ibid., chap. 51. Compared texts from first draft discards and SW, 62.

59. Bakhtin, *Rabelais,* 316.

60. *SW,* chap. 35 and throughout

61. Ibid., 156.

62. Michel Foucault, *Language, Counter-Memory, Practice,* ed. and trans. Donald F. Bouchard and Sherry Simon (Ithaca, N.Y.: Cornell Univ. Press, 1977), 161. The following discussion of carnivalized history is based on that of Foucault.

63. *SW,* 147-48.

64. Foucault, *Language, Counter-Memory, Practice,* 149.

65. Ibid., 147.

66. *SW,* chap. 24, 80.

67. Ibid., 158-59.

68. Ibid., 127.

69. See introduction, note 57, above.

70. *SW,* 156.

71. Bakhtin, *Rabelais,* 91; *SW,* 212.

72. *SW,* 192.

73. Nietzsche, "On Reading and Writing," pt. 1 of *Thus Spake Zarathustra,* in *Portable Nietzsche,* 153.

Morgan Harlow (essay date 2005)

SOURCE: Harlow, Morgan. "Martian Legacy: Ray Bradbury's *The Martian Chronicles.*" *War, Literature and the Arts* 17, nos. 1-2 (2005): 311-14.

[*In the following essay, Harlow finds* The Martian Chronicles *still relevant over fifty years after its initial publication.*]

Beyond providing pure enjoyment for space freaks and gadget geeks, one hallmark of the best science fiction is that it offers serious examination of the cultural and psychological landscapes and ethical questions raised by our changing times. In **The Martian Chronicles,** written in the late 1940s, published in 1950, Ray Bradbury reminds us that the world will become what we make of it, and each step in re-imagining ourselves brings us steadily closer to the future.

More than prediction, however, Bradbury claims that he is writing to "prevent the future," by pointing out the failings of society. To imagine an encounter with Martians is to see ourselves anew, an experience to be both hoped for and feared as it brings the knowledge that we, too, are the "other." This is the central idea of **The Martian Chronicles,** a meditation of self and other in the tradition of Walt Whitman's *Song of Myself,* where the encounter with the other becomes a means to knowing the self, an age-old theme basic to human nature and implicit in the experience of all art and literature.

While Whitman sought to unify and direct a nation divided by the politics of civil war, Bradbury, in the aftermath of WWII and the atomic bombings of Japan, sought to redirect the course of technology and prevent the human race from self-annihilation. Both Bradbury and Whitman concentrate not on the future but on the now, inviting us to come along with them, Whitman for a walk across America, Bradbury to Mars, to see the people as they are, for what they are—individuals with emotions, desires, hopes and fears.

Of his first published story, **"The Lake,"** Bradbury has said, "It was some sort of hybrid, something verging on the new." *The Martian Chronicles* may be seen as such a hybrid, one which resulted from the creative merging of a variety of literary techniques, steeped in the traditions of naturalism, romanticism and realism and suffused with a collage of allusions ranging from those which have been borrowed from and quoted outright—Lord Byron, Edgar Allan Poe, Sara Teasdale—to those which may or may not have been consciously assimilated into the text.

Bradbury set about his work in writing *The Martian Chronicles* with the cool critical eye of the naturalistic novelist, providing the laboratory conditions Emile Zola, in *Le roman experimental,* has set forth as necessary in order to observe the forces which work upon humans. The colonization of Mars, like the colonization of the Americas by Europeans, is characterized by greed and ignorance, fear of the natives, exploitation of the new world, and acts of genocide. This parallel is clearly drawn in the *Chronicles* episode, **"And the Moon Be Still as Bright,"** in which the Fourth Expedition to Mars arrives to discover that the Martian race has been killed off by a chicken pox virus brought to the red planet by a previous expedition, thus echoing the deadly smallpox epidemic which devastated Native American populations after the Europeans arrived on the scene. Spender, a member of the Fourth Expedition, sympathizes with the spirit of the Martians and seeks to avenge the death of the Martian race by raging against the earth crew in a manner bearing striking resemblance to the 1990's Unabomber case, in protest of the technology and greed that brought them to Mars. Spender invokes the poetry of romanticism by reciting Byron's "So We'll Go No More A-Roving," a poem, he says, that "might have been written by the last Martian poet." The Consul's assumption of the identity of William Blackstone, the white man who went to live with the Indians, in Malcolm Lowry's *Under the Volcano* comes to mind here, as does the romantic notion of spiritual vision gotten through an affinity, accidentally stumbled upon, for the land and the collective spirit of the inhabitants who lived there before. As with the Consul's drinking, Mars becomes a way of seeing, of being, a state of mind, a vision, an addiction.

The romantic notion of the power of the imagination to reinvent ourselves, to make the world over and to place ourselves in a history, in time, in the cosmos, is explored by Bradbury with the landing of Earth people on the Martian world. At first the core of the self for the Earth people, like the purple triangle that forms the core of Mrs. Ramsay in Virginia Woolf's *To the Lighthouse,* can be defined as an entity with a definite shape and color: the third planet from the sun, Earth. And yet the self has a way of spreading outward, and the core is, essentially, selfless. Mrs. Ramsay's self extends limitlessly through space, through time, to include the lives of other people, the lighthouse, the rooks gathering at twilight; beyond her own death to become the house, the sky, the neglected garden, the cleaning woman, the future of the cleaning woman's son, and so on, ad infinitum. In the same way, the people from Earth become part of the timeless haunted landscape of the Martian world and the dead yet still dreaming cities of the ancient Martian race. The knowledge of this slowly creeps into the consciousness, as when the captain of the Fourth Expedition wonders: were the Martians ancestors of humans ten thousand years removed? By the time the great intellectual leap is made, the flash of brilliance, Emerson's "transparent eye-ball," Borges's "The Aleph," the realization that *we* are the Martians, it has, more than likely, already become an accepted, matter of course fact of life.

And so one of Bradbury's transplanted Earth people looks back at Earth one day, trying to imagine the war he has heard about by radio and seeing nothing but a green light:

> "It's like when I was a boy," said Father Peregrine. "We heard about wars in China. But we never believed them. It was too far away. And there were too many people dying. It was impossible. Even when we saw the motion pictures we didn't believe it. Well, that's how it is now. Earth is China. It's so far away it's unbelievable. It's not here. You can't touch it. You can't even see it. All you see is a green light. Two billion people living on that light? Unbelievable! War? We don't hear the explosions."

Like the green light at the end of Daisy's dock in F. Scott Fitzgerald's *The Great Gatsby,* the green light of Earth is all that is left of a world that has been lost. We are woken up out of the dream. There is realism.

Even Bradbury can't avoid realism, that ugly but inevitable footnote to our existence. Realism is the spoiler of dreams, wrecker of homes, a death that extinguishes even desire. It brings with it the knowledge that ideas are not enough so we must act, it reduces music, however lovely, to the status of noise. Realism is the ultimate downer, as in songwriter Jimmy Webb's 1960's pop ballad, "MacArthur Park": "someone left the cake out in the rain . . . and we'll never have that recipe again," a feeling James Salter's character, Nedra, in the novel, *Light Years,* knows all too well.

In *The Martian Chronicles,* realism is the littering of the Martian landscape, the shattering of the beautiful crystal cities of the Martians with a single blast of gunshot, the 1940's-era plain-old-Americans transplanted to Mars, the humanity of the Martians, and the tragic awareness that mankind doesn't learn from its mistakes, that its failings loom large.

A decade after the publication of *The Martian Chronicles,* the war in Vietnam found Americans involved in the same pattern of genocidal colonization that had been inflicted on countless cultures over the course of history, a pattern Bradbury had warned against with realistic and what now seems tragically prophetic vision.

The Martian Chronicles represents an original and serious work of artistic invention and vision, firmly grounded in literary tradition. It remains a force to be reckoned with, a pivotal work which has influenced the course of literature and the thinking of scientists and of ordinary citizens who face the task—with nothing less than the biological imperative of an entire species at stake, and with it, all life as we know it—of advancing human nature and values into an age in which atomic warfare and space travel have become part of the human experience. The challenge of Mars, according to Bradbury, is to the mind.

Works Cited

Bradbury, Ray. *The Martian Chronicles.* New York: Doubleday, 1950.

Bradbury, Ray. "Run Fast, Stand Still . . ." (1986). In *Zen in the Art of Writing, Essays on Creativity.* Capra Press, 1990.

Bradbury, Ray, Arthur C. Clarke, Bruce Murray, Carl Sagan, and Walter Sullivan. *Mars and the Mind of Man,* New York: Harper & Row, 1973.

"*Playboy* Interview: Ray Bradbury," *Playboy,* 43.5, 1996.

Ray Bradbury and Ben P. Indick (interview date 21 August 2006)

SOURCE: Bradbury, Ray, and Ben P. Indick. "An Author of Many Ages." *Publishers Weekly* 253, no. 33 (21 August 2006): 48.

[*In the following interview, Bradbury recalls the writings of Robert Heinlein and Edgar Rice Burroughs as childhood influences.*]

[*Indick:*] *First, is it okay to mention your age?*

[Bradbury:] Sure, what the hell. I'm just 12 years old.

So you're a 12-year-old octogenarian. Are you keeping busy?

I have three books coming out this fall. Besides *Farewell Summer,* I have *Somewhere a Band Is Playing,* a fantasy, and *Leviathan 99,* a kind of *Moby-Dick* in outer space.

Why decades later did you write a sequel to **Dandelion Wine**?

Farewell Summer was originally part of the book I submitted to Doubleday 55 years ago. They said it was too long and cut it right in half. The first half they called *Dandelion Wine.* The second half was renamed *Wild Summer.* It just took me a little while to get it in shape under the title *Farewell Summer.*

Do you remember the sale of your very first story?

When I was 19 years old, I showed a story I had written to my teacher and friend, Robert Heinlein. I can't remember the name of it, or the name of the magazine. There was no pay, but I got free copies of the magazine. I ran around giving them to everybody. I was selling newspapers on a street corner in Los Angeles and even gave away copies to my customers. I was on that street for four years, every afternoon. I made $10 a week on that corner, and it gave me time to write my stories and go to the library.

Was there any one writer who especially influenced you?

Edgar Rice Burroughs. I read all the Tarzan books, and I followed the Tarzan cartoon strip in the Sunday newspapers. I was inspired to write a sequel to some of Burroughs's Martian books.

Was it ever published?

God, no, I was 12 years old!

Of course, you later wrote your **Martian Chronicles.**

Yes, that book reflects the Burroughs influence.

Did you think you would still be writing at 86?

When you're young and someone tells you that you're going to be 50 years old some day, that sounds old. Then all of a sudden you're 86. It's incredible.

What are you going to do when you're 100 years old?

Wait till I get there.

FURTHER READING

Biography

Bradbury, Ray. "Hunter of Metaphors." In *The Writing Life: Writers on How They Think and Work,* edited by Marie Arana, pp. 171-77. New York: PublicAffairs, 2003.

Autobiographical essay.

Criticism

Donaldson, Wendy C. "Heroism Defined and Mentors Divided: Ray Bradbury's *Fahrenheit 451.*" In *The Image of the Hero in Literature, Media, and Society,* edited

by Steven Kaplan, pp. 482-86. Pueblo, Colo.: Colorado State University, 2004.

Analysis of heroism and heroic characters in *Fahrenheit 451.*

McGiveron, Rafeeq O. "'Do You Know the Legend of Hercules and Antaeus?' The Wilderness in Ray Bradbury's *Fahrenheit 451.*" *Extrapolation* 38, no. 2 (summer 1997): 102-09.

Asserts that Bradbury's treatment of the natural world has been neglected in analysis of his fiction.

Tibbetts, John C. "The Illustrating Man." *Creative Screenwriting* 6, no. 1 (January-February 1999): 45-54.

Provides a consideration of Bradbury's screenplays.

Additional coverage of Bradbury's life and career is contained in the following sources published by Thomson Gale: *American Writers Supplement,* **Vol. 4;** *Authors and Artists for Young Adults,* **Vol. 15;** *Authors in the News,* **Vols. 1, 2;** *Beacham's Encyclopedia of Popular Fiction: Biography & Resources,* **Vol. 1;** *Beacham's Guide to Literature for Young Adults,* **Vols. 4, 5, 11;** *Concise Dictionary of American Literary Biography,* **1968-1988;** *Contemporary Authors,* **Vols. 1-4R;** *Contemporary Authors New Revision Series,* **Vols. 2, 30, 75, 125;** *Contemporary Literary Criticism,* **Vols. 1, 3, 10, 15, 42, 98;** *Contemporary Novelists,* **Eds. 1, 2, 3, 4, 5, 6, 7;** *Contemporary Popular Writers;* *Dictionary of Literary Biography,* **Vols. 2, 8;** *DISCovering Authors; DISCovering Authors: British; DISCovering Authors: Canadian; DISCovering Authors Modules: Most-studied Authors, Novelists,* **and** *Popular Fiction and Genre Authors; DISCovering Authors 3.0; Exploring Novels; Exploring Short Stories;* *Literary Movements for Students,* **Vol. 2;** *Literature and Its Times,* **Vols. 3, 5;** *Literature and Its Times Supplement,* **Eds. 1:2;** *Literature Resource Center; Major 20th-Century Writers,* **Eds. 1, 2;** *Major 21st-Century Writers,* **(eBook) 2005;** *Modern American Literature,* **Ed. 5;** *Novels for Students,* **Vols. 1, 22;** *Reference Guide to American Literature,* **Ed. 4;** *Reference Guide to Short Fiction,* **Ed. 2;** *Science Fiction Writers,* **Eds. 1, 2;** *Short Stories for Students,* **Vols. 1, 20;** *Short Story Criticism,* **Vols. 29, 53;** *Something About the Author,* **Vols. 11, 64, 123;** *St. James Guide to Horror, Ghost & Gothic Writers; St. James Guide to Science Fiction Writers,* **Ed. 4;** *St. James Guide to Young Adult Writers; Supernatural Fiction Writers,* **Vols. 1, 2;** *Twayne's United States Authors; World Literature Criticism,* **Vol. 1.**

China Miéville
1972-

English novelist, short story writer, and nonfiction writer.

The following entry presents an overview of Miéville's career through 2006.

INTRODUCTION

Miéville caught the attention of critics from the publication of his first novel, and by his third book was established as one of the most important speculative fiction writers currently at work. To date he has completed an award-winning trilogy (called the New Crobuzon series), a standalone novel titled *King Rat* (1998), a novella and collection of short stories, a nonfiction Marxist treatise, and a young-adult novel.

BIOGRAPHICAL INFORMATION

Miéville was born and raised in London, England. "China" is in fact his given name, not a pseudonym, chosen when his parents consulted a dictionary for a beautiful word with which to name their son. Miéville's studies have been extensive, including English and anthropology at Cambridge University, international relations at the London School of Economics, and a year abroad at Harvard University. He developed an interest in socialism which persists to the present and is evident in his writing, and completed a doctoral degree with a dissertation on Marxism and international law. Amid these efforts, he also found time to spend a year in Egypt teaching English. Miéville is the recipient of numerous awards including the Arthur C. Clarke Award (2001 and 2004) and the British Fantasy Award (2001). Miéville lives in London.

MAJOR WORKS

Miéville eschews traditional fantasy in favor of "weird fiction." His first novel, *King Rat,* concerns a man who learns he is genetically half-human and half-rat. When the man he believed to be his father dies mysteriously, his true father, the King Rat, appears and informs him that he is heir to the kingdom of rats, if he will only help to defeat the Pied Piper once and for all. *Perdido Street Station* (2001), Miéville's second novel, introduces the world of New Crobuzon, a place rife with monsters, mutants, and magical happenings but also filled with very human challenges and lessons for its characters and for readers. The protagonist, Isaac, is a scientist called upon to heal a garuda whose wings have been amputated as punishment for a crime Isaac does not understand until later. In *The Scar* (2002), ostracized linguist Bellis Coldwine attempts to escape New Crobuzon, only to be captured by pirates and pressed into service as their librarian and interpreter. *Iron Council* (2004), the final title in the New Crobuzon trilogy, relates the struggles of a slave-labor force building a desert railroad system and plotting to overthrow its corrupt government. In each of these works, which Miéville refers to as his "anti-trilogy," the depictions are detailed and encompassing, drawing readers into a uniquely populated, fully articulated parallel world. Similar attention to detail appears in the stories collected in *Looking for Jake* (2005), including the novella *The Tain,* in which the reflections created in mirrors are set free and take revenge on their human captors. In his first young-adult novel, *Un Lun Dun* (2007), Miéville presents "Un-London," another dystopia beset by strange and potentially fatal threats.

CRITICAL RECEPTION

Many reviewers have expressed awe at Miéville's intellectual depth, authorial intensity, and devotion to his craft. Recurring themes within critical evaluations of his work concern Miéville's disdain of traditional fantasy writing and his adherence to socialist principles, which are woven throughout much of his writing. Many commentators have asserted that Miéville's youth is remarkable when considered in the context of his scholarship and literary aptitude, making him a wunderkind who has already achieved a level of esteem more often reserved for authors with long-established careers.

PRINCIPAL WORKS

King Rat (novel) 1998
*Perdido Street Station (novel) 2001
*The Scar (novel) 2002
The Tain (novella) 2002

*These works comprise the New Crobuzon trilogy.

†This collection includes the novella *The Tain*.

CRITICISM

Charles De Lint (review date February 1999)

SOURCE: De Lint, Charles. Review of *King Rat*, by China Miéville. *Magazine of Fantasy and Science Fiction* 96, no. 2 (February 1999): 30.

[*Below, De Lint offers early praise for Miéville in a review of his first novel,* King Rat.]

Anyone familiar with the tropes of fantasy and fairy tales already knows the story: the young man who, all unbeknownst to him, is of royal lineage, something he only finds out when either mysterious people suddenly show up, trying to kill him, or he leaves his known life (of his own will or not) to go adventuring, often both. There's usually an elder figure involved from whom he learns of his lineage, responsibilities, special powers (if he has such), and the like.

In a general sense, that's the basic plot of *King Rat*. Saul Garamond returns to London from a vacation to find his father dead. He's arrested for the murder and rescued from jail by a mysterious figure, and then the fun begins.

You see, the royal blood Saul carries is rat blood. Unlike umpteen other fantasies, *King Rat* takes us out of the high courts of fairy tale, away from the romanticized city streets of many current fantasies, down into the sewers with the rats. And not cute, cuddly Muppet rats, either. No, these rats stink, eat garbage, urinate to mark their territory—in short, do all the things rats do. And so do humans with rat blood such as Saul realizes he is.

Mieville's perspective is, if you'll excuse the apparent paradox of this comment, such a refreshing change from the usual take on fantasy and otherworldly beings.

Of course, that's not all *King Rat* has going for it. Mieville explores the parts of London most of us won't see. He writes knowledgeably about the rooftops and crowded market streets, sewers and housing estates, the alternative club scene, jungle music, bass and drum. And his characters are fabulous, even the bit players such as Saul's friends from his previous life and those he meets in his new: Anansi the King of Spiders, Loplow the King of Birds, and the like. But he really shines with Saul, especially depicting the slow metamorphosis from a normal human disgusted by the idea of living in a sewer and eating garbage to one relishing it.

This is a riveting, brilliant novel. The language sings, the concepts are original and engrossing, and the villainy . . .

<Spoiler alert.>

Allow me, for once, to break tradition with this column and give away a few elements that spoil surprises, but show just how fresh Mieville's take on fantasy is. His antagonist is a flute-player named Peter, unassuming in appearance, mad as a hatter in temperament. He also happens to be the original Pied Piper. I loved the King of the Rats' retelling of the classic story—how it would appear from a rat's point of view—and how Mieville updates it all into the present. The Piper can control any species with his flute, but only one at a time. He hates Saul because Saul has both human and rat blood and so he can't touch Saul with his music. Now imagine how delighted he is to discover the wonders of modern recording technology, the ability to overdub and sample.

It's wonderful touches such as this, the inspired mingling of old mythic matter with the contemporary world, that make *King Rat* such an utter delight.

China Miéville and Charles Shaar Murray (interview date 18 March 2000)

SOURCE: Miéville, China, and Charles Shaar Murray. "The Lord of the Earrings." *Independent (London)* (18 March 2000): 9.

[*In the following interview, conducted on the eve of publication of Miéville's second novel,* Perdido Street Station, *the author discusses his politics and genre.*]

The next time somebody tries to sell you a copy of *Socialist Worker,* give the vendor a closer look. If you happen to be in West London and he's a tall, muscular, crop-haired guy with an unfeasibly ample allocation of earrings, there's a strong possibility that it's China Mieville. His second novel, *Perdido Street Station* is about to blow a very large hole in the stodgy complacencies of one of our most popular, and most conservative, literary genres.

These days, the term "fantasy" tends to mean interminable faux-epic quest trilogies: one part Jive Tolkien, one part Conan The Barbarian, one part either Norse or Arthurian cliche. It's escapism for people who yearn for an age before electricity, plumbing and democracy. Mieville has a different, and far bigger, kettle of fish to fry.

His 1998 debut, *King Rat,* was a "hidden London" novel in the tradition of Iain Sinclair, Michael Moorcock and Christopher Fowler; but *Perdido Street Station* is a post-grunge Gormenghast with nary an elf or a runesword to be seen. In this crowded, clamorous urban fever dream, a plethora of species live chitinous cheek to feathered jowl, the squalid and the poetic become inseparable, and a sculptor and a scientist must resolve a nightmare within a nightmare.

"*Perdido Street Station* is my attempt to simultaneously say, 'Fuck you' to fantasy, and to say to readers, 'Please read some fantasy,'" says Mieville. "It's a way of saying, 'I know you think you don't like fantasy, but maybe you could give this a try'."

He adds that "So much modern genre fantasy is so trite . . . When you read Tolkien's theory of fantasy in *On Fairy Tales,* he has a systematic theory of 'consolatory fantasy': that consolation is the function of fantasy. That whole idea makes me want to puke, and it stinks up the whole genre.

"That's why *Perdido Street Station* is a fuck-you to fantasy, as defined by totally predictable plots, rampant generalisation and stereotypes. It's one of the only genres in which the whole function of having characters of different races is to pigeonhole them.

"If you have an elf," he explains, "odds-on they're going to be noble, mysterious and good with their hands. A dwarf is going to be unimaginative and probably trustworthy and a bit stolid. And orcs are going to be evil. It's not just a paean to feudalism, but to a feudalism that never was: happy feudalism, nice feudalism, feudalism lite."

Mieville owns up to being a fantasy writer, but he prefers the descriptions "weird fiction" or "fantastic literature". "I use the term 'fantastic literature' as a way of bracketing the genres of supernatural horror, epic fantasy, low fantasy and science fiction. The term I would prefer to reinvigorate is 'weird fiction'."

He believes that "there's a radical moment in all weird fiction, and that moment is the positing of the impossible as true. Whether you make that what the story's all about or you simply have it as a starting-point, that to me is a radical moment. The problem with most genre fantasy is that it takes this radical moment of alienation and otherness and renders it as comfort food, like the seabirds which chew up food and regurgitate it into their babies' mouths when the babies can't really take the raw thing. It's pap, in the literal sense."

He's aware that "when you say 'fantasy', people think of Tolkien and his innumerable heirs". That's unfortunate, Mieville argues, as it masks the alternative tradition of weird fiction: authors such as "William Hope Hodgeson, Robert Chambers, Clark Ashton Smith, H P Lovecraft, and certainly the *Weird Tales* tradition with Fritz Leiber, and then Mervyn Peake, and up to date with people like M John Harrison.

"Essentially I'm a fantasy writer, though in a different tradition that stresses the macabre, the surreal, the alienating, the decadent, the lush, the grotesque—a tradition of grotesquerie, cruelty, sadness and alienation. The surrealist aesthetic is an alienating aesthetic, the opposite of Tolkien's consolatory, comforting aesthetic. Part of that means not shying away when the dynamic of the aesthetic is quite cruel. It doesn't dissolve into sadism. In real life I'm quite sentimental, so I overcompensate in my fiction. I have to be quite ruthless about sentimentality. Given the history of fantasy, you have to purge yourself of it."

Yet Mieville is a committed Marxist. So what kind of relationship does a dialectical materialist have with high fantasy? "Through the heritage of the surrealists and of weird fiction, 'the fantastic' has the potential to be a truly extraordinary, radical genre. The fact that it often isn't is frustrating and a shame, but that's not the genre's fault. My relationship with weird fiction stems from the fact that it's what I grew up on. I love it, and it's what I gravitate to when I'm in a bookshop.

"It's the opposite of cosy, but genre fantasy is by far the worst offender. Science fiction has far more serious, radical, interesting, questioning writing in it. Horror, although it's often denigrated, has a very good tradition of serious writing. Almost by definition, what it's about is rendering the everyday unsafe and unsettling. More than SF and more than horror, the fantasy field is awash with crap.

"It's not the case that as a socialist I'm going to write a particular book and get across a particular message. That's not my job . . . I want to tell weird, macabre stories involving strange species and I want to have fun inventing species and cities that couldn't possibly exist. I want to create the impossible as an aesthetic project. I'm a political writer of weird fiction; ergo I'm a writer of political weird fiction.

Yet his fiction can never serve as a vehicle for politics. "There's always going to be politics in there, but if I want to make the argument for socialism, I'm not going to do it in a fantasy novel. That would be a ridiculous medium for it. The relationship is inextricable—everything I ever write is informed by my politics—but not in a very immediate sense.

"Iain Banks said once that he'd love to write an explicitly political novel but whenever he tries it reads like the most awful Stalinist agitprop. That's basically how I feel. I put politics in my books, but that's not what they're for.

"The most important political things I can do I will do: things like leafleting, making political arguments, selling *Socialist Worker.* I think it would be foolish to suggest that because a story is left-wing, it's going to be better. One of my favourite writers is M R James, who was a High-Church Tory and wrote the best and most chilling ghost stories ever. I'm not going to say that those stories would have been improved if he'd been a socialist, because you don't judge writers as writers on their politics. Jeffrey Archer is scum. He is also a shit writer. Those are two separate things. Louis-Ferdinand Celine was scum, but a superb writer."

As for his own imaginative landscape in **Perdido Street Station,** he intends to stay there for a while. "I like this universe, and I've done a lot of work on it. The next book I'm writing is also set in it, but it is not a sequel. It is not number two in a trilogy: I promise.

"One of my biggest bugbears is fate. The trope I loathe most in genre fantasy is fate, prophecy and 'lo-it-is-written'—because, in narrative terms, what's interesting is the innate, enabling power of the individual and social forces. That's what narrative fucking is, you know what I mean?"

Finally, is "China Mieville" his real name? And if so, why? "Because my parents were hippies, and they looked through the dictionary for 'a beautiful word'. Apparently, they nearly settled on 'Banyan' but thankfully flicked forward a few pages—and also because it's Cockney rhyming slang for 'mate'." China Mieville a biography: "I was born in Norwich in 1972, but left sharpish and grew up in north-west London, in Willesden. Moved to Notting Hill about 10 years ago. I have no memory of anywhere other than London. I did anthropology at Cambridge: I started off doing English but changed after a term. Then I did a Masters in International Relations at LSE, followed by a year's scholarship at Harvard, the most boring year of my life. It was through being at university that I got interested in serious socialism, as opposed to flaky socialism, and started reading Marx, which had a huge effect on me. I'm doing this PhD in critical theory of international law, the philosophy of jurisprudence." China Mieville's

first novel was **King Rat** (1998); **Perdido Street Station** appears next week from Macmillan. It just topped the Amazon list of "future bestsellers".

Michael Moorcock (review date 6 May 2000)

SOURCE: Moorcock, Michael. "City of Dreadful Light." *Spectator* 284, no. 8961 (6 May 2000): 33-4.

[*In the following review, fellow fantasist Moorcock relates the literary acrobatics Miéville achieves in* Perdido Street Station.]

Imaginative fiction which refused to rationalise its flights of fantasy as dreams, visions or scientific speculation used to be called simply 'fantasy'. The description suited books as varied as Grant Allen's *The British Barbarians,* Wells's *The Wonderful Visit,* Garnett's *Lady into Fox,* Woolf's *Orlando,* White's *Mistress Masham's Repose,* Peake's *Titus Groan,* Richardson's *Exploits of Engelbrecht,* Carter's *The Magic Toyshop,* Amis's *The Alteration,* Harrison's *In Viriconium,* Ackroyd's *Hawksmoor* or Rushdie's *Satanic Verses.*

Today Tolkien-cloned 'Fantasy' has become a bookshop category like 'Mysteries' or 'Romance'. We know it has something to do with talking animals, elves, heroic quests or, if we're lucky, comical wizards but we have a problem distinguishing the individual, the literary, from the popular generic.

We once emphatically described J. G. Ballard as *speculative* fiction rather than science fiction because we needed to distinguish his work from a public perception, in spite of Kingsley Amis's puritan prescriptions, that SF was all spaceships, purple people eaters and pulp plot lines, an impression, of course, which television and movies have confirmed a millionfold since *New Maps of Hell* was published in 1960.

It's currently fashionable to call an unrationalised fantasy a parallel- or alternate-world story, terms borrowed from SF. Such stories began as ideas rather than backgrounds. The best known modern example is probably Philip K. Dick's *The Man in the High Castle* (1962), which proposed a present in which the Allies lost the second world war. Saki did it best, for my taste, in *When William Came* (1914), written before his death in the trenches, about Germany winning the first world war and a British ruling class coming to terms with its conquerors. In the hands of desperate professional writers this device quickly becomes an easy way of tarting up some shabby old plots. The exotic lost land adventure, which began with Defoe, if not with *Palmerin of England,* suffers badly from actual exploration. Mapped, logged and claimed, the mysterious becomes merely untrue. *She* or *Tarzan of the Apes* can no longer exist in the Africa we now know. They can, however, plug on happily in a 'parallel' Africa, where the sun never set on the empire, some Ruritania, or even Dickensian London.

A more ambitious kind of fiction creating a mysterious city or world, such as *Gormenghast,* has considerable irony and is only a shade away from Faulkner's Yawknapatawpha in intention and sensibility. This fiction tends to use its backgrounds as part of its narrative structure. The best is M. J. Harrison's *Viriconium* sequence, which indulges a Walpolean taste for the exotic and the antique. It's a romantic, knowing, postmodern version of the Gothic in which strange, ruined cities are not merely given soul, but achieve sentience, even senility. An often overlooked example is Brecht's *Threepenny Novel,* which offers a marvellously distorted Edwardian London. More recently there's Steve Beard's *Digital Leatherette.* Beard was published beside Melville, Steve Aylett and Tim Etchells in last year's *Britpulp* anthology edited by Tony White. All borrow elements from popular fiction, have their own invented worlds, with their own architecture, own history and own bizarre inhabitants. Aylett's absurdist thrillers (*Slaughtermatic, The Inflatable Volunteer*) mostly happen in the city of Beerlight, while Etchells's sardonic fables are set in *Endland,* a world of infinite rundown housing estates, boozers and fast food restaurants.

Like Alan Moore's or Grant Morrison's popular graphic stories, this fiction shares a Shelleyan suspicion of church and state. While finishing China Mieville's impressive second novel, set in the baroque, brooding, gaslit industrial city of New Crobuzon, I realised that he had a lot in common with the 14th-century muralist who decorated our local Oxfordshire church with pictures of the poor and meek ascending to heaven while the authorities, including kings and bishops, went headfirst into the maws of demonic beasts.

Mieville's first novel, **King Rat,** published last year, was an extraordinarily vivid, tactile tale of underground London. Set in the here and now, with subtle hints of the supernatural, it showed the author's empathy for creatures you would normally hope to poison. *Perdido Street Station,* a massive and gorgeously detailed parallel-world fantasy, offers us a range of rather more exotic creatures, all of whom are wonderfully drawn and reveal a writer with a rare descriptive gift, an unusually observant eye for physical detail, for the sensuality and beauty of the ordinarily human as well as the thoroughly alien.

By chapter one Mieville has graphically convinced us of the mutual sexual passion of a plump human chemist and his sculptor beetle mistress. By chapter two we're

feeling the pain of a proud hawkperson from the distant desert who has committed some abominable flock-crime and has had his wings sawn off in punishment. His yearning, elegiac voice becomes one of the most successful narrative threads in the book. When Mieville avoids generic plotlines and stock characters and writes about individual alienation and love, about difficult relationships and complex architecture, the book comes most thoroughly to life and takes on tremendous tensions.

Perdido Street Station (the name of the rail hub where vast numbers of lines meet) has a wonderfully emblematic setting in its vast, murky, steam-driven Victorian city, teeming with races and species of bewildering variety, in which electricity doesn't exist, where magic works, where elementals are part of everyday life, where Hell is an actual place and corrupt politicians make deals with Satan. There are spectacularly gripping scenes with terrifying fabulous beasts which stop you from eating or sleeping while you read and give you nightmares when you stop. There's a monstrous threat, a noble victory. Yet Mieville's determination to deliver value for money, a great page-turner, leads him to add genre borrowings which set up a misleading expectation of the kind of plot you're going to get and make individuals start behaving out of character, forcing the author into rationalisations at odds with the creative, intellectual and imaginative substance of the book.

That aside, Mieville's catholic contemporary sensibility, delivering generous Victorian value and a well-placed moral point or two, makes **Perdido Street Station** utterly absorbing and you won't get a better deal, pound for pound, for your holiday reading.

Edward James (review date 1 September 2000)

SOURCE: James, Edward. "Living with Golems." *Times Literary Supplement* (1 September 2000): 11.

[*Below, James offers a positive review of* Perdido Street Station.]

At one point in China Miéville's amazing narrative, the scientist Isaac tears an advertisement from a wall and reads:

> *MR BOMBADREZIL'S UNIQUE* and *WONDERFUL FAIR,* guaranteed to astound and enthral the most *JADED PALATE. THE PALACE OF LOVE; THE HALL OF TERRORS; THE VORTEX;* and many other attractions for reasonable prices. Also come to see the extraordinary freak-show, the *CIRCUS OF WEIRD.* . . . Some attractions not suitable for the easily shocked, or those of a *NERVOUS DISPOSITION.*

Mr. Bombadrezil is clearly Miéville himself; this book [**Perdido Street Station**], his second novel, a unique and wonderful fair; and its setting, New Crobuzon, an extraordinary freak-show, a circus of weird.

The city of New Crobuzon, judging by the map, resonates closely with Miéville's own London. Its level of technology is, very roughly, Dickensian. At its heart lies the Station, an "enormous mongrel building . . . the coagulate of miles of railway line and years of architectural styles and violations". The city oozes and pulsates with life: not just human life, above the streets as well as in and below them. "Wyrman clawed their way above the city leaving trails of defecation and profanity . . . Golems thrown together by drunken students beat mindlessly through the sky on wings made of paper or leather or fruit-rind, falling apart as they flew."

Some of these races we learn more about—particularly the insect-human khepri, the frog-like vodyanoi and the flying garuda. The necessity for co-existence with other beings, however strange their ways and incomprehensible their goals may seem, is one of the themes of *Perdido Street Station.* Isaac Grimnebolin is interested in devising a unified theory which will link physics with thaumaturgy and all the other sciences. But a mutilated garuda from the deserts to the north of the city visits him, and deflects Isaac's researches in different directions, as well as leading him unwittingly to release a terrifying danger into the city. As we follow the efforts of Isaac, his khepri lover Lin, and others to control this threat, we travel further into the festering recesses of New Crobuzon, and become more familiar with the estranging ways of its inhabitants. The threat is removed; the pain of the mutilated garuda, with which the book begins, is eased.

This is an astonishing novel, guaranteed to astound and enthral the most jaded palate. It is exhilarating, sometimes very moving, occasionally shocking, always humane and thought-provoking. Its exuberant and unflagging inventiveness, as well as the strong narrative, keep up interest throughout, despite its length. Half a century after first publication, Mervyn Peake's *Titus Groan* trilogy still has a growing number of devotees; I would not be surprised if, over the years, *Perdido Street Station* won itself an equally loyal following.

Kim Newman (review date 3 June 2002)

SOURCE: Newman, Kim. "Cactus Men, Mosquito People and a Disdain for Heroic Quests." *Independent (London)* (3 June 2002): 10.

[*In the following review, Newman finds Miéville's third novel,* The Scar, *refreshingly different from standard fantasy literature.*]

Though *The Scar* is China Miéville's third novel, it seems like a second book. *King Rat,* his debut, was set in a contemporary London shot through with fantastical elements. *Perdido Street Station,* his second novel, moved into a world which seemed entirely different, though its teeming city of New Crobuzon is a growth of *King Rat*'s London into a fantasy setting.

The Scar returns to Bas-Lag, Mieville's fantastical alternate Earth. It voyages away from the cityscape of Perdido Street towards the eponymous feature: a rift, ostensibly left behind by alien or extra-dimensional conquerors, which boils with possibilities and potentialities.

Bellis Coldwine, a linguist forced into exile as a side-effect of the vast plot of *Perdido Street Station,* is aboard a ship sailing for the equivalent of early-colonial America or Australia when the vessel is seized by pirates. They incorporate it, and everyone aboard, into Armada—a great floating township. A huge engineering project is being worked, and one of Bellis's fellow travellers is needed to provide expertise. Everyone else is press-ganged and found work in Armada.

The story advances in great, mind-stretching gallops. Concepts which would fuel a lesser trilogy (like the harnessing of a submarine being of Moby-Dick proportions) are stepping-stones to still larger concerns. The point is not the overarching skeleton of story, but the crowded flesh of imagined lives and societies that cling to it.

We meet cactus-men and vampires, spies and scholars, fish demons and mosquito people, but there is besides the sense of wonder a feeling for tangled, moving complexities. They would seem irritants for the standard find-the-ruby-and-kill-the-dragon fantasy tome, but are the pulsing life of a real book.

This audacious approach sets Mieville's project apart from the vast majority of fantasies. The generic post-Tolkien fantasist sets out a purpose by drawing a map, then fills in the gaps: the pleasures on offer are the domestication of wildwoods, with every level of human or non-human society set in stone and rules laid down for the workings of magic and science.

Mieville's Bas-Lag doesn't work like that. At the heart of *Perdido Street Station* was a city that at once was and was not London; at the end of *The Scar,* narrative itself must fray. The central characters question the underlying structure of most fantasy—the heroic quest—and set forth the point of view of all who had to be duped or forced to go along with the great voyage. The novel has a hero and a villain, but they are deliberately vague, secondary characters.

Like Mieville's first two novels, *The Scar* is a feat of the imagination, a rich reclamation of the pleasures of every genre. It's also a caution against imagination, a sobering look at the chaos left in the wake of every mad visionary.

Fantasy tends to work by furnishing worlds to which readers wish to return, as to a nursery or a garden. Mieville's Bas-Lag is the world we already live in—where stories can never be easily finished—but looked at in a way that we have never seen before.

Nick Hasted (review date 28 July 2002)

SOURCE: Hasted, Nick. "A Life on the Ocean Wave with Pirates and Punks." *Independent on Sunday (London)* (28 July 2002): 15.

[*In the following review, Hasted praises Miéville's development of a new world in* The Scar.]

One test of a fantasy novel is whether the world its author creates is fully imagined and provides you with new sensations, beyond the limits of the "real". With his third book [*The Scar*], the follow-up to the award-winning *Perdido Street Station,* young Londoner Mieville continues to build a planet of engrossing wonders, powered by a narrative thrust of clockwork intricacy and battleship force.

Perhaps unsurprisingly for an author only a letter away from Melville, he leaves the dark, industrial splendours of his world's major power, New Crobuzon, for the open seas. Bellis Coldwine, fleeing Crobuzon, is hijacked by pirates and taken to Armada, a centuries-old, mongrel city of stolen boats and peoples, roughly stitched together and slowly, astonishingly floating across the ocean. On board, Bellis witnesses a gradually unfolded plan to fish a monstrous sea-beast from a hole in the ocean, to pull the city towards a cosmic rent in a dead stretch of sea.

The fiercely self-sufficient Bellis is an unsentimental pair of eyes through which to view Armada's voyage. Still, Mieville uses her journey to fill your mind with histories and views which, whether mentioned in a sentence or gruesomely experienced, suggest a bursting, layered universe: from the Malarial Queendom to the Ghosthead Empire, the half-submerged city of the cray-men to the Liveside ghetto of New Cromlech's zombie town, even the carefully composed names fascinate.

Mieville is concerned with change, in all its forms. His work is anyway a hybrid, a mutant strain beginning in the Earth we know—with pirate tales, the Victorian London-like empire of New Crobuzon, and only half-strange words (like "chymical")—as if these books have appeared from a familiar but warped dimension. He extends this facet of the fantasy genre (itself infected here with steam-punk sf and the maritime novel) into a litany of bodies, minds, lovers, ships, species and even limits of space and time, which are haphazardly broken and remade by torture, surgery, experience, sword-strokes, sex, mining and vampirism. Scarring is his continual metaphor—seen as a disfigurement, but in fact a sign that the body, though altered, has healed. That is the lesson thick-skinned Bellis must learn.

Mieville communicates all this with an understanding of human need which grounds even his most far-fetched visions. He is capable of describing impressionistic, present-tense sea-battles of brutal immediacy, and the small, tingling sexual flush the lonely Bellis feels at a powerful man's glance. Though Mieville ignores the fairy tale, pure narrative favoured by the past decade's premier British fantasists, Neil Gaiman and Clive Barker, he happily shares their results: *The Scar* is a ripping, thoughtful yarn.

Carl Freedman (essay date winter 2003)

SOURCE: Freedman, Carl. "Towards a Marxist Urban Sublime: Reading China Miéville's *King Rat.*" *Extrapolation* 44, no. 4 (winter 2003): 395-408.

[*In the following essay, Freedman encourages attention to Miéville's first novel even as momentum builds in anticipation of his fourth and identifies components of Marxism and the sublime of the natural world in* King Rat.]

The multi-volume fictional work that China Miéville currently has in progress—the work that may eventually be known as the New Crobuzon sequence—promises to rank as one of the major achievements of early twenty-first-century Anglophone fiction; certainly the two thick volumes that have already appeared, *Perdido Street Station* (2000) and *The Scar* (2002), are both important novels in their own right. It is thus understandable that Miéville's more compact first novel, *King Rat* (1998), which immediately precedes the New Crobuzon books, should be somewhat overshadowed by its successors: understandable, but regrettable. For not only is *King Rat* an excellent piece of work in and of itself, but it also announces a good many of the themes and concerns that find ampler (but not necessarily more brilliant) development in the later books. In this paper I will sketch out the conceptual basis of the Miévillian fictional universe and will then focus on one particularly important theme, namely, the construction of what I call an urban sublime. "Sublime" is here meant in something very like its core Longinian sense, but with the major difference that the natural environment with which Longinus and his eighteenth-century followers like Hume, Burke, and Kant associate the awe and grandeur of sublimity usually gives way, in Miéville's work, to an emphatically urban setting; and I will also maintain that the Miévillian sublime strives to incorporate the specifically political sublimity of Marxism.

King Rat is an unusually complex book to classify generically; it includes elements of fantasy, science fiction, Dickensian urban realism, detective fiction, allegory, the beast fable, the superhero comic book, and the *Bildungsroman*. The neat formulation that Mark Bould has suggested to describe *Perdido Street Station*—"a science fiction story set in a fantasy sub-creation" (310)—does, however, seem to me somewhat applicable to the earlier novel as well, so long as we add that here the "fantasy sub-creation" looks partly like the actual end-of-millennium London in which Miéville himself happens to live. In any case, the plot of *King Rat* is cogent and streamlined, despite the apparent (although, as we will see, *only* apparent) generic eclecticism. The novel opens as Saul Garamond is returning, late at night, to the high-rise London flat that he shares with his father, from whom he is somewhat estranged emotionally and in whose earnest Marxist politics he has no interest whatever. Saul goes to bed without seeing his father and is rudely awakened in the morning by the police's pounding on the door. It turns out that Saul's father is dead, having fallen or jumped or been pushed out of the apartment window; and the police take Saul into custody as a possible suspect. Alone in a cell, Saul is joined by what seems to be a ratty-looking man, who helps Saul to escape. This "man" is actually King Rat—who is literally the king of the rats—and he claims Saul as his nephew; he explains that Saul is himself half rat, because his long-dead mother was King Rat's sister, who married, as it were, out of the species. Under King Rat's mentorship, Saul's rat nature awakens, and he develops many remarkable powers: superhuman strength and speed, and the ability to dash straight up a wall, to squeeze through tiny chinks and cracks, to make himself so inconspicuous as to become practically invisible to human eyes, and to digest and enjoy any sort of food, no matter how rotten or filthy.

The plot soon thickens. We learn that King Rat has not been able to exercise much authority over his subjects ever since failing to save them from the Pied Piper seven centuries ago; Miéville's novel is, in one of its many aspects, a sequel to Robert Browning's *The Pied Piper of Hamelin* (1842). King Rat and the Piper are still bitter enemies, and King Rat hopes that—with Saul's help, and also in alliance with his colleagues, Anansi, the king of the spiders, and Loplop, the king of the birds—he will yet be able to defeat the Piper and regain the loyalty of the common rats. The Piper's deadliest weapon is his music, which charms his victims into total submission; but a different tune is required for each species, and King Rat hopes that Saul, as a half-breed between two species, may prove immune. The Piper, we learn, is indeed a vicious killer, and one who has a special interest in getting rid of Saul, since he shares King Rat's suspicion that the rat-man may be impervious to his musical spells and hence extraordinar-

ily dangerous to him. But Saul also learns that King Rat is hardly superior, morally, to the Piper. It transpires that King Rat is not Saul's uncle at all, but his biological father, for King Rat raped Saul's (perfectly human) mother with the specific intention of fathering a half-breed for use against the Piper. In addition to being a rapist, King Rat is just as cold-blooded a murderer as the Piper himself; it was he, for instance, that forced Mr. Garamond (that is, the man who has raised Saul and treated him like a son; we never learn his first name) out the window. In the novel's climactic scene, which takes place in a London Drum 'n' Bass club—appropriately enough, since Drum 'n' Bass has all along provided the book's musical "soundtrack"—Saul defeats the Piper, but does so in such a way that King Rat not only fails to gain any credit for the victory but is disgraced yet further in the eyes of his subjects. The latter unanimously acclaim Saul as their true sovereign. But Saul, in a political awakening and self-conscious tribute to his late (and *real,* though not biological) father, proclaims the overthrow of the rat monarchy and the triumph of revolutionary egalitarianism. *"This one's for you, Dad"* (317; emphasis in original), he thinks to himself. In his final line of the novel, he announces himself as "Citizen Rat" (318).

In a subordinate narrative line, the Pied Piper (while concealing his real identity) has formed a collaborative musical relationship with Natasha Karadjian, a friend of Saul's and a Drum 'n' Bass composer and arranger popular throughout the clubs of London. His aim is to master the art of electronic music. For he calculates (in one of the novel's deftest science-fictional effects) that modern musical technology, which enables more than one distinct musical track to be played simultaneously, will allow him to overcome what had always been his most serious limitation, namely, his inability to charm more than one species with his flute at the same time. In the climactic battle at the nightclub, the strategy proves partly successful; multi-track recording does enable the Piper to control spiders and humans and rats simultaneously. But the Piper had expected that Saul, as half rat and half human, would be captivated by the combination of the two pertinent tunes; and he is not. "One plus one equals *one,* motherfucker," as Saul explains to his enemy. "I'm not rat plus man, get it? I'm bigger than either one *and I'm bigger than the two.* I'm a new thing. *You can't make me dance*" (301; emphasis in original). And so Saul triumphs over the Piper.

What makes Saul's victory possible, then, is that he is a figure of radical *hybridity*; the coupling of male rat and female human in the long-ago violence of rape produces not an additive mixture of the two but a fundamentally different kind of being with resources superior to those of either of his genetic lines. This point, crucial to the resolution of the novel's action-adventure plot, is also an expression of its most profound philosophical significance. For, on the conceptual plane, *King Rat* is above all a neo-Adornian celebration of heterogeneity and complexity, of overdetermined dialectical combination, and, correlatively, an attack on the totalitarian and, in the end, genocidal ideal of *purity.*

This is, we should note, one of Miéville's great themes in nearly all of his work to date. It is most extensively expressed in the fictional universe of New Crobuzon, with its usually more-or-less peaceful co-existence of a remarkable variety of sentient species, who are represented through detail more vivid and convincing than that to be found, perhaps, in any other such project in all of speculative fiction. It is significant, for instance, that the opening chapter of *Perdido Street Station* ends with an exquisite figure of difference and unity, namely the sexual union of Isaac, the novel's human protagonist, and his girlfriend Lin, who is a khepri, that is, a member of a species that appears to bear much the same sort of relationship to insects that our own species does to apes. The passage (14) delineates Isaac and Lin's passion with tenderness, excitement, and anatomical precision, and comes as close, I think, as any text has ever come to successfully resolving the all but insoluble representational problem posed by alien sexuality: I mean the problem of making clear the element of radical otherness, of graphically showing that different species are involved, while nonetheless preserving that sense of authentic sexual *frisson* that, for most of us, is exclusively associated with intra-species relations.[2] The heterosexual thrill of Isaac and Lin's lovemaking is made fully concrete for the reader, who, however, is never allowed to substitute a mental image of a human woman for that of the insectoid Lin. Opposed, in *Perdido Street Station,* to such joyous heterogeneity realized in unity are the monstrous slake-moths, figures of purity and mass murder, who with single-minded resolution voraciously suck the sentience out of as many of New Crobuzon's varied citizens as possible. It is no accident that the tragic climax of the novel occurs when a slake-moth attacks Lin and permanently maims her psyche, thus rendering forever impossible the sexual (and other) reciprocity between her and Isaac that had been celebrated in chapter 1 (though the catastrophe does not diminish Isaac's unselfish devotion to his now as-if-lobotomized lover).

The slake-moths of *Perdido Street Station,* with their inexorable rapacity and utter inability to deal with those different from themselves in any way except murderous incorporation, represent the most memorable image of purity in Miéville's fiction (one might also cite the mosquito-women of *The Scar,* though the gender politics at work there make that case somewhat different). But the same intellectual point conveyed by these "capitalist monsters" (see Shaviro 2002) is made, in both figural and in more expository form, in *King*

Rat. As Saul feels the rat side of his nature awakening, and as he thus becomes increasingly conscious of his own radical hybridity, he comes to understand the monstrous quality of non-hybridity and homogeneity: "*Purity is a negative state and contrary to nature,* Saul had once read. That made sense to him now. He could see the world clearly in all its natural and supernatural impurity. . . ." (81; emphasis in original). If Saul is himself the individual type of hybridity, his mortal enemy, the Piper, figures the precise philosophical opposite. Tall, blonde, and a perfect visual emblem of Nazi "Aryanism," the Piper is absolutely singular—the only one of his kind, and hence different from every other creature on earth—and explicitly enacts the literally genocidal ethic of purity, having no means of relating to those different from himself except murder. Though more apparently "human" in physical terms, he is, conceptually, the precise analogue of a slake-moth. One wonders whether the sentence about purity that Saul remembers reading is not actually a paraphrase of any of several celebrated passages by Adorno, for instance this one from *Negative Dialectics*:

> Genocide is the absolute integration. It is on its way wherever men are leveled off—"polished off," as the German military called it—until one exterminates them literally, as deviations from the concept of their total nullity. Auschwitz confirmed the philosopheme of pure identity as death.
>
> (Adorno 1983, 362)

Conversely, when Adorno offers one of his rare utopian glimpses into how a genuinely non-dominative state of heterogeneity might be understood—e.g., in his exaltation of "peace among men as well as between men and their Other," in which peace is defined as "distinctness without domination, with the distinct participating in each other" (Adorno 1978, 500)—one finds that the concept can hardly be better illustrated than, for instance, by the passage describing Isaac and Lin's lovemaking in *Perdido Street Station.*

Adorno offered such moments of utopian positivity very sparingly, in large part because he feared that any too explicit articulation of utopia might ultimately prove reductive and so unwittingly collude in the dialectic of identitarian domination that it was meant to stand against. But one thing that Miéville's work suggests, from *King Rat* onwards, is that speculative fiction may sometimes function as a more efficient genre than philosophical exposition for the overt expression of impurity and nonidentity, of "peace" in Adorno's sense. In Miéville's first novel, certainly, there is hardly a level of the text in which a neo-Adornian sense of hybridity is not powerfully and positively enforced. In addition to the character of the protagonist Saul, and to the climax of the narrative line in Saul's victory over the Pied Piper and the latter's genocidal schemes, we might cite, for example, the generic composition of the text itself. The remarkable variety of genres that make their presence felt in the novel has already been noted. But what needs to be stressed now is that this variousness is not a matter of adding and mixing eclectically but of a genuinely dialectical (and "peaceful") hybridity, of a true generic overdetermination. For the novel as for Saul, one plus one (plus one, plus one, and so forth) really does equal one. For example, the detective story of **King Rat**—that aspect of the text dominated by Detective Inspector Crowley, the surprisingly sympathetic policeman who attempts to solve some of the murders committed by the Piper and by King Rat, and whose shrewd intuitions lead him a significant distance toward the truth that the positivistic world-view of police work makes impossible to grasp completely—is by no means an undigested lump in a salad of literary kinds. On the contrary, it is organically interconnected with (for instance) the Dickensian realism, as the Crowley narrative helps to establish a vivid baseline reference for the "real," or mundane, London of empirical experience; and in this way the text virtually recapitulates that passage in nineteenth-century English literary history whereby Dickens's "realistic" urban representations gave birth to the detective fiction of Wilkie Collins and Sir Arthur Conan Doyle. At the same time, of course, the Sherlockian positivism of the realistic narrative baseline provides a sense of the mundane against which the fantastic and science-fictional elements of the novel can be defined.

It is the dialectical unity of science fiction and fantasy that provides perhaps the most remarkable aspect of the novel's generic hybridity. Many writers have simply dumped elements of these two normally opposed genres into the same text; but Miéville really connects them. Bould's useful notion of a science-fictional narrative unfolding within fantastic perimeters—so that (the example is mine) "thaumaturgy" in **Perdido Street Station** and, to a lesser degree, in **The Scar** appears as a reasonably straightforward and cognitively based skill, learnable and teachable like any other, even while there remains something magically inexplicable about its ultimate relation to the scientific rationality of our own empirical environment—needs to be somewhat complicated in the case of **King Rat.** For here the fictional environment is constituted not by fantasy *simpliciter* but by the dialectic of fantasy and realism, as the supernatural presuppositions of the text concerning the rats and the Piper do not cancel but rather, as we will see, enhance and expand the "realistic" London of the late 1990s; and within this imaginative problematic a properly cognitive, science-fictional narrative logic plays out. On the technical level, perhaps the most memorable single instance of this logic is the ingenious use, which we have already noted *en passant,* of modern (or "postmodern") electronic technology to concretize and extrapolate from the fantastic premises concerning

the Piper's music that Miéville's novel inherits from Browning's poem. But even more important, ultimately, in the science-fictional element of **King Rat** is its specifically utopian political dimension, something to be considered toward the end of this paper.

If the art that constitutes **King Rat** is one of overdetermined dialectical hybridity, the same is true of that art which the novel most emphatically exalts (in its acknowledgments and epigraph as well as in the main text), namely, the music of Drum 'n' Bass. The chief thematic function of the whole subplot that centers on the musician Natasha and her capture by the Piper is, surely, to provide an occasion for the text to represent an aesthetic experience as radically overdetermined as its own. As often, Miéville's mastery of vivid detail is stunning: in how many instances, aside from the supreme achievement of Thomas Mann's *Doctor Faustus* (1947), has the sound of music been so convincingly communicated through the silent medium of prose as it is in **King Rat**? But the point to be stressed here is that the sound of Drum 'n' Bass is an emphatically impure one; a totality of heterogeneous tones, it is held together in some at least provisional unity by the predominance of an African-American cultural tradition, on one level, and, on another, by the manipulations of the most sophisticated electronic technology. The novel describes Drum 'n' Bass as "the apotheosis of black music," with its rhythm "stolen from Hip Hop, born of Funk" (59)—thus suggesting vistas of musical history that go back to rhythm-and-blues and, ultimately, to the slave spirituals themselves. But the details of Natasha's compositional technique show her to range even more widely than that, as she synthesizes (in both the technological and philosophical senses) sounds and influences that range from Steve Reich to My Bloody Valentine.[3] Indeed, Natasha's remarkable Miéville-like creativity and her dominance within a clearly marked narrative strand might be taken to establish her as a kind of secondary protagonist of **King Rat,** thus fulfilling (as Saul does not) the later Miévillian pattern of the creative protagonist (the scientist Isaac in **Perdido Street Station,** the linguist Bellis in **The Scar**).

It is no accident that Natasha's most considerable musical creation is entitled *Wind City* and described by the text as the musical equivalent or evocation of "a huge metropolis" (210). For, of all the varied representations of hybridity, of impurity, in **King Rat,** the greatest and most overarching is surely the portrayal of the huge metropolis of London; and it is largely in the hybridity of Miéville's London that its sublimity lies. More than that even; the novel's apprehension of the sublime hybridity of London is itself in great part enabled by its *own* hybridity, its own generic overdetermination. Indeed, it is precisely the latter that enables **King Rat** to somewhat recapture an older tradition of representing London. I have elsewhere argued (see Freedman) that, as an aspect of the bourgeois cultural revolution—that is, during the earlier part of the epoch, not yet ended, of what Miéville himself calls, in both *King Rat* and in a scholarly article published the same year, the capitalist "conspiracy of architecture" (221; but see also Miéville 1998a)—London becomes a site of estranging epistemological nontransparency, productive of awe and Benjaminian shock. Among the writers who most powerfully record this sense of London as ungraspable are Blake, Wordsworth, and, a bit belatedly but perhaps most importantly of all, Dickens. Yet, as the world's first capitalist metropolis ages and becomes more familiar, and as newer cities (New York, Los Angeles, Tokyo) invent more novel forms of urban shock, London tends, perhaps inevitably, to lose a great deal of the awe-producing strangeness recorded in Dickens's *Little Dorrit* (1857) and Blake's "London" (1794). In more recent representations, London sometimes comes to seem almost quaint.

It is not the least of Miéville's many achievements to have practically reinvented something like a Blakean or Dickensian sense of London. This is not, indeed, Miéville's only mode of producing an urban sublime; there is perhaps even greater sublimity in New Crobuzon and (in *The Scar*) in Armada, two of the most extraordinary yet convincing imaginary cities in all of fiction. But in *King Rat* (and, in a more minor way, in Miéville's novella *The Tain* [2002]), the project of urban representation is differently inflected by being directly linked to an actual historical city that possesses one of the richest literary histories of any metropolis on the globe. Any modern capitalist city is, virtually by definition, a place of nontransparency and hybridity, a place structured more complexly and productive of more different kinds of experience than any single individual can truly take in. Wordsworth, for instance, expresses this then-new sense of London when, recording a stroll through Bartholomew Fair in Book VII of *The Prelude* (1850), he feels himself to be within "a phantasma, / Monstrous in colour, motion, shape, sight, sound!"—a locus of such hybridity, of such multivarious "prodigies," that "All moveables of wonder, from all parts, / Are here" (291-293). Depicting, in *King Rat,* the aging bourgeois London of the 1990s, Miéville captures this awe-struck experience of the city afresh by sublating the "realism" of Blake, Wordsworth, and Dickens into a hybrid generic totality partly determined by the resources of fantasy and science fiction.

It is partly a matter of sheer *spatial* expansion. As Saul comes into his rat nature, he feels his native city expand beyond the oppressive but familiar London he had known, with the "weight of ten million people so close to him [that it] seemed to make the air vibrate" (17), and to become an effectively new city, "infinitely vaster than he had imagined, unknowable and furtive" (53). The old London of the streets comes to seem ridiculously small, as the city acquires immense new depths in the labyrinthine sewer passages where the rats make their homes, passages navigable more by smell than by sight, and including such awesomely sublime monuments of grandeur as the huge underground chamber of "cathedral architecture, thirty feet high, like the fossilized belly of a whale long entombed under the city" (89). At the same time, Saul's London becomes an experience of new height as well as new depth, as he learns to move through the city with lightning speed across its rooftops and bridges. Of course, this massive expansion of London is intensive and qualitative as well as extensive and quantitative; the city of the rats offers to Saul "a new existence at right-angles to the world of people he had left behind" (147). London becomes for Saul what it once was for Wordsworth, a locus of the most estranging and heterogeneous "prodigies," from the humble, shrewd, determined proletarian rats, to the uncanny figure of the mass-murdering Piper, to such relatively sympathetic characters as Loplop and Anansi, the latter of whom, with his genial Afro-Jamaican accent and bearing, ratifies in a new, fantastic dimension the multicultural and multiracial hybridity of the really existing end-of-millennium London (a particular hybridity instanced more "realistically" by Saul's friend, the black artist and urban *flâneur* Fabian). The London constructed by the generic overdeterminations of *King Rat* is itself massively overdetermined, a city made emphatically new and strange, but in that way akin to the "classic" early-to-middle capitalist city of Blake, Wordsworth, and Dickens; like them, Saul is "captivated by London" (219), and with abundant good reason.

This, then, is the urban sublime of Miéville's first novel. Longinus defines the sublime as "a kind of height and conspicuous excellence in speeches and writings"; it is "[w]hat is wonderful, with its stunning power," and, as such, "prevails everywhere over that which aims merely at persuasion and at gracefulness" (8-9). In much the same vein, Burke—always the most influential writer on sublimity in English—sharply distinguishes between the sublime and the beautiful, associating the latter with the merely bright, small, and smooth. The urban sublime—the awe-inspiring (if frequently unbeautiful) grandeur of the modern capitalist metropolis, in all its unfathomable heterogeneity and hybridity—has been a frequent effect of literary representation from Blake onwards, but in recent literature it has rarely been attained more brilliantly than in *King Rat.* By exploiting the resources proper to science fiction and fantasy, the novel invokes a London more stunning and strange and various than any, perhaps, that unaided literary realism could any longer convey.

But a *Marxist* urban sublime? Though *King Rat* is in the end a deeply political novel, its politics are, so to speak, held somewhat at a distance throughout most of the text: a distance that partly corresponds to the emotional distance between Saul and his old-fashioned socialist father. Almost from Saul's birth until his own death, Mr. Garamond has conscientiously attempted to pass on to his son a certain tradition of English working-class Marxism. When Saul, for example, at the age of three, happens to pass by a cauldron of boiling tar that some workmen are using to repair a road, and is seized with terror at the thought of falling into it, his father sees an opportunity to instill in Saul the traditional socialist virtues of reason, clarity, knowledge, and bravery. He encourages Saul to approach the road workers and to ask them about the tar. Saul does so, receives their answers, and the results are essentially what his father seems to have intended: "He did not fall in. And he was still afraid, but not as much as he had been, and he knew why his father had made him find out about the tar, and he had been brave" (25). Much later, during the last Christmas he will ever see, Mr. Garamond gives his son an illustrated, leather-bound edition of Lenin's *What Is To Be Done?* (1902), inscribing it, with working-class modesty, *"To Saul, This always made sense to me. Love from the Old Leftie"* (69; emphasis in original). Yet, however attractive this mode of parenting may be to the reader—who can hardly fail to appreciate the elder Garamond's gracious humility and unselfish devotion to his son—it leaves Saul himself, after he comes of age, rather cold. He cares nothing for his father's ideas, is repelled by his father's earnestness and physical girth, and encourages his friends to regard Mr. Garamond as essentially a buffoon. It is characteristic that Saul deliberately avoids his father on what turns out to be the last night of the elder Garamond's life.

Apart from such direct flashback references to Saul's father, overtly political passages are fairly sparse until the final pages of *King Rat*. But an identifiable politics is at work in the text; and it is connected with Saul's changing attitude, during the time present of the novel, toward the now deceased Mr. Garamond. Saul's re-evaluation of his father is partly caused by the simple fact of violent loss; but much more important is his crucial discovery of King Rat's rape of his mother. Reading his father's journal, he is moved by the deep compassion and selfless devotion Mr. Garamond expresses towards his wife—attitudes, Saul realizes, that the elder Garamond then extended to Saul himself, despite his being genetically the son of a rapist and even, in a sense, his mother's murderer, since Mrs. Garamond died of complications arising from Saul's birth:

> He [Mr. Garamond] had had no truck with the awful, bloody vulgarity of genes. He had built fatherhood with his actions.

> Saul did not sob, but his cheeks were wet. Wasn't it odd and sad, he thought a little hysterically, that it was only on learning that his father was not his father, that he realized how completely his father he had been?

> *There's a dialectic for you, Dad,* he thought, and grinned fleetingly.

> It was only in losing him that he regained him, finally, after so many dry years.

> [183; emphasis in original]

Rarely, one supposes, has the philosophical concept of the Marxist dialectic been invoked in so emotionally affecting a way.

No less consequential, for the politics of the text, than Saul's changing attitude toward his father is his experience with the rats and with his own nature as half rat himself. Though *King Rat* is certainly not a strict allegory in the manner, say, of *The Pilgrim's Progress* (1684), it does contain numerous moments of powerfully allegorical significance, many involving the ordinary rank-and-file rats who grow increasingly loyal to Saul as the story progresses. Anonymously pervasive and oppressed throughout urban space like the industrial proletariat—and city-dwelling "vermin" like the Jews in the Nazi ideology partly symbolized by the Pied Piper—the rats are most evidently figures of victimhood; the text actually uses the term *holocaust* (130) to describe the Piper's genocidal assault against the rats of Hamelin. Yet, if the rats stand for those crushed beneath the iron heel of capitalism, especially in the latter's fascist form, they are also figures of a certain kind of freedom. The physical ease with which they are able to go practically anywhere throughout the vast metropolis corresponds to an autonomy they enjoy vis-à-vis capitalist ideology (and here the chief philosophical reference is less Adornian than Lukácsian—see Lukács, 83-222). Despite the fact that the rat city is much more immense and complex than the purely human city he had known before, Saul himself, once fully grown into his rat capabilities, is able to grasp it, in all its sublime heterogeneity, far more capably than any "normal" subject of bourgeois hegemony could. Unlike the Wordsworth of *The Prelude,* Saul becomes able to understand and resist the capitalist commodification of which London is the central (British) site:

> He realized that he had defeated the city. . . . He had defeated the conspiracy of architecture, the tyranny by which the buildings that women and men had built had taken control of them, circumscribed their relations, confined their movements. These monolithic products of human hands had turned on their creators, and defeated them with common sense, quietly installed themselves as rulers. They were as insubordinate as Frankenstein's monster, but they had waged a more subtle campaign, a war of position more effective by far.

> (221)

In this remarkable passage, a reference to the text with which Mary Shelley founded science fiction combines with classic Marxist language describing commodity fetishism (and with classic Gramscian language about political strategy) in order to describe the *nearly* insurmountable capitalist oppression that all of us are up against. But the hybrid rat-man Saul does, to a significant degree, surmount it.

In the book's final pages, then, Saul's newly found love and respect for his late father combines with his sense of relative freedom with regard to the capitalist city in order to produce an overtly political resolution of deeply utopian character. Strategizing during the final battle at the Drum 'n' Bass club, Saul poses the most urgent question in precisely the Leninist terms dear to the late Mr. Garamond—"What is to be done?" (286)—and after the victory over the genocidal Piper has been achieved he actually foments a revolution. As we have seen, he declines to substitute himself—though he would presumably prove a "good" king—for the bad King Rat, but instead announces the abolition of monarchy itself, and, with an explicit mental salute to his father, proclaims a new era of social equality. Revolution—the world turned upside down—is surely the ultimate instance of overdetermined hybrid totality, and the ultimate sublimity as well: no natural phenomenon has ever proven so awesome as the overthrow of tyranny and the dawn of freedom. The dominant note of the novel's ending is one of triumph, and if this mode of resolution carries any proper danger, it is—as Adorno would doubtless warn—the danger of a reductive or hyperbolic triumphal*ism*.

King Rat does avoid this danger—but at the cost of rendering somewhat ambiguous the Marxist character of its revolutionary sublimity. It is after all a *king,* not a capitalist system, that has been overthrown, and we should attend to the precise language by which Saul carries out his revolution—which, not incidentally, is a revolution from above, one that the common rats have to be persuaded to accept. "I declare this Year One of the Rat Republic" (317), announces Saul. The values he exalts are "Liberty, Equality . . . and let's put the 'rat' back into 'Fraternity'" (317; ellipsis in original). Finally, as we have noted, he designates himself as "Citizen Rat" (318). These are—very obviously—the slogans of 1789, not 1917; we are in the rhetorical universe of the Rights of Man, not of All Power to the Workers. Despite the Marxist (and Leninist) character of Saul's beloved father and of his own resistance to commodity fetishism, at the moment of actual revolutionary rupture he falls into the language of bourgeois rather than socialist democracy. Despite the clear Marxist tendency of Saul's development—most notably expressed in the passage on the "conspiracy of architecture"—at the end neither he nor the novel goes beyond the limits of bourgeois radicalism. Indeed, at the *very* end the novel hints that even the achievements of radical bourgeois democracy

may be insecure; for, on the text's final, unnumbered, italicized page, the "feudal" (or fascist) King Rat himself warns, *"I'll be back again."*

This warning may serve to remind us that the country in which *King Rat* was written is after all still a monarchy, and one where—more than three centuries after the bourgeois innovations of the Civil War and the Glorious Revolution—the power of the once-feudal landowning class remains immense; as of this writing, the wealthiest single individual in the United *Kingdom* is still the Duke of Westminster, with his vast real-estate holdings in central London and elsewhere. More generally, the way in which the novel moves towards a Marxist sublime but declines to consummate this tendency can usefully be taken to suggest the limits imposed on socialist imagining by the deeply reactionary political climate in Britain during the 1990s. After the devastations of Thatcherism, which pulled the entire British political spectrum so sharply to the right, especially in its fatal weakening of trade unionism, the repeal of Clause Four and the more general Blairite evacuation of social democracy from the Labour Party have resulted in a drastically reduced socialist field; the political grouping that once served, if always ambiguously, as the largest vehicle of socialist thought and action in the UK is now clearly to the right of the frankly pro-capitalist Liberal Democrats, and in many ways to the right of even the old Disraeli-to-Macmillan tradition of liberal Toryism (vestigially represented today by such marginal Conservative politicians as Kenneth Clarke). The predictable social effect has been one of extreme demoralization and depoliticization: a situation lucidly represented in the "realistic" side of *King Rat* itself. It is no accident that the only thoroughgoing socialist in the novel is old, fat Mr. Garamond, a survivor from an earlier era, and that even he is removed from the stage at the beginning of the text's time present. The younger characters—Fabian, Natasha, Saul before his transformation—are all instinctive rebels against the established order, but their rebelliousness is of the despairing, apolitical sort, wholly untethered to any positive socialist (or even bourgeois-radical) program. Yet, after all, their Britain corresponds, in the world beyond the text, to the Britain that produced the novel itself and that therefore cannot be considered altogether hopeless. If *King Rat* does not quite achieve a really Marxist sublime, it nonetheless keeps hope alive by stubbornly maintaining such an achievement on the agenda.

Notes

1. I should acknowledge a considerable debt to the uncommonly talented and engaged group of undergraduates at Louisiana State University who took my spring 2003 seminar on the fiction of China Miéville; many of the ideas in this paper were worked out in collaboration with them.

2. I am indebted here to the important (though not yet published) work of Dr. Alcena Rogan on alien sex in speculative fiction; but see her "Alien Sex Acts in Feminist Science Fiction: Heuristic Models for Thinking a Feminist Future of Desire," forthcoming in *PMLA*.

3. *Vide* Shaviro 1997, p. 26: "My Bloody Valentine's music leaves you with a strange post-coital feeling: as if you knew you'd had an orgasm recently, but you couldn't remember when, or even exactly how it felt. Maybe this is what sex with space aliens would be like."

Works Cited

Adorno, Theodor W. 1978. "Subject and Object." In *The Essential Frankfurt School Reader.* Ed. Andrew Arato and Eike Gebhardt. New York: Urizen.

———. 1983. *Negative Dialectics.* Tr. E. B. Ashton. New York: Continuum.

Bould, Mark. 2002. "On the British SF Boom." *Science Fiction Studies.* No. 87 (Vol. 29, Part 2).

Burke, Edmund. 1998. *A Philosophical Enquiry into the Origin of Our Ideas of the Sublime and Beautiful.* Ed. Adam Phillips. London: Oxford University Press.

Freedman, Carl. 2002. "London as Science Fiction: A Note on Some Images from Johnson, Blake, Wordsworth, Dickens, and Orwell." *Extrapolation.* Vol. 43, No. 3.

Longinus. 1985. *On the Sublime.* Tr. James Arieti and John Crossett. New York: Edwin Mellen.

Lukács, Georg. 1971. *History and Class Consciousness: Studies in Marxist Dialectics.* Tr. Rodney Livingstone. Cambridge, Mass.: MIT Press.

Miéville, China. 1998a. "The Conspiracy of Architecture: Notes on a Modern Anxiety." *Historical Materialism.* No. 2.

———. 1998b. *King Rat.* New York: Tor.

———. 2000. *Perdido Street Station.* New York: Ballantine.

———. 2002a. *The Scar.* New York: Ballantine.

———. 2002b. *The Tain.* PS Publishing.

Shaviro, Steven. 1997. *Doom Patrols: A Theoretical Fiction about Postmodernism.* New York: Serpent's Tail.

———. 2002. "Capitalist Monsters." *Historical Materialism.* Volume 10, Issue 4.

Wordsworth, William. 1971. *The Prelude: A Parallel Text.* Ed. J. C. Maxwell. Harmondsworth: Penguin.

Elizabeth Hand (review date March 2003)

SOURCE: Hand, Elizabeth. Review of *The Scar,* by China Miéville. *Magazine of Fantasy and Science Fiction* 104, no. 3 (March 2003): 38-42.

[*In the following excerpt, Hand notes the influence of M. John Harrison on Miéville and reviews* The Scar.]

> *Well you think you had a good time*
> *With the boy that you just met*
> *Kicking sand from beach to beach*
> *Your clothes all soaking wet*
> *But if you look around and see*
> *A shadow on the run*
> *Don't be too surprised if it's just*
> *a paper sun.*

—"Paper Sun," Traffic

Paper Suns

With the appearance of the collection *Things That Never Happen* and *Light,* a new novel, we seem to be having an M. John Harrison Moment. And about time, too. For more than twenty years, Harrison's work has anticipated the amphetamine buzz and bleak ardor of the early twenty-first century: it's just taken the world that long to catch up with him.

But now we have. An entire generation of writers has been influenced by Harrison or fallen somewhere within his remit; China Miéville, who provides a heartfelt and engaging introduction to *Things That Never Happen,* is perhaps the youngest and best known.

. . . . .

Raw Power

In his intro to *Things That Never Happen,* China Miéville mentions reading Harrison's "Egnaro" when he was fifteen. "We should all be so lucky," I thought (and, "Well, this explains a lot."). I will admit here that I have not yet read Miéville's first two novels, **King Rat** and last year's award-winning **Perdido Street Station.** But, based on his most recent book, **The Scar,** I'd say Miéville is coming pretty close to pitching a perfect season. **The Scar** returns to the vast and hallucinogenically imagined world of its predecessor, but this time the action moves from the febrile reaches of the city of New Crobuzon, to the febrile reaches of a floating city called Armada. The narrator, Bellis, is an unwilling conscript to Armada's population, and **The Scar**'s loose plot involves her efforts to escape and return to New Crobuzon. The notion of a floating city is delectable, but Miéville seems a bit uncomfortable away from dry land, or very, very deep water. The most gripping parts of **The Scar** are those that are set beneath the surface of various oceans: a gorgeous preface that takes place miles undersea; a fantastic battle with a gigantic bonefish; an absolutely wonderful, over-the-top sequence about the descent in a bathysphere to investigate an ailing, kraken-like monster called the avanc, a creature substantially larger than my hometown, which has been harnessed to tow Armada across the seas. This last gave me the same primal thrill I felt the first time I saw *Gorgo,* an experience I've spent decades trying to recapture. There is also a terrifying and extremely moving visit to the island of the anophelii, mosquito-men and -women whose cultural and sexual mores are beautifully detailed and described, though I felt that these chapters would have been better served if they'd been worked into a short story, rather than an onshore jaunt for the passenger-residents of Armada.

Still, for the most part, **The Scar** functions as a picturesque narrative, a tour de force that sometimes feels a bit like a prolonged march, or paddle, across an endless seascape. Miéville is a spectacular talent, but **The Scar** still feels like a young writer's book. Maybe a young reader's as well: I found its 600-plus pages, with their discursive rambles regarding Armadan politics, races, and intrigues, exhaustive and often exhausting. That beautiful, immense avanc seems like a nice metaphor for Miéville's extravagant gift as a writer. I am very interested in what he does with it next.

Scott Maisano (essay date spring 2004)

SOURCE: Maisano, Scott. "Reading Underwater; or, Fantasies of Fluency from Shakespeare to Miéville and Emshwiller." *Extrapolation* 45, no. 1 (spring 2004): 76-88.

[*In the following essay, Maisano places Miéville in context with other fantasy writers, historic and modern.*]

Why is it that, while reading good fantasy literature, one inevitably comes across an episode in the narrative where it has suddenly become impossible to read good fantasy literature? Take for example Shakespeare's *The Tempest,* a "taproot text" according to Clute and Grant (857), for fantastic fiction ranging from Rachel Ingalls *Mrs. Caliban* to Jan Siegel's *Prospero's Children.* In the play the erstwhile Duke of Milan, Prospero, neglects the affairs of government in order to immerse himself in the solitary pleasures of reading magic books, and as a result of this indulgence finds himself out of power and exiled to a desert island. During a conversation that Prospero has with his daughter, the audience learns that when the Duke and his helpless infant were first put to sea in a leaky, rat-infested vessel, a kindly though somewhat dim-witted bureaucrat loaded up their already sinking boat with the books that Prospero had prized above his dukedom. His life thus literally imperiled by his reading habits, Prospero becomes the first bibliophile

to prompt that tired old ice-breaker of a question: "if you were to be stranded on a desert island for a dozen years, what books would you want to have with you?" At the end of *The Tempest,* however, Prospero renounces his magic and drowns his books; the audience has absolutely no idea what the contents of those books were and, consequently, no clue as to how Prospero himself would have answered the very question his unfortunate situation gave rise to in the popular imagination.

Ordinarily, one would think of Prospero's studies as "an imaginary act of reading," i.e., either part of an actor's performance (if Prospero is seen leafing through a tome *qua* stage prop) or part of a character's conception (if other characters, like Caliban, make reference to the books so that, even if one never sees them, one associates with Prospero). However, the moment that I (as reader or audience member) begin to wonder about the content of the books themselves—a moment Shakespeare's text makes irresistible—Prospero's act of reading becomes the one that is 'real' (i.e., I know there were books of magic available in the seventeenth century, with which Shakespeare might have been familiar and perhaps had in mind when he conceived of Prospero), and mine the one that is 'imaginary' (in so far as I no longer make contact with 'the books behind the books,' the actual books to which Prospero himself would have had access). Read the scholarly articles being written today which promise access to the genuine, historical grimoires and incunabula that Shakespeare's magus *must have read,* and you will know how powerful—and how real—the fantasy of reading imaginary works can feel (Mowat).

The fantasy, I think, has everything to do with the way Prospero chooses to dispose of his library. If you think about it, drowning books is an odd phenomenon. The practice is not as easily understood as, say, the book-burnings which have spelled the end for other magical texts, most recently those of J. K. Rowling. The sight of a flaming mountain of children's books says something, and it says it quite directly with little room to confuse the message. But how does one read drowned texts? Answering that question, I'll suggest in this article, is tantamount to understanding how one reads—or, more to the point, how one imagines one reads—fantasy literature itself. To pursue this matter further, let's take up another example, one positioned at the receiving end of Prospero's drowning his books: that encyclopedic and aquatic virtuoso, Jules Verne's Captain Nemo. Like Prospero, Nemo resides in exile, for reasons more or less mysterious, though seemingly having something to do with the defeat of Villaret-Joyeuse by Captain Nelson on the so-called 'Glorious First of June.' More importantly, Nemo has a library a thousand times the size of Prospero's and many of his titles are read off to us by the inquisitive Professor Arronax: volumes of "science, morality, and literature . . . the most beautiful works history has produced . . . from Homer to Victor Hugo, from Xenophon to Michelet, from Rabelais to George Sand" (75). More astounding than Nemo's chauvinism, as evidenced by the suggestion that none but the ancient Greeks and modern French had produced a single volume worthy of preservation, is Jules Verne's own failure of imagination when it comes to describing underwater reading practices. Akin to the lists of 'great books' or 'essential reading' compiled by today's arbiters of high culture, such as Harold Bloom or William Bennett, there remains an element of predictability—even provinciality—in Nemo's collection, a standardized canon which belies his otherwise idiosyncratic genius. Can I ever fantasize about Nemo's reading—as we have seen it is possible to fantasize about Prospero's—if all his textual treasures are immediately identifiable, instantly recognizable? What would be the point of an academic setting out to read the books that Nemo himself has read, the real books which shaped this fictional character? Chances are that an undergraduate double-majoring in French and Classics will have read many, if not most, of these books already. One can't help feeling disappointed by the mere fact that it is possible to say whence Captain Nemo has acquired his education, from what books exactly: for, fantasy literature at its best inspires in the reader a sense of "knowingness" to rival that of both Prospero and Nemo, yet it does so without ever sharing with the reader precisely what it is that she is supposed to know.

Perhaps the best example I can give to illustrate this idea of having books 'at hand' but not 'in hand' came during a conversation that I had with China Miéville, who was himself a respondent to the session at which Carl Freedman and I presented analyses of his works at the Wis Con. China provided me with some insight into my own constitutive blind-spot in reading his novel, *The Scar*: namely, that all the pirated ships which together comprise the floating city of Armada take their names from literary texts. Thus, the characters in the novel are literally walking across, over, and through centuries of literature. Though I spotted a few of the more conspicuous references along the way, I confess that I was, for the most part, as oblivious as the characters themselves to the references which possessed meaning in my world but none in theirs. Among the references China was kind enough to email me afterwards were, in his words:

> The Pinchermarn—*Pincher Martin*, by William Golding. Lt. Cumbershum is a character from *Rights of Passage* also by William Golding. The Arronax labs is from *20,000 Leagues Under the Sea*. The Castor—ok, that is Latin for Beaver. Now, this is part of an extended reference to *The Hunting of the Snark* by Lewis Carroll, because Tintinnabulum is the Bellman, and his lieutenants, Faber, et al, are all the other people (the

banker, the boots, etc) from that poem. And one of their number was a Beaver. Hence Castor. The Jarvee—*The Haunted Jarvee,* a ghostly ship story featuring Carnacki the ghost finder, by William Hope Hodgson. Another Hodgson reference is Wintershaw Market—winterstraw being the surname of his protagonist in the maritime novel *Boats of the Glen Carrig.*

(email)

If only I had known! And yet not knowing did not prevent me from reading or from understanding the book; indeed, had I truly known all that I didn't know while reading *The Scar,* I might have enjoyed the book less.

A sense of "knowing-ness" constitutes the fantasy genre, I am suggesting, in the same way that the Kantian or Burkean "sublime" supplies the telltale sign of gothic fiction or the Suvinian element of "cognitive estrangement" marks a work as science fiction. These last two aesthetic criteria, the "sublime" and "cognitive estrangement," are not wholly dissimilar: for Kant, the pleasures of the sublime surpassed those of the beautiful because in the case of the sublime "the mind is not simply attracted" by something, as it is in the case of the beautiful, "but is also alternately repelled," which creates a discomforting but invigorating tension (Kant 91). For Suvin, by comparison, what distinguishes the peculiarly "cognitive estrangement" of science fiction from the (non-cognitive?) estrangement of the folktale and fantasy literature is that only the former invites us into an alternate world at the same time that it pushes us back onto such hard realities as gravity, electricity, and mortality. Both Kant and Suvin privilege moments of tension, of contest and indecision between the attraction toward something Other and the repulsion backward to the Self/Same. Suvin, however, also admits being directly influenced by modernist theories of literature—perhaps themselves indebted in some way to Kant's aesthetics—such as Shklovsky's formalist concept of *"ostranenie"* and Brecht's idea of "alienation" (Suvin 6). Prior to Suvin's definition of science fiction, in any case, Tzvetan Todorov had already delimited his own definition of the "fantastic," as it appears in literature, to the "duration of [an] uncertainty," to a more or less brief confusion between the world we know from quotidian experience and another world that defies all experience: "Once we choose one answer or the other," he explains, "we leave the fantastic for a neighboring genre, the uncanny [if we choose our own world] or the marvelous [if we do not]" (25). The result of such highly selective (and often arbitrary) definitions—that is, the result of reading only for those fleeting moments or those singularly "sublime" texts which, as Carl Freedman (*pace* Roland Barthes) puts it, produce a "cognition effect" in the reader—is that probably ninety-nine percent of the "strange," "weird," "impossible," and even "sublime" fiction being produced by writers and consumed by readers is not being reviewed, critiqued or analyzed by scholars. For want of a concept.

What academics who study science fiction and literature of the fantastic desperately need, with all due respect to the pioneering work of Todorov, Suvin and Freedman, is a word for discussing the countless encounters with weirdness that do not come under the rubrics of Brechtian "alienation" or of Formalist "estrangment" or Modernist "de-familiarization" and that are also not reducible to examples of "ideological duping," "the willing suspension of disbelief," or the simple act of "identifying" with a text. What is needed, then, is a word for the reader's sense of familiarity—and the facility with a reader adapts—even in the most "estranged" worlds of fiction. My word for such knowing-ness, derived from Diana Herald's primer to genre fantasy, is "fluency"; and I want to distinguish "fluency" from Suvin's "estrangement" not as modes of writing but as modes of reading (the imaginary relationship one forms with a text) without disparaging one at the expense of the other. The word "fluency" derives from the Latin "fluentia," whence we also get the word "fluid." The *Oxford English Dictionary* defines the meaning of fluency from the 17th century onwards as "an absence of rigidity . . . a readiness of utterance, a flow of words." Suvin and others might hasten to describe "fluency" as a sort of "non-cognitive" estrangement; I am enough of a Shklovskyite, however, to suspect that things which are truly "new and strange"—as fantasy literature, virtually by definition, is—possess, at least in latent form, the capacity to arouse us from our mental slumbers, dogmatic or otherwise.

The beginning of a science fiction or fantasy novel traditionally defies fluency because its insistence is elsewhere, on estrangement. As Carl Freedman observes in *Critical Theory and Science Fiction,* the opening paragraph of a book like Philip K. Dick's *Do Androids Dream of Electric Sheep* trips up its readers, catches them unawares; "the point to be stressed about the language is its profoundly critical, dialectical character" (32). With its technical neologisms such as Dick's "mood organ" designed to de-familiarize what is seemingly most familiar to us, our own feelings, the style precipitates what Freedman, following Suvin, calls "cognitive estrangement, a clear otherness vis-à-vis the mundane empirical world where the text was produced." Instead of emphasizing the provocative nouns, such as "estrangement" or "otherness," in Freedman's definition of the 'felt experience' of reading science fiction, I would call attention to the homely modifier, "clear." "Clear otherness"—the kind that lends itself to comprehension and rational analysis following our initial estrangement—might accurately describe the experience of first sitting down to read Dick's book, but what happens once the reader has grown accustomed to the "mood organs"? Is it possible to sustain the pleasurable

"tension" of "cognitive estrangement" or the high modernist demands of the "de-familiarization" indefinitely? In a few cases—*The Turn of the Screw,* "The Metamorphosis," *Giles, Goatboy*—perhaps. But fantasy literature on the whole (and here I would include science fiction) most often allows us to apprehend such otherness without ever completely coming to terms with it, without ever fully comprehending it.

In his own attempt to illustrate the "fantastic," in fact, Todorov supplies a wonderfully unwitting example of the idea of "fluency." Todorov's primary example of the fantastic, which (he claims) "lasts only as long as a certain hesitation . . . common to reader and character, who must decide whether or not what they perceive derives from 'reality' as it exists in common opinion" (41), comes from Cazotte's *Le Diable Amoureux.* According to Todorov's initial description, the story's main character, Alvaro, "hesitates, wonders (and the reader with him) whether what is happening to him is real, if what surrounds him is indeed reality . . . or whether it is no more than an illusion, which here assumes the form of a dream" (24). But, when Todorov later cites a passage from Cazotte's tale to illustrate his point, another possibility emerges (though perhaps unbeknownst to Todorov):

> Take for instance [writes Todorov] the scene in *Le Diable Amoureux* where Soberano gives proof of his magical powers:
>
> He raises his voice: 'Caldéron,' he says, 'get my pipe, light it, and bring it back to me.' No sooner has he uttered his command than I see the pipe vanish; and before I can figure out how this was done, or ask who this obedient Caldéron was, the lit pipe was back, and my interlocutor had resumed his occupation.
>
> (85)

Todorov uses this passage to underscore the fleeting sensation of hesitation between reality and illusion which, he suggests, is "common to reader and character" alike. But the passage also clearly contains, in its reference to "Caldéron," the means to distinguish reader from character: a reader might easily recognize the name of the servant as an allusion to the seventeenth-century Spanish dramatist, Pedro Calderón de la Barca (or simply Calderón), whose most famous work. *La vida es sueño (Life Is a Dream)* deals with precisely the same theme of mistaking reality for a dream-world. If a reader were to pause over the name "Caldéron" and to consider its potential relatedness to the author, Calderón, we would have here—would we not?—an example of "cognitive estrangement": a tension arising from the simultaneous overlap and discord between an alternate world of fiction and the world we recognize as our own. If, like Todorov, however, one does not hesitate at the name "Caldéron," does not recognize it as anything but part and parcel of the fictional environment, hasn't one (intentionally or not) then foreclosed on a moment of indecision, a moment of the "fantastic" itself, in favor of a moment of "fluency"? In other words, without fully comprehending or coming to terms with a crucial outcropping of the fictional environment into the real world, one simply goes on reading, (over)confident in her or his familiarity with a strange text.

I have placed the prefix "over" in parentheses to indicate that one's confidence and familiarity—in short, one's "fluency"—with a given text is always relative to another reader's, perhaps even to the author's, understanding of the words on the page. I also wish to clarify that the competing experiences of "fluency" and "estrangement" are not determined simply by the reader, but also by the texts themselves, which all have ways of thematizing estrangement at the expense of fluency, as well as the reverse. To illustrate this point, compare the initial shock of Professor Arronax at the sight of Captain Nemo's submarine library—"I'm really astounded to think that it travels with you into the ocean depths"—to the comparatively calm reaction of the children who discover not only books, but real live fictional characters, at the bottom of the ocean in E. Nesbitt's early twentieth-century fantasy, *Wet Magic*. When the five children in Nesbitt's novel for young readers go beneath the sea at the invitation of a mermaid, she attempts to acculturate them to the life of water nymphs, only to realize that they've already magically adapted themselves to this environment:

> 'And now I want to tell you one thing. What you're breathing isn't air, and it isn't water. It's something that both water people and air people can breathe.'
>
> 'The greatest common measure,' said Bernard.
>
> 'A simple equation,' said Mavis.
>
> 'Things which are equal to the same thing are equal to each other,' said Francis; and the three looked at each other and wondered why they had said such things.
>
> 'Don't worry,' said the [mer]lady, 'it's only the influence of the place. This is the Cave of Learning, you know, very dark at the beginning and getting lighter and lighter as you get nearer to the golden door. All these rocks are made of books really, and they exude learning from every crack . . . Let us all go through the gate or you'll all be talking Sanskrit before we know where we are.'
>
> (119)

Unlike Professor Aronnax, the children are not the least bit "astounded" to learn that "the rocks" in the deep sea "are made of books really"; rather they begin to quote the very books themselves in an effort make sense of their own situation. The books here "exude learning from every crack," not unlike the diploma granted to the scarecrow at the end of *The Wizard of Oz,* such that the children discover that they have 'always already

been fluent' in this discourse of magic and make-believe. Indeed, they'll soon "be talking Sanskrit"—soon have their own impenetrably complex language—if they remain immersed in this environment.

As Diana Herald notes in her primer for readers new to the genre: "avid fantasy readers have their own language, the language that is spoken in fantasy fiction" (9). The circularity of this explanation unfortunately offers very little to Herald's uninitiated readers, but it paradoxically explains a lot to any academic who finds herself or himself frustrated by the lack of sophisticated scholarship on most "genre fiction." Academics, it seems, can't quite stay submerged or remain underwater long enough to acquire the requisite 'fluency' for these fictional environments: they keep wanting to come up for air. And often the fantasy books themselves invite academics to return to the surface, to compare what they've found in the fictional depths with what they've already got 'onboard' their scholarship. As it turns out, for example, the books that comprise Nesbitt's Cave of Learning are all real books that many of us, adults, would recognize: indeed, unbeknownst to them even the incantatory hymn the children first used to conjure the mermaid is a verse from John Milton's masque, *Comus*. Lest one object that *Wet Magic* is simply 'a children's book' and therefore unworthy of discussion alongside Jules Verne, it's worth pointing out that Nesbitt does cue her readers to these intertextual resonances and allusions, and thus potentially troubles their sense of "fluency" with the burden of knowing that there are lots of things which they haven't yet read, and which might shed some light on the book's Atlantean misadventures. But, when war breaks out under water and the evil characters from the books in the Cave of Learning—including Shakespeare's Caliban—are set free to wage destruction and to "stupefy" their opponents, that which "protects" the fictional children is precisely their ignorance, the fact that they've read so very little. Nesbitt, therefore, may be winking at her audience, letting them in on her joke about academics who are easily "stupefied" and thus prone to drowning in a sea of ultimately meaningless references.

Given these circumstances, where should one situate Nesbitt's book on the continuum from "fluency" to "cognitive estrangement"? Certainly, the mermaids' environment is every bit as strange as the one aboard Captain Nemo's *Nautilus*—and every bit as "familiar," insofar as both contain what seems to be the complete *Time-Life* series of Western masterpieces—and yet the reader, like the children, feels eerily conversant and at ease in Nesbitt's world. Is it simply the case that what I'm calling "fluency" is the same as "estrangement," without the added factor of what Freedman refers to as the "cognition effect" of science fiction? Freedman, it seems, is willing to take that bet, as he equates the difference "between science fiction and the fantastic" to

Fluency	**Estrangement**
Wet Magic	*20,000 Leagues Under the Sea*
Fantasy	Science Fiction
Reading underwater—Familiarity	Reading underwater—Astonishment

Not-estrangement	**Not-fluency**
Man and Dolphin	*The Scar* and "The Circular Library of Stones"
Interspecies Communication	Intraspecies Communication Failure
Reading underwater— "A Sense of Weirdness"	Reading underwater—"rigorously weird"

the difference "between cognition and the admittedly irrational" (75). In order to get beyond such binary distinctions as "science fiction" versus "fantasy," or "cognition" versus "the admittedly irrational," I'd like to make use of a device that others have found useful for similar purposes: the Greimasian semiotic square.

If on the upper dimension of the square I place the dialectical tension between "fluency" and "estrangement"—that is, between the instant acceptance that the children grant to the underwater books in *Wet Magic* and the profound astonishment and desire for an explanation that Professor Arronax expresses at the sight of Nemo's library—then I can begin to flesh out some provocative middle ground between these two ostensibly antithetical modes of "reading underwater" by positing, on the lower dimension of the square, all the ways of negating "estrangement" that do not simply result in "fluency," and vice versa: hence the two terms at the bottom of the square, "not estrangement" and "not fluency" (See *Fig. 1*).

In the category of "not estrangement" I have placed the accomplishments, both real and imagined, of marine biologists who have worked on the problem of "interspecies communication." Recent science fiction is teeming with examples of aquatic animals communicating in ways that appear increasingly familiar—rather than alien—to us. To mention just a couple of examples, Ben Bova narrates part of his recent novel, *Jupiter*, from the perspective of a Jovian sea creature, named Leviathan; in *Manifold: Time*, meanwhile, Stephen Baxter has imagined a "gen-enged" Caribbean reef squid capable of "manning" a rocket flight into deep space. Both Bova and Baxter ascribe minds and even "souls" to these aquatic creatures in ways that effectively vex the issues of animal exploitation and experimentation by humans. What I find just as fascinating about the real-life accounts of scientists talking, for instance, to dolphins by means of hydrophones, is the way that others in the scientific community have reacted to such experiments, often condemning them for "anthropomorphizing" their non-human subjects. John Lilly, who spent decades working to communicate with dolphins, writes elegantly about his effort to challenge such objections, even as he internalized the criticism and began to have second thoughts about the 'objectivity' of his

scientific work. In his ground-breaking work, *Man and Dolphin,* Lilly speaks of "the experience of 'getting close' to an individual of another species" (29); and elsewhere, in "A Feeling of Weirdness," he comes back to this phraseology, emphasizing proximity rather than estrangement: "The feeling was that we were *up against the edge* of a vast uncharted region in which we were about to embark with a good deal of mistrust concerning the appropriateness of our own equipment" (71, emphasis mine). To speak of getting close, or getting up against the edge, in no way diminishes the "otherness" of the thing encountered; but it's not quite the same as "estrangement," either. As Lilly acknowledges, he and his fellow lab workers occasionally "committed the [scientific] sin of . . . anthropomorphizing," when, for instance, they would refer to the dolphins as "persons" and so forth. There's a genuine sense of mutual reciprocation and communication between humans and dolphins in Lilly's case studies that runs counter to the "cognition effect" deemed proper to most professional scientific journals: in such instances the dialogue is dismissed as "non-cognitive," because one group of humans' account of interspecies communication and comprehension proves ironically incommunicable and incomprehensible to another group of the *same* species.

There is also a talking dolphin in China Miéville's ***The Scar***. But when this dolphin, whose name is Bastard John, looks askance "with his liquid, piggy eyes" and barks "what were doubtless insults in his imbecilic cetacean chittering" (171), his unfamiliar "insults" sound strange to his present auditor not because they are, in fact, "imbecilic," but because the auditor—Tanner Sack, a "Remade" who has had two tentacles grafted to the front of his torso and speaks a language known as Ragamoll—has not yet acquired a proficiency in the dialect of Salt, the patois of welders and engineers (some of them dolphins) working below the sea. This unusual situation brings us to the remaining quadrant of our makeshift semiotic square, "non-fluency." Miéville's book, more spectacularly than any other "fantastic" text I've encountered, incorporates into its very narrative a range of hermeneutical difficulties and interpretive (im)possibilities so profound that it easily gives the lie to all formalist and structuralist (including Greimasian) illusions of textual mastery.

For those who haven't yet read it, **The Scar**'s main character, Bellis Coldwine, is a linguist *cum* translator *cum* librarian *cum* de facto historian of a civilization adrift. She is always at sea—and occasionally under it—when dealing with her enormous array of texts: in the following excerpt, Bellis finds herself working as a librarian for a pirate syndicate when suddenly the books that have been recently pilfered from her own boat begin to be processed and catalogued by her captors.

> She sat for a long time on the floor with her legs splayed, propped up against the shelves, staring at the copy of *Codexes of the Wormseye Scrub.* She felt the familiar fraying spine and the slightly embossed "B. Coldwine." It was her own copy: she recognized its wear. She gazed at it guardedly, as if it were a test she might fail.
>
> The cart did not contain her other work. *High Kettai Grammatology,* but she did find the Salkrikaltor Cray textbook she had brought to *Terpsichoria.*
>
> *Our stuff's finally coming through,* she thought.
>
> It affected her like a blow.
>
> *This was mine,* she thought. *This was taken.*
>
> What else from her ship? Was this Doctor Mollificatt's copy of *Future Tenses*? she wondered. Widow Cadomium's *Orthography and Hieroglyphs*?
>
> She could not be still. She stood and walked, tense, wandering vague and stricken through the library. She passed into the open air and over the bridges that linked the library's vessels, carrying her book clutched to her, above the water and then back into the darkness by the bookshelves.
>
> (109)

For me, this passage captures precisely the fantasy of fluency: it mirrors my own experience of reading genre fantasy, right down to the anxious sense of bewilderment and confusion; but it also transforms the very difficulty of reading into a fantasy, into precisely the kind of thing that I want to read *about*.

In order to fantasize about fluency, of course, we must first feel the full weight of what it means to be "non-fluent." Miéville gives us that sensation too. When Bellis begins to tutor another character, Shekel, in Ragamoll, he suddenly reads voraciously, everything he can get his hands on in the library. Until one day,

> he realized that he had taken a book from a shelf just to one side of the Ragmoll section; that it shared the alphabet that was now his, but pieced it together into a different language. Shekel was dumbstruck at the realization that these glyphs he had conquered could do the same job for so many peoples who could not understand each other at all. He grinned as he thought about it. He was glad to share.
>
> He opened more foreign volumes, making or trying to make the noises that the letters spelled out and laughing at how strange they sounded. He looked carefully

> at the pictures and cross-referenced them again. Tentatively he concluded that in this language, this particular clutch of letters meant *boat,* and this other set *moon . . .*
>
> For hours he found intrigue and astonishment by exploring the non-Ragamoll shelves. He found in those meaningless words and illegible alphabets not only an awe at the world, but the remnants of the fetishism to which he had been subjected before, when all books had existed for him as these did now, only as mute objects with mass and dimension and color, but without content . . .
>
> He gazed at the books in Base and High Kettai and Sunglari and Lubbock and Khadohi with a kind of fascinated nostalgia for his own illiteracy, without for a fraction of a moment missing it.
>
> (145-6)

Intrigue, astonishment, awe, fetishism, and fascination: again, Suvin and Freedman might dismiss these states of mind as simply "non-cognitive," but that's not how they function here. The astonishment, in this case, is at one's own ignorance; and heightened literacy remains a condition of possibility for Shekel's sense of "fascinated nostalgia." As a relative newcomer to the literature of fantasy and science fiction, Shekel's strange epiphany feels all too familiar to me: the sudden shift from the difficulty of reading fantasy ("what is 'thinning' *per se,* or a 'dying earth' venue, exactly?) to the fantasy of overcoming that difficulty is akin to the sense of reading an utterly foreign language and not being able to put it down. This is the quotidian—unrelenting and undeniably cognitive—"estrangement" which Suvin, Todorov, and Freedman, so far as I can tell, are at a loss to explain. This "estrangement" doesn't necessarily give way, upon further reflection, to comprehension; nor, I think, can readers afford to wait till it does: for this is an "estrangement" that never goes away, but one that gradually feels more and more natural, like talking (to) dolphins.

In Carol Emshwiller's short story, "The Circular Library of Stones," the narrator searches the scorched earth beneath a "(now dried up) river" for the ruins of an ancient library. In this heart-wrenching instance of "non-fluency"—in which a woman is institutionalized for her conviction that an entire world of books which was intended for (and perhaps even partly authored by) herself lies just out of reach, just beneath the desiccated surface of waters that once brought the library's cargo to port—I am returned to my opening dilemma, to the one that confronts me each time that I witness Prospero drowning his books in Shakespeare's *The Tempest.* "Real" reading has become impossible, a fantasy: whatever texts are put before us are simply props, poor stand-ins for the magical tomes we'll never have a chance to see. Half-sobbing for joy and remorse, Emshwiller's story begins thus:

Gaining access to their books! If I could find the library and learn to read their writing! If I could find, there, stories beyond my wildest dreams. A love story, for instance, where the love is of a totally different kind . . . a kind of ardor we have never even thought of, more long-lasting than our simple attachments, more world-shaking than our simple sexualities. Or a literature that is two things at once, which we can only do in drawings, where a body might be, at one and the same time, a face in which the breasts also equal eyes, or two naked ladies sitting side by side, arms raised, that also forms a skull, their black hair the eye sockets.

(1)

The desire which we're both chasing and postponing every time we read books of fantasy—like *The Scar,* "The Circular Library of Stones" and *The Tempest*—is the desire to, well, read more books of fantasy. Consider, if you will, the recent publication of "Classic Books from the Library of Hogwarts School of Witch-craft and Wizardry," books which are sold with dust jackets proclaiming "Property of Harry Potter." Now, at last, one has "access" to the very works once read by the fictional character himself; one has found the library and learned to read their writing. But, of course, this sort of spin-off product of the cottage industry can never meet the expectations of the devoted fan. And the inevitable disappointment at reading such a work—the feeling, upon first seeing the book, that one would rather kiss it, a la Caliban, than read it—is the surest sign that no real book will ever compare with those being read across the page, on the other side of the fictive wall. It is, however, only by making explicit this impossible desire *to read fictional works of fiction* that the limits to one's knowledge become enjoyable as such; and, subsequently, one is reminded of the essential fantasy underpinning every apparent instance of fluency.

Note

1. I'd like to thank both China and Carl Freedman for a wonderful and thought-provoking exchange.

Works Cited

Baxter, Stephen. *Manifold: Time*. New York: Del Rey, 2000.

Bova, Ben. *Jupiter*. New York: TOR, 2001.

Clute, John and John Grant, eds. *The Encyclopedia of Fantasy*. New York: St. Martin's Griffin, 1997.

Emshwiller, Carol. "The Circular Library of Stones." *Strange Horizons* <http://www.strangehorizons.com/2001/20010430/circular_library.shtml>.

"Fluency." *The Oxford English Dictionary*. 2nd ed., CD-ROM. Oxford: Oxford UP, 1992.

Freedman, Carl. *Critical Theory and Science Fiction*. Hanover, NH: Wesleyan UP, 2000.

Herald, Diana. *Fluent in Fantasy: A Guide to Reading Interests*. Englewood, CO: Libraries Unlimited, 1999.

Kant, Immanuel. *The Critique of Judgement*. Trans. James Creed Meredith. Oxford Clarendon Press, 1952.

Lilly, John. "A Feeling of Weirdness." *Mind in the Waters, A Book to Celebrate the Consciousness of Whales and Dolphins*. Ed. Joan McIntyre. New York: Scribner, 1974.

———. *Man and Dolphin*. Garden City, NY: Double-day, 1961.

Miéville, China. "RE: Fwd: Re: WisCon 27: Academic Session 01 China Miéville." E-mail to the author. 29 July, 2003.

———. *The Scar*. Del Rey, 2002.

Mowat, Barbara. "Prospero's Book." *Shakespeare Quarterly*. Vol. 52, no. 1 (2001): 1-33.

Nesbitt, E. *Wet Magic*. New York: Coward-McCann Inc., 1913.

Rowling, J. K. *Harry Potter Schoolbooks Box Set: Two Classic Books from the Library of Hogwarts School of Witchcraft and Wizardry*. New York: Scholastic, 2001.

Suvin, Darko. *Metamorphoses of Science Fiction: On the Poetics and History of a Literary Genre*. New Haven: Yale UP, 1979.

Todorov, Tzvetan. *The Fantastic: A Structural Approach to a Literary Genre*. Trans. Richard Howard. Ithaca: Cornell UP, 1975.

Verne, Jules. *20,000 Leagues Under the Sea*. Trans. Anthony Bonner. New York: Bantam Books, 1981.

Gerald Jonas (review date 18 July 2004)

SOURCE: Jonas, Gerald. Review of *Iron Council,* by China Miéville. *New York Times Book Review* (18 July 2004): 19.

[*In the following review of* Iron Council, *Jonas identifies Miéville as among the authors of the new Next Wave British literary movement.*]

Iron Council, by China Mieville, is an exemplar of what some are calling the Next Wave in British science fiction. The name is a sly reference to the New Wave of the 1960's, when English and American writers as varied as Michael Moorcock, J. G. Ballard, Harlan Ellison and Samuel R. Delany cast a suspicious eye on genre staples like space travel and future technology. The Next Wave—which, depending on who's counting, includes British novelists like M. John Harrison, Richard K. Morgan and Neal Asher—mixes left-leaning politics and a taste for horror into cautionary tales of societies gone wrong at the core.

Iron Council is set in an imaginary world dominated by the city of New Crobuzon, a corrupt center of power clearly inspired by Charles Dickens's London. Science and technology play an important role in New Crobuzon; the book's central metaphor is an attempt to drive a rail line through the unexplored continent beyond the city's borders. But real power lies in the wielding of magic. While golems and hexes and other conceits from European mythology figure prominently, these myths have been stripped of all traces of religious allegory. Without ever spelling out the details (any more than Isaac Asimov explained the intricacies of his robots' "positronic brains"), Mieville treats magic as another form of technology, one that follows dimly apprehended rules and that typically exacts a cost greater than its practitioners anticipate.

In an instructive parallel to slavery in the antebellum South, the economy of New Crobuzon seems to rely on the labor of the Remade—criminals "reconfigured in the city's punishment factories" into nightmare chimeras, part human, part animal, part machine. Chain gangs of Remades are sent to work on the transcontinental railway, side by side with human laborers and members of New Crobuzon's many "xenian" species—sentient creatures that resemble frogs and birds and insect-humanoid hybrids.

Mieville feels no need to explain the presence of the xenians in New Crobuzon; they are as much a part of his imaginary society as the magic-empowered militia that enforces the dictates of the ruling elite. What concerns him is the emergence of a serious resistance movement. When oppressed humans overcome their ingrained loathing of the Remade and the xenians to make common cause against the powers that be, Mieville invests their rising with a historical poignancy that by no means ensures its success. To convey both the weirdness and the familiarity of his vividly elaborated world, he peppers his sentences with unusual words ("serein," "strath," "atramentous," "cuneal") that will send most readers to a good unabridged dictionary—and back again to this challenging but deeply rewarding novel.

Roz Kaveney (review date 10 September 2004)

SOURCE: Kaveney, Roz. "Remade in Revolution." *Times Literary Supplement,* no. 5293 (10 September 2004): 20.

[In the following review, Kaveney identifies the recurrence of Marxist themes in Miéville's Iron Council.*]*

It is ironic that a fantasy genre the terms of which were in large part dictated by the socialist William Morris, should have acquired a set of political values in which human solidarity tends to be seen in feudal terms. Tolkien's Sam and Frodo are the most loyal of friends, but Frodo remains Sam's master. One of the tasks that China Miéville's fourth novel [*Iron Council*] sets itself is to write a heroic fantasy in which the assumed values are not merely not feudal, but actively Marxist.

This means that he has had to create, in the earlier New Crobuzon novels—*Perdido Street Station* (2001) and *The Scar* (2003)—a Fantasyland that has moved on from medievalism into something like high capitalism, even if the technologies involved have as much to do with magic as with science. This is a place in which deviants and rebels cannot even call their shapes their own; the standard punishment is to have your body whimsically "remade" into monstrosity. This would be crude symbolism were it not for the fact that Miéville takes such delight in multiplying grotesquerie. The first two books had plots whose main point was to take the reader on a guided tour of the city of New Crobuzon and the ocean where some of its worst enemies lurk. Having helped us understand this world, Miéville now has to show people trying to change it.

His literary model here is less *Lord of the Rings* than Jack London's novel of 1900, *The Iron Heel,* to which Miéville's title may allude. The ideal mode for a novel of revolution is the tragic, because if the revolution is the tragic, because if the revolution fails its chronicler does not have to deal with betrayal. The actual insurrection here owes much to the Paris Commune—the city is at war, and the rebels find themselves fighting its enemies as well as its ruling class. As revolution crumbles, hope keeps fighting; once, there was a rising that succeeded—the remade convict workers on an endless railroad across shifting nightmare lands found solidarity with unpaid whores and cynical engineers, and seized the tracklaying train. Somewhere out in deserts and swamps, they have the place to which they fled, pulling track and bridges up behind them.

This is not the most original of images, but it is a telling one—so telling that Miéville has to provide a lengthy back story which distorts the middle of the novel. We know, because Miéville does not allow us the consolation of suspense, that the perpetual revolution, the armoured train that is the Iron Council, will not make it back to the city in time; the question that faces the novel's principal characters is how to make final defeat worthwhile.

Most of the principals are as much case histories as characters—street urchins and tough whores radicalized by their situation. Most of the book's energy comes from the detached intellectual Judah Lowe, the Council's ally and muscle, whose name indicates both his strength—the ability to create golems from mud, air and ever more abstract concepts—and his eventual decision to commit what might be seen as a betrayal, for the greater good. The double service done by Judah Lowe's name is an example of Miéville's erudite wordplay, which sometimes betrays him into a clotted cleverness: "Godspit", a character curses, and it is a good fantasy curse. Too much of this—and there are often ten examples on a single page—suggests that the book was at least as much fun to write as it is to read. Sadly, this intense tale of revolt and solidarity is weakened by solipsism at its core.

Carl Freedman (essay date summer 2005)

SOURCE: Freedman, Carl. "To the Perdido Street Station: The Representation of Revolution in China Miéville's *Iron Council.*" *Extrapolation* 46, no. 2 (summer 2005): 235-48.

[*In the following essay, Freedman identifies* Iron Council *as the third work in Miéville's New Crobuzon trilogy, but also notes thematic similarities between* Iron Council *and Miéville's first novel,* King Rat.]

> The category of reflection, central to the Marxist problematic as we have shown, is concerned not with realism but with materialism, which is profoundly different.
>
> —Étienne Balibar and Pierre Macherey, "On Literature as an Ideological Form" (1974)

> Marxist reality means: reality plus the future within it.
>
> —Ernst Bloch, "Marxism and Poetry" (1935)

When China Miéville published *Iron Council* in 2004, the novel was widely and justly appreciated as the conclusion of a trilogy that the author had begun with *Perdido Street Station* (2000) and continued with *The Scar* (2002), both highly acclaimed books that quickly established Miéville as one of the most important writers of speculative fiction on either side of the Atlantic. To be sure, the three volumes form a trilogy in only a loose sense. There is no overarching narrative that spans the three installments, and there are no truly continuing dramatis personae, though a character or event prominently featured in one volume may be mentioned *en passant* in another. What really unites the novels is their common setting in the invented world of Bas-Lag, a kind of alternative Earth though one whose relationship in time or space to our own is never directly broached. In logical rigor and consistency, in almost endlessly inventive detail, and in general three-dimensional solidity, Bas-Lag is one of the most fully achieved imaginary worlds ever created; it is, for instance, vastly richer, more plausible, and more reward-

ing than Tolkien's Middle-earth. Furthermore, each volume significantly expands our sense of it. *Perdido Street Station* is set almost (though not quite) exclusively in the city-state of New Crobuzon—a diverse, authoritarian port city that, while stunningly original, owes something to Victorian London, something to modern Cairo, something to the Vieux Carré of New Orleans, and doubtless something to many other sources as well—whereas *The Scar* departs from the city at the outset and shows us the seaways and the seafaring life of Bas-Lag and also the latter's complex geopolitics in which New Crobuzon is only one powerful player. *Iron Council* returns to New Crobuzon, but also introduces a vast continental land mass traversed by the great railway project alluded to in the title. Miéville clearly knows a good deal more about Bas-Lag than he has needed to reveal in these three thick volumes; and one expects that at some point—though not, perhaps, immediately—he will return to it.

What has generally gone unnoticed, however, is that, in writing *Iron Council,* Miéville has not only completed the Bas-Lag trilogy but has also achieved a quite different literary consummation: namely, the completion of a fictional diptych about revolution begun with his first published novel, *King Rat* (1998). A work of smaller compass than the Bas-Lag trilogy, *King Rat* is also a novel of very different texture and mode. It is set not in an invented world but in the London of the 1990s, though a London invaded by fantastic forces and one that operates, in some ways, "at right angles" (to borrow one of the central metaphors of the text itself) to the empirical London we know. My crucial point here is not only that some continuing thematic and political concerns subsist despite the generic discontinuity, but also that, as we shall see, the generic discontinuity itself amounts to a political intervention of the highest importance. For the two novels are not simply about two different revolutions, but about two radically different *kinds* of revolution—and the political difference is so fundamental that it might well be described as a generic one.

It is thus necessary to recall, briefly, the substance of *King Rat,* though this is ground that I have elsewhere covered in much greater detail.[1] The text is structured on a certain antinomy: put simply, the novel is the story of a revolution but not the sort of revolution whose story it most ardently *wants* to tell. For *King Rat* is a radically left-wing book, investing heavily in a Marxist analysis of late-capitalist society and in a socialist ethics as well. A revolutionary-socialist stance is operative (if not always explicit) in every chapter, and is clear even without reference to the public politics of the author (who happens to be a Marxist scholar of international law, an editor of the learned Marxist journal *Historical Materialism,* a militant of the British Socialist Workers Party, and a one-time candidate for

Parliament on the Socialist Alliance ticket). Yet there is nothing at all socialist about the revolution with which the novel climaxes and concludes. The rats constitute a sort of proletariat, but there is no movement among them to overthrow the conditions of oppression and exploitation in which they live. Instead, the protagonist Saul Garamond (himself half rat and half human) single-handedly topples the monarchy of the title character, thus making a revolution from above and ushering in a new era that seems to promise (at best) bourgeois rather than socialist democracy. This is indeed progress, but not to the degree or of the kind implied by the Marxist intent of the text as a whole. The text is, however, entirely clear-sighted about what it finally settles for. "I declare this Year One of the Rat Republic" (317), announces Saul, who exalts the values of "Liberty, Equality . . . and let's put the 'rat' back into 'Fraternity'" (317; ellipsis in original). At the end, he designates himself as "Citizen Rat" (318). These are—quite obviously—the slogans of 1789, not 1917; we are in the world of the Rights of Man, not that of All Power to the Workers. Lenin (a particular hero for Saul's father) has been replaced by Robespierre. The socialist novel ends with a bourgeois revolution.

We need to be very clear that, when comparing socialist revolution with bourgeois revolution, we are by no means dealing with differing versions of the same essential thing. It would, indeed, be closer to the truth to say that the word *revolution* in the two phrases is at least as much a pun as a full-fledged political category. A bourgeois revolution is, in the nature of the case, a severely *limited* operation, however widespread the physical upheaval may become. For such a revolution is based on the struggle between rival power elites, typically pitting the increasing power of capital against a feudal or at any rate decisively pre-capitalist old regime of entrenched privilege.[2] The bourgeoisie or their (sometimes highly mediated) political representatives do indeed tend to espouse universalistic rather than admittedly class goals, and may accordingly "invite" the masses to fight on their side. But any serious effort to advance the economic interests of the masses at the expense of those of the rising new elite tends to be strictly, and not gently, curtailed—as the followers of Gracchus Babeuf learned in France during the 1790s, and as those of Gerard Winstanley learned in England during the 1640s and 1650s.

By contrast, the economic interests of the masses are precisely what a socialist revolution is all about. Its ultimate aim is not to substitute rule by a rising, more progressive class for rule by an exhausted and reactionary one, but instead to abolish class rule altogether. It strives to establish the structures not only of political democracy but also of economic democracy, so that equality before the law will be completed and guaranteed by equality of ownership of the total social wealth.[3] Whereas a bourgeois revolution is at bottom concerned with a choice of masters, and with the forms by which mastery is exercised, a socialist revolution is not complete until mastery itself has been rendered into a fading historical memory. Socialist revolution is thus an incomparably, indeed *generically,* more radical transformation than bourgeois revolution; and this radicality is surely the major reason that, despite some interesting and important (and sometimes terrifying) attempts, no fully successful socialist revolution has yet been consummated on our planet. But Miéville is not one to be limited by the philistine myopia that would forbid attempting (even in imagination) that which has never before been achieved; and the project of **Iron Council** is precisely to begin anew the attempt to imagine what socialist revolution might be like. As Edmund Wilson famously traced the socialist idea from its Enlightenment origins to Lenin's 1917 arrival at the Finland station, from which he assumed leadership of the October Revolution, Miéville now extends the story into an alternative future, pressing on to the Perdido Street Station, the geographical center of oppressive rule in despotic, capitalist New Crobuzon.[4]

Indeed, this is perhaps the main project for which New Crobuzon and Bas-Lag exist in the first place. Now that we can survey the Bas-Lag trilogy as a whole, it is evident that the creation of what is arguably the most boldly and meticulously realized alternative world in fiction serves the ultimate purpose of providing a locus where ideas of socialist revolution can be experimentally concretized. For **King Rat** is finally limited, politically, by its London setting. The contradiction between the Marxist ideals that the text tries to uphold, on the one hand, and, on the other, the Robespierrist slogans with which it climaxes and must finally content itself should be seen as in some measure a reflection of an actual social contradiction: namely, the contradiction in 1990s Britain between the will to maintain the socialist idea and the increasing marginalization of socialism (even in the tepid, reformist version of the old Labour Party before its current Blairite leadership renounced socialism altogether) within the actual socio-political arena. Yet few other current real-world settings provide a much more promising locale for socialist imagining: not, certainly, oligarchic post-Soviet Russia, nor roaringly state-capitalist China, nor the emphatically neo-liberal United States. In such a reactionary world environment, it is not surprising that the revolutionary-socialist imagination should migrate to the alternative worlds of speculative fiction. It should also be noted, though, that the world-wide movement for global justice (often defamed by its enemies as an "anti-globalization" movement) that was catalyzed by the Seattle anti-WTO demonstrations of 1999 (the year following the publication of **King Rat**) has in recent years provided a renewal of strong, though non-localizable, anti-capitalist energy; and that this political energy may to some degree lie behind the socialist project of the Bas-Lag trilogy and of *Iron Council* in particular.

While generically an instance of what Miéville calls "weird fiction"—his highly original version of specula- tive fiction that blends science fiction, Surrealism, fantasy, magical realism, and Lovecraftian horror, and in his latest effort with the whole tradition of the Western from Zane Grey to Cormac McCarthy thrown into the mix—*Iron Council* alludes to many historical movements of socialist and radical opposition: e.g., the labor struggles that attended the coming of the railroad to the American West; the Paris Commune; Narodnik terrorism in pre-Revolutionary Russia; the October Revolution; and modern struggles of black liberation and women's liberation, especially as the latter move- ment has focused on the dignity and organization of sex workers. But the result is not just a collection of fragmentary historical allegories but a coherent and autonomous, though multivalent and fictional, social formation: and, moreover, one constructed according to unswervingly materialist premises despite—or rather partly because of—the frequent departures of the text from literary realism (to adapt the crucial distinction invoked in the epigraph above by Balibar and Macherey). Indeed, the freedom and flexibility offered by arealistic modes of fiction have enabled Miéville to produce one of the most searching materialist medita- tions on socialist revolution—ontologically, ethically, and even aesthetically—in contemporary Anglophone fiction.

On the level of Marxist ontology (and epistemology), perhaps the most important point is that the complexity of Bas-Lag allows Miéville to suggest with particular force and clarity the material *overdetermination* (in the Freudian sense as recomplicated by Louis Althusser)[5] that is crucial to a socialist revolution. Probably more than any other sort of historical event, socialist revolu- tion is based on the conjuncture of a multiplicity of material determinations, all of them relatively autono- mous and none reducible to any of the others. In *Iron Council* the revolution that appears in the making depends, first of all, on two almost (if not quite) completely independent movements: on the one hand, the formation of a revolutionary Collective (reminiscent of the Paris Commune) that is able to precipitate a dual- power situation in New Crobuzon and then temporarily to take effective executive power in large sections of the city; and, on the other, the earlier takeover of the great rail project by its own workers, who reconstitute themselves as the Iron Council and maintain the train as a perpetually moving egalitarian city that succeeds in evading punitive action by the New Crobuzon Militia, the city-state's principal repressive apparatus. The chief

narrative line in the time present of the novel concerns the efforts by representatives of the Collective to locate the (by now legendary) Iron Council, which they regard as a precedent and inspiration and to whom they look for advice and assistance.

Furthermore, both the Council and the Collective are themselves vividly drawn formations of great internal dialectical complexity. The Collective is partly the work of the Caucus, a broad coalition of socialist and quasi- Marxist parties and underground newspapers (the best known of which, the *Runagate Rampant,* is, along with its heroic editor, Benjamin Flex, prominently featured in *Perdido Street Station*). The illegal Caucus competes with the more sensational and quasi-Narodnik terrorism of the followers of the mysterious Toro, who succeed in assassinating the Mayor of New Crobuzon. Whether this political killing (though justified in purely moral terms) makes a genuine revolutionary contribution is, however, more than dubious; the text seems to endorse the viewpoint of Ori (a former Caucus militant who leaves to join the anarchistic terrorism of the Toroans) when, after the Collective comes into being, he finds "in himself a drab certainty that the killing of the Mayor had done nothing at all" toward the goal of revolution (455). On the other hand, there is no doubt whatever that the building of the Collective is due in large part not only to the Caucus but also to a great many previ- ously unaffiliated citizens, whose rage has been build- ing over decades marked not only by grinding poverty but also by the (literally) fantastically cruel repression with which the Mayor's government has attempted to crush all stirrings of dissidence. It seems unlikely, however, that this rage would have boiled over without the additional toll taken by the exhausting foreign war that New Crobuzon has been fighting with the faraway Tesh, and the increasing disaffection of the city's soldiers; there is doubtless an allusion here to the exhaustion of the Russian Czarist state by the First World War and the important role played by Russian soldiers in the October Revolution.

As to the determinations of the Iron Council, some of them are less familiar within the classical Marxist problematic of the nineteenth and early-twentieth centuries. The revolutionary seizure of the train is in part a straightforward labor struggle, and an essential contribution to the formation of the Council is (finally) made by the free male workers employed by the Transcontinental Railroad Trust (the name instantly recalls the America of the Wild West). But this group of workers does not, in fact, take the lead in the uprising that leads to the Iron Council, and even displays, at first, some conservative tendencies in comparison to two other, distinct elements in the ultimate revolution- ary coalition. One is the contingent of female sex work- ers, who refuse to extend credit to their male customers and strike on the simple slogan, *No pay no lay.* At first the men respond with a myopic hostility fueled by the sexual frustration that has, of course, provided a market for the striking women's services in the first place. Not without difficulty, the women do, however, succeed in convincing the men (whose own wages are being withheld by the TRT) that class solidarity between them is more important than the gender differences; and the women's slogan assumes a more general significance, as the strike widens to include male workers and *lay,* in addition to its sexual meaning, comes to signify the laying of railroad track. But there is also a third distinct group in the uprising, and one that, unlike the ordinary male workers, supports and joins the women workers' strike without delay or hesitation: namely, the slave-labor force of Remade, both male and female. The Remade—one of the most memorably imaginative creations in the whole trilogy, figuring largely in *Perdido Street Station* and *The Scar* as well as in *Iron Council*—are New Crobuzoners who, having fallen afoul of the Mayor's government for one reason or another, are sentenced to "punishment factories" where their bodies are permanently reshaped in deliberately grotesque and humiliating ways. Maimed by all manner of amputations and mutilations and by the addition to their bodies of animal and mechanical parts, the Remade are typically looked upon with intense disgust by those who have not suffered the same fate. In the trilogy they serve in part to figure the situation of any group regarded as inferior and degraded in specifically *racial* ways; and, as ever, sexual taboos play a large role in enforcing such bigotry. A crucial point in the formation of the Iron Council is reached when Ann-Hari, the leader of the female strikers, grips a leading Remade militant and (to the spontaneous horror of many non-Remade men) kisses him squarely on the mouth. There is not necessarily any "natural" affinity among the sex workers, the Remade, and the free male laborers; but the novel vividly illustrates how such revolutionary coalitions are formed.

I have sketched out the overdeterminationism of *Iron Council*—and some of the particular overdeterminations of revolutionary activity by the Council and the Collective—in necessarily brief and hence somewhat schematic terms. But Miéville's mastery of psychological and thematic coherence and of abundant detail means that there is nothing schematic about the novel itself, whose account seems as "thick"—as rich and solid—as that of any existential history. Yet this fictional history does not, in fact, culminate in the triumph of socialism. The Collective meets much the same fate as its chief real-world model, the Paris Commune (though numerous other historical precedents could be cited, such as the Munich Soviet Republic of 1919 or revolutionary Barcelona in 1936). The dual-power situation endures long enough that a limited but authentically utopian zone of popular democracy is constituted, and the characteristic military heroism of proletarian revolution flourishes. Ultimately, though, support for the Collective is neither widespread nor well-organized enough to resist the massive physical power of the apparatuses of state repression—most importantly the New Crobuzon Militia, which gradually but decisively regains control of the city in atrociously bloody fighting. The golem-maker Judah Low, who is probably the most far-seeing theorist of revolution within the text, warns that the time present of the novel is the "wrong time" (548) for revolution. The text's attitude toward the heartbreakingly brief triumph of the Collective seems strictly parallel to the attitude Marx displays in his writings on the Paris Commune itself: namely, an unbounded admiration for the courage and sacrifice of the revolutionaries (Marx, in *The Civil War in France* [1871], describes the Commune as "the glorious harbinger of a new society" and the murdered Communards as "enshrined in the great heart of the working class" [233]) combined with a grim calculation that the objective balance of forces does not yet allow the overthrow of the repressive state followed by a popular seizure of the means of economic production. The Collective is smashed, but the Militia has had to wreck New Crobuzon itself to do it, and the ruling-class boast, "Order reigns in New Crobuzon!" (561) thus rings rather hollow. *Runagate Rampant* continues to publish, and revolutionary hope is not completely extinguished.

The fate of the Iron Council is rather different and more complicated than that of the Collective, and is foregrounded more prominently in the text. Indeed, the Council is really the collective protagonist of the whole novel; and it is deeply significant that in this final installment of the Bas-Lag trilogy, where collective socialist action is explicitly engaged, it is a *group* of characters who dominate the book in somewhat the same way that *Perdido Street Station* and *The Scar* are dominated by individual protagonists, namely the scientist Isaac Dan der Grimnebulin and the linguist Bellis Coldwine, respectively. But Judah (who, uniquely among the novel's characters, is directly and personally involved with both the Council and the Collective) is, if not the sole protagonist, still the single most important figure in *Iron Council*; and he plays the most decisive role in the final turn (within the novel) of the Council's story. In addition to being a revolutionary of saintly selflessness—and one who, like most saints (and perhaps most revolutionaries), has a touch of megalomania in his personality—Judah is notable for having advanced the technology of golem-making (or "golemetry") further than any practitioner of the art before him; and he has frequently used his talent in directly political ways, notably in assisting at the birth and the early defense of the Iron Council. Towards the end of the novel, as the Council is at last returning to

New Crobuzon to join the efforts of the Collective, Judah attempts—but fails—to dissuade his comrades from their course. The Collective, he believes, has already been sufficiently defeated that any attempt to join its revolutionary project is bound to fail; so that the Council, which for a full generation has managed to sustain itself as a moving space of classless democracy, would be entering New Crobuzon merely in order to commit collective suicide. Unable to convince his fellow Councillors of this conclusion, Judah takes matters into his own hands. In a supreme and unprecedented golemetric feat, he constructs a golem out of time itself and uses it to suspend the perpetual train in a kind of temporal limbo. At a stroke, the Iron Council's progress toward New Crobuzon is halted, and it is also rendered invulnerable to any retaliatory action by the Militia. Most of the Councillors are put into what seems to be some sort of suspended animation, thus to remain until an entirely uncertain future: "[p]erhaps till things are ready [i.e., for revolution]" (543), as Judah himself puts it.

The text's attitude toward Judah's *coup* is intensely complex, and helps to engage the novel's most searching consideration of revolutionary ethics. Judah faces a dilemma in some ways parallel to that confronted by Isaac in the final pages of **Perdido Street Station.** Early in that novel Isaac had promised to use his scientific and technological abilities to restore the lost wings of the garuda Yagharek; and towards the end of the story Isaac is particularly determined to fulfill his promise, since Yag has by this time become a loyal friend and a battle-tested comrade in the fight against the monstrous slake-moths. Before he can honor his commitment, however, he learns that Yagharek's wings had been amputated in a garuda judicial proceeding because of Yag's guilt in an especially vile crime. Isaac is thus faced with the awful choice between betraying his promise to a loyal friend and condoning that friend's earlier criminality, helping him to evade its consequences. Isaac chooses not to replace the wings, thus dooming Yagharek, a member of a species for whom flying is as integral to normal life as walking is to humans, to a flightless existence. But neither he nor the text can be certain if this is the right decision or, indeed, whether any "right" decision is even conceivable.

It is similar with Judah. The text gives us no reason to suspect that his estimation of the hopelessness of the Council's projected return to New Crobuzon is at all faulty. Since the golem-maker Judah uniquely possesses the power to save the Iron Council and all that it has achieved, does he not have, as he insists, the moral and political duty to do so? Yet Ann-Hari—perhaps Judah's only true peer among the revolutionary leaders as well as, at various times, his lover—is also persuasive when she maintains that Judah could not possibly *know* with

absolute certainty that the revolutionary cause was hopeless in the near term; and that, even more crucially, he had no moral right to take the decision away from a democratic collective process and arrogate it to himself alone: "You don't get to choose. You don't decide when is the right time, when it fits your story. *This was the time we were here*" (552; emphasis in original). On this point the comparison with **Perdido Street Station** is especially pertinent. For Yagharek's crime, as Isaac learns, was one which Isaac—and we—would understand as rape, but which is understood very differently in garuda society. As Yagharek's victim Kar'uchai explains, she does not consider herself to have been violated, or defiled, or ravished—all concepts indelibly marked by reactionary ideologies of patriarchal paternalism. Yagharek's crime against Kar'uchai was to *steal her choice,* and choice-theft, according to Kar'uchai, is among garudas "the only crime we *have*" (692; emphasis in original). It is also the crime that Judah has committed against the Iron Council: so that Judah, though in one way parallel to Isaac, is in another way parallel to Yagharek himself. He may have saved the Councillors physically, but only at the cost of depriving them of that autonomy of decision-making without which the revolutionary project becomes deeply problematic at best. Judah himself understands this point, and makes no attempt to evade the bullet (something his golemetric abilities would have easily enabled him to do) when Ann-Hari, with profound sadness but full determination, shoots him to death. Throughout the two novels Yagharek and Judah have become deeply sympathetic figures; yet the reader cannot feel certain that either Yag's mutilation or Judah's execution is necessarily unjust.

The major difference between the two cases is that Isaac faces a purely individual moral dilemma, whereas, with Judah, Ann-Hari, and the Council, Miéville has raised the whole question to a higher level by casting it in the collective terms of socialist revolution: so that **Iron Council** not only engages, in its overdeterminationism, the ontology and epistemology of revolution, but also amounts to a profound, complex interrogation of the tactics and ethics of revolution as well. Indeed, in this dimension of the novel Miéville continues a political-ethical discourse begun long ago by Trotsky, who, in his pre-Bolshevik phase, vehemently derided Lenin's theory of party organization as "substitutism" (*zamestitelstvo*), that is to say, the notion that it was sometimes permissible for a relatively small group to substitute its own judgment for that of the broader socialist movement: a practice that Trotsky attacked as undemocratic and likely to lead, ultimately, to the dictatorship of a single individual (see Deutscher 88-97). Whether Trotsky was right against Lenin (and against his own later, Leninist position) remains an open historical question. There are compelling arguments that Stalin's dictatorship was always implicit, to some degree, in even the earliest practices of Bolshevik organization—but also that, this side of the purest, most ineffectual anarchism, a certain degree of substitutism may remain an unavoidable practical necessity for a revolutionary movement. Miéville does not claim (even implicitly) to have settled the argument. But, in Judah's decisive act of quasi-Leninist substitutism and Ann-Hari's quasi-Trotskyist response to it, he has dramatized the ethical and strategic issues at stake with force and rigor.

So complicated is the incident of Judah's suspension of the train that it also helps to address a further and different set of issues too, issues that engage what might be called the *aesthetics,* or even the hermeneutics, of socialist revolution. In addition to raising urgent ethical questions, the temporal suspension that Judah effects also amounts, on a rather different level, to a metaphor for the preservation of revolutionary hope through such deeply unrevolutionary eras as that in which the novel itself is written. Here we need to consider not only this particular act of golemetry but also many other political interventions by literally fantastic forces throughout the novel. For there are many points at which the revolutionaries triumph only because of resources not actually available to socialists in the real world. Once, for example, the situation of the Iron Council is saved against attack by TRT gendarmes by the unexpected arrival of the borinatch, a "cavalry of striders" (258) with supernormal abilities like the power to reach and fight through dimensions unseen to humans; their rescue of the Council is not only fantastic but also amounts to a clear (though distant) generic echo of the near-miraculous arrival of the US Cavalry in many Western films, like John Ford's *Stagecoach* (1939). Then too, there are several instances where the Council is able to evade the Militia by taking refuge in the Cacotopic Stain, a mysterious and deeply feared area of Bas-Lag where the very structure of space-time seems unpredictable and malevolent: "Iron Council relied on the cacotopic zone. That was what would hide them" (406). Finally—to offer one more example out of many that could be cited—Judah's golemetry saves, or helps to save, the day on numerous occasions prior to his ultimate invention of the time-golem: as when he makes golems literally out of thin air to wage "a strange, near-invisible fight" (505) against the Council's enemies. We should remember that Miéville's character is named after Rabbi Judah Loew, who, according to the fantastic Jewish legend, invented a golem out of clay in the ghetto of sixteenth-century Prague in order to protect the Jews from Christian pogroms: protection that the Jews lacked, of course, in actuality.

By the strictest canons of realism—by Georg Lukács's definitive standards of socialist realism, for instance—

the use of plot devices like golems amounts to a kind of cheating. How can a novel honestly claim to engage the rigors of socialist revolution if it constantly has recourse to factors beyond the capacity of any conceivable real-world revolutionary movement? There are, however, several grounds on which Miéville's practice here can be defended. To begin with, the supermundane elements in *Iron Council* can be understood as metaphorical displacements, within the invented world of Bas-Lag, of phenomena familiar enough in actual earthly history. The timely arrival of the borinatch reminds us that revolutions have always proceeded in part by attracting unexpected allies, whose participation could not have been predicted in advance. And does not the Cacotopic Stain figure the importance of terrain for revolutionary guerilla movements, for instance the elaborate use of their country's landscape by the Vietnamese revolutionaries who defeated the French and American occupiers? As for golems, golemetry—like all magic or thaumaturgy in the Bas-Lag trilogy—is fundamentally a material *technology,* a learnable and teachable skill; and Judah's technical brilliance may serve to stress the importance, for revolutionaries, of mastering the most advanced technologies available (an interesting recent example is the use of computer networks by the Mexican Zapatistas to extend their organizational reach and overcome what might otherwise have been a disabling geographical isolation in Chiapas). Yet in reply to these points the uncompromising Lukácisan might insist that such displacements are after all required only by the more general and logically prior displacement of earth itself by Bas-Lag; and that the choice of such an "unrealistic" setting in the first place amounts to the betrayal of realism and a concomitant failure of authorial nerve. To answer this charge leads us to a deeper defense—indeed, *the* fundamental defense—of Miévillian "weird fiction."

As we have already suggested, the choice of an alternative-world rather than a real-world environment for a novel about socialist revolution cannot be understood apart from the singularly inhospitable circumstances for socialist revolution offered by the real world during the era in which *Iron Council* has been written. One might say that, in terms of individual talent, Miéville may be a better or a worse novelist than, say, Maxim Gorky (justly one of Lukács's particular heroes of socialist realism), but that what is certain is that Miéville could not possibly *be* Gorky, no matter what. The setting of this revolutionary novel in a fantastic world implicitly recognizes, in its very structure, the unavailability of socialist revolution in the immediate empirical world; and the use, in *Iron Council,* of some magical devices in the invented revolutionary struggle is best grasped as a series of utopian signs, or figures, or placeholders, for social forces whose precise nature cannot yet be identified but which must be in some way posited if the ultimate ideal of revolutionary social justice is to be maintained. The basic project of **Iron Council,** in other words, is to keep hope alive, to insist upon the horizon of socialist revolution even in the current absence of entirely specific particulars that could define the latter. The text's towering figure for such hope is the suspended train of the Iron Council, unable to effect immediate practical change but still charged with revolutionary energy that is to be discharged another day. As the novel's final paragraph puts it:

> Years might pass and we will tell the story of the Iron Council and how it was made, how it made itself and went, and how it came back, and is coming, is still coming. Women and men cut a line across the dirtland and dragged history out and back across the world. They are still with shouts setting their mouths and we usher them in. They are coming out of the trenches of rock toward the brick shadows. They are always coming.
>
> (564)

The key word of this passage is of course the adverb in the final sentence.

This is not, to be sure, realism in any normal generic sense. But it is a kind of material reality nonetheless. It is, precisely, the Marxist reality invoked in the epigraph above from Ernst Bloch, the greatest philosopher of utopia, who insisted that the real is never exhausted by the empirical content of any actually existing social formation but, on the contrary, always includes the revolutionary potential implicit in human activity—the potential to which we are driven by the never-destroyed (though often disappointed) principle of hope. To comprehend such potential in our future is for Bloch the chief function of the aesthetic imagination, including—emphatically including—the imagination of the fantastic. Miéville is here completely at one with Bloch, and both are at one with Marx. In a famous passage from Volume One of *Capital,* to which Miéville himself refers in one of his scholarly pieces (see Miéville 2002b), Marx defines human labor itself partly in terms of the imagining of that which does not yet exist. What distinguishes "the worst architect from the best of bees," says Marx, is that the architect "builds the cell in his mind before he constructs it in wax." Accordingly, "[a]t the end of every labour process, a result emerges which had already been conceived by the worker at the beginning, hence already existed ideally" (284). Especially if we bear in mind that the root Greek meaning of "fantastic" *(phantastikos)* is the making visible of something to the mind's eye, it is easy to concur with Miéville's gloss on this passage: "The fantastic is there at the most prosaic moment of production" (44). No less than any other form of material production—indeed, far more so—the production of a socialist society takes place first of all in the imagination.

Iron Council, then, completes the diptych begun with **King Rat** by transcending the intellectual and imaginative horizons of the earlier novel, fine as **King Rat** is. True enough, both texts ultimately fail to represent an achieved socialist revolution. But, because the later novel does engage the revolutionary-socialist problematic with great rigor and with scrupulously realized particulars—and because it keeps hope alive by keeping socialist revolution on the agenda despite all immediate setbacks—its "failure" takes place on a much more advanced level. In the celebrated opening pages of *The Eighteenth Brumaire of Louis Bonaparte* (1852), Marx explains that bourgeois revolutions, with their limited aims and their necessary bad faith, take their poetry from the past—"to deaden their awareness of their own content" (149). He adds that socialist revolutions, however, whose aims transcend any pre-existing rhetorical resources, must take their poetry from the future. In the early twenty-first century, perhaps no author can do more than China Miéville has done in **Iron Council**: which is to have made a brilliant preliminary sort of poetry out of the fact that, at a date whose lateness would have shocked Marx himself, the actual poetry of socialist revolution remains stubbornly in the future.[6]

Notes

1. The remainder of this paragraph provides a highly condensed recapitulation (with one or two new emphases) of Freedman 2003.

2. Some recent Marxist scholarship has begun to suggest that the category of bourgeois revolution—and even the relationship between the bourgeoisie and the early history of capitalism—may be more problematic than had previously been thought; e.g., see Wood 2002. But it seems to me that Miéville's work is coherent with the more traditional Marxist view assumed above.

3. Actually, Miéville, as a (critical) follower of the Soviet legal theorist Evgeny Pashukanis, would himself insist that socio-economic equality would not so much "complete and guarantee" equality before the law as *supersede* it: for the Pashukanisite position holds the legal form to be inseparable from the commodity form and hence from class exploitation. In his major work of scholarship thus far (Miéville 2005), Miéville argues, for instance, that, "[i]n its very neutrality, law maintains capitalist relations" (101) and that "[t]he political—the violent, the coercive—lies at the heart of the legal" (151). Most emphatically, he insists, "The chaotic and bloody world around us *is the rule of law*" (319; emphasis in original).

4. I wish I could claim to be the first to think of the title pun of this paper, which brings together *Iron Council* with *To the Finland Station* (1940), Wilson's classic "study in the writing and acting of history." Unfortunately, it can be found in Dirda 2004.

5. The chief reference here is to Althusser 1977, 87-116 and 161-218; see also Freud 1965, *passim*. In the current context it is relevant to note that the October Revolution is Althusser's privileged instance of over-determination (Althusser 99-101).

6. In preparing the final version of this paper, I have (as more than once in the past) received important and useful help from Mark Bould, Chris Kendrick, Steve Shaviro, and Sherryl Vint. I should also acknowledge a continuing debt to the students who several years ago took part in my undergraduate seminar on the fiction of China Miéville at Louisiana State University—and especially to Lee Abbott, Rich Cooper, and Anson Trahan, who re-united for a discussion of *Iron Council*, which had not yet been published when the seminar took place.

Works Cited

Althusser, Louis. *For Marx*. Trans. Ben Brewster. London: NLB. 1977.

Deutscher, Isaac. *The Prophet Armed—Trotsky: 1879-1921*. Volume I. New York: Vintage. 1965.

Dirda, Michael. "'Iron Council' by China Miéville." *The Washington Post*. 22 August 2004. BW15.

Freedman, Carl. "Towards a Marxist Urban Sublime: Reading China Miéville's *King Rat*." *Extrapolation*. Winter 2003. 395-408.

Freud, Sigmund. *The Interpretation of Dreams*. Ed. and Trans. James Strachey. New York: Avon. 1965.

Marx, Karl. *The Eighteenth Brumaire of Louis Bonaparte*. Trans. Ben Fowkes. In Karl Marx. *Surveys from Exile: Political Writings, Volume II*. Ed. David Fernbach. New York: Random House. 1973.

———. *The Civil War in France*. In Karl Marx. *The First International and After: Political Writings, Volume III*. Ed. David Fernbach. New York: Random House. 1974.

———. *Capital*. Volume One. Trans. Ben Fowkes. London: Penguin. 1976.

Miéville, China. *King Rat*. New York: Tor. 1998.

———. *Perdido Street Station*. New York: Ballantine. 2000.

———. *The Scar*. New York: Ballantine. 2002a.

———. "Editorial Introduction" to "Symposium: Marxism and Fantasy." *Historical Materialism*. Volume 10, Issue 4. 2002b.

———. *Iron Council*. New York: Ballantine. 2004.

———. *Between Equal Rights: A Marxist Theory of International Law*. Leiden: Brill. 2005.

Wilson, Edmund. *To the Finland Station: A Study in the Writing and Acting of History*. New York: Doubleday. 1940.

Wood, Ellen Meiksins. *The Origin of Capitalism: A Longer View*. London: Verso. 2002.

Sam Thompson (review date 14 October 2005)

SOURCE: Thompson, Sam. "Uncanny Invasions." *Times Literary Supplement*, no. 5350 (14 October 2005): 25.

[*Below, Thompson reviews the entries in* Looking for Jake and Other Stories, *finding that many of Miéville's favorite themes and techniques are included.*]

China Miéville is a writer original enough to work within the strictures of genre fiction. His novels are re-configurations of heroic fantasy-adventure, revelling in swashbuckling plots, outlandish scenery and spectacular set pieces, but rejecting post-Tolkien clichés in favour of a tradition of dark weirdness inherited from Mervyn Peake, Michael Moorcock and M. John Harrison. Miéville also brings an acute socialist agenda to a genre often accused of political backwardness. Three of his four novels take place in and around New Crobuzon, a fantastical megalopolis that looks like the dreaming unconscious of modern London: a violent, vibrant, techno-Gothic sprawl where science and magic drive the turbines of capitalism, and multiculturalism means a city shared between humans, cactuc-men, insect-women and still odder species.

Looking for Jake and Other Stories is a collection of fourteen, most of which have settings more recognizable than New Crobuzon. The collection contains many Londons, extrapolating the city into possible futures and satirical extremes, subjecting it to uncanny invasions and interdimensional visitations, and demolishing it in a variety of catastrophes. In the title story, London has suffered "a very inexact apocalypse". Cause and effect have been replaced by "vague entropy". Most of the population has inexplicably vanished, the sky is filled with monsters and the Underground system with lost souls. Refusing to make sense, the story becomes a manifesto for a kind of fiction that is devoted to the idea of the city, but committed to surrealistically remaking it. The narrator's house overlooks a drab vista, a "featureless crosshatching of brick and concrete", but, he says, "I learnt to see the view from my roof in the garish glow of fireworks, to hold it in the awe it deserved".

Miéville delights in the formalities of pulp fantasy. **"Reports of Certain Events in London"** is a stylish, well-crafted story presented as a sheaf of documentary evidence that has fallen into the hands of the narrator ("I, China Miéville") who proceeds to uncover a cabal dedicated to investigating occult urban phenomena called "Via Ferae". **"Different Skies"** is the diary of an old man who discovers that his study window looks into a parallel city. The distinctive trace of H. P. Lovecraft is evident in **"Details"**, the tale of a meddler in the supernatural who discovers that, indeed, "the devil's in the details". Another kind of pulp tradition appears in **"On the Way to the Front"**, a comic-strip story, illustrated by Liam Sharp, about mysterious soldiers passing through London; the sense of hybrid vigour created by the inclusion of a graphic tale is more satisfying than the slight, evasive story itself, however.

Often the stories are politically fuelled. **"'Tis the Season"** is a technicolor satire of privatization, in which citizens need an official YuleCo licence to celebrate Christmas, and riot police clash with the "Red-and-White Bloc" on protest marches. In **"An End to Hunger"**, a computer hacker tangles with a sinister charitable organization, while in **"Foundation"**, a Gulf War veteran is cursed with visions of the atrocities in which he was involved.

Miéville's best stories combine politicized verve with Gothic menace, and teeter uneasily on the line between the weird and the everyday. In **"Go-Between"**, Morley keeps finding sealed capsules inside his groceries, stamped with instructions for onward delivery. He knows he is a participant in some struggle, but has no idea who he is serving—or, when terrorists attack London, how he may be involved. Miéville's narrators are outsiders, skirting the edges of hidden worlds they cannot fully comprehend, and the stories in *Looking for Jake* trade heavily on ambiguity and suggestiveness. While this occasionally means that they leave their own promises unfulfilled, it also produces powerful tales of paranoid complicity like **"Go-Between"**.

The collection closes with **"The Tain"**, a novella whose source is an entry on "the fauna of mirrors" in *The Wood of Imaginary Beings* by Jorge Luis Borges. London is an eerie wasteland occupied by survivalists and military enclaves, and haunted by marauding, uncanny creatures. The long-imprisoned occupants of the world's mirrors have broken free and taken revenge on their captors: "your own faces came for you, your own arms crooked and pushing through the mirror". This spooky idea is realized in atmospheric detail, in a transformed urban landscape: "what had been the Post Office Tower, then Telecom Tower, and was now something else altogether: a distorted beacon in the killing fields of central London". The apocalyptic impulse runs through these stories. As all makers of good zombie movies know, nothing puts everyday life in perspective quite like seeing it wiped out by a plague of homicidal monsters. This, certainly, is part of China Miéville's purpose; but here the fantastical is not merely an oblique commentary on the real: the world through the mirror has its own agenda.

James Sallis (review date April 2006)

SOURCE: Sallis, James. Review of *Looking for Jake,* by China Miéville. *Magazine of Fantasy and Science Fiction* 110, no. 4 (April 2006): 36-41.

[*In the following excerpt, Sallis deems* Looking for Jake *a worthy addition to an already impressive oeuvre.*]

The field of fantastic literature has always been blessed with an extraordinary pool of talent, elders in the field maintaining their quality and volume of output even as those like Gene Wolfe and Neal Barrett, while growing a bit long in the tooth, also grow better with each year, the lot of them rushing out to the gate to greet newcomers like Ted Chiang, K. J. Bishop, and Richard K. Morgan. Then every so often there comes along a new writer—someone like Sturgeon, or Bester, say, in the field's adolescence—who just plain rocks us all back on our heels.

China Miéville started out that way four years ago with **Perdido Street Station,** followed up with **The Scar,** a brilliant take on (among much else) colonialism, then with **Iron Council**'s tale of a worker's revolution. All three novels are set in New Crobuzon, a land where high fantasy and the grittiest realism, medieval alchemy and modern technology, ancient and modern London, Mervyn Peake and Philip Farmer meet.

And now we have **Looking for Jake,** a collection of fourteen stories whose checkered pasts include venues ranging from independent publication by the UK's PS Publishing (**"The Tain"**) to the *Socialist Review* (**"'Tis the Season"**). Four stories are new. Only one, **"Jack,"** is set in New Crobuzon. And one, **"On the Way to the Front,"** is not a story at all but a story-sized graphic novel with artwork by Liam Sharp.

Like the novels, the stories are many-layered, multi-voiced, and intricately textured, possessed of an often stunning imaginative force. And like **King Rat** and **Perdido Street Station,** many of these stories are paeans to London, though a London transfigured, a London half-dissolved and—possibly—in the process of re-forming.

> The river was clogged with wrecks. Besides the mouldering barges that had always been there jutted the bows of police boats, and the decks and barrels of sunken gunships. Inverted tugs like rusting islands. The Thames flowed slowly around these impediments.
>
> Light's refusal to shimmer on its surface made the river matte as dried ink, overlaid on a cutout of London. Where the bridge's supports met the water, they disappeared into light and darkness.

That's from **"The Tain,"** the tale of a London besieged by creatures who have erupted from every reflective surface.

And this is from the collection's title story:

> The last time I picked up the receiver something whispered to me down the wires, asked me a question in a reverential tone, in a language I did not understand, all sibilants and dentals. I put the phone down carefully and have not lifted it since.

Miéville begins where many others leave off, with beautifully evocative language, social conscience, a clear sense of history, romantic longing, intelligence, despair—and a profound reverence for the past of fantastic fiction.

Art does not progress but forever circles back upon itself, reinventing itself and its vessels. Miéville's work, as I wrote here upon publication of *Perdido Street Station,* spreads its arms to take in much of what attracts us as readers to fantastic fiction, to what has always attracted us, and makes it new. These are books you sink into. This is a man putting everything he is—everything he has learned, everything he feels, everything he knows not to be true and everything he hopes can be—into his books.

This is, very possibly, greatness.

Bruce Allen (essay date 2007)

SOURCE: Allen, Bruce. "'Monsters Are the Main Thing': The Worlds of China Miéville." In *Contemporary Literary Criticism* 235, edited by Jeffrey W. Hunter. Farmington Hills, Mich.: Thomson Gale, 2007.

[In the following essay, Allen presents a global analysis of Miéville's oeuvre to date.]

China Miéville, with his unusual name and imposing appearance, is fascinating from the first glance. There are the shaved head, multiple earrings, the sneaky I-know-something-you-don't-know smile, and the brawny physique—all of which suggest nothing so much as a moonlighting professional football player auditioning for the role of household product symbol "Mr. Clean." Then there is his name. "China," as he has disclosed in numerous interviews, was the invention of "hippy" parents determined to adorn their offspring with a "beautiful name." Fortuitously enough, said name connotes exoticism, expansiveness, and a hint of mystery—all qualities lavishly exhibited by his ambitious fiction, which has, in a little less than a decade, boosted him to the pinnacle of the enduringly popular genre of adult fantasy.

But this punk-inflected H. G. Wells is a much more complex and interesting figure than the horde of virtually indistinguishable purveyors of faux-Arthurian quest tales rife with elves, dragons, wizards, and otherworldly what-have-you. He is in fact a highly visible public intellectual with a passionate interest in political history and theory and a commitment to social change so firm that it led him to run for Parliament—as a Socialist candidate—in 2001.

Miéville lost the election, but the reading world became the real winner, as he channeled his varied energies into a flood of vivid, edgy, and exciting fiction that has pushed the boundaries of genre to exhilarating extremes. His stories and novels shape tales of heroic adventure and mortal conflict into implacably onrushing vehicles for the expression of consistently challenging, often quite literally radical ideas.

A Londoner born (in 1972) and bred, Miéville is nevertheless an impressively cosmopolitan example of what poet William Blake called the mental traveler. He was educated at Cambridge, Harvard (briefly), and the London School of Economics, crowning his studies at the latter institution with a dissertation on Marxist political theory. He has contributed to numerous periodicals, anthologies, and online publications; given public readings throughout Great Britain and the United States; somehow found time to spend a year working and traveling in Egypt and Zimbabwe; and offers persuasive evidence (for example, in his annotated "Fifty Fantasy & Science Fiction Works That Socialists Should Read," published by *Fantastic Metropolis* [January 2002; www.fantasticmetropolis.com] and linked through the unofficial Miéville website "Runagate Rampant" [runagate-rampant.netfirms.com]) of having read and thoughtfully considered virtually every major work of politically inflected traditional and contemporary fantasy fiction.

His 1998 debut novel *King Rat,* a dark reimagining of the legend of the Pied Piper, was nominated for both an International Horror Guild Award and a Bram Stoker Prize. The three hefty blockbusters that followed it, *Perdido Street Station, The Scar,* and *Iron Council,* which comprise his (presumably uncompleted) New Crobuzon series and total nearly nineteen hundred pages, brought him nominations for the prestigious Hugo and Nebula Awards, and earned two equally prestigious British Fantasy Society and Arthur C. Clarke Awards. His short story collection *Looking for Jake* appeared in 2005, and was followed a year later by the nonfiction political study *Between Equal Rights: A Marxist Theory of International Law.* Seeking further worlds to conquer, Miéville has, most recently, written his first young adult fantasy novel, *Un Lun Dun* (2007).

Yet despite his range of interests, which both accommodate and range beyond purely literary concerns, Miéville is quick to acknowledge that he is the proud inheritor of several venerable traditions. While conceding both the achievement and the primacy of J. R. R. Tolkien, for example, he politely declines to follow the overused tropes and too often trodden byways of Middle Earth, instead aligning himself with the early twentieth-century masters of more abrasive, confrontational, and fatalistic fantasy: William Hope Hodgson, Robert W. Chambers, H. P. Lovecraft—inventors of perilous and threatening "worlds" which eerily mirror our own; practitioners of, as Miéville says, "the macabre, the surreal, the alienating, the decadent, the lush, the grotesque—a tradition of grotesquerie, cruelty, sadness, and alienation." Those words (from a year-2000 interview with *The Independent*) are echoed in numerous other public statements citing mentors and influences. As many critics and readers have pointed out, Miéville's haunted urban landscapes undoubtedly derive from the garish inventions of Mervyn Peake's gorgeously eccentric *Gormenghast* trilogy (1946-59) and the ongoing (1971-) *Viriconium* novels of Miéville's older contemporary M. John Harrison. He also tips his cap to fantasy masters Gene Wolfe and Michael Moorcock, their younger counterparts Neal Stephenson, Mary Gentle, and Susanna Clarke, and some of the more unconventional mainstream authors, such as Cormac McCarthy and Doris Lessing.

We can sense the presence of all these exemplars in Miéville's own fiction. And we catch occasional hints of H. Rider Haggard, Arthur Conan Doyle, and Rafael Sabatini, in the exuberance with which he declares (in that *Independent* interview), "I want to have fun inventing species and cities that couldn't possibly exist." Like the storytelling Fat Boy of Dickens's *The Pickwick Papers* who exclaims, "I wants to make your flesh creep," Miéville confesses (in a 2005 interview with *The Believer*), "The monsters are the main thing that I love about the fantastic."

Still, the mischievous boy who wants to scare the pants off you coexists productively (if not quite peacefully) with the socialist intellectual who urges you to share his fervent wish to topple existing governments and bring about radical social and economic reforms. Like Walt Whitman, Miéville is large, he contains multitudes. Like Doris Lessing (particularly in her often reviled "space fiction"), he dreams into being imperiled societies caught between the yearning for stability and enlightenment and the exigencies of social control. Like his near-namesake Herman Melville (whose *Moby-Dick* set his adolescent imagination afire), he envisions in claustrophobic microcosms the vastness of human possibility and elemental influence. And he wants to create fiction that encompasses all our experiences and all our possibilities. "So," he explained in a conversation with the internet magazine BookSense.com, "my aim would be precisely to write the ripping yarn that is also sociologically serious and avant-garde. I mean, that's the Holy Grail right there."

Most of the qualities of Miéville's precociously mature fiction are already present in his vivid, propulsively readable first novel. *King Rat* is both a scrupulously distorted urban novel (akin to, but considerably more mordant than his former countryman Neil Gaiman's popular fantasy novel *Neverwhere*) and a *bildungsroman* whose callow protagonist plunges into an ordeal that gradually discloses the mystery of his origins and the paradoxes of his nature. That protagonist is Saul Garamond, a young Londoner with a serious drug problem who is arrested and falsely accused of the murder of his estranged father (who had "fallen" to his death from a high window). Flashbacks to Saul's motherless childhood are juxtaposed with details of his interrogation by Detective Inspector Crowley—who suspects, as does the reader, that Saul's story is more complicated than it initially appears to be.

Enter the bizarre title character, a grungy, festering apparition (described by the narrator as "a figure skulking like a Victorian villain" who brusquely introduces himself (as "king" of the city's sewers), assures Saul that he too is "royalty," and, freeing the prisoner from jail, takes him to an underground "kingdom" (in the London sewers) offered to Saul as his eventual legacy.

Saul violently rejects the Rat King's explanation: that this bewhiskered Fagin (leader of the rodents that scurry to do his bidding) is his real father—the rapist of Saul's mother, who died giving birth to him. The "war" between prodigal parent and reluctant son escalates, and the novel branches out into several intriguingly interrelated subplots. But all narrative roads lead back to Saul—through his friend Natasha Karadjian, a musician and composer (whose work in progress, "Wind City," attempts to capture the roiling polyglot essence of London), their mutual acquaintance Fabian (a genial drug procurer), and putative fellow musician "Pete," whose friendly interest in Natasha masks his dogged pursuit of Saul. For Pete, you see, is the Pied Piper; and, as he explains to Saul when the two eventually face off, "you are going to die, because you won't dance when I tell you to." Being of mixed (i.e., human and rats') blood, Saul is impervious to the Piper's seductive rhythms.

In other words, it's all about control. D. I. Crowley needs answers to the mystery he's investigating. Saul needs confirmation of both his humanity and his distance from the Rat King's sardonic fatalism. The malodorous monarch needs to exert his power over his dominion, his recalcitrant heir, and such parallel power holders as his enemy the Piper and his mythic counterparts Anansi the Spider (who speaks in an engagingly loopy Caribbean patois) and Loplow, King of the Birds (both of whom, sad to say, really aren't given enough to do). Miéville throws them all together to colorful melodramatic effect, and brings his story to a deeply ironic conclusion in which both father and son realize the limits of their connection and collusion, and even of their freedom.

King Rat is of particular interest for its deft fusion of received material (from legends and fairy tales), complex atmospheric effects, and what might be called ultimate multiculturalism. (It is perhaps not too much to say that Miéville's baroque blendings of ethnic groups and races, not to mention humans and other species, incorporate a plea that we overcome the "differences" that divide us as pointed as do Salman Rushdie's celebrations of national, ethnic, and racial mixing.) Humans, rats, and hybrids—sentient beings, one and all—jostle ferociously for survival and identity in a grimly entertaining supra-human comedy. Its setting is likewise a hybrid—a late-Victorian London, populated by elegant swells, starving riffraff, and grotesquely mutated half-human beings; its industries driven by steam power, yet reaching out for beckoning new technologies and promising scientific discoveries. This is the world of "steampunk" fantasy (first so named in the late 1980s), as adumbrated in the clotted melodramas of (the aforementioned) Conan Doyle and Rider Haggard, Jules Verne, the young Robert Louis Stevenson, Bram Stoker, and G. K. Chesterton. The theme of urban nightmare embellished and endangered by technological promise and threat has proven wildly popular ever since, through the pulp fiction of the 1920s-1930s (particularly in the magnificently goofy Martian adventures penned by Tarzan creator Edgar Rice Burroughs), and culminating recently in the aggressively eclectic steampunk fiction of Tim Powers, Brian Stableford, Kim Newman, William Gibson, and Bruce Sterling. Miéville is very much a creature of this line of literary development—though he seems to eschew the steampunk label, preferring to classify himself as a practitioner of what he calls "the New Weird."

Nothing could have been newer, or weirder, following on the nipped heels of *King Rat,* than Miéville's mammoth second novel, *Perdido Street Station.* Its setting is an overcrowded, over-polluted city-state, New Crobuzon, part of an alternate "world" (identified more definitively in subsequent books as Bas-Lag), and renowned as a kind of crucible for the applications of various, and sometimes conflicting realities. Both steam power and magic, for example, "run" the city, and provide benefits enjoyed solely by New Crobuzon's wealthy ruling class. An oppressive Parliament enacts the will of these "haves," while New Crobuzon's countless poor are routinely scientifically altered, "enabling" them to perform more arduous labor or to provide additional sexual options for their "betters." They are thus known as remades. The city's corrupt mayor, Rudgutter, uses all the power he can amass to keep a step ahead of the crime lord Motley, who, like a human Rat King, controls a thriving criminal underground. As if all this isn't hellish enough, Hell itself literally exists—and New Crobuzon politicians frequently make deals with Satan.

In addition to remades (the nefarious Motley is one, incidentally: a bizarre construction assembled from incompatible organic and mechanical parts), the city is filled with xenians, including vodyani (semi-human frog-like amphibians), cactcae (part human, part cactus), and khepri (part human, part insect), among other beguiling amalgamations. And there are humans: notably, the novel's protagonist, Isaac Dan der Grimnebulin, a research scientist with a special interest in crisis theory and the ambition of devising a unified theory that will link all the known sciences with sociology, politics, and magic (one example: he's deeply invested in the hybrid discipline of bio-thaumaturgy).

As Isaac's studies lead him in initially promising, eventually compromising directions, other agendas and destinies assert themselves. Isaac's khepri lover, Lin, a gifted sculptress woman-beetle, is hired to sculpt a likeness of crime boss Motley. Meanwhile Isaac is visited by Yagharek, a (half-human, half-bird) garuda, whose wings have been sundered from his body for an unspecified crime against his species. Man agrees to help birdman, but the resulting commitment distracts Isaac's attention from his efforts to devise a perpetual motion machine.

Mistakes are made. In the process of attempting to graft new wings onto Yagharek, Isaac unknowingly releases a horrific destructive force: a weird caterpillar utilized as a laboratory specimen is fed a drug that increases its size alarmingly, creating a "monster" (and here fantasy addicts will surely catch an allusion to E. R. Eddison's 1922 classic *The Worm Ouroboros*) that menaces New Crobuzon's very survival. And that's not all, disaster fans. The city is further imperiled by hovering Slake-Moths, airborne mutants bearing the power to enter their victims' thoughts and senses, reducing them to vegetative states. And of course there is the overarching figure of the Weaver, a gigantic spider driven by a hunger to gather and control everything within its constantly expanding web (it is, presumably, the fully "animal" counterpart to the power-seekers Rudgutter and Motley). What's to be done? Well, things happen at the title location: the point at which multiple railroad lines gather together and meet, much like the strands of a web. Isaac—perhaps another Newton, perhaps another son of the biblical Abraham, chosen to be sacrificed—descends to the underworld, a Beatrice-deprived Dante guided by an affable Virgil named Lemuel Pigeon. New Crobuzon's fate indubitably hangs in the balance—and I am not the man to spoil your pleasure by revealing more than I have already spoken. This wonderfully deranged page-turner earned Miéville the Arthur C. Clarke and British Fantasy Society Awards, and put him on the map as one of the most creative fantasists at work today. The two novels that followed it confirmed that both Miéville and the brilliantly mad mad world of Bas-Lag are something special indeed.

The Scar (2001), which won both British Fantasy Society and Locus Awards, though not specifically a sequel to ***Perdido Street Station,*** develops from it a chronicle of adventure and conflict set in more distant parts of Bas-Lag, and of considerable genre interest for its clever echoes of Jules Verne's scientific romances and Rafael Sabatini's lusty swashbucklers. This big novel's central figure is, once again, of something less than conventional heroic stature. She is Bellis Coldwine, an accomplished linguist and former colleague of Isaac Dan der Grimnebulin who, having been declared an enemy of New Crobuzon's government for her association with Isaac and acting on inside information that the city may soon be under attack, has escaped it by traveling on the *Terpsichore*. This ship, sailing across the Swollen Ocean from New Crobuzon to its distant "colony" Nova Esperium, carries a cargo of criminal remades to be employed as slaves and for whom Bellis will function as interpreter.

Bellis's personal history is told in unsent letters she later writes, in between frustrated attempts to escape her new surroundings, after the *Terpsichore* is seized by pirates who murder its captain and crew, then tow the vessel to Armada, a floating city made out of hulls and miscellaneous parts of wrecked ships. The novel then becomes the story of Armada, a patchwork metropolis undergoing major structural changes and bent on developing itself into a superpower and taking over the faraway realm known as The Scar, where logic and probability are subject to the direction of those who rule there. The beings who aspire to such command are The Lovers, an eerie pair of consorts disfigured by bodily scars (as are most of Armada's inhabitants). The Lovers preach harmony and tolerance, declaring universal equality. But, as readers of China Miéville's fiction have learned, our very differences are what divide us and pit us against one another. The Lovers' preemptive platitudes ignore a burgeoning civil war led by their rebellious bodyguard Uther Doul and by a rival faction, the ab-dead, devoted to a disgruntled "vampir." Various other involved Armadans pursuing their own dreams and visions include a brooding naturalist (Johannes Tearfly), a remade (Tanner Sack) who embraces the possibility of transformation into a total amphibian, an ingenuous cabin boy (Shekel), and an Indiana Jones-like adventurer (Silas Fennec) who may not be the "good guy" he seems to be.

The Scar is not so much a unified narrative as it is a thing of fascinating fragments. It moves rather slowly at first, as Miéville labors to introduce an encyclopedic abundance of material. The early history of Bas-Lag is layered in at considerable—arguably, excessive—length. But its picaresque energy produces some wonderful stuff. The early sea battle between the *Terpsichore* and the attacking pirate ship is a jovially nasty fusion of C. S. Forester and an unkinder, less gentle Ray Bradbury. An attempt to harness the power of a huge leviathan

creature (the Avanc) that hides itself in a hole in the Swollen Ocean out-Vernes the immortal Jules, as does a marvelous description of an oceanic descent in a rudimentary bathysphere. The atmospheric power of Poe is felt in descriptions of threatening indistinct shapes that prowl Armada's waters. And even the prodigally gifted young H. G. Wells might have saluted a lengthy account of a journey to the island of the human-mosquito hybrids the anophelii, whose culture is analyzed in ingenious and fascinating detail. The novel's scattered emphases perhaps preclude definitive interpretation. But one does sense a sardonic caricature of Bas-Lag/Great Britain as a warmongering seafaring imperial power. And in the rigidly orchestrated inequities of Armada, there are both logical connection to and grim extrapolation from the seemingly intractable sociopolitical quandaries that afflict New Crobuzon and beyond.

The stakes are raised in Miéville's most overtly political novel, ***Iron Council,*** which appeared in 2004 and brought its author a second Arthur C. Clarke Award. It is part three of what Miéville has called his "anti-trilogy." This time around, in addition to detailing the provenance and complex interrelationships of New Crobuzon and its far-flung environs, Miéville dramatizes violent efforts to reshape them. ***Iron Council***'s protagonist, Cutter, is introduced as the de facto leader of a group of nomads who oppose their persecutors, the New Crobuzon Militia, the strong-arm arm of the city's mayor and Parliament. Cutter also leads a search for the man he loves (interestingly, many if not most of this novel's characters are matter-of-factly bisexual) Judah Lowe: a golem maker (like his historical namesake, Rabbi Loewe, creator of the first golem), who has refused to use his power for the government's purposes. Lowe has returned from the wilderness, where Cutter and his companions stew in their aggrieved juices, to preach the gospel of reform to New Crobuzon's huddled masses.

The city is at war with the rival city-state of Tesh, and is exhausting its resources in a manner that will not escape the notice of citizens of countries currently engaged in military actions in the all-too-real Middle East. It is simultaneously besieged by rebellious workers—exploited remades and xenians who proclaim themselves the Iron Council and protest their employment on chain gangs laboring to extend a transcontinental railroad line far into the unsettled and undeveloped wilderness beyond New Crobuzon's formal boundaries. The novel thus describes an unconventional spectrum showing multiple varieties of dissent and revolutionary action. Its supporting characters include an aged socialist visionary (Spiral) who communicates dreams of freedom to his hopeful comrades, an excessively angry young man (Uri) who moves from theoretical argument to homicidal terrorism, and an incendiary malcontent (Toro) who leads a plot to assassinate New Crobuzon's reactionary mayor (in whom resemblances to former British prime minister Margaret Thatcher are doubtless not coincidental).

Iron Council does succeed both as narrative and as argument, despite a ponderously long flashback (of nearly one hundred and fifty pages), placed in the middle of the book, which blithely interrupts the story to recount the history of the Iron Council's early days when it was led by Judah Lowe's former lover, Ann-Hari. Miéville gets away with this, against odds, because the novel's zealous energy is communicated in forceful prose studded with arcane verbiage and inventive neologisms, and it is unified by a superb central metaphor: that of the Perpetual Train, a conveyance assembled by the rebel workers from parts of other trains (similar, thus, to the ship-city of *The Scar*), which looms throughout the story as an image of judgment careening through the wilderness toward the complacent target of New Crobuzon.

This is a thriller that forces you to think. Its opening chapters hearken back to earlier fictionalizations of labor struggle and resistance to totalitarian control. If you've read widely enough in bad well-intentioned fiction, you may find yourself recalling with perverse fondness William Morris's hysterical Victorian utopian allegories, or even Jack London's crypto-fascist allegory *The Iron Heel*. (There is, just possibly, a buried allusion to London's classic story "To Build a Fire" in this novel's initial image, of a traveler building a fire in a wilderness.) There are elements of the classic American western novel and film as well, a not-terribly-subtle clarion call to rebellion in several somewhat forced references to the Paris Commune of 1968, and in the plight of the exploited "nobodies" a likely implicit comparison to the history of slavery in the American South.

Yes, *Iron Council* is preachy. It's also animated, ambitious, engrossing, and very much a book of its conflicted and perplexing time. Following as it did the expressionistic fantasy of *Perdido Street Station* and *The Scar*—as something truly new and different—it was, one guesses, destined to receive a mixed reaction from review media and readers with specific expectations. But the thing is alive on the page, and it is difficult not to believe that its confrontational let's-change-the-world momentum constitutes yet another gratifying step forward.

New Crobuzon awaits further exploration, while Miéville fries other fish. His first collection of shorter fiction, *Looking for Jake* (2005), contains fourteen stories, all but four of which are previously unpublished. Appropriately, these contents are otherwise "mixed" as well. One, **"On the Way to the Front,"** is a graphic short story, accompanied by the illustrations of fantasy comic book artist Liam Sharp. Another, **"The Tain,"** is

a novella previously published as a stand-alone chapbook in 2002. Connections, both implicit and explicit, to the matter of Miéville's enormous anti-trilogy are made in the plaintive title story (this volume's earliest, from 1998), in which the narrator who is "looking for Jake" wanders a destroyed London in the aftermath of "a very inexact apocalypse," its sky darkened by "hungry flapping things"; all changed utterly and catastrophically, as he writes a letter he knows will never be answered. The very absence of explanation effectively blends intimations of last things with the pain of a grievous personal loss. And there is another graceful echo of the New Crobuzon experience in **"Jack,"** the crisply told story of the remade Jack Half-a-Prayer (a featured character in *Iron Council*), who brazenly flouts authority, becomes a Robin Hood, and pays the ultimate price for his "crimes." Several slighter stories include a mischievous conte cruel depicting a haunted children's playroom in a large furniture store (**"The Ball Room"**); a mock history of the "progress" of a mysterious brain disease (**"Entry Taken from a Medical Encyclopedia"**); a monologue spoken by a witch's intemperate "familiar"; the Lovecraftian **"Details,"** in which a student of the occult discovers disturbingly more than he had aspired to learn; and the story of a computer hacker's misadventure when he happens upon compromising information about a little-known charitable organization (**"An End to Hunger"**). Current events are ominously transfigured in the nightmarish experience of an American Desert Storm veteran who, upon "safely" returning to a city at peace (albeit built on the site of a mass grave), is haunted by ghosts of the victims of a genocidal military attack. The reader senses something approximately parallel in the aforementioned illustrated story **"On the Way to the Front,"** which pictures battle-weary soldiers passing through London as if on march, their presence unexplained. Are they ghosts? Or veterans unable to adjust to life "back home"? The felt ambiguity is both teasing and stimulating, but the story's meanings appear to have been deliberately withheld. The impression of generic menace is more persuasively conveyed in **"Reports of Certain Events in London,"** in which evidence of both an unidentified cabal involved in investigating suspicious occult phenomena and a secret "underground" war is uncovered by the story's narrator—China Miéville—as he inadvertently reads somebody else's mail.

Generally, the stories whose details are most specific work best. In the futuristic satire of **"'Tis the Season,"** the culmination of strategies deployed by special-interest groups and ideologues who wish to adapt Christmas to their own ends is that authorities require anyone wishing to celebrate the holiday to apply for an official permit. Those who demur are addressed by riot police. In the suggestive **"Different Skies,"** an elderly man who has delightedly installed a handsome stained-glass window in his apartment quickly discovers that it presents a view of a disorganized parallel city. His "window" on the life around him brings to his reluctant attention the clamor of young people, whom he fears, and from whom he can now no longer absent himself. An even more disturbing impression of a world beyond one's control afflicts the nameless protagonist of the Kafkaesque **"Go Between."** He's an ordinary Londoner who finds sealed capsules hidden among the groceries he buys, and accepts the implied command to deliver them to destinations imprinted on the objects. He's a chosen messenger. But what is the message he bears? Is he a helper, a deliverer, or an agent of a terrorist plot? *Looking for Jake* concludes with **"The Tain,"** another vision of post-apocalyptic London. Its relation to its namesake, the medieval Irish tale (part of the celebrated Ulster Cycle) of "The Cattle Raid of Cooley," appears only tangential at best. In that earlier story, a renegade queen and her consort wage war on Ulster over possession of a potent prize bull and are defeated by the young hero Cuchulain, who gives his life for his homeland. In Miéville's **"Tain"** (inspired, as a concluding quotation acknowledges, by an entry in Jorge Luis Borges's *The Book of Imaginary Beings*), survivalists and paramilitary groups populate a future London under attack from mirror images that have escaped from their confines and have sworn revenge on the human "originals" whom they blame for imprisoning them within the mirrors' glass. Miéville articulates this fabulous premise with fiendish ingenuity, creating spectacular visual effects in a panoramic portrayal of quite literal self-destruction. It is probably not important that we understand the "Tain" connection. Perhaps an explanation is forthcoming in a future New Crobuzon story or novel. In any case, the metaphor of mirroring appears a particularly rich one, and we will surely encounter it again somewhere in the vast depths of Bas-Lag.

Most recently, Miéville has published his first novel for young adult readers: *Un Lun Dun* (2007). Early reviews describe this book as an adventure set in a more benign New Crobuzon: UnLondon, a place occupied by "broken" people and objects; the discarded flotsam and jetsam of a city in which all is disposable, and where the effluent legacy of industrialism has created a destructive cloud (the Smog) that threatens the city's populace, and tests the mettle of the novel's resourceful adolescent heroines.

From the Rat King to the Slake-Moths and the Avanc, the Iron Council and the accusatory armies of our combative present and undefined future, China Miéville has dreamed our common fears and premonitions into unforgettable images of sometimes sharply menacing, sometimes indistinct forces that seem bent on nothing less than universal annihilation. Still, there are phoenixes, strange things of all persuasions and potentialities that rise from ashes, and wherever a scar appears, the process of healing has begun. More than nightmare, something other than simple dystopian prophecy, the seductive hybrid creations of this brilliant young inventor's prodigious imagination lurk memorably on the fringes of our own consciousness, and seem to be whispering insistently that they have more, much more to tell us.

FURTHER READING

Biographies

Gordon, Joan. "Reveling in Genre: An Interview with China Miéville." *Science Fiction Studies* 30, no. 3 (November 2003): 355-73.

    Provides a lengthy interview with Miéville.

Page, Benedicte. "No Elves or Centaurs." *Bookseller* (1 March 2002): 32.

    Interview with Miéville in which he discusses the fantasy genre.

Criticism

Gordon, Joan. "Hybridity, Heterotopia, and Mateship in China Miéville's *Perdido Street Station*." *Science Fiction Studies* 30, no. 3 (November 2003): 456-76.

    Analysis of *Perdido Street Station*.

Halevi, Charles Chi. "On a Fast Track to Perdition." *Chicago Sun-Times* (29 April 2001): 12.

    Positive review of *Perdido Street Station*.

Bharati Mukherjee
1940-

Indian-born American novelist, short story writer, and nonfiction writer.

The following entry presents an overview of Mukherjee's career through 2006. For further information on her life and works, see *CLC,* Volumes 53 and 115.

INTRODUCTION

Mukherjee's writing, delivered in an understated prose style, portrays the humiliation and pain associated with Third World peoples acclimating to North American culture. Her protagonists are usually sensitive people, lacking a stable base for personal and cultural identity, and are victimized by racism, sexism, or other forms of social oppression. Several critics have compared her studies of cultural clashes to the works of V. S. Naipaul, while others have noted the influence of Bernard Malamud on her portrayal of minority individuals who experience difficulty adapting to their new surroundings.

BIOGRAPHICAL INFORMATION

Mukherjee was born in 1940 to an upper-middle-class Bengali Brahmin family in pre-independence India. As a child educated in colonial schools, she was encouraged to devalue her native culture, a process she reversed only later in life. Mukherjee received a B.A. in English in 1959 and an M.A. in English and ancient Indian culture two years later, both from the University of Calcutta. Also in 1961 Mukherjee came to the United States to study at the Iowa Writers' Workshop. There she met and married Canadian writer Clark Blaise, with whom she later collaborated on two nonfiction works. The couple attempted to establish a home in Canada, but Mukherjee met with such pervasive racism that they moved to the United States, where she settled into writing and teaching and became an American citizen in 1988. Mukherjee has been an English professor at the University of California at Berkeley since 1987. She received the National Book Critics Circle Award for *The Middleman and Other Stories* (1988) and was the winner of the Pushcart Prize in 1999.

MAJOR WORKS

Mukherjee's marriage to a member of another culture changed her life and writing dramatically. Her fiction portrays the delicate place of Indian and other Third World immigrants in North American culture. *The Tiger's Daughter* (1972) provides a satiric look at Indian society from the point of view of a young expatriate, Tara Banerjee Cartwright, who is caught between an American culture to which she is not yet accustomed and the culture of her native land from whose morals and values she is estranged. *Wife* (1975) tells the story of Dimple, who moves to the United States with her husband and becomes torn between Indian and American cultures. *Days and Nights in Calcutta* (1977), written with Mukherjee's husband, Clark Blaise, is a journal of the couple's 1973 visit to India. Mukherjee also collaborated with Blaise on *The Sorrow and the Terror* (1987) which recounts the bombing of an Air India flight that killed over 300 people. Mukherjee's short story collection *The Middleman and Other Stories* traces the lives of Third World immigrants and their adjustment to becoming Americans. The protagonists struggle to survive economically while facing alienation and racism. The stories celebrate "differentness" and express the value of maintaining distinction while also assimilating.

In the novel *Jasmine* (1989), based on Mukherjee's short story of the same name, the title character is widowed, which in her native Punjab means a life of sorrow and loneliness. She rejects this fate and leaves for America, where she undergoes a series of transformations. Her travels eventually lead her to a new identity as Jane with a common-law husband and child in the farm country of Iowa. The novel ends with the protagonist abandoning her life again for a new existence in California. The novel is a celebration of the American freedom to develop an individual identity, a freedom characterized by both pain and excitement. *The Holder of the World* (1993) traces the story of two women in two different time periods. A diamond called the Tear Drop connects Beigh Masters to a nineteenth-century Puritan, Hannah Easton. Most of the novel focuses on Beigh's narration of Hannah's story, which includes growing up in Massachusetts and eventually ending up in India as the lover of the Raja. When she returns to New England pregnant with the Raja's child, the reader learns that Hannah is actually Hester Prynne, the protagonist of Nathaniel Hawthorne's *The Scarlet Letter. Leave It to Me* (1997) traces the search of Debby DiMartino to find her origins and identity. Born to an American mother and Eurasian father, then abandoned and adopted by an Italian-American family in New York, Debby travels to California to find her birth parents and becomes an accessory to her mother's murder. *Desirable Daughters* (2002) relates the Americanization of two Indian sisters, Tara and Padma, in the context of Tara's experience as a rich divorcee in Silicon Valley. The traditional Indian tale of the Tree-Bride informs this novel and became the title of the sequel, *The Tree Bride* (2004), which delves more fully into the story of Tara's ancestor, the literal Tree-Bride, wedded by her father at age five to a tree deep in the forest to spite the greedy father of her intended bride-groom.

CRITICAL RECEPTION

Mukherjee has not yet achieved her wish to be recognized solely as an American writer. Many critics continue to examine her work for themes of immigration and assimilation, and some insist that Mukherjee is exploiting a fad of postcolonial literature and has become so immersed in American culture that she is no longer qualified to write about India from a first-person perspective. Nonetheless, Mukherjee has been recognized for developing her own style and message which are relevant within American literature.

PRINCIPAL WORKS

The Tiger's Daughter (novel) 1972
Wife (novel) 1975
Days and Nights in Calcutta [with Clark Blaise] (nonfiction) 1977
Darkness (short stories) 1985
The Sorrow and the Terror: The Haunting Legacy of the Air India Tragedy [with Blaise] (nonfiction) 1987
The Middleman and Other Stories (short stories) 1988
Jasmine (novel) 1989
Political Culture and Leadership in India (nonfiction) 1991
Regionalism in Indian Perspective (nonfiction) 1992
The Holder of the World (novel) 1993
Leave It to Me (novel) 1997
Desirable Daughters (novel) 2002
The Tree Bride (novel) 2004

CRITICISM

Abha Prakash Leard (review date winter 1997)

SOURCE: Leard, Abha Prakash. Review of *Jasmine*, by Bharati Mukherjee. *Explicator* 55, no. 2 (winter 1997): 114-17.

[*In the following review, Leard outlines Mukherjee's examination of identity in* Jasmine.]

Despite postcolonial readings of Bharati Mukherjee's novel *Jasmine,* Western critics have not placed in context the pivotal play of migrations, forced and voluntary, literal and figurative, found in the plural female subjectivity of the novel.[1] With the connotations of both dislocation and progress within the tangled framework of the narrator's personal history, journey as metaphor in the novel stands for the ever-moving, regenerating process of life itself. In presenting a woman capable of birthing more than one self during the course of her lifetime, Mukherjee invests her novel with the unique form of a Hindu bildungsroman, where the body is merely the shell for the inner being's journey toward a more enlightened and empowered subjectivity.

But the material self exists and is the site of oppression and transformation. Cognizant of the formidable interventions of gender, class, religion, and historical circumstance, Mukherjee shapes her heroine as a "fighter and adapter" (40), who is perpetually in the process of remaking her self and her destiny. Set in the seventies and eighties when the violent separatist demands of the militant Sikhs forced many Hindus to migrate from Punjab, *Jasmine* centers around the experiences of Jyoti, a teenage Hindu widow, who travels all the way from Hasnapur, India, her feudalistic village, to America. These experiences are told in first person by a woman who identifies herself as Jane Ripplemeyer, the pregnant, twenty-four-year-old, live-in girlfriend of Bud Ripplemeyer, a Jewish banker in Baden, Iowa. But the "I" in the past and present fragments of this first-person narrative belongs to a woman who sees herself as more than one person. Officially known as Jyoti Vijh in India, the narrator, in America, is a many-named immigrant with a fake passport and forged residency papers. By giving her protagonist more than one name, usually through the character of a husband/lover, Mukherjee subverts the notion of a fixed, uniform subject. Simultaneously, the narrator's plurality of names—Jasmine, Jazzy, Jase, Jane (which successively became more Westernized)—helps to mask her ethnic difference and enable her to survive in a hostile, alien land.

Jasmine's decision to leave her homeland coincides with her desire to escape the confines of her cultural identity. This desire, articulated in the dramatic recollection of the opening chapter, is a subtext that continually spurs the narrative's critique of the patriarchal underpinnings of Hindu culture and its social fabric. The little girl's refusal to accept the astrologer's prophecy translates into the adult narrator's unwillingness to imprison herself within traditional, predetermined codes of femininity. As Jyoti matures into a young woman, her resistance against a determinate existence continues in her unconventional marriage to Prakash, a "modern man" (76), who wants them to leave the backwardness of India for a more satisfying life in America. Within a cultural context that privileges arranged marriages, Jyoti's romance, that she has engineered, can indeed be seen not only as nontraditional but also as a subversive tactic against the established cultural norm. Her marriage is not only liberating but transforming as well. Comparing her husband to Professor Higgins, the benevolent patriarch of *Pygmalion,* the narrator recollects the early days of her marriage when Prakash, in an attempt to make her a "new kind of city woman" (77), changes her name to Jasmine. Although "shutt[ling] between identities" (77), the narrator is eager to transcend the name/identity of her child self in the hope of escaping the doomed prophecy lurking in her future. To leave the country of her birth would mean new beginnings, "new fates, new stars" (85). But before the seventeen-year-old bride can embark on a new life with her husband, he is killed in a terrorist bombing.

The motif of the broken pitcher in *Jasmine* epitomizes not only the temporality of one life journey within the ongoing Hindu cycle of rebirth, but also the fragility of constructed boundaries, whether of the self, the family, or the nation. The author parallels the violence of the Khalistan movement that is responsible for Jasmine's widowhood and her subsequent displacement and exile to the bloody communal riots between the Hindus and Muslims at the time of India's independence in 1947. Despite her distance from this historical event, which rendered millions of people homeless and destitute overnight, the narrator can still empathize with her parents' anguished memories of the Partition that forced them to leave their ancestral home in Lahore and flee to Punjab. The fragmentation of the nation and the family as well as the haunting journey from terror to refuge have seeped into Jasmine's subconscious—"the loss survives in the instant replay of family story: forever Lahore smokes, forever my parents flee" (41).

Directly or indirectly, historical conflicts (sparked by religious intolerance) within India determine the problematic constitution of Jasmine's shifting individuality. Her "illegal" (171) migrant life in America is an extension of an existence that began in the shadow of political refuge and later, with her husband's death, almost ended in her widowed status. Within the enclosures of the Hindu culture, a widow must atone the death of her husband for the rest of her life. Jasmine's widowhood cancels her right to material fulfillment. It entails a life of isolation in the "widow's dark hut" (96), on the margins of Hasnapur society. For Jasmine, to live the life of a widow is to live a fate worse than death.

Jasmine's difficult "odyssey" (101) to America and her initial experiences in an alien society parallel the emergence of a new selfhood despite the vulnerability

of her youth and material circumstances. Her brutal rape at the hands of Half-face, a man who represents the worst of America in his racist and inhuman treatment of the Asian and black refugees aboard his trawler, is a climactic moment in the text which signals the sudden awakening of Jasmine's "sense of mission" (117). Refusing to "balance [her] defilement with [her] death" (117), a traditional ending for most rape victims in orthodox Indian society, Jasmine, infused with the destructive energy of the goddess Kali,[2] murders the man who symbolizes the "underworld of evil" (116) and begins a new "journey, traveling light" (121).

Given a world where violence and bloodshed, exploitation and persecution are constants, Jasmine's plurality of selves is her only strategy for survival. Knowing only too well that there are "no harmless, compassionate ways to remake oneself" (29), Jasmine views her multiple selves with a detachment that has been forged in pain. But beneath this carefully maintained distance is the terrible agony of a woman who cannot free herself from the collective memory of her haunting past:

> Jyoti of Hasnapur was not Jasmine, Duff's day mummy and Taylor and Wylie's *au pair* in Manhattan: *that* Jasmine isn't *this* Jane Ripplemeyer. . . . And which of us is the undetected murderer of a half-faced monster, which of us has held a dying husband, and which of us was raped and raped and raped in boats and cars and motel rooms?

Having lived through "hideous times" (214), Jasmine, in her arduous journey of survival, has accomplished the rare mission of transcending the boundaries of a unitary self and identifying with all the nameless victims of gender, culture, class, and imperialism. The narrative ends on a note of optimism where Jasmine, "cocooning a cosmos" (224) in her pregnant belly, and about to "reposition her stars" (240) again, is ready to plunge into another life and another journey of transformation.

Notes

1. For a notable exception, see Kristin Carter Sanborn, "'We Murder Who We Were': Jasmine and the Violence of Identity," *American Literature* 66.3 (September 1994): 573-593.

2. The narrator acknowledges her affinity to the goddess later in the text where she lists a "husband" for "each of the women [she] [has] . . . Prakash for Jasmine, Taylor for Jase, Bud for Jane, Half-Face for Kali" (197). According to ancient Hindu belief, Kali was born from the brow of the supreme goddess Durga to annihilate "demonic male power and restore peace and equilibrium" (Mookerjee 8). For a detailed mythology of Kali, see Mookerjee.

Works Cited

Mookerjee, Ajit. *Kali: The Feminine Force.* Vermont: Destiny Books, 1988.

Mukherjee, Bharati. *Jasmine* (New Delhi: Penguin, 1990). All page references are to this edition.

Carmen Faymonville (review date fall 1997)

SOURCE: Faymonville, Carmen. Review of *Jasmine,* by Bharati Mukherjee. *Explicator* 56, no. 1 (fall 1997): 53-4.

[*In the following review, Faymonville reads* Jasmine *as an optimistic reframing of the traditional American frontier tale.*]

Bharati Mukherjee's novel *Jasmine* relies on frontier myths and the narratives of Americanization associated with western locales, mobility, and frontier-hero lifestyles. As a South Asian woman writer residing in the United States, Mukherjee explores the promise of American-style individualism and female liberation alongside the burden of Old World responsibilities and cultural ties signaling female oppression.

In the book, Jasmine comes from India, where she was bound by traditional views about women, to the United States, where gender roles have historically been more fluid. The American pioneer woman in particular stands out as a female role model of self-reliance and feminine courage. Mukherjee employs frontier myths to project the psychological and cultural development of Jasmine, who physically and metaphorically travels toward western philosophy. The protagonist moves from India to Florida, to New York, then to the Midwest, and finally to California. Metaphorically she moves from East to West and becomes an American "gold digger."

The Gold Rush mentality adopted by Jasmine makes her feel that she is able to profit from the uncharted country of America. Older Americans, however, see her as an exotic newcomer who disturbs the moral equilibrium of a fragile frontier society. Jasmine settles with Bud Ripplemeyer, a disabled banker, on an Iowa homestead. In doing so she creates a life that replicates that of earlier immigrants and their eventual assimilation. The Ripplemeyers, who are of European extraction, are now at home in the Midwest. Yet, coming from India and being of non-European origin, Jasmine is rejected because of her ethnicity. Nevertheless, the story presents Jasmine as a new pioneer who will follow the same fate as the earlier settlers: She, too, will be absorbed into the culture and become a true American.

By moving to California at the end of the novel, Jasmine hopes to find complete assimilation into the national culture; but on her way she must cross several borders and fight many obstacles. These obstacles are depicted as both physical and metaphorical. As many American authors before her, Mukherjee depicts, through wilderness legends, fears about the irrationality of the inner self once it is released from the laws of civilization. Specifically, Mukherjee explores Jasmine's moral adaptation of the laws of the land. After her husband is killed, Jasmine travels to America as they had originally planned but with the intention of committing "Sati," a Hindu widow's ritual immolation. Before reaching her destination, she is raped; Jasmine at first considers killing herself but instead turns on her attacker and kills him. This act of violence is that of the frontier outlaw who takes retribution into his own hands. As in the classic western novel, psychological issues of repression and guilt are central to an understanding of the frontier character of Jasmine. For Mukherjee's protagonist, the West liberates her inner self so that a chaotic unconscious can be calmed. Consequently, she is able to find a new morality that enables her to leave behind those things that limit her personal freedom. This new-found freedom also requires her to relinquish her ethnic roots and to cast her lot with other seekers and wanderers. In the end, Jasmine accepts the irrational as human and tries to integrate reality and fantasy.

Mukherjee incorporates the American West into the novel through allusions to the western novel *Shane*. Shane is a hero—a lone, rugged, mysterious individual. He arrives at the ranch of a struggling homesteader, and while he is there a transformation occurs. In the end, he rides off into the sunset, headed, one supposes, farther west. The transformation can be seen either as a restoration of an older moral order, or as a destruction of the existing social order. The novel depicts the battle between the old order, the sheepherders, and the new order of cattlemen. Similarly, in *Jasmine,* a new class of overlords threatens to alter the landscape of farms and agricultural order in the rural west in favor of golf courses and amusement parks. Jasmine had read *Shane* while in India and was thus ideologically prepared for the frontier lures: "I remember a thin one, *Shane* about an American village much like Punjab" (40). Significantly, her homeland already carried the traces of frontier society.

Jasmine's constructive tendencies can be seen in the effect her presence has on the small town of Baden, Iowa, as it begins to change from a monocultural enclave to a more multicultural place: Jasmine's presence causes locals to question their old certainties—whether about food or religion. Slowly, the older Americans come to understand that they have to accommodate Jasmine's differences, just as she tries to become a part of their way of life.

Overall, Jasmine's departure for a frontier even farther west parallels the American myth played out in the western novel, but with a distinctive gender difference.

Shane was a free individual because he was a man. Jasmine, who is given the name Jane by the banker, is more like Calamity Jane, but she is still bound by the feminine decorum that society expects. When she leaves town she does so with considerable guilt because she abandons the man who needs her to go to California with her former lover, Taylor. The novels ends with a scene in which Jasmine drives off with Taylor into the sunset, "greedy with wants and reckless from hope" (241).

Works Cited

Mukherjee, Bharati. *Jasmine*. New York: Fawcett Crest, 1989.

Schaefer, Jack. *Shane*. Ed. James C. Work. Lincoln: U of Nebraska P, 1984.

John K. Hoppe (essay date winter 1999)

SOURCE: Hoppe, John K. "The Technological Hybrid as Post-American: Cross-Cultural Genetics in *Jasmine*." *MELUS* 24, no. 4 (winter 1999): 137-56.

[*In the following essay, Hoppe notes the title character's perpetual exchange of identities in flight from the past and the perception of destiny in* Jasmine.]

By definition a postcolonial writer, Bharati Mukherjee is no multiculturalist. She took explicit aim at the term in 1994: "Multiculturalism emphasizes the differences between racial heritages. This emphasis on the differences has too often led to the dehumanization of the different. And dehumanization leads to discrimination. And discrimination can ultimately lead to genocide." Later she writes, "Parents express rage or despair at their U.S.-born children's forgetting of, or indifference to, some aspects of Indian culture. . . . I would ask: What is it we have lost if our children are acculturating into the culture in which we are living?" (**"Beyond Multiculturalism"** 2C). She is plainly disinterested in the preservation of cultures, the hallowing of tradition, obligations to the past; at least, she is not interested in the nostalgic aspects of such preservation. Rather, her current work forwards a distinction between "pioneers" and pitiable others for whom attachments to personal and cultural pasts foreclose possibilities. These pioneering characters undergo personal changes in their movements from culture to culture, changes that Mukherjee characterizes in the strongest terms. In an interview from 1988, she discussed the origins of her fictional characters' immigration experiences in her own (from Bengal to the U.S., and then to Canada before returning to the U.S.):

> We [immigrants] have experienced rapid changes in the history of the nations in which we lived. When we uproot ourselves from those countries and come here, either by choice or out of necessity, we suddenly must absorb 200 years of American history and learn to adapt to American society. Our lives are remarkable, often heroic. . . . Although they [the fictional immigrant characters] are often hurt or depressed by setbacks in their new lives and occupations, they do not give up. They take risks they wouldn't have taken in their old, comfortable worlds to solve their problems. As they change citizenship, they are reborn.

(1988 Interview 654)

Using the category of "rebirth" for these changes avows their thoroughness and also, by opposing rebirth to "comfort," implies a quality of anxiety and even violence therein. Mukherjee is so far from veneration of tradition that her works accept—indeed, embrace—the violence that accompanies cross-cultural revision and personal change. One of her most important and famous heroines, Jasmine, says: "There are no harmless, compassionate ways to remake ourselves. We murder who we were so we can rebirth ourselves in the image of dreams" (*Jasmine* 25). It is the willingness of Jasmine and others of Mukherjee's ethnic characters to murder their past selves that enables them to actively advance into unknown but promising futures. The futures they propel themselves toward—and even help to shape—are not guaranteed to be successful, but do have the potential for personal, material and spiritual success.

By contrast, those of her characters who hold onto history, the past, and their past places in their cultures simply for the sake of maintaining its traditions are doomed to failure, stasis, and often death. Most significantly for the student of American literature, she articulates her central subjects' productive violence quite closely with the ideology of American progress and risk—using such dearly held tropes as the frontier, the cowboy/pioneer, and the astronaut to mark her heroes and heroines. Just as importantly, however, she separates "America"—as an ideal space/temporality of continuous self-invention—from America's dominant citizens. In revisionary-subversive response to the nativist American ideology which holds that Anglo-Americans are the blessed children and international acolytes of this American ideal, Mukherjee turns the tables. In her works, many Anglo-Americans become spiritually, emotionally, and even physically crippled, overwhelmed by the obligations of living up to America's potent promises and traditions, while some first-generation immigrants—ethnic Americans, though she dislikes qualifying "American" in any way—accept the dangers and take the risks necessary to make the leap into a truly new future, a leap Mukherjee figures as specifically and quintessentially American. For Mukherjee, this revisionary immigrant "American" identity is inextricably intertwined with representations and tropings of modern technology. Interestingly, the inscription of technology in *Jasmine,* though pervasive, has received little critical commentary, an oversight it is my aim, in the last half of this essay, to correct.

Mukherjee's concept of violent personal, trans-cultural transformation is different from the attempts at total erasure practiced by the colonizing powers on their conquests. Mukherjee may disclaim allegiance to cultural pasts and traditions, but her characters do more than simply discard these. As in the Caribbean novelist Wilson Harris's works, dead selves and cultures do not vanish, but are always present. Jasmine murders herself in order to recreate different selves, but she can never wholly deny, forget, or escape the previous ones. Even at the end of the novel, as she prepares to transform herself again by leaving Bud and going to California with Taylor and Duff and the baby she's carrying, her past is with her: "Watch me reposition the stars, I whisper to the astrologer who floats cross-legged above my kitchen stove. . . . I cry into Taylor's shoulder, cry through all the lives I've given birth to, cry for my dead" (214). They are dead, but not gone, for they can never cease to frame, warn, and influence Jasmine. As much as Mukherjee figures Jasmine as a subject who makes fleeing her past (India, her family, her fate, even her names) a virtue, Jasmine is continually evoking that past and re-fashioning it and herself. Her continuous and aggressive revision of the fate foretold in her childhood by a Hindu seer and her ability to affect it, to attain agency in its dynamics, most clearly demonstrates this simultaneity of past, present and future. This emphasis on the dynamic interplay encompassing both change and preservation leads me to place Mukherjee in the field of cross-cultural writers like Harris, who coined the phrase and uses it to emphasize "the evolutionary thrust it restores to orders of the imagination, the ceaseless dialogue it inserts between hardened conventions and eclipsed or half-eclipsed otherness, within an intuitive self that moves endlessly into flexible patterns, arcs or bridges of community" (xviii). It is this ceaseless, flexible dialogue between cultures that is at the center of Mukherjee's work, and represents, in her view, the polar opposite of multiculturalism's aim to stabilize difference.

Jasmine tells the story of a young girl born in the village of Hasnapur, India, who undergoes enormous personal and cultural disruptions and revisions, changes which are not finished by the close of the action. A poor girl but a bright student, Jyoti is educated over the protests of her traditional father, and eventually marries a modern Indian husband, Prakash, whose dream becomes emigration to the U.S. to study and open an electronics business, a career which will include Jyoti, now re-named Jasmine by her husband. Already she has undergone major identity shifts, from feudal Hasnapur to urban Jullundhar, from her traditional cultural desire to have children early to Prakash's contempt for those desires: "We aren't going to spawn! We aren't ignorant

peasants!" (70), and already she feels the tensions of trying to accommodate these changes: "Jyoti, Jasmine: I shuttled between identities," she says, and ". . . I felt suspended between worlds" (69-70).

Soon Prakash is killed, by a bomb meant for Jasmine and hidden in a portable radio by Sikh terrorists. Jasmine vows to complete Prakash's dream, to go to his intended school in Tampa, Florida and sacrifice herself on the campus. She manages to smuggle herself into America using false passport papers. There she is raped by her smuggler, after which she kills him and abandons her holy journey. She is befriended by an American woman, Lillian, who helps her learn to pass as an American woman and evade the INS and who calls her "Jazzy." She moves to New York, moves in with Prakash's old professor and becomes a live-in domestic, feeling desperately that she has moved back to Hasnapur. She gets a green card and an *au pair* position in Manhattan, which allows her to complete her Americanization by becoming an integral part of an American family and also by learning how to consume, which she does gleefully. However, her husband's killer appears in New York as well, and she flees to Iowa, where she marries Bud, a rural banker, becomes Jane Ripplemeyer, and adopts a Vietnamese refugee son, Du. The novel closes as Taylor, her now-divorced former employer in Manhattan, asks her to come with him and his daughter to California, where Du has already gone. Pregnant from her time with Bud, she leaves him anyway to be with Taylor in California. Such are the bare bones of the narrative, but its unifying theme is Jyoti/Jasmine/Jane's mutability, her adaptation to circumstances, expressed as a change from passive, traditional object of fate to active, modern, cross-cultural shaper of her future.

From the beginning, Jyoti rebels against her cultural inscriptions. A seer foretells her future, pronouncing "my widowhood and exile . . . I was nothing, a speck in the solar system. . . . I was helpless, doomed" (1). In response she whispers "I don't believe you," and, claiming that a wound on her forehead is her "third eye" she proclaims herself a "sage," rewriting her position from passive object to empowered seer. Then, swimming in the river, she happens across "what I don't want to become," a dog's old, waterlogged carcass (3). This image of stasis, passivity, and rot establishes her negative horizon, the 'fate' she will succeed in avoiding. Mukherjee establishes this mortal stasis as a component of the past, and it becomes Jasmine's goal to move away from the past at all costs, including the cost of self-knowledge, a stable identity. In many places throughout the text, Jasmine refers to herself, and her past selves, as ghosts, phantoms, or to herself as an astronaut, moving between worlds, never solidly attached to any. Often, she adopts the trope of reincarnation, describing her various identities as separate lives,

lives which must be sealed off from each other: "For me, experience must be forgotten, or else it will kill" (29). She disdains her father's obsession with the vanished past, a past in which he was a wealthy farmer, before the Partition Riots.[1] The family was violently dispossessed of their property, but her father has never been able to accept his new status, preferring to imagine himself as he was. Jasmine says of him, "He'll never see Lahore again and I never have. Only a fool would let it rule his life" (37). In the end she is seen to continue this protean narrative, never sure what the future will bring, but always knowing that it is preferable to the past: "Time will tell if I am a tornado, rubble-maker, arising from nowhere and disappearing into a cloud. I am out the door and in the potholed and rutted driveway . . . greedy with wants and reckless from hope" (214).

It is important to note, however, that this self-determination is inflected with some of the same cultural narratives that Jasmine attempts to re-direct. Her present is a tense, contingent result of continual negotiations between her past and her future; her future self can never entirely escape her past inscriptions. In a recent article on *Jasmine,* "'We Murder Who We Were': *Jasmine* and the Violence of Identity," Kristin Carter-Sanborn reads Jasmine's "shuttling between identities" differently from Mukherjee's apparent desire to have them constructed as self-empowering. I disagree with this reading, as it de-emphasizes important elements in the text that are crucial in understanding its inscription of Jasmine/Jyoti as autonomous and independent, albeit within the parameters of certain cultural fields which I enumerate below.

Carter-Sanborn points out that Jasmine's near-euphoric sense of her (and other immigrants') ability to change and adapt to new circumstances is expressed in the highly ambiguous image, "We murder who we are so we can rebirth ourselves in the images of dreams," leading Carter-Sanborn to ask ". . . but of whose dreams?" (577). Under Carter-Sanborn's reading, each change or transformation that Jyoti/Jase/Jasmine goes through, from traditional village girl to modern Indian wife to avenging killer to nurturing day mummy to 'foreign' Iowa farm wife, all occur under the control—sometimes outright, as in Prakash's lectures on her new identity, sometimes more subtle, as with Bud's joking references to her as the "Jane" of Tarzan movies—of others, usually men.[2] Reincarnation, the text's central figure for these personal/subjective transformations, Carter-Sanborn believes,

> . . . may in fact disguise the imperial subject dreaming of and violently remaking its 'third world' Others to fit those dreams. . . . Bud, Taylor, and even her first husband Prakash, whom Jasmine characterizes as a

type of Professor Higgins, call upon these [Orientalist] vocabularies in order to speak the narrator's name and thus remake her in the shape of their own fantasies.

(579)

This is a perceptive but, I argue, incomplete reading of Jasmine's shifting subjectivity.

One of Carter-Sanborn's central pieces of evidence is her reading of the scene in which Jasmine is raped by a smuggler named Half-Face, whom she then kills. Carter-Sanborn notes an evacuation of agency from the character of Jasmine as she prepares to murder him. In the shower after the rape, the glass fogs so that her face becomes indistinct, and her revenge is figured not as her own, but rather as a result of the action of the goddess Kali, as Jasmine feels herself become "walking death" (106). This transformation Carter-Sanborn labels a "dissociative state," and claims that the recourse to the Hindu goddess "blocks access to agency" (589). As further evidence, she points to the section of Chapter Eight in which the young Jyoti kills a rabid dog, noting that in her description of the event agency transfers from the young girl to the staff: "The staff crushed the dog's snout while it was still in mid-air" (49). Carter-Sanborn says, "It is as if the staff has leaped out of Jyoti's hands and done its work alone; she describes the scene from the point of view of a prone and helpless observer" (587). For Carter-Sanborn, agency is thus displaced at crucial moments from Jasmine elsewhere, in a pattern that has been and will be repeated throughout the narrative. Carter-Sanborn is accurate when she sees Jane/Jasmine's chain of identities as divided, often as objects of others' desires and agendas:

> To act, for Jasmine, is to become entirely other. In an interesting inversion of the colonial project sketched by Bhabha, Jasmine can authoritatively impute the idea of "multiplicity" to her own character only retrospectively . . . from the perspective of a woman with an all-seeing "third eye." . . . In cataloging her selves Jasmine is able to conjoin them in the overarching "multiple" consciousness of the narrative. But in the very construction of that consciousness there is no "simultaneity" or even continuity to be found. The narrator is not the widow and the au pair; the Iowa wife and the undetected murderer. The continuity between one of these states and any other is either obscured or destroyed, her implicit argument goes, by the violence of the transformative moment. She abandons agency in this moment to her theoretical Other, and it is this Other who determines and delivers her into new forms.

(582-83)

There is no question that Jasmine does shift between identities and positions frequently. At the end of the novel, when Jane is leaving Bud to go to California with Taylor and Duff, at one discursive level Mukherjee makes an attempt to present her central character as autonomous and self-willed by having her leave Bud, with whose child she is pregnant. Here, Jane ceases obeying one form of responsibility—to Bud and their future family—and thus seems to move away from her pattern of conformity to dominant, male inscriptions of her. But here again she abandons agency in certain places. First, she thinks to herself, "I am not choosing between men. I am caught between the promise of America [choosing Taylor/California] and old-world dutifulness [Bud/Iowa]" (213-14). The verbs are significant. In the first sentence she is "not choosing between men," which may lead us to think she will announce that her choices are actually between different categories. But the next sentence reveals that she actually is not choosing at all; she is 'caught,' passively, between paths. Further down the page she expresses her sense of the change involved in leaving Iowa this way: ". . . the frontier is pushing indoors . . . ," another image that locates agency elsewhere, outside of Jane. She is the object, not the subject of these actions. The last paragraph reinforces this sense as she says, "Then *there is nothing I can do*. Time will tell if I am a tornado rubble-maker, arising from nowhere and disappearing into a cloud" (214, emphasis added). Her human agency is first disavowed, then dispersed and abandoned altogether in the image of the natural force, inscrutable and unpredictable, entirely beyond the category of will. Carter-Sanborn is entirely correct in questioning these absences of subjective agency in Jasmine's narratives, but she overlooks equally important parts of those episodes: their *useful effects*. I argue that Jasmine's subjectivity is not "erased," but rather that she enters new and empowering subjective possibilities, both with the aid of her originary culture's narratives and in other ways that are articulated through the twinned tropes of "America" and high technology.

Let us return to the rabid dog episode. As the reader can see, and as Carter-Sanborn herself acknowledges, Jyoti intends to defend herself: ". . . even as she recognizes 'fate' in the terrifying form of the rabid jackal she resists that doom: 'I wasn't ready to die'" (586). And before crushing the dog's head, Jyoti sets up the attack, plans her approach: "I took aim and waited for it to leap on me" (49). While it is true that the attack itself is described from a passive point of view, the effect is salutary: the dog is dead, Jyoti evades victimization. And in the other violent moments in the text, including Jasmine's revenge on Half-Face, the shifting of agency and the ambiguity of her identity does not in any way counteract the validity or efficacy of the actions. She succeeds. In the novel's last scene outlined above, Jasmine shifts from passive to active even within paragraphs. On the space of the last page, interspersed among the passive constructions noted earlier, Jasmine does assume a directive voice: "'I have to see Du' I announce," at one point, and then later "I'm not leaving Bud . . . I'm going somewhere" shows a clear shift of interpretation, from one which

sees her as object of others' narratives (Bud's) to one which shifts the focus of agency back to herself. Just before leaving, she reiterates this theme: "Watch me reposition the stars, I whisper to the astrologer who floats cross-legged above my kitchen stove" (214). This formulates Jasmine as an active participant in her fate, while leaving an altered version of the Hindu fate that attempts to name her at the beginning of the novel somewhat intact; she never fully escapes, but does successfully *negotiate*, her various pasts.

I read the transformations undergone in the space marked by "Jasmine" or her various names—what Mukherjee calls her "shuttling between identities"—as analogous, at the individual level, with the broader cultural dynamics Homi Bhabha observes obtain for the Other under conditions of postmodernity:

> Terms of cultural engagement, whether antagonistic or affiliative, are produced performatively. The representation of difference must not be hastily read as the reflection of pre-given ethnic or cultural traits set in the fixed tablet of tradition. The social articulation of difference, from the minority perspective, is a complex, on-going negotiation that seeks to authorize cultural hybridities that emerge in moments of historical transformation.
>
> (2)

It is here that I read significant analogs with Jyoti/Jasmine/Jane's episodic leaps between identities and "worlds," her continual negotiations with her past and its "fate" and the "images of dreams" she finds in ever more modern worlds, and in the mythologies of new places. Here Bhabha writes of the accompanying validity of tradition to be used, as Jasmine does, in working out new subjectivities that confront and surmount different and contradictory intersections of powers and cultures:

> The "right" to signify from the periphery of authorized power and privilege does not depend on the persistence of tradition; it is resourced by the power of tradition to be reinscribed through the conditions of contingency and contradictoriness that attend upon the lives of those who are "in the minority." The recognition that tradition bestows is a partial form of identification. In restaging the past it introduces other, incommensurable cultural temporalities into the invention of tradition.
>
> (2)

Put simply, it is Jasmine's right and power to call upon Indian cultural and religious traditions in this new setting, in a process which transforms those traditions into active tools of power for her, altering both. It is within this context that I contend the usage of the goddess Kali actually instantiates agency in Jasmine. Or, more precisely, there occurs a calling forth, in which Kali functions as an articulation of Jasmine and vice-versa, both inscribed upon and yet also different from each other. This is evidently a tense and anxious, only partial identification, an interstitial subjectivity which cannot be wholly one presence nor wholly another. It functions, importantly, in a multifaceted border space between Jasmine's proxy mission, the violence inflicted upon her by Half-Face's erasure of her identity as widow and his brutal subjection of her, and the new cultural cartography of America, in a hotel that, with its "Western shower" which Jasmine "had never used . . . with automatic hot water coming hard from a nozzle instead of cool water from a hand-dipped pitcher," is both torture chamber and ". . . a miracle. . . . It was a place that permitted a kind of purity" (104). Samir Dayal's assessment of Jasmine's identity accords with my own in emphasizing its radically unstable nature: "Jasmine instinctively grasps that self-assertion does not necessarily imply a confidence in a stable, reified self. Her struggle to maintain her precarious sense of self registers the effectivity of violence in the continual articulation of her precarious subjectivity in the world," a subjectivity he has provocatively called "violent self-transcendence" (80, 71). Both this reading and my own emphasize the inescapable excess of cultural interaction, the borderland postcolonial subjectivities that are multiple, and never thoroughly integrated into stable boundaries.

For Mukherjee, the mutually reinforcing tropes of technology and America serve as metaphors and vehicles for a version of the "revision and reconstruction" Bhabha speaks of as defining the postcolonial identity. Technology is a continual and highly ambiguous presence in *Jasmine,* and its functions and associations are crucial to our understanding of the new subjectivities achieved by the text's most highly-valorized characters, Jasmine and Du.

While technology is evident throughout the various cultural zones of the text, including even "feudal" Hasnapur, it is America that provides its most "natural" home, its most active locus. America and technology are reciprocal figures, each providing the optimum conditions and frame for the other, articulating each other along a borderline named "mutability." The mutability of technology subtends, allows, and reiterates the protean character of America in the novel, and the mutual interaction of this continual fluidity enables and inscribes Jasmine's own personal subjective changes. Early in the novel, Jane observes "They tell me I have no accent, but I don't sound Iowan, either. I'm like one of those voices on the telephone, very clear and soothing. Maybe Northern California, they say. Du says they're computer generated" (*Jasmine,* 10-11). Here, Jasmine/Jane's adaptability is underlined by her similarity to the dispersed and functional voice of the computer network.

Even before reaching Iowa, in Manhattan, the scene of an important identity shift (Jazzy to Jase) and stage for further Americanization, technology accompanies and

tropes the narrative's themes. After her departure from her traditional role as domestic female in the community of transplanted, unassimilated Indians in Queens, she goes to an American friend for help. Kate Gordon-Feldstein introduces her to her pet iguana Sam, brought in from the Galápagos, who "thinks he's a dog" (145). Sam thrives—in a Manhattan loft that had seen incarnations as a dance space and television studio before conversion into an apartment—because of a sun lamp and the puréed lettuce Kate feeds him. Holding him, Jasmine thinks "Truly, I had been reborn. Indian village girls do not hold large reptiles on their laps" (144). Both Jasmine and Sam have come a long way to meet in New York, a meeting that can only occur because technology can substitute for the Galápagos' environment and because Jasmine has transformed identities, an adaptation emphasized by the casual incongruity of the tropical lizard's existence in the northern city. Later, she moves into the Upper West Side apartment of Taylor, the man with and for whom she will eventually leave for California, but for whom she starts working as an *au pair.* Taylor's wife Wylie shows her around the kitchen and comes to the microwave. In an attempt at multicultural sympathy, Wylie says "If you have a thing about radiation, you don't have to use it. . . . You just let us know when we upset you, all right?" In reply, Jasmine says simply, "I don't have a thing about radiation" (150). Mukherjee strongly wants to contrast Wylie's stereotyping of Jasmine as a "primitive," "Third World Other" with Jasmine's actual affiliation with technology and its powers and possibilities, most notably possibilities for rapid change.

One of the most central images of the potency of this techno-cultural doubling occurs in Jasmine's first view of America, as she and other illegal immigrants land in the surf of the Gulf Coast:

> Then suddenly in the pinkening black of pre-dawn, America caromed off the horizon.
>
> The first thing I saw were the two cones of a nuclear plant, and smoke spreading from them in complicated but seemingly purposeful patterns, edges lit by the rising sun, like a gray, intricate map of an unexplored island continent, against the pale unscratched blue of the sky. I waded through Eden's waste: plastic bottles, floating oranges, boards, sodden boxes, white and green plastic sacks tied shut but picked open by birds and pulled apart by crabs.
>
> (95-96)

The map of the unknown continent etched into the sky can only remind us of the visions of the earliest European explorers, an echo reinforced by the "seemingly purposeful" design she reads into it. It is unknown but part of her destiny, blurry but fated, alien from and owned by the observer at one and the same time. It is an imperial vision, ironically re-written by an undreamed-of explorer, a visionary unauthorized by Western narratives of power and possession, an illegal Indian woman. It stems from the cooling towers of a nuclear plant, binding the image of the waiting continent to the field of technology and its ambiguous promises. Thus, her vision is unmistakably inflected with futurity as the scene of exploration merges with its nuclear frame. Yet this Eden is different, littered, already written over by prior conquests, including the technological; it is not the "virgin land" of her predecessors, but a thickly populated zone of confrontation. It is this subversive re-appropriation of the already exhausted American cultural narratives of newness, open possibilities, and unknown but promising futures by new, postcolonial immigrants that is, we shall see, at the core of *Jasmine*'s multiple narratives.

This previously unimagined re-appropriation from the margins has an important forerunner in the novel. On her way to America, Jasmine and other illegal aliens move via what she calls "phantom airlines," in the shadows and corners of the authorized networks. The very technological/transportation linkages—international airlines, airports—that support, at one level, the global capitalism that centers the West and performs economic and ideological neo-colonial operations on the "Third World," are also spaces of opportunity and re-fashioning for Jasmine and her fellow-travelers: "There is a shadow world of aircraft permanently aloft that share air lanes and radio frequencies with Pan Am and British Air and Air-India, portaging people who coexist with tourists and businessmen. But we are refugees and mercenaries and guest workers. . . ." (90). It is significant that Jasmine and her fellow "phantom" passengers are not written as being accepted into that system of legalized, valorized national citizenship available to the privileged subjects who can (like Mukherjee herself) afford it. Rather, they are "ghosts," unthinkable and diaphanous entities taking advantage of the liminal, unauthorized and interstitial spaces that are the inevitable possibilities—the remainders, the excesses—of those pathways hurled outward to draw global Others into the sphere of power of the modern West: "What country? What continent? We pass through wars, through plagues. . . . The zigzag route is the straightest. . . . I phantom my way through three continents" (91). Her inscription as phantom in this context underlines the danger and power of her interstitial position: the phantom is dangerously less real; she would have no defense if detected. Yet, at the same time it is this liminal position that allows her to mimic the centered subjects of this international system to her advantage.

Jasmine finds even in the hotel room of her brutalization a certain comfort in the modern technology of the Western shower. Mukherjee chooses this same hotel to expand on the marvelous mutability of America. It soon

becomes "something called Paradise Bay Complex: A Mixed-Use Vacation and Residence Community . . . hell turned into paradise—to me this seems very American" (122). Repeatedly, America is associated with swift change, passage into the future and the erasure of the past: "It is by now only a passing wave of nausea, this response to the speed of transformation, the fluidity of American character and the American landscape" (123). And even before her arrival, she and Prakash think of moving to America in terms that emphasize change and possibility: "We'd start with new fates, new stars" (77). It is this possibility for change that is the most salient feature of America for Jasmine; for many others, as we shall see, America cannot function in the same way.

The other major character whose experience of America involves taking advantage of American mutability is Du, Jasmine/Jane's and Bud's adoptive Vietnamese refugee son. And it is in his narrative that the strongest links between technological mutability and the promise of America are articulated. Du is linked to technology from the beginning of his appearance: "We bought ourselves a satellite dish the day after we first talked long distance to Du. There's no telling where this telecast is coming from" (14). Du scavenges electronic parts, taking things apart and reassembling them in new ways, for unimagined purposes:

> It's not engineering. It's recombinant electronics. I have altered the gene pool of the common American appliance. I have spliced the gene of a Black & Decker paint sprayer onto the gear drive of a repaired Mixmaster. I have created a multi-use super air blower with a variable-speed main-drive. . . . I didn't have to *learn* it, it's what I do.
>
> (139)

This technological mastery becomes a metaphor for Du's ability to adapt to his new circumstances, and to have survived the war and refugee camps of his childhood.

It is in this scene that Mukherjee links this technological adaptability again with the productive violence of their marginalized pasts and, very possibly, their futures. Jasmine uses her own electrical knowledge—learned from Prakash—to help Du in one of his creations: "'I understand circuitry.' . . . 'I've also killed a man, you know,'" to which Du responds "'So have I, More than one'" (139). Plainly, for Jasmine and Du technology's adaptable, amoral effectiveness is the most recognizable model for their own journeys, their cross-cultural negotiations. For Mukherjee, the postmodern, postcolonial subject should be like an electronic component: functional, modern, and entirely flexible.

Jasmine and Du have many foils in the novel, all of them characters whose choice of cultural values is traditional and rooted in the past. And, in a further re-appropriation of white American ideology by postcolonial ethnic characters, the authorized subjects of the American national narrative are those who fail to fulfill its destiny. Darrel Lutz, the mid-westerner, inheritor of the 'heartland of America,' hangs himself from his hog barn while the immigrants survive and push ahead, change, and grow stronger. Darrel is the clearest example in the novel of the enervating and stagnating effects of the national narrative—the same national mythology that provides opportunity for the immigrants—on its "chosen" subjects: Anglo-Americans. Darrel has inherited his father's farm, but is clearly unsatisfied to simply propagate that legacy. In one of his first appearances in the novel, Mukherjee makes it plain that Darrel is mis-matched to his fate. We see him sitting in his father's tractor, but he doesn't fit it. It is "too large" for him, signaling a sort of degeneration in the stock, and a reversal of the growth trajectory required by the American national narrative. Darrel's appearance in the out-sized tractor is more than coincidence, for Mukherjee will write Darrel's tragic maladjustment to American mythology on the field of agricultural technology. A sign of a more willful rejection of his patrimony is Darrel's painting over of the St. Louis Cardinals baseball team logo (his father's choice) with that of the Chicago Cubs, the Cardinals' archrivals. But it is a failed attempt, for the rebellion is contained within the terms of the father's values; to choose a different team is to remain tied to the original need to choose.

Darrel demonstrates dissatisfaction with and rebellion against his destined role as "heartland" farmer, proud husbandman of the land, in several ways. To Jane he reveals his secret desire: to sell the farm and open a Radio Shack in New Mexico. The choice of enterprise is significant, as it puts Darrel in the same general category as Du, Prakash, Professorji, and Jasmine herself, that of modernized characters who are attracted to and adept at handling electronic technology, a technological modernity viewed with suspicion by farmers who are, as Jasmine says, "the same everywhere." Darrel also engages in legal negotiations aimed at selling the farm to a company which would transform it into a golfing range, an idea that is anathema to Bud's notions of the proper disposition of farm lands, as well as to his respect for Darrel's dead father. Mukherjee makes it clear that Darrel would be better off to pursue this dream. Staying in Iowa and working his father's farm depresses him, driving him to drink heavily. One drunken evening he reveals to Jane his desire for her, and his wish that she should run away with him to the Radio Shack in the desert. In a practice which reflects both his desire to abandon his cultural narrative and his corollary desire for Jane—as she represents exotic possibilities to him—he experiments with Indian cooking, partially in hope of impressing her.

Darrel's suicide is both a striking climax to the Iowa section of the narrative and a powerful figure for Mukherjee's message of the dangers of tradition. Darrel in the end does not sell the farm to the golf company, partially because of Bud's denigration of the idea but largely because he cannot bring himself to entirely reject the powerful cultural expectations and narratives that cannot validate other vocations than farming: "With ground so cheap and farmers so desperate, they're snapping up huge packages for future non-ag use. . . . It breaks Bud's heart even to mention it" (7). As a sort of compromise, Darrel devotes his energies to building a high-tech hog barn, one that can feed a great number of hogs and circulate their waste back to the fields with little labor, another enterprise for which Bud has overt disdain. But this is clearly only a partial solution to Darrel's basic predicament; while he can attempt to modernize the farm, he is still following the path laid down by the several overlapping narratives that bind him: Midwestern "heartland" mythology, broader American agrarian/pastoral narratives, and the family history that is enforced by Bud, who functions as Darrel's (and the county's) surrogate financial "father." Ultimately, the contradictions become too great for Darrel to mediate, and he hangs himself from the beams of the unfinished structure. Jasmine/Jane describes him not as a farmer but as, significantly, an astronaut, "shamed by the failure of his liftoff" (209). The astronaut imagery inscribes Darrel into the narratives of progress and futurity, but negatively; he has failed, and his failure can be traced to his guilty attachment to the farm. His father's farm, but in many ways Iowa's farm and America's farm, its obligations foreclose other possibilities for Darrel, so that his attempt to start a high-tech adventure on it is doomed from the start. According to the logic of Mukherjee's past/future, farm/frontier dichotomy, Darrel's attempt to straddle both worlds is impossible.

> Darrel's already imagined himself in New Mexico selling Tandys: his will has muscled out his guilt, or his destiny. . . . Crazy, Darrel wants an Indian princess and a Radio Shack franchise in Santa Fe. Crazy, he's a recruit in some army of white Christian survivalists. Sane, he wants to baby-sit three hundred hogs and reinvent the fertilizer/pesticide wheel.
>
> (207)

The futility of the high-tech hog operation is communicated in Mukherjee's description of it as "reinvent[ing]" the wheel—the very cliché for useless and self-delusional action. Mukherjee's characters cannot be half-way astronauts and prosper. Darrel's attachment to the past, to the land and his/its cultural responsibilities, is clearly articulated on a structure of guilt and repression, leading directly to a doom that cannot be averted be technology.

Jasmine/Jane's husband Bud is equally clearly a representative of the dangers of tradition. He is in many ways analogous to Jyoti's own father, the gentleman farmer who refuses to accept his own loss of power and status, and therefore relevance, in the new India:

> In Lahore my parents had lived in a big stucco house with porticoes and gardens. They had owned farmland, shops. . . . Mataji, my mother, couldn't forget the Partition Riots. Muslims sacked our house. . . . I've never been to Lahore, but the loss survives in the instant replay of family story: forever Lahore smokes, forever my parents flee.
>
> (35-36)

Here again Mukherjee plays on the ambivalence of technology, as the horrific attachment to a past that is imagined as eternally present, a past which forms the ultimate horizon—in this case, the locked gate—of her parents' identities is figured as a tape, immutably and inevitably repeated in a process which flattens time into an eternally present past. A tape differs from a memory or a vision in its mechanical stasis, its stifling sameness. Memories and visions may alter to renew themselves and their dreamers. But here, as with Darrel's hog barn, technology is figuratively amenable to a useless and doomed cultural necromancy, but always to the detriment of the user.

Bud is not guilty in his relationship to the community, as Darrel is, but he too has paid a price for his involvement with the farm society. He was shot by a farmer who went mad as a result of changing conditions, economic tensions and changes not accounted for in the heartland cultural narrative of hard work and decent reward. Perhaps understanding Bud's exposed position as banker, and central node of this culture's "social symbolic orders," Jasmine/Jane wants to tell him "Don't make moral decisions for Darrel. . . . Bud gets too involved. It almost killed him two years ago" (16). Bud remains fixed to a static conception of the farm community, despite the fact that the community itself is changing against his wishes. Bud's ex-wife, Karin, runs a help hotline for the desperate, a modern remedy to the problems of new times that are still only dimly understood. "Something's gotten out of hand in the heartland," says a mental health consultant of the depression, shootings, and rising divorce rates the area is suffering (138). White supremacy is on the rise, as are one-world conspiracy theories. Even the heartland is coming unsettled, but Bud's solution shows his devotion to traditional wisdom: "You'll see, it'll rain" (9). Bud is crippled by a deranged farmer's bullet; his desire to organize the community's finances and land according to a stable narrative has not paid off.

Another group of characters who function to show the dangers of devotion to tradition are the Khalsa Lions, Sikh terrorists who eventually plant the bomb in the radio that kills Prakash, though it had been meant for Jasmine, as she does not conform to traditional dress codes. They are unmistakably symbols of cultural conservatism:

> There was a new Sikh boys' gang, the Khalsa Lions, who liked action. Khalsa means pure. As Lions of Purity, the gang dressed in white shirts and pajamas and indigo turbans, and all of them toted heavy·kirpans on bandoliers. They had money to zigzag through the bazaar on scooters, but since they were . . . farmers' sons, we assumed the money for scooters came from smuggling liquor and guns in and out of Pakistan. In villages close enough to the border, smuggling was not an unacceptable profession.
>
> (42)

Three things are significant here. The dedicated warriors for religious and cultural purity have no compunction about using motor-scooters, nor the transistor radios they will later use to kill Prakash. Second, as farmers' sons they bear immediate comparison to Darrel and to Jasmine's own father, the bitterly dispossessed farmer; as Jasmine says, farmers are the same everywhere, and Mukherjee's identification and equivalence of them begins to write the futile devotion to the past and its already-ossified materials in physical/geographical terms. The farm is the site of the past, the unhealthy space of repetition and stasis. Third, the Khalsa Lions' liquor and arms-trafficking activities, though outside the bounds of their strict religious dogma, nevertheless are necessary for the prosecution of those codes in the villages. And Mukherjee makes clear the specific terms of existence of the Khalsa Lions are conditioned by their proximity to the border; this proximity is what instantiates the attempts to push back that border, to return the here-and-now to an untroubled center, attempts which rely upon the very cultural and commercial hybridity they despise.

In Mukherjee's inscription, the Khalsa Lions' devotion to tradition is murderous, and that of the Iowans' is self-destructive and suicidal. Jasmine and Du are constructed to adapt, to change, to mediate the overlapping but often contradictory spaces of the postmodern world, and it is their ability to do this which establishes them as "Americanized": "My transformation has been genetic; Du's was hyphenated. We were so full of wonder at how fast he became American, but he's a hybrid, like the fantasy appliances he wants to build" (198). It is on the basis of this interpretation that I differ again from Kristin Carter-Sanborn, who finds Mukherjee's double construction of Jasmine as 'multiple' and as American to be impossible:

> . . . Her flirtation with "multiplicity" ironically resolves itself into a domestic and domesticated fantasy, a classic American dream of assimilation. Disguised as a call for revolution in our very understanding of the processes of identity in contemporary America, the narrative's lessons reveal a desire to invest American

identity itself with presence and authority. Thus the novel may more than anything demonstrate the very impossibility of an integrated subjecthood in the framework of Western notions of independence and individual accomplishment.

(582-83)

On the other hand, I argue that it is precisely Jasmine's *non-integration*—her ability and willingness to take up and cast off cultural, religious and other roles as she needs to, in pursuit of a potentially utopian future—that marks her, within the terms of the text, as most identifiably American. Mukherjee demonstrates that the most successful "selves" are mutable, shifting, postmodern next of various negotiated, contingent positions. It is the various farmers' inability to negotiate change and temporality, their fantasies of the land as permanent and therefore their own identities as fixed by that vision, that doom them to failure, futility, or death. Rather, Mukherjee forwards the useful mutability of technology as her metaphor for successful subjectivity, and technology is powerfully situated in the domain of the idea of "America." In this way, Mukherjee falls in line with a long tradition of writers who mythologize America as endlessly productive, and adds to the utopian tropology familiar from the earliest writings of the Age of Conquest a renewed emphasis on the powers of the machine. And like her pioneering forbears, Jasmine's actions show the disregard for conventional morality's finer points that flows from the doubled espousal of transformative violence and utilitarian technology.

Keeping in mind Mukherjee's understanding of this New World interplay of place and character, I read *Jasmine* as a textual production whose thematics propose precisely that new, contingent positionality that Bhabha has in mind when he describes the cultural significance of postmodernism and the postcolonial world's evaporating boundaries:

> The wider significance of the postmodern condition lies in the awareness that the epistemological "limits" of those ethnocentric ideas are also the enunciative boundaries of other dissonant, even dissident histories and voices—women, the colonized, minority groups, the bearers of policed sexualities. For the demography of the new internationalism is the history of postcolonial migration. . . .

(4)

The sign of Jasmine's flexibility is her ability to appropriate the "pioneer/explorer" rhetoric that had belonged to Anglo-Americans but which, in this novel, has become an ossified and impossible cultural weight for its intended heirs. Jasmine and Du re-combine, re-appropriate, and re-invent cultural traditions and subjectivities in new combinations, imagining the land as wilderness/frontier/open possibility imaginatively and thus claiming it for their use, in a mutated and shifting

echo of the process the European settlers used as they imaginatively emptied and re-wrote the New World to serve as their destiny. Mukherjee described the necessity for this process for her immigrant characters: "There isn't a role model for the 'Jasmines' or the 'Dimples.' They have to invent the roles, survive and revise as best as they can" (1990 Interview 23). *Jasmine*'s postcolonial, ethnic characters are post-American, carving out new spaces for themselves from among a constellation of available cultural narratives, never remaining bound by any one, and always fluidly negotiating the boundaries of their past, present, and futures.

Let me underline that the foregoing analysis should not be mistaken for a celebration of Mukherjee's own enthusiasm for the amoral and romanticized Americanization-via-technological-subjectivity that it uncovers. I find the criticisms of Mukherjee's problematically postmodern postcolonials offered by scholars such as Fred Pfeil and others highly persuasive.[3] In various ways, all these critics object to Mukherjee's mis-representations of the real circumstances of postcolonial subjects within cultural, economic, literary and ideological relationships between "First" and "Third" worlds. To (unavoidably) grossly oversimplify, these writers critique the way Mukherjee's texts, in the words of Anindyo Roy, "elide the deep contradictions built within the space of postcoloniality . . . [her aesthetic] forms are clearly indicative of the stabilization and commodification of a colonized culture by a postcolonial writer whose own authorial gaze corresponds to that of the Orientalizing West" (128-29). Such critiques may be, I believe, profitably supplemented by a fuller appreciation of the importance of figures of technology in her aesthetics. Mukherjee is unambiguous about her desire to be considered an American writer, not an Indian or Indian-American one.[4] And, as I have shown, *Jasmine* forwards a powerful linkage between an immigrant's personal progress and assimilation into a technologized America and an Americanized technological identity, a technological subjectivity that clearly has everything to do with the operations and contradictions of the new relationships of global capital.

Notes

1. The Partition Riots, in Spring-Summer 1947, were widespread violence between Muslim, Hindu and Sikh resulting from the political partition of Pakistan from India. For a fuller discussion, see Arthur Lall, who describes the impact: ". . . the partition led to over a million deaths, a refugee problem whose dimensions pale that of the Middle East refugee situation, and a property loss that has been too large ever to assess accurately" (136).

2. Other critics of Mukherjee's immigrant characters understand fully that the "fluid identities" she celebrates involve stresses and anxieties, but have

not read a lack of agency therein, as Carter-Sanborn does. Gurleen Grewal comes closest to this view, finding Jasmine's sati-motivated voyage to America both psychologically and culturally unrealistic. I am indebted to Carmen Wickramagamage's very useful 1992 article, "Relocation as Positive Act," on Mukherjee's connection of immigration with violence and empowerment. F. Timothy Ruppel's essay notes that *"Jasmine* is a novel that resists closure and suggests a strategy of continual transformation as a necessary and historical contingent ethic of survival" (182). Also see Brinda Bose ("There is a simultaneous fracturing and evolving of identity going on here, in terms of both ethnicity and gender, which is true of the experience of multiculturalism" (57)); Arvindra Sant-Wade and Karen Marguerite Radell, Samir Dayal; and Pushpa N. Parekh for various useful approaches to this view of identity in Mukherjee.

3. See Anindyo Roy, Alpana Sharma Knippling, Debjani Banerjee and Gurleen Grewal.

4. On her disavowal of "immigrant author" status, see, for example, her 1988 "Immigrant Writing: Give Us Your Maximialists."

Works Cited

Bhabha, Homi. "Locations of Culture," Introduction to *The Location of Culture.* New York: Routledge, 1994.

Bose, Brinda. "A Question of Identity: Where Gender, Race, and America Meet in Bharati Mukherjee," in Emmanuel S. Nelson, Ed., *Bharati Mukherjee: Critical Perspectives.* New York: Garland, 1993. 47-64.

Carter-Sanborn, Kristin. "'We Murder Who We Were': *Jasmine* and the Violence of Identity," *American Literature,* 66:3 (1994). 573-93.

Dayal, Samir. "Creating, Preserving, Destroying: Violence in Bharati Mukherjee's *Jasmine.*" in Emmanuel S. Nelson, Ed., *Bharati Mukherjee: Critical Perspectives.* New York: Garland, 1993. 65-88.

Grewal, Gurleen, "Born Again American: The Immigrant Consciousness in Jasmine." in Emmanuel S. Nelson, Ed., *Bharati Mukherjee: Critical Perspectives.* New York: Garland, 1993. 181-96.

Knippling, Alpana Sharma. "Toward an Investigation of the Subaltern in Bharati Mukherjee's *The Middleman and Other Stories* and *Jasmine.*" in Emmanuel S. Nelson, Ed., *Bharati Mukherjee: Critical Perspectives.* New York: Garland, 1993. 143-60.

Lall, Arthur. *The Emergence of Modern India.* New York: Columbia UP, 1981.

Mukhjeree, Bharati. "Beyond Multiculturalism." *Des Moines Register* 2 Oct. 1994, 1C+.

———. "Immigrant Writing: Give Us Your Maximialists." *New York Times Book Review* 28 August 1988: 1, 28-29.

———. Interview. *The Iowa Review* 20:3 (1990) 7-32.

———. Interview. *The Massachusetts Review* (1988): 645-54.

———. *Jasmine.* Fawcett Crest: New York, 1989.

———. *The Middleman and Other Stories.* Grove P: New York, 1988.

Parekh, Pushpa N. "Telling Her Tale: Narrative Voice and Gender Roles in Bharati Mukherjee's *Jasmine.*" *Bharati Mukherjee: Critical Perspectives.* Emmanuel S. Nelson, Ed., New York: Garland, 1993. 181-96.

Pfeil, Fred. "No Basta Teorizar: In-Difference to Solidarity in Contemporary Fiction, Theory, and Practice." *Scattered Hegemonies: Postmodernity and Transnational Feminist Practices.* Inderpal Grewal and Caren Kaplan, Eds., Minneapolis: U of Minneapolis P, 1994. 197-230.

Roy, Anindyo. "The Aesthetics of an (Un)willing Immigrant: Bharati Mukherjee's *Days and Nights in Calcutta* and *Jasmine.*" *Bharati Mukherjee: Critical Perspectives.* Emmanuel S. Nelson, Ed., New York: Garland, 1993. 127-42.

Ruppel, F. Timothy. "'Re-inventing Ourselves a Million Times': Narrative, Desire, Identity, and Bharati Mukherjee's *Jasmine.*" *College Literature* 22:1 (1995): 181-91.

Sant-Wade, Arvindra and Karen Marguerite Radell. "Refashioning the Self: Immigrant Women in Bharati Mukherjee's New World." *Studies in Short Fiction* 29 (1992): 11-17.

Wickramagamage, Carmen. "Relocation as Positive Act: The Immigrant Experience in Bharati Mukherjee's Novels," *Diaspora* 2:2 (1992): 171-200.

Jennifer Drake (essay date spring 1999)

SOURCE: Drake, Jennifer. "Looting American Culture: Bharati Mukherjee's Immigrant Narratives." *Contemporary Literature* 40, no. 1 (spring 1999): 60.

[*In the following essay, Drake examines Mukherjee's experience of America as depicted in her fiction and in the essay "A Four-Hundred-Year-Old Woman."*]

> We need another time of writing that will be able to inscribe the ambivalent and chiasmatic intersections of time and place that constitute the problematic "modern" experience of the western nation.
>
> How does one write the nation's modernity as the event of the everyday and the advent of the epochal?
>
> Homi Bhabha, "DissemiNation"

In the essay **"A Four-Hundred-Year-Old Woman,"** Bharati Mukherjee writes: "[M]y literary agenda begins by acknowledging that America has transformed me. It does not end until I show how I (and the hundreds of thousands like me) have transformed America" (25). Mukherjee's stories of American transformations create an unsettled "time of writing" that links "the event of the everyday and the advent of the epochal" so as to rethink American narratives of immigration. In her tales, people and nations scatter and gather. Assimilation is cultural looting, cultural exchange, or a willful and sometimes costly negotiation: an eye for an eye, a self for a self. People mix with gods and goddesses, or become gods and goddesses, reincarnating, translating narratives of coherence. Translated men and women make nations metaphorical, imagining homes in the cracks between nostalgia and frontier dreams. Violence roams, Kali's bloody tongue. Mayflower claims can't save anyone; we're all immigrants, strangers in a strange land.

Because Mukherjee employs familiar American narratives in order to transform them, and to make them transformative, her representations of America and Americans are easily misread. For example, Victoria Carchidi sidesteps the violence and anxiety in Mukherjee's fiction to read Mukherjee as insisting "that when such multiple worlds meet, the result can be a glorious freeing of the leaves of the kaleidoscope, that complexly intermix and produce a new pattern" (98). Susan Koshy suggests that Mukherjee's stories themselves elide the question of violence, arguing, "Mukherjee's celebration of assimilation is an insufficient confrontation of the historical circumstances of ethnicity and race in the United States and of the complexities of diasporic subject-formation" (69). But Mukherjee's stories do not simply promote American multiculture or celebrate assimilation; rather, precisely in order to confront "the historical circumstances of ethnicity and race in the United States" and "the complexities of diasporic subject-formation," Mukherjee fabulizes America, Hinduizes assimilation, and represents the real pleasures and violences of cultural exchange. Representing immigration through the logic of transformation, Mukherjee's project involves, as David Mura puts it, "a discovery and a creation, as well as a retrieval, of a new set of myths, heroes, and gods, and a history that has been occluded or ignored" (204).

To discover, create, and retrieve America's multicultural myths and histories, Mukherjee rejects the expatriate's nostalgia. She rejects the hyphen and the acceptable stories it generates—stories about immigrants struggling between two incommensurable worlds, finally choosing one or the other. Her immigrant characters are settlers, Americans—not sojourners, tourists, guest workers, foreigners. Arguing that "[w]herever I travel in the (very) Old World, I find 'Americans' in the making, whether or not they ever make it to these shores. . . . dreamers and conquerors, not afraid of transforming themselves, not afraid of abandoning some of their

principles along the way" (**"Four-Hundred-Year-Old Woman"** 27), Mukherjee holds America accountable for its promises and favorite myths about itself: this nation and its people are diverse dreamers, generous, heroic, hard-working, democratic, lovers of truth and defenders of equal opportunity for all. This American Dream offers possible worlds, unleashes the imagination. Despite its actual failures, this is its transformative power, and Mukherjee's work engages this most generous aspect. In her stories, hope's transformative violence—a gritty leap toward "freedom"—dialogues with the false hope offered by an American Dream premised on white supremacy and disseminated by global capitalism's exploitations.

Mukherjee's appropriation of powerful American myths and transnational American dreams to the rewriting of hyphenated "Americans" as Americans thus walks a critical tightrope. I understand this aspect of her project as aligned with Arjun Appadurai's view that "the United States is no longer the puppeteer of a world system of images, but is only one node of a complex transnational construction of imaginary landscapes. The world we live in today is characterized by a new role for the imagination in social life" (327). Appadurai continues:

> The image, the imagined, the imaginary—these are all terms which direct us to something critical and new in global cultural processes: the imagination as a social practice. No longer mere fantasy (opium for the masses whose real work is elsewhere), no longer simple escape (from a world defined principally by more concrete purposes and structures), no longer elite pastime (thus not relevant to the lives of ordinary people) and no longer mere contemplation (irrelevant for new forms of desire and subjectivity), the imagination has become an organized field of social practices, a form of work (both in the sense of labor and of culturally organized practice) and a form of negotiation between sites of agency ("individuals") and globally defined fields of possibility. It is this unleashing of the imagination which links the play of pastiche (in some settings) to the terror and coercion of states and their competitors. The imagination is now central to all forms of agency, is itself a social fact, and is the key component of the new global order.

The imagination as social practice and social fact works where myth logic meets fractals, chaos, fuzzy set theory; globalization is ineffectually understood purely in terms of Western or U.S. hegemony; narratives of Americanization here and abroad must be interrupted by narratives of indigenization; neither the center nor the periphery can hold, or hold on. How else to explain the people we meet and become, "individuals" living out complex collective histories? How to live as we have to live in the midst of everyday epochal violence, instantaneous change? As the main character of Mukherjee's novel *Jasmine* passionately argues:

I do believe that extraordinary events can jar the needle arm, jump tracks, rip across incarnations, and deposit a life into a groove that was not prepared to receive it.

I should never have been Jane Ripplemeyer of Baden, Iowa. I should have lived and died in that feudal village, perhaps making a monumental leap to modern Jullundhar. When Jyoti's future was blocked after the death of Prakash, Lord Yama should have taken her.

"Yes," I say, "I do believe you. We do keep revisiting the world. I have also traveled in time and space. It is possible."

Jyoti of Hasnapur was not Jasmine, Duff's day mummy and Taylor and Wylie's au pair in Manhattan; that Jasmine isn't this Jane Ripplemeyer having lunch with Mary Webb at the University Club today. And which of us is the undetected murderer of a half-faced monster, which of us has held a dying husband, which of us was raped and raped and raped in boats and cars and motel rooms?

(127)

David Mura's call for "a new set of myths, heroes, and gods, and a history that has been occluded or ignored" transforms, in Mukherjee's imagination, into stories of immigrants as active agents of change. These stories join, rather than replace, the histories of economic and physical violence that fuel immigration and that immigrants face upon reaching the New World. To bring these stories and histories together, Mukherjee marries the literal and the metaphorical. For example, in *Jasmine* she writes Jasmine as "a love goddess" (Interview [Connell et al.] 25)—both destroyer and preserver, powerful with want and wanting, facing and making violent change, moving through lives with tornado force, "in love with the country . . . revitalizing it, if it allows itself to be revitalized" (Interview [Connell et al.] 26). Like Vishnu the Preserver, who contains "our world inside his potbellied stomach," Jasmine "cocoon[s] a cosmos" (Jasmine 224); "Like creatures in fairy tales, we've shrunk and we've swollen and we've swallowed the cosmos whole" (*Jasmine* 240); like Kali the Destroyer, Jasmine kills to feed cycles of rebirth. Reading *Jasmine* too literally, or reading her only as an individual human being, ignores the work of metaphor: "The imagination is now central to all forms of agency, is itself a social fact, and is the key component of the new global order" (Appadurai 327). To read *Jasmine* only through the lens of assimilation ignores that when a goddess transforms, she doesn't lose herself: she is no singular self; she contains the cosmos. When a goddess transforms, she takes action, exerts great power. Hence "immigration" is transformation in multiples, "immigration" is a force of nature as transformative as global warming; "immigration" demands myth, imagination, metaphor.

Giving up the India that she was born into, and the India she initially (re)created to anchor her own New World anxiety, Mukherjee-the-writer determined to

"invent a more exciting—perhaps a more psychologically accurate a more precisely metaphoric India: many more Indias" (Mukherjee and Blaise 297). As part of this process, she also invents a more precisely metaphoric America, many more Americas—amnesiac, violent, free, possible. She filters her insistently American stories through what she describes as "a Hindu imagination; everything is a causeless, endless middle" (Mukherjee and Blaise 175). The violence and hope twinned in Mukherjee's writing must be understood in terms of this imaginative "Indianness," where "Indianness is now a metaphor, a particular way of partially comprehending the world" (Mukherjee, *Darkness* xv), where Indianness means that "different perceptions of reality converge without embarrassing anyone" (Mukherjee and Blaise 296). This metaphoric, imaginative Indianness fuels her desire, and her struggle, for an equally metaphoric America. Creating this America, she writes:

It is, of course, America that I love. Where history occurs with the dramatic swiftness and interest of half-hour television shows. America is sheer luxury, being touched more by the presentation of tragedy than by tragedy itself. History can be dealt with in thirty-second episodes; I need not suffer its drabness and continuum. . . .

In India, history is full of uninterrupted episodes; there is no one to create heroes and define our sense of loss, of right and wrong, tragedy and buffoonery. Events have no necessary causes; behavior no inevitable motive. Things simply are, because that is their nature.

(Mukherjee and Blaise 168)

In Mukherjee's imagination, America is a place in flux, a metaphor that represents freedom from Indian history-as-fate. She knows she should have ended up a Brahmin wife, privileged, angry, innocent, bored, dutiful, rebellious: "in Calcutta, we are rarely allowed to escape what our hands reveal us to be" (Mukherjee and Blaise 219). However, as Jessica Hagedorn observes, though America can offer a "profound sense of 'freedom' (to) a woman—a freedom of movement and choice. . . . Freedom (also) has its price" (175). For Mukherjee, American freedom costs her the clarity and stability of full-Brahmin status, sacrificed when she marries a white French-Canadian American. And she exchanges racial invisibility in India for "minority" status in North America. She gives up a certain kind of home, home-as-comfort, home-as-talisman, exchanging that stable *desh* for imagination's portability, its astonishing and insistent demolitions and reinventions, its work. In Mukherjee's America, "home" says "freedom," "home" says "war zone." "Home" is no consolation, no place to rest. There are too many Americas and Indias for that.

In an essay entitled "In a Free State: Postcolonialism and Postmodernism in Bharati Mukherjee's Fiction," Gail Ching-Liang Low describes a seminar she convened on the "politics of speech and representation, the creative ways in which women of colour countered racist and sexist erasure in mainstream white culture by reclaiming the right to tell their own stories" (8). The group emphasized the importance of what Toni Morrison and bell hooks, among others, have described as "re-memory," "the politicization of memory," and "the struggle of memory against forgetting," exploring the recovery of "lost ancestral and cultural lines" through the use of vernacular forms (8). But when the group turned to Mukherjee's work, Low writes, "we found that we could not fit her writing into the model of postcolonial and diasporic texts that we had collectively mapped out as important . . . There was real anger and dismay . . . at Mukherjee's easy dismissal of much of what we took to be necessary interventions in the cultural mainstream" (9-10). Low explains:

> Mukherjee seemed not to be concerned with preserving cultural identities and did not want to be labeled an "Indian" writer. She is whole-heartedly unapologetic about her celebration of cultural dislocation and opposes Indianness as "a fragile identity to be preserved against obliteration." Instead of consolidating cultural specificities against a dominant white urban America, she positively rejects it [sic].
>
> (9)

The struggle against historicocultural erasure and for collective voice that this group privileges is different from, though related to, Mukherjee's struggle to rewrite normative narratives of American identity through writing immigration stories about personal and cultural transformations. I would like to make two key points here to account for the differences between these projects.

First, Mukherjee's work resists a particular form of racist logic and practice that she associates with Canadian racial and national discourses, particularly in the 1970s. She describes "making a choice between two distinct New World myths of nationhood"—the Canadian ethnic mosaic and the American melting pot—after experiencing "racial harassment in increasingly crude forms . . . including removal to a seat in the back of an inter-city bus" and witnessing Canada's creation of "new official phrases—'visible minority,' 'absorptive capacity,' among others—to marginalize its non-white citizens exclusively on the basis of race" (Mukherjee and Blaise 302). Mukherjee also associates Canada, literally and metaphorically, with Britain, so that moving to Canada felt like "going to England, a step backward to an old world" (Interview [Connell et al.] 11), and taking Canadian citizenship meant undoing "the work of generations of martyred freedom fighters, pledg[ing] loyalty to the British Queen" (Mukherjee and Blaise 169). So even though Canada's ethnic mosaic model and its emphasis on cultural difference and racial tolerance sounds good to liberal ears, Mukherjee's move to

Canada meant replaying Old World colonial oppression, updated for a postcolonial world.

In his essay "Is There a Neo-Racism?" Etienne Balibar theorizes what he calls "the new racism," a concept that helps to clarify Mukherjee's position:

> The new racism is a racism of the era of "decolonization," of the reversal of population movements between the old colonies and the old metropolises, and the division of humanity within a singular political sphere. Ideologically, current racism, which in France centres upon the immigration complex, fits into a framework of "racism without races" which is already widely developed in other countries, particularly the Anglo-Saxon ones. It is a racism whose dominant theme is not biological heredity but the insurmountability of cultural differences, a racism which, at first sight, does not postulate the superiority of certain groups or peoples in relation to others but "only" the harmfulness of abolishing frontiers, the incompatibility of life-styles and traditions. . . .
>
> . . . We now move from the theory of races or the struggle between the races in human history, whether based on biological or psychological principles, to a theory of "race relations" within society, which naturalizes not racial belonging but racist conduct.
>
> (21-22)

Discourses that emphasize the insurmountability of cultural differences, then, naturalize racist conduct. Mukherjee's fictions, and her discussions of them, emphasize resistance to discourses of difference put to this use. Balibar argues that discourses of differential racism, mimicking (and sometimes confusing) more emancipatory takes on "difference," effectively cover over the fact that the dominant culture still demands assimilation before integration, and that this assimilation "is presented as progress, as an emancipation, a conceding of rights":

> The "different" cultures are those which constitute obstacles, or which are established as obstacles (by schools or the norms of international communication) to the acquisition of culture. And, conversely, the "cultural handicaps" of the dominated classes are presented as practical equivalents of alien status, or as ways of life particularly exposed to the destructive effects of mixing.
>
> (25)

Hence Mukherjee's argument that she and other immigrants are "Americans"—a metaphor/process/state of mind that signifies transforming selves, transforming the nation, rejecting the "mothering tyranny of nostalgia" (**"Four-Hundred-Year-Old Woman"** 25) for a worldview that knows culture is a live thing that cannot survive intact. For Mukherjee, U.S. complicity with the logic and practice of "new racism" is balanced, though not erased, by a strong history of civil rights activism and by the beckoning of the New World possibility that the United States represents:

I made my choice; I shouldered my way into the country in which I felt minority discourse empowered rather than enfeebled me. . . . This time I was repossessing a "homeland" I had willed into existence, not inherited.

(Mukherjee and Blaise 303)

Secondly, Mukherjee's "transformation—not preservation" chant (**"Four-Hundred-Year-Old Woman"** 27) must be located—entangled—in the imaginary worlds of Hindu epics and in the visual logic of the Moghul miniature paintings that so inform Mukherjee's aesthetic. Her writing feeds off the freedom that "America" allows her to imagine and the different perceptions of reality that "India" allows her to imagine. This complexity is made visible, given a form that can be used, in Moghul miniatures:

> My image of artistic structure and artistic excellence is Moghul miniature painting, with its crazy foreshortening of vanishing point, its insistence that everything happens simultaneously, bound only by shape and color. In the miniature paintings of India, there are a dozen separate foci, the most complicated stories can be rendered on a grain of rice, the corners are as elaborated as the centers. There is a sense of the interpenetration of all things.

("Four-Hundred-Year-Old Woman" 27-28)

Historically, Moghul miniatures signify cultural clash and exchange; this painting tradition was brought to India by Islamic invaders and conquerors. Unlike European medieval art, which shares some of the perspectival strategies of the miniatures but emphasizes God's-eye Christian narratives, and unlike Western painting during and after the Renaissance, which explores the visual organization of secular space from the perspective of a single viewer, Moghul miniature paintings gather stories together to create a multifocal field of vision, even as the different tableaux within each painting compete with each other for the viewer's attention: What's going on up in the right-hand corner? How is that scene related to the scene that seems centrally positioned? How to read the architectural spaces that divide yet connect these stories? How to read the painted renditions of woven patterns, their relationship to secular and sacred art-making? As Mukherjee suggests: "understanding this art is really a matter of learning to see it in a different way. This is what I'm trying to do in my novels and stories. I want many stories going on simultaneously to distract, to crowd the reader's consciousness" (Interview [Bonnie] 8). Mukherjee's stories are "about" every character and detail in them, no matter how small.

Even as Mukherjee's writing recalls Moghul miniature paintings, it also suggests modes of vision informed by computer technologies. For example, contemporary Mexican American artist Martina Lopez makes digital images, "photographs," using the computer to scan pictures she has taken of clouds and landscapes, then adding figures from old snapshots (Wolf, "Memory/Reference: The Digital Photography of Martina Lopez"). Lopez alters the dimensions, hues, and perspectives of these figures, playing with scale so that different-sized images are rendered in equal detail. The ancestors are present, lost; their stories gather with ours, make what dreams look like—vertigo, fear, clutter. In her novel *Holder of the World,* Mukherjee attempts to create the kinds of effects Lopez achieves with digital imaging, digital imaging recalling Moghul miniature paintings, both "like an Indian dessert, things fried that shouldn't be, hot that should be cold, sweet that should be tart. . . . an art that knows no limit, no perspective and vanishing point, no limit to extravagance, or to detail, that temperamentally cannot exclude" (Holder 19). Because unclutteredness is fatal, Mukherjee begins the novel this way:

> I [Beigh Masters] live in three time zones simultaneously, and I don't mean Eastern, Central and Pacific. I mean the past, the present and the future. . . .
>
> . . . Nothing is ever lost, but continents and centuries sometimes get in the way. . . .
>
> . . . [Venn] animates information. He's out there beyond virtual reality. . . .
>
> . . . he's establishing a grid, a data base. The program is called X-2989, which translates to October 29, 1989, the day his team decided, arbitrarily, to research. By "research" they mean the mass ingestion of all the world's newspapers, weather patterns, telephone directories, satellite passes, every arrest, every television show, political debate, airline schedule. . . .
>
> Finally, a use for sensory and informational overload.
>
> Every time-traveler will create a different reality—just as we all do now. No two travellers will be able to retrieve the same reality, or even a fraction of the available realities. History's a big savings bank, says Venn, we can all make infinite reality withdrawals. But we'll be able to compare our disparate experience in the same reality, and won't that be fun? . . .
>
> Every time-traveler will punch in the answers to a thousand personal questions . . . to construct a kind of personality genome. . . .
>
> With a thousand possible answers we can each create an infinity of possible characters. And so we contain a thousand variables, and history is a billion separate information bytes. Mathematically, the permutations do begin to resemble the randomness of life. Time will become as famous as place. . . .
>
> My life has gotten just a little more complicated than my ability to describe it. That used to be the definition of madness, now it's just discontinuous overload.

(5-7)

The vast sense of perspective that Mukherjee establishes here indicates what her writing attempts: to find narrative structures and American English sentences that signify, and act out, lives that have gotten a little more complex than our abilities to describe them. Like the Moghul miniatures and Lopez's digital images, Mukherjee's writing creates fullness in short takes, crams a world of detail into fragments of story, compresses constant motion, travel, discontinuous overload. This is how immigration feels; this is how America feels. As Mukherjee explains, contemporary Anglo-American fictions fail to provide forms, and vocabularies, that can do this detail-oriented, noncausal work:

> I'm interested in finding the right form for me and my characters, who are the kinds of Americans who haven't been written about before. So the characters of, say, an Ann Beattie are significantly different from mine because they've not been dislocated in such severe and traumatic ways. An oceanic or social view rarely creeps into contemporary American fiction. It is simply—well, not simply, predominantly—fiction about personal relationships. Even someone like Raymond Carver, whose work I admire very, very much, and whose stories are obviously meant to be tragic, is talking about small disappointments. Whereas in talking about Jasmine's life, I'm really talking about the history of current America too.
>
> (Interview [Connell et al.] 29)

Mukherjee's stories, then, represent the density of contemporary American experience. Her writing constructs interactive models—historical information bytes as scaffolding, a flexible and epic Hindu imagination as connective tissue. The participants in Low's seminar on the politics of speech and representation did not see how Mukherjee's work does participate, critically, noncausally, in the recovery of lost ancestral and cultural lines through the use of vernacular forms (8). Through vernacular and postmodern strategies of cultural dislocation, mythic transformation, and multifocal points of view, Mukherjee develops forms for writing capacious enough to meet contemporary American multiculture, and all its histories, head-on.

Through a complex plot that moves from New England to England to India, *The Holder of the World* insists that America's founders, the Puritans, should be understood as what Stuart Hall has called "translated" men and women, born/e across the world, "irrevocably the product of several interlocking histories and cultures" (qtd. in Mercer 27-28). This is why Mukherjee describes her contemporary immigrant characters as new Americans, and as so profoundly American—the twinned anxiety and exhilaration of translated men and women fuels the restless frontier search for a big-enough, new-enough home that has long defined the American experience. This condition comprises our common culture, our imagined community, our commonality of feeling, the (not) ground where "we" meet regardless of our race, ethnicity, whatever. In this context, it is interesting that critics and readers seem to focus on Mukherjee's immigrant Americans, Americans in the making, to the exclusion of the stories that represent "white" Americans as also Americans in the making, immigrants to a new and multicultural land. Mukherjee's *The Middleman and Other Stories* provides the most fertile ground for exploring the ways in which her writing represents white Americans as willing and not-so-willing immigrants to the New World.

As Priscilla Wald suggests in her reading of Gertrude Stein's *The Making of Americans*: "Immigrants, for Stein, were selves in transit, between narratives as much as between geopolitical locations. Their status at once manifested and provoked an anxiety of identity that Stein represented as a transition between states of consciousness. . . . The experience is one of alienation rather than transcendence" (238). Wald's reading of Stein clarifies the point that immigrants can be understood as persons "between narratives," "between states of consciousness," and it is this transitional state that Mukherjee explores through her white American characters. As the recent culture wars have demonstrated, an increasingly multicultural America confuses "settled" Americans, usually white—those of us who have been here long enough to develop amnesia about our own immigrant histories; those of us whose ancestors found it politically and economically expedient to become "white" and then deny that rebirth, calling it genetic fact instead. Transformation, from the perspective of whiteness and regardless of actual economic profile, most often signifies terror, fear of falling, loss. We imagine that we have something—power, money, security, whiteness—that change threatens, and we can't see beyond that threat to New World hope. Our myths feature hard work and determination, not whim or fate: "In America, at least in New Jersey, everyone . . . seems to acknowledge a connection between merit and reward. Everyone looks busy, distraught from overwork. . . . Such faith in causality can only lead to betrayal" (Mukherjee, *Darkness* 139). It's an indulgence to believe in God, so let's make God and his word literal too—miracles, yes, but no monkey-gods, no action without a moral, just cause, just deserts. But even though we're a literal people, we dissimulate; as Benjamin DeMott argues in *The Imperial Middle: Why Americans Can't Think Straight about Class,* "Intransigent bias and individualistic independence learned early, in America, to disguise themselves as each other" (159). Located within these worldviews, the question of contemporary America's (multi)cultural transformation becomes the question that made the December 1994 cover of *The Atlantic Monthly*: "Must it be the rest against the West? Whether it's racist fantasy or realistic concern, it's a question that just won't go away: As population and misery increase, will the wretched of the earth overwhelm the Western paradise?" (Connelly and Kennedy).

Jeb, white narrator of Mukherjee's story **"Loose Ends,"** turns to the particular narratives of coherence that *The Atlantic*'s question suggests: that he belongs here and "they" don't, that "they" are wretched and "we" are not, that the West is Paradise in its death throes and it is all "their" fault. But transformed—reincarnated—during his time in Vietnam, as America was transformed by the Vietnam War, Jeb now lives in an America defined by global exchange, cultural contact, violence. He's turned American hitman on home soil, works for Mr. "Haysoos" Velasquez, lives in a Miami like Havana, Beirut, Saigon: "It's life in the procurement belt, between those lines of tropical latitudes, where the world shops for its illicit goods and dumps its surplus parts, where it prefers to fight its wars, and once you've settled into its give and take, you find it's impossible to live anywhere else" (50). His life gives the lie to his narratives of coherence; the grammar of "we" and "they" won't parse; he's brought America's Vietnam home with him, re-creates "America" in the image of "his" Vietnam, a war zone:

> I like Miami. I like the heat. You can smell the fecund rot of the jungle in every headline. You can park your car in the shopping mall and watch the dope change hands, the Goldilockses and Peter Pans go off with new daddies, the dishwashers and short-order cooks haggle over fake passports, the Mr. Vees in limos huddle over arms-shopping lists, all the while gull guano drops on your car with the soothing steadiness of rain.
>
> (45)

This is Americanization translated by global travel, Americanization phantoming its way through airports, America's global project come home to roost.

To survive the Vietnam War, Jeb fed his working-class American hunger with the blood of "others" and the desire to live. He becomes his cinematic heroes, the stuff of legend, the American male outlaw:

> I liked the green spaces of Nam, too. In spite of the consequences. I was the Pit Bull—even the Marines backed off. I was Jesse James hunched tight in the gunship, trolling the jungle for hidden wonders.
>
> "If you want to stay alive," Doc Healy cautioned me the first day, "just keep consuming and moving like a locust. Do that, Jeb m'boy, and you'll survive to die a natural death."
>
> (45)

Jeb weaves American narratives of classlessness, white supremacy, and male heroism together to make nostalgia and success from his post-Vietnam rage and disfranchisement, embodying what DeMott calls "a patriotism of the scream"—the desperate need to love the romanticized, idealized America that sent its working-class young men to fight in Vietnam, the need to resurrect that America through devotion even after the fall (219). This takes a devotee's passion and depth of belief, and all the myths a person can muster.

Confused, anxious, between narratives and seeking sense, Jeb tells a story about Alice in Wonderland disappearing down the rabbit hole, taking America with her:

> Where did America go? . . . Down the rabbit hole, Doc Healy used to say. Alice knows, but she took it with her. Hard to know which one's the Wonderland. Back when me and my buddies were barricading the front door, who left the back door open?
>
> (48)

In Jeb's story, Alice leaves behind a pastel Florida house with a tiny yard, "a retirement bungalow like they used to advertise in the comic pages of the Sunday papers" (48), a piece of crappy swamp property not "quite surfaced from the slime, and the soil . . . too salty to take a planting" (48), crappy house and crappy property to appease people who had worked and worked and saved as much as they could which was not quite enough to get the Dream in hand. In Jeb's story, though, the retirees are gone, and Alice has left the pastel house to "a nice big friendly greaser like Mr. Chavez" (48), new seeker of the American Dream.

As Jeb tells his story, it is clear that he assumes that his reader or listener is white, assimilated, and the grandson or granddaughter of the old American working class (who were probably immigrants, or first generation, but Jeb forgets this part of the narrative). Jeb confirms his imagined reader's suspicions: that there was a "good Florida" and that your grandparents worked hard for it, and that your grandparents got their just deserts, which are now being denied to you:

> I keep two things in mind nowadays. First, Florida was built for your pappy and grammie. I remember them, I was a kid here, I remember the good Florida when only the pioneers came down and it was considered too hot and wet and buggy to ever come to much. I knew your pappy and grammie, I mowed their lawn, trimmed their hedges, washed their cars. I toted their golf bags. Nice people—they deserved a few years of golf, a garden to show off when their kids came down to visit, a white car that justified its extravagant air conditioning and never seemed to get dirty. That's the first thing about Florida; the nice thing. The second is this: Florida is run by locusts and behind them are sharks and even pythons and they've pretty well chewed up your mom and pop and all the other lawn bowlers and blue-haired ladies.
>
> (49-50)

Jeb longs for the first Florida but lives the second, consuming and moving like a locust; the second Florida makes much more sense to him now, though he still worships the coherence of the first. This dissonance scares him. A translated man, he's between narratives as much as between geopolitical locations. But he still likes to pretend that he's home and self-possessed, even though he knows he isn't, never was.

What to do, between narratives? Jeb hitches a ride to the farthest cheap motel, owned by new Americans working for their American Dream. And for them, the American Dream is working, more or less. But instead of taking the Patel family's success as a sign of hope for his longed-for America of just deserts, this is what he sees:

> Inside, in a room reeking of incense, are people eating. There are a lot of them. There are a lot of little brown people sitting cross-legged on the floor of a regular motel room and eating with their hands. Pappies with white beards, grammies swaddled in silk, men in dark suits, kids, and one luscious jailbait in blue jeans.
>
> They look at me. A bunch of aliens and they stare like I'm the freak.
>
> (52)

The America he sees in the motel room is actually more like the America for which he waxes nostalgic than it is like the America of locusts, pythons, and middlemen which he now inhabits and thinks killed off the America of the white grammies and pappies. Problem is, Jeb just can't renarrate what "we the people" might look like. He lives the logic of war, battle, the little brown enemy, self-hatred, racism disguised as nationalism, systematic class inequity disguised as "some people's" lack of motivation and ability: "They've forgotten me. I feel left out, left behind. While we were nailing up that big front door, these guys were sneaking in around back. They got their money, their family networks, and their secretive languages" (53). All Jeb's got is this story, confusing the desire to escape his own betrayal by America for hatred of a visibly different enemy.

As the "luscious jailbait in blue jeans" shows Jeb his motel room, he "catch[es] the look on her face. Disgust, isn't that what it is? Distaste for the likes of me" (54). Briefly seeing himself as "other" through this young American woman's eyes—very briefly seeing her, seeing with her, putting himself back in the picture by seeing himself as a failed American from her point of view—Jeb experiences this identification as estrangement from the narratives of self and other he's been struggling to maintain. Jeb "pounce[s] on Alice before she can drop down below, and take America with her" (54). He names her and writes her into his story; he rapes her to keep his story in the first person, to take his America back, to stop "Alice" and her family from transforming America as they transform themselves into Americans with more hope than he's felt in a very long time. He rapes "Alice" to mark himself as part of her transformation, and to transform her transformation, so he's still part of America's story.

As Jasmine says, "There are no harmless, compassionate ways to remake oneself. . . . We murder who we were so we can rebirth ourselves in the images of

dreams" (29). Jeb gives himself up to his new life; he goes down the rabbit hole and takes America with him. Stuck in Miami-Saigon's paddyfields, driving one of the Patels' cars, Jesse-Jeb becomes the reticulated python, "eyes brown and passionless as all of Vietnam":

> That snakeshit—all that coiled power—stays with me, always. That's what happened to us in the paddyfields. We drowned in our shit. An inscrutable humanoid python sleeping on a bed of turds: that's what I never want to be. . . .
>
> This is what I've become. I want to squeeze this state dry and swallow it whole.
>
> (49, 54)

In this Wonderland, Jeb-as-Jesse James becomes just Jeb—drowning, a man alone, a man who clings to the myths that kill any chance he's got of survival in the new world because they're all he's got. Narrating **"Loose Ends"** as the story of his transformation into the stuff of nightmare, Jeb embodies America's imperial violence; he is its offspring, its living dead.

The Vietnam War also comes home to America in **"Fathering,"** undoes stories about the American family as **"Loose Ends"** undoes stories about the American Dream, both undoing stories about American masculinity. As Priscilla Wald suggests, and as Jason and Sharon in **"Fathering"** believe, "[a]n official narrative of American identity . . . is a family narrative. . . . If genealogy supplies the logic and language of identity, family relations provide its structure. Identity is marked by and within the family, which is the cornerstone of socialization" (253). But the convention of explaining personal, familial, or national identities genealogically falls apart in this story, as "genealogy" transforms to mean something like Foucault's use of the term:

> Genealogy does not resemble the evolution of a species and does not map the destiny of a people. On the contrary, to follow the complex course of descent is to maintain passing events in their proper dispersion; it is to identify the accidents, the minute deviations—or conversely, the complete reversals—the errors, the false appraisals, and the faulty calculations that give birth to those things that continue to exist and have value for us; it is to discover that truth or being does not lie at the root of what we know and what we are, but the exteriority of accidents. . . . The search for descent is not the erecting of foundations: on the contrary, it disturbs what was previously considered immobile; it fragments what was thought unified; it shows the heterogeneity of what was imagined consistent with itself.
>
> (81-82)

In the context of Mukherjee's work, "genealogy" looks like "history" filtered through a Hindu imagination—history as accident, the everyday as epochal, perspective as multifocal view. **"Fathering"** filters American myths through a Hindu imagination to tell a story about the impossibility of possessing yourself, your child, your nation—a traumatic lesson for Americans who depend upon ownership (control, a logic of domination) for self-possession.

In **"Fathering,"** Jason decides to search for his Vietnamese daughter Eng. He hopes, believes, that materializing his experience in Vietnam by bringing Eng "home" will heal him, make him stop living like it didn't happen, make him remember the Jason that Vietnam (America) murdered, transformed. He's being a good father, taking responsibility for his daughter; he's being a good person, taking responsibility for healing himself: many American stories would reward him with a happy ending. But the story Jason winds up telling in **"Fathering"** is a story that the Broadway hit *Miss Saigon* avoids—what happens after the child of an American soldier and "the honeyest-skinned bar girl with the tiniest feet in Saigon" (117) lands on American soil. What happens is the failure of fathering as Dr. Spock would define it, fathering understood through narratives of ownership, or kinship, kinship signifying something besides a few genes and a lot of violence in common. What happens is the failure of patriarchy, the American family, the idea that "nation" equals "common culture." What happens is the dissolution of heterosexual coupling, as the "alien child" (123) displaces the white American almost-wife.

The child, Eng, is very sick and very unassimilated, unassimilable, crazy with post-traumatic stress syndrome and the violent stories she holds on to that are her genealogy, her narratives of coherence:

> "She bring me food," Eng's screaming. "She bring me food from the forest. They shoot Grandma! Bastards!"
>
> "Eng?" I don't dare touch her. I don't know how.
>
> "You shoot my grandmother?" She whacks the air with her bony arms. Now I see the bruises, the small welts all along the insides of her arms. Some have to be weeks old, they're that yellow. The twins' scrapes and cuts never turned that ochre. I can't help wondering if maybe Asian skin bruises differently from ours, even though I want to say skin is skin; especially hers is skin like mine.
>
> (121)

Jason struggles with Eng's difference, keeps trying to tamp it down, find common ground, assert the connection of "me and mine." He limns Eng's story with comments about "the twins" and their usual immunizations, sicknesses, things that happen to all little girls. But Eng is a kind of goddess, a pissed-off spirit, the return of the repressed. She can't be tied down. She's not just "a sick, frightened, foreign kid . . . a fighter" (119), though she is that too. And though she's Jason's kid, she'll never be. In Eng, the metaphorical and the literal converge.

To Jason, Eng is a foreignness he tries to tame, conquer, father, heal. When these patriarchal modes of connection don't work, he plays the only role he can, the only script they both share, part of the script that produced their relationship—soldier and child, "my Saigon kid and me":

> "Get the hell out, you bastard!" Eng yells. "Vamos! Bang bang?" She's pointing her arm like a semiautomatic, taking out Sharon, then the doctor. My Rambo. "Old way is good way. Money cure is good cure. When they shoot my grandma, you think pills do her any good? You Yankees, please go home." She looks straight at me. "Scram, Yankee bastard!" . . .
>
> Then, as in fairy tales, I know what has to be done. "Coming, pardner!" I whisper. "I got no end of coins." I jiggle the change in my pocket. I jerk her away from our enemies. My Saigon kid and me: we're a team. In five minutes we'll be safely away in the cold chariot of our van.
>
> (124)

Jason takes the leap into the violence of fairy tales and their shared history, because he has no access to other scripts that allow for difference-that-can't-be-grasped, and, simultaneously, intimacy as strong as family, the multiple meanings of blood. This is where the story ends for Jason and Eng: mutual dislocation, in between selves and countries, translated but not assimilated, clinging to the one coherent story they share.

Like Jason, Rindy in **"Orbiting"** both accommodates and resists the transformations a new American brings to her narratives of coherence. But unlike Jason and Jeb, Rindy herself has not undergone violent dislocation; her American story is about ethnic whiteness, about a multicultural assimilated family, about being changed by desire for a scarred immigrant revolutionary even while desiring to "Americanize" him. Rindy's story prompts questions concerning what bell hooks calls the "political possibilities" of desire, and Rindy's story provides a contradictory answer as to "whether or not desire for contact with the Other, for connection rooted in the longing for pleasure, can act as a critical intervention challenging and subverting racist domination, inviting and enabling critical resistance" (22).

The setting is Thanksgiving dinner, that all-American ritual family gathering, and the family certainly tells "all-American" stories. Rindy deMarco is a Jersey girl, first generation Italian American on her mother's side, third generation Italian American on her father's side. Her parents' stories illustrate the process of assimilation over time; her father is "very American, so Italy's a safe source of pride for him. . . . [He] had one big adventure in his life, besides fighting in the Pacific, and that was marrying a Calabrian peasant" (58). Rindy's mother took a while to "find herself," stayed in the house for years, but now she's taking a class at Paterson and has given up her stories about the wolves, unlit outdoor privies, and hard work of her mountain village. Not particularly upwardly mobile, content living in her studio apartment and selling funky jewelry she doesn't design, Rindy bucks her mother's immigrant faith that children will do quantifiably better than their parents. Rindy's sister Cindi (they used to be Renata and Carla—too Italian, too Old World) married Brent, who "in spite of the obvious hairpiece and the gold chain, is a rebel. He was born Schwartzendruber, but changed his name to Schwartz. . . . His father's never taken their buggy out of the county" (62). Rindy's ex-boyfriend, Vic, a romantic, macrobiotic, feminist man, just left her to follow a hunger for "places that get the Cubs on cable instead of the Mets" (63). And now Rindy has fallen in love with Ro (Roashan), whom the family will meet for the first time at Thanksgiving:

> He's been in the States three months, maybe less. . . .
>
> . . . . Ro has fled here from Kabul. He wants to take classes at NJIT and become an electrical engineer. He says he's lucky his father got him out. A friend of Ro's father, a man called Mumtaz, runs a flied chicken restaurant in Brooklyn in a neighborhood Ro calls "Little Kabul," though probably no one else has ever noticed.
>
> (64)

As this supposedly assimilated American family gathers for Thanksgiving dinner, they bring together many incarnations, many cultures and histories and names. The details that Mukherjee chooses to describe Rindy's family show that, in America, past selves and their stories don't disappear; they just emerge in the corners of rooms, or kaleidoscope into talk's subtext, creating new stories that, like Moghul miniature paintings, revel in detail and juxtaposition. What machinations of fate, or international violence twinned with international commerce, locate the deMarco family's stories in the same frame? How does a famed warrior from the Khyber Pass who keeps halal ever hook up with a Catholic Italian American from New Jersey?

Ro's "foreignness" disrupts the deMarco family's comfort zone, exposing their dependence on a narrow band of "American" narratives to make things make sense despite, or because of, the complex histories they themselves carry and forget. They're not quite sure where Afghanistan is, or what kind of tragedy might have brought Ro to America: famine? genocide? some sort of third world tribal skirmish? All those international sound bites blur. They are uncomfortable with Ro's culturally specific masculinity, his political passion, his Kabuli class privilege. He can't talk about the Celtics and the Knicks, though he could talk about squash or skiing at St. Moritz if Brent and Dad deMarco could. He isn't dressed quite right—"shows too much white collar and cuff"—and as Rindy observes,

he doesn't stand like an American man: "His hands hang kind of stiffly from the shoulder joints, and when he moves, his palms are tucked tight against his thighs, his stomach sticks out like a slightly pregnant woman's. Each culture establishes its own manly posture, different ways of claiming space" (70). Cordial yet uncomfortable with the deMarcos, Ro becomes animated when speaking about the Soviet menace in Kabul. For Rindy's father and Brent, "It's an unwelcome revelation . . . that a reasonably educated and rational man like Ro would die for things that [they have] never heard of and would rather laugh about. Ro was tortured in jail. . . . Dad looks sick. The meaning of Thanksgiving should not be so explicit" (72-73).

Rindy enjoys her family's discomfort with Ro, though it irritates her at the same time. Being with Ro makes her feel like a rebel, but she is embarrassed by what she perceives as Ro's social awkwardness. Rindy revels in the ways that Ro transforms her life; she glowingly describes her newfound familiarity with things like halal, whole nutmeg, Pashto words, the differences between Afghan tribes, political buzzwords like Babrak Karmal and Kandahar and Pamir. She makes his story hers, uses it to exoticize her own, and so participates in a form of domination that seeks contact with the Other "as a way to make the (self) over, to leave behind white 'innocence' and enter the world of 'experience'" (hooks 23). At the same time, Rindy's narratives of coherence are clearly being transformed in powerful ways, so that exploitative modes of relationship could change. She cannot just ignore that "[w]hen I'm with Ro I feel I am looking at America through the wrong end of a telescope. He makes it sound like a police state, with sudden raids, papers, detention centers, deportations, and torture and death waiting in the wings" (66).

Rindy takes pleasure in making her narratives of coherence less coherent, and she uses desire to fuel this undoing. But desire makes suspect moves. Even as Rindy constructs Ro as desirable, and masculine, and so refuses American stereotypes of unattractive and effeminate Asian men, she becomes mired in the language of "foreignness" and "exoticness" to articulate his desirability. In a passionate attempt to speak of Ro's difference differently, she compares him to Clint Eastwood, one of American pop culture's most manly men:

> I realize all in a rush how much I love this man with his blemished, tortured body. I will give him citizenship if he asks. Vic was beautiful, but Vic was self-sufficient. Ro's my chance to heal the world.
>
> I shall teach him how to walk like an American, how to dress like Brent but better, how to fill up a room as Dad does instead of melting and blending but sticking out in the Afghan way. In spite of the funny way he holds himself and the funny way he moves his head from side to side when he wants to say yes, Ro is Clint Eastwood, scarred hero and survivor.
>
> (74-75)

Rindy tries to understand Ro's masculinity, and the violence that marks his body, by translating him into a familiar American hero. And though this transformation is mutual—internationalized, Clint is not a completely familiar Clint—Rindy also falls into a culturally familiar language of domination. She writes Ro's difference as requiring assimilative change, and she plots her own heroic story by giving herself a mission: if she heals "her" man, she heals the world.

Patricia Wald writes, "Character and culture come together not in the fear of merging but in the fear of disappearing into incomprehensibility—into an identification . . . with an immigrant divested of the cultural narratives, and the familiar terms, that mark personhood" (239). Precisely because they interact and identify with new Americans, and are being changed by them, Jeb, Jason, and Rindy tell contradictory stories. They struggle to keep their stories comprehensible even as they tell stories about incomprehensibility and displacement. They attempt to resist incomprehensibility by animating narratives that constitute "self" and "other," in ways that make a comfortable and familiar sense. But their stories do not, and cannot, shore up a sense-making predicated on a logic of domination and on the incommensurability of "self" and "other," since (multi)cultural contact and exchange occasion their need for comprehensible stories. Jeb, Jason, and Rindy narrate a losing-self-sense that signifies "white" America's transformation. In a world where transformation has become more comprehensible than rigid notions of comprehensibility, Mukherjee's multifocal and multicultural American writing struggles for, and leads us toward, multiple models of comprehensibility.

Works Cited

Appadurai, Arjun. "Disjuncture and Difference in the Global Cultural Economy." *Colonial Discourse and Post-Colonial Theory.* Ed. Patrick Williams and Laura Chrisman. New York: Columbia UP, 1994. 324-39.

Balibar, Etienne. "Is There a 'Neo-Racism'?" *Race, Nation, Class: Ambiguous Identities.* By Etienne Balibar and Immanuel Wallerstein. Trans. Chris Turner. New York: Verso, 1991. 17-28.

Bhabha, Homi K. "DissemiNation: Time, Narrative, and the Margins of the Modern Nation." *Nation and Narration.* Ed. Homi K. Bhabha. New York: Routledge, 1990. 291-322.

Carchidi, Victoria. "'Orbiting': Bharati Mukherjee's Kaleidoscope Vision." *MELUS* 20 (1995): 91-101.

Connelly, Matthew, and Paul Kennedy. "Must It Be the Rest Against the West?" *Atlantic Monthly* Dec. 1994: 61+.

DeMott, Benjamin. *The Imperial Middle: Why Americans Can't Think Straight about Class.* New Haven, CT: Yale UP, 1992.

Foucault, Michel. "Nietzsche, Genealogy, History." *The Foucault Reader.* Ed. Paul Rabinow. New York: Pantheon, 1984. 76-100.

Hagedorn, Jessica. "The Exile Within/The Question of Identity." *The State of Asian America: Activism and Resistance in the 1990s.* Ed. Karin Aguilar-San Juan. Boston: South End, 1990. 173-82.

hooks, bell. *Black Looks: Race and Representation.* Boston: South End, 1992.

Koshy, Susan. "The Geography of Female Subjectivity: Ethnicity, Gender, and Diaspora." *Diaspora* 3.1 (1994): 69-84.

Low, Gail Ching-Liang. "In a Free State: Postcolonialism and Postmodernism in Bharati Mukherjee's Fiction." *Women: A Cultural Review* 4.1 (1993): 8-17.

Mercer, Kobena. *Welcome to the Jungle: New Positions in Black Cultural Studies.* New York: Routledge, 1994.

Mukherjee, Bharati. *Darkness.* New York: Fawcett-Columbine, 1985.

———. "A Four-Hundred-Year-Old Woman." *Critical Fictions: The Politics of Imaginative Writing.* Ed. Philomena Mariani. Seattle: Bay, 1991.

———. *Holder of the World.* New York: Fawcett-Columbine, 1993.

———. "An Interview with Bharati Mukherjee." With Fred Bonnie. *AWP Chronicle* 28.2 (Oct.-Nov. 1995): 1+.

———. Interview. With Michael Connell, Jessie Grearson, and Tom Grimes. *Iowa Review* 20 (1990): 7-32.

———. *Jasmine.* New York: Grove-Weidenfeld, 1989.

———. *The Middleman and Other Stories.* New York: Grove, 1988.

Mukherjee, Bharati, and Clark Blaise. *Days and Nights in Calcutta.* 1977. St. Paul: Hungry Mind, 1995.

Mura, David. "A Shift in Power, A Sea Change in the Arts: Asian American Constructions." *The State of Asian America: Activism and Resistance in the 1990s.* Ed. Karin Aguilar-San Juan. Boston: South End, 1994. 183-204.

Wald, Priscilla. *Constituting Americans: Cultural Anxiety and Narrative Form.* Durham, NC: Duke UP, 1995.

Wolf, Sylvia. "Memory/Reference: The Digital Photography of Martina Lopez." Exhibit brochure. The Art Institute of Chicago. 16 Sept. 1995-28 Jan. 1996. N. pag.

Shao-Pin Luo (essay date April 2003)

SOURCE: Luo, Shao-Pin. "Rewriting Travel: Ahdaf Soueif's *The Map of Love* and Bharati Mukherjee's *The Holder of the World*." *Journal of Commonwealth Literature* 38, no. 2 (April 2003): 77-104.

[*In the following essay, Luo perceives travel as a device in the fiction of Mukherjee and Ahdaf Soueif.*]

> We should begin by acknowledging that the map of the world has no divinely or dogmatically sanctioned spaces, essences, or privileges. . . . What matters a great deal more than the stable identity kept current in official discourse is the contestatory force of an interpretative method whose material is the disparate, but intertwined and interdependent, and above all overlapping streams of historical experience.[1]

Recent critical books on travel and travel writing cover a wide range of topics such as Orientalism and colonialism (Said 1978, Lowe 1991, Behdad 1994),[2] imperialism and globalization (Pratt 1992, Kaplan 1996, Clifford 1997),[3] and gender and sexual difference (Mills 1991, Blunt 1994, Grewal 1996).[4] The popular *Granta* special issues of travel writing in the 1980s and 1990s published creative pieces by, among others, Redmond O'Hanlon, Bruce Chatwin, and Amitav Ghosh. Additionally, a recent issue of *Wasafiri,* devoted to the topic of "Travellers' Tales: Alternative Traditions", focuses on "the far smaller body of travel writing, from the early modern period onwards, produced by travellers from 'new worlds', who journeyed *to* the European and colonial centres of authority".[5] This collection includes essays on the travels of the late eighteenth-century Persian Abu Taleb, and on a Moroccan traveller in nineteenth-century France; an interview with Bernardine Evaristo, whose book *The Emperor's Babe* recounts the story of a young girl of Sudanese parentage who grew up in Roman London 1,800 years ago; an excerpt from Caryl Phillips's book, *A New World Order,* which describes various journeys to sub-Saharan Africa, to Antigua, to New York, and puts forward the author's ambivalent view that wherever he may be, he is "of, and not of, this place".[6] James Duncan and Derek Gregory, the editors of *Writes of Passage: Reading Travel Writing,* explain this explosion of interest in travel writing as follows:

> This sense of re-imagining the world through its representation, describing spiralling circles between home and away, here and there, and reworking the connective between "travel" and "writing" gives much of this work a decidedly critical edge. At its very best, it raises urgent questions about the politics of representation and spaces of transculturation, about the continuities between a colonial past and a supposedly post-colonial present, and about the ecological, economic, and cultural implications of globalizing projects of modernity.[7]

Similarly, James Clifford describes travel as a metaphor for the contemporary postcolonial condition: it is "a figure for different modes of dwelling and displacement, for trajectories and identities, for storytelling and theorizing in a postcolonial world of global contacts".[8] In this sense, travel writing has become central to postcolonial studies. Homi Bhabha has thought about its potential for "the performance of identity as iteration, the re-creation of the self in the world of travel".[9] Graham Huggan, in his essay "Counter-Travel Writing and Post-Coloniality", explores "the possibilities inherent in travel writing as cultural critique".[10] And Said has written about the "pleasures of exile" in terms of travel: "Seeing 'the entire world as a foreign land' makes possible originality of vision. Most people are principally aware of one culture, one setting, one home; exiles are aware of at least two, and this plurality of vision gives rise to an awareness of simultaneous dimensions, an awareness that is contrapuntal".[11] With these postcolonial concerns in mind, my essay aims to "re-imagine the world" by exploring the connection between migration and interaction among cultures described in Ahdaf Soueif's *The Map of Love* (1999) and Bharati Mukherjee's *The Holder of the World* (1993). Both novels examine ideas of travel and transculturation, especially for women, by traversing through time and geography and illustrating the interconnectedness of different traditions.

"A story can start from the oddest things: a magic lamp, a conversation overheard, a shadow moving on a wall."[12] Thus Soueif begins *The Map of Love,* a story "conjured out of a box" (p. 11)—a leather trunk that travels from London to Cairo and back, to New York and to Cairo again, full of old papers in English, French, and Arabic (pp. 4, 7)—discovered in her dying mother's home by Isabel Parkman, a journalist living in New York. Isabel is falling in love with Omar al-Ghamwari, a famous music conductor, who thinks of himself as Egyptian, and American, and Palestinian—"I have no problem with identity" (p. 50)—and who sends her to visit his sister Amal in Cairo. Amal, he says, will help her unravel the contents of the trunk—journals and letters from the turn of last century. The writer is Anna Winterbourne, who travelled to Cairo and fell in love with Sharif Basha, an Egyptian, and who, Isabel discovers, is a link that connects her to Omar: both can trace their family histories to Anna's. Omar's sister Amal also becomes "obsessed with Anna Winterbourne's brown journal. She has become [so] real to me. . . . I need to fill in the gaps, to know who the people are of whom she speaks, to paint in the backdrop against which she is living her life here, on the page in front of me" (p. 26).

The Holder of the World begins in another place and another time, in seventeenth-century Mughal India, with a legendary diamond. Beigh Masters, the narrator, born in New England in the mid-twentieth century, is an "asset hunter" married to Venn Iyer, an Indian computer scientist working on a database to allow time travel into virtual reality. The title of the novel refers to the seventeenth-century Muslim emperor Aurangzeb, who once owned the "emperor's tear", a jewel that, for Beigh, "set in motion a hunger for connectedness, a belief that with sufficient passion and intelligence we can deconstruct the barriers of time and geography. Maybe that led, circuitously, . . . to the Salem Bibi and the tangled lines of India and New England".[13] Like Amal, piecing together the story of Anna Winterbourne through the contents of the trunk, Beigh reconstructs the life of Hannah Easton, the "Salem Bibi", through various texts and paintings; through museums in Massachusetts, graveyards in India and auctions in Bangkok; and through a computer simulation made by Venn. Beigh's passion to discover Hannah's life becomes more than professional; it consumes her: "For eleven years, I have been tracking the Salem Bibi, a woman from Salem who ended up in the Emperor's court" (p. 19).

Both novels are also inspired by paintings: John Frederick Lewis's watercolours in *The Map of Love* and Mughal miniature paintings in **The Holder of the World.** Anna Winterbourne, during her first husband's illness, takes to walking to the South Kensington Museum, where she discovers the watercolours of John Frederick Lewis[14] and "their world of light and colour" (p. 215). Anna writes, "When . . . I found those wonderful paintings by Frederick Lewis, I had, I believe, some sense of divine ordination. . . . And when the day came and it was deemed proper that I should travel . . . , it seemed the most natural thing in the world that my thoughts would turn to Egypt" (pp. 101-2). The scene shifts to a pre-auction viewing at Sotheby's in New York—and a seventeenth-century Indian miniature, in which a woman in ornate Mughal court dress is holding a lotus blossom. The woman is Caucasian and blonde: "a beautiful woman, more Pre-Raphaelite than I had imagined, with crinkly golden hair" (p. 281). "I thought, 'Who is this very confident-looking seventeenth-century woman, who sailed in some clumsy wooden boat across dangerous seas and then stayed there?'" says Mukherjee in an interview. "She had transplanted herself in what must have been a traumatically different culture. How did she survive?"[15] These questions prompted the novel. Compare the above portrait of Hannah Easton in **The Holder of the World** to the following of Anna Winterbourne in *The Map of Love*:

> The young woman's hair is blonde and is worn loose and crimped in the style made famous by the pre-Raphaelites. She has a smooth, clear brow, an oval face and a delicate chin. Her mouth is about to break into a smile. But her eyes are the strangest shade of blue, violet really, and they look straight at you and they

say—they say a lot of things. There's a strength in that look, a wilfulness; one would almost call it defiance except that it is so good-humoured.

(pp. 5-6)

The trunk and the diamond, the watercolours and the miniatures, traversing time and geography, bring us two tales of travel and transculturation. As K. Anthony Appiah puts it, in his review of **The Holder of the World**: "We live in a time of bad news for relations among communities. . . . men and women live and die within the shifting alliances and antagonisms of constantly reshaping identities. . . . In a world where a Bosnian Serb can murder a Muslim in-law, whose language he knows, whose table he has shared, we can find solace in even the fictional *idea* of a love that transcends more substantial cultural differences".[16] This idea of love celebrated in **The Holder of the World** is not dissimilar to Soueif's "love across countries and seas" (p. 351) between Anna and Sharif in *The Map of Love*. There are many parallels between the two novels. Both delve into history to find connections that have always bound all cultures, no matter how different, and suggest "that a more intricate phenomenon is in fact taking place, as in those 'border zones' where a complex syncretic cultural system comes to replace two or more ostensibly simpler cultures".[17] While Mukherjee illuminates the connections between seventeenth-century New England and pre-colonial India, Soueif represents the colonial history and nationalist politics in Egypt at the turn of last century. Beigh follows the steps of a woman ancestor and discovers her "secret" history; Amal unfolds the story of a Victorian woman traveller. Both narrators possess a sense of entitlement to their stories. The voice of Anna sets Amal dreaming: "Fragments of a life lived a long, long time ago. Across a hundred years the woman's voice speaks to her—so clearly that she cannot believe it is not possible to pick up her pen and answer" (p. 4). And Beigh is inspired to follow in her "almost" ancestor's footsteps: "*Go,* Salem Bibi whispers, her kohl-limned sapphire eyes cleaving a low-hanging sky. *Fly as long and as hard as you can, my co-dreamer! Scout a fresh site on another hill. Found with me a city where lions lie with lambs, where pity quickens knowledge, where desire dissipates despair!*" (p. 19). Further, both novels are discourses on women travellers (especially in earlier centuries) and female travel writing. What makes travel literature interesting is precisely the flexibility of its cultural images and hybrid forms. Alison Blunt, writing about Mary Kingsley's travels in West Africa, emphasizes the "textual polyphony" of Kingsley's travel writing;[18] Steve Clark writes that "postcolonial studies has seized upon this very impurity of the form as an exemplary record of cross-cultural encounters".[19] Both texts make extensive use of archival materials from museum records to testimonials, and both Anna in *The Map of Love* and Hannah in **The Holder of the World** express themselves not only through diaries and letters, but also through forms of storytelling, revisionist mythmaking, sketching and painting, and even weaving and gardening. Finally, in both texts, modern journeys parallel their historical ones, and there is a dialogic relation between past and present as both texts display their historical, transcultural worlds as mirrors for our modern world of migration and displacement and demonstrate that, as Clifford writes, "If we rethink culture and its science, anthropology, in terms of travel, then the organic, naturalizing bias of the term "culture"—seen as a rooted body that grows, lives, dies, and so on—is questioned. Constructed and disputed *historicities,* sites of displacement, interference, and interaction, come more sharply into view".[20] In the following sections, I will discuss how, in both novels, travel functions as forms of cultural translation and transformation, hybrid textual discourses serve as imaginative expressions of those transformations and, finally, how cross-cultural relationships become the vehicle for a transcultural vision.

I Travel, Translation, Transformation

Clifford has described terms such as travel as translations.[21] Mary Louise Pratt, in her influential *Imperial Eyes: Travel Writing and Transculturation,* explains that the term "contact zone", which she uses to refer to "the space in which peoples geographically and historically separated come into contact with each other and establish ongoing relations", comes from linguistics, "where the term contact language refers to improvised languages that develop among speakers of different native languages who need to communicate with each other . . . .".[22] Language and translation provide an important entry into Mukherjee's and Soueif's narratives. For Hannah in **The Holder of the World,** the journey to India is a form of translation. Beigh asks, on reaching the Coromandel Coast, "that misty January morning three hundred years ago, . . . what must Hannah, a child totally of the North Atlantic, have thought?" (p. 103). Hannah knows she has been "transported to the other side of the world, but the transportation was more than more 'conveyancing', . . . Many years later she called the trip, and her long residence in India, her 'translation'" (p. 104):

> The word did not exist ("traveller" was in common usage), but if it had, she might have used it: she was, in some original sense of the word (as a linguist is to language), a tourist. She was alert to novelty, but her voyage was mental, interior. Getting there was important, but savouring the comparison with London or Salem, and watching her life being transformed, that was the pleasure. She did not hold India up to inspection by the lamp of England, or of Christianity, nor did she aspire to return to England upon completion of Gabriel's tour. . . . She did not fear the unknown or the unexplored.
>
> (p. 104)

Language and translation play even more extensive roles in *The Map of Love.* In a review of Soueif's novels, Joseph Massad comments on Soueif's fascinating experiments with translation. He describes how Soueif "transforms English into Arabic and Arabic into English in revolutionary ways" by rendering "Arabic phrases into English without any syntactic compromises" and "in the very narrative structure of the novel", as well as in her "creative use of etymology in explaining Arabic words".[23] Soueif herself explains her intent in an interview: "In *The Map of Love,* there is a constant attempt to render Arabic into English, not just to translate phrases, but to render something of the dynamic of Arabic, how it works, into English. So, there is this question of how to open a window into another culture".[24] A very specific example of this attempt at not only linguistic, but also cultural translation occurs in the medium of communication between Anna and Sharif: it is neither English nor Arabic, the native tongue of the characters, but French. Sharif confides to an Egyptian friend: "We cannot speak each other's language. We have to use French" (p. 272), to which his friend replies, "Perhaps that is better. You make more effort, you make sure you understand—and are understood. Sometimes I think, because we use the same words, we assume we mean the same things—" (p. 272). In the following dialogue between Anna and Sharif, one even detects the hint of a Brechtian alienation effect:

> "Does it trouble you," she asks, "that we have to speak in French?"
>
> "I like French."
>
> "But does it trouble you that you cannot speak to me in Arabic?"
>
> "No. It makes foreigners of us both. It's good that I should have to come some way to meet you."
>
> (p. 157)

At the end of the novel, Amal recognizes the difficulties in the transferences of languages and cultures and ponders the (im)possibility of translation: "She has translated novels—or done her best to translate them. It is so difficult to truly translate from one language into another, from one culture into another; almost impossible really" (p. 515). Yet she remembers Anna's tireless effort at learning the Arabic language, and how Anna was eventually able to translate between English and Arabic for Sharif. And in the end, both novels explore what Pratt calls the "'contact' perspective", which foregrounds "the interactive, improvisational dimensions of colonial encounters" and "treats the relations among colonizers and colonized, or travellers and 'travellees', not in terms of separateness or apartheid, but in terms of copresence, interaction, interlocking understandings and practices, often within radically asymmetrical relations of power".[25]

The Map of Love and **The Holder of the World** are stories of women's travel and transformation. In his essay "Travelling Cultures", Clifford points out that "the discursive/imaginary topographies of Western travel are being revealed as systematically gendered": "'Good travel' (heroic, educational, scientific, adventurous, ennobling) is something men (should) do. Women are impeded from serious travel". Or if they do go to distant lands, it is "largely as companions or as 'exceptions', . . . forced to conform, masquerade, or rebel discreetly within a set of normatively male definitions and experiences".[26] As Trinh Minh-ha writes, "Unless economical necessity forces her to leave the home on a daily basis, she is likely to be restrained in her mobility—a transcultural, class-and gender-specific practice that for centuries has not only made travelling quasi impossible for women, but has also compelled every 'travelling' female creature to become a stranger to her own family, society, and gender".[27] Like many recent books that examine how women, in different traditions and histories, have travelled, Alison Blunt's *Travel, Gender, and Imperialism* attempts "not just . . . to correct or supplement an incomplete record of the past but a way of critically understanding how history operates as a site of the production of gender knowledge". Blunt's project is more than a matter of restructuring and recomposing history and adding a gendered subject: "The construction of subjectivity itself becomes a central point of inquiry".[28] She focuses on the travels of Mary Kingsley and situates her travel writing within the broader contexts of travel and imperialism. Emphasizing notions of ambivalence to undermine the dichotomization of a colonial self and colonized other, Blunt writes,

> It is important to recognize constructions of subjectivity along lines of gender, race, and class to deconstruct totalizing notions of difference because "the intersection of colonial and gender discourses involves a shifting, contradictory subject positioning, whereby Western women can simultaneously constitute 'centre' and 'periphery', identity and alterity. A Western woman, in these narratives, exists in a relation of subordination to Western man and in a relation of domination toward 'non-Western' men and women".[29]

Blunt describes Kingsley's "split position" as being "primarily constructed in terms of gender subordination while at home but able, while on her travels, temporarily to share in racial superiority in the context of imperial power and authority. Such constructions were, however, ambivalent rather than fixed, as reflected by the textual polyphony of her travel writing".[30] Both Mukherjee's story of Hannah Easton and Soueif's of Anna Winterbourne can be discussed in similar terms. As Hannah and Anna embark on their journeys of self-discovery and negotiate between cultures, they transform themselves as well as others. Both are believers in transculturation in their willingness to change and survive;

increasingly alienated and ostracized from their own societies, they immerse themselves in local cultures and gain gradual understanding both of themselves and of those around them.

Before Hannah leaves for her travels, "her life is at the crossroads of many worlds" (p. 60), and there is "a wildness about [her]" (p. 62). Orphaned after her widowed mother, Rebecca, disappears to join her Nipmuc lover, Hannah is adopted by Robert and Susanna Fitch of Salem. Then Hannah marries Gabriel Legge, an adventurer, who takes Hannah first to England and then to India, where he works for the East India Company on the Coromandel Coast. Hannah "thrilled" to Gabriel Legge's "tales of exotic adventure" (p. 69), "his sea-faring yarns . . . and longed for escape" (p. 67).

Once she arrives in India, however, Hannah feels she has entered a world that is a complete contrast to her own Puritanical world: it is filled with the fecundity of nature and multifarious languages, cultures and religions. Remarkably, she savours it all and takes "sheer pleasure" in "this vast new jungle" (p. 105) and in "the world's variety":

> They all spoke different languages, they owed fidelity to different masters, they worshipped different gods, and their ancestors had come from different countries. It had been inconceivable to a Puritan soul like Hannah's. Not just pagans and Muhammadans, but different gods and different ways of worshipping the same gods. Even putting a plural ending on the sacred word God: it became her secret blasphemy. *Gods.*
>
> (p. 100)

Hannah's travels along the Coromandel Coast change her perceptions, not only of herself, but also of the Indians around her. In one episode, she learns about the life of her servant, Bhagmati: "Bhagmati had had a vital life, distinct from waiting on *firangi* households. Why had Hannah not sensed that before? . . . They're humans; they have a richer life than I do" (p. 222). Yet, racial superiority is shown undisguisedly by the wives of the English factors, who "accepted cups of tea and biscuits from Bhagmati without seeing her. Bhagmati was invisible to the women of White Town" (p. 133). When Legge becomes a pirate and Hannah is shunned by white society, Bhagmati becomes her only friend and helper. Although Bhagmati's story remains secondary to that of Hannah, an interesting reversal of roles develops between Hannah and Bhagmati. When they are kept at the court of the Raja, Hannah feels that "now she was in a totally Hindu world, Bhagmati seemed no longer a servant. Perhaps she, Hannah, was about to become one" (p. 220). She is amazed when she sees that "the servant woman appeared young and beautiful, regal in her posture! She had changed into fresh, fragrant garments. The bared lustrous skin of her arms smelled of floral oils and woody essences. Her hair, still wet from a bath from the rain-churned river, cascaded in raven waves. Even her voice had a new confidence" (p. 218). As she watches Bhagmati transform from a lowly servant girl to a confident self, she learns humility and "felt herself the servant woman" (p. 221).

Hannah's is a life of metamorphosis and self-invention. During her sojourn in India, "She didn't feel bereft—of roots, of traditions. . . . Instead she felt unfinished, unformed. She was, she is, of course, a goddess-in-the-making" (p. 163). Her "going native" is a process of cultural translation and of transformation, an enabling rather than an alienating experience. When she falls in love with the Indian prince Jadav Singh, she realizes that she "was no longer the woman she'd been in Salem or London. The *qsbas* and villages of Roopconda bore no resemblance to the fading, phantom landscapes where she'd lived in Old and New England. Everything was in flux on the Coromandel coastline", and she proves again and again that "the survivor is the one who improvises, not follows, the rules" (p. 234). Indeed, there is "a new name for a new incarnation. Rebecca Easton was dead. Hannah Easton Fitch Legge was dying" (p. 222) and "in one rainy season, Hannah Legge had gone from woolen-clad English married woman on the Coromandel Coast to pregnant sari-wearing bibi of a raja; a murderer, a widow, a peacemaker turned prisoner of the most powerful man in India. . . . She wasn't Hannah anymore; she was Mukta, Bhagmati's word for 'pearl'" (p. 271).

Interestingly, *The Map of Love* makes numerous references not only to real historical figures in Egyptian nationalist politics, but also to actual women travellers at the turn of last century. For example, Anna reads *Letters from Egypt* by Lady Lucie Duff Gordon (p. 101), who "didn't like civilization so very much": "The letters she wrote home revealed an attitude hardly met with before in the English abroad: First of all she avoided the supposed comforts and security of Cape Town and took herself up-country to Caledon; secondly she chose the company of non-Europeans, preferring best to be with the poor Malay immigrants".[31] Though as pointed out by Massad, Anna is already influenced by her English father-in-law's opposition to imperial expansion and racism (in the context of the Boer War) and is receptive to liberal ideas of anticolonial nationalism,[32] she is obviously much affected by Lady Duff Gordon and other women travellers such as Lady Anne Blunt.[33] Both Lady Blunt and Sir Wilfrid Blunt, an explorer, Orientalist scholar and strong supporter of Arab nationalism, make appearances in the novel. Referring to Blunt's example, Anna writes, "Though I did not fancy running barefoot in the streets of Cairo, dressing as a man to go on an expedition did not seem so outlandish—it is said that Lady Anne Blunt does it and

other ladies besides" (p. 107). Anna wants to sit in the coffee shops and listen to storytellers. She is unwilling to travel with a tour group because "that would not have been the same thing at all. . . . I would have remained within the world I knew. I would have seen things through my companions' eyes, and my mind would have been too occupied in resisting their impressions to establish its own" (p. 212). So, just as Hannah puts on a sari in the Prince's Fort, Anna ventures into the desert, disguised as a French man, and later as an Arab woman (p. 192): "At the Agency certainly they do not believe an Englishwoman should go about unchaperoned. But I have never heard of any harm befalling a lady travelling alone—and I cannot help feeling that the letters of Lady Duff Gordon give a truer glimpse into the Native mind than do all the speeches of the gentlemen of Chancery" (p. 107). The "dialogic consciousness that seeks out local knowledge" that Ali Behdad in *Belated Travellers* attributes to Anne Blunt and her *Pilgrimage to Nejd* (1881) reflects Anna's frame of mind as well:

> Her marginal location as a woman in the field of Orientalism seems to have engendered a dialogic consciousness that marks in her representational practice an elusive shift away from some of the dominant strains of scientific Orientalism. Self-reflexivity in writing about culture, interest in local knowledge, and sensitivity to coevalness with Bedouins are instances of discontinuity from dominant Orientalist discourses.[34]

Anna puts on the veil and she feels exhilarated, rather than inhibited, by the freedom it provides: "Still, it is a most liberating thing, this veil. While I was wearing it, I could look wherever I wanted and nobody could look back at me. Nobody could find out who I was. I was one of many black-clad harem in the station and on the train and could have traded places with several of them and no one been the wiser" (p. 195). There is certainly an identification with the native, for when she encounters the English at the train station, she feels alienated from them: "The oddest thing of all was that I suddenly saw them as bright, exotic creatures, walking in a kind of magical space, oblivious to all around them; at ease, chattering to each other as though they were out for a stroll in the park, while the people, pushed aside, watched and waited for them to pass" (pp. 194-5). In discussing Isabelle Eberhardt and her travels, Behdad argues that for Eberhardt cross-dressing is, as it is also for Anna, "not merely a performative gesture", but also a demonstration of her belief in the idea of transculturation: "Her goal in travelling in North Africa was not only to be 'far from the profane banalities of the invading West', as an escapist traveller, but also to have an opportunity, as a believer of 'transculturation', to 'inspire [herself] with the great evocative ideas of Islamic faith, which is the peace of the soul'".[35]

As Bhagmati becomes Hannah's friend and guide in *The Holder of the World,* Anna's friendship with Layla,

Sharif's sister, is "one of the main bridges of cultural dialogue in the novel".[36] Because of Layla, Anna is able to visit the harem and other otherwise inaccessible domains. But Anna's representation of the harem, like Lady Blunt's, "is anything but erotic and violent". Of Lady Blunt's descriptions, Behdad writes, "Significantly, her narrative neither dramatizes the harem's inaccessibility nor valorizes her visit as a symbolic 'penetration' into a sacred and secretive domain, as do previous accounts by men".[37] Anna characterizes her visit to the "small jewel-like palace by the Nile" as an ordinary social event. She describes her host as being very serious and formidably well-educated: "I found the company and conversation most pleasing and quite contrary to the prevailing view of the life of the harem being one of indolence and torpor" (pp. 236-7). At these and other social gatherings that Anna attends with Layla, there are many discussions about the "woman question" (p. 236), education for girls, and the lifting of the veil (p. 375); Anna even "joked that the hareem had made a working woman of her, for she was constantly occupied in preparing for her classes [art classes for ladies at the University on Fridays], and writing for the magazine [a ladies' magazine on the woman question in both Arabic and French editions] (p. 355) and translating from and into English for Sharif" (p. 435).

Narratives of women's travel and transformation, both novels are also commentaries on women's travel writing, and in that sense, in Huggan's words, "counter-" travel narratives. There is no lack of satirical references to "Oriental tales" of abduction (p. 134) and of the harem as a place "of indolence and torpor" (p. 237) in *The Map of Love,* or mock travellers' tales of encounters with "cargos of freaks and monsters" and of "sea voyages too fantastic to have occurred" (p. 147) in ***The Holder of the World.*** Soueif refers to one Thomas Cook's tourist handbook to Egypt that Anna apparently reads and finds that "the book, like my friends at the Agency, has a fairer view of the land than of its inhabitants" (p. 209). Some analyses of women's travel writing, such as Sara Mills's *Discourses of Difference,* have been criticized for perceiving this writing as "different" from travel writing by men and describing it as "more tentative than male writing", more heterogeneous and inclined to present "people as individuals".[38] Clark argues that "Women writers cannot simply be assumed to have struggled with, rather than benefited from, the discourse of imperialism" and that "formal criteria for viewing women's travel writing 'on its own terms' are surprisingly difficult to establish".[39] Grewal, praising Lisa Lowe's and Pratt's discussions of the writings of Lady Mary Montague and Mary Kingsley for "their useful and measured understandings of the complex locations of Western women as they rewrite and participate in colonial discourses", stresses the importance of historicizing and contextualizing feminisms everywhere.[40] Mills herself acknowledges in a later essay, "Knowledge, Gender, Empire", this heated debate about "essentialist versus postmodernist feminisms". Still she insists that "knowledges produced within an imperial context are profoundly gendered" and that "gender shapes the parameters of the possible texture structures within which writers construct their work".[41] The following discussion focuses on the diverse expressions of Anna and Hannah as they reflect on their cultural translation, self-fashioning and transformation in their travels.

II "TEXTUAL HYBRIDIZATION"

An important aspect of ***The Holder of the World*** and *The Map of Love* is the "textual polyphony",[42] the heterogeneous forms of discourses in the texts. Both novels are "framed narratives", with stories told and retold in different versions. Both consist of fascinating collages of different texts as the two narrators, in their reconstructions of both personal lives and historical events, do enormous amounts of research through texts (diaries, letters, memoirs), translations, paintings, museums, family histories, historical archives, shipping records, commercial consultation books, newspaper clippings, myths and legends, oral stories and even emails and computer simulations. In Mukherjee, there is an obvious pairing of the scenes on Keats's Grecian Urn and the depictions in the Mughal miniature paintings. Mukherjee even names one painting after Keats: "In the largest of the series—its catalog name is *The Apocalypse,* but I call it *The Unravish'd Bride*—beautiful Salem Bibi stands on the cannon-breached rampart of a Hindu fort" (p. 17). Mukherjee's use of Keats's Ode for the epigraphs for each of the four parts of the novel will be discussed further later in the essay; suffice to say here that such intertextuality is an integral part of the text. Interestingly, Soueif also uses numerous texts as epigraphs for the chapters. These epigraphs consist of quotations, in Arabic, French and English, from poems, ancient Egyptian prayers, songs, novels, Shakespeare (*Othello*) and an opera (*Tosca*), and from a great variety of personages such as Gamal 'Abd el-Nasser, Agathon, Aphra Behn, Hilaire Belloc, Walt Whitman, Alexander Brome, an Egyptian scribe, Lord Cromer, Ama Ata Aidoo, George Young, Sabreen, W. B. Yeats, S. T. Coleridge, Boutros Ghali Basha, Arwa Salih and Mustafa Kamel. Discussing the "textual hybridization" in Soueif's book, Amin Malak examines both the linguistic and cultural translations the text performs. Malak finds that not only does Soueif render to perfection both the linguistic patterns of the fellaheen of Upper Egypt as well as the idiom of an aristocratic English lady, but also that the "hybrid metaphors" in the text—"a 1919 Egyptian flag emblazoned with the Crescent and the Cross, symbolizing the unity of the Egyptian Muslims and Christians in their uprising against British occupation; the mosque nestling inside a monastery, a heart-warming image of each holy sanctuary protecting the other from demolition at times of tension; and the three calendars followed simultaneously in Egypt: Gregorian, Islamic, and Coptic"—reveal the intention of the author to present a "narrative that is not only hybrid linguistically but also discursively, leading subtly towards humane, positive perspectives on Arab-Muslim culture in its most tolerant illustrations and in its openness towards the Other".[43] These varied literary techniques serve, in Massad's words, "to contextualize, layer, and interrupt the narrative, creating prose of shimmering complexity",[44] and further, to rewrite and reconstruct lives and histories, and to recreate transcultural spaces across time and geography.

A. DIARIES AND LETTERS

Mills argues that many women's travel accounts are written "in the form of letters or diaries because they are the only forms which are loose enough to contain their unstructured narratives".[45] Journals and letters play a central part in both narratives. In **The Holder of the World,** as soon as Hannah leaves Salem for her travels, initially to England, she becomes a travel writer and writes *London Sketches by an Anonymous Colonial Daughter,* "intended—or at least contrived—as epistles to a distant mother" (p. 74). What is interesting about these writings is that they are "addresses to Expatriates and Nativists" (p. 74), reflecting contemporary debates about "cosmopolitans" and "nativists", such as those in Salman Rushdie's *Imaginary Homelands,* for example. In her letters, she calls "those she had known in Salem who dreamed of a 'return' to England" "Desponders" (p. 74). Later, in India, she also makes a distinction between perpetual exiles and those determined to put down roots:

> Men like Higginbottham and the Marquis had no home, no loyalties except to themselves. Their homelands were imaginary. For them there was no going back, and no staying on. They were in a perpetual state of suspension, which was not the same as floating free. They were ghosts, trapped in space meant for full-fleshed and warm-blooded humans. She would need to root herself, she was not sure where nor how, before she too became ghostly.
>
> (p. 182)

Hannah's first impressions of life on the Coromandel Coast are tentative and "cautiously impersonal" (p. 122). Beigh regards these early writings as "reticent" and "ironic": "Maybe Hannah was still unready, unformed. Still afraid to discover herself disloyal" (p. 115). Both Gabriel Legge and Hannah keep diaries. Gabriel's diary entries reflect his way of thinking—matter-of-fact, objective and enterprising: "The ideal of England in India moved him. The idea of spreading enlightenment, science, sanitation and, as he understood it, Christian tolerance, and of absorbing the best in the culture around him, was a continual delight" (p. 142). They are

full of what Pratt calls "liberty, enlightenment, advancement, the universe—the official vocabulary of bourgeois humanitarianism".[46] Beigh pores over those diaries but "found only paltry recognition of the woman sewing just a few feet away" (p. 141). As for Hannah, half a year into her residence in India, "the diary entries become more disorderly, and personal" (p. 124) and begin to be full of haunting images and "thoughts of spirits and phantoms" (p. 125) and to reflect her desire to comprehend the different culture and world around her. Yet, though she "kept a journal of events", it was "through her embroidery, and much later through her stealthily penned *Memoirs,* she revealed to herself her deepest secrets" (p. 128).

In *The Map of Love,* the majority of Anna's story is retold by Amal through Anna's diaries and letters to her friend Caroline and her English father-in-law Sir Charles in England. The trunk contains several journals: one bound in brown leather that chronicles Anna's life in England before coming to Egypt, a large green one that depicts her life in Egypt, and a small blue one that tells of her adventures into the desert and her falling in love with Sharif Basha. Reading her first letters to Caroline, Amal finds Anna's "mannered approach . . . a little self-conscious perhaps, a little aware of the genre— *Letters from Egypt, A Nile Voyage, More Letters from Egypt*" (p. 58). Her first impressions of Egypt are superficial and romantic as shown in this description of the Bazaar: "It is exactly as I have pictured it; the merchandise so abundant, the colours so bold, the smells so distinct . . . the shelves and shelves of aromatic oils, the sacks of herbs and spices, their necks rolled down to reveal small hills of smooth red henna, lumpy ginger stems, shiny black carob sticks, all letting off their spicy, incensy perfume into the air" (p. 67). However, as she "learns a little more of native life" (p. 71) and desires to speak the Arabic language, and hears of Mr. Blunt's example, who has "gone over" and is regarded "as a crank who chooses to live in the desert" (p. 70), Anna feels "a sense of increased spaciousness within myself" (p. 90) and gradually reaches the transitional state of the "in-between: in the area of transformations" (p. 66).

After climbing the Pyramids, visiting the Bazaar, the Mosques, dancing at the Khedives Ball and playing croquet at the Club at Ghezirah, Anna is deeply discontented: "And yet—I sit here in my room at Shepherd's Hotel possessed by the strangest feeling that still I am not in Egypt. . . . There is something at the heart of it all which eludes me . . . and which . . . seems far, far from my grasp" (p. 102). The breakthrough, recorded in the small blue book, comes when Anna encounters Layla, Sharif's sister, when she is "abducted" while venturing alone into the desert. This compelling section of the novel interweaves a dialogue between Anna and Layla, each recording her first impressions of the other and their developing friendship, Anna in her blue journal and Layla in the grey volume of what Amal calls her "testimony" (p. 133). Layla is surprised to find Anna, under the circumstances, utterly composed and eagerly curious, with "none of the arrogance or the coldness we were used to imagining in her countrymen" (p. 372): "I was surprised that it did not seem that her first interest was the regaining of her liberty. She was completely natural in her looks and behaviour and so interested in her own abduction—in the events that led up to it, in the house in which she found herself, in my opinions with regard to the whole event—that I found myself quite forgetting that she was a stranger" (p. 136). On the other hand, Anna feels as if she has "stumbled" into "the world of those beloved paintings" of Lewis (p. 134), and immediately gains an "altered perspective" (p. 134) into Egyptian life. Her description of her first sight of Layla is in the language of Lewis's paintings, full of soft colour and gentle warmth: "She was Egyptian, and a lady—the first I had seen without the black cloak and the veil. She had pulled a cover of black silk up to her waist, her chemise above that was the purest white, and then again, her hair vied with the silken cover for the depth and lustre of its black. Her skin was the colour of gently toasted chestnut, and she lay on cushions of deep emerald and blue, and the whole tableau was framed, yet again, by the lattice of a mashrabiyya" (p. 134). There is genuine delight when they discover that they can converse with each other in French, as Layla herself is also a traveller and has travelled to France. And an immediate friendship is struck up between the two as they tell each other about their respective lives; Layla writes, "We . . . felt our way towards each other as though our ignorance, one of the other, were the one thing in the world that stood between us and friendship" (p. 136). As Anna learns Layla's name and finds out that "a woman here does not take her husband's name upon marriage" (p. 137), and as she is welcomed into the homes and gatherings of the ladies of Cairo, Amal finds Anna "changed and invigorated" (p. 237). Layla thus guides Anna towards compassion and understanding of Egyptian life, Egyptian women and Egyptian culture.

B. Transcultural Tapestries

Both women, Anna and Hannah, love to weave. In *The Holder of the World,* Hannah, even in her earlier days in Puritan colonial America, discovers "in herself an obsessive love of needlework, which was, she suspected, an overflow of a nascent fascination with—or failing for—finer things. A stray sunbeam on her workbasket, kindling the weakest combustion of colours among twisted skeins of coloured thread, could raise indecent palpitations in her heart" (pp. 41-2). This inner "conflict she tried so hard to deny or suppress" (p. 42) is given expression in what Beigh describes as "one of the great colonial samplers" that Hannah creates, titled "uttermost shore": "A twelve-year-old Puritan orphan who had

never been out of Massachusetts imagined an ocean, palm trees, thatched cottages, and black-skinned men casting nets and colourfully garbed bare-breasted women mending them; native barks and, on the horizon, high-masted schooners" (p. 44). The embroidery provides an outlet for Hannah's emotions and flights of imagination and, with a pun on embroidery as the "embellishment of tales",[47] for the stories of her memories and fantasies; most importantly, it is a remarkable expression of a transcultural vision: "That little embroidery is the embodiment of desire . . . a pure vision. It is the first native American response to a world that could be African or Indian or anything not American. It employs the same economy, the same apparently naive sophistication as the Mughal paintings that would later feature her" (p. 44). And not only is that sampler extraordinary, so is Hannah, in that period and society: Hannah is a person "undreamed of in Puritan society. Of course she must suffer 'spells' and be judged an invalid. . . . Either she will take society with her to a new level, or she will perish in the attempt. Either people will follow, or they will kill her" (p. 59).

In *The Map of Love,* Amal finds in Anna's trunk "folded once, and rolled in muslin, a curious woven tapestry showing a pharaonic image and an Arabic inscription" (p. 6). Her whole research, in a way, is to piece together the three panels of the tapestry that Anna wove in Egypt. Weaving for Anna is a way of immersing herself in the Egyptian life around her; by then, she is happily married to Sharif and surrounded by Egyptian friends. In one of her letters, Anna writes, "I still paint and sketch but my new passion is weaving. . . . I find that when I work at it I am still a part of everything that surrounds me. . . . When I work at the loom I am still part of things and it seems as if the sounds and the smells and the people coming and going all somehow get into the weave" (p. 385). The tapestry is "a most wonderful work", made up of three panels. Anna proudly describes it as her "contribution to the Egyptian Renaissance": "It shall depict the Goddess Isis, with her brother consort the God Osiris and between them the Infant Horus,[48] and above them a Quranic verse. . . . I have already prepared a sketch of it and for the colours I will use the deep turquoises, gold and terracotta of the Ancient Egyptians and the deep green that I have never seen anywhere except in Egypt's fields" (p. 403). The tapestry, with its interesting juxtaposition of "pagan" images of the pharaohs and the sacred inscription of an Islamic verse, is already a convergence of traditions; it is also Anna's transculturation in the Egyptian world, her way of rewriting the classical myth with her own love story. The novel ends with Amal going back in time, the tapestry representing the love and the child Nur shared between Anna and Sharif: "Once more Amal sees Anna sitting in the sunshine, working at her loom . . . , the baby in the basket, the sounds from the house drifting into the courtyard. She sees Sharif Basha coming through the doorway, pausing to take in the scene and to feel his heart flood once again with love" (pp. 515-16). She reads the inscription on the tapestry, "He brings forth the living from the dead", as she herself writes down and brings forth the story of Anna and Sharif al-Baroundi.

C. Rewriting Myth and History

Just as Amal goes back in time and shares a moment with her beloved heroine in *The Map of Love,* Beigh time travels to the seventeenth-century and catches a glimpse of the fabled diamond at the end of *The Holder of the World.* And just as Anna rewrites the Egyptian story of the Goddess Isis with her tapestry, Hannah retells the Hindu story of Sita. According to Mukherjee, the "frozen beauty" of the Grecian Urn and the Keatsian romance are one illustration of history and art: freezing and freeing time, as much in Keats's poem as in a Mughal miniature painting:

> My image of artistic structure and artistic excellence is Moghul miniature painting, with its crazy foreshortening of vanishing point, its insistence that everything happens simultaneously, bound only by shape and colour. In the miniature paintings of India, there are a dozen separate foci, the most complicated stories can be rendered on a grain of rice, the corners are as elaborated as the centres. There is a sense of the interpenetration of all things.[49]

Mukherjee's intention is to create new conventions for writing history, and she calls her work a "postmodernist historical novel".[50] Her vision of history is so to speak crystallized in the symbol of the diamond: "In its reflective, prismatic qualities, the diamond has stood as an image of the ways in which history can be reflected, refracted, retrieved or revised".[51] Further, Venn and his computer science, with its compression of the time-space continuum, enables the disruption of a linear view of history: "In the long run, the technology will enable any of us to insert ourselves anywhere and anytime on the time-space continuum for as long as the grid can hold" (p. 6). Beigh is indeed transported for a few seconds back into Hannah's last violent days in India and enabled to locate the fabulous but lost diamond. But Mukherjee's emphasis is on the writer's creative process and the manipulation of "neutral data" in the "reconstruction not just of a time and a place, but also of a person" (p. 138). And the reconstructed Hannah, "a life through three continents and thirty years" (p. 279), is precisely the woman needed to change history.

Thus, a poem, a painting, a diamond and a computer simulation, all converge to form a complex postmodernist historiography. Yet in Mukherjee's rewriting of myth and history, technology is further fused with the narrative form of orality, *"a complex narrative tradi-*

tion": Hannah discovers that "reciters . . . indulge themselves with closures that suit the mood of their times and their regions" (p. 176). On the Coromandel Coast, Hannah finds "a world of stories and recitations" (p. 170): "With Bhagmati as guide, Hannah felt she had tumbled headlong into a brilliantly hued subterranean world peopled with shape-changing monsters and immortals that exaggerated or parodied hers" (p. 171). Bhagmati tells the story of Sita, and into her retelling and rewriting of the epic poem, Beigh weaves the life-stories of Rebecca, Hannah, Bhagmati and herself. In the epic, the god Vishnu comes down to earth for the seventh time to save mortals from demons, assuming the bodily form of Prince Rama, the heir to the throne of the aged King Dasaratha, and husband of an orphan named Sita. Prince Rama is unjustly banished to a forest, and the demon-king Ravanna abducts the beautiful Sita.[52] Hannah finds that the story of Sita resonates with her own experience of being an orphan and in captivity: "In Bhagmati's honey-toned recitation Sita is the self-sacrificing ideal Hindu wife. But the shape she assumes in Hannah's fantasies is of a woman impatient to test herself, to explore and survive in an alien world" (pp. 173-4). There are naturally many versions of the story: "Sita's story doesn't end with her rescue. The complications, the variations, are only beginning" (p. 175). But Beigh is interested in Sita's own version of her captivity: "I want to hear Sita tell me of her resistance to or accommodation with the multiheaded, multilimbed carnivorous captor. . . . I may not have Sita's words, but I have the Salem Bibi's; I know from her own captivity narrative what Sita would have written" (p. 177).

The novel also rewrites Nathaniel Hawthorne's *The Scarlet Letter.* There are obvious parallels between Hester Prynne and Rebecca/Hannah Easton.[53] Rebecca runs off with her lover into the forest, just as Hester does. Hannah uses her needlework to express her desire and vision, again as Hester does. Hawthorne describes Hester's dress thus: "Her attire, which, indeed, she had wrought for the occasion, in prison, and had modelled much after her own fancy, seemed to express the attitude of her spirit, the desperate recklessness of her mood, by its wild and picturesque peculiarity". And later, "She had in her nature a rich, voluptuous, Oriental characteristic—a taste for the gorgeously beautiful, which, save in the exquisite productions of her needle, found nothing else in all the possibilities of her life to exercise itself upon. . . . To Hester Prynne, it [needlework] might have been a mode of expressing, and therefore soothing, the passion of her life".[54] On the other hand, for Hannah, "her embroidery gave away the conflict she tried so hard to deny or suppress. . . . Her needle spoke; it celebrated the trees, flowers, birds, fish . . . all the more forceful because it was unacknowledged, was augmented with fancy. Flora and fauna grew wild on fecund and voluptuous terrain" (p. 42). Hester, because she is "so kind to the poor, so helpful to the sick, so comforting to the afflicted", is "self-ordained a Sister of Mercy".[55] We remember that Hannah is very good at scalp-healing and is called "the World-Healer" (p. 8), and during the infamous witch trials, she plays a role as "counsellor of women" (p. 61). Hester Prynne is outlawed from society. Yet, even though she exists as if in "a sort of magic circle" where people avoid her, somehow, "the tendency of her fate and fortunes had been to set her free". She looks critically from this "estranged point of view at human institutions", and "the scarlet letter was her passport into regions where other women dared not tread".[56] In the epic story, Sita also has a white circle drawn around her, within which she is to "confine herself, and be safe, while she is alone" (p. 175). Does Sita step out of the circle to defy the rules, to be free and to embrace alien life, just like Hester Prynne, Rebecca, Hannah, Bhagmati and Beigh? Beigh asks, "Could a woman who had strayed leagues and sea channels away from restrictive protection of the white circle, who had travelled in flying chariots, resisted the heady courtship of a ten-headed demon, discovered the potency of self-reliance, return to the passive domesticities of her very young girlhood?" (p. 176). Ultimately, both Hester Prynne and Hannah Easton are women "undreamed of in Puritan society"; either they will "take society . . . to a new level, or . . . perish in the attempt" (p. 59).

Finally, this is another version of the "real story of the brave Salem mother and her illegitimate daughter" (p. 284). As Anthony Appiah writes, Mukherjee "has the hubris, the chutzpah, the sheer unmitigated gall, to connect her book with Hawthorne's novel which 'many call our greatest work' [p. 286]: it is a connection she has earned. Nathaniel Hawthorne is a relative of hers. And like Hannah Easton, she has every right to claim her kinship across the centuries".[57] One may still wonder about the impetus behind the rewriting of a novel of Puritan origin, but of course Mukherjee is taking American history at its "purist" moment and has revealed such a moment to be conflicted and even constructed. *The Holder of the World* is "an alternative history which could revise forever the imaginative relations between immigrants and 'natives' in Mukherjee's America".[58] The following important detail reveals a counter-writing of another kind. Mukherjee writes of a fisherman's child on the Coromandel Coast, observing and taking note of all that is happening around him. As he watches Hannah and Gabriel Legge walking on his beach, "he saw a vision of himself on another shore by another ocean, an adventurer without family, without caste, without country, cantering into worlds without rules" (pp. 160-61). Indeed, he realizes his dream and finds his way to William III's court in London where he chances upon John Dryden's play *Aureng-Zebe*[59] and

"was incensed by its Eurocentric falsity" (p. 161). Thereupon he composes his own heroic play, *The World-Taker,* "in rhyming couplets as a corrective" (p. 161).

III TRANSCULTURAL CONNECTIONS

When Beigh's research takes her to the obscure maritime museum in Massachusetts, amid the Mughal treasures that contain miniature paintings, she witnesses "the Old World's first vision of the New" (p. 16). As the museum displays mostly Puritan history, the "crude and blackened objects glower as reproaches to Mughal opulence, glow as tributes to Puritan practicality. As in the kingdom of tropical birds, the Mughal men were flashy with decoration, slow moving in their cosmetic masculinity" (p. 12). Beigh wonders, "What must these worlds have thought, colliding with each other? How mutually staggered they must have been; one wonders which side first thought the other one mad" (p. 12). However, the exhibits allow her to have the opportunity of seeing with at least two points of view, "slaloming between *us* and *them,* imagine *our* wonder and *their* dread, now as a freebooter from colonial Rehoboth or Marblehead, and now as a Hindu king or Mughal emperor watching the dawn of a dreadful future through the bloody prism of a single perfect ruby, through an earring or a jewel from the heavy necklace" (p. 13).

Mukherjee describes seventeenth-century Salem as a busy port town, its wharves "raucous with sailors, whores and drunks": "The world's races were represented, and a mini-congerie of languages. Spanish and French coins were in circulation; it mattered little which regal head graced the ducat. The finished products of the civilized world were being unloaded in Salem, while holds were stuffed with barbarian ballast, lumber and hides and salted foodstuffs for the journey home" (p. 39). In her essay "Spaces In-Between", Judie Newman discusses how Salem, despite its reputation as "the witch city", has another quite different history, whose wealth and prosperity were entirely founded on trade with the East. She writes of its Peabody Museum, "with its enormous collections of Asian art, porcelain, textiles, and precious objects from India, China and Japan, its maritime collections, and a mass of souvenirs of the East. In the days of its prosperity, Salem was not 'the witch city'. Its city seal bore a palm-tree, a Parsee, and a ship, with the motto *'Divitis indiae usque ad ultimum sinum'* (To the farthest port of the rich East)".[60] Mukherjee describes port cities like Salem as "nerve centres of their time" (p. 47); and in the same way, she compares the seventeenth-century Coromandel Coast of the Bay of Bengal to "Manhattan in the mid-eighties" (pp. 101-2), as "a kind of late-stage capitalism" (p. 101), and her account of the Indian trade is also a story of European plunder: "They had not come to India in order to breed and colonize, or even to convert. They were here to plunder, to enrich themselves (under the guise of a Royal Charter) and pay their fees to the ruling nawabs" (pp. 99-100).

The references to the diamonds and jewellery serve an important purpose in the text. They stand as a metaphor for an intrinsic desire for beauty, which contrasts with Puritan austerity: "How they yearned for beauty, these nomads of central Asia perched on Delhi's throne, how endless the bounty must have seemed, a gravel of jewels to encrust every surface, gems to pave their clothes, their plates, their swords. Peacocks of display, helpless sybarites, consumed not with greed but its opposite: exhibition" (p. 8). For the Puritans, "to admire a thing in and of itself, to honour an activity merely for being, these were alien and uncomfortable concepts" (p. 77). There is abundant contrast between the New World and the Old, but this opposition is never stark. There are contradictory accounts in England of the New World: "New World Man was either an ungrateful wretch wallowing in moral regression, or the upright angel of God's green promise, reaping the rewards of sober rectitude" (pp. 71-2). But there is also this paradoxical description: "The New World was hard and savage; it was soft and bountiful. It was evil, it was innocent. England was refined and cultured; it was soiled and sinful. Probably every colonialist and every Englishman ascribed to one or many of those views, serially or simultaneously, whatever the nature of their mutual contradiction" (p. 72). The West is shown here to be complex, contradictory and heterogeneous. And just as the Salem world is full of paradoxes, so is the Mughal world.

Although India seems the opposite of Salem, Hannah makes a significant observation during her stay at the court of Raja Jadav Singh, the Lion of Devgad, that the religious divisions and conflicts in India are no different from the religious intolerance and conflicts of Puritan society. At one point, Hannah shows her incomprehension of her Indian lover's zeal and passion for war: "He did not seem an especially pious man, not by the standards of Salem and the Coromandel, yet he was waging a war against the Great Mughal, a religious purist, on religious principles of his own" (p. 232). Toward the end of the novel, the great Mughal emperor explains the origins of the name of the diamond and his will to kill infidels on behalf of Allah: "I do not fight for treasure and glory in this life. This diamond is the tear I shed as I discharge my duty. That is why it is called the Emperor's Tear. The dutiful and the innocent, if they are pure and if they submit, will be judged by the all-seeing, all-merciful Allah. The sum of their lives will be weighed in the scales of judgment" (p. 269). Yet Hannah's is a vision that looks beyond divisions of race, religion or nation, and "the manichean world of Puritan morality, . . . the internecine rivalries of

European freebooters and factors, and . . . the remorseless blood-feuds of Hindu and Muslim kingdoms".[61] It is then perhaps not so naive of Hannah to beg for love and mercy, because the gods that "controlled the universe had conspired to put her Christian-Hindu-Muslim self, her American-English-Indian self, her orphaned, abandoned, widowed, pregnant self, her *firangi* and bibi self, into a single message" (p. 268):

> I have come late in my life to the feeling of love. Love for a man, love for a place, love for a people. They are not Devgad people or Roopconda people, not Hindu people or Muslim people, not Sunni or Shia, priests or untouchables, servants or kings. If all is equal in the eye of Brahma as the Hindus say, if Allah is all-seeing and all-merciful as you say, then who has committed atrocities on the children, the women, the old people? Who has poisoned the hearts of men?
>
> (p. 268)

Hannah "would offer her life, if necessary, to end the war. Only a person outside the pale of the two civilizations could do it. Only a woman, a pregnant woman, a pregnant white woman, had the confidence or audacity to try it" (p. 259).

Soueif's intention of rewriting and setting history "on a different course" (p. 481) is made clear in the epigraph through Gamal 'Abd el-Nasser's words from *The Covenant* (1962): "It is strange that this period (1900-1914) when the Colonialists and their collaborators thought everything was quiet—was one of the most fertile in Egypt's history. A great examination of the self took place, and a great recharging of energy in preparation for a new Renaissance". *The Map of Love* is a fictional love story that is set against the context of real historical events of the anti-colonial and nationalist struggles in Egypt at the turn of last century. The love shared between Anna and Sharif is not an easy one: there are doubts, questions and uncertainties. At first, Sharif would not permit himself to think that an understanding between them would even be possible: for her "he would have receded into an exotic part—a remote part—of her Egyptian journey. A better kind of 'Native' she had travelled with in the desert and spoken with one night in a moonlit garden. And now she is back where she belongs" (p. 262). They are both afraid that they are inventing each other:

> The desert and the stars and an ancient monastery with a mosque nestling within its walls. Those were his settings. Those and the old house out of the paintings that had brought her to Egypt in the first place. And what would she make of his doubt, his despair? Of how he sometimes hated himself for piecing a life together under a rule not of his choosing? "A citizen life, ruled by an alien lord." Could she ever know him? Could he ever know her? Or would they always hold fast to what they imagined of each other so that life together would for each be more lonely than life alone?
>
> (pp. 271-2)

This cross-cultural relationship is explored in the context of politics, history and geography. In her interview with Massad, Soueif explains that what she is trying to explore in her characters are "the possibilities and limitations of their personal life under particular historical circumstances—what happens when a man, who has lived his life by nationalist principles, falls in love with a member of the force that is occupying his country, for example?"[62] On his wedding day to Anna, Sharif's mother reminds him that the obstacles and ostracism facing Anna would be much greater than those for him, and she offers him such moving advice:

> Her whole life will change. Her people will be angry with her. And the British will shun her. . . . She will be torn off from her own people. Even her language she will not be able to use. . . . You will be everything to her. If you make her unhappy, who will she go to? No mother, no sister, no friend. Nobody. It means if she angers you, you forgive her. If she crosses you, you make it up with her. And whatever the English do, you will never burden her with the guilt of her country. She will be not only your wife and the mother of your children—insha' Allah—but she will be your guest and a stranger under your protection and if you are unjust to her God will never forgive you.

(pp. 281-2)

Yet in the end, this personal relationship stands in stark contrast to general Western attitudes towards the East. In an essay Sharif writes that the East holds economic, religious, historical and romantic attractions for Europe, yet "when [the European] comes here, he finds that the land is inhabited by people he does not understand and possibly does not much like" (p. 481), and "Europe simply does not see the people of the countries it wishes to annex—and when it does, it sees them in accordance with its own old and accepted definitions: backward people, lacking rational abilities and subject to religious fanaticism. People whose countries—the holy and picturesque lands of the East—are too good for them" (p. 483). In Amal's eyes, the article is relevant even to the contemporary scene, and she copies it out for her brother Omar to have it published again with only "a few small amendments" (p. 488). As Massad points out, Soueif is very much aware that the predominant Western journalistic interest in the Arab world is not aimed at cultural dialogue and understanding, but rather at exoticizing the Arab and Muslim Other through covering topics like "the fundamentalists, the veil, the cold peace, polygamy, women's status in Islam, female genital mutilation . . ." (p. 6).[63] However, Sharif sees that "the only hope . . . lies in a unity of conscience between the people of the world" (p. 484).

Moving across time-lines and between cultures, both Mukherjee and Soueif demonstrate the "intertwined and interdependent, and above all overlapping streams of historical experience".[64] In the end Soueif finds a touch-ing metaphor for her transcultural vision in Anna's tapestry, a symbol for the love Anna and Sharif share, which shows that "In fact, there can be generosity, and vision, and overcoming barriers, and finally, human existential integrity".[65] Mukherjee reimagines Hannah's identity "through three continents and thirty years" as a "Christian-Hindu-Muslim self" and an "American-English-Indian self" (p. 265), beyond divisions of race, religion, and nation. Iain Chambers writes, "To live in another place, is to begin to inhabit the ambiguous territories that draw us out of our actual being towards a way of becoming in which no one history or identity is immune from a new and diverse 'worldling of the world'".[66] Ultimately, this essay has endeavoured to explore aspects of this "worldling of the world". It is about re-writing travel, re-reading and re-imagining nations and narrations as forms of translation and transculturation. It is about travelling and transforming, traversing time and space as well as words and ideas: "The translator transforms while being transformed. Imperfection thus leads to new realms of exploration, and travelling as a practice of bold omission and minute description allows one to (become) shamelessly hybridize(d) as one shuttles back and forth between critical blindness and critical insight".[67]

I am deeply grateful to Dr. Victor Li for reading draft versions of this article and for offering invaluable advice. I also wish to thank The Social Sciences and Humanities Research Council of Canada for funding this project.

Notes

1. Edward Said, *Culture and Imperialism*, New York: Knopf, 1993, pp. 311-12.

2. Edward Said, *Orientalism*, New York: Vintage Books, 1978; Lisa Lowe, *Critical Terrains: French and British Orientalisms*, Ithaca: Cornell UP, 1991; Ali Behdad, *Belated Travellers: Orientalism in the Age of Colonial Dissolution*, Durham, NC: Duke UP, 1994.

3. Mary Louise Pratt, *Imperial Eyes: Travel Writing and Transculturation*, London: Routledge, 1992; Caren Kaplan, *Questions of Travel: Postmodern Discourses of Displacement*, Durham, NC: Duke UP, 1996; James Clifford, *Routes: Travel and Translation in the Late Twentieth Century*, Cambridge, MA: Harvard UP, 1997.

4. Sara Mills, *Discourses of Difference: An Analysis of Women's Travel Writing and Colonialism*, London: Routledge, 1991; Alison Blunt, *Travel, Gender, and Imperialism: Mary Kingsley and West Africa*, New York: The Guilford Press, 1994; Inderpal Grewal, *Home and Harem: Nation, Gender, Empire, and the Cultures of Travel*, Durham, NC: Duke UP, 1996.

5. Susheila Nasta, "Editorial: Travellers' Tales: Alternative Traditions", *Wasafiri*, 34 (2001), 3.

6. Caryl Phillips, "A New World Order", *Wasafiri,* 34 (2001), 39.

7. James Duncan and Derek Gregory, eds., *Writes of Passage: Reading Travel Writing,* London: Routledge, 1999, p. 1.

8. James Clifford, "Notes on Travel and Theory", *Travelling Theories, Travelling Theorists,* eds. James Clifford and Vivek Dhareshwar, Inscriptions 5, Santa Cruz: Centre for Cultural Studies, UCSC, 1989, p. 177.

9. Homi K. Bhabha, *The Location of Culture,* London: Routledge, 1994, p. 9.

10. Graham Huggan, "Counter-Travel Writing and Post-Coloniality", *Being/s in Transit: Travelling, Migration, Dislocation,* ed. Liselotte Glage, ASNEL Papers 5, Amsterdam: Rodopi, 2000, p. 39.

11. Edward Said, *Reflections on Exile and Other Essays,* Cambridge, MA: Harvard UP, 2000, p. 186.

12. Ahdaf Soueif, *The Map of Love,* London: Bloomsbury, 1999, p. 6. All subsequent references are to this edition and appear in parentheses in the text.

13. Bharati Mukherjee, *The Holder of the World,* New York: Knopf, 1993, p. 11. All subsequent references are to this edition and appear in parentheses in the text.

14. John Frederick Lewis (1805-1876) lived in Cairo from 1842-1850. Thackeray, the most notable of his English visitors, published an amusing account of Lewis's life style in *Notes of a Journey from Cornhill to Grand Cairo* (1846). In 1850, Lewis sent *The Harem* (Japan, priv.col.; partial replica, London, V&A) to London for exhibition at the Old Water-Colour Society. Its exotic oriental theme caused a sensation. The following year, Lewis returned to England and success; in 1856 he was made president of the Water-Colour Society.

15. Joseph A. Cincotti, "Same Trip, Opposite Direction", *The New York Times Book Review,* 10 October 1993, p. 7.

16. K. Anthony Appiah, "Giving Up the Perfect Diamond", review of *The Holder of the World* by Bharati Mukherjee, *The New York Times Book Review,* 10 October 1993, p. 7.

17. Françoise Lionnet, *Postcolonial Representations: Women, Literature, Identity,* Ithaca: Cornell UP, 1995, p. 8.

18. *Travel, Gender, and Imperialism,* p. 161.

19. Steve Clark, ed., *Travel Writing and Empire: Postcolonial Theory in Transit,* London: Zed Books, 1999, p. 2.

20. *Routes,* p. 25.

21. *ibid.,* pp. 11, 39.

22. *Imperial Eyes,* p. 6.

23. Joseph Massad, "The Politics of Desire in the Writings of Ahdaf Soueif", *Journal of Palestine Studies,* 28, 4 (1999), 75, 80.

24. Ahdaf Soueif, "Interview with Joseph Massad", *Journal of Palestine Studies,* 28,4 (1999), 85.

25. *Imperial Eyes,* p. 7.

26. *Routes,* pp. 31, 32.

27. Trinh T. Minh-ha, "Other Than Myself/My Other Self", *Travellers' Tales: Narratives of Home and Displacement,* ed. George Robertson *et al.,* London: Routledge, 1994, p. 15.

28. *Travel, Gender, and Imperialism,* pp. 3-4, 3.

29. *ibid.,* p. 37.

30. *ibid.,* p. 161.

31. Jane Robinson, *Wayward Women: A Guide to Women Travellers,* Oxford: OUP, 1990, p. 279.

32. "The Politics of Desire", 80.

33. Lady Lucie Duff Gordon (1821-1869): *Letters from Egypt* (1865), *Last Letters from Egypt* (1875). Lady Anne Blunt (1837-1917), granddaughter of Lord Byron: *Bedouin Tribes of the Euphrates* (1879), *A Pilgrimage to Nejd, the Cradle of the Arab Race* (1881). See Robinson, *Wayward Women: A Guide to Women Travellers* for entries on Lady Duff Gordon, p. 278, and Lady Blunt, p. 6.

34. *Belated Travellers,* pp. 107, 111.

35. *ibid.,* pp. 124, 125.

36. "The Politics of Desire", 80.

37. *Belated Travellers,* p. 107.

38. *Discourses of Difference,* p. 3.

39. *Travel Writing and Empire,* pp. 23, 22.

40. *Home and Harem,* p. 11.

41. Sara Mills, "Knowledge, Gender, and Empire", *Writing Women and Space: Colonial and Postcolonial Geographies,* ed. Alison Blunt and Gillian Rose, New York: The Guilford Press, 1994, pp. 36, 29, 30.

42. *Travel, Gender, and Imperialism,* p. 136.

43. Amin Malak, "Arab-Muslim Feminism and the Narrative of Hybridity: The Fiction of Ahdaf Soueif", *Alif: Journal of Comparative Poetics,* 20 (2000), 157.

44. "The Politics of Desire", 78.

45. *Discourses of Difference,* p. 104.

46. *Imperial Eyes,* p. 105.

47. Nalini Iyer, "American/Indian: Metaphors of the Self in Bharati Mukherjee's *The Holder of the World*", *ARIEL,* 17,4 (1996), 36.

48. For the story of Isis and Osiris, see Roger Lancelyn Green's *Tales of Ancient Egypt,* New York: Henry Z. Walck, 1968.

49. Bharati Mukherjee, "A Four-Hundred-Year-Old Woman", *Critical Fictions: The Politics of Imaginative Writing,* ed. Philomena Mariani, Seattle: Bay, 1991, pp. 27-8.

50. Bharati Mukherjee, "Interview with Eleanor Wachtel", *Writers & Company,* CBC Radio, Toronto, 14 November 1993.

51. Judie Newman, "Spaces In-Between: Hester Prynne as the Salem Bibi in Bharati Mukherjee's *The Holder of the World*", *Borderlands: Negotiating Boundaries in Post-Colonial Writing,* ed. Monika Reif-Hülser, Amsterdam: Rodopi, p. 85.

52. The story of Sita is told in detail in *The Holder of the World,* p. 172. See also Nalini Iyer, "American/Indian: Metaphors of the Self", 43-4. In Note 6, Iyer explains a combination of the various versions of the story, a popular part of Hindu mythology. See also Paula Richman, ed., *Many Rāmāyanas: The Diversity of Narrative Tradition in South Asia,* Berkeley: University of California Press, 1991.

53. See also Judie Newman's comparison of Hester and Hannah in her excellent study of Hawthorne's Puritan New England, "Spaces In-Between", 78.

54. Nathaniel Hawthorne, *The Scarlet Letter,* New York: New American Library, 1980, pp. 61, 87.

55. *ibid.,* pp. 157, 156.

56. *ibid.,* pp. 220, 190, 190.

57. "Giving Up the Perfect Diamond", 7.

58. Claire Messud, "The Emperor's Tear", review of *The Holder of the World* by Bharati Mukherjee, *Times Literary Supplement,* 12 November 1993, p. 23.

59. Regarding John Dryden's *Tragedy of Aureng-Zebe* and "the identity of the 'Great Mogul's diamond'", see the appendices in François Bernier's *Travels in the Mogul Empire, AD 1656-1668,* trans. and ed. Archibald Constable; second edn., revised by Vincent A. Smith, London: OUP, 1934; first Indian edn., New Delhi: Oriental Books, repr. 1983.

60. "Spaces In-Between", p. 72.

61. Susan Koshy, review of *The Holder of the World,* *Amerasia Journal,* 20, 1 (1994), 189.

62. "Interview with Joseph Massad", 87.

63. "The Politics of Desire", 79.

64. *Culture and Imperialism,* p. 312.

65. *Reflections on Exile,* p. 410.

66. Iain Chambers, "Signs of Silence, Lines of Listening", *The Post-Colonial Question: Common Skies, Divided Horizons,* eds. Iain Chambers and Lidia Curti, London: Routledge, 1996, p. 59.

67. "Other Than Myself", p. 24.

Bharati Mukherjee and Sharmani Patricia Gabriel (interview date 29 May-3 June 2003)

SOURCE: Mukherjee, Bharati, and Sharmani Patricia Gabriel. "'Routes of Identity': In Conversation with Bharati Mukherjee." *ARIEL* 34, no. 4 (October 2003): 125-38.

[*In the following interview, conducted May 29 and June 3, 2003, Mukherjee engages in a lengthy discussion of her writing and critics' reactions to her work.*]

Bharati Mukherjee was in Kuala Lumpur, Malaysia in June 2003 as a guest of the United States Embassy to deliver a series of public lectures on a "Writers on America" project. The following interview had its beginnings as a digital video conference on 29 May 2003, with me speaking from the US Embassy in Kuala Lumpur to the author in San Francisco. This "virtual" conversation was followed up with a personal meeting with Professor Mukherjee at the Mandarin Oriental, Kuala Lumpur on 3 June 2003.

Mukherjee is author of six novels—***The Tiger's Daughter*** (1971), ***Wife*** (1975), ***Jasmine*** (1989), ***The Holder of the World*** (1993), ***Leave It to Me*** (1997) and ***Desirable Daughters*** (2002)—and two collections of short fiction—***Darkness*** (1985) and ***The Middleman and Other Stories*** (1988), for which she was awarded the National Book Critics Circle Award for Best Fiction in 1988. She has also written several pieces of social commentary, many of which share the ideological concerns of her fiction.

Over the course of her thirty-year creative and critical career, Mukherjee has energetically been engaged in redefining American national identity from the perspective of immigration, which she construes as a cultural process that keeps the meaning of America alive to continual re-invention.

Bharati Mukherjee lives in San Francisco and is currently Professor of English at the University of California at Berkeley.

[*Gabriel*]: *In a much publicized, front-page article for* The New York Times Book Review *in 1988, you elucidated with great passion and enthusiasm that the primary goal of your critical and creative project was to write about the making of the "new" Americans, whom you define as Americans from non-traditional immigrant countries who have never been written about before in American literature. Do you continue to see your goal as a writer in those terms today?*

[Mukherjee]: Yes, very much so. Since 1965, when the late Robert Kennedy, who was Attorney General at that time, changed the immigration laws, making it easier for people from non-European countries to come into the United States, there has been a steady and visible growth in the population of non-European Americans. However, the literary traditions of the 1960s, and prior to the 1960s, did not have the vocabulary, the discourse, for talking about the particular kinds of experiences or identity crises that the non-Europeans encountered once they had made the circuitous journey to the United States, which is where their real odyssey started. And it is that particular passion, the messiness of immigration and the triumphant but, at the same time, raw messiness of becoming part of the larger social fabric of the United States that I'm interested in fictionalising and dramatizing. I think right now the big story in the United States is multiculturalism rather than the racial black-white discourse that gave rise to standard, although sometimes exciting, fiction prior to the mid-1960s.

Much of the force of your immigrant narratives comes from your portrayal of characters who are determined to construct new identities and a new sense of belonging for themselves from "the hurly-burly of the unsettled magma between two worlds," as you describe it in your essay "A Four-Hundred-Year-Old Woman." That sense of danger and adventure is evident even in your recent works. Hasn't your romance with the United States been dimmed by forty years of living and writing in America?

I am a romantic, and my passion just gets more intense. But mine is a clear-eyed love of immigration and reformation of personality that the United States has offered me. And, so, in the last forty years, just as the society of the United States has become more nuanced in political terms, especially in its attitude to its non-European naturalized citizens, I too have become more nuanced in the ways in which I know what I want and how I want to fit in American society.

Do you see the migrant perspective as still being capable of telling fresh, new stories about cultural change and transformation?

Yes, absolutely. I believe that it is the fact of being "in between," of having a fresh angle on the narrative of remaking the self in the new world, that keeps the immigrant writer, the naturalized American writer, at her or his most fervent, intense and sensitive.

While you have been received favourably by publishers and the reading public, you have faced a good deal of criticism, particularly from India-born critics in the

United States for neglecting issues of race, education and gender in your tales of survivors, particularly in the novel, **Jasmine.** *What is your response to such criticism?*

I have given a long response to such criticism in an online journal of post-colonial literature called *Jouvert* that comes out of Columbia University where some postcolonial scholars who were born in Asia congregate. I have said this before, the writer can only write about the individual self. Only fifteenth-rate literature will come out of writers who want, first, to have a political agenda and then write to fulfill that agenda. My romance is with the ways in which the individual even when faced with adversity responds to that adversity. I think fiction writers, serious literary fiction writers, and Marxist postcolonial critics are always going to be at loggerheads. What the scholars want is theory, they want to have a particular theory to impose on fiction and they look to the socio-economic status of the writer rather than the text itself. I'm sure that many of these critics whom you refer to have actually not read my books. But they have read each other on Mukherjee. And also, I take issue with scholars who need for someone who looks like me—I'm talking about skin colour and particular accent in English—to write about "postcolonial" issues. Postcolonial critics like Spivak and her disciples would want me to participate in a kind of gender writing where the women characters should be seen as being oppressed. In the short story, **"Jasmine,"** the protagonist knows exactly what she wants—she has grown up in the multicultural society of the New World—she knows what she is willing to barter for what kind of private pleasure and so the ending of the story where she is seen making love to her white employer on the rug in front of the fireplace was seen initially by American women critics as, "Look, Mukherjee is showing Third World women being exploited by white male Americans," whereas I am saying that Jasmine is a much stronger and smarter character. She sets out to get what she wants. She may be misguided, but she knows what she wants. Postcolonial scholars would like me to dramatize all white people as villains and oppressors and all non-white characters as the oppressed and victimized. I refuse to do that because it is not the way my characters respond to circumstances in life, it is not the way I see people around me respond necessarily to circumstances.

What you are saying then is, as a writer of immigrant literature, your goal is to construct a new narrative of Americanness, in contrast to the postcolonial writer who is more interested in creating a new mythology of postcolonial nationhood?

Yes, definitely. I'm saying that I am an American writer. If I were to define myself as a "postcolonial" writer, I would still have to be writing about Indo-British relationships.

While you make clear your reasons for not wanting to be called a "postcolonial" writer, as a formerly colonized subject yourself do you not view the term or concept of "postcolonial" serving any usefulness?

Only to the extent that I realize I would have been a very different kind of writer if destiny had deposited me in Britain rather than in the United States. In that case, if I had lived my entire adult life in Great Britain, I would have been concerned not only with postcolonial issues and the need for race relations to be worked out in terms of brown and white in Britain, I would also be writing a very different kind of English. The liberation for me personally was that through accidents of love—I fell in love with a fellow student of the [Iowa] Writers' Workshop when I was 23 years old and got married to him in a five-minute lunchtime wedding—I realized that my life had changed and that I was going to have to lead my entire life in the United States, the New World. Slowly, gradually, I realized that there had been, whether I had wanted it or not, a great deal of erosion in the language structure, the syntax and the choice of point of view that as a novelist I felt comfortable with. When I first arrived in the United States, I was very much a postcolonial writer who thought of the omniscient point of view as being the most comfortable. I was playing in my first novel, **The Tiger's Daughter,** with parodying Forster and Jane Austen and all the great British novelists who had been held up to me in my school and college days as the ones to imitate. I would have, if I had considered myself a postcolonial writer, been mimicking and bettering those British narrative models. But the accident of suddenly being deposited in the New World meant there are no rules and so I had to find not only ways of identifying myself as a newcomer in the New World, but also find new forms of novel writing, of short story writing, in order to articulate all these new feelings. So the language and the form became very, very different. I see myself in the tradition of other immigrant groups, of the post-1965 non-Europeans who have had additional factors or stresses to deal with or address in their finding a spot in the American social fabric. But my personal interest is in totally deleting the academic postcolonial discourse about centre and periphery. I'm saying, "We are all, no matter where we might have come from originally, equal partners here and United States society has to change in order to accommodate this new sense of who we are."

Your work in this sense, as a writer and a social and cultural commentator, collectively presents a profile that is almost unique in America. Among writers who belong to the South Asian diaspora in the United States (I'm thinking here of the more established names such as Anita Desai and Bapsi Sidhwa as well as newer voices such as Jhumpa Lahiri), yours seems to be a more strident voice in the American literary scene. How would you compare or contrast your work with that of these other writers of South Asian ancestry who also deal with the immigrant experience in America?

There is a critical mass of writers now [in America], and many of them happen to be women writers, who either were born in India or are of Indian ancestry. The majority, the Anita Desais, the Bapsi Sidhwas, are expatriate Indian writers whose inspiration is still derived from experiences that happened in India and at a time perhaps when they were not personal witnesses to those incidents. So theirs is a virtual experience of the homeland. They are writing about nostalgia, they are producing expatriate fiction, which is perfectly fine, but that's not American fiction. They are not constructing themselves, they are not seeing themselves as American writers. I think Jhumpa Lahiri and I are among the very few who are writing not about the India we left behind but the here and now, the daily life that we encounter and that many hundreds and thousands of other South Asians or other immigrant groups are facing in the United States right now. We are writing immigrant fiction, whereas writers like Anita Desai and Bapsi Sidhwa, marvellous though their writing is, are writing nostalgic expatriate fiction.

Professor Mukherjee, you were born into a prominent Bengali family of wealth and standing—

That was all a long time ago [laughter]—and that is why I get attacked so much by postcolonial critics. . . . (laughter)

*—and protected by the strict caste system of India. In a recent essay called **"On Being an American Writer,"** you write that Indian immigrant writers like you arrived in America "after the cultural and political wars of the 1960's and never experienced the civil rights battles or the Vietnamese resistance." What is interesting, however, is that for a person who had led a very sheltered existence, you went on to vigorously participate in social and political causes in America. What particular moment or incident was responsible for bringing about your active involvement in social issues?*

There were many different moments rather than a single moment. When I arrived in the fall of 1961 as a student of the Iowa Writers' Workshop, there were very few Indian women in America—many of the professional women from South Asia came as a result of a change in immigration laws in 1965 and the 1970's. So I was present as the Americans my age got involved in women's movements—Doris Lessing's *The Golden Notebook* was out in 1962 and Sylvia Plath's *The Bell Jar* in 1963. If I had married, let us say, the perfect Bengali bridegroom, the kind that my father would have picked for me, I think probably I would have been less politicized and writing very different kinds of fiction. But because I married an American—I got married and had my first child when I was 23—I became absorbed in my husband Clark's kinds of interests. I knew more about American sports because he was a sports fan, I knew about Trivial Pursuit simply because I was a young, dutiful wife. I took over, I shared all those interests in ways that American women my age may not have. And so I was also learning to change my sympathies, learning to sensitize myself to minority problems while at the same time experiencing social demotion. I learned to gain a theoretical as well as emotional feel for the underclass. I was no longer Dr. Mukherjee's daughter living in a walled, princess-like setting. No one knew or cared about what my family was like. And then, in Canada, around 1973, 1974, when the policy papers about Canada were out, racism was targeted primarily at South Asian immigrants, the professionals who had kids in private schools, more than the poor labourers from other groups. That Canadian experience of institutional and physical violence—I was sent to sit at the back of the Greyhound bus—made me a far more political citizen and a far more politicized writer, politicized in the sense that I could not write about a love story, about a man and a woman as a white American writer might about personal relationships. My stories are always set in the context of social and racial conflicts. But I also, because I came from a privileged background in my formative years, whether I wanted it or not, because I was a privileged member of the establishment in Calcutta, I had the confidence to say, "I will not put up with this kind of injustice." But mine was a lone voice in the late 1970's, in those years of incredibly violent race relations. My experience of virulent and unabashed racism, without the support or relief of the Constitution or constitutive agencies of redress, in Canada is what made me a strong, outspoken person. My prologue to the collection of stories in **Darkness** is one of the most important essays I have written about racism in Canada. I wrote it because the series editor wanted a prologue. But it gave me the chance to suddenly articulate to myself the difference I felt between writing in Canada and writing in the United States about the "coloured" immigrants, about the hundreds and thousands of people like me.

Professor Mukherjee, the texts, **Jasmine** *and* **The Middleman and Other Stories,** *are on the primary reading list of the American Literature course offered by the English Department of the University of Malaya, where I teach. While my students sympathized with the difficulties of displacement that confronted your women characters, the female students especially felt rather uncomfortable with the choices made by some of your protagonists—such as Nafisa in* **"The Lady from Lucknow"** *[from the* **Darkness** *collection], Maya in* **"The Tenant"** *[from* **The Middleman and Other Stories**]*, and especially Jasmine of the short story and novel—*

whose growing empowerment in America was articulated in primarily sexual terms. Does the sexual freedom of your characters function as an index of their Americanization?

I do not know if I would call it [the sexual empowerment of my characters] an index of their Americanization. To me and for the characters you have just mentioned, the breaking out of that world of taboos is not equivalent to or the exact equal of Americanization. But it is interesting saying, "I am no longer that old given self, the one that was governed by social dictates. But I am not running out of control. I am someone willing to change myself and take risks, though some of those risks may be silly or excessive and the fallout of those adventures can be harmful." So for me and my authorial vision, having had the guts to take that step outside the safe parameters of the old self is in itself a kind of progress. It is positive, it is saying that change is possible, it is saying, "I'm willing to look for a new identity." The risk-taking of some of these characters and their self-discovery can take many forms, but in the case of these women characters, because they have been so confined in terms of gender, their form of self-control takes the form of sexual liberation. But in my head, I never equated that with Americanization because I do not believe as an author, as an individual and as a citizen that there is any such thing as a fixed "Americannness."

Does that risk-taking by your characters explain the preponderance of violence in your fiction?

Yes. There are many kinds of transformation, especially for those of us who have come out of traditional societies, out of very, very sheltered backgrounds, as I did, and then landing in an alien culture where there are no rules that you recognize, where you do not know any of the rules of the new country. Risk-taking and the consequences of that risk-taking can be very, very violent. That uprooting from what you know to land somewhere where you have no clue as to what is expected of you, let alone what you expect of yourself, is a traumatizing experience. And so, as a writer, I have to find metaphors for talking about the psychic violence of up-rooting and re-rooting. That is why there is so much physical violence in my fiction. This physical violence can take either the form of sexual violence or of actual homes burning down, as in [the novel] **Leave It to Me.** I grew up in a Calcutta that first had to fight the colonialists, and then go through the bloody violence of Partition and the language riots. So violence has been the condition for writers like me, though now it has gotten more prevalent. I'm talking about violence as a psychic, social and physical condition.

Your work revolves around the idea of people being dispersed from their homeland and in showing how the "original" culture that the immigrant subject brings with her or him gets transformed through active interaction with American culture, which itself is transformed by that interaction. This results, as you have defined it, in the formation of a new "immigrant" American culture. While you privilege the term "immigrant" to refer to the context which makes identity and cultural change and renewal possible, how amenable are you to your works being explored in the context of "diaspora"? I refer here to the idea of diaspora as articulated by cultural theorists such as James Clifford and Stuart Hall, who view diaspora as dynamic communities that shape and reshape their own ancestral culture as well as the cultures with which they come into contact.

I try to stay away from the vocabulary of theorists as much as possible. So, if you had not put it so clearly, I probably would not have understood what is meant by diaspora! [laughter]. Anyway, I think I have always been very clear about cultural change. In fact, I was attacked by cultural theorists when the prologue to **Darkness** came out saying that we are a series of fluid identities, that culture never stops. What I say in my essay in the book called *Letters of Transit [Reflections on Exile, Identity, Language and Loss]* edited by Andre Aciman, which also has essays by Edward Said and Eva Hoffman, is that those who have self-fashioned themselves as expatriate South Asian writers, even though they may carry American passports, are creating an India that is imaginary, an India that is totally shaped by nostalgia. It is not the India that Indians of 2003 live in. "Diaspora" means that you have reshaped yourself to your private purposes, to suit what you want to do with your original culture. Now I'm not sure if that is consonant with what people like Hall and the others are saying but that is what I am saying. Diaspora is only one part of my concern and my characters' concern. Diaspora is the end of that zigzag route—when you think the journey is over it is only just beginning.

The term "assimilation" generally carries negative connotations in many national contexts. Certainly, here in Malaysia, the dominant cultures' tacit expectation that immigrant communities shed every vestige of their past and cultural history if they are to be accommodated has met with considerable resistance from minority communities. Do you see any similarities with this position and how you treat or speak of assimilation in your writings?

A cherished strategy of mine, a very well thought-out strategy of mine, especially when I'm writing a first-person novel as in **Jasmine** is to have other minor characters who are also experiencing immigration or sexual rebellion but with very different responses. So while Jasmine breaks away from the ghetto and lights out for other kinds of experiences, I have also included other groups like the Kannibal Indians who never get

the chance—the establishment does not give them a chance—or the Caribbean day-care workers who have to leave their children behind in the islands in order to be underpaid housekeepers so that white American women can become professional directors and lawyers. And so these characters are going to have a very different response to America. And I hope I have made it clear that Jasmine, while she is a very lovable character, has wants, however reckless, has hopes and that there are others who are critiquing her particular desire and persistence, her hope. So it is not that I am for assimilation against retention, but I'm saying that natural erosion will take place unless you artificially—I'm putting this in the American context—unless you artificially over many generations hang on to an identity that you claim is stable rather than mutable. The authorial vision must always be wiser and detached enough to make the protagonist a part of a much larger scene. It seems to be the need of cultural theorists like Spivak to attack me as an assimilationist because I have said that I am an American writer. My fight is with even Black Americans who feel they need to exoticize in order to be seen as multicultural. For me saying that you are not part of the centre is not being multicultural. Multicultural is not about saying "I am no longer Indian" but about each of us, even within the South Asian group, finding in ourselves signs of mongrelization, syncretism, synthesis.

In Malaysia, a diasporic nation like many other formerly colonized countries, those of us who position ourselves as "Malaysian" reject the state's identification of us as "immigrants." For to be immigrant, in state ideology, is to belong "elsewhere," to not fully belong "here." However, you privilege the term "immigrant" in your cultural and political aesthetic as an American writer. How do you explain the difference between these positions?

The word, the concept "immigrant" is true of me because I came as an immigrant to the States. I am not a first-generation American. I am an immigrant who is a naturalized United States citizen. In those nation states where the concept of citizenship is worked out in terms of either religious, linguistic or ethnic criteria, it becomes harder for the individual who does not belong in those officially designated "national" categories to say, "I am one of you, treat me as a first-class citizen." I don't know much about Malaysia to make parallel contrasts but in a society like the United States, where the mythology, never mind how it converts into practice, where the mythology says, "We are all like minded. You are American if you subscribe to the specific values articulated in the American Bill of Rights and the Constitution," it becomes much easier for those first-generation, second-generation minority groups to claim membership, full membership, in that society because the rhetoric gives us the chance.

Do you write with a particular readership in mind?

I think my primary readership is going to be American because I have never written a book about any other country, except for my first novel, *The Tiger's Daughter*. But that does not mean that I write with an American readership in mind. I'm writing for people like me who have gone through that experience of dislocation, and I'm writing for people like you as well who can take something out of the stories of individuals whose particulars may be very different but whose conflicts may have some resemblance to the facts of their own lives.

In **The Middleman and Other Stories** *and the works that follow, the scope of your fiction was broadened to encompass the narrative of the other, non-Indian, minority groups in America. However, in your latest novel,* **Desirable Daughters,** *apart from the character of the Hungarian refugee, Andy, your characters are principally from the Indian immigrant community, that of New York in particular. In this sense, the novel seems to me to carry strong echoes of the pre-***Middleman*** phase of your writing; I'm thinking in particular of your early novel* **Wife.** *It seems to me that in your latest novel you are very concerned with showing the heterogeneities within the Indian immigrant community in America rather than showcasing the diversity of American groups.*

I think that the setting and the American adventures are all dictated by the particular character and his or her circumstances. In my last novel, I wanted to write about three sisters, much like my own sisters and myself, who, when deposited in America, responded very differently to the experience of being outside rules, outside the country, outside family protection. So, because I did that and I was writing at the end of the millennium when the Indian immigrant group had gathered critical mass, it is a very different kind of America in which Tara finds herself than, say, Jasmine did, or like I did when I was writing *Darkness.* When I first arrived in America, if you saw an Indian on the street of Manhattan, you would say "Hello!" [laughter]. As a result, the kind of groups that the two United States-based sisters, Tara and Padma, deal with are very much within their own South Asian immigrant, naturalized, American community—a community that someone like Jasmine would have wished to belong to, or that was necessary for someone like Dimple [in *Wife*] to belong to. And so, you're quite right, I wanted to get across the sense that being a South Asian American is not a monolithic identity. It was even worse when they would lump all Asian writers together. Now that there is enough fiction being written about the Indian diaspora, it is important for people to realize that one character does not represent the range of identities and experiences.

One of the first things that struck me when I started reading **Desirable Daughters** *is that the main character is called Tara, also the name of the protagonist of your first novel,* **The Tiger's Daughter.** *Is there a story behind this?*

[laughter] It was only after I was quite well into the novel that I realized my first protagonist was also a Tara. So, no, it was purely unintentional.

In **Desirable Daughters,** *the sense of languor with which you recreate personal, family and cultural history, and the lushness of detail with which you evoke East Bengal in the opening section of the book seems to jar with the speed and violence of the concluding sections of the novel. Are you contrasting Tara's ancestral past with her quest for self discovery in the American present?*

Yes, because the beginning comes back to the end and the ending comes back to the beginning. This is the family memory, memoir, that Tara is constructing for herself. She who had been anxious to leave the control of her husband, Bish Chatterjee, whom she had misjudged as another patriarch, and get out of the gated community of Atherton to go find herself, to go pursue her personal happiness in the Upper Haight area of San Francisco, has to come back to realize what it is that she has cut off from herself. She has to discover and reassess her family history, she has to try to understand her national history. And it is in doing so that she understands her ex-husband Bish, understands why they are very different. Tara needs to immerse herself in that lushness to rediscover within herself all the sensory details that she had rejected, all that she had not wanted to know, as a young woman.

You portray your women characters as being adaptable due to their upbringing and cultural conditioning, and therefore more resilient and innovative in facing the pressure of constructing new identities. In this context, your male characters, the Indian husbands—carriers of patriarchal constructs into America—tend to suffer the stigma of stereotype. However, Bish [in **Desirable Daughters***] seems to have broken away from this mould, for through him you show, for the first time, the kinds of pressures that Indian men also face in America. Is there any particular reason for this?*

I guess I fell in love with Bish [laughter]. Bish is someone who never really yields the core part of himself. He can integrate American football—he watches Joe Montana [an American football star] on TV and gets the brainwave for CHATTEE—and other aspects of American culture into his Bengali identity, which is seen in the kind of clothes that he wears. This strategy may not work out for Tara or the other Silicon Valley wives that get together in the mall. Yes, I thought I understood Bish much better as I got into the first draft. He becomes in a way the novel's hero. He suffers. Tara doesn't realize during the course of her adventures in America that it is Bish who is the target of the assassins.

How has this book been received in India?

It made the top 10 publisher's listing in India—finally! My last couple of books did not interest Indians so much. They felt I was merely writing about the trauma of dislocation and relocation in the New World, although in **The Holder of the World,** I use India as one third of the world. But they were very interested in **Desirable Daughters,** where the idea of the contemporary models of transformative identity processes in America, as experienced by two sisters in America, has struck a resonance in India. After all, almost every middle-class family has a relation in New Jersey.

A final question. What are you working on at the moment?

I am working on a sequel to my last novel, which I hope to complete by the end of the year. The title of this book is going to be **The Tree Bride.** Here Tara recounts in fuller detail the story of the transformation of her ancestor, Tara Lata, from five-year-old child bride to sanctuary provider for the freedom fighters who fought the British.

[**The Tree Bride** was published by Harper Perennial in July 2005.]

Professor Mukherjee, thank you.

Ramlal Agarwal (review date October-December 2003)

SOURCE: Agarwal, Ramlal. Review of *Desirable Daughters,* by Bharati Mukherjee. *World Literature Today* 77, nos. 3-4 (October-December 2003): 86-7.

[*In the following review, Agarwal declares the characters of* Desirable Daughters *insipid and their stories often appalling.*]

In **Desirable Daughters,** Bharati Mukherjee sets herself a dual task: she wants to tell her Indian readers about Indian expatriates in America and her American readers about weird customs and traditions of Indian society. It is a difficult undertaking, and Tara, the novel's narrator admits as much. "It is one of those San Francisco things I can't begin to explain in India," she says, "just like I can't explain my Indian life to the women I know in California. I have told my Calcutta stories many times, and Americans seem to find them endlessly amusing and appalling." Incidentally, so are her American stories for Indian readers.

Mukherjee begins the novel by telling the story of "The Tree-Bride," which has a pervasive influence on the rest of the book. Jai Krishna Gangooly was a pleader at Decca High Court. A Bengali Brahmin, he was a staunch believer in Hindu culture. He had three daughters, the youngest named Tara Lata. When Tara was five years old, he arranged her marriage. Just before the wedding, however, the bride-groom's father increased his demands for the dowry. Refusing to be cowed into submission, Jai Krishna took his daughter into a deep forest and married her to a tree, and thus Tara became known as Tree-Bride. But that was decades ago. Several generations down the line, Tara, the narrator, marries the best available man and goes to America, where her new husband, Bishwapriya Chatterjee, makes millions in the Silicon Valley. In due course, she gets a divorce and walks away with millions following the settlement. She lives independently with her son, Rabindra, and freely sleeps with Andy, her carpenter, as well as with friends of her ex-husband. In short, unlike her ancestress, she enjoys complete social, financial, and sexual freedom. But the strange behavior of her son and the emergence of Chris Dey claiming to be the son of her sister Padma begin to disrupt her safe haven. Naturally, she turns to her family and wants to be reconciled with her ex-husband, but an explosion destroys her house and wounds Bishwapriya very badly. In the end, Tara returns to Mishtigunj, where the Tree-Bride lived "not for rest but to follow the Ganges to its source." The narrator and the Tree-Bride reach the same dead end, although through different routes.

Obviously, **Desirable Daughters** deals with America and its liberties, individualism, and money power and with India and its gods, ghosts, and curious social practices. American readers may find the Indian stories amusing and appalling, but Indian readers will find the American stories more appalling than amusing. This is because Mukherjee presents a set of totally insipid characters.

Tara is what a tabloid portrayed her as being: a woman living off a generous divorce settlement from one man while playing around with another and still keeping the first one on a leash. Her sister Padma is a brash hypocrite and an unabashed flirt. Bishwapriya, her husband, behaves like an American, which he regrets. Small wonder if these characters with no likeable qualities or strong personalities fail to impress the reader, notwithstanding Bharati Mukherjee's many felicities of language.

Lawrence Buell (essay date 2005)

SOURCE: Buell, Lawrence.[1] "Hawthorne and the Problem of 'American' Fiction: The Example of *The Scarlet Letter.*" In *Hawthorne and the Real: Bicenten-*

nial Essays, edited by Millicent Bell, pp. 70-87. Columbus, Ohio: Ohio State University Press, 2005.

[*In the following essay, Buell examines Mukherjee's rewriting of Hawthorne's* Scarlet Letter *in* The Holder of the World.]

This essay is intended as a kind of contemporary equivalent to Lionel Trilling's (1964) landmark centennial assessment of changing conceptions of the tenor of Hawthorne's work. Trilling's "Our Hawthorne" concentrated on a particular shift in critical perception from the delicate ironist imaged by Henry James to the troubled Kafka-esque Hawthorne descried by Herman Melville but not prevalent until the twentieth century. Hawthorne emerges from this analysis both as a moving target fascinating in and of itself and as a barometer of changing dispensations of critical inquiry (Trilling). Since Trilling wrote, the variability and contestedness of the "essential" Hawthorne and his legacy, or legacies, have been further underscored by such excellent influence/reception studies as Richard Brodhead's *The School of Hawthorne* (1986) and by a plethora of fictive reworkings of his plots, particularly *The Scarlet Letter.* Not only is the issue of what ought to count as "our" Hawthorne far more problematic now than it seemed in 1964. To reflect seriously about the issue through a turn-of-the-twenty-first-century lens also requires engaging the much vaster question of what ought to count as "American" literary history. The case of Hawthorne's masterpiece demonstrates this especially.

1

The Scarlet Letter holds a unique place in Anglo-American literary history. It was the book that made Hawthorne famous, his most incontestably "perfect" book, the book most crucial in establishing him as the most consummate artist in American fiction before James. James was not alone in looking back upon it as a landmark event in U.S. literary emergence: "Something might at last be sent to Europe as exquisite in quality as anything that had been received" (James [1878] 1984, 403).

The Scarlet Letter's exquisite self-circumscription has been held against it as well. James thought it lacked passion. New historicists have seen it as evading the slavery issue, or giving aid and comfort to a conservative con-sensualism through some of the very strategies of ambiguation that make it so aesthetically resplendent (Arac 1986). Fault has been found with the practice of making this text and/or "Hawthorne" generally so central to the narrative U.S. literary history, as in Jane Tompkins's argument that Hawthorne's high critical reputation relative to the "scribbling woman" he denigrated is an artifact of a "dynastic cultural elite" (Tompkins 1985, 30).[2] Yet *The Scarlet Letter* will surely

continue to be a key reference point for U.S. literary history. It remains the single most taught long work of premodern American literature. Although far from being the earliest U.S. novel of consequence, it is widely looked upon as "the inaugural text of the indigenous canon" (Gilmore 2003, 84). Were a vote taken among Americanist critics as to the first indisputable Anglo-American classic in the genre, *The Scarlet Letter* would almost surely win.

This status derives not just from its qualities as a freestanding text but from its historical representation and historical impact. Among major premodern U.S. fictions, *The Scarlet Letter* comes closest to rendering a myth of national origins. It has also become a masterplot for American writers, from Harold Frederic (*The Damnation of Theron Ware*) and Henry James to Toni Morrison (*Beloved*) and Bharati Mukherjee (*The Holder of the World*). In this sense James was prophetic in his explanation of why, in addition to its craftsmanship, *The Scarlet Letter* seemed "in the United States a literary event of the first importance." For "the best of it was that the thing was absolutely American; it belonged to the soil, to the air; it came out of the very heart of New England" (James [1878] 1984, 402, 403).

Some have not found the connection between Americanness and Hawthornian romance so self-evident. In a contentious essay as significant in its own way as James's assessment a decade later, novelist J. W. DeForest looked in vain for "The Great American Novel" he wished to call into being. Hawthorne, "the greatest of American imaginations," was part of the problem. His "personages" seemed to "belong to the wide realm of art rather than to our nationality," to be "as probably natives of the furthest mountains of Cathay or of the moon as of the United States of America" (DeForest 1868, 28). This was actually quite close to the view Hawthorne himself expressed in his Preface to *The House of the Seven Gables* (3):

> The personages of the tale—though they give themselves out to be of ancient stability and considerable prominence—are really of the author's own making, or, at all events, of his own mixing. . . . He would be glad, therefore, if . . . the book may be read strictly as a Romance, having a great deal more to do with the clouds overhead than with any portion of the actual soil of the County of Essex.

Of course, in *this* instance Hawthorne had a special interest in distancing himself from actual personages and locale (to ward off charges of libel), whereas "The Custom-House" makes the opposite appeal—to loco-centricity and provincial antiquarianism—under the guise of observing the law of literary "propriety" that justifies an account of how the "authentic" manuscript came into the author's possession (4). Hawthorne scholarship has demonstrated the accuracy of *The*

Scarlet Letter's historical geography (Ryskamp 1959), and the uncanny correspondence of its plot and two main protagonists with those of the Antinomian Controversy (Colacurcio 1972). But these meticulous historical readings also presuppose a detached cosmopolitan intelligence. It wasn't *just* a dodge for Hawthorne to claim that *Seven Gables* came from cloudland, nor was he concealing his dependence on documentary sources in affirming of *The Scarlet Letter* that, save for "the authenticity of the outline," he had allowed himself "nearly or altogether as much license as if the facts had been entirely of my own invention" (33).

Americanists, who constitute the overwhelming majority of Hawthorne scholars, have generally read such disclaimers in the spirit of James rather than of DeForest: as attempts to claim elbow room for romantic stylization without taking his protestations of detachment from native place and history too seriously. Even if Hawthorne invokes New England and/or national ideology only to dismantle it, surely the cultural reference point remains U.S.-ness, New England-ness, post-Puritanness, antebellum ideological ferment.

Lately, however, a more quizzical conception of *The Scarlet Letter*'s investment in the national has begun to emerge. "Underlying the primary attention given to New England history in the novel," has been descried "a subsurface of English history that Hawthorne has carefully structured in order to examine American Puritans within a framework larger than the provincial boundaries of New England" (Newberry 1987, 168). Again and again "residual attachments to Old World culture and theology" seem to "permeate the consciousness of these emigrant characters" (Giles 1962, 178), making *The Scarlet Letter* as much a text about cultural migration and diaspora as a text about settlement, founding, and the Puritan origins of national culture. Hester and Pearl seem more like creatures of the author's fascination with the "Orient" than figures who belong in a Puritan colonial setting (Luedtke 1989, 181-87). And what are we to make of the oddity that a text so influential for national letters as *The Scarlet Letter* should be so tenuously affiliated, so tenuously committed in its own cultural allegiances? We need to rethink once more that penultimate flourish in "The Custom-House," "I am a citizen of somewhere else" (44).

The old, now widely discredited way of thinking about such a remark only takes us back to Americanness again: Hawthorne was declaring allegiance to the romance mode because the cultural "thinness" of the comparatively young, open country made impossible the thick social representations of the novel. From such fictions as his (and Cooper's and Melville's and others), the distinctive shape of the "American novel" took form.[3] So it was once thought. We can do better than

that, better too than anti-romance revisionist theory has done. To do so, at the risk of seeming perverse I should like to start at the very end of *The Scarlet Letter* and work back from there.

The Scarlet Letter confirms its residual skepticism about the possibility of radical breaks and new departures by ending with a glimpse of the spot where Hester Prynne is buried, next to the "old and sunken grave" of Arthur Dimmesdale, with a space between but a single tombstone marking both, those markings worn by the weathering of two hundred years. "On this simple slab of slate,

> —as the curious investigator may still discern, and perplex himself with the purport—there appeared the semblance of an engraved escutcheon. It bore a device, a herald's wording of which might serve for a motto and brief description of our now concluded legend; so sombre is it, and relieved only by one ever-glowing point of light gloomier than the shadow:—

"ON A FIELD SABLE, THE LETTER A, GULES"

Well indeed might "the curious investigator" be perplexed, so encrypted is this passage. To be sure, there is an obvious return-to-starting-point fitness to the book's ending: Chapter 1 mentions the cemetery, in the same breath as the prison, as being among a colonial government's first allotments of space for public use; and "The Custom-House" is suffused with elegiac images of burial, exhumation, and mystified musing *à propos* the musty packet containing the "original narrative" of Surveyor Pue. But so strange a return! What seems as if it ought to be a distinct visual image cannot be visualized. The basic *idea* is plain enough: a red letter against a black background. But the rhetoric is teasingly oblique. The carving on the gravestone is rendered neither quite as language nor quite as picture, but *via* the arcane semiotics of heraldry.

To be sure, it is typical of Hawthorne's colonial tales to proliferate emblematic schemata and instill a sense of remoteness of past from present. They squint back at quaint old tombstones, houses, furniture, and other colonial artifacts from an immense aesthetic distance, like Henry Thoreau prompted by an old painting of seventeenth-century Concord to wonder whether real people could truly have existed then. In this Hawthorne and Thoreau were both engaging in a familiar ritual of romanticized gothicization of the Puritan primordium and revealing themselves—more than they let on—as children of the early industrial age, the first generation to undergo what we now call future shock. Yet *The Scarlet Letter*'s closing scene feels alien even by that standard. Though identified as a particular burying-ground, the colony's first, it feels more like an English graveyard than a New England one, whose old slabs generally sported no such adornments.[4] Is the reader to assume the design is the work of the grown-up Pearl, the new world's richest heiress long since resocialized into old-world elegance? Might it also, or alternatively, be a potshot at the rising interest in pedigree among northeastern elite families as the nineteenth century unfolded? (The New England Historic Genealogical Society, the nation's first such organization, had been founded just five years before the novel's publication.) In any case, the inscription is atypical of standard colonial and antebellum funerary design.

But I want to concentrate especially on a still more occluded element: the intertextual palimpsest the heraldic reference creates. The text here recalls two passages by classic English writers that turn on the symbolic contrast of sable and gules. One is the concluding stanza of the English Puritan poet Andrew Marvell's "The Unfortunate Lover," a weirdly contorted metaphysical lyric that dates from the approximate time of Hawthorne's plot. The other is a passage from Walter Scott's "Introduction" to *Waverley,* the first in the series of fictionalized renderings of Scottish history from the mid-seventeenth to the mid-eighteenth century that secured his reputation as the father of the historical romance, Hawthorne's own genre. Neither of these texts is unknown to Hawthorne criticism, but neither have they been much discussed (cf. Gale 315, Stubbs 175-76).

> This is the only *Banneret*
> That ever Love created yet:
> Who though, by the Malignant Starrs,
> Forced to live in Storms and Warrs;
> Yet dying leave a Perfume here,
> And Musick within every Ear:
> And he in Story only rules
> In a Field *Sable* a Lover *Gules.*
>
> (Marvell 1: 29)

[My story will emphasize] those passions common to men in all stages of society, and which have alike agitated the human heart, whether it throbbed under the steel corslet of the fifteenth century, the brocaded coat of the eighteenth, or the blue rock and white dimity waistcoat of the present day. Upon these passions it is no doubt true that the state of manners and laws casts a necessary colouring; but the bearings, to use the language of heraldry, remain the same. . . . The wrath of our ancestors, for example, was colored *gules*; it broke forth in acts of open and sanguinary violence against the objects of its fury. Our malignant feelings, which must seek gratification through more indirect channels, and undermine the obstacles which they cannot openly bear down, may be rather said to be tinctured *sable.* But the deep-ruling impulse is the same in both cases; and the proud peer who can now only ruin his neighbor according to law, by protracted suits, is the genuine descendant of the baron, who wrapped the castle of his competitor in flames, and knocked him on the head as he endeavoured to escape from the conflagration. It is from the great book of Nature, the

same through a thousand editions, whether of blackletter, or wire-wove and hot-pressed, that I have venturously essayed to read a chapter to the public.

> (Scott 1901, 1:13-14)

We cannot be sure if Hawthorne had either passage consciously in mind, though almost certainly he knew them both. He was an attentive reader of Renaissance allegorical poetry, and he read and reread Scott, "his boyhood favorite among novelists" (Dekker 1987, 131), from youth until near his death.[5] In any case, the passages underscore fundamental implications of the main plot: that love-longing is fulfilled in fantasy, not in real life, and that ancient and modern forms of deviance and oppression are nonidentical but akin. Hawthorne's romance fuses the discrepant sable-gules polarities from the two pre-texts. Marvell and Scott use heraldry to achieve a stylized diagnostic control over very different passions. For Marvell, the passion of love; for Scott, aggression. Marvell's sable/gules antithesis refers to violently conflicted emotions within the lover, which can be resolved only in a certain kind of idealizing story. Scott's antithesis is between different kinds of revenge. *The Scarlet Letter* subsumes both antitheses within *its* dominant polarity between the one passion and the other: love versus patriarchal repression, whether exerted from without or from within.

Would the author of *The Scarlet Letter*—supposing him to have had these pre-texts in mind—have expected readers to catch the allusions? I suspect not, seeing that a basic *gestalt* of some sort can be grasped without perceiving the esoterica, although it piquantly enhances the effect when you do. You're bound to feel a sense of the story of Hester and Dimmesdale being converted into "legend" even if you remain oblivious to the antecedent realms of legend—all the more so given that the scene of graveyard pondering was a stock memorial and literary device in the eighteenth and nineteenth centuries, Thomas Gray's "Elegy Written in a Country Churchyard" and the frame narrative of Scott's *Old Mortality* being familiar to most middle-class readers of Hawthorne's day.

To catch the two more deeply buried allusions helps make better sense of the ending's strangeness, however. The injection of heraldry seems less freakish, seems indeed a sophisticated preemption of tradition by a mind steeped in the Anglo-European inheritance. For Marvell, the device urbanely evokes such courtly love topoi as the typical lover's proverbial throes. Only in nevernever land can he attain the apotheosis of the banneret (knighthood on the spot for valor in the field of battle). Abstraction underscores the remoteness of the prospect. Scott's invocation of the topos is more complex, simultaneously bringing the past nearer and exoticizing the bourgeois present by the parallel to bygone feudalism. But here, too, the formal sable versus gules contrast urbanely rises above and displaces the phenomenon of aggression by rendering it as design. In *The Scarlet Letter,* the two levels of signification merge (the contortions of love and the aggressions of patriarchy), and on Scott's complex terms, dramatizing a counterpoint of opposition versus affinity between the then and the now.

In so doing, Hawthorne and his precursors also emphasize something timeless, perennial, about their stories. Costumes differ, emotions remain the same. Marvell's hapless wight is a perennial lover-loser. *The Scarlet Letter*'s quiet affiliation with these texts helps establish *its* story not just as a Puritan tale but also as part and parcel of Euro-diasporic collective memory stretching back to the Middle Ages. Hawthorne's redeployment of the sable-gules schema is no more hermetically American than filmmaker Akira Kurosawa's retelling of Shakespeare's *King Lear* in *Ran* is hermetically Japanese.

The more we start to think of Hawthorne in relation to figures like Scott and Marvell, the less *The Scarlet Letter* looks like a text firmly and unshakeably embedded within a line of American descent from Puritan history or as a critique of American Transcendentalism or nineteenth-century American Victorian moralism. The more it makes sense that the precursor to which Henry James thought to liken it was Scottish writer John Gibson Lockhart's *Adam Blair* (1822), a novel of ministerial adultery in an old-world puritanical culture. The more it begins to make sense that the first rewriting of *The Scarlet Letter* was not an American novel but George Eliot's *Adam Bede*. It, too, is a historical fiction that features a pair of illicit lovers named Hester and Arthur, with an illegitimate child—also in a provincial social context that intensifies the mixture of guilt, suffering, and repression. Why should not an English country town of the turn of the nineteenth century be every bit as promising a venue for a Hester-Arthur story as seventeenth-century New England?

That is not the way the majority of Hawthorne scholars, who are mostly Americanists, have been conditioned to think about Hawthorne's legacy. We are much more inclined to think of Hawthorne in relation to William Faulkner or John Updike or Toni Morrison than to compare him to George Eliot, even though Eliot is on record as declaring Hawthorne "a grand favorite of mine" (Eliot 1954-78, 2: 52). The underlying assumption is that Hawthorne was a classic American writer chiefly of importance to "our" literary history as an agent of U.S. literary emergence and the propagation of distinctive strains in national fiction thereafter.

With one side of his mind this was also how Hawthorne himself thought. He was attracted to the idea of writing "tales of my native land" (the working title of an early, uncompleted project). He was one of the several dozen antebellum New England authors who answered lawyer-orator Rufus Choate's call for a series of New England-based fictions—in a lecture given in Hawthorne's native Salem, Massachusetts—that would rival Scott's Waverley novels (Choate 1852, 1: 319-46). Hawthorne was by far the most talented of the lot (Bell). Historically ordered, his colonial tales together with his first three book-length romances constitute an episodic epic of New England history from the first generation of settlement through Transcendentalist communitarianism.

Yet with another side of his mind, Hawthorne doubted whether a distinctively national fiction or narrative was possible or even desirable. Much of his late writing was devoted to the Anglo-American connection and unfinished romances of ancestral linkage and/or inheritance. His American masterpiece indicates a hesitancy about the viability of the story of an autonomous American history repeated soon afterward in seriocomic form in his last published historical tale, "Main-Street," in which an earnest, voluble, but self-undermining showman attempts to stage a series of tableaux of colonial history to a marginally invested audience of townsmen, only to break down during the Great Snow of 1717 when his crude mechanical contrivance fails. So much for the patriotic boosterism of Rufus Choate.

In *The Scarlet Letter,* likewise, the story of Hester and Arthur is not shown as having any lasting American issue. The mother country is pictured wistfully as a place of healthy vitality and merriment, the new world of Puritan Boston seen as a diminished shadowland by contrast. "We have yet to learn again the forgotten art of gaiety," the narrator sighs (232) as he describes the book's one festive scene. "The Custom-House" portrays a nineteenth-century America already moribund. That this was an age of unparalleled national expansion and economic growth one could never tell from Hawthorne's essay. The author's home town is in decay. The country doesn't seem to be going anywhere. That is perhaps the most strikingly idiosyncratic aspect of this novel's vision of history: not its representation of Puritan nostalgia for the mother country (for many Puritans *did* return home, as Hawthorne would have known); not the comparison between Puritan austerity and latter-day lightening-up (already a cliché in Hawthorne's day), but rather the sense that the whole new world experiment may be fizzling out. Two centuries of New England history end in the anticlimax of the aptly named Custom-House.

This was not, of course, the biographical Hawthorne's full view of the matter. In other moods, George Dekker usefully reminds us, "Hawthorne could argue earnestly that the sadly imperfect liberal democracy nurtured in the United States, and especially in New England, was the best hope of mankind" (Dekker 1987, 170). This may even have been his prevailing view as a citizen. But it was not a view that Hawthorne could make prevail in either his fictive renditions of New England or in his history for children, *Grandfather's Chair,* neither of which manages to draw the line between colonial New England and the present-day national efflorescence that was axiomatic to the likes of Choate and Daniel Webster, not to mention the New England-dominated schoolbook industry of Hawthorne's day. In *The Scarlet Letter,* the one moment during either the introduction or the romance proper that the grand narrative is told with any enthusiasm, it remains inaudible and suspect. That is the point before the denouement when Dimmesdale sermonizes on the glorious destiny of New England—a standard topic for ministers on certain ceremonial occasions, then and (even more) in Hawthorne's day. *The Scarlet Letter* makes sure to put the reader at a great distance from this performance—outside the church alongside Hester, who doesn't catch a word of it. All we know for sure is that Dimmesdale is in an abnormal and agitated state. His rapturous prophecy is not to be believed.

The skepticism Hawthorne generally evinces toward historical pieties in both "The Custom-House" and *The Scarlet Letter* has generally been explained in Americanist terms. Lauren Berlant brilliantly reads Hawthorne as offering "a counter-National Symbolic marked by a hermeneutic of negativity and defamiliarization" (Berlant 1991, 34). Catherine Jones, in a thoughtful comparative discussion of the uses of history and tradition in Hawthorne and Scott, sees in Hawthorne a distinctly American tendency to disown the past. ("The self-definition of America precludes direct access to a continuous folk memory" [Jones 2000, 136].) There is much to be said for these views of the case: the image of Hawthornian narrative practice as a process of wily skeptical negotiation within certain forms of ideological blockage attendant upon his inevitable embeddedness within his national and/or regional culture at a particular point in time. But we also need to question the prior assumption that the most fruitful way to situate Hawthorne should be in terms of his or his text's standing as an "American" discourse, whether acquiescent or dissenting. The cosmopolitanism of perspective that his historical fictions imply in the course of engaging in their provincial struggles—as with *The Scarlet Letter*'s glimpses backward to the motherland, or the intertextual knot at the close—may indeed be so construed, but it is hardly imperative so to construe them. Hester's return to Boston to her old role as letter-wearer, which Sacvan Bercovitch reads—thoughtfully, subtly, learnedly—as an enactment of the national covenant of consent (Bercovitch 1991),[6] might also be conceived as confirmation of the impoverished options to which the decision to emigrate condemns one. The old world past cannot be disowned in this romance because the new world avatar is only a diminished version of the old.

The reduction of the protagonists to ghosts of their former selves shows this plainly enough. Dimmesdale "had come from one of the great English universities, bringing all the learning of the new age into our wild forest-land" (66). It's all downhill from there. Internalization of the provincial thought police socializes him into such timidity that Hester's challenge in the forest ("[B]e a scholar and a sage among the wisest and the most renowned of the cultivated world. Preach! Write! Act!") sickens rather than invigorates him (198). Hester's mind, by contrast, expands to the point that she assumes "a freedom of speculation, then common enough on the other side of the Atlantic." But by colonial Puritan standards this is "a deadlier crime than that stigmatized by the scarlet letter" (164). In this brave new world, what Hester has become cannot socially exist. Despite the fact that *The Scarlet Letter* takes place entirely on American soil, despite its attention to colonial culture and institutions, despite its having been written in the heyday of national expansion, it remains at heart a diasporic rather than a nativized imagination of place, in the sense that the standard of cultural vitality remains transatlantic and colonial life and culture by contrast diminished, underactualized, and without issue—with characters, narrator, author all self-consciously detached from the new world place that is supposed to be their habitat.

As such, *The Scarlet Letter* seems less a reflection on issues of national consensus and less a template for narratives of American nationalization than a story of transnational dislocation whose investment in issues of nationhood is peripheral at best. To the extent that we take it as a barometric indicator or reference point for new world imagination, its closest affiliations are narratives of rebuffed or imperfect assimilation of a place conceived through unassimilated eyes as alien ground, from the narratives of Mary Rowlandson and Olaudah Equiano to James's *The Europeans* to Cather's *O Pioneers!* and Flannery O'Connor's "The Displaced Person" to Chang Rae Lee's *Native Speaker* and *A Gesture Life.* Like all these texts and others like them, *The Scarlet Letter* does not so much insinuate "Here is national fiction" as pose the question: "Can there be such a thing?" or "Why should there be?"

2

Here, then, is the "problem of 'American' fiction" *The Scarlet Letter* exemplifies and to which the title of this essay alludes. The cultural work that *The Scarlet Letter* has been made to perform is not quite the work it undertakes to perform. The book is arguably not an "American" performance so much as one that critical and creative repossessions have by and large tended to Americanize in ways that play down its cosmopolitan and deracinated aspects. In this respect, it is hardly unique among the canonical writings of our literary history. On the contrary, the larger significance of belaboring the point at hand is precisely that it is exemplary of a much larger-scale foreshortening of vista. The foreshortening I have described is akin to the centripetalism that leads Americanists to claim Equiano as an "American" writer or to block out the transnationalism of (say) Melville's account of business culture in "Bartleby the Scrivener" (Why not Dickens? Why not Gogol? Why not Joyce's "Counterparts"?). The examples are endless, especially for immigrant and expatriate writing. But *The Scarlet Letter* is an especially imposing case, insofar as more than any other premodern American novel it has come to stand as a point of origin in the history of American literary-cultural emergence and as a point of textual origin for later artists. Few other novels have seemed for so many critics so pivotal for the solidification of national historical imagination.

Indeed, the sequence of American reinventions of *The Scarlet Letter* plot from Frederic and James to Updike and Mukherjee—the legacy of Hawthorne's masterpiece as a master-plot for national writers—has unquestionably helped to create a solider sense of national literary tradition than Hawthorne could ever have felt. The ironic effect of this remarkable success story is its tendency to distract one from how desolidifying a text *The Scarlet Letter* is—although the plethora of rewritings testifies to that, too. "Most persons of ability," Emerson remarks, "meet in society with a kind of tacit appeal," as if to imply "I am not all there" (Emerson 1971-, 3: 127). *The Scarlet Letter* imparts just such an impression through its structural tightness, its laconic restraint of emotional tone, and its oscillation of narrative judgment—suggesting tortuous, self-conflicted operation within the reluctant confines of the mind's own making. Among the various explanations for the amount of exegesis and reenactment that *The Scarlet Letter* has provoked, *one* is that its uneasy, self-conscious narratorial reticence invites second-guessing reappraisal and active rewriting of the author's version of his own tale. That is why it is not *utterly* outrageous for the 1990s Hollywood adaptation of *The Scarlet Letter* to end with the Indians rescuing Hester, Dimmesdale, and Pearl and burning down Boston. For the narrator repeatedly emits signals to the effect that he might wish that things could work out differently, even though he fears they can't and (in some moods, particularly near the end) agrees they shouldn't.

One of the book's early reviewers praised *The Scarlet Letter* on just such grounds: for the author's ethical restraint, allowing "his guilty parties to end, not as his own fancy or his own benevolent sympathies might dictate, but as the spiritual laws, lying back of all persons dictated to him" (Whipple 346). Modern readers have tended by contrast to long for a breakaway from the book's self-imposed emotional/ethical/

ideological confines—most especially as they constrain its heroine. So Frederic I. Carpenter, in the classic essay in this vein, assigns Hawthorne a grade of A-minus for inability to get past "emotional" to full "intellectual" realization of Hester's potential for "embodying the authentic American dream of freedom and independence in the new world" (Carpenter 1944, 180). Since the advent of critical feminist studies, debate around the general issue of whether the narrative undercuts Hester has continued—at a far higher level of sophistication—as in Nina Baym's defenses of *The Scarlet Letter*'s feminism ("Hester has certainly changed the Puritans more than they have changed her") and David Leverenz's critique of its misogyny (Baym 1986, 29; cf. Baym 1976, 142-51; Leverenz 1983). Even more variable have been the fictive rewritings of Hester, such as Frederic's flirtatiously sophisticated Celia Madden; Faulkner's matriarch-victim Addie Bundren; Updike's wily, self-indulgent, misnamed Sarah Worth; and Mukherjee's picaresque world-traveling Hannah Easton. Read them in a series, throw in for good measure the filmic Hesters from Lilian Gish to Demi Moore, and well might the curious interpreter perplex him or herself with the question: "Whose Hawthorne?"

Even if one agrees that *The Scarlet Letter* is the kind of text that provokes revision, it does not follow that the revisions thereby provoked will question the legitimacy of reading Hawthorne in Americanist terms. Indeed, few of the just-mentioned texts do so. One that does, however, and with a metahistorical self-consciousness whose perspicacity compensates for its intervals of zany froth, is Mukherjee's ***The Holder of the World*** (1993). This novel is equally instructive for its resistance to *The Scarlet Letter*'s status as a founding document in the history of imagined nationness and for the form in which it eventually succumbs to a version of the temptation that it critiques in Hawthorne.

The Holder of the World features a female latter-day narrator, Beigh Masters, who, like Hawthorne, is a skilled historian conscious of her family's New England antecedence, nominally engaged in money-making ("asset management") but overtaken—more wholeheartedly than Surveyor Hawthorne—by an identification with the novel's primary Hester-figure, Hannah. (***Holder*** also features two other characters provocatively named Hester.) This Hannah is not an immigrant but a Massachusetts frontier child whose widowed still-youthful mother deserts her during King Philip's War for the sake of her Indian lover. Thus begins a picaresque plot that takes Hannah through a Puritan girlhood in Salem, brief residence in London, then to the original India—the obverse transit from that of the Indo-American author. There she becomes the mistress of the ruler of a Hindu state, fleeing it after his death (which she unintentionally helps bring about) at the hands of the Moghul emperor in order to return to New England with her unborn child, predictably named Pearl. The shady merchant-pirate who whisks her from Salem to England to India is a blow-up of the swashbuckling sea captain who makes a cameo appearance near the end of *The Scarlet Letter*, contracting to take Hester, Dimmesdale, and Pearl back to England. Hannah's marriage to Gabriel Legge, in order to escape stultifying Salem, is one of several exploitations of *The Scarlet Letter*'s fleeting glimpses of the wider, livelier world beyond—and behind—the infant colony.[7]

Hannah's extrication from her stiff, monitorial Puritan foster-parents does not save her from a series of irksome domestic enclosures thereafter. But it makes for a vertiginous and mind-expanding *peripeteia* starkly different from *The Scarlet Letter*'s intense confinement. Hawthorne multiculturalized, Hawthorne transnationalized, Hawthorne in technicolor. *Holder* wants to put the New England experiment in the global Anglophone context just barely visible in Hawthorne's text: to connect the remotest ends of Empire, and dramatize in the process the hyperactive, raffish fortuity of colonial enterprise, as against the tightly regimented affair *The Scarlet Letter* foregrounds. Significantly, two of the clues by means of which the narrator reconstructs Hannah's lifeline are a youthful fantasy-sampler of "the uttermost shore"—yes, like Hester Prynne, Hannah is deft with the needle—and an Indian artist's renditions of "the Salem Bibi": two happenstance mirror images of the termini of the Anglophone world.

In all this one sees a more lighthearted version of Carpenter's judgmentalism: *The Scarlet Letter* lacked the courage of its best convictions. Hawthorne "sh[ied] away from the real story of the brave Salem mother and her illegitimate daughter," even though it was Hannah's "stories of the China and India trade" that induced Hawthorne's great-grandfather to become the first of the clan to go to sea (Mukherjee 1993, 283-85). In applying her corrective, Mukherjee's narrator far outdoes "The Custom-House"'s ponderously whimsical anecdote of imagined reconnection with the past, when the surveyor puts the moth-eaten letter to his chest and feels that strange, unexpected pulsation of heat. With the aid of virtual reality simulation software designed by her Indian boyfriend, an MIT researcher, Beigh is transported back to the moment Hannah and her servant-companion Bhagmati (whom she has renamed Hester after a childhood friend) are fleeing the emperor with "the world's most perfect diamond." One-upping Hawthorne, Beigh feels the diamond as it is handed off by faltering Hannah to the fleeing Bhagmati/Hester, feels herself mowed down by the sharpshooter's bullets that mortally wound Bhagmati, then feels herself wield Bhagmati's knife and "plunge the diamond into the deepest part of me" (283). The boyfriend's program

doesn't get Beigh precisely where she'd expected—into *Hannah's* mind/body—but at least she meets Hannah (virtually) face to face.

Given *Holder*'s insistence on deterritorializing Hawthorne, one of its most arresting moves is its Americanization of the denouement. Mukherjee's Hester *and* Pearl come back to New England to stay. What's more, they come back as proto-republican libertarians. "'We are Americans to freedom born!' White Pearl and Black Pearl [their local nicknames] were heard to mutter, the latter even in school." *Holder* here sets itself against Hawthorne's "morbid introspection into guilt and repression that many call our greatest work. . . . He wrote," she adds, "against the fading of the light, the dying of the old program, the distant memory of a shameful, heroic time," whereas *this* novel seeks to "bring alive the first letter of an alphabet of hope and of horror stretching out, and back to the uttermost shores" (285, 286). This is intriguingly congruent with Colacurco's and Bercovitch's diagnoses of a Hawthorne fascinated by America's Puritan origins—although *Holder* posits a(n even) more culturally embedded Hawthorne and arrives at the diagnosis through a very different route: locating national beginnings in the experience of global roaming rather than in the localized Puritan experiment per se.

Holder might have given *The Scarlet Letter* more credit for anticipatory resistance to Americanist-centripetal historical criticism. For *The Scarlet Letter* anticipates something of Mukherjee's geocultural plenitude at those moments when it pauses to wonder whether "we perhaps exaggerate the gray or sable tinge" of early Puritan manners, when, after all, these "were native Englishmen, whose fathers had lived in the sunny richness of the Elizabethan epoch; a time when the life of England, viewed as one great mass, would appear to have been as stately, magnificent, and joyous, as the world has ever witnessed" (230). Asides like this one show that the author was aware—as was his heroine—that *The Scarlet Letter*'s here and now was not the whole seventeenth-century world, certainly not the whole Anglo-phone world and indeed not even the whole world of early Massachusetts settlement culture. Such passages are calculated fissures in the seeming monolith, standing invitations to tell this provincial tale differently if one feels so moved. But nothing more than hints. *The Scarlet Letter* finally leaves it to the curious inquirer to decide whether to read the book more as an open secret (deliberately a fragment of all that it knows might be said) or as a closed book (a resolutely self-contained local tale "of human frailty and sorrow" [48] notwithstanding whatever cracks and fissures). *The Holder of the World* seems—too hastily—to have presumed the latter intent, at least for the purpose of establishing by contrast its own wider geocultural horizon.

Mukherjee is not alone in this sort of rewriting. English novelist Christopher Bigbsy's concurrent *Hester* (1994) is in some ways an even more de-centered retelling than *The Holder of the World.* Its best energies are devoted to the in-England, voyage-over, and pre-*Scarlet Letter* back-story of Hester's involvements with Chillingworth and Dimmesdale. Bigsby's elaboration of Hawthorne's Hester's memory-snatches, on the scaffold, of her former family and married life are comparable to Mukherjee's exfoliation of Hawthorne's skipper into Gabriel Legge; and the result is almost as much of a re-Englishing of *The Scarlet Letter* as *Adam Bede.* The New England phase of the novel, particularly the recapitulation of *The Scarlet Letter* plotline, is perfunctory by comparison to the earlier life and adventures of the three principals. *Holder of the World* expends an even smaller percentage of text than *Hester* on American shores; but it is careful to begin in New England initially so as to make its protagonist an American original whose idiosyncracies are brought out, broadened, then returned home through globalization. The contrast makes sense in light of Mukherjee's insistence that "I am an American writer, in the American mainstream, trying to extend it . . . I am not an Indian writer, not an exile, not an expatriate. I am an immigrant" (Alam 1996, 11). So *Holder of the World,* relative to *Hester,* participates in the "Americanization" of *The Scarlet Letter,* even as it critiques Hawthorne for Yankee parochialism. Participates not only in the sense that *Holder* finally becomes still another self-identified American writer's rewriting of an American classic, but also in that it strives to makes its version of *The Scarlet Letter* into an image of/reflection on Americanness no less strenuously than do (say) Updike or Berlant or Bercovitch in their own quite different ways. So too with Toni Morrison's *Beloved,* whose reweaving of the tropes of the pariah-mother, the elf-child, and remembered diaspora turned potential cul de sac constitute in its own way perhaps the single most brilliant contemporary heterodox re-Americanization of *The Scarlet Letter* plot, though less to my purpose here since for Morrison *The Scarlet Letter* is a secondary and more occluded pretext.[8]

Altogether, the 500-year palimpsest from Marvell to Mukherjee reviewed here shows, I hope, that the absorption of *The Scarlet Letter* as American discourse makes cultural-historical sense, but that it is not the only plausible outcome. The romance offers itself as a portable archetype. "The Puritan community in *The Scarlet Letter,*" as Baym declares, can be thought of as "a symbol of society in general" (Baym 1976, 141). Solemn visitants to Hester's grave who "on a certain day still lay blood-red roses in the tangled grass," opines Bigsby's narrator in similarly generalizing fashion, "tell the story of a woman's love and of man's capacity for good and ill" (Bigsby 1994, 186). England, New England, India, the essential story is the same, one might argue. This is not to deny the presence of cultural particularities. Bercovitch writes no less cogently that "Hawthorne rendered Puritan intolerance more vividly than any other historical novelist," because "better than any other" he understood the complexities of Puritanism *"as an interpretive community"* (emphasis in original)—as well as both the dead and living dimensions of that legacy for the nineteenth century (Bercovitch 1991, 48). But then again, insofar as Puritanism itself is diasporic, one might reply that Hawthorne's chief glory is of a transcultural kind: to have represented Puritan doctrines "as an expression of an enduring states of the human soul," or to have rendered Puritanism "lyrically, with a purity of intensity of focus which makes it, for the time, inescapable" (Manning 1990, 181). And beyond that, insofar as the Puritan experiment in Massachusetts was but a variant manifestation of the Anglophone diaspora generally, an experiment itself fissiparous and pluriform, should not a more sprawling and unglued diasporic rendition like Mukherjee's be prized, however fanciful at certain points?

There is no end to such rumination. No end to the reinterpretations and the retellings. After 150 years, it is clear that the percolation effect of *The Scarlet Letter* won't diminish anytime soon, and with it the multiplication of possible Hawthornes. Lionel Trilling anticipated this, though somewhat grudgingly. For Trilling, some versions (the modernist) were undeniably closer to the true Hawthorne than others (James's), and there seemed something wrong with Hawthorne's artistry "in the degree that he does not dominate us" but leaves us with unresolved questions. In closing, Trilling went so far as to blame Hawthorne for instilling in readers the "sensation of having been set at liberty. . . . We find ourselves at a loss and uncertain in the charge of an artist so little concerned to impose upon us the structure of his imagination." Yet in final qualification Trilling speculates that even though "our judgment of Hawthorne may have to be that he is not for today, or perhaps not even tomorrow," he may nonetheless, as Nietzsche remarks in another context, be "one of the spirits of yesterday—and the day after tomorrow" (Trilling 1964, 457). Early-twenty-first-century postmodern transnationalism bears this speculation out. Today Hawthornian indeterminacy (at the heart of James's admiration for Hawthorne's delicacy, I think) is more in phase. No longer does it seem necessary to posit, much less to defend, *an* essential Hawthorne. We can feel more at home with the kind of interpretative liberty *The Scarlet Letter* invites, even while holding its narration under restraint.

The particular form of liberty for which this essay has argued, is willingness to suspend, even if not to scrap, the assumption that *The Scarlet Letter* must be read as a symptomatically "American" tale, as a cornerstone of "American literature." It can, of course, be so read. It will continue to be so read. But it is neither necessary nor desirable that it should inevitably be so read. And if it is to be so read, it should be in consciousness of the extraterritorial circles of discourse, history, and migration lurking—often unseen by Americanist eyes—in such underexplored portions of the text as the encrypted closing allusions, and elaborated in transnational readings and repossessions of Hawthorne of the past dozen years or so. Reimagining in such terms a text like *The Scarlet Letter*—so salient and durable a cornerstone in the organization of Americanist thinking about national narrative imagination—might go a long way toward a more expansive understanding of how "American" narratives actually do take form and work.

Notes

1. For preparation of this essay I am grateful to Jared Hickman.

2. It is important to stress that Tompkins does not deny the excellence of Hawthorne or *The Scarlet Letter*; her concern is rather to demonstrate the contingency as against the inevitability of what counts as literary merit. As such she provides a more self-consciously theoretical account than Trilling does—though by no means the only possibly account—of the instability of what counts as "our Hawthorne."

3. The first comprehensive critical formulation of the romance-as-American-fictional-difference hypothesis was Chase. The most influential attack has been Baym (1976, 1981). The two most significant recent attempts at reviving a more critically scrupulous version of the romance hypothesis, in both of which Hawthorne figures significantly, are Budick and Thompson/Link.

4. An earlier scene, however, offers a glimpse of Pearl skipping among the tombstones of the same burying ground, stopping to dance upon "the broad, flat, armorial tombstone of a departed worthy,—perhaps of Isaac Johnson himself," the lot's first owner.

5. Hawthorne wrote his sister Elizabeth in 1820 that he had read all of Scott's books except for *Lord of the Isles* (*Letters, 1813-1843*, 132). His son Julian Hawthorne remembered his father reading aloud to the family "the whole of Walter Scott's novels" a few years before his death (J. Hawthorne 2: 9).

6. Like Berlant's serendipitously concurrent study, Bercovitch argues that "Hawthorne sought to rise above [party] politics not by escaping history, but by representing it ironically" (Bercovitch 1991, 107).

7. Of the several critical discussions of Mukherjee as a reviser of Hawthorne, the most helpfully informative and satisfyingly complex to my mind is Newman, although I disagree with its argument that the novel attempts a "deconstruction" of new historicism.

8. For published discussions of Hawthorne-Morrison, see especially Stryz. I am especially indebted, however, to a comparative study still in ms. by C. Namwali Serpell, "Ghostly Secrecy and Palimpsest Secrecy."

Rocío G. Davis (essay date 2006)

SOURCE: Davis, Rocío G. "Performing Dialogic Subjectivities: The Aesthetic Project of Autobiographical Collaboration in *Days and Nights in Calcutta*." In *Literary Gestures: The Aesthetic in Asian American Writing*, edited by Rocío G. Davis and Sue-Im Lee, pp. 159-72. Philadelphia, Pa.: Temple University Press, 2006.

[*In the following essay, Davis identifies* Days and Nights in Calcutta *as a dual-perspective collaborative autobiography.*]

Subverting traditional autobiographical structure to deploy originative formal and aesthetic concerns—a correlate to revised perceptions on subjectivity, identity, and ethnicity—is a prevalent strategy in contemporary Asian American life writing. The increasingly dialogic nature of life writing reflects a multi-voiced cultural situation that allows the subject to control the tensions between personal and communal dialogues within texts that signify discursively. Issues of self-representation—with its attendant concerns with identity politics, the rewriting of history, and the attempt to validate personal and social experience—become central to the autobiographical strategies employed by many Asian American writers as they perform individual and relational processes of self-awareness. Maxine Hong Kingston's *The Woman Warrior* and Michael Ondaatje's *Running in the Family,* for example, articulate physical and psychological disruption through postmodern collagic texts. Similarly, Sara Suleri's *Meatless Days* and Garrett Hongo's *Volcano: A Memoir of Hawai'i* use the short-story cycle to enact their accounts of personal and locational affiliation.[1] In this essay, I read Clark Blaise and Bharati Mukherjee's collaborative autobiography, ***Days and Nights in Calcutta,*** as a formal subversion of genre that occasions a renewed aesthetic.[2] Via a doubled journal that offers contradictory/complementary perspectives on the experience of a year in India, Blaise and Mukherjee enact a regenerated formal and aesthetic experience based on a dialogue between two independent texts, suggesting an alternative model for self-inscription.

Collaborative autobiographies challenge the fundamental paradigm of the unified self of traditional autobiography, as well as the concept of monologic representation. Indeed, the renewed formal and aesthetic experience of these autobiographical texts stems precisely from the tension created by a dialogue. Collaborative writing, defined succinctly as a text composed by more than one person—as-told-to, ghostwritten, and coproduced or collectively produced texts—is the clearest textual manifestation of this phenomenon.[3] Asian American collaborative life writing exercises illustrate how this strategy was, on occasion, fundamental to the writing and/or publication of the text. Jeanne Wakatsuki Houston's story of Japanese American internment, *Farewell to Manzanar,* was written with her husband, James.[4] The role of the editor was crucial to the publication of Mary Paik Lee's *Quiet Odyssey: A Pioneer Korean Woman in America,* as it was Sucheng Chan's enthusiasm for Lee's story that led her to revise, complete, and publish it.[5] Autobiographic collaboration also features ostensibly equal participation of both subjects, such as that evidenced in Blaise and Mukherjee's texts, or enacted by Maylee Chai and Winberg Chai in *The Girl from Purple Mountain,* a dialogue between a father and daughter about his mother, where familial, historical, and diasporic concerns are woven into the story of three generations of a Chinese American family.[6] The interaction between the participants in this autobiographic act reconfigures the traditional idea of a monologic narrative as it interrogates the relationship between lives and narrative construction, stressing the discursive potential behind generic choice.

Collaborative texts that enact a dialogue between two voices—two positions—radically alter not only the idea of individual self-representation but also that of autobiographical form and process. To authorize a dialogue, rather than the traditional monologue, as the central discursive strategy in life writing texts suggests a multilayered project with formal and cultural resonances. One of the constitutive thematic/textual markers of this renewed autobiographical exercise involves an emphasis on the intersection of biography and autobiography, locating the narrating subject most often in a community—family or ethnic group.[7] The relational configuration of autobiography controls the shape of the text, leading to originative formal choices. By reading Blaise's and Mukherjee's *Days and Nights in Calcutta,* I address the project of collaborative autobiography as a performative act that renegotiates critical concepts of the self-in-autobiography and proposes a new literary form of negotiating the transcultural position of Asian American writers.[8] Deploying an innovative formal operation, *Days and Nights in Calcutta* advocates a renewed aesthetic mode of performing the narrative processes of subjectivity: the text *enacts* the relation as it/that it *narrates.* Moreover, this form of collaboration is increasingly being reinterpreted, as Sidonie Smith and Julia Watson suggest, "as arenas and occasions of a dialogical process shared among two or more voices."[9] As Susanna Egan notes:

> Parallels between life and text become even closer when both subjects are involved in the preparation of the text. Narration then takes the form of dialogue; it

becomes interactive, and (auto)biographical identification becomes reciprocal, adaptive, corrective, affirmative, as is also common in life among people who are close to each other. . . . These autobiographies, in other words, do not reflect life so much as they reflect (upon) their own processes of making meaning out of life.[10]

Days and Nights in Calcutta illustrates the writers' negotiation of immigration and ethnic affiliation, as these inform their relationship and their writerly processes. Blaise and Mukherjee combine their journals to emphasize the intersection of ethnic, social, familial, and personal positions precisely because each of them, as individuals, occupy differing locations in the structure. Questions of position, power, and agency are assessed through dialogue. As separate but significantly linked individuals with different perspectives on the manner in which racial and ethnic identity functions in their societies, the dialogic structure of the text dramatizes the processes that lead Blaise and Mukherjee to rethink their positions. These autobiographical documents factor their innovative formal process through simultaneous operations of conflict and dialogue, and by providing a sense of both performance and mutual spectatorship. To have one's opinions, perspectives, and stories complemented or challenged by an (ostensibly) equally authoritative voice *within the text itself* stresses the dialogic element, making the relationship, rather than the individuals, the center of the text. Blaise's and Mukherjee's chronicles—written independently but structured in the published text to perform the dialogue—gives the reader a renewed life-reading experience that promotes the potential of narrative structuring in transcultural contexts. Importantly, it also requires us to reexamine autobiography, as Albert Stone suggests, as "*occasion, script, performance, process* rather than simply as form or literary genre."[11] Collaborative autobiography illustrates the points that Stone notes in superlative ways, and this paradigm allows us to discern the nuances of Blaise and Mukherjee's formal and aesthetic project. By privileging the relational and the dialogic, the text acquires elevated discursive potential. Moreover, the dialogue textually enacts the complicated transcultural positioning that the writers have to engage in their lives. This collaborative autobiographical act becomes, simultaneously: an *occasion* for dialogue, the negotiation of the *script* of that dialogue, the *performance* of subjectivity, and a discursive *process.* The analysis of *Days and Nights in Calcutta* will proceed according to the approach Stone proposes and that I negotiate paradigmatically in the context of both formal renovation and transcultural position. This approach organically deploys the literary, critical, and cultural concerns of the texts as they intersect with personal and social issues in the context of self-representation.

In the first place, the *occasion* is, as Egan notes, the "real presence" of the speakers, confirmed "by the responsiveness of each to the other and by the fact that their dialogue is comprehensible only in terms of the involvement of both"[12] and authorized by the autobiographical pact. ***Days and Nights in Calcutta*** is composed of journals that Blaise and Mukherjee kept on a year's sabbatical in India, after a series of unfortunate accidents (Blaise breaks his wrist, their house burns down, and their car is wrecked) led them to leave Canada with their two young sons. The journals are framed by a prologue by Blaise and epilogues, written for the book's publication in 1977 and reissue in 1995. The first part of the text is written by Blaise and the second by Mukherjee; similar events, themes, questions, and changing perspectives are engaged by each. Notably, the two sections do not directly refer to each other and there is no textual evidence that the two writers read each other's journals. This structure evinces how Blaise and Mukherjee posit the center of their autobiographical exercise as occurring precisely in the space between their individual positions and independent texts. The autobiographical occasion occurs in writing that creates a dialogue, opening up a third space for relational selfhood. Their contrasted positions on cultural and ethnic affiliation, family obligations, the role of the writer, and questions of diasporic belonging obliges them to reexamine the basis of their marriage. The challenge of a journal, and the tension that characterizes it, derives from the writers' lack of foreknowledge about outcomes of the plot: there is no critical reworking of events nuanced by hindsight, and the reader accompanies Blaise and Mukherjee on this doubled journey of rediscovery of India and of themselves.

India is the central focus of both diaries, and the force that compels them to reappraise their social, cultural, and personal positions. Blaise claims that "From the moment we landed, India conspired to write this journal" (10). As a white Canadian married to a Bengali Brahmin, Blaise is welcomed by his wife's relatives and given privileged access to cultural and intellectual events. But Mukherjee has to rethink Blaise's position in her life and what she gave up when she married him. In a sense, Blaise's account might be read as a travel journal, as he continually reexamines and rewrites himself in transit. He explains his position in these terms:

> I had my books, my notes, and my husband's heart to say yes to anything my wife's city offered me. Not to hold back, not to judge, not to be shocked, never to say no. I was the *jamai*, the son-in-law, collecting all his wedding gifts ten years late. Though we'd been married ten years, it has been ten years of knowing Bharati on my terms and in my language. The only big adjustment in my life (accomplished with all the groans of a youthful identity crisis) had been a thirty-mile drive over the border to Montreal, the dropping of an accidental American passport, and the reassertion of the Canadian.
>
> (96)

Barry Fruchter suggests that Blaise "at least semiconsciously recuperates the traditional narrative of the Orientalist traveler . . . he uses his senses of irony and ambiguity . . . both as markers to distinguish the writer from his complacent ethnocentric compatriots at home and as badges of pride to keep him aloof from the 'natives' abroad."[13] His eagerness to engage the multifariousness of India reality reinscribes the rhetoric of the "European Grand Tour," where traveling subjects "recorded their observations as educational journeys through successive cultures."[14] Yet, due to his conjugal connection to India, Blaise's intention is more urgent, even if as naïve. Moreover, because of his own history of cultural displacement, Blaise believes that his biracial children also need to connect with India and their family there.

Mukherjee's position is more complex: her marriage to a non-Bengali and, perhaps more important, her economic independence, alienate her from the traditional society she was raised to belong to. The return to her family home and city becomes a painful journey of tentative and frustrated reconnection. The couple's processes are contrasting: Blaise looks outward and moves forward, in a stimulating voyage of discovery as Mukherjee journeys inward and to the past. She finds herself reviewing, reworking, and rewriting the inherited texts of the configuration of the Bengali Brahmin woman she was and has become. In her 1995 epilogue, she admits that the project she had originally embarked upon, "a communal autobiography of the women of my age and my vanishing class who had stayed on in the riot-pocked hometown," was transformed in the process into the "real" story about North America (301-2). Her journal reports her difficult process of trying to reenter that world and the impossibility of belonging to what she had left behind. Her ambivalence is resolved at the end, with her decision to return to Canada, albeit temporarily.

Interestingly, the few published essays on ***Days and Nights in Calcutta*** read the book as unilaterally Mukherjee's autobiography. Barry Fruchter, Pramila Venkateswaran, and Anindyo Roy, for example, discuss the text primarily from the point of view of Mukherjee, relegating her husband's text to, at best, a 164-page introduction.[15] But to discuss Mukherjee's text independently of her husband's is to disregard their generic choice in their life writing exercise. To read this text as anything *but* a carefully constructed collaborative autobiography disables the discursive potential of the text, and fails to acknowledge dialogism as constitutive of the couple's formal and aesthetic strategy. Though

Fruchter does acknowledge, without further discussion, that we cannot discuss Mukherjee's "contribution" to the volume without "[at] least touching on her husband's section, which in a sense sets up a pattern to be answered by hers,"[16] Venkateswaran, obsessed with locating Mukherjee in the context of Indian women believes that the text "derives its power by allowing the collective voices of Calcutta women to take over the narrative."[17] This critical perspective, though it provides fascinating insights to the situation of Indian women and does negotiate the issue of collectivity and collaboration, limits this notion only to the context of the polyphony of voices pertaining to Mukherjee's interactions with women, really only a minor section of her account. Blaise's role as "witness" to his wife's narrative is interpreted in the narrowest possible sense by Venkateswaran. This narrow reading might be explained by Mukherjee's position as a leading Asian American writer, and a political need to privilege her contribution and foreground her section.[18] Roy's essay focuses on Mukherjee's complex aesthetic project, but ignores the evidence that the formal strategy is radically collaborative. Surprisingly, none of these critical articles foreground the fundamental paradigm set up by the writers: the performance of subjectivity precisely *in the act of dialogue* through a specific formal process.

In the second place, the *script* of both dialogues centers on the question of immigration, as well as ethnic, cultural, social, and national affiliation.[19] The experience of India requires both Blaise and Mukherjee to reexamine their views of belonging in society. Blaise's strategy consists of deploying literary and/or journalistic conventions: his acute observations and critical analyses attest to a curious and well-informed intellect at work. His sincere attempts to understand and, in a sense, find a home in his wife's culture illustrate his own perspectives on ethnic affiliation. Yet, having lived all his life in mainstream (read *white*) North America, he cannot comprehend the intricate nuances of Indian cultural and societal norms. He is uncomfortable with his imposed sahib status, the fluidity of social relations, and easy connections with celebrities like Satyajit Ray—the effortless entrance into high society motivate his ambivalence.

The issue of the Indian definition of identity and the manner it is negotiated on a personal and national level fascinates Blaise. "In India, of course," he explains, "identity never has to be sought; it is the lone certainty, and one's identity determines nearly everything. The father decides the son's career as surely as he chooses his daughter's husband. It is his duty to do so, and duty in India is discharged guiltlessly" (93). The peaceful coexistence of apparent contradictions confound him: the position of family servants, the role of parents in organizing their children's lives, the sanctioned separation between classes and castes. This ambivalence, and

the equilibrium between things that appeared diametrically opposed, is partially resolved as Blaise negotiates the nature of Hinduism. Astonished by "moment-by-moment inventiveness within the rigidity" (161) in the elaborate ritual of a relative's wedding, he comprehends: "Of course there was order, even precision, to the ritual, but it was the order and precision of oriental carpetry, of intricate design endlessly repeated and varied, without a clear vanishing point or center of attention" (159). As Egan notes, "emblematic of space absorbing difference and time, Hindu rituals absorb all the contradictions of this composite travelogue."[20] Blaise watches his two sons "praying" with their grandfather, young Bernie transforming the Hindu prayers into his own multilingual chatter: *"Lufthansa, Lufthansa, let down your hair"* (38), to the delight of both Canadian father and Hindu grandfather.

Mukherjee's journey of self-examination yields a painful conflict. She is angered by Westerners' (including her husband's) attitudes toward India, even as she chafes under the restrictions imposed upon her by a position she had abandoned years before. Aware that she is simultaneously envied and pitied—for similar reasons—she finds herself needing to find a place to belong, to call her *desh*, her homeland. She explores the motivations of her immigration, and what her marriage to Blaise has implied—culturally, socially, and personally. She describes herself as a "late-blooming colonial who writes in a borrowed language (English), lives permanently in an alien country (Canada), and publishes in and is read, when read at all, in another alien country, the United States. My Indianness is fragile; it has to be professed and fought for, even though I look so unmistakably Indian" (170). Because of her family history—education abroad and at an elite school run by Irish nuns—Mukherjee and her sisters had grown into another version of the traditional Bengali Brahmin woman. These multiple locations lead her to uncomfortably occupy a liminal position wherever she finds herself. Though Mukherjee makes her home in Canada, it continues to be alien to her, and, as she insists, she to it. She argues that Canada has relegated her to second-class citizenship—she cannot hope to achieve the writerly recognition her husband easily enjoys because of her status as a visible minority. "I am tired of being exotic, being complimented for qualities of voice, education, bearing, appearance, that are not extraordinary," she complains (169). Because of her painful awareness of her multiple liminality, in this time of "sliding convictions," Mukherjee renounces the attitudes of well-meaning scholars at the residence in Calcutta as patronizing or even contemptuous of India; even her husband was not "exempt from my growing disgust" (220). Her suspicions derive from her growing insecurity. As her foreign husband becomes more and more comfortable, she, the native, occupies a more precarious position.

This gap weights more deeply as Mukherjee's narrative progresses and she faces the contradictions of her current intellectual and social dispositions with what she finds in India, within her family and among friends like her. Interestingly, one of the many contradictions of India that this text illustrates is the manner in which, as Egan explains, Mukherjee's conversations with friends "expose both the rigid structures of possibility for women and the permeable nature of boundaries encountered by the talented, the beautiful, the rich, or the lucky."[21] The social formation of high-class Bengalis— outwardly elastic, open, and friendly—was "simultaneously rigid, hierarchical, and exclusive" (213). As Mukherjee reacquaints herself with old friends and finds new ones, she is repeatedly astonished by the flexibility and inconsistency of their concerns: a conversation about Mother Teresa segues easily into a discussion about hairstyles, each one just as passionate. Her eagerness to explore "the social life I had once regarded with irony" (199), marks a crucial point of ambivalence. Her reintroduction into this world requires a complex retrospection of cultural and social awareness. Mukherjee knows that ethnic affiliation in India is inextricably linked to social position, and her place will be defined by the latter as much as by the color of her skin: "In a city [Calcutta] where there are no natural outsides and insides, the phenomenon of the party, like the walls of the compound, is a strategy of self-definition" (213). This phenomenon, unknown and unimaginable in Montreal—and beyond her husband's understanding—modifies preconceptions harbored from a distance. The paradox of her own position—insider/outsider, daughter/prodigal—seen through the eyes of others, begins to significantly alter her own view. She regards the question of leaving India, and returning to it, from the prism of possibilities of reconnecting and reconfiguring a selfhood from a lost history.

This dilemma leads to the third point in the analysis: as Blaise and Mukherjee negotiate the inherited scripts of national and ethnic affiliation, they perform highly unique itineraries of subjectivity. Smith and Watson explain that "a *performative* view of life narratives theorizes autobiographical occasions as dynamic sites for the performance of identities constitutive of subjectivity. In this view, identities are not fixed or essentialized attributes of autobiographical subjects; rather they are produced and reiterated through cultural norms, and thus remain provisional and unstable."[22] Another way of understanding the performative quality of life writing centers on the "act of composition," as Eakin proposes when he posits life writing as a process of "narratively constituted identity."[23] Eakin invites us, in the analysis of these texts, to note the "performance of the collaboration . . . , the relation between the two individuals involved."[24] The roles each writer plays and how one's narrative stance and perspective nuances the other's account must be addressed. This process has implications for Asian American formal negotiations of life writing, which recurrently engages multiply positioned itineraries of subjectivity, as Blaise and Mukherjee demonstrate.

Their differing cultural histories and ethnic posturing are the subtext of Blaise and Mukherjee's performances. In Canada, an officially multicultural nation, Mukherjee's Indianness was an issue negotiated daily, particularly in her professional life. In India, this ethnic affiliation is again subject to interrogation as it intersects with social position. But both writers enact ideas of evolving selfhood in their journals, as individuals and in dialogue. This doubled journal stresses the separate individuals Blaise and Mukherjee are and how their self-revelations, linked to how differing perspectives on ethnic affiliation, torment their relationship. She now confronts the questions that Blaise often asked visiting Bengalis in Montreal: "'What have you given up? Is it worth it?' For the next year, I was to hear her answers, and it has shaken our marriage to its core," he says (104). As the couple examines their relationship through the prisms of ethnic and national affiliation and social class, their text becomes a performance of their evolving perspectives. The experience of India, viewed almost as a rebirth after their Canadian home is consumed in flames, allows them to engage in a significant act of self-invention, a re-presentation in writing. As both had renounced citizenships and made their place in other countries, their multi-locationality contributes to their processes of liminality. To perform these processes in a journal—the form that most clearly rejects finality—signifies discursively.

G. Thomas Couser asserts that collaborative autobiography is "inherently ventriloquistic", obliging us to consider the positions of power in transcultural dual-authored texts.[25] As much as a collaborative text of this nature ostensibly presents a relationship of symmetry and balance, subtle manipulations appear that might correspond to the writers' public roles. Before the writing of the *Days and Nights in Calcutta,* Blaise and Mukherjee were—to differing degrees—already recognized public figures in Canada, the United States, and India. Blaise was a renowned Canadian writer; Mukherjee was denied access to this recognition there. In India, she was the star, he the consort. Perhaps because this book was written in India and deals primarily with India, Mukherjee appears to dominate the text. Her presumably authoritative position leads her to, consciously or not, control the dialogue and performance in the act of collaboration. This point is arguable on many levels: specifically, Blaise's narrative comes first and is longer than his wife's. Yet there is a sense in the text that his account functions as a frame, or even introduction, to hers. In India, Blaise's identity as Mukherjee's husband opens doors and allows him to be accepted as an equal. The identity he performs is, in a sense, intact—he leaves India basically as the same person he was when he arrived. Indeed, the most significant transformations in the text are Mukherjee's revisions of her own ethnic and social position. Blaise returns to Montreal much skinnier (though he gleefully notes that his wife has gained thirty pounds), but essentially the same Canadian intellectual, satisfied by the productivity of his experience.[26]

Mukherjee's performance of identity is much more vexed, and remains unresolved, as her epilogue assures us. The titles of her chapters—"Emblems," "Intimations," "Calcutta"—suggest a romantic impulse to reclaim memories, to find the self she had lost or invented, and reconcile herself with the scripted performance expected of her as a middle-class educated woman of Ballygunge and Calcutta. But her trajectory has subverted that script: she defines "three disproportionate parts"—the traditional joint family, life as a single family, and her reincarnation in the West—where "[e]ach phase required a repudiation of all previous avatars; an almost total rebirth" (179). The third avatar is the most crucial: it signals, in Blaise's words, her obligation to trade in "something in the bargain—their innocence, perhaps, their *place* in some ongoing, creative flow" (75). This is precisely where Mukherjee's complex struggle for position lies: in her attempt to find her place in that "family"—nuclear, joint, and national. Interestingly, some of Blaise's observations elucidate his wife's dilemmas and hint at an important point of contention between them. His initial enthusiasm for his wife's family in Ballygunge ends in frustration. "In India all is finally family," he complains, "If we in the West suffer the nausea of disconnectedness, alienation, anomy, the Indian suffers the oppression of kinship" (92). He likens their stay in her father's house as "a *No Exit,* a closet drama of resentment and dependence among people who, like cellmates, know each other too well to hide a thing" (80). Mukherjee, because of her sense of continual dislocation, yearns for that sense of comfortable stability. She writes that she envies her acquaintances in Montreal, capable of effortlessly enacting image changes, their "confident attempts to remake themselves" (175), something she cannot conceive for herself because she knows that "excess of passion leads only to trouble. I am, I insist, well mannered, discreet, secretive and above all, pliable" (175). Yet she acknowledges her awareness of how an acute sense of irony—developed from her years of study of British novels and membership in English departments—has altered her perspective. Reinserting herself in that place and that family, Mukherjee again falls into the timeless routine of family visits, gossiping with aunts and cousins, listening to All-India Radio. In Calcutta, where they escape to, she occupies another position, that of an Indian memsahib. These separate and contiguous lives "impinged but did not collide" (239). She learns to perform the roles that place demands and expects of her, even as she watches herself, gauging her reactions carefully and analyzing her actions.

Identification with family links with connection to the city, and location in India plays a pivotal role in self-identification. Blaise and Mukherjee's descriptions of Calcutta's streets, alleys, marketplaces, hotels, and homes necessarily limn the intricate relationship of the city with its inhabitants. As Blaise notes, "Bengalis love to explain Calcutta; the identification with the city is so complete that the standard question put to an outsider—'What do you think of Calcutta?'—is a shorthand way of asking, 'What do you think of Bengalis? What do you think of me?'" (64-5). Mukherjee's observations of her husband's way of functioning in her city reflects this identification: he is stereotyped as the typical foreigner, and she observes him as though a stranger, from a distance, appropriating the perspective of her friends who do not understand her choice. More important, propelled by this "misplaced bitterness," she accuses him of forcing expatriation on her, in a desperate fight for her "sanity," understood as her increasingly fragile position (221). As her husband happily performs his role as consort—"[m]y idea of hospitality while in Calcutta would be to give the largest number of people the greatest number of opportunities to entertain me" (95)—he tries to understand her increasing insecurity. Mukherjee reads his well-meaning interest and support as critical interventions to her increasingly complex process of self-negotiation.

This aspect dramatizes the suitability of the collaborative text as a vehicle for the concerns of transcultural subjects: by privileging individual voices as they occupy diverse positions in the retelling of their own history, the genre enacts as it signifies. The discursive process, the fourth element in the analysis, is evidenced as the shifting voices illustrate the negotiation of perspectives, power relations, and the adjustments required in this dialogue. Each voice represents a different position, and the text itself enacts the process of adjustment that Blaise and Mukherjee—Canadian and Indian, white and brown, writer and writer, husband and wife—experience in their year in India. As Mukherjee seeks redefinition by measuring herself against the world she left behind, positing this as "a time to subvert memory, to hunt down sly conciliatory impulses," Blaise's role is that of "witness" to his wife's process (221). But this concept must be interpreted in complex sense—as he watches, his presence interrogates and his conversations provide crucial counterpoints to Mukherjee's engagement with liminality. Significantly, the narrative enactment of that process requires the participation of both parties—a formal and aesthetic choice made consciously by the writers. As Egan argues, "Adjustments between the two narrators also establish each one as the critical reader of the other. . . . Just as this journey calls into question the cultural securities of the

Western white man, requiring him to listen in new ways to his Bengali wife, so too the qualities of narrative, shifting significantly from part one to part two, function responsively, pointing up both harmony and dissonance."[27]

Ultimately, both Blaise and Mukherjee realize that the immigrant positions they have chosen make them outsiders, both in Canada and in India. Moreover, their complacent acknowledgement of the superiority of the West is undermined by the dialogues they have with many in India. After a long conversation with a groom-to-be, one of Mukherjee's cousins, Blaise perceives a concurrent thread of understanding, as he and the boy smile, "doubtless pitying the cultural constrictions of the other's society" (95). Mukherjee repeatedly asks her friends if they would rather live elsewhere, and the answers were inevitably the same: they considered themselves "the luckiest people in the world" (201). After analyzing in detail these women's lives, which continued where hers left off after she immigrated to the United States, Mukherjee increasingly comes to see things from their point of view—acknowledging, for instance, that Western critiques of the Indian system are forms of political and cultural imperialism. These renewed perspectives become weapons that defend her right to self-definition in her marriage, and, in arguments with her husband, she notes that "[t]o defend my friends was to assert my right to differ with him" (202). For Blaise, as for Mukherjee, time in India exposes their different brands of Eurocentrism and deepens their understanding of each other. In her discussion of Mukherjee's aesthetic project, Roy notes the writer's determined amalgamation in limning the possibilities of accommodating "a decidedly Hindu imagination with an Americanized sense of the craft of fiction."[28] In these assertions, Roy argues, Mukherjee negotiates the aesthetic to construct a scheme that readily locates forms of "identity" and "difference": "[t]hese forms are clearly indicative of the stabilization and commodification of a colonized culture by a postcolonial writer whose own authorial gaze corresponds to that of the Orientalizing West."[29] The ambivalences they negotiate require them to refocus their perspectives on the West and India, and the fundamental relations between the two, enacted in their marriage, a microcosm of immigrant complexity. As Egan notes, in this transaction, "center and periphery shift, providing critiques for each other."[30] This is precisely the location of the dialogic enactment of subjectivity, exhibited textually to stress the advantages of the formal mode they deploy.

Mukherjee's section ends with a conciliatory note that illustrates the middle ground arrived at after a painful journey of antithetical and contradictory cultural and social negotiations. Her fervent examination of the malady of the culturally dispossessed and socially dis-

enfranchized becomes muted by the erosion of time. She acknowledges that her idealized—"faintly Chekhovian" (297)—image of India, which had sustained her in cold Canada, had buckled under the reality of the heat and dust. The journal—her "accidental autobiography"—traces her journey "from exile to settler and claimant," secure once more in the decision to return "home" to a city she knows herself displaced from (302). In a sense, it marks a closure to her vexed self-definition as a Bengali and an Indian, as she acknowledges the limitations of the society she had, in immigration, idealized.[31] Her conclusion in the final epilogue promotes a renewed definition of affiliation, wrought out of the processes of the palimpsestic movement: "I want to think that our story—Clark's, our sons', and mine, braided together—is a happy one. Happy because we made our fates out of the many possibilities offered us by destiny. We build our 'homeland' out of expectation, not memory" (303).

For Blaise and Mukherjee, therefore, the construction of their story—individual, interacting, and intersecting lives—enacts a fundamental aspect of their distinct processes of selfhood. This collaborative autobiography charts itineraries of subject dialogue and positionality that obliges us to reevaluate formal and aesthetic paradigms. The resulting text becomes a dynamic chronicle that charts their writers' individual processes of adaptation and renegotiation of previously accepted models, prejudices, and stances. Readers witness the formal dialogue that makes this change happen, participating in the evolution of this relationship. ***Days and Nights in Calcutta*** demonstrates how collaboration as a generic strategy effectively augments possibilities of inscribing the autobiographical project, attending to the relational quality of our lives. Albert Stone has suggested that, if we approach collaboration having abandoned "the belief in literature as a collection of autonomous aesthetic icons and sacred texts, . . . dual-authorship may cease being a literary problem to become rather a cultural solution."[32] The plural positions of these writers, performed though their dialogic life-writing exercise, reflects the shifting boundaries of immigrant representation and illustrates the possibilities of the autobiographical form. ***Days and Nights in Calcutta*** functions as a powerful tool for cultural criticism because of the discursive possibilities of the act of dialogue as the principal strategy life writing exercise that multiplies meaning. As writers explore the genre as *occasion, script, performance,* and *process,* the dialogue signifies on a literary and cultural level. In the context of Asian American life writing, collaborative texts, emblematic of the transcultural position, accommodates not only issues of ethnicity, culture, or nation but, importantly, limn the formal approaches to the narrated subject in his or her act of inscription.

Notes

1. Sara Suleri, *Meatless Days* (Chicago: University of Chicago Press, 1987); Garrett Hongo, *Volcano: A Memoir of Hawai'i* (New York: Alfred A. Knopf, 1995); Maxine Hong Kingston, *The Woman Warrior: Memoir of a Girlhood Among Ghosts* (New York: Knopf, 1975); Michael Ondaatje, *Running in the Family* (New York: Penguin, 1982). See my *Transcultural Reinventions: Asian American and Asian Canadian Short-Story Cycles* (Toronto: TSAR, 2001) for a discussion of Suleri and Hongo.

2. Clark Blaise and Bharati Mukherjee, *Days and Nights in Calcutta* (1977. St. Paul, MN: Hungry Mind Press, 1995). All quotations from this edition will be cited parenthetically within the text.

3. G. Thomas Couser posits a continuum between "ethnographic autobiography, in which the writer outranks the generally anonymous subject, to celebrity autobiography, in which the famous subject outranks the generally anonymous writer. . . . At the very centre are those texts produced by partners who are true peers—for example, dual autobiographies, in which each partner contributes a separate narrative, and truly co-authored (rather than "as-told-to") autobiographies. . . . In these texts there is more than one subject, and the act of collaboration may itself be presented in the foreground of the narrative rather than confined to the background or to supplementary texts" ("Collaborative Autobiography," in *Encyclopedia of Life Writing: Autobiographical and Biographical Forms,* ed. Margaretta Jolly (London: Fitzroy Dearborn Publishers, 2001): Vol. 1, 222.

4. Jeanne Wakatsuki Houston and James D. Houston, *Farewell to Manzanar.* (1973. New York: Bantam, 1995).

5. In her introduction, Chan relates how she encountered Lee's text, and worked with the author to expand the material (*Quiet Odyssey: A Pioneer Korean Woman in America* [Seattle: University of Washington Press, 1990]). Other collaborative texts include Le Ly Hayslip's two volumes of her autobiography—*When Heaven and Earth Changed Places* (New York: Plume, 1990) and *Child of War, Woman of Peace* (New York: Anchor Books, 1993)—the first written with Jay Wurts, and the second with her son, James Hayslip. In *Child of War,* Hayslip speaks briefly about her processes of collaboration (300).

6. *The Girl from Purple Mountain: Love, Honor, War, and One Family's Journey from China to America* (New York: Thomas Dunne Books, 2001).

7. Paul John Eakin, in *How Our Lives Become Stories: Making Selves* (Ithaca, NY: Cornell University Press, 1999), highlights the relational component of life writing, which often intersects with collaboration in autobiography. In Asian American writing, the relational component limned in Kingston's text marks the development of subsequent auto/biographies—in Suleri's *Meatless Days* and Helie Lee's *Still Life with Rice* (New York: Touchstone, 1996), for example—and this concern offers a renewed aesthetic that complicates the concept of the individuality and autonomy of the narrator.

8. I use the term "performative" as Sidonie Smith does in her work on autobiographical storytelling ("Performativity, Autobiographical Practice, Resistance," *A/b: Auto/Biography Studies* 10. [1995]: 18).

9. Sidonie Smith and Julia Watson, *Reading Autobiography: A Guide for Interpreting Narratives* (Minneapolis, MN: University of Minnesota Press, 2001): 149.

10. Susanna Egan, *Mirror Talk: Genres of Crisis in Contemporary Autobiography,* (Chapel Hill, NC: University of North Carolina Press, 1999): 7-8.

11. Albert E. Stone, "Collaboration in Contemporary American Autobiography," *Revue Francaise D'Etudes Americaines* 14 (May 1982): 164.

12. Egan, *Mirror Talk*: 9-10.

13. Barry Fruchter, "Bharati Mukherjee," in *Asian American Autobiographers: A Bio-Bibliographical Critical Sourcebook,* ed. Guiyou Huang (Westport, CT: Greenwood Press, 2001): 258.

14. Smith and Watson, *Reading Autobiography*: 94.

15. Pramila Venkateswaran, "Bharati Mukherjee as Autobiographer," in *Bharati Mukherjee: Critical Perspectives,* ed. Emmanuel S. Nelson (New York: Garland Publishing, 1993): 23-45; Anindyo Roy, "The Aesthetics of an (Un)Willing Immigrant: Bharati Mukherjee's *Days and Nights in Calcutta* and *Jasmine,*" in *Bharati Mukherjee: Critical Perspectives,* ed. Emmanuel S. Nelson (New York: Garland Publishing, 1993): 127-41.

16. Fruchter, "Bharati Mukherjee": 258.

17. Venkateswaran, "Bharati Mukherjee as Autobiographer": 24.

18. Another point concerns the book's editorial history: *Days and Nights in Calcutta* was published first in the United States in 1977 (it was published in Canada in 1986, and reissued with a new prologue and epilogue in the United States in 1995), where Mukherjee's popularity outshines her husband, and where her position as an Asian American subject has made her the focus of critical interest. This editorial consideration, and the desire of Asian American scholars to engage in issues of immigrant and ethnic identity, have led to what I believe is still an unjustified emphasis on Mukherjee in U.S readings of this book.

19. Because my discussion centers primarily on Blaise and Mukherjee's formal and aesthetic project, I will

not discuss the nuances of their positions on ethnicity and nationhood. For a discussion of these issues, see Egan.

20. Egan, *Mirror Talk*: 135.

21. Ibid., 141.

22. Smith and Watson, *Reading Autobiography*: 143.

23. Eakin, *How Our Lives Become Stories*: 139.

24. Ibid., 59.

25. Couser, "Collaborative Autobiography": 223.

26. In his 1995 prologue to the volume, Blaise acknowledges his naïve superiority, his "imperial confidence" that justified his perspective on his experience, and led to some misguided conclusions and predictions about India.

27. Egan, *Mirror Talk*: 138.

28. Roy, "The Aesthetics of an (Un)Willing Immigrant": 198.

29. Ibid., 128-9.

30. Egan, *Mirror Talk*: 136.

31. Fruchter, "Bharati Mukherjee": 262.

32. Stone, "Collaboration in Contemporary American Autobiography": 153.

FURTHER READING

Criticism

Johnson, Robert. "Orbiting Identities: Bharati Mukherjee's Short Stories and the Defamiliarization of Nature." *MAWA Review* 12, no. 2 (December 1997): 87-91.

> Examination of the theme of identity in Mukherjee's short fiction.

Miller, Katherine. "Mobility and Identity Construction in Bharati Mukherjee's *Desirable Daughters*: The Tree Wife and Her Rootless Namesake." *Studies in Canadian Literature* 29, no. 1 (2004): 63-73.

> Consideration of the implications of the Tree-Wife story on the development of identity.

Sarkar, Farida. "Suppression, Frustration, Anger, and the Identity Crisis of Dimple Dasgupta in Bharati Mukherjee's *Wife*." In *Contributions to Bengal Studies: An Interdisciplinary and International Approach,* edited by Enayetur Rahim and Henry Schwarz, pp. 452-62. Dhaka, Bangladesh: Beximco, 1998.

> Provides an extended analysis of Mukherjee's novel *Wife*.

Aleksandr Solzhenitsyn
1918-

(Full name Aleksandr Isaevich Solzhenitsyn) Russian novelist, short story writer, essayist, poet, and nonfiction writer.

The following entry presents an overview of Solzhenitsyn's career through 2006. For further information on his life and works, see *CLC*, Volumes 1, 2, 4, 7, 9, 10, 18, 26, 34, 78, and 134.

INTRODUCTION

Solzhenitsyn is a Nobel prize-winning Russian author and political icon. He is best known for the novella *Odin den' Ivana Denisovicha* (1963; *One Day in the Life of Ivan Denisovich*) and the memoir *Arkhipelag GULag* (1973; *The Gulag Archipelago*), both brutal and, at the time of their publication, shocking accounts of the Soviet labor camps under Communist leader Josef Stalin. Solzhenitsyn was imprisoned for eight years but survived to document the stories he had carefully memorized, not daring to commit them to paper until he was free.

BIOGRAPHICAL INFORMATION

Solzhenitsyn was born in 1918 in Kislovodsk, Russia, and raised by his widowed mother. The family lived in poverty due to the Soviet government's refusal to grant Solzhenitsyn's mother sufficient employment. Early on, Solzhenitsyn became determined to write a great novel about the Bolshevik Revolution which occurred the year before his birth, but first he earned degrees in philology, mathematics, and physics, and in 1941 became a physics professor. In 1945, Solzhenitsyn committed the indiscretion that set the course for his now-fabled life: he criticized Stalin in personal letters which were discovered by counter-intelligence agents and was promptly convicted of conspiring against the State and sentenced to prison. Solzhenitsyn survived eight years in the gulag system and a brush with death due to intestinal cancer, but lived to be released in 1953 into exile in Kok-Terek in Central Asia. There he was able to resume teaching and begin recording and expanding upon all of the works he had previously carried in memory. Three years later, freed from exile, Solzhenitsyn returned to central Russia and, during a brief period of political openness fostered by Nikita Khrushchev, published *One Day in the Life of Ivan Denisovich* to popular success. The fall of the Khrushchev regime brought intolerance for Solzhenitsyn's literary outspokenness, however. He was denied the opportunity to receive his 1970 Nobel Prize in person, and was expelled from Russia in 1974 upon the French publication of *The Gulag Archipelago*. He settled in the United States, establishing a home in Vermont with his wife, Natalia, and did not return to Russia for twenty years. When he did go back, his arrival was not the watershed some might have expected. Boris Yeltsin welcomed him with open arms and Russia's highest honor, the Order of St. Andrew, which Solzhenitsyn refused to accept on the grounds that his mother country was in too much disarray for him to allow himself the indulgence of a prize. After a brief flurry of respectful interest, the populace became largely bored or disillusioned with Solzhenitsyn, and he settled into a daily life of being known by all, grudgingly tolerated by some, yet largely ignored in comparison with previous years where he was relentlessly pursued by the press. Now near 90 years old and in declining health, he continues to write.

MAJOR WORKS

Set in Stalinist Russia, *One Day in the Life of Ivan Denisovich* focuses on a simple prisoner who wants only to serve his sentence of hard labor with Christian integrity. In the novel Solzhenitsyn strove to avoid the aims of Socialist Realism, which reflected the official directives of the state and so imposed thoughts and feelings on its readers. Instead he rendered his tale in an ironic, understated, elliptical manner intended to elicit spontaneous feelings. Despite this book's popular success, most critics consider *V kruge pervom* (1968; *The First Circle*) and *Rakovyl korpus* (1968; *The Cancer Ward*) Solzhenitsyn's principal achievements of the 1960s. Both works are set in institutions isolated from society, feature characters with diverse backgrounds and philosophies, and incorporate Solzhenitsyn's experiences as a prisoner and cancer patient. *The Gulag Archipelago,* a detailed account of Stalinist repression that is widely considered Solzhenitsyn's most important work of nonfiction, emphasizes the fact that arrest and torture were common practices in the Soviet Union. Solzhenitsyn approached the work in a scientific manner, creating a taxonomy of arrests and tortures and inviting readers to participate with him in categorizing forms of physical punishment. Solzhenitsyn also includes accounts of his arrest and confinement in different prisons and concentration camps, as well as many personal narratives from other victims of arbitrary violence. In *The Gulag Archipelago,* Solzhenitsyn finds all Russians—including himself—accountable for the evils of Stalinism. "We didn't love freedom enough," he writes. "We purely and simply deserved everything that happened afterward." *Krasnoe koleso (The Red Wheel),* its first volume published in 1971, is the project Solzhenitsyn dreamed of in his relatively carefree younger years: a series of historic novels chronicling the events leading up to the Bolshevik Revolution.

CRITICAL RECEPTION

Analysis of Solzhenitsyn's work reaches far beyond literary criticism. His influence is significant to those studying the writing of fiction, the critical analysis of literature, the history of Russia, and the politics of resistance. In recent years, many critics have taken a position of respectful indulgence toward Solzhenitsyn's *Red Wheel* series. Such scholars have found it inaccessible to all but the most devoted of scholars while acknowledging the incalculable human effort Solzhenitsyn has devoted to the completion of a project that impassioned him from adolescence, was deferred for decades, and has finally been realized.

PRINCIPAL WORKS

Odin den' Ivana Denisovicha (novella) 1962; translation by Ralph Parker published as *One Day in the Life of Ivan Denisovich,* 1963

Dlya polzy'dela (novella) 1963; translation by David Floyd and Max Hayward published as *For the Good of the Cause,* 1964

Sluchai na stantsii Krechetovka [and] *Matrenin dvor* (novellas; titles mean "An Incident at Krechetovka Station" and "Matryona's House") 1963; translation by Paul W. Blackstock published as *We Never Make Mistakes,* 1963

V kruge pervom (novel) 1968; translation by Thomas P. Whitney published as *The First Circle,* 1968

Rakovyi korpus (novel) 1968; translation by Nicholas Bethell and David Burg published in two volumes as *Cancer Ward,* 1968-69; published as *The Cancer Ward,* 1969

Olen'i shalashovka (play) 1968; translation by Nicholas Bethell and David Burg published as *The Love Girl and the Innocent,* 1969

Svecha na vetru (play) 1968; translation by Keith Armes and Arthur Hudgins published as *Candle in the Wind,* 1973

Krasnoe koleso (novel; title means "The Red Wheel"), Volume 1: *Avgust chetyrnadtsatogo,* 1971, translation by Michael Glenny published as *August 1914,* 1972, revised edition, 1983; Volume 2: *Oktiabr' shestnatsatogo,* 1984, translation by Harry Willetts published

as *November 1916: The Red Wheel, Knot II,* 1999; Volume 3: *Mart semnadtsatogo* (title means "March 1917"), 1986; Volume 4: *Aprel' semnadtsatogo* (title means "April 1917"), 1991

Stories and Prose Poems by Aleksandr Solzhenitsyn (short stories and poems; translated by Michael Glenny) 1971

Nobelevskara lektsira po literature (lecture) 1972; translation by F. D. Reeve published as *Nobel Lecture by Aleksandr Solzhenitsyn,* 1972

*Arkhipelag GULag, 1918-1956: Opyt khudozhestvennego issledovaniia (memoir) 1973; translation published as *The Gulag Archipelago, 1918-1956: An Experiment in Literary Investigation,* Volume 1 (translated by Thomas P. Whitney) 1974, Volume 2 (translated by Whitney) 1976, Volume 3 (translated by Willetts) 1979

Prusskie nochi: pozma napisappaja v lagere v 1950 (poems; title means *Prussian Nights: Epic Poems Written at the Forced Labor Camp, 1950*) 1974

Pis'mo vozhdram Sovetskogo Soruza (nonfiction) 1974; translation by Hilary Sternberg published as *Letter to the Soviet Leaders,* 1974

Solzhenitsyn: A Pictorial Autobiography (autobiography) 1974

Bodalsia telёnok s dubom (memoir) 1975; translation published as *The Oak and the Calf,* 1975; translation by Harry Willetts published as *The Oak and the Calf: Sketches of Literary Life in the Soviet Union,* 1980

Lenin v Tsiurikhe (nonfiction) 1975; translation by Harry Willetts published as *Lenin in Zurich,* 1976

Iz-pod glyb [*From under the Rubble*] (essays, with others; translated by Michael Scammell) 1975; published as *From under the Ruins,* 1975

Rasskazy (short stories) 1976

Kak nam obustroit' Rossiiu? (essay) 1990; translation published as *Rebuilding Russia: Reflections and Tentative Proposals,* 1991

Les Invisibles (memoir) 1992; translation published as *Invisible Allies,* 1995

The Russian Question toward the End of the Century (nonfiction) 1995

Dvesti let vmeste (1795-1995) (history) 2001

*Also published as *Arkhipelag Gulag*; the capitalization in the word GU-Lag derives from an acronym denoting the Russian term for the Chief Administration for Corrective Labor Camps.

CRITICISM

Michael Scammell (essay date 3 December 1998)

SOURCE: Scammell, Michael. "The Solzhenitsyn Archipelago." *New York Review of Books* 45, no. 19 (3 December 1998): 36-40.

[*Below, Scammell offers a comprehensive analysis of Solzhenitsyn's literary and political impact as he reviews D. M. Thomas's biography,* Alexander Solzhenitsyn: A Century in His Life.]

In June 1978, some twenty-two thousand people sat or stood in the rain at Harvard's commencement ceremonies to listen to a keynote speaker denounce them as lacking in courage, morally adrift, and self-deluded. The speaker, whose identity had been kept secret until just two days beforehand, was the celebrated Russian novelist Aleksandr Solzhenitsyn, and the title he chose for his impassioned lecture was **"A World Split Apart."**

Solzhenitsyn's themes were the decline of the West, the moral emptiness of modern society, the excesses of liberal democracy, and the mortal threat to the world of Communist domination. His target was not just modernism but the Enlightenment values that had spawned it, and behind those values the heritage of the Renaissance. Echoing Tocqueville's misgivings at the birth of the American republic, Solzhenitsyn scorned the idea that a government's first duty is to serve the people. "The pursuit of happiness," be argued, had led only to a soulless materialism, a cold and mechanical reliance on the law, and unpardonable license on the part of the citizenry. "In today's Western society, there has opened up a disequilibrium between the freedom to do good deeds and the freedom to do bad."

The ruling classes of the West, according to Solzhenitsyn, had lost their moral bearings and were guilty of a collapse of courage. Eastern Europe was spiritually far in advance of the decadent West. The "complex and deadly pressures" there had developed characters that were "stronger, more profound, and more interesting" than those in the "prosperous, ordered life of the West." For the East to become like the West, he argued, would be for it to lose more than it gained.

I watched Solzhenitsyn's speech on television with a group of friends in a summer house in Connecticut. The people around me had all admired Solzhenitsyn's novels and been immensely impressed by his courage in publishing **The Gulag Archipelago.** They had been outraged by his forcible expulsion from the Soviet Union in 1974. They were also used to having their society excoriated by visitors from other parts of the world, and inclined to agree with them that Americans should be doing more to improve their society.

So they were not surprised when the Harvard audience honored Solzhenitsyn with a tumultuous ovation, acknowledging the Russian's personal magnetism, his literary achievements, and his civic courage. The entire occasion was a kind of public apotheosis, covered extensively in the press and on television afterward. James Reston, George Will, Arthur Schlesinger, Jr., and Archibald MacLeish were among those who commented immediately on Solzhenitsyn's message, and a book of their responses was published later, with additional reflections by Sidney Hook, Richard Pipes, and Michael Novak, among others.[1]

* * *

From the immediate reaction Solzhenitsyn might have been forgiven for thinking that he had influenced American thinking. But most commentators held that although he was an inspiring figure who deserved a hearing, his judgments were too sweeping to bear close examination. His knowledge of American life seemed superficial at best. His claims for Russian spiritual superiority sounded preposterous in the light of what was actually happening in the Soviet Union; his claim of Soviet military superiority flatly contradicted what was known of American arms. As for reversing the Renaissance and the Enlightenment, what did Solzhenitsyn want—a return to the Middle Ages? His speech seemed to express superpatriotism in a new guise, born of the conviction that Russia had to be better than America at something.

The intellectual shortcomings of the speech were all too apparent, and Solzhenitsyn's reputation in the US was badly damaged. He had given similar speeches before, but to less prestigious audiences and with less attention, and he had somehow been given the benefit of the doubt. No longer. Solzhenitsyn, who, despite his expressed contempt for the press and television, paid close attention to what they were saying about him, attributed the precipitous drop in his popularity to American (and Western) resentment of his criticisms. Concluding that their very accuracy had made him unpopular, he withdrew to his Vermont retreat and into silence.

Public silence, that is, for he was heavily engaged in working on his sequence of historical novels collectively entitled **The Red Wheel.** Planned as an epic chronicle of the events leading from World War I to the October Revolution, the series had been inaugurated by **August 1914,** published while Solzhenitsyn was still in the Soviet Union. Since his exile he had returned to the series with renewed energy. The historical archives of the West were now open to him and contained a wealth of material inaccessible inside the Soviet Union. His notebooks were bursting with his research, and he set out to incorporate the new material into his grand scheme.

The work went very slowly. Ten years after the appearance of the original **August 1914,** he brought out an enlarged and revised edition twice the length. A year later he published **October 1916,** also in two volumes. Between 1986 and 1988 he brought out **March 1917,** in four volumes, and then in 1991, **April 1917** in two volumes. His original intention had been to complete the series in twenty volumes covering the period from 1914 to 1922, but after finishing half this number, each running to between 500 and 750 pages, he was on the brink of exhaustion. In an epilogue to **April 1917** he stated that he was stopping the series six months short of the October Revolution, partly because of lack of time, but also because it was now clear to him that after the February Revolution in 1917, the Bolsheviks were the "only decisive force" left in the country. But even then he couldn't resist summarizing the remaining volumes planned to take the story to the spring of 1922, and adding the titles of five epilogues continuing to 1945.

One reason for Solzhenitsyn's reluctance to continue *The Red Wheel* must have been his realization that the Russian present was rapidly becoming more interesting than the Russian past. The ill-fated experiment whose beginnings Solzhenitsyn was exploring in such detail was about to disintegrate. Gorbachev had tried to stave off collapse with the reform policies of perestroika and glasnost, but after the Berlin Wall came down in 1989 it was all over. The attempted coup by Soviet generals in 1991 was the last gasp of a dying regime. Yeltsin rode to power on the back of the tanks that shelled the Russian parliament, but he also stepped into a political vacuum, much as Lenin had done in 1917. The vaunted Soviet system collapsed without a whimper.

The parallel with Lenin was probably not lost on Solzhenitsyn. More to the point, for all his laborious study of Russian history, his political prophesies had been proven wrong. The "decadent West" had triumphed over the "evil empire," and neither Soviet military might nor Russian spirituality seemed much in evidence in his country's defeat. On the other hand, Solzhenitsyn could justly claim credit for having shaken up the Soviet system himself, and in the aftermath of communism's demise, nobody was disposed to remind him of his recent speeches. He now had enormous authority inside Russia, and when his books began to be published there in 1989 and 1990 (while Gorbachev was still in power), some seven million copies were sold.

Friends and admirers pleaded with him to come back and take his rightful place in the life of the country. His enormous reputation would give him considerable influence. But Solzhenitsyn hesitated. Technically there was still a charge of treason against him, and *The Red Wheel* was unfinished. While Gorbachev was in power Solzhenitsyn published a long political essay, **"Rebuilding Russia,"** in response to perestroika (which also means "rebuilding"), in which he again attacked America's "cultural imperialism" and warned that "the more energetic the political activity in a country, the greater is the loss to spiritual life."

This was not what most Russians wanted to hear, especially after 1991, when they were given their first chance in seventy years to take an active part in politics. Far from abhorring the West, they were dazzled by it and couldn't get enough of its consumer economy. Yet Solzhenitsyn's reputation remained high. On a state visit to Washington, Yeltsin called him in Vermont to invite him to return to Russia, but still the great man dawdled. In 1992 he dispatched his wife, Natalya, to prepare the way for his return, but it was another two years before he finally went back himself, choosing to do so by way of Vladivostok and a two-month train journey across Russia.

* * *

By the time he arrived in Moscow, on July 21, 1994, only a small crowd braved the rain to meet him at the station—some twenty thousand fewer than at Harvard all those years earlier. He addressed them with conviction. He had met students and farmers and factory workers across the country, people living in slums and working without pay, and he hoped to "bring their message to the ears of the leaders in Moscow." But it was too late. When he addressed the Russian Duma a few months later, the deputies stifled their yawns. He became the host of a fifteen-minute talk show on despised television, but it was canceled after a year for lack of interest.

Solzhenitsyn's stock had sunk precipitously. A new edition of his collected works had only fifteen thousand subscribers. For many Russian writers he became a subject of mockery. Tatyana Tolstaya pilloried him in these pages as an angry misanthrope and pious hypocrite.[2] One critic, Grigori Amelin, likened the "Voltaire from Vermont" to "a hat-rack in an entrance hall." Another wrote that Solzhenitsyn's "humanistic pathos" was just as comic and outdated as socialist realism, while the writer Dmitri Prigov held he was as much an icon of the Communist period as Lenin.

He retired behind a new stockade in the exclusive district of Troitse Lykovo, on the outskirts of Moscow, building a new dacha with his Western royalties. That it was in a district much favored by Kremlin grandees and on the site of an earlier dacha belonging to Stalin's crony, Lazar Kaganovich, was not lost on his critics. More important to Solzhenitsyn was its proximity to the seventeenth-century baroque Church of the Dormition on the site of a former convent. A favored spot for Solzhenitsyn's strolls, it is a melancholy reminder of Russia's once splendid religious life.

* * *

How are we to account for the speed of Solzhenitsyn's descent from revered sage and prophet, from "great writer" in the grand Russian tradition, to irrelevant political dinosaur and target of jokes? And what are we now to think of the novels, stories, plays, and that great hybrid of memoir and nonfiction, *The Gulag Archipelago,* that rocked the world with the stark truthfulness of its testimony when Soviet power seemed unstoppable? What, for that matter, are we to make of the ten lengthy tomes of *The Red Wheel,* which Solzhenitsyn himself thought of as his life's work?

Such are the questions that have impelled the British novelist D. M. Thomas to reexamine Solzhenitsyn. In his recent biography, *Alexander Solzhenitsyn: A Century in His Life,* Thomas argues that it is now possible to assess Solzhenitsyn's life and work "freed" from the ongoing struggle against tyranny. . . . He is now, more distinctly, a writer than a fighter for rights; though that superhuman struggle will always be an essential factor in any assessment of him." The project seems a plausible one. In the fourteen years since the last biography appeared, Russia has changed more dramatically then at any time since the October Revolution. And Solzhenitsyn is no longer a writer in exile.

The last biography, of course, was mine, and Thomas opens his book with a tribute to my own "monumental" work on Solzhenitsyn,[3] whose scope, he says, he does not intend to rival with his own. For fully three quarters of his book, Thomas follows the trail I laid down rather too faithfully. It is all here: Solzhenitsyn's nouveau-riche ancestry (later camouflaged), his poverty-stricken childhood, his brilliant record as a student at Rostov University, military service in World War II, arrest, imprisonment in the labor camps, and meteoric rise to world fame as bard of the camps and chief scourge of the Soviet government after Khrushchev's thaw, followed by banishment to the West in 1974.

Thomas draws on the same sources and cites the originals. Since the English translations he quotes are either identical to mine or slightly paraphrased, and his interpretation usually no different, the borrowing is pretty obvious.[4] It might be argued that close parallels are inevitable, given the sameness of so many of the sources and the basic facts of the life described, but in practice this rarely happens. Studies of all sorts of literary figures have shown that each new biographer, even scrutinizing the same documents as other biographers, can draw radically different conclusions. The point of a new biography should be to give a new perspective, not to recast an old one.

* * *

What is most disconcerting about Thomas's book is the opportunities it misses. It contains virtually no interviews with anyone in Russia who knew or worked with Solzhenitsyn (and very few with anyone in the West). Thomas traveled to southern Russia to see the hovel in which Solzhenitsyn spent much of his childhood in the city of Rostov; but for some reason he did not go the extra three hundred miles to visit Solzhenitsyn's native village and interview the surviving cousin who lives

there. He describes Solzhenitsyn's birthplace from guidebooks and memoirs, and speculates about the wealth of Solzhenitsyn's grandfather Semyon on the basis of newspaper reports. Had he gone to their village, he could have seen for himself the palatial house that Semyon Solzhenitsyn built there.[5]

Thomas refers to his subject throughout using the intimate nickname "Sanya." Natalya Reshetovskaya, Solzhenitsyn's first wife, becomes "Natasha," Solzhenitsyn's second wife, Natalya Svetlova, is "Alya," and the redoubtable critic and writer Elena Chukovskaya is "Liusha." This is like calling him "Al" Solzhenitsyn, or like writing about "Johnny" Updike and "Phil" Roth. Thomas excuses himself by saying that he is "a novelist and poet, not a biographer," which also allows him to pass off Solzhenitsyn's fiction as fact, and to make up for gaps in his knowledge by interpreting scenes preceded by the words "I imagine."

In writing about Soviet history and politics, Thomas relies heavily on hindsight. It is easy now to thunder about the iniquities of the purges and the Stalinist terror, but Thomas is wholly unable to explain the attraction of Communist ideals for the young Solzhenitsyn (and others of his generation) in the Thirties, or why Solzhenitsyn was reluctant to abandon communism until long after he had been flung into the labor camps. Since he fails to understand such convictions, Thomas does a serious injustice to Lev Kopelev, Solzhenitsyn's fellow prisoner and comrade. A seasoned dissident, Kopelev wrote courageously about the brutal events in which he had taken part as a young Party member during the Thirties. Thomas cites Kopelev's account of the arrests and killing that took place at that time without acknowledging Kopelev's subsequent remorse. Thomas also fails to consider whether the true believer Solzhenitsyn might also have taken part in such activities had he been ten years older and in Kopelev's place. As a result, the reader might conclude that Kopelev was merely a soulless apparatchik, whereas he was an example of a familiar intellectual figure of our century (Solzhenitsyn was another), an idealist blinded by his faith.

In the last quarter of his book, Thomas is able to bring something new to his story. He draws adroitly, for example, on Solzhenitsyn's brief addendum to his memoirs, *Invisible Allies,* published in 1995, and on a collection of Soviet government documents on Solzhenitsyn, *The Solzhenitsyn Files,* that I edited and published the same year. He is also able to quote from the memoirs of Galina Vishnevskaya Rostropovich about the efforts she and her husband made to protect Solzhenitsyn, as well as from memoirs by Solzhenitsyn's first wife, Natalya Reshetovskaya. He also makes good use of press reports of Solzhenitsyn's return to Russia in 1994, and the brief period of his life there since.

But here, too, there are problems, which are best illustrated by his dealings with Reshetovskaya. Thomas appears to have interviewed her twice, with meager results. He refers briefly to her third volume of memoirs, *Ottachenye* ("Excommunication"), published in Moscow in 1994, but most of his references to her role in Solzhenitsyn's life come from her KGB-doctored memoir, *Sanya,* published in 1975. One guesses that this is because *Sanya* was published in English, since Thomas's bibliography is limited to works in English; but *Sanya* was superseded eight years ago by its Russian original, *Sol'zhenitryn i charyushchaya Rossiya* ("Solzhenitsyn and Russian Readers"), published in serial form in Rostov in 1990, and as a book in Moscow the same year. As we would expect, the original memoirs are far fuller, more interesting, and more accurate than the distorted English version. Reshetovskaya gives far more weight to Solzhenitsyn's literary achievements than in the later volume, and comes across as far less shrill and vengeful.

* * *

Thomas promises a revaluation of Solzhenitsyn "freed from the ongoing struggle against tyranny." This would entail a discussion of Solzhenitsyn's literary work as a whole, above all of the ten volumes that make up **The Red Wheel** (to which Solzhenitsyn devoted nearly thirty years of his life—not just the seventeen in Vermont mentioned by Thomas). But no such analysis can be found in his book. Thomas's devotion to English-language sources suggests that his Russian may not be up to it. *October 1916* is touched upon briefly for some autobiographical tidbits concerning Solzhenitsyn's love life, but the only work in the series that is discussed in any detail is *August 1914,* the only one translated into English when Thomas was writing his book.

To earlier discussions of this novel Thomas brings little new. Like others he notes that it starts out bravely, in "Tolstoyan" fashion, with some family scenes based on the life of Solzhenitsyn's mother and grandparents, before lapsing into a historical treatise, which is briefly brought to life by stirring descriptions of General Samsonov's campaign on the Eastern front during World War I, and Samsonov's suicide after his defeat (which many critics think the strongest episode in the novel). Thomas does advance the interesting idea that in loading himself down with historical research, Solzhenitsyn "stopped listening to the muse." In effect, he abandoned his imagination in order to recreate historical events in suffocating detail and at interminable length, thus throttling his talent.

What is true of *August 1914* applies also to the later novels, and this may explain Thomas's refusal to give even a cursory account of the several thousand pages in the series. In these novels, while following the family life and love affairs of his main character, the scientifically minded officer Vorotyntsev, and including isolated scenes from the private lives of a few other characters, Solzhenitsyn concentrates overwhelmingly on the social and political events of the era, and their lesson for the present. This is obviously where his true interest lies, and it plays havoc with his literary intentions: we get a dry commentary on Russian history and military failure, not an imaginative story we can follow with interest.

Here, it seems to me, and not in reactions to his unpalatable political views, lie the real causes of the decline in Solzhenitsyn's reputation. *August 1914* has never been popular with readers either in the Soviet Union or in the West. Its lack of immediacy and urgency, its leisurely narrative techniques—despite the clumsy deployment of cinematic scenes, headlines, and similar "modernist" devices borrowed from Dos Passos and others—and its structural weaknesses have all disappointed admirers of his earlier work. When the first version of *August 1914* appeared it was possible to hope that its lopsided architecture and its long-winded historical reconstructions formed only one corner of an edifice whose impressive shape would emerge as the later volumes were published. Unfortunately the volumes we now have form a structure whose upper stories appear stunted and disproportionately small, with almost no windows.

In an interview long ago Solzhenitsyn showed he was aware of widespread disappointment with *August 1914* when he said that it was from the appearance of that novel that he dated the "schism" among his readers. His use of the word "schism" is characteristic, for Solzhenitsyn is a born schismatic of a peculiarly Russian type, much like Dostoevsky (Raskolnikov's name means "schismatic") and Lenin (who created a schism between Bolsheviks and Mensheviks). His use of this term to describe his audience indicated that he still took an ideological view of readers' responses to *August 1914,* choosing to interpret them as hostile reactions to his politics, rather than criticism of his art.

The enlarged version of *August 1914,* published in English in 1989, was just as much a disappointment as the original one. The English translation sank with hardly a trace, and it will be interesting to see what happens when "Knot II," *November 1916,* appears early next year from Farrar, Straus and Giroux. Though still formidably long at just under a thousand pages, this volume pays rather more attention to the domestic and private lives of the characters than did volume one, and interweaves them more successfully with the public and historical events of the time. There are still plenty of historical digressions, but nothing to equal the 70 pages of small print devoted to Prime Minister Stolypin's early life in *August 1914.* So, too, the cinematic and headline sections have been reduced in number. An interesting feature of the new work is the introduction of a lightly fictionalized portrait of the Don Cossack writer Fyodor Kryukov, whom Solzhenitsyn regards as the real author of large parts of Sholokhov's *The Quiet Don.*[6]

* * *

Generally speaking, it seems as if Solzhenitsyn listened to the critics of *August 1914* and made a genuine attempt to modify and lighten subsequent volumes in *The Red Wheel,* but it was not enough to win his Russian audience back. When Radio Liberty started broadcasting the novels into the Soviet Union in the 1980s, the number of people listening to the station is said to have plummeted. Solzhenitsyn had lost a large part of his audience well before he ever set foot in the country again, and the unpopularity of the later works eventually turned readers away from the earlier ones.

Thomas does not discuss the implications of this development, nor does he attempt to assess Solzhenitsyn's literary achievement throughout his career. Such powerful works as *One Day in the Life of Ivan Denisovich, The First Circle,* and *The Gulag Archipelago* do not get the close attention they deserve. Instead, at every possible opportunity, Thomas resorts to strained comparisons with Akhmatova, Pasternak, Mandelstam, Trvetayeva, and even Pushkin. Thomas shows that he is familiar with the work of these writers—he has translated Pushkin and Akhmatova—but the only thing the four twentieth-century poets have in common with Solzhenitsyn is that they were persecuted by the same Soviet tyranny and resisted it. In every other respect, their experimental poetry could hardly be farther removed from the naturalistic realism of Solzhenitsyn.

More to the point is Solzhenitsyn's affinity with Tolstoy, so obvious in the early novels and stories and so clearly the inspiration for *The Red Wheel.* Thomas acknowledges Tolstoy's influence on *August 1914,* in which the great writer actually appears as a character. But he does not notice that Solzhenitsyn's affinity is more with the late biblical and patriarchal Tolstoy than with the classic novelist in his sensuous prime. In Solzhenitsyn the reader will find no Natasha Rostova, Anna Karenina, or Pierre Berukhov. At best he will find modern counterparts of the self-centered Andrei Volkonsky, the cunning peasant Platon Karatayev, and a shadow of Napoleon in the figure of Stalin in *The First Circle.*

Solzhenitsyn has encouraged the comparison with Tolstoy. It was himself he had in mind when he wrote, in *The First Circle,* that "a great writer is like a second government," but he also knew that he was echoing Alexin Suvorin's remark at the turn of the century that "we have two tsars in Russia: Nicholas II and Tolstoy."

However, the self-identification with Tolstoy has worked to Solzhenitsyn's detriment, especially in the case of *The Red Wheel.*

* * *

The Red Wheel was clearly inspired by the same fanatical determination to tell the truth that has motivated Solzhenitsyn from the very outset of his career. The urge to bear witness made him into an incomparable chronicler of some of the worst cruelties of the twentieth century, and was the driving force behind all his best work. *One Day in the Life of Ivan Denisovich, The First Circle, Cancer Ward,* and above all *The Gulag Archipelago* were written with a fiery conviction that transformed history into poetry. *The Gulag Archipelago* even became a sort of model for *The Red Wheel*—even though the outline of the novel was conceived in the 1930s, before Solzhenitsyn had ever heard of the labor camps. Solzhenitsyn's aim in both books, he once told his Paris publisher, Nikita Struve, was to "reconstruct history in its fullness, authenticity and complexity," using "an artist's vision" to bring documentary material to life.

But there was a problem that Solzhenitsyn did not reckon with. Having conceived while still a student a series of historical novels about the events leading up to the Revolution, Solzhenitsyn held doggedly to his plan for thirty years—through the world war, a term in the labor camps, a life of provincial obscurity, sudden fame, and exile to the West—even though his original vision had become an anachronism. The ideological purpose of the epic was entirely reversed: initially conceived as a celebration of the Revolution, it became an account of the Revolution as a tragic disaster. But that did not persuade Solzhenitsyn to reexamine his conception. He seems to have perceived his arrest and incarceration in the labor camps, and the great series of works he wrote recapturing his experiences, as a detour from the main task of his life, which was to write *The Red Wheel.* It was as though one part of his mental clock had stopped in about 1936. Perhaps he thought he would betray his youthful self if he did not persist with his great project.

In the Thirties, it should be recalled, Tolstoy was force-fed to Soviet students as one of the great harbingers of the Communist revolution, and held up in literary circles as the best classical model for Soviet writers to emulate. This canonization of a protorevolutionary Tolstoy showed a profound misunderstanding of his art. That an eighteen-year-old neophyte should fall under its influence and be swept away by visions of imitating Tolstoy is understandable, but that a mature writer in his fifties, with a distinguished body of writing behind him, should return to that adolescent vision suggests a triumph of will over common sense. It was too late even in 1936 to be dreaming of Tolstoyan epics, let alone after the world-shattering events of World War II.

The example of Tolstoy affected Solzhenitsyn in other ways as well. His Vermont retreat struck many visitors as self-consciously reminiscent of Tolstoy's estate Yasnaya Polyana, where he lived during the last decades of his life. When I was in Vermont in 1977, I couldn't help noticing the scythe leaning against the wall of his summer house, a reminder that Tolstoy liked to use his scythe in his spare time in imitation of his beloved peasants (but Solzhenitsyn's scythe was of stainless steel).

Tolstoy's Yasnaya Polyana, however, was open and welcoming. Visitors came liberally from Russia and abroad, and Tolstoy maintained vigorous contacts with other thinkers and writers of his time. Cavendish was walled off from the rest of the world by a chain-link fence and closed-circuit television at the main gate. It seemed as though Solzhenitsyn had shut himself off in a private compound, a substitute for the harsher one in which he had spent the formative years of his life.

Solzhenitsyn, in my view, could more usefully be compared to Maxim Gorky, another Soviet idol during Solzhenitsyn's youth (a doting uncle even sent Gorky some of the young Solzhenitsyn's stories). Like Solzhenitsyn, Gorky was a provincial autodidact who became a world literary sensation, rocked the literary and political establishments of his day, and in the last part of his career became a legend, an icon, and a "rule-giver." Gorky is remembered more for his nonfiction autobiographies and memoirs than for his many novels and short stories, and the same may well prove to be true of Solzhenitsyn.

* * *

The more one looks at his work, the more it seems that *The Gulag Archipelago* will last as his one incontrovertible masterpiece. Infusing the dry facts of political history with liberal doses of autobiography and hundreds of personal stories brought to him by fellow prisoners and helpers, Solzhenitsyn created, at great speed and in the white heat of inspiration, a unique polyphonic saga, an epic chronicle of cruelty and courage that has no precedent in Russian or in any other literature.[7] *The Gulag Archipelago* also has a unique narrative voice, which Solzhenitsyn permitted himself only here and in his memoir, *The Oak and the Calf.* It is a sinuous, flexible, often harsh instrument that ranges from intimate reflection to stentorian revelation, from quiet prayer to magnificent exhortation, from deadpan description to ruthless irony; in its power it far surpasses the quickly ironic voice of even his best novel, *The First Circle.*

The inspired quality of *The Gulag Archipelago* has gone largely unrecognized in the English-speaking world owing to the hasty publication of volumes one and two in a badly flawed translation. The haste was a result of Solzhenitsyn's demand that the work be published as soon as a copy fell into the hands of the KGB, and the task became even more urgent when Solzhenitsyn was arrested. Thomas takes note of the difficulties surrounding the book's publication and concedes the poor quality of the translation, but instead of considering the consequences for Solzhenitsyn's literary reputation, he gets tangled in the details of the fiasco.[8] The only part of *The Gulag Archipelago* that now exists in a readable English version is volume three, translated by Harry Willetts. That, however, did not appear until 1978, the year of Solzhenitsyn's Harvard speech, and like volume two, it went largely unread. Solzhenitsyn's supreme work is thus largely unknown to English speakers.

Looking back, one is astonished at how short the period of Solzhenitsyn's literary eminence was. He burst into world consciousness with *One Day in the Life of Ivan Denisovich* in 1961; fourteen years later, in 1975, his last acknowledged major work, *The Oak and the Calf,* was published in Russian. Future readers may still revalue *The Red Wheel,* and there is probably a second volume of memoirs to come. Some hopes were raised after Solzhenitsyn's return to Russia with the announcement that he planned to publish some new short stories. Two came out in the May 1995 issue of *Novy Mir,* and three more in October. One is a sympathetic account of the life of Marshall Zhukov, another a satirical portrait of a prominent Soviet writer, told in the realist style of Solzhenitsyn's late work. They are of interest more for their subject matter than for any special literary qualities, and give every appearance of being offshoots from the later volumes of *The Red Wheel.*

* * *

Of more topical interest is a 1996 story, **"Rough Times,"** which contrasts the tough morality of a Soviet industrialist with the corrupt financial maneuvers of a Yeltsinite banker, very much to the industrialist's favor. Last year, Solzhenitsyn published in *Novy Mir* some "miniature stories"—his name for poems in prose. Their lyrical tone came as a relief from the relentless social commentary of the longer stories, but both the miniatures and the longer stories are very far from having the bloom of Tolstoy's late works, such as his peasant parables and *Khadji Murat.*

Still, nothing that Solzhenitsyn has published in the last quarter of his life can detract from the quality of the works written in his prime. That even they have been eclipsed in recent times owes more to declining interest in his great theme of the labor camps than to any inherent deficiencies. The crimes and enormities of the recent past get little attention in today's shallow and materialistic Russia. Unlike after World War II, when the defeated Axis powers were obliged to confront their governments' crimes and to re-educate their populations under pressure from their conquerors, the Russians now seem to have emerged from party dictatorship untroubled by the horrors of the past. With no external force to pressure them, they prefer almost total amnesia, at least for the time being. And for them Solzhenitsyn is part of the tragic history they want to forget.

The wheel (if not **The Red Wheel**) will undoubtedly turn again. When the contemporary urge to bury the past abates, Solzhenitsyn's contribution to Russian letters (not to speak of his influence on the history of our century) will be evaluated anew. His reputation will probably never quite regain the luster that it possessed between 1962 and 1972, but he will still be recognized as one of the most important Russian writers of the twentieth century.

Notes

1. Ronald Berman, editor, *Solzhenitsyn at Harvard: The Address, Twelve Early Responses, and Six Later Reflections* (Washington, D.C.: Ethics and Public Policy Center, 1980).

2. *The New York Review,* October 19, 1995.

3. *Solzhenitsyn, A Biography* (Norton, 1984).

4. For example, a translation I made from the memoirs of a White Cossack officer, Colonel A. G. Shkuro, published in Argentina in 1946, is quoted word for word, yet the attribution is made to Shkuro. The translation I made of a more obscure Danish pamphlet, *Hvem er Solzhenitsyn?* ("Who Is Solzhenitsyn?"), by one of Solzhenitsyn's school friends, Kirill Simonyan, is paraphrased by Thomas, yet the Danish original is cited. There are numerous other examples of such unattributed "borrowings."

5. I had seen photographs of Semyon's big house when writing my account of Solzhenitsyn's childhood, but did not mention it because allegations about Solzhenitsyn's well-to-do grandparents were being used to discredit him (and his work) in the eyes of Soviet readers.

6. See D., *Stremya Tikhogo Dona* ("The Stream of 'The Quiet Don'"), with an introduction by Solzhenitsyn (Paris: YMCA Press, 1973).

7. Curiously enough, *The Gulag Archipelago* was conceived as a riposte to a superficially similar work, edited by Gorky, *The White Sea-Baltic, Stalin Canal,* about the glories of Stalinist "re-education through labor."

8. The full story of the publication of this flawed translation, in which I was involved by trying first to stop it, and then to edit it, remains to be told. The writer Olga Carlisle has commented on it twice, in *Solzhenitsyn and the Secret Circle* (Holt, 1978) and

Under a New Sky (Ticknor and Fields, 1993), but the picture remains unclear. According to Thomas, she was in possession of a complete edited version of Thomas Whitney's translation of volume one of *The Gulag Archipelago,* but declined to show it to Solzhenitsyn's Swiss lawyer on the grounds that he did not ask for it. Given the intense pressure to publish volume one after its discovery by the KGB in the summer of 1973, and the extraordinary measures taken by Frances McCullough and myself to edit Whitney's first draft at top speed, it is extraordinary that Carlisle never came forward. So far as I can make out, her edited translation was not made available to Harper and Row, and has never seen the light of day.

Michael Nicholson (essay date 1999)

SOURCE: Nicholson, Michael. "Solzhenitsyn, Exile and the *Genius Loci.*" *Canadian-American Slavic Studies* 33, nos. 2-4 (1999): 307-34.

[*In the following essay, Nicholson considers the impact of emigration and exile on Solzhenitsyn's writing.*]

> Сыт Лондон, пирует Вена,
> Нарядсн и весел Стокгольм
> и нам бы туда,
> Эабывши лачужню голь . . .
>
> Так нет, не забыть же, на поди!
>
> Вот едут,—эачем, спроси . . .
> Не жить им покойно на Эападе,
> Оставив сердца на Руси . . .[1]
>
> (1951, *Ekibastuz labour camp*)

Emigration, and particularly exile, entail processes of dislocation and deracination which, whatever their accompanying compensations, throw notions of home, borders and separation into stark relief. The émigré, it has been suggested, does not so much cross the boundary between one home and another as enter a space between 'the periphery of the alien culture and of his own—hence, a region within which various semiotic fields intersect'.[2] The openness of the individual expatriate writer to these ambiguities and the trace they leave upon his literary output are not uniform or predictable. At one extreme, Zinovy Zinik has chosen to thematize the very processes involved, not merely recording the paradoxes of emigration, but tracing the mechanics of their perception.

> When you look from the outside into a house, you have to press your face against the window, so your face becomes distorted. So as a result you always get a caricature.
>
> Q[uestion]. But of yourself?

> Of course, of myself. The moment I start writing, it is already a part of me, but a caricatured part of me.[3]

No such susceptibility to the charms of polysemy and cultural intertextuality troubled those elderly writers of the First Emigration irreverently limned by Vladislav Khodasevich in 1933:

> [They] brought with them from Russia the same set of ready-made images and ideas on which their reputation had been based. . . . In exile their creative work ran along the familiar old tracks, never drawing renewal from any quarter. . . . Their books bear the imprimature of Berlin or Paris, but might just as easily have been written in Moscow or St Petersburg. It was as if their writing desks had been shipped from the Arbat to Auteuil, arriving by some miracle without so much as an inkwell or pencil out of place.[4]

On the face of it Aleksandr Solzhenitsyn would seem to be closer to this latter category of émigré writers. By the time he was forced out of Russia, he was already an established author in his late fifties. Far from seeking new themes and impressions upon his arrival, he promptly undertook never to write a serious work of literature about the West.[5] In an interview to mark his first five years in exile he elaborated:

> You need to develop a feeling for your own native language, your native soil and its history, and together they will provide more than enough material, while the interaction between writer and material will suggest the appropriate form.[6]

Thanks to the extraordinary efforts of his wife, he had with him, in the shape of *Krasnoe koleso,* not just work in progress, but enough of it to see out even a prospective centenarian. Had this not been so, he wrote soon after he reached the West, he would have found himself in exile 'with a gaping hole in my side and anguish in my heart—not a writer, but a cripple'.[7] As for the actual writing desk to house this treasure—it, too, swiftly followed him from Moscow.

However, in caricaturing the self-sufficiency of established émigré writers in 1933 Khodasevich had a particular aim in mind. His essay is concerned with the dissolution of an émigré sense of identity.

> Without some higher sense of a mission, of being an envoy [*poslannichestvo*]—there is no emigration, but just a clutch of refugees looking for somewhere to settle down and have a better life.[8]

As we know from his remarks on the subject of emigration, Solzhenitsyn would respect the spirit of the slogan to which Khodasevich is alluding ('My ne v izgnan'i, a v poslan'i'[9]), yet the last thing that he himself wished to do in the 1970s and 1980s was to cultivate an 'emigrantskaia dusha', to become identified with the Third Wave of Russian emigration. The self-containment of

Solzhenitsyn's years in exile was rooted not in complacency, but in an active determination to remain an outcast,[10] in a belief that somehow he might yet return to Russia, and a refusal in the meantime to wear the label 'émigré' with pride, or, indeed, at all. Almost from the moment of his arrival in the West he searched for a secluded temporary home—in the Sternenberg Hills near Zürich, around Lillehammer in Norway and, eventually, in Cavendish, Vermont—which would hinder assimilation and physically remind him of Russia. In the West his dogged hopes of repatriation so flouted common sense that they aroused at best sympathy and a patronising smile—until, that is, the embarrassingly under-predicted collapse of the Soviet Union flouted it rather more spectacularly. Thereupon Solzhenitsyn duly set about winding up his affairs in the West. Almost uniquely among major Russian literary figures living in emigration, he had declared his intention to lay his bones on Russian soil, to return to Russia not as a 'tourist', but once and for all. Though his removal in 1994 was not swift enough for some, there is no evidence that he swerved from that resolve. Viewers of the BBC Television film *The Homecoming* in 1995 were treated to a fine coup de théâtre when, as almost his last act in his place of exile and with undisguised satisfaction, he cleared his writing desk for shipment back to Russia, before setting off to meet it there.

The bid to preserve a Russian identity through decades of foreign exile required powerful sustaining images and to this extent could hardly escape mythicizing processes. In Solzhenitsyn's case appropriate mythopoetic constructs, manifest not least in the form of recurrent spatial patterns and affinities, were already at hand to shape and legitimize his detachment in exile. At the same time, his prominence and the contrast between acerbic, well-publicized polemical forays and the often no less controversial reclusivity of his life in Cavendish caused other, exogenous, myths to be spun around him. Both of these aspects will be considered in the following pages.

Dom and antidom

The singlemindedness with which Solzhenitsyn has pursued his literary aspirations and obligations dates back at least to the 1930s. War, the camps and drastic political reorientation tempered an edge which was already present in the young man. It went far beyond that prudent determination to exclude external and domestic distractions which every writer possesses or sighs for. Its conscious, almost ruthless, intensity is something that Solzhenitsyn has never sought to deny. It included an early decision not to have children (which he held to for some thirty years). In contributing to the calamities of his first marriage and the alienation of former friends, this sternness of character has provided much grist for the biographers' mill. Yet without it—to state the very obvious—there would have been neither the works, nor the response, nor, in short, the phenomenon to set those mill-wheels turning.[11]

However great his powers of concentration, Solzhenitsyn quickly came to value physical locations which could guarantee tranquillity and isolation. As he grew up, he and his mother rarely knew a secure home.[12] The importance to him of improvising a haven to write in is attested as early as 1943 in a letter from the front:

> In one of the houses the Germans have destroyed I've patched up such a room as I never dreamed of back in Rostov. . . . It's the peace and solitude I longed for![13]

Prison and camp could offer occasional lulls and the warmth of camaraderie.[14] They could even, at least with hindsight, come to constitute a kind of spiritual *katorga-rodina*, for 'this is the place of your spiritual birth, and a secret part of your soul will remain here for ever'.[15] But in the camps the chance to write, even in one's head, had to be snatched where it could, and anything resembling hearth and home as a place of creative seclusion remained a remote fantasy.

Whatever the hardships of Solzhenitsyn's exile 'in perpetuity' to the Kazakhstan village of Kok-Terek in 1953 (and these included strategically inevitable bachelorhood, as well as a life-threatening cancer), it eventually brought him something approaching that 'distant dwelling place of toil and pleasures pure' for which Pushkin had yearned in vain.[16] Solzhenitsyn was able to purchase his own clay hut, standing comparatively isolated on the edge of the settlement, with a solid table to work at when the coast was clear, a camera for microfilming his seditious works, and staunch friends and fellow-conspirators in the Zubov couple. He returns several times in his fiction and memoirs to this unforgettable, if spartan idyll.[17]

Solzhenitsyn's subsequent biography is dotted with such islands of tranquillity.[18] Before his literary début, they included the *izba* of Matrena Vasil'evna Zakharova at Mil'tsevo, immortalized in 'Matrenin dvor'; and a rustic table in the cramped garden of Reshetovskaia's Riazan' home amidst the revving trucks on Kasimovskii Lane. It was at this table that ***Ivan Denisovich*** was written in 1959. When the story was published three years later, Solzhenitsyn had greater need than ever of hiding places for his seditious writing. He would disappear to the rudimentary and splendidly remote *kha-lupka* of his 'second Matrena', Agaf'ia Ivanovna Folomkina, in the forest village of Davydovo near Solotcha.[19] Later, his favourite refuge would be 'Borzovka', the tiny summer house he purchased in 1965, with its view of the decapitated church in the village of Rozhdestvo-na-lst'e.[20] In two successive winters (1965-1967), quite unbeknown to the KGB (and on one occasion shaving off

his beard to confuse them further), he slipped away to his Estonian 'hideaway' [*ukryvishche*], a farmhouse near Tartu, and completed the major part of his work on ***Gulag***.[21] These, together with the unrealized dream of building an ecologically sound house in the hills on the edge of Lake Baikal in Siberia,[22] are the precursors of his Cavendish 'home' and his new house outside Moscow at Troitse-Lykovo.

Solzhenitsyn's chosen locations tend to be sturdily rooted in nature. Features which he prizes are forest, water and some elevation or undulation of terrain. We might recall his autobiographical narrator entering an idyllically named village in 'Matrenin dvor':

> Vysokoe Pole did not belie its name. It stood on rising ground, with gentle hollows and other little hills around it. It was enclosed by an un-broken ring of forest. There was a pool behind a weir. Just the place you wouldn't mind living and dying in.
>
> (III, 124)[23]

Self-sufficiency is highly regarded, and into the long writing day he would squeeze such practical chores as plain cooking, chopping wood, building himself a work table under the trees, or draining his frequently flooded plot of land at Borzovka. Expulsion to the West did not weaken his habits or diminish the significance he attached to the isolated, simple working home.[24] The house in which he settled in Vermont may have been well-appointed, but until the winter drove him back into the main house he would write in a shack beside a deep, cold pool on a forested slope in the grounds.

Solzhenitsyn's favourite *topoi* have little in common with Zinik's self-reflexive image of a distorted face peering into the window of an alien house. They tend to follow more archaic patterns.[25] Lotman reminds us how venerable and universal a modelling system is the juxtaposition of home with 'anti-home' or 'forest home': the former demarcates one's own native space, safe, cultured, watched over by benevolent *lares* or *domovye*; the latter is alien, demonized space, a gateway to the underworld.[26] What could be more natural for one in Solzhenitsyn's circumstances than to identify the hostile outside world with the political system to which he had fallen victim? After all, concealing himself in order to write and hiding away the products of his pen were for a quarter of a century a way of life to him. In the rhetoric of *Bodalsia telenok s dubom* 'outside' becomes an exposed heath, seared by the breath of the searching Dragon, while homes and temporary refuges are for ever probed by the Allseeing Eye. Even a plain plywood box with a skilfully concealed false bottom, a gift from the arch-conspirator Nikolai Zubov, opens up a fourth-dimensional, enchanted space beyond space:

> . . . the secret cavity—those dark hundred cubic centimeters of space that I had dreamed about and that, though technically within the USSR, were yet beyond the control of the Soviet regime.[27]

It would not be surprising if two decades of exile, with their relative physical security,[28] should have weakened Solzhenitsyn's perception of home as a political refuge. However, in his autobiographical and fictional writings, house and home had long tended to figure in schematic arrangements which go beyond this simple antithesis. Apart from the bulwark against political unfreedom, we encounter the notion of home as coherence and self-limitation in the face of chaotic 'freedom'.

A striking instance in **Arkhipelag GULag** pits the 'home' of clarity and concentrated self-control against an 'outside' world which by virtue of its very freedom is diffuse, opaque and dysphonic. The released prisoner does not simply exchange the misery of slavery for the joys of liberty but, at one point, leaves his 'spiritual birth-place', his bitter-sweet *katorga-rodina* to 'trudge aimlessly into the mute and unresponsive expanse of *freedom*' (VII, 451).[29] In the same book, the author-narrator's decision to indulge his yearning for Central Russia in the wake of Khrushchev's 'de-Stalinization' and leave the cocoon of exile is acknowledged as 'weakness': 'I abandoned my pellucid exile and set off into a muddied world' (VII, 440). There is an apolitical or suprapolitical aspect to such thinking, and it helps us to understand why in the popular scenario of a Solzhenitsyn released from the 'prison house' of Brezhnev's Russia and clutched to the bosom of the 'free' West, he eventually came to be recast as a perplexing ingrate. His own preoccupation with the fate of Russia as he envisaged it and his impatience with Western obtuseness in its dealings with Communism played their part, of course. But the personal challenge of sustaining ideals of focused self-limitation in the midst of a formless expanse of apparently frivolous freedom should not be underestimated as a motivating force. The 'forest house' is associated not with political tyranny but with the tyranny of distraction.[30]

Another long-standing topological variant in Solzhenitsyn's writing involves not the antithesis of good home *versus* bad outside, but a spatial alternation within the potential of home itself:

—home as intimacy with the soil and cycles of nature, providing a *horizontal* integration into the Russian landscape, and

—home as tranquil detachment from and elevation above the quotidian, occasionally allowing a commanding perspective and spiritual lucidity—movement along an essentially *vertical* axis.

Apart from its role as a place to nestle in for protection and sustenance, home can thus become the springboard for a flight out of time and space. Here, for example, is the recollection of a blissful summer of work in 1964:[31]

. . . I stayed on a pine-covered hillside a little way off. A worktable had been set into the ground, there was a

trail that led to the spot, a tent for protection from the rain and, through the silent forest, access to a mysterious lake.[32]

The worktable may be rooted in the soil, but particularly suggestive in this context is the path through silence towards mystery. We shall meet this landscape again. The occasion for the second example is a brief night-time journey which Solzhenitsyn made in the middle of another reclusive and productive burst of writing the following winter. The accumulated intellectual and spiritual[33] intensity of his experience turns a bus-ride into a cosmic, vaguely mythical metaphor:

. . . I seemed to be alone in the darkened bus as it raced through the emptiness of night, engine growling and headlights sweeping across patches of snow on the road ahead. . . . an empty bus was carrying me through the darkness across the whole world . . . , or even out of this world entirely.[34]

Solzhenitsyn might have been compelled in exile to find a substitute for the Russian landscape itself, but these topological variants continue to attract him, especially the tension between an ensconced, earth-bound state and, growing out of it, a mystical, solipsistic encapsulation accompanied by weightless soaring motion. With this is mind, let us turn to his fictional writing before, during and after the years of exile.

'*KHOROSH BY DOM, DA CHERT ZHIVET V NEM.*'[35]

There is a particular attraction in taking as our starting point Solzhenitsyn's prose poems or **Krokhotki**. The original cycle was written between 1958 and 1960. Some thirty-six years would elapse, including all twenty spent in exile, before Solzhenitsyn returned to Russia and to this genre. Moreover, with a brevity and simplicity that allow no complications of plot beyond ironic antithesis or a wryly pointed ending, and with their lyrical intonation and allegorical, axiological design, they offer particularly clear examples of the kind of spatial relationships enumerated above. Recurring reference points are the home, church and lake; expansive vistas tend to be circumscribed; linear movement is subverted in favour of symbolically-charged vertically. And, to borrow Ernst Cassirer's words:

Here each place has its own peculiar atmosphere, surrounds itself, so to speak, with its own magical-mythical haze.[36]

Home is ostensibly plain and constricted. In '**Na rodine Esenina**' epithets are chosen to emphasize drabness, poverty and physical decrepitude (*odnoobraznyi, oby-knovennyi, ubogii, khilyi*), while the rooms of the *izba* where the poet was born are poky (*kletushki*). Even the distant view from the high bank of the Oka, which inspired Esenin's famous lines, seems dull. Yet into the unlikely receptacle of an unruly peasant lad in a dreary village, the Creator casts a genius for revealing the mystery of the mundane, the unsuspected beauty of stove, barn and hayrick (III, 177-78). The pattern whereby the humble and unprepossessing dwelling opens up to afford a glimpse of something higher can be seen in chapter 61 of *V kruge pervom* ('Tverskoi diadushka').[37] It is famously reproduced in 'Matrena's Home', written at the same time as the *Krokhotki.* There the ex-zek, newly returned to Central Russia and hoping to lose and immerse himself in 'inmost Russia, if such a thing happened to exist' (III, 123), finds his refuge in the best known of all Solzhenitsyn's homes.[38] The muddied world laps at and partly destroys its ancient timbers, but the ravaged narrator does indeed find his *nutrianaia Rus'* there, and Matrena and her smile survive death as a kind of *nerukot-vornyi* icon.[39]

Even a physically hostile *rodina* can attract irresistibly. In '**Koster i murav'i**' the narrator is struck by the strange force which draws ants to their deaths in a bid to regain their 'abandoned homeland', a rotten log now ablaze in the campfire (III, 180). The verses which stand as epigraph to the present essay are among the earliest available writings by Solzhenitsyn. In their fuller version[40] they show the human equivalent of these scorched ants pouring back to Stalin's Russia at the end of the war, there to trade German occupation, captivity and emigration for the welcome of a Soviet labour camp. The watchword of *Krasnoe koleso*—'Rossiiu zhalko'—is anticipated in the arrestee's bemused refrain, as he asks his beloved/repellent homeland: 'Za chto ia tebia liubliu?'?[41]

Particularly rich in spatial references and in associations with Solzhenitsyn's fiction at large are '**Putesh-estvuia vdol' Oki**' and '**Ozero Segden**'. The promise of linear movement in the title of the first is reinforced—and at once withdrawn—by the opening words: 'When you've walked along the country roads of Central Russia, you begin to understand . . .' (III, 184). What follows is an image of the understanding attained, and not at all an itinerary or quest for understanding. As so often in Solzhenitsyn's fiction journeys incline more towards the pilgrimage than the odyssey.[42] In '**Putesh-estvuia . . .**' the focus is no longer upon individual homes but on the church around which they cluster. Churches, and particularly their bell-towers, are shown as reaching outwards across the Russian *prostor,* 'nodding to one another from afar'. This they do more or less literally by dint of being built frequently within sight of another church or monastery, and in this sense they become the 'key to the soothing Russian landscape', giving meaning to its vast formlessness. Yet even when the 'next' bell-tower is invisible or inaudible, the link is sustained—no longer on the horizontal axis, but on the vertical. For in 'villages which are separated from and invisible to one another,' we are told, the bell-towers still 'rise up towards a single heaven' (III, 184).

This comforting tract is interrupted when, on closer inspection, the churches reveal themselves as 'dead', as 'skeletons'. The closure and desecration of churches in Soviet times has locked people in the cares of the day. Human avarice and malevolence are not an invention of the twentieth century, but the evening bells had once distracted men from their immediate concerns, raising them above the level of beasts and briefly reinstating an elevated, eternal perspective. Now the bells are gone. They are mourned no less poignantly in chapter 44 of *V kruge pervom* ('Na prostore'), where the church and bell-tower of Rozhdestvo beckon to Innokentii from the far side of a quintessentially Russian expanse, but turn out, as he draws closer, to be a stinking ruin in a crippled *kolkhoz* village. Elsewhere in the same novel, the inextricably compromised Iakonov grasps too late the meaning of the peal in the Church of Nikita the Martyr: since he was last here the belltower has been demolished, he has sold his soul, and the view down over the winding River Moscow affords no epiphany (chapter 25). Solzhenitsyn's interest in this unifying trinity of 'vysota, krasota, obzor' (XX, 555) does not diminish over the following thirty years.

Lake Segden, in the eponymous prose poem, will serve as a final topological permutation of the ethical, mythical and political. Perfectly circular and framed by dense forest, the clear, tranquil, almost primordial lake seems to commune with the sky above:

> The water is smooth and even as can be, dotted with duckweed near the shore, but otherwise limpid white, and the lake bottom—white.
>
> The water is enclosed. The forest too. The lake gazes into the sky, the sky into the lake. . . . Oh, to settle here for good. . . . Here your soul would flow between sky and water like the shimmering air. . . .
>
> (III, 164-65)

So far the lake functions as a metaphor for a perfect clarity of understanding unattainable in life, obscured as it inevitably is by the movement and ripples of living.[43] But quietude and contemplative passivity are not the dominant mood of this piece. Lake Segden is also presented as a symbol of Russia itself. 'Rodina . . .' the narrator sighs, but the idyllic scene is illusory. A powerful figure has taken the lake for his own and, while the local people sweat and toil, has built his *dacha* on its shore and set his guards over every path. The usurpation is mythically intensified: the lake/*rodina* becomes an 'enchanted castle' in the grip of 'a cruel prince, a squint-eyed villain' (III, 164-65). The narrator can barely creep close enough to steal a furtive, longing glance at the lake.

There is no crusade to retake the castle in '**Ozero Segden**'. Later myth-makers would allot to Solzhenitsyn the exile a more prominent role in just such a fairy tale—as the vengeful *bogatyr'* on a prancing white steed, poised to expel the usurper and release Segden/ Russia from its spell; or even as the cruel prince himself, snarling defiantly behind his ensorcelled ramparts. For now we note in his own texts the inseparability of the public (national/patriotic) impulse from the individual endeavour so to withdraw from the public arena (if not from life itself) as to glimpse a reflection of the divine purpose of the universe, and a tendency to shape the spaces of his fiction to this design.

FROM FORTRESS CAVENDISH UPON A WHITE CHARGER

Mythicizations of Solzhenitsyn in his Vermont exile came from three broad directions. In the Soviet Union the KGB and the Novosti Press Agency worked energetically to vilify him and neutralize his influence, especially in the West. This involved such items as a book-length exposé by a Czech defector, the doctored memoirs of Solzhenitsyn's first wife, orthodox antidotes to his *Avgust Chetyrnadtsatogo,* a two-volume East German novelization of his career as a CIA puppet, a labour camp denunciation elaborately forged in his hand and fed to a gullible Swiss crime writer, together with other such exotica. All of this, however, was merely the prolongation of a campaign well in hand before his expulsion. In Europe and America admirers who had assumed Solzhenitsyn the gallant dissident to be a Prague Spring socialist or a Western-style democrat were forced to revamp their images of him. Even for those swathes of American opinion which were not automatically alienated by the new labels 'conservative, religious, nationalist' Solzhenitsyn's reservations about the ideals of the land of the free and the American dream led to his being branded a churlish ingrate by the wife of President Carter and, in rather different idiom, by *Hustler* magazine.[44] The third area which generated obloquy and caricature was the Russian émigré community, notably the Third Emigration, from which Solzhenitsyn especially endeavoured to distance himself.

There is much in this phase of Solzhenitsyn's reception that is bizarre and delightful. As a single example, Robert Asprey capitalized on American liberal confusion as to who was the 'real' Solzhenitsyn in a novel which has an expelled Nobel Prize-winning writer with Solzhenitsyn's biography spirited off his plane during an unscheduled stopover in Berlin and imprisoned by an unholy alliance of neo-Nazis and rogue elements of the KGB. Meanwhile a trained double carries on to Frankfurt in his place and is soon stalking about the rostra of the West deliberately nudging it towards nuclear confrontation with the evil empire. Happily, the nice Solzhenitsyn-figure is released in the nick of time by a CIA super-spook with luxuriant golden tresses who, when clothed at all, is most at home, we learn, in

mauve sunglasses, red striped shirt, blue denim bell-bottoms, cowboy boots and 'a neatly knotted necktie of blue silk overprinted with open books [which] showed him a member of Oxford University'.[45] Closer, however, to the spatial concerns of the present essay is the myth of 'Fortress Cavendish'.

Solzhenitsyn's clearest repudiation of the designation 'émigré' came in an interview five years after his arrival in the West:

> . . . I am not an émigré, I did not follow an inner impulse [*dushevnoe dvizhenie*] to leave my homeland, did not decide to start a new life and settle properly somewhere else. So I have a different mental attitude.[46]

Even allowing for the many gradations of duress which may attend a decision to leave one's chosen country, there are few who would grudge Solzhenitsyn the distinction he makes between emigration and exile in his own case.[47] Nevertheless, this demarcation and the tenor of some of his other remarks on emigration were symptomatic of a process of isolation even within exile. On Solzhenitsyn's side this meant that cautious acknowledgement of the worthy intentions of former dissidents who continued their struggle in emigration gave way to mounting indignation at what he saw as false, even russophobic prophets in their ranks. By 1982 he presented himself in a vitriolic essay as the victim of increasingly concerted vilification by these 'pluralists':

> Acres of print rang with their ranting. Two dozen tar-brushes bedaubed me from head to foot. . . . In recent years they have all joined in emptying their slop-pails on me—the whole servile, yapping Soviet press, in the space of twenty years, never bespattered me so copiously and so furiously.[48]

His ire was unstintingly reciprocated. Not long afterwards, Vadim Belotserkovsky set out to refute this image of a Solzhenitsyn beleaguered by yapping émigré democrats. Quite the contrary—it was Solzhenitsyn and his coterie who had *them* surrounded:

> Through a network of Russian-language radio stations, presses and publishing houses in the West, the Nobel Prize-winning novelist and his émigré followers . . . disseminate a steady stream of propaganda. . . . In contrast to the well-funded Solzhenitsyn apparat, democratic émigré groups lack financial resources and have few publications and poor distribution in the Soviet Union. . . . Soviet propaganda would be toothless were it not for the support of Solzhenitsyn's 'fifth column' in the West.[49]

Solzhenitsyn took exception to being presented as the dictatorial Secretary General of some émigré Central Committee, manipulating the gullible Western press through his own Agitprop Department. He ridiculed the very idea that 'that there really exist any such fearsome covert cohorts, mobilized and trained by me'.[50] Certainly there was justice in his indignation at some of the extravagantly abusive labels being applied to him, which included 'frenzied advocate of clerical totalitarianism . . . Russia's Ayatollah . . . the Grand Inquisitor . . . programmed by political mummies who once supported Hitler. . . .'[51]

A particular metaphorical target was the family home on the outskirts of the small Vermont village of Cavendish. Solzhenitsyn's secluded existence, abetted by townsfolk who declined to give directions to his house, quickly became a legend.[52] He worked almost entirely at home, bringing his children up in as Russian an environment as he and his wife could contrive. Even his occasional forays into the outside world for speaking engagements or to conduct research seemed to preserve something of this domestic encapsulation: hotel rooms became workplaces and headquarters, with sightseeing rather a low priority; a heartening impression of a healthy grassroots America was gleaned not least from a cross-country car trip with his wife.

The curiosity, disdain and irony of outsiders—émigrés and Western journalists alike—quickly made of his temporary home a 'portable Gulag'.[53] A great blessing was the fence which he built around his property:

> High above town above Windy Hill Road . . . Alexander Solzhenitsyn's perimeter fence begins. Every few yards, painted signs declare private property, brook no trespassing. At the gate, a camera's eye is vigilant. . . . Soviet Russia's most prominent exile bought *and fortified* this 50-acre estate in 1976.[54]

Although apologetic for having inconvenienced local snowmobilers, Solzhenitsyn was not unhappy that journalists and uninvited guests might be put off by reports of a formidable towering stronghold. The reality—that the TV monitor often did not work, that the chainlink fence would not greatly have challenged even a portly KGB agent and could be bought at Sears—was hardly the stuff of legend. But the legend knew better.

For émigré commentators Solov'ev and Klepikova the fence captured the parodoxical, crippled psyche of a dangerous neo-Stalinist:

> This is the yearning for prison of a man who was set free, but wishes to return—to prison. . . . Is it any wonder that Solzhenitsyn who spent some years in Stalin's camps should ring his Vermont home with an impenetrable fence and even set up TV monitors at the entrance—just like a watch-tower?[55]

Lev Navrozov's elegant variation threw in profligacy and anti-Semitism for good measure:

> He has invested much of his money into the building of his self-imposed one-family concentration camp which is to protect him from his enemies (Jews?).[56]

Back in Russia Tatiana Tolstaia, though scathing, at least kept her feet on the ground. For her the fence evoked smug rectitude and dogmatism, masquerading as 'self-limitation':

> the long exile has seen him construct round himself 'the mythopoetic model of the wise old man behind the fence . . . he supposes that there is one single truth and the combined evidence of his work suggests that he believes that it is known to him alone.'[57]

With the perimeter fence well established, it was not surprising that preternatural guard dogs should be spotted through the mists. In 1977 Elizabeth Hardwick shared with readers of *Time* magazine her vision of encountering the

> doom-faced writer, . . . the striding Armaggedon on the road, glowing, as I imagine him to be, with eschatological fires and accompanied by menacing dogs.[58]

These faithful companions (perhaps named Cerberus and Pluto) may have been spirited back to Russia in 1994 to guard Solzhenitsyn's new 'fortress' at Troitse-Lykovo, for, as Anne McElvoy reports:

> I was recently told by a former Communist functionary that Solzhenitsyn's dogs have razor teeth and can only be discouraged from sinking them into the flesh of any passing Communist by being called off in Old Church Slavonic.[59]

Beside the hut where the real Solzhenitsyn preferred to do his writing is a pond with a small rock promontory. In the BBC TV documentary *The Homecoming* Stepan Solzhenitsyn recalls his father telling him and his brothers, when they were still small, that this stone was in fact an enchanted horse, which would awaken when Russia was free and carry them back to Russia 'Pegasus-style', as he puts it.[60] This endearing anecdote has its more fanciful parallel in the myth of 'Solzhenitsyn on a white horse'. The primary associations of such an equestrian pose are positive, suggesting the valour of St George (Egorii or Georgii, patron saint of Russia) as he tramples the dragon under hoof, or the figure of Il'ia Muromets, bravest and wisest of the *bogatyri* and most loyal in his defence of Kiev ('Стар был на коне наусед седой, / лод старым был конь наубел белой'). In more recent folklore devoted to Solzhenitsyn, however, this once chivalrous image is used to convey sinister motives and comic pretentiousness. The former aspect may be seen in Solov'ev and Klepikova's conspiracy-scenario of 1980. Not content with echoing widespread fears of 'national bolshevist' tendencies in the Soviet establishment, they promote them to the status of an organized clandestine Russian nationalist party, enjoying protection at the highest level, and implicate Solzhenitsyn by hearsay:

> Solzhenitsyn is sanctifying with his prestige some of the most vicious ideas harbored in Russian minds. One of his Moscow followers—not a dissident, an *of-*

ficial!—told us in the spring of 1977: 'Mind my words! Solzhenitsyn will still come back to Moscow as a conqueror on a white horse. . . .'[61]

In the 1970s and 1980s there were members of the Third Emigration as well as metropolitan Russians who would assure all who cared to listen that Solzhenitsyn was the puppet master behind the *Pamiat'* movement, that he was the ghost writer of Shafarevich's xenophobic 'Russophobia', and, later, that he was deliberately delaying his return to Russia until the nationalist forces were ready for their figurehead.

For those less self-deluding, but who nevertheless viewed Solzhenitsyn's Russian patriotism with apprehension and distaste, the image of Solzhenitsyn on a white horse was used ironically, emphasizing the pompous, quixotic and anachronistic as much as the threatening. This tendency is epitomized by the Solzhenitsyn parody in Vladimir Voinovich's satirical novel *Moskva 2042*:

> on the path running from the distant outbuildings there appeared a wondrous horseman, clad all in white and mounted on a white horse. . . . A white cloak, white camisole, white trousers, white boots, white beard and at his side a long sword in a white scabbard.[62]

This is Sim Simych Karnavalov, a broad caricature of Solzhenitsyn as self-exalting nationalistic graphomaniac and idol of a growing underground monarchist party in the Soviet Union. Hidden away in his North American retreat and working on the 'glyby' of his vast opus, he breaks off at noon every day to enact the moment when, mounted on his horse Glagol, he will cross the Soviet frontier to rout the 'satanicheskie zaglotchiki',[63] receive the traditional gift of bread and salt, and assume his rightful place as Russia's tsar and saviour. The appearances of Sim Simych are more amusing than the bulk of the text, which involves a rather laboured journey to a dystopian future Russia, but Solzhenitsyn, feeling himself nowhere more misquoted and misrepresented than in the area of his national views, might be forgiven for not relishing the joke. However, it is time to turn from the myth-enshrouded fence and its chthonic canine guardians to the comparatively palpable world of historical fiction.

THE RED WHEEL

A vital focus for Solzhenitsyn's efforts to make Cavendish a nourishing enclave and to keep at bay the muddied expanse of freedom was *Krasnoe koleso.* For many years it kept him effectively locked in the Russia of 1917, a period which he had chosen for its bearing upon the present state of Russia:

> I lived in 1917 with the people I was writing about, so much so that I felt myself in every sense their contemporary. In many ways they were more alive to

me than people with whom I have been involved in the present day. I was totally wrapped up in them and no one disturbed me.[64]

But while *Krasnoe koleso* functioned as a kind of time capsule and survival module in one, as a literary undertaking it strained Solzhenitsyn's condensing impulse to the utmost.[65]

Indeed, he never completed this historical epopee which he had tentatively begun as a student in Rostov-on-the-Don in the 1930s, and which aimed at nothing less than an understanding, by historical and literary means, of the causes of the October Revolution. The fourth and last completed instalment, *Aprel' Semnadtsatogo,* bears the dates 1984-1989 and was published in 1991 as volume 20 of his *Collected Works.* It is followed by a summary of the continuation as it might have been, entitled **'Where the Narrative Breaks off'** ['Na obryve povestvovan'ia']. Even that synopsis omits the more fictional strands in the book. What we have then is an amputation and partial cauterization, though Solzhenitsyn took comfort in the fact that the crucial lesson of the February Revolution and the conduct of the liberal intelligentsia had been communicated within the 6,400 pages actually published.

The system of 'knots' [*uzly*] into which these pages were organized was intended to capture both the density and the underlying movement of history by focusing upon a series of decisive periods, each of two or three weeks duration.[66] In reducing the number of knots, as it became clear that twenty was too ambitious for one of his age, Solzhenitsyn found it difficult to protect the survivors against compensatory inflation. Thus, the third *uzel, Mart Semnadtsatogo* eventually covered approximately the same number of 'historical' days as had the preceding *Oktiabr' Shestnadtsatogo,* but was more than twice as long, approaching 3,000 pages. Of greater structural significance is the disproportional increase in the number of chapters in the later *uzly.* Again **Mart** provides the extreme example, with no less than 656 chapters, whose average length has dropped from almost sixteen pages in *Oktiabr'* to barely four and a half pages. It was statistics like these which convinced some that Solzhenitsyn had been steamrollered by his own material, and had lost his sense of genre.[67]

In *Krasnoe koleso* the flurry of events is intensifying, the spokes of the red wheel are whirring faster, and time is slipping out of joint. We would not expect the function of space and, particularly, enclosures to be unaffected. Rooms and locations are still described with an eye to creating a particular atmosphere and may still become coextensive with characteristics of their occupants. An example in *Oktiabr' Shestnadtsatogo* is the return of the peasant soldier Arsenii Blagodarev to his village near Tambov and to his family *izba.* The home under threat in *Krasnoe koleso* is Russia, as it was in **'Matrenin dvor'**, but in a work of this scale Russia cannot be equated with any one principal physical location from which a deeper meaning gradually emanates, nor yet, as in earlier long works, with a system of enclosures which organizes the work as a whole. Instead of the contrasting and interlocking circles of *V kruge pervom* and the concentric locations of *Rakovyi korpus* (bed, ward, clinic, Tashkent, post-Stalin Russia, universal human dimension), we have a wheel which rolls, gains momentum and slips out of control, its revolutions containing, organizing and creating nothing.

Onto the sprawling chaotic panorama of Russia at war and in revolution are superimposed the irrational 'Rossiiu zhalko' of Sania Lazhenitsyn and the doomed efforts of Vorotyntsev to find a stable point from which to 'spasat' Rossiiu'. In this violent whirl a dominant spatial organizer is—untypically for Solzhenitsyn hitherto[68]—the path or road. Vorotyntsev's belief that the right man in the right place can decisively affect the course of a campaign sent him and the reader of *Avgust Chetyrnadtsatogo* on a peripatetic canter through the battlefields of East Prussia. By *Mart Shestnadtsatogo* this becomes a hagridden gallop (albeit by rail) from St Petersburg to Moscow with the revolution snapping at his heels, thence to Kiev, the Romanian front, and finally to Mogilev in Belorussia, scene of the last act of the Romanov dynasty and the grave [*mogila*] of the Russia he seems powerless to preserve.

But the *put'* represents not simply the broad course of military and political events and the historical destiny of Russia. Intertwined with them, as never before in Solzhenitsyn's fiction, is the muddy path of human life and affairs. In *Oktiabr'* and *Mart* Vorotyntsev's acuity, dynamism and high ideals do not save him from confusion and remorse. After betraying his wife, then abandoning his lover, he is cripplingly aware of having bungled his private life for years. In the final *uzel* his poisoned marriage is dying in the grave of Mogilev no less surely than the Russia he mourns. The same jumble of near clairvoyance and massive human fallibility besets Varsonof'ev, the eccentric *zvezdochet* who in chapter 42 of *Avgust Chetyrnadtsatogo* had teased Sania and Kostia with the riddle of history and the elusiveness of 'every true path'.[69] But Varsonof'ev turns out to be more than just a puckish sage, deftly steering us through the symbolic reaches of the book from his 'sturdy old-world' house (XX, 528). He is visited almost nightly by onerous, sometimes terrifying dreams whose riddle he cannot decipher and by memories of the 'mangled mess' [*miasorubnoe mesivo*] of his failed marriage. In *Mart* he has to conclude that, on closer inspection, his 'whole life consists almost entirely of mistakes', and only 'through the enfeebled eyes of an old man can we discern all that we have left undone' (XVII, 45).[70] Convinced as he is of the intimate web of

interconnections in all things, he is unable for much of the time to 'make sense of Russia's path and [his] own life' (XVII, 48).

Without this background the final two chapters of *Aprel'* and, thus, of the entire discontinued *Krasnoe koleso* might recall at a fairly glib level the lyrical, contemplative moments of Solzhenitsyn's earlier fiction. The penultimate chapter sees Varsonof'ev initially buffeted by fears and hopes following his recent meeting with the young couple Sania and Ksen'ia. Two related and familiar motifs then emerge. Thirty years earlier the narrator of **'Zakhar-Kalita'** had longed to sweep away the quibbles of historians and grasp the 'integral and irreversible' meaning of the Battle of Kulikovo (III, 312). Now, at the end of *Krasnoe koleso*, Varsonof'ev laments that the very frenzy of revolutionary events obscures the 'supreme vantage point' from which the magnificent curve, the overall design of history reveals itself (XX, 553). Again, in the mid-1960s Solzhenitsyn had the old Doctor Oreshchenkov in *Rakovyi korpus* reflecting that the true purpose of life, lost in the bustle of daily events, is:

> . . . to preserve, as far as possible, untarnished and undistorted, the image of eternity lodged within each individual.
>
> Like a silver moon in a calm, still pond.
>
> (IV, 403)

Varsonof'ev, too, finds that the proximity of death, far from oppressing him, increases the 'elevating capacity of the spirit' and releases 'a great, free vertical dimension which he had been unable to attain in life' (XX, 553-54).

This does not mean, however, that we leave Varsonof'ev in a haze of abstractions and bucolic allegories. He is resigned to the paradox that 'only through earthly events may cosmic battles be waged' (XX, 553), and with a diffident sigh he girds his loins for the struggle to come. He will dedicate his pen to containing a revolution which threatens to roll unchecked ('raskatyvat'sia po prostranstvam' [XX, 554]), but is realistic enough to expect soon to be uprooted from home, if not from homeland. There is no simple correlation between the position of Varsonof'ev in 1917 and of his author seventy years later contemplating a new liberation and a new Time of Troubles in distant Russia, but compared with earlier works such ideas and dilemmas seem in *Krasnoe koleso* to have been more searchingly tested by doubt and disillusionment, and we must suppose that exile as well as age has been at work in this process.[71]

The final chapter of the epopee sees Vorotyntsev similarly bogged down yet drawn aloft. The disorder of his personal life has its equivalent in the public arena, where he is unsure whose alliance to seek and even against whom—'such a hellish, vertiginous state of affairs' (XX, 554). By the closing lines of the book he will have regained his resolve, if not his confidence of victory.

> And his shoulders straightened again. No, there is some light ahead. Not everything has been squandered yet.
>
> But what fork in the road shall we head for? And under what stone shall we lay our bones to rest?
>
> (XX, 557)

Just before that point, however, he pauses in a moment of lassitude, on a bench at the easternmost edge of the earthen rampart around Mogilev.

> What a delight—the broad view out over the river below, over the floodlands and away into the distance. It's like rising up above your own life.
>
> (556)

And Vorotyntsev dreams of being buried on the raised western bank of a Russian river where he can watch the morning sun rise over the water for all time. On the one hand this elegiac moment recalls the enviable resting place chosen by the poet Polonsky, in the prose poem 'Prakh poeta':

> We all like to think our spirit will hover above our grave and gaze at the peaceful expanses all around.
>
> (III, 167)

At the same time, there is something 'external', even valedictory, about Vorotyntsev's affectionate gaze over the Dnieper and the villages stretching away into the Russian heartland.

> My dear, sad, cheated Kostroma homeland.[72] Why have I stayed away from you for so very, very long?
>
> . . . and the yearning reached him even here, tugging at his heart.
>
> Or did he sense that he would never go back there again? . . .
>
> O, my motherland. We have failed you, served you badly.
>
> And now—we have served our last.
>
> (XX, 556)

In 1994 Solzhenitsyn returned, an émigré *malgré lui,* to a Russia startlingly different from the one he had left in 1974. His strenuous efforts to keep abreast of events in his homeland, the many letters he received advising him against returning, cannot have fully prepared him for what he would find. To another returning émigré, Zinovy Zinik, Russia in the nineties seemed like a land full of disorientated immigrants:

> The people there [have] emigrated to a new country. The old country slipped off from under their feet, and they are now in the new one. And it is as alien to them as it is to me.[73]

The fact that Solzhenitsyn had contributed more than most to the collapse of the Soviet Union did not ensure his assimilation into a new Russia, which he knew, even before his departure, to be bored and embarrassed by the monumental features of its past—the heroic no less than the villainous.[74] Literary Russia had become more sympathetic towards postmodernism than to *engagement,* to pluralism than to truthseeking, while the legendary voracity of the Soviet reading public had evaporated with the Soviet Union itself, leaving ***Krasnoe koleso*** unable to compete with pamphlets on erotic mushrooms and the sequel to *Gone with the Wind.* As for the overlapping political, commercial and criminal face of the new Russia, Solzhenitsyn's loathing was unrestrained. In one despondent moment he observed:

> We are holding together now as a single unified country, but our cultural space is in shreds *[kul'turnoe prostranstvo u nas razorvano].* . . .[75]

Some comfort was to be drawn, however, from the awareness of a reservoir of common sense and decency in the ordinary people whom he had met in large numbers during his whistle-stop tour of Siberia in 1994 and in subsequent travels within Russia. Different as they were from the bicycle trips he made through Russia in the 1950s and 1960s, they triggered a return to a genre associated with those experiences—the *Krokhotki.* This, as he told the editor-in-chief of *Novyi mir,* was a form in which he had found it impossible to write during his years outside the frontiers of Russia.[76] The new *Krokhotki* show obvious similarities with the old: one is a reflection on approaching death, suggestive of Turgenev's *Senilia,* two take natural phenomena as allegories for types of human behaviour; in two more bells and bell towers figure prominently. But these are heavier pieces than before—somewhat longer, less simply expressed and decidedly more fierce in their lunges at Russia's latest oppressors. One, indeed, **'Pozor'**, voices fears for the very survival of Russia as a nation and utters a sustained malediction against those who preside over her ruin.[77]

The most typical in its 'spiritual optimism' is **'Kolokol'nia'**,[78] in which a lone bell-tower is seen protruding high above the waves of the Volga, while what survives of the half-flooded town of Kaliazin has the air of a ghost-town populated by deceived abandoned souls. Though Kaliazin suggests a gloomy *pars pro toto,* the bell-tower stands nevertheless:

> As our hope. As our prayer: no, the Lord will not permit *all* of Russia to be drowned beneath the waves.

The link with the homes, churches and bell-towers of Solzhenitsyn's earlier fiction does not need further elaboration. More intriguing and poignant is **'Kolokol Uglicha'**.[79]

This piece takes us back four hundred years to the Russia of Boris Godunov and his alleged assassination of the young Tsarevich Dmitrii in Uglich in 1591. An uprising of the townspeople of Uglich in revulsion at the murder was summarily dealt with. Not only were hundreds of protesters executed, mutilated and exiled, but the bell which sounded the call to arms shared their fate. Its mountings damaged so that it should never hang again, it was whipped for its insubordination and taken off to Siberia in a cart hauled by its fellow rebels. In 1994, when Solzhenitsyn was returning across Siberia from his twenty-year exile, he visited the chapel in Tobol'sk where the exiled bell of Uglich had served three hundred years of 'solitary confinement'. Not long afterwards their paths crossed again when he visited Uglich and saw the bell, newly installed in the Church of Dmitrii-in-Blood. The parallels become irresistible when the narrator is invited to ring the bell. 'Long suffering had dulled its bronze to grey,' he writes, but there is an eloquence to this deep resonance reaching out from the remote past to our 'foolishly scurrying, sullied [*zamutnennye*] souls'.

There are familiar patterns here, but the simple ascending curve is absent. The reflection (or echo) of a timeless wisdom imperfectly rendered by the turbid waters of the present grows out of a specific historical object lesson: 'the lamentation and horror of the people of Uglich rose aloft, the bell proclaimed a universal fear for Russia's safety'. And it is that fear which dominates the ending, rather than the soaring timeless thrust of **'Kolokol'nia'**. The original alarm bell had rung out on the threshold of the Time of Troubles.

> And now it has fallen to me to ring this bell so full of suffering amidst the lingering decay of a Third Time of Troubles. There is no avoiding the comparison: the prophetic alarm of the people is but a minor irritant to the throne and to the thick-skinned boyars around it. This was true four hundred years ago, and it is no less true today.

Solzhenitsyn's very concept of literature is rooted in a belief in the communicability of experience, though at times in exile that faith was shaken.[80] Now, back in Russia, he finds that the muddied waters of freedom have silted up the space once occupied by Communism, or, to use another of his images, an evil prince still casts his spell over Lake Segden, and the people still scuttle about in his shadow denied access to the healing lucidity of its waters. As for Solzhenitsyn, he finds himself sounding a tocsin that has pealed through centuries of Russian history and grappling in his declining years with the fear that perhaps he rings in vain.

Notes

1. Approximate translation: 'London is sated, / Vienna is feasting, / While Stockholm's dolled up to the nines. / It wouldn't be bad to go off there ourselves, / And to leave Russia's squalour behind . . . / But there's no forgetting—just try it! / Why is it that back they all come? / For the West's peace and plenty can never be bought / At the price of a heart left at home.'

2. Anja Pülsch, *Emigration als literarisches Verfahren bei Zinovij Zinik* (München: Otto Sagner, 1995), p. 25.

3. Zinik, interviewed in English by Pülsch, *ibid.,* pp. 179-80.

4. Vladislav Khodasevich, 'Literatura v izgnanii' (1933) in his *Koleblemyi trenozhnik: Izbrannoe* (Moskva: Sov. pisatel', 1991), p. 469. The reference is to the Porte d'Auteuil district of Paris.

5. French TV discussion, 11 April 1975, conducted by Bernard Pivot for the programme 'Apostrophes'. The transcript records Solzhenitsyn as saying: 'Je puis vous jurer que jamais je n'écrirai une seule oeuvre sérieuse, artistique sur l'Occident', and this remark is reproduced in the published French version, 'Soljenitsyne en direct', *Contrepoint*, no. 21 (1976), p. 156. The words in question are not included in the somewhat abridged Russian variant published in Solzhenitsyn's authorized collected works or in the fuller, three-volume *Publitsistika* (see note 6). Announcements for the forthcoming volume of memoirs devoted to his time in the West (see note 11) suggest, perhaps in the same spirit, that the subtitle 'sketches from *literary* life', will not be used, as it had been with the first volume, *Bodalsia telenok s dubom*. V. Radzishevskii, 'Chitaem Solzhenitsyna', *Literaturnaia gazeta,* 31 July 1996.

6. BBC Radio interview with Janis Sapiets, February 1979. Aleksandr Solzhenitsyn, *Publitsistika v trekh tomakh*, vol. 2 (Iaroslavl': Verkhne-volzhskoe knizhnoe izdatel'stvo, 1996), p. 491.

7. *Bodalsia telenok s dubom: Ocherki literaturnoi zhizni* (Moskva: Soglasie, 1996), p. 400.

8. *Koleblemyi trenozhnik*, p. 468.

9. 'We come as envoys, not as exiles.'

10. He is not squeamish about the literal sense of 'outcast': 'When our family was chucked out [and sent] abroad (*vyshvyrnuli za granitsu*) . . .', cited in L. Aleinik, 'Bestsennyi podarok Aleksandra Solzhenitsyna', *Russkaia mysl'* 20-26 June 1996.

11. Since the appearance of Michael Scammell's biography, *Solzhenitsyn: A Biography* (New York/London: Norton, 1984), Solzhenitsyn has released a substantial section of his autobiography, *Nevidimki*, hitherto suppressed for conspiratorial reasons. First published in *Novyi mir*, nos. 11 & 12 (1991), it was incorporated into the 'Soglasie' edition of *Bodalsia telenok s dubom* (see note 7). *Nevidimki* was separately published in English as *Invisible Allies* (Washington, DC: Counterpoint, 1995 and London:

Harvill, 1997). The sequel to *Bodalsia telenok,* covering the years of exile and entitled *Ugodilo zernyshko promezh dvukh zhernovov: Ocherki izgnaniia,* was announced in 1996 by 'Soglasie', Moscow, and a third volume devoted to the years after Solzhenitsyn's return to Russia is reportedly in preparation. The unambiguously KGB-tainted memoirs of his first wife Natal'ia Reshetovskaia have been superseded by her three more recent publications: *Aleksandr Solzhenitsyn i chitaiushchaia Rossiia* (Moskva: Sov. Rossiia, 1990), *Razryv* (Irkutsk: ML "LIK" Vostochno-Sibirskogo knizhnogo izdatel'stva, 1992) and *Otluchenie—iz zhizni Aleksandra Solzhenitsyna: Vospominaniia zheny* (Moskva: MGAP "Mir knigi", 1994). The available documentation was spectacularly augmented by *Kremlevskii samosud: Sekretnye dokumenty Politbiuro o pisatele A. Solzhenitsyne* (Moskva: Biblioteka zhurnala "Istochnik"/Edition q, 1994); abridged English translation, as *The Solzhenitsyn Files,* ed. and with an introduction by Michael Scammell (Chicago: edition q, 1995). Poised to take advantage of these more recent publications, as well as from the cooperation of Reshetovskaia and others, is D. M. Thomas's new biography, *Alexander Solzhenitsyn: A Century in His Life* (New York: St Martin's Press, 1998).

12. 'We lived in Rostov for nineteen years up until the war—and for fifteen of them we couldn't get a room from the state, but had to keep renting various ramshackle huts from private owners at high prices. When we were given a room at last, it was in a converted stable, constantly cold and drafty, heated by coal that was hard to get hold of, and with a good walk to fetch water.' Interview with *The New York Times* and *Washington Post,* 30 March 1972; in *Bodalsia telenok,* p. 647.

13. Letter of 9 March 1943 to N. Reshetovskaia, cited in her *Otluchenie,* p. 115.

14. Part 1, chapter 5 of *Arkhipelag GULag* bears the title 'First Celi—First Love'. At the close of the early play *Plenniki* the prison, a microcosm of Russia in 1945, becomes a 'house' or 'home' and its incumbents a close-knit fellowship ['zhili plotno'], Aleksandr Solzhenitsyn, *Sobranie sochinenii,* vol. 8 (Vermont/ Paris: YMCA Press, 1981), pp. 248 and 250. [All references to this edition are given henceforth in the form (VIII, 248-50).] In *V kruge pervom* the massive stone cell of the Marfino *sharashka* floats free above Stalin's Moscow, an ark bearing aloft its Rosicrucian brotherhood of zeks (II, 9). At the central point of *Odin den' Ivana Denisovicha,* Shukhov's work gang huddles round the stove in a half-built power station with its window embrasures blocked with stolen roofing-felt and becomes, all too briefly, a family, sustained by its own mythic memory (III, 60-64).

15. *Gulag* (VII, 451).

16. '[. . . pobeg] / V obitel' dal'nuiu trudov i chistykh neg'.

17. See *Gulag* (VII, 437-40); chapter 1 of *Nevidimki* ('Nikolai Ivanovich Zubov'), *Bodalsia telenok,* especially pp. 401-09; and the pages in *Rakovyi korpus* devoted to the Kadmins (alias the Zubovs) and the settlement of Ush-Terek (Kok-Terek), particularly chapter 20.

18. The clearest photographs of most of these homes are to be found in *Bodalsia telenok,* between pp. 162 and 163.

19. Reshetovskaia, *Otluchenie,* p. 3.

20. It was here, in 1968, according to Reshetovskaia, that he wrote the Rozhdestvo chapter of *V kruge pervom* (chapter 44 of the authorized edition, 'Na prostore'), saying: 'Everything seems boxed in, there isn't enough space [in the novel]—this will be the chapter that provides it,' *Otluchenie,* p. 64.

21. See chapter 4 of *Nevidimki* ('Estontsy'), in *Bodalsia telenok,* p. 429 ff.

22. Early excerpts from Reshetovskaia's memoirs, published in the *samizdat* journal *Veche,* no. 5, 25 May 1972, included an account and quotations from correspondence relating to this half-humorous 'plan'. See also Scammell, *Solzhenitsyn,* p. 428.

23. English slightly adapted from Harry Willetts's version in *Encounter,* no. 116 (May 1963), p. 28.

24. Victor Sparre, who helped Solzhenitsyn in his abortive search for a house in Norway, recalls his criteria as quiet, simplicity, anonymity and the possibility of keeping his finger on the pulse of the West (and, one might add, of Russia). The luxury he could have afforded figured nowhere in Solzhenitsyn's *desiderata* ('I have no feeling for it'). See the section 'Solzhenitsyn on the Bridge' in Victor Sparre, *The Flame in the Darkness* (London: Grosvenor Books, 1979), pp. 34-56.

25. Among the more recent essays treating topological aspects of Solzhenitsyn's writing are: Willi Beitz, 'Raum und Zeit in A. Solženicyns Roman *V kruge pervom*: Zum Verhältnis von Poetik und Weltsicht', *Zeitschrift für Slawistik,* vol. 39, no. 1 (1994), 66-81; Richard Tempest, 'The Geometry of Hell: The Poetics of Space and Time in *One Day in the Life of Ivan Denisovich,*' in Alexis Klimoff, ed., *One Day in the Life of Ivan Denisovich: A Critical Companion* (Evanston, IL: Northwestern Univ. Press, 1997), pp. 54-69; M. Brewer, 'Izobrazhenie prostranstva i vremeni v lagernoi literature: *Odin den' Ivana Denisovicha i Kolymskie rasskazy, Graduate Essays in Slavic Languages and Literatures* (Pittsburgh), vol. 8 (1995), 92-100; Oleg Lekmanov's brief but cogent 'Ot zheleznoi dorogi podale, k ozeram: O tom, kak ustroeno prostranstvo v rasskaze A. I. Solzhenitsyna "Matrenin dvor"', *Russkaia mysl',* 7-13 May 1998,

p. 13. See also Catherine V. Chvany's careful study of Solzhenitsyn's mythic sense of historical truth in her 'The Poetics of Truth in Solženitsyn's "Zaxar-Kalita" (Zakhar-the-Pouch)', in E. Semeka-Pankratov, ed., *Studies in Poetics: Commemorative Volume Krystyna Pomorska (1928-1986)* (Columbus, Ohio: Slavica, 1995), pp. 191-206.

26. Iu. M. Lotman, 'Zametki o khudozhestvennom prostranstve', in his *Izbrannye stat'i v trekh tomakh* (Tallinn: Aleksandra, 1992), vol. 1, p. 457. For a clear survey of writing on spatial form, see K. Hansen Löve, *The Evolution of Space in Russian Literature: A Spatial Reading of 19th and 20th Century Narrative Literature* (Amsterdam: Rodopi, 1994), especially chapter 2 ('On the Notion of Space in Literature').

27. *Bodalsia telenok*, p. 405.

28. This is not to belittle the realistic fear, especially in the early years in the West, of KGB retaliation. Details of a failed KGB assassination attempt upon Solzhenitsyn's life in Novocherkassk in 1971 became known in 1992: see *Bodalsia telenok*, p. 508 and the testimony of retired KGB Lieutenant-Colonel Boris Ivanov, pp. 675-84. The original publication abridged Ivanov's statement, but incorporated it into a wider investigative report by Dmitrii Likhanov. See 'Smertel'naia zhara', *Sovershenno sekretno*, no. 4 1992), pp. 10-13.

29. The circle structure of *V kruge pervom* is based on a similar de-coupling of captivity and unfreedom.

30. In comparable, if ironic, vein, Solzhenitsyn noted in 1990 that the Iron Curtain had done an excellent job of protecting Russia from all that was positive in Western culture, while doing nothing to contain the seeping 'liquid manure' of Western popular culture. *Publitsistika*, vol. 1, pp. 561-62.

31. The landscape behind this and the following example is, strictly speaking, Finnish, but in the present context Solzhenitsyn's Finnish refuges of the mid-sixties may be seen as co-extensive with his Russian hideaways.

32. *Bodalsia telenok*, p. 431.

33. He writes at the same point that it was during this stay at his Finnish refuge that, still reeling from the disastrous seizure of his papers by the KGB, he composed three prayers. The best known of them includes the line: 'From the heights of earthly fame I look back / in wonder at the road that led / through hopelessness to this place whence I can send / mankind a reflection of Your radiance.' He objected to the publication of this prayer as tactless, but its relevance to the motifs of elevation and reflection in these pages is obvious.

34. *Bodalsia telenok*, p. 436.

35. 'The house would be fine, but the devil lives inside'. *Poslovitsy russkogo naroda: Sbornik V. Dalia* (Moskva: Khudozhestvennaia literatura, 1984), vol. 2, p. 83.

36. Cited in Hansen Löve, *The Evolution of Space*, p. 39.

37. 'Never had Innokentii been in such a crushed and twisted old building, starved of light and air, furniture all warped and askew; never had he experienced such dismal poverty . . .' (II, 79).

38. This unlikely epiphany affects another putative ex-zek in the prose poem 'Dykhanie', who can conceive of no greater freedom than to stand beneath a solitary apple tree in a cramped garden, hemmed in by houses and the din of passing trucks, and to breathe in the freshness left by a shower of rain (III, 163).

39. In 1994 Solzhenitsyn revisited Matrena's *izba*, now restored as a *dom-muzei* in his and her honour. See Irina Petrova, 'V Rossii snova est' gde zateriat'sia', *Novaia ezhednevnaia gazeta*, 10 June 1994, p. 3 and the photograph in *The Times*, 3 Sept. 1994, p. 11.

40. 'Na Sovetskoi granitse' (iz stikhotvornoi povesti *Shosse Entuziastov*), *Vestnik RKhD*, no. 117 (1-1976), pp. 148-54.

41. *Ibid.*, p. 151.

42. The terminology is that used by Lotman in contrasting the journeys of Dante and Ulysses in the *Divine Comedy*. Dante's quest for knowledge is marked by the vertical axis of morality. His *put'* thus becomes a 'pilgrimage', whereas that of Ulysses remains but a journey. Lotman, *Izbrannye stat'i*, p. 456.

43. The prose poem 'Otrazhen'e v vode' spells out this very allegory (III, 170).

44. For a survey of such responses, see my 'Solzhenitsyn: Effigies and Oddities', in J. B. Dunlop, *et al.*, eds., *Solzhenitsyn in Exile: Critical Essays and Documentary Materials* (Stanford, CA: Hoover Institution Press, 1985), pp. 109-42.

45. Robert B. Asprey, *Operation Prophet* (New York: Doubleday, 1977), p. 17.

46. *Publitsistika*, vol. 2, p. 494.

47. Seven KGB agents surrounded Solzhenitsyn on his involuntary journey from a Russian jail to a destination which had not even been disclosed to him. This was not an 'emigration' in any normal and natural sense of the word, *pace* Daniel Rancour-Laferriere: 'Whether he likes it or not, Solzhenitsyn is an émigré.' See his 'Solzhenitsyn and the Jews: A Psychoanalytic View,' *Soviet Jewish Affairs*, vol. 15, no. 3 (1985), 48.

48. 'Nashi pliuralisty', *Publitsistika*, vol. 1, pp. 406 and 441. English in *Survey*, vol. 29, no. 2 (125), 1 and 26.

49. 'Undoing the West in the Soviet Union', *The Nation*, 16 March 1985, front cover and pp. 306-08.

50. 'Nashi pliuralisty', p. 443.

51. *Ibid.*, p. 442.

52. The cinematographic potential of the approach to Solzhenitsyn's Cavendish retreat was most obviously exploited in Stanislav Govorukhin's 1991 TV-documentary *Aleksandr Solzhenitsyn* for the programme 'Krupnyi plan'. See also Jean Cazenave's film of Bernard Pivot interviewing the writer in Cavendish for French TV's *Apostrophes* in 1983, and the first part of Archie Baron's *The Homecoming* for BBC TV, 1995.

53. Cf. Vadim Belotserkovskii, *Iz portativnogo GULAGA rossiiskoi emigratsii* (München; author's edn., 1983), which includes an essay on Solzhenitsyn.

54. Bill Keller, 'The Vintage Actor Gets Great Reviews', *The New York Times,* 1 June 1988. (Emphasis added—M.N.)

55. V. Solov'ev and E. Klepikova, 'Solzhenitsyn, vypusknik Gulaga', *Novyi Amerikanets,* 15-20 Sept. 1980), pp. 26-27; cited after *Solzhenitsyn Studies* (Lancaster), vol. 1, No. 4 (1980), 167.

56. 'Solzhenitsyn: A Double-faced Totalitarian of Stalin's Vintage', *New York City Tribune,* 1 July 1985, p. 4B.

57. Cited in Anne McElvoy, 'The Second Circle', *Times,* 21 May 1994, Magazine Section, p. 19.

58. 'On the Record', *Time,* 19 Dec. 1977, p. 25 (but adjacent pagination inconsistent).

59. 'The Second Circle', p. 18.

60. In the BBC TV documentary *The Homecoming.* Victor Sparre is evidently alluding to the same story in *The Flame in the Darkness,* pp. 51-52.

61. E. Klepikova and V. Solovyov, 'The Secret Russian Party', *Midstream,* vol. 26, No. 8 (Oct. 1980), 18.

62. Vladimir Voinovich, *Moskva 2042* (Ann Arbor, MI: Ardis, 1987), p. 70. First publication in Russia was by 'Vsia Moskva' in 1990.

63. There is much linguistic play in the novel. Thus the 'knots' [*uzly*] of *Krasnoe koleso* become 'lumps' or 'clods' in allusion to the collection of essays *Iz-pod glyb* [From under the Rubble] of which Solzhenitsyn was co-editor. The 'satanic ingurgitators' and the horse's name 'Word' (or perhaps 'Logos') parody archaizing and apocalyptic tendencies in Solzhenitsyn's language.

64. Transcript of *The Homecoming.*

65. Cf. his 1976 interview with Nikita Struve: 'This passion for condensation (*uplotnenie*) is obviously a personal thing, not simply inherent in the material. . . . perhaps it is a habit that comes from living in a cell. I cannot cope with a novel if the material is arranged too freely'. *Publitsistika,* vol. 2, p. 422.

66. The *uzel* structure may be seen as an elaboration upon a technique first used in *Rakovyi korpus.* Since the progressive effects of illness had to be shown, he could not fall back on the single day of *Ivan Denisovich,* or the handful of days covered in *V kruge pervom.* Rejecting on unbroken linear extension over time, Solzhenitsyn split the *povest'* (novella) into two parts, two stations, of short duration but rich in associations. This is consistent with his statement that the structural division of *Krasnoe koleso* into *uzly* dates from 1967 (XII, 545).

67. See in this context Petr Vail' and Aleksandr Genis, 'Poiski zhanra. Aleksandr Solzhenitsyn', *Oktiabr',* no. 6 (1990), pp. 197-202.

68. This generalization could be defended against the claims of an entire section of *Arkhipelag GULag* devoted to 'vechnoe dvizhenie' (Part II), or, more cautiously, against the momentum of the early *Dorozhen'ka,* of which the careering *Prusskie nochi* was once a chapter.

69. In the final *uzel* we learn that the answer to the riddle he had set the boys at their first meeting is, in fact, *Doroga*—the Road of Life and of History. At the same time, he concedes the 'terrible' truth that 'wheels' can roll along without a road (XX, 532).

70. Varsonof'ev's age of sixty-one in *Mart Semnadtsatogo* coincides with that of Solzhenitsyn when he was finishing *Oktiabr' Shestnadtsatogo* and had already embarked upon *Mart.*

71. Interestingly, the 'supreme vantage point' affords Varsonof'ev a sense of Russian history not on its own, but as part of 'a single conception involving the West' (XX, 553).

72. Solzhenitsyn had studied at an artillery training school in Kostroma in 1941.

73. Pülsch, *Emigration,* p. 185,

74. His impatience with the *Zeitgeist* not long before his return may be judged by, e.g., 'Otvetnoe slovo na prisuzhdenie literaturnoi nagrady Amerikanskogo natsional'nogo kluba iskusstv, N'iu-Iork, 19 ianvaria 1993', *Novyi mir,* no. 4 (1993), pp. 3-6.

75. Speech at Saratov University, 13 Sept. 1995, in Aleksandr Solzhenitsyn, *Po minute v den'* (Moskva: Argumenty i fakty, 1995), p. 140.

76. *Novyi mir,* no. 1 (1997), p. 99.

77. In the early 1970s Solzhenitsyn could still hope that Russia would emerge *From Under the Rubble [Iz-pod glyb].* Preparing to return home at the end of the 1980s he left the hero of his epopee poised at the brink of the abyss of 1917 ('na obryve'). As the fol-

lowing decade drew to a close he would mourn a contemporary Russia now 'caving in', subsiding into ruin: *Rossiia v obvale* (Moskva: Russkii put', 1998).

78. *Novyi mir,* no. 3 (1997), p. 70.

79. *Ibid.,* no.1 (1997), p. 100.

80. 'But your society recoils from our warning voices. I suppose we have to face the sad fact that experience is generally incommunicable, leaving everyone to experience everything for themselves.' BBC Radio talk, 24 March 1976, in *Publitsistika,* vol. 1, pp. 296-97.

Natal'ia Ivanova (essay date summer 2001)

SOURCE: Ivanova, Natal'ia. "'I've Been Faulted for Everything but the Weather . . .': Aleksandr Isaevich on Iosif Aleksandrovich." *Russian Studies in Literature* 37, no. 3 (summer 2001): 25-43.

[In the following essay, Ivanova relates Solzhenitsyn's professional dislike of Joseph Brodsky.]

Two Russian Nobel Prize winners, two expellees, a poet and a prose writer, Joseph Brodsky and Aleksandr Solzhenitsyn—yet more separates them than brings them together. Though what brings them together is the continent of the Russian language, thanks to which Russian literature exists and, as a special feature of it, Russian Nobel Laureates. The Russian language is multicomponent; it hides within itself numerous ways, roads, and paths along which one can travel. Here, even geniuses and titans can live and virtually never meet, as Tolstoy and Dostoyevsky never met. Such a nonmeeting was, it seemed, destined for Solzhenitsyn and Brodsky. At least, in Brodsky's lifetime there was no meeting, neither face-to-face nor in absentia, with the exception of one letter, about which Lev Losev wrote recently ("Solzhenitsyn and Brodsky as neighbors" [Solzhenitsyn i Brodskii kak sosedi], *Zvezda,* no. 5 [2000]). But then several years passed after the poet's untimely demise, and something unexpected and, in the literary sense, rather remarkable happened: Solzhenitsyn *met* Brodsky. He attentively read Brodsky's poetry when preparing his *Literary Collection* [*Literaturnaia kollektsiia*].

And he did not like Brodsky.

Solzhenitsyn did not like him to such a degree that, though usually thorough, accurate, and even pedantic, in his references and reservations, he allows—whether unintentionally or intentionally—an inaccuracy, even a factual mistake, by ascribing compilation of the 1989 book *Part of Speech: Selected Poems, 1962-1989* [*Chast' rechi. Izbrannye stikhi 1962-1989*] to the poet.

Actually, the collection was compiled not by Brodsky (who, as is known, was averse to this kind of work) but by E. Beznosov. The copyright mark © indicates that the compilation rights belong not to the author but to the publishers—Khudozhestvennaia literatura—who put out the poorly bound volume in a printing of 50,000.

"This little volume of selected poems, if one reads it all successively . . . But I will stop here. In what order are the poems arranged? Not strictly chronologically; Brodsky does not trust this order," Solzhenitsyn writes in the first paragraph of his article (from *Literary Collection*) **"Joseph Brodsky—Selected Poems" ["Iosif Brodskii—izbrannye stikhi"]** (*Novyi mir,* no. 12 [1999]).

Nothing in Solzhenitsyn's written and oral speech is ever unintentional, and it is not unintentionally that he uses the epithet *strictly*: This word actually defines the position of the article's author. He is *strict*; from the very outset he adopts the stance not of a reader, who may even be exacting, thorough, and seeking to understand, but of one sternly demanding of the poet: Explain why, and in what order, are your poems arranged? Then comes another question, this time with a follow-up assumption and presumption: "Is this to say that he has found some other internal organic link and course of development? Not at all, because we see that the sequence of the poems varies from book to book. Hence it has not been found." Teacher to pupil: Sit down, you got a "D." The answer is unsatisfactory. And it does not matter to the teacher that the pupil and even his shadow have long since left the classroom and, more likely, were never even there. Moreover, the "pupil" actually had nothing to do with the subject—the "composition" of the collection that had aroused such strict questions.

However, this is a popular polemical method frequently adopted by out-of-the-ordinary, "monological" individuals. If there is no basis for a polemical discourse, if there is nothing initially to grasp at, while the person has clearly gone against one's grain and arouses a clawing hostility, so as to push off and get afloat such a basis must be conjured up. Thus Solzhenitsyn begins to polemize with an imaginary Brodsky who had *inappropriately,* from Solzhenitsyn's point of view, arranged his collection.

From here, Solzhenitsyn takes on the role of a critic in the same mode, imagining and mentally adding on to the target of his criticism and polemic.

The target is certainly powerful and vivid, and he arouses in Solzhenitsyn an appropriately energetic response. Energetically negative: Solzhenitsyn does not accept Brodsky.

Well, you may say, it is a matter of taste.

But this is one aspect. The other and more significant one is that Solzhenitsyn exposes Brodsky. And this is most interesting, because actually this exposé, so impassioned and energetic, presents a picture not so much of the target of the critical attack as *a portrait of the critic,* who is out to denounce and expose.

The article is not only and not so much a portrait of Brodsky as a self-portrait of Solzhenitsyn.

(I could add, however, that it would be interesting to read through Solzhenitsyn's "literary collection" precisely so as to understand Solzhenitsyn—certainly not to get, with his help, closer to the work of Lipkin, Lisnianskaia, Svetov, and others, whom Solzhenitsyn treats much more warmly and condescendingly, if not lovingly, than his Nobel neighbor.)

* * *

In light of all the aforesaid, let us begin not with Brodsky but with language. I will not repeat what everyone already knows about Solzhenitsyn's predilection for expanding (and at the same time deepening) the Russian literary vocabulary. But expanding the vocabulary in prose or journalism is one thing, whereas in a critical literary essay it is something entirely different. Here, after all, we simply cannot get away from Brodsky: Against the background of his lyrical poetry, the language Solzhenitsyn employs as a literary critical tool seems especially expressive—because of its *incompatibility* with Brodsky's poetry.

I will list but a few, and perhaps not most remarkable, examples:[1] "Izzhazhdano li okunanie v khliabi" [a longing to immerse in the depths], "bravadno" [bravada-ceously], "iadche vsego iz' 'iavit'" [express most caustically], "sdergi" [flailings], "prosocheno" [leaked, seeped through], "proskkvoznet" [pass through; pierce], "peretiok nachalsia" [(over)flow has begun], "petushinstvo" [act cockily], "apofeoz . . . rassudlivosti" [apotheosis of . . . reasonableness], "iznevol'no" [involuntarily, unwittingly], "zanozhonnost'" [the root here could be from "zanoza"—"splinter," or "noga"—"foot," or "nozh"—"knife"]. And this is but a small part of Solzhenitsyn's *archaeneologisms.* Most interesting, however, is not the vocabulary itself but also the syntactic and phraseological structure, the architecture of the phrase into which Solzhenitsyn blithely inserts his pet word, for example: "And this fashion could not but *zapolonit'* ["fill" or "capture"] Joseph Brodsky, possibly given his apparent personal vulnerability—as a form of self-defense as well." So what if the word *zapolonit'* stumps the reader, because its contemporary meaning is closer to "fill to the brim" rather than "take prisoner"? Solzhenitsyn, with his energy of negation, couldn't care less about trifles. Or, for example, he writes: "An entirely different pole of sincere feeling of

the poet *prokolot' sia* in the highly cantankerous 'Speeches on Spilt Milk' [Rechi na prolitom moloke]" (320 more lines). Again, in modern usage, the word *prokolot' sia* means to reveal one's true colors; so what has this to do with "pole of sincere feeling"?

I have chosen these examples from Solzhenitsyn's text not for bone picking but for clarity: They are indicative of the incompatibility of Solzhenitsyn's vocabulary principles with the subject he has undertaken to judge. These linguistic forays—over difficult obstacles—do not achieve their goal, or, rather, miss it, because the region of their linguistic habitat is located elsewhere.

Nevertheless, if there is one thing one cannot deny Solzhenitsyn, it is persistence. If a fortress does not surrender, it is starved out. If the enemy does not surrender, he is destroyed.

Russian literature of the second half of the twentieth century has been so rich in internal subject matter, including ideology, that even in the "camp" of those who had left the country—whether of their own free will or expelled from it—fights and battles have been (and still are) going on—words like *arguments* or *polemics* would be too mild. These clashes of opinions, considerations, and ideas did not bypass Solzhenitsyn. Indeed, as often as not, he himself instigated them. In Brodsky's case, he reveals a persistent temperament combined with didactic sternness (incidentally, in the article there is one rather droll passage, where Solzhenitsyn castigates Brodsky for incorrectly using terms from a geometry school textbook (something about the legs or hypotenuse of a right triangle). Here, to use an expression from his own text, he has revealed himself [*prokolot' sia*]: the math teacher from the Ryazan school is still alive in Solzhenitsyn).

All this may, of course, seem to be just incidental, so to say coastal beacons and indicators. Actually, where is the main watershed between Solzhenitsyn and Brodsky?

Solzhenitsyn quotes with indignation a phrase of Brodsky's, which is important for an understanding of them both: In the twentieth century, for a writer "it is impossible to take [even] oneself absolutely seriously."

Brodsky is quite convinced of this. His entire poetry, filled as it is with bitter self-irony and not precluding the posing of the most serious, "damned" questions of existence, confirms this.

Solzhenitsyn is equally convinced of the reverse: In the twentieth century, every writer *must* take oneself seriously and carry this burden.

Both feel responsibility before "the time and the place," but each embodies this responsibility differently.

But it is precisely *irony* that Solzhenitsyn refuses to forgive Brodsky for: Because irony can be directed at anything and anyone, it has no boundaries or limits. Every single creature, occurrence, person, country, or people can fall under its corrosive (or vivifying, depending on what one thinks) influence. No one, even the most gifted, the most talented writer, is guaranteed against attacks of such irony.

Solzhenitsyn, however, categorically rejects both irony and self-irony, assuming that this evil, this "fashion," "irony as a way of looking at things," has, like everything negative and destructive, come from the West. And if, as Solzhenitsyn declares, "For Brodsky invariable irony becomes almost an obligation of poetic service," then that *poetic service* of his is destructive for Russian culture and the Russian language.

But this has to be somehow proved!—while maintaining outward respect, but without literary politesse, which is absolutely alien to Solzhenitsyn. In general, Solzhenitsyn did not have to go out and prove anything: The complete difference, not just distance between, or different directions of, their fates, biographies, and poetics, is apparent.

Solzhenitsyn, however, stubbornly wants to proffer proof, to argue and confirm that he is right. To him, Brodsky is an impediment in the literary and social universe of the second half of the twentieth century. And not only Brodsky but his readers as well, having adopted this irony, are capable of assailing (joking, ironizing, ridiculing, even shocking) values that Solzhenitsyn considers immutable.

Whereas for Solzhenitsyn the world must be regulated by authority, and that authority is Solzhenitsyn himself, in Brodsky's world authorities are deceptive. A single line of Brodsky's—"I am sitting on a chair, mad with anger"—is already destructive for a literary world subordinated to values and authorities established by someone else.

To destroy the influence of Brodsky, which is destructive for the authoritatively hierarchic perception of the world, it is necessary to destroy his image and his authority—the whole myth of Brodsky's greatness, which keeps getting in Solzhenitsyn's way.

Solzhenitsyn begins his destruction with . . . love for a woman. He realizes only too well that this is a honing tool for a poetic world of any complexity. If feeling for a woman is subjected to ironic analysis, if it cools and becomes "the apotheosis of coldness and reasonableness [*khladnosti i rassudlivosti*]," manifested in this test (a Russian on a date) are the essential qualities not only of a person but also of a poet (and of poetry). Brodsky's "love fabric" is (according to Solzhenitsyn) "sup-

purated" [*iz'' iazvlena*] by irony, "romanticism for him is in bad taste," he "profanes [*profaniruet*] the text with abrupt flailings [*rezkimi sdergami*] . . . descending to mockery." To be sure, even Solzhenitsyn cannot fail to note how "wonderful" some poems are, but he immediately supplements the compliment with persistent pointers to "irrepressible aloofness, coldness, jejune statement of fact." "Chills in longness" [*zastuzhivaet v dolgote*], "chilling [*kholodeiushchie*] reflections"—actually, basic *qualities* and merits of Brodsky's poetry noted by many researchers and memoir writers are perceived by Solzhenitsyn as fundamental *defects*. Yakov Gordin, for example, credits Brodsky with a genre discovery and a genre achievement: the *long verse-work* [*bol' shoe stikhotvorenie*] ("Hills" [*Kholmy*], "Isaac and Abraham" [*Isaak i Avraam*], "Gorbunov and Gorchakov," and other poems), as distinct from the *poema*:

> He has at his disposal all that is needed for the fashioning of genre, which may become genres in their own right. If Pushkin, in fact, introduced the *poema* genre, then Brodsky, already at the beginning of the 1960s, was introducing a new kind of poem—the long verse-work.[2]

As for irony, here, too, there is a point of view contrary to Solzhenitsyn's:

> There was this cleansing of life through irony, self-deprecation, sarcasm. It was a sort of pick-me-up for his romantic hangover. An attempt to rid his poems of their farcical histrionics by looking at it from on high with an ironical vision. . . . [G]iven this broadness of vision—not angry, perhaps, but bitter is, alas, trivial an epithet—the irony verges on sarcasm which is clothed in a very down-to-earth vocabulary.[3]

A distinctive feature of Brodsky's poetry is in the combination of irony with "allure" and "charm" (Anatoly Naiman). But all this proves nothing to Solzhenitsyn and cannot make him change his mind: rather, he is once again convinced of the correctness of his approach, of "debunking."

Solzhenitsyn's purpose and task precludes debate, argumentation, or proof of another's point of view, because the statement (already after an analysis of the subject of "love," in the course of which Brodsky is showered with not so much literary as ethical accusations) that "because of a core, all-pervading coldness, Brodsky's poetry in most cases does not grip the heart" leaves no room for debate.

An argument appealing "to the heart" does not require anything: It takes nothing into account but personal conviction.

Actually all literature is divided, not only by Solzhenitsyn but by all his followers (imitators—both mentally and spiritually), into "heartfelt" [*serdechnaia*] and "heartless" [*besserdechnaia*]. So Brodsky's poetry has no "heart." It is heartless.

By denying Brodsky any "heartfelt" feelings [*serdech-nost'*], he actually thereby places the poet outside the confines of culture: "His poems go from poetry to intellectual and rhetorical gymnastics." The logic here is this: If there is no heart, there is no "simplicity" or "spiritual accessibility"; hence it is outside the confines of "poetry." But following this logic, the "confines of poetry" are filled with tear-jerking romances, while Russian poetry, from Baratynskii to Mandelstam, from Pasternak to Kharms, is left to wait outside the gate. If one is looking for "simplicity," Russian poetry—complex and certainly not always "spiritually accessible"—is hardly the place to turn to: "accessible" are L. Shchipakhina and L. Vasil'eva, and it is certainly hard to decide where to place Oleg Chukhontsev or the young Maksim Amelin. It is not Brodsky's *poems* that Solzhenitsyn *doesn't like*—and it is not poems (as poems) that he writes about; what he doesn't like is the *perception of the world,* he is repulsed by a *poetry* he calls "snobbish posturing," he is turned off by *behavior*: "He views the world not even condescendingly but with a disgust for being, with a kind of grimace of hostility, dislike for the existing, and sometimes loathing of it." All these are mental deductions—*outside* literature and *outside* poetry—but, for Solzhenitsyn, with his understanding of literary tasks and purposes, it is precisely feelings of the heart and the love of being ("the existing") that not simply color (or do not color) our literature but are literature. "There are quite a few poems in which Brodsky expresses loathing for whatever catches his glance." For Solzhenitsyn, as Solzhenitsyn sees it, *poetry* must be *beautiful, heartfelt,* and *kind*: Anything else is not of it (or of culture). For example, if a landscape in a poem is without people, that is bad, a negative quality: "And, in truth, his landscapes are mostly deserted and lack motion or are even clots of despondency ("San-P'etro")." That means, if a still life depicts a lot of good food it is good, if there are only a couple of empty oyster shells and a lemon, it is bad; if a landscape depicts a sumptuous palace with a manicured park, that is excellent, but if it is a swamp with a few blades of grass and no people, or even frogs—that is very bad.

But Solzhenitsyn does not stop there: Brodsky's poetry (and his position) are such a powerful irritant that he denies Brodsky any intellectual depth, which Solzhenitsyn usually refers to as civilization.

What Solzhenitsyn does not deny Brodsky is technical ability: "In his rhymes Brodsky is inexhaustible and highly inventive, he extracts them from the language even where they seem not to exist." This is a compliment but, in a way, questionable, if one reads into it (it may imply *violation* of the language: "He extracts them from the language even where they seem not to exist"). But this is immediately followed by a "downgrading" comment: "He also, of course, goes to extremes" and

"for these expansive rhymes and the construction of these refined strophes (additionally complicated by the unwinding consequences of rhyming) Brodsky must pay a high price." Solzhenitsyn continues to press on, "destroying" Brodsky's technical skills as well: "Hyphenating from one line to the next . . . becomes a worn-out cliché, these hyphenations no longer carry any emotional luster, they cease to serve any artistic purpose and are only needlessly tiresome," "become annoying and ingenuous," are "no longer artful but careless." And more: "The sticky form of the verse loses [*zabluzhi-vaet*] the author among unnecessary objects, circumstances, excrescencies, and even tumors, brought in from outside." Brodsky is castigated for "deliberate misarticulation [*kosnoiazychie*]," "rebuses" and "conundrums": "So many corrupted, lacerated phrases—rearrange and decipher them." "The inner unity . . . is lost, dissipated"; "capricious fluttering of thoughts"; "far-fetched conglomerates." Conclusion: "The verse does not pour out, it was deliberately *manufactured*. The poet occasionally demonstrates heights of tightrope walking, without, however, offering us (I would like to know who those "we" are.—N. I.) any musical, heartfelt, or mental joy." Solzhenitsyn also denies Brodsky musicality in everything, leaving nothing of his poetry, denying it existentially [*sushchnostno*], in whole and in part.

This is not just an effort to bring him down: The objective here is destruction. It is a serious objective and a serious task, because in the highest sense, "up there" they—Solzhenitsyn and Brodsky—do not even coexist: They reject each other.

So: feelings, love are absent—instead, there is deadening coldness; there is no heart—instead, there is heartlessness; there is no beauty—instead of it there is ugliness; intellect, too, is lacking: "At times one fails to find in these poems a thought of any magnitude."

After such a diagnosis, or such a sentence—I do not know what word is more appropriate for Solzhenitsyn's operation on the poems—the author of the article proceeds with analysis (or a search for biographical reasons for the *crime*—because Brodsky is a criminal, a Raskolnikov of Russian poetry, who has overstepped the commanded limits assigned to it. And, in general, he is hardly a *poet*. In this sense, Judge Savel'eva may be a little amnestied: Indeed, who ever told Brodsky that he was a poet?).

And so, analysis.

It is considered that Brodsky suffered from trial and exile?

Solzhenitsyn shrugs his shoulders.

"He expressed these impressions in exaggeratedly wrathful poems . . ."

"Quite a mild sentence, by Gulag standards . . ."

"Initially Brodsky's worldwide fame over his trial went far beyond the reputation of his poems . . ."

"[D]igressed from a correct self-assessment . . ."

"He began to imagine that he had engaged in a titanic struggle against the communist regime."

Anna Akhmatova, who was concerned for the young poet, in whom she had immediately seen an exceptional talent, could, with her involvement in Brodsky's fate, allow herself to joke: "What a biography they are making for our redhead!" The only positive aspect Solzhenitsyn sees in Brodsky's biography and poetry is his days in exile, where, of course, "the breath of the land, the Russian village, and nature suddenly produce shoots of initial understanding"; "the vivifying effects of the land, of everything growing, horses and village work" are all wonderfully positive. Solzhenitsyn, for some reason, dwells especially on horses, recalling the remarkable impact on himself—a city student at the time—of a horse-drawn military transport, when he "experienced much the same and was already inhaling it joyously." Although he, fastidiously, does not mention it, he implies, of course, the smell. So manure plus horse carts, or vice versa, and also, "had Brodsky lived a little longer in exile, that component of his development could have significantly extended. But he was shortly after pardoned . . ."

Indeed, what a pity!

Manure and horses and a lengthy exile, at least five years or so, and who knows, Brodsky might still have become a poet with whom Solzhenitsyn could empathize. Someone like, say, Primerov or at least Peredreev . . . After all, there were all the prerequisites—opportunities, as Solzhenitsyn sensed them—"vividly expressed, with sincere feeling, without posturing"! But alas, he was retrieved by those damned educatees [*obrazovantsy*] ("growing up in that peculiar Leningrad intellectual circle, Brodsky barely touched the vast Russian soil. In fact, his entire spirit is international, he has, by nature, a multilateral, cosmopolitan heritage"). So, at the educatees' request, the authorities let him go from exile to the city, and thereby doomed the poet.

And that, after all this, Brodsky left the confines of his homeland is nothing great, either.

And he has no God, no Christian faith.

In all his life, he never expressed "a single weighty political judgment."

And there is no metaphysics: "And then, after towering for so many years in the pose of a metaphysical poet, to get so 'physically' soiled!" A Russophobe.

In general, whatever you look for, he has nothing.

The conclusion is quite hypocritical: "One cannot but feel sorry for him."

Actually, one cannot but feel sorry for Solzhenitsyn. For one, to get so irritated and continuously try to keep in reign one's percolating rage is extremely harmful for one's own feelings (especially if they are Christian). Second (or perhaps, actually, first) one should feel sorry for a writer who has apparently failed to acquire an ear and a sense, a taste and understanding for genuine poetry. Explaining it to him is useless, so I will not undertake such a hopeless task.

I would only like to remind the reader that Solzhenitsyn, too, had composed verses and showed his compositions to Akhmatova, who advised him not to make them public for reasons of complete poetic hopelessness. However, I totally reject the idea of revenge—so intricate—against Akhmatova for failing to understand his poems through a *critique* of Brodsky's poetry: How much Akhmatova had been mistaken about what her favorite protégé was actually worth—because, unlike Solzhenitsyn, I have no desire to draw conclusions from irritated reading. As I see it, perhaps the main reason for such a sudden attack, which actually stems from Solzhenitsyn's entire world outlook, lies in his specific artistic tastes, which developed more based on the *peredvizhniki* than on twentieth-century art, more based on literature of a highly didactic and dictatorial prophetic nature than on the festively diverse, motley, and even luxuriant poetics of Pushkin or Gogol (for all their differences). Essentially, Solzhenitsyn in all his artistic tastes and predilections, follows the much later Tolstoy, who had renounced much and was not moved by much. Solzhenitsyn the artist is one matter, Solzhenitsyn the judge of tastes is another, so please do not confuse them (and I do not want to confuse them myself). The poetics of Solzhenitsyn's prose writing can be (and sometimes is) very contemporary, even modern; his compositional constructs may be unexpected; in prose writing, he has often employed montage principles of the cinema; in the poetics of his essays, investigative writing, and novels, he captured and used different narrative styles, refashioning them enormously with his inimitable, individual intonations. I will not be like Solzhenitsyn, who refused to see in his subject (Brodsky) anything of merit at all—well, there were, of course, some merits, but these merits are more double-faced qualities, like Janus, which can easily turn into their opposite. The artistic and ideological type of personality personified by Solzhenitsyn precludes viewing any "outsider" or "stranger" as an equal partner, it precludes questioning as a position, it precludes any problems in relationships. He is very definite in his evaluations, certainly unambiguous and direct in his summaries and conclusions; for him, there is no such thing as many points of view ("pluralism" in the artistic sphere, and not only in the ideological, is unacceptable and even hostile to Solzhenitsyn). He is comfortable only with those writers who share his value system: religiousness, reverence for the people, historicism. A friend of mine once had a lady friend who would occasionally remark: "Sex precludes humor." In Solzhenitsyn's case, his literary workshop, which manufactures not only essays from the *Literary Collection,* completely precludes anything even slightly related to the culture of laughter: The only exception may be bitter sarcasm and irony that destroys the opponent. Laughter cannot, by definition, be directed at oneself, ever.

I would like to say: One cannot help pitying him . . .

. . . although Solzhenitsyn's world precludes not only humor but pity as well.

In Brodsky's case, what is involved is not only a deliberate unacceptance of his position, ethics, and poetics. Also present, of course, is the fact that, as they say in Russian, "two bears cannot live in the same den." It is also rather difficult to accommodate two such personalities as Solzhenitsyn and Brodsky on one (Russian-Nobel) Olympus. (Although, we may note in parentheses, Brodsky never attempted an assault on Solzhenitsyn.)

If one reads the interviews assembled by Valentina Polukhina in her book, *Brodsky through the Eyes of His Contemporaries* [Brodskii glazami sovremennikov],[4] the watershed between those who accept and those who reject Brodsky is fairly clear: As a rule it is, after all, a matter of ideology and not just an irritating "dissimilitude" of poetics. But, curiously, his rejection via ideology is not direct: It starts out first with poetics. Yury Kublanovsky, in his interview, says:

> And very often I know, before I read him, what he's going to tell me—that is, as far as ideas are concerned. He twists metaphors, he twists his impressions and sets the taut flywheel of his inspiration into motion. And with some of his poems, not that many, somewhere in the middle, they start to tire one, because I know, as a reader, that there are no surprises lying in store for me.[5]

In the "negative" system, the very same qualities that others discuss as positive will be evaluated negatively, for example, long versified texts ("ersatz *poemas,*" "too tiresome"). Whereas Bella Akhmadulina and Gordin treat Brodsky as, in a certain sense, an heir of the Pushkin tradition, comparable with Pushkin in his efforts for the benefit of the development of the Russian language

and Russian poetry ("It is a miracle, an absolute miracle. In this sense we can absolutely compare Brodsky to Pushkin. . . . His language is unexampled, unheard of. It is an absolute discovery of his. And in this sense . . . that is, an absolutely fateful person for some new time, right? This loftiness and the lowliness! It is simply wonderful!"—Akhmadulina), Viktor Krivulin and Kublanovskii, as well as Nadezhda Mandelstam, whom the latter quotes, are not at all enthralled by Brodsky's "contribution" ("The Yankee of Russian poetry").

As well as that notorious "coldness."

Polukhina asks:

> "How would you defend Brodsky from those writers and critics who accuse him of being a cold poet, who say he has few poems about love and that he despises the reader?"
>
> "I have never even seen or heard such fools."
>
> "You don't feel that he is a cold poet"
>
> "Oh, no! . . ."
>
> "You think such accusations should be brushed aside and not considered seriously?"
>
> "Whatever can he be accused of? He certainly should arouse different feelings toward himself, but, you know, why should we talk about fools now?"

Akhmadulina's complete emotional *acceptance* of Brodsky is poles apart from Solzhenitsyn—and she, too, does not need any arguments. Viktor Krivulin, on the other hand, considers Brodsky a "removed" poet.

There is a similar situation with "the soil." That quality of Brodsky's that some define as openness to world culture and, in particular, European culture, and, even more specifically, English-language culture (Yevgeny Rein, Gordin, and, to a certain degree, Aleksandr Kushner), in others arouses wrathful denunciation: "as it were, cultivating almost contempt, an effort to separate oneself from Russian culture and enter American culture"; characteristic of him is "a linguistic gesture of alienation and reserved constraint, a sense of shame for being Russian"; "one cannot be a world-class poet and break with the soil or be in such a position of ambiguity" (Krivulin); "Pushkin, as you know, grew closer and closer to the 'back-to-the-soil' movement's standpoint; that is, he developed in a completely opposite direction to Brodsky" (Kublanovsky).[6]

Let us look again for the boundary, the watershed.

Whatever one says, the boundary is ideology, and only afterward, as a consequence, the nonacceptance of his poetics.

The ideology is, of course, not always openly expressed and sometimes exists latently. Say, the issue is one of Brodsky's religion—or nonreligion.

Opinions, statements, and responses to this question are divided just as on all other aspects of Brodsky's work. Only some express themselves more diplomatically and circumspectly, others more sharply and definitively. Most distinct here was, perhaps, Kublanovsky. While graciously conceding that Brodsky was "a religious poet" (the highest point), he notes sternly that, nevertheless, "sometimes Brodsky lacks religious feeling, tact, and taste," as a consequence of which he suffers from "spiritual shortcomings," which "mar, [and] even, to some extent, vulgarize his poetic landscape"[7] (the point is lowered and Brodsky's "religiousness," which had been noted before, is subjected to skeptical analysis). And, finally, his Brodsky is not a Christian. Not that he is a "bad" Christian, or even has his "lapses"—no, he is not a Christian, and that is totally unacceptable.

Polukhina asks—after my above quotes of Kublanovsky regarding the "landscape": "To what extent does his Jewishness play a role here?"

And although Kublanovsky denies any "fault" of Jewishness ("It is not his Jewishness that is at fault"), the logic of his thought leads, alas, precisely to that accursed Jewish issue. After stressing, once again, that "his Jewish blood plays a secondary role" (ah, but still it does? If only secondary?), Kublanovsky then goes on, rather meaningfully, to recall:

> He wrote to me once that his anticlericalism was a product of the fact that he lived near the Church of the Transfiguration, and when he ran past it, without fail, the smell of the incense would make him want to puke. And we know of pure-blooded Jews, like his friend Anatoly Naiman, who have overcome all that and entered the church.[8]

So it seems that if a *pure-blooded Jew could overcome* his Jewishness, that is an indisputable plus and example worth following; but if one remains oneself, that is *arrogance* (in that same interview). Let us try to draw some at least intermediate conclusions. Let us draw a chart.

Some fairly extensive responses to Solzhenitsyn's article have already appeared in the press (L. Shtern—*Exlibris NG*, April 13, 2000; I. Efimov—*Novyi mir*, no. 5 [2000]). However, the driving emotional forces in these responses were the desire to *defend* and *deny*, and if to explain, then this: Brodsky does not correspond to the portrait drawn by Solzhenitsyn, whose reflections clearly remind one of *Soviet* (including legal) claims against the poet.

In my opinion, however, Solzhenitsyn's article should not be viewed as a sentence pronounced that has to be challenged (although in the eyes of our public, this

Brodsky	
For	**Against**
Individualism	Indivdualism
Aloofness	Coldness, absence of personal warmth
Irony	Irony
Philosophical features	Absence thereof
Intelligence	Intellect
Profundity of thought	Superficiality
Culture	Civilization
Openess to world, European culture	Cosmopolitanism, internationalism
Complex strophe system	Mutilation of Russian speech
Dissolving in the language, use of its wealth and possibilities	Distortion of Russian language
Grandiloquence	Grandiloquence
Lowly speech (use of "low" lexical layers alongside "elevated" elements)	Vulgarity
Aristocratic features	Elitism
Churchly features	Religious freedom
"The urge to neutralize every lyrical element, to bring it closer to the sound of a pendulum"	Lack of spontaneous lyricism
"Art is art"	"Art is not to serve"
Thoughtfulness	Mechanistic elements
Tragic elements	Spiritual emptiness
Metaphysical features	Pseudo-metaphysical features

could be useful) but rather as a symptom that requires clear understanding. It is a symptom of a disease that has gone deeper than anyone—socialists, communists, capitalists—ever thought. The split in Russian culture, as this symptom testifies, continues. The "giant" (Solzhenitsyn) and the "titan" (Brodsky) only crystallize around themselves already existing—no, not differences—completely different, juxtaposing views of the world, Russia, and, in fact, themselves.

What can one explain to Solzhenitsyn, who judges, sharply denounces, and totally denigrates both the personality and the poetry of Brodsky, when it was Brodsky who said: "Do not pronounce judgment, especially when dealing with fellow writers. 'Don't throw stones in another person's garden,' and so on, and so forth" (see interview of David Bethea with Joseph Brodsky in *Novaia Iunost'*, no. 1 [2000]). The difference lies not only in poetics, world outlook, and philosophy of life; their very ethics differ. To Solzhenitsyn, Brodsky is not a "fellow writer," he is not a literary colleague and not a member of the company of "Nobelists"; rather, he is an enemy who should be destroyed. Solzhenitsyn's weapon is the word, and he uses it to destroy.

To be sure, there are many others, poets and prose writers, who are incapable of a favorable "understanding" of Brodsky, and, in different cases, there are different explanations of this. Elena Shvarts says that this is like "cat and dog," and there are any number of oppositions (Viktor Kulle arranges them as follows: Brodsky—Aigi,

Brodsky—Nekrasov, Brodsky—Rubinshtein. Variants are possible, although, to my taste, these are certainly figures of a different scale). Solzhenitsyn's task, however, as well as his attitude as a stimulus for solving the problem, lies beyond the confines of literature itself. Brodsky's "alienness" harbors a threat: His path and his poetics are tempting because of their success. I am afraid of the analogy that comes to mind, but in all that arouses Solzhenitsyn's wrath and rage there is much of Pushkin's Mozart: love of street music, an insouciance, irony (including self-irony), indifference to essentially serious tasks. But here is what is so curious: Under Solzhenitsyn's pen, Brodsky is transformed into Salieri (cold, calculating, etc.)! What Solzhenitsyn does is to transfer the Mozart of our poetry of the end of the century into a Salieri "register"—and for what? After all, Brodsky is no rival of his! And if he is so different, why not leave him with his difference? But no, the effort to "shoot down" is nurtured by a subconscious desire to *get rid of* Brodsky (What, of the same rank? A Nobel Prize winner, an exile, a "genius," with his own "myth"? Spare me). It was hardly worth the efforts of such a *giant* as Solzhenitsyn to "rip into" Brodsky's poetry: It will withstand this anyway, and also because it (and he) is gone, they are up there, beyond the clouds, where they are beyond any stern judgment. Brodsky will never be able to respond to Solzhenitsyn's attacks, and Solzhenitsyn will forever remain in unexpected company vis-à-vis the forever silenced poet.

Notes

1. Translator's note: The examples are presented as they appear in the Russian text, followed in brackets by an English translation, which may or may not convey Solzhenitsyn's precise meaning, since the words are, as the author indicates, "archaeneologisms" and are not defined in any dictionary known to me. They are also presented out of context, which makes it additionally difficult to understand their intended meaning.

2. Yakov Gordin, "A Tragic Perception of the World" [Tragediinost' mirovospriiatiia], in Valentina Polukhina, *Brodsky through the Eyes of His Contemporaries* [Brodskii glazami sovremennikov] (New York: St. Martin's, 1992), p. 47.

3. Ibid., p. 38.

4. Polukhina, *Brodsky through the Eyes of His Contemporaries.*

5. Yury Kublanovsky. "A Yankee in Russian Poetry" [Amerikashka v russkoi poezii], in Polukhina, *Brodsky through the Eyes of His Contemporaries,* p. 203.

6. Ibid., p. 207.

7. Ibid.

8. Ibid.

Daniel J. Mahoney (essay date 2001)

SOURCE: Mahoney, Daniel J. "Introductory Note: Taking Solzhenitsyn Seriously." In *Aleksandr Solzhenitsyn: The Ascent from Ideology,* pp. 1-17. Lanham, Md.: Rowman & Littlefield, 2001.

[*In the following essay, Mahoney discusses Solzhenitsyn's credibility as a political voice.*]

The second volume of Aleksandr Solzhenitsyn's *The Gulag Archipelago* begins with what Martin Malia has rightly called a "magnificent metaphor" evoking Homer and setting the stage for a full-scale indictment of communist totalitarianism "and all its works."[1] Solzhenitsyn traces the origin of the system of party dictatorship, systematic lawlessness, ideological mendacity, class terror, and "corrective labor" in the Soviet Union "relentlessly back to 1917 and the Founder"[2] of Soviet socialism himself, Vladimir Lenin. Solzhenitsyn writes:

> Rosy-fingered Eos, so often mentioned in Homer and called Aurora by the Romans, caressed, too, with those fingers the first early morning of the Archipelago.
>
> When our compatriots heard via the BBC that M. Mihajlov claimed to have discovered that concentration camps had existed in our country as far back as 1921, many of us (and many in the West too) were astonished: That early really? Even in 1921?
>
> Of course not! Of course Mihajlov was in error. . . . It would be far more accurate to say that the Archipelago was born with the shots of the cruiser *Aurora.*[3]

The three volumes of *The Gulag Archipelago* are a comprehensive indictment of communism, establishing that the system of state coercion and concentration camp repression dates from the founding moment of the Bolshevik regime. The "archipelago" of repression is coextensive with the opening salvo unleashed by the cruiser *Aurora,* the shots that signaled the beginning of the Bolshevik coup in St. Petersburg in October 1917. It was Lenin who inaugurated the one-party state, established Feliks Dzerzhinsky's Cheka or secret police as the "sword and shield" of the Communist Party, and set in motion "extrajudicial reprisals" against purported enemies of the Revolution. It was Lenin who began the systematic persecution of believers and initiated the barbaric practice of taking innocent *hostages* "to terrorize or wreak vengeance on a military enemy or a rebellious population."[4] It was Lenin, not Joseph Stalin, who established the Soviet Union's first forced labor camps, perversely preferring monasteries and other church establishments for these first manifestations of the *Gulag* system. Solzhenitsyn, of course, recognizes that Lenin did not immediately create the full apparatus of developed totalitarianism. Rather, he laid the institutional and psychological foundations of the monopolistic party regime governing through force and ideological fiat.

Solzhenitsyn traces the totalitarian character of the Bolshevik regime to Lenin's fanatical determination to "purg(e) the Russian land of all kinds of harmful insects."[5] A wide range of Russia's population fell within the "broad definition of *insects*": members of opposition parties, of course, but also participants in the prerevolutionary zemstvo or self-governing provincial bodies, members of the cooperative movement, believers of all sorts, Tolstoyans, members of suspect professions or classes, and independent-minded intellectuals who criticized the communists or denied the truth of the Marxist-Leninist worldview.[6] The dehumanization—even the "animalization"—of real and imagined opposition is, as Solzhenitsyn powerfully shows, a defining feature of Leninist political culture. Lenin denied the legitimacy of an independent civil society and strove to eliminate any manifestation of democratic self-government, individual initiative, or intellectual and spiritual independence. It was Lenin, not Stalin, who began the practice of eliminating individuals or groups of peoples simply on the basis of their *class* origins. Stalinism thus is a logical if not strictly speaking inevitable development of Lenin's original totalitarianism.

Like Karl Marx, Lenin believed that "the dictatorship of the proletariat," "the suppression of the minority of exploiters by the majority of the hired slaves of yesterday," would be a "comparatively easy" affair.[7] This was a fundamental delusion. Marx and Lenin ignored the fact that "love of one's own" was deeply rooted in human nature and that the desire for political liberty could not be satisfied through ideological word games that pretended that a totalitarian state was in fact a *democratic* dictatorship.[8] In Solzhenitsyn's view, the majority of human beings want to own something of their own, to think freely, and to have a say in their own governance. Thus, these and other aspects of human nature were the enduring enemy that the revolutionaries ultimately had to overcome. Solzhenitsyn caustically observes that this "comparatively easy" internal repression cost the people of the Soviet Union up to sixty-six million lives between 1918 and 1956.[9] Solzhenitsyn's estimates of the demographic consequences of Soviet communism are undoubtedly on the high side, but the magnitude of Soviet repression under Lenin and Stalin (surely totaling tens of millions of lives lost) has been confirmed by such sources as Academician Aleksandr Yakovlev, chairman of the official Commission for the Rehabilitation of the Victims of Political Repression in the Russian Republic, and the authors of the famous *The Black Book of Communism* originally published in France in November 1997.[10]

Upon the publication of the three volumes of **The Gulag** in the West between 1974 and 1978, a large part of left-liberal intellectual opinion summarily dismissed Solzhenitsyn's claim that Stalinism was a natural development of Leninism. They even more adamantly rejected his view that the Soviet regime in its ideological heyday under Lenin and Stalin matched Nazi Germany in unalloyed political Evil and surpassed it in terror and repression. Even many anticommunist scholars disagreed with Solzhenitsyn's claim that the root of the Soviet tragedy lay in *ideology*—in the impulse to create a world without conflict or evil, governed according to the laws of Historical Necessity. Instead, they emphasized the "Russian" sources of Soviet despotism or the merely cynical use of ideology by the Kremlin elite.

Today, Solzhenitsyn's conclusions are much less controversial. While some "revisionist" scholars such as J. Arch Getty still attribute crimes such as collectivization in the Soviet Union or the Great Leap Forward in China to mere "policy blunders"[11] and thus leave the honor of socialism intact, many intellectuals and commentators in the West have quietly abandoned the old distinction between a well-intentioned Leninism and its Stalinist "perversion." Even Solzhenitsyn's indictment of ideology is widely if by no means universally shared. The aforementioned *The Black Book of Communism* is an instructive case in point.

SOLZHENITSYN AND THE BLACK BOOK OF COMMUNISM

The Black Book of Communism is unthinkable without Solzhenitsyn and his **Gulag Archipelago.** Its principal contributors are French and hail from the Left—either as former communists and Trotskyites or graduates of the revolutionary "psychodrama" of May 1968—and to various degrees remain men of the Left. Its authors belong to that generation of ex-radicals whose ideological confidence was shaken to the core by the publication of **The Gulag Archipelago.**

The Black Book is the first systematic and comparative analysis of the "crimes, terror and repression" that accompanied communism everywhere and that seems to define its "genetic code."[12] The book's centerpiece is a relentlessly documented narrative of political violence and repression in the Soviet Union under Lenin and Stalin,[13] drawing on extensive archival materials made available to researchers since the collapse of communist rule in 1991. But *The Black Book* also contains absorbing accounts of communist repression in eastern Europe, Asia ("between reeducation and massacre"), and the Third World.

Sophisticated observers mock the notion of a unitary or monolithic communism and this book indeed richly displays the diverse local variants of communism throughout the twentieth century. But if Josip Tito, Mao

Zedong, and Enver Hoxha eventually broke with Moscow and followed independent "national communist" paths, they always looked to Lenin as the source of their inspiration and legitimacy. Orthodox communist regimes, from Petrograd to the China Seas (as historian Martin Malia puts it in his introduction to the book),[14] reveal a strikingly similar ideological profile. Everywhere communism became entrenched, one discovers a single-party regime, a mendacious ideology, a "wooden" rhetoric that demonized real and imagined enemies. Communist regimes engaged in large-scale social engineering and systematically ignored the concerns of ordinary, ideologically "unenlightened" human beings, especially peasants. This "fanatical faith in the surgeon's knife,"[15] as Russian novelist Vasily Grossman once put it, led to full-scale tragedy, even genocide, in the case of the Soviet "war against the kulaks" (1929-1934), the Chinese "Great Leap Forward" (1958-1961), and the Khmer Rouge's massacre of a quarter of Cambodia's population between 1975 and 1979.

The book's original publication in France created a scandal, not least because its cumulative effect is to establish that communism was the twentieth century's fiercest practitioner of state violence and "crimes against humanity." It forthrightly challenges the claim that Nazism holds a monopoly on "absolute political evil"[16] in our time. *The Black Book* provides careful, scholarly confirmation of Solzhenitsyn's most controversial claims.

The chapters on the Soviet Union and China in *The Black Book* are as powerful as they are in large part because their authors, Nicolas Werth and Jean-Louis Margolin, avoid excessive polemics and allow the evidence to simply speak for itself. If anything, Werth is excessively conservative in his estimates, drawing almost exclusively from not always reliable "official" party and state archival materials to verify politically inspired deaths and incarcerations in the Soviet Union under Lenin and Stalin. Still, despite the limits of this method, Werth concludes that the Bolshevik regime was responsible directly or indirectly for the deaths of at least twenty million people between 1918 and 1956 and for the imprisonment in camps and labor colonies of millions more. In addition, he demolishes the widespread notion of a good Lenin and a bad Stalin by showing that terror defined the Soviet regime from its inception. While too indebted to the revisionist Sovietology of the 1970s and 1980s, which mocked the notion of totalitarianism as a Cold War term of abuse, Werth nonetheless concludes that there is no basis for the revisionist claim that the terror of the 1930s was driven by overzealous party and police officials acting largely independently of Stalin's orders. This perverse denial of intentionality, so widespread in the academy today, is

the product of wishful thinking, of leftist prejudices, and of a dogmatic emphasis on social history that denies a place for politics and ideology in the unfolding of the communist tragedy.

Likewise, Margolin's chapter on China shows that the crimes of Maoism are rooted in ideological hubris and in a denial of the humanity of those on the wrong side of the "class struggle." Margolin refutes the widely held superstition that Mao was just another cruel Chinese emperor, though one who at least fed his people and put them on the road to development. He demonstrates that Mao committed crimes unprecedented in Chinese history and was guided by an ideology that was at war with China's best national and ethical principles. Like Solzhenitsyn, Margolin denies the "national" origins of revolutionary terror and repression. The devastating consequences of Mao's rule stagger the mind: sixty-five million lost lives.[17]

Perhaps the deepest reason *The Black Book* has sparked controversy is that it argues that communism, an ideology of the humanitarian or "progressive" Left, is intrinsically perverse. In fact, the book shows, communism is as intrinsically perverse as Nazism. Without denying the unique criminality of the Nazi regime, the volume's editor, Stéphane Courtois, argues that communist crimes, like Nazi crimes, partake of the desire to eliminate groups of people on the basis of their origins, not because of any individual culpability or responsibility. He denies that communism's crimes have any right to be excused or mitigated because they were committed in the name of universal principles or for the attainment of an egalitarian future. Drawing on the arguments of Solzhenitsyn and Vasily Grossman, Courtois shows that communism is an *eliminationist* or *exterminationist* ideology. But in contrast to Nazism, it selects its enemies on the basis of class rather than race.[18]

In an argument foreshadowing that of *The Black Book,* Solzhenitsyn suggested in **The Gulag Archipelago** that the USSR's war against the independent peasantry—the so-called de-kulakization campaign and its accompanying deportations and famine—was the first systematic effort to eliminate an entire class of people for ideological reasons. In some real sense, Solzhenitsyn suggests, Adolf Hitler was Lenin's and Stalin's faithful pupil. In a moving passage, Solzhenitsyn adamantly denies the humanistic or universalist inspiration of Bolshevik policy:

> Like raging beasts, abandoning every concept of "humanity," abandoning all humane principles which had evolved through the millennia, they began to round up the very best farmers and their families, and to drive them, stripped of their possessions, naked, into the northern wastes, into the tundra and the taiga.[19]

Courtois quotes the eloquent reflections of Grossman on the ways in which communist rhetoric dehumanized those it set out to eliminate. In his poignant, but little-known novel *Forever Flowing,* Grossman writes: "To massacre them, it was necessary to proclaim that kulaks are not human beings, just as the Germans proclaimed that Jews are not human beings. Thus did Lenin and Stalin say: kulaks are not human beings."[20] It is impossible after reading *The Black Book,* or Solzhenitsyn or Grossman for that matter, to repeat the insidious but commonplace sophistry that communism is good in theory, but a failure in practice.

To be sure, there still remain several enduring obstacles to communism receiving its moral due as one of the two essentially criminal political enterprises of the past century. Historians and political theorists resist the kind of comparative analysis of communism that *The Black Book* exemplifies, and tend to write off its crimes as due to contingent factors. Those crimes are blamed (much to Solzhenitsyn's consternation) on everything—Stalin's excesses, age-old Russian despotism, Mao's cruelty, Fidel Castro's vanity—except communism itself. Second, there are few photographic or cinematic images of communism's misdeeds. In an age dominated by media images, this is a major obstacle to a public recognition of the enormity of communism's crimes. And we probably cannot expect any help from Hollywood on this score. The last obstacle is the most subtle and important. As Malia points out in his splendid introduction to *The Black Book,* "any realistic accounting of communist crime would effectively shut the door on Utopia; and too many good souls in this unjust world cannot abandon hope for an absolute end to inequality."[21] Many scholars and intellectuals will likely continue to ignore the ideological foundations of communist totalitarianism and will continue to blame its criminality on accidental features such as "Stalinism." Communism may be dead, but the utopian or ideological impulse persists.

But after Solzhenitsyn that impulse will never be credible again. In that sense, Solzhenitsyn was undoubtedly right to ponder in *The Oak and the Calf* if the publication of *The Gulag Archipelago* was the moment foretold by the "foul midnight hags" of *Macbeth,* the moment "when Birnham Wood shall walk."[22] The Politburo's decision to exile Solzhenitsyn to the West after the publication of *Gulag* in Paris in December 1973 could not prevent Birnham Wood from beginning its march. With *Gulag,* Solzhenitsyn initiated a "war on two fronts": he aimed to convince public opinion in both Russia and the West that communism deserved the same universal opprobrium to which Nazism had rightly been subjected.[23] If Solzhenitsyn has not exactly won his war, communism has certainly lost the decisive battles. With the *Gulag,* Solzhenitsyn initiated the final struggle—the decisive blow against communism—that allowed others such as Pope John Paul II, Ronald Reagan, Mikhail Gorbachev, and Václav Havel to play their crucial roles in the denouement of European communism.

The "Discrediting" of a Great Writer

Even so, Solzhenitsyn is rarely given credit for his monumental contribution to the cause of human liberty in our time. In fact, there has been no more successful effort to discredit a great writer and thinker than that carried out against Solzhenitsyn over the past twenty-five years. In his **"Letter to the Soviet Leaders"** (1974), published in the West shortly after he was sent into exile, Solzhenitsyn searingly criticized the role played by Marxist-Leninist ideology in the destruction of Russia and recommended that the government jettison communism while gradually altering the country's political and social life.[24] His measured advice was thoroughly misunderstood in the West and by a large part of the Russian intelligentsia. His call for gradualism was perversely read as an endorsement of authoritarianism. His recognition of Christianity as a spiritual force that could contribute to the healing of Russia was transformed into "theocracy" (despite his repeated claim that he wished no special privileges for his own faith). Soon, Solzhenitsyn was denounced as a Russian ayatollah—the "Persian trick,"[25] as he angrily called it.

By the time of his famous commencement address at Harvard in 1978, a legend was firmly in place that he was some combination of theocrat, tsarist, antisemite, and imperialist.[26] His criticism in that speech of the "anthropocentric humanism" of the Enlightenment and of the rampant litigiousness of the West was taken as further evidence of his antidemocratic politics, despite his accompanying defense of the rule of law and his expression of respect for the American founding. As the great Sovietologist Adam Ulam has written, with the Harvard address Solzhenitsyn "became for much of the liberal establishment a reactionary whose praiseworthy struggle against communist oppression was not matched by an understanding and attachment to the democratic principles of the twentieth century."[27] Truth be told, many in the West at the time did not share Solzhenitsyn's deep and abiding opposition to communism. His sometimes intemperate chiding of the Free World during the 1970s and 1980s for its vacillation before communist expansion did not help matters in journalistic and academic circles, where anti-anticommunism was a ruling passion. By the mid-1980s, Solzhenitsyn had lost much of what had once been a vast readership.

Yet over the past fifteen years, the writer has provided ample material for the definitive rebuttal of his critics. In the revised *August 1914* (published in English in

1989), Solzhenitsyn sketches his own model of Russian statesmanship in the figure of Pyotr Stolypin, a principled centrist who fought for constitutional monarchy and land reform against opposition in both the tsarist and revolutionary camps.[28] (Solzhenitsyn's portrait of Stolypin's statesmanship is explored in detail in chapter 4 of this work). Stolypin paid for these efforts with his life—assassinated, quite fittingly, by a double agent of the tsarist secret police and revolutionary terrorists. Solzhenitsyn emphasizes Stolypin's vision of a nation of individuals freed from the corruption of absolutism and the tyranny of the village collective, individuals whose love of Russia is not mystical but rather rooted in their status as property-owning, self-determining citizens. But Solzhenitsyn's critics ignore his portrait of Stolypin and continue to label him a Slavophile "mystic" enamored of "Orthodoxy, Nationalism, and Autocracy."[29] Solzhenitsyn's explicit criticisms of tsarist autocracy and his eloquent defenses of political liberty and the rule of law do not deter his critics from putting forward old or new misrepresentations.

In **Rebuilding Russia** (1990), Solzhenitsyn draws on Aristotle, Charles-Louis Montesquieu, and Alexis de Tocqueville in an exploration of the preconditions of political freedom. In so doing, he reveals himself to be a partisan of a complex political system combining a Gaullist-style presidency with local councils and assemblies. He acknowledges enthusiastically the liberties evident in the Swiss and New England towns of his exile.[30] This "Tocquevillian" defense of local self-government is forcefully reiterated in his 1998 work **Russia in Collapse**[31] and is the subject of chapter 6 of this book.

Repeatedly, Solzhenitsyn has demanded that Russians at all levels repent for the crimes and lies of the communist period in which every inhabitant played some part. In **"The Russian Question" at the End of the Twentieth Century** (1995), he denounced pan-Slavic imperialism and noted: "There is some truth in the reproaches leveled at Russian ruling and intellectual elites for their belief in Russian exclusiveness and messianism."[32] For Solzhenitsyn, the country must find its own path of development, one that avoids imitation of the worst features of the increasingly relativist and decadent West. Yet he also praises what is truly universal in the Western purpose: "its historically unique stability of civic life under the rule of law—a hard-won stability which grants independence and space to every private citizen."[33]

SOLZHENITSYN AND POSTCOMMUNIST RUSSIA

Solzhenitsyn was among the first to see through the "democratic" pretensions of Boris Yeltsin's Russia. In fact, he was the first to call the new regime an "oligarchy" (in his speech to the Duma in the fall of 1994), a term subsequently adopted by almost everyone, but without attribution. Solzhenitsyn's aversion to Yeltsin even led the writer to reject the Order of Andrei of the First Rank, the Russian Republic's highest award bestowed on him by Yeltsin on the occasion of his eightieth birthday in December 1998.[34] It can be plausibly argued that Solzhenitsyn gives Yeltsin too little credit for dismantling communist totalitarianism. The great Russian writer understates the positive features of the new order—the institutionalization of civic and political liberties and the unleashing of entrepreneurial energies—that accompany its omnipresent corruption and its cruel impoverishment of millions of ordinary Russian citizens. But Solzhenitsyn is surely right to chastise Yeltsin for allowing organized thievery to become the ideology of the new Russian state and for associating the name of anticommunism with a rapacious and immoral ruling elite.

Solzhenitsyn initially responded quite warily to Yeltsin's selection of Vladimir Putin as his successor as president of Russia, undoubtedly seeing him as a product of the Communist secret services as well as a product of Yeltsin's "family" of self-serving oligarchs. More recently, Solzhenitsyn has expressed confidence in Putin's personal integrity and judgment, and in his willingness to take on the corruption of the hitherto untouchable governmental and business elite. After Putin met with Solzhenitsyn at the writer's house in October 2000, critics such as the "reformer" Anatoly Chubais even accused Putin of being under the influence of Solzhenitsyn's "antidemocratic" ideology.[35] But in early December 2000, Solzhenitsyn confounded critics by strongly criticizing Putin for reinstating the old Soviet anthem (with new lyrics) as Russia's national hymn, calling the decision "extremely inappropriate and ill-timed."[36] So much for Solzhenitsyn's supposed alliance with "the most reactionary part of the Russian secret services and the Communist party," to cite Chubais's particularly egregious formulation.

Over the past decade, Solzhenitsyn has made his practical political position clear enough: he remains an inveterate anticommunist; he favors strong grassroots democracy; he is for a market economy and real land reform but is adamantly opposed to a kleptocracy that lives off the nation, using its political connections to perpetuate its social dominance and to impoverish a people already victimized by communism. Like George Orwell, Solzhenitsyn envisions a decent society where the ordinary man is protected from the sophisticated abstractions of the Left ("socialist utopia") and the Right ("the market" as an end in itself unrestrained by law and morality). Solzhenitsyn firmly opposes calls for a reinvigorated Russian empire but also warns the West against triumphalism and complacency. He harshly criticized the NATO bombing of Serbian cities during the so-called Kosovo war as a cruel inversion of humanitarian criteria.[37] He denounced the first Chechen war as senseless and self-defeating, but believed that Putin had little choice but to intervene again in Chechnya in 1999 once Islamic rebels attacked Russian Dagestan.[38] His positions on Chechnya and the NATO bombing of Serbia are sometimes mistakenly seen as evidence of Solzhenitsyn's extreme nationalism and hostility to the West. In truth, Solzhenitsyn advises "self-limitation," that is principled and prudent restraint, as the wisest path for Russia and the West alike.

SOLZHENITSYN AND THE IDOLATRY OF PROGRESS

In my view, Solzhenitsyn still has something important, even profound, to impart to us. He is a teacher of moderation, a chronicler of modern faith in progress gone awry, an anti-ideologue par excellence. His work illustrates the moral and intellectual vulnerability of the modern intellectual before the sirens of progressive ideology. In *The First Circle*, he provides a devastating portrait of Eleanor Roosevelt (the "Mrs. R" of chapter 54, "Buddha's Smile") as a naive political pilgrim hoodwinked about the rehabilitative possibilities of the Butyrskaya Gulag prison during a trip to the Soviet Union in 1944.[39] In addition, the second volume of *The Gulag* contains a scathing indictment of the famous writer Maxim Gorky's whitewashing of Soviet repression in the 1920s and 1930s. In 1929, Gorky traveled to the Special Purpose Camp on the Solovetsky Islands. The visit was part of a larger literary tour of the USSR that aimed to highlight the social achievements of the revolution. Despite the best efforts of the authorities to whitewash the truth about the camps, Gorky saw and heard enough to discern the essential facts. (A courageous young boy, in particular, risked his life to tell Gorky about the various tortures and deprivations that characterized life at Solovki. He was later shot.) Gorky, however, did not allow the truth to get in his way. Courting favor with Stalin and committed to the cause of socialist transformation, Gorky issued a statement praising Solovki's GPU or secret police administrators as "vigilant and tireless sentinels of the Revolution" as well as "bold creators of culture."[40] Gorky later was the driving force behind a collaborative effort of thirty-six Soviet writers called *The White Sea-Baltic Stalin Canal*, "a disgraceful book on the White Sea Canal which was the first to glorify slave labor."[41] The Belomor or White Sea Canal—the "most savage construction project of the twentieth century"—was built with "wheelbarrow and pick" and took up to a quarter-million lives in the brief twenty months of its construction between the fall of 1931 and the spring of 1933.[42] In Solzhenitsyn's view, Gorky is the literary exemplar of the *lie*—of the spiritual corruption that accompanies the revolutionary displacement of standards of good and evil by ideological criteria of progress and reaction.

For Solzhenitsyn, the other great literary practitioner of the ideological lie was the French existentialist writer Jean-Paul Sartre. The self-proclaimed philosopher of "freedom" repeatedly extolled Soviet socialism in its Stalinist and post-Stalinist forms as the representative of the cause of humanity on the march. He reserved his vituperation for anticommunists (such as Raymond Aron) whom he contemptuously dismissed as "dogs." This "wandering minstrel of humanism," as Solzhenitsyn called him, saw in one of the most inhumane regimes in history the first necessary step in the reconciliation of man with man.[43]

From these instructive examples, Solzhenitsyn draws a wider conclusion: because the leftist intellectual genuflects before the altar of "History," he is easily taken in by the most fatuous claims of "progressive" despotism. Solzhenitsyn is an incisive critic of the superstitions lurking behind the "rationalism" of modern Enlightenment. But Solzhenitsyn's alternative to the chimera of Historical Progress is not some choice for "reaction," as is commonly supposed. Instead, Solzhenitsyn defends the commonsense appraisal of good and evil rooted in a natural order of things. This old-fashioned message provokes mockery in certain intellectual corners although its good sense is amply confirmed by the tragic experience of the twentieth century.

Solzhenitsyn is an elegant and moving writer and a penetrating guide to the political and spiritual dislocations of our time. But will anyone still read him? It is for those willing to do so—whose minds have not been dulled by the intellectual "consensus" about him or the mistaken belief that the nature of communism is now but a historical question—that the present book is addressed.

In the next chapter, we will reconsider the much misunderstood Harvard address in light of Solzhenitsyn's important clarification of its themes in his 1993 Liechtenstein address. The latter address was Solzhenitsyn's final word to a West that had had so much difficulty making sense of his message during his twenty years of exile. It is a remarkable overview of the political and spiritual condition of humankind at the end of the twentieth century, as well as a searching meditation on the nature and limits of modern "progress." In subsequent chapters, we will examine his dissection of the ideological distortion of reality as well as the positive—and life affirming—alternatives to it that he limns in his work as a whole. Our goal is nothing less than to take Solzhenitsyn seriously as a discerning teacher about politics and the human soul.

Notes

1. Martin Malia, "A War on Two Fronts: Solzhenitsyn and the Gulag Archipelago," *The Russian Review* (January 1977): 53 and 58-59.

2. Malia, "A War on Two Fronts," 59.

3. Aleksandr I. Solzhenitsyn, *The Gulag Archipelago,* vol. 2, trans. Thomas P. Whitney (New York: Harper & Row, 1975), 9. For a comprehensive discussion of Solzhenitsyn's account of Lenin, see James F. Pontuso, "Solzhenitsyn's Lenin" in *Solzhenitsyn's Political Thought* (Charlottesville: University Press of Virginia, 1990), 51-71.

4. Aleksandr I. Solzhenitsyn, *The Gulag Archipelago,* vol. 1, trans. Thomas P. Whitney (New York: Harper & Row, 1974), 29.

5. Solzhenitsyn, *Gulag,* vol. 1, 27.

6. Solzhenitsyn, *Gulag,* vol. 1, 28.

7. Solzhenitsyn, *Gulag,* vol. 2, 10.

8. On the natural foundations of human freedom and "love of one's own" see Pontuso, *Solzhenitsyn's Political Thought,* 89-118, and my discussion in chapter 7 of this book. See also Solzhenitsyn's remarks about "the dictatorship of the proletariat" in *The Gulag Archipelago,* vol. 3, trans. H. T. Willetts (New York: Harper & Row, 1978), 23.

9. Solzhenitsyn, *Gulag,* vol. 2, 10. For a lucid discussion of Solzhenitsyn's monumental contribution to "the development of a political understanding of genocide and its consequences" see Irving Louis Horowitz, *Taking Lives: Genocide and State Power,* 4th edition (New Brunswick, N.J.: Transaction, 1997), 179-206.

10. Aleksandr Yakovlev, a former adviser to Mikhail Gorbachev, is preparing a major "official" report on the extent of the repressions under Lenin and Stalin. In numerous public statements he has made clear that in his view politically induced deaths under communism totaled tens of millions and that state terror is coextensive with Leninism itself. The on-line news service of Radio Free Europe/Radio Liberty (RFE/RL) cites a March 9 story in Toronto's *Globe and Mail* that summarizes some of Yakovlev's preliminary conclusions in a newly published book, *Maelstrom of Memory.* Yakovlev writes that "Russia is covered up to its horizons with bones and nameless graves." He estimates that as many as thirty-five million victims were killed "as the direct result of Soviet decisions" (RFE/RL citation). Yakovlev also concluded that more than forty-one million citizens were imprisoned between 1923 and 1954, and that eighty-five thousand Orthodox priests were shot in 1937 alone. See also Stéphane Courtois et al., *The Black Book of Communism: Crimes, Terror, Repression,* trans. Jonathan Murphy, consulting ed. Mark Kramer, with a foreword by Martin Malia (Cambridge: Harvard University Press, 1999).

11. J. Arch Getty, "The Future Did Not Work," *The Atlantic Monthly* (March 2000): 115.

12. See Stéphane Courtois's discussion of the "genetic code" of communism in *The Black Book,* 754.

13. See Nicolas Werth's section entitled "A State Against Its People: Violence, Repression, and Terror in the Soviet Union" in *The Black Book,* 33-268.

14. *The Black Book,* xix.

15. Quoted in Courtois, "Conclusion: Why?" in *The Black Book,* 753.

16. *The Black Book,* xx.

17. *The Black Book,* 4, 463-546, esp. 463-65.

18. *The Black Book,* 8-17, 734-57.

19. Solzhenitsyn, *Gulag,* vol. 1, 56.

20. Quoted in *The Black Book,* 16.

21. *The Black Book,* xx.

22. Solzhenitsyn, *The Oak and the Calf: A Memoir* (New York: Harper & Row, 1980), 379.

23. For a penetrating account of Solzhenitsyn's struggle to influence "public opinion" in the East and West, see Martin Malia, "A War on Two Fronts."

Irving Louis Horowitz suggestively remarks that by placing communism in the same class as German Nazism, Solzhenitsyn "stepped over a psychological threshold of commentary few others dared to cross; at least prior to the collapse and exposure of the Communist system." See Horowitz, *Taking Lives,* p. 184.

24. See Solzhenitsyn, "Letter to the Soviet Leaders" in *East and West,* trans. Hilary Sternberg (New York: Harper & Row, 1980), 120-42.

25. See Solzhenitsyn's denunciation of "the Persian trick" in "I Am No Russian Ayatollah," *Encounter* (February 1980): 34-35.

26. For the text of the Harvard address as well as a representative selection of early and late responses see *Solzhenitsyn at Harvard: The Address, Twelve Early Responses, Six Later Reflections,* ed. Ronald Berman (Washington, D.C.: Ethics and Public Policy Center, 1980) and Aleksandr Solzhenitsyn, *Détente: Prospects for Democracy and Dictatorship,* 2nd edition (New Brunswick, N.J.: Transaction, 1980), 1-18.

27. Adam Ulam, *Understanding the Cold War: A Historian's Personal Reflections* (Charlottesville, Va.: Leopolis Press, 2000), 178.

28. See chapters 8 and 60-73 of Solzhenitsyn, *The Red Wheel I: August 1914,* trans. H. T. Willetts (New York: Farrar, Straus and Giroux, 1989).

29. For a representative example, see Eduard Ponarin, "Alexander Solzhenitsyn as a Mirror of the Russian Counter-Revolution," part of the "Program on New Approaches to Russian Security" available at http://www.fas.harvard.edu/~ponars. Ponarin, an associate professor of sociology at the European University in

St. Petersburg, admits that Solzhenitsyn favors "a bottoms-up vertical line of local government" but then associates this position with "the classic 'Orthodoxy, Autocracy and Nationalism.'" Ponarin presents no evidence that Solzhenitsyn favors a special political status for Orthodoxy or supports any form of autocratic politics whatsoever. These calumnies are simply presupposed as self-evident and thus in no need of textual confirmation.

30. See Solzhenitsyn, *Rebuilding Russia: Reflections and Tentative Proposals,* trans. Alexis Klimoff (New York: Farrar, Straus and Giroux, 1991).

31. An English-language edition of *Russia in Collapse* will appear in 2002 from ISI Books. Throughout this book, I have drawn on the French translation, *La Russie sous l'Avalanche* (Paris: Fayard, 1998).

32. Solzhenitsyn, *"The Russian Question" at the End of the Twentieth Century* (New York: Farrar, Straus and Giroux, 1995), 60.

33. This quotation is drawn from Solzhenitsyn's address delivered to the International Academy of Philosophy in the principality of Liechtenstein, reprinted as an appendix to *"The Russian Question,"* 125.

34. For Yeltsin's account of this dispute, see his *Midnight Diaries* (New York: Public Affairs, 2000), 122-23.

35. I have drawn on various news wire accounts (BBC, Reuters, AP) available on the Internet.

36. I have drawn on the *Moscow Times* of December 6, 2000, and various news wire accounts, especially AP and Reuters. For a balanced appraisal of "the present activities of President Putin," see Aleksandr Solzhenitsyn, "Neither Gulag Nor Eden: Freedom of Two Kinds" in *World Press Review* (March 2001): 10-12.

37. Solzhenitsyn reiterated that criticism in his address of December 13, 2000, on the occasion of receiving the Grand Prize of the French Academy of Moral and Political Sciences at the French Embassy in Moscow.

38. Solzhenitsyn has proposed negotiations with Chechen village chieftains rather than with the fanatical and deeply anti-Russian Islamic rebels.

39. See Solzhenitsyn, chapter 54, "Buddha's Smile" in *The First Circle,* trans. Thomas P. Whitney (Evanston, Ill.: Northwestern University Press, 1997), 327-37.

40. Solzhenitsyn, *Gulag,* vol. 2, 60-63. The quotations are drawn from 63. For a remarkable account of Gorky's justifications of Soviet slave labor, see Darius Tolczyk, *See No Evil: Literary Cover-ups & Discoveries of the Soviet Camp Experience* (New Haven: Yale University Press, 1999).

41. Solzhenitsyn, *Gulag,* vol. 1, xii.

42. Solzhenitsyn, *Gulag,* vol. 2, 91, 98-99.

43. For Solzhenitsyn's evaluation of "'the master of men's minds' in France and throughout Europe," see *Gulag,* vol. 3, 319, 328n, and *The Oak and the Calf,* 119n.

Daniel J. Mahoney (essay date 2001)

SOURCE: Mahoney, Daniel J. "True and False Liberalism: Stolypin and His Enemies in *August 1914.*" In *Aleksandr Solzhenitsyn: The Ascent from Ideology,* pp. 65-97. Lanham, Md.: Rowman & Littlefield, 2001.

[*In the following essay, Mahoney considers in detail Solzhenitsyn's treatment of Pyotr Stolypin in* August 1914, *the first volume of* The Red Wheel.]

The Russian Revolution of 1917 had an undeniably dramatic impact on the destiny of the twentieth century. The first, ostensibly democratic, revolution of 1917, in February, overthrew the *ancien régime* and closed off the possibility of a peaceful Russian evolution toward European-style constitutional monarchy. In the midst of war, it pushed Russian politics irrevocably to the Left, and created a power vacuum that was filled by the most militant and "totalitarian" of the revolutionary sects. With the second revolution of 1917, in October, the Bolsheviks, under the leadership of Lenin, withstood the opposition of almost every stratum of society and began their monumental effort at establishing "utopia in power." In the process they undid all of the principal reforms introduced in the final period of the tsarist regime (1860-1917). They eliminated the hard-won acquisition of rule of law, destroyed the independence of civil society, abolished the constitutional order established in the aftermath of an earlier revolution, and ferociously attacked the legitimacy of the churches, the aristocracy, the bourgeoisie, and the independent peasantry. They even managed to do what the Tsars had never come close to doing: destroying the proud socialist and revolutionary parties of the noncommunist Left. With war, communism, and later the full-scale collectivization of agriculture, the Leninist regime restored serfdom, but in a new ideological guise and accompanied by rivers of blood. In addition to its devastating impact on the possibility of a humane modernization of Russia in continuity with national traditions and solicitous of the independence of civil society, the October Revolution opened up this century's great ideological schism. It gave rise to the heated triangular conflict between liberal democracy and Left and Right totalitarianisms, the first phase of which ended with the defeat of Nazi Germany in 1945, the second only with the unexpected implosion of European communism between 1989 and 1991.

In the Marxist-Leninist vulgate, the collapse of the Russian old regime and the victory of communism were *inevitable,* preordained by the laws of historical dialectic. But the communists could never anticipate that their long revolutionary project would culminate seventy years later in a desperate effort to restore constitutional politics and a "normal" civil society, a "restoration" made all the more difficult by the pernicious legacy of Red October.[1] Today, only a few diehard leftists believe that the Bolshevik Revolution was in any way preordained by the laws of history. In contrast, the majority of analysts in Russia and the West alike still welcome the February Revolution as an unqualified victory for democracy over absolutism. They forget that there could be no October Revolution without the February one and that it was the February Revolution that put an end to the prospects for stable constitutional development in Russia.

In his great cycle of historical novels, *The Red Wheel,* beginning with *August 1914,* Aleksandr Solzhenitsyn sets out to examine and "de-construct" claims made on behalf of the inevitability of the communist revolution. *The Red Wheel* is first and foremost an attempt to restore Russian national memory, but it is also an effort to explore through the medium of literature fundamental historical and philosophical questions that have implications beyond the Russian tragedy. Some Western observers have been perplexed by the historical character of *The Red Wheel* and have denied that it is a novel in any recognizable sense of the term.[2] This perplexity is the result of what Alexis Klimoff has called "the Western tendency to draw a sharp distinction between fiction and non-fiction" in contrast to the Russian tradition's emphasis on the simultaneously "cognitive, ethical and aesthetic goals" of great literature. In the Russian tradition, "literary achievement was not seen in the ability of a powerful imagination to create a vivid world ex nihilo, but rather in the writer's skill in selecting, shaping, and ordering the data of reality, in this sense re-creating it in aesthetically compelling ways."[3] Solzhenitsyn explicitly identifies with this ethical/realist understanding of the literary enterprise. In response to a particularly ferocious attack on *Lenin in Zurich* (whose chapters are culled from several volumes of *The Red Wheel*), Solzhenitsyn emphatically affirmed "that I am not simply a belletristic writer, but . . . in all my books I place myself in the service of historical truth."[4]

At present, only two of the five volumes of *The Red Wheel* have appeared in English, the augmented *August 1914* published in 1989 as well as *November 1916,* published in 1999.[5] What is apparent on the basis of these two massive volumes alone is that, in Solzhenitsyn's view, the decadence and decrepitude of the Russian old regime in no way suggests that Russia was predestined to experience communist totalitarianism. Not that Solzhenitsyn has any illusions, whatsoever, about the solidity of the old order. *The Red Wheel* is a powerful indictment of the senile petrification of the old regime in its final period, marked by incompetent military leadership, a propensity to fatalism on the part of its leaders,[6] a mediocre Tsar, a meddling and superstitious Tsarina, and an uncomprehending bureaucracy that failed to see that Russia's only hope lay in far-reaching reforms. But Russia's problems in that period are in no way attributable to the blindness of the regime alone. Russian society, too, failed to appreciate sufficiently that its real interest lay not in indulgence toward violent revolutionaries but in a prudent reconciliation with those healthy forces in the regime committed to a free, prosperous, and civilized Russia. Alas, the liberals "were as immoderate as only Russian liberals could be" (541) [All internal citations are to Aleksandr Solzhenitsyn, *The Red Wheel I: August 1914,* trans. H. T. Willetts (New York: Farrar, Straus and Giroux, 1989).] and generally sided with revolution over reform. The genuinely progressive elements in Russia, represented in *August 1914* by Solzhenitsyn's fictional hero, Georgi Vorotyntsev, supported the reform of the regime in a manner compatible with inherited traditions and constitutional government, but they were increasingly isolated and outmaneuvered by the extremists on the Left and Right. Yet Solzhenitsyn suggests that Russia knew one exceptional statesman, her greatest in perhaps two centuries, who set out "to steer Russia along this new and strange middle channel" (541) that was the road of her salvation. That statesman was Pyotr Stolypin, prime minister of Russia between 1906 and 1911. Stolypin combined repression of revolutionary terrorism with far-reaching reforms and tried to govern in conjunction with society's representatives in the elective Duma. After five years of tumultuous rule, he fell victim to an assassin's bullet in September 1911. For Solzhenitsyn, the death of Stolypin meant the effective end of the prospects for constitutional government and social progress in Russia. Solzhenitsyn dramatically concludes that what the assassin's bullet had slain was nothing less than the dynasty itself. The assassin Dmitri Bogrov's bullets "were the opening shots of the fusillade at Yekaterinburg" (606) that brutally destroyed the historic monarchy once and for all in July 1918.

THE STOLYPIN CYCLE

The fifteen chapters in what the author calls the "Stolypin cycle" (see opening Publisher's Note) in the augmented *August 1914* (chapters 8, 60 to 73), are a veritable tractate on statesmanship. Solzhenitsyn tells the story of Stolypin's courageous efforts to save Russia and the dynasty within the context of the ongoing conflict between Russian state and society. Respectable representatives of society, such as the progressive-minded Aunts Adalia and Agnessa in *August 1914,* mindlessly celebrated the moral heroism of the populist and socialist terrorists. The extreme Russian Right and the tsarist courtiers were equally resistant to political good sense and the requirements of social progress. They "did not want to know about reform and progress, about new ideas, and above all about concessions, [and] which believed in nothing but prayerful prostration before the Tsar, in petrified immobility, century after century" (653). Solzhenitsyn is equally scornful of Russian reactionaries as he is of Russian liberals and, contrary to legend, expresses no nostalgia whatsoever for tsarist immobility or absolutism.

The Red Wheel is written as a series of "knots," what Solzhenitsyn calls "narrative(s) in discrete periods of time." The original edition of *August 1914,* published in Russian in Paris in 1971 and in English in 1972, limited itself to the immediate events leading up to the very earliest stage (e.g., the Battle of Tannenburg) of World War I.[7] But Solzhenitsyn soon concluded that it was impossible to address the question of the supposed inevitability of October 1917 without examining in detail the most sustained effort to reform the old regime. He concluded that it was necessary to closely examine Stolypin's five-year tenure as prime minister. He thus introduced a series of flashbacks to previous knots, including a dense historical chapter (65) on Stolypin's life and statecraft, as well as riveting accounts of the assassin's plot, the attack on Stolypin at the Kiev Opera, Stolypin's death, and the reaction of both the regime and society to it. The fourteen chapters of the Stolypin cycle, while undoubtedly interruptions in the orderly flow of the novel, are justified by the fact that Russia's prospects in the war, and more broadly, her hopes for peaceful, piecemeal and humane political development, were dealt a crushing blow by the assassination of Stolypin.

While Solzhenitsyn's portrait of Stolypin is unquestionably admiring, it in no way departs from the fundamental facts or overwhelmingly positive evaluations of his talents expressed by the best non-Marxist historians in the West. For example, a well-known historian of Russia, Richard Pipes, whose work, in radical contrast to Solzhenitsyn's, affirms the essential continuity between age-old Russian "patrimonialism" and Soviet despotism, nonetheless emphasizes Stolypin's exceptional character as a statesman and human being. In his monumental *The Russian Revolution,* published in 1990, Pipes writes that Stolypin "was arguably the most outstanding statesman of Imperial Russia. For all their remarkable gifts, his only possible rivals—Speranskii and Witte—lacked his combination of the statesman's vision and the politician's skill."[8] Pipes does not dispute Solzhenitsyn's account of the wisdom of Stolypin's proposed reforms, especially his commitment to replacing the peasant commune with individual proprietorship, as well as his visionary support for the expansion of civil rights, the reform of the bureaucracy, and the introduction of advanced social legislation. Nor does he deny that Stolypin remained at heart a convinced constitutionalist despite his conviction that the state must vigorously defend itself against the terrorism of leftist revolutionar-

ies. But Pipes sharply challenges Solzhenitsyn's account of the assassin Bogrov's motives in killing Stolypin, denying that Bogrov's Judaism played any role whatsoever in his decision to strike at Stolypin, (and tendentiously suggesting a whiff of antisemitism in Solzhenitsyn's account).[9] Otherwise, there is no fundamental divergence in their account of the facts nor in their extraordinarily high evaluations of Stolypin's statesmanship. In words that could have been written by Solzhenitsyn, Pipes concludes that Stolypin "towered over the Russian statesmen of his era. . . . He gave Russia, traumatized by the Revolution of 1905, a sense of national purpose and hope."[10] Pipes agrees with Solzhenitsyn about Stolypin's undeniable "personal greatness."[11] This greatness is linked not only to his extraordinary character but also to his determination to steer a middle path of political development "above partisanship and utopianism."[12] Where Pipes finally differs from Solzhenitsyn is in his conviction that Stolypin was already "politically finished" in September 1911, "destroyed by the very people whom he had tried to save."[13] In Pipes's view, if Stolypin had lived he would not have been able to "prevent a revolution."[14] He lacked sufficient backing from the principal moderate parties on whom he had to rely for support and his "grand project of political and social reform remained largely on paper."[15] Even his program of agrarian reform, as profound as it was in its appreciation of the sources of Russian backwardness, was at best a limited success, "wiped out in 1917 by the spontaneous action of communal peasants."[16]

Solzhenitsyn, for his part, does not deny that Stolypin was politically finished *in the fall of 1911.* His precipitous and illegal actions over the western zemstvo bill had alienated him from the crown, turned both the Duma and the State Council against him, and led to a break with the Octobrists, the principal constitutionalist grouping in the Duma (587-97). Solzhenitsyn judges rather harshly Stolypin's behavior during this affair.[17] Why then does Solzhenitsyn suggest that Stolypin might have saved the regime, and the prospects for constitutional government in Russia, if he had not been gunned down by Bogrov in Kiev in the fall of 1911? Unlike Pipes, he refuses to believe that the career of a man of Stolypin's extraordinary talents and vision could be irrevocably finished despite the extraordinary opposition he had confronted during his final months in office. Even the most decadent political order has been known to turn to extraordinary men during times of crisis, as, in fact, the Tsar did in 1906 with Stolypin (one thinks also of the tumultuous political careers of Churchill and de Gaulle). It is not impossible that the monarchy and Duma would have seen Stolypin in a different light once World War I had broken out, and that Stolypin's extraordinary skills might have helped save Russia from the revolutionary precipice.

Chapter 65 of the augmented *August 1914* is entitled **"Pyotr Arkadievich Stolypin."** It is a long, somewhat dense, but fascinating biographical and historical account of Stolypin's life and statesmanship. The first pages of the chapter are an integral part of the "novel" itself, eloquently discussing the central idea that gave "high purpose" (529) to Stolypin's statecraft, namely, the liberation of the peasant from the tyranny and penury of the repartitional commune. The final five or six pages of the chapter provide a riveting account of Stolypin's premonition of his impending death and of the final, dramatic moments at the Kiev Opera on September 14, 1911, when Stolypin was shot in the presence of the Tsar. The eighty or so pages in between are in small print and are intended for "the most indefatigably curious readers" (531). These pages provide a detailed account of Stolypin's career from 1905 until 1911. Solzhenitsyn apologizes for "such a crude distortion of the novel form." It is justified, he writes, only because "Russia's whole history, her very memory" had been "distorted in the past, and her historians silenced" (531). But this apology should not mislead the reader. The historical character of the "small printed" section of chapter 65 does not take away from the clarity or eloquence of Solzhenitsyn's account. His is a carefully limned portrait of a "great-souled man" worthy of Plutarch's *Lives.* In addition to its salutary character, the chapter is an essential element in Solzhenitsyn's dissection of the Marxist-Leninist dogma that the revolution was somehow historically inevitable. Solzhenitsyn challenges the leftist dogma that communism, whatever its defects, was an advance over the "absolutism" that preceded it.

Solzhenitsyn admires Stolypin both for his manly character and for his well-grounded but visionary ideas. He describes Stolypin as "firm" and "self-possessed," "a figure of epic presence" (560). He embodied authority in a natural and unforced way, and his unapologetic defense of his principles as well as of the regime's unequivocal right to defend itself against its armed opponents, impressed even his most inveterate critics. Stolypin's impressive qualities startled an intelligentsia that habitually "revell(ed) in their intellectual superiority to an obtuse and decrepit government which had never, as far as anyone could remember, produced an orator, a thinker, or statesman" (536).

Stolypin was a constitutionalist and a convinced monarchist. But he was not scrupulous in his attachment to constitutional forms as were some otherwise like-minded leaders such as the zemstvo leader D. M. Shipov.[18] Stolypin did not believe that Russia could afford such moralism in the face of a genuine revolutionary challenge to the existence of the regime. In contrast to the mediocrity of Tsar Nikolai II he was "the pillar (stolp) of the Russian state" and "his qualities were, in truth, kingly" (582). Solzhenitsyn subtly suggests the superiority of natural aristocracy to conventional or hereditary monarchy. Stolypin tried to be faithful to the mediocre but decent monarch and he was appalled by advanced society's ridiculous caricature of him as "shortsighted, stupid, malicious, vengeful, callous" (578). In truth, Tsar Nikolai II "diverged no farther from the mean of mediocrity than the average monarch" and his mediocrity was made up for, in some part, by his abundant "goodness of heart" (578). But Stolypin's magnanimity was not reciprocated by the hangers-on at the royal court. They did not hesitate to attribute the most self-serving motives to Stolypin since they knew nothing of statesmanship or service to the common good. Stolypin had tried to build a far-reaching coalition in the Duma on the model of George III's alliance of "the King's Friends."[19] In Stolypin's view, this coalition would include a range of liberals and conservatives loyal to constitutional monarchy and committed to sensible reforms. The petty reactionaries in the court could see in such farsighted prudence only personal self-aggrandizement.

Stolypin had "three favorite lines of policy" (589) that defined his "liberal conservatism" (544) as Solzhenitsyn calls it. He was committed to "advancement of the peasant" through his liberation from the traditional commune, he supported the zemstvo or local self-government as the best means to promote civic consciousness among the people, and he encouraged patriotism or "Russian national awareness," although not imperialism or pan-Slavism. These policies remain pillars of Solzhenitsyn's own practical political agenda as outlined in **Rebuilding Russia,** an agenda that might reasonably be called neo-Stolypinite in character and inspiration.[20]

STOLYPIN'S CENTRAL IDEA

The centerpiece of Stolypin's vision was his deep conviction that the Russian peasant could not be free and that Russia could not be a great and prosperous nation if the peasant did not own his own land. If Stolypin (and his latter-day partisan Solzhenitsyn) share a "Slavophile" conviction that the land is sacred, if they share a "feeling for the land, for the upturned soil" they most certainly do not uphold the traditionalist view of the peasant commune, with its "compulsory egalitarianism," as the embodiment of that feeling and sense of responsibility. Stolypin was convinced, "sure as holy writ," that the Russian peasant "would never prosper while he was shackled by the commune." The peasant or repartitional commune, which survived the emancipation of the serfs by Tsar Aleksandr II in 1861, required the peasants to redivide their lands in a way that made improvements "senseless." The compulsory repartition of the land "made it impossible for the peasant and his land to grow together, perpetuated holdings each consisting of widely separated, long, narrow strips of arable land and meadow." Stolypin certainly admired the skill and communal solidarity of Russian peasants. But the Russian strip-farming system was "excruciatingly wasteful" (in contrast to the enclosed farms of peasant proprietors in Belorussia and Ukraine) and it stifled peasant initiative and independence. Stolypin was rightly convinced that neither the maintenance of the communal system nor the redistribution of the gentry's land to a "land-hungry" peasantry could begin to address the problems of the Russian countryside. All the redistribution in the world could not outpace the dramatic increases in the peasant population of European Russia in recent decades (for quotations in this paragraph, see 530).

Solzhenitsyn states that "Stolypin's idea was one of shining simplicity—yet too complicated to be grasped or accepted." It was opposed by traditionalists, Slavophile romantics, by selfish gentry who feared a self-reliant peasantry, and by revolutionaries and leftists who associated the commune with "socialism." Yet Stolypin was determined to break the back of the repartitional commune and to give the peasant "permanent property" in the land. Only then could the peasant have "freedom and prosperity." Stolypin (and Solzhenitsyn) know all the romantic, "Slavophile" arguments for the commune. In this romantic rendering, the commune demands self-denial and "the harmonization of the will of the individual with that of the commune." Stolypin was certainly convinced that there is something higher than freedom and prosperity, namely spiritual greatness, and that it ultimately lies in the "eternal subordination" of the individual to the common good. But Stolypin, clearly speaking for the author, knows that such spiritualism ultimately "makes action impossible." Human beings need to live with property and prosperity "as we live with all the temptations of this life" (530-31 for this and preceding quotations). The failure to distinguish between a general recognition of the primacy of spiritual goods and the advocacy of a utopian "spiritualist" politics, is at the source of the systematic misunderstanding in the West of Solzhenitsyn's major public pronouncements, such as the Harvard address of 1978. And Solzhenitsyn's Stolypin appreciates that the real-life commune has little in common with the subordination of the individual to spiritual concerns. Much as Aristotle insisted that the abolition of private property in the name of civic unity would paradoxically undermine virtue and sow discord among citizens (*Politics* book 2, chapter 5) so Stolypin believed that in practice the supposedly 'communal' commune "created a good deal of discord amongst the peasants" (531).

Stolypin had not only thought long and hard about the pressing peasant problem, he had also immersed himself in the details of agricultural policy since his days as a student studying science at Petersburg University. As a provincial governor in the western provinces he had seen first hand the superiority of an agricultural sector "where peasant land was as a rule held by each household separately" (532). He took a keen interest in agricultural policy and became a kind of crusader for agricultural reform when he became governor of Saratov in 1904. This was not an ideal location for introducing innovations of any kind. Saratov was a hotbed of antiregime activity. Educated "society" was filled with "white-hot hostility" (532) to authority as well as with general indulgence toward left-wing parties and even revolutionaries and terrorists. Solzhenitsyn writes that on the eve of the 1905 Revolution, Russia was "in the grip of a chill which would soon be a raging fever" and the unwise Russo-Japanese War of 1904-1905 did nothing to moderate her ailments. In the midst of revolutionary upheaval, several attempts were made on Stolypin's life (533-34). In the fall of 1905, the adjutant-general in Saratov was blown up by a bomb in Stolypin's home. But none of this deterred Stolypin from his tasks. He was determined to stand up to the terrorist assault; to challenge the indulgence of society toward revolution; and to *explain* to all who would listen his thoughts about the absolute necessity of land reform. In his view, there was "a deep-seated fault in the structure of peasant life" (534) that was feeding revolutionary unrest and turning the peasantry, the traditional base of tsarism, against the regime. But neither the peasants nor society at large, with its relentless clamoring for land redistribution from the gentry and thoughtless romanticism about the commune, understood the nature of the Russian disease. Stolypin's mission was to convince all who would listen that the repartitional commune "was an unsurmountable barrier" to the establishment of an order of "independent and prosperous farmers" (534). One of Stolypin's provincial reports as governor, laying out his modernizing vision, was read by the Tsar himself (Solzhenitsyn suggests wryly that this was something of a miracle since the Tsar was "not noted for his assiduity as a reader or thinker" [535]). The result was that Stolypin was brought to St. Petersburg to become minister of the interior in 1906.

FIGHTING REVOLUTION AS A STATESMAN

It is during this period that Stolypin would begin his determined campaign against revolutionary terrorism, a campaign that would continue during his first years as prime minister. Solzhenitsyn makes clear that Stolypin's "thoughts were those of a statesman" (535). Ultimately, one had to fight the revolution "as a statesman not as a head of the police" (554), as Solzhenitsyn eloquently suggests. But there could be no constitutional order in Russia if revolutionaries were free to murder government officials and civilians alike, to rob banks, to destroy the economic infrastructure of the country, to encourage peasants to destroy estates, and to set the countryside on fire. On August 25, 1906, a little more than a month after replacing the uninspired Ivan Goremykin as prime minister, Stolypin himself was the target of yet another assassination attempt. Terrorists, disguised as gendarmes, threw briefcases with explosives into his home on Aptekarsky Island in St. Petersburg, while he was receiving visitors. As a result, twenty-seven people, including ordinary petitioners, were killed and another thirty-two were injured. Stolypin's three-year-old son and one of his daughters were badly wounded. These attacks made Stolypin all the more determined to stamp out revolutionary terrorism as the sine qua non for the success of his reformist program. In the course of the misnamed "Stolypin terror," "field courts" were introduced for "specially serious . . . cases of looting, murder, and attacks on the police, on the civil authorities and on peaceful citizens, so as to bring trial and sentence closer to the time and place of the crime" (548). As the historian Richard Pipes notes, governors and military officials in eighty-two of Russia's eighty-seven provinces were given the authority to turn civilians "whose guilt was so obvious as to require no investigation" over to military courts for the administration of summary justice.[21] The field courts had "to convene within twenty-four hours of the crime and read a verdict in forty-eight hours. There was no appeal from their sentences, which were to be carried out within twenty-four hours.[22] According to Pipes, about 4,680 people were sentenced to death for violent political crimes between September, 1906, when the policy was decreed under Article 87 of the constitution, and the end of 1909.[23]

Stolypin's "first task, a strange one to him, was to lead the police into battle—such a battle as Russia's revolutionaries had never encountered or expected" (535). Without order, there could be no rule of law nor prospects for social development. Stolypin believed that firmness at the beginning would save many lives and prevent a full-scale revolutionary upheaval in Russia. "He would use conciliatory methods where persuasion was possible" (546). But in a situation where so-called liberals such as the Kadets or Constitutional Democrats were positively "pant(ing) for revolution" (559), excusing terrorist attacks and fighting salutary reforms, the regime had a duty to maintain public order. At the same time, it needed to remain scrupulously committed to the path of constitutional government, laid out in the Tsar's Manifesto of October 30, 1905, and the constitution or "Fundamental Laws" of May 6, 1906. The constitution may have been hurriedly adopted, unwisely imitating English and French models of universal manhood suffrage and parliamentary procedure (538). But "there could be no back-tracking. . . . A constitution had been granted: the country had to learn to live by it" (563). Many, even most, of the same liberal and leftist parliamentarians and publicists who condemned "Stolypin's terror" and fulminated against "Stolypin's neckties" (the noose) remained silent about and even applauded revolutionary terror. It was in these difficult

circumstances, so impropitious to constitutional political development, that Stolypin had to pursue his precarious "middle channel," surrounded by "swarms of enemies . . . on both wings" (541).

Solzhenitsyn reflects at some length on the following paradox: Stolypin often had to pursue his centrist, constitutional path through extraconstitutional or at least questionably constitutional means (591). Solzhenitsyn criticizes Stolypin for excessive use of Article 87, which granted the government the power to promulgate laws when the Duma was not in session, even if the use of such an extraordinary step was sometimes necessary. He attributes this propensity to Stolypin's impatience about the long-standing resistance of nearly all segments of Russian society to necessary reforms. He also sympathetically notes that all of Stolypin's reform efforts, from the dismissal of the ineffectual and Left-dominated First and Second Dumas to the introduction of far-reaching agrarian reforms, initially got off the ground as a result of the invocation of Article 87 (591).

In discussing Stolypin's use of Article 87, Solzhenitsyn raises the problem of political founding and the related question of the statesman's handling of extreme situations. The wise founder of a political order, even a constitutional one, must have a certain freedom, at least at the beginning, "to legislate without parliament" (591). This is especially true in the Russian case where the center confronted an unholy alliance of reactionary anticonstitutionalists and revolutionaries of various stripes. Solzhenitsyn observes that even long-established parliamentary systems have been confronted "with great trials" in the twentieth century sometimes calling for the resort to extraconstitutional means to preserve liberty. "Russia was overtaken by these trials earlier than any other country and at a time when she was less well prepared" (591). Solzhenitsyn is warning against a doctrinaire liberalism that ignores the essential preconditions of a free society and demands moral purity from those statesmen trying to preserve a civilized order from fundamental assault. Stolypin's and Russia's dilemma raises a question of political philosophy that is incapable of any simple or universal resolution, namely the question of "the correct relation between parliamentary procedure and the individual will of the responsible statesman" (591). Writing in 1976 (the year of the composition of chapter 65)[24] Solzhenitsyn suggests that it would be "more discrete" of him to postpone pronouncement on the problem "until the beginning of the twenty-first century" (591). In truth, it is a theoretically and practically insoluble problem of statecraft, as Solzhenitsyn clearly appreciates. Solzhenitsyn's Stolypin eschews both a Machiavellian disregard for constitutional government and a liberal legalism or formalism that, under Russian circumstances of the time, would only aid the cause of those who preferred revolution to reform. Throughout **The Red Wheel,**

Solzhenitsyn suggests that many so-called Russian liberals tactically appealed to a scrupulous understanding of the law in order to undermine the prospects for ordered liberty in Russia. The aversion of many liberals to the requirements of legitimate authority, and their concomitant indulgence toward revolutionaries of the Left, are not distinctively Russian phenomena. This problem first arose in classic form in Russia in the final half of the nineteenth century but would become a commonplace dilemma of liberalism throughout the world in the twentieth.

On July 21, 1906, Stolypin, acting as the new prime minister, utilized the authority of Article 87 and dissolved the First Duma elected after the institution of constitutional government in Russia. The Duma was dominated by leftist parties who opposed any and all cooperation with the regime. Its tone was set by the Kadets who were still imbued with the absurdly illiberal notion that there could be "no enemies to the Left." They refused to accept the fact that the October 1905 Manifesto had radically changed the nature of Russian politics. The leaders of the First Duma had appealed directly to the population in the name of the representative parliament and, for all intents and purposes, were fomenting revolution among the population at large. Stolypin believed he had one fundamental choice, a choice not anticipated by democratic purists: he could "seize the bridles of the runaway horses already pawing the abyss, or watch the Russian chariot plunge to destruction" (543). He dismissed the First Duma while simultaneously calling for a great social effort "to accomplish the *most important* of our monarchy's tasks—which is to raise the prosperity of the peasantry" (543). The Kadets responded with their Vyborg Manifesto, calling on the Russian people to refuse to pay taxes or serve in the armed forces. Some militant Social Revolutionaries and Social Democrats (Bolsheviks) went further and issued a "Manifesto to the Army and Navy," calling on soldiers and sailors "to liberate the people from this traitorous government" (544). Both appeals went unheeded by the public at large.

After the Second Duma turned out to be "even more radical" and irresponsible than the First, the government dissolved it on June 16, 1907. Recognizing the political immaturity of the workers and peasants (too easily manipulated by leftist demagogues) Stolypin introduced a weighted suffrage that increased the representation of the more politically experienced middle and upper classes. This change in the electoral law was, strictly speaking, illegal under the October Manifesto. But Stolypin was convinced that "only by illegally changing the electoral law could the electoral principle and the national representation be saved" (564). He must choose "the true path" between "two rivals concentrations of mediocrity and philistinism" (564) even at the price of legal purity. His gamble paid

off. The result of the change in the electoral law was the more politically balanced Third Duma, which would serve out its full term until 1912 (surviving Stolypin himself). Stolypin was able to work first with Aleksandr Guchkov's center-right Octobrists, so named for their commitment to the principles of constitutional monarchy affirmed by the October Manifesto, and later with Russian nationalists committed to his idea of a reinvigorated Russia. Stolypin was committed to cooperation with the new Duma and desired to make them full participants in his project of political and economic reform. He addressed the Duma on a regular basis, dazzling its representatives with his rhetoric and putting them off guard with his carefully thought-out program of balanced reform. He thus won the enmity of courtiers and reactionaries who hoped to restore full-blown autocratic rule. Stolypin walked a precipice of sorts. He made every effort to lay the framework for a genuine constitutional order while utilizing tenuously constitutional means to overcome the opposition of the illiberal Left and Right and the inertia of often self-serving parliamentarians. He pursued his course with a delicate mixture of moderation and determination that is the hallmark of the true statesman.

A Second Petrine Revolution

Stolypin was determined to break free from the cycle of repression and reform that had dominated Russia's politics since the reign of Tsar Aleksandr I at the beginning of the nineteenth century. In modern Russia, reform had always been introduced when the regime was weak or on the verge of collapse, "while stern measures to restore order were taken to indicate a renunciation of reform" (549). Stolypin was determined to combine order with an unflagging commitment to fundamental reforms. His greatness lay in his characteristic ability to follow such a path with courage and without hesitation or regret.

In Stolypin's view, a strong, Russian state should not be confused with a repressive or immobile one. But the prospects for shaking up the sedentary court and bureaucracy were limited indeed. Instead, "the cure must begin below, with the peasants" (552). The hundred million Russian peasantry must be given a stake in the political order. They must be given the opportunity to become genuine proprietors and citizens. Stolypin's agrarian reforms began with a modest step to cede state, appanage, and Church land to peasants. This reform, introduced by decree the same day as the explosion on Apterkarsky Island, not surprisingly met "concerted opposition" from a major segment of the nobility (552). Stolypin also eased "restrictions on the sale of land held in trust or entailed" and "reduc(ed) loan payments and offer(ed) more generous credits to the peasants" (552). But his major reform was without doubt the decree of November 22, 1906, granting the peasant the right to leave the commune (552-55). Solzhenitsyn explains that previous governmental enactments had all aimed at freezing the commune in place. Solzhenitsyn points out that the reactionaries, such as the Tsarist Prime Minister Pobedonostsev (who lost power with the Revolution of 1905) thought like Socialist Revolutionaries when it came to the commune. They were mindlessly committed to equal land endowment, and "periodic redistribution in accordance with census returns" (552). In announcing his reform to the Duma, Stolypin lashed out at this consensus across the ideological spectrum, a consensus that guaranteed the permanent impoverishment and marginalization of Russia's peasantry. He eloquently articulated the pernicious economic and moral effects of the repartitional commune:

> The obligation for all to conform to a single pattern of farming can be tolerated no longer. It is intolerable for a peasant with initiative to invest his talents and efforts in land which is only temporarily his. Continual redistribution begets carelessness and indifference in the cultivator. Equal shares in the land mean equal shares in ruin. Egalitarian land-use lowers agricultural standards and the general cultural level of the country at large. (quoted on 552)

Stolypin believed that the paternalism of both the Left and Right obscured the real causes of the peasants' discontent: the peasant's "lack of land that was truly his, land that he felt to be his, was what undermined *his* respect for everyone else's property" (553). The true barrier against revolutionary socialism was a peasantry whose *natural* desire for property was satisfied. Stolypin rejected the argument of leading "liberals" that ordinary Russian peasants were incapable of handling the responsibility of proprietorship free from the guidance of the commune. These liberals feared that too many peasants would squander their resources on drinking and leave their families destitute. Stolypin told the Duma that such thinking was needlessly paternalistic and ignored the inherent strength of the majority of the Russian population. Stolypin famously argued that Russia must wager on "the sensible and the strong, not the drunken and weak" (575). He did not place his hopes on "land-grabbing Kulaks" as revolutionary and communist propaganda would later insist, but rather on hardworking and energetic farmers who were willing to take risks for their families and country.

Stolypin's wager on the independent and self-reliant peasant bore immediate fruit in his resettlement policy that allowed peasants to settle on unoccupied lands east of the Ural Mountains (583-84). Not only did resettlement relieve rural poverty and overcrowding in European Russia, but it allowed peasants to operate in complete independence from the residual tyranny of the peasant commune. With the help of government loans for building homes and buying machinery and with

many other incentives in place, over four million peasants had resettled in Siberia, the Kirghiz lands, and Semirechye by 1914. For Stolypin, the Siberian resettlement was proof of what "the strong and sober" were capable of if they were liberated from the restraints imposed by antiquated tradition and counterproductive, egalitarian passions. Stolypin liked to say that "another ten or fifteen years and the revolutionaries won't have a chance" (562). Solzhenitsyn clearly shares this view although others are less sanguine about the long-term impact that Stolypin's reforms would have had absent war and revolution. Historians do not differ much about the facts, only in their interpretations of their import. In addition to the over four million people who took advantage of the opportunities for resettlement, Stolypin's agrarian reforms allowed for what Richard Pipes has called "the emergence in central Russia of an independent peasantry of a Western type."[25] By 1916, 22 percent of communal households with 14.5 percent of acreage had filed petitions in order to free themselves from the commune. About 10 percent of European Russian peasants in 1917 farmed on private, enclosed lands; the rest still practiced strip farming linked to the repartitional commune.[26] Despite the deep-seated resistance to innovation on the part of the bulk of Russia's peasantry, the debilitating stranglehold of the commune on Russian agriculture had finally been broken. Solzhenitsyn is not wrong to inquire as to what might have been "achieved in twenty years of unhampered development" (584). Tragically, history was not to grant Russia the luxury of such leisurely, uninterrupted national development.

Stolypin wished "to follow a specifically *Russian* line" (567) of social development. He supported an ambitious program of social and political reforms and was committed to general principles of civil rights and constitutional government. But like Solzhenitsyn himself, Stolypin opposed slavish imitation of western European models of liberal democracy. He hoped that Russia could combine a commitment to self-government, especially that local self-government that educates citizens in the give-and-take of political life, with a recognition of the central role that Christianity has historically played in giving shape to Russian national consciousness (Stolypin actively opposed what he saw as senseless and cruel disabilities against Russia's Jewish population [see 555 and 599]). On this front, he met opposition from an obdurate Tsar who seemed to think that the maintenance of petty antisemitic laws was an obligation of Christian monarchy (see 555).

Above all, Stolypin believed Russia needed time in order to successfully navigate her own path to modernity, one that would not foolishly squander her national inheritance. The radical liberals believed that uneducated, inexperienced people could become citizens at one stroke and hence supported and manipulated universal suffrage. In contrast, Stolypin believed that the peasants needed to be given a real stake in the social order and then encouraged to responsibly defend and articulate their interests through institutions of local self-government (see 566). Stolypin was a Russian nationalist but one who rejected the ideological chimera of panSlavism and the temptation of an imperialist foreign policy (580-82 and 600). In his view, Russia must limit herself in order to become strong, and one mark of Russian national greatness was the capacity for prudent self-restraint. His "policy became the rallying point for all those educated people—as yet alas, so few—in whom some unchilled remnant, or some hesitant beginning of Russian natural sentiment and Orthodox belief could be detected" (582-83). Stolypin supported a synthesis of tradition and modernity, of conservatism and liberalism, that offered Russia an opportunity to escape the futile "civil war" between regime and society that had hampered Russia's development since the Decembrist revolt of 1825. In Solzhenitsyn's view, "a second Peter ruled Russia . . . as radical a reformer, but with ideas that distinguished him from Peter the Great" (582). The first Peter had destroyed the independence of the Church, continued the persecution of the Old Believers, pursued a policy of relentless imperial expansion, and modernized Russia through despotic means and with contempt for many of her best traditions. Stolypin, like Solzhenitsyn, is deeply ambivalent about many aspects of the Petrine inheritance. But the ambivalence of these Russian patriots is that of conservative liberals concerned with the strength and freedom of the Russian nation and not that of reactionaries nostalgic for a premodern or feudal Russia.

STOLYPIN'S VISIONARY PROGRAM

After his confrontation with the State Council and Duma over the western zemstvo bill, Stolypin set out to confront the enemy from within, the intransigent bureaucracy that had been suspicious of his every move. "The healing of the legs, the lower limbs, the peasantry, was proceeding splendidly; the time had now come to heal the bureaucracy" (598). In May 1911, he dictated a visionary program of reform to his secretary, a program confiscated by the government after his death. His program was arranged systematically and laid out changes for each of the branches of the state administration. A new ministry would give support to the zemstvos in carrying out administrative, welfare, and educational tasks. A new ministry of labor would "draft laws to improve (the position) of Russian workers, and to make the rootless proletarian a partner in the constructive work of the state and the zemstvos" (598-99). Stolypin outlined plans for greater financial backing for the education of clergy and expressed support for the restoration of the Patriarchate—and hence the establishment of a genuinely independent Orthodox

Church (599). Special emphasis was placed on education, including the goal of universal free primary education by the year 1922 and a huge expansion in the number of state-supported intermediate educational institutions and high schools. At the summit of the educational system, Stolypin wished to establish a national academy to train civil servants. "A dazzling array of specialists and experts would take their place in the Russian government machine" (600). The Tsar would then be able to draw on competent professionals in government and would not be dependent on the advice of courtiers for the choice of ministers. Stolypin insisted that the precondition of his reform program was peace abroad and a rejection of grandiose projects of Russian territorial expansion (600). Russian national greatness depended on a reform of the state apparatus and active efforts to improve the lives of ordinary people. Maintenance of a European peace, and the cultivation of good relations with the United States were also important pillars of his program (600).

Stolypin's reform agenda aimed at nothing less than the comprehensive reconstruction of Russia by 1927-32. Of course, Solzhenitsyn's readers know that a very different plan was imposed on "Soviet" society during those years—a plan that relied upon class struggle, collectivization, and forced industrialization and that utilized terror as its instrument. Solzhenitsyn leaves no doubt which was the genuinely humane and "progressive" plan for Russia's reconstruction. Solzhenitsyn sadly notes that Stolypin's project "vanished, was never published, discussed, exhibited, or indeed recovered— all that survived was the testimony of the man who helped Stolypin to draft it" (601). Tragically, the communists' first Five-Year plan "coincided with what would have been the last five-year period of Stolypin's project" (601).

DYING ALONE

The final pages of chapter 65 (no longer in "small print") follow immediately upon the description of Stolypin's remarkable reform program. The reader sees a Stolypin apprehensive about Russia's future, and "full of foreboding of his own death" (601).

Officials in the tsarist inner circle and bureaucracy already acted as if he was a *former* prime minister. Stolypin was required to attend a major ceremony in Kiev with the Tsar, commemorating the fiftieth anniversary of Aleksandr II's emancipation of the serfs, but he was left out of the official Court program on the occasion and was not even given a bodyguard. The time-serving Interior Minister General Kurlov had picked up the appropriate signs from the Court and was convinced "that Stolypin was no longer worthy of respect, or even of attention" (603). Even though the duplicitous Bogrov had sent a letter to the police on

September 8 warning them of an impending attempt on Stolypin's life, Stolypin was informed belatedly on September 14 and without any details about the threat to his life. No additional security precautions were taken and Stolypin himself did not take the threat seriously since no bomb (the chosen weapon of Russian terrorists) had been discovered. To make matters worse, the Okhrana informer and terrorist Bogrov was admitted to the Kiev Opera on the evening of September 14, 1911, *with the knowledge of Russian police officials.* During the second intermission of the program, Bogrov shot Stolypin within eyeshot of the Tsar.

For several days, Stolypin precariously hung on to life and for a short while even seemed to be improving. He learned from his doctor that he had been shot by Bogrov, the terrorist and sometime secret police informer. He spent several days anxiously waiting for the Tsar to appear. But the Tsar remained mindlessly committed to his itinerary despite the extraordinary assassination attempt against his prime minister. Stolypin desperately wanted to speak to the Tsar, to convey to him for one last time the absolute necessity to proceed with reforms for the sake of Russia and the dynasty (645). Solzhenitsyn's Stolypin is overwhelmed by a sense of the tragedy of having to depart "at forty-nine, and still at the height of his power" (646). He knew that he was "leaving behind a Russia still rent by the radical hostility of civil society towards the imperial power" (646). After taking a turn for the worse, Stolypin died on September 18, fearful for his country and mindful of the Tsar's "weakness," his terrible inability "to face unpleasant realities" (651). Stolypin accepted his death with "rare equanimity and self-possession" (652). Solzhenitsyn concludes chapter 69, which culminates in Stolypin's death, with explicitly biblical language to describe the great statesman: "He Brought Light To The World And The World Rejected Him." Stolypin offered Russia *political* salvation, a middle channel between absolutism and revolution, a path that aimed to respect the mutual requirements of liberty, social progress, and national greatness. He respected Russia's Christian traditions and he brought a sense of religious obligation to his tasks as a statesman. He was a statesman and Christian who respected the autonomy of politics without ever forgetting its moral underpinnings.

Stolypin was despised by "progressive" society that feared he might succeed in defeating the revolution with statesmanship. He was equally hated by the reactionaries and courtiers who could not forgive his support for constitutionalism, his refusal to jettison the October Manifesto or the difficult task of working with the Duma. The Tsar, in a supreme act of indifference and ingratitude, managed to miss Stolypin's funeral. "Everybody could see that the Autocrat of All the Russias had shown no pity for the wounded man" (654). Only a few foreign newspapers captured the nature of

Stolypin's greatness and the true extent of Russia's loss. The *Times* of London rightly observed that he "had adapted the political life of Russia to representative institutions more quickly and in a more orderly fashion than it had ever been done in any country" (655). A Viennese paper noted that Russia's terrorist socialists "called themselves freedom fighters in an attempt to conceal their revolting barbarism but succeeded only in hindering the work of peaceful development" (655). Only fifty parliamentarians, including "a penitent Guchkov," attended Stolypin's funeral (656). The same Left-Right consensus that came together in defense of the regressive peasant commune, united once again in one final expression of contempt for Stolypin's heroic efforts to save the honor of Russia. Solzhenitsyn ends chapter 70 with a final, fitting tribute to Stolypin's courage. He writes that Stolypin's enemies "had never succeeded in frightening him. Only in killing him" (657).

BOGROV AND "THE JEWISH QUESTION"

In Solzhenitsyn's view, Stolypin's statesmanship offered the last fundamental opportunity for Russia to avert the revolutionary cataclysm. In an interview with David Aikman in *Time* magazine on July 24, 1989, published to coincide with the American publication of the augmented *August 1914,* Solzhenitsyn compared the "Red Wheel," the profound and seemingly unstoppable movement toward the revolutions of 1917, to "a gigantic cosmic wheel" in which "everybody including those who turn it, becomes a helpless atom."[27] With the death of Stolypin, Russia effectively lost control of her destiny. Some critics have been alarmed by the fact that Solzhenitsyn emphasizes that Stolypin's assassin, Dmitri Bogrov, was a Jew, and that his resentment against the antisemitic character of the Russian regime played a major role in this decision to strike at Stolypin. Some critics have suggested, on the basis of the Bogrov chapters in *August 1914* (especially chapter 63), that Solzhenitsyn is an antisemite who blames the Jews for provoking Russia's descent into the totalitarian abyss.[28]

But this interpretation does profound injustice to Solzhenitsyn. For one thing, Solzhenitsyn has repeatedly rejected, and even mocked, the anti-Jewish obsessions of the extreme Russian Right and has never expressed an iota of sympathy for antisemitism in any form.[29] In addition, Solzhenitsyn admires Stolypin in no small part for his humane attitude toward the Jews and his desire to eliminate all legal disabilities against them. But Solzhenitsyn insists that there was a "Jewish question" in Russia on the eve of the revolution that needs to be addressed by the conscientious historian.[30] In his view, the analysis of that problem demands more than ritualistic denunciations of antisemitism. Solzhenitsyn gives a balanced analysis of Bogrov's motives, even doing justice to his undoubted, if misguided, heroism. He draws on reputable accounts of Bogrov's life and motives, such as that provided by Bogrov's brother.[31] He locates two principal motives behind Bogrov's decision to strike at Stolypin. The first is that Bogrov, like many revolutionaries, feared the impact of Stolypin's reforms on the prospects for revolutionary action in Russia. Stolypin gave "the regime an unnatural appearance of solidity when it is not solid at all." As a result, "the people no longer have any enthusiasm for political reform" (498). Solzhenitsyn also speculates that Bogrov believed that Stolypin was effectually antisemitic, not because he promoted anti-Jewish measures but because he was single-mindedly concerned with promoting the *Russian* character of the state. In Bogrov's view, "The development of the country along Stolypin's lines promised no golden age for the Jews" (494). Solzhenitsyn may overstate Bogrov's "Jewish" motive in shooting Stolypin, but the entire context of these chapters suggests absolutely no antisemitic attribution of "guilt" to the Jews on Solzhenitsyn's part. Solzhenitsyn makes clear that the blindness of the regime, as much as anything else, was responsible for the revolutionary propensity of many intellectually minded Jews in Russia in the period before the revolution.

CONCLUSION

The "Stolypin cycle" in *August 1914* is a defense of moderation and public-spirited statesmanship in a context in which both regime and society were driving "Russia toward the abyss."[32]

Russia needed an intelligent and courageous politics of the center that had the foresight to mold together order and liberty, tradition and modernity, social innovation with enduring national and religious principles. The intellectuals, even the so-called liberals such as the Kadets, were in fact radicals who opposed constructive reforms if they would in any way strengthen the existing regime and social order.

These false liberals could see no enemies on the Left and failed to appreciate that liberalism must defend itself against the impatience of "progressives" as well as the inertia of reactionaries. The partisans of autocracy rejected the sensible conservative insight, best articulated by Aristotle and Burke, that balanced reform is the best means of conserving a political order.[33] Russia's "civil war" was the first of several in the twentieth century in which an ossified old regime confronted the forces of hyper- or radical modernity with a weak center marginalized on the edge of the battle.[34] In a memorable passage in *November 1916,* Solzhenitsyn pays tribute to the difficulty of pursuing "a middle line" of social development, particularly in an age of ideological politics. "The loud mouth, the big fist, the bomb, the prison bars are of no help to you, as they are to those at the two extremes. Following the middle line demands the utmost self-control, the most inflexible courage, the

most patient calculation, the most precise knowledge."[35] This passage beautifully captures the character of Stolypin's achievement. His greatness is in no way negated by the fact that his prudent statesmanship was finally insufficient to prevent the Red Wheel from churning relentlessly forward.

ADDENDUM

AFTER STOLYPIN: THE CORRUPTION OF STATE AND SOCIETY AND THE DRIFT TOWARD REVOLUTION IN NOVEMBER 1916

In *August 1914,* Solzhenitsyn created a remarkable portrait of the statesman Pyotr Stolypin, scourge of the revolutionary Left and reactionary Right alike and the last best hope, according to Solzhenitsyn, for Russia's salvation. In *November 1916,* the reader feels the gaping nonpresence of Stolypin (even Tsar Nikolai II seems momentarily to feel the loss of the great man and statesman). By concentrating on the superficial quiescence of the period from October 27 to November 16, 1916, Solzhenitsyn allows his readers to see the mutually reinforcing corruption of Russian state and society as well as the absence of any statesmanlike figures who might have helped stem the revolutionary tide. Those moderate and patriotic figures who, broadly speaking, shared Stolypin's desire for reform without revolution, lack the judgment and finesse or a sufficient position of responsibility to make a real difference. The book is strewn with sympathetic figures, from the spiritually sensitive Sanya Lazhenitsyn to the army chaplain Father Severyan (who seems to speak for Solzhenitsyn when he criticizes Tolstoy's "Voltairian" humanitarianism[36]) to the profound but hapless zemstvo leader D. M. Shipov, who shares many of Stolypin's political ideas but lacks his fortitude and his nuanced appreciation of the limits of abstract moralism in politics.[37] Above all, there is the fictional Georgi Vorotyntsev, demoted to an isolated front and still a colonel late in the war. As the readers of *August 1914* will know, Vorotyntsev had the temerity to defend General A. V. Samsonov after the disastrous Battle of Tannenberg when the regime was looking for scapegoats to blame for its generalized corruption and incompetence.[38]

Vorotyntsev is the fictional hero of *The Red Wheel,* Stolypin its historical one. Vorotyntsev clearly represents the best of modern Russia. He is patriotic and religious-minded and a military strategist of some note, but with scientific interests and a keen appreciation of the need to reform radically a deeply sclerotic regime. Personally and intellectually, he blends tradition and modernity. During the time in question, he is on leave in Petersburg and Moscow and actively pursues the prospects with Aleksandr Guchkov, head of the Octobrist opposition party, of a "palace revolution" against the inept Tsar, a revolution aiming to save, not destroy, the monarchy and regime.[39] In the process of his conversations and investigations he discovers to his consternation the multiplying signs of approaching revolution.

Vorotyntsev, speaking for Solzhenitsyn himself, has arrived at the conclusion that Russia's continued involvement in World War I can only undermine the confidence of the Russian people in their ineffectual regime. He is increasingly sympathetic to the "treasonous" possibility of a "separate peace" with Germany.[40] He is nearly desperate to act, to do something, *anything* to save his beloved Russia. But he is distracted by marital problems with his wife, Alina, and by a dizzying and life-restoring affair with the remarkable historian Olda Andozerskaya whom he meets at a Petersburg dinner party. Olda's striking blend of femininity and independent-mindedness (in the company of fashionable society she dares defend the superiority of constitutional monarchy, even law-abiding autocracy, over republicanism and socialism in all their forms)[41] immediately wins Vorotyntsev's heart. But it also deflects him from the path of personal and political obligation. Vorotyntsev's infidelity, and the personal crisis that accompanies it, mirrors Russia's spiritual and political crisis. In the penultimate chapter, his moving expression of regret for the deep harm he has caused Alina suggests the need that Russia has for spiritual healing on the eve of her confrontation with the abyss.[42]

In its symbolism and sensibility, *November 1916* is perhaps the most Christian of Solzhenitsyn's books, though it is never didactic or sectarian.[43] Sanya and Father Severyan do not hesitate to criticize the Orthodox Church for its complicity in the persecution of the Old Believers and Vorotyntsev is critical of the senseless oppression of the Jews.[44] But Solzhenitsyn is convinced that the Church, freed from slavish attachment to the state, can play a particularly vital role in the spiritual regeneration of Russia. In the moving final chapter a forlorn woman, Zina, who has a disastrous affair and a child out of wedlock, and whose self-preoccupation has contributed indirectly to the death of her child, finds herself drawn ineluctably to an Orthodox Church. There, through the act of confession, she begins to experience unconditional forgiveness. As the political theorist David Walsh has suggested, the impetuous Zina seems to symbolize Russia herself in her agony and need for divine solace.[45] In this book, Solzhenitsyn never loses sight of the spiritual nature of the crisis that continues to afflict Russia.

One salient dimension of that crisis, on constant display in *November 1916,* is the moral and political corruption of the intellectuals. The Russian intellectual class might have played a salutary social role by contributing to the gradual liberalization and modernization of Russian state and society, but instead it largely became a "subversive," even nihilistic, force. Solzhenitsyn's unmistakable hostility to the juvenile leftism of the pre-revolutionary Russian intelligentsia has greatly damaged his reputation among "liberals" in Russia today. In contrast to them, he believes that the first, ostensibly democratic, Russian Revolution of February 1917 marks the crucial event in the spiritual and political decomposition of Russia. In Solzhenitsyn's view, the liberals were incapable of governing or acting in a politically responsible way.

Several of *November 1916*'s "historical" chapters offer probing and polemical analyses of Russian liberalism, especially the Left-leaning Constitutional Democratic, or Kadet, Party and the so-called "Progressive Bloc" within the last Duma, the tsarist parliament.[46] Seven chapters focus on Lenin, plotting and quarreling with Parvus and fantastically planning for the outbreak of proletarian revolution in that bastion of bourgeois repression, Switzerland! (Some historians, such as the great biographer of Stalin, the ex-communist Boris Souvarine, questioned the historical accuracy of Solzhenitsyn's portrait of Lenin while others, including Robert Conquest, applauded his skillful artistic rendition of Lenin's monstrous attachment to revolution at all costs. These interpretations are, of course, not necessarily mutually exclusive). These chapters had already appeared in *Lenin in Zurich* in 1975.[47] Let me conclude by highlighting Solzhenitsyn's searing indictment of Russian liberalism in *November 1916,* an indictment all the more important since the Russian liberals became the founders of the provisional government of 1917 and are the prototype of contemporary Russian "westernizing" intellectuals.

Solzhenitsyn never attacks the Kadets for being liberal per se. Instead, he criticizes them for being "not in fact really liberal"[48] at all. In the great conflict between a reactionary state and the revolutionary Left, the liberals always managed "to caress the left," Solzhenitsyn notes. He continues: "their sympathies always with the left, their feet are capable of shuffling only leftward, their heads bob busily as they listen to leftist arguments—but they feel disgraced if they take a step to or listen to a word from the right."[49] For Solzhenitsyn, it is clear that indulging the Left is not a peculiarity or monopoly of Russian liberalism.

The Red Wheel establishes with great eloquence and luminous clarity (reinforced by H. T. Willett's superb translation) that Russia desperately needed a politics of the realistic and principled center to overcome the blindness of the imperial authorities as well as the nihilistic impatience and destructiveness of the revolutionary Left. Statesmen such as Stolypin and, to a lesser extent, Guchkov, who courageously supported the suppression of revolutionary terror even as they encouraged extensive land reform, a responsible system of representation, and the rule of law, were despised by the liberals who should have recognized in them Russia's and liberalism's salvation. *November 1916,* like the "Stolypin cycle" of *August 1914,* is a defense of civic courage and moderation, of an authentic liberalism that can see enemies on the Left as well as the Right.

Notes

1. On the "ideological" character of the Soviet regime as the key to the entire communist misadventure, see Martin Malia, *The Soviet Tragedy: A History of Socialism in Russia, 1917-1991* (New York: Free Press, 1994). On communism as a fundamental obstacle to genuine modernization, see Malia, *Russia under Western Eyes: From the Bronze Horseman to the Lenin Mausoleum* (Cambridge: Harvard University Press, 1998), especially parts 4 and 5.

2. See for example, D. M. Thomas, *Alexander Solzhenitsyn: A Century in His Life* (New York: St. Martin's Press, 1998), 479.

3. Alexis Klimoff, "The Sober Eye: Ivan Denisovich and the Peasant Perspective" in *One Day in the Life of Ivan Denisovich: A Critical Companion,* ed. Alexis Klimoff (Evanston, Ill: Northwestern University Press, 1997), 6-7.

4. Aleksandr Solzhenitsyn, "An Exchange with Boris Souvarine on *Lenin in Zurich*" in *Solzhenitsyn in Exile: Critical Essays and Documentary Materials,* ed. John B. Dunlop, Richard S. Haugh, and Michael Nicholson (Stanford: Hoover Institution Press, 1985), 338.

5. See Aleksandr Solzhenitsyn, *August 1914: The Red Wheel I,* trans. Harry T. Willetts (New York: Farrar, Straus and Giroux, 1989), with paperback versions available from Noonday Press and Penguin, and *November 1916: The Red Wheel II,* trans. Harry T. Willetts (New York: Farrar, Straus and Giroux, 1999). Subsequent volumes, already available in Russian, include two volumes of *March 1917* as well as *April 1917,* which concludes with a long excursus covering events through the year 1922.

6. For excellent accounts of Solzhenitsyn's critique in the augmented *August 1914* of both Tolstoyan and Marxist historicism and pietistic fatalism, see Vladislav Krasnov, "Wrestling with Lev Tolstoi: War, Peace and Revolution in Aleksandr Solzhenitsyn's New *August Chetyrnadtsatogo,*" in *Slavic Review* (45, 4, Winter 1986), 707-19 and Alexis Klimoff, "Inevitability vs. Will: A Theme and Its Variations in Solzhenitsyn's *August 1914*" in *Transactions of the Association of Russian-American Scholars in the U.S.A.* (Vol. 29, 1998), 305-12.

7. For the original version of the book, see Solzhenitsyn, *August 1914,* trans. Michael Glenny (New York: Farrar, Straus and Giroux, 1972).

8. Richard Pipes, *The Russian Revolution* (New York: Knopf, 1990), 166.

9. Pipes, *The Russian Revolution,* 188-89. Elsewhere, Pipes makes the fantastic claim that "Solzhenitsyn is undoubtedly in the grip of the Russian extreme right's view of the Revolution, which is that it was the doing of Jews." The remark by Pipes is quoted in Richard Grenier, "Solzhenitsyn and Anti-Semitism: A New Debate," *New York Times,* November 13, 1985, 24. See also Edward E. Ericson Jr., *Solzhenitsyn and the Modern World* (Washington, D.C.: Regnery, 1993), 202-4.

It is remarkable that in his discussion of Solzhenitsyn and Stolypin in *The Russian Revolution,* Pipes makes no mention of Solzhenitsyn's powerful defense of political moderation in *August 1914* and fails to consider his sustained critique of the (antisemitic) Russian Right throughout *The Red Wheel.* Nor does Pipes mention the remarkable affinities between his own and Solzhenitsyn's ultimate judgments about the character, policies, and achievement of Stolypin.

10. Pipes, *The Russian Revolution,* 190.

11. Pipes, *The Russian Revolution,* 190.

12. Pipes, *The Russian Revolution,* 190.

13. Pipes, *The Russian Revolution,* 191.

14. Pipes, *The Russian Revolution,* 190.

15. Pipes, *The Russian Revolution,* 190.

16. Pipes, *The Russian Revolution,* 190.

17. Stolypin wished to change the old zemstvo law in order to give greater representation in the western provinces of the Russian empire to Russian peasants over against the Polish gentry who were the chief beneficiaries of the differential franchise. He was chiefly motivated by a patriotic desire to maintain the Russian character of these provinces. In Solzhenitsyn's view, Stolypin underestimated the commitment of the regime to the principle of aristocracy (it not unsurprisingly preferred the conservative rule of Polish aristocrats to the potentially disruptive dominance of Russian peasants open to manipulation by intellectuals). He also showed a "stubborn" disregard for the importance of constitutional forms by insisting that the Duma and State Council be suspended for three days so that the Western Zemstvo Act could be promulgated under Article 87 (591). Solzhenitsyn is uncharacteristically harsh in his judgment: "The occasion did not warrant his [Stolypin's] resignation, or the wrecking of the Council, or the application of Article 87" (591).

18. For a sympathetic account of Shipov's strengths and limits as a leader, and an implicit critique of his moralistic approach to politics see *November 1916,* 60-80, esp. 65-66.

19. On this point see Pipes, *The Russian Revolution,* 169.

20. See Solzhenitsyn, *Rebuilding Russia: Reflections and Tentative Proposals* (New York: Farrar, Straus, and Giroux, 1991).

21. Pipes, *The Russian Revolution,* 170.

22. Pipes, *The Russian Revolution,* 170.

23. Pipes, *The Russian Revolution,* 170. All dates in this chapter are given according to the Gregorian or Western calendar rather than the Julian calendar (thirteen days behind the former) in use in Russia until 1918. I have continued, however, to refer to February and October Revolutions (old-style references) since they remain standard terms for the Russian Revolutions of 1917.

24. See "Publisher's Note" to the augmented *August 1914,* vi in the Penguin edition.

25. Pipes, *The Russian Revolution,* 174.

26. Pipes, *The Russian Revolution,* 175.

27. See "Interview: Russia's Prophet in Exile," *Time* (July 24, 1989), 56-60. The quote is from 58.

28. See note 9. For a particularly authoritative response to one of the most irresponsible attributions of anti-semitic motives to Solzhenitsyn, see Alexis Klimoff, "Solzhenitsyn and the Jews," *Midstream* (June/July 1986), 38-41.

29. See for example, Solzhenitsyn, *La Russie sous l'Avalanche,* translated from the Russian by Georges Philippenko and Nikita Struve (Paris: Fayard, 1998), chapter 25, "Les maladies du nationalisme russe," where Solzhenitsyn laments the "unhealthy and aggressive extremisms" that came to dominate much of the Russian nationalist Right in the 1970s and 1980s. He writes of the propensity of the extremist elements to interpret "all the events of the world and of Russian history as following from the intrigues of Free Masons and Jews" (252).

30. See the Grenier article cited in note 9.

31. "Interview," *Time* (July 24, 1989), 58.

32. Solzhenitsyn, *November 1916,* 57.

33. See Book V of Aristotle's *Politics* and Edmund Burke, *Reflections on the Revolution in France* (Oxford: Oxford University Press/World Classics, 1993) esp. 21-23. Burke writes: "A state without the means of some change is without the means of its conservation. Without such means it might even risk the loss of that part of the constitution which it wished the most religiously to preserve."

34. The Spanish Civil War of 1936-1939 is perhaps the classic example of a civil conflict where the party of the constitutionalist center was almost completely marginalized by the forces of the authoritarian (Carlist and Falangist) Right and the proto-totalitarian (Stalinist) Left.

35. Solzhenitsyn, *November 1916,* 59.

36. Solzhenitsyn, *November 1916,* 48-50.

37. See note 18.

38. See chapter 82 of *August 1914,* 784-95.

39. See *November 1916,* 560-74. For a detailed account of Guchkov's political career see *November 1916,* chapter 41, 534-60.

40. See Vorotyntsev's exchange with Svechin about the desirability of a "separate peace" in *November 1916,* 512-13.

41. Like his sympathetic fictional character Andozer-skaya, Solzhenitsyn is not "doctrinaire" about forms of government.

42. Solzhenitsyn, *November 1916,* 977-84.

43. On the "Christian" character of *November 1916,* see Edward E. Ericson Jr., "For Love of Russia: Review of *November 1916*" in *Modern Age* (Spring 2000): 205-9.

44. For Sanya's and Father Severyan's criticism of the Orthodox Church's role in the persecution of the Old Believers, see *November 1916,* 43-46. For Vorotyntsev's humane and balanced view of "the Jewish question," see 528-30. In both cases the characters express positions identical with Solzhenitsyn's own.

45. See David Walsh, *After Ideology: Recovering the Spiritual Foundations of Freedom* (Washington, D.C.: Catholic University of America Press, 1995), 167-68.

46. See especially chapter 7 of *November 1916,* "The Origin of the Kadets," 57-81, and chapter 62, "The Progressive Bloc," 766-90.

47. Solzhenitsyn, *Lenin in Zurich,* trans. Harry T. Willetts (New York: Farrar, Straus and Giroux, 1976). The Russian edition appeared in Paris from YMCA Press in 1975.

48. Solzhenitsyn, *November 1916,* 59.

49. Solzhenitsyn, *November 1916,* 59.

Pamela S. Saur (essay date winter 2004)

SOURCE: Saur, Pamela S. "Solzhenitsyn's *Matryona's Home.*" *Explicator* 62, no. 2 (winter 2004): 118-21.

[*Below, Saur presents a detailed evaluation of the short story "Matryona's Home."*]

Alexander Solzhenitsyn's well-known story **"Matryona's Home"** (1963) reflects the author's Christianity and moral commitment, his skill at traditional storytelling, and his love of the "Old Mother Russia," which he contrasts bitterly with the USSR. The story is autobiographical in that its narrator, Ignatich, like the author himself, was allowed to work as a teacher in a remote village after being released from imprisonment for his political views. As Cheryl A. Spitz says of Ignatich:

He is depicted in the very process of groping for his psychological and spiritual roots, for the manner of how best to live in uniformity with his nature as a Russian. He believes that this process requires leaping backwards over the disjuncture of Stalin's regime and of the whole Soviet experiment. It involves digging below the surface of Soviet culture to the base soil of the ancient Russian culture and below that, to the ideal of that culture.

(174)

In a superb literary achievement, Solzhenitsyn weaves together a compelling narrative; a Christian, antimaterialistic testimony; a nostalgic tribute to his homeland; and a political exposé. Although the political exposé remains in the background, when one assembles all the details of Soviet life and institutions included in the story, a remarkably thorough, quite negative portrait of Soviet society emerges. The story is set in 1953, in the early cold war era, just a few years before the USSR launched "Sputnik" (the first manmade satellite), handing the United States a disturbing defeat in the emerging "Space Race." At this time, the Soviet Union was waging a successful public relations campaign about its educational, scientific, and technological progress and the efficiency of its centralized economy. **"Matryona's Home"** takes place on a *kolkhoz* (collective farm), a supposedly glorious achievement of the Soviet system. Despite its modern setting, the people in this story live in poverty and without modern conveniences or communication. The story reveals their very low standard of living and takes a critical view not only of their work and living conditions, but of the Soviet institutions in the realms of education, medicine, social welfare, and justice. Far from a socialist utopia enjoyed by equal "comrades," the environment of the story is permeated with privation, inequality, bureaucracy, and corruption. In fact, so harsh is the regime under which the people live that imprisonment brings no disgrace, for the people accept Ignatich as a neighbor and teacher without question. Because of the appallingly low standard of living, people resort to scheming, bartering, and even theft and lawbreaking merely to acquire meager supplies of food, warm clothing, shelter, and fuel to survive the harsh winters. Solzhenitsyn's critique of the Soviet system is all the more scathing in that the story shows that the new age has not brought modern technology, equality, and efficiency at the cost of religious and economic freedom; it has brought the people no advantages.

Upon his release from prison, as the story opens, Ignatich encounters the world-famous Soviet bureaucracy: "They passed every dot and comma in my document through a fine comb, went from one room to another, made telephone calls" (2544). Authority also impinges very directly on the life of Matryona, Ignatich's landlady, who is central in the story. She makes several long trips in an attempt to get a pension but encounters instead one bureaucratic hurdle after another. She is sick, but not categorized as "disabled"; she is not entitled to benefits of factory workers because she worked for a farm; and she cannot document her husband's military service to qualify for widow's benefits. As the story says, "Injustices had piled up, one on top of another" (2550-51). To add insult to injury, she is asked to work voluntarily, with her pitchfork, for the same *kolkhoz* that provides her no pension. As suggested by the pitchfork, the farming here is anything but modern. Matryona's garden is sandy, has not been manured for years, and she plants only potatoes. Not even the "modern" concept of crop rotation is followed.

Inequality and class privilege, anathema to the ideology of communism, also appear: "[T]here was no peat on sale to the villagers. It was delivered, free, to the bosses and to the people round the bosses. [. . .] So, just as in the old days they used to steal the squire's wood, now they pinched peat from the trust" (2552). It seems that hierarchy and privilege have not disappeared with the tsars. The seeking of medical attention, as well as another indication of class inequality, receives the brief comment: "To call in the doctor from the clinic [. . .] would have seemed strange in Talnovo and would have given the neighbors something to talk about—what does she think she is, a lady?" (2555). Nor is education ideal. Ignatich reveals that the practice of "social promotion" runs rampant. Students pass because "the school had to make an effort to keep its record up" (2559).

Harsh authorities and rules also figure prominently in the events of the story that lead up to Matryona's death after a terrible train accident. Matryona decides to give part of her house to her foster daughter Kira and her husband, because they are facing a typical bureaucratic Catch 22: "To get and keep a plot of land [. . .] the young couple had to put up some sort of building" (2553). Operating in the flourishing underground economy of the Soviet era. Matryona hires a tractor driver to work illegally in his free time. To avoid being discovered by the authorities, the driver makes hurried trips in a dangerously overloaded tractor. According to custom, Matryona also has to make liquor to pay the workers, and the narrator worries, "Matryona could do time for making hooch" (2566). In the end, the attempts by various characters and officials trying to avoid responsibility for the terrible accident provide insight into the Soviet system of justice. One of the men present at the accident hides "so that they won't know he was at the crossing. If they find out they'll drag him in as a witness. [. . .] 'Don't know lies up, and do know gets tied up'" (2568).

After Matryona's death, the remaining family members argue about the house. We learn: "They were on the verge of taking it to court, but made peace because they realized that the court would hand over the house to neither side, but to the Rural District Council. A bargain was struck" (2574). Once again, the people's well-being and survival depend on "working outside the system." Being law-abiding and surviving seem to be incompatible in this environment, a situation well represented by the narrator Ignatich, a good man who becomes a convict in this society.

At the story's conclusion, the narrator praises Matryona's saintliness and righteousness, using a quotation from Genesis. Appropriately enough, the story's structure, the tragedy of Matryona's death, and the overtly religious and very unambiguous ending all draw the reader's attention to Matryona and to the author's religious and moral didacticism. However, Matryona's life story, as told by Ignatich, is very strongly determined by its specific milieu: woven into the story is a strong and thorough commentary on the reality of everyday life in the post-war Soviet Union.

Works Cited

Spitz, Sheryl A. "The Impact of Structure in Solzhenitsyn's 'Matryona's Home,'" *The Russian Review* 36 (1977): 167-83.

Solzhenitsyn, Alexander. "Matryona's Home." Trans. H. T. Willetts. *The Norton Anthology of World Masterpieces.* Ed. Maynard Mack. 5th Continental edition. New York: W. W. Norton, 1987, 2539-75.

Daniel J. Mahoney (essay date August-September 2004)

SOURCE: Mahoney, Daniel J. "Traducing Solzhenitsyn." *First Things* 145 (August-September 2004): 14-17.

[*In the following essay, Mahoney discusses the remarkably negative slant that characterizes much of the journalism written about Solzhenitsyn.*]

Aleksandr Solzhenitsyn is one of the great souls of the age. He is also among its most maligned and misunderstood figures. It is hard to think of another prominent writer whose thought and character have been subjected to as many willful distortions and vilifications over the past thirty years.

Things were not always so. Until the early 1970s Solzhenitsyn was widely admired in the West as a dissident and as a critic of Communist totalitarianism. On the left he was appreciated as a defender of human rights against an undeniably illiberal and autocratic regime. But with the publication of works such as *August 1914* (1972), the *Letter to the Soviet Leaders,* and the cultural-spiritual anthology *From Under the Rubble* (both published in the West in 1974), it became

impossible to claim Solzhenitsyn as a champion of left-liberal secularism. He continued to be, of course, a ferocious critic of the ideological "lie" and a tenacious defender of fundamental human liberties. But this anti-totalitarian writer clearly did not believe that a free Russia should become a slavish imitator of the secular, postmodern West. It became increasingly clear that he was both an old-fashioned patriot and a committed Christian—but here also he was perplexing to some, because he adamantly rejected "blood and soil" nationalism, expressed no desire to return to the Tsarist past, and asked for no special privileges for Christianity in a post-totalitarian Russia.

Some of his critics soon reasoned that if Solzhenitsyn was not a conventional liberal, then he must be an enemy of liberty. The legend grew that he was, at best, a "Slavophile" and a romantic critic of decadent Western political institutions, and that he was, at worst, an authoritarian and even, perhaps, an anti-Semite and a theocrat. Even those Western critics who admired Solzhenitsyn's courage in confronting the Communist behemoth and who drew upon his dissections of ideological tyranny tended to slight his contribution to the renewal of the spiritual foundations of human liberty in a post-totalitarian world. In a memorable article published in *Commentary* in 1985 ("The Terrible Question of Aleksandr Solzhenitsyn"), Norman Podhoretz praised Solzhenitsyn as an anti-Communist and as the author of *The Gulag Archipelago,* while largely taking for granted the accuracy of the caricature about him that had taken shape over the previous decade and a half. Podhoretz simply assumed that Solzhenitsyn was an authoritarian or anti-democratic thinker, though he did acquit Solzhenitsyn, a strong supporter of the state of Israel, of the charge of anti-Semitism. He also cavalierly dismissed as a literary failure *The Red Wheel,* Solzhenitsyn's magnum opus that explores the events leading up to the Bolshevik revolution. (Podhoretz was in no position to do so at the time since he did not have access to any of the finished volumes of that great work.) The anti-Communist Podhoretz, however, never denied Solzhenitsyn's greatness or his enduring commitment to human dignity.

Unfortunately, other American conservatives have succumbed to the facile consensus that has developed about Solzhenitsyn—a consensus that has, as we shall see, little connection with reality. The same tiresome distortions are recycled ad nauseam and contribute to a willful refusal to consider Solzhenitsyn's thinking about the political and spiritual condition of modern man. My experience has been that even those who are well disposed toward Solzhenitsyn are genuinely surprised to learn that he is, in fact, an indefatigable advocate of democratic self-government, a critic of illiberal nationalism in all its forms, an erudite historian who has defended authentic Russian liberalism against its reactionary and revolutionary opponents, and an Orthodox Christian who does not take an exclusivist view toward other Christians and recognizes the wisdom inherent in all the great religions of the world. There is, to be sure, a good deal of impressive scholarship about Solzhenitsyn in all the major European languages, but such work rarely gains the kind of public hearing that would alter the reigning public perceptions about the Russian Nobel laureate.

Serious, informed, and measured engagement with Solzhenitsyn's writing is all too rare in America. Some of Solzhenitsyn's critics are content to sneer at him without bothering to produce quotations that would support their characterizations of his thought. The distinguished historian Richard Pipes has used this tendentious mode in his recent memoir, *Vixi,* in which Pipes calls Solzhenitsyn "quite innocent of historical knowledge" and declares, without offering any evidence, that Solzhenitsyn is committed to an impossible "'Holy Russia' of his imagination." After acknowledging Solzhenitsyn's "courage in standing up to the equally hate-filled and equally fanatical Communist regime," Pipes goes on to dismiss him as a "false prophet" full of "hate-driven intellectual intolerance." Thus Pipes fabricates a moral equivalence between the author of *The Gulag Archipelago* and the inhuman regime he did so much to bring to its knees. This shameful comparison dishonors Pipes, who here lends his considerable authority to the vituperative campaign against Solzhenitsyn.

* * *

The Russian-born libertarian journalist Cathy Young provides an equally shoddy account of the writings of Solzhenitsyn in the May 2004 issue of *Reason* magazine ("Traditional Prejudices: The Anti-Semitism of Alexander Solzhenitsyn"). Her subject is *Dvesti let vmeste (Two Hundred Years Together)*, Solzhenitsyn's monumental study of Russian-Jewish relations. (Volume one was published in 2001 and volume two in 2003; there is as yet no English translation. See the July-August 2004 issue of *Society* for my extensive discussion of this work.) In a calm and authoritative-sounding tone, Young engages in nothing less than character assassination, eschewing anything that resembles *explication de texte* and ignoring everything in Solzhenitsyn's writings that might militate against her claims.

A reader of her essay, for example, would never learn about Solzhenitsyn's condemnation of "scandalous restrictions" against Jews under the Russian old regime, his criticisms of the Russian state for its "unpardonable inaction" in failing to anticipate and respond to brutal anti-Jewish pogroms, his admiration for the great Russian statesman Pyotr Stolypin's efforts to end the Jewish disabilities, or his criticism of the White forces during the Russian Civil War for their inexcusable

toleration of anti-Semitic violence in territories under their control. Nor would one learn about his moving and somber discussion in chapter twenty-one of *Two Hundred Years Together* of the Holocaust unleashed against Jews on Soviet territory. In that chapter Solzhenitsyn narrates the truly mind-boggling facts regarding the extermination of Soviet Jews in the western territories of the Soviet Union. It is true that he refuses to choose between the two terrible totalitarianisms of the twentieth century: this is because Communist and Nazi totalitarianism are equally deserving of unqualified condemnation by all decent people. Solzhenitsyn refuses to set the sufferings of Russians and Jews against each other. The "totality of suffering" experienced by both at the hands of the Communist and Nazi regimes was "so great, the weight of the lessons inflicted by History so unsupportable, the anguish for the future so gnawing" that it is imperative that such suffering give rise to empathy and understanding between Russians and Jews.

Throughout these two volumes, Solzhenitsyn is emphatic in his condemnation of all bigoted and hostile depictions of Jews *qua* Jews, and he expresses the deepest respect for the spiritual greatness of the Jewish people. He never attributes "collective guilt" to Jews or any other people. To be sure, he calls on Russians and Jews alike to take "collective responsibility" for their respective sins and omissions. In his view, Russians and Jews must both come to terms with the members of their peoples who acted in complicity with the Communist regime. They should also stop blaming others for all of their misfortunes and discontents. Jews must not pretend that every Jew was a victim, that there were no "revolutionary assassins" in their midst. And Russians must admit that they were the "authors of [their own revolutionary] shipwreck" and resist the deluded inclination "to blame everything on the Jews."

Instead of accurately reporting Solzhenitsyn's published views, Young resurrects several discredited indictments, perhaps the most egregious one being that the author of *The Gulag Archipelago* is not a true friend of human liberty but is instead a partisan of a traditionalist collectivism. She shows no awareness of Solzhenitsyn's eloquent defenses of the rule of law and the importance of local self-government to a healthy and well-constituted civic life. The third and final volume of *The Gulag Archipelago,* for example, ends with a stirring denunciation of the absence of the rule of law in Soviet Russia, and all of Solzhenitsyn's recent political writings invoke the crucial importance of local self-government for the consolidation of political liberty and civic virtue in post-Communist Russia. Solzhenitsyn does not slight what Russians can learn from the Western and American experiences of democratic self-government. Addressing the town meeting of Cavendish, Vermont (his home from 1976 until 1994), shortly before returning to his native Russia, he spoke thoughtfully about how in Cavendish and its neighboring communities he had "observed the sensible and sure process of grassroots democracy, in which the local population solves most of its problems on its own, not waiting for the decisions of higher authorities. Unfortunately, we do not have this in Russia, and that is still our greatest shortcoming."

More fundamentally, Young shows no appreciation of the personalism that informs nearly every page of *The Gulag Archipelago.* This is a remarkable lacuna since the book is nothing less than "a celebration of personality," to cite the apt formulation of the distinguished Russianist John B. Dunlop. The *Gulag*'s portraits of freedom-loving individuals and indomitable souls such as the young Zoya Leshcheva (who fearlessly defended her religious faith against her atheistic persecutors), the defiant Anna Skripnikova (who had the self-respect to act as a free citizen in a totalitarian state and spent the years from 1918 to 1959 in and out of prison), the committed escaper Georgi Tenno, and the religious poet Anatoli Silin, are unforgettable encomia to the human spirit. As any charitable reader of the *Gulag* will discern, Solzhenitsyn is no collectivist. But neither is he a "libertarian" who ignores the indispensable moral foundations of human liberty. Of course, Young has every right to quarrel with Solzhenitsyn's account of Russian history or with his understanding of the moral and religious foundations of human liberty. But it is dishonest, and worse, to accuse him of anti-Semitism or to label him an enemy of human freedom.

* * *

How does one begin to break out of this interminable recycling of distortions and misrepresentations? To begin with, it is necessary to recognize that the defense of human liberty and dignity is not exhausted by the categories or assumptions of late modernity. Solzhenitsyn is a liberal in the sense that he is acutely aware of the myriad moral and cultural prerequisites of human liberty. In particular, he belongs to a noble Russian tradition that attempts to breathe "only the best air from the West" while "feeding ourselves only with the best milk from our own Mother Russia." These words of the prerevolutionary Russian journalist M. O. Menshikov are highlighted in James H. Billington's excellent new book *Russia in Search of Itself.* As Billington points out, the most illuminating Russian thought of the past 125 years—from Soloviev, Bulgakov, and Berdiaev, to Solzhenitsyn and D. M. Likhachev today—has attempted to draw on the best of the Western *and* Russian philosophical, theological, literary, and political traditions. This synthesizing current, which is suspicious of Western nihilism and scientism as well as of Eastern despotism, is all but ignored by Western elites today, who reflexively identify liberalism with materialism, relativism, and political correctness.

Solzhenitsyn has meditated on this problem of conjugating Russia and the West, liberty and the moral contents of life, with great penetration and finesse in the various volumes of *The Red Wheel.* These books include profound reflections on the character of political moderation and the requirements of a statesmanship that would unite Christian attentiveness to the spiritual dignity of man with an appreciation of the need to respect the unceasing evolution of society. Solzhenitsyn takes aim at reactionaries who ignore the inexorability of human "progress," at revolutionaries who take nihilistic delight in destroying the existing order, and at "false liberals" who refuse to explore prudently the necessarily difficult relations between order and liberty, progress and tradition.

In nearly all of his major writings, Solzhenitsyn appeals to the indispensability of the spiritual qualities of "repentance" and "self-limitation" for a truly balanced individual and collective life. But he never turns the classical or Christian virtues into an antimodern ideology that would escape the reality of living with the tensions inherent in a dynamic, modern society. He is not, however, unduly sanguine about the prospects for these virtues in the contemporary scene. As he writes in *November 1916,* "In the life of nations, even more than in private life, the rule is that concessions and self-limitation are ridiculed as naive and stupid." Solzhenitsyn thus has no illusions about repentance and self-limitation becoming the explicit and unchallenged foundation of free political life. His more modest hope is to claim a hearing for the Good amidst the cacophony of claims that vie for public notice. Neither genuflecting before progress nor irresponsibly rejecting it, Solzhenitsyn insists that we must "seek and expand ways of directing its might towards the perpetration of good." Solzhenitsyn's moral vision has too often been politicized in ways that mistake his rejection of progressivist illusions for a reactionary refusal to admit the possibility of progress.

Solzhenitsyn is, in truth, a conservative liberal who wants to temper the one-sided modern preoccupation with individual freedom with a salutary reminder of the moral ends that ought to inform responsible human choice. Like the best classical and Christian thinkers of the past, he believes that human beings should not "neglect their spiritual essence" or "show an exaggerated concern for man's material needs." Thus, while he displays a rich appreciation of the limits of politics, he also recognizes that "a Christian must . . . actively endeavor to improve the holders of power and the state system." And when Solzhenitsyn addresses specifically political questions he does so as a principled advocate of political moderation. His portrait in *August 1914* of Prime Minister Pyotr Stolypin's efforts to establish a constitutional order that would be consistent with Russia's spiritual traditions and that would keep Russia from falling into the revolutionary abyss contains some of the wisest pages ever written about statesmanship.

The shamefully one-sided journalistic and critical reception too often accorded to Solzhenitsyn's work thus serves as an unintended confirmation of the difficulty of pursuing what he has called the "middle line" in the service of human liberty and human dignity. Solzhenitsyn has used his literary gifts and moral witness to teach us, as he says in **The Gulag Archipelago,** "that the line separating good and evil passes not through states, nor between classes, nor between political parties either—but through all human hearts." Today, though he is eighty-five years old and has had some physical setbacks, he remains committed to his writing. Moreover, his stature and moral authority remain high where it most counts: in his native Russia. In response to the recent awarding of the Solzhenitsyn Prize to the actor and the director of the television series that brought Dostoevski's *The Idiot* to the screen, the popular writer Darya Dontsova commented that "the great Solzhenitsyn is in reality a very modern man, and young of heart." Most importantly, amidst the corruption and moral drift of the post-Communist transition, he has never ceased to remind his compatriots that they "must build a moral Russia or none at all." He remains an intrepid defender of a freedom that is worthy of man and has thus maintained faith with the best in both Russian and Western traditions. He merits our continuing gratitude, respect, and admiration.

Miriam Dobson (essay date fall 2005)

SOURCE: Dobson, Miriam. "Contesting the Paradigms of De-Stalinization: Readers' Responses to *One Day in the Life of Ivan Denisovich*." *Slavic Review* 64, no. 3 (fall 2005): 580-600.

[*In the following essay, Dobson outlines the impact of* One Day in the Life of Ivan Denisovich.]

"In Khar'kov I have seen all kinds of queues—for the film *Tarzan,* butter, women's drawers, chicken giblets, and horse-meat sausage," wrote a certain Mark Konenko, describing urban life under Nikita Khrushchev. He continued, "But I cannot remember a queue as long as the one for your book in the libraries. . . . I waited six months on the list and to no avail. By chance I got hold of it for forty-eight hours."[1] The author he addressed was Aleksandr Solzhenitsyn; the book was **Odin den' Ivana Denisovicha (One Day in the Life of Ivan Denisovich**), published in the November 1962 issue of the literary journal *Novyi Mir.*[2] A former prisoner himself, Konenko perhaps had vested interest in the

work, yet his comments suggest that his fascination was far from unique. According to Konenko, the urge to read about life in Iosif Stalin's prison camps proved stronger than even the usual hunger for sausage and American movies. The struggle to obtain a copy of the coveted text required stamina, luck, and connections. Another of Solzhenitsyn's correspondents wrote: "I am only a nurse, and there were professors and university teachers in the queue for the book. But because I know someone in the library, and because I was there myself, I was given it for the New Year without waiting in the queue."[3]

In the winter of 1962-63, citizens across the Soviet Union voraciously read Solzhenitsyn's bleak depiction of life in one of Stalin's labor camps. Whether incensed by Solzhenitsyn's audacity or by the horrors he revealed, few could respond with indifference. Many felt compelled to set their reactions down on paper. As established writers, literary critics, and leading party members wrote reviews for a variety of Soviet newspapers and journals, the pages of *Novyi mir, Ogonek, Literaturnaia gazeta, Izvestiia, Literaturnaia Rossiia, Oktiabr', Don,* and *Pravda* became the site of a major polemic between what Ivan Lakshin, a contemporary critic, dubbed the "friends and foes of Ivan Denisovich."[4] The nation's leading literati and politicians may have battled it out publicly in the Soviet press, but ordinary citizens were no less opinionated. The journal *Novyi mir* received an unprecedented number of letters from readers who wished to articulate their views on the controversial new work. As readers sought to understand its significance, they discussed not only the text itself but also the important political and social changes that had occurred in the decade since Stalin's death. Although other pieces of fiction on the "camp theme" were being published, Solzhenitsyn's novella became the focal point for broader debates about Soviet politics and history.[5]

Scholars of the Khrushchev era have long paid particular attention to literature. Released from some of the constraints of the Stalinist era, the intelligentsia used fiction as a vehicle to discuss political and social change. According to received wisdom, "the story of Thaw politics is about culture. The story of Thaw culture is about politics."[6] The polemic that followed the publication of **One Day in the Life of Ivan Denisovich** has generated particular interest in the west. Anna Krylova recently claimed that when he appeared on the literary scene in 1962, Solzhenitsyn was eagerly greeted as the "long awaited rebel."[7] Arguing that throughout the postwar period the American academic and political community yearned for the rebirth of the "liberal man" in Soviet Russia, Krylova maintains that the west seized on Solzhenitsyn so enthusiastically because he seemed to prove that "disbelief" was possible within the Soviet world. Indeed, the fact that his first work engendered such passionate responses from the cultural and political elite seemed to suggest that Solzhenitsyn was not alone in his capacity to challenge the Soviet system. It encouraged western observers to think that there were significant numbers of Soviet citizens who condemned the Stalinist past and desired—at the very least—liberalization.

As early as 1964, Max Hayward wrote in *Slavic Review* that the discussion of Solzhenitsyn's work "has now become the main arena for the ever more bitter feud between the 'conservatives' and the 'liberals,'"[8] Hayward viewed the polemic as a conflict between two well-defined factions, those advocating change and those defending the status quo. This binary model became dominant in Sovietology, explored most fully in an article written by Stephen Cohen in the late 1970s. Borrowing terms from Lakshin's 1964 article "The Friends and Foes of Ivan Denisovich," Cohen followed Hayward in suggesting that after Stalin's death Soviet political life coalesced around the "two poles" of reformism and conservatism, but he now extended the scope of this model to include not only literary experts and political figures, but also the ordinary Soviet citizen. At this time Cohen could, of course, only base his argument on published sources largely produced by members of the artistic or political elite, but he suggested both "trends are expressed below, in society, in popular sentiments and attitudes."[9]

Access to unpublished citizens' letters now allows us to probe popular opinion more fully. The *Novyi mir* mailbag contains letters from lawyers, teachers, party members, purge victims and their relatives, self-confessed thieves, prisoners, camp workers, pensioners, an army captain, a collective farmer, a worker in a chemical laboratory, and simply "young people." These letters reflect a broad spectrum of opinion. On the one hand, jubilant readers lavished praise on Solzhenitsyn, Aleksandr Tvardovskii, and all that seemed to truly promise a "new world";[10] on the other hand, skeptical voices remained convinced that the camps had been populated by inveterate enemies of the Soviet people.[11] Yet in the extant corpus of citizens' letters, such stark positions appear relatively rare.[12] Without denying that potential for conflict along the lines suggested by Cohen existed within Khrushchev's society, I argue that the reformer/conservative paradigm imposes excessively fixed identities onto its subjects. The beliefs held by any one individual cannot always be so neatly categorized. Individuals might welcome some of the changes occurring in the post-Stalin years while opposing others. Although Lakshin had maintained that an individual's attitude towards Ivan Denisovich was a reliable gauge of his political attitudes more broadly, close examination of readers' letters suggests that those who

embraced reform in other areas did not always praise Solzhenitsyn's work. The discussion that followed the publication of *One Day in the Life of Ivan Denisovich* was in fact part of a rather more complex dialogue about the nature of change in the post-Stalin era.

Solzhenitsyn's tale of life in a labor camp led many readers to reflect not only on the crimes of the past but also on current issues, in particular the changing status of the gulag since Stalin's death. Between 1953 and 1959, the Soviet government had introduced a raft of measures intended to radically scale down the gulag. By 1960 the camp population was little more than a fifth of its 1953 size.[13] Contrary to traditional understandings of de-Stalinization, repressed party members were by no means the only returnees.[14] In addition to those legally rehabilitated, many made it home as a result either of one of the amnesties decreed in these years or of the new measures introduced to allow early release.[15] The enormous exodus from the camps taking place in the first seven years of de-Stalinization thus included prisoners who had served time for the entire spectrum of offences, including not only anti-Soviet activity but also hooliganism, theft, and murder. Although the downsizing of the gulag was already being reversed by the early 1960s, massive releases had generated significant anxiety amongst citizens who worried that the Soviet collective was under threat from highly destructive elements, hitherto contained and isolated in the camp zone.

By the time the censors allowed Solzhenitsyn's work to be published in 1962, readers had established clear ideas about how these former exiles were to be regarded. This article first explores how victims of 1937-38 were able to craft effective narratives of their suffering and martyrdom that—far from threatening the status quo—in fact served to confirm the righteousness of the party and the Soviet cause. The right of *Ezhovshchina* victims to rejoin the Soviet collective was rarely contested in the letters preserved. Other returning prisoners faced a rather less warm homecoming, however. In their objections to the "vulgarity" of Solzhenitsyn's characters, I suggest Soviet readers voiced a deep fear of former *zeks,* in particular those they associated with the criminal underworld. Their texts articulate a determined opposition to the policies that had allowed such large numbers of the camp population to be set free. Exploring letters written by prisoners themselves, moreover, we find that by 1962 zeks had become bitterly aware of this resentment and understood the deeply unpopular nature of the releases. Recognizing the intractable nature of Soviet attitudes towards the criminal population, *Novyi mir* readers corresponding from within the gulag had come to realize how strongly this aspect of de-Stalinization was being contested on the outside.

FROM ENEMIES TO HEROES?

One Day in the Life of Ivan Denisovich was published almost exactly one year after the Twenty-Second Party Congress. Held in the autumn of 1961, the Congress had made Khrushchev's earlier condemnation of the cult of personality public and sanctioned the removal of Stalin's body from the Mausoleum on Red Square. Claiming that the moment had come to tell the truth about the past, Khrushchev promised that past miscarriages of justice had now been corrected. In his concluding speech at the Congress, he pronounced: "The time will come when we will all die, for we are all mortal. Until then we must do our work, and we can and must tell the party and the people the truth. We need to do this so that nothing like this can ever be repeated."[16] Truth was the byword of the moment. Disclosing the errors of the past was not to be a source of shame but was instead embraced as a return to the true revolutionary path.[17] Former "enemies of the people" were now praised for their revolutionary heroism and hailed as martyrs to the Bolshevik cause. One was even invited to speak of her ordeal at the Congress. A Leningrad party member since 1902, D. A. Lazurkina explained that she had "shared the lot" of many old Bolsheviks. As she retold her life story, she created the narrative of a heroic martyr to the revolutionary cause. Imprisoned as a political enemy under both tsarism and Stalinism, she ascribed her survival to an unshakeable belief in the party. Her ordeals, she maintained, had only served to confirm her faith in the communist creed.[18]

In the wake of the Twenty-Second Party Congress, no one publicly contested the desirability of "fighting against the cult of personality and its consequences" nor openly challenged the right of Ezhovshchina victims of 1937-38 such as Lazurkina to full rehabilitation. As Nanci Adler recognizes, the thick journals "propagated 'heroic epoch' tales which extolled the virtue of victims of the terror who, despite it all, 'returned home having preserved the flame of their devotion to the revolution.'"[19] Former political prisoners were thus invited to think of themselves as shining examples of the Bolshevik spirit.

In response to the publication of ***One Day in the Life of Ivan Denisovich,*** many purge victims contributed their memoirs to the editors of *Novyi mir.* When one purge victim, a certain Aleksandr Zuev, sent off a copy of his recollections to the journal, he received a response from Tvardovskii in which the editor explained that the journal was simply inundated with such memoirs.[20] Boris Oliker received a similar reply from Tvardovskii's deputy in which he was told that the journal had received "hundreds" of such memoirs over the past year.[21] This urge on the part of purge victims to recollect and recount appears widespread, and in the Institute of Marxism-Leninism a special repository (*fond*) was created for "manuscript materials relating to miscarriages of justice committed during the cult of Stalin's personality." Having spent much of the 1950s composing petitions for release, rehabilitation, housing, and work, many purge victims were not ready to lay down their pens. As they wrote, they hoped to bring meaning to their distressing ordeals, linking their own resurrection with the rebirth of the party. They wrote not to indict or condemn the party for its errors but to prove its courage in righting the wrongs of the past.[22]

No longer considering themselves outsiders to society, the memoirists added their voices to those celebrating the restoration of "truth" from the tribune of the Twenty-Second Party Congress and on the pages of the Soviet press.[23] Both Oliker and Zuev were uncertain whether their memoirs were publishable, but neither had any doubt that their work was in keeping with the party line. They firmly believed that the pariah status they had endured for so long was now unequivocally revoked. Oliker recounted how a leading party official in his hometown of Minsk had invited him in for a "free and friendly chat," even encouraging him to seek out a publisher. *Novyi mir* encouraged this impression. Although they rejected the manuscripts, the editors were insistent that the victims' experiences were not being disregarded: Oliker was told that even if it remained unpublished, "the manuscript was worth writing," while Zuev was assured it was still "correct and necessary" that "these pages" had been written.

Significantly, there is little in surviving letters to suggest that the revived status of these former "enemies of people" was a source of conflict for a broader public. Following Khrushchev and the party leadership, they regarded their rehabilitation as a necessary step on the revolutionary journey. Documents preserved in the *Novyi mir* archive do, however, indicate that the question of readmission might prove controversial in other ways. Some seemed to suggest that not all Stalin's outcasts could be welcomed home and exonerated in this way. Did everyone who had been banished under Stalin deserve the same kind of privileged status, they queried. Could *all* former enemies become heroes?

With relatively few characters fitting the profile of the noble party victim, Solzhenitsyn's work brought such issues to a head. In her letter to *Novyi mir,* E. A. Ignatovich, a worker in a chemical laboratory in Tula oblast, put the case trenchantly: "With regard to Solzhenitsyn, I want to ask the question: Why? Why did you write in the introduction to ***One Day in the Life of Ivan Denisovich*** that it was about 1937 people? No, there wasn't even one 1937 person here. From my point of view they were wartime deserters, criminals, and cowards. To my mind, the story was well written but the heroes are trash [*drian'*]."[24] Ignatovich, it seems, might have welcomed a story detailing the ordeals of those repressed in 1937, but she found any rewriting of the war myth problematic. Her letter continued, "I will say one thing—these prisoners were enemies [*vragi*], and they still are. The man who became the captain of English ships doesn't arouse any kind of sympathy in me. Why didn't he go to the Soviet embassy and return to his motherland? On the English front they fed him up and there was little danger to his life—that's why he stayed in the West. The captain is trash."[25] In the final paragraph of her letter, we begin to glean some understanding of why Ignatovich took such a hostile position towards the characters arrested for their wartime "crimes." Ignatovich concluded with a few lines from her own autobiography: "I was a fourteen-year-old girl when I was taken to Germany. I ran away three times, and I got to know all of the prisons. As a result of this I was eventually taken to the concentration camp at Ravensbruck in 1943. Because I was a stupid girl, the Germans were able to catch me, but if I had been able to escape to a friendly country, I would have asked to be returned to my motherland. The captain on the other hand didn't do this. He's simply a coward."[26] While she seemed to accept the rehabilitation of Ezhovshchina victims, Ignatovich found the readmission of wartime prisoners far more problematic, for it implicitly undermined her own heroic status. If failure to be repatriated was no longer considered a crime, then Ignatovich's own fight to resist captivity perhaps began to seem less impressive. *One Day in the Life of Ivan Denisovich* raised the question of who, in this new de-Stalinized world, might be considered heroes. For those whose own life story and self-esteem were so firmly rooted in their wartime experience, the threat that established myths might change—and with them the recognized cast of heroes and enemies—could be highly disturbing.

Gal'chenko and Petrov, party members from Zagorsk, also objected to the characters Solzhenitsyn created. The pair recoiled not only at the invidious depiction of prison guards ("who are shown to be worse than the SS commanders in a fascist concentration camp"), but also at the prisoners' personalities.[27] They produced a blistering tirade: "Can they really be Soviet people who simply fell into the camps as a result of Stalin's cult of personality? Where are their organization, ideas, culture, and humanity? Ivan Denisovich Shukhov—the main hero of the 'story'—is supposed to be seen as a good person, but in actual fact he is shown to be a petty crook/odd-jobber [*mel'kii zhulik/masterok*] who swindles two extra bowls of soup from hungry comrades, a glutton, a toady (in his relations towards Tsezar'), who doesn't have a single friend or a single honest thought. Is this really a 'hero,' is this realism? This is in fact an alien [*chuzhak*]!" Like Ignatovich, Gal'chenko and Petrov were anxious to define who could be considered "heroes." Where Ignatovich had challenged the life stories of Solzhenitsyn's protagonists,

these two party loyalists chose to attack the moral traits Solzhenitsyn ascribed to his characters. In their eyes, Shukhov was so lacking in positive attributes he could not even be identified as a Soviet person. He should remain an outsider and an alien, belonging not to the Soviet collective but to some unnamed "other" (*chuzhoi*).

In both letters, the authors worried that Khrushchev's de-Stalinizing rhetoric was being applied too broadly. Criticism of the "cult of personality," they maintained, should not be used to revise the status of all those cast out during the Stalinist era. Readmission into Soviet society should be granted only to party members victimized at the height of the Terror. Setting themselves up as defenders of Soviet moral values, the letter writers intimated that many who "fell into the camps" were indeed there for a reason—they were not truly Soviet people.

The publication of *One Day in the Life of Ivan Denisovich* invited Soviet readers to think more fully about the transformation of social boundaries that had occurred in the first post-Stalin decade. As formulated by Gal'chenko and Petrov, key issues included: Who was Soviet, and who was "alien"? How were such identities to be decided? In the corpus of letters preserved, such questions appeared frequently. Fearful of the impact of recent changes, some citizens continued to regard the majority of the gulag inhabitants as individuals who had failed to meet the profile of the "new Soviet man," and who, as such, were unfit to be included in the Soviet collective.

The Threat of Poshlost'

One of the defining aspects of Stalinism was the state's drive to mold its subjects into new Soviet men and women. Current work on the Stalinist era stresses the centrality of this "civilizing mission."[28] In the late 1930s, the Terror was not only a means to destroy perceived enemies within the political elite but also to cleanse society of those who failed to meet with the regime's strict demands for "cultured" behavior. According to Paul Hagenloh, "The Terror was also the culmination of a decade-long radicalization of policing practice against 'recidivist' criminals, social marginals, and all manner of lower-class individuals who did not or could not fit into the emerging Stalinist system."[29] Through education and propaganda, Soviet people were encouraged to turn themselves into cultured and respectable citizens, while the gulag became an outpost for those who failed, for those who remained uncultured and dissolute.[30] The effect of the mass releases from the gulag was to erode the fixed boundaries between these two worlds, a process that some found disturbing. Rising crime levels in the 1950s seemed to substantiate their anxieties.[31] The publication of Solzhenitsyn's story provided anxious readers with an opportunity to reassert a collective identity as respectable and cultured citizens, an identity that they considered threatened by the allegedly uncivilized contingent returning from the gulag.

Introducing Solzhenitsyn's work in the November 1962 issue of *Novyi mir,* the journal's editor, Aleksandr Tvardovskii, seemed to predict some aspects of this forthcoming debate. In the opening paragraph of his preface, he encouraged readers to approve the work as a necessary part of breaking with the past, citing from Khrushchev's speech at the Twenty-Second Party Congress: "[W]e can and must explain all and tell the truth to the party and people. . . . This must be done so that nothing similar can ever be repeated."[32] Extolling Solzhenitsyn's work as a necessary contribution to the party's quest for "truth," he appeared unable to countenance any fundamental opposition to the work. No one, he seemed to claim, could deny the necessity of speaking openly about the horrors of Stalin's gulag. Yet in the closing words of his preface, Tvardovskii did acknowledge that some might be shocked, and even angered, by Solzhenitsyn's text. Some overly "persnickety" [*priveredlivyi*] people, he feared, would object to some words and expressions taken from the "milieu" in which the story takes place. Tvardovskii already realized that the issue of language would be central.

Though initial reviews had been positive, dissenting voices emerged by the new year, and the question of language did indeed prove important.[33] Writing in the literary journal *Don* in January, the critic Fedor Chapchakhov criticized Solzhenitsyn's use of "convict slang," or literally "convict music" (*blatnaia muzika*).[34] Nevertheless, none of the published critics focused on the problem of language with quite the tenacity shown by ordinary readers. In the letters located in the *Novyi mir* archive, language appears to be the single most distressing aspect of **One Day in the Life of Ivan Denisovich.** One pensioner described how he almost laughed at the made-up criminal (*blatnoi*) words, but was then overcome with confusion as to how this kind of "concoction" came to be published.[35] A Russian teacher complained that in all sixty-five pages the reader would not find a single phrase written in the literary language he had been taught.[36] Meanwhile, a captain in the Soviet army expressed his indignation that someone who had received higher education, served as an officer, and was now a teacher and novice author, should use words that most readers would take "years to learn."[37] For him, Solzhenitsyn's status identified him as a respectable member of Soviet society, and this fact should have been reflected in the language the author employed.

Even readers who passionately denounced the atrocities committed under Stalin were nonetheless aghast at the author's use of slang and profanity. Such a response is best illustrated by a letter from a certain Z. G. Grinberg, a *Novyi mir* reader from the city of Ukhta in the republic of Komi. Grinberg identified himself as a keen follower of both Khrushchev and of the journal's liberal editor, Tvardovskii.[38] He welcomed the repudiation of the cult of personality and believed that the new openness was valuable: he expressed admiration for the recent film *Chistoe nebo* (*Clear Skies*), in which an innocent victim of repression endured all his suffering without losing faith in the party.[39] He also praised a short story recently printed in *Izvestiia,* in which the heroes—communists consigned to one of Stalin's prison camps—displayed great fortitude and "moral cleanliness."[40] Grinberg had good reason to appreciate Khrushchev's policies: once a leading party cadre, he had been repressed in 1937 and endured eight years in the camps.

A purge victim himself, Grinberg hardly fits the profile of a conservative pro-Stalinist, but he was, nonetheless, deeply concerned by the publication of **One Day in the Life of Ivan Denisovich.** For him, the work represented a distortion of Khrushchev's new rhetoric: "N. S. Khrushchev did not mean in any way for all this dirt to be raked up under the guise of truth." Though a "foe" of Solzhenitsyn and **Ivan Denisovich,** Grinberg presented himself as a friend of Khrushchev and a defender of the "truth." He believed that Solzhenitsyn had exploited the current quest for truth in order "rake up" dirt, and, as Tvardovskii had predicted, it was indeed the language of the text that he contested. The whole tale, wrote Grinberg, was composed in the jargon of the "thief, the recidivist, and the bandit." He cited various examples of this slang, which, he claimed, "makes you sick." Why, he asked, do we need to make a cult out of thieves' jargon? In addition to labeling Solzhenitsyn's language "the lexicon of thieves and bandits," he also repeatedly designated it as vulgar (*poshlyi*) and called the terms vulgarities (*poshliatina*). *Poshlost'*—derived from the Russian word *poshlo,* originally meaning "traditional" or "ancient"—represented a direct challenge to the "new" Soviet values.[41] Grinberg's dread of vulgarity revealed both the significance he attached to the new mores of Soviet society and his deep anxiety that they were now under threat.

Grinberg feared the appearance of bad language as a threat to Soviet *kul'turnost',* especially as this "vulgarity" was now apparently condoned by the nation's cultural luminaries. Throughout the Soviet era, literature had been one of the prime sites for the promotion of "cultured" behavior and language. "The culture of speech derived from good literature," writes Vadim Volkov in his study of the campaigns for kul'turnost' in the 1930s, and "reading was also directly connected with the acquisition of culturedness."[42] It was no surprise then that Grinberg was so aghast to discover examples of the criminal jargon promoted in a leading literary journal. He asked the editors of *Novyi mir,* "Do you really have to be a 'persnickety' person to disapprove of an approach to literature that flaunts the most vulgar [*samye poshlye*] examples of the thieves' lexicon in our high-minded Soviet literature?" A few lines later he again questioned why Tvardovskii encouraged "actual vulgarity" (*nastoiashaia poshliatina*) in literature.

Grinberg's linguistic quibbles reflected the broader anxieties engulfing Soviet society in the 1950s. Many feared that if the millions of prisoners released from the gulag spoke and thought in the same way as Ivan Denisovich, the cultured behavior that the party had fought so hard to inculcate was now under threat. Grinberg apparently believed the boundaries between respectable Soviet society and the dirty underworld of the criminal should remain sealed. Expressing his concerns that "this jargon and vulgarity [*poshlost'*]" would reach "the lexicon of callow youths," he argued that poshlost' represented the "harmful influence of an alien ideology [*chuzhaia ideologiia*]." If the jargon spoken within the camp was "alien," its use—according to Grinberg—exposed Soviet youth to dangerously foreign influences. Soviet respectability was thus at risk from a foreign culture that had been fostered within the segregated zone of the gulag and that the process of de-Stalinization was now allowing to filter back into society.

Such anxieties were even more explicit in a letter addressed to the Chairman of the Supreme Court by a certain A. Mel'nikov. Mel'nikov opened fire on Solzhenitsyn's use of "criminal words" (*blatnye slovechki*), words that he found shameful and disgusting. With echoes of Grinberg, he wrote: "This kind of vulgarity [*poshlost'*] is clearly only permissible abroad, but here in the USSR the man of the future is being raised, and not the man of the obsolete past, when the older children taught the younger ones to say disgusting swear words to their own mothers. . . . Why then is the journal *Novyi mir* not pulling the reader towards the good, but instead dragging him towards the mire [*boloto*]?"[43] Mel'nikov structured his text on certain oppositions, between the good and the "mire," here and abroad, the new and the old. Abroad "vulgarity" might flourish, but there was no place for it here in the Soviet Union. Similarly, in the "old" Russia children had been raised in the uncouth and vulgar ways of their older brothers and sisters, but now, according to Mel'nikov, they were raised as citizens of the communist future.[44] Believing the nuclear family was no longer able to pass on unsavory behavior to the new generation, Mel'nikov cherished the Soviet state's interest in child rearing. For him, the publication of *One Day in the Life of Ivan Denisovich* was thus at odds with the official commitment to raising this new man. He found it contradictory that, even as it struggled to combat the problem of hooliganism, the state allowed this work full of foul words, written by a "malicious hoodlum" (*zlostnyi khuligan*), to be published. In choosing to address his

letter to the Supreme Court, Mel'nikov intimated that this was not a matter only for the literary experts at *Novyi mir* but also one for the government bodies responsible for maintaining law and order.[45]

In another letter, this time addressed to the editors of the satirical journal *Krokodil*, a lawyer praised Solzhenitsyn for "telling the truth," but condemned his use of bad language, writing graphically: "Some phrases in the book are disgusting, like typhus lice on the human body."[46] With Soviet citizens fearful that the immoral behavior of the gulag was set to contaminate society, criminal argot was repudiated as the means by which this dreaded contagion might spread.

The publication of *One Day in the Life of Ivan Denisovich* ignited a passionate debate in which the most aggressive attacks came not from unrepentant "Stalinists" as such, but from citizens convinced that Soviet society was experiencing a major social crisis. The polemic points to a "moral panic." In the late 1950s and early 1960s, citizens were highly concerned about the erosion of key Soviet values, fearing that the emptying of the gulag endangered the purity of Soviet society. Anxiety about the "blatnoi" lexicon in Solzhenitsyn's novel played into broader fears about the gulag releases and rising levels of crime, and the letters addressed to the editors of *Novyi mir* were part of a more general letter-writing practice. Over the course of the 1950s, central bodies such as the Supreme Soviet were inundated with correspondence from ordinary citizens who railed against the criminals allegedly terrorizing the city streets and pleaded for the authorities to take more punitive measures when dealing with the culprits.[47] Solzhenitsyn's apparent infatuation with "blatnaia muzika" enraged a community already deeply fearful that criminal culture might soon drown out their own respectable voices.

DEMANDING REEDUCATION

Despite the concerns of the Soviet public, the party had spent much of the 1950s loudly proclaiming its commitment to transforming all criminals into decent Soviet citizens. In 1959, in a speech made at the Third Writers' Congress, Khrushchev went so far as to claim that "we believe that no such thing exists as a person who cannot be corrected."[48] In this high-profile forum, Khrushchev recounted at the length the story of one criminal's conversion from criminal to good family man and respected colleague. He told how a certain Konstantin Nogovitsin had come under the influence of a criminal gang after losing his father at a young age (presumably as a result of war), falling into a cycle of repeat offending and prison sentences, until Khrushchev's recent reforms had enabled him to start a new life. Khrushchev's story referred to the 2 March 1959 decree "On the participation of workers in the maintenance of public order," which promoted the use of non-custodial sentences to allow the reeducation of prisoners within society.[49] A "collective"—such as a workplace or housing block—could now save an offender from incarceration by offering to become his guardian;[50] likewise, a prisoner might be granted early release if a collective guaranteed to take responsibility for his "probation." This repudiation of prison sentences in favor of the reeducation and correction of offenders *within* society meant that the emptying of the gulag, begun in 1953, accelerated greatly in 1959. When the total number of prisoners dipped to 550,000 in 1960, the population was at its lowest since 1935.[51]

Yet by 1962 when *One Day in the Life of Ivan Denisovich* was published, this policy was already being reversed. In a matter of just two years, the party had sanctioned a return to a more severe approach to criminal justice. Aside from the more notorious "de-Stalinizing" aspects of his speeches at the Twenty-Second Party Congress, Khrushchev had also articulated a new intolerance for those who refused work, lamenting that "some people seem to think that under communism, man won't have to sow or reap, but just sit about eating pies." In a break with his speeches of 1959, he no longer claimed that all could be saved, but instead called for a more aggressive "battle against idlers and parasites, hooligans, and drunkards." Instead of wishing to see them reformed within the Soviet community, he now advocated their banishment, affirming that "there is no place for these weeds in our life."[52]

With the tide already turning against the notion of reeducation, the responses to *One Day in the Life of Ivan Denisovich* are all the more noteworthy. Mel'nikov for one welcomed the changes, admitting that there had recently been some successes in the fight against crime and that "you don't see the rampant hell-raisers who spew out foul language [*razbushe-vavshikhsia deboshirov izvergaiushchikh skvernosloviia*] on the streets any more. Now they quickly take them off to sober up at the police station."[53] However, the state's volte-face did not receive support from all quarters. Several prisoners wrote to the editors of *Novyi mir* over the course of 1962-63, perhaps inspired by a letter published in *Literaturnaia gazeta*, allegedly from a former recidivist thief named Minaev.[54] Yet where Minaev was full of disgust for the criminal world he had once inhabited, the prisoners who dispatched letters to the editors of *Novyi mir* sought some kind of vindication. Seizing on the publication of Solzhenitsyn's novella as an opportunity to express their own views on the subject of crime and punishment, they railed against their renewed exclusion from Soviet society. Of the five prisoners whose letters survive in the *Novyi mir* archive, only one believed that the Soviet system might still welcome him home. Singularly optimistic, Aleksandr Sergachev asked the editors to find him a ghostwriter willing to transform

his experiences—which included a series of sentences for theft and hooliganism—into a publishable autobiography.[55] All serving time for nonpolitical crimes, the four other prisoners no longer believed that the Soviet regime would engage in the rewriting of their life stories. Unlike a purge victim such as Lazurkina, whose autobiography ended triumphantly with full rehabilitation, these prisoners recognized their chances of a new life to be slim. Increasingly convinced that their readmission to society had become impossible, they knew the days when reintegration and rehabilitation was promised to *all* were now over. One prisoner, a certain Mikhail Fadeev, commented pointedly that prisoners were now "doomed not to correction, but to physical destruction by means of hunger, calculated deprivation, and suffering in the camps of the USSR."[56]

A fellow prisoner, V. A. Lovtsov, firmly believed that the government now lacked any kind of commitment to its erstwhile goal of reeducation. Describing in detail the barbarity of life in the camps, he was highly critical of the Soviet penal system for failing to "correct" prisoners. According to Lovtsov, prisoners in 1951—the year in which *One Day in the Life of Ivan Denisovich* was set—would commonly say that as soon as they were free they would try to steal a little bit more money, commit a robbery, or even kill someone. "Neither reeducation nor correction had touched them," averred Lovtsov. While the gulag allowed them to become master card-players, it denied them access to newspapers, study, or training. Penal reform was still painfully slow in the post-Stalin years, he said, and not until Khrushchev's speech at the Third Writers' Congress in 1959 did the prisoner begin to hope for change. Hearing Khrushchev's promises of "faith in man" (*vera v chelovek*), every prisoner felt that he too "could become a human being" (*stat' chelovekom*).[57] Soon, however, this too became another broken promise. Commenting on the failure of the amnesties and the high levels of repeat offences, he argued that the authorities had betrayed their own pledge to "correct" prisoners. Applied only to petty offenders, the amnesties ignored those serving longer terms, effectively suggesting that the more dangerous criminals could not in fact be "reforged." Denouncing this approach, Lovtsov emotionally claimed that the criminal should be "forgiven," however grave his first offence had been. "If you believe in him once, if you forgive him, he will never be a criminal again." According to Lovtsov, Khrushchev's promises of "faith in man" had never materialized, and the practices of the gulag remained sharply at odds with the advertised rhetoric of 1959. Lovtsov had grown despondent, and at one point wrote: "I am a son of the Gulag, if you can put it that way."[58] Although the reforms of the early Khrushchev era had promised "reforging," it seems Lovtsov thought of himself as an innate outsider, his membership to the other world of the gulag almost a birthmark, a part of his identity that he would never be allowed to shed.

Railing against his exclusion, Lovtsov realized the difficulty inherent in proving that he had reacquired the moral qualities needed to participate in Soviet life once more. He wrote: "Do you really think that I don't want to be respectable [*chestnym*], that I don't want to live well, like millions of Soviet citizens? But how to obtain this? How and to whom shall I prove that I want to live respectably [*chestno*], that I won't commit any more crimes? . . . Nobody wants to deal with my case."[59] Lovtsov repeatedly used the adjective "chestnyi" in his letter. As he understood it, *chestnost'* was the prime quality used to distinguish members of Soviet society from those banished as outcasts. Although *chestnyi* literally means honest or honorable, Soviet citizens invariably used the term to describe an upstanding member of the community more broadly. Indeed, anyone who worked hard, who spoke politely, and who abided by the moral codes governing Soviet society could readily be identified as chestnyi.[60] Chestnost' can perhaps be read as an antonym for poshlost'. With Soviet citizens loudly insisting on the poshlost' of gulag culture, those inhabiting this other world realized that their chances of being recognized as a "chestnyi chelovek" were increasingly remote.

The unobtainable nature of chestnost' was also a key theme for a prisoner named A. Makarov, who was serving a twenty-five-year sentence in the Komi ASSR. From the outset, he problematized the notion of "correction" and "reeducation": "Having read [Solzhenitsyn]'s story, one can't but help thinking not only about those who endured those TERRIBLE YEARS, but also about those who are now enduring the TORTURES [*MUKI*] of 'Correction' even now. In addition to this book, I have also read many books and brochures on moral education [*vospitanie*], and I have decided to use these brochures in writing this letter, so that with your help I can find answers to some of the questions which as a prisoner I somehow can't work out."[61] Well-versed in Soviet theories on reeducation, he began by citing at length from a brochure by A. Kovalev entitled *Psikhologiia lichnosti zakliuchennogo i individual'nyi podkhod v protsess perevospitaniia* (The psychology and personality of the prisoner and the individual approach to the process of reeducation). Using the regime's own texts to condemn it, he noted its failure to live up to the grand claims of the 1950s. Having repeatedly read that Soviet justice was committed to returning prisoners to life within the Soviet collective, Makarov asked sardonically: "In a few years' time, will I really be working in some collective or other, if out of the forty-three years of my life, I've spent five and a half of them serving in the army and seventeen in prison?" Concluding that redemption was simply not possible, he

dismissed the notion of correction as merely a "pretext" (*predlog*) that hid the gulag's true function as a site of infinite suffering. "I can't find any answer to the question," he wrote. "Who needs these camps, why do they exist? Are they really a method of 'reeducation,' or a means of spiritual and physical corruption?"[62] By the end of the letter he came to the radical conclusion that he would never be allowed back: "There's only one way out: death! To die is far simpler than meeting the daily norms. The only pity is that so many still have to meet the norms and I have to ask: What is all this for, and who needs it? If I have still not become respectable [*chestnyi*] in the eyes of the people and atoned for my crime with seventeen years of imprisonment then are the people respectable [*chestnyi*] in my eyes?" Makarov had already reached the bitter conclusion that a return to Soviet society was impossible, the regime's promises of reeducation empty. He would never be recognized as chestnyi. And if readmission into the Soviet community was not possible, he renounced life.

One of the most astute writers, Makarov clearly realized that by the early 1960s two different approaches were being taken: one approach for criminals, another for party members. Later in his letter, he cited from a 1963 tract on crime that already embodied the regime's new course. In this work, entitled *V obshchestve, stroiashchem kommunizm, ne dolzhno byt' mesta pravonarusheniiam i prestupnosti* (In a society building communism, there should be no place for law-breaking and crime), A. L. Remenson had even begun to undermine the notion of vospitanie, a fact which Makarov was quick to note. The passage identified by Makarov read: "Some prisoners claim that 'I'm not the one who's guilty: it was the war, my poor upbringing [*plokhoe moe vospitanie*], the wrong kind of teachers, and so on. Poor, unhappy old me—I'm not to blame.' We should say straight out to these people: 'Don't deceive yourself!' The war brought almost everyone unhappiness and there were shortcomings in the way millions of people were raised [*nedostatki vospitaniia vstrelis' milliony liudei*]. But the absolute majority of Soviet people overcame [*peredolet'*] the difficulties, rather than bowing down before them."[63] Makarov went on to argue that the same line should logically be taken to purge victims. Reworking the passage cited above, Makarov suggested that even purge victims like Solzhenitsyn himself could be told: "Don't deceive yourself; not all communists ended up in camps under Stalin. In fact, many were able to 'overcome' these difficulties, rather than bowing down before them and so they didn't end up in a camp." Makarov was deeply bitter that political prisoners were vindicated [*opravdanyi*], while those sentenced under Stalin for nonpolitical sentences were still doomed to eternal incarceration. In dealing with the great body of Stalin's outcasts, the state was now making significant distinctions between different categories. As Makarov noted, the promise of readmission was no longer universal but restricted primarily to political prisoners such as Solzhenitsyn.

A. G. Baev took a slightly different approach, but the beliefs underpinning his letter were similar. Writing on 22 December 1962, whilst serving his fifth sentence, Baev opened his letter with a long description of conditions in a labor camp. In it he hoped to prove to his reader that the hardships and injustices endured by Ivan Denisovich had not yet been eradicated.[64] Rotten meat, neglect for the sick, and official corruption were still the staple of camp life. Such experiences led Baev to believe that no prisoner could emerge reformed. A prisoner was typically so corrupted by his ordeals in the camps and by the loss of his family and home, he wrote, that there was little chance he would do anything other than offend again upon release. Baev realized that a different narrative strategy must be fashioned for the new era. In recognition of the fact that the "conversion" story of the ordinary criminal had now lost its appeal, he instead sought to be reclassified as one of Stalin's victims. According to Baev, his errors—which he did not deny—had been grossly exaggerated by an unjust system that wanted to turn him into an "eternal '*zek*.'" Denying that he was born a criminal, Baev sketched out his life story: "During the war, I lost my parents and became a street child at the age of twelve. While I was still a minor, I joined the army and received many awards. I was in the partisan forces. But after the war, a 'crack' [*treshchina*] appeared, and the stamp of Stalin's cult of personality was imprinted on my life. And so I served fifteen years in prison, experiencing all the 'joys' of a life without any happiness and without any hope for the future."[65] Where a few years earlier a tale of childhood suffering and of wartime loss might have received a sympathetic hearing, Baev seems aware that this was insufficient in itself to invoke official interest. In Baev's eyes, his only chance to rejoin the Soviet collective was to align himself with the regime's new priorities. In the wake of the Twenty-Second Party Congress, it seemed that the only credential for a successful readmission into Soviet society was to be a victim of Stalin's cult of personality. But Baev's attempt at reclassification was not entirely successful. A reply from the *Novyi mir* editors noted pointedly: "It seems to us that you wrongly compare your life in the camps with the life of the prisoners in Solzhenitsyn's story **One Day in the Life of Ivan Denisovich.** Ivan Denisovich and his comrades were sentenced unlawfully, whereas you have been sentenced five times and you don't deny that you were guilty. What kind of victim of the cult were you? Did the period of the cult really lead people to commit crimes?"[66] Baev wrote a second angry letter.[67] Again he asserted that as someone born and raised under Soviet power, he should not have become a criminal; the fact that he did reflected the inadequacies of the Stalinist period. This time the editors did not reply. Having determined that Baev was a criminal and not a victim of political repression, the editors closed the dialogue.

These prisoners concurred that the promises of redemption blazoned across the newspapers in the 1950s had now been broken. None of them could really cherish any hope that they would emerge from the camps as new men or be taken on by a collective within Soviet society for reeducation. While the purge victims could share in the euphoric mood of 1961-62, the "criminal," who had been wooed with notions of correction throughout the 1950s, remained isolated and excluded.

Some prisoners even realized that it was not only the state that had rejected them, but also—and perhaps most vociferously—the Soviet public. One prisoner wrote to Solzhenitsyn: "We who are serving twenty-five years are the bread and butter for those who are supposed to teach us virtue, corrupt though they are themselves. Did not the colonizers make out that Indians and Negroes were not fully human in this way? . . . It takes nothing at all to arouse public opinion against us. It is enough to write an article in the paper called 'Man in a Cage,' or to describe how a degenerate criminal violated a five-month-old baby girl, and tomorrow the people will organize meetings to demand that we be burnt in furnaces."[68] The perceived dynamic here between the press and popular opinion is revealing. While acknowledging the role the media might play, the prisoner also appreciated the high levels of collective anger emanating from Soviet citizens. According to this prisoner-correspondent, the reluctance to view outcasts as fully human came not only from the state but also from deep within society itself. The identification and branding of outcasts was not just a state-led enterprise but one in which the newspaper-reading public also played an important part.

These letters provide an unexpected angle to the Ivan Denisovich debate. As the post-Stalinist world sought to redefine the boundary between insiders and outsiders, those cast out did not always remain silent. Instead of accepting their renewed exclusion, they used the notions of "reeducation" and "reforging" promoted during the 1950s in order to claim their rightful return to society. But with the state engineering a dramatic turn away from a rhetoric that had never successfully caught the public imagination, the prisoners built their protest on promises that were already being retracted.

* * *

In early 1963, a man named Kuterev submitted a short story to the editors of *Novyi mir*. Having served in the army since the age of seventeen, Kuterev was now the deputy commander of a labor camp and an active member of the party at the oblast level. He identified himself as an innovator deeply committed to the penal reforms introduced under Khrushchev. In the form of his protagonist, an "educator" (*vospitatel'*) named Denis Ivanovich, Kuterev created a shining example of how in the Khrushchev era a commander might transform his camp into a site of humane learning for those in need of special guidance. Naming his work *Odna noch' Denisa Ivanovicha* (*One Night in the Life of Denis Ivanovich*), Kuterev explicitly set up a series of oppositions to Solzhenitsyn's novella. Ivan Denisovich's name is reversed to become Denis Ivanovich, day becomes night, prisoner becomes camp official. Although he considered himself a reformer, Kuterev was evidently deeply hostile to Solzhenitsyn's tale, deliberately crafting his riposte as its mirror image and presenting his dialogue with Solzhenitsyn as a dualistic conflict between two antagonistic positions.[69]

Kuterev's work returns us to the idea of the Khrushchev era as one of binary conflict, as suggested by Cohen. To describe this clash, Cohen drew on the words of the poet Anna Akhmatova, who poignantly wrote of "two Russias eyeball to eyeball—those who were imprisoned and those who put them there."[70] Yet in the correspondence explored here, this does not appear such an important fault-line. Assigning guilt for the crimes of the past was not a high priority for *Novyi mir* readers. Nor did individuals readily identify themselves as either pro or contra change. The oppositions citizens constructed were rather different—between purity and contamination, respectability (*chestnost'*) and vulgarity (*poshlost'*), culturedness and criminality. Some Soviet citizens found the official sponsorship of a text that embodied the language and subculture of society's outcasts disturbing, for it threatened the civilized and cultured self-image that Soviet society pursued. Fearing that an important opposition within the Soviet belief system was being eroded, some citizens wrote letters to preserve an absolute partition between two Russias: a Soviet Russia where people spoke and behaved as citizens of the communist future and another where the ways and customs of "old" Russia still lingered.

By providing access to aspects of popular opinion, the sources used here suggest that the Khrushchev era did not simply witness a struggle between two clearly defined factions, as has so often been supposed. Indeed, individuals might embrace some aspects of de-Stalinization whilst fiercely contesting others.[71] For many readers, it was the release of less "cultured" prisoners that proved the most distressing element of de-Stalinization. By introducing elements from the "alien" world of the gulag into the respectable realm of literature, **One Day in the Life of Ivan Denisovich** had challenged what many readers considered core Soviet values.

Stalinism certainly left complex legacies. On the one hand, the Stalinist civilizing drive apparently penetrated the thinking of many Soviet citizens, creating vocal sectors of the population who stridently believed in the importance of maintaining "cultured" behavior. On the other, the punitive nature of the Stalinist regime brought into being the enormous gulag monolith, where those banished from society became part of a community with very different values and modes of behavior. (Indeed, later in his career Solzhenitsyn would suggest that the zeks became a separate nation, with their own economy, psychology, manners, and language: "*matiorshchina.*"[72]) By releasing large numbers from the camps and reviving notions such as correction and reeducation, Khrushchev made a radical attempt to reconcile these two opposing worlds.

This enterprise ran aground, however. According to prisoners who composed letters in response to **One Day in the Life of Ivan Denisovich,** the public's anxieties were already outdated. Still banished to the gulag for a variety of criminal offences, these men were increasingly convinced that the Soviet state had abandoned them once more, already reerecting insurmountable barriers between Soviet citizens and their undesirable outcasts. According to statistics from the archives, such claims were not unfounded. The year 1960 was already the last in the gulag's decline, and between the end of 1960 and the beginning of 1962 the size of the gulag population had almost doubled, reaching a figure of almost a million once more.[73] With the number of prisoners already escalating dramatically, some of Khrushchev's most daring policies were being reversed a full three years before he was ousted from power. Important aspects of the de-Stalinizing project were thus defeated, not by Khrushchev's successors, but, at least in part, by the vehement resistance of a Soviet public resentful of any threats to their "imagined community" and deeply fearful of men like Ivan Denisovich, whom they still envisaged as embodiments of an uncultured, alien "other."

A grant from the Arts and Humanities Research Board supported the research and writing of this article. I would like to thank those who commented on earlier versions of this paper presented at the AAASS 34th National Convention in Pittsburgh and at the School of Slavonic and East European Studies (University College London) in November 2002, in particular Geoffrey Hosking, Pete Duncan, Wendy Slater, Maya Haber, Bettina Weichert, and Sheila Fitzpatrick. Especial thanks go to Susan Morrissey who read and commented on this article in several earlier forms. I am also grateful to the two anonymous referees at *Slavic Review* for their helpful suggestions.

Notes

1. Aleksandr Solzhenitsyn, "How People Read *One Day*: A Survey of Letters," in Leopold Labedz, ed., *Solzhenitsyn: A   Documentary   Record*

(Harmondsworth, 1974), 50. While many readers addressed letters to the editors of *Novyi mir* (now preserved at the Russian State Archive of Literature and Art), others wrote directly to the author himself. Small snippets of these letters are printed in Labedz's collection.

2. Aleksandr Solzhenitsyn, "Odin den' Ivana Denisovicha," *Novyi mir,* 1962, no. 11: 8-74.

3. Solzhenitsyn, "How People Read *One Day,*" 50.

4. See for example Konstantin Simonov, "O proshlom vo imia budushchego," *Izvestiia,* 18 November 1962, 5; "Vo imia pravdy, vo imia zhizni," *Pravda,* 23 November 1962, 7-8; N. Kruzhkov, "Tak bylo, tak ne budet," *Ogonek,* 2 December 1962, 28-29; Lidiia Fomenko, "Bol'shie ozhidaniia," *Literaturnaia Rossiia,* 11 January 1963, 6-7; "V redaktsiiu Literaturnoi gazety," *Literaturnaia gazeta,* 22 January 1963, 3; Fedor Chapchakhov, "Nomera i liudi," *Don* 7, no. 1 (January 1963): 155-159; N. Sergovantsev, "Tragediia odinochestva i 'sploshnoi byt,'" *Oktiabr'* 40, no. 4 (April 1963): 198-206; V. Lakshin, "Ivan Denisovich, ego druz'ia i nedrugi," *Novyi mir,* 1964, no. 1:223-245.

5. A year earlier, *Novyi mir* had already published Viktor Nekrasov's *Kira Grigorievna,* a tale recounting the difficulties encountered by a gulag survivor upon returning home. Viktor Nekrasov, "Kira Grigorievna," *Novyi mir,* 1961, no. 6:70-126.

6. Nancy Condee, "Cultural Codes of the Thaw," in William Taubman, Sergei Khrushchev, and Abbott Gleason, eds., *Nikita Khrushchev* (New Haven, 2000), 160.

7. Anna Krylova, "The Tenacious Liberal Subject in Soviet Studies," *Kritika: Explorations in Russian and Eastern European Studies* 1, no. 1 (Winter 2000): 119-46.

8. Max Hayward, "Solzhenitsyn's Place in Contemporary Soviet Literature," *Slavic Review* 23, no. 3 (September 1964): 433.

9. Stephen F. Cohen, "The Friends and Foes of Change: Reformism and Conservatism in the Soviet Union," in Stephen F. Cohen, Alexander Rabinowitch, and Robert Sharlet, eds., *The Soviet Union Since Stalin* (Bloomington, 1980), 14.

10. Rossiiskii gosudarstvennyi arkhiv literatury i iskusstva (RGALI), f. 1702 (*Novyi mir*), op. 9, d. 109 (Readers' letters about works published in the journal), l. 123.

11. Rossiiskii gosudarstvennyi arkhiv sotsial'no-politicheskoi istorii (RGASPI), f. 560 (Special *fond* of manuscript materials relating to the violation of legality in the years of Stalin's cult of personality), op. 1, d.44, l. 1. Having worked as a prison guard for fifteen years, this party member wrote to the Central Committee, convinced that in the camps where he had served there were indeed significant numbers of "inveterate [*ot'iavlennye*] enemies of Soviet power, traitors, German collaborators [*nemetskie posobniki*], henchmen [*karateli*], bandits," and not only the innocent victims he found in Solzhenitsyn's work.

12. This article primarily uses three *dela* from the *Novyi mir* fond at RGALI, f. 1702 (*Novyi mir*), op. 9, d. 107-109, which contain letters from the very end of 1962 through to the summer of 1963. Letters continued to be received in the second half of 1963, but these were often more general responses to Solzhenitsyn's publications and reputation, rather than specifically related to his first work, "Odin den' Ivana Denisovicha." In the three dela explored, about twenty letters were copied. Of these twenty, only two supported the work unequivocally, while one questioned the necessity of publishing such works at all (the sister of a purge victim, Comrade Spasskaia was distressed to read of the horrors her brother had endured, d. 107, ll. 34-35). The majority, however, were more equivocal. The other seventeen letters examined all claimed to accept the process of de-Stalinization, whilst challenging certain important aspects of Solzhenitsyn's work. At least eight of the letters criticized Solzhenitsyn's use of language. Five letters came from men still serving prison sentences for nonpolitical crimes.

13. The camp population was 2,466,914 on 1 April 1953, falling to 781,630 by January of 1956 and as low as 550,000 in 1960. See Gosudarstvennyi arkhiv Rossiiskoi Federatsii (GARF), f. 7523 (Supreme Soviet), op. 89 (Documents relating to the review of pardon appeals), d. 4408, l. 82; and GARF, f. 7523, op. 95 (Group for the preparation of pardon appeals), d. 109, l. 27.

14. In the Secret Speech, Khrushchev depicts the returnees almost exclusively as high-ranking party members victimized by Stalin's terror. Western observers have tended to follow his example, focusing predominantly on the rehabilitation of political prisoners and paying only fleeting attention to the millions of nonpolitical *zeks* (*zakliuchennye*: prisoners, slang) allowed to return in the first post-Stalin years. For a recent example of this focus, see Nanci Adler, *The Gulag Survivor: Beyond the Soviet System* (New Brunswick, N.J., 2002).

15. Amnesties were passed in 1953, 1954, 1955, 1957, and 1959. In addition, the "work-day" system, established in 1919 but abandoned under Stalin, was reintroduced in July 1954, allowing prisoners who met their targets to win early release. On the "work-day" system, see GARF, f. 7523, op. 89, d. 4403, ll. 12-17.

16. Cited in Aleksandr Tvardovskii's preface to "Odin den' Ivana Denisovicha," *Novyi mir,* 1962, no. 11:8.

17. Two Russian émigrés later wrote that "the undoubted bestseller of the Soviet press of the 1960s was

Khrushchev's concluding speech at the Twenty-Second Party Congress, which drew on the dramatic conflict between his desire to tell the truth and the intention of Molotov-Kaganovich to hide it." Petr Vail' and Aleksandr Genis, *60-e: Mir sovetskogo cheloveka* (Ann Arbor, 1988), 139.

18. "Rech' tovarishcha D. A. Lazurkinoi," *Pravda,* 31 October 1961, 2.

19. The main thrust of Adler's work is to demonstrate the ongoing difficulties endured by "the Gulag survivor," but she admits that in the early 1960s, the Soviet press was ready to print returnees' memoirs. The texts chosen for publication invariably showed a communist who had never lost faith in the party that had rejected him. See for example the memoirs of Boris D'iakov, published in the March 1963 issue of *Zvezda.* He began by saying, "My chief aim is to show true communists always remain communists no matter what terrible experiences are thrown at them." The recollections of A. V. Gorbatov, published in 1964 in *Novyi mir,* embody a similarly heroic martyrdom. A Red Army general briefly repressed at the height of the purges, Gorbatov had returned to take up a leading position in the Soviet Army. Adler, *Gulag Survivor,* 215; Boris D'iakov, "Perezhitoe," *Zvezda,* 1963, no. 3:177; A. V. Gorbatov, "Gody i voiny," *Novyi mir,* 1964, no. 3:133-56; no. 4:99-138; no. 5:106-53.

20. Arkhiv "Memoriala," Moscow, f. 2 (Memoir collection), op. 1, d. 68 (personal file of Aleksandr Nikonorovich Zuev), l. 2.

21. Aleksei Kondratovich wrote to Boris Oliker, a rehabilitated party member from Minsk, in May 1963. RGALI, f. 1702, op. 9, d. 109, l. 20.

22. The fond mentioned is now housed at RGASPI, f. 560, op. 1. For a fuller exploration of these memoirs, see Miriam Dobson, "Refashioning the Enemy: Popular Beliefs and the Rhetoric of Destalinisation, 1953-1964" (PhD diss., University of London, 2003), 225-41.

23. "Doklad N. S. Khrushcheva," *Pravda,* 18 October 1961: 9; "Doklad N. S. Khrushcheva," *Pravda,* 19 October 1961, 1; "Rech' tovarishcha G. D. Dzhavakhishvili," *Pravda,* 31 October 1961, 2; "Rech' tovarishcha P. N. Demicheva," *Pravda,* 20 October 1961, 2; "Rech'N. V. Podgornogo," *Pravda,* 20 October 1961, 4.

24. RGALI, f. 1702, op. 9, d. 109, l. 152.

25. Ibid., l. 153.

26. Ibid.

27. Ibid., d. 107, ll. 97-100.

28. See David L. Hoffmann, *Stalinist Values: The Cultural Norms of Soviet Modernity, 1917-1941* (Ithaca, 2003).

29. Paul M. Hagenloh, "'Socially Harmful Elements' and the Great Terror," in Sheila Fitzpatrick, ed., *Stalinism: New Directions* (London, 2000), 286-87.

30. The gulag had initially been imagined as a site of redemption. Katerina Clark identifies the years 1931 to 1935 as the period in which this vision of the gulag prevailed. Under Maksim Gor'kii's tutelage, there appeared several accounts of how social aliens were dispatched to hard labor within the camp system, given intensive reeducation, thereby "re-forged" as decent citizens. *Belomor,* the literary work edited by Gor'kii, contained the bold claim that "as the result of twenty months of work, the country has a few thousand skilled builders who have gone through a hard but formative experience and have been cured of the creeping infection of petty bourgeois society." The motif of redemption was to recede, however, with the escalation of terror in the second half of the decade. See Katerina Clark, *The Soviet Novel: History As Ritual,* 3d ed. (Bloomington, 2000), 118-19; Maksim Gor'kii, L. Auerbach, and S. G. Firin, *Belomor: An Account of the Construction of the New Canal between the White Sea and the Baltic Sea,* trans. Amabel Williams-Ellis (London, 1935), 338.

31. Statistics from the Ministry of the Interior suggest increased criminal activity in the years following Stalin's death. As a result of the March amnesty, 1953 witnessed a particularly grave crime wave, and though 1954 saw a brief lull, there was a steady rise in crimes recorded over the coming years. By 1957, the overall number of crimes registered was 39 percent higher than in even 1953. The figures for murder are particularly startling, with the number doubling between 1953 and 1957. GARF, f. 7523, op. 89, d. 7494, l. 54.

32. Tvardovskii's preface to "Odin den'Ivana Denisovicha," *Novyi mir,* 1962, no. 11:9.

33. Fomenko, "Bol'shie ozhidaniia."

34. Chapchakhov, "Nomera i liudi."

35. RGALI, f. 1702, op. 9, d. 108, ll. 10-12.

36. Ibid., d. 107, l. 71.

37. Ibid., l. 65.

38. Ibid., ll. 58-61.

39. Grigorii Chukhrai, director, *Chistoe nebo* (Moscow: Mosfil'm, 1961).

40. Georgii Shelest', "Samorodok," *Izvestiia,* 6 November 1962, 6. In the story, four purged party members sent to the Kolyma gold mines exhibit true communist behavior. Having unearthed a huge nugget of gold, they are tempted to hide it in order to then sliver off small pieces each day, thus meeting their targets with less exertion. They resist, however, and hand it all in immediately in order to help the war effort.

41. Svetlana Boym, *Common Places: Mythologies of Everyday Life in Russia* (Cambridge, Mass., 1994), 42, 64.

42. Vadim Volkov, "The Concept of *Kul'turnost'*: Notes on the Stalinist Civilizing Process," in Fitzpatrick, *Stalinism: New Directions,* 223.

43. RGALI, f. 1702, op. 9, d. 107, l. 76.

44. In his work on swearing in late imperial Russia, Steve Smith has suggested that for "conscious" workers striving to acquire kul'turnost', swearing was so strongly associated with a perceived "*lack* of culture" it came to serve as a "recognised marker of Russian ethnicity." It is revealing that half a century after the revolution, Mel'nikov associated bad language with a hangover from the past, an unsavory kind of behavior that was Russian and not Soviet. See S. A. Smith, "The Social Meanings of Swearing: Workers and Bad Language in Late Imperial and Early Soviet Russia," *Past and Present,* no. 160 (August 1998): 181.

45. The Supreme Court simply forwarded the letter to the *Novyi mir* editors.

46. RGALI, f. 1702, op. 9, d. 109, l. 66.

47. Many citizens set pen to paper to contest the regime's commitment to "correction" and "reeducation." The growing tide of letters was frequently noted in reports from government officials. In March 1961, Kalinychev and Savel'ev, senior figures within the Supreme Soviet, wrote to its chairman, Leonid Brezhnev, voicing concerns not only about rising crime but also the outcry it had generated. They noted that the number of crimes reported had again risen steeply in 1960 and with it the influx of letters. See GARF, f. 7523, op. 107 (Documentary materials from the structural subdivision of the Presidium of the Supreme Soviet), d. 189, l. 73; GARF, f. 7523, op. 95, d. 99, ll. 49-53.

48. "Rech' N. S. Khrushcheva na III s'ezde pisatelei 22 maia 1959 goda," *Pravda,* 24 May 1959, 1-3.

49. "Voluntary Militia and Courts," *Soviet Studies* 11, no. 2 (October 1959): 214-17.

50. The "community organization" could apply for "guardianship" of an offender during the police investigation, or if the matter came to trial, the judge could decide on this as a form of social rehabilitation.

51. GARF, f. 7523, op. 95, d. 109, l. 27.

52. "Doklad N. S. Khrushcheva," *Pravda,* 18 October 1961, 11.

53. RGALI, f. 1702, op. 9, d. 107, l. 76.

54. "V redaktsiiu Literaturnoi gazety," *Literaturnaia gazeta,* 22 January 1963, 3.

55. RGALI, f. 1702, op. 9, d. 107, ll. 49-51.

56. Ibid., l. 79.

57. Ibid., d. 108, l. 5.

58. Ibid., l. 2.

59. Ibid., l. 7.

60. Jeffrey Brooks's comments on the importance of honor (*chest'*) within Soviet culture are astute. He notes that "every society sets boundaries to identify insiders and outsiders" and considers chest' as a key marker in the setting of these social boundaries. However, Brooks goes on to interpret Soviet honor in rather exclusive terms, discussing the role of official honors such as state prizes and titles. I would like to suggest instead that the adjective *chestnyi* was often used in the Soviet context to denote ordinary, decent colleagues and neighbors, not those singled out for their achievements. Jeffrey Brooks, *Thank You, Comrade Stalin! Soviet Public Culture from Revolution to Cold War* (Princeton, 2000), 127.

61. RGALI, f. 1702, op. 9, d. 109, l. 139.

62. Ibid., l. 141.

63. A. L. Remenson, *V obshchestve, stroiashchem kommunizm, ne dolzhno byt'mesta pravonarusheniiam i prestupnosti* (Moscow, 1963), 19.

64. RGALI, f. 1702, op. 9, d. 107, ll. 8-14.

65. Ibid., l. 12.

66. Ibid., l. 7.

67. Ibid., ll. 1-6.

68. Solzhenitsyn, "How People Read *One Day*," 56.

69. RGALI, f. 1702, op. 9, d. 109, ll. 10-17.

70. Cited in Stephen F. Cohen, "The Stalin Question since Stalin," in Stephen F. Cohen, ed., *An End to Silence: Uncensored Opinion in the Soviet Union from Roy Medvedev's Underground Magazine "Political Diary"* (New York, 1982), 27.

71. Another key aspect of de-Stalinization was, of course, the revised status of Stalin himself. The year 1956 saw the Soviet public respond extremely passionately to his dethronement. Here too, however, reactions cannot be easily categorized as either pro or contra de-Stalinization. For a more detailed exploration of this, see Dobson, "Refashioning the Enemy," 129-72.

72. Aleksandr I. Solzhenitsyn, *The Gulag Archipelago, 1918-1956: An Experiment in Literary Investigation,* trans. Thomas P. Whitney, 3 vols. (New York, 1974-78), 2:505.

73. GARF, f. 7523, op. 95, d. 109, ll. 25-27.

Rimgaila Salys (essay date winter 2006)

SOURCE: Salys, Rimgaila. "Solzhenitsyn's *One Day in the Life of Ivan Denisovich*." *Explicator* 64, no. 2 (winter 2006): 104-07.

[*In the following essay, Salys examines Solzhenitsyn's treatment of two films by Sergei Eisenstein in* One Day in the Life of Ivan Denisovich.]

> These ideas did not come from books, neither were they imported for the sake of coherence. They were formed in conversations with people now dead, in prison cells and by forest fires, they were tested against THAT life, they grew out of THAT existence.
>
> —Alexander Solzhenitsyn, Nobel Lecture, 1970

On two separate occasions, Tsezar, the imprisoned film-maker of Solzhenitsyn's novel [***One Day in the Life of Ivan Denisovich***], engages fellow inmates Kh-123 and Captain Buinovskii in conversations on the merits of Sergei Eisenstein's films *Battleship Potemkin* (1925) and *Ivan the Terrible* (1946). Critics have read these passages from two perspectives—first as exposés of the moral insensitivity of well-fed camp intellectuals who discuss arcane issues in front of starving zeks; second, in the case of *Ivan the Terrible,* as critiques of Eisenstein's questionable artistic ethics under the pressure of Stalinist coercion—and therefore representative of Solzhenitsyn's own views on the moral duty of the artist to speak the Truth, regardless of circumstances.[1] But these interpretations do not explain Solzhenitsyn's choice of specific episodes from the two films for the inmates' discussion. When resituated in their context (the events of camp life that frame the two conversations), it becomes apparent that the Eisenstein passages display further imbrications of meaning as historical metaphors bearing directly on the central narrative line of the novel.

Both passages turn on the "how" and "what" of art, as Tsezar calls them—issues of form and content, the aesthetics and ethics of art. The first conversation takes place at the end of the working day, as the brigades wait for a missing zek, when Tsezar engages the exhausted Buinovskii in conversation on the merits of *Potemkin.* When Tsezar praises the "how" (the artistic qualities) of the film, in the famous pince-nez and baby carriage episodes, the former naval officer responds with a criticism of both the "how" and the "what" (the message) of the film: "[. . .] in that film, life on board ship is like a puppet show. [. . .] The officers are rotters to a man." Tsezar responds, "That's true to history!" The captain counters, "So who do you think led the men into battle? Then again, those maggots crawling on the meat look as big as earthworms. Surely there were never any maggots like that?" Tsezar explains,

"The camera can't show them any smaller!" The captain concludes, "I tell you what, if they brought that meat to our camp today instead of the shitty fish we get and chucked it in the pot without washing or scraping it, I think we'd . . ." (122).

Buinovskii thus rejects as false Eisenstein's message of universally villainous czarist officers and the poorly fed, oppressed working classes. In the preceding scene of ***One Day,*** Solzhenitsyn makes an exactly congruent point about zeks imprisoned as "enemies of the people." Just as czarist officers were not all villains, zeks are not all spies: "There were five spies in every gang, but those were made-up spies, make-believe spies. Their papers had them down as spies, but they were just ex-prisoners of war. Shukhov was one of those himself" (120). Buinovskii's remark about the desirability of the film's maggoty meat in the camps both neutralizes Eisenstein's social critique of prerevolutionary oppression—the zeks will gladly devour the meat rejected by the *Potemkin*'s sailors—and hints at Tsezar's insensitivity. Finally, the captain's comment on supersized cinematic maggots argues for realism in film over formalist devices: the "how" of magnified maggots serves to legitimize the falsified "what" of oppression.

Earlier in the day Ivan Denisovich was an accidental witness to another of Tsezar's intellectual exercises, his argument with Kh-123 over the merits of Eisenstein's *Ivan the Terrible, Part 2:* "Objectively, you will have to admit that Eisenstein is a genius. Surely you can't deny that *Ivan the Terrible* is a work of genius? The dance of the oprichniki with the mask! The scene in the cathedral!" (85).[2] Kh-123 objects angrily: "So much art in it that it ceases to be art. Pepper and poppy seed instead of good honest bread. And the political motive behind it is utterly loathsome—an attempt to justify a tyrannical individual. An insult to the memory of three generations of the Russian intelligentsia!" Tsezar responds, "Yes, but art isn't what you do, it's how you do it" (86). Ivan Denisovich has already tried once to interrupt the conversation, hoping that Tsezar would reward him with a cigarette for delivering his lunchtime gruel. But the preoccupied Tsezar has completely forgotten about Shukhov, who then slips out quietly to go to work: "Never mind, it wasn't all that cold outside. A great day for bricklaying" (86).

Kh-123's attack on *Ivan the Terrible* as an unethical glorification of a tyrant is largely misdirected. Stalin, who considered the medieval czar a great historical hero and his predecessor, saw part 2 of the film in August 1946, did not like it, and *Ivan* was among four films banned by Central Committee decree in September: "Eisenstein in the second part of *Ivan the Terrible* displayed his ignorance of historical facts by portraying the progressive army of the *oprichniki* as a band of degenerates similar to the American Ku Klux Klan, and Ivan, a man of strong will and character, as a man of no will and little character, something like Hamlet" (qtd. in Leyda 391).[3] The czar is, in fact, portrayed as a calculating murderer in the film, albeit in service of his country, with the *oprichniki* as his bloodthirsty, unprincipled accomplices. With his nineteenth-century utilitarian aesthetics of critical realism, uncompromising position, and twenty-year prison term, Kh-123 is most likely an old radical, perhaps a member of the outlawed Social Revolutionary Party. Ivan Denisovich inwardly criticizes him for not devoting sufficient attention to his food: "He was eating his gruel without savoring it. It wouldn't do him any good" (85)—in the same way, Eisenstein's artistic achievements in *Ivan the Terrible* are wasted on Kh-123 (Toker 278).

The argument between Tsezar and Kh-123 is left unresolved because it is filtered through Ivan's consciousness, which registers only indifference and incomprehension of the "educated conversation" (85). However, Ivan's thoughts about his work ("A great day for bricklaying") conclude the scene because Tsezar's advocacy of "how" over "what" in the case of Eisenstein also bears directly on Ivan's labor, as described in the bricklaying scenes that follow the argument with Kh-123. The zeks build for others, the camp authorities and free citizens of the area, or construct prisons for themselves, yet Ivan is unable to do shoddy work, even toward an immoral end. The workday has ended, yet Ivan Denisovich risks guard dogs and punishment to check the quality of his bricklaying: "He moved quickly back from the wall to take a good look. All right. Then quickly up to the wall to look over the top from right to left. Outside straight as could be. Hands weren't past it yet. Eye as good as any spirit level" (113). For Ivan Denisovich, work is the most profound means of self-expression available to him in the repressive environment of the camp. In performing good work, albeit toward an unethical end that strengthens a coercive system, Ivan reaffirms himself as a creative human being (Klimoff 20-21). In his own world, then, Ivan Denisovich makes exactly the same choice for "how" over "what," as did Eisenstein in his *Ivan the Terrible*, which had been commissioned by Stalin as a glorification of the brutal czar. The argument between Tsezar and Kh-123 is therefore resolved in Eisenstein's favor via the parallel message of self-realization in the bricklaying episode.[4]

Solzhenitsyn ultimately judges both Eisenstein films against the strictest ethical measure of all—the Truth of the camps. *Potemkin,* created with voluntary ideological élan during the less brutal 1920s, is rejected in both its "what" and "how," for its falsified content (the villainous officers and oppressed sailors), mirrored in the false charges against Gulag inmates, and for its technique (the magnified maggots) that serves to justify a false message. Conversely, *Ivan the Terrible,* created under the pressure of Stalinism, is accepted because it argues a creative, responsible "how" in the face of an unethical, coercive "what" as a necessary affirmation of humanity that is seconded by Ivan Denisovich's conscientious, even inspired, manual labor in the camps.

Notes

1. Most recently, Porter (97) and Klimoff (14-15).

2. I have slightly modified the Willetts translation of "masked oprichniki" here. The Russian original ("Pliaska oprichnikov s lichinoi!") refers to the feast at which the *oprichniki* dance as a group, led by Fedor Basmanov wearing a female mask. The novel's reference to part 2 of *Ivan the Terrible* is somewhat anachronistic. The film was banned in 1946 and not released until 1958. Although Tsezar, as a beginning filmmaker, might have seen it in-house, Kh-123, who has done twenty years in the camps, would not have had such an opportunity.

3. Barry points out the film's political peripaties as evidence for Tsezar's view (9).

4. Kh-123's two accusations (preoccupation with technique in art and unethical art that justifies a tyrant) can also be seen as self-referential on the part of Solzhenitsyn. Toker has read the second accusation as an oblique reference to Solzhenitsyn's own literary muting of the horrors of camp life in order to pass the censor (278). Klimoff has summarized Solzhenitsyn's personal views on the paradox of good work performed toward an unethical end (21-22).

Works Cited

Barry, Minako. "The References to Eisenstein in *One Day in the Life of Ivan Denisovich.*" *Notes on Contemporary Literature* 5 (1990): 9-10.

Klimoff, Alexis. "The Sober Eye: Ivan Denisovich and the Peasant Perspective." *One Day in the Life of Ivan Denisovich. A Critical Companion.* Ed. Alexis Klimoff. Evanston. IL: Northwestern UP, 1997. 3-31.

Leyda, Jay, Kino. *A History of the Russian and Soviet Film,* 3rd ed. Princeton, NJ: Princeton UP, 1983.

Porter, Robert. *Solzhenitsyn's* One Day in the Life of Ivan Denisovich. London: Bristol Classical P, 1997.

Solzhenitsyn, Aleksandr. *One Day in the Life of Ivan Denisovich.* Trans. H. T. Willetts. New York: Noonday, 1991.

Toker, L. "On Some Aspects of the Narrative Method in *One Day in the Life of Ivan Denisovich.*" *Russian Philology and History. In Honour of Professor Victor Levin.* Ed. W. Moskovich. Jerusalem: Hebrew University, 1992.

FURTHER READING

Biographies

Remnick, David. "Deep in the Woods: Solzhenitsyn, a New Book, and the New Russia." *New Yorker* 77, no. 22 (6 August 2001): 32-40.

Extended analysis of Solzhenitsyn's influence in Russia and the U.S., and interview in which Solzhenitsyn and Remnick reflect on their past conversations and the author's perception of his role and literary legacy.

Thomas, D. M. *Alexander Solzhenitsyn: A Century in His Life*. New York: St. Martin's, 1998, 583 p.

Biography of Solzhenitsyn examining his life and work from a post-oppression perspective.

Additional coverage of Solzhenitsyn's life and career is contained in the following sources published by Thomson Gale: *Authors and Artists for Young Adults,* **Vol. 49;** *Authors in the News,* **Vol. 1;** *Beacham's Encyclopedia of Popular Fiction: Biography & Resources,* **Vol. 3;** *Contemporary Authors,* **Vols. 69-72;** *Contemporary Authors New Revision Series,* **Vols. 40, 65, 116;** *Contemporary Literary Criticism,* **Vols. 1, 2, 4, 7, 9, 10, 18, 26, 78, 134;** *Contemporary World Writers,* **Ed. 2;** *Dictionary of Literary Biography,* **Vol. 302;** *DISCovering Authors; DISCovering Authors: British; DISCovering Authors: Canadian; DISCovering Authors Modules: Most-studied* **and** *Novelists; DISCovering Authors 3.0; Encyclopedia of World Literature in the 20th Century,* **Ed. 3;** *European Writers* **Vol. 13;** *Exploring Short Stories; Literature and Its Times,* **Vol. 4;** *Literature Resource Center; Major 20th-Century Writers,* **Eds. 1, 2;** *Major 21st-Century Writers,* **(eBook) 2005;** *Novels for Students,* **Vol. 6;** *Reference Guide to Short Fiction,* **Ed. 2;** *Reference Guide to World Literature,* **Eds. 2, 3;** *Short Stories for Students,* **Vol. 9;** *Short Story Criticism,* **Vol. 32;** *Twayne's World Authors;* **and** *World Literature Criticism,* **Vol. 5.**

How to Use This Index

The main references

list all author entries in the following Gale Literary Criticism series:

AAL = *Asian American Literature*
BG = *The Beat Generation: A Gale Critical Companion*
BLC = *Black Literature Criticism*
BLCS = *Black Literature Criticism Supplement*
CLC = *Contemporary Literary Criticism*
CLR = *Children's Literature Review*
CMLC = *Classical and Medieval Literature Criticism*
DC = *Drama Criticism*
HLC = *Hispanic Literature Criticism*
HLCS = *Hispanic Literature Criticism Supplement*
HR = *Harlem Renaissance: A Gale Critical Companion*
LC = *Literature Criticism from 1400 to 1800*
NCLC = *Nineteenth-Century Literature Criticism*
NNAL = *Native North American Literature*
PC = *Poetry Criticism*
SSC = *Short Story Criticism*
TCLC = *Twentieth-Century Literary Criticism*
WLC = *World Literature Criticism, 1500 to the Present*
WLCS = *World Literature Criticism Supplement*

The cross-references

list all author entries in the following Gale biographical and literary sources:

AAYA = *Authors & Artists for Young Adults*
AFAW = *African American Writers*
AFW = *African Writers*
AITN = *Authors in the News*
AMW = *American Writers*
AMWR = *American Writers Retrospective Supplement*
AMWS = *American Writers Supplement*
ANW = *American Nature Writers*
AW = *Ancient Writers*
BEST = *Bestsellers*
BPFB = *Beacham's Encyclopedia of Popular Fiction: Biography and Resources*
BRW = *British Writers*
BRWS = *British Writers Supplement*
BW = *Black Writers*
BYA = *Beacham's Guide to Literature for Young Adults*
CA = *Contemporary Authors*
CAAS = *Contemporary Authors Autobiography Series*
CABS = *Contemporary Authors Bibliographical Series*
CAD = *Contemporary American Dramatists*
CANR = *Contemporary Authors New Revision Series*
CAP = *Contemporary Authors Permanent Series*
CBD = *Contemporary British Dramatists*
CCA = *Contemporary Canadian Authors*
CD = *Contemporary Dramatists*
CDALB = *Concise Dictionary of American Literary Biography*
CDALBS = *Concise Dictionary of American Literary Biography Supplement*
CDBLB = *Concise Dictionary of British Literary Biography*

CMW = *St. James Guide to Crime & Mystery Writers*
CN = *Contemporary Novelists*
CP = *Contemporary Poets*
CPW = *Contemporary Popular Writers*
CSW = *Contemporary Southern Writers*
CWD = *Contemporary Women Dramatists*
CWP = *Contemporary Women Poets*
CWRI = *St. James Guide to Children's Writers*
CWW = *Contemporary World Writers*
DA = *DISCovering Authors*
DA3 = *DISCovering Authors 3.0*
DAB = *DISCovering Authors: British Edition*
DAC = *DISCovering Authors: Canadian Edition*
DAM = *DISCovering Authors: Modules*
   DRAM: *Dramatists Module;* **MST:** *Most-studied Authors Module;*
   MULT: *Multicultural Authors Module;* **NOV:** *Novelists Module;*
   POET: *Poets Module;* **POP:** *Popular Fiction and Genre Authors Module*
DFS = *Drama for Students*
DLB = *Dictionary of Literary Biography*
DLBD = *Dictionary of Literary Biography Documentary Series*
DLBY = *Dictionary of Literary Biography Yearbook*
DNFS = *Literature of Developing Nations for Students*
EFS = *Epics for Students*
EXPN = *Exploring Novels*
EXPP = *Exploring Poetry*
EXPS = *Exploring Short Stories*
EW = *European Writers*
FANT = *St. James Guide to Fantasy Writers*
FW = *Feminist Writers*
GFL = *Guide to French Literature,* Beginnings to 1789, 1798 to the Present
GLL = *Gay and Lesbian Literature*
HGG = *St. James Guide to Horror, Ghost & Gothic Writers*
HW = *Hispanic Writers*
IDFW = *International Dictionary of Films and Filmmakers: Writers and Production Artists*
IDTP = *International Dictionary of Theatre: Playwrights*
LAIT = *Literature and Its Times*
LAW = *Latin American Writers*
JRDA = *Junior DISCovering Authors*
MAICYA = *Major Authors and Illustrators for Children and Young Adults*
MAICYAS = *Major Authors and Illustrators for Children and Young Adults Supplement*
MAWW = *Modern American Women Writers*
MJW = *Modern Japanese Writers*
MTCW = *Major 20th-Century Writers*
NCFS = *Nonfiction Classics for Students*
NFS = *Novels for Students*
PAB = *Poets: American and British*
PFS = *Poetry for Students*
RGAL = *Reference Guide to American Literature*
RGEL = *Reference Guide to English Literature*
RGSF = *Reference Guide to Short Fiction*
RGWL = *Reference Guide to World Literature*
RHW = *Twentieth-Century Romance and Historical Writers*
SAAS = *Something about the Author Autobiography Series*
SATA = *Something about the Author*
SFW = *St. James Guide to Science Fiction Writers*
SSFS = *Short Stories for Students*
TCWW = *Twentieth-Century Western Writers*
WLIT = *World Literature and Its Times*
WP = *World Poets*
YABC = *Yesterday's Authors of Books for Children*
YAW = *St. James Guide to Young Adult Writers*

Literary Criticism Series
Cumulative Author Index

Anand, Mulk Raj 1905-2004 ...... **CLC 23, 93**
    See also CA 65-68; CAAS 231; CANR 32,
    64; CN 1, 2, 3, 4, 5, 6, 7; DAM NOV;
    DLB 323; EWL 3; MTCW 1, 2; MTFW
    2005; RGSF 2
Anatol
    See Schnitzler, Arthur
Anaximander c. 611B.C.-c.
    546B.C. .... **CMLC 22**
Anaya, Rudolfo A. 1937- .... **CLC 23, 148;**
    HLC 1
    See also AAYA 20; BYA 13; CA 45-48; 4;
    CANR 1, 32, 51, 124; CN 4, 5, 6, 7; DAM
    MULT, NOV; DLB 82, 206, 278; HW 1;
    LAIT 4; LLW; MAL 5; MTCW 1, 2;
    MTFW 2005; NFS 12; RGAL 4; RGSF 2;
    TCWW 2; WLIT 1
Andersen, Hans Christian
    1805-1875 .... **NCLC 7, 79; SSC 6, 56;**
    WLC 1
    See also AAYA 57; CLR 6, 113; DA; DA3;
    DAB; DAC; DAM MST, POP; EW 6;
    MAICYA 1, 2; RGSF 2; RGWL 2, 3;
    SATA 100; TWA; WCH; YABC 1
Anderson, C. Farley
    See Mencken, H(enry) L(ouis); Nathan,
    George Jean
Anderson, Jessica (Margaret) Queale
    1916- .... **CLC 37**
    See also CA 9-12R; CANR 4, 62; CN 4, 5,
    6, 7; DLB 325
Anderson, Jon (Victor) 1940- .... **CLC 9**
    See also CA 25-28R; CANR 20; CP 1, 3, 4,
    5; DAM POET
Anderson, Lindsay (Gordon)
    1923-1994 .... **CLC 20**
    See also CA 128; CAAE 125; CAAS 146;
    CANR 77
Anderson, Maxwell 1888-1959 .... **TCLC 2,**
    144
    See also CA 152; CAAE 105; DAM
    DRAM; DFS 16, 20; DLB 7, 228; MAL
    5; MTCW 2; MTFW 2005; RGAL 4
Anderson, Poul 1926-2001 .... **CLC 15**
    See also AAYA 5, 34; BPFB 1; BYA 6, 8,
    9; CA 181; 1-4R, 181; 2; CAAS 199;
    CANR 2, 15, 34, 64, 110; CLR 58; DLB
    8; FANT; INT CANR-15; MTCW 1, 2;
    MTFW 2005; SATA 90; SATA-Brief 39;
    SATA-Essay 106; SCFW 1, 2; SFW 4;
    SUFW 1, 2
Anderson, Robert (Woodruff)
    1917- .... **CLC 23**
    See also AITN 1; CA 21-24R; CANR 32;
    CD 6; DAM DRAM; DLB 7; LAIT 5
Anderson, Roberta Joan
    See Mitchell, Joni
Anderson, Sherwood 1876-1941 ... **SSC 1, 46,**
    91; TCLC 1, 10, 24, 123; WLC 1
    See also AAYA 30; AMW; AMWC 2; BPFB
    1; CA 121; CAAE 104; CANR 61;
    CDALB 1917-1929; DA; DA3; DAB;
    DAC; DAM MST, NOV; DLB 4, 9, 86;
    DLBD 1; EWL 3; EXPS; GLL 2; MAL 5;
    MTCW 1, 2; MTFW 2005; NFS 4; RGAL
    4; RGSF 2; SSFS 4, 10, 11; TUS
Anderson, Wes 1969- .... **CLC 227**
    See also CA 214
Andier, Pierre
    See Desnos, Robert
Andouard
    See Giraudoux, Jean(-Hippolyte)
Andrade, Carlos Drummond de ..... **CLC 18**
    See Drummond de Andrade, Carlos
    See also EWL 3; RGWL 2, 3
Andrade, Mario de .... **TCLC 43**
    See de Andrade, Mario
    See also DLB 307; EWL 3; LAW; RGWL
    2, 3; WLIT 1

Andreae, Johann V(alentin)
    1586-1654 .... **LC 32**
    See also DLB 164
Andreas Capellanus fl. c. 1185- .... **CMLC 45**
    See also DLB 208
Andreas-Salome, Lou 1861-1937 ... **TCLC 56**
    See also CA 178; DLB 66
Andreev, Leonid
    See Andreyev, Leonid (Nikolaevich)
    See also DLB 295; EWL 3
Andress, Lesley
    See Sanders, Lawrence
Andrewes, Lancelot 1555-1626 .... **LC 5**
    See also DLB 151, 172
Andrews, Cicily Fairfield
    See West, Rebecca
Andrews, Elton V.
    See Pohl, Frederik
Andrews, Peter
    See Soderbergh, Steven
Andreyev, Leonid (Nikolaevich)
    1871-1919 .... **TCLC 3**
    See Andreev, Leonid
    See also CA 185; CAAE 104
Andric, Ivo 1892-1975 .... **CLC 8; SSC 36;**
    TCLC 135
    See also CA 81-84; CAAS 57-60; CANR
    43, 60; CDWLB 4; DLB 147, 329; EW
    11; EWL 3; MTCW 1; RGSF 2; RGWL
    2, 3
Androvar
    See Prado (Calvo), Pedro
Angela of Foligno 1248(?)-1309 .... **CMLC 76**
Angelique, Pierre
    See Bataille, Georges
Angell, Roger 1920- .... **CLC 26**
    See also CA 57-60; CANR 13, 44, 70, 144;
    DLB 171, 185
Angelou, Maya 1928- ... **BLC 1; CLC 12, 35,**
    64, 77, 155; PC 32; WLCS
    See also AAYA 7, 20; AMWS 4; BPFB 1;
    BW 2, 3; BYA 2; CA 65-68; CANR 19,
    42, 65, 111, 133; CDALBS; CLR 53; CP
    4, 5, 6, 7; CPW; CSW; CWP; DA; DA3;
    DAB; DAC; DAM MST, MULT, POET,
    POP; DLB 38; EWL 3; EXPN; EXPP; FL
    1:5; LAIT 4; MAICYA 2; MAICYAS 1;
    MAL 5; MBL; MTCW 1, 2; MTFW 2005;
    NCFS 2; NFS 2; PFS 2, 3; RGAL 4;
    SATA 49, 136; TCLE 1:1; WYA; YAW
Angouleme, Marguerite d'
    See de Navarre, Marguerite
Anna Comnena 1083-1153 .... **CMLC 25**
Annensky, Innokentii Fedorovich
    See Annensky, Innokenty (Fyodorovich)
    See also DLB 295
Annensky, Innokenty (Fyodorovich)
    1856-1909 .... **TCLC 14**
    See also CA 155; CAAE 110; EWL 3
Annunzio, Gabriele d'
    See D'Annunzio, Gabriele
Anodos
    See Coleridge, Mary E(lizabeth)
Anon, Charles Robert
    See Pessoa, Fernando (Antonio Nogueira)
Anouilh, Jean 1910-1987 ..... **CLC 1, 3, 8, 13,**
    40, 50; DC 8, 21
    See also AAYA 67; CA 17-20R; CAAS 123;
    CANR 32; DAM DRAM; DFS 9, 10, 19;
    DLB 321; EW 13; EWL 3; GFL 1789 to
    the Present; MTCW 1, 2; MTFW 2005;
    RGWL 2, 3; TWA
Anselm of Canterbury
    1033(?)-1109 .... **CMLC 67**
    See also DLB 115
Anthony, Florence
    See Ai
Anthony, John
    See Ciardi, John (Anthony)

Anthony, Peter
    See Shaffer, Anthony; Shaffer, Peter
Anthony, Piers 1934- .... **CLC 35**
    See also AAYA 11, 48; BYA 7; CA 200;
    200; CANR 28, 56, 73, 102, 133; CLR
    118; CPW; DAM POP; DLB 8; FANT;
    MAICYA 2; MAICYAS 1; MTCW 1, 2;
    MTFW 2005; SAAS 22; SATA 84, 129;
    SATA-Essay 129; SFW 4; SUFW 1, 2;
    YAW
Anthony, Susan B(rownell)
    1820-1906 .... **TCLC 84**
    See also CA 211; FW
Antiphon c. 480B.C.-c. 411B.C. .... **CMLC 55**
Antoine, Marc
    See Proust, (Valentin-Louis-George-Eugene)
    Marcel
Antoninus, Brother
    See Everson, William (Oliver)
    See also CP 1
Antonioni, Michelangelo 1912- .... **CLC 20,**
    144
    See also CA 73-76; CANR 45, 77
Antschel, Paul 1920-1970
    See Celan, Paul
    See also CA 85-88; CANR 33, 61; MTCW
    1; PFS 21
Anwar, Chairil 1922-1949 .... **TCLC 22**
    See Chairil Anwar
    See also CA 219; CAAE 121; RGWL 3
Anzaldua, Gloria (Evanjelina)
    1942-2004 .... **CLC 200; HLCS 1**
    See also CA 175; CAAS 227; CSW; CWP;
    DLB 122; FW; LLW; RGAL 4; SATA-
    Obit 154
Apess, William 1798-1839(?) .... **NCLC 73;**
    NNAL
    See also DAM MULT; DLB 175, 243
Apollinaire, Guillaume 1880-1918 .... **PC 7;**
    TCLC 3, 8, 51
    See Kostrowitzki, Wilhelm Apollinaris de
    See also CA 152; DAM POET; DLB 258,
    321; EW 9; EWL 3; GFL 1789 to the
    Present; MTCW 2; PFS 24; RGWL 2, 3;
    TWA; WP
Apollonius of Rhodes
    See Apollonius Rhodius
    See also AW 1; RGWL 2, 3
Apollonius Rhodius c. 300B.C.-c.
    220B.C. .... **CMLC 28**
    See Apollonius of Rhodes
    See also DLB 176
Appelfeld, Aharon 1932- ... **CLC 23, 47; SSC**
    42
    See also CA 133; CAAE 112; CANR 86,
    160; CWW 2; DLB 299; EWL 3; RGHL;
    RGSF 2; WLIT 6
Appelfeld, Aron
    See Appelfeld, Aharon
Apple, Max (Isaac) 1941- .... **CLC 9, 33; SSC**
    50
    See also CA 81-84; CANR 19, 54; DLB
    130
Appleman, Philip (Dean) 1926- .... **CLC 51**
    See also CA 13-16R; 18; CANR 6, 29, 56
Appleton, Lawrence
    See Lovecraft, H. P.
Apteryx
    See Eliot, T(homas) S(tearns)
Apuleius, (Lucius Madaurensis) c. 125-c.
    164 .... **CMLC 1, 84**
    See also AW 2; CDWLB 1; DLB 211;
    RGWL 2, 3; SUFW; WLIT 8
Aquin, Hubert 1929-1977 .... **CLC 15**
    See also CA 105; DLB 53; EWL 3
Aquinas, Thomas 1224(?)-1274 ..... **CMLC 33**
    See also DLB 115; EW 1; TWA

Aragon, Louis 1897-1982 .... **CLC 3, 22; TCLC 123**
See also CA 69-72; CAAS 108; CANR 28, 71; DAM NOV, POET; DLB 72, 258; EW 11; EWL 3; GFL 1789 to the Present; GLL 2; LMFS 2; MTCW 1, 2; RGWL 2, 3

Arany, Janos 1817-1882 .... **NCLC 34**

Aranyos, Kakay 1847-1910
See Mikszath, Kalman

Aratus of Soli c. 315B.C.-c. 240B.C. .... **CMLC 64**
See also DLB 176

Arbuthnot, John 1667-1735 .... **LC 1**
See also DLB 101

Archer, Herbert Winslow
See Mencken, H(enry) L(ouis)

Archer, Jeffrey 1940- .... **CLC 28**
See also AAYA 16; BEST 89:3; BPFB 1; CA 77-80; CANR 22, 52, 95, 136; CPW; DA3; DAM POP; INT CANR-22; MTFW 2005

Archer, Jeffrey Howard
See Archer, Jeffrey

Archer, Jules 1915- .... **CLC 12**
See also CA 9-12R; CANR 6, 69; SAAS 5; SATA 4, 85

Archer, Lee
See Ellison, Harlan

Archilochus c. 7th cent. B.C.- .... **CMLC 44**
See also DLB 176

Arden, John 1930- .... **CLC 6, 13, 15**
See also BRWS 2; CA 13-16R; 4; CANR 31, 65, 67, 124; CBD; CD 5, 6; DAM DRAM; DFS 9; DLB 13, 245; EWL 3; MTCW 1

Arenas, Reinaldo 1943-1990 .. **CLC 41; HLC 1**
See also CA 128; CAAE 124; CAAS 133; CANR 73, 106; DAM MULT; DLB 145; EWL 3; GLL 2; HW 1; LAW; LAWS 1; MTCW 2; MTFW 2005; RGSF 2; RGWL 3; WLIT 1

Arendt, Hannah 1906-1975 .... **CLC 66, 98**
See also CA 17-20R; CAAS 61-64; CANR 26, 60; DLB 242; MTCW 1, 2

Aretino, Pietro 1492-1556 .... **LC 12**
See also RGWL 2, 3

Arghezi, Tudor .... **CLC 80**
See Theodorescu, Ion N.
See also CA 167; CDWLB 4; DLB 220; EWL 3

Arguedas, Jose Maria 1911-1969 .... **CLC 10, 18; HLCS 1; TCLC 147**
See also CA 89-92; CANR 73; DLB 113; EWL 3; HW 1; LAW; RGWL 2, 3; WLIT 1

Argueta, Manlio 1936- .... **CLC 31**
See also CA 131; CANR 73; CWW 2; DLB 145; EWL 3; HW 1; RGWL 3

Arias, Ron 1941- .... **HLC 1**
See also CA 131; CANR 81, 136; DAM MULT; DLB 82; HW 1, 2; MTCW 2; MTFW 2005

Ariosto, Lodovico
See Ariosto, Ludovico
See also WLIT 7

Ariosto, Ludovico 1474-1533 ... **LC 6, 87; PC 42**
See Ariosto, Lodovico
See also EW 2; RGWL 2, 3

Aristides
See Epstein, Joseph

Aristophanes 450B.C.-385B.C. .... **CMLC 4, 51; DC 2; WLCS**
See also AW 1; CDWLB 1; DA; DA3; DAB; DAC; DAM DRAM, MST; DFS 10; DLB 176; LMFS 1; RGWL 2, 3; TWA; WLIT 8

Aristotle 384B.C.-322B.C. .... **CMLC 31; WLCS**
See also AW 1; CDWLB 1; DA; DA3; DAB; DAC; DAM MST; DLB 176; RGWL 2, 3; TWA; WLIT 8

Arlt, Roberto (Godofredo Christophersen) 1900-1942 .... **HLC 1; TCLC 29**
See also CA 131; CAAE 123; CANR 67; DAM MULT; DLB 305; EWL 3; HW 1, 2; IDTP; LAW

Armah, Ayi Kwei 1939- . **BLC 1; CLC 5, 33, 136**
See also AFW; BRWS 10; BW 1; CA 61-64; CANR 21, 64; CDWLB 3; CN 1, 2, 3, 4, 5, 6, 7; DAM MULT, POET; DLB 117; EWL 3; MTCW 1; WLIT 2

Armatrading, Joan 1950- .... **CLC 17**
See also CA 186; CAAE 114

Armin, Robert 1568(?)-1615(?) .... **LC 120**

Armitage, Frank
See Carpenter, John (Howard)

Armstrong, Jeannette (C.) 1948- .... **NNAL**
See also CA 149; CCA 1; CN 6, 7; DAC; SATA 102

Arnette, Robert
See Silverberg, Robert

Arnim, Achim von (Ludwig Joachim von Arnim) 1781-1831 .. **NCLC 5, 159; SSC 29**
See also DLB 90

Arnim, Bettina von 1785-1859 ...... **NCLC 38, 123**
See also DLB 90; RGWL 2, 3

Arnold, Matthew 1822-1888 ..... **NCLC 6, 29, 89, 126; PC 5; WLC 1**
See also BRW 5; CDBLB 1832-1890; DA; DAB; DAC; DAM MST, POET; DLB 32, 57; EXPP; PAB; PFS 2; TEA; WP

Arnold, Thomas 1795-1842 .... **NCLC 18**
See also DLB 55

Arnow, Harriette (Louisa) Simpson 1908-1986 .... **CLC 2, 7, 18**
See also BPFB 1; CA 9-12R; CAAS 118; CANR 14; CN 2, 3, 4; DLB 6; FW; MTCW 1, 2; RHW; SATA 42; SATA-Obit 47

Arouet, Francois-Marie
See Voltaire

Arp, Hans
See Arp, Jean

Arp, Jean 1887-1966 .... **CLC 5; TCLC 115**
See also CA 81-84; CAAS 25-28R; CANR 42, 77; EW 10

Arrabal
See Arrabal, Fernando

Arrabal (Teran), Fernando
See Arrabal, Fernando
See also CWW 2

Arrabal, Fernando 1932- ... **CLC 2, 9, 18, 58**
See Arrabal (Teran), Fernando
See also CA 9-12R; CANR 15; DLB 321; EWL 3; LMFS 2

Arreola, Juan Jose 1918-2001 .... **CLC 147; HLC 1; SSC 38**
See also CA 131; CAAE 113; CAAS 200; CANR 81; CWW 2; DAM MULT; DLB 113; DNFS 2; EWL 3; HW 1, 2; LAW; RGSF 2

Arrian c. 89(?)-c. 155(?) .... **CMLC 43**
See also DLB 176

Arrick, Fran .... **CLC 30**
See Gaberman, Judie Angell
See also BYA 6

Arrley, Richmond
See Delany, Samuel R., Jr.

Artaud, Antonin (Marie Joseph) 1896-1948 .... **DC 14; TCLC 3, 36**
See also CA 149; CAAE 104; DA3; DAM DRAM; DFS 22; DLB 258, 321; EW 11; EWL 3; GFL 1789 to the Present; MTCW 2; MTFW 2005; RGWL 2, 3

Arthur, Ruth M(abel) 1905-1979 ..... **CLC 12**
See also CA 9-12R; CAAS 85-88; CANR 4; CWRI 5; SATA 7, 26

Artsybashev, Mikhail (Petrovich) 1878-1927 .... **TCLC 31**
See also CA 170; DLB 295

Arundel, Honor (Morfydd) 1919-1973 .... **CLC 17**
See also CA 21-22; CAAS 41-44R; CAP 2; CLR 35; CWRI 5; SATA 4; SATA-Obit 24

Arzner, Dorothy 1900-1979 .... **CLC 98**

Asch, Sholem 1880-1957 .... **TCLC 3**
See also CAAE 105; DLB 333; EWL 3; GLL 2; RGHL

Ascham, Roger 1516(?)-1568 .... **LC 101**
See also DLB 236

Ash, Shalom
See Asch, Sholem

Ashbery, John 1927- ... **CLC 2, 3, 4, 6, 9, 13, 15, 25, 41, 77, 125, 221; PC 26**
See Berry, Jonas
See also AMWS 3; CA 5-8R; CANR 9, 37, 66, 102, 132; CP 1, 2, 3, 4, 5, 6, 7; DA3; DAM POET; DLB 5, 165; DLBY 1981; EWL 3; INT CANR-9; MAL 5; MTCW 1, 2; MTFW 2005; PAB; PFS 11; RGAL 4; TCLE 1:1; WP

Ashdown, Clifford
See Freeman, R(ichard) Austin

Ashe, Gordon
See Creasey, John

Ashton-Warner, Sylvia (Constance) 1908-1984 .... **CLC 19**
See also CA 69-72; CAAS 112; CANR 29; CN 1, 2, 3; MTCW 1, 2

Asimov, Isaac 1920-1992 ..... **CLC 1, 3, 9, 19, 26, 76, 92**
See also AAYA 13; BEST 90:2; BPFB 1; BYA 4, 6, 7, 9; CA 1-4R; CAAS 137; CANR 2, 19, 36, 60, 125; CLR 12, 79; CMW 4; CN 1, 2, 3, 4, 5; CPW; DA3; DAM POP; DLB 8; DLBY 1992; INT CANR-19; JRDA; LAIT 5; LMFS 2; MAICYA 1, 2; MAL 5; MTCW 1, 2; MTFW 2005; RGAL 4; SATA 1, 26, 74; SCFW 1, 2; SFW 4; SSFS 17; TUS; YAW

Askew, Anne 1521(?)-1546 .... **LC 81**
See also DLB 136

Assis, Joaquim Maria Machado de
See Machado de Assis, Joaquim Maria

Astell, Mary 1666-1731 .... **LC 68**
See also DLB 252; FW

Astley, Thea (Beatrice May) 1925-2004 .... **CLC 41**
See also CA 65-68; CAAS 229; CANR 11, 43, 78; CN 1, 2, 3, 4, 5, 6, 7; DLB 289; EWL 3

Astley, William 1855-1911
See Warung, Price

Aston, James
See White, T(erence) H(anbury)

Asturias, Miguel Angel 1899-1974 .... **CLC 3, 8, 13; HLC 1; TCLC 184**
See also CA 25-28; CAAS 49-52; CANR 32; CAP 2; CDWLB 3; DA3; DAM MULT, NOV; DLB 113, 290, 329; EWL 3; HW 1; LAW; LMFS 2; MTCW 1, 2; RGWL 2, 3; WLIT 1

Atares, Carlos Saura
See Saura (Atares), Carlos

Athanasius c. 295-c. 373 .... **CMLC 48**

Atheling, William
See Pound, Ezra (Weston Loomis)

Atheling, William, Jr.
See Blish, James (Benjamin)

Atherton, Gertrude (Franklin Horn)
1857-1948 .... **TCLC 2**
See also CA 155; CAAE 104; DLB 9, 78,
186; HGG; RGAL 4; SUFW 1; TCWW 1,
2
Atherton, Lucius
See Masters, Edgar Lee
Atkins, Jack
See Harris, Mark
Atkinson, Kate 1951- .... **CLC 99**
See also CA 166; CANR 101, 153; DLB
267
Attaway, William (Alexander)
1911-1986 .... **BLC 1; CLC 92**
See also BW 2, 3; CA 143; CANR 82;
DAM MULT; DLB 76; MAL 5
Atticus
See Fleming, Ian; Wilson, (Thomas) Wood-
row
Atwood, Margaret 1939- . **CLC 2, 3, 4, 8, 13,**
15, 25, 44, 84, 135, 232; PC 8; SSC 2,
46; WLC 1
See also AAYA 12, 47; AMWS 13; BEST
89:2; BPFB 1; CA 49-52; CANR 3, 24,
33, 59, 95, 133; CN 2, 3, 4, 5, 6, 7; CP 1,
2, 3, 4, 5, 6, 7; CPW; CWP; DA; DA3;
DAB; DAC; DAM MST, NOV, POET;
DLB 53, 251, 326; EWL 3; EXPN; FL
1:5; FW; GL 2; INT CANR-24; LAIT 5;
MTCW 1, 2; MTFW 2005; NFS 4, 12,
13, 14, 19; PFS 7; RGSF 2; SATA 50,
170; SSFS 3, 13; TCLE 1:1; TWA; WWE
1; YAW
Atwood, Margaret Eleanor
See Atwood, Margaret
Aubigny, Pierre d'
See Mencken, H(enry) L(ouis)
Aubin, Penelope 1685-1731(?) .... **LC 9**
See also DLB 39
Auchincloss, Louis 1917- ..... **CLC 4, 6, 9, 18,**
45; SSC 22
See also AMWS 4; CA 1-4R; CANR 6, 29,
55, 87, 130; CN 1, 2, 3, 4, 5, 6, 7; DAM
NOV; DLB 2, 244; DLBY 1980; EWL 3;
INT CANR-29; MAL 5; MTCW 1; RGAL
4
Auchincloss, Louis Stanton
See Auchincloss, Louis
Auden, W(ystan) H(ugh) 1907-1973 . **CLC 1,**
2, 3, 4, 6, 9, 11, 14, 43, 123; PC 1;
WLC 1
See also AAYA 18; AMWS 2; BRW 7;
BRWR 1; CA 9-12R; CAAS 45-48;
CANR 5, 61, 105; CDBLB 1914-1945;
CP 1, 2; DA; DA3; DAB; DAC; DAM
DRAM, MST, POET; DLB 10, 20; EWL
3; EXPP; MAL 5; MTCW 1, 2; MTFW
2005; PAB; PFS 1, 3, 4, 10; TUS; WP
Audiberti, Jacques 1899-1965 .... **CLC 38**
See also CA 252; CAAS 25-28R; DAM
DRAM; DLB 321; EWL 3
Audubon, John James 1785-1851 . **NCLC 47**
See also AMWS 16; ANW; DLB 248
Auel, Jean M(arie) 1936- .... **CLC 31, 107**
See also AAYA 7, 51; BEST 90:4; BPFB 1;
CA 103; CANR 21, 64, 115; CPW; DA3;
DAM POP; INT CANR-21; NFS 11;
RHW; SATA 91
Auerbach, Berthold 1812-1882 .... **NCLC 171**
See also DLB 133
Auerbach, Erich 1892-1957 .... **TCLC 43**
See also CA 155; CAAE 118; EWL 3
Augier, Emile 1820-1889 .... **NCLC 31**
See also DLB 192; GFL 1789 to the Present
August, John
See De Voto, Bernard (Augustine)
Augustine, St. 354-430 .... **CMLC 6; WLCS**
See also DA; DA3; DAB; DAC; DAM
MST; DLB 115; EW 1; RGWL 2, 3;
WLIT 8

Aunt Belinda
See Braddon, Mary Elizabeth
Aunt Weedy
See Alcott, Louisa May
Aurelius
See Bourne, Randolph S(illiman)
Aurelius, Marcus 121-180 .... **CMLC 45**
See Marcus Aurelius
See also RGWL 2, 3
Aurobindo, Sri
See Ghose, Aurabinda
Aurobindo Ghose
See Ghose, Aurabinda
Ausonius, Decimus Magnus c. 310-c.
394 .... **CMLC 88**
See also RGWL 2, 3
Austen, Jane 1775-1817 ...... **NCLC 1, 13, 19,**
33, 51, 81, 95, 119, 150; WLC 1
See also AAYA 19; BRW 4; BRWC 1;
BRWR 2; BYA 3; CDBLB 1789-1832;
DA; DA3; DAB; DAC; DAM MST, NOV;
DLB 116; EXPN; FL 1:2; GL 2; LAIT 2;
LATS 1:1; LMFS 1; NFS 1, 14, 18, 20,
21; TEA; WLIT 3; WYAS 1
Auster, Paul 1947- .... **CLC 47, 131, 227**
See also AMWS 12; CA 69-72; CANR 23,
52, 75, 129; CMW 4; CN 5, 6, 7; DA3;
DLB 227; MAL 5; MTCW 2; MTFW
2005; SUFW 2; TCLE 1:1
Austin, Frank
See Faust, Frederick (Schiller)
Austin, Mary (Hunter) 1868-1934 . **TCLC 25**
See also ANW; CA 178; CAAE 109; DLB
9, 78, 206, 221, 275; FW; TCWW 1, 2
Averroes 1126-1198 .... **CMLC 7**
See also DLB 115
Avicenna 980-1037 .... **CMLC 16**
See also DLB 115
Avison, Margaret (Kirkland) 1918- .. **CLC 2,**
4, 97
See also CA 17-20R; CANR 134; CP 1, 2,
3, 4, 5, 6, 7; DAC; DAM POET; DLB 53;
MTCW 1
Axton, David
See Koontz, Dean R.
Ayckbourn, Alan 1939- ...... **CLC 5, 8, 18, 33,**
74; DC 13
See also BRWS 5; CA 21-24R; CANR 31,
59, 118; CBD; CD 5, 6; DAB; DAM
DRAM; DFS 7; DLB 13, 245; EWL 3;
MTCW 1, 2; MTFW 2005
Aydy, Catherine
See Tennant, Emma (Christina)
Ayme, Marcel (Andre) 1902-1967 ... **CLC 11;**
SSC 41
See also CA 89-92; CANR 67, 137; CLR
25; DLB 72; EW 12; EWL 3; GFL 1789
to the Present; RGSF 2; RGWL 2, 3;
SATA 91
Ayrton, Michael 1921-1975 .... **CLC 7**
See also CA 5-8R; CAAS 61-64; CANR 9,
21
Aytmatov, Chingiz
See Aitmatov, Chingiz (Torekulovich)
See also EWL 3
Azorin .... **CLC 11**
See Martinez Ruiz, Jose
See also DLB 322; EW 9; EWL 3
Azuela, Mariano 1873-1952 .. **HLC 1; TCLC**
3, 145
See also CA 131; CAAE 104; CANR 81;
DAM MULT; EWL 3; HW 1, 2; LAW;
MTCW 1, 2; MTFW 2005
Ba, Mariama 1929-1981 .... **BLCS**
See also AFW; BW 2; CA 141; CANR 87;
DNFS 2; WLIT 2
Baastad, Babbis Friis
See Friis-Baastad, Babbis Ellinor

Bab
See Gilbert, W(illiam) S(chwenck)
Babbis, Eleanor
See Friis-Baastad, Babbis Ellinor
Babel, Isaac
See Babel, Isaak (Emmanuilovich)
See also EW 11; SSFS 10
Babel, Isaak (Emmanuilovich)
1894-1941(?) . **SSC 16, 78; TCLC 2, 13,**
171
See Babel, Isaac
See also CA 155; CAAE 104; CANR 113;
DLB 272; EWL 3; MTCW 2; MTFW
2005; RGSF 2; RGWL 2, 3; TWA
Babits, Mihaly 1883-1941 .... **TCLC 14**
See also CAAE 114; CDWLB 4; DLB 215;
EWL 3
Babur 1483-1530 .... **LC 18**
Babylas 1898-1962
See Ghelderode, Michel de
Baca, Jimmy Santiago 1952- . **HLC 1; PC 41**
See also CA 131; CANR 81, 90, 146; CP 6,
7; DAM MULT; DLB 122; HW 1, 2;
LLW; MAL 5
Baca, Jose Santiago
See Baca, Jimmy Santiago
Bacchelli, Riccardo 1891-1985 .... **CLC 19**
See also CA 29-32R; CAAS 117; DLB 264;
EWL 3
Bach, Richard 1936- .... **CLC 14**
See also AITN 1; BEST 89:2; BPFB 1; BYA
5; CA 9-12R; CANR 18, 93, 151; CPW;
DAM NOV, POP; FANT; MTCW 1;
SATA 13
Bach, Richard David
See Bach, Richard
Bache, Benjamin Franklin
1769-1798 .... **LC 74**
See also DLB 43
Bachelard, Gaston 1884-1962 ...... **TCLC 128**
See also CA 97-100; CAAS 89-92; DLB
296; GFL 1789 to the Present
Bachman, Richard
See King, Stephen
Bachmann, Ingeborg 1926-1973 .... **CLC 69**
See also CA 93-96; CAAS 45-48; CANR
69; DLB 85; EWL 3; RGHL; RGWL 2, 3
Bacon, Francis 1561-1626 ..... **LC 18, 32, 131**
See also BRW 1; CDBLB Before 1660;
DLB 151, 236, 252; RGEL 2; TEA
Bacon, Roger 1214(?)-1294 .... **CMLC 14**
See also DLB 115
Bacovia, George 1881-1957 .... **TCLC 24**
See Vasiliu, Gheorghe
See also CDWLB 4; DLB 220; EWL 3
Badanes, Jerome 1937-1995 .... **CLC 59**
See also CA 234
Bage, Robert 1728-1801 .... **NCLC 182**
See also DLB 39; RGEL 2
Bagehot, Walter 1826-1877 .... **NCLC 10**
See also DLB 55
Bagnold, Enid 1889-1981 .... **CLC 25**
See also AAYA 75; BYA 2; CA 5-8R;
CAAS 103; CANR 5, 40; CBD; CN 2;
CWD; CWRI 5; DAM DRAM; DLB 13,
160, 191, 245; FW; MAICYA 1, 2; RGEL
2; SATA 1, 25
Bagritsky, Eduard .... **TCLC 60**
See Dzyubin, Eduard Georgievich
Bagrjana, Elisaveta
See Belcheva, Elisaveta Lyubomirova
Bagryana, Elisaveta .... **CLC 10**
See Belcheva, Elisaveta Lyubomirova
See also CA 178; CDWLB 4; DLB 147;
EWL 3
Bailey, Paul 1937- .... **CLC 45**
See also CA 21-24R; CANR 16, 62, 124;
CN 1, 2, 3, 4, 5, 6, 7; DLB 14, 271; GLL
2

CDBLB 1945-1960; CN 1, 2, 3, 4; CP 1, 2, 3, 4; DA; DA3; DAB; DAC; DAM DRAM, MST, NOV; DFS 2, 7, 18; DLB 13, 15, 233, 319, 321, 329; DLBY 1990; EWL 3; GFL 1789 to the Present; LATS 1:2; LMFS 2; MTCW 1, 2; MTFW 2005; RGSF 2; RGWL 2, 3; SSFS 15; TEA; WLIT 4

Beckford, William 1760-1844 .... **NCLC 16**
   See also BRW 3; DLB 39, 213; GL 2; HGG; LMFS 1; SUFW

Beckham, Barry (Earl) 1944- .... **BLC 1**
   See also BW 1; CA 29-32R; CANR 26, 62; CN 1, 2, 3, 4, 5, 6; DAM MULT; DLB 33

Beckman, Gunnel 1910- .... **CLC 26**
   See also CA 33-36R; CANR 15, 114; CLR 25; MAICYA 1, 2; SAAS 9; SATA 6

Becque, Henri 1837-1899 .... **DC 21; NCLC 3**
   See also DLB 192; GFL 1789 to the Present

Becquer, Gustavo Adolfo 1836-1870 .... **HLCS 1; NCLC 106**
   See also DAM MULT

Beddoes, Thomas Lovell 1803-1849 .. **DC 15; NCLC 3, 154**
   See also BRWS 11; DLB 96

Bede c. 673-735 .... **CMLC 20**
   See also DLB 146; TEA

Bedford, Denton R. 1907-(?) .... **NNAL**

Bedford, Donald F.
   See Fearing, Kenneth (Flexner)

Beecher, Catharine Esther 1800-1878 .... **NCLC 30**
   See also DLB 1, 243

Beecher, John 1904-1980 .... **CLC 6**
   See also AITN 1; CA 5-8R; CAAS 105; CANR 8; CP 1, 2, 3

Beer, Johann 1655-1700 .... **LC 5**
   See also DLB 168

Beer, Patricia 1924- .... **CLC 58**
   See also CA 61-64; CAAS 183; CANR 13, 46; CP 1, 2, 3, 4, 5, 6; CWP; DLB 40; FW

Beerbohm, Max
   See Beerbohm, (Henry) Max(imilian)

Beerbohm, (Henry) Max(imilian) 1872-1956 .... **TCLC 1, 24**
   See also BRWS 2; CA 154; CAAE 104; CANR 79; DLB 34, 100; FANT; MTCW 2

Beer-Hofmann, Richard 1866-1945 .... **TCLC 60**
   See also CA 160; DLB 81

Beg, Shemus
   See Stephens, James

Begiebing, Robert J(ohn) 1946- .... **CLC 70**
   See also CA 122; CANR 40, 88

Begley, Louis 1933- .... **CLC 197**
   See also CA 140; CANR 98; DLB 299; RGHL; TCLE 1:1

Behan, Brendan (Francis) 1923-1964 .... **CLC 1, 8, 11, 15, 79**
   See also BRWS 2; CA 73-76; CANR 33, 121; CBD; CDBLB 1945-1960; DAM DRAM; DFS 7; DLB 13, 233; EWL 3; MTCW 1, 2

Behn, Aphra 1640(?)-1689 .. **DC 4; LC 1, 30, 42, 135; PC 13; WLC 1**
   See also BRWS 3; DA; DA3; DAB; DAC; DAM DRAM, MST, NOV, POET; DFS 16; DLB 39, 80, 131; FW; TEA; WLIT 3

Behrman, S(amuel) N(athaniel) 1893-1973 .... **CLC 40**
   See also CA 13-16; CAAS 45-48; CAD; CAP 1; DLB 7, 44; IDFW 3; MAL 5; RGAL 4

Bekederemo, J. P. Clark
   See Clark Bekederemo, J.P.
   See also CD 6

Belasco, David 1853-1931 .... **TCLC 3**
   See also CA 168; CAAE 104; DLB 7; MAL 5; RGAL 4

Belcheva, Elisaveta Lyubomirova 1893-1991 .... **CLC 10**
   See Bagryana, Elisaveta

Beldone, Phil "Cheech"
   See Ellison, Harlan

Beleno
   See Azuela, Mariano

Belinski, Vissarion Grigoryevich 1811-1848 .... **NCLC 5**
   See also DLB 198

Belitt, Ben 1911- .... **CLC 22**
   See also CA 13-16R; 4; CANR 7, 77; CP 1, 2, 3, 4, 5, 6; DLB 5

Belknap, Jeremy 1744-1798 .... **LC 115**
   See also DLB 30, 37

Bell, Gertrude (Margaret Lowthian) 1868-1926 .... **TCLC 67**
   See also CA 167; CANR 110; DLB 174

Bell, J. Freeman
   See Zangwill, Israel

Bell, James Madison 1826-1902 .... **BLC 1; TCLC 43**
   See also BW 1; CA 124; CAAE 122; DAM MULT; DLB 50

Bell, Madison Smartt 1957- ..... **CLC 41, 102, 223**
   See also AMWS 10; BPFB 1; CA 183; 111, 183; CANR 28, 54, 73, 134; CN 5, 6, 7; CSW; DLB 218, 278; MTCW 2; MTFW 2005

Bell, Marvin (Hartley) 1937- .... **CLC 8, 31**
   See also CA 21-24R; 14; CANR 59, 102; CP 1, 2, 3, 4, 5, 6, 7; DAM POET; DLB 5; MAL 5; MTCW 1; PFS 25

Bell, W. L. D.
   See Mencken, H(enry) L(ouis)

Bellamy, Atwood C.
   See Mencken, H(enry) L(ouis)

Bellamy, Edward 1850-1898 ..... **NCLC 4, 86, 147**
   See also DLB 12; NFS 15; RGAL 4; SFW 4

Belli, Gioconda 1948- .... **HLCS 1**
   See also CA 152; CANR 143; CWW 2; DLB 290; EWL 3; RGWL 3

Bellin, Edward J.
   See Kuttner, Henry

Bello, Andres 1781-1865 .... **NCLC 131**
   See also LAW

Belloc, (Joseph) Hilaire (Pierre Sebastien Rene Swanton) 1870-1953 .... **PC 24; TCLC 7, 18**
   See also CA 152; CAAE 106; CLR 102; CWRI 5; DAM POET; DLB 19, 100, 141, 174; EWL 3; MTCW 2; MTFW 2005; SATA 112; WCH; YABC 1

Belloc, Joseph Peter Rene Hilaire
   See Belloc, (Joseph) Hilaire (Pierre Sebastien Rene Swanton)

Belloc, Joseph Pierre Hilaire
   See Belloc, (Joseph) Hilaire (Pierre Sebastien Rene Swanton)

Belloc, M. A.
   See Lowndes, Marie Adelaide (Belloc)

Belloc-Lowndes, Mrs.
   See Lowndes, Marie Adelaide (Belloc)

Bellow, Saul 1915-2005 ...... **CLC 1, 2, 3, 6, 8, 10, 13, 15, 25, 33, 34, 63, 79, 190, 200; SSC 14; WLC 1**
   See also AITN 2; AMW; AMWC 2; AMWR 2; BEST 89:3; BPFB 1; CA 5-8R; CAAS 238; CABS 1; CANR 29, 53, 95, 132; CDALB 1941-1968; CN 1, 2, 3, 4, 5, 6, 7; DA; DA3; DAB; DAC; DAM MST, NOV, POP; DLB 2, 28, 299, 329; DLBD 3; DLBY 1982; EWL 3; MAL 5; MTCW

1, 2; MTFW 2005; NFS 4, 14; RGAL 4; RGHL; RGSF 2; SSFS 12, 22; TUS

Belser, Reimond Karel Maria de 1929-
   See Ruyslinck, Ward
   See also CA 152

Bely, Andrey .... **PC 11; TCLC 7**
   See Bugayev, Boris Nikolayevich
   See also DLB 295; EW 9; EWL 3

Belyi, Andrei
   See Bugayev, Boris Nikolayevich
   See also RGWL 2, 3

Bembo, Pietro 1470-1547 .... **LC 79**
   See also RGWL 2, 3

Benary, Margot
   See Benary-Isbert, Margot

Benary-Isbert, Margot 1889-1979 .... **CLC 12**
   See also CA 5-8R; CAAS 89-92; CANR 4, 72; CLR 12; MAICYA 1, 2; SATA 2; SATA-Obit 21

Benavente (y Martinez), Jacinto 1866-1954 .... **DC 26; HLCS 1; TCLC 3**
   See also CA 131; CAAE 106; CANR 81; DAM DRAM, MULT; DLB 329; EWL 3; GLL 2; HW 1, 2; MTCW 1, 2

Benchley, Peter 1940-2006 .... **CLC 4, 8**
   See also AAYA 14; AITN 2; BPFB 1; CA 17-20R; CAAS 248; CANR 12, 35, 66, 115; CPW; DAM NOV, POP; HGG; MTCW 1, 2; MTFW 2005; SATA 3, 89, 164

Benchley, Peter Bradford
   See Benchley, Peter

Benchley, Robert (Charles) 1889-1945 .... **TCLC 1, 55**
   See also CA 153; CAAE 105; DLB 11; MAL 5; RGAL 4

Benda, Julien 1867-1956 .... **TCLC 60**
   See also CA 154; CAAE 120; GFL 1789 to the Present

Benedict, Ruth 1887-1948 .... **TCLC 60**
   See also CA 158; CANR 146; DLB 246

Benedict, Ruth Fulton
   See Benedict, Ruth

Benedikt, Michael 1935- .... **CLC 4, 14**
   See also CA 13-16R; CANR 7; CP 1, 2, 3, 4, 5, 6, 7; DLB 5

Benet, Juan 1927-1993 .... **CLC 28**
   See also CA 143; EWL 3

Benet, Stephen Vincent 1898-1943 ..... **PC 64; SSC 10, 86; TCLC 7**
   See also AMWS 11; CA 152; CAAE 104; DA3; DAM POET; DLB 4, 48, 102, 249, 284; DLBY 1997; EWL 3; HGG; MAL 5; MTCW 2; MTFW 2005; RGAL 4; RGSF 2; SSFS 22; SUFW; WP; YABC 1

Benet, William Rose 1886-1950 ..... **TCLC 28**
   See also CA 152; CAAE 118; DAM POET; DLB 45; RGAL 4

Benford, Gregory (Albert) 1941- ..... **CLC 52**
   See also BPFB 1; CA 175; 69-72, 175; 27; CANR 12, 24, 49, 95, 134; CN 7; CSW; DLBY 1982; MTFW 2005; SCFW 2; SFW 4

Bengtsson, Frans (Gunnar) 1894-1954 .... **TCLC 48**
   See also CA 170; EWL 3

Benjamin, David
   See Slavitt, David R(ytman)

Benjamin, Lois
   See Gould, Lois

Benjamin, Walter 1892-1940 .... **TCLC 39**
   See also CA 164; DLB 242; EW 11; EWL 3

Ben Jelloun, Tahar 1944-
   See Jelloun, Tahar ben
   See also CA 135; CWW 2; EWL 3; RGWL 3; WLIT 2

Benn, Gottfried 1886-1956 .. **PC 35; TCLC 3**
See also CA 153; CAAE 106; DLB 56;
EWL 3; RGWL 2, 3
Bennett, Alan 1934- .... **CLC 45, 77**
See also BRWS 8; CA 103; CANR 35, 55,
106, 157; CBD; CD 5, 6; DAB; DAM
MST; DLB 310; MTCW 1, 2; MTFW
2005
Bennett, (Enoch) Arnold
1867-1931 .... **TCLC 5, 20**
See also BRW 6; CA 155; CAAE 106; CD-
BLB 1890-1914; DLB 10, 34, 98, 135;
EWL 3; MTCW 2
Bennett, Elizabeth
See Mitchell, Margaret (Munnerlyn)
Bennett, George Harold 1930-
See Bennett, Hal
See also BW 1; CA 97-100; CANR 87
Bennett, Gwendolyn B. 1902-1981 .... **HR 1:2**
See also BW 1; CA 125; DLB 51; WP
Bennett, Hal .... **CLC 5**
See Bennett, George Harold
See also CA 13; DLB 33
Bennett, Jay 1912- .... **CLC 35**
See also AAYA 10, 73; CA 69-72; CANR
11, 42, 79; JRDA; SAAS 4; SATA 41, 87;
SATA-Brief 27; WYA; YAW
Bennett, Louise 1919-2006 .. **BLC 1; CLC 28**
See also BW 2, 3; CA 151; CAAS 252; CD-
WLB 3; CP 1, 2, 3, 4, 5, 6, 7; DAM
MULT; DLB 117; EWL 3
Bennett, Louise Simone
See Bennett, Louise
Bennett-Coverley, Louise
See Bennett, Louise
Benoit de Sainte-Maure fl. 12th cent.
- .... **CMLC 90**
Benson, A. C. 1862-1925 .... **TCLC 123**
See also DLB 98
Benson, E(dward) F(rederic)
1867-1940 .... **TCLC 27**
See also CA 157; CAAE 114; DLB 135,
153; HGG; SUFW 1
Benson, Jackson J. 1930- .... **CLC 34**
See also CA 25-28R; DLB 111
Benson, Sally 1900-1972 .... **CLC 17**
See also CA 19-20; CAAS 37-40R; CAP 1;
SATA 1, 35; SATA-Obit 27
Benson, Stella 1892-1933 .... **TCLC 17**
See also CA 154, 155; CAAE 117; DLB
36, 162; FANT; TEA
Bentham, Jeremy 1748-1832 .... **NCLC 38**
See also DLB 107, 158, 252
Bentley, E(dmund) C(lerihew)
1875-1956 .... **TCLC 12**
See also CA 232; CAAE 108; DLB 70;
MSW
Bentley, Eric 1916- .... **CLC 24**
See also CA 5-8R; CAD; CANR 6, 67;
CBD; CD 5, 6; INT CANR-6
Bentley, Eric Russell
See Bentley, Eric
ben Uzair, Salem
See Horne, Richard Henry Hengist
Beranger, Pierre Jean de
1780-1857 .... **NCLC 34**
Berdyaev, Nicolas
See Berdyaev, Nikolai (Aleksandrovich)
Berdyaev, Nikolai (Aleksandrovich)
1874-1948 .... **TCLC 67**
See also CA 157; CAAE 120
Berdyayev, Nikolai (Aleksandrovich)
See Berdyaev, Nikolai (Aleksandrovich)
Berendt, John 1939- .... **CLC 86**
See also CA 146; CANR 75, 83, 151
Berendt, John Lawrence
See Berendt, John

Beresford, J(ohn) D(avys)
1873-1947 .... **TCLC 81**
See also CA 155; CAAE 112; DLB 162,
178, 197; SFW 4; SUFW 1
Bergelson, David (Rafailovich)
1884-1952 .... **TCLC 81**
See Bergelson, Dovid
See also CA 220; DLB 333
Bergelson, Dovid
See Bergelson, David (Rafailovich)
See also EWL 3
Berger, Colonel
See Malraux, (Georges-)Andre
Berger, John (Peter) 1926- .... **CLC 2, 19**
See also BRWS 4; CA 81-84; CANR 51,
78, 117; CN 1, 2, 3, 4, 5, 6, 7; DLB 14,
207, 319, 326
Berger, Melvin H. 1927- .... **CLC 12**
See also CA 5-8R; CANR 4, 142; CLR 32;
SAAS 2; SATA 5, 88, 158; SATA-Essay
124
Berger, Thomas 1924- .... **CLC 3, 5, 8, 11, 18,
38**
See also BPFB 1; CA 1-4R; CANR 5, 28,
51, 128; CN 1, 2, 3, 4, 5, 6, 7; DAM
NOV; DLB 2; DLBY 1980; EWL 3;
FANT; INT CANR-28; MAL 5; MTCW
1, 2; MTFW 2005; RHW; TCLE 1:1;
TCWW 1, 2
Bergman, (Ernst) Ingmar 1918- ...... **CLC 16,
72, 210**
See also AAYA 61; CA 81-84; CANR 33,
70; CWW 2; DLB 257; MTCW 2; MTFW
2005
Bergson, Henri(-Louis) 1859-1941 . **TCLC 32**
See also CA 164; DLB 329; EW 8; EWL 3;
GFL 1789 to the Present
Bergstein, Eleanor 1938- .... **CLC 4**
See also CA 53-56; CANR 5
Berkeley, George 1685-1753 .... **LC 65**
See also DLB 31, 101, 252
Berkoff, Steven 1937- .... **CLC 56**
See also CA 104; CANR 72; CBD; CD 5, 6
Berlin, Isaiah 1909-1997 .... **TCLC 105**
See also CA 85-88; CAAS 162
Bermant, Chaim (Icyk) 1929-1998 ... **CLC 40**
See also CA 57-60; CANR 6, 31, 57, 105;
CN 2, 3, 4, 5, 6
Bern, Victoria
See Fisher, M(ary) F(rances) K(ennedy)
Bernanos, (Paul Louis) Georges
1888-1948 .... **TCLC 3**
See also CA 130; CAAE 104; CANR 94;
DLB 72; EWL 3; GFL 1789 to the
Present; RGWL 2, 3
Bernard, April 1956- .... **CLC 59**
See also CA 131; CANR 144
Bernard, Mary Ann
See Soderbergh, Steven
Bernard of Clairvaux 1090-1153 .. **CMLC 71**
See also DLB 208
Bernard Silvestris fl. c. 1130-fl. c.
1160 .... **CMLC 87**
See also DLB 208
Berne, Victoria
See Fisher, M(ary) F(rances) K(ennedy)
Bernhard, Thomas 1931-1989 ..... **CLC 3, 32,
61; DC 14; TCLC 165**
See also CA 85-88; CAAS 127; CANR 32,
57; CDWLB 2; DLB 85, 124; EWL 3;
MTCW 1; RGHL; RGWL 2, 3
Bernhardt, Sarah (Henriette Rosine)
1844-1923 .... **TCLC 75**
See also CA 157
Bernstein, Charles 1950- .... **CLC 142,**
See also CA 129; 24; CANR 90; CP 4, 5, 6,
7; DLB 169
Bernstein, Ingrid
See Kirsch, Sarah

Beroul fl. c. 12th cent. - .... **CMLC 75**
Berriault, Gina 1926-1999 .... **CLC 54, 109;
SSC 30**
See also CA 129; CAAE 116; CAAS 185;
CANR 66; DLB 130; SSFS 7,11
Berrigan, Daniel 1921- .... **CLC 4**
See also CA 187; 33-36R, 187; 1; CANR
11, 43, 78; CP 1, 2, 3, 4, 5, 6, 7; DLB 5
Berrigan, Edmund Joseph Michael, Jr.
1934-1983
See Berrigan, Ted
See also CA 61-64; CAAS 110; CANR 14,
102
Berrigan, Ted .... **CLC 37**
See Berrigan, Edmund Joseph Michael, Jr.
See also CP 1, 2, 3; DLB 5, 169; WP
Berry, Charles Edward Anderson 1931-
See Berry, Chuck
See also CA 115
Berry, Chuck .... **CLC 17**
See Berry, Charles Edward Anderson
Berry, Jonas
See Ashbery, John
See also GLL 1
Berry, Wendell 1934- .... **CLC 4, 6, 8, 27, 46;
PC 28**
See also AITN 1; AMWS 10; ANW; CA
73-76; CANR 50, 73, 101, 132; CP 1, 2,
3, 4, 5, 6, 7; CSW; DAM POET; DLB 5,
6, 234, 275; MTCW 2; MTFW 2005;
TCLE 1:1
Berryman, John 1914-1972 ... **CLC 1, 2, 3, 4,
6, 8, 10, 13, 25, 62; PC 64**
See also AMW; CA 13-16; CAAS 33-36R;
CABS 2; CANR 35; CAP 1; CDALB
1941-1968; CP 1; DAM POET; DLB 48;
EWL 3; MAL 5; MTCW 1, 2; MTFW
2005; PAB; RGAL 4; WP
Bertolucci, Bernardo 1940- ...... **CLC 16, 157**
See also CA 106; CANR 125
Berton, Pierre (Francis de Marigny)
1920-2004 .... **CLC 104**
See also CA 1-4R; CAAS 233; CANR 2,
56, 144; CPW; DLB 68; SATA 99; SATA-
Obit 158
Bertrand, Aloysius 1807-1841 .... **NCLC 31**
See Bertrand, Louis oAloysiusc
Bertrand, Louis oAloysiusc
See Bertrand, Aloysius
See also DLB 217
Bertran de Born c. 1140-1215 .... **CMLC 5**
Besant, Annie (Wood) 1847-1933 ..... **TCLC 9**
See also CA 185; CAAE 105
Bessie, Alvah 1904-1985 .... **CLC 23**
See also CA 5-8R; CAAS 116; CANR 2,
80; DLB 26
Bestuzhev, Aleksandr Aleksandrovich
1797-1837 .... **NCLC 131**
See also DLB 198
Bethlen, T. D.
See Silverberg, Robert
Beti, Mongo .... **BLC 1; CLC 27**
See Biyidi, Alexandre
See also AFW; CANR 79; DAM MULT;
EWL 3; WLIT 2
Betjeman, John 1906-1984 ...... **CLC 2, 6, 10,
34, 43; PC 75**
See also BRW 7; CA 9-12R; CAAS 112;
CANR 33, 56; CDBLB 1945-1960; CP 1,
2, 3; DA3; DAB; DAM MST, POET;
DLB 20; DLBY 1984; EWL 3; MTCW 1,
2
Bettelheim, Bruno 1903-1990 .... **CLC 79;
TCLC 143**
See also CA 81-84; CAAS 131; CANR 23,
61; DA3; MTCW 1, 2; RGHL
Betti, Ugo 1892-1953 .... **TCLC 5**
See also CA 155; CAAE 104; EWL 3;
RGWL 2, 3

Blount, Roy (Alton), Jr. 1941- .... **CLC 38**
 See also CA 53-56; CANR 10, 28, 61, 125;
 CSW; INT CANR-28; MTCW 1, 2;
 MTFW 2005

Blowsnake, Sam 1875-(?) .... **NNAL**

Bloy, Leon 1846-1917 .... **TCLC 22**
 See also CA 183; CAAE 121; DLB 123;
 GFL 1789 to the Present

Blue Cloud, Peter (Aroniawenrate)
 1933- .... **NNAL**
 See also CA 117; CANR 40; DAM MULT

Bluggage, Oranthy
 See Alcott, Louisa May

Blume, Judy (Sussman) 1938- .... **CLC 12, 30**
 See also AAYA 3, 26; BYA 1, 8, 12; CA 29-
 32R; CANR 13, 37, 66, 124; CLR 2, 15,
 69; CPW; DA3; DAM NOV, POP; DLB
 52; JRDA; MAICYA 1, 2; MAICYAS 1;
 MTCW 1, 2; MTFW 2005; NFS 24;
 SATA 2, 31, 79, 142; WYA; YAW

Blunden, Edmund (Charles)
 1896-1974 .... **CLC 2, 56; PC 66**
 See also BRW 6; BRWS 11; CA 17-18;
 CAAS 45-48; CANR 54; CAP 2; CP 1, 2;
 DLB 20, 100, 155; MTCW 1; PAB

Bly, Robert (Elwood) 1926- .... **CLC 1, 2, 5,**
 10, 15, 38, 128; PC 39
 See also AMWS 4; CA 5-8R; CANR 41,
 73, 125; CP 1, 2, 3, 4, 5, 6, 7; DA3; DAM
 POET; DLB 5; EWL 3; MAL 5; MTCW
 1, 2; MTFW 2005; PFS 6, 17; RGAL 4

Boas, Franz 1858-1942 .... **TCLC 56**
 See also CA 181; CAAE 115

Bobette
 See Simenon, Georges (Jacques Christian)

Boccaccio, Giovanni 1313-1375 ... **CMLC 13,**
 57; SSC 10, 87
 See also EW 2; RGSF 2; RGWL 2, 3; TWA;
 WLIT 7

Bochco, Steven 1943- .... **CLC 35**
 See also AAYA 11, 71; CA 138; CAAE 124

Bode, Sigmund
 See O'Doherty, Brian

Bodel, Jean 1167(?)-1210 .... **CMLC 28**

Bodenheim, Maxwell 1892-1954 .... **TCLC 44**
 See also CA 187; CAAE 110; DLB 9, 45;
 MAL 5; RGAL 4

Bodenheimer, Maxwell
 See Bodenheim, Maxwell

Bodker, Cecil 1927-
 See Bodker, Cecil

Bodker, Cecil 1927- .... **CLC 21**
 See also CA 73-76; CANR 13, 44, 111;
 CLR 23; MAICYA 1, 2; SATA 14, 133

Boell, Heinrich (Theodor)
 1917-1985 ..... **CLC 2, 3, 6, 9, 11, 15, 27,**
 32, 72; SSC 23; WLC 1
 See Boll, Heinrich (Theodor)
 See also CA 21-24R; CAAS 116; CANR
 24; DA; DA3; DAB; DAC; DAM MST,
 NOV; DLB 69; DLBY 1985; MTCW 1,
 2; MTFW 2005; SSFS 20; TWA

Boerne, Alfred
 See Doeblin, Alfred

Boethius c. 480-c. 524 .... **CMLC 15**
 See also DLB 115; RGWL 2, 3; WLIT 8

Boff, Leonardo (Genezio Darci)
 1938- .... **CLC 70; HLC 1**
 See also CA 150; DAM MULT; HW 2

Bogan, Louise 1897-1970 .... **CLC 4, 39, 46,**
 93; PC 12
 See also AMWS 3; CA 73-76; CAAS 25-
 28R; CANR 33, 82; CP 1; DAM POET;
 DLB 45, 169; EWL 3; MAL 5; MBL;
 MTCW 1, 2; PFS 21; RGAL 4

Bogarde, Dirk
 See Van Den Bogarde, Derek Jules Gaspard
 Ulric Niven
 See also DLB 14

Bogosian, Eric 1953- .... **CLC 45, 141**
 See also CA 138; CAD; CANR 102, 148;
 CD 5, 6

Bograd, Larry 1953- .... **CLC 35**
 See also CA 93-96; CANR 57; SAAS 21;
 SATA 33, 89; WYA

Boiardo, Matteo Maria 1441-1494 .... **LC 6**

Boileau-Despreaux, Nicolas 1636-1711 . **LC 3**
 See also DLB 268; EW 3; GFL Beginnings
 to 1789; RGWL 2, 3

Boissard, Maurice
 See Leautaud, Paul

Bojer, Johan 1872-1959 .... **TCLC 64**
 See also CA 189; EWL 3

Bok, Edward W(illiam)
 1863-1930 .... **TCLC 101**
 See also CA 217; DLB 91; DLBD 16

Boker, George Henry 1823-1890 . **NCLC 125**
 See also RGAL 4

Boland, Eavan 1944- ... **CLC 40, 67, 113; PC**
 58
 See also BRWS 5; CA 207; 143, 207;
 CANR 61; CP 1, 6, 7; CWP; DAM POET;
 DLB 40; FW; MTCW 2; MTFW 2005;
 PFS 12, 22

Boll, Heinrich (Theodor) .... **TCLC 185**
 See Boell, Heinrich (Theodor)
 See also BPFB 1; CDWLB 2; DLB 329;
 EW 13; EWL 3; RGHL; RGSF 2; RGWL
 2, 3

Bolt, Lee
 See Faust, Frederick (Schiller)

Bolt, Robert (Oxton) 1924-1995 ...... **CLC 14;**
 TCLC 175
 See also CA 17-20R; CAAS 147; CANR
 35, 67; CBD; DAM DRAM; DFS 2; DLB
 13, 233; EWL 3; LAIT 1; MTCW 1

Bombal, Maria Luisa 1910-1980 .... **HLCS 1;**
 SSC 37
 See also CA 127; CANR 72; EWL 3; HW
 1; LAW; RGSF 2

Bombet, Louis-Alexandre-Cesar
 See Stendhal

Bomkauf
 See Kaufman, Bob (Garnell)

Bonaventura .... **NCLC 35**
 See also DLB 90

Bonaventure 1217(?)-1274 .... **CMLC 79**
 See also DLB 115; LMFS 1

Bond, Edward 1934- .... **CLC 4, 6, 13, 23**
 See also AAYA 50; BRWS 1; CA 25-28R;
 CANR 38, 67, 106; CBD; CD 5, 6; DAM
 DRAM; DFS 3, 8; DLB 13, 310; EWL 3;
 MTCW 1

Bonham, Frank 1914-1989 .... **CLC 12**
 See also AAYA 1, 70; BYA 1, 3; CA 9-12R;
 CANR 4, 36; JRDA; MAICYA 1, 2;
 SAAS 3; SATA 1, 49; SATA-Obit 62;
 TCWW 1, 2; YAW

Bonnefoy, Yves 1923- . **CLC 9, 15, 58; PC 58**
 See also CA 85-88; CANR 33, 75, 97, 136;
 CWW 2; DAM MST, POET; DLB 258;
 EWL 3; GFL 1789 to the Present; MTCW
 1, 2; MTFW 2005

Bonner, Marita . **HR 1:2; PC 72; TCLC 179**
 See Occomy, Marita (Odette) Bonner

Bonnin, Gertrude 1876-1938 .... **NNAL**
 See Zitkala-Sa
 See also CA 150; DAM MULT

Bontemps, Arna(ud Wendell)
 1902-1973 .. **BLC 1; CLC 1, 18; HR 1:2**
 See also BW 1; CA 1-4R; CAAS 41-44R;
 CANR 4, 35; CLR 6; CP 1; CWRI 5;
 DA3; DAM MULT, NOV, POET; DLB
 48, 51; JRDA; MAICYA 1, 2; MAL 5;
 MTCW 1, 2; SATA 2, 44; SATA-Obit 24;
 WCH; WP

Boot, William
 See Stoppard, Tom

Booth, Martin 1944-2004 .... **CLC 13**
 See also CA 188; 93-96, 188; 2; CAAS 223;
 CANR 92; CP 1, 2, 3, 4

Booth, Philip 1925- .... **CLC 23**
 See also CA 5-8R; CANR 5, 88; CP 1, 2, 3,
 4, 5, 6, 7; DLBY 1982

Booth, Wayne C. 1921-2005 .... **CLC 24**
 See also CA 1-4R; 5; CAAS 244; CANR 3,
 43, 117; DLB 67

Booth, Wayne Clayson
 See Booth, Wayne C.

Borchert, Wolfgang 1921-1947 .... **TCLC 5**
 See also CA 188; CAAE 104; DLB 69, 124;
 EWL 3

Borel, Petrus 1809-1859 .... **NCLC 41**
 See also DLB 119; GFL 1789 to the Present

Borges, Jorge Luis 1899-1986 .... **CLC 1, 2, 3,**
 4, 6, 8, 9, 10, 13, 19, 44, 48, 83; HLC 1;
 PC 22, 32; SSC 4, 41; TCLC 109;
 WLC 1
 See also AAYA 26; BPFB 1; CA 21-24R;
 CANR 19, 33, 75, 105, 133; CDWLB 3;
 DA; DA3; DAB; DAC; DAM MST,
 MULT; DLB 113, 283; DLBY 1986;
 DNFS 1, 2; EWL 3; HW 1, 2; LAW;
 LMFS 2; MSW; MTCW 1, 2; MTFW
 2005; RGHL; RGSF 2; RGWL 2, 3; SFW
 4; SSFS 17; TWA; WLIT 1

Borowski, Tadeusz 1922-1951 .... **SSC 48;**
 TCLC 9
 See also CA 154; CAAE 106; CDWLB 4;
 DLB 215; EWL 3; RGHL; RGSF 2;
 RGWL 3; SSFS 13

Borrow, George (Henry)
 1803-1881 .... **NCLC 9**
 See also BRWS 12; DLB 21, 55, 166

Bosch (Gavino), Juan 1909-2001 ..... **HLCS 1**
 See also CA 151; CAAS 204; DAM MST,
 MULT; DLB 145; HW 1, 2

Bosman, Herman Charles
 1905-1951 .... **TCLC 49**
 See Malan, Herman
 See also CA 160; DLB 225; RGSF 2

Bosschere, Jean de 1878(?)-1953 ... **TCLC 19**
 See also CA 186; CAAE 115

Boswell, James 1740-1795 ... **LC 4, 50; WLC**
 1
 See also BRW 3; CDBLB 1660-1789; DA;
 DAB; DAC; DAM MST; DLB 104, 142;
 TEA; WLIT 3

Bottomley, Gordon 1874-1948 ..... **TCLC 107**
 See also CA 192; CAAE 120; DLB 10

Bottoms, David 1949- .... **CLC 53**
 See also CA 105; CANR 22; CSW; DLB
 120; DLBY 1983

Boucicault, Dion 1820-1890 .... **NCLC 41**

Boucolon, Maryse
 See Conde, Maryse

Bourdieu, Pierre 1930-2002 .... **CLC 198**
 See also CA 130; CAAS 204

Bourget, Paul (Charles Joseph)
 1852-1935 .... **TCLC 12**
 See also CA 196; CAAE 107; DLB 123;
 GFL 1789 to the Present

Bourjaily, Vance (Nye) 1922- .... **CLC 8, 62**
 See also CA 1-4R; 1; CANR 2, 72; CN 1,
 2, 3, 4, 5, 6, 7; DLB 2, 143; MAL 5

Bourne, Randolph S(illiman)
 1886-1918 .... **TCLC 16**
 See also AMW; CA 155; CAAE 117; DLB
 63; MAL 5

Bova, Ben 1932- .... **CLC 45**
 See also AAYA 16; CA 5-8R; 18; CANR
 11, 56, 94, 111, 157; CLR 3, 96; DLBY
 1981; INT CANR-11; MAICYA 1, 2;
 MTCW 1; SATA 6, 68, 133; SFW 4

Bova, Benjamin William
 See Bova, Ben

Brown, Christy 1932-1981 .... **CLC 63**
See also BYA 13; CA 105; CAAS 104; CANR 72; DLB 14

Brown, Claude 1937-2002 ... **BLC 1; CLC 30**
See also AAYA 7; BW 1, 3; CA 73-76; CAAS 205; CANR 81; DAM MULT

Brown, Dan 1964- .... **CLC 209**
See also AAYA 55; CA 217; MTFW 2005

Brown, Dee 1908-2002 .... **CLC 18, 47**
See also AAYA 30; CA 13-16R; 6; CAAS 212; CANR 11, 45, 60, 150; CPW; CSW; DA3; DAM POP; DLBY 1980; LAIT 2; MTCW 1, 2; MTFW 2005; NCFS 5; SATA 5, 110; SATA-Obit 141; TCWW 1, 2

Brown, Dee Alexander
See Brown, Dee

Brown, George
See Wertmueller, Lina

Brown, George Douglas
1869-1902 .... **TCLC 28**
See Douglas, George
See also CA 162

Brown, George Mackay 1921-1996 ... **CLC 5, 48, 100**
See also BRWS 6; CA 21-24R; 6; CAAS 151; CANR 12, 37, 67; CN 1, 2, 3, 4, 5, 6; CP 1, 2, 3, 4, 5, 6; DLB 14, 27, 139, 271; MTCW 1; RGSF 2; SATA 35

Brown, Larry 1951-2004 .... **CLC 73**
See also CA 134; CAAE 130; CAAS 233; CANR 117, 145; CSW; DLB 234; INT CA-134

Brown, Moses
See Barrett, William (Christopher)

Brown, Rita Mae 1944- .... **CLC 18, 43, 79**
See also BPFB 1; CA 45-48; CANR 2, 11, 35, 62, 95, 138; CN 5, 6, 7; CPW; CSW; DA3; DAM NOV, POP; FW; INT CANR-11; MAL 5; MTCW 1, 2; MTFW 2005; NFS 9; RGAL 4; TUS

Brown, Roderick (Langmere) Haig-
See Haig-Brown, Roderick (Langmere)

Brown, Rosellen 1939- .... **CLC 32, 170**
See also CA 77-80; 10; CANR 14, 44, 98; CN 6, 7

Brown, Sterling Allen 1901-1989 ...... **BLC 1; CLC 1, 23, 59; HR 1:2; PC 55**
See also AFAW 1, 2; BW 1, 3; CA 85-88; CAAS 127; CANR 26; CP 3, 4; DA3; DAM MULT, POET; DLB 48, 51, 63; MAL 5; MTCW 1, 2; MTFW 2005; RGAL 4; WP

Brown, Will
See Ainsworth, William Harrison

Brown, William Hill 1765-1793 .... **LC 93**
See also DLB 37

Brown, William Larry
See Brown, Larry

Brown, William Wells 1815-1884 ...... **BLC 1; DC 1; NCLC 2, 89**
See also DAM MULT; DLB 3, 50, 183, 248; RGAL 4

Browne, (Clyde) Jackson 1948(?)- ... **CLC 21**
See also CA 120

Browne, Sir Thomas 1605-1682 .... **LC 111**
See also BRW 2; DLB 151

Browning, Robert 1812-1889 . **NCLC 19, 79; PC 2, 61; WLCS**
See also BRW 4; BRWC 2; BRWR 2; CD-BLB 1832-1890; CLR 97; DA; DA3; DAB; DAC; DAM MST, POET; DLB 32, 163; EXPP; LATS 1:1; PAB; PFS 1, 15; RGEL 2; TEA; WLIT 4; WP; YABC 1

Browning, Tod 1882-1962 .... **CLC 16**
See also CA 141; CAAS 117

Brownmiller, Susan 1935- .... **CLC 159**
See also CA 103; CANR 35, 75, 137; DAM NOV; FW; MTCW 1, 2; MTFW 2005

Brownson, Orestes Augustus
1803-1876 .... **NCLC 50**
See also DLB 1, 59, 73, 243

Bruccoli, Matthew J(oseph) 1931- ... **CLC 34**
See also CA 9-12R; CANR 7, 87; DLB 103

Bruce, Lenny .... **CLC 21**
See Schneider, Leonard Alfred

Bruchac, Joseph 1942- .... **NNAL**
See also AAYA 19; CA 33-36R; CANR 13, 47, 75, 94, 137, 161; CLR 46; CWRI 5; DAM MULT; JRDA; MAICYA 2; MAIC-YAS 1; MTCW 2; MTFW 2005; SATA 42, 89, 131, 176; SATA-Essay 176

Bruin, John
See Brutus, Dennis

Brulard, Henri
See Stendhal

Brulls, Christian
See Simenon, Georges (Jacques Christian)

Brunetto Latini c. 1220-1294 .... **CMLC 73**

Brunner, John (Kilian Houston)
1934-1995 .... **CLC 8, 10**
See also CA 1-4R; 8; CAAS 149; CANR 2, 37; CPW; DAM POP; DLB 261; MTCW 1, 2; SCFW 1, 2; SFW 4

Bruno, Giordano 1548-1600 .... **LC 27**
See also RGWL 2, 3

Brutus, Dennis 1924- ... **BLC 1; CLC 43; PC 24**
See also AFW; BW 2, 3; CA 49-52; 14; CANR 2, 27, 42, 81; CDWLB 3; CP 1, 2, 3, 4, 5, 6, 7; DAM MULT, POET; DLB 117, 225; EWL 3

Bryan, C(ourtlandt) D(ixon) B(arnes)
1936- .... **CLC 29**
See also CA 73-76; CANR 13, 68; DLB 185; INT CANR-13

Bryan, Michael
See Moore, Brian
See also CCA 1

Bryan, William Jennings
1860-1925 .... **TCLC 99**
See also DLB 303

Bryant, William Cullen 1794-1878 . **NCLC 6, 46; PC 20**
See also AMWS 1; CDALB 1640-1865; DA; DAB; DAC; DAM MST, POET; DLB 3, 43, 59, 189, 250; EXPP; PAB; RGAL 4; TUS

Bryusov, Valery Yakovlevich
1873-1924 .... **TCLC 10**
See also CA 155; CAAE 107; EWL 3; SFW 4

Buchan, John 1875-1940 .... **TCLC 41**
See also CA 145; CAAE 108; CMW 4; DAB; DAM POP; DLB 34, 70, 156; HGG; MSW; MTCW 2; RGEL 2; RHW; YABC 2

Buchanan, George 1506-1582 .... **LC 4**
See also DLB 132

Buchanan, Robert 1841-1901 .... **TCLC 107**
See also CA 179; DLB 18, 35

Buchheim, Lothar-Guenther
1918-2007 .... **CLC 6**
See also CA 85-88

Buchner, (Karl) Georg
1813-1837 .... **NCLC 26, 146**
See also CDWLB 2; DLB 133; EW 6; RGSF 2; RGWL 2, 3; TWA

Buchwald, Art 1925-2007 .... **CLC 33**
See also AITN 1; CA 5-8R; CANR 21, 67, 107; MTCW 1, 2; SATA 10

Buchwald, Arthur
See Buchwald, Art

Buck, Pearl S(ydenstricker)
1892-1973 .... **CLC 7, 11, 18, 127**
See also AAYA 42; AITN 1; AMWS 2; BPFB 1; CA 1-4R; CAAS 41-44R; CANR 1, 34; CDALBS; CN 1; DA; DA3; DAB;

DAC; DAM MST, NOV; DLB 9, 102, 329; EWL 3; LAIT 3; MAL 5; MTCW 1, 2; MTFW 2005; RGAL 4; RHW; SATA 1, 25; TUS

Buckler, Ernest 1908-1984 .... **CLC 13**
See also CA 11-12; CAAS 114; CAP 1; CCA 1; CN 1, 2, 3; DAC; DAM MST; DLB 68; SATA 47

Buckley, Christopher 1952- .... **CLC 165**
See also CA 139; CANR 119

Buckley, Christopher Taylor
See Buckley, Christopher

Buckley, Vincent (Thomas)
1925-1988 .... **CLC 57**
See also CA 101; CP 1, 2, 3, 4; DLB 289

Buckley, William F., Jr. 1925- ..... **CLC 7, 18, 37**
See also AITN 1; BPFB 1; CA 1-4R; CANR 1, 24, 53, 93, 133; CMW 4; CPW; DA3; DAM POP; DLB 137; DLBY 1980; INT CANR-24; MTCW 1, 2; MTFW 2005; TUS

Buechner, Frederick 1926- ..... **CLC 2, 4, 6, 9**
See also AMWS 12; BPFB 1; CA 13-16R; CANR 11, 39, 64, 114, 138; CN 1, 2, 3, 4, 5, 6, 7; DAM NOV; DLBY 1980; INT CANR-11; MAL 5; MTCW 1, 2; MTFW 2005; TCLE 1:1

Buell, John (Edward) 1927- .... **CLC 10**
See also CA 1-4R; CANR 71; DLB 53

Buero Vallejo, Antonio 1916-2000 ... **CLC 15, 46, 139, 226; DC 18**
See also CA 106; CAAS 189; CANR 24, 49, 75; CWW 2; DFS 11; EWL 3; HW 1; MTCW 1, 2

Bufalino, Gesualdo 1920-1996 .... **CLC 74**
See also CA 209; CWW 2; DLB 196

Bugayev, Boris Nikolayevich
1880-1934 .... **PC 11; TCLC 7**
See Bely, Andrey; Belyi, Andrei
See also CA 165; CAAE 104; MTCW 2; MTFW 2005

Bukowski, Charles 1920-1994 ... **CLC 2, 5, 9, 41, 82, 108; PC 18; SSC 45**
See also CA 17-20R; CAAS 144; CANR 40, 62, 105; CN 4, 5; CP 1, 2, 3, 4, 5; CPW; DA3; DAM NOV, POET; DLB 5, 130, 169; EWL 3; MAL 5; MTCW 1, 2; MTFW 2005

Bulgakov, Mikhail 1891-1940 .... **SSC 18; TCLC 2, 16, 159**
See also AAYA 74; BPFB 1; CA 152; CAAE 105; DAM DRAM, NOV; DLB 272; EWL 3; MTCW 2; MTFW 2005; NFS 8; RGSF 2; RGWL 2, 3; SFW 4; TWA

Bulgakov, Mikhail Afanasevich
See Bulgakov, Mikhail

Bulgya, Alexander Alexandrovich
1901-1956 .... **TCLC 53**
See Fadeev, Aleksandr Aleksandrovich; Fadeev, Alexandr Alexandrovich; Fadeyev, Alexander
See also CA 181; CAAE 117

Bullins, Ed 1935- ... **BLC 1; CLC 1, 5, 7; DC 6**
See also BW 2, 3; CA 49-52; 16; CAD; CANR 24, 46, 73, 134; CD 5, 6; DAM DRAM, MULT; DLB 7, 38, 249; EWL 3; MAL 5; MTCW 1, 2; MTFW 2005; RGAL 4

Bulosan, Carlos 1911-1956 .... **AAL**
See also CA 216; DLB 312; RGAL 4

Bulwer-Lytton, Edward (George Earle Lytton) 1803-1873 .... **NCLC 1, 45**
See also DLB 21; RGEL 2; SFW 4; SUFW 1; TEA

Bunin, Ivan
See Bunin, Ivan Alexeyevich

Caeiro, Alberto
See Pessoa, Fernando (Antonio Nogueira)

Caesar, Julius .... **CMLC 47**
See Julius Caesar
See also AW 1; RGWL 2, 3; WLIT 8

Cage, John (Milton), (Jr.)
1912-1992 .... **CLC 41; PC 58**
See also CA 13-16R; CAAS 169; CANR 9, 78; DLB 193; INT CANR-9; TCLE 1:1

Cahan, Abraham 1860-1951 .... **TCLC 71**
See also CA 154; CAAE 108; DLB 9, 25, 28; MAL 5; RGAL 4

Cain, G.
See Cabrera Infante, G.

Cain, Guillermo
See Cabrera Infante, G.

Cain, James M(allahan) 1892-1977 .. **CLC 3, 11, 28**
See also AITN 1; BPFB 1; CA 17-20R; CAAS 73-76; CANR 8, 34, 61; CMW 4; CN 1, 2; DLB 226; EWL 3; MAL 5; MSW; MTCW 1; RGAL 4

Caine, Hall 1853-1931 .... **TCLC 97**
See also RHW

Caine, Mark
See Raphael, Frederic (Michael)

Calasso, Roberto 1941- .... **CLC 81**
See also CA 143; CANR 89

Calderon de la Barca, Pedro
1600-1681 . **DC 3; HLCS 1; LC 23, 136**
See also DFS 23; EW 2; RGWL 2, 3; TWA

Caldwell, Erskine 1903-1987 .. **CLC 1, 8, 14, 50, 60; SSC 19; TCLC 117**
See also AITN 1; AMW; BPFB 1; CA 1-4R; 1; CAAS 121; CANR 2, 33; CN 1, 2, 3, 4; DA3; DAM NOV; DLB 9, 86; EWL 3; MAL 5; MTCW 1, 2; MTFW 2005; RGAL 4; RGSF 2; TUS

Caldwell, (Janet Miriam) Taylor (Holland)
1900-1985 .... **CLC 2, 28, 39**
See also BPFB 1; CA 5-8R; CAAS 116; CANR 5; DA3; DAM NOV, POP; DLBD 17; MTCW 2; RHW

Calhoun, John Caldwell
1782-1850 .... **NCLC 15**
See also DLB 3, 248

Calisher, Hortense 1911- ..... **CLC 2, 4, 8, 38, 134; SSC 15**
See also CA 1-4R; CANR 1, 22, 117; CN 1, 2, 3, 4, 5, 6, 7; DA3; DAM NOV; DLB 2, 218; INT CANR-22; MAL 5; MTCW 1, 2; MTFW 2005; RGAL 4; RGSF 2

Callaghan, Morley Edward
1903-1990 ..... **CLC 3, 14, 41, 65; TCLC 145**
See also CA 9-12R; CAAS 132; CANR 33, 73; CN 1, 2, 3, 4; DAC; DAM MST; DLB 68; EWL 3; MTCW 1, 2; MTFW 2005; RGEL 2; RGSF 2; SSFS 19

Callimachus c. 305B.C.-c.
240B.C. .... **CMLC 18**
See also AW 1; DLB 176; RGWL 2, 3

Calvin, Jean
See Calvin, John
See also DLB 327; GFL Beginnings to 1789

Calvin, John 1509-1564 .... **LC 37**
See Calvin, Jean

Calvino, Italo 1923-1985 .... **CLC 5, 8, 11, 22, 33, 39, 73; SSC 3, 48; TCLC 183**
See also AAYA 58; CA 85-88; CAAS 116; CANR 23, 61, 132; DAM NOV; DLB 196; EW 13; EWL 3; MTCW 1, 2; MTFW 2005; RGHL; RGSF 2; RGWL 2, 3; SFW 4; SSFS 12; WLIT 7

Camara Laye
See Laye, Camara
See also EWL 3

Camden, William 1551-1623 .... **LC 77**
See also DLB 172

Cameron, Carey 1952- .... **CLC 59**
See also CA 135

Cameron, Peter 1959- .... **CLC 44**
See also AMWS 12; CA 125; CANR 50, 117; DLB 234; GLL 2

Camoens, Luis Vaz de 1524(?)-1580
See Camoes, Luis de
See also EW 2

Camoes, Luis de 1524(?)-1580 . **HLCS 1; LC 62; PC 31**
See Camoens, Luis Vaz de
See also DLB 287; RGWL 2, 3

Campana, Dino 1885-1932 .... **TCLC 20**
See also CA 246; CAAE 117; DLB 114; EWL 3

Campanella, Tommaso 1568-1639 .... **LC 32**
See also RGWL 2, 3

Campbell, John W(ood, Jr.)
1910-1971 .... **CLC 32**
See also CA 21-22; CAAS 29-32R; CANR 34; CAP 2; DLB 8; MTCW 1; SCFW 1, 2; SFW 4

Campbell, Joseph 1904-1987 .... **CLC 69; TCLC 140**
See also AAYA 3, 66; BEST 89:2; CA 1-4R; CAAS 124; CANR 3, 28, 61, 107; DA3; MTCW 1, 2

Campbell, Maria 1940- .... **CLC 85; NNAL**
See also CA 102; CANR 54; CCA 1; DAC

Campbell, (John) Ramsey 1946- ..... **CLC 42; SSC 19**
See also AAYA 51; CA 228; 57-60, 228; CANR 7, 102; DLB 261; HGG; INT CANR-7; SUFW 1, 2

Campbell, (Ignatius) Roy (Dunnachie)
1901-1957 .... **TCLC 5**
See also AFW; CA 155; CAAE 104; DLB 20, 225; EWL 3; MTCW 2; RGEL 2

Campbell, Thomas 1777-1844 .... **NCLC 19**
See also DLB 93, 144; RGEL 2

Campbell, Wilfred .... **TCLC 9**
See Campbell, William

Campbell, William 1858(?)-1918
See Campbell, Wilfred
See also CAAE 106; DLB 92

Campbell, William Edward March
1893-1954
See March, William
See also CAAE 108

Campion, Jane 1954- .... **CLC 95, 229**
See also AAYA 33; CA 138; CANR 87

Campion, Thomas 1567-1620 .... **LC 78**
See also CDBLB Before 1660; DAM POET; DLB 58, 172; RGEL 2

Camus, Albert 1913-1960 ...... **CLC 1, 2, 4, 9, 11, 14, 32, 63, 69, 124; DC 2; SSC 9, 76; WLC 1**
See also AAYA 36; AFW; BPFB 1; CA 89-92; CANR 131; DA; DA3; DAB; DAC; DAM DRAM, MST, NOV; DLB 72, 321, 329; EW 13; EWL 3; EXPN; EXPS; GFL 1789 to the Present; LATS 1:2; LMFS 2; MTCW 1, 2; MTFW 2005; NFS 6, 16; RGHL; RGSF 2; RGWL 2, 3; SSFS 4; TWA

Canby, Vincent 1924-2000 .... **CLC 13**
See also CA 81-84; CAAS 191

Cancale
See Desnos, Robert

Canetti, Elias 1905-1994 .. **CLC 3, 14, 25, 75, 86; TCLC 157**
See also CA 21-24R; CAAS 146; CANR 23, 61, 79; CDWLB 2; CWW 2; DA3; DLB 85, 124, 329; EW 12; EWL 3; MTCW 1, 2; MTFW 2005; RGWL 2, 3; TWA

Canfield, Dorothea F.
See Fisher, Dorothy (Frances) Canfield

Canfield, Dorothea Frances
See Fisher, Dorothy (Frances) Canfield

Canfield, Dorothy
See Fisher, Dorothy (Frances) Canfield

Canin, Ethan 1960- .... **CLC 55; SSC 70**
See also CA 135; CAAE 131; MAL 5

Cankar, Ivan 1876-1918 .... **TCLC 105**
See also CDWLB 4; DLB 147; EWL 3

Cannon, Curt
See Hunter, Evan

Cao, Lan 1961- .... **CLC 109**
See also CA 165

Cape, Judith
See Page, P(atricia) K(athleen)
See also CCA 1

Capek, Karel 1890-1938 .... **DC 1; SSC 36; TCLC 6, 37; WLC 1**
See also CA 140; CAAE 104; CDWLB 4; DA; DA3; DAB; DAC; DAM DRAM, MST, NOV; DFS 7, 11; DLB 215; EW 10; EWL 3; MTCW 2; MTFW 2005; RGSF 2; RGWL 2, 3; SCFW 1, 2; SFW 4

Capella, Martianus fl. 4th cent. - .. **CMLC 84**

Capote, Truman 1924-1984 . **CLC 1, 3, 8, 13, 19, 34, 38, 58; SSC 2, 47, 93; TCLC 164; WLC 1**
See also AAYA 61; AMWS 3; BPFB 1; CA 5-8R; CAAS 113; CANR 18, 62; CDALB 1941-1968; CN 1, 2, 3; CPW; DA; DA3; DAB; DAC; DAM MST, NOV, POP; DLB 2, 185, 227; DLBY 1980, 1984; EWL 3; EXPS; GLL 1; LAIT 3; MAL 5; MTCW 1, 2; MTFW 2005; NCFS 2; RGAL 4; RGSF 2; SATA 91; SSFS 2; TUS

Capra, Frank 1897-1991 .... **CLC 16**
See also AAYA 52; CA 61-64; CAAS 135

Caputo, Philip 1941- .... **CLC 32**
See also AAYA 60; CA 73-76; CANR 40, 135; YAW

Caragiale, Ion Luca 1852-1912 ...... **TCLC 76**
See also CA 157

Card, Orson Scott 1951- .... **CLC 44, 47, 50**
See also AAYA 11, 42; BPFB 1; BYA 5, 8; CA 102; CANR 27, 47, 73, 102, 106, 133; CLR 116; CPW; DA3; DAM POP; FANT; INT CANR-27; MTCW 1, 2; MTFW 2005; NFS 5; SATA 83, 127; SCFW 2; SFW 4; SUFW 2; YAW

Cardenal, Ernesto 1925- .... **CLC 31, 161; HLC 1; PC 22**
See also CA 49-52; CANR 2, 32, 66, 138; CWW 2; DAM MULT, POET; DLB 290; EWL 3; HW 1, 2; LAWS 1; MTCW 1, 2; MTFW 2005; RGWL 2, 3

Cardinal, Marie 1929-2001 .... **CLC 189**
See also CA 177; CWW 2; DLB 83; FW

Cardozo, Benjamin N(athan)
1870-1938 .... **TCLC 65**
See also CA 164; CAAE 117

Carducci, Giosue (Alessandro Giuseppe)
1835-1907 .... **PC 46; TCLC 32**
See also CA 163; DLB 329; EW 7; RGWL 2, 3

Carew, Thomas 1595(?)-1640 . **LC 13; PC 29**
See also BRW 2; DLB 126; PAB; RGEL 2

Carey, Ernestine Gilbreth
1908-2006 .... **CLC 17**
See also CA 5-8R; CAAS 254; CANR 71; SATA 2

Carey, Peter 1943- .... **CLC 40, 55, 96, 183**
See also BRWS 12; CA 127; CAAE 123; CANR 53, 76, 117, 157; CN 4, 5, 6, 7; DLB 289, 326; EWL 3; INT CA-127; MTCW 1, 2; MTFW 2005; RGSF 2; SATA 94

Carleton, William 1794-1869 .... **NCLC 3**
See also DLB 159; RGEL 2; RGSF 2

Ciardi, John (Anthony) 1916-1986 . **CLC 10, 40, 44, 129; PC 69**
See also CA 5-8R; 2; CAAS 118; CANR 5, 33; CLR 19; CP 1, 2, 3, 4; CWRI 5; DAM POET; DLB 5; DLBY 1986; INT CANR-5; MAICYA 1, 2; MAL 5; MTCW 1, 2; MTFW 2005; RGAL 4; SAAS 26; SATA 1, 65; SATA-Obit 46

Cibber, Colley 1671-1757 .... **LC 66**
See also DLB 84; RGEL 2

Cicero, Marcus Tullius
106B.C.-43B.C. .... **CMLC 3, 81**
See also AW 1; CDWLB 1; DLB 211; RGWL 2, 3; WLIT 8

Cimino, Michael 1943- .... **CLC 16**
See also CA 105

Cioran, E(mil) M. 1911-1995 .... **CLC 64**
See also CA 25-28R; CAAS 149; CANR 91; DLB 220; EWL 3

Cisneros, Sandra 1954- .... **CLC 69, 118, 193; HLC 1; PC 52; SSC 32, 72**
See also AAYA 9, 53; AMWS 7; CA 131; CANR 64, 118; CN 7; CWP; DA3; DAM MULT; DLB 122, 152; EWL 3; EXPN; FL 1:5; FW; HW 1, 2; LAIT 5; LATS 1:2; LLW; MAICYA 2; MAL 5; MTCW 2; MTFW 2005; NFS 2; PFS 19; RGAL 4; RGSF 2; SSFS 3, 13; WLIT 1; YAW

Cixous, Helene 1937- .... **CLC 92**
See also CA 126; CANR 55, 123; CWW 2; DLB 83, 242; EWL 3; FL 1:5; FW; GLL 2; MTCW 1, 2; MTFW 2005; TWA

Clair, Rene .... **CLC 20**
See Chomette, Rene Lucien

Clampitt, Amy 1920-1994 ... **CLC 32; PC 19**
See also AMWS 9; CA 110; CAAS 146; CANR 29, 79; CP 4, 5; DLB 105; MAL 5

Clancy, Thomas L., Jr. 1947-
See Clancy, Tom
See also CA 131; CAAE 125; CANR 62, 105; DA3; INT CA-131; MTCW 1, 2; MTFW 2005

Clancy, Tom .... **CLC 45, 112**
See Clancy, Thomas L., Jr.
See also AAYA 9, 51; BEST 89:1, 90:1; BPFB 1; BYA 10, 11; CANR 132; CMW 4; CPW; DAM NOV, POP; DLB 227

Clare, John 1793-1864 .. **NCLC 9, 86; PC 23**
See also BRWS 11; DAB; DAM POET; DLB 55, 96; RGEL 2

Clarin
See Alas (y Urena), Leopoldo (Enrique Garcia)

Clark, Al C.
See Goines, Donald

Clark, Brian (Robert)
See Clark, (Robert) Brian
See also CD 6

Clark, (Robert) Brian 1932- .... **CLC 29**
See Clark, Brian (Robert)
See also CA 41-44R; CANR 67; CBD; CD 5

Clark, Curt
See Westlake, Donald E.

Clark, Eleanor 1913-1996 .... **CLC 5, 19**
See also CA 9-12R; CAAS 151; CANR 41; CN 1, 2, 3, 4, 5, 6; DLB 6

Clark, J. P.
See Clark Bekederemo, J.P.
See also CDWLB 3; DLB 117

Clark, John Pepper
See Clark Bekederemo, J.P.
See also AFW; CD 5; CP 1, 2, 3, 4, 5, 6, 7; RGEL 2

Clark, Kenneth (Mackenzie)
1903-1983 .... **TCLC 147**
See also CA 93-96; CAAS 109; CANR 36; MTCW 1, 2; MTFW 2005

Clark, M. R.
See Clark, Mavis Thorpe

Clark, Mavis Thorpe 1909-1999 ...... **CLC 12**
See also CA 57-60; CANR 8, 37, 107; CLR 30; CWRI 5; MAICYA 1, 2; SAAS 5; SATA 8, 74

Clark, Walter Van Tilburg
1909-1971 .... **CLC 28**
See also CA 9-12R; CAAS 33-36R; CANR 63, 113; CN 1; DLB 9, 206; LAIT 2; MAL 5; RGAL 4; SATA 8; TCWW 1, 2

Clark Bekederemo, J.P. 1935- . **BLC 1; CLC 38; DC 5**
See Bekederemo, J. P. Clark; Clark, J. P.; Clark, John Pepper
See also BW 1; CA 65-68; CANR 16, 72; DAM DRAM, MULT; DFS 13; EWL 3; MTCW 2; MTFW 2005

Clarke, Arthur C. 1917- .... **CLC 1, 4, 13, 18, 35, 136; SSC 3**
See also AAYA 4, 33; BPFB 1; BYA 13; CA 1-4R; CANR 2, 28, 55, 74, 130; CLR 119; CN 1, 2, 3, 4, 5, 6, 7; CPW; DA3; DAM POP; DLB 261; JRDA; LAIT 5; MAICYA 1, 2; MTCW 1, 2; MTFW 2005; SATA 13, 70, 115; SCFW 1, 2; SFW 4; SSFS 4, 18; TCLE 1:1; YAW

Clarke, Austin 1896-1974 .... **CLC 6, 9**
See also CA 29-32; CAAS 49-52; CAP 2; CP 1, 2; DAM POET; DLB 10, 20; EWL 3; RGEL 2

Clarke, Austin C. 1934- . **BLC 1; CLC 8, 53; SSC 45**
See also BW 1; CA 25-28R; 16; CANR 14, 32, 68, 140; CN 1, 2, 3, 4, 5, 6, 7; DAC; DAM MULT; DLB 53, 125; DNFS 2; MTCW 2; MTFW 2005; RGSF 2

Clarke, Gillian 1937- .... **CLC 61**
See also CA 106; CP 3, 4, 5, 6, 7; CWP; DLB 40

Clarke, Marcus (Andrew Hislop)
1846-1881 .... **NCLC 19; SSC 94**
See also DLB 230; RGEL 2; RGSF 2

Clarke, Shirley 1925-1997 .... **CLC 16**
See also CA 189

Clash, The
See Headon, (Nicky) Topper; Jones, Mick; Simonon, Paul; Strummer, Joe

Claudel, Paul (Louis Charles Marie)
1868-1955 .... **TCLC 2, 10**
See also CA 165; CAAE 104; DLB 192, 258, 321; EW 8; EWL 3; GFL 1789 to the Present; RGWL 2, 3; TWA

Claudian 370(?)-404(?) .... **CMLC 46**
See also RGWL 2, 3

Claudius, Matthias 1740-1815 .... **NCLC 75**
See also DLB 97

Clavell, James 1925-1994 .... **CLC 6, 25, 87**
See also BPFB 1; CA 25-28R; CAAS 146; CANR 26, 48; CN 5; CPW; DA3; DAM NOV, POP; MTCW 1, 2; MTFW 2005; NFS 10; RHW

Clayman, Gregory .... **CLC 65**

Cleaver, (Leroy) Eldridge
1935-1998 .... **BLC 1; CLC 30, 119**
See also BW 1, 3; CA 21-24R; CAAS 167; CANR 16, 75; DA3; DAM MULT; MTCW 2; YAW

Cleese, John (Marwood) 1939- .... **CLC 21**
See Monty Python
See also CA 116; CAAE 112; CANR 35; MTCW 1

Cleishbotham, Jebediah
See Scott, Sir Walter

Cleland, John 1710-1789 .... **LC 2, 48**
See also DLB 39; RGEL 2

Clemens, Samuel Langhorne 1835-1910
See Twain, Mark
See also CA 135; CAAE 104; CDALB 1865-1917; DA; DA3; DAB; DAC; DAM

MST, NOV; DLB 12, 23, 64, 74, 186, 189; JRDA; LMFS 1; MAICYA 1, 2; NCFS 4; NFS 20; SATA 100; YABC 2

Clement of Alexandria
150(?)-215(?) .... **CMLC 41**

Cleophil
See Congreve, William

Clerihew, E.
See Bentley, E(dmund) C(lerihew)

Clerk, N. W.
See Lewis, C.S.

Cleveland, John 1613-1658 .... **LC 106**
See also DLB 126; RGEL 2

Cliff, Jimmy .... **CLC 21**
See Chambers, James
See also CA 193

Cliff, Michelle 1946- .... **BLCS; CLC 120**
See also BW 2; CA 116; CANR 39, 72; CD-WLB 3; DLB 157; FW; GLL 2

Clifford, Lady Anne 1590-1676 .... **LC 76**
See also DLB 151

Clifton, Lucille 1936- ... **BLC 1; CLC 19, 66, 162; PC 17**
See also AFAW 2; BW 2, 3; CA 49-52; CANR 2, 24, 42, 76, 97, 138; CLR 5; CP 2, 3, 4, 5, 6, 7; CSW; CWP; CWRI 5; DA3; DAM MULT, POET; DLB 5, 41; EXPP; MAICYA 1, 2; MTCW 1, 2; MTFW 2005; PFS 1, 14; SATA 20, 69, 128; WP

Clinton, Dirk
See Silverberg, Robert

Clough, Arthur Hugh 1819-1861 .. **NCLC 27, 163**
See also BRW 5; DLB 32; RGEL 2

Clutha, Janet Paterson Frame 1924-2004
See Frame, Janet
See also CA 1-4R; CAAS 224; CANR 2, 36, 76, 135; MTCW 1, 2; SATA 119

Clyne, Terence
See Blatty, William Peter

Cobalt, Martin
See Mayne, William (James Carter)

Cobb, Irvin S(hrewsbury)
1876-1944 .... **TCLC 77**
See also CA 175; DLB 11, 25, 86

Cobbett, William 1763-1835 .... **NCLC 49**
See also DLB 43, 107, 158; RGEL 2

Coburn, D(onald) L(ee) 1938- .... **CLC 10**
See also CA 89-92; DFS 23

Cocteau, Jean 1889-1963 ... **CLC 1, 8, 15, 16, 43; DC 17; TCLC 119; WLC 2**
See also AAYA 74; CA 25-28; CANR 40; CAP 2; DA; DA3; DAB; DAC; DAM DRAM, MST, NOV; DLB 65, 258, 321; EW 10; EWL 3; GFL 1789 to the Present; MTCW 1, 2; RGWL 2, 3; TWA

Cocteau, Jean Maurice Eugene Clement
See Cocteau, Jean

Codrescu, Andrei 1946- .... **CLC 46, 121**
See also CA 33-36R; 19; CANR 13, 34, 53, 76, 125; CN 7; DA3; DAM POET; MAL 5; MTCW 2; MTFW 2005

Coe, Max
See Bourne, Randolph S(illiman)

Coe, Tucker
See Westlake, Donald E.

Coen, Ethan 1958- .... **CLC 108**
See also AAYA 54; CA 126; CANR 85

Coen, Joel 1955- .... **CLC 108**
See also AAYA 54; CA 126; CANR 119

The Coen Brothers
See Coen, Ethan; Coen, Joel

Coetzee, J.M. 1940- ..... **CLC 23, 33, 66, 117, 161, 162**
See also AAYA 37; AFW; BRWS 6; CA 77-80; CANR 41, 54, 74, 114, 133; CN 4, 5, 6, 7; DA3; DAM NOV; DLB 225, 326,

Currie, Ellen 19(?)- .... **CLC 44**

Curtin, Philip
   See Lowndes, Marie Adelaide (Belloc)

Curtin, Phillip
   See Lowndes, Marie Adelaide (Belloc)

Curtis, Price
   See Ellison, Harlan

Cusanus, Nicolaus 1401-1464 .... **LC 80**
   See Nicholas of Cusa

Cutrate, Joe
   See Spiegelman, Art

Cynewulf c. 770- .... **CMLC 23**
   See also DLB 146; RGEL 2

Cyrano de Bergerac, Savinien de
   1619-1655 .... **LC 65**
   See also DLB 268; GFL Beginnings to
   1789; RGWL 2, 3

Cyril of Alexandria c. 375-c. 430 . **CMLC 59**

Czaczkes, Shmuel Yosef Halevi
   See Agnon, S(hmuel) Y(osef Halevi)

Dabrowska, Maria (Szumska)
   1889-1965 .... **CLC 15**
   See also CA 106; CDWLB 4; DLB 215;
   EWL 3

Dabydeen, David 1955- .... **CLC 34**
   See also BW 1; CA 125; CANR 56, 92; CN
   6, 7; CP 5, 6, 7

Dacey, Philip 1939- .... **CLC 51**
   See also CA 231; 37-40R, 231; 17; CANR
   14, 32, 64; CP 4, 5, 6, 7; DLB 105

Dacre, Charlotte c. 1772-1825(?) . **NCLC 151**

Dafydd ap Gwilym c. 1320-c. 1380 ..... **PC 56**

Dagerman, Stig (Halvard)
   1923-1954 .... **TCLC 17**
   See also CA 155; CAAE 117; DLB 259;
   EWL 3

D'Aguiar, Fred 1960- .... **CLC 145**
   See also CA 148; CANR 83, 101; CN 7;
   CP 5, 6, 7; DLB 157; EWL 3

Dahl, Roald 1916-1990 ...... **CLC 1, 6, 18, 79;**
   TCLC 173
   See also AAYA 15; BPFB 1; BRWS 4; BYA
   5; CA 1-4R; CAAS 133; CANR 6, 32,
   37, 62; CLR 1, 7, 41, 111; CN 1, 2, 3, 4;
   CPW; DA3; DAB; DAC; DAM MST,
   NOV, POP; DLB 139, 255; HGG; JRDA;
   MAICYA 1, 2; MTCW 1, 2; MTFW 2005;
   RGSF 2; SATA 1, 26, 73; SATA-Obit 65;
   SSFS 4; TEA; YAW

Dahlberg, Edward 1900-1977 .. **CLC 1, 7, 14**
   See also CA 9-12R; CAAS 69-72; CANR
   31, 62; CN 1, 2; DLB 48; MAL 5; MTCW
   1; RGAL 4

Daitch, Susan 1954- .... **CLC 103**
   See also CA 161

Dale, Colin .... **TCLC 18**
   See Lawrence, T(homas) E(dward)

Dale, George E.
   See Asimov, Isaac

d'Alembert, Jean Le Rond
   1717-1783 .... **LC 126**

Dalton, Roque 1935-1975(?) ..... **HLCS 1; PC**
   36
   See also CA 176; DLB 283; HW 2

Daly, Elizabeth 1878-1967 .... **CLC 52**
   See also CA 23-24; CAAS 25-28R; CANR
   60; CAP 2; CMW 4

Daly, Mary 1928- .... **CLC 173**
   See also CA 25-28R; CANR 30, 62; FW;
   GLL 1; MTCW 1

Daly, Maureen 1921-2006 .... **CLC 17**
   See also AAYA 5, 58; BYA 6; CAAS 253;
   CANR 37, 83, 108; CLR 96; JRDA; MAI-
   CYA 1, 2; SAAS 1; SATA 2, 129; SATA-
   Obit 176; WYA; YAW

Damas, Leon-Gontran 1912-1978 .... **CLC 84**
   See also BW 1; CA 125; CAAS 73-76;
   EWL 3

Dana, Richard Henry Sr.
   1787-1879 .... **NCLC 53**

Daniel, Samuel 1562(?)-1619 .... **LC 24**
   See also DLB 62; RGEL 2

Daniels, Brett
   See Adler, Renata

Dannay, Frederic 1905-1982 .... **CLC 11**
   See Queen, Ellery
   See also CA 1-4R; CAAS 107; CANR 1,
   39; CMW 4; DAM POP; DLB 137;
   MTCW 1

D'Annunzio, Gabriele 1863-1938 ... **TCLC 6,**
   40
   See also CA 155; CAAE 104; EW 8; EWL
   3; RGWL 2, 3; TWA; WLIT 7

Danois, N. le
   See Gourmont, Remy(-Marie-Charles) de

Dante 1265-1321 .... **CMLC 3, 18, 39, 70; PC**
   21; WLCS
   See Alighieri, Dante
   See also DA; DA3; DAB; DAC; DAM
   MST, POET; EFS 1; EW 1; LAIT 1;
   RGWL 2, 3; TWA; WP

d'Antibes, Germain
   See Simenon, Georges (Jacques Christian)

Danticat, Edwidge 1969- ... **CLC 94, 139, 228**
   See also AAYA 29; CA 192; 152, 192;
   CANR 73, 129; CN 7; DNFS 1; EXPS;
   LATS 1:2; MTCW 2; MTFW 2005; SSFS
   1; YAW

Danvers, Dennis 1947- .... **CLC 70**

Danziger, Paula 1944-2004 .... **CLC 21**
   See also AAYA 4, 36; BYA 6, 7, 14; CA
   115; CAAE 112; CAAS 229; CANR 37,
   132; CLR 20; JRDA; MAICYA 1, 2;
   MTFW 2005; SATA 36, 63, 102, 149;
   SATA-Brief 30; SATA-Obit 155; WYA;
   YAW

Da Ponte, Lorenzo 1749-1838 .... **NCLC 50**

d'Aragona, Tullia 1510(?)-1556 .... **LC 121**

Dario, Ruben 1867-1916 .... **HLC 1; PC 15;**
   TCLC 4
   See also CA 131; CANR 81; DAM MULT;
   DLB 290; EWL 3; HW 1, 2; LAW;
   MTCW 1, 2; MTFW 2005; RGWL 2, 3

Darley, George 1795-1846 .... **NCLC 2**
   See also DLB 96; RGEL 2

Darrow, Clarence (Seward)
   1857-1938 .... **TCLC 81**
   See also CA 164; DLB 303

Darwin, Charles 1809-1882 .... **NCLC 57**
   See also BRWS 7; DLB 57, 166; LATS 1:1;
   RGEL 2; TEA; WLIT 4

Darwin, Erasmus 1731-1802 .... **NCLC 106**
   See also DLB 93; RGEL 2

Daryush, Elizabeth 1887-1977 ...... **CLC 6, 19**
   See also CA 49-52; CANR 3, 81; DLB 20

Das, Kamala 1934- .... **CLC 191; PC 43**
   See also CA 101; CANR 27, 59; CP 1, 2, 3,
   4, 5, 6, 7; CWP; DLB 323; FW

Dasgupta, Surendranath
   1887-1952 .... **TCLC 81**
   See also CA 157

Dashwood, Edmee Elizabeth Monica de la
   Pasture 1890-1943
   See Delafield, E. M.
   See also CA 154; CAAE 119

da Silva, Antonio Jose
   1705-1739 .... **NCLC 114**

Daudet, (Louis Marie) Alphonse
   1840-1897 .... **NCLC 1**
   See also DLB 123; GFL 1789 to the Present;
   RGSF 2

Daudet, Alphonse Marie Leon
   1867-1942 .... **SSC 94**
   See also CA 217

d'Aulnoy, Marie-Catherine c.
   1650-1705 .... **LC 100**

Daumal, Rene 1908-1944 .... **TCLC 14**
   See also CA 247; CAAE 114; EWL 3

Davenant, William 1606-1668 .... **LC 13**
   See also DLB 58, 126; RGEL 2

Davenport, Guy (Mattison, Jr.)
   1927-2005 .... **CLC 6, 14, 38; SSC 16**
   See also CA 33-36R; CAAS 235; CANR
   23, 73; CN 3, 4, 5, 6; CSW; DLB 130

David, Robert
   See Nezval, Vitezslav

Davidson, Avram (James) 1923-1993
   See Queen, Ellery
   See also CA 101; CAAS 171; CANR 26;
   DLB 8; FANT; SFW 4; SUFW 1, 2

Davidson, Donald (Grady)
   1893-1968 .... **CLC 2, 13, 19**
   See also CA 5-8R; CAAS 25-28R; CANR
   4, 84; DLB 45

Davidson, Hugh
   See Hamilton, Edmond

Davidson, John 1857-1909 .... **TCLC 24**
   See also CA 217; CAAE 118; DLB 19;
   RGEL 2

Davidson, Sara 1943- .... **CLC 9**
   See also CA 81-84; CANR 44, 68; DLB
   185

Davie, Donald (Alfred) 1922-1995 .... **CLC 5,**
   8, 10, 31; PC 29
   See also BRWS 6; CA 1-4R; 3; CAAS 149;
   CANR 1, 44; CP 1, 2, 3, 4, 5, 6; DLB 27;
   MTCW 1; RGEL 2

Davie, Elspeth 1918-1995 .... **SSC 52**
   See also CA 126; CAAE 120; CAAS 150;
   CANR 141; DLB 139

Davies, Ray(mond Douglas) 1944- ... **CLC 21**
   See also CA 146; CAAE 116; CANR 92

Davies, Rhys 1901-1978 .... **CLC 23**
   See also CA 9-12R; CAAS 81-84; CANR
   4; CN 1, 2; DLB 139, 191

Davies, Robertson 1913-1995 .. **CLC 2, 7, 13,**
   25, 42, 75, 91; WLC 2
   See Marchbanks, Samuel
   See also BEST 89:2; BPFB 1; CA 33-36R;
   CAAS 150; CANR 17, 42, 103; CN 1, 2,
   3, 4, 5, 6; CPW; DA; DA3; DAB; DAC;
   DAM MST, NOV, POP; DLB 68; EWL 3;
   HGG; INT CANR-17; MTCW 1, 2;
   MTFW 2005; RGEL 2; TWA

Davies, Sir John 1569-1626 .... **LC 85**
   See also DLB 172

Davies, Walter C.
   See Kornbluth, C(yril) M.

Davies, William Henry 1871-1940 ... **TCLC 5**
   See also BRWS 11; CA 179; CAAE 104;
   DLB 19, 174; EWL 3; RGEL 2

Davies, William Robertson
   See Davies, Robertson

Da Vinci, Leonardo 1452-1519 ..... **LC 12, 57,**
   60
   See also AAYA 40

Davis, Angela (Yvonne) 1944- .... **CLC 77**
   See also BW 2, 3; CA 57-60; CANR 10,
   81; CSW; DA3; DAM MULT; FW

Davis, B. Lynch
   See Bioy Casares, Adolfo; Borges, Jorge
   Luis

Davis, Frank Marshall 1905-1987 ...... **BLC 1**
   See also BW 2, 3; CA 125; CAAS 123;
   CANR 42, 80; DAM MULT; DLB 51

Davis, Gordon
   See Hunt, E. Howard

Davis, H(arold) L(enoir) 1896-1960 . **CLC 49**
   See also ANW; CA 178; CAAS 89-92; DLB
   9, 206; SATA 114; TCWW 1, 2

Davis, Hart
   See Poniatowska, Elena

192; EW 6; GFL 1789 to the Present;
LAIT 1, 2; NFS 14, 19; RGWL 2, 3;
SATA 18; TWA; WCH

Dumas, Alexandre (fils) 1824-1895 ...... **DC 1;
NCLC 9**
See also DLB 192; GFL 1789 to the Present;
RGWL 2, 3

Dumas, Claudine
See Malzberg, Barry N(athaniel)

Dumas, Henry L. 1934-1968 .... **CLC 6, 62**
See also BW 1; CA 85-88; DLB 41; RGAL
4

du Maurier, Daphne 1907-1989 .. **CLC 6, 11,
59; SSC 18**
See also AAYA 37; BPFB 1; BRWS 3; CA
5-8R; CAAS 128; CANR 6, 55; CMW 4;
CN 1, 2, 3, 4; CPW; DA3; DAB; DAC;
DAM MST, POP; DLB 191; GL 2; HGG;
LAIT 3; MSW; MTCW 1, 2; NFS 12;
RGEL 2; RGSF 2; RHW; SATA 27;
SATA-Obit 60; SSFS 14, 16; TEA

Du Maurier, George 1834-1896 ..... **NCLC 86**
See also DLB 153, 178; RGEL 2

Dunbar, Paul Laurence 1872-1906 ... **BLC 1;
PC 5; SSC 8; TCLC 2, 12; WLC 2**
See also AAYA 75; AFAW 1, 2; AMWS 2;
BW 1, 3; CA 124; CAAE 104; CANR 79;
CDALB 1865-1917; DA; DA3; DAC;
DAM MST, MULT, POET; DLB 50, 54,
78; EXPP; MAL 5; RGAL 4; SATA 34

Dunbar, William 1460(?)-1520(?) .... **LC 20;
PC 67**
See also BRWS 8; DLB 132, 146; RGEL 2

Dunbar-Nelson, Alice .... **HR 1:2**
See Nelson, Alice Ruth Moore Dunbar

Duncan, Dora Angela
See Duncan, Isadora

Duncan, Isadora 1877(?)-1927 .... **TCLC 68**
See also CA 149; CAAE 118

Duncan, Lois 1934- .... **CLC 26**
See also AAYA 4, 34; BYA 6, 8; CA 1-4R;
CANR 2, 23, 36, 111; CLR 29; JRDA;
MAICYA 1, 2; MAICYAS 1; MTFW
2005; SAAS 2; SATA 1, 36, 75, 133, 141;
SATA-Essay 141; WYA; YAW

Duncan, Robert 1919-1988 ... **CLC 1, 2, 4, 7,
15, 41, 55; PC 2, 75**
See also BG 1:2; CA 9-12R; CAAS 124;
CANR 28, 62; CP 1, 2, 3, 4; DAM POET;
DLB 5, 16, 193; EWL 3; MAL 5; MTCW
1, 2; MTFW 2005; PFS 13; RGAL 4; WP

Duncan, Sara Jeannette
1861-1922 .... **TCLC 60**
See also CA 157; DLB 92

Dunlap, William 1766-1839 .... **NCLC 2**
See also DLB 30, 37, 59; RGAL 4

Dunn, Douglas (Eaglesham) 1942- .... **CLC 6,
40**
See also BRWS 10; CA 45-48; CANR 2,
33, 126; CP 1, 2, 3, 4, 5, 6, 7; DLB 40;
MTCW 1

Dunn, Katherine 1945- .... **CLC 71**
See also CA 33-36R; CANR 72; HGG;
MTCW 2; MTFW 2005

Dunn, Stephen 1939- .... **CLC 36, 206**
See also AMWS 11; CA 33-36R; CANR
12, 48, 53, 105; CP 3, 4, 5, 6, 7; DLB
105; PFS 21

Dunn, Stephen Elliott
See Dunn, Stephen

Dunne, Finley Peter 1867-1936 ...... **TCLC 28**
See also CA 178; CAAE 108; DLB 11, 23;
RGAL 4

Dunne, John Gregory 1932-2003 ..... **CLC 28**
See also CA 25-28R; CAAS 222; CANR
14, 50; CN 5, 6, 7; DLBY 1980

Dunsany, Lord .... **TCLC 2, 59**
See Dunsany, Edward John Moreton Drax
Plunkett
See also DLB 77, 153, 156, 255; FANT;
IDTP; RGEL 2; SFW 4; SUFW 1

**Dunsany, Edward John Moreton Drax
Plunkett** 1878-1957
See Dunsany, Lord
See also CA 148; CAAE 104; DLB 10;
MTCW 2

Duns Scotus, John 1266(?)-1308 ... **CMLC 59**
See also DLB 115

du Perry, Jean
See Simenon, Georges (Jacques Christian)

Durang, Christopher 1949- .... **CLC 27, 38**
See also CA 105; CAD; CANR 50, 76, 130;
CD 5, 6; MTCW 2; MTFW 2005

Durang, Christopher Ferdinand
See Durang, Christopher

Duras, Claire de 1777-1832 .... **NCLC 154**

Duras, Marguerite 1914-1996 . **CLC 3, 6, 11,
20, 34, 40, 68, 100; SSC 40**
See also BPFB 1; CA 25-28R; CAAS 151;
CANR 50; CWW 2; DFS 21; DLB 83,
321; EWL 3; FL 1:5; GFL 1789 to the
Present; IDFW 4; MTCW 1, 2; RGWL 2,
3; TWA

Durban, (Rosa) Pam 1947- .... **CLC 39**
See also CA 123; CANR 98; CSW

Durcan, Paul 1944- .... **CLC 43, 70**
See also CA 134; CANR 123; CP 1, 5, 6, 7;
DAM POET; EWL 3

d'Urfe, Honore
See Urfe, Honore d'

Durfey, Thomas 1653-1723 .... **LC 94**
See also DLB 80; RGEL 2

Durkheim, Emile 1858-1917 .... **TCLC 55**
See also CA 249

Durrell, Lawrence (George)
1912-1990 ..... **CLC 1, 4, 6, 8, 13, 27, 41**
See also BPFB 1; BRWS 1; CA 9-12R;
CAAS 132; CANR 40, 77; CDBLB 1945-
1960; CN 1, 2, 3, 4; CP 1, 2, 3, 4, 5; DAM
NOV; DLB 15, 27, 204; DLBY 1990;
EWL 3; MTCW 1, 2; RGEL 2; SFW 4;
TEA

Durrenmatt, Friedrich
See Duerrenmatt, Friedrich
See also CDWLB 2; EW 13; EWL 3;
RGHL; RGWL 2, 3

Dutt, Michael Madhusudan
1824-1873 .... **NCLC 118**

Dutt, Toru 1856-1877 .... **NCLC 29**
See also DLB 240

Dwight, Timothy 1752-1817 .... **NCLC 13**
See also DLB 37; RGAL 4

Dworkin, Andrea 1946-2005 ..... **CLC 43, 123**
See also CA 77-80; 21; CAAS 238; CANR
16, 39, 76, 96; FL 1:5; FW; GLL 1; INT
CANR-16; MTCW 1, 2; MTFW 2005

Dwyer, Deanna
See Koontz, Dean R.

Dwyer, K. R.
See Koontz, Dean R.

Dybek, Stuart 1942- .... **CLC 114; SSC 55**
See also CA 97-100; CANR 39; DLB 130;
SSFS 23

Dye, Richard
See De Voto, Bernard (Augustine)

Dyer, Geoff 1958- .... **CLC 149**
See also CA 125; CANR 88

Dyer, George 1755-1841 .... **NCLC 129**
See also DLB 93

Dylan, Bob 1941- .... **CLC 3, 4, 6, 12, 77; PC
37**
See also CA 41-44R; CANR 108; CP 1, 2,
3, 4, 5, 6, 7; DLB 16

Dyson, John 1943- .... **CLC 70**
See also CA 144

Dzyubin, Eduard Georgievich 1895-1934
See Bagritsky, Eduard
See also CA 170

E. V. L.
See Lucas, E(dward) V(errall)

Eagleton, Terence (Francis) 1943- .. **CLC 63,
132**
See also CA 57-60; CANR 7, 23, 68, 115;
DLB 242; LMFS 2; MTCW 1, 2; MTFW
2005

Eagleton, Terry
See Eagleton, Terence (Francis)

Early, Jack
See Scoppettone, Sandra
See also GLL 1

East, Michael
See West, Morris L(anglo)

Eastaway, Edward
See Thomas, (Philip) Edward

Eastlake, William (Derry)
1917-1997 .... **CLC 8**
See also CA 5-8R; 1; CAAS 158; CANR 5,
63; CN 1, 2, 3, 4, 5, 6; DLB 6, 206; INT
CANR-5; MAL 5; TCWW 1, 2

Eastman, Charles A(lexander)
1858-1939 .... **NNAL; TCLC 55**
See also CA 179; CANR 91; DAM MULT;
DLB 175; YABC 1

Eaton, Edith Maude 1865-1914 .... **AAL**
See Far, Sui Sin
See also CA 154; DLB 221, 312; FW

Eaton, (Lillie) Winnifred 1875-1954 .... **AAL**
See also CA 217; DLB 221, 312; RGAL 4

Eberhart, Richard 1904-2005 ...... **CLC 3, 11,
19, 56; PC 76**
See also AMW; CA 1-4R; CAAS 240;
CANR 2, 125; CDALB 1941-1968; CP 1,
2, 3, 4, 5, 6, 7; DAM POET; DLB 48;
MAL 5; MTCW 1; RGAL 4

Eberhart, Richard Ghormley
See Eberhart, Richard

Eberstadt, Fernanda 1960- .... **CLC 39**
See also CA 136; CANR 69, 128

**Echegaray (y Eizaguirre), Jose (Maria
Waldo)** 1832-1916 .... **HLCS 1; TCLC 4**
See also CAAE 104; CANR 32; DLB 329;
EWL 3; HW 1; MTCW 1

Echeverria, (Jose) Esteban (Antonino)
1805-1851 .... **NCLC 18**
See also LAW

Echo
See Proust, (Valentin-Louis-George-Eugene)
Marcel

Eckert, Allan W. 1931- .... **CLC 17**
See also AAYA 18; BYA 2; CA 13-16R;
CANR 14, 45; INT CANR-14; MAICYA
2; MAICYAS 1; SAAS 21; SATA 29, 91;
SATA-Brief 27

Eckhart, Meister 1260(?)-1327(?) .. **CMLC 9,
80**
See also DLB 115; LMFS 1

Eckmar, F. R.
See de Hartog, Jan

Eco, Umberto 1932- .... **CLC 28, 60, 142**
See also BEST 90:1; BPFB 1; CA 77-80;
CANR 12, 33, 55, 110, 131; CPW; CWW
2; DA3; DAM NOV, POP; DLB 196, 242;
EWL 3; MSW; MTCW 1, 2; MTFW
2005; NFS 22; RGWL 3; WLIT 7

Eddison, E(ric) R(ucker)
1882-1945 .... **TCLC 15**
See also CA 156; CAAE 109; DLB 255;
FANT; SFW 4; SUFW 1

Eddy, Mary (Ann Morse) Baker
1821-1910 .... **TCLC 71**
See also CA 174; CAAE 113

Edel, (Joseph) Leon 1907-1997 .. **CLC 29, 34**
See also CA 1-4R; CAAS 161; CANR 1,
22, 112; DLB 103; INT CANR-22

Eden, Emily 1797-1869 .... **NCLC 10**

Edgar, David 1948- .... **CLC 42**
See also CA 57-60; CANR 12, 61, 112;
CBD; CD 5, 6; DAM DRAM; DFS 15;
DLB 13, 233; MTCW 1

Edgerton, Clyde (Carlyle) 1944- ...... **CLC 39**
See also AAYA 17; CA 134; CAAE 118;
CANR 64, 125; CN 7; CSW; DLB 278;
INT CA-134; TCLE 1:1; YAW

Edgeworth, Maria 1768-1849 ... **NCLC 1, 51,
158; SSC 86**
See also BRWS 3; DLB 116, 159, 163; FL
1:3; FW; RGEL 2; SATA 21; TEA; WLIT
3

Edmonds, Paul
See Kuttner, Henry

Edmonds, Walter D(umaux)
1903-1998 .... **CLC 35**
See also BYA 2; CA 5-8R; CANR 2; CWRI
5; DLB 9; LAIT 1; MAICYA 1, 2; MAL
5; RHW; SAAS 4; SATA 1, 27; SATA-
Obit 99

Edmondson, Wallace
See Ellison, Harlan

Edson, Margaret 1961- ...... **CLC 199; DC 24**
See also CA 190; DFS 13; DLB 266

Edson, Russell 1935- .... **CLC 13**
See also CA 33-36R; CANR 115; CP 2, 3,
4, 5, 6, 7; DLB 244; WP

Edwards, Bronwen Elizabeth
See Rose, Wendy

Edwards, G(erald) B(asil)
1899-1976 .... **CLC 25**
See also CA 201; CAAS 110

Edwards, Gus 1939- .... **CLC 43**
See also CA 108; INT CA-108

Edwards, Jonathan 1703-1758 .... **LC 7, 54**
See also AMW; DA; DAC; DAM MST;
DLB 24, 270; RGAL 4; TUS

Edwards, Sarah Pierpont 1710-1758 .. **LC 87**
See also DLB 200

Efron, Marina Ivanovna Tsvetaeva
See Tsvetaeva (Efron), Marina (Ivanovna)

Egeria fl. 4th cent. - .... **CMLC 70**

Egoyan, Atom 1960- .... **CLC 151**
See also AAYA 63; CA 157; CANR 151

Ehle, John (Marsden, Jr.) 1925- ...... **CLC 27**
See also CA 9-12R; CSW

Ehrenbourg, Ilya (Grigoryevich)
See Ehrenburg, Ilya (Grigoryevich)

Ehrenburg, Ilya (Grigoryevich)
1891-1967 .... **CLC 18, 34, 62**
See Erenburg, Il'ia Grigor'evich
See also CA 102; CAAS 25-28R; EWL 3

Ehrenburg, Ilyo (Grigoryevich)
See Ehrenburg, Ilya (Grigoryevich)

Ehrenreich, Barbara 1941- .... **CLC 110**
See also BEST 90:4; CA 73-76; CANR 16,
37, 62, 117; DLB 246; FW; MTCW 1, 2;
MTFW 2005

Eich, Gunter
See Eich, Gunter
See also RGWL 2, 3

Eich, Gunter 1907-1972 .... **CLC 15**
See Eich, Gunter
See also CA 111; CAAS 93-96; DLB 69,
124; EWL 3

Eichendorff, Joseph 1788-1857 .... **NCLC 8**
See also DLB 90; RGWL 2, 3

Eigner, Larry .... **CLC 9**
See Eigner, Laurence (Joel)
See also CA 23; CP 1, 2, 3, 4, 5, 6; DLB 5;
WP

Eigner, Laurence (Joel) 1927-1996
See Eigner, Larry
See also CA 9-12R; CAAS 151; CANR 6,
84; CP 7; DLB 193

Eilhart von Oberge c. 1140-c.
1195 .... **CMLC 67**
See also DLB 148

Einhard c. 770-840 .... **CMLC 50**
See also DLB 148

Einstein, Albert 1879-1955 .... **TCLC 65**
See also CA 133; CAAE 121; MTCW 1, 2

Eiseley, Loren
See Eiseley, Loren Corey
See also DLB 275

Eiseley, Loren Corey 1907-1977 .... **CLC 7**
See Eiseley, Loren
See also AAYA 5; ANW; CA 1-4R; CAAS
73-76; CANR 6; DLBD 17

Eisenstadt, Jill 1963- .... **CLC 50**
See also CA 140

Eisenstein, Sergei (Mikhailovich)
1898-1948 .... **TCLC 57**
See also CA 149; CAAE 114

Eisner, Simon
See Kornbluth, C(yril) M.

Ekeloef, (Bengt) Gunnar
1907-1968 .... **CLC 27; PC 23**
See Ekelof, (Bengt) Gunnar
See also CA 123; CAAS 25-28R; DAM
POET

Ekelof, (Bengt) Gunnar 1907-1968
See Ekeloef, (Bengt) Gunnar
See also DLB 259; EW 12; EWL 3

Ekelund, Vilhelm 1880-1949 .... **TCLC 75**
See also CA 189; EWL 3

Ekwensi, C. O. D.
See Ekwensi, Cyprian (Odiatu Duaka)

Ekwensi, Cyprian (Odiatu Duaka)
1921- .... **BLC 1; CLC 4**
See also AFW; BW 2, 3; CA 29-32R;
CANR 18, 42, 74, 125; CDWLB 3; CN 1,
2, 3, 4, 5, 6; CWRI 5; DAM MULT; DLB
117; EWL 3; MTCW 1, 2; RGEL 2; SATA
66; WLIT 2

Elaine .... **TCLC 18**
See Leverson, Ada Esther

El Crummo
See Crumb, R.

Elder, Lonne III 1931-1996 ..... **BLC 1; DC 8**
See also BW 1, 3; CA 81-84; CAAS 152;
CAD; CANR 25; DAM MULT; DLB 7,
38, 44; MAL 5

Eleanor of Aquitaine 1122-1204 ... **CMLC 39**

Elia
See Lamb, Charles

Eliade, Mircea 1907-1986 .... **CLC 19**
See also CA 65-68; CAAS 119; CANR 30,
62; CDWLB 4; DLB 220; EWL 3; MTCW
1; RGWL 3; SFW 4

Eliot, A. D.
See Jewett, (Theodora) Sarah Orne

Eliot, Alice
See Jewett, (Theodora) Sarah Orne

Eliot, Dan
See Silverberg, Robert

Eliot, George 1819-1880 ...... **NCLC 4, 13, 23,
41, 49, 89, 118; PC 20; SSC 72; WLC 2**
See Evans, Mary Ann
See also BRW 5; BRWC 1, 2; BRWR 2;
CDBLB 1832-1890; CN 7; CPW; DA;
DA3; DAB; DAC; DAM MST, NOV;
DLB 21, 35, 55; FL 1:3; LATS 1:1; LMFS
1; NFS 17, 20; RGEL 2; RGSF 2; SSFS
8; TEA; WLIT 3

Eliot, John 1604-1690 .... **LC 5**
See also DLB 24

Eliot, T(homas) S(tearns)
1888-1965 ...... **CLC 1, 2, 3, 6, 9, 10, 13,
15, 24, 34, 41, 55, 57, 113; PC 5, 31;
WLC 2**
See also AAYA 28; AMW; AMWC 1;
AMWR 1; BRW 7; BRWR 2; CA 5-8R;
CAAS 25-28R; CANR 41; CBD; CDALB

1929-1941; DA; DA3; DAB; DAC; DAM
DRAM, MST, POET; DFS 4, 13; DLB 7,
10, 45, 63, 245, 329; DLBY 1988; EWL
3; EXPP; LAIT 3; LATS 1:1; LMFS 2;
MAL 5; MTCW 1, 2; MTFW 2005; NCFS
5; PAB; PFS 1, 7, 20; RGAL 4; RGEL 2;
TUS; WLIT 4; WP

Elisabeth of Schonau c.
1129-1165 .... **CMLC 82**

Elizabeth 1866-1941 .... **TCLC 41**

Elizabeth I 1533-1603 .... **LC 118**
See also DLB 136

Elkin, Stanley L. 1930-1995 ...... **CLC 4, 6, 9,
14, 27, 51, 91; SSC 12**
See also AMWS 6; BPFB 1; CA 9-12R;
CAAS 148; CANR 8, 46; CN 1, 2, 3, 4,
5, 6; CPW; DAM NOV, POP; DLB 2, 28,
218, 278; DLBY 1980; EWL 3; INT
CANR-8; MAL 5; MTCW 1, 2; MTFW
2005; RGAL 4; TCLE 1:1

Elledge, Scott .... **CLC 34**

Eller, Scott
See Shepard, Jim

Elliott, Don
See Silverberg, Robert

Elliott, George P(aul) 1918-1980 .... **CLC 2**
See also CA 1-4R; CAAS 97-100; CANR
2; CN 1, 2; CP 3; DLB 244; MAL 5

Elliott, Janice 1931-1995 .... **CLC 47**
See also CA 13-16R; CANR 8, 29, 84; CN
5, 6, 7; DLB 14; SATA 119

Elliott, Sumner Locke 1917-1991 ..... **CLC 38**
See also CA 5-8R; CAAS 134; CANR 2,
21; DLB 289

Elliott, William
See Bradbury, Ray

Ellis, A. E. .... **CLC 7**

Ellis, Alice Thomas .... **CLC 40**
See Haycraft, Anna
See also CN 4, 5, 6; DLB 194

Ellis, Bret Easton 1964- ..... **CLC 39, 71, 117,
229**
See also AAYA 2, 43; CA 123; CAAE 118;
CANR 51, 74, 126; CN 6, 7; CPW; DA3;
DAM POP; DLB 292; HGG; INT CA-
123; MTCW 2; MTFW 2005; NFS 11

Ellis, (Henry) Havelock
1859-1939 .... **TCLC 14**
See also CA 169; CAAE 109; DLB 190

Ellis, Landon
See Ellison, Harlan

Ellis, Trey 1962- .... **CLC 55**
See also CA 146; CANR 92; CN 7

Ellison, Harlan 1934- .... **CLC 1, 13, 42, 139;
SSC 14**
See also AAYA 29; BPFB 1; BYA 14; CA
5-8R; CANR 5, 46, 115; CPW; DAM
POP; DLB 8; HGG; INT CANR-5;
MTCW 1, 2; MTFW 2005; SCFW 2;
SFW 4; SSFS 13, 14, 15, 21; SUFW 1, 2

Ellison, Ralph 1914-1994 . **BLC 1; CLC 1, 3,
11, 54, 86, 114; SSC 26, 79; WLC 2**
See also AAYA 19; AFAW 1, 2; AMWC 2;
AMWR 2; AMWS 2; BPFB 1; BW 1, 3;
BYA 2; CA 9-12R; CAAS 145; CANR
24, 53; CDALB 1941-1968; CN 1, 2, 3,
4, 5; CSW; DA; DA3; DAB; DAC; DAM
MST, MULT, NOV; DLB 2, 76, 227;
DLBY 1994; EWL 3; EXPN; EXPS;
LAIT 4; MAL 5; MTCW 1, 2; MTFW
2005; NCFS 3; NFS 2, 21; RGAL 4;
RGSF 2; SSFS 1, 11; YAW

Ellmann, Lucy 1956- .... **CLC 61**
See also CA 128; CANR 154

Ellmann, Lucy Elizabeth
See Ellmann, Lucy

Everett, Percival L. 1956- .... **CLC 57**
    See Everett, Percival
    See also BW 2; CA 129; CANR 94, 134;
        CN 7; MTFW 2005
Everson, R(onald) G(ilmour)
    1903-1992 .... **CLC 27**
    See also CA 17-20R; CP 1, 2, 3, 4; DLB 88
Everson, William (Oliver)
    1912-1994 .... **CLC 1, 5, 14**
    See Antoninus, Brother
    See also BG 1:2; CA 9-12R; CAAS 145;
        CANR 20; CP 2, 3, 4, 5; DLB 5, 16, 212;
        MTCW 1
Evtushenko, Evgenii Aleksandrovich
    See Yevtushenko, Yevgeny (Alexandrovich)
    See also CWW 2; RGWL 2, 3
Ewart, Gavin (Buchanan)
    1916-1995 .... **CLC 13, 46**
    See also BRWS 7; CA 89-92; CAAS 150;
        CANR 17, 46; CP 1, 2, 3, 4, 5, 6; DLB
        40; MTCW 1
Ewers, Hanns Heinz 1871-1943 ..... **TCLC 12**
    See also CA 149; CAAE 109
Ewing, Frederick R.
    See Sturgeon, Theodore (Hamilton)
Exley, Frederick (Earl) 1929-1992 .... **CLC 6,
    11**
    See also AITN 2; BPFB 1; CA 81-84;
        CAAS 138; CANR 117; DLB 143; DLBY
        1981
Eynhardt, Guillermo
    See Quiroga, Horacio (Sylvestre)
Ezekiel, Nissim (Moses) 1924-2004 .. **CLC 61**
    See also CA 61-64; CAAS 223; CP 1, 2, 3,
        4, 5, 6, 7; DLB 323; EWL 3
Ezekiel, Tish O'Dowd 1943- .... **CLC 34**
    See also CA 129
Fadeev, Aleksandr Aleksandrovich
    See Bulgya, Alexander Alexandrovich
    See also DLB 272
Fadeev, Alexandr Alexandrovich
    See Bulgya, Alexander Alexandrovich
    See also EWL 3
Fadeyev, A.
    See Bulgya, Alexander Alexandrovich
Fadeyev, Alexander .... **TCLC 53**
    See Bulgya, Alexander Alexandrovich
Fagen, Donald 1948- .... **CLC 26**
Fainzil'berg, Il'ia Arnol'dovich
    See Fainzilberg, Ilya Arnoldovich
Fainzilberg, Ilya Arnoldovich
    1897-1937 .... **TCLC 21**
    See Il'f, Il'ia
    See also CA 165; CAAE 120; EWL 3
Fair, Ronald L. 1932- .... **CLC 18**
    See also BW 1; CA 69-72; CANR 25; DLB
        33
Fairbairn, Roger
    See Carr, John Dickson
Fairbairns, Zoe (Ann) 1948- .... **CLC 32**
    See also CA 103; CANR 21, 85; CN 4, 5,
        6, 7
Fairfield, Flora
    See Alcott, Louisa May
Fairman, Paul W. 1916-1977
    See Queen, Ellery
    See also CAAS 114; SFW 4
Falco, Gian
    See Papini, Giovanni
Falconer, James
    See Kirkup, James
Falconer, Kenneth
    See Kornbluth, C(yril) M.
Falkland, Samuel
    See Heijermans, Herman
Fallaci, Oriana 1930-2006 .... **CLC 11, 110**
    See also CA 77-80; CAAS 253; CANR 15,
        58, 134; FW; MTCW 1

Faludi, Susan 1959- .... **CLC 140**
    See also CA 138; CANR 126; FW; MTCW
        2; MTFW 2005; NCFS 3
Faludy, George 1913- .... **CLC 42**
    See also CA 21-24R
Faludy, Gyoergy
    See Faludy, George
Fanon, Frantz 1925-1961 ... **BLC 2; CLC 74;
    TCLC 188**
    See also BW 1; CA 116; CAAS 89-92;
        DAM MULT; DLB 296; LMFS 2; WLIT
        2
Fanshawe, Ann 1625-1680 .... **LC 11**
Fante, John (Thomas) 1911-1983 .... **CLC 60;
    SSC 65**
    See also AMWS 11; CA 69-72; CAAS 109;
        CANR 23, 104; DLB 130; DLBY 1983
Far, Sui Sin .... **SSC 62**
    See Eaton, Edith Maude
    See also SSFS 4
Farah, Nuruddin 1945- ...... **BLC 2; CLC 53,
    137**
    See also AFW; BW 2, 3; CA 106; CANR
        81, 148; CDWLB 3; CN 4, 5, 6, 7; DAM
        MULT; DLB 125; EWL 3; WLIT 2
Fargue, Leon-Paul 1876(?)-1947 .... **TCLC 11**
    See also CAAE 109; CANR 107; DLB 258;
        EWL 3
Farigoule, Louis
    See Romains, Jules
Farina, Richard 1936(?)-1966 .... **CLC 9**
    See also CA 81-84; CAAS 25-28R
Farley, Walter (Lorimer)
    1915-1989 .... **CLC 17**
    See also AAYA 58; BYA 14; CA 17-20R;
        CANR 8, 29, 84; DLB 22; JRDA; MAI-
        CYA 1, 2; SATA 2, 43, 132; YAW
Farmer, Philip Jose 1918- .... **CLC 1, 19**
    See also AAYA 28; BPFB 1; CA 1-4R;
        CANR 4, 35, 111; DLB 8; MTCW 1;
        SATA 93; SCFW 1, 2; SFW 4
Farquhar, George 1677-1707 .... **LC 21**
    See also BRW 2; DAM DRAM; DLB 84;
        RGEL 2
Farrell, J(ames) G(ordon)
    1935-1979 .... **CLC 6**
    See also CA 73-76; CAAS 89-92; CANR
        36; CN 1, 2; DLB 14, 271, 326; MTCW
        1; RGEL 2; RHW; WLIT 4
Farrell, James T(homas) 1904-1979 . **CLC 1,
    4, 8, 11, 66; SSC 28**
    See also AMW; BPFB 1; CA 5-8R; CAAS
        89-92; CANR 9, 61; CN 1, 2; DLB 4, 9,
        86; DLBD 2; EWL 3; MAL 5; MTCW 1,
        2; MTFW 2005; RGAL 4
Farrell, Warren (Thomas) 1943- ..... **CLC 70**
    See also CA 146; CANR 120
Farren, Richard J.
    See Betjeman, John
Farren, Richard M.
    See Betjeman, John
Fassbinder, Rainer Werner
    1946-1982 .... **CLC 20**
    See also CA 93-96; CAAS 106; CANR 31
Fast, Howard 1914-2003 .... **CLC 23, 131**
    See also AAYA 16; BPFB 1; CA 181; 1-4R,
        181; 18; CAAS 214; CANR 1, 33, 54, 75,
        98, 140; CMW 4; CN 1, 2, 3, 4, 5, 6, 7;
        CPW; DAM NOV; DLB 9; INT CANR-
        33; LATS 1:1; MAL 5; MTCW 2; MTFW
        2005; RHW; SATA 7; SATA-Essay 107;
        TCWW 1, 2; YAW
Faulcon, Robert
    See Holdstock, Robert
Faulkner, William (Cuthbert)
    1897-1962 .... **CLC 1, 3, 6, 8, 9, 11, 14,
    18, 28, 52, 68; SSC 1, 35, 42, 92, 97;
    TCLC 141; WLC 2**
    See also AAYA 7; AMW; AMWR 1; BPFB
        1; BYA 5, 15; CA 81-84; CANR 33;

CDALB 1929-1941; DA; DA3; DAB;
        DAC; DAM MST, NOV; DLB 9, 11, 44,
        102, 316, 330; DLBD 2; DLBY 1986,
        1997; EWL 3; EXPN; EXPS; GL 2; LAIT
        2; LATS 1:1; LMFS 2; MAL 5; MTCW
        1, 2; MTFW 2005; NFS 4, 8, 13, 24;
        RGAL 4; RGSF 2; SSFS 2, 5, 6, 12; TUS
Fauset, Jessie Redmon
    1882(?)-1961 .. **BLC 2; CLC 19, 54; HR
    1:2**
    See also AFAW 2; BW 1; CA 109; CANR
        83; DAM MULT; DLB 51; FW; LMFS 2;
        MAL 5; MBL
Faust, Frederick (Schiller)
    1892-1944 .... **TCLC 49**
    See Brand, Max; Dawson, Peter; Frederick,
        John
    See also CA 152; CAAE 108; CANR 143;
        DAM POP; DLB 256; TUS
Faust, Irvin 1924- .... **CLC 8**
    See also CA 33-36R; CANR 28, 67; CN 1,
        2, 3, 4, 5, 6, 7; DLB 2, 28, 218, 278;
        DLBY 1980
Fawkes, Guy
    See Benchley, Robert (Charles)
Fearing, Kenneth (Flexner)
    1902-1961 .... **CLC 51**
    See also CA 93-96; CANR 59; CMW 4;
        DLB 9; MAL 5; RGAL 4
Fecamps, Elise
    See Creasey, John
Federman, Raymond 1928- .... **CLC 6, 47**
    See also CA 208; 17-20R, 208; 8; CANR
        10, 43, 83, 108; CN 3, 4, 5, 6; DLBY
        1980
Federspiel, J.F. 1931- .... **CLC 42**
    See also CA 146
Federspiel, Juerg F.
    See Federspiel, J.F.
Feiffer, Jules 1929- .... **CLC 2, 8, 64**
    See also AAYA 3, 62; CA 17-20R; CAD;
        CANR 30, 59, 129, 161; CD 5, 6; DAM
        DRAM; DLB 7, 44; INT CANR-30;
        MTCW 1; SATA 8, 61, 111, 157
Feiffer, Jules Ralph
    See Feiffer, Jules
Feige, Hermann Albert Otto Maximilian
    See Traven, B.
Feinberg, David B. 1956-1994 .... **CLC 59**
    See also CA 135; CAAS 147
Feinstein, Elaine 1930- .... **CLC 36**
    See also CA 69-72; 1; CANR 31, 68, 121;
        CN 3, 4, 5, 6, 7; CP 2, 3, 4, 5, 6, 7; CWP;
        DLB 14, 40; MTCW 1
Feke, Gilbert David .... **CLC 65**
Feldman, Irving (Mordecai) 1928- ..... **CLC 7**
    See also CA 1-4R; CANR 1; CP 1, 2, 3, 4,
        5, 6, 7; DLB 169; TCLE 1:1
Felix-Tchicaya, Gerald
    See Tchicaya, Gerald Felix
Fellini, Federico 1920-1993 .... **CLC 16, 85**
    See also CA 65-68; CAAS 143; CANR 33
Felltham, Owen 1602(?)-1668 .... **LC 92**
    See also DLB 126, 151
Felsen, Henry Gregor 1916-1995 ..... **CLC 17**
    See also CA 1-4R; CAAS 180; CANR 1;
        SAAS 2; SATA 1
Felski, Rita .... **CLC 65**
**Fenelon, Francois de Pons de Salignac de la
    Mothe-** 1651-1715 .... **LC 134**
    See also DLB 268; EW 3; GFL Beginnings
        to 1789
Fenno, Jack
    See Calisher, Hortense
Fenollosa, Ernest (Francisco)
    1853-1908 .... **TCLC 91**
Fenton, James 1949- .... **CLC 32, 209**
    See also CA 102; CANR 108, 160; CP 2, 3,
        4, 5, 6, 7; DLB 40; PFS 11

Francis, Robert (Churchill)
  1901-1987 .... **CLC 15; PC 34**
  See also AMWS 9; CA 1-4R; CAAS 123;
  CANR 1; CP 1, 2, 3, 4; EXPP; PFS 12;
  TCLE 1:1

Francis, Lord Jeffrey
  See Jeffrey, Francis
  See also DLB 107

Frank, Anne(lies Marie)
  1929-1945 .... **TCLC 17; WLC 2**
  See also AAYA 12; BYA 1; CA 133; CAAE
  113; CANR 68; CLR 101; DA; DA3;
  DAB; DAC; DAM MST; LAIT 4; MAI-
  CYA 2; MAICYAS 1; MTCW 1, 2;
  MTFW 2005; NCFS 2; RGHL; SATA 87;
  SATA-Brief 42; WYA; YAW

Frank, Bruno 1887-1945 .... **TCLC 81**
  See also CA 189; DLB 118; EWL 3

Frank, Elizabeth 1945- .... **CLC 39**
  See also CA 126; CAAE 121; CANR 78,
  150; INT CA-126

Frankl, Viktor E(mil) 1905-1997 ...... **CLC 93**
  See also CA 65-68; CAAS 161; RGHL

Franklin, Benjamin
  See Hasek, Jaroslav (Matej Frantisek)

Franklin, Benjamin 1706-1790 .. **LC 25, 134;**
  WLCS
  See also AMW; CDALB 1640-1865; DA;
  DA3; DAB; DAC; DAM MST; DLB 24,
  43, 73, 183; LAIT 1; RGAL 4; TUS

Franklin, (Stella Maria Sarah) Miles
  (Lampe) 1879-1954 .... **TCLC 7**
  See also CA 164; CAAE 104; DLB 230;
  FW; MTCW 2; RGEL 2; TWA

Franzen, Jonathan 1959- .... **CLC 202**
  See also AAYA 65; CA 129; CANR 105

Fraser, Antonia 1932- .... **CLC 32, 107**
  See also AAYA 57; CA 85-88; CANR 44,
  65, 119; CMW; DLB 276; MTCW 1, 2;
  MTFW 2005; SATA-Brief 32

Fraser, George MacDonald 1925- ...... **CLC 7**
  See also AAYA 48; CA 180; 45-48, 180;
  CANR 2, 48, 74; MTCW 2; RHW

Fraser, Sylvia 1935- .... **CLC 64**
  See also CA 45-48; CANR 1, 16, 60; CCA
  1

Frayn, Michael 1933- .... **CLC 3, 7, 31, 47,**
  176; DC 27
  See also AAYA 69; BRWC 2; BRWS 7; CA
  5-8R; CANR 30, 69, 114, 133; CBD; CD
  5, 6; CN 1, 2, 3, 4, 5, 6, 7; DAM DRAM,
  NOV; DFS 22; DLB 13, 14, 194, 245;
  FANT; MTCW 1, 2; MTFW 2005; SFW
  4

Fraze, Candida (Merrill) 1945- .... **CLC 50**
  See also CA 126

Frazer, Andrew
  See Marlowe, Stephen

Frazer, J(ames) G(eorge)
  1854-1941 .... **TCLC 32**
  See also BRWS 3; CAAE 118; NCFS 5

Frazer, Robert Caine
  See Creasey, John

Frazer, Sir James George
  See Frazer, J(ames) G(eorge)

Frazier, Charles 1950- .... **CLC 109, 224**
  See also AAYA 34; CA 161; CANR 126;
  CSW; DLB 292; MTFW 2005

Frazier, Ian 1951- .... **CLC 46**
  See also CA 130; CANR 54, 93

Frederic, Harold 1856-1898 ... **NCLC 10, 175**
  See also AMW; DLB 12, 23; DLBD 13;
  MAL 5; NFS 22; RGAL 4

Frederick, John
  See Faust, Frederick (Schiller)
  See also TCWW 2

Frederick the Great 1712-1786 .... **LC 14**

Fredro, Aleksander 1793-1876 .... **NCLC 8**

Freeling, Nicolas 1927-2003 .... **CLC 38**
  See also CA 49-52; 12; CAAS 218; CANR
  1, 17, 50, 84; CMW 4; CN 1, 2, 3, 4, 5,
  6; DLB 87

Freeman, Douglas Southall
  1886-1953 .... **TCLC 11**
  See also CA 195; CAAE 109; DLB 17;
  DLBD 17

Freeman, Judith 1946- .... **CLC 55**
  See also CA 148; CANR 120; DLB 256

Freeman, Mary E(leanor) Wilkins
  1852-1930 .... **SSC 1, 47; TCLC 9**
  See also CA 177; CAAE 106; DLB 12, 78,
  221; EXPS; FW; HGG; MBL; RGAL 4;
  RGSF 2; SSFS 4, 8; SUFW 1; TUS

Freeman, R(ichard) Austin
  1862-1943 .... **TCLC 21**
  See also CAAE 113; CANR 84; CMW 4;
  DLB 70

French, Albert 1943- .... **CLC 86**
  See also BW 3; CA 167

French, Antonia
  See Kureishi, Hanif

French, Marilyn 1929- .. **CLC 10, 18, 60, 177**
  See also BPFB 1; CA 69-72; CANR 3, 31,
  134; CN 5, 6, 7; CPW; DAM DRAM,
  NOV, POP; FL 1:5; FW; INT CANR-31;
  MTCW 1, 2; MTFW 2005

French, Paul
  See Asimov, Isaac

Freneau, Philip Morin 1752-1832 .. **NCLC 1,**
  111
  See also AMWS 2; DLB 37, 43; RGAL 4

Freud, Sigmund 1856-1939 .... **TCLC 52**
  See also CA 133; CAAE 115; CANR 69;
  DLB 296; EW 8; EWL 3; LATS 1:1;
  MTCW 1, 2; MTFW 2005; NCFS 3; TWA

Freytag, Gustav 1816-1895 .... **NCLC 109**
  See also DLB 129

Friedan, Betty 1921-2006 .... **CLC 74**
  See also CA 65-68; CAAS 248; CANR 18,
  45, 74; DLB 246; FW; MTCW 1, 2;
  MTFW 2005; NCFS 5

Friedan, Betty Naomi
  See Friedan, Betty

Friedlander, Saul 1932- .... **CLC 90**
  See also CA 130; CAAE 117; CANR 72;
  RGHL

Friedman, B(ernard) H(arper)
  1926- .... **CLC 7**
  See also CA 1-4R; CANR 3, 48

Friedman, Bruce Jay 1930- ...... **CLC 3, 5, 56**
  See also CA 9-12R; CAD; CANR 25, 52,
  101; CD 5, 6; CN 1, 2, 3, 4, 5, 6, 7; DLB
  2, 28, 244; INT CANR-25; MAL 5; SSFS
  18

Friel, Brian 1929- .... **CLC 5, 42, 59, 115; DC**
  8; SSC 76
  See also BRWS 5; CA 21-24R; CANR 33,
  69, 131; CBD; CD 5, 6; DFS 11; DLB
  13, 319; EWL 3; MTCW 1; RGEL 2; TEA

Friis-Baastad, Babbis Ellinor
  1921-1970 .... **CLC 12**
  See also CA 17-20R; CAAS 134; SATA 7

Frisch, Max 1911-1991 ...... **CLC 3, 9, 14, 18,**
  32, 44; TCLC 121
  See also CA 85-88; CAAS 134; CANR 32,
  74; CDWLB 2; DAM DRAM, NOV; DLB
  69, 124; EW 13; EWL 3; MTCW 1, 2;
  MTFW 2005; RGHL; RGWL 2, 3

Fromentin, Eugene (Samuel Auguste)
  1820-1876 .... **NCLC 10, 125**
  See also DLB 123; GFL 1789 to the Present

Frost, Frederick
  See Faust, Frederick (Schiller)

Frost, Robert 1874-1963 . **CLC 1, 3, 4, 9, 10,**
  13, 15, 26, 34, 44; PC 1, 39, 71; WLC 2
  See also AAYA 21; AMW; AMWR 1; CA
  89-92; CANR 33; CDALB 1917-1929;
  CLR 67; DA; DA3; DAB; DAC; DAM
  MST, POET; DLB 54, 284; DLBD 7;
  EWL 3; EXPP; MAL 5; MTCW 1, 2;
  MTFW 2005; PAB; PFS 1, 2, 3, 4, 5, 6,
  7, 10, 13; RGAL 4; SATA 14; TUS; WP;
  WYA

Frost, Robert Lee
  See Frost, Robert

Froude, James Anthony
  1818-1894 .... **NCLC 43**
  See also DLB 18, 57, 144

Froy, Herald
  See Waterhouse, Keith (Spencer)

Fry, Christopher 1907-2005 ... **CLC 2, 10, 14**
  See also BRWS 3; CA 17-20R; 23; CAAS
  240; CANR 9, 30, 74, 132; CBD; CD 5,
  6; CP 1, 2, 3, 4, 5, 6, 7; DAM DRAM;
  DLB 13; EWL 3; MTCW 1, 2; MTFW
  2005; RGEL 2; SATA 66; TEA

Frye, (Herman) Northrop
  1912-1991 .... **CLC 24, 70; TCLC 165**
  See also CA 5-8R; CAAS 133; CANR 8,
  37; DLB 67, 68, 246; EWL 3; MTCW 1,
  2; MTFW 2005; RGAL 4; TWA

Fuchs, Daniel 1909-1993 .... **CLC 8, 22**
  See also CA 81-84; 5; CAAS 142; CANR
  40; CN 1, 2, 3, 4, 5; DLB 9, 26, 28;
  DLBY 1993; MAL 5

Fuchs, Daniel 1934- .... **CLC 34**
  See also CA 37-40R; CANR 14, 48

Fuentes, Carlos 1928- .. **CLC 3, 8, 10, 13, 22,**
  41, 60, 113; HLC 1; SSC 24; WLC 2
  See also AAYA 4, 45; AITN 2; BPFB 1;
  CA 69-72; CANR 10, 32, 68, 104, 138;
  CDWLB 3; CWW 2; DA; DA3; DAB;
  DAC; DAM MST, MULT, NOV; DLB
  113; DNFS 2; EWL 3; HW 1, 2; LAIT 3;
  LATS 1:2; LAW; LAWS 1; LMFS 2;
  MTCW 1, 2; MTFW 2005; NFS 8; RGSF
  2; RGWL 2, 3; TWA; WLIT 1

Fuentes, Gregorio Lopez y
  See Lopez y Fuentes, Gregorio

Fuertes, Gloria 1918-1998 .... **PC 27**
  See also CA 178, 180; DLB 108; HW 2;
  SATA 115

Fugard, (Harold) Athol 1932- . **CLC 5, 9, 14,**
  25, 40, 80, 211; DC 3
  See also AAYA 17; AFW; CA 85-88; CANR
  32, 54, 118; CD 5, 6; DAM DRAM; DFS
  3, 6, 10; DLB 225; DNFS 1, 2; EWL 3;
  LATS 1:2; MTCW 1; MTFW 2005; RGEL
  2; WLIT 2

Fugard, Sheila 1932- .... **CLC 48**
  See also CA 125

Fujiwara no Teika 1162-1241 .... **CMLC 73**
  See also DLB 203

Fukuyama, Francis 1952- .... **CLC 131**
  See also CA 140; CANR 72, 125

Fuller, Charles (H.), (Jr.) 1939- .... **BLC 2;**
  CLC 25; DC 1
  See also BW 2; CA 112; CAAE 108; CAD;
  CANR 87; CD 5, 6; DAM DRAM,
  MULT; DFS 8; DLB 38, 266; EWL 3;
  INT CA-112; MAL 5; MTCW 1

Fuller, Henry Blake 1857-1929 .... **TCLC 103**
  See also CA 177; CAAE 108; DLB 12;
  RGAL 4

Fuller, John (Leopold) 1937- .... **CLC 62**
  See also CA 21-24R; CANR 9, 44; CP 1, 2,
  3, 4, 5, 6, 7; DLB 40

Fuller, Margaret
  See Ossoli, Sarah Margaret (Fuller)
  See also AMWS 2; DLB 183, 223, 239; FL
  1:3

Fuller, Roy (Broadbent) 1912-1991 ... **CLC 4, 28**
See also BRWS 7; CA 5-8R; 10; CAAS 135; CANR 53, 83; CN 1, 2, 3, 4, 5; CP 1, 2, 3, 4, 5; CWRI 5; DLB 15, 20; EWL 3; RGEL 2; SATA 87

Fuller, Sarah Margaret
See Ossoli, Sarah Margaret (Fuller)

Fuller, Sarah Margaret
See Ossoli, Sarah Margaret (Fuller)
See also DLB 1, 59, 73

Fuller, Thomas 1608-1661 .... **LC 111**
See also DLB 151

Fulton, Alice 1952- .... **CLC 52**
See also CA 116; CANR 57, 88; CP 5, 6, 7; CWP; DLB 193; PFS 25

Furphy, Joseph 1843-1912 .... **TCLC 25**
See Collins, Tom
See also CA 163; DLB 230; EWL 3; RGEL 2

Fuson, Robert H(enderson) 1927- .... **CLC 70**
See also CA 89-92; CANR 103

Fussell, Paul 1924- .... **CLC 74**
See also BEST 90:1; CA 17-20R; CANR 8, 21, 35, 69, 135; INT CANR-21; MTCW 1, 2; MTFW 2005

Futabatei, Shimei 1864-1909 .... **TCLC 44**
See Futabatei Shimei
See also CA 162; MJW

Futabatei Shimei
See Futabatei, Shimei
See also DLB 180; EWL 3

Futrelle, Jacques 1875-1912 .... **TCLC 19**
See also CA 155; CAAE 113; CMW 4

Gaboriau, Emile 1835-1873 .... **NCLC 14**
See also CMW 4; MSW

Gadda, Carlo Emilio 1893-1973 ...... **CLC 11; TCLC 144**
See also CA 89-92; DLB 177; EWL 3; WLIT 7

Gaddis, William 1922-1998 ... **CLC 1, 3, 6, 8, 10, 19, 43, 86**
See also AMWS 4; BPFB 1; CA 17-20R; CAAS 172; CANR 21, 48, 148; CN 1, 2, 3, 4, 5, 6; DLB 2, 278; EWL 3; MAL 5; MTCW 1, 2; MTFW 2005; RGAL 4

Gage, Walter
See Inge, William (Motter)

Gaiman, Neil 1960- .... **CLC 195**
See also AAYA 19, 42; CA 133; CANR 81, 129; CLR 109; DLB 261; HGG; MTFW 2005; SATA 85, 146; SFW 4; SUFW 2

Gaiman, Neil Richard
See Gaiman, Neil

Gaines, Ernest J. 1933- .. **BLC 2; CLC 3, 11, 18, 86, 181; SSC 68**
See also AAYA 18; AFAW 1, 2; AITN 1; BPFB 2; BW 2, 3; BYA 6; CA 9-12R; CANR 6, 24, 42, 75, 126; CDALB 1968-1988; CLR 62; CN 1, 2, 3, 4, 5, 6, 7; CSW; DA3; DAM MULT; DLB 2, 33, 152; DLBY 1980; EWL 3; EXPN; LAIT 5; LATS 1:2; MAL 5; MTCW 1, 2; MTFW 2005; NFS 5, 7, 16; RGAL 4; RGSF 2; RHW; SATA 86; SSFS 5; YAW

Gaitskill, Mary 1954- .... **CLC 69**
See also CA 128; CANR 61, 152; DLB 244; TCLE 1:1

Gaitskill, Mary Lawrence
See Gaitskill, Mary

Gaius Suetonius Tranquillus
See Suetonius

Galdos, Benito Perez
See Perez Galdos, Benito
See also EW 7

Gale, Zona 1874-1938 .... **TCLC 7**
See also CA 153; CAAE 105; CANR 84; DAM DRAM; DFS 17; DLB 9, 78, 228; RGAL 4

Galeano, Eduardo (Hughes) 1940- . **CLC 72; HLCS 1**
See also CA 29-32R; CANR 13, 32, 100; HW 1

Galiano, Juan Valera y Alcala
See Valera y Alcala-Galiano, Juan

Galilei, Galileo 1564-1642 .... **LC 45**

Gallagher, Tess 1943- .... **CLC 18, 63; PC 9**
See also CA 106; CP 3, 4, 5, 6, 7; CWP; DAM POET; DLB 120, 212, 244; PFS 16

Gallant, Mavis 1922- ..... **CLC 7, 18, 38, 172; SSC 5, 78**
See also CA 69-72; CANR 29, 69, 117; CCA 1; CN 1, 2, 3, 4, 5, 6, 7; DAC; DAM MST; DLB 53; EWL 3; MTCW 1, 2; MTFW 2005; RGEL 2; RGSF 2

Gallant, Roy A(rthur) 1924- .... **CLC 17**
See also CA 5-8R; CANR 4, 29, 54, 117; CLR 30; MAICYA 1, 2; SATA 4, 68, 110

Gallico, Paul (William) 1897-1976 .... **CLC 2**
See also AITN 1; CA 5-8R; CAAS 69-72; CANR 23; CN 1, 2; DLB 9, 171; FANT; MAICYA 1, 2; SATA 13

Gallo, Max Louis 1932- .... **CLC 95**
See also CA 85-88

Gallois, Lucien
See Desnos, Robert

Gallup, Ralph
See Whitemore, Hugh (John)

Galsworthy, John 1867-1933 .... **SSC 22; TCLC 1, 45; WLC 2**
See also BRW 6; CA 141; CAAE 104; CANR 75; CDBLB 1890-1914; DA; DA3; DAB; DAC; DAM DRAM, MST, NOV; DLB 10, 34, 98, 162, 330; DLBD 16; EWL 3; MTCW 2; RGEL 2; SSFS 3; TEA

Galt, John 1779-1839 .... **NCLC 1, 110**
See also DLB 99, 116, 159; RGEL 2; RGSF 2

Galvin, James 1951- .... **CLC 38**
See also CA 108; CANR 26

Gamboa, Federico 1864-1939 .... **TCLC 36**
See also CA 167; HW 2; LAW

Gandhi, M. K.
See Gandhi, Mohandas Karamchand

Gandhi, Mahatma
See Gandhi, Mohandas Karamchand

Gandhi, Mohandas Karamchand
1869-1948 .... **TCLC 59**
See also CA 132; CAAE 121; DA3; DAM MULT; DLB 323; MTCW 1, 2

Gann, Ernest Kellogg 1910-1991 ..... **CLC 23**
See also AITN 1; BPFB 2; CA 1-4R; CAAS 136; CANR 1, 83; RHW

Gao Xingjian 1940- .... **CLC 167**
See Xingjian, Gao
See also MTFW 2005

Garber, Eric 1943(?)-
See Holleran, Andrew
See also CANR 89

Garcia, Cristina 1958- .... **CLC 76**
See also AMWS 11; CA 141; CANR 73, 130; CN 7; DLB 292; DNFS 1; EWL 3; HW 2; LLW; MTFW 2005

Garcia Lorca, Federico 1898-1936 ...... **DC 2; HLC 2; PC 3; TCLC 1, 7, 49, 181; WLC 2**
See Lorca, Federico Garcia
See also AAYA 46; CA 131; CAAE 104; CANR 81; DA; DA3; DAB; DAC; DAM DRAM, MST, MULT, POET; DFS 4, 10; DLB 108; EWL 3; HW 1, 2; LATS 1:2; MTCW 1, 2; MTFW 2005; TWA

Garcia Marquez, Gabriel 1928- .... **CLC 2, 3, 8, 10, 15, 27, 47, 55, 68, 170; HLC 1; SSC 8, 83; WLC 3**
See also AAYA 3, 33; BEST 89:1, 90:4; BPFB 2; BYA 12, 16; CA 33-36R; CANR 10, 28, 50, 75, 82, 128; CDWLB 3; CPW;

CWW 2; DA; DA3; DAB; DAC; DAM MST, MULT, NOV, POP; DLB 113, 330; DNFS 1, 2; EWL 3; EXPN; EXPS; HW 1, 2; LAIT 2; LATS 1:2; LAW; LAWS 1; LMFS 2; MTCW 1, 2; MTFW 2005; NCFS 3; NFS 1, 5, 10; RGSF 2; RGWL 2, 3; SSFS 1, 6, 16, 21; TWA; WLIT 1

Garcia Marquez, Gabriel Jose
See Garcia Marquez, Gabriel

Garcilaso de la Vega, El Inca
1539-1616 .... **HLCS 1; LC 127**
See also DLB 318; LAW

Gard, Janice
See Latham, Jean Lee

Gard, Roger Martin du
See Martin du Gard, Roger

Gardam, Jane (Mary) 1928- .... **CLC 43**
See also CA 49-52; CANR 2, 18, 33, 54, 106; CLR 12; DLB 14, 161, 231; MAICYA 1, 2; MTCW 1; SAAS 9; SATA 39, 76, 130; SATA-Brief 28; YAW

Gardner, Herb(ert George)
1934-2003 .... **CLC 44**
See also CA 149; CAAS 220; CAD; CANR 119; CD 5, 6; DFS 18, 20

Gardner, John, Jr. 1933-1982 ... **CLC 2, 3, 5, 7, 8, 10, 18, 28, 34; SSC 7**
See also AAYA 45; AITN 1; AMWS 6; BPFB 2; CA 65-68; CAAS 107; CANR 33, 73; CDALBS; CN 2, 3; CPW; DA3; DAM NOV, POP; DLB 2; DLBY 1982; EWL 3; FANT; LATS 1:2; MAL 5; MTCW 1, 2; MTFW 2005; NFS 3; RGAL 4; RGSF 2; SATA 40; SATA-Obit 31; SSFS 8

Gardner, John (Edmund) 1926- .... **CLC 30**
See also CA 103; CANR 15, 69, 127; CMW 4; CPW; DAM POP; MTCW 1

Gardner, Miriam
See Bradley, Marion Zimmer
See also GLL 1

Gardner, Noel
See Kuttner, Henry

Gardons, S. S.
See Snodgrass, W.D.

Garfield, Leon 1921-1996 .... **CLC 12**
See also AAYA 8, 69; BYA 1, 3; CA 17-20R; CAAS 152; CANR 38, 41, 78; CLR 21; DLB 161; JRDA; MAICYA 1, 2; MAICYAS 1; SATA 1, 32, 76; SATA-Obit 90; TEA; WYA; YAW

Garland, (Hannibal) Hamlin
1860-1940 .... **SSC 18; TCLC 3**
See also CAAE 104; DLB 12, 71, 78, 186; MAL 5; RGAL 4; RGSF 2; TCWW 1, 2

Garneau, (Hector de) Saint-Denys
1912-1943 .... **TCLC 13**
See also CAAE 111; DLB 88

Garner, Alan 1934- .... **CLC 17**
See also AAYA 18; BYA 3, 5; CA 178; 73-76, 178; CANR 15, 64, 134; CLR 20; CPW; DAB; DAM POP; DLB 161, 261; FANT; MAICYA 1, 2; MTCW 1, 2; MTFW 2005; SATA 18, 69; SATA-Essay 108; SUFW 1, 2; YAW

Garner, Hugh 1913-1979 .... **CLC 13**
See Warwick, Jarvis
See also CA 69-72; CANR 31; CCA 1; CN 1, 2; DLB 68

Garnett, David 1892-1981 .... **CLC 3**
See also CA 5-8R; CAAS 103; CANR 17, 79; CN 1, 2; DLB 34; FANT; MTCW 2; RGEL 2; SFW 4; SUFW 1

Garnier, Robert c. 1545-1590 .... **LC 119**
See also DLB 327; GFL Beginnings to 1789

Garrett, George (Palmer, Jr.) 1929- . **CLC 3, 11, 51; SSC 30**
See also AMWS 7; BPFB 2; CA 202; 1-4R, 202; 5; CANR 1, 42, 67, 109; CN 1, 2, 3,

4, 5, 6, 7; CP 1, 2, 3, 4, 5, 6, 7; CSW;
DLB 2, 5, 130, 152; DLBY 1983

Garrick, David 1717-1779 .... **LC 15**
See also DAM DRAM; DLB 84, 213;
RGEL 2

Garrigue, Jean 1914-1972 .... **CLC 2, 8**
See also CA 5-8R; CAAS 37-40R; CANR
20; CP 1; MAL 5

Garrison, Frederick
See Sinclair, Upton

Garrison, William Lloyd
1805-1879 .... **NCLC 149**
See also CDALB 1640-1865; DLB 1, 43,
235

Garro, Elena 1920(?)-1998 .. **HLCS 1; TCLC
153**
See also CA 131; CAAS 169; CWW 2;
DLB 145; EWL 3; HW 1; LAWS 1; WLIT
1

Garth, Will
See Hamilton, Edmond; Kuttner, Henry

Garvey, Marcus (Moziah, Jr.)
1887-1940 ... **BLC 2; HR 1:2; TCLC 41**
See also BW 1; CA 124; CAAE 120; CANR
79; DAM MULT

Gary, Romain .... **CLC 25**
See Kacew, Romain
See also DLB 83, 299; RGHL

Gascar, Pierre .... **CLC 11**
See Fournier, Pierre
See also EWL 3; RGHL

Gascoigne, George 1539-1577 .... **LC 108**
See also DLB 136; RGEL 2

Gascoyne, David (Emery)
1916-2001 .... **CLC 45**
See also CA 65-68; CAAS 200; CANR 10,
28, 54; CP 1, 2, 3, 4, 5, 6, 7; DLB 20;
MTCW 1; RGEL 2

Gaskell, Elizabeth Cleghorn
1810-1865 .... **NCLC 5, 70, 97, 137; SSC
25, 97**
See also BRW 5; CDBLB 1832-1890; DAB;
DAM MST; DLB 21, 144, 159; RGEL 2;
RGSF 2; TEA

Gass, William H. 1924- . **CLC 1, 2, 8, 11, 15,
39, 132; SSC 12**
See also AMWS 6; CA 17-20R; CANR 30,
71, 100; CN 1, 2, 3, 4, 5, 6, 7; DLB 2,
227; EWL 3; MAL 5; MTCW 1, 2;
MTFW 2005; RGAL 4

Gassendi, Pierre 1592-1655 .... **LC 54**
See also GFL Beginnings to 1789

Gasset, Jose Ortega y
See Ortega y Gasset, Jose

Gates, Henry Louis, Jr. 1950- ... **BLCS; CLC
65**
See also BW 2, 3; CA 109; CANR 25, 53,
75, 125; CSW; DA3; DAM MULT; DLB
67; EWL 3; MAL 5; MTCW 2; MTFW
2005; RGAL 4

Gatos, Stephanie
See Katz, Steve

Gautier, Theophile 1811-1872 .. **NCLC 1, 59;
PC 18; SSC 20**
See also DAM POET; DLB 119; EW 6;
GFL 1789 to the Present; RGWL 2, 3;
SUFW; TWA

Gay, John 1685-1732 .... **LC 49**
See also BRW 3; DAM DRAM; DLB 84,
95; RGEL 2; WLIT 3

Gay, Oliver
See Gogarty, Oliver St. John

Gay, Peter 1923- .... **CLC 158**
See also CA 13-16R; CANR 18, 41, 77,
147; INT CANR-18; RGHL

Gay, Peter Jack
See Gay, Peter

Gaye, Marvin (Pentz, Jr.)
1939-1984 .... **CLC 26**
See also CA 195; CAAS 112

Gebler, Carlo 1954- .... **CLC 39**
See also CA 133; CAAE 119; CANR 96;
DLB 271

Gee, Maggie 1948- .... **CLC 57**
See also CA 130; CANR 125; CN 4, 5, 6,
7; DLB 207; MTFW 2005

Gee, Maurice 1931- .... **CLC 29**
See also AAYA 42; CA 97-100; CANR 67,
123; CLR 56; CN 2, 3, 4, 5, 6, 7; CWRI
5; EWL 3; MAICYA 2; RGSF 2; SATA
46, 101

Gee, Maurice Gough
See Gee, Maurice

Geiogamah, Hanay 1945- .... **NNAL**
See also CA 153; DAM MULT; DLB 175

Gelbart, Larry
See Gelbart, Larry (Simon)
See also CAD; CD 5, 6

Gelbart, Larry (Simon) 1928- .... **CLC 21, 61**
See Gelbart, Larry
See also CA 73-76; CANR 45, 94

Gelber, Jack 1932-2003 ...... **CLC 1, 6, 14, 79**
See also CA 1-4R; CAAS 216; CAD;
CANR 2; DLB 7, 228; MAL 5

Gellhorn, Martha (Ellis)
1908-1998 .... **CLC 14, 60**
See also CA 77-80; CAAS 164; CANR 44;
CN 1, 2, 3, 4, 5, 6 7; DLBY 1982, 1998

Genet, Jean 1910-1986 .. **CLC 1, 2, 5, 10, 14,
44, 46; DC 25; TCLC 128**
See also CA 13-16R; CANR 18; DA3;
DAM DRAM; DFS 10; DLB 72, 321;
DLBY 1986; EW 13; EWL 3; GFL 1789
to the Present; GLL 1; LMFS 2; MTCW
1, 2; MTFW 2005; RGWL 2, 3; TWA

Genlis, Stephanie-Felicite Ducrest
1746-1830 .... **NCLC 166**
See also DLB 313

Gent, Peter 1942- .... **CLC 29**
See also AITN 1; CA 89-92; DLBY 1982

Gentile, Giovanni 1875-1944 .... **TCLC 96**
See also CAAE 119

Geoffrey of Monmouth c.
1100-1155 .... **CMLC 44**
See also DLB 146; TEA

George, Jean
See George, Jean Craighead

George, Jean Craighead 1919- .... **CLC 35**
See also AAYA 8, 69; BYA 2, 4; CA 5-8R;
CANR 25; CLR 1; 80; DLB 52; JRDA;
MAICYA 1, 2; SATA 2, 68, 124, 170;
WYA; YAW

George, Stefan (Anton) 1868-1933 . **TCLC 2,
14**
See also CA 193; CAAE 104; EW 8; EWL
3

Georges, Georges Martin
See Simenon, Georges (Jacques Christian)

Gerald of Wales c. 1146-c. 1223 ... **CMLC 60**

Gerhardi, William Alexander
See Gerhardie, William Alexander

Gerhardie, William Alexander
1895-1977 .... **CLC 5**
See also CA 25-28R; CAAS 73-76; CANR
18; CN 1, 2; DLB 36; RGEL 2

Gerson, Jean 1363-1429 .... **LC 77**
See also DLB 208

Gersonides 1288-1344 .... **CMLC 49**
See also DLB 115

Gerstler, Amy 1956- .... **CLC 70**
See also CA 146; CANR 99

Gertler, T. .... **CLC 34**
See also CA 116

Gertsen, Aleksandr Ivanovich
See Herzen, Aleksandr Ivanovich

Ghalib .... **NCLC 39, 78**
See Ghalib, Asadullah Khan

Ghalib, Asadullah Khan 1797-1869
See Ghalib
See also DAM POET; RGWL 2, 3

Ghelderode, Michel de 1898-1962 ..... **CLC 6,
11; DC 15; TCLC 187**
See also CA 85-88; CANR 40, 77; DAM
DRAM; DLB 321; EW 11; EWL 3; TWA

Ghiselin, Brewster 1903-2001 .... **CLC 23**
See also CA 13-16R; 10; CANR 13; CP 1,
2, 3, 4, 5, 6, 7

Ghose, Aurabinda 1872-1950 .... **TCLC 63**
See Ghose, Aurobindo
See also CA 163

Ghose, Aurobindo
See Ghose, Aurabinda
See also EWL 3

Ghose, Zulfikar 1935- .... **CLC 42, 200**
See also CA 65-68; CANR 67; CN 1, 2, 3,
4, 5, 6, 7; CP 1, 2, 3, 4, 5, 6, 7; DLB 323;
EWL 3

Ghosh, Amitav 1956- .... **CLC 44, 153**
See also CA 147; CANR 80, 158; CN 6, 7;
DLB 323; WWE 1

Giacosa, Giuseppe 1847-1906 .... **TCLC 7**
See also CAAE 104

Gibb, Lee
See Waterhouse, Keith (Spencer)

Gibbon, Edward 1737-1794 .... **LC 97**
See also BRW 3; DLB 104; RGEL 2

Gibbon, Lewis Grassic .... **TCLC 4**
See Mitchell, James Leslie
See also RGEL 2

Gibbons, Kaye 1960- .... **CLC 50, 88, 145**
See also AAYA 34; AMWS 10; CA 151;
CANR 75, 127; CN 7; CSW; DA3; DAM
POP; DLB 292; MTCW 2; MTFW 2005;
NFS 3; RGAL 4; SATA 117

Gibran, Kahlil 1883-1931 . **PC 9; TCLC 1, 9**
See also CA 150; CAAE 104; DA3; DAM
POET, POP; EWL 3; MTCW 2; WLIT 6

Gibran, Khalil
See Gibran, Kahlil

Gibson, Mel 1956- .... **CLC 215**

Gibson, William 1914- .... **CLC 23**
See also CA 9-12R; CAD; CANR 9, 42, 75,
125; CD 5, 6; DA; DAB; DAC; DAM
DRAM, MST; DFS 2; DLB 7; LAIT 2;
MAL 5; MTCW 2; MTFW 2005; SATA
66; YAW

Gibson, William 1948- .... **CLC 39, 63, 186,
192; SSC 52**
See also AAYA 12, 59; AMWS 16; BPFB
2; CA 133; CAAE 126; CANR 52, 90,
106; CN 6, 7; CPW; DA3; DAM POP;
DLB 251; MTCW 2; MTFW 2005; SCFW
2; SFW 4

Gibson, William Ford
See Gibson, William

Gide, Andre (Paul Guillaume)
1869-1951 ...... **SSC 13; TCLC 5, 12, 36,
177; WLC 3**
See also CA 124; CAAE 104; DA; DA3;
DAB; DAC; DAM MST, NOV; DLB 65,
321, 330; EW 8; EWL 3; GFL 1789 to
the Present; MTCW 1, 2; MTFW 2005;
NFS 21; RGSF 2; RGWL 2, 3; TWA

Gifford, Barry (Colby) 1946- .... **CLC 34**
See also CA 65-68; CANR 9, 30, 40, 90

Gilbert, Frank
See De Voto, Bernard (Augustine)

Gilbert, W(illiam) S(chwenck)
1836-1911 .... **TCLC 3**
See also CA 173; CAAE 104; DAM DRAM,
POET; RGEL 2; SATA 36

Gold, Herbert 1924- ... **CLC 4, 7, 14, 42, 152**
See also CA 9-12R; CANR 17, 45, 125; CN
1, 2, 3, 4, 5, 6, 7; DLB 2; DLBY 1981;
MAL 5

Goldbarth, Albert 1948- .... **CLC 5, 38**
See also AMWS 12; CA 53-56; CANR 6,
40; CP 3, 4, 5, 6, 7; DLB 120

Goldberg, Anatol 1910-1982 .... **CLC 34**
See also CA 131; CAAS 117

Goldemberg, Isaac 1945- .... **CLC 52**
See also CA 69-72; 12; CANR 11, 32; EWL
3; HW 1; WLIT 1

Golding, Arthur 1536-1606 .... **LC 101**
See also DLB 136

Golding, William 1911-1993 . **CLC 1, 2, 3, 8,
10, 17, 27, 58, 81; WLC 3**
See also AAYA 5, 44; BPFB 2; BRWR 1;
BRWS 1; BYA 2; CA 5-8R; CAAS 141;
CANR 13, 33, 54; CD 5; CDBLB 1945-
1960; CLR 94; CN 1, 2, 3, 4; DA; DA3;
DAB; DAC; DAM MST, NOV; DLB 15,
100, 255, 326, 330; EWL 3; EXPN; HGG;
LAIT 4; MTCW 1, 2; MTFW 2005; NFS
2; RGEL 2; RHW; SFW 4; TEA; WLIT
4; YAW

Golding, William Gerald
See Golding, William

Goldman, Emma 1869-1940 .... **TCLC 13**
See also CA 150; CAAE 110; DLB 221;
FW; RGAL 4; TUS

Goldman, Francisco 1954- .... **CLC 76**
See also CA 162

Goldman, William 1931- .... **CLC 1, 48**
See also BPFB 2; CA 9-12R; CANR 29,
69, 106; CN 1, 2, 3, 4, 5, 6, 7; DLB 44;
FANT; IDFW 3, 4

Goldman, William W.
See Goldman, William

Goldmann, Lucien 1913-1970 .... **CLC 24**
See also CA 25-28; CAP 2

Goldoni, Carlo 1707-1793 .... **LC 4**
See also DAM DRAM; EW 4; RGWL 2, 3;
WLIT 7

Goldsberry, Steven 1949- .... **CLC 34**
See also CA 131

Goldsmith, Oliver 1730(?)-1774 .... **DC 8; LC
2, 48, 122; PC 77; WLC 3**
See also BRW 3; CDBLB 1660-1789; DA;
DAB; DAC; DAM DRAM, MST, NOV,
POET; DFS 1; DLB 39, 89, 104, 109, 142;
IDTP; RGEL 2; SATA 26; TEA; WLIT 3

Goldsmith, Peter
See Priestley, J(ohn) B(oynton)

Gombrowicz, Witold 1904-1969 .... **CLC 4, 7,
11, 49**
See also CA 19-20; CAAS 25-28R; CANR
105; CAP 2; CDWLB 4; DAM DRAM;
DLB 215; EW 12; EWL 3; RGWL 2, 3;
TWA

Gomez de Avellaneda, Gertrudis
1814-1873 .... **NCLC 111**
See also LAW

Gomez de la Serna, Ramon
1888-1963 .... **CLC 9**
See also CA 153; CAAS 116; CANR 79;
EWL 3; HW 1, 2

Goncharov, Ivan Alexandrovich
1812-1891 .... **NCLC 1, 63**
See also DLB 238; EW 6; RGWL 2, 3

Goncourt, Edmond (Louis Antoine Huot) de
1822-1896 .... **NCLC 7**
See also DLB 123; EW 7; GFL 1789 to the
Present; RGWL 2, 3

Goncourt, Jules (Alfred Huot) de
1830-1870 .... **NCLC 7**
See also DLB 123; EW 7; GFL 1789 to the
Present; RGWL 2, 3

Gongora (y Argote), Luis de
1561-1627 .... **LC 72**
See also RGWL 2, 3

Gontier, Fernande 19(?)- .... **CLC 50**

Gonzalez Martinez, Enrique
See Gonzalez Martinez, Enrique
See also DLB 290

Gonzalez Martinez, Enrique
1871-1952 .... **TCLC 72**
See Gonzalez Martinez, Enrique
See also CA 166; CANR 81; EWL 3; HW
1, 2

Goodison, Lorna 1947- .... **PC 36**
See also CA 142; CANR 88; CP 5, 6, 7;
CWP; DLB 157; EWL 3; PFS 25

Goodman, Paul 1911-1972 ..... **CLC 1, 2, 4, 7**
See also CA 19-20; CAAS 37-40R; CAD;
CANR 34; CAP 2; CN 1; DLB 130, 246;
MAL 5; MTCW 1; RGAL 4

GoodWeather, Harley
See King, Thomas

Googe, Barnabe 1540-1594 .... **LC 94**
See also DLB 132; RGEL 2

Gordimer, Nadine 1923- ...... **CLC 3, 5, 7, 10,
18, 33, 51, 70, 123, 160, 161; SSC 17,
80; WLCS**
See also AAYA 39; AFW; BRWS 2; CA
5-8R; CANR 3, 28, 56, 88, 131; CN 1, 2,
3, 4, 5, 6, 7; DA; DA3; DAB; DAC; DAM
MST, NOV; DLB 225, 326, 330; EWL 3;
EXPS; INT CANR-28; LATS 1:2; MTCW
1, 2; MTFW 2005; NFS 4; RGEL 2;
RGSF 2; SSFS 2, 14, 19; TWA; WLIT 2;
YAW

Gordon, Adam Lindsay
1833-1870 .... **NCLC 21**
See also DLB 230

Gordon, Caroline 1895-1981 . **CLC 6, 13, 29,
83; SSC 15**
See also AMW; CA 11-12; CAAS 103;
CANR 36; CAP 1; CN 1, 2; DLB 4, 9,
102; DLBD 17; DLBY 1981; EWL 3;
MAL 5; MTCW 1, 2; MTFW 2005;
RGAL 4; RGSF 2

Gordon, Charles William 1860-1937
See Connor, Ralph
See also CAAE 109

Gordon, Mary 1949- .. **CLC 13, 22, 128, 216;
SSC 59**
See also AMWS 4; BPFB 2; CA 102;
CANR 44, 92, 154; CN 4, 5, 6, 7; DLB 6;
DLBY 1981; FW; INT CA-102; MAL 5;
MTCW 1

Gordon, Mary Catherine
See Gordon, Mary

Gordon, N. J.
See Bosman, Herman Charles

Gordon, Sol 1923- .... **CLC 26**
See also CA 53-56; CANR 4; SATA 11

Gordone, Charles 1925-1995 .. **CLC 1, 4; DC
8**
See also BW 1, 3; CA 180; 93-96, 180;
CAAS 150; CAD; CANR 55; DAM
DRAM; DLB 7; INT CA-93-96; MTCW
1

Gore, Catherine 1800-1861 .... **NCLC 65**
See also DLB 116; RGEL 2

Gorenko, Anna Andreevna
See Akhmatova, Anna

Gorky, Maxim .... **SSC 28; TCLC 8; WLC 3**
See Peshkov, Alexei Maximovich
See also DAB; DFS 9; DLB 295; EW 8;
EWL 3; TWA

Goryan, Sirak
See Saroyan, William

Gosse, Edmund (William)
1849-1928 .... **TCLC 28**
See also CAAE 117; DLB 57, 144, 184;
RGEL 2

Gotlieb, Phyllis (Fay Bloom) 1926- .. **CLC 18**
See also CA 13-16R; CANR 7, 135; CN 7;
CP 1, 2, 3, 4; DLB 88, 251; SFW 4

Gottesman, S. D.
See Kornbluth, C(yril) M.; Pohl, Frederik

Gottfried von Strassburg fl. c.
1170-1215 .... **CMLC 10**
See also CDWLB 2; DLB 138; EW 1;
RGWL 2, 3

Gotthelf, Jeremias 1797-1854 .... **NCLC 117**
See also DLB 133; RGWL 2, 3

Gottschalk, Laura Riding
See Jackson, Laura (Riding)

Gould, Lois 1932(?)-2002 .... **CLC 4, 10**
See also CA 77-80; CAAS 208; CANR 29;
MTCW 1

Gould, Stephen Jay 1941-2002 .... **CLC 163**
See also AAYA 26; BEST 90:2; CA 77-80;
CAAS 205; CANR 10, 27, 56, 75, 125;
CPW; INT CANR-27; MTCW 1, 2;
MTFW 2005

Gourmont, Remy(-Marie-Charles) de
1858-1915 .... **TCLC 17**
See also CA 150; CAAE 109; GFL 1789 to
the Present; MTCW 2

Gournay, Marie le Jars de
See de Gournay, Marie le Jars

Govier, Katherine 1948- .... **CLC 51**
See also CA 101; CANR 18, 40, 128; CCA
1

Gower, John c. 1330-1408 .... **LC 76; PC 59**
See also BRW 1; DLB 146; RGEL 2

Goyen, (Charles) William
1915-1983 .... **CLC 5, 8, 14, 40**
See also AITN 2; CA 5-8R; CAAS 110;
CANR 6, 71; CN 1, 2, 3; DLB 2, 218;
DLBY 1983; EWL 3; INT CANR-6; MAL
5

Goytisolo, Juan 1931- .... **CLC 5, 10, 23, 133;
HLC 1**
See also CA 85-88; CANR 32, 61, 131;
CWW 2; DAM MULT; DLB 322; EWL
3; GLL 2; HW 1, 2; MTCW 1, 2; MTFW
2005

Gozzano, Guido 1883-1916 .... **PC 10**
See also CA 154; DLB 114; EWL 3

Gozzi, (Conte) Carlo 1720-1806 .... **NCLC 23**

Grabbe, Christian Dietrich
1801-1836 .... **NCLC 2**
See also DLB 133; RGWL 2, 3

Grace, Patricia Frances 1937- .... **CLC 56**
See also CA 176; CANR 118; CN 4, 5, 6,
7; EWL 3; RGSF 2

Gracian y Morales, Baltasar
1601-1658 .... **LC 15**

Gracq, Julien .... **CLC 11, 48**
See Poirier, Louis
See also CWW 2; DLB 83; GFL 1789 to
the Present

Grade, Chaim 1910-1982 .... **CLC 10**
See also CA 93-96; CAAS 107; DLB 333;
EWL 3; RGHL

Grade, Khayim
See Grade, Chaim

Graduate of Oxford, A
See Ruskin, John

Grafton, Garth
See Duncan, Sara Jeannette

Grafton, Sue 1940- .... **CLC 163**
See also AAYA 11, 49; BEST 90:3; CA 108;
CANR 31, 55, 111, 134; CMW 4; CPW;
CSW; DA3; DAM POP; DLB 226; FW;
MSW; MTFW 2005

Graham, John
See Phillips, David Graham

Graham, Jorie 1950- .... **CLC 48, 118; PC 59**
See also AAYA 67; CA 111; CANR 63, 118;
CP 4, 5, 6, 7; CWP; DLB 120; EWL 3;
MTFW 2005; PFS 10, 17; TCLE 1:1

Graham, R(obert) B(ontine) Cunninghame
See Cunninghame Graham, Robert (Gallnigad) Bontine
See also DLB 98, 135, 174; RGEL 2; RGSF 2

Graham, Robert
See Haldeman, Joe

Graham, Tom
See Lewis, (Harry) Sinclair

Graham, W(illiam) S(ydney)
1918-1986 .... CLC 29
See also BRWS 7; CA 73-76; CAAS 118; CP 1, 2, 3, 4; DLB 20; RGEL 2

Graham, Winston (Mawdsley)
1910-2003 .... CLC 23
See also CA 49-52; CAAS 218; CANR 2, 22, 45, 66; CMW 4; CN 1, 2, 3, 4, 5, 6, 7; DLB 77; RHW

Grahame, Kenneth 1859-1932 ...... TCLC 64, 136
See also BYA 5; CA 136; CAAE 108; CANR 80; CLR 5; CWRI 5; DA3; DAB; DLB 34, 141, 178; FANT; MAICYA 1, 2; MTCW 2; NFS 20; RGEL 2; SATA 100; TEA; WCH; YABC 1

Granger, Darius John
See Marlowe, Stephen

Granin, Daniil 1918- .... CLC 59
See also DLB 302

Granovsky, Timofei Nikolaevich
1813-1855 .... NCLC 75
See also DLB 198

Grant, Skeeter
See Spiegelman, Art

Granville-Barker, Harley
1877-1946 .... TCLC 2
See Barker, Harley Granville
See also CA 204; CAAE 104; DAM DRAM; RGEL 2

Granzotto, Gianni
See Granzotto, Giovanni Battista

Granzotto, Giovanni Battista
1914-1985 .... CLC 70
See also CA 166

Grass, Guenter
See Grass, Gunter
See also CWW 2; DLB 330; RGHL

Grass, Gunter 1927- .. CLC 1, 2, 4, 6, 11, 15, 22, 32, 49, 88, 207; WLC 3
See Grass, Guenter
See also BPFB 2; CA 13-16R; CANR 20, 75, 93, 133; CDWLB 2; DA; DA3; DAB; DAC; DAM MST, NOV; DLB 75, 124; EW 13; EWL 3; MTCW 1, 2; MTFW 2005; RGWL 2, 3; TWA

Grass, Gunter Wilhelm
See Grass, Gunter

Gratton, Thomas
See Hulme, T(homas) E(rnest)

Grau, Shirley Ann 1929- .... CLC 4, 9, 146; SSC 15
See also CA 89-92; CANR 22, 69; CN 1, 2, 3, 4, 5, 6, 7; CSW; DLB 2, 218; INT CA-89-92; CANR-22; MTCW 1

Gravel, Fern
See Hall, James Norman

Graver, Elizabeth 1964- .... CLC 70
See also CA 135; CANR 71, 129

Graves, Richard Perceval
1895-1985 .... CLC 44
See also CA 65-68; CANR 9, 26, 51

Graves, Robert 1895-1985 ... CLC 1, 2, 6, 11, 39, 44, 45; PC 6
See also BPFB 2; BRW 7; BYA 4; CA 5-8R; CAAS 117; CANR 5, 36; CDBLB 1914-1945; CN 1, 2, 3; CP 1, 2, 3, 4; DA3; DAB; DAC; DAM MST, POET; DLB 20, 100, 191; DLBD 18; DLBY 1985; EWL

3; LATS 1:1; MTCW 1, 2; MTFW 2005; NCFS 2; NFS 21; RGEL 2; RHW; SATA 45; TEA

Graves, Valerie
See Bradley, Marion Zimmer

Gray, Alasdair 1934- .... CLC 41
See also BRWS 9; CA 126; CANR 47, 69, 106, 140; CN 4, 5, 6, 7; DLB 194, 261, 319; HGG; INT CA-126; MTCW 1, 2; MTFW 2005; RGSF 2; SUFW 2

Gray, Amlin 1946- .... CLC 29
See also CA 138

Gray, Francine du Plessix 1930- ..... CLC 22, 153
See also BEST 90:3; CA 61-64; 2; CANR 11, 33, 75, 81; DAM NOV; INT CANR-11; MTCW 1, 2; MTFW 2005

Gray, John (Henry) 1866-1934 ...... TCLC 19
See also CA 162; CAAE 119; RGEL 2

Gray, John Lee
See Jakes, John

Gray, Simon (James Holliday)
1936- .... CLC 9, 14, 36
See also AITN 1; CA 21-24R; 3; CANR 32, 69; CBD; CD 5, 6; CN 1, 2, 3; DLB 13; EWL 3; MTCW 1; RGEL 2

Gray, Spalding 1941-2004 .... CLC 49, 112; DC 7
See also AAYA 62; CA 128; CAAS 225; CAD; CANR 74, 138; CD 5, 6; CPW; DAM POP; MTCW 2; MTFW 2005

Gray, Thomas 1716-1771 .... LC 4, 40; PC 2; WLC 3
See also BRW 3; CDBLB 1660-1789; DA; DA3; DAB; DAC; DAM MST; DLB 109; EXPP; PAB; PFS 9; RGEL 2; TEA; WP

Grayson, David
See Baker, Ray Stannard

Grayson, Richard (A.) 1951- .... CLC 38
See also CA 210; 85-88, 210; CANR 14, 31, 57; DLB 234

Greeley, Andrew M. 1928- .... CLC 28
See also BPFB 2; CA 5-8R; 7; CANR 7, 43, 69, 104, 136; CMW 4; CPW; DA3; DAM POP; MTCW 1, 2; MTFW 2005

Green, Anna Katharine
1846-1935 .... TCLC 63
See also CA 159; CAAE 112; CMW 4; DLB 202, 221; MSW

Green, Brian
See Card, Orson Scott

Green, Hannah
See Greenberg, Joanne (Goldenberg)

Green, Hannah 1927(?)-1996 .... CLC 3
See also CA 73-76; CANR 59, 93; NFS 10

Green, Henry .... CLC 2, 13, 97
See Yorke, Henry Vincent
See also BRWS 2; CA 175; DLB 15; EWL 3; RGEL 2

Green, Julian .... CLC 3, 11, 77
See Green, Julien (Hartridge)
See also EWL 3; GFL 1789 to the Present; MTCW 2

Green, Julien (Hartridge) 1900-1998
See Green, Julian
See also CA 21-24R; CAAS 169; CANR 33, 87; CWW 2; DLB 4, 72; MTCW 1, 2; MTFW 2005

Green, Paul (Eliot) 1894-1981 .... CLC 25
See also AITN 1; CA 5-8R; CAAS 103; CAD; CANR 3; DAM DRAM; DLB 7, 9, 249; DLBY 1981; MAL 5; RGAL 4

Greenaway, Peter 1942- .... CLC 159
See also CA 127

Greenberg, Ivan 1908-1973
See Rahv, Philip
See also CA 85-88

Greenberg, Joanne (Goldenberg)
1932- .... CLC 7, 30
See also AAYA 12, 67; CA 5-8R; CANR 14, 32, 69; CN 6, 7; NFS 23; SATA 25; YAW

Greenberg, Richard 1959(?)- .... CLC 57
See also CA 138; CAD; CD 5, 6

Greenblatt, Stephen J(ay) 1943- ...... CLC 70
See also CA 49-52; CANR 115

Greene, Bette 1934- .... CLC 30
See also AAYA 7, 69; BYA 3; CA 53-56; CANR 4, 146; CLR 2; CWRI 5; JRDA; LAIT 4; MAICYA 1, 2; NFS 10; SAAS 16; SATA 8, 102, 161; WYA; YAW

Greene, Gael .... CLC 8
See also CA 13-16R; CANR 10

Greene, Graham 1904-1991 .. CLC 1, 3, 6, 9, 14, 18, 27, 37, 70, 72, 125; SSC 29; WLC 3
See also AAYA 61; AITN 2; BPFB 2; BRWR 2; BRWS 1; BYA 3; CA 13-16R; CAAS 133; CANR 35, 61, 131; CBD; CDBLB 1945-1960; CMW 4; CN 1, 2, 3, 4; DA; DA3; DAB; DAC; DAM MST, NOV; DLB 13, 15, 77, 100, 162, 201, 204; DLBY 1991; EWL 3; MSW; MTCW 1, 2; MTFW 2005; NFS 16; RGEL 2; SATA 20; SSFS 14; TEA; WLIT 4

Greene, Robert 1558-1592 .... LC 41
See also BRWS 8; DLB 62, 167; IDTP; RGEL 2; TEA

Greer, Germaine 1939- .... CLC 131
See also AITN 1; CA 81-84; CANR 33, 70, 115, 133; FW; MTCW 1, 2; MTFW 2005

Greer, Richard
See Silverberg, Robert

Gregor, Arthur 1923- .... CLC 9
See also CA 25-28R; 10; CANR 11; CP 1, 2, 3, 4, 5, 6, 7; SATA 36

Gregor, Lee
See Pohl, Frederik

Gregory, Lady Isabella Augusta (Persse)
1852-1932 .... TCLC 1, 176
See also BRW 6; CA 184; CAAE 104; DLB 10; IDTP; RGEL 2

Gregory, J. Dennis
See Williams, John A(lfred)

Gregory of Nazianzus, St.
329-389 .... CMLC 82

Grekova, I. .... CLC 59
See Ventsel, Elena Sergeevna
See also CWW 2

Grendon, Stephen
See Derleth, August (William)

Grenville, Kate 1950- .... CLC 61
See also CA 118; CANR 53, 93, 156; CN 7; DLB 325

Grenville, Pelham
See Wodehouse, P(elham) G(renville)

Greve, Felix Paul (Berthold Friedrich)
1879-1948
See Grove, Frederick Philip
See also CA 141, 175; CAAE 104; CANR 79; DAC; DAM MST

Greville, Fulke 1554-1628 .... LC 79
See also BRWS 11; DLB 62, 172; RGEL 2

Grey, Lady Jane 1537-1554 .... LC 93
See also DLB 132

Grey, Zane 1872-1939 .... TCLC 6
See also BPFB 2; CA 132; CAAE 104; DA3; DAM POP; DLB 9, 212; MTCW 1, 2; MTFW 2005; RGAL 4; TCWW 1, 2; TUS

Griboedov, Aleksandr Sergeevich
1795(?)-1829 .... NCLC 129
See also DLB 205; RGWL 2, 3

Grieg, (Johan) Nordahl (Brun)
1902-1943 .... TCLC 10
See also CA 189; CAAE 107; EWL 3

Gurney, A(lbert) R(amsdell), Jr.
1930- .... **CLC 32, 50, 54**
See Gurney, A. R.
See also AMWS 5; CA 77-80; CAD; CANR
32, 64, 121; CD 5, 6; DAM DRAM; EWL
3

Gurney, Ivor (Bertie) 1890-1937 ... **TCLC 33**
See also BRW 6; CA 167; DLBY 2002;
PAB; RGEL 2

Gurney, Peter
See Gurney, A(lbert) R(amsdell), Jr.

Guro, Elena (Genrikhovna)
1877-1913 .... **TCLC 56**
See also DLB 295

Gustafson, James M(oody) 1925- ... **CLC 100**
See also CA 25-28R; CANR 37

Gustafson, Ralph (Barker)
1909-1995 .... **CLC 36**
See also CA 21-24R; CANR 8, 45, 84; CP
1, 2, 3, 4, 5, 6; DLB 88; RGEL 2

Gut, Gom
See Simenon, Georges (Jacques Christian)

Guterson, David 1956- .... **CLC 91**
See also CA 132; CANR 73, 126; CN 7;
DLB 292; MTCW 2; MTFW 2005; NFS
13

Guthrie, A(lfred) B(ertram), Jr.
1901-1991 .... **CLC 23**
See also CA 57-60; CAAS 134; CANR 24;
CN 1, 2, 3; DLB 6, 212; MAL 5; SATA
62; SATA-Obit 67; TCWW 1, 2

Guthrie, Isobel
See Grieve, C(hristopher) M(urray)

Guthrie, Woodrow Wilson 1912-1967
See Guthrie, Woody
See also CA 113; CAAS 93-96

Guthrie, Woody .... **CLC 35**
See Guthrie, Woodrow Wilson
See also DLB 303; LAIT 3

Gutierrez Najera, Manuel
1859-1895 .... **HLCS 2; NCLC 133**
See also DLB 290; LAW

Guy, Rosa (Cuthbert) 1925- .... **CLC 26**
See also AAYA 4, 37; BW 2; CA 17-20R;
CANR 14, 34, 83; CLR 13; DLB 33;
DNFS 1; JRDA; MAICYA 1, 2; SATA 14,
62, 122; YAW

Gwendolyn
See Bennett, (Enoch) Arnold

H. D. .... **CLC 3, 8, 14, 31, 34, 73; PC 5**
See Doolittle, Hilda
See also FL 1:5

H. de V.
See Buchan, John

Haavikko, Paavo Juhani 1931- .. **CLC 18, 34**
See also CA 106; CWW 2; EWL 3

Habbema, Koos
See Heijermans, Herman

Habermas, Juergen 1929- .... **CLC 104**
See also CA 109; CANR 85; DLB 242

Habermas, Jurgen
See Habermas, Juergen

Hacker, Marilyn 1942- ...... **CLC 5, 9, 23, 72,
91; PC 47**
See also CA 77-80; CANR 68, 129; CP 3,
4, 5, 6, 7; CWP; DAM POET; DLB 120,
282; FW; GLL 2; MAL 5; PFS 19

Hadewijch of Antwerp fl. 1250- ... **CMLC 61**
See also RGWL 3

Hadrian 76-138 .... **CMLC 52**

Haeckel, Ernst Heinrich (Philipp August)
1834-1919 .... **TCLC 83**
See also CA 157

Hafiz c. 1326-1389(?) .... **CMLC 34**
See also RGWL 2, 3; WLIT 6

Hagedorn, Jessica T(arahata)
1949- .... **CLC 185**
See also CA 139; CANR 69; CWP; DLB
312; RGAL 4

Haggard, H(enry) Rider
1856-1925 .... **TCLC 11**
See also BRWS 3; BYA 4, 5; CA 148;
CAAE 108; CANR 112; DLB 70, 156,
174, 178; FANT; LMFS 1; MTCW 2;
RGEL 2; RHW; SATA 16; SCFW 1, 2;
SFW 4; SUFW 1; WLIT 4

Hagiosy, L.
See Larbaud, Valery (Nicolas)

Hagiwara, Sakutaro 1886-1942 .... **PC 18;
TCLC 60**
See Hagiwara Sakutaro
See also CA 154; RGWL 3

Hagiwara Sakutaro
See Hagiwara, Sakutaro
See also EWL 3

Haig, Fenil
See Ford, Ford Madox

Haig-Brown, Roderick (Langmere)
1908-1976 .... **CLC 21**
See also CA 5-8R; CAAS 69-72; CANR 4,
38, 83; CLR 31; CWRI 5; DLB 88; MAI-
CYA 1, 2; SATA 12; TCWW 2

Haight, Rip
See Carpenter, John (Howard)

Haij, Vera
See Jansson, Tove (Marika)

Hailey, Arthur 1920-2004 .... **CLC 5**
See also AITN 2; BEST 90:3; BPFB 2; CA
1-4R; CAAS 233; CANR 2, 36, 75; CCA
1; CN 1, 2, 3, 4, 5, 6, 7; CPW; DAM
NOV, POP; DLB 88; DLBY 1982; MTCW
1, 2; MTFW 2005

Hailey, Elizabeth Forsythe 1938- ..... **CLC 40**
See also CA 188; 93-96, 188; 1; CANR 15,
48; INT CANR-15

Haines, John (Meade) 1924- .... **CLC 58**
See also AMWS 12; CA 17-20R; CANR
13, 34; CP 1, 2, 3, 4, 5; CSW; DLB 5,
212; TCLE 1:1

Ha Jin 1956- .... **CLC 109**
See Jin, Xuefei
See also CA 152; CANR 91, 130; DLB 244,
292; MTFW 2005; SSFS 17

Hakluyt, Richard 1552-1616 .... **LC 31**
See also DLB 136; RGEL 2

Haldeman, Joe 1943- .... **CLC 61**
See Graham, Robert
See also AAYA 38; CA 179; 53-56, 179;
25; CANR 6, 70, 72, 130; DLB 8; INT
CANR-6; SCFW 2; SFW 4

Haldeman, Joe William
See Haldeman, Joe

Hale, Janet Campbell 1947- .... **NNAL**
See also CA 49-52; CANR 45, 75; DAM
MULT; DLB 175; MTCW 2; MTFW 2005

Hale, Sarah Josepha (Buell)
1788-1879 .... **NCLC 75**
See also DLB 1, 42, 73, 243

Halevy, Elie 1870-1937 .... **TCLC 104**

Haley, Alex(ander Murray Palmer)
1921-1992 .... **BLC 2; CLC 8, 12, 76;
TCLC 147**
See also AAYA 26; BPFB 2; BW 2, 3; CA
77-80; CAAS 136; CANR 61; CDALBS;
CPW; CSW; DA; DA3; DAB; DAC;
DAM MST, MULT, POP; DLB 38; LAIT
5; MTCW 1, 2; NFS 9

Haliburton, Thomas Chandler
1796-1865 .... **NCLC 15, 149**
See also DLB 11, 99; RGEL 2; RGSF 2

Hall, Donald 1928- .. **CLC 1, 13, 37, 59, 151;
PC 70**
See also AAYA 63; CA 5-8R; 7; CANR 2,
44, 64, 106, 133; CP 1, 2, 3, 4, 5, 6, 7;
DAM POET; DLB 5; MAL 5; MTCW 2;
MTFW 2005; RGAL 4; SATA 23, 97

Hall, Donald Andrew, Jr.
See Hall, Donald

Hall, Frederic Sauser
See Sauser-Hall, Frederic

Hall, James
See Kuttner, Henry

Hall, James Norman 1887-1951 ..... **TCLC 23**
See also CA 173; CAAE 123; LAIT 1;
RHW 1; SATA 21

Hall, Joseph 1574-1656 .... **LC 91**
See also DLB 121, 151; RGEL 2

Hall, Marguerite Radclyffe
See Hall, Radclyffe

Hall, Radclyffe 1880-1943 .... **TCLC 12**
See also BRWS 6; CA 150; CAAE 110;
CANR 83; DLB 191; MTCW 2; MTFW
2005; RGEL 2; RHW

Hall, Rodney 1935- .... **CLC 51**
See also CA 109; CANR 69; CN 6, 7; CP
1, 2, 3, 4, 5, 6, 7; DLB 289

Hallam, Arthur Henry
1811-1833 .... **NCLC 110**
See also DLB 32

Halldor Laxness .... **CLC 25**
See Gudjonsson, Halldor Kiljan
See also DLB 293; EW 12; EWL 3; RGWL
2, 3

Halleck, Fitz-Greene 1790-1867 .... **NCLC 47**
See also DLB 3, 250; RGAL 4

Halliday, Michael
See Creasey, John

Halpern, Daniel 1945- .... **CLC 14**
See also CA 33-36R; CANR 93; CP 3, 4, 5,
6, 7

Hamburger, Michael (Peter Leopold)
1924- .... **CLC 5, 14**
See also CA 196; 5-8R, 196; 4; CANR 2,
47; CP 1, 2, 3, 4, 5, 6, 7; DLB 27

Hamill, Pete 1935- .... **CLC 10**
See also CA 25-28R; CANR 18, 71, 127

Hamilton, Alexander
1755(?)-1804 .... **NCLC 49**
See also DLB 37

Hamilton, Clive
See Lewis, C.S.

Hamilton, Edmond 1904-1977 .... **CLC 1**
See also CA 1-4R; CANR 3, 84; DLB 8;
SATA 118; SFW 4

Hamilton, Elizabeth 1758-1816 ... **NCLC 153**
See also DLB 116, 158

Hamilton, Eugene (Jacob) Lee
See Lee-Hamilton, Eugene (Jacob)

Hamilton, Franklin
See Silverberg, Robert

Hamilton, Gail
See Corcoran, Barbara (Asenath)

Hamilton, (Robert) Ian 1938-2001 . **CLC 191**
See also CA 106; CAAS 203; CANR 41,
67; CP 1, 2, 3, 4, 5, 6, 7; DLB 40, 155

Hamilton, Jane 1957- .... **CLC 179**
See also CA 147; CANR 85, 128; CN 7;
MTFW 2005

Hamilton, Mollie
See Kaye, M.M.

Hamilton, (Anthony Walter) Patrick
1904-1962 .... **CLC 51**
See also CA 176; CAAS 113; DLB 10, 191

Hamilton, Virginia 1936-2002 .... **CLC 26**
See also AAYA 2, 21; BW 2, 3; BYA 1, 2,
8; CA 25-28R; CAAS 206; CANR 20, 37,
73, 126; CLR 1, 11, 40; DAM MULT;
DLB 33, 52; DLBY 2001; INT CANR-
20; JRDA; LAIT 5; MAICYA 1, 2; MAI-
CYAS 1; MTCW 1, 2; MTFW 2005;
SATA 4, 56, 79, 123; SATA-Obit 132;
WYA; YAW

Hammett, (Samuel) Dashiell
1894-1961 .... **CLC 3, 5, 10, 19, 47; SSC
17; TCLC 187**
See also AAYA 59; AITN 1; AMWS 4;
BPFB 2; CA 81-84; CANR 42; CDALB

1929-1941; CMW 4; DA3; DLB 226, 280; DLBD 6; DLBY 1996; EWL 3; LAIT 3; MAL 5; MSW; MTCW 1, 2; MTFW 2005; NFS 21; RGAL 4; RGSF 2; TUS

Hammon, Jupiter 1720(?)-1800(?) .... **BLC 2; NCLC 5; PC 16**
See also DAM MULT, POET; DLB 31, 50

Hammond, Keith
See Kuttner, Henry

Hamner, Earl (Henry), Jr. 1923- ...... **CLC 12**
See also AITN 2; CA 73-76; DLB 6

Hampton, Christopher 1946- .... **CLC 4**
See also CA 25-28R; CD 5, 6; DLB 13; MTCW 1

Hampton, Christopher James
See Hampton, Christopher

Hamsun, Knut .... **TCLC 2, 14, 49, 151**
See Pedersen, Knut
See also DLB 297, 330; EW 8; EWL 3; RGWL 2, 3

Handke, Peter 1942- .... **CLC 5, 8, 10, 15, 38, 134; DC 17**
See also CA 77-80; CANR 33, 75, 104, 133; CWW 2; DAM DRAM, NOV; DLB 85, 124; EWL 3; MTCW 1, 2; MTFW 2005; TWA

Handy, W(illiam) C(hristopher)
1873-1958 .... **TCLC 97**
See also BW 3; CA 167; CAAE 121

Hanley, James 1901-1985 ..... **CLC 3, 5, 8, 13**
See also CA 73-76; CAAS 117; CANR 36; CBD; CN 1, 2, 3; DLB 191; EWL 3; MTCW 1; RGEL 2

Hannah, Barry 1942- .. **CLC 23, 38, 90; SSC 94**
See also BPFB 2; CA 110; CAAE 108; CANR 43, 68, 113; CN 4, 5, 6, 7; CSW; DLB 6, 234; INT CA-110; MTCW 1; RGSF 2

Hannon, Ezra
See Hunter, Evan

Hansberry, Lorraine (Vivian)
1930-1965 ... **BLC 2; CLC 17, 62; DC 2**
See also AAYA 25; AFAW 1, 2; AMWS 4; BW 1, 3; CA 109; CAAS 25-28R; CABS 3; CAD; CANR 58; CDALB 1941-1968; CWD; DA; DA3; DAB; DAC; DAM DRAM, MST, MULT; DFS 2; DLB 7, 38; EWL 3; FL 1:6; FW; LAIT 4; MAL 5; MTCW 1, 2; MTFW 2005; RGAL 4; TUS

Hansen, Joseph 1923-2004 .... **CLC 38**
See Brock, Rose; Colton, James
See also BPFB 2; CA 29-32R; 17; CAAS 233; CANR 16, 44, 66, 125; CMW 4; DLB 226; GLL 1; INT CANR-16

Hansen, Karen V. 1955- .... **CLC 65**
See also CA 149; CANR 102

Hansen, Martin A(lfred)
1909-1955 .... **TCLC 32**
See also CA 167; DLB 214; EWL 3

Hanson, Kenneth O(stlin) 1922- .... **CLC 13**
See also CA 53-56; CANR 7; CP 1, 2, 3, 4, 5

Hardwick, Elizabeth 1916- .... **CLC 13**
See also AMWS 3; CA 5-8R; CANR 3, 32, 70, 100, 139; CN 4, 5, 6; CSW; DA3; DAM NOV; DLB 6; MBL; MTCW 1, 2; MTFW 2005; TCLE 1:1

Hardy, Thomas 1840-1928 .... **PC 8; SSC 2, 60; TCLC 4, 10, 18, 32, 48, 53, 72, 143, 153; WLC 3**
See also AAYA 69; BRW 6; BRWC 1, 2; BRWR 1; CA 123; CAAE 104; CDBLB 1890-1914; DA; DA3; DAB; DAC; DAM MST, NOV, POET; DLB 18, 19, 135, 284; EWL 3; EXPN; EXPP; LAIT 2; MTCW 1, 2; MTFW 2005; NFS 3, 11, 15, 19; PFS 3, 4, 18; RGEL 2; RGSF 2; TEA; WLIT 4

Hare, David 1947- . **CLC 29, 58, 136; DC 26**
See also BRWS 4; CA 97-100; CANR 39, 91; CBD; CD 5, 6; DFS 4, 7, 16; DLB 13, 310; MTCW 1; TEA

Harewood, John
See Van Druten, John (William)

Harford, Henry
See Hudson, W(illiam) H(enry)

Hargrave, Leonie
See Disch, Thomas M.

Hariri, Al- al-Qasim ibn 'Ali Abu Muhammad al-Basri
See al-Hariri, al-Qasim ibn 'Ali Abu Muhammad al-Basri

Harjo, Joy 1951- ..... **CLC 83; NNAL; PC 27**
See also AMWS 12; CA 114; CANR 35, 67, 91, 129; CP 6, 7; CWP; DAM MULT; DLB 120, 175; EWL 3; MTCW 2; MTFW 2005; PFS 15; RGAL 4

Harlan, Louis R(udolph) 1922- .... **CLC 34**
See also CA 21-24R; CANR 25, 55, 80

Harling, Robert 1951(?)- .... **CLC 53**
See also CA 147

Harmon, William (Ruth) 1938- .... **CLC 38**
See also CA 33-36R; CANR 14, 32, 35; SATA 65

Harper, F. E. W.
See Harper, Frances Ellen Watkins

Harper, Frances E. W.
See Harper, Frances Ellen Watkins

Harper, Frances E. Watkins
See Harper, Frances Ellen Watkins

Harper, Frances Ellen
See Harper, Frances Ellen Watkins

Harper, Frances Ellen Watkins
1825-1911 ..... **BLC 2; PC 21; TCLC 14**
See also AFAW 1, 2; BW 1, 3; CA 125; CAAE 111; CANR 79; DAM MULT, POET; DLB 50, 221; MBL; RGAL 4

Harper, Michael S(teven) 1938- ... **CLC 7, 22**
See also AFAW 2; BW 1; CA 224; 33-36R, 224; CANR 24, 108; CP 2, 3, 4, 5, 6, 7; DLB 41; RGAL 4; TCLE 1:1

Harper, Mrs. F. E. W.
See Harper, Frances Ellen Watkins

Harpur, Charles 1813-1868 .... **NCLC 114**
See also DLB 230; RGEL 2

Harris, Christie
See Harris, Christie (Lucy) Irwin

Harris, Christie (Lucy) Irwin
1907-2002 .... **CLC 12**
See also CA 5-8R; CANR 6, 83; CLR 47; DLB 88; JRDA; MAICYA 1, 2; SAAS 10; SATA 6, 74; SATA-Essay 116

Harris, Frank 1856-1931 .... **TCLC 24**
See also CA 150; CAAE 109; CANR 80; DLB 156, 197; RGEL 2

Harris, George Washington
1814-1869 .... **NCLC 23, 165**
See also DLB 3, 11, 248; RGAL 4

Harris, Joel Chandler 1848-1908 ..... **SSC 19; TCLC 2**
See also CA 137; CAAE 104; CANR 80; CLR 49; DLB 11, 23, 42, 78, 91; LAIT 2; MAICYA 1, 2; RGSF 2; SATA 100; WCH; YABC 1

Harris, John (Wyndham Parkes Lucas) Beynon 1903-1969
See Wyndham, John
See also CA 102; CAAS 89-92; CANR 84; SATA 118; SFW 4

Harris, MacDonald .... **CLC 9**
See Heiney, Donald (William)

Harris, Mark 1922- .... **CLC 19**
See also CA 5-8R; 3; CANR 2, 55, 83; CN 1, 2, 3, 4, 5, 6, 7; DLB 2; DLBY 1980

Harris, Norman .... **CLC 65**

Harris, (Theodore) Wilson 1921- .... **CLC 25, 159**
See also BRWS 5; BW 2, 3; CA 65-68; 16; CANR 11, 27, 69, 114; CDWLB 3; CN 1, 2, 3, 4, 5, 6, 7; CP 1, 2, 3, 4, 5, 6, 7; DLB 117; EWL 3; MTCW 1; RGEL 2

Harrison, Barbara Grizzuti
1934-2002 .... **CLC 144**
See also CA 77-80; CAAS 205; CANR 15, 48; INT CANR-15

Harrison, Elizabeth (Allen) Cavanna
1909-2001
See Cavanna, Betty
See also CA 9-12R; CAAS 200; CANR 6, 27, 85, 104, 121; MAICYA 2; SATA 142; YAW

Harrison, Harry (Max) 1925- .... **CLC 42**
See also CA 1-4R; CANR 5, 21, 84; DLB 8; SATA 4; SCFW 2; SFW 4

Harrison, James
See Harrison, Jim

Harrison, James Thomas
See Harrison, Jim

Harrison, Jim 1937- .... **CLC 6, 14, 33, 66, 143; SSC 19**
See also AMWS 8; CA 13-16R; CANR 8, 51, 79, 142; CN 5, 6; CP 1, 2, 3, 4, 5, 6; DLBY 1982; INT CANR-8; RGAL 4; TCWW 2; TUS

Harrison, Kathryn 1961- .... **CLC 70, 151**
See also CA 144; CANR 68, 122

Harrison, Tony 1937- .... **CLC 43, 129**
See also BRWS 5; CA 65-68; CANR 44, 98; CBD; CD 5, 6; CP 2, 3, 4, 5, 6, 7; DLB 40, 245; MTCW 1; RGEL 2

Harriss, Will(ard Irvin) 1922- .... **CLC 34**
See also CA 111

Hart, Ellis
See Ellison, Harlan

Hart, Josephine 1942(?)- .... **CLC 70**
See also CA 138; CANR 70, 149; CPW; DAM POP

Hart, Moss 1904-1961 .... **CLC 66**
See also CA 109; CAAS 89-92; CANR 84; DAM DRAM; DFS 1; DLB 7, 266; RGAL 4

Harte, (Francis) Bret(t)
1836(?)-1902 ... **SSC 8, 59; TCLC 1, 25; WLC 3**
See also AMWS 2; CA 140; CAAE 104; CANR 80; CDALB 1865-1917; DA; DA3; DAC; DAM MST; DLB 12, 64, 74, 79, 186; EXPS; LAIT 2; RGAL 4; RGSF 2; SATA 26; SSFS 3; TUS

Hartley, L(eslie) P(oles) 1895-1972 ... **CLC 2, 22**
See also BRWS 7; CA 45-48; CAAS 37-40R; CANR 33; CN 1; DLB 15, 139; EWL 3; HGG; MTCW 1, 2; MTFW 2005; RGEL 2; RGSF 2; SUFW 1

Hartman, Geoffrey H. 1929- .... **CLC 27**
See also CA 125; CAAE 117; CANR 79; DLB 67

Hartmann, Sadakichi 1869-1944 ... **TCLC 73**
See also CA 157; DLB 54

Hartmann von Aue c. 1170-c. 1210 .... **CMLC 15**
See also CDWLB 2; DLB 138; RGWL 2, 3

Hartog, Jan de
See de Hartog, Jan

Haruf, Kent 1943- .... **CLC 34**
See also AAYA 44; CA 149; CANR 91, 131

Harvey, Caroline
See Trollope, Joanna

Harvey, Gabriel 1550(?)-1631 .... **LC 88**
See also DLB 167, 213, 281

Harwood, Ronald 1934- .... **CLC 32**
See also CA 1-4R; CANR 4, 55, 150; CBD; CD 5, 6; DAM DRAM, MST; DLB 13

Hasegawa Tatsunosuke
See Futabatei, Shimei

Hasek, Jaroslav (Matej Frantisek) 1883-1923 .... **SSC 69; TCLC 4**
See also CA 129; CAAE 104; CDWLB 4; DLB 215; EW 9; EWL 3; MTCW 1, 2; RGSF 2; RGWL 2, 3

Hass, Robert 1941- ... **CLC 18, 39, 99; PC 16**
See also AMWS 6; CA 111; CANR 30, 50, 71; CP 3, 4, 5, 6, 7; DLB 105, 206; EWL 3; MAL 5; MTFW 2005; RGAL 4; SATA 94; TCLE 1:1

Hastings, Hudson
See Kuttner, Henry

Hastings, Selina .... **CLC 44**

Hathorne, John 1641-1717 .... **LC 38**

Hatteras, Amelia
See Mencken, H(enry) L(ouis)

Hatteras, Owen .... **TCLC 18**
See Mencken, H(enry) L(ouis); Nathan, George Jean

Hauptmann, Gerhart (Johann Robert) 1862-1946 .... **SSC 37; TCLC 4**
See also CA 153; CAAE 104; CDWLB 2; DAM DRAM; DLB 66, 118, 330; EW 8; EWL 3; RGSF 2; RGWL 2, 3; TWA

Havel, Vaclav 1936- ..... **CLC 25, 58, 65, 123; DC 6**
See also CA 104; CANR 36, 63, 124; CD-WLB 4; CWW 2; DA3; DAM DRAM; DFS 10; DLB 232; EWL 3; LMFS 2; MTCW 1, 2; MTFW 2005; RGWL 3

Haviaras, Stratis .... **CLC 33**
See Chaviaras, Strates

Hawes, Stephen 1475(?)-1529(?) .... **LC 17**
See also DLB 132; RGEL 2

Hawkes, John 1925-1998 .. **CLC 1, 2, 3, 4, 7, 9, 14, 15, 27, 49**
See also BPFB 2; CA 1-4R; CAAS 167; CANR 2, 47, 64; CN 1, 2, 3, 4, 5, 6; DLB 2, 7, 227; DLBY 1980, 1998; EWL 3; MAL 5; MTCW 1, 2; MTFW 2005; RGAL 4

Hawking, S. W.
See Hawking, Stephen W.

Hawking, Stephen W. 1942- ..... **CLC 63, 105**
See also AAYA 13; BEST 89:1; CA 129; CAAE 126; CANR 48, 115; CPW; DA3; MTCW 2; MTFW 2005

Hawkins, Anthony Hope
See Hope, Anthony

Hawthorne, Julian 1846-1934 .... **TCLC 25**
See also CA 165; HGG

Hawthorne, Nathaniel 1804-1864 ... **NCLC 2, 10, 17, 23, 39, 79, 95, 158, 171; SSC 3, 29, 39, 89; WLC 3**
See also AAYA 18; AMW; AMWC 1; AMWR 1; BPFB 2; BYA 3; CDALB 1640-1865; CLR 103; DA; DA3; DAB; DAC; DAM MST, NOV; DLB 1, 74, 183, 223, 269; EXPN; EXPS; GL 2; HGG; LAIT 1; NFS 1, 20; RGAL 4; RGSF 2; SSFS 1, 7, 11, 15; SUFW 1; TUS; WCH; YABC 2

Hawthorne, Sophia Peabody 1809-1871 .... **NCLC 150**
See also DLB 183, 239

Haxton, Josephine Ayres 1921-
See Douglas, Ellen
See also CA 115; CANR 41, 83

Hayaseca y Eizaguirre, Jorge
See Echegaray (y Eizaguirre), Jose (Maria Waldo)

Hayashi, Fumiko 1904-1951 .... **TCLC 27**
See Hayashi Fumiko
See also CA 161

Hayashi Fumiko
See Hayashi, Fumiko
See also DLB 180; EWL 3

Haycraft, Anna 1932-2005
See Ellis, Alice Thomas
See also CA 122; CAAS 237; CANR 90, 141; MTCW 2; MTFW 2005

Hayden, Robert E(arl) 1913-1980 ..... **BLC 2; CLC 5, 9, 14, 37; PC 6**
See also AFAW 1, 2; AMWS 2; BW 1, 3; CA 69-72; CAAS 97-100; CABS 2; CANR 24, 75, 82; CDALB 1941-1968; CP 1, 2, 3; DA; DAC; DAM MST, MULT, POET; DLB 5, 76; EWL 3; EXPP; MAL 5; MTCW 1, 2; PFS 1; RGAL 4; SATA 19; SATA-Obit 26; WP

Haydon, Benjamin Robert 1786-1846 .... **NCLC 146**
See also DLB 110

Hayek, F(riedrich) A(ugust von) 1899-1992 .... **TCLC 109**
See also CA 93-96; CAAS 137; CANR 20; MTCW 1, 2

Hayford, J(oseph) E(phraim) Casely
See Casely-Hayford, J(oseph) E(phraim)

Hayman, Ronald 1932- .... **CLC 44**
See also CA 25-28R; CANR 18, 50, 88; CD 5, 6; DLB 155

Hayne, Paul Hamilton 1830-1886 . **NCLC 94**
See also DLB 3, 64, 79, 248; RGAL 4

Hays, Mary 1760-1843 .... **NCLC 114**
See also DLB 142, 158; RGEL 2

Haywood, Eliza (Fowler) 1693(?)-1756 .... **LC 1, 44**
See also BRWS 12; DLB 39; RGEL 2

Hazlitt, William 1778-1830 ...... **NCLC 29, 82**
See also BRW 4; DLB 110, 158; RGEL 2; TEA

Hazzard, Shirley 1931- .... **CLC 18, 218**
See also CA 9-12R; CANR 4, 70, 127; CN 1, 2, 3, 4, 5, 6, 7; DLB 289; DLBY 1982; MTCW 1

Head, Bessie 1937-1986 ...... **BLC 2; CLC 25, 67; SSC 52**
See also AFW; BW 2, 3; CA 29-32R; CAAS 119; CANR 25, 82; CDWLB 3; CN 1, 2, 3, 4; DA3; DAM MULT; DLB 117, 225; EWL 3; EXPS; FL 1:6; FW; MTCW 1, 2; MTFW 2005; RGSF 2; SSFS 5, 13; WLIT 2; WWE 1

Headon, (Nicky) Topper 1956(?)- .... **CLC 30**

Heaney, Seamus 1939- . **CLC 5, 7, 14, 25, 37, 74, 91, 171, 225; PC 18; WLCS**
See also AAYA 61; BRWR 1; BRWS 2; CA 85-88; CANR 25, 48, 75, 91, 128; CD-BLB 1960 to Present; CP 1, 2, 3, 4, 5, 6, 7; DA3; DAB; DAM POET; DLB 40, 330; DLBY 1995; EWL 3; EXPP; MTCW 1, 2; MTFW 2005; PAB; PFS 2, 5, 8, 17; RGEL 2; TEA; WLIT 4

Hearn, (Patricio) Lafcadio (Tessima Carlos) 1850-1904 .... **TCLC 9**
See also CA 166; CAAE 105; DLB 12, 78, 189; HGG; MAL 5; RGAL 4

Hearne, Samuel 1745-1792 .... **LC 95**
See also DLB 99

Hearne, Vicki 1946-2001 .... **CLC 56**
See also CA 139; CAAS 201

Hearon, Shelby 1931- .... **CLC 63**
See also AITN 2; AMWS 8; CA 25-28R; 11; CANR 18, 48, 103, 146; CSW

Heat-Moon, William Least .... **CLC 29**
See Trogdon, William (Lewis)
See also AAYA 9

Hebbel, Friedrich 1813-1863 . **DC 21; NCLC 43**
See also CDWLB 2; DAM DRAM; DLB 129; EW 6; RGWL 2, 3

Hebert, Anne 1916-2000 .... **CLC 4, 13, 29**
See also CA 85-88; CAAS 187; CANR 69, 126; CCA 1; CWP; CWW 2; DA3; DAC; DAM MST, POET; DLB 68; EWL 3; GFL 1789 to the Present; MTCW 1, 2; MTFW 2005; PFS 20

Hecht, Anthony (Evan) 1923-2004 .... **CLC 8, 13, 19; PC 70**
See also AMWS 10; CA 9-12R; CAAS 232; CANR 6, 108; CP 1, 2, 3, 4, 5, 6, 7; DAM POET; DLB 5, 169; EWL 3; PFS 6; WP

Hecht, Ben 1894-1964 ..... **CLC 8; TCLC 101**
See also CA 85-88; DFS 9; DLB 7, 9, 25, 26, 28, 86; FANT; IDFW 3, 4; RGAL 4

Hedayat, Sadeq 1903-1951 .... **TCLC 21**
See also CAAE 120; EWL 3; RGSF 2

Hegel, Georg Wilhelm Friedrich 1770-1831 .... **NCLC 46, 151**
See also DLB 90; TWA

Heidegger, Martin 1889-1976 .... **CLC 24**
See also CA 81-84; CAAS 65-68; CANR 34; DLB 296; MTCW 1, 2; MTFW 2005

Heidenstam, (Carl Gustaf) Verner von 1859-1940 .... **TCLC 5**
See also CAAE 104; DLB 330

Heidi Louise
See Erdrich, Louise

Heifner, Jack 1946- .... **CLC 11**
See also CA 105; CANR 47

Heijermans, Herman 1864-1924 .... **TCLC 24**
See also CAAE 123; EWL 3

Heilbrun, Carolyn G(old) 1926-2003 .... **CLC 25, 173**
See Cross, Amanda
See also CA 45-48; CAAS 220; CANR 1, 28, 58, 94; FW

Hein, Christoph 1944- .... **CLC 154**
See also CA 158; CANR 108; CDWLB 2; CWW 2; DLB 124

Heine, Heinrich 1797-1856 .... **NCLC 4, 54, 147; PC 25**
See also CDWLB 2; DLB 90; EW 5; RGWL 2, 3; TWA

Heinemann, Larry 1944- .... **CLC 50**
See also CA 110; 21; CANR 31, 81, 156; DLBD 9; INT CANR-31

Heinemann, Larry Curtiss
See Heinemann, Larry

Heiney, Donald (William) 1921-1993
See Harris, MacDonald
See also CA 1-4R; CAAS 142; CANR 3, 58; FANT

Heinlein, Robert A. 1907-1988 .. **CLC 1, 3, 8, 14, 26, 55; SSC 55**
See also AAYA 17; BPFB 2; BYA 4, 13; CA 1-4R; CAAS 125; CANR 1, 20, 53; CLR 75; CN 1, 2, 3, 4; CPW; DA3; DAM POP; DLB 8; EXPS; JRDA; LAIT 5; LMFS 2; MAICYA 1, 2; MTCW 1, 2; MTFW 2005; RGAL 4; SATA 9, 69; SATA-Obit 56; SCFW 1, 2; SFW 4; SSFS 7; YAW

Helforth, John
See Doolittle, Hilda

Heliodorus fl. 3rd cent. - .... **CMLC 52**
See also WLIT 8

Hellenhofferu, Vojtech Kapristian z
See Hasek, Jaroslav (Matej Frantisek)

Heller, Joseph 1923-1999 . **CLC 1, 3, 5, 8, 11, 36, 63; TCLC 131, 151; WLC 3**
See also AAYA 24; AITN 1; AMWS 4; BPFB 2; BYA 1; CA 5-8R; CAAS 187; CABS 1; CANR 8, 42, 66, 126; CN 1, 2, 3, 4, 5, 6; CPW; DA; DA3; DAB; DAC; DAM MST, NOV, POP; DLB 2, 28, 227; DLBY 1980, 2002; EWL 3; EXPN; INT CANR-8; LAIT 4; MAL 5; MTCW 1, 2; MTFW 2005; NFS 1; RGAL 4; TUS; YAW

Hellman, Lillian 1906-1984 . **CLC 2, 4, 8, 14, 18, 34, 44, 52; DC 1; TCLC 119**
See also AAYA 47; AITN 1, 2; AMWS 1; CA 13-16R; CAAS 112; CAD; CANR 33; CWD; DA3; DAM DRAM; DFS 1, 3, 14; DLB 7, 228; DLBY 1984; EWL 3; FL 1:6; FW; LAIT 3; MAL 5; MBL; MTCW 1, 2; MTFW 2005; RGAL 4; TUS

Helprin, Mark 1947- .... **CLC 7, 10, 22, 32**
See also CA 81-84; CANR 47, 64, 124; CDALBS; CN 7; CPW; DA3; DAM NOV, POP; DLBY 1985; FANT; MAL 5; MTCW 1, 2; MTFW 2005; SUFW 2

Helvetius, Claude-Adrien 1715-1771 .. **LC 26**
See also DLB 313

Helyar, Jane Penelope Josephine 1933-
See Poole, Josephine
See also CA 21-24R; CANR 10, 26; CWRI 5; SATA 82, 138; SATA-Essay 138

Hemans, Felicia 1793-1835 ...... **NCLC 29, 71**
See also DLB 96; RGEL 2

Hemingway, Ernest (Miller)
1899-1961 .... **CLC 1, 3, 6, 8, 10, 13, 19, 30, 34, 39, 41, 44, 50, 61, 80; SSC 1, 25, 36, 40, 63; TCLC 115; WLC 3**
See also AAYA 19; AMW; AMWC 1; AMWR 1; BPFB 2; BYA 2, 3, 13, 15; CA 77-80; CANR 34; CDALB 1917-1929; DA; DA3; DAB; DAC; DAM MST, NOV; DLB 4, 9, 102, 210, 308, 316, 330; DLBD 1, 15, 16; DLBY 1981, 1987, 1996, 1998; EWL 3; EXPN; EXPS; LAIT 3, 4; LATS 1:1; MAL 5; MTCW 1, 2; MTFW 2005; NFS 1, 5, 6, 14; RGAL 4; RGSF 2; SSFS 17; TUS; WYA

Hempel, Amy 1951- .... **CLC 39**
See also CA 137; CAAE 118; CANR 70; DA3; DLB 218; EXPS; MTCW 2; MTFW 2005; SSFS 2

Henderson, F. C.
See Mencken, H(enry) L(ouis)

Henderson, Sylvia
See Ashton-Warner, Sylvia (Constance)

Henderson, Zenna (Chlarson)
1917-1983 .... **SSC 29**
See also CA 1-4R; CAAS 133; CANR 1, 84; DLB 8; SATA 5; SFW 4

Henkin, Joshua .... **CLC 119**
See also CA 161

Henley, Beth .... **CLC 23; DC 6, 14**
See Henley, Elizabeth Becker
See also AAYA 70; CABS 3; CAD; CD 5, 6; CSW; CWD; DFS 2, 21; DLBY 1986; FW

Henley, Elizabeth Becker 1952-
See Henley, Beth
See also CA 107; CANR 32, 73, 140; DA3; DAM DRAM, MST; MTCW 1, 2; MTFW 2005

Henley, William Ernest 1849-1903 .. **TCLC 8**
See also CA 234; CAAE 105; DLB 19; RGEL 2

Hennissart, Martha 1929-
See Lathen, Emma
See also CA 85-88; CANR 64

Henry VIII 1491-1547 .... **LC 10**
See also DLB 132

Henry, O. . **SSC 5, 49; TCLC 1, 19; WLC 3**
See Porter, William Sydney
See also AAYA 41; AMWS 2; EXPS; MAL 5; RGAL 4; RGSF 2; SSFS 2, 18; TCWW 1, 2

Henry, Patrick 1736-1799 .... **LC 25**
See also LAIT 1

Henryson, Robert 1430(?)-1506(?) ..... **LC 20, 110; PC 65**
See also BRWS 7; DLB 146; RGEL 2

Henschke, Alfred
See Klabund

Henson, Lance 1944- .... **NNAL**
See also CA 146; DLB 175

Hentoff, Nat(han Irving) 1925- .... **CLC 26**
See also AAYA 4, 42; BYA 6; CA 1-4R; 6; CANR 5, 25, 77, 114; CLR 1, 52; INT CANR-25; JRDA; MAICYA 1, 2; SATA 42, 69, 133; SATA-Brief 27; WYA; YAW

Heppenstall, (John) Rayner
1911-1981 .... **CLC 10**
See also CA 1-4R; CAAS 103; CANR 29; CN 1, 2; CP 1, 2, 3; EWL 3

Heraclitus c. 540B.C.-c. 450B.C. ... **CMLC 22**
See also DLB 176

Herbert, Frank 1920-1986 ... **CLC 12, 23, 35, 44, 85**
See also AAYA 21; BPFB 2; BYA 4, 14; CA 53-56; CAAS 118; CANR 5, 43; CDALBS; CPW; DAM POP; DLB 8; INT CANR-5; LAIT 5; MTCW 1, 2; MTFW 2005; NFS 17; SATA 9, 37; SATA-Obit 47; SCFW 1, 2; SFW 4; YAW

Herbert, George 1593-1633 . **LC 24, 121; PC 4**
See also BRW 2; BRWR 2; CDBLB Before 1660; DAB; DAM POET; DLB 126; EXPP; PFS 25; RGEL 2; TEA; WP

Herbert, Zbigniew 1924-1998 ..... **CLC 9, 43; PC 50; TCLC 168**
See also CA 89-92; CAAS 169; CANR 36, 74; CDWLB 4; CWW 2; DAM POET; DLB 232; EWL 3; MTCW 1; PFS 22

Herbst, Josephine (Frey)
1897-1969 .... **CLC 34**
See also CA 5-8R; CAAS 25-28R; DLB 9

Herder, Johann Gottfried von
1744-1803 .... **NCLC 8**
See also DLB 97; EW 4; TWA

Heredia, Jose Maria 1803-1839 .... **HLCS 2**
See also LAW

Hergesheimer, Joseph 1880-1954 ... **TCLC 11**
See also CA 194; CAAE 109; DLB 102, 9; RGAL 4

Herlihy, James Leo 1927-1993 .... **CLC 6**
See also CA 1-4R; CAAS 143; CAD; CANR 2; CN 1, 2, 3, 4, 5

Herman, William
See Bierce, Ambrose (Gwinett)

Hermogenes fl. c. 175- .... **CMLC 6**

Hernandez, Jose 1834-1886 .... **NCLC 17**
See also LAW; RGWL 2, 3; WLIT 1

Herodotus c. 484B.C.-c. 420B.C. .. **CMLC 17**
See also AW 1; CDWLB 1; DLB 176; RGWL 2, 3; TWA; WLIT 8

Herr, Michael 1940(?)- .... **CLC 231**
See also CA 89-92; CANR 68, 142; DLB 185; MTCW 1

Herrick, Robert 1591-1674 .... **LC 13; PC 9**
See also BRW 2; BRWC 2; DA; DAB; DAC; DAM MST, POP; DLB 126; EXPP; PFS 13; RGAL 4; RGEL 2; TEA; WP

Herring, Guilles
See Somerville, Edith Oenone

Herriot, James 1916-1995 .... **CLC 12**
See Wight, James Alfred
See also AAYA 1, 54; BPFB 2; CAAS 148; CANR 40; CLR 80; CPW; DAM POP; LAIT 3; MAICYA 2; MAICYAS 1; MTCW 2; SATA 86, 135; TEA; YAW

Herris, Violet
See Hunt, Violet

Herrmann, Dorothy 1941- .... **CLC 44**
See also CA 107

Herrmann, Taffy
See Herrmann, Dorothy

Hersey, John 1914-1993 .. **CLC 1, 2, 7, 9, 40, 81, 97**
See also AAYA 29; BPFB 2; CA 17-20R; CAAS 140; CANR 33; CDALBS; CN 1, 2, 3, 4, 5; CPW; DAM POP; DLB 6, 185,

278, 299; MAL 5; MTCW 1, 2; MTFW 2005; RGHL; SATA 25; SATA-Obit 76; TUS

Herzen, Aleksandr Ivanovich
1812-1870 .... **NCLC 10, 61**
See Herzen, Alexander

Herzen, Alexander
See Herzen, Aleksandr Ivanovich
See also DLB 277

Herzl, Theodor 1860-1904 .... **TCLC 36**
See also CA 168

Herzog, Werner 1942- .... **CLC 16**
See also CA 89-92

Hesiod c. 8th cent. B.C.- .... **CMLC 5**
See also AW 1; DLB 176; RGWL 2, 3; WLIT 8

Hesse, Hermann 1877-1962 ... **CLC 1, 2, 3, 6, 11, 17, 25, 69; SSC 9, 49; TCLC 148; WLC 3**
See also AAYA 43; BPFB 2; CA 17-18; CAP 2; CDWLB 2; DA; DA3; DAB; DAC; DAM MST, NOV; DLB 66, 330; EW 9; EWL 3; EXPN; LAIT 1; MTCW 1, 2; MTFW 2005; NFS 6, 15, 24; RGWL 2, 3; SATA 50; TWA

Hewes, Cady
See De Voto, Bernard (Augustine)

Heyen, William 1940- .... **CLC 13, 18**
See also CA 220; 33-36R, 220; 9; CANR 98; CP 3, 4, 5, 6, 7; DLB 5; RGHL

Heyerdahl, Thor 1914-2002 .... **CLC 26**
See also CA 5-8R; CAAS 207; CANR 5, 22, 66, 73; LAIT 4; MTCW 1, 2; MTFW 2005; SATA 2, 52

Heym, Georg (Theodor Franz Arthur)
1887-1912 .... **TCLC 9**
See also CA 181; CAAE 106

Heym, Stefan 1913-2001 .... **CLC 41**
See also CA 9-12R; CAAS 203; CANR 4; CWW 2; DLB 69; EWL 3

Heyse, Paul (Johann Ludwig von)
1830-1914 .... **TCLC 8**
See also CA 209; CAAE 104; DLB 129, 330

Heyward, (Edwin) DuBose
1885-1940 .... **HR 1:2; TCLC 59**
See also CA 157; CAAE 108; DLB 7, 9, 45, 249; MAL 5; SATA 21

Heywood, John 1497(?)-1580(?) .... **LC 65**
See also DLB 136; RGEL 2

Heywood, Thomas 1573(?)-1641 .... **LC 111**
See also DAM DRAM; DLB 62; LMFS 1; RGEL 2; TEA

Hibbert, Eleanor Alice Burford
1906-1993 .... **CLC 7**
See Holt, Victoria
See also BEST 90:4; CA 17-20R; CAAS 140; CANR 9, 28, 59; CMW 4; CPW; DAM POP; MTCW 2; MTFW 2005; RHW; SATA 2; SATA-Obit 74

Hichens, Robert (Smythe)
1864-1950 .... **TCLC 64**
See also CA 162; DLB 153; HGG; RHW; SUFW

Higgins, Aidan 1927- .... **SSC 68**
See also CA 9-12R; CANR 70, 115, 148; CN 1, 2, 3, 4, 5, 6, 7; DLB 14

Higgins, George V(incent)
1939-1999 .... **CLC 4, 7, 10, 18**
See also BPFB 2; CA 77-80; 5; CAAS 186; CANR 17, 51, 89, 96; CMW 4; CN 2, 3, 4, 5, 6; DLB 2; DLBY 1981, 1998; INT CANR-17; MSW; MTCW 1

Higginson, Thomas Wentworth
1823-1911 .... **TCLC 36**
See also CA 162; DLB 1, 64, 243

Higgonet, Margaret .... **CLC 65**

Highet, Helen
See MacInnes, Helen (Clark)

Highsmith, Patricia 1921-1995 ...... **CLC 2, 4, 14, 42, 102**
See Morgan, Claire
See also AAYA 48; BRWS 5; CA 1-4R; CAAS 147; CANR 1, 20, 48, 62, 108; CMW 4; CN 1, 2, 3, 4, 5; CPW; DA3; DAM NOV, POP; DLB 306; MSW; MTCW 1, 2; MTFW 2005

Highwater, Jamake (Mamake)
1942(?)-2001 .... **CLC 12**
See also AAYA 7, 69; BPFB 2; BYA 4; CA 65-68; 7; CAAS 199; CANR 10, 34, 84; CLR 17; CWRI 5; DLB 52; DLBY 1985; JRDA; MAICYA 1, 2; SATA 32, 69; SATA-Brief 30

Highway, Tomson 1951- ...... **CLC 92; NNAL**
See also CA 151; CANR 75; CCA 1; CD 5, 6; CN 7; DAC; DAM MULT; DFS 2; MTCW 2

Hijuelos, Oscar 1951- .... **CLC 65; HLC 1**
See also AAYA 25; AMWS 8; BEST 90:1; CA 123; CANR 50, 75, 125; CPW; DA3; DAM MULT, POP; DLB 145; HW 1, 2; LLW; MAL 5; MTCW 2; MTFW 2005; NFS 17; RGAL 4; WLIT 1

Hikmet, Nazim 1902-1963 .... **CLC 40**
See Nizami of Ganja
See also CA 141; CAAS 93-96; EWL 3; WLIT 6

Hildegard von Bingen 1098-1179 . **CMLC 20**
See also DLB 148

Hildesheimer, Wolfgang 1916-1991 .. **CLC 49**
See also CA 101; CAAS 135; DLB 69, 124; EWL 3; RGHL

Hill, Geoffrey (William) 1932- ...... **CLC 5, 8, 18, 45**
See also BRWS 5; CA 81-84; CANR 21, 89; CDBLB 1960 to Present; CP 1, 2, 3, 4, 5, 6, 7; DAM POET; DLB 40; EWL 3; MTCW 1; RGEL 2; RGHL

Hill, George Roy 1921-2002 .... **CLC 26**
See also CA 122; CAAE 110; CAAS 213

Hill, John
See Koontz, Dean R.

Hill, Susan (Elizabeth) 1942- ...... **CLC 4, 113**
See also CA 33-36R; CANR 29, 69, 129; CN 2, 3, 4, 5, 6, 7; DAB; DAM MST, NOV; DLB 14, 139; HGG; MTCW 1; RHW

Hillard, Asa G. III .... **CLC 70**

Hillerman, Tony 1925- .... **CLC 62, 170**
See also AAYA 40; BEST 89:1; BPFB 2; CA 29-32R; CANR 21, 42, 65, 97, 134; CMW 4; CPW; DA3; DAM POP; DLB 206, 306; MAL 5; MSW; MTCW 2; MTFW 2005; RGAL 4; SATA 6; TCWW 2; YAW

Hillesum, Etty 1914-1943 .... **TCLC 49**
See also CA 137; RGHL

Hilliard, Noel (Harvey) 1929-1996 ... **CLC 15**
See also CA 9-12R; CANR 7, 69; CN 1, 2, 3, 4, 5, 6

Hillis, Rick 1956- .... **CLC 66**
See also CA 134

Hilton, James 1900-1954 .... **TCLC 21**
See also CA 169; CAAE 108; DLB 34, 77; FANT; SATA 34

Hilton, Walter (?)-1396 .... **CMLC 58**
See also DLB 146; RGEL 2

Himes, Chester (Bomar) 1909-1984 .. **BLC 2; CLC 2, 4, 7, 18, 58, 108; TCLC 139**
See also AFAW 2; AMWS 16; BPFB 2; BW 2; CA 25-28R; CAAS 114; CANR 22, 89; CMW 4; CN 1, 2, 3; DAM MULT; DLB 2, 76, 143, 226; EWL 3; MAL 5; MSW; MTCW 1, 2; MTFW 2005; RGAL 4

Himmelfarb, Gertrude 1922- .... **CLC 202**
See also CA 49-52; CANR 28, 66, 102

Hinde, Thomas .... **CLC 6, 11**
See Chitty, Thomas Willes
See also CN 1, 2, 3, 4, 5, 6; EWL 3

Hine, (William) Daryl 1936- .... **CLC 15**
See also CA 1-4R; 15; CANR 1, 20; CP 1, 2, 3, 4, 5, 6, 7; DLB 60

Hinkson, Katharine Tynan
See Tynan, Katharine

Hinojosa, Rolando 1929- .... **HLC 1**
See Hinojosa-Smith, Rolando
See also CA 131; 16; CANR 62; DAM MULT; DLB 82; HW 1, 2; LLW; MTCW 2; MTFW 2005; RGAL 4

Hinton, S.E. 1950- .... **CLC 30, 111**
See also AAYA 2, 33; BPFB 2; BYA 2, 3; CA 81-84; CANR 32, 62, 92, 133; CDALBS; CLR 3, 23; CPW; DA; DA3; DAB; DAC; DAM MST, NOV; JRDA; LAIT 5; MAICYA 1, 2; MTCW 1, 2; MTFW 2005; NFS 5, 9, 15, 16; SATA 19, 58, 115, 160; WYA; YAW

Hippius, Zinaida (Nikolaevna) .... **TCLC 9**
See Gippius, Zinaida (Nikolaevna)
See also DLB 295; EWL 3

Hiraoka, Kimitake 1925-1970
See Mishima, Yukio
See also CA 97-100; CAAS 29-32R; DA3; DAM DRAM; GLL 1; MTCW 1, 2

Hirsch, E.D., Jr. 1928- .... **CLC 79**
See also CA 25-28R; CANR 27, 51, 146; DLB 67; INT CANR-27; MTCW 1

Hirsch, Edward 1950- .... **CLC 31, 50**
See also CA 104; CANR 20, 42, 102; CP 6, 7; DLB 120; PFS 22

Hirsch, Eric Donald, Jr.
See Hirsch, E.D., Jr.

Hitchcock, Alfred (Joseph)
1899-1980 .... **CLC 16**
See also AAYA 22; CA 159; CAAS 97-100; SATA 27; SATA-Obit 24

Hitchens, Christopher 1949- .... **CLC 157**
See also CA 152; CANR 89, 155

Hitchens, Christopher Eric
See Hitchens, Christopher

Hitler, Adolf 1889-1945 .... **TCLC 53**
See also CA 147; CAAE 117

Hoagland, Edward (Morley) 1932- .. **CLC 28**
See also ANW; CA 1-4R; CANR 2, 31, 57, 107; CN 1, 2, 3, 4, 5, 6, 7; DLB 6; SATA 51; TCWW 2

Hoban, Russell 1925- .... **CLC 7, 25**
See also BPFB 2; CA 5-8R; CANR 23, 37, 66, 114, 138; CLR 3, 69; CN 4, 5, 6, 7; CWRI 5; DAM NOV; DLB 52; FANT; MAICYA 1, 2; MTCW 1, 2; MTFW 2005; SATA 1, 40, 78, 136; SFW 4; SUFW 2; TCLE 1:1

Hobbes, Thomas 1588-1679 .... **LC 36**
See also DLB 151, 252, 281; RGEL 2

Hobbs, Perry
See Blackmur, R(ichard) P(almer)

Hobson, Laura Z(ametkin)
1900-1986 .... **CLC 7, 25**
See also BPFB 2; CA 17-20R; CAAS 118; CANR 55; CN 1, 2, 3, 4; DLB 28; SATA 52

Hoccleve, Thomas c. 1368-c. 1437 ...... **LC 75**
See also DLB 146; RGEL 2

Hoch, Edward D(entinger) 1930-
See Queen, Ellery
See also CA 29-32R; CANR 11, 27, 51, 97; CMW 4; DLB 306; SFW 4

Hochhuth, Rolf 1931- .... **CLC 4, 11, 18**
See also CA 5-8R; CANR 33, 75, 136; CWW 2; DAM DRAM; DLB 124; EWL 3; MTCW 1, 2; MTFW 2005; RGHL

Hochman, Sandra 1936- .... **CLC 3, 8**
See also CA 5-8R; CP 1, 2, 3, 4, 5; DLB 5

Hochwaelder, Fritz 1911-1986 .... **CLC 36**
See Hochwalder, Fritz
See also CA 29-32R; CAAS 120; CANR 42; DAM DRAM; MTCW 1; RGWL 3

Hochwalder, Fritz
See Hochwaelder, Fritz
See also EWL 3; RGWL 2

Hocking, Mary (Eunice) 1921- .... **CLC 13**
See also CA 101; CANR 18, 40

Hodgins, Jack 1938- .... **CLC 23**
See also CA 93-96; CN 4, 5, 6, 7; DLB 60

Hodgson, William Hope
1877(?)-1918 .... **TCLC 13**
See also CA 164; CAAE 111; CMW 4; DLB 70, 153, 156, 178; HGG; MTCW 2; SFW 4; SUFW 1

Hoeg, Peter 1957- .... **CLC 95, 156**
See also CA 151; CANR 75; CMW 4; DA3; DLB 214; EWL 3; MTCW 2; MTFW 2005; NFS 17; RGWL 3; SSFS 18

Hoffman, Alice 1952- .... **CLC 51**
See also AAYA 37; AMWS 10; CA 77-80; CANR 34, 66, 100, 138; CN 4, 5, 6, 7; CPW; DAM NOV; DLB 292; MAL 5; MTCW 1, 2; MTFW 2005; TCLE 1:1

Hoffman, Daniel (Gerard) 1923- . **CLC 6, 13, 23**
See also CA 1-4R; CANR 4, 142; CP 1, 2, 3, 4, 5, 6, 7; DLB 5; TCLE 1:1

Hoffman, Eva 1945- .... **CLC 182**
See also AMWS 16; CA 132; CANR 146

Hoffman, Stanley 1944- .... **CLC 5**
See also CA 77-80

Hoffman, William 1925- .... **CLC 141**
See also CA 21-24R; CANR 9, 103; CSW; DLB 234; TCLE 1:1

Hoffman, William M.
See Hoffman, William M(oses)
See also CAD; CD 5, 6

Hoffman, William M(oses) 1939- ..... **CLC 40**
See Hoffman, William M.
See also CA 57-60; CANR 11, 71

Hoffmann, E(rnst) T(heodor) A(madeus)
1776-1822 .... **NCLC 2; SSC 13, 92**
See also CDWLB 2; DLB 90; EW 5; GL 2; RGSF 2; RGWL 2, 3; SATA 27; SUFW 1; WCH

Hofmann, Gert 1931-1993 .... **CLC 54**
See also CA 128; CANR 145; EWL 3; RGHL

Hofmannsthal, Hugo von 1874-1929 ... **DC 4; TCLC 11**
See also CA 153; CAAE 106; CDWLB 2; DAM DRAM; DFS 17; DLB 81, 118; EW 9; EWL 3; RGWL 2, 3

Hogan, Linda 1947- ..... **CLC 73; NNAL; PC 35**
See also AMWS 4; ANW; BYA 12; CA 226; 120, 226; CANR 45, 73, 129; CWP; DAM MULT; DLB 175; SATA 132; TCWW 2

Hogarth, Charles
See Creasey, John

Hogarth, Emmett
See Polonsky, Abraham (Lincoln)

Hogarth, William 1697-1764 .... **LC 112**
See also AAYA 56

Hogg, James 1770-1835 .... **NCLC 4, 109**
See also BRWS 10; DLB 93, 116, 159; GL 2; HGG; RGEL 2; SUFW 1

Holbach, Paul-Henri Thiry
1723-1789 .... **LC 14**
See also DLB 313

Holberg, Ludvig 1684-1754 .... **LC 6**
See also DLB 300; RGWL 2, 3

Holcroft, Thomas 1745-1809 .... **NCLC 85**
See also DLB 39, 89, 158; RGEL 2

Holden, Ursula 1921- .... **CLC 18**
See also CA 101; 8; CANR 22

DAM MULT, POET; DLB 38; GLL 2;
LAIT 5; MAICYA 1, 2; MTCW 1; SATA
4, 136; YAW

Jordan, June Meyer
See Jordan, June

Jordan, Neil 1950- .... **CLC 110**
See also CA 130; CAAE 124; CANR 54,
154; CN 4, 5, 6, 7; GLL 2; INT CA-130

Jordan, Neil Patrick
See Jordan, Neil

Jordan, Pat(rick M.) 1941- .... **CLC 37**
See also CA 33-36R; CANR 121

Jorgensen, Ivar
See Ellison, Harlan

Jorgenson, Ivar
See Silverberg, Robert

Joseph, George Ghevarughese .... **CLC 70**

Josephson, Mary
See O'Doherty, Brian

Josephus, Flavius c. 37-100 .... **CMLC 13**
See also AW 2; DLB 176; WLIT 8

Josiah Allen's Wife
See Holley, Marietta

Josipovici, Gabriel (David) 1940- ...... **CLC 6,
43, 153**
See also CA 224; 37-40R, 224; 8; CANR
47, 84; CN 3, 4, 5, 6, 7; DLB 14, 319

Joubert, Joseph 1754-1824 .... **NCLC 9**

Jouve, Pierre Jean 1887-1976 .... **CLC 47**
See also CA 252; CAAS 65-68; DLB 258;
EWL 3

Jovine, Francesco 1902-1950 .... **TCLC 79**
See also DLB 264; EWL 3

Joyce, James (Augustine Aloysius)
1882-1941 .... **DC 16; PC 22; SSC 3, 26,
44, 64; TCLC 3, 8, 16, 35, 52, 159;
WLC 3**
See also AAYA 42; BRW 7; BRWC 1;
BRWR 1; BYA 11, 13; CA 126; CAAE
104; CDBLB 1914-1945; DA; DA3;
DAB; DAC; DAM MST, NOV, POET;
DLB 10, 19, 36, 162, 247; EWL 3; EXPN;
EXPS; LAIT 3; LMFS 1, 2; MTCW 1, 2;
MTFW 2005; NFS 7; RGSF 2; SSFS 1,
19; TEA; WLIT 4

Jozsef, Attila 1905-1937 .... **TCLC 22**
See also CA 230; CAAE 116; CDWLB 4;
DLB 215; EWL 3

Juana Ines de la Cruz, Sor
1651(?)-1695 ... **HLCS 1; LC 5, 136; PC
24**
See also DLB 305; FW; LAW; RGWL 2, 3;
WLIT 1

Juana Inez de La Cruz, Sor
See Juana Ines de la Cruz, Sor

Juan Manuel, Don 1282-1348 .... **CMLC 88**

Judd, Cyril
See Kornbluth, C(yril) M.; Pohl, Frederik

Juenger, Ernst 1895-1998 .... **CLC 125**
See Junger, Ernst
See also CA 101; CAAS 167; CANR 21,
47, 106; DLB 56

Julian of Norwich 1342(?)-1416(?) . **LC 6, 52**
See also BRWS 12; DLB 146; LMFS 1

Julius Caesar 100B.C.-44B.C.
See Caesar, Julius
See also CDWLB 1; DLB 211

Junger, Ernst
See Juenger, Ernst
See also CDWLB 2; EWL 3; RGWL 2, 3

Junger, Sebastian 1962- .... **CLC 109**
See also AAYA 28; CA 165; CANR 130;
MTFW 2005

Juniper, Alex
See Hospital, Janette Turner

Junius
See Luxemburg, Rosa

Junzaburo, Nishiwaki
See Nishiwaki, Junzaburo
See also EWL 3

Just, Ward 1935- .... **CLC 4, 27**
See also CA 25-28R; CANR 32, 87; CN 6,
7; INT CANR-32

Just, Ward Swift
See Just, Ward

Justice, Donald (Rodney)
1925-2004 .... **CLC 6, 19, 102; PC 64**
See also AMWS 7; CA 5-8R; CAAS 230;
CANR 26, 54, 74, 121, 122; CP 1, 2, 3, 4,
5, 6, 7; CSW; DAM POET; DLBY 1983;
EWL 3; INT CANR-26; MAL 5; MTCW
2; PFS 14; TCLE 1:1

Juvenal c. 60-c. 130 .... **CMLC 8**
See also AW 2; CDWLB 1; DLB 211;
RGWL 2, 3; WLIT 8

Juvenis
See Bourne, Randolph S(illiman)

K., Alice
See Knapp, Caroline

Kabakov, Sasha .... **CLC 59**

Kabir 1398(?)-1448(?) .... **LC 109; PC 56**
See also RGWL 2, 3

Kacew, Romain 1914-1980
See Gary, Romain
See also CA 108; CAAS 102

Kadare, Ismail 1936- .... **CLC 52, 190**
See also CA 161; EWL 3; RGWL 3

Kadohata, Cynthia (Lynn)
1956(?)- .... **CLC 59, 122**
See also AAYA 71; CA 140; CANR 124;
SATA 155

Kafka, Franz 1883-1924 ... **SSC 5, 29, 35, 60;
TCLC 2, 6, 13, 29, 47, 53, 112, 179;
WLC 3**
See also AAYA 31; BPFB 2; CA 126;
CAAE 105; CDWLB 2; DA; DA3; DAB;
DAC; DAM MST, NOV; DLB 81; EW 9;
EWL 3; EXPS; LATS 1:1; LMFS 2;
MTCW 1, 2; MTFW 2005; NFS 7; RGSF
2; RGWL 2, 3; SFW 4; SSFS 3, 7, 12;
TWA

Kahanovitch, Pinchas
See Der Nister

Kahanovitsch, Pinkhes
See Der Nister

Kahanovitsh, Pinkhes
See Der Nister

Kahn, Roger 1927- .... **CLC 30**
See also CA 25-28R; CANR 44, 69, 152;
DLB 171; SATA 37

Kain, Saul
See Sassoon, Siegfried (Lorraine)

Kaiser, Georg 1878-1945 .... **TCLC 9**
See also CA 190; CAAE 106; CDWLB 2;
DLB 124; EWL 3; LMFS 2; RGWL 2, 3

Kaledin, Sergei .... **CLC 59**

Kaletski, Alexander 1946- .... **CLC 39**
See also CA 143; CAAE 118

Kalidasa fl. c. 400-455 .... **CMLC 9; PC 22**
See also RGWL 2, 3

Kallman, Chester (Simon)
1921-1975 .... **CLC 2**
See also CA 45-48; CAAS 53-56; CANR 3;
CP 1, 2

Kaminsky, Melvin .... **CLC 12, 217**
See Brooks, Mel
See also AAYA 13, 48; DLB 26

Kaminsky, Stuart M. 1934- .... **CLC 59**
See also CA 73-76; CANR 29, 53, 89, 161;
CMW 4

Kaminsky, Stuart Melvin
See Kaminsky, Stuart M.

Kamo no Chomei 1153(?)-1216 .... **CMLC 66**
See also DLB 203

Kamo no Nagaakira
See Kamo no Chomei

Kandinsky, Wassily 1866-1944 .... **TCLC 92**
See also AAYA 64; CA 155; CAAE 118

Kane, Francis
See Robbins, Harold

Kane, Henry 1918-
See Queen, Ellery
See also CA 156; CMW 4

Kane, Paul
See Simon, Paul

Kanin, Garson 1912-1999 .... **CLC 22**
See also AITN 1; CA 5-8R; CAAS 177;
CAD; CANR 7, 78; DLB 7; IDFW 3, 4

Kaniuk, Yoram 1930- .... **CLC 19**
See also CA 134; DLB 299; RGHL

Kant, Immanuel 1724-1804 ..... **NCLC 27, 67**
See also DLB 94

Kantor, MacKinlay 1904-1977 .... **CLC 7**
See also CA 61-64; CAAS 73-76; CANR
60, 63; CN 1, 2; DLB 9, 102; MAL 5;
MTCW 2; RHW; TCWW 1, 2

Kanze Motokiyo
See Zeami

Kaplan, David Michael 1946- .... **CLC 50**
See also CA 187

Kaplan, James 1951- .... **CLC 59**
See also CA 135; CANR 121

Karadzic, Vuk Stefanovic
1787-1864 .... **NCLC 115**
See also CDWLB 4; DLB 147

Karageorge, Michael
See Anderson, Poul

Karamzin, Nikolai Mikhailovich
1766-1826 .... **NCLC 3, 173**
See also DLB 150; RGSF 2

Karapanou, Margarita 1946- .... **CLC 13**
See also CA 101

Karinthy, Frigyes 1887-1938 .... **TCLC 47**
See also CA 170; DLB 215; EWL 3

Karl, Frederick R(obert)
1927-2004 .... **CLC 34**
See also CA 5-8R; CAAS 226; CANR 3,
44, 143

Karr, Mary 1955- .... **CLC 188**
See also AMWS 11; CA 151; CANR 100;
MTFW 2005; NCFS 5

Kastel, Warren
See Silverberg, Robert

Kataev, Evgeny Petrovich 1903-1942
See Petrov, Evgeny
See also CAAE 120

Kataphusin
See Ruskin, John

Katz, Steve 1935- .... **CLC 47**
See also CA 25-28R; 14, 64; CANR 12;
CN 4, 5, 6, 7; DLBY 1983

Kauffman, Janet 1945- .... **CLC 42**
See also CA 117; CANR 43, 84; DLB 218;
DLBY 1986

Kaufman, Bob (Garnell)
1925-1986 .... **CLC 49; PC 74**
See also BG 1:3; BW 1; CA 41-44R; CAAS
118; CANR 22; CP 1; DLB 16, 41

Kaufman, George S. 1889-1961 ...... **CLC 38;
DC 17**
See also CA 108; CAAS 93-96; DAM
DRAM; DFS 1, 10; DLB 7; INT CA-108;
MTCW 2; MTFW 2005; RGAL 4; TUS

Kaufman, Moises 1964- .... **DC 26**
See also CA 211; DFS 22; MTFW 2005

Kaufman, Sue .... **CLC 3, 8**
See Barondess, Sue K(aufman)

Kavafis, Konstantinos Petrou 1863-1933
See Cavafy, C(onstantine) P(eter)
See also CAAE 104

Kavan, Anna 1901-1968 .... **CLC 5, 13, 82**
See also BRWS 7; CA 5-8R; CANR 6, 57;
DLB 255; MTCW 1; RGEL 2; SFW 4

Keyber, Conny
See Fielding, Henry
Keyes, Daniel 1927- .... **CLC 80**
See also AAYA 23; BYA 11; CA 181; 17-
20R, 181; CANR 10, 26, 54, 74; DA;
DA3; DAC; DAM MST, NOV; EXPN;
LAIT 4; MTCW 2; MTFW 2005; NFS 2;
SATA 37; SFW 4
Keynes, John Maynard
1883-1946 .... **TCLC 64**
See also CA 162, 163; CAAE 114; DLBD
10; MTCW 2; MTFW 2005
Khanshendel, Chiron
See Rose, Wendy
Khayyam, Omar 1048-1131 ... **CMLC 11; PC 8**
See Omar Khayyam
See also DA3; DAM POET; WLIT 6
Kherdian, David 1931- .... **CLC 6, 9**
See also AAYA 42; CA 192; 21-24R, 192;
2; CANR 39, 78; CLR 24; JRDA; LAIT
3; MAICYA 1, 2; SATA 16, 74; SATA-
Essay 125
Khlebnikov, Velimir .... **TCLC 20**
See Khlebnikov, Viktor Vladimirovich
See also DLB 295; EW 10; EWL 3; RGWL
2, 3
Khlebnikov, Viktor Vladimirovich 1885-1922
See Khlebnikov, Velimir
See also CA 217; CAAE 117
Khodasevich, V.F.
See Khodasevich, Vladislav
Khodasevich, Vladislav
1886-1939 .... **TCLC 15**
See also CAAE 115; DLB 317; EWL 3
Khodasevich, Vladislav Felitsianovich
See Khodasevich, Vladislav
Kielland, Alexander Lange
1849-1906 .... **TCLC 5**
See also CAAE 104
Kiely, Benedict 1919-2007 . **CLC 23, 43; SSC 58**
See also CA 1-4R; CANR 2, 84; CN 1, 2,
3, 4, 5, 6, 7; DLB 15, 319; TCLE 1:1
Kienzle, William X. 1928-2001 .... **CLC 25**
See also CA 93-96; 1; CAAS 203; CANR
9, 31, 59, 111; CMW 4; DA3; DAM POP;
INT CANR-31; MSW; MTCW 1, 2;
MTFW 2005
Kierkegaard, Soren 1813-1855 ..... **NCLC 34, 78, 125**
See also DLB 300; EW 6; LMFS 2; RGWL
3; TWA
Kieslowski, Krzysztof 1941-1996 .... **CLC 120**
See also CA 147; CAAS 151
Killens, John Oliver 1916-1987 .... **CLC 10**
See also BW 2; CA 77-80; 2; CAAS 123;
CANR 26; CN 1, 2, 3, 4; DLB 33; EWL
3
Killigrew, Anne 1660-1685 .... **LC 4, 73**
See also DLB 131
Killigrew, Thomas 1612-1683 .... **LC 57**
See also DLB 58; RGEL 2
Kim
See Simenon, Georges (Jacques Christian)
Kincaid, Jamaica 1949- ...... **BLC 2; CLC 43, 68, 137, 234; SSC 72**
See also AAYA 13, 56; AFAW 2; AMWS 7;
BRWS 7; BW 2, 3; CA 125; CANR 47,
59, 95, 133; CDALBS; CDWLB 3; CLR
63; CN 4, 5, 6, 7; DA3; DAM MULT,
NOV; DLB 157, 227; DNFS 1; EWL 3;
EXPS; FW; LATS 1:2; LMFS 2; MAL 5;
MTCW 2; MTFW 2005; NCFS 1; NFS 3;
SSFS 5, 7; TUS; WWE 1; YAW

King, Francis (Henry) 1923- .... **CLC 8, 53, 145**
See also CA 1-4R; CANR 1, 33, 86; CN 1,
2, 3, 4, 5, 6, 7; DAM NOV; DLB 15, 139;
MTCW 1
King, Kennedy
See Brown, George Douglas
King, Martin Luther, Jr. 1929-1968 . **BLC 2; CLC 83; WLCS**
See also BW 2, 3; CA 25-28; CANR 27,
44; CAP 2; DA; DA3; DAB; DAC; DAM
MST, MULT; LAIT 5; LATS 1:2; MTCW
1, 2; MTFW 2005; SATA 14
King, Stephen 1947- .... **CLC 12, 26, 37, 61, 113, 228; SSC 17, 55**
See also AAYA 1, 17; AMWS 5; BEST
90:1; BPFB 2; CA 61-64; CANR 1, 30,
52, 76, 119, 134; CN 7; CPW; DA3; DAM
NOV, POP; DLB 143; DLBY 1980; HGG;
JRDA; LAIT 5; MTCW 1, 2; MTFW
2005; RGAL 4; SATA 9, 55, 161; SUFW
1, 2; WYAS 1; YAW
King, Stephen Edwin
See King, Stephen
King, Steve
See King, Stephen
King, Thomas 1943- .... **CLC 89, 171; NNAL**
See also CA 144; CANR 95; CCA 1; CN 6,
7; DAC; DAM MULT; DLB 175; SATA
96
Kingman, Lee .... **CLC 17**
See Natti, (Mary) Lee
See also CWRI 5; SAAS 3; SATA 1, 67
Kingsley, Charles 1819-1875 .... **NCLC 35**
See also CLR 77; DLB 21, 32, 163, 178,
190; FANT; MAICYA 2; MAICYAS 1;
RGEL 2; WCH; YABC 2
Kingsley, Henry 1830-1876 .... **NCLC 107**
See also DLB 21, 230; RGEL 2
Kingsley, Sidney 1906-1995 .... **CLC 44**
See also CA 85-88; CAAS 147; CAD; DFS
14, 19; DLB 7; MAL 5; RGAL 4
Kingsolver, Barbara 1955- .... **CLC 55, 81, 130, 216**
See also AAYA 15; AMWS 7; CA 134;
CAAE 129; CANR 60, 96, 133;
CDALBS; CN 7; CPW; CSW; DA3;
DAM POP; DLB 206; INT CA-134; LAIT
5; MTCW 2; MTFW 2005; NFS 5, 10,
12, 24; RGAL 4; TCLE 1:1
Kingston, Maxine Hong 1940- .... **AAL; CLC 12, 19, 58, 121; WLCS**
See also AAYA 8, 55; AMWS 5; BPFB 2;
CA 69-72; CANR 13, 38, 74, 87, 128;
CDALBS; CN 6, 7; DA3; DAM MULT,
NOV; DLB 173, 212, 312; DLBY 1980;
EWL 3; FL 1:6; FW; INT CANR-13;
LAIT 5; MAL 5; MBL; MTCW 1, 2;
MTFW 2005; NFS 6; RGAL 4; SATA 53;
SSFS 3; TCWW 2
Kinnell, Galway 1927- ..... **CLC 1, 2, 3, 5, 13, 29, 129; PC 26**
See also AMWS 3; CA 9-12R; CANR 10,
34, 66, 116, 138; CP 1, 2, 3, 4, 5, 6, 7;
DLB 5; DLBY 1987; EWL 3; INT CANR-
34; MAL 5; MTCW 1, 2; MTFW 2005;
PAB; PFS 9; RGAL 4; TCLE 1:1; WP
Kinsella, Thomas 1928- .... **CLC 4, 19, 138; PC 69**
See also BRWS 5; CA 17-20R; CANR 15,
122; CP 1, 2, 3, 4, 5, 6, 7; DLB 27; EWL
3; MTCW 1, 2; MTFW 2005; RGEL 2;
TEA
Kinsella, W.P. 1935- .... **CLC 27, 43, 166**
See also AAYA 7, 60; BPFB 2; CA 222;
97-100, 222; 7; CANR 21, 35, 66, 75,
129; CN 4, 5, 6, 7; CPW; DAC; DAM
NOV, POP; FANT; INT CANR-21; LAIT
5; MTCW 1, 2; MTFW 2005; NFS 15;
RGSF 2

Kinsey, Alfred C(harles)
1894-1956 .... **TCLC 91**
See also CA 170; CAAE 115; MTCW 2
Kipling, (Joseph) Rudyard 1865-1936 . **PC 3; SSC 5, 54; TCLC 8, 17, 167; WLC 3**
See also AAYA 32; BRW 6; BRWC 1, 2;
BYA 4; CA 120; CAAE 105; CANR 33;
CDBLB 1890-1914; CLR 39, 65; CWRI
5; DA; DA3; DAB; DAC; DAM MST,
POET; DLB 19, 34, 141, 156, 330; EWL
3; EXPS; FANT; LAIT 3; LMFS 1; MAI-
CYA 1, 2; MTCW 1, 2; MTFW 2005;
NFS 21; PFS 22; RGEL 2; RGSF 2; SATA
100; SFW 4; SSFS 8, 21, 22; SUFW 1;
TEA; WCH; WLIT 4; YABC 2
Kircher, Athanasius 1602-1680 .... **LC 121**
See also DLB 164
Kirk, Russell (Amos) 1918-1994 .. **TCLC 119**
See also AITN 1; CA 1-4R; 9; CAAS 145;
CANR 1, 20, 60; HGG; INT CANR-20;
MTCW 1, 2
Kirkham, Dinah
See Card, Orson Scott
Kirkland, Caroline M. 1801-1864 . **NCLC 85**
See also DLB 3, 73, 74, 250, 254; DLBD
13
Kirkup, James 1918- .... **CLC 1**
See also CA 1-4R; 4; CANR 2; CP 1, 2, 3,
4, 5, 6, 7; DLB 27; SATA 12
Kirkwood, James 1930(?)-1989 .... **CLC 9**
See also AITN 2; CA 1-4R; CAAS 128;
CANR 6, 40; GLL 2
Kirsch, Sarah 1935- .... **CLC 176**
See also CA 178; CWW 2; DLB 75; EWL
3
Kirshner, Sidney
See Kingsley, Sidney
Kis, Danilo 1935-1989 .... **CLC 57**
See also CA 118; CAAE 109; CAAS 129;
CANR 61; CDWLB 4; DLB 181; EWL 3;
MTCW 1; RGSF 2; RGWL 2, 3
Kissinger, Henry A(lfred) 1923- ..... **CLC 137**
See also CA 1-4R; CANR 2, 33, 66, 109;
MTCW 1
Kittel, Frederick August
See Wilson, August
Kivi, Aleksis 1834-1872 .... **NCLC 30**
Kizer, Carolyn 1925- ..... **CLC 15, 39, 80; PC 66**
See also CA 65-68; 5; CANR 24, 70, 134;
CP 1, 2, 3, 4, 5, 6, 7; CWP; DAM POET;
DLB 5, 169; EWL 3; MAL 5; MTCW 2;
MTFW 2005; PFS 18; TCLE 1:1
Klabund 1890-1928 .... **TCLC 44**
See also CA 162; DLB 66
Klappert, Peter 1942- .... **CLC 57**
See also CA 33-36R; CSW; DLB 5
Klein, A(braham) M(oses)
1909-1972 .... **CLC 19**
See also CA 101; CAAS 37-40R; CP 1;
DAB; DAC; DAM MST; DLB 68; EWL
3; RGEL 2; RGHL
Klein, Joe
See Klein, Joseph
Klein, Joseph 1946- .... **CLC 154**
See also CA 85-88; CANR 55
Klein, Norma 1938-1989 .... **CLC 30**
See also AAYA 2, 35; BPFB 2; BYA 6, 7,
8; CA 41-44R; CAAS 128; CANR 15, 37;
CLR 2, 19; INT CANR-15; JRDA; MAI-
CYA 1, 2; SAAS 1; SATA 7, 57; WYA;
YAW
Klein, T(heodore) E(ibon) D(onald)
1947- .... **CLC 34**
See also CA 119; CANR 44, 75; HGG
Kleist, Heinrich von 1777-1811 ...... **NCLC 2, 37; SSC 22**
See also CDWLB 2; DAM DRAM; DLB
90; EW 5; RGSF 2; RGWL 2, 3

Klima, Ivan 1931- .... **CLC 56, 172**
See also CA 25-28R; CANR 17, 50, 91;
CDWLB 4; CWW 2; DAM NOV; DLB
232; EWL 3; RGWL 3

Klimentev, Andrei Platonovich
See Klimentov, Andrei Platonovich

Klimentov, Andrei Platonovich
1899-1951 .... **SSC 42; TCLC 14**
See Platonov, Andrei Platonovich; Platonov,
Andrey Platonovich
See also CA 232; CAAE 108

Klinger, Friedrich Maximilian von
1752-1831 .... **NCLC 1**
See also DLB 94

Klingsor the Magician
See Hartmann, Sadakichi

Klopstock, Friedrich Gottlieb
1724-1803 .... **NCLC 11**
See also DLB 97; EW 4; RGWL 2, 3

Kluge, Alexander 1932- .... **SSC 61**
See also CA 81-84; DLB 75

Knapp, Caroline 1959-2002 .... **CLC 99**
See also CA 154; CAAS 207

Knebel, Fletcher 1911-1993 .... **CLC 14**
See also AITN 1; CA 1-4R; 3; CAAS 140;
CANR 1, 36; CN 1, 2, 3, 4, 5; SATA 36;
SATA-Obit 75

Knickerbocker, Diedrich
See Irving, Washington

Knight, Etheridge 1931-1991 ... **BLC 2; CLC
40; PC 14**
See also BW 1, 3; CA 21-24R; CAAS 133;
CANR 23, 82; CP 1, 2, 3, 4, 5; DAM
POET; DLB 41; MTCW 2; MTFW 2005;
RGAL 4; TCLE 1:1

Knight, Sarah Kemble 1666-1727 .... **LC 7**
See also DLB 24, 200

Knister, Raymond 1899-1932 .... **TCLC 56**
See also CA 186; DLB 68; RGEL 2

Knowles, John 1926-2001 ... **CLC 1, 4, 10, 26**
See also AAYA 10, 72; AMWS 12; BPFB
2; BYA 3; CA 17-20R; CAAS 203; CANR
40, 74, 76, 132; CDALB 1968-1988; CLR
98; CN 1, 2, 3, 4, 5, 6, 7; DA; DAC;
DAM MST, NOV; DLB 6; EXPN; MTCW
1, 2; MTFW 2005; NFS 2; RGAL 4;
SATA 8, 89; SATA-Obit 134; YAW

Knox, Calvin M.
See Silverberg, Robert

Knox, John c. 1505-1572 .... **LC 37**
See also DLB 132

Knye, Cassandra
See Disch, Thomas M.

Koch, C(hristopher) J(ohn) 1932- .... **CLC 42**
See also CA 127; CANR 84; CN 3, 4, 5, 6,
7; DLB 289

Koch, Christopher
See Koch, C(hristopher) J(ohn)

Koch, Kenneth 1925-2002 .... **CLC 5, 8, 44**
See also AMWS 15; CA 1-4R; CAAS 207;
CAD; CANR 6, 36, 57, 97, 131; CD 5, 6;
CP 1, 2, 3, 4, 5, 6, 7; DAM POET; DLB
5; INT CANR-36; MAL 5; MTCW 2;
MTFW 2005; PFS 20; SATA 65; WP

Kochanowski, Jan 1530-1584 .... **LC 10**
See also RGWL 2, 3

Kock, Charles Paul de 1794-1871 . **NCLC 16**

Koda Rohan
See Koda Shigeyuki

Koda Rohan
See Koda Shigeyuki
See also DLB 180

Koda Shigeyuki 1867-1947 .... **TCLC 22**
See Koda Rohan
See also CA 183; CAAE 121

Koestler, Arthur 1905-1983 ... **CLC 1, 3, 6, 8,
15, 33**
See also BRWS 1; CA 1-4R; CAAS 109;
CANR 1, 33; CDBLB 1945-1960; CN 1,

2, 3; DLBY 1983; EWL 3; MTCW 1, 2;
MTFW 2005; NFS 19; RGEL 2

Kogawa, Joy Nozomi 1935- ...... **CLC 78, 129**
See also AAYA 47; CA 101; CANR 19, 62,
126; CN 6, 7; CP 1; CWP; DAC; DAM
MST, MULT; FW; MTCW 2; MTFW
2005; NFS 3; SATA 99

Kohout, Pavel 1928- .... **CLC 13**
See also CA 45-48; CANR 3

Koizumi, Yakumo
See Hearn, (Patricio) Lafcadio (Tessima
Carlos)

Kolmar, Gertrud 1894-1943 .... **TCLC 40**
See also CA 167; EWL 3; RGHL

Komunyakaa, Yusef 1947- .. **BLCS; CLC 86,
94, 207; PC 51**
See also AFAW 2; AMWS 13; CA 147;
CANR 83; CP 6, 7; CSW; DLB 120; EWL
3; PFS 5, 20; RGAL 4

Konrad, George
See Konrad, Gyorgy

Konrad, Gyorgy 1933- .... **CLC 4, 10, 73**
See also CA 85-88; CANR 97; CDWLB 4;
CWW 2; DLB 232; EWL 3

Konwicki, Tadeusz 1926- .... **CLC 8, 28, 54,
117**
See also CA 101; 9; CANR 39, 59; CWW
2; DLB 232; EWL 3; IDFW 3; MTCW 1

Koontz, Dean R. 1945- .... **CLC 78, 206**
See also AAYA 9, 31; BEST 89:3, 90:2; CA
108; CANR 19, 36, 52, 95, 138; CMW 4;
CPW; DA3; DAM NOV, POP; DLB 292;
HGG; MTCW 1; MTFW 2005; SATA 92,
165; SFW 4; SUFW 2; YAW

Koontz, Dean Ray
See Koontz, Dean R.

Kopernik, Mikolaj
See Copernicus, Nicolaus

Kopit, Arthur (Lee) 1937- ...... **CLC 1, 18, 33**
See also AITN 1; CA 81-84; CABS 3;
CAD; CD 5, 6; DAM DRAM; DFS 7, 14;
DLB 7; MAL 5; MTCW 1; RGAL 4

Kopitar, Jernej (Bartholomaeus)
1780-1844 .... **NCLC 117**

Kops, Bernard 1926- .... **CLC 4**
See also CA 5-8R; CANR 84, 159; CBD;
CN 1, 2, 3, 4, 5, 6, 7; CP 1, 2, 3, 4, 5, 6,
7; DLB 13; RGHL

Kornbluth, C(yril) M. 1923-1958 .... **TCLC 8**
See also CA 160; CAAE 105; DLB 8;
SCFW 1, 2; SFW 4

Korolenko, V.G.
See Korolenko, Vladimir G.

Korolenko, Vladimir
See Korolenko, Vladimir G.

Korolenko, Vladimir G.
1853-1921 .... **TCLC 22**
See also CAAE 121; DLB 277

Korolenko, Vladimir Galaktionovich
See Korolenko, Vladimir G.

Korzybski, Alfred (Habdank Skarbek)
1879-1950 .... **TCLC 61**
See also CA 160; CAAE 123

Kosinski, Jerzy 1933-1991 ..... **CLC 1, 2, 3, 6,
10, 15, 53, 70**
See also AMWS 7; BPFB 2; CA 17-20R;
CAAS 134; CANR 9, 46; CN 1, 2, 3, 4;
DA3; DAM NOV; DLB 2, 299; DLBY
1982; EWL 3; HGG; MAL 5; MTCW 1,
2; MTFW 2005; NFS 12; RGAL 4;
RGHL; TUS

Kostelanetz, Richard (Cory) 1940- .. **CLC 28**
See also CA 13-16R; 8; CANR 38, 77; CN
4, 5, 6; CP 2, 3, 4, 5, 6, 7

Kostrowitzki, Wilhelm Apollinaris de
1880-1918
See Apollinaire, Guillaume
See also CAAE 104

Kotlowitz, Robert 1924- .... **CLC 4**
See also CA 33-36R; CANR 36

Kotzebue, August (Friedrich Ferdinand) von
1761-1819 .... **NCLC 25**
See also DLB 94

Kotzwinkle, William 1938- ..... **CLC 5, 14, 35**
See also BPFB 2; CA 45-48; CANR 3, 44,
84, 129; CLR 6; CN 7; DLB 173; FANT;
MAICYA 1, 2; SATA 24, 70, 146; SFW
4; SUFW 2; YAW

Kowna, Stancy
See Szymborska, Wislawa

Kozol, Jonathan 1936- .... **CLC 17**
See also AAYA 46; CA 61-64; CANR 16,
45, 96; MTFW 2005

Kozoll, Michael 1940(?)- .... **CLC 35**

Kramer, Kathryn 19(?)- .... **CLC 34**

Kramer, Larry 1935- .... **CLC 42; DC 8**
See also CA 126; CAAE 124; CANR 60,
132; DAM POP; DLB 249; GLL 1

Krasicki, Ignacy 1735-1801 .... **NCLC 8**

Krasinski, Zygmunt 1812-1859 .... **NCLC 4**
See also RGWL 2, 3

Kraus, Karl 1874-1936 .... **TCLC 5**
See also CA 216; CAAE 104; DLB 118;
EWL 3

Kreve (Mickevicius), Vincas
1882-1954 .... **TCLC 27**
See also CA 170; DLB 220; EWL 3

Kristeva, Julia 1941- .... **CLC 77, 140**
See also CA 154; CANR 99; DLB 242;
EWL 3; FW; LMFS 2

Kristofferson, Kris 1936- .... **CLC 26**
See also CA 104

Krizanc, John 1956- .... **CLC 57**
See also CA 187

Krleza, Miroslav 1893-1981 .... **CLC 8, 114**
See also CA 97-100; CAAS 105; CANR
50; CDWLB 4; DLB 147; EW 11; RGWL
2, 3

Kroetsch, Robert (Paul) 1927- .... **CLC 5, 23,
57, 132**
See also CA 17-20R; CANR 8, 38; CCA 1;
CN 2, 3, 4, 5, 6, 7; CP 6, 7; DAC; DAM
POET; DLB 53; MTCW 1

Kroetz, Franz
See Kroetz, Franz Xaver

Kroetz, Franz Xaver 1946- .... **CLC 41**
See also CA 130; CANR 142; CWW 2;
EWL 3

Kroker, Arthur (W.) 1945- .... **CLC 77**
See also CA 161

Kroniuk, Lisa
See Berton, Pierre (Francis de Marigny)

Kropotkin, Peter (Alekseievich)
1842-1921 .... **TCLC 36**
See Kropotkin, Petr Alekseevich
See also CA 219; CAAE 119

Kropotkin, Petr Alekseevich
See Kropotkin, Peter (Alekseievich)
See also DLB 277

Krotkov, Yuri 1917-1981 .... **CLC 19**
See also CA 102

Krumb
See Crumb, R.

Krumgold, Joseph (Quincy)
1908-1980 .... **CLC 12**
See also BYA 1, 2; CA 9-12R; CAAS 101;
CANR 7; MAICYA 1, 2; SATA 1, 48;
SATA-Obit 23; YAW

Krumwitz
See Crumb, R.

Krutch, Joseph Wood 1893-1970 ..... **CLC 24**
See also ANW; CA 1-4R; CAAS 25-28R;
CANR 4; DLB 63, 206, 275

Krutzch, Gus
See Eliot, T(homas) S(tearns)

Krylov, Ivan Andreevich
 1768(?)-1844 .... **NCLC 1**
 See also DLB 150
Kubin, Alfred (Leopold Isidor)
 1877-1959 .... **TCLC 23**
 See also CA 149; CAAE 112; CANR 104;
 DLB 81
Kubrick, Stanley 1928-1999 .... **CLC 16;**
 TCLC 112
 See also AAYA 30; CA 81-84; CAAS 177;
 CANR 33; DLB 26
Kumin, Maxine 1925- .... **CLC 5, 13, 28, 164;**
 PC 15
 See also AITN 2; AMWS 4; ANW; CA
 1-4R; 8; CANR 1, 21, 69, 115, 140; CP 2,
 3, 4, 5, 6, 7; CWP; DA3; DAM POET;
 DLB 5; EWL 3; EXPP; MTCW 1, 2;
 MTFW 2005; PAB; PFS 18; SATA 12
Kundera, Milan 1929- . **CLC 4, 9, 19, 32, 68,**
 115, 135, 234; SSC 24
 See also AAYA 2, 62; BPFB 2; CA 85-88;
 CANR 19, 52, 74, 144; CDWLB 4; CWW
 2; DA3; DAM NOV; DLB 232; EW 13;
 EWL 3; MTCW 1, 2; MTFW 2005; NFS
 18; RGSF 2; RGWL 3; SSFS 10
Kunene, Mazisi 1930-2006 .... **CLC 85**
 See also BW 1, 3; CA 125; CAAS 252;
 CANR 81; CP 1, 6, 7; DLB 117
Kunene, Mazisi Raymond
 See Kunene, Mazisi
Kunene, Mazisi Raymond Fakazi Mngoni
 See Kunene, Mazisi
Kung, Hans .... **CLC 130**
 See Kung, Hans
Kung, Hans 1928-
 See Kung, Hans
 See also CA 53-56; CANR 66, 134; MTCW
 1, 2; MTFW 2005
Kunikida Doppo 1869(?)-1908
 See Doppo, Kunikida
 See also DLB 180; EWL 3
Kunitz, Stanley 1905-2006 ..... **CLC 6, 11, 14,**
 148; PC 19
 See also AMWS 3; CA 41-44R; CAAS 250;
 CANR 26, 57, 98; CP 1, 2, 3, 4, 5, 6, 7;
 DA3; DLB 48; INT CANR-26; MAL 5;
 MTCW 1, 2; MTFW 2005; PFS 11;
 RGAL 4
Kunitz, Stanley Jasspon
 See Kunitz, Stanley
Kunze, Reiner 1933- .... **CLC 10**
 See also CA 93-96; CWW 2; DLB 75; EWL
 3
Kuprin, Aleksander Ivanovich
 1870-1938 .... **TCLC 5**
 See Kuprin, Aleksandr Ivanovich; Kuprin,
 Alexandr Ivanovich
 See also CA 182; CAAE 104
Kuprin, Aleksandr Ivanovich
 See Kuprin, Aleksander Ivanovich
 See also DLB 295
Kuprin, Alexandr Ivanovich
 See Kuprin, Aleksander Ivanovich
 See also EWL 3
Kureishi, Hanif 1954- .. **CLC 64, 135; DC 26**
 See also BRWS 11; CA 139; CANR 113;
 CBD; CD 5, 6; CN 6, 7; DLB 194, 245;
 GLL 2; IDFW 4; WLIT 4; WWE 1
Kurosawa, Akira 1910-1998 ..... **CLC 16, 119**
 See also AAYA 11, 64; CA 101; CAAS 170;
 CANR 46; DAM MULT
Kushner, Tony 1956- .... **CLC 81, 203; DC 10**
 See also AAYA 61; AMWS 9; CA 144;
 CAD; CANR 74, 130; CD 5, 6; DA3;
 DAM DRAM; DFS 5; DLB 228; EWL 3;
 GLL 1; LAIT 5; MAL 5; MTCW 2;
 MTFW 2005; RGAL 4; RGHL; SATA 160
Kuttner, Henry 1915-1958 .... **TCLC 10**
 See also CA 157; CAAS 107; DLB 8;
 FANT; SCFW 1, 2; SFW 4

Kutty, Madhavi
 See Das, Kamala
Kuzma, Greg 1944- .... **CLC 7**
 See also CA 33-36R; CANR 70
Kuzmin, Mikhail (Alekseevich)
 1872(?)-1936 .... **TCLC 40**
 See also CA 170; DLB 295; EWL 3
Kyd, Thomas 1558-1594 .. **DC 3; LC 22, 125**
 See also BRW 1; DAM DRAM; DFS 21;
 DLB 62; IDTP; LMFS 1; RGEL 2; TEA;
 WLIT 3
Kyprianos, Iossif
 See Samarakis, Antonis
L. S.
 See Stephen, Sir Leslie
Labe, Louise 1521-1566 .... **LC 120**
 See also DLB 327
Labrunie, Gerard
 See Nerval, Gerard de
La Bruyere, Jean de 1645-1696 .... **LC 17**
 See also DLB 268; EW 3; GFL Beginnings
 to 1789
LaBute, Neil 1963- .... **CLC 225**
 See also CA 240
Lacan, Jacques (Marie Emile)
 1901-1981 .... **CLC 75**
 See also CA 121; CAAS 104; DLB 296;
 EWL 3; TWA
Laclos, Pierre-Ambroise Francois
 1741-1803 .... **NCLC 4, 87**
 See also DLB 313; EW 4; GFL Beginnings
 to 1789; RGWL 2, 3
Lacolere, Francois
 See Aragon, Louis
La Colere, Francois
 See Aragon, Louis
La Deshabilleuse
 See Simenon, Georges (Jacques Christian)
Lady Gregory
 See Gregory, Lady Isabella Augusta (Persse)
Lady of Quality, A
 See Bagnold, Enid
La Fayette, Marie-(Madelaine Pioche de la
 Vergne) 1634-1693 .... **LC 2**
 See Lafayette, Marie-Madeleine
 See also GFL Beginnings to 1789; RGWL
 2, 3
Lafayette, Marie-Madeleine
 See La Fayette, Marie-(Madelaine Pioche de
 la Vergne)
 See also DLB 268
Lafayette, Rene
 See Hubbard, L. Ron
La Flesche, Francis 1857(?)-1932 ...... **NNAL**
 See also CA 144; CANR 83; DLB 175
La Fontaine, Jean de 1621-1695 .... **LC 50**
 See also DLB 268; EW 3; GFL Beginnings
 to 1789; MAICYA 1, 2; RGWL 2, 3;
 SATA 18
LaForet, Carmen 1921-2004 .... **CLC 219**
 See also CA 246; CWW 2; DLB 322; EWL
 3
LaForet Diaz, Carmen
 See LaForet, Carmen
Laforgue, Jules 1860-1887 . **NCLC 5, 53; PC**
 14; SSC 20
 See also DLB 217; EW 7; GFL 1789 to the
 Present; RGWL 2, 3
Lagerkvist, Paer (Fabian)
 1891-1974 ..... **CLC 7, 10, 13, 54; TCLC**
 144
 See Lagerkvist, Par
 See also CA 85-88; CAAS 49-52; DA3;
 DAM DRAM, NOV; MTCW 1, 2; MTFW
 2005; TWA
Lagerkvist, Par .... **SSC 12**
 See Lagerkvist, Paer (Fabian)
 See also DLB 259, 331; EW 10; EWL 3;
 RGSF 2; RGWL 2, 3

Lagerloef, Selma (Ottiliana Lovisa)
 .... **TCLC 4, 36**
 See Lagerlof, Selma (Ottiliana Lovisa)
 See also CAAE 108; MTCW 2
Lagerlof, Selma (Ottiliana Lovisa)
 1858-1940
 See Lagerloef, Selma (Ottiliana Lovisa)
 See also CA 188; CLR 7; DLB 259, 331;
 RGWL 2, 3; SATA 15; SSFS 18
La Guma, Alex 1925-1985 .. **BLCS; CLC 19;**
 TCLC 140
 See also AFW; BW 1, 3; CA 49-52; CAAS
 118; CANR 25, 81; CDWLB 3; CN 1, 2,
 3; CP 1; DAM NOV; DLB 117, 225; EWL
 3; MTCW 1, 2; MTFW 2005; WLIT 2;
 WWE 1
Lahiri, Jhumpa 1967- .... **SSC 96**
 See also AAYA 56; CA 193; CANR 134;
 DLB 323; MTCW 2005; SSFS 19
Laidlaw, A. K.
 See Grieve, C(hristopher) M(urray)
Lainez, Manuel Mujica
 See Mujica Lainez, Manuel
 See also HW 1
Laing, R(onald) D(avid) 1927-1989 . **CLC 95**
 See also CA 107; CAAS 129; CANR 34;
 MTCW 1
Laishley, Alex
 See Booth, Martin
Lamartine, Alphonse (Marie Louis Prat) de
 1790-1869 .... **NCLC 11; PC 16**
 See also DAM POET; DLB 217; GFL 1789
 to the Present; RGWL 2, 3
Lamb, Charles 1775-1834 ..... **NCLC 10, 113;**
 WLC 3
 See also BRW 4; CDBLB 1789-1832; DA;
 DAB; DAC; DAM MST; DLB 93, 107,
 163; RGEL 2; SATA 17; TEA
Lamb, Lady Caroline 1785-1828 ... **NCLC 38**
 See also DLB 116
Lamb, Mary Ann 1764-1847 .... **NCLC 125**
 See also DLB 163; SATA 17
Lame Deer 1903(?)-1976 .... **NNAL**
 See also CAAS 69-72
Lamming, George (William) 1927- ... **BLC 2;**
 CLC 2, 4, 66, 144
 See also BW 2, 3; CA 85-88; CANR 26,
 76; CDWLB 3; CN 1, 2, 3, 4, 5, 6, 7; CP
 1; DAM MULT; DLB 125; EWL 3;
 MTCW 1, 2; MTFW 2005; NFS 15;
 RGEL 2
L'Amour, Louis 1908-1988 .... **CLC 25, 55**
 See also AAYA 16; AITN 2; BEST 89:2;
 BPFB 2; CA 1-4R; CAAS 125; CANR 3,
 25, 40; CPW; DA3; DAM NOV, POP;
 DLB 206; DLBY 1980; MTCW 1, 2;
 MTFW 2005; RGAL 4; TCWW 1, 2
Lampedusa, Giuseppe (Tomasi) di
 .... **TCLC 13**
 See Tomasi di Lampedusa, Giuseppe
 See also CA 164; EW 11; MTCW 2; MTFW
 2005; RGWL 2, 3
Lampman, Archibald 1861-1899 ... **NCLC 25**
 See also DLB 92; RGEL 2; TWA
Lancaster, Bruce 1896-1963 .... **CLC 36**
 See also CA 9-10; CANR 70; CAP 1; SATA
 9
Lanchester, John 1962- .... **CLC 99**
 See also CA 194; DLB 267
Landau, Mark Alexandrovich
 See Aldanov, Mark (Alexandrovich)
Landau-Aldanov, Mark Alexandrovich
 See Aldanov, Mark (Alexandrovich)
Landis, Jerry
 See Simon, Paul
Landis, John 1950- .... **CLC 26**
 See also CA 122; CAAE 112; CANR 128

Leacock, Stephen (Butler)
1869-1944 .... **SSC 39; TCLC 2**
See also CA 141; CAAE 104; CANR 80;
DAC; DAM MST; DLB 92; EWL 3;
MTCW 2; MTFW 2005; RGEL 2; RGSF
2

Lead, Jane Ward 1623-1704 .... **LC 72**
See also DLB 131

Leapor, Mary 1722-1746 .... **LC 80**
See also DLB 109

Lear, Edward 1812-1888 ..... **NCLC 3; PC 65**
See also AAYA 48; BRW 5; CLR 1, 75;
DLB 32, 163, 166; MAICYA 1, 2; RGEL
2; SATA 18, 100; WCH; WP

Lear, Norman (Milton) 1922- .... **CLC 12**
See also CA 73-76

Leautaud, Paul 1872-1956 .... **TCLC 83**
See also CA 203; DLB 65; GFL 1789 to the
Present

Leavis, F(rank) R(aymond)
1895-1978 .... **CLC 24**
See also BRW 7; CA 21-24R; CAAS 77-
80; CANR 44; DLB 242; EWL 3; MTCW
1, 2; RGEL 2

Leavitt, David 1961- .... **CLC 34**
See also CA 122; CAAE 116; CANR 50,
62, 101, 134; CPW; DA3; DAM POP;
DLB 130; GLL 1; INT CA-122; MAL 5;
MTCW 2; MTFW 2005

Leblanc, Maurice (Marie Emile)
1864-1941 .... **TCLC 49**
See also CAAE 110; CMW 4

Lebowitz, Fran(ces Ann) 1951(?)- ... **CLC 11,
36**
See also CA 81-84; CANR 14, 60, 70; INT
CANR-14; MTCW 1

Lebrecht, Peter
See Tieck, (Johann) Ludwig

le Carre, John 1931- .... **CLC 9, 15**
See also AAYA 42; BEST 89:4; BPFB 2;
BRWS 2; CA 5-8R; CANR 13, 33, 59,
107, 132; CDBLB 1960 to Present; CMW
4; CN 1, 2, 3, 4, 5, 6, 7; CPW; DA3;
DAM POP; DLB 87; EWL 3; MSW;
MTCW 1, 2; MTFW 2005; RGEL 2; TEA

Le Clezio, J. M.G. 1940- .... **CLC 31, 155**
See also CA 128; CAAE 116; CANR 147;
CWW 2; DLB 83; EWL 3; GFL 1789 to
the Present; RGSF 2

Le Clezio, Jean Marie Gustave
See Le Clezio, J. M.G.

Leconte de Lisle, Charles-Marie-Rene
1818-1894 .... **NCLC 29**
See also DLB 217; EW 6; GFL 1789 to the
Present

Le Coq, Monsieur
See Simenon, Georges (Jacques Christian)

Leduc, Violette 1907-1972 .... **CLC 22**
See also CA 13-14; CAAS 33-36R; CANR
69; CAP 1; EWL 3; GFL 1789 to the
Present; GLL 1

Ledwidge, Francis 1887(?)-1917 .... **TCLC 23**
See also CA 203; CAAE 123; DLB 20

Lee, Andrea 1953- .... **BLC 2; CLC 36**
See also BW 1, 3; CA 125; CANR 82;
DAM MULT

Lee, Andrew
See Auchincloss, Louis

Lee, Chang-rae 1965- .... **CLC 91**
See also CA 148; CANR 89; CN 7; DLB
312; LATS 1:2

Lee, Don L. .... **CLC 2**
See Madhubuti, Haki R.
See also CP 2, 3, 4, 5

Lee, George W(ashington)
1894-1976 .... **BLC 2; CLC 52**
See also BW 1; CA 125; CANR 83; DAM
MULT; DLB 51

Lee, Harper 1926- ... **CLC 12, 60, 194; WLC
4**
See also AAYA 13; AMWS 8; BPFB 2;
BYA 3; CA 13-16R; CANR 51, 128;
CDALB 1941-1968; CSW; DA; DA3;
DAB; DAC; DAM MST, NOV; DLB 6;
EXPN; LAIT 3; MAL 5; MTCW 1, 2;
MTFW 2005; NFS 2; SATA 11; WYA;
YAW

Lee, Helen Elaine 1959(?)- .... **CLC 86**
See also CA 148

Lee, John .... **CLC 70**

Lee, Julian
See Latham, Jean Lee

Lee, Larry
See Lee, Lawrence

Lee, Laurie 1914-1997 .... **CLC 90**
See also CA 77-80; CAAS 158; CANR 33,
73; CP 1, 2, 3, 4, 5, 6; CPW; DAB; DAM
POP; DLB 27; MTCW 1; RGEL 2

Lee, Lawrence 1941-1990 .... **CLC 34**
See also CAAS 131; CANR 43

Lee, Li-Young 1957- .... **CLC 164; PC 24**
See also AMWS 15; CA 153; CANR 118;
CP 6, 7; DLB 165, 312; LMFS 2; PFS 11,
15, 17

Lee, Manfred B. 1905-1971 .... **CLC 11**
See Queen, Ellery
See also CA 1-4R; CAAS 29-32R; CANR
2, 150; CMW 4; DLB 137

Lee, Manfred Bennington
See Lee, Manfred B.

Lee, Nathaniel 1645(?)-1692 .... **LC 103**
See also DLB 80; RGEL 2

Lee, Shelton Jackson
See Lee, Spike
See also AAYA 4, 29

Lee, Spike 1957(?)- .... **BLCS; CLC 105**
See Lee, Shelton Jackson
See also BW 2, 3; CA 125; CANR 42;
DAM MULT

Lee, Stan 1922- .... **CLC 17**
See also AAYA 5, 49; CA 111; CAAE 108;
CANR 129; INT CA-111; MTFW 2005

Lee, Tanith 1947- .... **CLC 46**
See also AAYA 15; CA 37-40R; CANR 53,
102, 145; DLB 261; FANT; SATA 8, 88,
134; SFW 4; SUFW 1, 2; YAW

Lee, Vernon .... **SSC 33, 98; TCLC 5**
See Paget, Violet
See also DLB 57, 153, 156, 174, 178; GLL
1; SUFW 1

Lee, William
See Burroughs, William S.
See also GLL 1

Lee, Willy
See Burroughs, William S.
See also GLL 1

Lee-Hamilton, Eugene (Jacob)
1845-1907 .... **TCLC 22**
See also CA 234; CAAE 117

Leet, Judith 1935- .... **CLC 11**
See also CA 187

Le Fanu, Joseph Sheridan
1814-1873 .... **NCLC 9, 58; SSC 14, 84**
See also CMW 4; DA3; DAM POP; DLB
21, 70, 159, 178; GL 3; HGG; RGEL 2;
RGSF 2; SUFW 1

Leffland, Ella 1931- .... **CLC 19**
See also CA 29-32R; CANR 35, 78, 82;
DLBY 1984; INT CANR-35; SATA 65;
SSFS 24

Leger, Alexis
See Leger, (Marie-Rene Auguste) Alexis
Saint-Leger

Leger, (Marie-Rene Auguste) Alexis
Saint-Leger 1887-1975 .. **CLC 4, 11, 46;
PC 23**
See Perse, Saint-John; Saint-John Perse
See also CA 13-16R; CAAS 61-64; CANR
43; DAM POET; MTCW 1

Leger, Saintleger
See Leger, (Marie-Rene Auguste) Alexis
Saint-Leger

Le Guin, Ursula K. 1929- ...... **CLC 8, 13, 22,
45, 71, 136; SSC 12, 69**
See also AAYA 9, 27; AITN 1; BPFB 2;
BYA 5, 8, 11, 14; CA 21-24R; CANR 9,
32, 52, 74, 132; CDALB 1968-1988; CLR
3, 28, 91; CN 2, 3, 4, 5, 6, 7; CPW; DA3;
DAB; DAC; DAM MST, POP; DLB 8,
52, 256, 275; EXPS; FANT; FW; INT
CANR-32; JRDA; LAIT 5; MAICYA 1,
2; MAL 5; MTCW 1, 2; MTFW 2005;
NFS 6, 9; SATA 4, 52, 99, 149; SCFW 1,
2; SFW 4; SSFS 2; SUFW 1, 2; WYA;
YAW

Lehmann, Rosamond (Nina)
1901-1990 .... **CLC 5**
See also CA 77-80; CAAS 131; CANR 8,
73; CN 1, 2, 3, 4; DLB 15; MTCW 2;
RGEL 2; RHW

Leiber, Fritz (Reuter, Jr.)
1910-1992 .... **CLC 25**
See also AAYA 65; BPFB 2; CA 45-48;
CAAS 139; CANR 2, 40, 86; CN 2, 3, 4,
5; DLB 8; FANT; HGG; MTCW 1, 2;
MTFW 2005; SATA 45; SATA-Obit 73;
SCFW 1, 2; SFW 4; SUFW 1, 2

Leibniz, Gottfried Wilhelm von
1646-1716 .... **LC 35**
See also DLB 168

Leimbach, Martha 1963-
See Leimbach, Marti
See also CA 130

Leimbach, Marti .... **CLC 65**
See Leimbach, Martha

Leino, Eino .... **TCLC 24**
See Lonnbohm, Armas Eino Leopold
See also EWL 3

Leiris, Michel (Julien) 1901-1990 ..... **CLC 61**
See also CA 128; CAAE 119; CAAS 132;
EWL 3; GFL 1789 to the Present

Leithauser, Brad 1953- .... **CLC 27**
See also CA 107; CANR 27, 81; CP 5, 6, 7;
DLB 120, 282

le Jars de Gournay, Marie
See de Gournay, Marie le Jars

Lelchuk, Alan 1938- .... **CLC 5**
See also CA 45-48; 20; CANR 1, 70, 152;
CN 3, 4, 5, 6, 7

Lem, Stanislaw 1921-2006 ..... **CLC 8, 15, 40,
149**
See also AAYA 75; CA 105; 1; CAAS 249;
CANR 32; CWW 2; MTCW 1; SCFW 1,
2; SFW 4

Lemann, Nancy (Elise) 1956- .... **CLC 39**
See also CA 136; CAAE 118; CANR 121

Lemonnier, (Antoine Louis) Camille
1844-1913 .... **TCLC 22**
See also CAAE 121

Lenau, Nikolaus 1802-1850 .... **NCLC 16**

L'Engle, Madeleine 1918- .... **CLC 12**
See also AAYA 28; AITN 2; BPFB 2; BYA
2, 4, 5, 7; CA 1-4R; CANR 3, 21, 39, 66,
107; CLR 1, 14, 57; CPW; CWRI 5; DA3;
DAM POP; DLB 52; JRDA; MAICYA 1,
2; MTCW 1, 2; MTFW 2005; SAAS 15;
SATA 1, 27, 75, 128; SFW 4; WYA; YAW

Lengyel, Jozsef 1896-1975 .... **CLC 7**
See also CA 85-88; CAAS 57-60; CANR
71; RGSF 2

Lenin 1870-1924
See Lenin, V. I.
See also CA 168; CAAE 121

Lieberman, Laurence (James)
    1935- .... **CLC 4, 36**
    See also CA 17-20R; CANR 8, 36, 89; CP
    1, 2, 3, 4, 5, 6, 7
Lieh Tzu fl. 7th cent. B.C.-5th cent.
    B.C. .... **CMLC 27**
Lieksman, Anders
    See Haavikko, Paavo Juhani
Lifton, Robert Jay 1926- .... **CLC 67**
    See also CA 17-20R; CANR 27, 78, 161;
    INT CANR-27; SATA 66
Lightfoot, Gordon 1938- .... **CLC 26**
    See also CA 242; CAAE 109
Lightfoot, Gordon Meredith
    See Lightfoot, Gordon
Lightman, Alan P(aige) 1948- .... **CLC 81**
    See also CA 141; CANR 63, 105, 138;
    MTFW 2005
Ligotti, Thomas (Robert) 1953- ...... **CLC 44;
    SSC 16**
    See also CA 123; CANR 49, 135; HGG;
    SUFW 2
Li Ho 791-817 .... **PC 13**
Li Ju-chen c. 1763-c. 1830 .... **NCLC 137**
Lilar, Francoise
    See Mallet-Joris, Francoise
Liliencron, Detlev
    See Liliencron, Detlev von
Liliencron, Detlev von 1844-1909 .. **TCLC 18**
    See also CAAE 117
Liliencron, Friedrich Adolf Axel Detlev von
    See Liliencron, Detlev von
Liliencron, Friedrich Detlev von
    See Liliencron, Detlev von
Lille, Alain de
    See Alain de Lille
Lillo, George 1691-1739 .... **LC 131**
    See also DLB 84; RGEL 2
Lilly, William 1602-1681 .... **LC 27**
Lima, Jose Lezama
    See Lezama Lima, Jose
Lima Barreto, Afonso Henrique de
    1881-1922 .... **TCLC 23**
    See Lima Barreto, Afonso Henriques de
    See also CA 181; CAAE 117; LAW
Lima Barreto, Afonso Henriques de
    See Lima Barreto, Afonso Henrique de
    See also DLB 307
Limonov, Eduard
    See Limonov, Edward
    See also DLB 317
Limonov, Edward 1944- .... **CLC 67**
    See Limonov, Eduard
    See also CA 137
Lin, Frank
    See Atherton, Gertrude (Franklin Horn)
Lin, Yutang 1895-1976 .... **TCLC 149**
    See also CA 45-48; CAAS 65-68; CANR 2;
    RGAL 4
Lincoln, Abraham 1809-1865 .... **NCLC 18**
    See also LAIT 2
Lind, Jakov .... **CLC 1, 2, 4, 27, 82**
    See Landwirth, Heinz
    See also CA 4; DLB 299; EWL 3; RGHL
Lindbergh, Anne Morrow
    1906-2001 .... **CLC 82**
    See also BPFB 2; CA 17-20R; CAAS 193;
    CANR 16, 73; DAM NOV; MTCW 1, 2;
    MTFW 2005; SATA 33; SATA-Obit 125;
    TUS
Lindsay, David 1878(?)-1945 .... **TCLC 15**
    See also CA 187; CAAE 113; DLB 255;
    FANT; SFW 4; SUFW 1
Lindsay, (Nicholas) Vachel
    1879-1931 .... **PC 23; TCLC 17; WLC 4**
    See also AMWS 1; CA 135; CAAE 114;
    CANR 79; CDALB 1865-1917; DA;

DA3; DAC; DAM MST, POET; DLB 54;
    EWL 3; EXPP; MAL 5; RGAL 4; SATA
    40; WP
Linke-Poot
    See Doeblin, Alfred
Linney, Romulus 1930- .... **CLC 51**
    See also CA 1-4R; CAD; CANR 40, 44,
    79; CD 5, 6; CSW; RGAL 4
Linton, Eliza Lynn 1822-1898 .... **NCLC 41**
    See also DLB 18
Li Po 701-763 .... **CMLC 2, 86; PC 29**
    See also PFS 20; WP
Lipsius, Justus 1547-1606 .... **LC 16**
Lipsyte, Robert 1938- .... **CLC 21**
    See also AAYA 7, 45; CA 17-20R; CANR
    8, 57, 146; CLR 23, 76; DA; DAC; DAM
    MST, NOV; JRDA; LAIT 5; MAICYA 1,
    2; SATA 5, 68, 113, 161; WYA; YAW
Lipsyte, Robert Michael
    See Lipsyte, Robert
Lish, Gordon 1934- .... **CLC 45; SSC 18**
    See also CA 117; CAAE 113; CANR 79,
    151; DLB 130; INT CA-117
Lish, Gordon Jay
    See Lish, Gordon
Lispector, Clarice 1925(?)-1977 .... **CLC 43;
    HLCS 2; SSC 34, 96**
    See also CA 139; CAAS 116; CANR 71;
    CDWLB 3; DLB 113, 307; DNFS 1; EWL
    3; FW; HW 2; LAW; RGSF 2; RGWL 2,
    3; WLIT 1
Littell, Robert 1935(?)- .... **CLC 42**
    See also CA 112; CAAE 109; CANR 64,
    115; CMW 4
Little, Malcolm 1925-1965
    See Malcolm X
    See also BW 1, 3; CA 125; CAAS 111;
    CANR 82; DA; DA3; DAB; DAC; DAM
    MST, MULT; MTCW 1, 2; MTFW 2005
Littlewit, Humphrey Gent.
    See Lovecraft, H. P.
Litwos
    See Sienkiewicz, Henryk (Adam Alexander
    Pius)
Liu, E. 1857-1909 .... **TCLC 15**
    See also CA 190; CAAE 115; DLB 328
Lively, Penelope 1933- .... **CLC 32, 50**
    See also BPFB 2; CA 41-44R; CANR 29,
    67, 79, 131; CLR 7; CN 5, 6, 7; CWRI 5;
    DAM NOV; DLB 14, 161, 207, 326;
    FANT; JRDA; MAICYA 1, 2; MTCW 1,
    2; MTFW 2005; SATA 7, 60, 101, 164;
    TEA
Lively, Penelope Margaret
    See Lively, Penelope
Livesay, Dorothy (Kathleen)
    1909-1996 .... **CLC 4, 15, 79**
    See also AITN 2; CA 25-28R; 8; CANR 36,
    67; CP 1, 2, 3, 4, 5; DAC; DAM MST,
    POET; DLB 68; FW; MTCW 1; RGEL 2;
    TWA
Livy c. 59B.C.-c. 12 .... **CMLC 11**
    See also AW 2; CDWLB 1; DLB 211;
    RGWL 2, 3; WLIT 8
Lizardi, Jose Joaquin Fernandez de
    1776-1827 .... **NCLC 30**
    See also LAW
Llewellyn, Richard
    See Llewellyn Lloyd, Richard Dafydd Viv-
    ian
    See also DLB 15
Llewellyn Lloyd, Richard Dafydd Vivian
    1906-1983 .... **CLC 7, 80**
    See Llewellyn, Richard
    See also CA 53-56; CAAS 111; CANR 7,
    71; SATA 11; SATA-Obit 37
Llosa, Jorge Mario Pedro Vargas
    See Vargas Llosa, Mario
    See also RGWL 3

Llosa, Mario Vargas
    See Vargas Llosa, Mario
Lloyd, Manda
    See Mander, (Mary) Jane
Lloyd Webber, Andrew 1948-
    See Webber, Andrew Lloyd
    See also AAYA 1, 38; CA 149; CAAE 116;
    DAM DRAM; SATA 56
Llull, Ramon c. 1235-c. 1316 .... **CMLC 12**
Lobb, Ebenezer
    See Upward, Allen
Locke, Alain (Le Roy)
    1886-1954 .... **BLCS; HR 1:3; TCLC 43**
    See also AMWS 14; BW 1, 3; CA 124;
    CAAE 106; CANR 79; DLB 51; LMFS
    2; MAL 5; RGAL 4
Locke, John 1632-1704 .... **LC 7, 35, 135**
    See also DLB 31, 101, 213, 252; RGEL 2;
    WLIT 3
Locke-Elliott, Sumner
    See Elliott, Sumner Locke
Lockhart, John Gibson 1794-1854 .. **NCLC 6**
    See also DLB 110, 116, 144
Lockridge, Ross (Franklin), Jr.
    1914-1948 .... **TCLC 111**
    See also CA 145; CAAE 108; CANR 79;
    DLB 143; DLBY 1980; MAL 5; RGAL
    4; RHW
Lockwood, Robert
    See Johnson, Robert
Lodge, David 1935- .... **CLC 36, 141**
    See also BEST 90:1; BRWS 4; CA 17-20R;
    CANR 19, 53, 92, 139; CN 1, 2, 3, 4, 5,
    6, 7; CPW; DAM POP; DLB 14, 194;
    EWL 3; INT CANR-19; MTCW 1, 2;
    MTFW 2005
Lodge, Thomas 1558-1625 .... **LC 41**
    See also DLB 172; RGEL 2
Loewinsohn, Ron(ald William)
    1937- .... **CLC 52**
    See also CA 25-28R; CANR 71; CP 1, 2, 3,
    4
Logan, Jake
    See Smith, Martin Cruz
Logan, John (Burton) 1923-1987 .... **CLC 5**
    See also CA 77-80; CAAS 124; CANR 45;
    CP 1, 2, 3, 4; DLB 5
Lo Kuan-chung 1330(?)-1400(?) .... **LC 12**
Lombard, Nap
    See Johnson, Pamela Hansford
Lombard, Peter 1100(?)-1160(?) ... **CMLC 72**
Lombino, Salvatore
    See Hunter, Evan
London, Jack 1876-1916 .. **SSC 4, 49; TCLC
    9, 15, 39; WLC 4**
    See London, John Griffith
    See also AAYA 13; AITN 2; AMW; BPFB
    2; BYA 4, 13; CDALB 1865-1917; CLR
    108; DLB 8, 12, 78, 212; EWL 3; EXPS;
    LAIT 3; MAL 5; NFS 8; RGAL 4; RGSF
    2; SATA 18; SFW 4; SSFS 7; TCWW 1,
    2; TUS; WYA; YAW
London, John Griffith 1876-1916
    See London, Jack
    See also AAYA 75; CA 119; CAAE 110;
    CANR 73; DA; DA3; DAB; DAC; DAM
    MST, NOV; JRDA; MAICYA 1, 2;
    MTCW 1, 2; MTFW 2005; NFS 19
Long, Emmett
    See Leonard, Elmore
Longbaugh, Harry
    See Goldman, William
Longfellow, Henry Wadsworth
    1807-1882 .... **NCLC 2, 45, 101, 103; PC
    30; WLCS**
    See also AMW; AMWR 2; CDALB 1640-
    1865; CLR 99; DA; DA3; DAB; DAC;

DAM MST, POET; DLB 1, 59, 235; EXPP; PAB; PFS 2, 7, 17; RGAL 4; SATA 19; TUS; WP

Longinus c. 1st cent. - .... **CMLC 27**
See also AW 2; DLB 176

Longley, Michael 1939- .... **CLC 29**
See also BRWS 8; CA 102; CP 1, 2, 3, 4, 5, 6, 7; DLB 40

Longstreet, Augustus Baldwin
1790-1870 .... **NCLC 159**
See also DLB 3, 11, 74, 248; RGAL 4

Longus fl. c. 2nd cent. - .... **CMLC 7**

Longway, A. Hugh
See Lang, Andrew

Lonnbohm, Armas Eino Leopold 1878-1926
See Leino, Eino
See also CAAE 123

Lonnrot, Elias 1802-1884 .... **NCLC 53**
See also EFS 1

Lonsdale, Roger .... **CLC 65**

Lopate, Phillip 1943- .... **CLC 29**
See also CA 97-100; CANR 88, 157; DLBY 1980; INT CA-97-100

Lopez, Barry (Holstun) 1945- .... **CLC 70**
See also AAYA 9, 63; ANW; CA 65-68; CANR 7, 23, 47, 68, 92; DLB 256, 275; INT CANR-7, CANR-23; MTCW 1; RGAL 4; SATA 67

Lopez de Mendoza, Inigo
See Santillana, Inigo Lopez de Mendoza, Marques de

Lopez Portillo (y Pacheco), Jose
1920-2004 .... **CLC 46**
See also CA 129; CAAS 224; HW 1

Lopez y Fuentes, Gregorio
1897(?)-1966 .... **CLC 32**
See also CA 131; EWL 3; HW 1

Lorca, Federico Garcia
See Garcia Lorca, Federico
See also DFS 4; EW 11; PFS 20; RGWL 2, 3; WP

Lord, Audre
See Lorde, Audre
See also EWL 3

Lord, Bette Bao 1938- .... **AAL; CLC 23**
See also BEST 90:3; BPFB 2; CA 107; CANR 41, 79; INT CA-107; SATA 58

Lord Auch
See Bataille, Georges

Lord Brooke
See Greville, Fulke

Lord Byron
See Byron, George Gordon (Noel)

Lorde, Audre 1934-1992 .... **BLC 2; CLC 18, 71; PC 12; TCLC 173**
See Domini, Rey; Lord, Audre
See also AFAW 1, 2; BW 1, 3; CA 25-28R; CAAS 142; CANR 16, 26, 46, 82; CP 2, 3, 4, 5; DA3; DAM MULT, POET; DLB 41; FW; MAL 5; MTCW 1, 2; MTFW 2005; PFS 16; RGAL 4

Lorde, Audre Geraldine
See Lorde, Audre

Lord Houghton
See Milnes, Richard Monckton

Lord Jeffrey
See Jeffrey, Francis

Loreaux, Nichol .... **CLC 65**

Lorenzini, Carlo 1826-1890
See Collodi, Carlo
See also MAICYA 1, 2; SATA 29, 100

Lorenzo, Heberto Padilla
See Padilla (Lorenzo), Heberto

Loris
See Hofmannsthal, Hugo von

Loti, Pierre .... **TCLC 11**
See Viaud, (Louis Marie) Julien
See also DLB 123; GFL 1789 to the Present

Lou, Henri
See Andreas-Salome, Lou

Louie, David Wong 1954- .... **CLC 70**
See also CA 139; CANR 120

Louis, Adrian C. .... **NNAL**
See also CA 223

Louis, Father M.
See Merton, Thomas (James)

Louise, Heidi
See Erdrich, Louise

Lovecraft, H. P. 1890-1937 .... **SSC 3, 52; TCLC 4, 22**
See also AAYA 14; BPFB 2; CA 133; CAAE 104; CANR 106; DA3; DAM POP; HGG; MTCW 1, 2; MTFW 2005; RGAL 4; SCFW 1, 2; SFW 4; SUFW

Lovecraft, Howard Phillips
See Lovecraft, H. P.

Lovelace, Earl 1935- .... **CLC 51**
See also BW 2; CA 77-80; CANR 41, 72, 114; CD 5, 6; CDWLB 3; CN 1, 2, 3, 4, 5, 6, 7; DLB 125; EWL 3; MTCW 1

Lovelace, Richard 1618-1657 . **LC 24; PC 69**
See also BRW 2; DLB 131; EXPP; PAB; RGEL 2

Lowe, Pardee 1904- .... **AAL**

Lowell, Amy 1874-1925 ... **PC 13; TCLC 1, 8**
See also AAYA 57; AMW; CA 151; CAAE 104; DAM POET; DLB 54, 140; EWL 3; EXPP; LMFS 2; MAL 5; MBL; MTCW 2; MTFW 2005; RGAL 4; TUS

Lowell, James Russell 1819-1891 ... **NCLC 2, 90**
See also AMWS 1; CDALB 1640-1865; DLB 1, 11, 64, 79, 189, 235; RGAL 4

Lowell, Robert (Traill Spence, Jr.)
1917-1977 .... **CLC 1, 2, 3, 4, 5, 8, 9, 11, 15, 37, 124; PC 3; WLC 4**
See also AMW; AMWC 2; AMWR 2; CA 9-12R; CAAS 73-76; CABS 2; CAD; CANR 26, 60; CDALBS; CP 1, 2; DA; DA3; DAB; DAC; DAM MST, NOV; DLB 5, 169; EWL 3; MAL 5; MTCW 1, 2; MTFW 2005; PAB; PFS 6, 7; RGAL 4; WP

Lowenthal, Michael (Francis)
1969- .... **CLC 119**
See also CA 150; CANR 115

Lowndes, Marie Adelaide (Belloc)
1868-1947 .... **TCLC 12**
See also CAAE 107; CMW 4; DLB 70; RHW

Lowry, (Clarence) Malcolm
1909-1957 .... **SSC 31; TCLC 6, 40**
See also BPFB 2; BRWS 3; CA 131; CAAE 105; CANR 62, 105; CDBLB 1945-1960; DLB 15; EWL 3; MTCW 1, 2; MTFW 2005; RGEL 2

Lowry, Mina Gertrude 1882-1966
See Loy, Mina
See also CA 113

Lowry, Sam
See Soderbergh, Steven

Loxsmith, John
See Brunner, John (Kilian Houston)

Loy, Mina .... **CLC 28; PC 16**
See Lowry, Mina Gertrude
See also DAM POET; DLB 4, 54; PFS 20

Loyson-Bridet
See Schwob, Marcel (Mayer Andre)

Lucan 39-65 .... **CMLC 33**
See also AW 2; DLB 211; EFS 2; RGWL 2, 3

Lucas, Craig 1951- .... **CLC 64**
See also CA 137; CAD; CANR 71, 109, 142; CD 5, 6; GLL 2; MTFW 2005

Lucas, E(dward) V(errall)
1868-1938 .... **TCLC 73**
See also CA 176; DLB 98, 149, 153; SATA 20

Lucas, George 1944- .... **CLC 16**
See also AAYA 1, 23; CA 77-80; CANR 30; SATA 56

Lucas, Hans
See Godard, Jean-Luc

Lucas, Victoria
See Plath, Sylvia

Lucian c. 125-c. 180 .... **CMLC 32**
See also AW 2; DLB 176; RGWL 2, 3

Lucilius c. 180B.C.-102B.C. .... **CMLC 82**
See also DLB 211

Lucretius c. 94B.C.-c. 49B.C. .... **CMLC 48**
See also AW 2; CDWLB 1; DLB 211; EFS 2; RGWL 2, 3; WLIT 8

Ludlam, Charles 1943-1987 .... **CLC 46, 50**
See also CA 85-88; CAAS 122; CAD; CANR 72, 86; DLB 266

Ludlum, Robert 1927-2001 .... **CLC 22, 43**
See also AAYA 10, 59; BEST 89:1, 90:3; BPFB 2; CA 33-36R; CAAS 195; CANR 25, 41, 68, 105, 131; CMW 4; CPW; DA3; DAM NOV, POP; DLBY 1982; MSW; MTCW 1, 2; MTFW 2005

Ludwig, Ken 1950- .... **CLC 60**
See also CA 195; CAD; CD 6

Ludwig, Otto 1813-1865 .... **NCLC 4**
See also DLB 129

Lugones, Leopoldo 1874-1938 .... **HLCS 2; TCLC 15**
See also CA 131; CAAE 116; CANR 104; DLB 283; EWL 3; HW 1; LAW

Lu Hsun .... **SSC 20; TCLC 3**
See Shu-Jen, Chou
See also EWL 3

Lukacs, George .... **CLC 24**
See Lukacs, Gyorgy (Szegeny von)

Lukacs, Gyorgy (Szegeny von) 1885-1971
See Lukacs, George
See also CA 101; CAAS 29-32R; CANR 62; CDWLB 4; DLB 215, 242; EW 10; EWL 3; MTCW 1, 2

Luke, Peter (Ambrose Cyprian)
1919-1995 .... **CLC 38**
See also CA 81-84; CAAS 147; CANR 72; CBD; CD 5, 6; DLB 13

Lunar, Dennis
See Mungo, Raymond

Lurie, Alison 1926- ..... **CLC 4, 5, 18, 39, 175**
See also BPFB 2; CA 1-4R; CANR 2, 17, 50, 88; CN 1, 2, 3, 4, 5, 6, 7; DLB 2; MAL 5; MTCW 1; NFS 24; SATA 46, 112; TCLE 1:1

Lustig, Arnost 1926- .... **CLC 56**
See also AAYA 3; CA 69-72; CANR 47, 102; CWW 2; DLB 232, 299; EWL 3; RGHL; SATA 56

Luther, Martin 1483-1546 .... **LC 9, 37**
See also CDWLB 2; DLB 179; EW 2; RGWL 2, 3

Luxemburg, Rosa 1870(?)-1919 ..... **TCLC 63**
See also CAAE 118

Luzi, Mario (Egidio Vincenzo)
1914-2005 .... **CLC 13**
See also CA 61-64; CAAS 236; CANR 9, 70; CWW 2; DLB 128; EWL 3

L'vov, Arkady .... **CLC 59**

Lydgate, John c. 1370-1450(?) .... **LC 81**
See also BRW 1; DLB 146; RGEL 2

Lyly, John 1554(?)-1606 .... **DC 7; LC 41**
See also BRW 1; DAM DRAM; DLB 62, 167; RGEL 2

L'Ymagier
See Gourmont, Remy(-Marie-Charles) de

Lynch, B. Suarez
See Borges, Jorge Luis

Maepenn, Hugh
See Kuttner, Henry
Maepenn, K. H.
See Kuttner, Henry
Maeterlinck, Maurice 1862-1949 ..... **TCLC 3**
See also CA 136; CAAE 104; CANR 80;
DAM DRAM; DLB 192, 331; EW 8;
EWL 3; GFL 1789 to the Present; LMFS
2; RGWL 2, 3; SATA 66; TWA
Maginn, William 1794-1842 .... **NCLC 8**
See also DLB 110, 159
Mahapatra, Jayanta 1928- .... **CLC 33**
See also CA 73-76; 9; CANR 15, 33, 66,
87; CP 4, 5, 6, 7; DAM MULT; DLB 323
Mahfouz, Nagib
See Mahfouz, Naguib
Mahfouz, Naguib 1911(?)-2006 ..... **CLC 153;**
SSC 66
See Mahfuz, Najib
See also AAYA 49; BEST 89:2; CA 128;
CAAS 253; CANR 55, 101; DA3; DAM
NOV; MTCW 1, 2; MTFW 2005; RGWL
2, 3; SSFS 9
Mahfouz, Naguib Abdel Aziz Al-Sabilgi
See Mahfouz, Naguib
Mahfouz, Najib
See Mahfouz, Naguib
Mahfuz, Najib .... **CLC 52, 55**
See Mahfouz, Naguib
See also AFW; CWW 2; DLB 331; DLBY
1988; EWL 3; RGSF 2; WLIT 6
Mahon, Derek 1941- .... **CLC 27; PC 60**
See also BRWS 6; CA 128; CAAE 113;
CANR 88; CP 1, 2, 3, 4, 5, 6, 7; DLB 40;
EWL 3
Maiakovskii, Vladimir
See Mayakovski, Vladimir (Vladimirovich)
See also IDTP; RGWL 2, 3
Mailer, Norman 1923- ... **CLC 1, 2, 3, 4, 5, 8,**
11, 14, 28, 39, 74, 111, 234
See also AAYA 31; AITN 2; AMW; AMWC
2; AMWR 2; BPFB 2; CA 9-12R; CABS
1; CANR 28, 74, 77, 130; CDALB 1968-
1988; CN 1, 2, 3, 4, 5, 6, 7; CPW; DA;
DA3; DAB; DAC; DAM MST, NOV,
POP; DLB 2, 16, 28, 185, 278; DLBD 3;
DLBY 1980, 1983; EWL 3; MAL 5;
MTCW 1, 2; MTFW 2005; NFS 10;
RGAL 4; TUS
Mailer, Norman Kingsley
See Mailer, Norman
Maillet, Antonine 1929- .... **CLC 54, 118**
See also CA 120; CAAE 115; CANR 46,
74, 77, 134; CCA 1; CWW 2; DAC; DLB
60; INT CA-120; MTCW 2; MTFW 2005
Maimonides, Moses 1135-1204 ..... **CMLC 76**
See also DLB 115
Mais, Roger 1905-1955 .... **TCLC 8**
See also BW 1, 3; CA 124; CAAE 105;
CANR 82; CDWLB 3; DLB 125; EWL 3;
MTCW 1; RGEL 2
Maistre, Joseph 1753-1821 .... **NCLC 37**
See also GFL 1789 to the Present
Maitland, Frederic William
1850-1906 .... **TCLC 65**
Maitland, Sara (Louise) 1950- .... **CLC 49**
See also BRWS 11; CA 69-72; CANR 13,
59; DLB 271; FW
Major, Clarence 1936- ... **BLC 2; CLC 3, 19,**
48
See also AFAW 2; BW 2, 3; CA 21-24R; 6;
CANR 13, 25, 53, 82; CN 3, 4, 5, 6, 7;
CP 2, 3, 4, 5, 6, 7; CSW; DAM MULT;
DLB 33; EWL 3; MAL 5; MSW
Major, Kevin (Gerald) 1949- .... **CLC 26**
See also AAYA 16; CA 97-100; CANR 21,
38, 112; CLR 11; DAC; DLB 60; INT
CANR-21; JRDA; MAICYA 1, 2; MAIC-
YAS 1; SATA 32, 82, 134; WYA; YAW

Maki, James
See Ozu, Yasujiro
Makin, Bathsua 1600-1675(?) .... **LC 137**
Makine, Andrei 1957- .... **CLC 198**
See also CA 176; CANR 103; MTFW 2005
Malabaila, Damiano
See Levi, Primo
Malamud, Bernard 1914-1986 .. **CLC 1, 2, 3,**
5, 8, 9, 11, 18, 27, 44, 78, 85; SSC 15;
TCLC 129, 184; WLC 4
See also AAYA 16; AMWS 1; BPFB 2;
BYA 15; CA 5-8R; CAAS 118; CABS 1;
CANR 28, 62, 114; CDALB 1941-1968;
CN 1, 2, 3, 4; CPW; DA; DA3; DAB;
DAC; DAM MST, NOV, POP; DLB 2,
28, 152; DLBY 1980, 1986; EWL 3;
EXPS; LAIT 4; LATS 1:1; MAL 5;
MTCW 1, 2; MTFW 2005; NFS 4, 9;
RGAL 4; RGHL; RGSF 2; SSFS 8, 13,
16; TUS
Malan, Herman
See Bosman, Herman Charles; Bosman,
Herman Charles
Malaparte, Curzio 1898-1957 .... **TCLC 52**
See also DLB 264
Malcolm, Dan
See Silverberg, Robert
Malcolm, Janet 1934- .... **CLC 201**
See also CA 123; CANR 89; NCFS 1
Malcolm X .... **BLC 2; CLC 82, 117; WLCS**
See Little, Malcolm
See also LAIT 5; NCFS 3
Malebranche, Nicolas 1638-1715 .... **LC 133**
See also GFL Beginnings to 1789
Malherbe, Francois de 1555-1628 .... **LC 5**
See also DLB 327; GFL Beginnings to 1789
Mallarme, Stephane 1842-1898 ...... **NCLC 4,**
41; PC 4
See also DAM POET; DLB 217; EW 7;
GFL 1789 to the Present; LMFS 2; RGWL
2, 3; TWA
Mallet-Joris, Francoise 1930- .... **CLC 11**
See also CA 65-68; CANR 17; CWW 2;
DLB 83; EWL 3; GFL 1789 to the Present
Malley, Ern
See McAuley, James Phillip
Mallon, Thomas 1951- .... **CLC 172**
See also CA 110; CANR 29, 57, 92
Mallowan, Agatha Christie
See Christie, Agatha (Mary Clarissa)
Maloff, Saul 1922- .... **CLC 5**
See also CA 33-36R
Malone, Louis
See MacNeice, (Frederick) Louis
Malone, Michael (Christopher)
1942- .... **CLC 43**
See also CA 77-80; CANR 14, 32, 57, 114
Malory, Sir Thomas 1410(?)-1471(?) . **LC 11,**
88; WLCS
See also BRW 1; BRWR 2; CDBLB Before
1660; DA; DAB; DAC; DAM MST; DLB
146; EFS 2; RGEL 2; SATA 59; SATA-
Brief 33; TEA; WLIT 3
Malouf, David 1934- .... **CLC 28, 86**
See also BRWS 12; CA 124; CANR 50, 76;
CN 3, 4, 5, 6, 7; CP 1, 3, 4, 5, 6, 7; DLB
289; EWL 3; MTCW 2; MTFW 2005;
SSFS 24
Malouf, George Joseph David
See Malouf, David
Malraux, (Georges-)Andre
1901-1976 .... **CLC 1, 4, 9, 13, 15, 57**
See also BPFB 2; CA 21-22; CAAS 69-72;
CANR 34, 58; CAP 2; DA3; DAM NOV;
DLB 72; EW 12; EWL 3; GFL 1789 to
the Present; MTCW 1, 2; MTFW 2005;
RGWL 2, 3; TWA

Malthus, Thomas Robert
1766-1834 .... **NCLC 145**
See also DLB 107, 158; RGEL 2
Malzberg, Barry N(athaniel) 1939- ... **CLC 7**
See also CA 61-64; 4; CANR 16; CMW 4;
DLB 8; SFW 4
Mamet, David 1947- .. **CLC 9, 15, 34, 46, 91,**
166; DC 4, 24
See also AAYA 3, 60; AMWS 14; CA 81-
84; CABS 3; CAD; CANR 15, 41, 67, 72,
129; CD 5, 6; DA3; DAM DRAM; DFS
2, 3, 6, 12, 15; DLB 7; EWL 3; IDFW 4;
MAL 5; MTCW 1, 2; MTFW 2005;
RGAL 4
Mamet, David Alan
See Mamet, David
Mamoulian, Rouben (Zachary)
1897-1987 .... **CLC 16**
See also CA 25-28R; CAAS 124; CANR 85
Mandelshtam, Osip
See Mandelstam, Osip (Emilievich)
See also EW 10; EWL 3; RGWL 2, 3
Mandelstam, Osip (Emilievich)
1891(?)-1943(?) .... **PC 14; TCLC 2, 6**
See Mandelshtam, Osip
See also CA 150; CAAE 104; MTCW 2;
TWA
Mander, (Mary) Jane 1877-1949 ... **TCLC 31**
See also CA 162; RGEL 2
Mandeville, Bernard 1670-1733 .... **LC 82**
See also DLB 101
Mandeville, Sir John fl. 1350- ...... **CMLC 19**
See also DLB 146
Mandiargues, Andre Pieyre de .... **CLC 41**
See Pieyre de Mandiargues, Andre
See also DLB 83
Mandrake, Ethel Belle
See Thurman, Wallace (Henry)
Mangan, James Clarence
1803-1849 .... **NCLC 27**
See also RGEL 2
Maniere, J.-E.
See Giraudoux, Jean(-Hippolyte)
Mankiewicz, Herman (Jacob)
1897-1953 .... **TCLC 85**
See also CA 169; CAAE 120; DLB 26;
IDFW 3, 4
Manley, (Mary) Delariviere
1672(?)-1724 .... **LC 1, 42**
See also DLB 39, 80; RGEL 2
Mann, Abel
See Creasey, John
Mann, Emily 1952- .... **DC 7**
See also CA 130; CAD; CANR 55; CD 5,
6; CWD; DLB 266
Mann, (Luiz) Heinrich 1871-1950 ... **TCLC 9**
See also CA 164, 181; CAAE 106; DLB
66, 118; EW 8; EWL 3; RGWL 2, 3
Mann, (Paul) Thomas 1875-1955 . **SSC 5, 80,**
82; TCLC 2, 8, 14, 21, 35, 44, 60, 168;
WLC 4
See also BPFB 2; CA 128; CAAE 104;
CANR 133; CDWLB 2; DA; DA3; DAB;
DAC; DAM MST, NOV; DLB 66, 331;
EW 9; EWL 3; GLL 1; LATS 1:1; LMFS
1; MTCW 1, 2; MTFW 2005; NFS 17;
RGSF 2; RGWL 2, 3; SSFS 4, 9; TWA
Mannheim, Karl 1893-1947 .... **TCLC 65**
See also CA 204
Manning, David
See Faust, Frederick (Schiller)
Manning, Frederic 1882-1935 .... **TCLC 25**
See also CA 216; CAAE 124; DLB 260
Manning, Olivia 1915-1980 .... **CLC 5, 19**
See also CA 5-8R; CAAS 101; CANR 29;
CN 1, 2; EWL 3; FW; MTCW 1; RGEL 2
Mannyng, Robert c. 1264-c.
1340 .... **CMLC 83**
See also DLB 146

Mano, D. Keith 1942- .... **CLC 2, 10**
  See also CA 25-28R; 6; CANR 26, 57; DLB
  6

Mansfield, Katherine .... **SSC 9, 23, 38, 81;**
  TCLC 2, 8, 39, 164; WLC 4
  See Beauchamp, Kathleen Mansfield
  See also BPFB 2; BRW 7; DAB; DLB 162;
  EWL 3; EXPS; FW; GLL 1; RGEL 2;
  RGSF 2; SSFS 2, 8, 10, 11; WWE 1

Manso, Peter 1940- .... **CLC 39**
  See also CA 29-32R; CANR 44, 156

Mantecon, Juan Jimenez
  See Jimenez (Mantecon), Juan Ramon

Mantel, Hilary 1952- .... **CLC 144**
  See also CA 125; CANR 54, 101, 161; CN
  5, 6, 7; DLB 271; RHW

Mantel, Hilary Mary
  See Mantel, Hilary

Manton, Peter
  See Creasey, John

Man Without a Spleen, A
  See Chekhov, Anton (Pavlovich)

Manzano, Juan Franciso
  1797(?)-1854 .... **NCLC 155**

Manzoni, Alessandro 1785-1873 ... **NCLC 29,**
  98
  See also EW 5; RGWL 2, 3; TWA; WLIT 7

Map, Walter 1140-1209 .... **CMLC 32**

Mapu, Abraham (ben Jekutiel)
  1808-1867 .... **NCLC 18**

Mara, Sally
  See Queneau, Raymond

Maracle, Lee 1950- .... **NNAL**
  See also CA 149

Marat, Jean Paul 1743-1793 .... **LC 10**

Marcel, Gabriel Honore 1889-1973 . **CLC 15**
  See also CA 102; CAAS 45-48; EWL 3;
  MTCW 1, 2

March, William .... **TCLC 96**
  See Campbell, William Edward March
  See also CA 216; DLB 9, 86, 316; MAL 5

Marchbanks, Samuel
  See Davies, Robertson
  See also CCA 1

Marchi, Giacomo
  See Bassani, Giorgio

Marcus Aurelius
  See Aurelius, Marcus
  See also AW 2

Marguerite
  See de Navarre, Marguerite

Marguerite d'Angouleme
  See de Navarre, Marguerite
  See also GFL Beginnings to 1789

Marguerite de Navarre
  See de Navarre, Marguerite
  See also RGWL 2, 3

Margulies, Donald 1954- .... **CLC 76**
  See also AAYA 57; CA 200; CD 6; DFS 13;
  DLB 228

Marie de France c. 12th cent. - ..... **CMLC 8;**
  PC 22
  See also DLB 208; FW; RGWL 2, 3

Marie de l'Incarnation 1599-1672 ...... **LC 10**

Marier, Captain Victor
  See Griffith, D(avid Lewelyn) W(ark)

Mariner, Scott
  See Pohl, Frederik

Marinetti, Filippo Tommaso
  1876-1944 .... **TCLC 10**
  See also CAAE 107; DLB 114, 264; EW 9;
  EWL 3; WLIT 7

Marivaux, Pierre Carlet de Chamblain de
  1688-1763 .... **DC 7; LC 4, 123**
  See also DLB 314; GFL Beginnings to
  1789; RGWL 2, 3; TWA

Markandaya, Kamala .... **CLC 8, 38**
  See Taylor, Kamala
  See also BYA 13; CN 1, 2, 3, 4, 5, 6, 7;
  DLB 323; EWL 3

Markfield, Wallace (Arthur)
  1926-2002 .... **CLC 8**
  See also CA 69-72; 3; CAAS 208; CN 1, 2,
  3, 4, 5, 6, 7; DLB 2, 28; DLBY 2002

Markham, Edwin 1852-1940 .... **TCLC 47**
  See also CA 160; DLB 54, 186; MAL 5;
  RGAL 4

Markham, Robert
  See Amis, Kingsley

Marks, J.
  See Highwater, Jamake (Mamake)

Marks-Highwater, J.
  See Highwater, Jamake (Mamake)

Markson, David M. 1927- .... **CLC 67**
  See also CA 49-52; CANR 1, 91, 158; CN
  5, 6

Markson, David Merrill
  See Markson, David M.

Marlatt, Daphne (Buckle) 1942- .... **CLC 168**
  See also CA 25-28R; CANR 17, 39; CN 6,
  7; CP 4, 5, 6, 7; CWP; DLB 60; FW

Marley, Bob .... **CLC 17**
  See Marley, Robert Nesta

Marley, Robert Nesta 1945-1981
  See Marley, Bob
  See also CA 107; CAAS 103

Marlowe, Christopher 1564-1593 . **DC 1; LC**
  22, 47, 117; PC 57; WLC 4
  See also BRW 1; BRWR 1; CDBLB Before
  1660; DA; DA3; DAB; DAC; DAM
  DRAM, MST; DFS 1, 5, 13, 21; DLB 62;
  EXPP; LMFS 1; PFS 22; RGEL 2; TEA;
  WLIT 3

Marlowe, Stephen 1928- .... **CLC 70**
  See Queen, Ellery
  See also CA 13-16R; CANR 6, 55; CMW
  4; SFW 4

Marmion, Shakerley 1603-1639 .... **LC 89**
  See also DLB 58; RGEL 2

Marmontel, Jean-Francois 1723-1799 .. **LC 2**
  See also DLB 314

Maron, Monika 1941- .... **CLC 165**
  See also CA 201

Marot, Clement c. 1496-1544 .... **LC 133**
  See also DLB 327; GFL Beginnings to 1789

Marquand, John P(hillips)
  1893-1960 .... **CLC 2, 10**
  See also AMW; BPFB 2; CA 85-88; CANR
  73; CMW 4; DLB 9, 102; EWL 3; MAL
  5; MTCW 2; RGAL 4

Marques, Rene 1919-1979 .. **CLC 96; HLC 2**
  See also CA 97-100; CAAS 85-88; CANR
  78; DAM MULT; DLB 305; EWL 3; HW
  1, 2; LAW; RGSF 2

Marquez, Gabriel Garcia
  See Garcia Marquez, Gabriel

Marquis, Don(ald Robert Perry)
  1878-1937 .... **TCLC 7**
  See also CA 166; CAAE 104; DLB 11, 25;
  MAL 5; RGAL 4

Marquis de Sade
  See Sade, Donatien Alphonse Francois

Marric, J. J.
  See Creasey, John
  See also MSW

Marryat, Frederick 1792-1848 .... **NCLC 3**
  See also DLB 21, 163; RGEL 2; WCH

Marsden, James
  See Creasey, John

Marsh, Edward 1872-1953 .... **TCLC 99**

Marsh, (Edith) Ngaio 1895-1982 .. **CLC 7, 53**
  See also CA 9-12R; CANR 6, 58; CMW 4;
  CN 1, 2, 3; CPW; DAM POP; DLB 77;
  MSW; MTCW 1, 2; RGEL 2; TEA

Marshall, Allen
  See Westlake, Donald E.

Marshall, Garry 1934- .... **CLC 17**
  See also AAYA 3; CA 111; SATA 60

Marshall, Paule 1929- .. **BLC 3; CLC 27, 72;**
  SSC 3
  See also AFAW 1, 2; AMWS 11; BPFB 2;
  BW 2, 3; CA 77-80; CANR 25, 73, 129;
  CN 1, 2, 3, 4, 5, 6, 7; DA3; DAM MULT;
  DLB 33, 157, 227; EWL 3; LATS 1:2;
  MAL 5; MTCW 1, 2; MTFW 2005;
  RGAL 4; SSFS 15

Marshallik
  See Zangwill, Israel

Marsten, Richard
  See Hunter, Evan

Marston, John 1576-1634 .... **LC 33**
  See also BRW 2; DAM DRAM; DLB 58,
  172; RGEL 2

Martel, Yann 1963- .... **CLC 192**
  See also AAYA 67; CA 146; CANR 114;
  DLB 326; MTFW 2005

Martens, Adolphe-Adhemar
  See Ghelderode, Michel de

Martha, Henry
  See Harris, Mark

Marti, Jose .... **PC 76**
  See Marti (y Perez), Jose (Julian)
  See also DLB 290

Marti (y Perez), Jose (Julian)
  1853-1895 .... **HLC 2; NCLC 63**
  See Marti, Jose
  See also DAM MULT; HW 2; LAW; RGWL
  2, 3; WLIT 1

Martial c. 40-c. 104 .... **CMLC 35; PC 10**
  See also AW 2; CDWLB 1; DLB 211;
  RGWL 2, 3

Martin, Ken
  See Hubbard, L. Ron

Martin, Richard
  See Creasey, John

Martin, Steve 1945- .... **CLC 30, 217**
  See also AAYA 53; CA 97-100; CANR 30,
  100, 140; DFS 19; MTCW 1; MTFW
  2005

Martin, Valerie 1948- .... **CLC 89**
  See also BEST 90:2; CA 85-88; CANR 49,
  89

Martin, Violet Florence 1862-1915 .. **SSC 56;**
  TCLC 51

Martin, Webber
  See Silverberg, Robert

Martindale, Patrick Victor
  See White, Patrick (Victor Martindale)

Martin du Gard, Roger
  1881-1958 .... **TCLC 24**
  See also CAAE 118; CANR 94; DLB 65,
  331; EWL 3; GFL 1789 to the Present;
  RGWL 2, 3

Martineau, Harriet 1802-1876 ...... **NCLC 26,**
  137
  See also DLB 21, 55, 159, 163, 166, 190;
  FW; RGEL 2; YABC 2

Martines, Julia
  See O'Faolain, Julia

Martinez, Enrique Gonzalez
  See Gonzalez Martinez, Enrique

Martinez, Jacinto Benavente y
  See Benavente (y Martinez), Jacinto

Martinez de la Rosa, Francisco de Paula
  1787-1862 .... **NCLC 102**
  See also TWA

Martinez Ruiz, Jose 1873-1967
  See Azorin; Ruiz, Jose Martinez
  See also CA 93-96; HW 1

Martinez Sierra, Gregorio
  See Martinez Sierra, Maria

Martinez Sierra, Gregorio
1881-1947 .... **TCLC 6**
See also CAAE 115; EWL 3
Martinez Sierra, Maria 1874-1974 .. **TCLC 6**
See also CA 250; CAAS 115; EWL 3
Martinsen, Martin
See Follett, Ken
Martinson, Harry (Edmund)
1904-1978 .... **CLC 14**
See also CA 77-80; CANR 34, 130; DLB
259, 331; EWL 3
Martyn, Edward 1859-1923 .... **TCLC 131**
See also CA 179; DLB 10; RGEL 2
Marut, Ret
See Traven, B.
Marut, Robert
See Traven, B.
Marvell, Andrew 1621-1678 .... **LC 4, 43; PC
10; WLC 4**
See also BRW 2; BRWR 2; CDBLB 1660-
1789; DA; DAB; DAC; DAM MST,
POET; DLB 131; EXPP; PFS 5; RGEL 2;
TEA; WP
Marx, Karl (Heinrich)
1818-1883 .... **NCLC 17, 114**
See also DLB 129; LATS 1:1; TWA
Masaoka, Shiki -1902 .... **TCLC 18**
See Masaoka, Tsunenori
See also RGWL 3
Masaoka, Tsunenori 1867-1902
See Masaoka, Shiki
See also CA 191; CAAE 117; TWA
Masefield, John (Edward)
1878-1967 .... **CLC 11, 47**
See also CA 19-20; CAAS 25-28R; CANR
33; CAP 2; CDBLB 1890-1914; DAM
POET; DLB 10, 19, 153, 160; EWL 3;
EXPP; FANT; MTCW 1, 2; PFS 5; RGEL
2; SATA 19
Maso, Carole 1955(?)- .... **CLC 44**
See also CA 170; CANR 148; CN 7; GLL
2; RGAL 4
Mason, Bobbie Ann 1940- ... **CLC 28, 43, 82,
154; SSC 4**
See also AAYA 5, 42; AMWS 8; BPFB 2;
CA 53-56; CANR 11, 31, 58, 83, 125;
CDALBS; CN 5, 6, 7; CSW; DA3; DLB
173; DLBY 1987; EWL 3; EXPS; INT
CANR-31; MAL 5; MTCW 1, 2; MTFW
2005; NFS 4; RGAL 4; RGSF 2; SSFS 3,
8, 20; TCLE 1:2; YAW
Mason, Ernst
See Pohl, Frederik
Mason, Hunni B.
See Sternheim, (William Adolf) Carl
Mason, Lee W.
See Malzberg, Barry N(athaniel)
Mason, Nick 1945- .... **CLC 35**
Mason, Tally
See Derleth, August (William)
Mass, Anna .... **CLC 59**
Mass, William
See Gibson, William
Massinger, Philip 1583-1640 .... **LC 70**
See also BRWS 11; DLB 58; RGEL 2
Master Lao
See Lao Tzu
Masters, Edgar Lee 1868-1950 ...... **PC 1, 36;
TCLC 2, 25; WLCS**
See also AMWS 1; CA 133; CAAE 104;
CDALB 1865-1917; DA; DAC; DAM
MST, POET; DLB 54; EWL 3; EXPP;
MAL 5; MTCW 1, 2; MTFW 2005;
RGAL 4; TUS; WP
Masters, Hilary 1928- .... **CLC 48**
See also CA 217; 25-28R, 217; CANR 13,
47, 97; CN 6, 7; DLB 244
Mastrosimone, William 1947- .... **CLC 36**
See also CA 186; CAD; CD 5, 6

Mathe, Albert
See Camus, Albert
Mather, Cotton 1663-1728 .... **LC 38**
See also AMWS 2; CDALB 1640-1865;
DLB 24, 30, 140; RGAL 4; TUS
Mather, Increase 1639-1723 .... **LC 38**
See also DLB 24
Mathers, Marshall
See Eminem
Mathers, Marshall Bruce
See Eminem
Matheson, Richard (Burton) 1926- .. **CLC 37**
See also AAYA 31; CA 97-100; CANR 88,
99; DLB 8, 44; HGG; INT CA-97-100;
SCFW 1, 2; SFW 4; SUFW 2
Mathews, Harry 1930- .... **CLC 6, 52**
See also CA 21-24R; 6; CANR 18, 40, 98,
160; CN 5, 6, 7
Mathews, John Joseph 1894-1979 .. **CLC 84;
NNAL**
See also CA 19-20; CAAS 142; CANR 45;
CAP 2; DAM MULT; DLB 175; TCWW
1, 2
Mathias, Roland (Glyn) 1915- .... **CLC 45**
See also CA 97-100; CANR 19, 41; CP 1,
2, 3, 4, 5, 6, 7; DLB 27
Matsuo Basho 1644(?)-1694 ...... **LC 62; PC 3**
See Basho, Matsuo
See also DAM POET; PFS 2, 7, 18
Mattheson, Rodney
See Creasey, John
Matthews, (James) Brander
1852-1929 .... **TCLC 95**
See also CA 181; DLB 71, 78; DLBD 13
Matthews, Greg 1949- .... **CLC 45**
See also CA 135
Matthews, William (Procter III)
1942-1997 .... **CLC 40**
See also AMWS 9; CA 29-32R; 18; CAAS
162; CANR 12, 57; CP 2, 3, 4, 5, 6; DLB
5
Matthias, John (Edward) 1941- .... **CLC 9**
See also CA 33-36R; CANR 56; CP 4, 5, 6,
7
Matthiessen, F(rancis) O(tto)
1902-1950 .... **TCLC 100**
See also CA 185; DLB 63; MAL 5
Matthiessen, Peter 1927- ... **CLC 5, 7, 11, 32,
64**
See also AAYA 6, 40; AMWS 5; ANW;
BEST 90:4; BPFB 2; CA 9-12R; CANR
21, 50, 73, 100, 138; CN 1, 2, 3, 4, 5, 6,
7; DA3; DAM NOV; DLB 6, 173, 275;
MAL 5; MTCW 1, 2; MTFW 2005; SATA
27
Maturin, Charles Robert
1780(?)-1824 .... **NCLC 6, 169**
See also BRWS 8; DLB 178; GL 3; HGG;
LMFS 1; RGEL 2; SUFW
Matute (Ausejo), Ana Maria 1925- .. **CLC 11**
See also CA 89-92; CANR 129; CWW 2;
DLB 322; EWL 3; MTCW 1; RGSF 2
Maugham, W. S.
See Maugham, W(illiam) Somerset
Maugham, W(illiam) Somerset
1874-1965 .. **CLC 1, 11, 15, 67, 93; SSC
8, 94; WLC 4**
See also AAYA 55; BPFB 2; BRW 6; CA
5-8R; CAAS 25-28R; CANR 40, 127;
CDBLB 1914-1945; CMW 4; DA; DA3;
DAB; DAC; DAM DRAM, MST, NOV;
DFS 22; DLB 10, 36, 77, 100, 162, 195;
EWL 3; LAIT 3; MTCW 1, 2; MTFW
2005; NFS 23; RGEL 2; RGSF 2; SATA
54; SSFS 17
Maugham, William Somerset
See Maugham, W(illiam) Somerset

Maupassant, (Henri Rene Albert) Guy de
1850-1893 . **NCLC 1, 42, 83; SSC 1, 64;
WLC 4**
See also BYA 14; DA; DA3; DAB; DAC;
DAM MST; DLB 123; EW 7; EXPS; GFL
1789 to the Present; LAIT 2; LMFS 1;
RGSF 2; RGWL 2, 3; SSFS 4, 21; SUFW;
TWA
Maupin, Armistead 1944- .... **CLC 95**
See also CA 130; CAAE 125; CANR 58,
101; CPW; DA3; DAM POP; DLB 278;
GLL 1; INT CA-130; MTCW 2; MTFW
2005
Maupin, Armistead Jones, Jr.
See Maupin, Armistead
Maurhut, Richard
See Traven, B.
Mauriac, Claude 1914-1996 .... **CLC 9**
See also CA 89-92; CAAS 152; CWW 2;
DLB 83; EWL 3; GFL 1789 to the Present
Mauriac, Francois (Charles)
1885-1970 .... **CLC 4, 9, 56; SSC 24**
See also CA 25-28; CAP 2; DLB 65, 331;
EW 10; EWL 3; GFL 1789 to the Present;
MTCW 1, 2; MTFW 2005; RGWL 2, 3;
TWA
Mavor, Osborne Henry 1888-1951
See Bridie, James
See also CAAE 104
Maxwell, William (Keepers, Jr.)
1908-2000 .... **CLC 19**
See also AMWS 8; CA 93-96; CAAS 189;
CANR 54, 95; CN 1, 2, 3, 4, 5, 6, 7; DLB
218, 278; DLBY 1980; INT CA-93-96;
MAL 5; SATA-Obit 128
May, Elaine 1932- .... **CLC 16**
See also CA 142; CAAE 124; CAD; CWD;
DLB 44
Mayakovski, Vladimir (Vladimirovich)
1893-1930 .... **TCLC 4, 18**
See Maiakovskii, Vladimir; Mayakovsky,
Vladimir
See also CA 158; CAAE 104; EWL 3;
MTCW 2; MTFW 2005; SFW 4; TWA
Mayakovsky, Vladimir
See Mayakovski, Vladimir (Vladimirovich)
See also EW 11; WP
Mayhew, Henry 1812-1887 .... **NCLC 31**
See also DLB 18, 55, 190
Mayle, Peter 1939(?)- .... **CLC 89**
See also CA 139; CANR 64, 109
Maynard, Joyce 1953- .... **CLC 23**
See also CA 129; CAAE 111; CANR 64
Mayne, William (James Carter)
1928- .... **CLC 12**
See also AAYA 20; CA 9-12R; CANR 37,
80, 100; CLR 25; FANT; JRDA; MAI-
CYA 1, 2; MAICYAS 11; SATA
6, 68, 122; SUFW 2; YAW
Mayo, Jim
See L'Amour, Louis
Maysles, Albert 1926- .... **CLC 16**
See also CA 29-32R
Maysles, David 1932-1987 .... **CLC 16**
See also CA 191
Mazer, Norma Fox 1931- .... **CLC 26**
See also AAYA 5, 36; BYA 1, 8; CA 69-72;
CANR 12, 32, 66, 129; CLR 23; JRDA;
MAICYA 1, 2; SAAS 1; SATA 24, 67,
105, 168; WYA; YAW
Mazzini, Guiseppe 1805-1872 .... **NCLC 34**
McAlmon, Robert (Menzies)
1895-1956 .... **TCLC 97**
See also CA 168; CAAE 107; DLB 4, 45;
DLBD 15; GLL 1
McAuley, James Phillip 1917-1976 .. **CLC 45**
See also CA 97-100; CP 1, 2; DLB 260;
RGEL 2

McBain, Ed
See Hunter, Evan
See also MSW

McBrien, William (Augustine)
1930- .... **CLC 44**
See also CA 107; CANR 90

McCabe, Patrick 1955- .... **CLC 133**
See also BRWS 9; CA 130; CANR 50, 90;
CN 6, 7; DLB 194

McCaffrey, Anne 1926- .... **CLC 17**
See also AAYA 6, 34; AITN 2; BEST 89:2;
BPFB 2; BYA 5; CA 227; 25-28R, 227;
CANR 15, 35, 55, 96; CLR 49; CPW;
DA3; DAM NOV, POP; DLB 8; JRDA;
MAICYA 1, 2; MTCW 1, 2; MTFW 2005;
SAAS 11; SATA 8, 70, 116, 152; SATA-
Essay 152; SFW 4; SUFW 2; WYA; YAW

McCaffrey, Anne Inez
See McCaffrey, Anne

McCall, Nathan 1955(?)- .... **CLC 86**
See also AAYA 59; BW 3; CA 146; CANR
88

McCann, Arthur
See Campbell, John W(ood, Jr.)

McCann, Edson
See Pohl, Frederik

McCarthy, Charles, Jr.
See McCarthy, Cormac

McCarthy, Cormac 1933- .... **CLC 4, 57, 101,**
204
See also AAYA 41; AMWS 8; BPFB 2; CA
13-16R; CANR 10, 42, 69, 101, 161; CN
6, 7; CPW; CSW; DA3; DAM POP; DLB
6, 143, 256; EWL 3; LATS 1:2; MAL 5;
MTCW 2; MTFW 2005; TCLE 1:2;
TCWW 2

McCarthy, Mary (Therese)
1912-1989 .. **CLC 1, 3, 5, 14, 24, 39, 59;**
SSC 24
See also AMW; BPFB 2; CA 5-8R; CAAS
129; CANR 16, 50, 64; CN 1, 2, 3, 4;
DA3; DLB 2; DLBY 1981; EWL 3; FW;
INT CANR-16; MAL 5; MBL; MTCW 1,
2; MTFW 2005; RGAL 4; TUS

McCartney, James Paul
See McCartney, Paul

McCartney, Paul 1942- .... **CLC 12, 35**
See also CA 146; CANR 111

McCauley, Stephen (D.) 1955- .... **CLC 50**
See also CA 141

McClaren, Peter .... **CLC 70**

McClure, Michael (Thomas) 1932- ... **CLC 6,**
10
See also BG 1:3; CA 21-24R; CAD; CANR
17, 46, 77, 131; CD 5, 6; CP 1, 2, 3, 4, 5,
6, 7; DLB 16; WP

McCorkle, Jill (Collins) 1958- .... **CLC 51**
See also CA 121; CANR 113; CSW; DLB
234; DLBY 1987; SSFS 24

McCourt, Frank 1930- .... **CLC 109**
See also AAYA 61; AMWS 12; CA 157;
CANR 97, 138; MTFW 2005; NCFS 1

McCourt, James 1941- .... **CLC 5**
See also CA 57-60; CANR 98, 152

McCourt, Malachy 1931- .... **CLC 119**
See also SATA 126

McCoy, Horace (Stanley)
1897-1955 .... **TCLC 28**
See also AMWS 13; CA 155; CAAE 108;
CMW 4; DLB 9

McCrae, John 1872-1918 .... **TCLC 12**
See also CAAE 109; DLB 92; PFS 5

McCreigh, James
See Pohl, Frederik

McCullers, (Lula) Carson (Smith)
1917-1967 .... **CLC 1, 4, 10, 12, 48, 100;**
SSC 9, 24, 99; TCLC 155; WLC 4
See also AAYA 21; AMW; AMWC 2; BPFB
2; CA 5-8R; CAAS 25-28R; CABS 1, 3;

CANR 18, 132; CDALB 1941-1968; DA;
DA3; DAB; DAC; DAM MST, NOV;
DFS 5, 18; DLB 2, 7, 173, 228; EWL 3;
EXPS; FW; GLL 1; LAIT 3, 4; MAL 5;
MBL; MTCW 1, 2; MTFW 2005; NFS 6,
13; RGAL 4; RGSF 2; SATA 27; SSFS 5;
TUS; YAW

McCulloch, John Tyler
See Burroughs, Edgar Rice

McCullough, Colleen 1937- ...... **CLC 27, 107**
See also AAYA 36; BPFB 2; CA 81-84;
CANR 17, 46, 67, 98, 139; CPW; DA3;
DAM NOV, POP; MTCW 1, 2; MTFW
2005; RHW

McCunn, Ruthanne Lum 1946- .... **AAL**
See also CA 119; CANR 43, 96; DLB 312;
LAIT 2; SATA 63

McDermott, Alice 1953- .... **CLC 90**
See also CA 109; CANR 40, 90, 126; CN
7; DLB 292; MTFW 2005; NFS 23

McElroy, Joseph 1930- .... **CLC 5, 47**
See also CA 17-20R; CANR 149; CN 3, 4,
5, 6, 7

McElroy, Joseph Prince
See McElroy, Joseph

McEwan, Ian 1948- .... **CLC 13, 66, 169**
See also BEST 90:4; BRWS 4; CA 61-64;
CANR 14, 41, 69, 87, 132; CN 3, 4, 5, 6,
7; DAM NOV; DLB 14, 194, 319, 326;
HGG; MTCW 1, 2; MTFW 2005; RGSF
2; SUFW 2; TEA

McFadden, David 1940- .... **CLC 48**
See also CA 104; CP 1, 2, 3, 4, 5, 6, 7; DLB
60; INT CA-104

McFarland, Dennis 1950- .... **CLC 65**
See also CA 165; CANR 110

McGahern, John 1934-2006 .... **CLC 5, 9, 48,**
156; SSC 17
See also CA 17-20R; CAAS 249; CANR
29, 68, 113; CN 1, 2, 3, 4, 5, 6, 7; DLB
14, 231, 319; MTCW 1

McGinley, Patrick (Anthony) 1937- . **CLC 41**
See also CA 127; CAAE 120; CANR 56;
INT CA-127

McGinley, Phyllis 1905-1978 .... **CLC 14**
See also CA 9-12R; CAAS 77-80; CANR
19; CP 1, 2; CWRI 5; DLB 11, 48; MAL
5; PFS 9, 13; SATA 2, 44; SATA-Obit 24

McGinniss, Joe 1942- .... **CLC 32**
See also AITN 2; BEST 89:2; CA 25-28R;
CANR 26, 70, 152; CPW; DLB 185; INT
CANR-26

McGivern, Maureen Daly
See Daly, Maureen

McGivern, Maureen Patricia Daly
See Daly, Maureen

McGrath, Patrick 1950- .... **CLC 55**
See also CA 136; CANR 65, 148; CN 5, 6,
7; DLB 231; HGG; SUFW 2

McGrath, Thomas (Matthew)
1916-1990 .... **CLC 28, 59**
See also AMWS 10; CA 9-12R; CAAS 132;
CANR 6, 33, 95; CP 1, 2, 3, 4, 5; DAM
POET; MAL 5; MTCW 1; SATA 41;
SATA-Obit 66

McGuane, Thomas 1939- .. **CLC 3, 7, 18, 45,**
127
See also AITN 2; BPFB 2; CA 49-52;
CANR 5, 24, 49, 94; CN 2, 3, 4, 5, 6, 7;
DLB 2, 212; DLBY 1980; EWL 3; INT
CANR-24; MAL 5; MTCW 1; MTFW
2005; TCWW 1, 2

McGuckian, Medbh 1950- .... **CLC 48, 174;**
PC 27
See also BRWS 5; CA 143; CP 4, 5, 6, 7;
CWP; DAM POET; DLB 40

McHale, Tom 1942(?)-1982 .... **CLC 3, 5**
See also AITN 1; CA 77-80; CAAS 106;
CN 1, 2, 3

McHugh, Heather 1948- .... **PC 61**
See also CA 69-72; CANR 11, 28, 55, 92;
CP 4, 5, 6, 7; CWP; PFS 24

McIlvanney, William 1936- .... **CLC 42**
See also CA 25-28R; CANR 61; CMW 4;
DLB 14, 207

McIlwraith, Maureen Mollie Hunter
See Hunter, Mollie
See also SATA 2

McInerney, Jay 1955- .... **CLC 34, 112**
See also AAYA 18; BPFB 2; CA 123;
CAAE 116; CANR 45, 68, 116; CN 5, 6,
7; CPW; DA3; DAM POP; DLB 292; INT
CA-123; MAL 5; MTCW 2; MTFW 2005

McIntyre, Vonda N. 1948- .... **CLC 18**
See also CA 81-84; CANR 17, 34, 69;
MTCW 1; SFW 4; YAW

McIntyre, Vonda Neel
See McIntyre, Vonda N.

McKay, Claude .... **BLC 3; HR 1:3; PC 2;**
TCLC 7, 41; WLC 4
See McKay, Festus Claudius
See also AFAW 1, 2; AMWS 10; DAB;
DLB 4, 45, 51, 117; EWL 3; EXPP; GLL
2; LAIT 3; LMFS 2; MAL 5; PAB; PFS
4; RGAL 4; WP

McKay, Festus Claudius 1889-1948
See McKay, Claude
See also BW 1, 3; CA 124; CAAE 104;
CANR 73; DA; DAC; DAM MST, MULT,
NOV, POET; MTCW 1, 2; MTFW 2005;
TUS

McKuen, Rod 1933- .... **CLC 1, 3**
See also AITN 1; CA 41-44R; CANR 40;
CP 1

McLoughlin, R. B.
See Mencken, H(enry) L(ouis)

McLuhan, (Herbert) Marshall
1911-1980 .... **CLC 37, 83**
See also CA 9-12R; CAAS 102; CANR 12,
34, 61; DLB 88; INT CANR-12; MTCW
1, 2; MTFW 2005

McManus, Declan Patrick Aloysius
See Costello, Elvis

McMillan, Terry 1951- .. **BLCS; CLC 50, 61,**
112
See also AAYA 21; AMWS 13; BPFB 2;
BW 2, 3; CA 140; CANR 60, 104, 131;
CN 7; CPW; DA3; DAM MULT, NOV,
POP; MAL 5; MTCW 2; MTFW 2005;
RGAL 4; YAW

McMurtry, Larry 1936- .... **CLC 2, 3, 7, 11,**
27, 44, 127
See also AAYA 15; AITN 2; AMWS 5;
BEST 89:2; BPFB 2; CA 5-8R; CANR
19, 43, 64, 103; CDALB 1968-1988; CN
2, 3, 4, 5, 6, 7; CPW; CSW; DA3; DAM
NOV, POP; DLB 2, 143, 256; DLBY
1980, 1987; EWL 3; MAL 5; MTCW 1,
2; MTFW 2005; RGAL 4; TCWW 1, 2

McMurtry, Larry Jeff
See McMurtry, Larry

McNally, Terrence 1939- ... **CLC 4, 7, 41, 91;**
DC 27
See also AAYA 62; AMWS 13; CA 45-48;
CAD; CANR 2, 56, 116; CD 5, 6; DA3;
DAM DRAM; DFS 16, 19; DLB 7, 249;
EWL 3; GLL 1; MTCW 2; MTFW 2005

McNally, Thomas Michael
See McNally, T.M.

McNally, T.M. 1961- .... **CLC 82**
See also CA 246

McNamer, Deirdre 1950- .... **CLC 70**
See also CA 188

McNeal, Tom .... **CLC 119**
See also CA 252

McNeile, Herman Cyril 1888-1937
See Sapper
See also CA 184; CMW 4; DLB 77

McNickle, (William) D'Arcy
1904-1977 .... CLC 89; NNAL
See also CA 9-12R; CAAS 85-88; CANR
5, 45; DAM MULT; DLB 175, 212;
RGAL 4; SATA-Obit 22; TCWW 1, 2

McPhee, John 1931- .... CLC 36
See also AAYA 61; AMWS 3; ANW; BEST
90:1; CA 65-68; CANR 20, 46, 64, 69,
121; CPW; DLB 185, 275; MTCW 1, 2;
MTFW 2005; TUS

McPherson, James Alan 1943- . BLCS; CLC
19, 77; SSC 95
See also BW 1, 3; CA 25-28R; 17; CANR
24, 74, 140; CN 3, 4, 5, 6; CSW; DLB
38, 244; EWL 3; MTCW 1, 2; MTFW
2005; RGAL 4; RGSF 2; SSFS 23

McPherson, William (Alexander)
1933- .... CLC 34
See also CA 69-72; CANR 28; INT
CANR-28

McTaggart, J. McT. Ellis
See McTaggart, John McTaggart Ellis

McTaggart, John McTaggart Ellis
1866-1925 .... TCLC 105
See also CAAE 120; DLB 262

Mead, George Herbert 1863-1931 . TCLC 89
See also CA 212; DLB 270

Mead, Margaret 1901-1978 .... CLC 37
See also AITN 1; CA 1-4R; CAAS 81-84;
CANR 4; DA3; FW; MTCW 1, 2; SATA-
Obit 20

Meaker, Marijane 1927-
See Kerr, M. E.
See also CA 107; CANR 37, 63, 145; INT
CA-107; JRDA; MAICYA 1, 2; MAIC-
YAS 1; MTCW 1; SATA 20, 61, 99, 160;
SATA-Essay 111; YAW

Medoff, Mark (Howard) 1940- .... CLC 6, 23
See also AITN 1; CA 53-56; CAD; CANR
5; CD 5, 6; DAM DRAM; DFS 4; DLB
7; INT CANR-5

Medvedev, P. N.
See Bakhtin, Mikhail Mikhailovich

Meged, Aharon
See Megged, Aharon

Meged, Aron
See Megged, Aharon

Megged, Aharon 1920- .... CLC 9
See also CA 49-52; 13; CANR 1, 140; EWL
3; RGHL

Mehta, Deepa 1950- .... CLC 208

Mehta, Gita 1943- .... CLC 179
See also CA 225; CN 7; DNFS 2

Mehta, Ved 1934- .... CLC 37
See also CA 212; 1-4R, 212; CANR 2, 23,
69; DLB 323; MTCW 1; MTFW 2005

Melanchthon, Philipp 1497-1560 .... LC 90
See also DLB 179

Melanter
See Blackmore, R(ichard) D(oddridge)

Meleager c. 140B.C.-c. 70B.C. ...... CMLC 53

Melies, Georges 1861-1938 .... TCLC 81

Melikow, Loris
See Hofmannsthal, Hugo von

Melmoth, Sebastian
See Wilde, Oscar (Fingal O'Flahertie Wills)

Melo Neto, Joao Cabral de
See Cabral de Melo Neto, Joao
See also CWW 2; EWL 3

Meltzer, Milton 1915- .... CLC 26
See also AAYA 8, 45; BYA 2, 6; CA 13-
16R; CANR 38, 92, 107; CLR 13; DLB
61; JRDA; MAICYA 1, 2; SAAS 1; SATA
1, 50, 80, 128; SATA-Essay 124; WYA;
YAW

Melville, Herman 1819-1891 ..... NCLC 3, 12,
29, 45, 49, 91, 93, 123, 157, 181; SSC 1,
17, 46, 95; WLC 4
See also AAYA 25; AMW; AMWR 1;
CDALB 1640-1865; DA; DA3; DAB;
DAC; DAM MST, NOV; DLB 3, 74, 250,
254; EXPN; EXPS; GL 3; LAIT 1, 2; NFS
7, 9; RGAL 4; RGSF 2; SATA 59; SSFS
3; TUS

Members, Mark
See Powell, Anthony

Membreno, Alejandro .... CLC 59

Menand, Louis 1952- .... CLC 208
See also CA 200

Menander c. 342B.C.-c. 293B.C. .... CMLC 9,
51; DC 3
See also AW 1; CDWLB 1; DAM DRAM;
DLB 176; LMFS 1; RGWL 2, 3

Menchu, Rigoberta 1959- .. CLC 160; HLCS
2
See also CA 175; CANR 135; DNFS 1;
WLIT 1

Mencken, H(enry) L(ouis)
1880-1956 .... TCLC 13
See also AMW; CA 125; CAAE 105;
CDALB 1917-1929; DLB 11, 29, 63, 137,
222; EWL 3; MAL 5; MTCW 1, 2;
MTFW 2005; NCFS 4; RGAL 4; TUS

Mendelsohn, Jane 1965- .... CLC 99
See also CA 154; CANR 94

Mendoza, Inigo Lopez de
See Santillana, Inigo Lopez de Mendoza,
Marques de

Menton, Francisco de
See Chin, Frank (Chew, Jr.)

Mercer, David 1928-1980 .... CLC 5
See also CA 9-12R; CAAS 102; CANR 23;
CBD; DAM DRAM; DLB 13, 310;
MTCW 1; RGEL 2

Merchant, Paul
See Ellison, Harlan

Meredith, George 1828-1909 .. PC 60; TCLC
17, 43
See also CA 153; CAAE 117; CANR 80;
CDBLB 1832-1890; DAM POET; DLB
18, 35, 57, 159; RGEL 2; TEA

Meredith, William (Morris) 1919- .... CLC 4,
13, 22, 55; PC 28
See also CA 9-12R; 14; CANR 6, 40, 129;
CP 1, 2, 3, 4, 5, 6, 7; DAM POET; DLB
5; MAL 5

Merezhkovsky, Dmitrii Sergeevich
See Merezhkovsky, Dmitry Sergeyevich
See also DLB 295

Merezhkovsky, Dmitry Sergeevich
See Merezhkovsky, Dmitry Sergeyevich
See also EWL 3

Merezhkovsky, Dmitry Sergeyevich
1865-1941 .... TCLC 29
See Merezhkovsky, Dmitrii Sergeevich;
Merezhkovsky, Dmitry Sergeevich
See also CA 169

Merimee, Prosper 1803-1870 ... NCLC 6, 65;
SSC 7, 77
See also DLB 119, 192; EW 6; EXPS; GFL
1789 to the Present; RGSF 2; RGWL 2,
3; SSFS 8; SUFW

Merkin, Daphne 1954- .... CLC 44
See also CA 123

Merleau-Ponty, Maurice
1908-1961 .... TCLC 156
See also CA 114; CAAS 89-92; DLB 296;
GFL 1789 to the Present

Merlin, Arthur
See Blish, James (Benjamin)

Mernissi, Fatima 1940- .... CLC 171
See also CA 152; FW

Merrill, James 1926-1995 ...... CLC 2, 3, 6, 8,
13, 18, 34, 91; PC 28; TCLC 173
See also AMWS 3; CA 13-16R; CAAS 147;
CANR 10, 49, 63, 108; CP 1, 2, 3, 4;
DA3; DAM POET; DLB 5, 165; DLBY
1985; EWL 3; INT CANR-10; MAL 5;
MTCW 1, 2; MTFW 2005; PAB; PFS 23;
RGAL 4

Merrill, James Ingram
See Merrill, James

Merriman, Alex
See Silverberg, Robert

Merriman, Brian 1747-1805 .... NCLC 70

Merritt, E. B.
See Waddington, Miriam

Merton, Thomas (James)
1915-1968 . CLC 1, 3, 11, 34, 83; PC 10
See also AAYA 61; AMWS 8; CA 5-8R;
CAAS 25-28R; CANR 22, 53, 111, 131;
DA3; DLB 48; DLBY 1981; MAL 5;
MTCW 1, 2; MTFW 2005

Merwin, W.S. 1927- ..... CLC 1, 2, 3, 5, 8, 13,
18, 45, 88; PC 45
See also AMWS 3; CA 13-16R; CANR 15,
51, 112, 140; CP 1, 2, 3, 4, 5, 6, 7; DA3;
DAM POET; DLB 5, 169; EWL 3; INT
CANR-15; MAL 5; MTCW 1, 2; MTFW
2005; PAB; PFS 5, 15; RGAL 4

Metastasio, Pietro 1698-1782 .... LC 115
See also RGWL 2, 3

Metcalf, John 1938- .... CLC 37; SSC 43
See also CA 113; CN 4, 5, 6, 7; DLB 60;
RGSF 2; TWA

Metcalf, Suzanne
See Baum, L(yman) Frank

Mew, Charlotte (Mary) 1870-1928 .. TCLC 8
See also CA 189; CAAE 105; DLB 19, 135;
RGEL 2

Mewshaw, Michael 1943- .... CLC 9
See also CA 53-56; CANR 7, 47, 147;
DLBY 1980

Meyer, Conrad Ferdinand
1825-1898 .... NCLC 81; SSC 30
See also DLB 129; EW; RGWL 2, 3

Meyer, Gustav 1868-1932
See Meyrink, Gustav
See also CA 190; CAAE 117

Meyer, June
See Jordan, June

Meyer, Lynn
See Slavitt, David R(ytman)

Meyers, Jeffrey 1939- .... CLC 39
See also CA 186; 73-76, 186; CANR 54,
102, 159; DLB 111

**Meynell, Alice (Christina Gertrude
Thompson)** 1847-1922 .... TCLC 6
See also CA 177; CAAE 104; DLB 19, 98;
RGEL 2

Meyrink, Gustav .... TCLC 21
See Meyer, Gustav
See also DLB 81; EWL 3

Michaels, Leonard 1933-2003 ..... CLC 6, 25;
SSC 16
See also AMWS 16; CA 61-64; CAAS 216;
CANR 21, 62, 119; CN 3, 45, 6, 7; DLB
130; MTCW 1; TCLE 1:2

Michaux, Henri 1899-1984 .... CLC 8, 19
See also CA 85-88; CAAS 114; DLB 258;
EWL 3; GFL 1789 to the Present; RGWL
2, 3

Micheaux, Oscar (Devereaux)
1884-1951 .... TCLC 76
See also BW 3; CA 174; DLB 50; TCWW
2

Michelangelo 1475-1564 .... LC 12
See also AAYA 43

Michelet, Jules 1798-1874 .... NCLC 31
See also EW 5; GFL 1789 to the Present

Michels, Robert 1876-1936 .... **TCLC 88**
See also CA 212

Michener, James A. 1907(?)-1997 . **CLC 1, 5, 11, 29, 60, 109**
See also AAYA 27; AITN 1; BEST 90:1; BPFB 2; CA 5-8R; CAAS 161; CANR 21, 45, 68; CN 1, 2, 3, 4, 5, 6; CPW; DA3; DAM NOV, POP; DLB 6; MAL 5; MTCW 1, 2; MTFW 2005; RHW; TCWW 1, 2

Mickiewicz, Adam 1798-1855 . **NCLC 3, 101; PC 38**
See also EW 5; RGWL 2, 3

Middleton, (John) Christopher 1926- .... **CLC 13**
See also CA 13-16R; CANR 29, 54, 117; CP 1, 2, 3, 4, 5, 6, 7; DLB 40

Middleton, Richard (Barham) 1882-1911 .... **TCLC 56**
See also CA 187; DLB 156; HGG

Middleton, Stanley 1919- .... **CLC 7, 38**
See also CA 25-28R; 23; CANR 21, 46, 81, 157; CN 1, 2, 3, 4, 5, 6, 7; DLB 14, 326

Middleton, Thomas 1580-1627 ...... **DC 5; LC 33, 123**
See also BRW 2; DAM DRAM, MST; DFS 18, 22; DLB 58; RGEL 2

Mieville, China 1972(?)- .... **CLC 235**
See also AAYA 52; CA 196; CANR 138; MTFW 2005

Migueis, Jose Rodrigues 1901-1980 . **CLC 10**
See also DLB 287

Mikszath, Kalman 1847-1910 .... **TCLC 31**
See also CA 170

Miles, Jack .... **CLC 100**
See also CA 200

Miles, John Russiano
See Miles, Jack

Miles, Josephine (Louise) 1911-1985 .... **CLC 1, 2, 14, 34, 39**
See also CA 1-4R; CAAS 116; CANR 2, 55; CP 1, 2, 3, 4; DAM POET; DLB 48; MAL 5; TCLE 1:2

Militant
See Sandburg, Carl (August)

Mill, Harriet (Hardy) Taylor 1807-1858 .... **NCLC 102**
See also FW

Mill, John Stuart 1806-1873 ... **NCLC 11, 58, 179**
See also CDBLB 1832-1890; DLB 55, 190, 262; FW 1; RGEL 2; TEA

Millar, Kenneth 1915-1983 .... **CLC 14**
See Macdonald, Ross
See also CA 9-12R; CAAS 110; CANR 16, 63, 107; CMW 4; CPW; DA3; DAM POP; DLB 2, 226; DLBD 6; DLBY 1983; MTCW 1, 2; MTFW 2005

Millay, E. Vincent
See Millay, Edna St. Vincent

Millay, Edna St. Vincent 1892-1950 ..... **PC 6, 61; TCLC 4, 49, 169; WLCS**
See Boyd, Nancy
See also AMW; CA 130; CAAE 104; CDALB 1917-1929; DA; DA3; DAB; DAC; DAM MST, POET; DLB 45, 249; EWL 3; EXPP; FL 1:6; MAL 5; MBL; MTCW 1, 2; MTFW 2005; PAB; PFS 3, 17; RGAL 4; TUS; WP

Miller, Arthur 1915-2005 ..... **CLC 1, 2, 6, 10, 15, 26, 47, 78, 179; DC 1; WLC 4**
See also AAYA 15; AITN 1; AMW; AMWC 1; CA 1-4R; CAAS 236; CABS 3; CAD; CANR 2, 30, 54, 76, 132; CD 5, 6; CDALB 1941-1968; DA; DA3; DAB; DAC; DAM DRAM, MST; DFS 1, 3, 8; DLB 7, 266; EWL 3; LAIT 1, 4; LATS 1:2; MAL 5; MTCW 1, 2; MTFW 2005; RGAL 4; RGHL; TUS; WYAS 1

Miller, Henry (Valentine) 1891-1980 .... **CLC 1, 2, 4, 9, 14, 43, 84; WLC 4**
See also AMW; BPFB 2; CA 9-12R; CAAS 97-100; CANR 33, 64; CDALB 1929-1941; CN 1, 2; DA; DA3; DAB; DAC; DAM MST, NOV; DLB 4, 9; DLBY 1980; EWL 3; MAL 5; MTCW 1, 2; MTFW 2005; RGAL 4; TUS

Miller, Hugh 1802-1856 .... **NCLC 143**
See also DLB 190

Miller, Jason 1939(?)-2001 .... **CLC 2**
See also AITN 1; CA 73-76; CAAS 197; CAD; CANR 130; DFS 12; DLB 7

Miller, Sue 1943- .... **CLC 44**
See also AMWS 12; BEST 90:3; CA 139; CANR 59, 91, 128; DA3; DAM POP; DLB 143

Miller, Walter M(ichael, Jr.) 1923-1996 .... **CLC 4, 30**
See also BPFB 2; CA 85-88; CANR 108; DLB 8; SCFW 1, 2; SFW 4

Millett, Kate 1934- .... **CLC 67**
See also AITN 1; CA 73-76; CANR 32, 53, 76, 110; DA3; DLB 246; FW; GLL 1; MTCW 1, 2; MTFW 2005

Millhauser, Steven 1943- ... **CLC 21, 54, 109; SSC 57**
See also CA 111; CAAE 110; CANR 63, 114, 133; CN 6, 7; DA3; DLB 2; FANT; INT CA-111; MAL 5; MTCW 2; MTFW 2005

Millhauser, Steven Lewis
See Millhauser, Steven

Millin, Sarah Gertrude 1889-1968 ... **CLC 49**
See also CA 102; CAAS 93-96; DLB 225; EWL 3

Milne, A. A. 1882-1956 .... **TCLC 6, 88**
See also BRWS 5; CA 133; CAAE 104; CLR 1, 26, 108; CMW 4; CWRI 5; DA3; DAB; DAC; DAM MST; DLB 10, 77, 100, 160; FANT; MAICYA 1, 2; MTCW 1, 2; MTFW 2005; RGEL 2; SATA 100; WCH; YABC 1

Milne, Alan Alexander
See Milne, A. A.

Milner, Ron(ald) 1938-2004 ..... **BLC 3; CLC 56**
See also AITN 1; BW 1; CA 73-76; CAAS 230; CAD; CANR 24, 81; CD 5, 6; DAM MULT; DLB 38; MAL 5; MTCW 1

Milnes, Richard Monckton 1809-1885 .... **NCLC 61**
See also DLB 32, 184

Milosz, Czeslaw 1911-2004 .... **CLC 5, 11, 22, 31, 56, 82; PC 8; WLCS**
See also AAYA 62; CA 81-84; CAAS 230; CANR 23, 51, 91, 126; CDWLB 4; CWW 2; DA3; DAM MST, POET; DLB 215, 331; EW 13; EWL 3; MTCW 1, 2; MTFW 2005; PFS 16; RGHL; RGWL 2, 3

Milton, John 1608-1674 ..... **LC 9, 43, 92; PC 19, 29; WLC 4**
See also AAYA 65; BRW 2; BRWR 2; CDBLB 1660-1789; DA; DA3; DAB; DAC; DAM MST, POET; DLB 131, 151, 281; EFS 1; EXPP; LAIT 1; PAB; PFS 3, 17; RGEL 2; TEA; WLIT 3; WP

Min, Anchee 1957- .... **CLC 86**
See also CA 146; CANR 94, 137; MTFW 2005

Minehaha, Cornelius
See Wedekind, Frank

Miner, Valerie 1947- .... **CLC 40**
See also CA 97-100; CANR 59; FW; GLL 2

Minimo, Duca
See D'Annunzio, Gabriele

Minot, Susan (Anderson) 1956- ...... **CLC 44, 159**
See also AMWS 6; CA 134; CANR 118; CN 6, 7

Minus, Ed 1938- .... **CLC 39**
See also CA 185

Mirabai 1498(?)-1550(?) .... **PC 48**
See also PFS 24

Miranda, Javier
See Bioy Casares, Adolfo
See also CWW 2

Mirbeau, Octave 1848-1917 .... **TCLC 55**
See also CA 216; DLB 123, 192; GFL 1789 to the Present

Mirikitani, Janice 1942- .... **AAL**
See also CA 211; DLB 312; RGAL 4

Mirk, John (?)-c. 1414 .... **LC 105**
See also DLB 146

Miro (Ferrer), Gabriel (Francisco Victor) 1879-1930 .... **TCLC 5**
See also CA 185; CAAE 104; DLB 322; EWL 3

Misharin, Alexandr .... **CLC 59**

Mishima, Yukio ... **CLC 2, 4, 6, 9, 27; DC 1; SSC 4; TCLC 161; WLC 4**
See Hiraoka, Kimitake
See also AAYA 50; BPFB 2; GLL 1; MJW; RGSF 2; RGWL 2, 3; SSFS 5, 12

Mistral, Frederic 1830-1914 .... **TCLC 51**
See also CA 213; CAAE 122; DLB 331; GFL 1789 to the Present

Mistral, Gabriela
See Godoy Alcayaga, Lucila
See also DLB 283, 331; DNFS 1; EWL 3; LAW; RGWL 2, 3; WP

Mistry, Rohinton 1952- ... **CLC 71, 196; SSC 73**
See also BRWS 10; CA 141; CANR 86, 114; CCA 1; CN 6, 7; DAC; SSFS 6

Mitchell, Clyde
See Ellison, Harlan

Mitchell, Emerson Blackhorse Barney 1945- .... **NNAL**
See also CA 45-48

Mitchell, James Leslie 1901-1935
See Gibbon, Lewis Grassic
See also CA 188; CAAE 104; DLB 15

Mitchell, Joni 1943- .... **CLC 12**
See also CA 112; CCA 1

Mitchell, Joseph (Quincy) 1908-1996 .... **CLC 98**
See also CA 77-80; CAAS 152; CANR 69; CN 1, 2, 3, 4, 5, 6; CSW; DLB 185; DLBY 1996

Mitchell, Margaret (Munnerlyn) 1900-1949 .... **TCLC 11, 170**
See also AAYA 23; BPFB 2; BYA 1; CA 125; CAAE 109; CANR 55, 94; CDALBS; DA3; DAM NOV, POP; DLB 9; LAIT 2; MAL 5; MTCW 1, 2; MTFW 2005; NFS 9; RGAL 4; RHW; TUS; WYAS 1; YAW

Mitchell, Peggy
See Mitchell, Margaret (Munnerlyn)

Mitchell, S(ilas) Weir 1829-1914 .... **TCLC 36**
See also CA 165; DLB 202; RGAL 4

Mitchell, W(illiam) O(rmond) 1914-1998 .... **CLC 25**
See also CA 77-80; CAAS 165; CANR 15, 43; CN 1, 2, 3, 4, 5, 6; DAC; DAM MST; DLB 88; TCLE 1:2

Mitchell, William (Lendrum) 1879-1936 .... **TCLC 81**
See also CA 213

Mitford, Mary Russell 1787-1855 ... **NCLC 4**
See also DLB 110, 116; RGEL 2

Mitford, Nancy 1904-1973 .... **CLC 44**
See also BRWS 10; CA 9-12R; CN 1; DLB 191; RGEL 2

Nekrasov, Nikolai Alekseevich
1821-1878 .... **NCLC 11**
See also DLB 277

Nelligan, Emile 1879-1941 .... **TCLC 14**
See also CA 204; CAAE 114; DLB 92;
EWL 3

Nelson, Willie 1933- .... **CLC 17**
See also CA 107; CANR 114

Nemerov, Howard 1920-1991 .... **CLC 2, 6, 9,
36; PC 24; TCLC 124**
See also AMW; CA 1-4R; CAAS 134;
CABS 2; CANR 1, 27, 53; CN 1, 2, 3;
CP 1, 2, 3, 4, 5; DAM POET; DLB 5, 6;
DLBY 1983; EWL 3; INT CANR-27;
MAL 5; MTCW 1, 2; MTFW 2005; PFS
10, 14; RGAL 4

Nepos, Cornelius c. 99B.C.-c.
24B.C. .... **CMLC 89**
See also DLB 211

Neruda, Pablo 1904-1973 .. **CLC 1, 2, 5, 7, 9,
28, 62; HLC 2; PC 4, 64; WLC 4**
See also CA 19-20; CAAS 45-48; CANR
131; CAP 2; DA; DA3; DAB; DAC;
DAM MST, MULT, POET; DLB 283,
331; DNFS 2; EWL 3; HW 1; LAW;
MTCW 1, 2; MTFW 2005; PFS 11;
RGWL 2, 3; TWA; WLIT 1; WP

Nerval, Gerard de 1808-1855 ... **NCLC 1, 67;
PC 13; SSC 18**
See also DLB 217; EW 6; GFL 1789 to the
Present; RGSF 2; RGWL 2, 3

Nervo, (Jose) Amado (Ruiz de)
1870-1919 .... **HLCS 2; TCLC 11**
See also CA 131; CAAE 109; DLB 290;
EWL 3; HW 1; LAW

Nesbit, Malcolm
See Chester, Alfred

Nessi, Pio Baroja y
See Baroja, Pio

Nestroy, Johann 1801-1862 .... **NCLC 42**
See also DLB 133; RGWL 2, 3

Netterville, Luke
See O'Grady, Standish (James)

Neufeld, John (Arthur) 1938- .... **CLC 17**
See also AAYA 11; CA 25-28R; CANR 11,
37, 56; CLR 52; MAICYA 1, 2; SAAS 3;
SATA 6, 81, 131; SATA-Essay 131; YAW

Neumann, Alfred 1895-1952 .... **TCLC 100**
See also CA 183; DLB 56

Neumann, Ferenc
See Molnar, Ferenc

Neville, Emily Cheney 1919- .... **CLC 12**
See also BYA 2; CA 5-8R; CANR 3, 37,
85; JRDA; MAICYA 1, 2; SAAS 2; SATA
1; YAW

Newbound, Bernard Slade 1930-
See Slade, Bernard
See also CA 81-84; CANR 49; CD 5; DAM
DRAM

Newby, P(ercy) H(oward)
1918-1997 .... **CLC 2, 13**
See also CA 5-8R; CAAS 161; CANR 32,
67; CN 1, 2, 3, 4, 5, 6; DAM NOV; DLB
15, 326; MTCW 1; RGEL 2

Newcastle
See Cavendish, Margaret Lucas

Newlove, Donald 1928- .... **CLC 6**
See also CA 29-32R; CANR 25

Newlove, John (Herbert) 1938- .... **CLC 14**
See also CA 21-24R; CANR 9, 25; CP 1, 2,
3, 4, 5, 6, 7

Newman, Charles 1938-2006 .... **CLC 2, 8**
See also CA 21-24R; CAAS 249; CANR
84; CN 3, 4, 5, 6

Newman, Charles Hamilton
See Newman, Charles

Newman, Edwin (Harold) 1919- ...... **CLC 14**
See also AITN 1; CA 69-72; CANR 5

Newman, John Henry 1801-1890 . **NCLC 38,
99**
See also BRWS 7; DLB 18, 32, 55; RGEL
2

Newton, (Sir) Isaac 1642-1727 ...... **LC 35, 53**
See also DLB 252

Newton, Suzanne 1936- .... **CLC 35**
See also BYA 7; CA 41-44R; CANR 14;
JRDA; SATA 5, 77

New York Dept. of Ed. .... **CLC 70**

Nexo, Martin Andersen
1869-1954 .... **TCLC 43**
See also CA 202; DLB 214; EWL 3

Nezval, Vitezslav 1900-1958 .... **TCLC 44**
See also CAAE 123; CDWLB 4; DLB 215;
EWL 3

Ng, Fae Myenne 1957(?)- .... **CLC 81**
See also BYA 11; CA 146

Ngema, Mbongeni 1955- .... **CLC 57**
See also BW 2; CA 143; CANR 84; CD 5,
6

Ngugi, James T(hiong'o) . **CLC 3, 7, 13, 182**
See Ngugi wa Thiong'o
See also CN 1, 2

Ngugi wa Thiong'o
See Ngugi wa Thiong'o
See also CD 3, 4, 5, 6, 7; DLB 125; EWL 3

Ngugi wa Thiong'o 1938- ... **BLC 3; CLC 36,
182**
See Ngugi, James T(hiong'o); Ngugi wa
Thiong'o
See also AFW; BRWS 8; BW 2; CA 81-84;
CANR 27, 58; CDWLB 3; DAM MULT,
NOV; DNFS 2; MTCW 1, 2; MTFW
2005; RGEL 2; WWE 1

Niatum, Duane 1938- .... **NNAL**
See also CA 41-44R; CANR 21, 45, 83;
DLB 175

Nichol, B(arrie) P(hillip) 1944-1988 . **CLC 18**
See also CA 53-56; CP 1, 2, 3, 4; DLB 53;
SATA 66

Nicholas of Cusa 1401-1464 .... **LC 80**
See also DLB 115

Nichols, John 1940- .... **CLC 38**
See also AMWS 13; CA 190; 9-12R, 190;
2; CANR 6, 70, 121; DLBY 1982; LATS
1:2; MTFW 2005; TCWW 1, 2

Nichols, Leigh
See Koontz, Dean R.

Nichols, Peter (Richard) 1927- .... **CLC 5, 36,
65**
See also CA 104; CANR 33, 86; CBD; CD
5, 6; DLB 13, 245; MTCW 1

Nicholson, Linda .... **CLC 65**

Ni Chuilleanain, Eilean 1942- .... **PC 34**
See also CA 126; CANR 53, 83; CP 5, 6, 7;
CWP; DLB 40

Nicolas, F. R. E.
See Freeling, Nicolas

Niedecker, Lorine 1903-1970 ..... **CLC 10, 42;
PC 42**
See also CA 25-28; CAP 2; DAM POET;
DLB 48

Nietzsche, Friedrich (Wilhelm)
1844-1900 .... **TCLC 10, 18, 55**
See also CA 121; CAAE 107; CDWLB 2;
DLB 129; EW 7; RGWL 2, 3; TWA

Nievo, Ippolito 1831-1861 .... **NCLC 22**

Nightingale, Anne Redmon 1943-
See Redmon, Anne
See also CA 103

Nightingale, Florence 1820-1910 ... **TCLC 85**
See also CA 188; DLB 166

Nijo Yoshimoto 1320-1388 .... **CMLC 49**
See also DLB 203

Nik. T. O.
See Annensky, Innokenty (Fyodorovich)

Nin, Anais 1903-1977 ..... **CLC 1, 4, 8, 11, 14,
60, 127; SSC 10**
See also AITN 2; AMWS 10; BPFB 2; CA
13-16R; CAAS 69-72; CANR 22, 53; CN
1, 2; DAM NOV, POP; DLB 2, 4, 152;
EWL 3; GLL 2; MAL 5; MBL; MTCW 1,
2; MTFW 2005; RGAL 4; RGSF 2

Nisbet, Robert A(lexander)
1913-1996 .... **TCLC 117**
See also CA 25-28R; CAAS 153; CANR
17; INT CANR-17

Nishida, Kitaro 1870-1945 .... **TCLC 83**

Nishiwaki, Junzaburo 1894-1982 .... **PC 15**
See Junzaburo, Nishiwaki
See also CA 194; CAAS 107; MJW; RGWL
3

Nissenson, Hugh 1933- .... **CLC 4, 9**
See also CA 17-20R; CANR 27, 108, 151;
CN 5, 6; DLB 28

Nister, Der
See Der Nister
See also DLB 333; EWL 3

Niven, Larry 1938-
See Niven, Laurence VanCott
See also CA 207; 21-24R, 207; 12; CANR
14, 44, 66, 113, 155; CPW; DAM POP;
MTCW 1, 2; SATA 95, 171; SFW 4

Niven, Laurence VanCott .... **CLC 8**
See Niven, Larry
See also AAYA 27; BPFB 2; BYA 10; DLB
8; SCFW 1, 2

Nixon, Agnes Eckhardt 1927- .... **CLC 21**
See also CA 110

Nizan, Paul 1905-1940 .... **TCLC 40**
See also CA 161; DLB 72; EWL 3; GFL
1789 to the Present

Nkosi, Lewis 1936- .... **BLC 3; CLC 45**
See also BW 1, 3; CA 65-68; CANR 27,
81; CBD; CD 5, 6; DAM MULT; DLB
157, 225; WWE 1

Nodier, (Jean) Charles (Emmanuel)
1780-1844 .... **NCLC 19**
See also DLB 119; GFL 1789 to the Present

Noguchi, Yone 1875-1947 .... **TCLC 80**

Nolan, Christopher 1965- .... **CLC 58**
See also CA 111; CANR 88

Noon, Jeff 1957- .... **CLC 91**
See also CA 148; CANR 83; DLB 267;
SFW 4

Norden, Charles
See Durrell, Lawrence (George)

Nordhoff, Charles Bernard
1887-1947 .... **TCLC 23**
See also CA 211; CAAE 108; DLB 9; LAIT
1; RHW 1; SATA 23

Norfolk, Lawrence 1963- .... **CLC 76**
See also CA 144; CANR 85; CN 6, 7; DLB
267

Norman, Marsha (Williams) 1947- . **CLC 28,
186; DC 8**
See also CA 105; CABS 3; CAD; CANR
41, 131; CD 5, 6; CSW; CWD; DAM
DRAM; DFS 2; DLB 266; DLBY 1984;
FW; MAL 5

Normyx
See Douglas, (George) Norman

Norris, (Benjamin) Frank(lin, Jr.)
1870-1902 .... **SSC 28; TCLC 24, 155**
See also AAYA 57; AMW; AMWC 2; BPFB
2; CA 160; CAAE 110; CDALB 1865-
1917; DLB 12, 71, 186; LMFS 2; MAL
5; NFS 12; RGAL 4; TCWW 1, 2; TUS

Norris, Leslie 1921-2006 .... **CLC 14**
See also CA 11-12; CAAS 251; CANR 14,
117; CAP 1; CP 1, 2, 3, 4, 5, 6, 7; DLB
27, 256

North, Andrew
See Norton, Andre

Ohiyesa
See Eastman, Charles A(lexander)

Okada, John 1923-1971 .... **AAL**
See also BYA 14; CA 212; DLB 312

Okigbo, Christopher 1930-1967 .... **BLC 3;
CLC 25, 84; PC 7; TCLC 171**
See also AFW; BW 1, 3; CA 77-80; CANR
74; CDWLB 3; DAM MULT, POET; DLB
125; EWL 3; MTCW 1, 2; MTFW 2005;
RGEL 2

Okigbo, Christopher Ifenayichukwu
See Okigbo, Christopher

Okri, Ben 1959- .... **CLC 87, 223**
See also AFW; BRWS 5; BW 2, 3; CA 130;
CAAE 130; CANR 65, 128; CN 5, 6, 7;
DLB 157, 231, 319, 326; EWL 3; INT
CA-138; MTCW 2; MTFW 2005; RGSF
2; SSFS 20; WLIT 2; WWE 1

Olds, Sharon 1942- .. **CLC 32, 39, 85; PC 22**
See also AMWS 10; CA 101; CANR 18,
41, 66, 98, 135; CP 5, 6, 7; CPW; CWP;
DAM POET; DLB 120; MAL 5; MTCW
2; MTFW 2005; PFS 17

Oldstyle, Jonathan
See Irving, Washington

Olesha, Iurii
See Olesha, Yuri (Karlovich)
See also RGWL 2

Olesha, Iurii Karlovich
See Olesha, Yuri (Karlovich)
See also DLB 272

Olesha, Yuri (Karlovich) 1899-1960 . **CLC 8;
SSC 69; TCLC 136**
See Olesha, Iurii; Olesha, Iurii Karlovich;
Olesha, Yury Karlovich
See also CA 85-88; EW 11; RGWL 3

Olesha, Yury Karlovich
See Olesha, Yuri (Karlovich)
See also EWL 3

Oliphant, Mrs.
See Oliphant, Margaret (Oliphant Wilson)
See also SUFW

Oliphant, Laurence 1829(?)-1888 .. **NCLC 47**
See also DLB 18, 166

Oliphant, Margaret (Oliphant Wilson)
1828-1897 .... **NCLC 11, 61; SSC 25**
See Oliphant, Mrs.
See also BRWS 10; DLB 18, 159, 190;
HGG; RGEL 2; RGSF 2

Oliver, Mary 1935- ... **CLC 19, 34, 98; PC 75**
See also AMWS 7; CA 21-24R; CANR 9,
43, 84, 92, 138; CP 4, 5, 6, 7; CWP; DLB
5, 193; EWL 3; MTFW 2005; PFS 15

Olivier, Laurence (Kerr) 1907-1989 . **CLC 20**
See also CA 150; CAAE 111; CAAS 129

Olsen, Tillie 1912-2007 .... **CLC 4, 13, 114;
SSC 11**
See also AAYA 51; AMWS 13; BYA 11;
CA 1-4R; CANR 1, 43, 74, 132;
CDALBS; CN 2, 3, 4, 5, 6, 7; DA; DA3;
DAB; DAC; DAM MST; DLB 28, 206;
DLBY 1980; EWL 3; EXPS; FW; MAL
5; MTCW 1, 2; MTFW 2005; RGAL 4;
RGSF 2; SSFS 1; TCLE 1:2; TCWW 2;
TUS

Olson, Charles (John) 1910-1970 .. **CLC 1, 2,
5, 6, 9, 11, 29; PC 19**
See also AMWS 2; CA 13-16; CAAS 25-
28R; CABS 2; CANR 35, 61; CAP 1; CP
1; DAM POET; DLB 5, 16, 193; EWL 3;
MAL 5; MTCW 1, 2; RGAL 4; WP

Olson, Toby 1937- .... **CLC 28**
See also CA 65-68; 11; CANR 9, 31, 84;
CP 3, 4, 5, 6, 7

Olyesha, Yuri
See Olesha, Yuri (Karlovich)

Olympiodorus of Thebes c. 375-c.
430 .... **CMLC 59**

Omar Khayyam
See Khayyam, Omar
See also RGWL 2, 3

Ondaatje, Michael 1943- ..... **CLC 14, 29, 51,
76, 180; PC 28**
See also AAYA 66; CA 77-80; CANR 42,
74, 109, 133; CN 5, 6, 7; CP 1, 2, 3, 4, 5,
6, 7; DA3; DAB; DAC; DAM MST; DLB
60, 323, 326; EWL 3; LATS 1:2; LMFS
2; MTCW 2; MTFW 2005; NFS 23; PFS
8, 19; TCLE 1:2; TWA; WWE 1

Ondaatje, Philip Michael
See Ondaatje, Michael

Oneal, Elizabeth 1934-
See Oneal, Zibby
See also CA 106; CANR 28, 84; MAICYA
1, 2; SATA 30, 82; YAW

Oneal, Zibby .... **CLC 30**
See Oneal, Elizabeth
See also AAYA 5, 41; BYA 13; CLR 13;
JRDA; WYA

O'Neill, Eugene (Gladstone)
1888-1953 ... **DC 20; TCLC 1, 6, 27, 49;
WLC 4**
See also AAYA 54; AITN 1; AMW; AMWC
1; CA 132; CAAE 110; CAD; CANR 131;
CDALB 1929-1941; DA; DA3; DAB;
DAC; DAM DRAM, MST; DFS 2, 4, 5,
6, 9, 11, 12, 16, 20; DLB 7, 331; EWL 3;
LAIT 3; LMFS 2; MAL 5; MTCW 1, 2;
MTFW 2005; RGAL 4; TUS

Onetti, Juan Carlos 1909-1994 ... **CLC 7, 10;
HLCS 2; SSC 23; TCLC 131**
See also CA 85-88; CAAS 145; CANR 32,
63; CDWLB 3; CWW 2; DAM MULT,
NOV; DLB 113; EWL 3; HW 1, 2; LAW;
MTCW 1, 2; MTFW 2005; RGSF 2

O Nuallain, Brian 1911-1966
See O'Brien, Flann
See also CA 21-22; CAAS 25-28R; CAP 2;
DLB 231; FANT; TEA

Ophuls, Max
See Ophuls, Max

Ophuls, Max 1902-1957 .... **TCLC 79**
See also CAAE 113

Opie, Amelia 1769-1853 .... **NCLC 65**
See also DLB 116, 159; RGEL 2

Oppen, George 1908-1984 ..... **CLC 7, 13, 34;
PC 35; TCLC 107**
See also CA 13-16R; CAAS 113; CANR 8,
82; CP 1, 2, 3; DLB 5, 165

Oppenheim, E(dward) Phillips
1866-1946 .... **TCLC 45**
See also CA 202; CAAE 111; CMW 4; DLB
70

Oppenheimer, Max
See Ophuls, Max

Opuls, Max
See Ophuls, Max

Orage, A(lfred) R(ichard)
1873-1934 .... **TCLC 157**
See also CAAE 122

Origen c. 185-c. 254 .... **CMLC 19**

Orlovitz, Gil 1918-1973 .... **CLC 22**
See also CA 77-80; CAAS 45-48; CN 1;
CP 1, 2; DLB 2, 5

O'Rourke, Patrick Jake
See O'Rourke, P.J.

O'Rourke, P.J. 1947- .... **CLC 209**
See also CA 77-80; CANR 13, 41, 67, 111,
155; CPW; DAM POP; DLB 185

Orris
See Ingelow, Jean

Ortega y Gasset, Jose 1883-1955 ...... **HLC 2;
TCLC 9**
See also CA 130; CAAE 106; DAM MULT;
EW 9; EWL 3; HW 1, 2; MTCW 1, 2;
MTFW 2005

Ortese, Anna Maria 1914-1998 .... **CLC 89**
See also DLB 177; EWL 3

Ortiz, Simon J(oseph) 1941- ... **CLC 45, 208;
NNAL; PC 17**
See also AMWS 4; CA 134; CANR 69, 118;
CP 3, 4, 5, 6, 7; DAM MULT, POET;
DLB 120, 175, 256; MAL 5; PFS
4, 16; RGAL 4; SSFS 22; TCWW 2

Orton, Joe ...... **CLC 4, 13, 43; DC 3; TCLC
157**
See Orton, John Kingsley
See also BRWS 5; CBD; CDBLB 1960 to
Present; DFS 3, 6; DLB 13, 310; GLL 1;
RGEL 2; TEA; WLIT 4

Orton, John Kingsley 1933-1967
See Orton, Joe
See also CA 85-88; CANR 35, 66; DAM
DRAM; MTCW 1, 2; MTFW 2005

Orwell, George ...... **SSC 68; TCLC 2, 6, 15,
31, 51, 128, 129; WLC 4**
See Blair, Eric (Arthur)
See also BPFB 3; BRW 7; BYA 5; CDBLB
1945-1960; CLR 68; DAB; DLB 15, 98,
195, 255; EWL 3; EXPN; LAIT 4, 5;
LATS 1:1; NFS 3, 7; RGEL 2; SCFW 1,
2; SFW 4; SSFS 4; TEA; WLIT 4; YAW

Osborne, David
See Silverberg, Robert

Osborne, George
See Silverberg, Robert

Osborne, John 1929-1994 .... **CLC 1, 2, 5, 11,
45; TCLC 153; WLC 4**
See also BRWS 1; CA 13-16R; CAAS 147;
CANR 21, 56; CBD; CDBLB 1945-1960;
DA; DAB; DAC; DAM DRAM, MST;
DFS 4, 19; DLB 13; EWL 3; MTCW 1,
2; MTFW 2005; RGEL 2

Osborne, Lawrence 1958- .... **CLC 50**
See also CA 189; CANR 152

Osbourne, Lloyd 1868-1947 .... **TCLC 93**

Osgood, Frances Sargent
1811-1850 .... **NCLC 141**
See also DLB 250

Oshima, Nagisa 1932- .... **CLC 20**
See also CA 121; CAAE 116; CANR 78

Oskison, John Milton
1874-1947 .... **NNAL; TCLC 35**
See also CA 144; CANR 84; DAM MULT;
DLB 175

Ossian c. 3rd cent. - .... **CMLC 28**
See Macpherson, James

Ossoli, Sarah Margaret (Fuller)
1810-1850 .... **NCLC 5, 50**
See Fuller, Margaret; Fuller, Sarah Margaret
See also CDALB 1640-1865; FW; LMFS 1;
SATA 25

Ostriker, Alicia (Suskin) 1937- .... **CLC 132**
See also CA 25-28R; 24; CANR 10, 30, 62,
99; CWP; DLB 120; EXPP; PFS 19

Ostrovsky, Aleksandr Nikolaevich
See Ostrovsky, Alexander
See also DLB 277

Ostrovsky, Alexander 1823-1886 .. **NCLC 30,
57**
See Ostrovsky, Aleksandr Nikolaevich

Otero, Blas de 1916-1979 .... **CLC 11**
See also CA 89-92; DLB 134; EWL 3

O'Trigger, Sir Lucius
See Horne, Richard Henry Hengist

Otto, Rudolf 1869-1937 .... **TCLC 85**

Otto, Whitney 1955- .... **CLC 70**
See also CA 140; CANR 120

Otway, Thomas 1652-1685 ... **DC 24; LC 106**
See also DAM DRAM; DLB 80; RGEL 2

Parshchikov, Aleksei 1954- .... **CLC 59**
See Parshchikov, Aleksei Maksimovich

Parshchikov, Aleksei Maksimovich
See Parshchikov, Aleksei
See also DLB 285

Parson, Professor
See Coleridge, Samuel Taylor

Parson Lot
See Kingsley, Charles

Parton, Sara Payson Willis
1811-1872 .... **NCLC 86**
See also DLB 43, 74, 239

Partridge, Anthony
See Oppenheim, E(dward) Phillips

Pascal, Blaise 1623-1662 .... **LC 35**
See also DLB 268; EW 3; GFL Beginnings
to 1789; RGWL 2, 3; TWA

Pascoli, Giovanni 1855-1912 .... **TCLC 45**
See also CA 170; EW 7; EWL 3

Pasolini, Pier Paolo 1922-1975 .. **CLC 20, 37,
106; PC 17**
See also CA 93-96; CAAS 61-64; CANR
63; DLB 128, 177; EWL 3; MTCW 1;
RGWL 2, 3

Pasquini
See Silone, Ignazio

Pastan, Linda (Olenik) 1932- .... **CLC 27**
See also CA 61-64; CANR 18, 40, 61, 113;
CP 3, 4, 5, 6, 7; CSW; CWP; DAM
POET; DLB 5; PFS 8, 25

Pasternak, Boris 1890-1960 ... **CLC 7, 10, 18,
63; PC 6; SSC 31; TCLC 188; WLC 4**
See also BPFB 3; CA 127; CAAS 116; DA;
DA3; DAB; DAC; DAM MST, NOV,
POET; DLB 302, 331; EW 10; MTCW 1,
2; MTFW 2005; RGSF 2; RGWL 2, 3;
TWA; WP

Patchen, Kenneth 1911-1972 .... **CLC 1, 2, 18**
See also BG 1:3; CA 1-4R; CAAS 33-36R;
CANR 3, 35; CN 1; CP 1; DAM POET;
DLB 16, 48; EWL 3; MAL 5; MTCW 1;
RGAL 4

Pater, Walter (Horatio) 1839-1894 . **NCLC 7,
90, 159**
See also BRW 5; CDBLB 1832-1890; DLB
57, 156; RGEL 2; TEA

Paterson, A(ndrew) B(arton)
1864-1941 .... **TCLC 32**
See also CA 155; DLB 230; RGEL 2; SATA
97

Paterson, Banjo
See Paterson, A(ndrew) B(arton)

Paterson, Katherine 1932- .... **CLC 12, 30**
See also AAYA 1, 31; BYA 1, 2, 7; CA 21-
24R; CANR 28, 59, 111; CLR 7, 50;
CWRI 5; DLB 52; JRDA; LAIT 4; MAI-
CYA 1, 2; MAICYAS 1; MTCW 1; SATA
13, 53, 92, 133; WYA; YAW

Paterson, Katherine Womeldorf
See Paterson, Katherine

Patmore, Coventry Kersey Dighton
1823-1896 .... **NCLC 9; PC 59**
See also DLB 35, 98; RGEL 2; TEA

Paton, Alan 1903-1988 ..... **CLC 4, 10, 25, 55,
106; TCLC 165; WLC 4**
See also AAYA 26; AFW; BPFB 3; BRWS
2; BYA 1; CA 13-16; CAAS 125; CANR
22; CAP 1; CN 1, 2, 3, 4; DA; DA3;
DAB; DAC; DAM MST, NOV; DLB 225;
DLBD 17; EWL 3; EXPN; LAIT 4;
MTCW 1, 2; MTFW 2005; NFS 3, 12;
RGEL 2; SATA 11; SATA-Obit 56; TWA;
WLIT 2; WWE 1

Paton Walsh, Gillian
See Paton Walsh, Jill
See also AAYA 47; BYA 1, 8

Paton Walsh, Jill 1937- .... **CLC 35**
See Paton Walsh, Gillian; Walsh, Jill Paton
See also AAYA 11; CANR 38, 83, 158; CLR
2, 65; DLB 161; JRDA; MAICYA 1, 2;
SAAS 3; SATA 4, 72, 109; YAW

Patsauq, Markoosie 1942- .... **NNAL**
See also CA 101; CLR 23; CWRI 5; DAM
MULT

Patterson, (Horace) Orlando (Lloyd)
1940- .... **BLCS**
See also BW 1; CA 65-68; CANR 27, 84;
CN 1, 2, 3, 4, 5, 6

Patton, George S(mith), Jr.
1885-1945 .... **TCLC 79**
See also CA 189

Paulding, James Kirke 1778-1860 ... **NCLC 2**
See also DLB 3, 59, 74, 250; RGAL 4

Paulin, Thomas Neilson
See Paulin, Tom

Paulin, Tom 1949- .... **CLC 37, 177**
See also CA 128; CAAE 123; CANR 98;
CP 3, 4, 5, 6, 7; DLB 40

Pausanias c. 1st cent. - .... **CMLC 36**

Paustovsky, Konstantin (Georgievich)
1892-1968 .... **CLC 40**
See also CA 93-96; CAAS 25-28R; DLB
272; EWL 3

Pavese, Cesare 1908-1950 .... **PC 13; SSC 19;
TCLC 3**
See also CA 169; CAAE 104; DLB 128,
177; EW 12; EWL 3; PFS 20; RGSF 2;
RGWL 2, 3; TWA; WLIT 7

Pavic, Milorad 1929- .... **CLC 60**
See also CA 136; CDWLB 4; CWW 2; DLB
181; EWL 3; RGWL 3

Pavlov, Ivan Petrovich 1849-1936 . **TCLC 91**
See also CA 180; CAAE 118

Pavlova, Karolina Karlovna
1807-1893 .... **NCLC 138**
See also DLB 205

Payne, Alan
See Jakes, John

Payne, Rachel Ann
See Jakes, John

Paz, Gil
See Lugones, Leopoldo

Paz, Octavio 1914-1998 . **CLC 3, 4, 6, 10, 19,
51, 65, 119; HLC 2; PC 1, 48; WLC 4**
See also AAYA 50; CA 73-76; CAAS 165;
CANR 32, 65, 104; CWW 2; DA; DA3;
DAB; DAC; DAM MST, MULT, POET;
DLB 290, 331; DLBY 1990, 1998; DNFS
1; EWL 3; HW 1, 2; LAW; LAWS 1;
MTCW 1, 2; MTFW 2005; PFS 18;
RGWL 2, 3; SSFS 13; TWA; WLIT 1

p'Bitek, Okot 1931-1982 .... **BLC 3; CLC 96;
TCLC 149**
See also AFW; BW 2, 3; CA 124; CAAS
107; CANR 82; CP 1, 2, 3; DAM MULT;
DLB 125; EWL 3; MTCW 1, 2; MTFW
2005; RGEL 2; WLIT 2

Peabody, Elizabeth Palmer
1804-1894 .... **NCLC 169**
See also DLB 1, 223

Peacham, Henry 1578-1644(?) .... **LC 119**
See also DLB 151

Peacock, Molly 1947- .... **CLC 60**
See also CA 103; 21; CANR 52, 84; CP 5,
6, 7; CWP; DLB 120, 282

Peacock, Thomas Love
1785-1866 .... **NCLC 22**
See also BRW 4; DLB 96, 116; RGEL 2;
RGSF 2

Peake, Mervyn 1911-1968 .... **CLC 7, 54**
See also CA 5-8R; CAAS 25-28R; CANR
3; DLB 15, 160, 255; FANT; MTCW 1;
RGEL 2; SATA 23; SFW 4

Pearce, Philippa 1920-2006
See Christie, Philippa
See also CA 5-8R; CANR 4, 109; CWRI 5;
FANT; MAICYA 2

Pearl, Eric
See Elman, Richard (Martin)

Pearson, T. R. 1956- .... **CLC 39**
See also CA 130; CAAE 120; CANR 97,
147; CSW; INT CA-130

Pearson, Thomas Reid
See Pearson, T. R.

Peck, Dale 1967- .... **CLC 81**
See also CA 146; CANR 72, 127; GLL 2

Peck, John (Frederick) 1941- .... **CLC 3**
See also CA 49-52; CANR 3, 100; CP 4, 5,
6, 7

Peck, Richard 1934- .... **CLC 21**
See also AAYA 1, 24; BYA 1, 6, 8, 11; CA
85-88; CANR 19, 38, 129; CLR 15; INT
CANR-19; JRDA; MAICYA 1, 2; SAAS
2; SATA 18, 55, 97, 110, 158; SATA-
Essay 110; WYA; YAW

Peck, Richard Wayne
See Peck, Richard

Peck, Robert Newton 1928- .... **CLC 17**
See also AAYA 3, 43; BYA 1, 6; CA 182;
81-84, 182; CANR 31, 63, 127; CLR 45;
DA; DAC; DAM MST; JRDA; LAIT 3;
MAICYA 1, 2; SAAS 1; SATA 21, 62,
111, 156; SATA-Essay 108; WYA; YAW

Peckinpah, David Samuel
See Peckinpah, Sam

Peckinpah, Sam 1925-1984 .... **CLC 20**
See also CA 109; CAAS 114; CANR 82

Pedersen, Knut 1859-1952
See Hamsun, Knut
See also CA 119; CAAE 104; CANR 63;
MTCW 1, 2

Peele, George 1556-1596 .... **DC 27; LC 115**
See also BRW 1; DLB 62, 167; RGEL 2

Peeslake, Gaffer
See Durrell, Lawrence (George)

Peguy, Charles (Pierre)
1873-1914 .... **TCLC 10**
See also CA 193; CAAE 107; DLB 258;
EWL 3; GFL 1789 to the Present

Peirce, Charles Sanders
1839-1914 .... **TCLC 81**
See also CA 194; DLB 270

Pellicer, Carlos 1897(?)-1977 .... **HLCS 2**
See also CA 153; CAAS 69-72; DLB 290;
EWL 3; HW 1

Pena, Ramon del Valle y
See Valle-Inclan, Ramon (Maria) del

Pendennis, Arthur Esquir
See Thackeray, William Makepeace

Penn, Arthur
See Matthews, (James) Brander

Penn, William 1644-1718 .... **LC 25**
See also DLB 24

PEPECE
See Prado (Calvo), Pedro

Pepys, Samuel 1633-1703 ... **LC 11, 58; WLC
4**
See also BRW 2; CDBLB 1660-1789; DA;
DA3; DAB; DAC; DAM MST; DLB 101,
213; NCFS 4; RGEL 2; TEA; WLIT 3

Percy, Thomas 1729-1811 .... **NCLC 95**
See also DLB 104

Percy, Walker 1916-1990 .... **CLC 2, 3, 6, 8,
14, 18, 47, 65**
See also AMWS 3; BPFB 3; CA 1-4R;
CAAS 131; CANR 1, 23, 64; CN 1, 2, 3,
4; CPW; CSW; DA3; DAM NOV, POP;
DLB 2; DLBY 1980, 1990; EWL 3; MAL
5; MTCW 1, 2; MTFW 2005; RGAL 4;
TUS

Ronsard, Pierre de 1524-1585 . **LC 6, 54; PC 11**
See also DLB 327; EW 2; GFL Beginnings to 1789; RGWL 2, 3; TWA

Rooke, Leon 1934- .... **CLC 25, 34**
See also CA 25-28R; CANR 23, 53; CCA 1; CPW; DAM POP

Roosevelt, Franklin Delano
1882-1945 .... **TCLC 93**
See also CA 173; CAAE 116; LAIT 3

Roosevelt, Theodore 1858-1919 ..... **TCLC 69**
See also CA 170; CAAE 115; DLB 47, 186, 275

Roper, William 1498-1578 .... **LC 10**

Roquelaure, A. N.
See Rice, Anne

Rosa, Joao Guimaraes 1908-1967 ... **CLC 23; HLCS 1**
See Guimaraes Rosa, Joao
See also CAAS 89-92; DLB 113, 307; EWL 3; WLIT 1

Rose, Wendy 1948- . **CLC 85; NNAL; PC 13**
See also CA 53-56; CANR 5, 51; CWP; DAM MULT; DLB 175; PFS 13; RGAL 4; SATA 12

Rosen, R. D.
See Rosen, Richard (Dean)

Rosen, Richard (Dean) 1949- .... **CLC 39**
See also CA 77-80; CANR 62, 120; CMW 4; INT CANR-30

Rosenberg, Isaac 1890-1918 .... **TCLC 12**
See also BRW 6; CA 188; CAAE 107; DLB 20, 216; EWL 3; PAB; RGEL 2

Rosenblatt, Joe .... **CLC 15**
See Rosenblatt, Joseph
See also CP 3, 4, 5, 6, 7

Rosenblatt, Joseph 1933-
See Rosenblatt, Joe
See also CA 89-92; CP 1, 2; INT CA-89-92

Rosenfeld, Samuel
See Tzara, Tristan

Rosenstock, Sami
See Tzara, Tristan

Rosenstock, Samuel
See Tzara, Tristan

Rosenthal, M(acha) L(ouis)
1917-1996 .... **CLC 28**
See also CA 1-4R; 6; CAAS 152; CANR 4, 51; CP 1, 2, 3, 4, 5, 6; DLB 5; SATA 59

Ross, Barnaby
See Dannay, Frederic; Lee, Manfred B.

Ross, Bernard L.
See Follett, Ken

Ross, J. H.
See Lawrence, T(homas) E(dward)

Ross, John Hume
See Lawrence, T(homas) E(dward)

Ross, Martin 1862-1915
See Martin, Violet Florence
See also DLB 135; GLL 2; RGEL 2; RGSF 2

Ross, (James) Sinclair 1908-1996 ... **CLC 13; SSC 24**
See also CA 73-76; CANR 81; CN 1, 2, 3, 4, 5, 6; DAC; DAM MST; DLB 88; RGEL 2; RGSF 2; TCWW 1, 2

Rossetti, Christina 1830-1894 ... **NCLC 2, 50, 66; PC 7; WLC 5**
See also AAYA 51; BRW 5; BYA 4; CLR 115; DA; DA3; DAB; DAC; DAM MST, POET; DLB 35, 163, 240; EXPP; FL 1:3; LATS 1:1; MAICYA 1, 2; PFS 10, 14; RGEL 2; SATA 20; TEA; WCH

Rossetti, Christina Georgina
See Rossetti, Christina

Rossetti, Dante Gabriel 1828-1882 . **NCLC 4, 77; PC 44; WLC 5**
See also AAYA 51; BRW 5; CDBLB 1832-1890; DA; DAB; DAC; DAM MST, POET; DLB 35; EXPP; RGEL 2; TEA

Rossi, Cristina Peri
See Peri Rossi, Cristina

Rossi, Jean-Baptiste 1931-2003
See Japrisot, Sebastien
See also CA 201; CAAS 215

Rossner, Judith 1935-2005 .... **CLC 6, 9, 29**
See also AITN 2; BEST 90:3; BPFB 3; CA 17-20R; CAAS 242; CANR 18, 51, 73; CN 4, 5, 6, 7; DLB 6; INT CANR-18; MAL 5; MTCW 1, 2; MTFW 2005

Rossner, Judith Perelman
See Rossner, Judith

Rostand, Edmond (Eugene Alexis)
1868-1918 .... **DC 10; TCLC 6, 37**
See also CA 126; CAAE 104; DA; DA3; DAB; DAC; DAM DRAM, MST; DFS 1; DLB 192; LAIT 1; MTCW 1; RGWL 2, 3; TWA

Roth, Henry 1906-1995 ..... **CLC 2, 6, 11, 104**
See also AMWS 9; CA 11-12; CAAS 149; CANR 38, 63; CAP 1; CN 1, 2, 3, 4, 5, 6; DA3; DLB 28; EWL 3; MAL 5; MTCW 1, 2; MTFW 2005; RGAL 4

Roth, (Moses) Joseph 1894-1939 ... **TCLC 33**
See also CA 160; DLB 85; EWL 3; RGWL 2, 3

Roth, Philip 1933- ... **CLC 1, 2, 3, 4, 6, 9, 15, 22, 31, 47, 66, 86, 119, 201; SSC 26; WLC 5**
See also AAYA 67; AMWR 2; AMWS 3; BEST 90:3; BPFB 3; CA 1-4R; CANR 1, 22, 36, 55, 89, 132; CDALB 1968-1988; CN 3, 4, 5, 6, 7; CPW 1; DA; DA3; DAB; DAC; DAM MST, NOV, POP; DLB 2, 28, 173; DLBY 1982; EWL 3; MAL 5; MTCW 1, 2; MTFW 2005; RGAL 4; RGHL; RGSF 2; SSFS 12, 18; TUS

Roth, Philip Milton
See Roth, Philip

Rothenberg, Jerome 1931- .... **CLC 6, 57**
See also CA 45-48; CANR 1, 106; CP 1, 2, 3, 4, 5, 6, 7; DLB 5, 193

Rotter, Pat .... **CLC 65**

Roumain, Jacques (Jean Baptiste)
1907-1944 .... **BLC 3; TCLC 19**
See also BW 1; CA 125; CAAE 117; DAM MULT; EWL 3

Rourke, Constance Mayfield
1885-1941 .... **TCLC 12**
See also CA 200; CAAE 107; MAL 5; YABC 1

Rousseau, Jean-Baptiste 1671-1741 ...... **LC 9**

Rousseau, Jean-Jacques 1712-1778 .... **LC 14, 36, 122; WLC 5**
See also DA; DA3; DAB; DAC; DAM MST; DLB 314; EW 4; GFL Beginnings to 1789; LMFS 1; RGWL 2, 3; TWA

Roussel, Raymond 1877-1933 .... **TCLC 20**
See also CA 201; CAAE 117; EWL 3; GFL 1789 to the Present

Rovit, Earl (Herbert) 1927- .... **CLC 7**
See also CA 5-8R; CANR 12

Rowe, Elizabeth Singer 1674-1737 ..... **LC 44**
See also DLB 39, 95

Rowe, Nicholas 1674-1718 .... **LC 8**
See also DLB 84; RGEL 2

Rowlandson, Mary 1637(?)-1678 .... **LC 66**
See also DLB 24, 200; RGAL 4

Rowley, Ames Dorrance
See Lovecraft, H. P.

Rowley, William 1585(?)-1626 ... **LC 100, 123**
See also DFS 22; DLB 58; RGEL 2

Rowling, J.K. 1965- .... **CLC 137, 217**
See also AAYA 34; BYA 11, 13, 14; CA 173; CANR 128, 157; CLR 66, 80, 112; MAICYA 2; MTFW 2005; SATA 109, 174; SUFW 2

Rowling, Joanne Kathleen
See Rowling, J.K.

Rowson, Susanna Haswell
1762(?)-1824 .... **NCLC 5, 69, 182**
See also AMWS 15; DLB 37, 200; RGAL 4

Roy, Arundhati 1960(?)- .... **CLC 109, 210**
See also CA 163; CANR 90, 126; CN 7; DLB 323, 326; DLBY 1997; EWL 3; LATS 1:2; MTFW 2005; NFS 22; WWE 1

Roy, Gabrielle 1909-1983 .... **CLC 10, 14**
See also CA 53-56; CAAS 110; CANR 5, 61; CCA 1; DAB; DAC; DAM MST; DLB 68; EWL 3; MTCW 1; RGWL 2, 3; SATA 104; TCLE 1:2

Royko, Mike 1932-1997 .... **CLC 109**
See also CA 89-92; CAAS 157; CANR 26, 111; CPW

Rozanov, Vasilii Vasil'evich
See Rozanov, Vassili
See also DLB 295

Rozanov, Vasily Vasilyevich
See Rozanov, Vassili
See also EWL 3

Rozanov, Vassili 1856-1919 .... **TCLC 104**
See Rozanov, Vasilii Vasil'evich; Rozanov, Vasily Vasilyevich

Rozewicz, Tadeusz 1921- ...... **CLC 9, 23, 139**
See also CA 108; CANR 36, 66; CWW 2; DA3; DAM POET; DLB 232; EWL 3; MTCW 1, 2; MTFW 2005; RGHL; RGWL 3

Ruark, Gibbons 1941- .... **CLC 3**
See also CA 33-36R; 23; CANR 14, 31, 57; DLB 120

Rubens, Bernice (Ruth) 1923-2004 . **CLC 19, 31**
See also CA 25-28R; CAAS 232; CANR 33, 65, 128; CN 1, 2, 3, 4, 5, 6, 7; DLB 14, 207, 326; MTCW 1

Rubin, Harold
See Robbins, Harold

Rudkin, (James) David 1936- .... **CLC 14**
See also CA 89-92; CBD; CD 5, 6; DLB 13

Rudnik, Raphael 1933- .... **CLC 7**
See also CA 29-32R

Ruffian, M.
See Hasek, Jaroslav (Matej Frantisek)

Ruiz, Jose Martinez .... **CLC 11**
See Martinez Ruiz, Jose

Ruiz, Juan c. 1283-c. 1350 .... **CMLC 66**

Rukeyser, Muriel 1913-1980 . **CLC 6, 10, 15, 27; PC 12**
See also AMWS 6; CA 5-8R; CAAS 93-96; CANR 26, 60; CP 1, 2, 3; DA3; DAM POET; DLB 48; EWL 3; FW; GLL 2; MAL 5; MTCW 1, 2; PFS 10; RGAL 4; SATA-Obit 22

Rule, Jane (Vance) 1931- .... **CLC 27**
See also CA 25-28R; 18; CANR 12, 87; CN 4, 5, 6, 7; DLB 60; FW

Rulfo, Juan 1918-1986 .. **CLC 8, 80; HLC 2; SSC 25**
See also CA 85-88; CAAS 118; CANR 26; CDWLB 3; DAM MULT; DLB 113; EWL 3; HW 1, 2; LAW; MTCW 1, 2; RGSF 2; RGWL 2, 3; WLIT 1

Rumi, Jalal al-Din 1207-1273 ...... **CMLC 20; PC 45**
See also AAYA 64; RGWL 2, 3; WLIT 6; WP

CDALB 1941-1968; CLR 18; CN 1, 2, 3, 4, 5, 6, 7; CPW 1; DA; DA3; DAB; DAC; DAM MST, NOV, POP; DLB 2, 102, 173; EWL 3; EXPN; LAIT 4; MAICYA 1, 2; MAL 5; MTCW 1, 2; MTFW 2005; NFS 1; RGAL 4; RGSF 2; SATA 67; SSFS 17; TUS; WYA; YAW

Salisbury, John
See Caute, (John) David

Sallust c. 86B.C.-35B.C. .... **CMLC 68**
See also AW 2; CDWLB 1; DLB 211; RGWL 2, 3

Salter, James 1925- .. **CLC 7, 52, 59; SSC 58**
See also AMWS 9; CA 73-76; CANR 107, 160; DLB 130

Saltus, Edgar (Everton) 1855-1921 . **TCLC 8**
See also CAAE 105; DLB 202; RGAL 4

Saltykov, Mikhail Evgrafovich
1826-1889 .... **NCLC 16**
See also DLB 238:

Saltykov-Shchedrin, N.
See Saltykov, Mikhail Evgrafovich

Samarakis, Andonis
See Samarakis, Antonis
See also EWL 3

Samarakis, Antonis 1919-2003 .... **CLC 5**
See Samarakis, Andonis
See also CA 25-28R; 16; CAAS 224; CANR 36

Sanchez, Florencio 1875-1910 .... **TCLC 37**
See also CA 153; DLB 305; EWL 3; HW 1; LAW

Sanchez, Luis Rafael 1936- .... **CLC 23**
See also CA 128; DLB 305; EWL 3; HW 1; WLIT 1

Sanchez, Sonia 1934- .... **BLC 3; CLC 5, 116, 215; PC 9**
See also BW 2, 3; CA 33-36R; CANR 24, 49, 74, 115; CLR 18; CP 2, 3, 4, 5, 6, 7; CSW; CWP; DA3; DAM MULT; DLB 41; DLBD 8; EWL 3; MAICYA 1, 2; MAL 5; MTCW 1, 2; MTFW 2005; SATA 22, 136; WP

Sancho, Ignatius 1729-1780 .... **LC 84**

Sand, George 1804-1876 ..... **NCLC 2, 42, 57, 174; WLC 5**
See also DA; DA3; DAB; DAC; DAM MST, NOV; DLB 119, 192; EW 6; FL 1:3; FW; GFL 1789 to the Present; RGWL 2, 3; TWA

Sandburg, Carl (August) 1878-1967 . **CLC 1, 4, 10, 15, 35; PC 2, 41; WLC 5**
See also AAYA 24; AMW; BYA 1, 3; CA 5-8R; CAAS 25-28R; CANR 35; CDALB 1865-1917; CLR 67; DA; DA3; DAB; DAC; DAM MST, POET; DLB 17, 54, 284; EWL 3; EXPP; LAIT 2; MAICYA 1, 2; MAL 5; MTCW 1, 2; MTFW 2005; PAB; PFS 3, 6, 12; RGAL 4; SATA 8; TUS; WCH; WP; WYA

Sandburg, Charles
See Sandburg, Carl (August)

Sandburg, Charles A.
See Sandburg, Carl (August)

Sanders, (James) Ed(ward) 1939- .... **CLC 53**
See also BG 1:3; CA 13-16R; 21; CANR 13, 44, 78; CP 1, 2, 3, 4, 5, 6, 7; DAM POET; DLB 16, 244

Sanders, Edward
See Sanders, (James) Ed(ward)
See also DLB 244

Sanders, Lawrence 1920-1998 .... **CLC 41**
See also BEST 89:4; BPFB 3; CA 81-84; CAAS 165; CANR 33, 62; CMW 4; CPW; DA3; DAM POP; MTCW 1

Sanders, Noah
See Blount, Roy (Alton), Jr.

Sanders, Winston P.
See Anderson, Poul

Sandoz, Mari(e Susette) 1900-1966 .. **CLC 28**
See also CA 1-4R; CAAS 25-28R; CANR 17, 64; DLB 9, 212; LAIT 2; MTCW 1, 2; SATA 5; TCWW 1, 2

Sandys, George 1578-1644 .... **LC 80**
See also DLB 24, 121

Saner, Reg(inald Anthony) 1931- .... **CLC 9**
See also CA 65-68; CP 3, 4, 5, 6, 7

Sankara 788-820 .... **CMLC 32**

Sannazaro, Jacopo 1456(?)-1530 .... **LC 8**
See also RGWL 2, 3; WLIT 7

Sansom, William 1912-1976 . **CLC 2, 6; SSC 21**
See also CA 5-8R; CAAS 65-68; CANR 42; CN 1, 2; DAM NOV; DLB 139; EWL 3; MTCW 1; RGEL 2; RGSF 2

Santayana, George 1863-1952 .... **TCLC 40**
See also AMW; CA 194; CAAE 115; DLB 54, 71, 246, 270; DLBD 13; EWL 3; MAL 5; RGAL 4; TUS

Santiago, Danny .... **CLC 33**
See James, Daniel (Lewis)
See also DLB 122

Santillana, Inigo Lopez de Mendoza, Marques de 1398-1458 .... **LC 111**
See also DLB 286

Santmyer, Helen Hooven
1895-1986 .... **CLC 33; TCLC 133**
See also CA 1-4R; CAAS 118; CANR 15, 33; DLBY 1984; MTCW 1; RHW

Santoka, Taneda 1882-1940 .... **TCLC 72**

Santos, Bienvenido N(uqui)
1911-1996 ... **AAL; CLC 22; TCLC 156**
See also CA 101; CAAS 151; CANR 19, 46; CP 1; DAM MULT; DLB 312; EWL; RGAL 4; SSFS 19

Sapir, Edward 1884-1939 .... **TCLC 108**
See also CA 211; DLB 92

Sapper .... **TCLC 44**
See McNeile, Herman Cyril

Sapphire
See Sapphire, Brenda

Sapphire, Brenda 1950- .... **CLC 99**

Sappho fl. 6th cent. B.C.- ... **CMLC 3, 67; PC 5**
See also CDWLB 1; DA3; DAM POET; DLB 176; FL 1:1; PFS 20; RGWL 2, 3; WLIT 8; WP

Saramago, Jose 1922- ..... **CLC 119; HLCS 1**
See also CA 153; CANR 96; CWW 2; DLB 287, 332; EWL 3; LATS 1:2; SSFS 23

Sarduy, Severo 1937-1993 .... **CLC 6, 97; HLCS 2; TCLC 167**
See also CA 89-92; CAAS 142; CANR 58, 81; CWW 2; DLB 113; EWL 3; HW 1, 2; LAW

Sargeson, Frank 1903-1982 ..... **CLC 31; SSC 99**
See also CA 25-28R; CAAS 106; CANR 38, 79; CN 1, 2, 3; EWL 3; GLL 2; RGEL 2; RGSF 2; SSFS 20

Sarmiento, Domingo Faustino
1811-1888 .... **HLCS 2; NCLC 123**
See also LAW; WLIT 1

Sarmiento, Felix Ruben Garcia
See Dario, Ruben

Saro-Wiwa, Ken(ule Beeson)
1941-1995 .... **CLC 114**
See also BW 2; CA 142; CAAS 150; CANR 60; DLB 157

Saroyan, William 1908-1981 ... **CLC 1, 8, 10, 29, 34, 56; SSC 21; TCLC 137; WLC 5**
See also AAYA 66; CA 5-8R; CAAS 103; CAD; CANR 30; CDALBS; CN 1, 2; DA; DA3; DAB; DAC; DAM DRAM, MST, NOV; DFS 17; DLB 7, 9, 86; DLBY 1981; EWL 3; LAIT 4; MAL 5; MTCW

1, 2; MTFW 2005; RGAL 4; RGSF 2; SATA 23; SATA-Obit 24; SSFS 14; TUS

Sarraute, Nathalie 1900-1999 .... **CLC 1, 2, 4, 8, 10, 31, 80; TCLC 145**
See also BPFB 3; CA 9-12R; CAAS 187; CANR 23, 66, 134; CWW 2; DLB 83, 321; EW 12; EWL 3; GFL 1789 to the Present; MTCW 1, 2; MTFW 2005; RGWL 2, 3

Sarton, May 1912-1995 ... **CLC 4, 14, 49, 91; PC 39; TCLC 120**
See also AMWS 8; CA 1-4R; CAAS 149; CANR 1, 34, 55, 116; CN 1, 2, 3, 4, 5, 6; CP 1, 2, 3, 4, 5, 6; DAM POET; DLB 48; DLBY 1981; EWL 3; FW; INT CANR-34; MAL 5; MTCW 1, 2; MTFW 2005; RGAL 4; SATA 36; SATA-Obit 86; TUS

Sartre, Jean-Paul 1905-1980 . **CLC 1, 4, 7, 9, 13, 18, 24, 44, 50, 52; DC 3; SSC 32; WLC 5**
See also AAYA 62; CA 9-12R; CAAS 97-100; CANR 21; DA; DA3; DAB; DAC; DAM DRAM, MST, NOV; DFS 5; DLB 72, 296, 321, 332; EW 12; EWL 3; GFL 1789 to the Present; LMFS 2; MTCW 1, 2; MTFW 2005; NFS 21; RGHL; RGSF 2; RGWL 2, 3; SSFS 9; TWA

Sassoon, Siegfried (Lorraine)
1886-1967 .... **CLC 36, 130; PC 12**
See also BRW 6; CA 104; CAAS 25-28R; CANR 36; DAB; DAM MST, NOV, POET; DLB 20, 191; DLBD 18; EWL 3; MTCW 1, 2; MTFW 2005; PAB; RGEL 2; TEA

Satterfield, Charles
See Pohl, Frederik

Satyremont
See Peret, Benjamin

Saul, John (W. III) 1942- .... **CLC 46**
See also AAYA 10, 62; BEST 90:4; CA 81-84; CANR 16, 40, 81; CPW; DAM NOV, POP; HGG; SATA 98

Saunders, Caleb
See Heinlein, Robert A.

Saura (Atares), Carlos 1932-1998 .... **CLC 20**
See also CA 131; CAAE 114; CANR 79; HW 1

Sauser, Frederic Louis
See Sauser-Hall, Frederic

Sauser-Hall, Frederic 1887-1961 ...... **CLC 18**
See Cendrars, Blaise
See also CA 102; CAAS 93-96; CANR 36, 62; MTCW 1

Saussure, Ferdinand de
1857-1913 .... **TCLC 49**
See also DLB 242

Savage, Catharine
See Brosman, Catharine Savage

Savage, Richard 1697(?)-1743 .... **LC 96**
See also DLB 95; RGEL 2

Savage, Thomas 1915-2003 .... **CLC 40**
See also CA 132; 15; CAAE 126; CAAS 218; CN 6, 7; INT CA-132; SATA-Obit 147; TCWW 2

Savan, Glenn 1953-2003 .... **CLC 50**
See also CA 225

Sax, Robert
See Johnson, Robert

Saxo Grammaticus c. 1150-c.
1222 .... **CMLC 58**

Saxton, Robert
See Johnson, Robert

Sayers, Dorothy L(eigh) 1893-1957 . **SSC 71; TCLC 2, 15**
See also BPFB 3; BRWS 3; CA 119; CAAE 104; CANR 60; CDBLB 1914-1945; CMW 4; DAM POP; DLB 10, 36, 77, 100; MSW; MTCW 1, 2; MTFW 2005; RGEL 2; SSFS 12; TEA

Seabrook, John
See Hubbard, L. Ron
Seacole, Mary Jane Grant
1805-1881 .... NCLC 147
See also DLB 166
Sealy, I(rwin) Allan 1951- .... CLC 55
See also CA 136; CN 6, 7
Search, Alexander
See Pessoa, Fernando (Antonio Nogueira)
Sebald, W(infried) G(eorg)
1944-2001 .... CLC 194
See also BRWS 8; CA 159; CAAS 202;
CANR 98; MTFW 2005; RGHL
Sebastian, Lee
See Silverberg, Robert
Sebastian Owl
See Thompson, Hunter S.
Sebestyen, Igen
See Sebestyen, Ouida
Sebestyen, Ouida 1924- .... CLC 30
See also AAYA 8; BYA 7; CA 107; CANR
40, 114; CLR 17; JRDA; MAICYA 1, 2;
SAAS 10; SATA 39, 140; WYA; YAW
Sebold, Alice 1963(?)- .... CLC 193
See also AAYA 56; CA 203; MTFW 2005
Second Duke of Buckingham
See Villiers, George
Secundus, H. Scriblerus
See Fielding, Henry
Sedges, John
See Buck, Pearl S(ydenstricker)
Sedgwick, Catharine Maria
1789-1867 .... NCLC 19, 98
See also DLB 1, 74, 183, 239, 243, 254; FL
1:3; RGAL 4
Sedulius Scottus 9th cent. -c. 874 .. CMLC 86
Seelye, John (Douglas) 1931- .... CLC 7
See also CA 97-100; CANR 70; INT CA-
97-100; TCWW 1, 2
Seferiades, Giorgos Stylianou 1900-1971
See Seferis, George
See also CA 5-8R; CAAS 33-36R; CANR
5, 36; MTCW 1
Seferis, George .... CLC 5, 11; PC 66
See Seferiades, Giorgos Stylianou
See also DLB 332; EW 12; EWL 3; RGWL
2, 3
Segal, Erich (Wolf) 1937- .... CLC 3, 10
See also BEST 89:1; BPFB 3; CA 25-28R;
CANR 20, 36, 65, 113; CPW; DAM POP;
DLBY 1986; INT CANR-20; MTCW 1
Seger, Bob 1945- .... CLC 35
Seghers, Anna .... CLC 7
See Radvanyi, Netty
See also CDWLB 2; DLB 69; EWL 3
Seidel, Frederick (Lewis) 1936- .... CLC 18
See also CA 13-16R; CANR 8, 99; CP 1, 2,
3, 4, 5, 6, 7; DLBY 1984
Seifert, Jaroslav 1901-1986 . CLC 34, 44, 93;
PC 47
See also CA 127; CDWLB 4; DLB 215,
332; EWL 3; MTCW 1, 2
Sei Shonagon c. 966-1017(?) ..... CMLC 6, 89
Sejour, Victor 1817-1874 .... DC 10
See also DLB 50
Sejour Marcou et Ferrand, Juan Victor
See Sejour, Victor
Selby, Hubert, Jr. 1928-2004 ..... CLC 1, 2, 4,
8; SSC 20
See also CA 13-16R; CAAS 226; CANR
33, 85; CN 1, 2, 3, 4, 5, 6, 7; DLB 2, 227;
MAL 5
Selzer, Richard 1928- .... CLC 74
See also CA 65-68; CANR 14, 106
Sembene, Ousmane
See Ousmane, Sembene
See also AFW; EWL 3; WLIT 2

Senancour, Etienne Pivert de
1770-1846 .... NCLC 16
See also DLB 119; GFL 1789 to the Present
Sender, Ramon (Jose) 1902-1982 ...... CLC 8;
HLC 2; TCLC 136
See also CA 5-8R; CAAS 105; CANR 8;
DAM MULT; DLB 322; EWL 3; HW 1;
MTCW 1; RGWL 2, 3
Seneca, Lucius Annaeus c. 4B.C.-c.
65 .... CMLC 6; DC 5
See also AW 2; CDWLB 1; DAM DRAM;
DLB 211; RGWL 2, 3; TWA; WLIT 8
Senghor, Leopold Sedar 1906-2001 ... BLC 3;
CLC 54, 130; PC 25
See also AFW; BW 2; CA 125; CAAE 116;
CAAS 203; CANR 47, 74, 134; CWW 2;
DAM MULT, POET; DNFS 2; EWL 3;
GFL 1789 to the Present; MTCW 1, 2;
MTFW 2005; TWA
Senior, Olive (Marjorie) 1941- .... SSC 78
See also BW 3; CA 154; CANR 86, 126;
CN 6; CP 6, 7; CWP; DLB 157; EWL 3;
RGSF 2
Senna, Danzy 1970- .... CLC 119
See also CA 169; CANR 130
Serling, (Edward) Rod(man)
1924-1975 .... CLC 30
See also AAYA 14; AITN 1; CA 162; CAAS
57-60; DLB 26; SFW 4
Serna, Ramon Gomez de la
See Gomez de la Serna, Ramon
Serpieres
See Guillevic, (Eugene)
Service, Robert
See Service, Robert W(illiam)
See also BYA 4; DAB; DLB 92
Service, Robert W(illiam)
1874(?)-1958 ... PC 70; TCLC 15; WLC
5
See Service, Robert
See also CA 140; CAAE 115; CANR 84;
DA; DAC; DAM MST, POET; PFS 10;
RGEL 2; SATA 20
Seth, Vikram 1952- .... CLC 43, 90
See also BRWS 10; CA 127; CAAE 121;
CANR 50, 74, 131; CN 6, 7; CP 5, 6, 7;
DA3; DAM MULT; DLB 120, 271, 282,
323; EWL 3; INT CA-127; MTCW 2;
MTFW 2005; WWE 1
Seton, Cynthia Propper 1926-1982 .. CLC 27
See also CA 5-8R; CAAS 108; CANR 7
Seton, Ernest (Evan) Thompson
1860-1946 .... TCLC 31
See also ANW; BYA 3; CA 204; CAAE
109; CLR 59; DLB 92; DLBD 13; JRDA;
SATA 18
Seton-Thompson, Ernest
See Seton, Ernest (Evan) Thompson
Settle, Mary Lee 1918-2005 .... CLC 19, 61
See also BPFB 3; CA 89-92; 1; CAAS 243;
CANR 44, 87, 126; CN 6, 7; CSW; DLB
6; INT CA-89-92
Seuphor, Michel
See Arp, Jean
Sevigne, Marie (de Rabutin-Chantal)
1626-1696 .... LC 11
See Sevigne, Marie de Rabutin Chantal
See also GFL Beginnings to 1789; TWA
Sevigne, Marie de Rabutin Chantal
See Sevigne, Marie (de Rabutin-Chantal)
See also DLB 268
Sewall, Samuel 1652-1730 .... LC 38
See also DLB 24; RGAL 4
Sexton, Anne (Harvey) 1928-1974 ..... CLC 2,
4, 6, 8, 10, 15, 53, 123; PC 2; WLC 5
See also AMWS 2; CA 1-4R; CAAS 53-56;
CABS 2; CANR 3, 36; CDALB 1941-
1968; CP 1, 2; DA; DA3; DAB; DAC;
DAM MST, POET; DLB 5, 169; EWL 3;
EXPP; FL 1:6; FW; MAL 5; MBL;

MTCW 1, 2; MTFW 2005; PAB; PFS 4,
14; RGAL 4; RGHL; SATA 10; TUS
Shaara, Jeff 1952- .... CLC 119
See also AAYA 70; CA 163; CANR 109;
CN 7; MTFW 2005
Shaara, Michael 1929-1988 .... CLC 15
See also AAYA 71; AITN 1; BPFB 3; CA
102; CAAS 125; CANR 52, 85; DAM
POP; DLBY 1983; MTFW 2005
Shackleton, C. C.
See Aldiss, Brian W.
Shacochis, Bob .... CLC 39
See Shacochis, Robert G.
Shacochis, Robert G. 1951-
See Shacochis, Bob
See also CA 124; CAAE 119; CANR 100;
INT CA-124
Shadwell, Thomas 1641(?)-1692 .... LC 114
See also DLB 80; IDTP; RGEL 2
Shaffer, Anthony 1926-2001 .... CLC 19
See also CA 116; CAAE 110; CAAS 200;
CBD; CD 5, 6; DAM DRAM; DFS 13;
DLB 13
Shaffer, Anthony Joshua
See Shaffer, Anthony
Shaffer, Peter 1926- ... CLC 5, 14, 18, 37, 60;
DC 7
See also BRWS 1; CA 25-28R; CANR 25,
47, 74, 118; CBD; CD 5, 6; CDBLB 1960
to Present; DA3; DAB; DAM DRAM,
MST; DFS 5, 13; DLB 13, 233; EWL 3;
MTCW 1, 2; MTFW 2005; RGEL 2; TEA
Shakespeare, William 1564-1616 .... WLC 5
See also AAYA 35; BRW 1; CDBLB Before
1660; DA; DA3; DAB; DAC; DAM
DRAM, MST, POET; DFS 20, 21; DLB
62, 172, 263; EXPP; LAIT 1; LATS 1:1;
LMFS 1; PAB; PFS 1, 2, 3, 4, 5, 8, 9;
RGEL 2; TEA; WLIT 3; WP; WS; WYA
Shakey, Bernard
See Young, Neil
Shalamov, Varlam (Tikhonovich)
1907-1982 .... CLC 18
See also CA 129; CAAS 105; DLB 302;
RGSF 2
Shamloo, Ahmad
See Shamlu, Ahmad
Shamlou, Ahmad
See Shamlu, Ahmad
Shamlu, Ahmad 1925-2000 .... CLC 10
See also CA 216; CWW 2
Shammas, Anton 1951- .... CLC 55
See also CA 199
Shandling, Arline
See Berriault, Gina
Shange, Ntozake 1948- ... BLC 3; CLC 8, 25,
38, 74, 126; DC 3
See also AAYA 9, 66; AFAW 1, 2; BW 2;
CA 85-88; CABS 3; CAD; CANR 27, 48,
74, 131; CD 5, 6; CP 5, 6, 7; CWD; CWP;
DA3; DAM DRAM, MULT; DFS 2, 11;
DLB 38, 249; FW; LAIT 4, 5; MAL 5;
MTCW 1, 2; MTFW 2005; NFS 11;
RGAL 4; SATA 157; YAW
Shanley, John Patrick 1950- .... CLC 75
See also AAYA 74; AMWS 14; CA 133;
CAAE 128; CAD; CANR 83, 154; CD 5,
6; DFS 23
Shapcott, Thomas W(illiam) 1935- .. CLC 38
See also CA 69-72; CANR 49, 83, 103; CP
1, 2, 3, 4, 5, 6, 7; DLB 289
Shapiro, Jane 1942- .... CLC 76
See also CA 196
Shapiro, Karl 1913-2000 ... CLC 4, 8, 15, 53;
PC 25
See also AMWS 2; CA 1-4R; 6; CAAS 188;
CANR 1, 36, 66; CP 1, 2, 3, 4, 5, 6; DLB
48; EWL 3; EXPP; MAL 5; MTCW 1, 2;
MTFW 2005; PFS 3; RGAL 4

Sokolov, Alexander V(sevolodovich) 1943-
   See Sokolov, Sasha
   See also CA 73-76

Sokolov, Raymond 1941- .... **CLC 7**
   See also CA 85-88

Sokolov, Sasha .... **CLC 59**
   See Sokolov, Alexander V(sevolodovich)
   See also CWW 2; DLB 285; EWL 3; RGWL
   2, 3

Solo, Jay
   See Ellison, Harlan

Sologub, Fyodor .... **TCLC 9**
   See Teternikov, Fyodor Kuzmich
   See also EWL 3

Solomons, Ikey Esquir
   See Thackeray, William Makepeace

Solomos, Dionysios 1798-1857 .... **NCLC 15**

Solwoska, Mara
   See French, Marilyn

Solzhenitsyn, Aleksandr I. 1918- .. **CLC 1, 2, 4, 7, 9, 10, 18, 26, 34, 78, 134, 235; SSC 32; WLC 5**
   See Solzhenitsyn, Aleksandr Isayevich
   See also AAYA 49; AITN 1; BPFB 3; CA
   69-72; CANR 40, 65, 116; DA; DA3;
   DAB; DAC; DAM MST, NOV; DLB 302,
   332; EW 13; EXPS; LAIT 4; MTCW 1,
   2; MTFW 2005; NFS 6; RGSF 2; RGWL
   2, 3; SSFS 9; TWA

Solzhenitsyn, Aleksandr Isayevich
   See Solzhenitsyn, Aleksandr I.
   See also CWW 2; EWL 3

Somers, Jane
   See Lessing, Doris

Somerville, Edith Oenone
   1858-1949 .... **SSC 56; TCLC 51**
   See also CA 196; DLB 135; RGEL 2; RGSF
   2

Somerville & Ross
   See Martin, Violet Florence; Somerville,
   Edith Oenone

Sommer, Scott 1951- .... **CLC 25**
   See also CA 106

Sommers, Christina Hoff 1950- ...... **CLC 197**
   See also CA 153; CANR 95

Sondheim, Stephen (Joshua) 1930- . **CLC 30, 39, 147; DC 22**
   See also AAYA 11, 66; CA 103; CANR 47,
   67, 125; DAM DRAM; LAIT 4

Sone, Monica 1919- .... **AAL**
   See also DLB 312

Song, Cathy 1955- .... **AAL; PC 21**
   See also CA 154; CANR 118; CWP; DLB
   169, 312; EXPP; FW; PFS 5

Sontag, Susan 1933-2004 ... **CLC 1, 2, 10, 13, 31, 105, 195**
   See also AMWS 3; CA 17-20R; CAAS 234;
   CANR 25, 51, 74, 97; CN 1, 2, 3, 4, 5, 6,
   7; CPW; DA3; DAM POP; DLB 2, 67;
   EWL 3; MAL 5; MBL; MTCW 1, 2;
   MTFW 2005; RGAL 4; RHW; SSFS 10

Sophocles 496(?)B.C.-406(?)B.C. .... **CMLC 2, 47, 51, 86; DC 1; WLCS**
   See also AW 1; CDWLB 1; DA; DA3;
   DAB; DAC; DAM DRAM, MST; DFS 1,
   4, 8; DLB 176; LAIT 1; LATS 1:1; LMFS
   1; RGWL 2, 3; TWA; WLIT 8

Sordello 1189-1269 .... **CMLC 15**

Sorel, Georges 1847-1922 .... **TCLC 91**
   See also CA 188; CAAE 118

Sorel, Julia
   See Drexler, Rosalyn

Sorokin, Vladimir .... **CLC 59**
   See Sorokin, Vladimir Georgievich

Sorokin, Vladimir Georgievich
   See Sorokin, Vladimir
   See also DLB 285

Sorrentino, Gilbert 1929-2006 .... **CLC 3, 7, 14, 22, 40**
   See also CA 77-80; CAAS 250; CANR 14,
   33, 115, 157; CN 3, 4, 5, 6, 7; CP 1, 2, 3,
   4, 5, 6, 7; DLB 5, 173; DLBY 1980; INT
   CANR-14

Soseki
   See Natsume, Soseki
   See also MJW

Soto, Gary 1952- ... **CLC 32, 80; HLC 2; PC 28**
   See also AAYA 10, 37; BYA 11; CA 125;
   CAAE 119; CANR 50, 74, 107, 157; CLR
   38; CP 4, 5, 6, 7; DAM MULT; DLB 82;
   EWL 3; EXPP; HW 1, 2; INT CA-125;
   JRDA; LLW; MAICYA 2; MAICYAS 1;
   MAL 5; MTCW 2; MTFW 2005; PFS 7;
   RGAL 4; SATA 80, 120, 174; WYA; YAW

Soupault, Philippe 1897-1990 .... **CLC 68**
   See also CA 147; CAAE 116; CAAS 131;
   EWL 3; GFL 1789 to the Present; LMFS
   2

Souster, (Holmes) Raymond 1921- .... **CLC 5, 14**
   See also CA 13-16R; 14; CANR 13, 29, 53;
   CP 1, 2, 3, 4, 5, 6, 7; DA3; DAC; DAM
   POET; DLB 88; RGEL 2; SATA 63

Southern, Terry 1924(?)-1995 .... **CLC 7**
   See also AMWS 11; BPFB 3; CA 1-4R;
   CAAS 150; CANR 1, 55, 107; CN 1, 2,
   3, 4, 5, 6; DLB 2; IDFW 3, 4

Southerne, Thomas 1660-1746 .... **LC 99**
   See also DLB 80; RGEL 2

Southey, Robert 1774-1843 .... **NCLC 8, 97**
   See also BRW 4; DLB 93, 107, 142; RGEL
   2; SATA 54

Southwell, Robert 1561(?)-1595 .... **LC 108**
   See also DLB 167; RGEL 2; TEA

Southworth, Emma Dorothy Eliza Nevitte
   1819-1899 .... **NCLC 26**
   See also DLB 239

Souza, Ernest
   See Scott, Evelyn

Soyinka, Wole 1934- .. **BLC 3; CLC 3, 5, 14, 36, 44, 179; DC 2; WLC 5**
   See also AFW; BW 2, 3; CA 13-16R;
   CANR 27, 39, 82, 136; CD 5, 6; CDWLB
   3; CN 6, 7; CP 1, 2, 3, 4, 5, 6 ,7; DA;
   DA3; DAB; DAC; DAM DRAM, MST,
   MULT; DFS 10; DLB 125, 332; EWL 3;
   MTCW 1, 2; MTFW 2005; RGEL 2;
   TWA; WLIT 2; WWE 1

Spackman, W(illiam) M(ode)
   1905-1990 .... **CLC 46**
   See also CA 81-84; CAAS 132

Spacks, Barry (Bernard) 1931- .... **CLC 14**
   See also CA 154; CANR 33, 109; CP 3, 4,
   5, 6, 7; DLB 105

Spanidou, Irini 1946- .... **CLC 44**
   See also CA 185

Spark, Muriel 1918-2006 .... **CLC 2, 3, 5, 8, 13, 18, 40, 94; PC 72; SSC 10**
   See also BRWS 1; CA 5-8R; CAAS 251;
   CANR 12, 36, 76, 89, 131; CDBLB 1945-
   1960; CN 1, 2, 3, 4, 5, 6, 7; CP 1, 2, 3, 4,
   5, 6, 7; DA3; DAB; DAC; DAM MST,
   NOV; DLB 15, 139; EWL 3; FW; INT
   CANR-12; LAIT 4; MTCW 1, 2; MTFW
   2005; NFS 22; RGEL 2; TEA; WLIT 4;
   YAW

Spark, Muriel Sarah
   See Spark, Muriel

Spaulding, Douglas
   See Bradbury, Ray

Spaulding, Leonard
   See Bradbury, Ray

Speght, Rachel 1597-c. 1630 .... **LC 97**
   See also DLB 126

Spence, J. A. D.
   See Eliot, T(homas) S(tearns)

Spencer, Anne 1882-1975 ...... **HR 1:3; PC 77**
   See also BW 2; CA 161; DLB 51, 54

Spencer, Elizabeth 1921- .... **CLC 22; SSC 57**
   See also CA 13-16R; CANR 32, 65, 87; CN
   1, 2, 3, 4, 5, 6, 7; CSW; DLB 6, 218;
   EWL 3; MTCW 1; RGAL 4; SATA 14

Spencer, Leonard G.
   See Silverberg, Robert

Spencer, Scott 1945- .... **CLC 30**
   See also CA 113; CANR 51, 148; DLBY
   1986

Spender, Stephen 1909-1995 ..... **CLC 1, 2, 5, 10, 41, 91; PC 71**
   See also BRWS 2; CA 9-12R; CAAS 149;
   CANR 31, 54; CDBLB 1945-1960; CP 1,
   2, 3, 4, 5, 6; DA3; DAM POET; DLB 20;
   EWL 3; MTCW 1, 2; MTFW 2005; PAB;
   PFS 23; RGEL 2; TEA

Spengler, Oswald (Arnold Gottfried)
   1880-1936 .... **TCLC 25**
   See also CA 189; CAAE 118

Spenser, Edmund 1552(?)-1599 ...... **LC 5, 39, 117; PC 8, 42; WLC 5**
   See also AAYA 60; BRW 1; CDBLB Before
   1660; DA; DA3; DAB; DAC; DAM MST,
   POET; DLB 167; EFS 2; EXPP; PAB;
   RGEL 2; TEA; WLIT 3; WP

Spicer, Jack 1925-1965 .... **CLC 8, 18, 72**
   See also BG 1:3; CA 85-88; DAM POET;
   DLB 5, 16, 193; GLL 1; WP

Spiegelman, Art 1948- .... **CLC 76, 178**
   See also AAYA 10, 46; CA 125; CANR 41,
   55, 74, 124; DLB 299; MTCW 2; MTFW
   2005; RGHL; SATA 109, 158; YAW

Spielberg, Peter 1929- .... **CLC 6**
   See also CA 5-8R; CANR 4, 48; DLBY
   1981

Spielberg, Steven 1947- .... **CLC 20, 188**
   See also AAYA 8, 24; CA 77-80; CANR
   32; SATA 32

Spillane, Frank Morrison .... **CLC 3, 13**
   See Spillane, Mickey
   See also BPFB 3; CMW 4; DLB 226; MSW

Spillane, Mickey 1918-2006
   See Spillane, Frank Morrison
   See also CA 25-28R; CAAS 252; CANR
   28, 63, 125; DA3; MTCW 1, 2; MTFW
   2005; SATA 66; SATA-Obit 176

Spinoza, Benedictus de 1632-1677 .. **LC 9, 58**

Spinrad, Norman (Richard) 1940- ... **CLC 46**
   See also BPFB 3; CA 233; 37-40R, 233;
   19; CANR 20, 91; DLB 8; INT CANR-
   20; SFW 4

Spitteler, Carl 1845-1924 .... **TCLC 12**
   See also CAAE 109; DLB 129, 332; EWL
   3

Spitteler, Karl Friedrich Georg
   See Spitteler, Carl

Spivack, Kathleen (Romola Drucker)
   1938- .... **CLC 6**
   See also CA 49-52

Spivak, Gayatri Chakravorty
   1942- .... **CLC 233**
   See also CA 154; CAAE 110; CANR 91;
   FW; LMFS 2

Spofford, Harriet (Elizabeth) Prescott
   1835-1921 .... **SSC 87**
   See also CA 201; DLB 74, 221

Spoto, Donald 1941- .... **CLC 39**
   See also CA 65-68; CANR 11, 57, 93

Springsteen, Bruce 1949- .... **CLC 17**
   See also CA 111

Springsteen, Bruce F.
   See Springsteen, Bruce

Spurling, Hilary 1940- .... **CLC 34**
   See also CA 104; CANR 25, 52, 94, 157

Spurling, Susan Hilary
   See Spurling, Hilary

Spyker, John Howland
See Elman, Richard (Martin)
Squared, A.
See Abbott, Edwin A.
Squires, (James) Radcliffe
1917-1993 .... **CLC 51**
See also CA 1-4R; CAAS 140; CANR 6,
21; CP 1, 2, 3, 4, 5
Srivastava, Dhanpat Rai 1880(?)-1936
See Premchand
See also CA 197; CAAE 118
Stacy, Donald
See Pohl, Frederik
Stael
See Stael-Holstein, Anne Louise Germaine
Necker
See also EW 5; RGWL 2, 3
Stael, Germaine de
See Stael-Holstein, Anne Louise Germaine
Necker
See also DLB 119, 192; FL 1:3; FW; GFL
1789 to the Present; TWA
Stael-Holstein, Anne Louise Germaine
Necker 1766-1817 ...... **NCLC 3, 91**
See Stael; Stael, Germaine de
Stafford, Jean 1915-1979 .. **CLC 4, 7, 19, 68;**
SSC 26, 86
See also CA 1-4R; CAAS 85-88; CANR 3,
65; CN 1, 2; DLB 2, 173; MAL 5; MTCW
1, 2; MTFW 2005; RGAL 4; RGSF 2;
SATA-Obit 22; SSFS 21; TCWW 1, 2;
TUS
Stafford, William (Edgar)
1914-1993 .... **CLC 4, 7, 29; PC 71**
See also AMWS 11; CA 5-8R; 3; CAAS
142; CANR 5, 22; CP 1, 2, 3, 4, 5; DAM
POET; DLB 5, 206; EXPP; INT CANR-
22; MAL 5; PFS 2, 8, 16; RGAL 4; WP
Stagnelius, Eric Johan 1793-1823 . **NCLC 61**
Staines, Trevor
See Brunner, John (Kilian Houston)
Stairs, Gordon
See Austin, Mary (Hunter)
Stalin, Joseph 1879-1953 .... **TCLC 92**
Stampa, Gaspara c. 1524-1554 .. **LC 114; PC**
43
See also RGWL 2, 3; WLIT 7
Stampflinger, K. A.
See Benjamin, Walter
Stancykowna
See Szymborska, Wislawa
Standing Bear, Luther
1868(?)-1939(?) .... **NNAL**
See also CA 144; CAAE 113; DAM MULT
Stanislavsky, Constantin
1863(?)-1938 .... **TCLC 167**
See also CAAE 118
Stanislavsky, Konstantin
See Stanislavsky, Constantin
Stanislavsky, Konstantin Sergeievich
See Stanislavsky, Constantin
Stanislavsky, Konstantin Sergeivich
See Stanislavsky, Constantin
Stanislavsky, Konstantin Sergeyevich
See Stanislavsky, Constantin
Stannard, Martin 1947- .... **CLC 44**
See also CA 142; DLB 155
Stanton, Elizabeth Cady
1815-1902 .... **TCLC 73**
See also CA 171; DLB 79; FL 1:3; FW
Stanton, Maura 1946- .... **CLC 9**
See also CA 89-92; CANR 15, 123; DLB
120
Stanton, Schuyler
See Baum, L(yman) Frank
Stapledon, (William) Olaf
1886-1950 .... **TCLC 22**
See also CA 162; CAAE 111; DLB 15, 255;
SCFW 1, 2; SFW 4

Starbuck, George (Edwin)
1931-1996 .... **CLC 53**
See also CA 21-24R; CAAS 153; CANR
23; CP 1, 2, 3, 4, 5, 6; DAM POET
Stark, Richard
See Westlake, Donald E.
Staunton, Schuyler
See Baum, L(yman) Frank
Stead, Christina (Ellen) 1902-1983 ... **CLC 2,**
5, 8, 32, 80
See also BRWS 4; CA 13-16R; CAAS 109;
CANR 33, 40; CN 1, 2, 3; DLB 260;
EWL 3; FW; MTCW 1, 2; MTFW 2005;
RGEL 2; RGSF 2; WWE 1
Stead, William Thomas
1849-1912 .... **TCLC 48**
See also CA 167
Stebnitsky, M.
See Leskov, Nikolai (Semyonovich)
Steele, Richard 1672-1729 .... **LC 18**
See also BRW 3; CDBLB 1660-1789; DLB
84, 101; RGEL 2; WLIT 3
Steele, Timothy (Reid) 1948- .... **CLC 45**
See also CA 93-96; CANR 16, 50, 92; CP
5, 6, 7; DLB 120, 282
Steffens, (Joseph) Lincoln
1866-1936 .... **TCLC 20**
See also CA 198; CAAE 117; DLB 303;
MAL 5
Stegner, Wallace (Earle) 1909-1993 .. **CLC 9,**
49, 81; SSC 27
See also AITN 1; AMWS 4; ANW; BEST
90:3; BPFB 3; CA 1-4R; 9; CAAS 141;
CANR 1, 21, 46; CN 1, 2, 3, 4, 5; DAM
NOV; DLB 9, 206, 275; DLBY 1993;
EWL 3; MAL 5; MTCW 1, 2; MTFW
2005; RGAL 4; TCWW 1, 2; TUS
Stein, Gertrude 1874-1946 .... **DC 19; PC 18;**
SSC 42; TCLC 1, 6, 28, 48; WLC 5
See also AAYA 64; AMW; AMWC 2; CA
132; CAAE 104; CANR 108; CDALB
1917-1929; DA; DA3; DAB; DAC; DAM
MST, NOV, POET; DLB 4, 54, 86, 228;
DLBD 15; EWL 3; EXPS; FL 1:6; GLL
1; MAL 5; MBL; MTCW 1, 2; MTFW
2005; NCFS 4; RGAL 4; RGSF 2; SSFS
5; TUS; WP
Steinbeck, John (Ernst) 1902-1968 ... **CLC 1,**
5, 9, 13, 21, 34, 45, 75, 124; SSC 11, 37,
77; TCLC 135; WLC 5
See also AAYA 12; AMW; BPFB 3; BYA 2,
3, 13; CA 1-4R; CAAS 25-28R; CANR 1,
35; CDALB 1929-1941; DA; DA3; DAB;
DAC; DAM DRAM, MST, NOV; DLB 7,
9, 212, 275, 309, 332; DLBD 2; EWL 3;
EXPS; LAIT 3; MAL 5; MTCW 1, 2;
MTFW 2005; NFS 1, 5, 7, 17, 19; RGAL
4; RGSF 2; RHW; SATA 9; SSFS 3, 6,
22; TCWW 1, 2; TUS; WYA; YAW
Steinem, Gloria 1934- .... **CLC 63**
See also CA 53-56; CANR 28, 51, 139;
DLB 246; FL 1:1; FW; MTCW 1, 2;
MTFW 2005
Steiner, George 1929- .... **CLC 24, 221**
See also CA 73-76; CANR 31, 67, 108;
DAM NOV; DLB 67, 299; EWL 3;
MTCW 1, 2; MTFW 2005; RGHL; SATA
62
Steiner, K. Leslie
See Delany, Samuel R., Jr.
Steiner, Rudolf 1861-1925 .... **TCLC 13**
See also CAAE 107
Stendhal 1783-1842 .... **NCLC 23, 46, 178;**
SSC 27; WLC 5
See also DA; DA3; DAB; DAC; DAM
MST, NOV; DLB 119; EW 5; GFL 1789
to the Present; RGWL 2, 3; TWA
Stephen, Adeline Virginia
See Woolf, (Adeline) Virginia

Stephen, Sir Leslie 1832-1904 .... **TCLC 23**
See also BRW 5; CAAE 123; DLB 57, 144,
190
Stephen, Sir Leslie
See Stephen, Sir Leslie
Stephen, Virginia
See Woolf, (Adeline) Virginia
Stephens, James 1882(?)-1950 .... **SSC 50;**
TCLC 4
See also CA 192; CAAE 104; DLB 19, 153,
162; EWL 3; FANT; RGEL 2; SUFW
Stephens, Reed
See Donaldson, Stephen R(eeder)
Stephenson, Neal 1959- .... **CLC 220**
See also AAYA 38; CA 122; CANR 88, 138;
CN 7; MTFW 2005; SFW 4
Steptoe, Lydia
See Barnes, Djuna
See also GLL 1
Sterchi, Beat 1949- .... **CLC 65**
See also CA 203
Sterling, Brett
See Bradbury, Ray; Hamilton, Edmond
Sterling, Bruce 1954- .... **CLC 72**
See also CA 119; CANR 44, 135; CN 7;
MTFW 2005; SCFW 2; SFW 4
Sterling, George 1869-1926 .... **TCLC 20**
See also CA 165; CAAE 117; DLB 54
Stern, Gerald 1925- .... **CLC 40, 100**
See also AMWS 9; CA 81-84; CANR 28,
94; CP 3, 4, 5, 6, 7; DLB 105; RGAL 4
Stern, Richard (Gustave) 1928- ... **CLC 4, 39**
See also CA 1-4R; CANR 1, 25, 52, 120;
CN 1, 2, 3, 4, 5, 6, 7; DLB 218; DLBY
1987; INT CANR-25
Sternberg, Josef von 1894-1969 .... **CLC 20**
See also CA 81-84
Sterne, Laurence 1713-1768 .... **LC 2, 48;**
WLC 5
See also BRW 3; BRWC 1; CDBLB 1660-
1789; DA; DAB; DAC; DAM MST, NOV;
DLB 39; RGEL 2; TEA
Sternheim, (William Adolf) Carl
1878-1942 .... **TCLC 8**
See also CA 193; CAAE 105; DLB 56, 118;
EWL 3; IDTP; RGWL 2, 3
Stevens, Margaret Dean
See Aldrich, Bess Streeter
Stevens, Mark 1951- .... **CLC 34**
See also CA 122
Stevens, Wallace 1879-1955 . **PC 6; TCLC 3,**
12, 45; WLC 5
See also AMW; AMWR 1; CA 124; CAAE
104; CDALB 1929-1941; DA; DA3;
DAB; DAC; DAM MST, POET; DLB 54;
EWL 3; EXPP; MAL 5; MTCW 1, 2;
PAB; PFS 13, 16; RGAL 4; TUS; WP
Stevenson, Anne (Katharine) 1933- .. **CLC 7,**
33
See also BRWS 6; CA 17-20R; 9; CANR 9,
33, 123; CP 3, 4, 5, 6, 7; CWP; DLB 40;
MTCW 1; RHW
Stevenson, Robert Louis (Balfour)
1850-1894 ...... **NCLC 5, 14, 63; SSC 11,**
51; WLC 5
See also AAYA 24; BPFB 3; BRW 5;
BRWC 1; BRWR 1; BYA 1, 2, 4, 13; CD-
BLB 1890-1914; CLR 10, 11, 107; DA;
DA3; DAB; DAC; DAM MST, NOV;
DLB 18, 57, 141, 156, 174; DLBD 13;
GL 3; HGG; JRDA; LAIT 1, 3; MAICYA
1, 2; NFS 11, 20; RGEL 2; RGSF 2;
SATA 100; SUFW; TEA; WCH; WLIT 4;
WYA; YABC 2; YAW
Stewart, J(ohn) I(nnes) M(ackintosh)
1906-1994 .... **CLC 7, 14, 32**
See Innes, Michael
See also CA 85-88; 3; CAAS 147; CANR
47; CMW 4; CN 1, 2, 3, 4, 5; MTCW 1,
2

Stewart, Mary (Florence Elinor)
1916- .... **CLC 7, 35, 117**
See also AAYA 29, 73; BPFB 3; CA 1-4R; CANR 1, 59, 130; CMW 4; CPW; DAB; FANT; RHW; SATA 12; YAW
Stewart, Mary Rainbow
See Stewart, Mary (Florence Elinor)
Stifle, June
See Campbell, Maria
Stifter, Adalbert 1805-1868 .. **NCLC 41; SSC 28**
See also CDWLB 2; DLB 133; RGSF 2; RGWL 2, 3
Still, James 1906-2001 .... **CLC 49**
See also CA 65-68; 17; CAAS 195; CANR 10, 26; CSW; DLB 9; DLBY 01; SATA 29; SATA-Obit 127
Sting 1951-
See Sumner, Gordon Matthew
See also CA 167
Stirling, Arthur
See Sinclair, Upton
Stitt, Milan 1941- .... **CLC 29**
See also CA 69-72
Stockton, Francis Richard 1834-1902
See Stockton, Frank R.
See also AAYA 68; CA 137; CAAE 108; MAICYA 1, 2; SATA 44; SFW 4
Stockton, Frank R. .... **TCLC 47**
See Stockton, Francis Richard
See also BYA 4, 13; DLB 42, 74; DLBD 13; EXPS; SATA-Brief 32; SSFS 3; SUFW; WCH
Stoddard, Charles
See Kuttner, Henry
Stoker, Abraham 1847-1912
See Stoker, Bram
See also CA 150; CAAE 105; DA; DA3; DAC; DAM MST, NOV; HGG; MTFW 2005; SATA 29
Stoker, Bram . **SSC 62; TCLC 8, 144; WLC 6**
See Stoker, Abraham
See also AAYA 23; BPFB 3; BRWS 3; BYA 5; CDBLB 1890-1914; DAB; DLB 304; GL 3; LATS 1:1; NFS 18; RGEL 2; SUFW; TEA; WLIT 4
Stolz, Mary 1920-2006 .... **CLC 12**
See also AAYA 8, 73; AITN 1; CA 5-8R; CANR 13, 41, 112; JRDA; MAICYA 1, 2; SAAS 3; SATA 10, 71, 133; YAW
Stolz, Mary Slattery
See Stolz, Mary
Stone, Irving 1903-1989 .... **CLC 7**
See also AITN 1; BPFB 3; CA 1-4R; 3; CAAS 129; CANR 1, 23; CN 1, 2, 3, 4; CPW; DA3; DAM POP; INT CANR-23; MTCW 1, 2; MTFW 2005; RHW; SATA 3; SATA-Obit 64
Stone, Oliver 1946- .... **CLC 73**
See also AAYA 15, 64; CA 110; CANR 55, 125
Stone, Oliver William
See Stone, Oliver
Stone, Robert 1937- .... **CLC 5, 23, 42, 175**
See also AMWS 5; BPFB 3; CA 85-88; CANR 23, 66, 95; CN 4, 5, 6, 7; DLB 152; EWL 3; INT CANR-23; MAL 5; MTCW 1; MTFW 2005
Stone, Ruth 1915- .... **PC 53**
See also CA 45-48; CANR 2, 91; CP 5, 6, 7; CSW; DLB 105; PFS 19
Stone, Zachary
See Follett, Ken
Stoppard, Tom 1937- ... **CLC 1, 3, 4, 5, 8, 15, 29, 34, 63, 91; DC 6; WLC 6**
See also AAYA 63; BRWC 1; BRWR 2; BRWS 1; CA 81-84; CANR 39, 67, 125; CBD; CD 5, 6; CDBLB 1960 to Present;

DA; DA3; DAB; DAC; DAM DRAM, MST; DFS 2, 5, 8, 11, 13, 16; DLB 13, 233; DLBY 1985; EWL 3; LATS 1:2; MTCW 1, 2; MTFW 2005; RGEL 2; TEA; WLIT 4
Storey, David (Malcolm) 1933- . **CLC 2, 4, 5, 8**
See also BRWS 1; CA 81-84; CANR 36; CBD; CD 5, 6; CN 1, 2, 3, 4, 5, 6; DAM DRAM; DLB 13, 14, 207, 245, 326; EWL 3; MTCW 1; RGEL 2
Storm, Hyemeyohsts 1935- ... **CLC 3; NNAL**
See also CA 81-84; CANR 45; DAM MULT
Storm, (Hans) Theodor (Woldsen)
1817-1888 .... **NCLC 1; SSC 27**
See also CDWLB 2; DLB 129; EW; RGSF 2; RGWL 2, 3
Storni, Alfonsina 1892-1938 . **HLC 2; PC 33; TCLC 5**
See also CA 131; CAAE 104; DAM MULT; DLB 283; HW 1; LAW
Stoughton, William 1631-1701 .... **LC 38**
See also DLB 24
Stout, Rex (Todhunter) 1886-1975 ..... **CLC 3**
See also AITN 2; BPFB 3; CA 61-64; CANR 71; CMW 4; CN 2; DLB 306; MSW; RGAL 4
Stow, (Julian) Randolph 1935- ... **CLC 23, 48**
See also CA 13-16R; CANR 33; CN 1, 2, 3, 4, 5, 6, 7; CP 1, 2, 3, 4; DLB 260; MTCW 1; RGEL 2
Stowe, Harriet (Elizabeth) Beecher
1811-1896 ..... **NCLC 3, 50, 133; WLC 6**
See also AAYA 53; AMWS 1; CDALB 1865-1917; DA; DA3; DAB; DAC; DAM MST, NOV; DLB 1, 12, 42, 74, 189, 239, 243; EXPN; FL 1:3; JRDA; LAIT 2; MAICYA 1, 2; NFS 6; RGAL 4; TUS; YABC 1
Strabo c. 64B.C.-c. 25 .... **CMLC 37**
See also DLB 176
Strachey, (Giles) Lytton
1880-1932 .... **TCLC 12**
See also BRWS 2; CA 178; CAAE 110; DLB 149; DLBD 10; EWL 3; MTCW 2; NCFS 4
Stramm, August 1874-1915 .... **PC 50**
See also CA 195; EWL 3
Strand, Mark 1934- .. **CLC 6, 18, 41, 71; PC 63**
See also AMWS 4; CA 21-24R; CANR 40, 65, 100; CP 1, 2, 3, 4, 5, 6, 7; DAM POET; DLB 5; EWL 3; MAL 5; PAB; PFS 9, 18; RGAL 4; SATA 41; TCLE 1:2
Stratton-Porter, Gene(va Grace) 1863-1924
See Porter, Gene(va Grace) Stratton
See also ANW; CA 137; CLR 87; DLB 221; DLBD 14; MAICYA 1, 2; SATA 15
Straub, Peter 1943- .... **CLC 28, 107**
See also BEST 89:1; BPFB 3; CA 85-88; CANR 28, 65, 109; CPW; DAM POP; DLBY 1984; HGG; MTCW 1, 2; MTFW 2005; SUFW 2
Straub, Peter Francis
See Straub, Peter
Strauss, Botho 1944- .... **CLC 22**
See also CA 157; CWW 2; DLB 124
Strauss, Leo 1899-1973 .... **TCLC 141**
See also CA 101; CAAS 45-48; CANR 122
Streatfeild, (Mary) Noel
1897(?)-1986 .... **CLC 21**
See also CA 81-84; CAAS 120; CANR 31; CLR 17, 83; CWRI 5; DLB 160; MAI-CYA 1, 2; SATA 20; SATA-Obit 48
Stribling, T(homas) S(igismund)
1881-1965 .... **CLC 23**
See also CA 189; CAAS 107; CMW 4; DLB 9; RGAL 4

Strindberg, (Johan) August
1849-1912 ... **DC 18; TCLC 1, 8, 21, 47; WLC 6**
See also CA 135; CAAE 104; DA; DA3; DAB; DAC; DAM DRAM, MST; DFS 4, 9; DLB 259; EW 7; EWL 3; IDTP; LMFS 2; MTCW 2; MTFW 2005; RGWL 2, 3; TWA
Stringer, Arthur 1874-1950 .... **TCLC 37**
See also CA 161; DLB 92
Stringer, David
See Roberts, Keith (John Kingston)
Stroheim, Erich von 1885-1957 ..... **TCLC 71**
Strugatskii, Arkadii (Natanovich)
1925-1991 .... **CLC 27**
See Strugatsky, Arkadii Natanovich
See also CA 106; CAAS 135; SFW 4
Strugatskii, Boris (Natanovich)
1933- .... **CLC 27**
See Strugatsky, Boris (Natanovich)
See also CA 106; SFW 4
Strugatsky, Arkadii Natanovich
See Strugatskii, Arkadii (Natanovich)
See also DLB 302
Strugatsky, Boris (Natanovich)
See Strugatskii, Boris (Natanovich)
See also DLB 302
Strummer, Joe 1952-2002 .... **CLC 30**
Strunk, William, Jr. 1869-1946 ...... **TCLC 92**
See also CA 164; CAAE 118; NCFS 5
Stryk, Lucien 1924- .... **PC 27**
See also CA 13-16R; CANR 10, 28, 55, 110; CP 1, 2, 3, 4, 5, 6, 7
Stuart, Don A.
See Campbell, John W(ood, Jr.)
Stuart, Ian
See MacLean, Alistair (Stuart)
Stuart, Jesse (Hilton) 1906-1984 ... **CLC 1, 8, 11, 14, 34; SSC 31**
See also CA 5-8R; CAAS 112; CANR 31; CN 1, 2, 3; DLB 9, 48, 102; DLBY 1984; SATA 2; SATA-Obit 36
Stubblefield, Sally
See Trumbo, Dalton
Sturgeon, Theodore (Hamilton)
1918-1985 .... **CLC 22, 39**
See Queen, Ellery
See also AAYA 51; BPFB 3; BYA 9, 10; CA 81-84; CAAS 116; CANR 32, 103; DLB 8; DLBY 1985; HGG; MTCW 1, 2; MTFW 2005; SCFW; SFW 4; SUFW
Sturges, Preston 1898-1959 .... **TCLC 48**
See also CA 149; CAAE 114; DLB 26
Styron, William 1925-2006 .. **CLC 1, 3, 5, 11, 15, 60, 232; SSC 25**
See also AMW; AMWC 2; BEST 90:4; BPFB 3; CA 5-8R; CANR 6, 33, 74, 126; CDALB 1968-1988; CN 1, 2, 3, 4, 5, 6, 7; CPW; CSW; DA3; DAM NOV, POP; DLB 2, 143, 299; DLBY 1980; EWL 3; INT CANR-6; LAIT 2; MAL 5; MTCW 1, 2; MTFW 2005; NCFS 1; NFS 22; RGAL 4; RGHL; RHW; TUS
Su, Chien 1884-1918
See Su Man-shu
See also CAAE 123
Suarez Lynch, B.
See Bioy Casares, Adolfo; Borges, Jorge Luis
Suassuna, Ariano Vilar 1927- .... **HLCS 1**
See also CA 178; DLB 307; HW 2; LAW
Suckert, Kurt Erich
See Malaparte, Curzio
Suckling, Sir John 1609-1642 . **LC 75; PC 30**
See also BRW 2; DAM POET; DLB 58, 126; EXPP; PAB; RGEL 2
Suckow, Ruth 1892-1960 .... **SSC 18**
See also CA 193; CAAS 113; DLB 9, 102; RGAL 4; TCWW 2

Tanizaki Jun'ichiro
See Tanizaki, Jun'ichiro
See also DLB 180; EWL 3

Tannen, Deborah 1945- .... **CLC 206**
See also CA 118; CANR 95

Tannen, Deborah Frances
See Tannen, Deborah

Tanner, William
See Amis, Kingsley

Tante, Dilly
See Kunitz, Stanley

Tao Lao
See Storni, Alfonsina

Tapahonso, Luci 1953- .... **NNAL; PC 65**
See also CA 145; CANR 72, 127; DLB 175

Tarantino, Quentin (Jerome)
1963- .... **CLC 125, 230**
See also AAYA 58; CA 171; CANR 125

Tarassoff, Lev
See Troyat, Henri

Tarbell, Ida M(inerva) 1857-1944 . **TCLC 40**
See also CA 181; CAAE 122; DLB 47

Tarkington, (Newton) Booth
1869-1946 .... **TCLC 9**
See also BPFB 3; BYA 3; CA 143; CAAE
110; CWRI 5; DLB 9, 102; MAL 5;
MTCW 2; RGAL 4; SATA 17

Tarkovskii, Andrei Arsen'evich
See Tarkovsky, Andrei (Arsenyevich)

Tarkovsky, Andrei (Arsenyevich)
1932-1986 .... **CLC 75**
See also CA 127

Tartt, Donna 1964(?)- .... **CLC 76**
See also AAYA 56; CA 142; CANR 135;
MTFW 2005

Tasso, Torquato 1544-1595 .... **LC 5, 94**
See also EFS 2; EW 2; RGWL 2, 3; WLIT
7

Tate, (John Orley) Allen 1899-1979 .. **CLC 2,
4, 6, 9, 11, 14, 24; PC 50**
See also AMW; CA 5-8R; CAAS 85-88;
CANR 32, 108; CN 1, 2; CP 1, 2; DLB 4,
45, 63; DLBD 17; EWL 3; MAL 5;
MTCW 1, 2; MTFW 2005; RGAL 4;
RHW

Tate, Ellalice
See Hibbert, Eleanor Alice Burford

Tate, James (Vincent) 1943- ..... **CLC 2, 6, 25**
See also CA 21-24R; CANR 29, 57, 114;
CP 1, 2, 3, 4, 5, 6, 7; DLB 5, 169; EWL
3; PFS 10, 15; RGAL 4; WP

Tate, Nahum 1652(?)-1715 .... **LC 109**
See also DLB 80; RGEL 2

Tauler, Johannes c. 1300-1361 ...... **CMLC 37**
See also DLB 179; LMFS 1

Tavel, Ronald 1940- .... **CLC 6**
See also CA 21-24R; CAD; CANR 33; CD
5, 6

Taviani, Paolo 1931- .... **CLC 70**
See also CA 153

Taylor, Bayard 1825-1878 .... **NCLC 89**
See also DLB 3, 189, 250, 254; RGAL 4

Taylor, C(ecil) P(hilip) 1929-1981 .... **CLC 27**
See also CA 25-28R; CAAS 105; CANR
47; CBD

Taylor, Edward 1642(?)-1729 . **LC 11; PC 63**
See also AMW; DA; DAB; DAC; DAM
MST, POET; DLB 24; EXPP; RGAL 4;
TUS

Taylor, Eleanor Ross 1920- .... **CLC 5**
See also CA 81-84; CANR 70

Taylor, Elizabeth 1912-1975 ..... **CLC 2, 4, 29**
See also CA 13-16R; CANR 9, 70; CN 1,
2; DLB 139; MTCW 1; RGEL 2; SATA
13

Taylor, Frederick Winslow
1856-1915 .... **TCLC 76**
See also CA 188

Taylor, Henry (Splawn) 1942- .... **CLC 44**
See also CA 33-36R; 7; CANR 31; CP 6, 7;
DLB 5; PFS 10

Taylor, Kamala 1924-2004
See Markandaya, Kamala
See also CA 77-80; CAAS 227; MTFW
2005; NFS 13

Taylor, Mildred D. 1943- .... **CLC 21**
See also AAYA 10, 47; BW 1; BYA 3, 8;
CA 85-88; CANR 25, 115, 136; CLR 9,
59, 90; CSW; DLB 52; JRDA; LAIT 3;
MAICYA 1, 2; MTFW 2005; SAAS 5;
SATA 135; WYA; YAW

Taylor, Peter (Hillsman) 1917-1994 .. **CLC 1,
4, 18, 37, 44, 50, 71; SSC 10, 84**
See also AMWS 5; BPFB 3; CA 13-16R;
CAAS 147; CANR 9, 50; CN 1, 2, 3, 4,
5; CSW; DLB 218, 278; DLBY 1981,
1994; EWL 3; EXPS; INT CANR-9;
MAL 5; MTCW 1, 2; MTFW 2005; RGSF
2; SSFS 9; TUS

Taylor, Robert Lewis 1912-1998 .... **CLC 14**
See also CA 1-4R; CAAS 170; CANR 3,
64; CN 1, 2; SATA 10; TCWW 1, 2

Tchekhov, Anton
See Chekhov, Anton (Pavlovich)

Tchicaya, Gerald Felix 1931-1988 .. **CLC 101**
See Tchicaya U Tam'si
See also CA 129; CAAS 125; CANR 81

Tchicaya U Tam'si
See Tchicaya, Gerald Felix
See also EWL 3

Teasdale, Sara 1884-1933 .... **PC 31; TCLC 4**
See also CA 163; CAAE 104; DLB 45;
GLL 1; PFS 14; RGAL 4; SATA 32; TUS

Tecumseh 1768-1813 .... **NNAL**
See also DAM MULT

Tegner, Esaias 1782-1846 .... **NCLC 2**

Teilhard de Chardin, (Marie Joseph) Pierre
1881-1955 .... **TCLC 9**
See also CA 210; CAAE 105; GFL 1789 to
the Present

Temple, Ann
See Mortimer, Penelope (Ruth)

Tennant, Emma (Christina) 1937- .. **CLC 13,
52**
See also BRWS 9; CA 65-68; 9; CANR 10,
38, 59, 88; CN 3, 4, 5, 6, 7; DLB 14;
EWL 3; SFW 4

Tenneshaw, S. M.
See Silverberg, Robert

Tenney, Tabitha Gilman
1762-1837 .... **NCLC 122**
See also DLB 37, 200

Tennyson, Alfred 1809-1892 ... **NCLC 30, 65,
115; PC 6; WLC 6**
See also AAYA 50; BRW 4; CDBLB 1832-
1890; DA; DA3; DAB; DAC; DAM MST,
POET; DLB 32; EXPP; PAB; PFS 1, 2, 4,
11, 15, 19; RGEL 2; TEA; WLIT 4; WP

Teran, Lisa St. Aubin de .... **CLC 36**
See St. Aubin de Teran, Lisa

Terence c. 184B.C.-c. 159B.C. ...... **CMLC 14;
DC 7**
See also AW 1; CDWLB 1; DLB 211;
RGWL 2, 3; TWA; WLIT 8

Teresa de Jesus, St. 1515-1582 .... **LC 18**

Teresa of Avila, St.
See Teresa de Jesus, St.

Terkel, Louis .... **CLC 38**
See Terkel, Studs
See also AAYA 32; AITN 1; MTCW 2; TUS

Terkel, Studs 1912-
See Terkel, Louis
See also CA 57-60; CANR 18, 45, 67, 132;
DA3; MTCW 1, 2; MTFW 2005

Terry, C. V.
See Slaughter, Frank G(ill)

Terry, Megan 1932- .... **CLC 19; DC 13**
See also CA 77-80; CABS 3; CAD; CANR
43; CD 5, 6; CWD; DFS 18; DLB 7, 249;
GLL 2

Tertullian c. 155-c. 245 .... **CMLC 29**

Tertz, Abram
See Sinyavsky, Andrei (Donatevich)
See also RGSF 2

Tesich, Steve 1943(?)-1996 .... **CLC 40, 69**
See also CA 105; CAAS 152; CAD; DLBY
1983

Tesla, Nikola 1856-1943 .... **TCLC 88**

Teternikov, Fyodor Kuzmich 1863-1927
See Sologub, Fyodor
See also CAAE 104

Tevis, Walter 1928-1984 .... **CLC 42**
See also CA 113; SFW 4

Tey, Josephine .... **TCLC 14**
See Mackintosh, Elizabeth
See also DLB 77; MSW

Thackeray, William Makepeace
1811-1863 ...... **NCLC 5, 14, 22, 43, 169;
WLC 6**
See also BRW 5; BRWC 2; CDBLB 1832-
1890; DA; DA3; DAB; DAC; DAM MST,
NOV; DLB 21, 55, 159, 163; NFS 13;
RGEL 2; SATA 23; TEA; WLIT 3

Thakura, Ravindranatha
See Tagore, Rabindranath

Thames, C. H.
See Marlowe, Stephen

Tharoor, Shashi 1956- .... **CLC 70**
See also CA 141; CANR 91; CN 6, 7

Thelwall, John 1764-1834 .... **NCLC 162**
See also DLB 93, 158

Thelwell, Michael Miles 1939- .... **CLC 22**
See also BW 2; CA 101

Theobald, Lewis, Jr.
See Lovecraft, H. P.

Theocritus c. 310B.C.- .... **CMLC 45**
See also AW 1; DLB 176; RGWL 2, 3

Theodorescu, Ion N. 1880-1967
See Arghezi, Tudor
See also CAAS 116

Theriault, Yves 1915-1983 .... **CLC 79**
See also CA 102; CANR 150; CCA 1;
DAC; DAM MST; DLB 88; EWL 3

Theroux, Alexander (Louis) 1939- .... **CLC 2,
25**
See also CA 85-88; CANR 20, 63; CN 4, 5,
6, 7

Theroux, Paul 1941- .... **CLC 5, 8, 11, 15, 28,
46, 159**
See also AAYA 28; AMWS 8; BEST 89:4;
BPFB 3; CA 33-36R; CANR 20, 45, 74,
133; CDALBS; CN 1, 2, 3, 4, 5, 6, 7; CP
1; CPW 1; DA3; DAM POP; DLB 2, 218;
EWL 3; HGG; MAL 5; MTCW 1, 2;
MTFW 2005; RGAL 4; SATA 44, 109;
TUS

Thesen, Sharon 1946- .... **CLC 56**
See also CA 163; CANR 125; CP 5, 6, 7;
CWP

Thespis fl. 6th cent. B.C.- .... **CMLC 51**
See also LMFS 1

Thevenin, Denis
See Duhamel, Georges

Thibault, Jacques Anatole Francois
1844-1924
See France, Anatole
See also CA 127; CAAE 106; DA3; DAM
NOV; MTCW 1, 2; TWA

Thiele, Colin 1920-2006 .... **CLC 17**
See also CA 29-32R; CANR 12, 28, 53,
105; CLR 27; CP 1, 2; DLB 289; MAI-
CYA 1, 2; SAAS 2; SATA 14, 72, 125;
YAW

Thistlethwaite, Bel
See Wetherald, Agnes Ethelwyn

Tomlinson, (Alfred) Charles 1927- .... **CLC 2, 4, 6, 13, 45; PC 17**
See also CA 5-8R; CANR 33; CP 1, 2, 3, 4, 5, 6, 7; DAM POET; DLB 40; TCLE 1:2

Tomlinson, H(enry) M(ajor)
1873-1958 .... **TCLC 71**
See also CA 161; CAAE 118; DLB 36, 100, 195

Tonna, Charlotte Elizabeth
1790-1846 .... **NCLC 135**
See also DLB 163

Tonson, Jacob fl. 1655(?)-1736 .... **LC 86**
See also DLB 170

Toole, John Kennedy 1937-1969 ..... **CLC 19, 64**
See also BPFB 3; CA 104; DLBY 1981; MTCW 2; MTFW 2005

Toomer, Eugene
See Toomer, Jean

Toomer, Eugene Pinchback
See Toomer, Jean

Toomer, Jean 1894-1967 .. **BLC 3; CLC 1, 4, 13, 22; HR 1:3; PC 7; SSC 1, 45; TCLC 172; WLCS**
See also AFAW 1, 2; AMWS 3, 9; BW 1; CA 85-88; CDALB 1917-1929; DA3; DAM MULT; DLB 45, 51; EWL 3; EXPP; EXPS; LMFS 2; MAL 5; MTCW 1, 2; MTFW 2005; NFS 11; RGAL 4; RGSF 2; SSFS 5

Toomer, Nathan Jean
See Toomer, Jean

Toomer, Nathan Pinchback
See Toomer, Jean

Torley, Luke
See Blish, James (Benjamin)

Tornimparte, Alessandra
See Ginzburg, Natalia

Torre, Raoul della
See Mencken, H(enry) L(ouis)

Torrence, Ridgely 1874-1950 .... **TCLC 97**
See also DLB 54, 249; MAL 5

Torrey, E. Fuller 1937- .... **CLC 34**
See also CA 119; CANR 71, 158

Torrey, Edwin Fuller
See Torrey, E. Fuller

Torsvan, Ben Traven
See Traven, B.

Torsvan, Benno Traven
See Traven, B.

Torsvan, Berick Traven
See Traven, B.

Torsvan, Berwick Traven
See Traven, B.

Torsvan, Bruno Traven
See Traven, B.

Torsvan, Traven
See Traven, B.

Tourneur, Cyril 1575(?)-1626 .... **LC 66**
See also BRW 2; DAM DRAM; DLB 58; RGEL 2

Tournier, Michel 1924- .... **CLC 6, 23, 36, 95; SSC 88**
See also CA 49-52; CANR 3, 36, 74, 149; CWW 2; DLB 83; EWL 3; GFL 1789 to the Present; MTCW 1, 2; SATA 23

Tournier, Michel Edouard
See Tournier, Michel

Tournimparte, Alessandra
See Ginzburg, Natalia

Towers, Ivar
See Kornbluth, C(yril) M.

Towne, Robert (Burton) 1936(?)- ..... **CLC 87**
See also CA 108; DLB 44; IDFW 3, 4

Townsend, Sue .... **CLC 61**
See Townsend, Susan Lilian
See also AAYA 28; CA 127; CAAE 119; CANR 65, 107; CBD; CD 5, 6; CPW;

CWD; DAB; DAC; DAM MST; DLB 271; INT CA-127; SATA 55, 93; SATA-Brief 48; YAW

Townsend, Susan Lilian 1946-
See Townsend, Sue

Townshend, Pete
See Townshend, Peter (Dennis Blandford)

Townshend, Peter (Dennis Blandford)
1945- .... **CLC 17, 42**
See also CA 107

Tozzi, Federigo 1883-1920 .... **TCLC 31**
See also CA 160; CANR 110; DLB 264; EWL 3; WLIT 7

Tracy, Don(ald Fiske) 1905-1970(?)
See Queen, Ellery
See also CA 1-4R; CAAS 176; CANR 2

Trafford, F. G.
See Riddell, Charlotte

Traherne, Thomas 1637(?)-1674 .. **LC 99; PC 70**
See also BRW 2; BRWS 11; DLB 131; PAB; RGEL 2

Traill, Catharine Parr 1802-1899 .. **NCLC 31**
See also DLB 99

Trakl, Georg 1887-1914 .... **PC 20; TCLC 5**
See also CA 165; CAAE 104; EW 10; EWL 3; LMFS 2; MTCW 2; RGWL 2, 3

Trambley, Estela Portillo .... **TCLC 163**
See Portillo Trambley, Estela
See also CA 77-80; RGAL 4

Tranquilli, Secondino
See Silone, Ignazio

Transtroemer, Tomas Gosta
See Transtromer, Tomas (Goesta)

Transtromer, Tomas (Gosta)
See Transtromer, Tomas (Goesta)
See also CWW 2

Transtromer, Tomas (Goesta)
1931- .... **CLC 52, 65**
See Transtromer, Tomas (Goesta)
See also CA 129; 17; CAAE 117; CANR 115; DAM POET; DLB 257; EWL 3; PFS 21

Transtromer, Tomas Gosta
See Transtromer, Tomas (Goesta)

Traven, B. 1882(?)-1969 .... **CLC 8, 11**
See also CA 19-20; CAAS 25-28R; CAP 2; DLB 9, 56; EWL 3; MTCW 1; RGAL 4

Trediakovsky, Vasilii Kirillovich
1703-1769 .... **LC 68**
See also DLB 150

Treitel, Jonathan 1959- .... **CLC 70**
See also CA 210; DLB 267

Trelawny, Edward John
1792-1881 .... **NCLC 85**
See also DLB 110, 116, 144

Tremain, Rose 1943- .... **CLC 42**
See also CA 97-100; CANR 44, 95; CN 4, 5, 6, 7; DLB 14, 271; RGSF 2; RHW

Tremblay, Michel 1942- .... **CLC 29, 102, 225**
See also CA 128; CAAE 116; CCA 1; CWW 2; DAC; DAM MST; DLB 60; EWL 3; GLL 1; MTCW 1, 2; MTFW 2005

Trevanian .... **CLC 29**
See Whitaker, Rod

Trevor, Glen
See Hilton, James

Trevor, William .. **CLC 7, 9, 14, 25, 71, 116; SSC 21, 58**
See Cox, William Trevor
See also BRWS 4; CBD; CD 5, 6; CN 1, 2, 3, 4, 5, 6, 7; DLB 14, 139; EWL 3; LATS 1:2; RGEL 2; RGSF 2; SSFS 10; TCLE 1:2

Trifonov, Iurii (Valentinovich)
See Trifonov, Yuri (Valentinovich)
See also DLB 302; RGWL 2, 3

Trifonov, Yuri (Valentinovich)
1925-1981 .... **CLC 45**
See Trifonov, Iurii (Valentinovich); Trifonov, Yury Valentinovich
See also CA 126; CAAS 103; MTCW 1

Trifonov, Yury Valentinovich
See Trifonov, Yuri (Valentinovich)
See also EWL 3

Trilling, Diana (Rubin) 1905-1996 . **CLC 129**
See also CA 5-8R; CAAS 154; CANR 10, 46; INT CANR-10; MTCW 1, 2

Trilling, Lionel 1905-1975 ..... **CLC 9, 11, 24; SSC 75**
See also AMWS 3; CA 9-12R; CAAS 61-64; CANR 10, 105; CN 1, 2; DLB 28, 63; EWL 3; INT CANR-10; MAL 5; MTCW 1, 2; RGAL 4; TUS

Trimball, W. H.
See Mencken, H(enry) L(ouis)

Tristan
See Gomez de la Serna, Ramon

Tristram
See Housman, A(lfred) E(dward)

Trogdon, William (Lewis) 1939-
See Heat-Moon, William Least
See also AAYA 66; CA 119; CAAE 115; CANR 47, 89; CPW; INT CA-119

Trollope, Anthony 1815-1882 .... **NCLC 6, 33, 101; SSC 28; WLC 6**
See also BRW 5; CDBLB 1832-1890; DA; DA3; DAB; DAC; DAM MST, NOV; DLB 21, 57, 159; RGEL 2; RGSF 2; SATA 22

Trollope, Frances 1779-1863 .... **NCLC 30**
See also DLB 21, 166

Trollope, Joanna 1943- .... **CLC 186**
See also CA 101; CANR 58, 95, 149; CN 7; CPW; DLB 207; RHW

Trotsky, Leon 1879-1940 .... **TCLC 22**
See also CA 167; CAAE 118

Trotter (Cockburn), Catharine
1679-1749 .... **LC 8**
See also DLB 84, 252

Trotter, Wilfred 1872-1939 .... **TCLC 97**

Trout, Kilgore
See Farmer, Philip Jose

Trow, George W.S. 1943-2006 .... **CLC 52**
See also CA 126; CANR 91

Troyat, Henri 1911-2007 .... **CLC 23**
See also CA 45-48; CANR 2, 33, 67, 117; GFL 1789 to the Present; MTCW 1

Trudeau, Garry B. .... **CLC 12**
See Trudeau, G.B.
See also AAYA 10; AITN 2

Trudeau, G.B. 1948-
See Trudeau, Garry B.
See also AAYA 60; CA 81-84; CANR 31; SATA 35, 168

Truffaut, Francois 1932-1984 ... **CLC 20, 101**
See also CA 81-84; CAAS 113; CANR 34

Trumbo, Dalton 1905-1976 .... **CLC 19**
See also CA 21-24R; CAAS 69-72; CANR 10; CN 1, 2; DLB 26; IDFW 3, 4; YAW

Trumbull, John 1750-1831 .... **NCLC 30**
See also DLB 31; RGAL 4

Trundlett, Helen B.
See Eliot, T(homas) S(tearns)

Truth, Sojourner 1797(?)-1883 ...... **NCLC 94**
See also DLB 239; FW; LAIT 2

Tryon, Thomas 1926-1991 .... **CLC 3, 11**
See also AITN 1; BPFB 3; CA 29-32R; CAAS 135; CANR 32, 77; CPW; DA3; DAM POP; HGG; MTCW 1

Tryon, Tom
See Tryon, Thomas

Waldo, E. Hunter
See Sturgeon, Theodore (Hamilton)

Waldo, Edward Hamilton
See Sturgeon, Theodore (Hamilton)

Walker, Alice 1944- ...... **BLC 3; CLC 5, 6, 9, 19, 27, 46, 58, 103, 167; PC 30; SSC 5; WLCS**
See also AAYA 3, 33; AFAW 1, 2; AMWS 3; BEST 89:4; BPFB 3; BW 2, 3; CA 37-40R; CANR 9, 27, 49, 66, 82, 131; CDALB 1968-1988; CN 1, 4, 5, 6, 7; CPW; CSW; DA; DA3; DAB; DAC; DAM MST, MULT, NOV, POET, POP; DLB 6, 33, 143; EWL 3; EXPN; EXPS; FL 1:6; FW; INT CANR-27; LAIT 3; MAL 5; MBL; MTCW 1, 2; MTFW 2005; NFS 5; RGAL 4; RGSF 2; SATA 31; SSFS 2, 11; TUS; YAW

Walker, Alice Malsenior
See Walker, Alice

Walker, David Harry 1911-1992 ...... **CLC 14**
See also CA 1-4R; CAAS 137; CANR 1; CN 1, 2; CWRI 5; SATA 8; SATA-Obit 71

Walker, Edward Joseph 1934-2004
See Walker, Ted
See also CA 21-24R; CAAS 226; CANR 12, 28, 53

Walker, George F(rederick) 1947- .. **CLC 44, 61**
See also CA 103; CANR 21, 43, 59; CD 5, 6; DAB; DAC; DAM MST; DLB 60

Walker, Joseph A. 1935-2003 .... **CLC 19**
See also BW 1, 3; CA 89-92; CAD; CANR 26, 143; CD 5, 6; DAM DRAM, MST; DFS 12; DLB 38

Walker, Margaret 1915-1998 .. **BLC; CLC 1, 6; PC 20; TCLC 129**
See also AFAW 1, 2; BW 2, 3; CA 73-76; CAAS 172; CANR 26, 54, 76, 136; CN 1, 2, 3, 4, 5, 6; CP 1, 2, 3, 4, 5, 6; CSW; DAM MULT; DLB 76, 152; EXPP; FW; MAL 5; MTCW 1, 2; MTFW 2005; RGAL 4; RHW

Walker, Ted .... **CLC 13**
See Walker, Edward Joseph
See also CP 1, 2, 3, 4, 5, 6, 7; DLB 40

Wallace, David Foster 1962- ... **CLC 50, 114; SSC 68**
See also AAYA 50; AMWS 10; CA 132; CANR 59, 133; CN 7; DA3; MTCW 2; MTFW 2005

Wallace, Dexter
See Masters, Edgar Lee

Wallace, (Richard Horatio) Edgar 1875-1932 .... **TCLC 57**
See also CA 218; CAAE 115; CMW 4; DLB 70; MSW; RGEL 2

Wallace, Irving 1916-1990 .... **CLC 7, 13**
See also AITN 1; BPFB 3; CA 1-4R; 1; CAAS 132; CANR 1, 27; CPW; DAM NOV, POP; INT CANR-27; MTCW 1, 2

Wallant, Edward Lewis 1926-1962 ... **CLC 5, 10**
See also CA 1-4R; CANR 22; DLB 2, 28, 143, 299; EWL 3; MAL 5; MTCW 1, 2; RGAL 4; RGHL

Wallas, Graham 1858-1932 .... **TCLC 91**

Waller, Edmund 1606-1687 .... **LC 86; PC 72**
See also BRW 2; DAM POET; DLB 126; PAB; RGEL 2

Walley, Byron
See Card, Orson Scott

Walpole, Horace 1717-1797 .... **LC 2, 49**
See also BRW 3; DLB 39, 104, 213; GL 3; HGG; LMFS 1; RGEL 2; SUFW 1; TEA

Walpole, Hugh (Seymour) 1884-1941 .... **TCLC 5**
See also CA 165; CAAE 104; DLB 34; HGG; MTCW 2; RGEL 2; RHW

Walrond, Eric (Derwent) 1898-1966 . **HR 1:3**
See also BW 1; CA 125; DLB 51

Walser, Martin 1927- .... **CLC 27, 183**
See also CA 57-60; CANR 8, 46, 145; CWW 2; DLB 75, 124; EWL 3

Walser, Robert 1878-1956 ..... **SSC 20; TCLC 18**
See also CA 165; CAAE 118; CANR 100; DLB 66; EWL 3

Walsh, Gillian Paton
See Paton Walsh, Jill

Walsh, Jill Paton .... **CLC 35**
See Paton Walsh, Jill
See also CLR 2, 65; WYA

Walter, Villiam Christian
See Andersen, Hans Christian

Walters, Anna L(ee) 1946- .... **NNAL**
See also CA 73-76

Walther von der Vogelweide c. 1170-1228 .... **CMLC 56**

Walton, Izaak 1593-1683 .... **LC 72**
See also BRW 2; CDBLB Before 1660; DLB 151, 213; RGEL 2

Wambaugh, Joseph (Aloysius), Jr. 1937- .... **CLC 3, 18**
See also AITN 1; BEST 89:3; BPFB 3; CA 33-36R; CANR 42, 65, 115; CMW 4; CPW 1; DA3; DAM NOV, POP; DLB 6; DLBY 1983; MSW; MTCW 1, 2

Wang Wei 699(?)-761(?) .... **PC 18**
See also TWA

Warburton, William 1698-1779 .... **LC 97**
See also DLB 104

Ward, Arthur Henry Sarsfield 1883-1959
See Rohmer, Sax
See also CA 173; CAAE 108; CMW 4; HGG

Ward, Douglas Turner 1930- .... **CLC 19**
See also BW 1; CA 81-84; CAD; CANR 27; CD 5, 6; DLB 7, 38

Ward, E. D.
See Lucas, E(dward) V(errall)

Ward, Mrs. Humphry 1851-1920
See Ward, Mary Augusta
See also RGEL 2

Ward, Mary Augusta 1851-1920 ... **TCLC 55**
See Ward, Mrs. Humphry
See also DLB 18

Ward, Nathaniel 1578(?)-1652 .... **LC 114**
See also DLB 24

Ward, Peter
See Faust, Frederick (Schiller)

Warhol, Andy 1928(?)-1987 .... **CLC 20**
See also AAYA 12; BEST 89:4; CA 89-92; CAAS 121; CANR 34

Warner, Francis (Robert Le Plastrier) 1937- .... **CLC 14**
See also CA 53-56; CANR 11; CP 1, 2, 3, 4

Warner, Marina 1946- .... **CLC 59, 231**
See also CA 65-68; CANR 21, 55, 118; CN 5, 6, 7; DLB 194; MTFW 2005

Warner, Rex (Ernest) 1905-1986 ...... **CLC 45**
See also CA 89-92; CAAS 119; CN 1, 2, 3, 4; CP 1, 2, 3, 4; DLB 15; RGEL 2; RHW

Warner, Susan (Bogert) 1819-1885 .... **NCLC 31, 146**
See also DLB 3, 42, 239, 250, 254

Warner, Sylvia (Constance) Ashton
See Ashton-Warner, Sylvia (Constance)

Warner, Sylvia Townsend 1893-1978 .. **CLC 7, 19; SSC 23; TCLC 131**
See also BRWS 7; CA 61-64; CAAS 77-80; CANR 16, 60, 104; CN 1, 2; DLB 34, 139; EWL 3; FANT; FW; MTCW 1, 2; RGEL 2; RGSF 2; RHW

Warren, Mercy Otis 1728-1814 ..... **NCLC 13**
See also DLB 31, 200; RGAL 4; TUS

Warren, Robert Penn 1905-1989 .. **CLC 1, 4, 6, 8, 10, 13, 18, 39, 53, 59; PC 37; SSC 4, 58; WLC 6**
See also AITN 1; AMW; AMWC 2; BPFB 3; BYA 1; CA 13-16R; CAAS 129; CANR 10, 47; CDALB 1968-1988; CN 1, 2, 3, 4; CP 1, 2, 3, 4; DA; DA3; DAB; DAC; DAM MST, NOV, POET; DLB 2, 48, 152, 320; DLBY 1980, 1989; EWL 3; INT CANR-10; MAL 5; MTCW 1, 2; MTFW 2005; NFS 13; RGAL 4; RGSF 2; RHW; SATA 46; SATA-Obit 63; SSFS 8; TUS

Warrigal, Jack
See Furphy, Joseph

Warshofsky, Isaac
See Singer, Isaac Bashevis

Warton, Joseph 1722-1800 ... **LC 128; NCLC 118**
See also DLB 104, 109; RGEL 2

Warton, Thomas 1728-1790 .... **LC 15, 82**
See also DAM POET; DLB 104, 109; RGEL 2

Waruk, Kona
See Harris, (Theodore) Wilson

Warung, Price .... **TCLC 45**
See Astley, William
See also DLB 230; RGEL 2

Warwick, Jarvis
See Garner, Hugh
See also CCA 1

Washington, Alex
See Harris, Mark

Washington, Booker T(aliaferro) 1856-1915 .... **BLC 3; TCLC 10**
See also BW 1; CA 125; CAAE 114; DA3; DAM MULT; LAIT 2; RGAL 4; SATA 28

Washington, George 1732-1799 .... **LC 25**
See also DLB 31

Wassermann, (Karl) Jakob 1873-1934 .... **TCLC 6**
See also CA 163; CAAE 104; DLB 66; EWL 3

Wasserstein, Wendy 1950-2006 . **CLC 32, 59, 90, 183; DC 4**
See also AAYA 73; AMWS 15; CA 129; CAAE 121; CAAS 247; CABS 3; CAD; CANR 53, 75, 128; CD 5, 6; CWD; DA3; DAM DRAM; DFS 5, 17; DLB 228; EWL 3; FW; INT CA-129; MAL 5; MTCW 2; MTFW 2005; SATA 94; SATA-Obit 174

Waterhouse, Keith (Spencer) 1929- . **CLC 47**
See also CA 5-8R; CANR 38, 67, 109; CBD; CD 6; CN 1, 2, 3, 4, 5, 6, 7; DLB 13, 15; MTCW 1, 2; MTFW 2005

Waters, Frank (Joseph) 1902-1995 .. **CLC 88**
See also CA 5-8R; 13; CAAS 149; CANR 3, 18, 63, 121; DLB 212; DLBY 1986; RGAL 4; TCWW 1, 2

Waters, Mary C. .... **CLC 70**

Waters, Roger 1944- .... **CLC 35**

Watkins, Frances Ellen
See Harper, Frances Ellen Watkins

Watkins, Gerrold
See Malzberg, Barry N(athaniel)

Watkins, Gloria Jean
See hooks, bell

Watkins, Paul 1964- .... **CLC 55**
See also CA 132; CANR 62, 98

Watkins, Vernon Phillips 1906-1967 .... **CLC 43**
See also CA 9-10; CAAS 25-28R; CAP 1; DLB 20; EWL 3; RGEL 2

Watson, Irving S.
See Mencken, H(enry) L(ouis)

Watson, John H.
See Farmer, Philip Jose

Watson, Richard F.
See Silverberg, Robert

Watts, Ephraim
See Horne, Richard Henry Hengist

Watts, Isaac 1674-1748 .... **LC 98**
See also DLB 95; RGEL 2; SATA 52

Waugh, Auberon (Alexander)
1939-2001 .... **CLC 7**
See also CA 45-48; CAAS 192; CANR 6,
22, 92; CN 1, 2, 3; DLB 14, 194

Waugh, Evelyn (Arthur St. John)
1903-1966 .. **CLC 1, 3, 8, 13, 19, 27, 44,**
107; SSC 41; WLC 6
See also BPFB 3; BRW 7; CA 85-88; CAAS
25-28R; CANR 22; CDBLB 1914-1945;
DA; DA3; DAB; DAC; DAM MST, NOV,
POP; DLB 15, 162, 195; EWL 3; MTCW
1, 2; MTFW 2005; NFS 13, 17; RGEL 2;
RGSF 2; TEA; WLIT 4

Waugh, Harriet 1944- .... **CLC 6**
See also CA 85-88; CANR 22

Ways, C. R.
See Blount, Roy (Alton), Jr.

Waystaff, Simon
See Swift, Jonathan

Webb, Beatrice (Martha Potter)
1858-1943 .... **TCLC 22**
See also CA 162; CAAE 117; DLB 190;
FW

Webb, Charles (Richard) 1939- .... **CLC 7**
See also CA 25-28R; CANR 114

Webb, Frank J. .... **NCLC 143**
See also DLB 50

Webb, James, Jr.
See Webb, James

Webb, James 1946- .... **CLC 22**
See also CA 81-84; CANR 156

Webb, James H.
See Webb, James

Webb, James Henry
See Webb, James

Webb, Mary Gladys (Meredith)
1881-1927 .... **TCLC 24**
See also CA 182; CAAS 123; DLB 34; FW;
RGEL 2

Webb, Mrs. Sidney
See Webb, Beatrice (Martha Potter)

Webb, Phyllis 1927- .... **CLC 18**
See also CA 104; CANR 23; CCA 1; CP 1,
2, 3, 4, 5, 6, 7; CWP; DLB 53

Webb, Sidney (James) 1859-1947 .. **TCLC 22**
See also CA 163; CAAE 117; DLB 190

Webber, Andrew Lloyd .... **CLC 21**
See Lloyd Webber, Andrew
See also DFS 7

Weber, Lenora Mattingly
1895-1971 .... **CLC 12**
See also CA 19-20; CAAS 29-32R; CAP 1;
SATA 2; SATA-Obit 26

Weber, Max 1864-1920 .... **TCLC 69**
See also CA 189; CAAE 109; DLB 296

Webster, John 1580(?)-1634(?) ...... **DC 2; LC**
33, 84, 124; WLC 6
See also BRW 2; CDBLB Before 1660; DA;
DAB; DAC; DAM DRAM, MST; DFS
17, 19; DLB 58; IDTP; RGEL 2; WLIT 3

Webster, Noah 1758-1843 .... **NCLC 30**
See also DLB 1, 37, 42, 43, 73, 243

Wedekind, Benjamin Franklin
See Wedekind, Frank

Wedekind, Frank 1864-1918 .... **TCLC 7**
See also CA 153; CAAE 104; CANR 121,
122; CDWLB 2; DAM DRAM; DLB 118;
EW 8; EWL 3; LMFS 2; RGWL 2, 3

Wehr, Demaris .... **CLC 65**

Weidman, Jerome 1913-1998 .... **CLC 7**
See also AITN 2; CA 1-4R; CAAS 171;
CAD; CANR 1; CD 1, 2, 3, 4, 5; DLB 28

Weil, Simone (Adolphine)
1909-1943 .... **TCLC 23**
See also CA 159; CAAE 117; EW 12; EWL
3; FW; GFL 1789 to the Present; MTCW
2

Weininger, Otto 1880-1903 .... **TCLC 84**

Weinstein, Nathan
See West, Nathanael

Weinstein, Nathan von Wallenstein
See West, Nathanael

Weir, Peter (Lindsay) 1944- .... **CLC 20**
See also CA 123; CAAE 113

Weiss, Peter (Ulrich) 1916-1982 .. **CLC 3, 15,**
51; TCLC 152
See also CA 45-48; CAAS 106; CANR 3;
DAM DRAM; DFS 3; DLB 69, 124;
EWL 3; RGHL; RGWL 2, 3

Weiss, Theodore (Russell)
1916-2003 .... **CLC 3, 8, 14**
See also CA 189; 9-12R, 189; 2; CAAS
216; CANR 46, 94; CP 1, 2, 3, 4, 5, 6, 7;
DLB 5; TCLE 1:2

Welch, (Maurice) Denton
1915-1948 .... **TCLC 22**
See also BRWS 8, 9; CA 148; CAAE 121;
RGEL 2

Welch, James (Phillip) 1940-2003 ..... **CLC 6,**
14, 52; NNAL; PC 62
See also CA 85-88; CAAS 219; CANR 42,
66, 107; CN 5, 6, 7; CP 2, 3, 4, 5, 6, 7;
CPW; DAM MULT, POP; DLB 175, 256;
LATS 1:1; NFS 23; RGAL 4; TCWW 1,
2

Weldon, Fay 1931- . **CLC 6, 9, 11, 19, 36, 59,**
122
See also BRWS 4; CA 21-24R; CANR 16,
46, 63, 97, 137; CDBLB 1960 to Present;
CN 3, 4, 5, 6, 7; CPW; DAM POP; DLB
14, 194, 319; EWL 3; FW; HGG; INT
CANR-16; MTCW 1, 2; MTFW 2005;
RGEL 2; RGSF 2

Wellek, Rene 1903-1995 .... **CLC 28**
See also CA 5-8R; 7; CAAS 150; CANR 8;
DLB 63; EWL 3; INT CANR-8

Weller, Michael 1942- .... **CLC 10, 53**
See also CA 85-88; CAD; CD 5, 6

Weller, Paul 1958- .... **CLC 26**

Wellershoff, Dieter 1925- .... **CLC 46**
See also CA 89-92; CANR 16, 37

Welles, (George) Orson 1915-1985 .. **CLC 20,**
80
See also AAYA 40; CA 93-96; CAAS 117

Wellman, John McDowell 1945-
See Wellman, Mac
See also CA 166; CD 5

Wellman, Mac .... **CLC 65**
See Wellman, John McDowell; Wellman,
John McDowell
See also CAD; CD 6; RGAL 4

Wellman, Manly Wade 1903-1986 ... **CLC 49**
See also CA 1-4R; CAAS 118; CANR 6,
16, 44; FANT; SATA 6; SATA-Obit 47;
SFW 4; SUFW

Wells, Carolyn 1869(?)-1942 .... **TCLC 35**
See also CA 185; CAAE 113; CMW 4;
DLB 11

Wells, H(erbert) G(eorge) 1866-1946 . **SSC 6,**
70; TCLC 6, 12, 19, 133; WLC 6
See also AAYA 18; BPFB 3; BRW 6; CA
121; CAAE 110; CDBLB 1914-1945;
CLR 64; DA; DA3; DAB; DAC; DAM
MST, NOV; DLB 34, 70, 156, 178; EWL
3; EXPS; HGG; LAIT 3; LMFS 2; MTCW
1, 2; MTFW 2005; NFS 17, 20; RGEL 2;
RGSF 2; SATA 20; SCFW 1, 2; SFW 4;
SSFS 3; SUFW; TEA; WCH; WLIT 4;
YAW

Wells, Rosemary 1943- .... **CLC 12**
See also AAYA 13; BYA 7, 8; CA 85-88;
CANR 48, 120; CLR 16, 69; CWRI 5;
MAICYA 1, 2; SAAS 1; SATA 18, 69,
114, 156; YAW

Wells-Barnett, Ida B(ell)
1862-1931 .... **TCLC 125**
See also CA 182; DLB 23, 221

Welsh, Irvine 1958- .... **CLC 144**
See also CA 173; CANR 146; CN 7; DLB
271

Welty, Eudora 1909-2001 .... **CLC 1, 2, 5, 14,**
22, 33, 105, 220; SSC 1, 27, 51; WLC 6
See also AAYA 48; AMW; AMWR 1; BPFB
3; CA 9-12R; CAAS 199; CABS 1; CANR
32, 65, 128; CDALB 1941-1968; CN 1,
2, 3, 4, 5, 6, 7; CSW; DA; DA3; DAB;
DAC; DAM MST, NOV; DLB 2, 102,
143; DLBD 12; DLBY 1987, 2001; EWL
3; EXPS; HGG; LAIT 3; MAL 5; MBL;
MTCW 1, 2; MTFW 2005; NFS 13, 15;
RGAL 4; RGSF 2; RHW; SSFS 2, 10;
TUS

Welty, Eudora Alice
See Welty, Eudora

Wen I-to 1899-1946 .... **TCLC 28**
See also EWL 3

Wentworth, Robert
See Hamilton, Edmond

Werfel, Franz (Viktor) 1890-1945 ... **TCLC 8**
See also CA 161; CAAE 104; DLB 81, 124;
EWL 3; RGWL 2, 3

Wergeland, Henrik Arnold
1808-1845 .... **NCLC 5**

Wersba, Barbara 1932- .... **CLC 30**
See also AAYA 2, 30; BYA 6, 12, 13; CA
182; 29-32R, 182; CANR 16, 38; CLR 3,
78; DLB 52; JRDA; MAICYA 1, 2; SAAS
2; SATA 1, 58; SATA-Essay 103; WYA;
YAW

Wertmueller, Lina 1928- .... **CLC 16**
See also CA 97-100; CANR 39, 78

Wescott, Glenway 1901-1987 .. **CLC 13; SSC**
35
See also CA 13-16R; CAAS 121; CANR
23, 70; CN 1, 2, 3, 4; DLB 4, 9, 102;
MAL 5; RGAL 4

Wesker, Arnold 1932- .... **CLC 3, 5, 42**
See also CA 1-4R; 7; CANR 1, 33; CBD;
CD 5, 6; CDBLB 1960 to Present; DAB;
DAM DRAM; DLB 13, 310, 319; EWL
3; MTCW 1; RGEL 2; TEA

Wesley, Charles 1707-1788 .... **LC 128**
See also DLB 95; RGEL 2

Wesley, John 1703-1791 .... **LC 88**
See also DLB 104

Wesley, Richard (Errol) 1945- .... **CLC 7**
See also BW 1; CA 57-60; CAD; CANR
27; CD 5, 6; DLB 38

Wessel, Johan Herman 1742-1785 .... **LC 7**
See also DLB 300

West, Anthony (Panther)
1914-1987 .... **CLC 50**
See also CA 45-48; CAAS 124; CANR 3,
19; CN 1, 2, 3, 4; DLB 15

West, C. P.
See Wodehouse, P(elham) G(renville)

West, Cornel 1953- .... **BLCS; CLC 134**
See also CA 144; CANR 91, 159; DLB 246

West, Cornel Ronald
See West, Cornel

West, Delno C(loyde), Jr. 1936- .... **CLC 70**
See also CA 57-60

West, Dorothy 1907-1998 ...... **HR 1:3; TCLC**
108
See also BW 2; CA 143; CAAS 169; DLB
76

Wilson, Harriet
See Wilson, Harriet E. Adams
See also DLB 239
Wilson, Harriet E.
See Wilson, Harriet E. Adams
See also DLB 243
Wilson, Harriet E. Adams
1827(?)-1863(?) .... **BLC 3; NCLC 78**
See Wilson, Harriet; Wilson, Harriet E.
See also DAM MULT; DLB 50
Wilson, John 1785-1854 .... **NCLC 5**
Wilson, John (Anthony) Burgess 1917-1993
See Burgess, Anthony
See also CA 1-4R; CAAS 143; CANR 2,
46; DA3; DAC; DAM NOV; MTCW 1,
2; MTFW 2005; NFS 15; TEA
Wilson, Katharina .... **CLC 65**
Wilson, Lanford 1937- .. **CLC 7, 14, 36, 197;**
DC 19
See also CA 17-20R; CABS 3; CAD; CANR
45, 96; CD 5, 6; DAM DRAM; DFS 4, 9,
12, 16, 20; DLB 7; EWL 3; MAL 5; TUS
Wilson, Robert M. 1941- .... **CLC 7, 9**
See also CA 49-52; CAD; CANR 2, 41; CD
5, 6; MTCW 1
Wilson, Robert McLiam 1964- .... **CLC 59**
See also CA 132; DLB 267
Wilson, Sloan 1920-2003 .... **CLC 32**
See also CA 1-4R; CAAS 216; CANR 1,
44; CN 1, 2, 3, 4, 5, 6
Wilson, Snoo 1948- .... **CLC 33**
See also CA 69-72; CBD; CD 5, 6
Wilson, William S(mith) 1932- .... **CLC 49**
See also CA 81-84
Wilson, (Thomas) Woodrow
1856-1924 .... **TCLC 79**
See also CA 166; DLB 47
Winchilsea, Anne (Kingsmill) Finch
1661-1720
See Finch, Anne
See also RGEL 2
Winckelmann, Johann Joachim
1717-1768 .... **LC 129**
See also DLB 97
Windham, Basil
See Wodehouse, P(elham) G(renville)
Wingrove, David 1954- .... **CLC 68**
See also CA 133; SFW 4
Winnemucca, Sarah 1844-1891 .... **NCLC 79;**
NNAL
See also DAM MULT; DLB 175; RGAL 4
Winstanley, Gerrard 1609-1676 .... **LC 52**
Wintergreen, Jane
See Duncan, Sara Jeannette
Winters, Arthur Yvor
See Winters, Yvor
Winters, Janet Lewis .... **CLC 41**
See Lewis, Janet
See also DLBY 1987
Winters, Yvor 1900-1968 .... **CLC 4, 8, 32**
See also AMWS 2; CA 11-12; CAAS 25-
28R; CAP 1; DLB 48; EWL 3; MAL 5;
MTCW 1; RGAL 4
Winterson, Jeanette 1959- .... **CLC 64, 158**
See also BRWS 4; CA 136; CANR 58, 116;
CN 5, 6, 7; CPW; DA3; DAM POP; DLB
207, 261; FANT; FW; GLL 1; MTCW 2;
MTFW 2005; RHW
Winthrop, John 1588-1649 .... **LC 31, 107**
See also DLB 24, 30
Wirth, Louis 1897-1952 .... **TCLC 92**
See also CA 210
Wiseman, Frederick 1930- .... **CLC 20**
See also CA 159
Wister, Owen 1860-1938 .... **TCLC 21**
See also BPFB 3; CA 162; CAAE 108;
DLB 9, 78, 186; RGAL 4; SATA 62;
TCWW 1, 2

Wither, George 1588-1667 .... **LC 96**
See also DLB 121; RGEL 2
Witkacy
See Witkiewicz, Stanislaw Ignacy
Witkiewicz, Stanislaw Ignacy
1885-1939 .... **TCLC 8**
See also CA 162; CAAE 105; CDWLB 4;
DLB 215; EW 10; EWL 3; RGWL 2, 3;
SFW 4
Wittgenstein, Ludwig (Josef Johann)
1889-1951 .... **TCLC 59**
See also CA 164; CAAE 113; DLB 262;
MTCW 2
Wittig, Monique 1935-2003 .... **CLC 22**
See also CA 135; CAAE 116; CAAS 212;
CANR 143; CWW 2; DLB 83; EWL 3;
FW; GLL 1
Wittlin, Jozef 1896-1976 .... **CLC 25**
See also CA 49-52; CAAS 65-68; CANR 3;
EWL 3
Wodehouse, P(elham) G(renville)
1881-1975 . **CLC 1, 2, 5, 10, 22; SSC 2;**
TCLC 108
See also AAYA 65; AITN 2; BRWS 3; CA
45-48; CAAS 57-60; CANR 3, 33; CD-
BLB 1914-1945; CN 1, 2; CPW 1; DA3;
DAB; DAC; DAM NOV; DLB 34, 162;
EWL 3; MTCW 1, 2; MTFW 2005; RGEL
2; RGSF 2; SATA 22; SSFS 10
Woiwode, L.
See Woiwode, Larry (Alfred)
Woiwode, Larry (Alfred) 1941- ... **CLC 6, 10**
See also CA 73-76; CANR 16, 94; CN 3, 4,
5, 6, 7; DLB 6; INT CANR-16
Wojciechowska, Maia (Teresa)
1927-2002 .... **CLC 26**
See also AAYA 8, 46; BYA 3; CA 183;
9-12R, 183; CAAS 209; CANR 4, 41;
CLR 1; JRDA; MAICYA 1, 2; SAAS 1;
SATA 1, 28, 83; SATA-Essay 104; SATA-
Obit 134; YAW
Wojtyla, Karol (Jozef)
See John Paul II, Pope
Wojtyla, Karol (Josef)
See John Paul II, Pope
Wolf, Christa 1929- .... **CLC 14, 29, 58, 150**
See also CA 85-88; CANR 45, 123; CD-
WLB 2; CWW 2; DLB 75; EWL 3; FW;
MTCW 1; RGWL 2, 3; SSFS 14
Wolf, Naomi 1962- .... **CLC 157**
See also CA 141; CANR 110; FW; MTFW
2005
Wolfe, Gene 1931- .... **CLC 25**
See also AAYA 35; CA 57-60; 9; CANR 6,
32, 60, 152; CPW; DAM POP; DLB 8;
FANT; MTCW 2; MTFW 2005; SATA
118, 165; SCFW 2; SFW 4; SUFW 2
Wolfe, Gene Rodman
See Wolfe, Gene
Wolfe, George C. 1954- .... **BLCS; CLC 49**
See also CA 149; CAD; CD 5, 6
Wolfe, Thomas (Clayton)
1900-1938 ...... **SSC 33; TCLC 4, 13, 29,**
61; WLC 6
See also AMW; BPFB 3; CA 132; CAAE
104; CANR 102; CDALB 1929-1941;
DA; DA3; DAB; DAC; DAM MST, NOV;
DLB 9, 102, 229; DLBD 2, 16; DLBY
1985, 1997; EWL 3; MAL 5; MTCW 1,
2; NFS 18; RGAL 4; SSFS 18; TUS
Wolfe, Thomas Kennerly, Jr.
1931- .... **CLC 147**
See Wolfe, Tom
See also CA 13-16R; CANR 9, 33, 70, 104;
DA3; DAM POP; DLB 185; EWL 3; INT
CANR-9; MTCW 1, 2; MTFW 2005; TUS

Wolfe, Tom .... **CLC 1, 2, 9, 15, 35, 51**
See Wolfe, Thomas Kennerly, Jr.
See also AAYA 8, 67; AITN 2; AMWS 3;
BEST 89:1; BPFB 3; CN 5, 6, 7; CPW;
CSW; DLB 152; LAIT 5; RGAL 4
Wolff, Geoffrey 1937- .... **CLC 41**
See also CA 29-32R; CANR 29, 43, 78, 154
Wolff, Geoffrey Ansell
See Wolff, Geoffrey
Wolff, Sonia
See Levitin, Sonia (Wolff)
Wolff, Tobias 1945- .... **CLC 39, 64, 172; SSC**
63
See also AAYA 16; AMWS 7; BEST 90:2;
BYA 12; CA 117; 22; CAAE 114; CANR
54, 76, 96; CN 5, 6, 7; CSW; DA3; DLB
130; EWL 3; INT CA-117; MTCW 2;
MTFW 2005; RGAL 4; RGSF 2; SSFS 4,
11
Wolitzer, Hilma 1930- .... **CLC 17**
See also CA 65-68; CANR 18, 40; INT
CANR-18; SATA 31; YAW
Wollstonecraft, Mary 1759-1797 .... **LC 5, 50,**
90
See also BRWS 3; CDBLB 1789-1832;
DLB 39, 104, 158, 252; FL 1:1; FW;
LAIT 1; RGEL 2; TEA; WLIT 3
Wonder, Stevie 1950- .... **CLC 12**
See also CAAE 111
Wong, Jade Snow 1922-2006 .... **CLC 17**
See also CA 109; CAAS 249; CANR 91;
SATA 112; SATA-Obit 175
Wood, Mrs. Henry 1814-1887 ...... **NCLC 178**
See also CMW 4; DLB 18; SUFW
Woodberry, George Edward
1855-1930 .... **TCLC 73**
See also CA 165; DLB 71, 103
Woodcott, Keith
See Brunner, John (Kilian Houston)
Woodruff, Robert W.
See Mencken, H(enry) L(ouis)
Woolf, (Adeline) Virginia 1882-1941 .. **SSC 7,**
79; TCLC 1, 5, 20, 43, 56, 101, 123,
128; WLC 6
See also AAYA 44; BPFB 3; BRW 7;
BRWC 2; BRWR 1; CA 130; CAAE 104;
CANR 64, 132; CDBLB 1914-1945; DA;
DA3; DAB; DAC; DAM MST, NOV;
DLB 36, 100, 162; DLBD 10; EWL 3;
EXPS; FL 1:6; FW; LAIT 3; LATS 1:1;
LMFS 2; MTCW 1, 2; MTFW 2005;
NCFS 2; NFS 8, 12; RGEL 2; RGSF 2;
SSFS 4, 12; TEA; WLIT 4
Woollcott, Alexander (Humphreys)
1887-1943 .... **TCLC 5**
See also CA 161; CAAE 105; DLB 29
Woolrich, Cornell .... **CLC 77**
See Hopley-Woolrich, Cornell George
See also MSW
Woolson, Constance Fenimore
1840-1894 .... **NCLC 82; SSC 90**
See also DLB 12, 74, 189, 221; RGAL 4
Wordsworth, Dorothy 1771-1855 . **NCLC 25,**
138
See also DLB 107
Wordsworth, William 1770-1850 .. **NCLC 12,**
38, 111, 166; PC 4, 67; WLC 6
See also AAYA 70; BRW 4; BRWC 1; CD-
BLB 1789-1832; DA; DA3; DAB; DAC;
DAM MST, POET; DLB 93, 107; EXPP;
LATS 1:1; LMFS 1; PAB; PFS 2; RGEL
2; TEA; WLIT 3; WP
Wotton, Sir Henry 1568-1639 .... **LC 68**
See also DLB 121; RGEL 2
Wouk, Herman 1915- .... **CLC 1, 9, 38**
See also BPFB 2, 3; CA 5-8R; CANR 6,
33, 67, 146; CDALBS; CN 1, 2, 3, 4, 5,
6; CPW; DA3; DAM NOV, POP; DLBY
1982; INT CANR-6; LAIT 4; MAL 5;
MTCW 1, 2; MTFW 2005; NFS 7; TUS

Literary Criticism Series
Cumulative Topic Index

This index lists all topic entries in Thompson Gale's *Children's Literature Review* (CLR), *Classical and Medieval Literature Criticism* (CMLC), *Contemporary Literary Criticism* (CLC), *Drama Criticism* (DC), *Literature Criticism from 1400 to 1800* (LC), *Nineteenth-Century Literature Criticism* (NCLC), *Short Story Criticism* (SSC), and *Twentieth-Century Literary Criticism* (TCLC). The index also lists topic entries in the Gale Critical Companion Collection, which includes the following publications: *The Beat Generation* (BG), *Feminism in Literature* (FL), *Gothic Literature* (GL), and *Harlem Renaissance* (HR).

Topic Index

CLC Cumulative Nationality Index

Nationality Index

Nationality Index

Nationality Index

Nationality Index

CLC-235 Title Index